WEBSTER'S
Spanish~English
Dictionary
for Students

Created in Cooperation with the Editors of
MERRIAM~WEBSTER

FEDERAL
STREET
PRESS

A Division of Merriam~Webster, Incorporated
Springfield, Massachusetts

This 2013 edition published by
Federal Street press
A Division of Merriam-Webster, Incorporated
P.O. Box 281
Springfield, MA 01102

ISBN 978-1-59695-096-2

8th Printing   Craftline, Ft. Wayne, IN   5/2013

Printed in the United States of America

Contents

Preface

This Spanish-English Dictionary is a concise reference to the core vocabulary of Spanish and English. Its 40,000 entries and over 50,000 translations provide up-to-date coverage of the basic vocabulary and idioms in both languages. In addition, the book includes many specifically Latin-American words and phrases.

This book shares many details of presentation with larger Spanish-English dictionaries, but for reasons of conciseness it also has a number of features uniquely its own. Users need to be familiar with the following major features of this dictionary.

Main entries follow one another in strict alphabetical order, without regard to intervening spaces or hyphens. The Spanish letter combinations *ch* and *ll* are alphabetized within the letters *C* and *L;* however, the Spanish letter *ñ* is alphabetized separately between *N* and *O.*

Homographs (words spelled the same but having different meanings or parts of speech) are run on at a single main entry if they are closely related. Run-on homograph entries are replaced in the text by a boldfaced swung dash (as **haber** . . . *v aux* . . . — ~ *nm* . . .). Homographs of distinctly different origin (as **date**[1] and **date**[2]) are given separate entries.

Run-on entries for related words that are not homographs may also follow the main entry. Thus we have the main entry **calcular** *vt* followed by run-on entries for — **calculador, -dora** *adj* . . . — **calculadora** *nf* . . . and — **cálculo** *nm.* However, if a related word falls later in the alphabet than a following unrelated main entry, it will be entered at its own place; **ear** and its run-on — **eardrum** precede the main entry **earl** which is followed by the main entry **earlobe.**

Variant spellings appear at the main entry separated by *or* (as **judgment** *or* **judgement, paralyze** *or Brit* **paralyse,** or **cacahuate** *or* **cacahuete**).

Inflected forms of English verbs, adjectives, adverbs, and nouns are shown when they are irregular (as **wage** . . . **waged, waging; ride** . . . **rode, ridden; good** . . . **better, best;** or **fly** . . . *n, pl* **flies**) or when there might be doubt about their spelling (as **ego** . . . *n, pl* **egos**). Inflected forms of Spanish irregular verbs are shown in the section Conjugation of Spanish Verbs on page v; numerical references to this table are included at the main entry (as **poseer** {20} *vt*). Irregular plurals of Spanish nouns or adjectives are shown at the main entry (as **ladrón, -drona** *n, mpl* **-drones**).

Cross-references are provided to lead the user to the appropriate main entry (as **mice** → **mouse** or **sobrestimar** → **sobreestimar**).

The grammatical function of entry words is indicated by an italic **functional label** (as *vt, adj, or nm*). Italic **usage labels** may be added at the entry or sense as well (as **timbre** *nm* . . . 4 *Lat* : postage stamp, **center** *or Brit* **centre** . . . *n* . . ., or **garra** *nf* . . . 2 *fam* : hand, paw). These labels are also included in the translations (as **bag** *n* . . . 2 HANDBAG : bolso *m*, cartera *f Lat*).

Usage notes are occasionally placed before a translation to clarify meaning or use (as **que** *conj* . . . 2 (*in comparisons*) : than).

Synonyms may appear before the translation word(s) in order to provide context for the meaning of an entry word or sense (as **sitio** *nm* . . . 2 ESPACIO : room, space; or **meet** . . . *vt* . . . 2 SATISFY : satisfacer).

Bold notes are sometimes used before a translation to introduce a plural sense or a common phrase using the main entry word (as **mueble** *nm* . . . 2 ~s *nmpl* : furniture, furnishings, or **call** . . . *vt* . . . 2 ~ **off** : cancelar). Note that when an entry word is repeated in a bold note, it is replaced by a swung dash.

Conjugation of Spanish Verbs

Simple Tenses

-AR Verbs (hablar)		-ER Verbs (comer)		-IR Verbs (vivir)	
PRESENT INDICATIVE TENSE					
hablo	hablamos	como	comemos	vivo	vivimos
hablas	habláis	comes	coméis	vives	vivís
habla	hablan	come	comen	vive	viven
PRESENT SUBJUNCTIVE TENSE					
hable	hablemos	coma	comamos	viva	vivamos
hables	habléis	comas	comáis	vivas	viváis
hable	hablen	coma	coman	viva	vivan
PRETERIT INDICATIVE TENSE					
hablé	hablamos	comí	comimos	viví	vivimos
hablaste	hablasteis	comiste	comisteis	viviste	vivisteis
habló	hablaron	comió	comieron	vivió	vivieron
IMPERFECT INDICATIVE TENSE					
hablaba	hablábamos	comía	comíamos	vivía	vivíamos
hablabas	hablabais	comías	comíais	vivías	vivíais
hablaba	hablaban	comía	comían	vivía	vivían
IMPERFECT SUBJUNCTIVE TENSE					
hablara	habláramos	comiera	comiéramos	viviera	viviéramos
hablaras	hablarais	comieras	comierais	vivieras	vivierais
hablara	hablaran	comiera	comieran	viviera	vivieran
or		*or*		*or*	
hablase	hablásemos	comiese	comiésemos	viviese	viviésemos
hablases	hablaseis	comieses	comieseis	vivieses	vivieseis
hablase	hablasen	comiese	comiesen	viviese	viviesen
FUTURE INDICATIVE TENSE					
hablaré	hablaremos	comeré	comeremos	viviré	viviremos
hablarás	hablaréis	comerás	comeréis	vivirás	viviréis
hablará	hablarán	comerá	comerán	vivirá	vivirán
FUTURE SUBJUNCTIVE TENSE					
hablare	habláremos	comiere	comiéremos	viviere	viviéremos
hablares	hablareis	comieres	comiereis	vivieres	viviereis
hablare	hablaren	comiere	comieren	viviere	vivieren
CONDITIONAL TENSE					
hablaría	hablaríamos	comería	comeríamos	viviría	viviríamos
hablarías	hablaríais	comerías	comeríais	vivirías	viviríais
hablaría	hablarían	comería	comerían	viviría	vivirían
IMPERATIVE TENSE					
	hablemos		comamos		vivamos
habla	hablad	come	comed	vive	vivid
hable	hablen	coma	coman	viva	vivan
PRESENT PARTICIPLE (GERUND) TENSE					
hablando		comiendo		viviendo	
PAST PARTICIPLE TENSE					
hablado		comido		vivido	

Compound Tenses

1. Perfect Tenses

The perfect tenses are formed with *haber* and the past participle:

PRESENT PERFECT
> he hablado, etc. (*indicative*);
> haya hablado, etc. (*subjunctive*)

PAST PERFECT
> había hablado, etc. (*indicative*);
> hubiera hablado, etc. (*subjunctive*)
> *or*
> hubiese hablado, etc. (*subjunctive*)

PRETERIT PERFECT
> hube hablado, etc. (*indicative*)

FUTURE PERFECT
> habré hablado, etc. (*indicative*)

CONDITIONAL PERFECT
> habría hablado, etc. (*indicative*)

2. Progressive Tenses

The progressive tenses are formed with *estar* and the present participle:

PRESENT PROGRESSIVE
> estoy llamando, etc. (*indicative*);
> esté llamando, etc. (*subjunctive*)

IMPERFECT PROGRESSIVE
> estaba llamando, etc. (*indicative*);
> estuviera llamando, etc. (*subjunctive*)
> *or*
> estuviese llamando, etc. (*subjunctive*)

PRETERIT PROGRESSIVE
> estuve llamando, etc. (*indicative*)

FUTURE PROGRESSIVE
> estaré llamando, etc. (*indicative*)

CONDITIONAL PROGRESSIVE
> estaría llamando, etc. (*indicative*)

PRESENT PERFECT PROGRESSIVE
> he estado llamando, etc. (*indicative*);
> haya estado llamando, etc. (*subjunctive*)

PAST PERFECT PROGRESSIVE
> había estado llamando, etc. (*indicative*);
> hubiera estado llamando, etc. (*subjunctive*)
> *or*
> hubiese estado llamando, etc. (*subjunctive*)

Irregular Verbs

The *imperfect subjunctive*, the *future subjunctive*, the *conditional*, and most forms of the *imperative* are not included in the model conjugations, but can be derived as follows:

The *imperfect subjunctive* and the *future subjunctive* are formed from the third person plural form of the preterit tense by removing the last syllable (*-ron*) and adding the appropriate suffix:

PRETERIT INDICATIVE, THIRD PERSON PLURAL (querer)	quisieron
IMPERFECT SUBJUNCTIVE (querer)	quisiera, quisieras, etc. *or* quisiese, quisieses, etc.
FUTURE SUBJUNCTIVE (querer)	quisiere, quisieres, etc.

The conditional uses the same stem as the future indicative:

FUTURE INDICATIVE (poner)	pondré, pondrás, etc.
CONDITIONAL (poner)	pondría, pondrías, etc.

The third person singular, first person plural, and third person plural forms of the *imperative* are the same as the corresponding forms of the present subjunctive.

The second person singular form of the *imperative* is generally the same as the third person singular of the present indicative. Exceptions are noted in the model conjugations list.

The second person plural *(vosotros)* form of the *imperative* is formed by removing the final *-r* of the infinitive form and adding a *-d* (ex.: *oír* → *oíd*).

Model Conjugations of Irregular Verbs

The model conjugations below include the following simple tenses: the *present indicative* (*IND*), the *present subjunctive* (*SUBJ*), the *preterit indicative* (*PRET*), the *imperfect indicative* (*IMPF*), the *future indicative* (*FUT*), the second person singular form of the *imperative* (*IMPER*) when it differs from the third person singular of the present indicative, the *gerund* or *present participle* (*PRP*), and the *past participle* (*PP*). Each set of conjugations is preceded by the corresponding infinitive form of the verb, shown in bold type. Only tenses containing irregularities are listed, and the irregular verb forms within each tense are displayed in bold type.

Each irregular verb entry in the Spanish-English section of this dictionary is cross-referenced by number to one of the following model conjugations. These cross-reference numbers are shown in curly braces { } immediately following the entry's functional label.

1 **abolir** *(defective verb)* : *IND* abolimos, abolís *(other forms not used); SUBJ (not used); IMPER (only second person plural is used)*

2 **abrir** : *PP* abierto

3 **actuar** : *IND* **actúo, actúas, actúa,** actuamos, actuáis, **actúan;** *SUBJ* **actúe, actúes, actúe,** actuemos, actuéis, **actúen;** *IMPER* **actúa**

4 **adquirir** : *IND* **adquiero, adquieres, adquiere,** adquirimos, adquirís, **adquieren;** *SUBJ* **adquiera, adquieras, adquiera,** adquiramos, adquiráis, **adquieran;** *IMPER* **adquiere**

5 **airar** : *IND* **aíro, aíras, aíra,** airamos, airáis, **aíran;** *SUBJ* **aíre, aíres, aíre,** airemos, airéis, **aíren;** *IMPER* **aíra**

6 **andar** : *PRET* **anduve, anduviste, anduvo, anduvimos, anduvisteis, anduvieron**

7 **asir** : *IND* **asgo,** ases, ase, asimos, asís, asen; *SUBJ* **asga, asgas, asga, asgamos, asgáis, asgan**

8 **aunar** : *IND* **aúno, aúnas, aúna,** aunamos, aunáis, **aúnan;** *SUBJ* **aúne, aúnes, aúne,** aunemos, aunéis, **aúnen;** *IMPER* **aúna**

9 **avergonzar** : *IND* **avergüenzo, avergüenzas, avergüenza,** avergonzamos, avergonzáis, **avergüenzan;** *SUBJ* **avergüence, avergüences, avergüence, avergoncemos, avergoncéis, avergüencen;** *PRET* **avergoncé;** *IMPER* **avergüenza**

10 **averiguar** : *SUBJ* **averigüe, averigües, averigüe, averigüemos, averigüéis, averigüen;** *PRET* **averigüé,** averiguaste, averiguó, averiguamos, averiguasteis, averiguaron

11 **bendecir** : *IND* **bendigo, bendices, bendice,** bendecimos, bendecís, **bendicen;** *SUBJ* **bendiga, bendigas, bendiga, bendigamos, bendigáis, bendigan;** *PRET* **bendije, bendijiste, bendijo, bendijimos, bendijisteis, bendijeron;** *IMPER* **bendice**

12 **caber** : *IND* **quepo,** cabes, cabe, cabemos, cabéis, caben; *SUBJ* **quepa, quepas, quepa, quepamos, quepáis, quepan;** *PRET* **cupe, cupiste, cupo, cupimos, cupisteis, cupieron;** *FUT* **cabré, cabrás, cabrá, cabremos, cabréis, cabrán**

13 **caer** : *IND* **caigo,** caes, cae, caemos, caéis, caen; *SUBJ* **caiga, caigas, caiga, caigamos, caigáis, caigan;** *PRET* caí, **caíste, cayó, caímos, caísteis, cayeron;** *PRP* **cayendo;** *PP* **caído**

14 **cocer** : *IND* **cuezo, cueces, cuece,** cocemos, cocéis, **cuecen;** *SUBJ* **cueza, cuezas, cueza,** cozamos, cozáis, **cuezan;** *IMPER* **cuece**

15 **coger** : *IND* **cojo,** coges, coge, cogemos, cogéis, cogen; *SUBJ* **coja, cojas, coja, cojamos, cojáis, cojan**

16 **colgar** : *IND* **cuelgo, cuelgas, cuelga,** colgamos, colgáis, **cuelgan;** *SUBJ* **cuelgue, cuelgues, cuelgue,** colguemos, colguéis, **cuelguen;** *PRET* **colgué,** colgaste, colgó, colgamos, colgasteis, colgaron; *IMPER* **cuelga**

17 **concernir** *(defective verb; used only in the third person singular and plural of the present indicative, present subjunctive, and imperfect subjunctive) see* 25 **discernir**

18 **conocer** : *IND* **conozco,** conoces, conoce, conocemos, conocéis, conocen; *SUBJ* **conozca, conozcas, conozca, conozcamos, conozcáis, conozcan**

19 **contar** : *IND* **cuento, cuentas, cuenta,** contamos, contáis, **cuentan;** *SUBJ* **cuente, cuentes, cuente,** contemos, contéis, **cuenten;** *IMPER* **cuenta**

20 **creer** : *PRET* creí, **creíste, creyó, creímos, creísteis, creyeron;** *PRP* **creyendo;** *PP* **creído**

21 **cruzar** : *SUBJ* **cruce, cruces, cruce, crucemos, crucéis, crucen;** *PRET* **crucé,** cruzaste, cruzó, cruzamos, cruzasteis, cruzaron

22 **dar** : *IND* **doy,** das, da, damos, **dais,** dan; *SUBJ* **dé,** des, **dé,** demos, **deis,** den; *PRET* **di, diste, dio, dimos, disteis, dieron**

23 **decir** : *IND* **digo, dices, dice,** decimos, decís, **dicen;** *SUBJ* **diga, digas, diga, digamos, digáis, digan;** *PRET* **dije, dijiste, dijo, dijimos, dijisteis, dijeron;** *FUT* **diré, dirás, dirá, diremos, diréis, dirán;** *IMPER* **di;** *PRP* **diciendo;** *PP* **dicho**

24 **delinquir** : *IND* **delinco,** delinques, delinque, delinquimos, delinquís, delinquen; *SUBJ* **delinca, delincas, delinca, delincamos, delincáis, delincan**

25 **discernir** : *IND* **discierno, disciernes, discierne,** discernimos, discernís, **disciernen;** *SUBJ* **discierna, disciernas, discierna,** discernamos, discernáis, **disciernan;** *IMPER* **discierne**

26 **distinguir** : *IND* **distingo,** distingues, distingue, distinguimos, distinguís, distinguen; *SUBJ* **distinga, distingas, distinga, distingamos, distingáis, distingan**

27 **dormir** : *IND* **duermo, duermes, duerme,** dormimos, dormís, **duermen;** *SUBJ* **duerma, duermas, duerma,** durmamos, durmáis, **duerman;** *PRET* dormí, dormiste, **durmió,** dormimos, dormisteis, **durmieron;** *IMPER* **duerme;** *PRP* **durmiendo**

28 **elegir** : *IND* **elijo, eliges, elige,** elegimos, elegís, **eligen;** *SUBJ* **elija, elijas, elija, elijamos, elijáis, elijan;** *PRET* elegí, elegiste, **eligió,** elegimos, elegisteis, **eligieron;** *IMPER* **elige;** *PRP* **eligiendo**

29 **empezar** : *IND* **empiezo, empiezas, empieza,** empezamos, empezáis, **empiezan;** *SUBJ* **empiece, empieces, empiece,** empecemos, empecéis, **empiecen;** *PRET* **empecé,** empezaste, empezó, empezamos, empezasteis, empezaron; *IMPER* **empieza**

30 **enraizar** : *IND* **enraízo, enraízas, enraíza,** enraizamos, enraizáis, **enraízan;** *SUBJ* **enraíce, enraíces, enraíce,** enraicemos, enraicéis, **enraícen;** *PRET* **enraicé,** enraizaste, enraizó, enraizamos, enraizasteis, enraizaron; *IMPER* **enraíza**

31 **erguir** : *IND* **irgo** or **yergo, irgues** or **yergues, irgue** or **yergue,** erguimos, erguís, **irguen** or **yerguen;** *SUBJ* **irga** or **yerga, irgas** or **yergas, irga** or **yerga,** irgamos, irgáis, **irgan** or **yergan;** *PRET* erguí, erguiste, **irguió,** erguimos, erguisteis, **irguieron;** *IMPER* **irgue** or **yergue;** *PRP* **irguiendo**

32 **errar** : *IND* **yerro, yerras, yerra,** erramos, erráis, **yerran;** *SUBJ* **yerre, yerres, yerre,** erremos, erréis, **yerren;** *IMPER* **yerra**

33 **escribir** : *PP* **escrito**

34 **estar** : *IND* **estoy, estás, está,** estamos, estáis, **están;** *SUBJ* **esté, estés, esté,** estemos, estéis, **estén;** *PRET* **estuve, estuviste, estuvo, estuvimos, estuvisteis, estuvieron;** *IMPER* **está**

35 **exigir** : *IND* **exijo,** exiges, exige, exigimos, exigís, exigen; *SUBJ* **exija, exijas, exija, exijamos, exijáis, exijan**

36 **forzar** : *IND* **fuerzo, fuerzas, fuerza,** forzamos, forzáis, **fuerzan;** *SUBJ* **fuerce, fuerces, fuerce,** forcemos, forcéis, **fuercen;** *PRET* **forcé,** forzaste, forzó, forzamos, forzasteis, forzaron; *IMPER* **fuerza**

37 **freír** : *IND* **frío, fríes, fríe, freímos,** freís, **fríen;** *SUBJ* **fría, frías, fría, friamos, friáis, frían;** *PRET* freí, **freíste, frió, freímos, freísteis, frieron;** *IMPER* **fríe;** *PRP* **friendo;** *PP* **frito**

38 **gruñir** : *PRET* gruñí, gruñiste, **gruñó,** gruñimos, gruñisteis, **gruñeron;** *PRP* **gruñendo**

39 **haber** : *IND* **he, has, ha, hemos,** habéis, **han;** *SUBJ* **haya, hayas, haya, hayamos, hayáis, hayan;** *PRET* **hube, hubiste, hubo, hubimos, hubisteis, hubieron;** *FUT* **habré, habrás, habrá, habremos, habréis, habrán;** *IMPER* **he**

40 **hacer** : *IND* **hago,** haces, hace, hacemos, hacéis, hacen; *SUBJ* **haga, hagas, haga, hagamos, hagáis, hagan;** *PRET* **hice, hiciste, hizo, hicimos, hicisteis, hicieron;** *FUT* **haré, harás, hará, haremos, haréis, harán;** *IMPER* **haz;** *PP* **hecho**

41 **huir** : *IND* **huyo, huyes, huye,** huimos, huís, **huyen;** *SUBJ* **huya, huyas, huya, huyamos, huyáis, huyan;** *PRET* huí, huiste, **huyó,** huimos, huisteis, **huyeron;** *IMPER* **huye;** *PRP* **huyendo**

42 **imprimir** : *PP* **impreso**

43 **ir** : *IND* **voy, vas, va, vamos, vais, van;** *SUBJ* **vaya, vayas, vaya, vayamos, vayáis, vayan;** *PRET* **fui, fuiste, fue, fuimos, fuisteis, fueron;** *IMPF* **iba, ibas, iba, íbamos, ibais, iban;** *IMPER* **ve;** *PRP* **yendo;** *PP* **ido**

44 **jugar** : *IND* **juego, juegas, juega,** jugamos, jugáis, **juegan;** *SUBJ* **juegue, juegues, juegue,** juguemos, juguéis, **jueguen;** *PRET* **jugué,** jugaste, jugó, jugamos, jugasteis, jugaron; *IMPER* **juega**

45 **lucir** : *IND* **luzco,** luces, luce, lucimos, lucís, lucen; *SUBJ* **luzca, luzcas, luzca, luzcamos, luzcáis, luzcan**

46 **morir** : *IND* **muero, mueres, muere,** morimos, morís, **mueren;** *SUBJ* **muera, mueras, muera,** muramos, muráis, **mueran;** *PRET* morí, moriste, **murió,** morimos, moristeis, **murieron;** *IMPER* **muere;** *PRP* **muriendo;** *PP* **muerto**

47 **mover** : *IND* **muevo, mueves, mueve,** movemos, movéis, **mueven;** *SUBJ* **mueva, muevas, mueva,** movamos, mováis, **muevan;** *IMPER* **mueve**

48 **nacer** : *IND* **nazco,** naces, nace, nacemos, nacéis, nacen; *SUBJ* **nazca, nazcas, nazca, nazcamos, nazcáis, nazcan**

49 **negar** : *IND* **niego, niegas, niega,** negamos, negáis, **niegan;** *SUBJ* **niegue, niegues, niegue,** neguemos, neguéis, **nieguen;** *PRET* **negué,** negaste, negó, negamos, negasteis, negaron; *IMPER* **niega**

50 **oír** : *IND* **oigo, oyes, oye,** oímos, oís, **oyen;** *SUBJ* **oiga, oigas, oiga, oigamos, oigáis, oigan;** *PRET* oí, **oíste, oyó,** oímos, oísteis, **oyeron;** *IMPER* **oye;** *PRP* **oyendo;** *PP* **oído**

51 **oler** : *IND* **huelo, hueles, huele,** olemos, oléis, **huelen;** *SUBJ* **huela, huelas, huela,** olamos, oláis, **huelan;** *IMPER* **huele**

52 **pagar** : *SUBJ* **pague, pagues, pague, paguemos, paguéis, paguen;** *PRET* **pagué,** pagaste, pagó, pagamos, pagasteis, pagaron

53 **parecer** : *IND* **parezco,** pareces, parece, parecemos, parecéis, parecen; *SUBJ* **parezca, parezcas, parezca, parezcamos, parezcáis, parezcan**

54 **pedir** : *IND* **pido, pides, pide,** pedimos, pedís, **piden;** *SUBJ* **pida, pidas, pida, pidamos, pidáis, pidan;** *PRET* pedí, pediste, **pidió,** pedimos, pedisteis, **pidieron;** *IMPER* **pide;** *PRP* **pidiendo**

55 **pensar** : *IND* **pienso, piensas, piensa,** pensamos, pensáis, **piensan;** *SUBJ* **piense, pienses, piense,** pensemos, penséis, **piensen;** *IMPER* **piensa**

56 **perder** : *IND* **pierdo, pierdes, pierde,** perdemos, perdéis, **pierden;** *SUBJ* **pierda, pierdas, pierda,** perdamos, perdáis, **pierdan;** *IMPER* **pierde**

57 **placer** : *IND* **plazco,** places, place, placemos, placéis, placen; *SUBJ* **plazca, plazcas, plazca, plazcamos, plazcáis, plazcan;** *PRET* plací, placiste, plació *or* **plugo,** placimos, placisteis, placieron *or* **pluguieron**

58 **poder** : *IND* **puedo, puedes, puede,** podemos, podéis, **pueden;** *SUBJ* **pueda, puedas, pueda,** podamos, podáis, **puedan;** *PRET* **pude, pudiste, pudo, pudimos, pudisteis, pudieron;** *FUT* **podré, podrás, podrá, podremos, podréis, podrán;** *IMPER* **puede;** *PRP* **pudiendo**

59 **podrir** *or* **pudrir** : *PP* **podrido** *(all other forms based on* pudrir*)*

60 **poner** : *IND* **pongo,** pones, pone, ponemos, ponéis, ponen; *SUBJ* **ponga, pongas, ponga, pongamos, pongáis, pongan;** *PRET* **puse, pusiste, puso, pusimos, pusisteis, pusieron;** *FUT* **pondré, pondrás, pondrá, pondremos, pondréis, pondrán;** *IMPER* **pon;** *PP* **puesto**

61 **producir** : *IND* **produzco,** produces, produce, producimos, producís, producen; *SUBJ* **produzca, produzcas, produzca, produzcamos, produzcáis, produzcan;** *PRET* **produje, produjiste, produjo, produjimos, produjisteis, produjeron**

62 **prohibir** : *IND* **prohíbo, prohíbes, prohíbe,** prohibimos, prohibís, **prohíben;** *SUBJ* **prohíba, prohíbas, prohíba,** prohibamos, prohibáis, **prohíban;** *IMPER* **prohíbe**

63 **proveer** : *PRET* proveí, **proveíste, proveyó, proveímos, proveísteis, proveyeron;** *PRP* **proveyendo;** *PP* **provisto**

64 **querer** : *IND* **quiero, quieres, quiere,** queremos, queréis, **quieren;** *SUBJ* **quiera, quieras, quiera,** queramos, queráis, **quieran;** *PRET* **quise, quisiste, quiso, quisimos, quisisteis, quisieron;** *FUT* **querré, querrás, querrá, querremos, querréis, querrán;** *IMPER* **quiere**

65 **raer** : *IND* **rao** *or* **raigo** *or* **rayo,** raes, rae, raemos, raéis, raen; *SUBJ* **raiga** *or* **raya, raigas** *or* **rayas, raiga** *or* **raya, raigamos** *or* **rayamos, raigáis** *or* **rayáis, raigan** *or* **rayan;** *PRET* raí, raíste, rayó, raímos, raísteis, rayeron; *PRP* **rayendo;** *PP* **raído**

66 **reír** : *IND* **río, ríes, ríe, reímos,** reís, **ríen;** *SUBJ* **ría, rías, ría, riamos, riáis, rían;** *PRET* reí, reíste, rió, reímos, reísteis, rieron; *IMPER* **ríe;** *PRP* **riendo;** *PP* **reído**

67 **reñir** : *IND* **riño, riñes, riñe,** reñimos, reñís, **riñen;** *SUBJ* **riña, riñas, riña, riñamos, riñáis, riñan;** *PRET* reñí, reñiste, **riñó,** reñimos, reñisteis, **riñeron;** *PRP* **riñendo**

68 **reunir** : *IND* **reúno, reúnes, reúne,** reunimos, reunís, **reúnen;** *SUBJ* **reúna, reúnas, reúna,** reunamos, reunáis, **reúnan;** *IMPER* **reúne**

69 **roer** : *IND* **roo** *or* **roigo** *or* **royo,** roes, roe, roemos, roéis, roen; *SUBJ* **roa** *or* **roiga** *or* **roya,** roas *or* **roigas** *or* **royas, roa** *or* **roiga** *or* **roya,** roamos *or* **roigamos** *or* **royamos,** roáis *or* **roigáis** *or* **royáis,** roan *or* **roigan** *or* **royan;** *PRET* roí, roíste, royó, roímos, roísteis, royeron; *PRP* **royendo;** *PP* **roído**

70 **romper** : *PP* **roto**

71 **saber** : *IND* **sé,** sabes, sabe, sabemos, sabéis, saben; *SUBJ* **sepa, sepas, sepa, sepamos, sepáis, sepan;** *PRET* **supe, supiste, supo, supimos, supisteis, supieron;** *FUT* **sabré, sabrás, sabrá, sabremos, sabréis, sabrán**

72 **sacar** : *SUBJ* **saque, saques, saque, saquemos, saquéis, saquen;** *PRET* **saqué,** sacaste, sacó, sacamos, sacasteis, sacaron

73 **salir** : *IND* **salgo**, sales, sale, salimos, salís, salen; *SUBJ* **salga, salgas, salga, salgamos, salgáis, salgan**; *FUT* **saldré, saldrás, saldrá, saldremos, saldréis, saldrán**; *IMPER* **sal**

74 **satisfacer** : *IND* **satisfago**, satisfaces, satisface, satisfacemos, satisfacéis, satisfacen; *SUBJ* **satisfaga, satisfagas, satisfaga, satisfagamos, satisfagáis, satisfagan**; *PRET* **satisfice, satisficiste, satisfizo, satisficimos, satificisteis, satisficieron**; *FUT* **satisfaré, satisfarás, satisfará, satisfaremos, satisfaréis, satisfarán**; *IMPER* **satisfaz** or **satisface**; *PP* **satisfecho**

75 **seguir** : *IND* **sigo, sigues, sigue**, seguimos, seguís, **siguen**; *SUBJ* **siga, sigas, siga, sigamos, sigáis, sigan**; *PRET* seguí, seguiste, **siguió**, seguimos, seguisteis, **siguieron**; *IMPER* **sigue**; *PRP* **siguiendo**

76 **sentir** : *IND* **siento, sientes, siente**, sentimos, sentís, **sienten**; *SUBJ* **sienta, sientas, sienta**, sintamos, **sintáis, sientan**; *PRET* sentí, sentiste, **sintió**, sentimos, sentisteis, **sintieron**; *IMPER* **siente**; *PRP* **sintiendo**

77 **ser** : *IND* **soy, eres, es, somos, sois, son**; *SUBJ* **sea, seas, sea, seamos, seáis, sean**; *PRET* **fui, fuiste, fue, fuimos, fuisteis, fueron**; *IMPF* **era, eras, era, éramos, erais, eran**; *IMPER* **sé**; *PRP* **siendo**; *PP* **sido**

78 **soler** *(defective verb; used only in the present, preterit, and imperfect indicative, and the present and imperfect subjunctive)* see 47 **mover**

79 **tañer** : *PRET* **tañí**, tañiste, **tañó**, tañimos, tañisteis, **tañeron**; *PRP* **tañendo**

80 **tener** : *IND* **tengo, tienes, tiene**, tenemos, tenéis, **tienen**; *SUBJ* **tenga, tengas, tenga, tengamos, tengáis, tengan**; *PRET* **tuve, tuviste, tuvo, tuvimos, tuvisteis, tuvieron**; *FUT* **tendré, tendrás, tendrá, tendremos, tendréis, tendrán**; *IMPER* **ten**

81 **traer** : *IND* **traigo**, traes, trae, traemos, traéis, traen; *SUBJ* **traiga, traigas, traiga, traigamos, traigáis, traigan**; *PRET* **traje, trajiste, trajo, trajimos, trajisteis, trajeron**; *PRP* **trayendo**; *PP* **traído**

82 **trocar** : *IND* **trueco, truecas, trueca**, trocamos, trocáis, **truecan**; *SUBJ* **trueque, trueques, trueque**, troquemos, **troquéis, truequen**; *PRET* **troqué**, trocaste, trocó, trocamos, trocasteis, trocaron; *IMPER* **trueca**

83 **uncir** : *IND* **unzo**, unces, unce, uncimos, uncís, uncen; *SUBJ* **unza, unzas, unza, unzamos, unzáis, unzan**

84 **valer** : *IND* **valgo**, vales, vale, valemos, valéis, valen; *SUBJ* **valga, valgas, valga, valgamos, valgáis, valgan**; *FUT* **valdré, valdrás, valdrá, valdremos, valdréis, valdrán**

85 **variar** : *IND* **varío, varías, varía**, variamos, variáis, **varían**; *SUBJ* **varíe, varíes, varíe**, variemos, variéis, **varíen**; *IMPER* **varía**

86 **vencer** : *IND* **venzo**, vences, vence, vencemos, vencéis, vencen; *SUBJ* **venza, venzas, venza, venzamos, venzáis, venzan**

87 **venir** : *IND* **vengo, vienes, viene**, venimos, venís, **vienen**; *SUBJ* **venga, vengas, venga, vengamos, vengáis, vengan**; *PRET* **vine, viniste, vino, vinimos, vinisteis, vinieron**; *FUT* **vendré, vendrás, vendrá, vendremos, vendréis, vendrán**; *IMPER* **ven**; *PRP* **viniendo**

88 **ver** : *IND* **veo, ves, ve**, vemos, veis, ven; *PRET* **vi, viste, vio, vimos, visteis, vieron**; *IMPER* **ve**; *PRP* **viendo**; *PP* **visto**

89 **volver** : *IND* **vuelvo, vuelves, vuelve**, volvemos, volvéis, **vuelven**; *SUBJ* **vuelva, vuelvas, vuelva**, volvamos, volváis, **vuelvan**; *IMPER* **vuelve**; *PP* **vuelto**

90 **yacer** : *IND* **yazco** or **yazgo** or **yago**, yaces, yace, yacemos, yacéis, yacen; *SUBJ* **yazca** or **yazga** or **yaga, yazcas** or **yazgas** or **yagas, yazca** or **yazga** or **yaga, yazcamos** or **yazgamos** or **yagamos, yazcáis** or **yazgáis** or **yagáis, yazcan** or **yazgan** or **yagan**; *IMPER* **yace** or **yaz**

Irregular English Verbs

INFINITIVE	PAST	PAST PARTICIPLE
arise	arose	arisen
awake	awoke	awoken *or* awaked
be	was, were	been
bear	bore	borne
beat	beat	beaten *or* beat
become	became	become
befall	befell	befallen
begin	began	begun
behold	beheld	beheld
bend	bent	bent
beseech	beseeched *or* besought	beseeched *or* besought
beset	beset	beset
bet	bet	bet
bid	bade *or* bid	bidden *or* bid
bind	bound	bound
bite	bit	bitten
bleed	bled	bled
blow	blew	blown
break	broke	broken
breed	bred	bred
bring	brought	brought
build	built	built
burn	burned *or* burnt	burned *or* burnt
burst	burst	burst
buy	bought	bought
can	could	—
cast	cast	cast
catch	caught	caught
choose	chose	chosen
cling	clung	clung
come	came	come
cost	cost	cost
creep	crept	crept
cut	cut	cut
deal	dealt	dealt
dig	dug	dug
do	did	done
draw	drew	drawn
dream	dreamed *or* dreamt	dreamed *or* dreamt
drink	drank	drunk *or* drank
drive	drove	driven
dwell	dwelled *or* dwelt	dwelled *or* dwelt
eat	ate	eaten
fall	fell	fallen
feed	fed	fed
feel	felt	felt
fight	fought	fought
find	found	found
flee	fled	fled
fling	flung	flung
fly	flew	flown

Irregular English Verbs

INFINITIVE	PAST	PAST PARTICIPLE
forbid	forbade	forbidden
forecast	forecast	forecast
forego	forewent	foregone
foresee	foresaw	foreseen
foretell	foretold	foretold
forget	forgot	forgotten *or* forgot
forgive	forgave	forgiven
forsake	forsook	forsaken
freeze	froze	frozen
get	got	got *or* gotten
give	gave	given
go	went	gone
grind	ground	ground
grow	grew	grown
hang	hung	hung
have	had	had
hear	heard	heard
hide	hid	hidden *or* hid
hit	hit	hit
hold	held	held
hurt	hurt	hurt
keep	kept	kept
kneel	knelt *or* kneeled	knelt *or* kneeled
know	knew	known
lay	laid	laid
lead	led	led
lean	leaned	leaned
leap	leaped *or* leapt	leaped *or* leapt
learn	learned	learned
leave	left	left
lend	lent	lent
let	let	let
lie	lay	lain
light	lit *or* lighted	lit *or* lighted
lose	lost	lost
make	made	made
may	might	—
mean	meant	meant
meet	met	met
mow	mowed	mowed *or* mown
pay	paid	paid
put	put	put
quit	quit	quit
read	read	read
rend	rent	rent
rid	rid	rid
ride	rode	ridden
ring	rang	rung
rise	rose	risen
run	ran	run
saw	sawed	sawed *or* sawn
say	said	said
see	saw	seen
seek	sought	sought
sell	sold	sold

INFINITIVE	PAST	PAST PARTICIPLE
send	sent	sent
set	set	set
shake	shook	shaken
shall	should	—
shear	sheared	sheared *or* shorn
shed	shed	shed
shine	shone *or* shined	shone *or* shined
shoot	shot	shot
show	showed	shown *or* showed
shrink	shrank *or* shrunk	shrunk *or* shrunken
shut	shut	shut
sing	sang *or* sung	sung
sink	sank *or* sunk	sunk
sit	sat	sat
slay	slew	slain
sleep	slept	slept
slide	slid	slid
sling	slung	slung
smell	smelled *or* smelt	smelled *or* smelt
sow	sowed	sown *or* sowed
speak	spoke	spoken
speed	sped *or* speeded	sped *or* speeded
spell	spelled	spelled
spend	spent	spent
spill	spilled	spilled
spin	spun	spun
spit	spit *or* spat	spit *or* spat
split	split	split
spoil	spoiled	spoiled
spread	spread	spread
spring	sprang *or* sprung	sprung
stand	stood	stood
steal	stole	stolen
stick	stuck	stuck
sting	stung	stung
stink	stank *or* stunk	stunk
stride	strode	stridden
strike	struck	struck
swear	swore	sworn
sweep	swept	swept
swell	swelled	swelled *or* swollen
swim	swam	swum
swing	swung	swung
take	took	taken
teach	taught	taught
tear	tore	torn
tell	told	told
think	thought	thought
throw	threw	thrown
thrust	thrust	thrust
tread	trod	trodden *or* trod
wake	woke	woken *or* waked
waylay	waylaid	waylaid
wear	wore	worn
weave	wove *or* weaved	woven *or* weaved

Irregular English Verbs

INFINITIVE	PAST	PAST PARTICIPLE
wed	wedded	wedded
weep	wept	wept
will	would	—
win	won	won
wind	wound	wound
withdraw	withdrew	withdrawn
withhold	withheld	withheld
withstand	withstood	withstood
wring	wrung	wrung
write	wrote	written

Abbreviations in this Work

adj	adjective	*nmf*	masculine or feminine noun
adv	adverb		
adv	adverbial phrase	*nmfpl*	plural noun invariable for gender
algn	alguien (someone)		
art	article	*nmfs & pl*	noun invariable for both gender and number
Brit	Great Britain		
conj	conjunction	*nmpl*	masculine plural noun
conj phr	conjunctive phrase	*nms & pl*	invariable singular or plural masculine noun
esp	especially		
etc	et cetera	*npl*	plural noun
f	feminine	*ns & pl*	noun invariable for plural
fam	familiar or colloquial		
fpl	feminine plural	*pl*	plural
interj	interjection	*pp*	past participle
Lat	Latin America	*prep*	preposition
m	masculine	*prep phr*	prepositional phrase
mf	masculine or feminine	*pron*	pronoun
mpl	masculine plural	*s.o.*	someone
n	noun	*sth*	something
nf	feminine noun	*usu*	usually
nfpl	feminine plural noun	*v*	verb
nfs & pl	invariable singular or plural feminine noun	*v aux*	auxiliary verb
		vi	intransitive verb
nm	masculine noun	*v impers*	impersonal verb
		vr	reflexive verb
		vt	transitive verb

Spanish-English
Dictionary

A

a¹ *nf* : a, first letter of the Spanish alphabet
a² *prep* **1** : to **2** ~ **las dos** : at two o'clock **3 al día siguiente** : (on) the following day **4** ~ **pie** : on foot **5 de lunes** ~ **viernes** : from Monday until Friday **6 tres veces** ~ **la semana** : three times per week **7** ~ **la** : in the manner of, like
abadía *nf* : abbey
abajo *adv* **1** : down, below, downstairs **2** ~ **de** *Lat* : under, beneath **3 de** ~ : (at the) bottom **4 hacia** ~ : downwards
abalanzarse {21} *vr* : hurl oneself, rush
abandonar *vt* **1** : abandon, leave **2** RENUNCIAR A : give up — **abandonarse** *vr* **1** : neglect oneself **2** ~ **a** : give oneself over to — **abandonado, -da** *adj* **1** : abandoned, deserted **2** DESCUIDADO : neglected **3** DESALIÑADO : slovenly — **abandono** *nm* **1** : abandonment, neglect **2 por** ~ : by default
abanico *nm* : fan — **abanicar** {72} *vt* : fan
abaratar *vt* : lower the price of — **abaratarse** *vr* : become cheaper
abarcar {72} *vt* **1** : cover, embrace **2** *Lat* : monopolize
abarrotar *vt* : pack, cram — **abarrotes** *nmpl* *Lat* **1** : groceries **2 tienda de** ~ : grocery store
abastecer {53} *vt* : supply, stock — **abastecimiento** *nm* : supply, provisions — **abasto** *nm* **1** : supply **2 no dar** ~ **a** : be unable to cope with
abatir *vt* **1** : knock down, shoot down **2** DEPRIMIR : depress — **abatirse** *vr* **1** : get depressed **2** ~ **sobre** : swoop down on — **abatido, -da** *adj* : dejected, depressed — **abatimiento** *nm* : depression, dejection
abdicar {72} *v* : abdicate — **abdicación** *nf, pl* **-ciones** : abdication
abdomen *nm, pl* **-dómenes** : abdomen — **abdominal** *adj* : abdominal
abecé *nm* : ABC — **abecedario** *nm* : alphabet
abedul *nm* : birch
abeja *nf* : bee — **abejorro** *nm* : bumblebee
aberración *nf, pl* **-ciones** : aberration
abertura *nf* : opening
abeto *nm* : fir (tree)
abierto, -ta *adj* : open
abigarrado, -da *adj* : multicolored
abismo *nm* : abyss, chasm — **abismal** *adj* : vast, enormous
abjurar *vi* ~ **de** : abjure

ablandar *vt* : soften (up) — **ablandarse** *vr* : soften
abnegarse {49} *vr* : deny oneself — **abnegado, -da** *adj* : self-sacrificing — **abnegación** *nf, pl* **-ciones** : self-denial
abochornar *vt* : embarrass — **abochornarse** *vr* : get embarrassed
abofetear *vt* : slap
abogado, -da *n* : lawyer — **abogacía** *nf* : legal profession — **abogar** {52} *vi* ~ **por** : plead for, defend
abolengo *nm* : lineage
abolir {1} *vt* : abolish — **abolición** *nf, pl* **-ciones** : abolition
abollar *vt* : dent — **abolladura** *nf* : dent
abominar *vt* : abominate — **abominable** *adj* : abominable — **abominación** *nf, pl* **-ciones** : abomination
abonar *vt* **1** : pay (a bill, etc.) **2** : fertilize (the soil) — **abonarse** *vr* : subscribe — **abonado, -da** *n* : subscriber — **abono** *nm* **1** : payment, installment **2** FERTILIZANTE : fertilizer **3** : season ticket (to the theater, etc.)
abordar *vt* **1** : tackle (a problem) **2** : accost, approach (a person) **3** *Lat* : board — **abordaje** *nm* : boarding
aborigen *nmf, pl* **-rígenes** : aborigine — ~ *adj* : aboriginal, native
aborrecer {53} *vt* : abhor, detest — **aborrecible** *adj* : hateful — **aborrecimiento** *nm* : loathing
abortar *vi* : have a miscarriage — *vt* : abort — **aborto** *nm* : abortion, miscarriage
abotonar *vt* : button — **abotonarse** *vr* : button up
abovedado, -da *adj* : vaulted
abrasar *vt* : burn, scorch — **abrasarse** *vr* : burn up — **abrasador, -dora** *adj* : burning
abrasivo, -va *adj* : abrasive — **abrasivo** *nm* : abrasive
abrazar {21} *vt* : hug, embrace — **abrazarse** *vr* : embrace — **abrazadera** *nf* : clamp — **abrazo** *nm* : hug, embrace
abrebotellas *nms & pl* : bottle opener — **abrelatas** *nms & pl* : can opener
abrevadero *nm* : watering trough
abreviar *vt* **1** : shorten, abridge **2** : abbreviate (a word) — **abreviación** *nf, pl* **-ciones** : shortening — **abreviatura** *nf* : abbreviation
abridor *nm* : bottle opener, can opener
abrigar {52} *vt* **1** : wrap up (in clothing) **2** ALBERGAR : cherish, harbor — **abrigarse** *vr*

abril   **2**

: dress warmly — **abrigado, -da** *adj* **1**
: sheltered **2** : warm, wrapped up (of persons) — **abrigo** *nm* **1** : coat, overcoat **2**
REFUGIO : shelter, refuge
abril *nm* : April
abrillantar *vt* : polish, shine
abrir {2} *vt* **1** : open **2** : unlock, undo — *vi*
: open up — **abrirse** *vr* **1** : open up **2**
: clear up (of weather)
abrochar *vt* : button, fasten — **abrocharse**
vr : fasten, do up
abrogar {52} *vt* : annul, repeal
abrumar *vt* : overwhelm — **abrumador,**
-dora *adj* : overwhelming, oppressive
abrupto, -ta *adj* **1** ESCARPADO : steep **2**
ÁSPERO : rugged, harsh **3** REPENTINO
: abrupt
absceso *nm* : abscess
absolución *nf, pl* **-ciones 1** : absolution **2**
: acquittal (in law)
absoluto, -ta *adj* **1** : absolute, unconditional
2 en absoluto : not at all — **absoluta-**
mente *adv* : absolutely
absolver {89} *vt* **1** : absolve **2** : acquit (in
law)
absorber *vt* **1** : absorb **2** : take up (time, energy, etc.) — **absorbente** *adj* **1** : absorbent
2 INTERESANTE : absorbing — **absorción**
nf, pl **-ciones** : absorption — **absorto, -ta**
adj : absorbed, engrossed
abstemio, -mia *adj* : abstemious — ∼ *n*
: teetotaler
abstenerse {80} *vr* : abstain, refrain — **ab-**
stención *nf, pl* **-ciones** : abstention — **ab-**
stinencia *nf* : abstinence
abstracción *nf, pl* **-ciones** : abstraction —
abstracto, -ta *adj* : abstract — **abstraer**
{81} *vt* : abstract — **abstraerse** *vr* : lose
oneself in thought — **abstraído, -da** *adj*
: preoccupied
absurdo, -da *adj* : absurd, ridiculous — **ab-**
surdo *nm* : absurdity
abuchear *vt* : boo, jeer — **abucheo** *nm*
: booing
abuelo, -la *n* **1** : grandfather, grandmother **2**
abuelos *nmpl* : grandparents
abulia *nf* : apathy, lethargy
abultar *vi* : bulge, be bulky — *vt* : enlarge,
expand — **abultado, -da** *adj* : bulky
abundar *vi* : abound, be plentiful — **abun-**
dancia *nf* : abundance — **abundante** *adj*
: abundant
aburrir *vt* : bore — **aburrirse** *vr* : get bored
— **aburrido, -da** *adj* **1** : bored **2** TEDIOSO
: boring — **aburrimiento** *nm* : boredom
abusar *vi* **1** : go too far **2** ∼ **de** : abuse —
abusivo, -va *adj* : outrageous, excessive —
abuso *nm* : abuse
abyecto, -ta *adj* : abject, wretched

acá *adv* : here, over here
acabar *vi* **1** : finish, end **2** ∼ **de** : have just
(done something) **3** ∼ **con** : put an end to
4 ∼ **por** : end up (doing sth) — *vt* : finish —
acabarse *vr* : come to an end — **acabado,**
-da *adj* **1** : finished, perfect **2** AGOTADO
: old, worn-out — **acabado** *nm* : finish
academia *nf* : academy — **académico, -ca**
adj : academic
acaecer {53} *vi* : happen, occur
acallar *vt* : quiet, silence
acalorar *vt* : stir up, excite — **acalorarse** *vr*
: get worked up — **acalorado, -da** *adj*
: emotional, heated
acampar *vi* : camp — **acampada** *nf* **ir de** ∼
: go camping
acanalado, -da *adj* **1** : grooved **2** : corrugated (of iron, etc.)
acantilado *nm* : cliff
acaparar *vt* **1** : hoard **2** MONOPOLIZAR
: monopolize
acápite *nm Lat* : paragraph
acariciar *vt* **1** : caress **2** : cherish (hopes,
ideas, etc.)
ácaro *nm* : mite
acarrear *vt* **1** : haul, carry **2** OCASIONAR
: give rise to — **acarreo** *nm* : transport
acaso *adv* **1** : perhaps, maybe **2 por si** ∼
: just in case
acatar *vt* : comply with, respect —
acatamiento *nm* : compliance, respect
acatarrarse *vr* : catch a cold
acaudalado, -da *adj* : wealthy, rich
acaudillar *vt* : lead
acceder *vi* **1** : agree **2** ∼ **a** : gain access to,
enter
acceso *nm* **1** : access **2** ENTRADA : entrance
3 : attack, bout (of an illness) — **accesible**
adj : accessible
accesorio *nm* : accessory — **accesorio, -ria**
adj : incidental
accidentado, -da *adj* **1** : eventful, turbulent
2 : rough, uneven (of land, etc.) **3** HERIDO
: injured — ∼ *n* : accident victim
accidental *adj* : accidental — **accidentarse**
vr : have an accident — **accidente** *nm* **1**
: accident **2** : unevenness (of land)
acción *nf, pl* **-ciones 1** : action **2** ACTO
: act, deed **3** : share, stock (in finance) —
accionar *vt* : activate — *vi* : gesticulate —
accionista *nmf* : stockholder
acebo *nm* : holly
acechar *vt* : watch, stalk — **acecho** *nm*
estar al ∼ **por** : be on the lookout for
aceite *nm* : oil — **aceitar** *vt* : oil — **aceitera**
nf **1** : oilcan **2** : cruet (in cookery) **3** *Lat*
: oil refinery — **aceitoso, -sa** *adj* : oily
aceituna *nf* : olive
acelerar *v* : accelerate — **acelerarse** *vr*

: hurry up — **aceleración** *nf, pl* -**ciones** : acceleration — **acelerador** *nm* : accelerator
acelga *nf* : (Swiss) chard
acentuar {3} *vt* **1** : accent **2** ENFATIZAR : emphasize, stress — **acentuarse** *vr* : stand out — **acento** *nm* **1** : accent **2** ÉNFASIS : stress, emphasis
acepción *nf, pl* -**ciones** : sense, meaning
aceptar *vt* : accept — **aceptable** *adj* : acceptable — **aceptación** *nf, pl* -**ciones** **1** : acceptance **2** ÉXITO : success
acequia *nf* : irrigation ditch
acera *nf* : sidewalk
acerbo, -ba *adj* : harsh, caustic
acerca *prep* ~ **de** : about, concerning
acercar {72} *vt* : bring near or closer — **acercarse** *vr* : approach, draw near
acero *nm* **1** : steel **2** ~ **inoxidable** : stainless steel
acérrimo, -ma *adj* **1** : staunch, steadfast **2** : bitter (of an enemy)
acertar {55} *vt* : guess correctly — *vi* **1** ATINAR : be accurate **2** ~ **a** : manage to — **acertado, -da** *adj* : correct, accurate
acertijo *nm* : riddle
acervo *nm* : heritage
acetona *nf* : acetone, nail-polish remover
achacar {72} *vt* : attribute, impute
achacoso, -sa *adj* : sickly
achaparrado, -da *adj* : squat, stocky
achaque *nm* : aches and pains
achatar *vt* : flatten
achicar {72} *vt* **1** : make smaller **2** ACOBARDAR : intimidate **3** : bail out (water) — **achicarse** *vr* : become intimidated
achicharrar *vt* : scorch, burn to a crisp
achicoria *nf* : chicory
aciago, -ga *adj* : fateful, unlucky
acicalar *vt* : dress up, adorn — **acicalarse** *vr* : get dressed up
acicate *nm* **1** : spur **2** INCENTIVO : incentive
ácido, -da *adj* : acid, sour — **acidez** *nf, pl* -**deces** : acidity — **ácido** *nm* : acid
acierto *nm* **1** : correct answer **2** HABILIDAD : skill, sound judgment
aclamar *vt* : acclaim — **aclamación** *nf, pl* -**ciones** : acclaim, applause
aclarar *vt* **1** CLARIFICAR : clarify, explain **2** : rinse (clothing) **3** ~ **la voz** : clear one's throat — *vi* : clear up — **aclararse** *vr* : become clear — **aclaración** *nf, pl* -**ciones** : explanation — **aclaratorio, -ria** *adj* : explanatory
aclimatar *vt* : acclimatize — **aclimatarse** *vr* ~ **a** : get used to — **aclimatación** *nf, pl* -**ciones** : acclimatization
acné *nm* : acne
acobardar *vt* : intimidate — **acobardarse** *vr* : become frightened

acodarse *vr* ~ **en** : lean (one's elbows) on
acoger {15} *vt* **1** REFUGIAR : shelter **2** RECIBIR : receive, welcome — **acogerse** *vr* **1** : take refuge **2** ~ **a** : resort to — **acogedor, -dora** *adj* : cozy, welcoming — **acogida** *nf* **1** : welcome **2** REFUGIO : refuge
acolchar *vt* : pad
acólito *nm* MONAGUILLO : altar boy
acometer *vt* **1** : attack **2** EMPRENDER : undertake — *vi* ~ **contra** : rush against — **acometida** *nf* : attack, assault
acomodar *vt* **1** ADAPTAR : adjust **2** COLOCAR : put, make a place for — **acomodarse** *vr* **1** : settle in **2** ~ **a** : adapt to — **acomodado, -da** *adj* : well-to-do — **acomodaticio, -cia** *adj* : accommodating, obliging — **acomodo** *nm* : job, position
acompañar *vt* **1** : accompany **2** ADJUNTAR : enclose — **acompañamiento** *nm* : accompaniment — **acompañante** *nmf* **1** COMPAÑERO : companion **2** : accompanist (in music)
acompasado, -da *adj* : rhythmic, measured
acondicionar *vt* : fit out, equip — **acondicionado, -da** *adj* : equipped
acongojar *vt* : distress, upset — **acongojarse** *vr* : get upset
aconsejar *vt* : advise — **aconsejable** *adj* : advisable
acontecer {53} *vi* : occur, happen — **acontecimiento** *nm* : event
acopiar *vt* : gather, collect — **acopio** *nm* : collection, stock
acoplar *vt* : couple, connect — **acoplarse** *vr* : fit together — **acoplamiento** *nm* : connection, coupling
acorazado, -da *adj* : armored — **acorazado** *nm* : battleship
acordar {19} *vt* **1** : agree (on) **2** *Lat* : award — **acordarse** *vr* : remember
acorde *adj* **1** : in agreement **2** ~ **con** : in keeping with — ~ *nm* : chord (in music)
acordeón *nm, pl* -**deones** : accordion
acordonar *vt* **1** : cordon off **2** : lace up (shoes)
acorralar *vt* : corner, corral
acortar *vt* : shorten, cut short — **acortarse** *vr* : get shorter
acosar *vt* : hound, harass — **acoso** *nm* : harassment
acostar {19} *vt* : put to bed — **acostarse** *vr* **1** : go to bed **2** TUMBARSE : lie down
acostumbrar *vt* : accustom — *vi* ~ **a** : be in the habit of — **acostumbrarse** *vr* ~ **a** : get used to — **acostumbrado, -da** *adj* **1** HABITUADO : accustomed **2** HABITUAL : usual
acotar *vt* **1** ANOTAR : annotate **2** DELIMITAR : mark off (land) — **acotación** *nf, pl*

-ciones : marginal note — **acotado, -da** *adj* : enclosed

acre *adj* **1** : pungent **2** MORDAZ : harsh, biting

acrecentar {55} *vt* : increase — **acrecentamiento** *nm* : growth, increase

acreditar *vt* **1** : accredit, authorize **2** PROBAR : prove — **acreditarse** *vr* : prove oneself — **acreditado, -da** *adj* **1** : reputable **2** : accredited (in politics, etc.)

acreedor, -dora *adj* : worthy — ~ *n* : creditor

acribillar *vt* **1** : riddle, pepper **2** ~ **a** : harass with

acrílico *nm* : acrylic

acrimonia *nf or* **acritud** *nf* **1** : pungency **2** RESENTIMIENTO : bitterness, acrimony

acrobacia *nf* : acrobatics — **acróbata** *nmf* : acrobat — **acrobático, -ca** *adj* : acrobatic

acta *nf* **1** : certificate **2** : minutes *pl* (of a meeting)

actitud *nf* **1** : attitude **2** POSTURA : posture, position

activar *vt* **1** : activate **2** ESTIMULAR : stimulate, speed up — **actividad** *nf* : activity — **activo, -va** *adj* : active — **activo** *nm* : assets *pl*

acto *nm* **1** ACCIÓN : act, deed **2** : act (in theater) **3 en el** ~ : right away

actor *nm* : actor — **actriz** *nf, pl* **-trices** : actress

actual *adj* : present, current — **actualidad** *nf* **1** : present time **2** ~**es** *nfpl* : current affairs — **actualizar** {21} *vt* : modernize — **actualización** *nf, pl* **-ciones** : modernization — **actualmente** *adv* : at present, nowadays

actuar {3} *vi* **1** : act, perform **2** ~ **de** : act as

acuarela *nf* : watercolor

acuario *nm* : aquarium

acuartelar *vt* : quarter (troops)

acuático, -ca *adj* : aquatic, water

acuchillar *vt* : knife, stab

acudir *vi* **1** : go, come **2** ~ **a** : be present at, attend **3** ~ **a** : turn to

acueducto *nm* : aqueduct

acuerdo *nm* **1** : agreement **2 de** ~ : OK, all right **3 de** ~ **con** : in accordance with **4 estar de** ~ : agree

acumular *vt* : accumulate — **acumularse** *vr* : pile up — **acumulación** *nf, pl* **-ciones** : accumulation — **acumulador** *nm* : storage battery — **acumulativo, -va** *adj* : cumulative

acunar *vt* : rock

acuñar *vt* **1** : mint (money) **2** : coin (a word)

acuoso, -sa *adj* : watery

acupuntura *nf* : acupuncture

acurrucarse {72} *vr* : curl up, nestle

acusar *vt* **1** : accuse **2** MOSTRAR : reveal, show — **acusación** *nf, pl* **-ciones** : accusation, charge — **acusado, -da** *adj* : prominent, marked — ~ *n* : defendant

acuse *nm* ~ **de recibo** : acknowledgment of receipt

acústica *nf* : acoustics — **acústico, -ca** *adj* : acoustic

adagio *nm* **1** REFRÁN : adage, proverb **2** : adagio (in music)

adaptar *vt* **1** : adapt **2** AJUSTAR : adjust, fit — **adaptarse** *vr* ~ **a** : adapt to — **adaptable** *adj* : adaptable — **adaptación** *nf, pl* **-ciones** : adaptation — **adaptador** *nm* : adapter (in electricity)

adecuar {8} *vt* : adapt, make suitable — **adecuarse** *vr* ~ **a** : be appropriate for — **adecuado, -da** *adj* : suitable, appropriate

adelantar *vt* **1** : advance, move forward **2** PASAR : overtake **3** : pay in advance — **adelantarse** *vr* **1** : move forward, get ahead **2** : be fast (of a clock) — **adelantado, -da** *adj* **1** : advanced, ahead **2** : fast (of a clock) **3 por** ~ : in advance — **adelante** *adv* **1** : ahead, forward **2** ¡~! : come in! **3 más** ~ : later on, further on — **adelanto** *nm* **1** : advance **2** *or* ~ **de dinero** : advance payment

adelgazar {21} *vt* : make thin — *vi* : lose weight

ademán *nm, pl* **-manes 1** GESTO : gesture **2** ~**es** *nmpl* : manners **3 en** ~ **de** : as if to

además *adv* **1** : besides, furthermore **2** ~ **de** : in addition to, as well as

adentro *adv* : inside, within — **adentrarse** *vr* ~ **en** : go into, get inside of

adepto, -ta *n* : follower, supporter

aderezar {21} *vt* : season, dress — **aderezo** *nm* : dressing, seasoning

adeudar *vt* **1** : debit **2** DEBER : owe — **adeudo** *nm* **1** DÉBITO : debit **2** *Lat* : debt

adherirse {76} *vr* **1** : adhere, stick — **adherencia** *nf* : adherence — **adhesión** *nf, pl* **-siones 1** : adhesion **2** APOYO : support — **adhesivo, -va** *adj* : adhesive — **adhesivo** *nm* : adhesive

adición *nf, pl* **-ciones** : addition — **adicional** *adj* : additional

adicto, -ta *adj* : addicted — ~ *n* : addict

adiestrar *vt* : train

adinerado, -da *adj* : wealthy

adiós *nm, pl* **adioses 1** : farewell **2** ¡~! : good-bye!

aditamento *nm* : attachment, accessory

aditivo *nm* : additive

adivinar *vt* **1** : guess **2** PREDECIR : foretell — **adivinación** *nf, pl* **-ciones** : guessing, pre-

diction — **adivinanza** *nf* : riddle — **adivino, -na** *n* : fortune-teller
adjetivo *nm* : adjective
adjudicar {72} *vt* : award — **adjudicarse** *vr* : appropriate — **adjudicación** *nf, pl* **-ciones** : awarding
adjuntar *vt* : enclose (with a letter, etc.) — **adjunto, -ta** *adj* : enclosed, attached — ~ *n* : assistant
administración *nf, pl* **-ciones** 1 : administration 2 : administering (of a drug, etc.) 3 DIRECCIÓN : management — **administrador, -dora** *n* : administrator, manager — **administrar** *vt* 1 : manage, run 2 : administer (a drug, etc.) — **administrativo, -va** *adj* : administrative
admirar *vt* : admire — **admirarse** *vr* : be amazed — **admirable** *adj* : admirable — **admiración** *nf, pl* **-ciones** 1 : admiration 2 ASOMBRO : amazement — **admirador, -dora** *n* : admirer
admitir *vt* 1 : admit 2 ACEPTAR : accept — **admisible** *adj* : admissible, acceptable — **admisión** *nf, pl* **-siones** 1 : admission 2 ACEPTACIÓN : acceptance
ADN *nm* : DNA
adobe *nm* : adobe
adobo *nm* : marinade
adoctrinar *vt* : indoctrinate — **adoctrinamiento** *nm* : indoctrination
adolecer {53} *vi* ~ **de** : suffer from
adolescente *adj & nmf* : adolescent — **adolescencia** *nf* : adolescence
adonde *conj* : where
adónde *adv* : where
adoptar *vt* : adopt (a child), take (a decision) — **adopción** *nf, pl* **-ciones** : adoption — **adoptivo, -va** *adj* : adopted, adoptive
adoquín *nm, pl* **-quines** : cobblestone
adorar *vt* : adore, worship — **adorable** *adj* : adorable — **adoración** *nf, pl* **-ciones** : adoration, worship
adormecer {53} *vt* 1 : make sleepy 2 ENTUMECER : numb — **adormecerse** *vr* : doze off — **adormecimiento** *nm* : drowsiness — **adormilarse** *vr* : doze
adornar *vt* : decorate, adorn — **adorno** *nm* : ornament, decoration
adquirir {4} *vt* 1 : acquire 2 COMPRAR : purchase — **adquisición** *nf, pl* **-ciones** 1 : acquisition 2 COMPRA : purchase
adrede *adv* : intentionally, on purpose
adscribir {33} *vt* : assign, appoint
aduana *nf* : customs (office) — **aduanero, -ra** *adj* : customs — ~ *n* : customs officer
aducir {61} *vt* : cite, put forward
adueñarse *vr* ~ **de** : take possession of
adular *vt* : flatter — **adulación** *nf, pl*
-ciones : adulation, flattery — **adulador, -dora** *adj* : flattering — ~ *n* : flatterer
adulterar *vt* : adulterate
adulterio *nm* : adultery — **adúltero, -ra** *n* : adulterer
adulto, -ta *adj & n* : adult
adusto, -ta *adj* : stern, severe
advenedizo, -za *n* : upstart
advenimiento *nm* : advent, arrival
adverbio *nm* : adverb — **adverbial** *adj* : adverbial
adversario, -ria *n* : adversary, opponent — **adverso, -sa** *adj* : adverse — **adversidad** *nf* : adversity
advertir {76} *vt* 1 AVISAR : warn 2 NOTAR : notice — **advertencia** *nf* : warning
adviento *nm* : Advent
adyacente *adj* : adjacent
aéreo, -rea *adj* : aerial, air
aerobic *nm* : aerobics *pl*
aerodinámico, -ca *adj* : aerodynamic
aeródromo *nm* : airfield
aerolínea *nf* : airline
aeromozo, -za *n* : flight attendant, steward *m*, stewardess *f*
aeronave *nf* : aircraft
aeropuerto *nm* : airport
aerosol *nm* : aerosol, spray
afable *adj* : affable — **afabilidad** *nf* : affability
afán *nm, pl* **afanes** 1 ANHELO : eagerness 2 EMPEÑO : effort, hard work — **afanarse** *vr* : toil — **afanosamente** *adv* : industriously, busily — **afanoso, -sa** *adj* 1 : eager 2 TRABAJOSO : arduous
afear *vt* : make ugly, disfigure
afección *nf, pl* **-ciones** : ailment, complaint
afectar *vt* : affect — **afectación** *nf, pl* **-ciones** : affectation — **afectado, -da** *adj* : affected
afectivo, -va *adj* : emotional
afecto *nm* : affection — **afecto, -ta** *adj* ~ **a** : fond of — **afectuoso, -sa** *adj* : affectionate, caring
afeitar *vt* : shave — **afeitarse** *vr* : shave — **afeitada** *nf* : shave
afeminado, -da *adj* : effeminate
aferrarse {55} *vr* : cling, hold on
afianzar {21} *vt* : secure, strengthen — **afianzarse** *vr* : become established
afiche *nm* Lat : poster
afición *nf, pl* **-ciones** 1 : penchant, fondness 2 PASATIEMPO : hobby — **aficionado, -da** *n* 1 ENTUSIASTA : enthusiast, fan 2 AMATEUR : amateur — **aficionarse** *vr* ~ **a** : become interested in
afilar *vt* : sharpen — **afilado, -da** *adj* : sharp — **afilador** *nm* : sharpener
afiliarse *vr* ~ **a** : join, become a member of

— **afiliación** *nf, pl* **-ciones** : affiliation —
afiliado, -da *adj* : affiliated
afín *adj, pl* **afines** : related, similar —
afinidad *nf* : affinity, similarity
afinar *vt* **1** : tune **2** PULIR : perfect, refine
afirmar *vt* **1** : state, affirm **2** REFORZAR
: strengthen — **afirmación** *nf, pl* **-ciones**
: statement, affirmation — **afirmativo, -va**
adj : affirmative
afligir {35} *vt* **1** : afflict **2** APENAR : distress
— **afligirse** *vr* : grieve — **aflicción** *nf, pl*
-ciones : grief, sorrow — **afligido -da** *adj*
: sorrowful, distressed
aflojar *vt* : loosen, slacken — *vi* : ease up —
aflojarse *vr* : become loose, slacken
aflorar *vi* : come to the surface, emerge —
afloramiento *nm* : outcrop
afluencia *nf* : influx — **afluente** *nm* : tributary
afortunado, -da *adj* : fortunate, lucky —
afortunadamente *adv* : fortunately
afrentar *vt* : insult — **afrenta** *nf* : affront, insult
africano, -na *adj* : African
afrontar *vt* : confront, face
afuera *adv* **1** : out **2** : outside, outdoors —
afueras *nfpl* : outskirts
agachar *vt* : lower — **agacharse** *vr*
: crouch, stoop
agalla *nf* **1** BRANQUIA : gill **2 tener ~s**
fam : have guts
agarrar *vt* **1** ASIR : grasp **2** *Lat* : catch —
agarrarse *vr* : hold on, cling — **agarradera**
nf Lat : handle — **agarrado, -da** *adj fam*
: stingy — **agarre** *nm* : grip, grasp — **agar-
rón** *nm, pl* **-rones** : tug, pull
agasajar *vt* : fête, wine and dine — **agasajo**
nm : lavish attention
agave *nm* : agave
agazaparse *vr* : crouch down
agencia *nf* : agency, office — **agente** *nmf*
: agent, officer
agenda *nf* **1** : agenda **2** LIBRETA : notebook
ágil *adj* : agile — **agilidad** *nf* : agility
agitar *vt* **1** : agitate, shake **2** : wave, flap
(wings, etc.) **3** PERTURBAR : stir up — **agitarse** *vr* **1** : toss about **2** INQUIETARSE : get
upset — **agitación** *nf, pl* **-ciones 1** : agitation, shaking **2** INTRANQUILIDAD : restless-
ness — **agitado, -da** *adj* **1** : agitated, excited **2** : choppy, rough (of the sea)
aglomerar *vt* : amass — **aglomerarse** *vr*
: crowd together
agnóstico, -ca *adj & n* : agnostic
agobiar *vt* **1** : oppress **2** ABRUMAR : overwhelm — **agobiado, -da** *adj* : weary,
weighed down — **agobiante** *adj* : oppress-
ing, oppressive
agonizar {21} *vi* : be dying — **agonía** *nf* **1**

: death throes **2** PENA : agony — **agoni-
zante** *adj* : dying
agorero, -ra *adj* : ominous
agostar *vt* : wither
agosto *nm* : August
agotar *vt* **1** : deplete, use up **2** CANSAR : exhaust, weary — **agotarse** *vr* **1** : run out,
give out **2** CANSARSE : get tired — **agotado, -da** *adj* **1** CANSADO : exhausted **2**
: sold out — **agotador, -dora** *adj* : exhaust-
ing — **agotamiento** *nm* : exhaustion
agraciado, -da *adj* **1** : attractive **2** AFORTU-
NADO : fortunate
agradar *vi* : be pleasing — **agradable** *adj*
: pleasant, agreeable — **agrado** *nm* **1**
: taste, liking **2 con ~** : with pleasure
agradecer {53} *vt* : be grateful for, thank —
agradecido, -da *adj* : grateful — **agradecimiento** *nm* : gratitude
agrandar *vt* : enlarge — **agrandarse** *vr*
: grow larger
agrario, -ria *adj* : agrarian, agricultural
agravar *vt* **1** : make heavier **2** EMPEORAR
: aggravate, worsen — **agravarse** *vr* : get
worse
agraviar *vt* : insult — **agravio** *nm* : insult
agredir {1} *vt* : attack
agregar {52} *vt* : add, attach — **agregado,
-da** *n* : attaché — **agregado** *nm* : aggregate
agresión *nf, pl* **-siones** : aggression, attack
— **agresividad** *nf* : aggressiveness — **agresivo, -va** *adj* : aggressive — **agresor, -sora**
n : aggressor, attacker
agreste *adj* : rugged, wild
agriar *vt* : sour — **agriarse** *vr* **1** : turn sour
(of milk, etc.) **2** : become embittered
agrícola *adj* : agricultural — **agricultura** *nf*
: agriculture, farming — **agricultor, -tora** *n*
: farmer
agridulce *adj* **1** : bittersweet **2** : sweet-and-
sour (in cooking)
agrietar *vt* : crack — **agrietarse** *vr* **1** : crack
2 : chap
agrimensor, -sora *n* : surveyor
agrio, agria *adj* : sour
agrupar *vt* : group together — **agruparse** *vr*
: form a group — **agrupación** *nf, pl*
-ciones : group, association — **agru-
pamiento** *nm* : grouping
agua *nf* **1** : water **2 ~ oxigenada** : hydrogen peroxide **3 ~s negras** *or* **~s resid-
uales** : sewage
aguacate *nm* : avocado
aguacero *nm* : downpour
aguado, -da *adj* **1** : watery **2** *Lat fam* : soft,
flabby — **aguar** {10} *vt* **1** : water down, dilute **2 ~ la fiesta** *fam* : spoil the party
aguafuerte *nm* : etching
aguanieve *nf* : sleet

aguantar *vt* **1** SOPORTAR : bear, withstand **2** SOSTENER : hold — *vi* : hold out, last — **aguantarse** *vr* **1** : resign oneself **2** CONTENERSE : restrain oneself — **aguante** *nm* **1** : patience **2** RESISTENCIA : endurance
aguardar *vt* : await
aguardiente *nm* : clear brandy
aguarrás *nm* : turpentine
agudo, -da *adj* **1** : acute, sharp **2** : shrill, high-pitched (in music) — **agudeza** *nf* **1** : sharpness **2** : witticism
agüero *nm* : augury, omen
aguijón *nm, pl* **-jones** **1** : stinger (of an insect) **2** ESTÍMULO : goad, stimulus — **aguijonear** *vt* : goad
águila *nf* : eagle
aguja *nf* **1** : needle **2** : hand (of a clock) **3** : spire (of a church)
agujero *nm* : hole
agujeta *nf* **1** *Lat* : shoelace **2** ~s *nfpl* : (muscular) stiffness
aguzar {21} *vt* **1** : sharpen **2** ~ **el oído** : prick up one's ears
ahí *adv* **1** : there **2 por** ~ : somewhere, thereabouts
ahijado, -da *n* : godchild, godson *m*, goddaughter *f*
ahínco *nm* : eagerness, zeal
ahogar {52} *vt* **1** : drown **2** ASFIXIAR : smother — **ahogarse** *vr* : drown — **ahogo** *nm* : breathlessness
ahondar *vt* : deepen — *vi* : elaborate, go into detail
ahora *adv* **1** : now **2** ~ **mismo** : right now
ahorcar {72} *vt* : hang, kill by hanging — **ahorcarse** *vr* : hang oneself
ahorita *adv Lat fam* : right now
ahorrar *vt* : save, spare — *vi* : save up — **ahorrarse** *vr* : spare oneself — **ahorro** *nm* : saving
ahuecar {72} *vt* **1** : hollow out **2** : cup (one's hands)
ahumar {8} *vt* : smoke, cure — **ahumado, -da** *adj* : smoked
ahuyentar *vt* : scare away, chase away
airado, -da *adj* : irate, angry
aire *nm* **1** : air **2** ~ **acondicionado** : air-conditioning **3 al** ~ **libre** : in the open air, outdoors — **airear** *vt* : air, air out
aislar {5} *vt* **1** : isolate **2** : insulate (in electricity) — **aislamiento** *nm* **1** : isolation **2** : (electrical) insulation
ajar *vt* **1** : crumple, wrinkle **2** ESTROPEAR : spoil
ajedrez *nm* : chess
ajeno, -na *adj* **1** : someone else's **2** EXTRAÑO : alien **3** ~ **a** : foreign to
ajetreado, -da *adj* : hectic, busy — **aje-**

trearse *vr* : bustle about — **ajetreo** *nm* : hustle and bustle
ají *nm, pl* **ajíes** *Lat* : chili pepper
ajo *nm* : garlic
ajustar *vt* **1** : adjust, adapt **2** ACORDAR : agree on **3** SALDAR : settle — **ajustarse** *vr* : fit, conform — **ajustable** *adj* : adjustable — **ajustado, -da** *adj* **1** : close, tight **2** CEÑIDO : tight-fitting — **ajuste** *nm* : adjustment
ajusticiar *vt* : execute, put to death
al (*contraction of* **a** *and* **el**) → **a²**
ala *nf* **1** : wing **2** : brim (of a hat)
alabanza *nf* : praise — **alabar** *vt* : praise
alacena *nf* : cupboard, larder
alacrán *nm, pl* **-cranes** : scorpion
alado, -da *adj* : winged
alambre *nm* : wire
alameda *nf* **1** : poplar grove **2** : tree-lined avenue — **álamo** *nm* : poplar
alarde *nm* : show, display — **alardear** *vi* : boast
alargar {52} *vt* **1** : extend, lengthen **2** PROLONGAR : prolong — **alargarse** *vr* : become longer — **alargador** *nm* : extension cord
alarido *nm* : howl, shriek
alarmar *vt* : alarm — **alarma** *nf* : alarm — **alarmante** *adj* : alarming
alba *nf* : dawn
albahaca *nf* : basil
albañil *nm* : bricklayer, mason
albaricoque *nm* : apricot
albedrío *nm* **libre** ~ : free will
alberca *nf* **1** : reservoir, tank **2** *Lat* : swimming pool
albergar {52} *vt* : house, lodge — **albergue** *nm* **1** : lodging **2** REFUGIO : shelter **3** ~ **juvenil** : youth hostel
albóndiga *nf* : meatball
alborear *v impers* : dawn — **albor** *nm* : dawning — **alborada** *nf* : dawn
alborotar *vt* : excite, stir up — *vi* : make a racket — **alborotarse** *vr* : get excited — **alborotado, -da** *adj* : excited, agitated — **alborotador, -dora** *n* : agitator, rioter — **alboroto** *nm* : ruckus
alborozar {21} *vt* : gladden — **alborozo** *nm* : joy
álbum *nm* : album
alcachofa *nf* : artichoke
alcalde, -desa *n* : mayor
alcance *nm* **1** : reach **2** ÁMBITO : range, scope
alcancía *nf* : money box
alcantarilla *nf* : sewer, drain
alcanzar {21} *vt* **1** : reach **2** LLEGAR A : catch up with **3** LOGRAR : achieve, attain — *vi* **1** : suffice, be enough **2** ~ **a** : manage to

alcaparra *nf* : caper
alcázar *nm* : fortress, castle
alce *nm* : moose, European elk
alcoba *nf* : bedroom
alcohol *nm* : alcohol — **alcohólico, -ca** *adj & n* : alcoholic — **alcoholismo** *nm* : alcoholism
aldaba *nf* : door knocker
aldea *nf* : village — **aldeano, -na** *n* : villager
aleación *nf, pl* **-ciones** : alloy
aleatorio, -ria *adj* : random
aleccionar *vt* : instruct, teach
aledaño, -ña *adj* : bordering — **aledaños** *nmpl* : outskirts
alegar {52} *vt* : assert, allege — *vi Lat* : argue — **alegato** *nm* **1** : allegation (in law) **2** *Lat* : argument
alegoría *nf* : allegory — **alegórico, -ca** *adj* : allegorical
alegrar *vt* : make happy, cheer up — **alegrarse** *vr* : be glad — **alegre** *adj* **1** CONTENTO : glad, happy **2** : colorful, bright — **alegremente** *adv* : happily — **alegría** *nf* : joy, cheer
alejar *vt* **1** : remove, move away **2** ENAJENAR : estrange — **alejarse** *vr* : move away, drift apart — **alejado, -da** *adj* : remote — **alejamiento** *nm* **1** : removal **2** : estrangement (of persons)
alemán, -mana *adj, mpl* **-manes** : German — **alemán** *nm* : German (language)
alentar {55} *vt* : encourage — **alentador, -dora** *adj* : encouraging
alergia *nf* : allergy — **alérgico, -ca** *adj* : allergic
alero *nm* : eaves *pl*
alertar *vt* : alert — **alerta** *adv* : on the alert — **alerta** *adj & nf* : alert
aleta *nf* **1** : fin, flipper **2** : small wing
alevosía *nf* : treachery — **alevoso, -sa** *adj* : treacherous
alfabeto *nm* : alphabet — **alfabético, -ca** *adj* : alphabetical — **alfabetismo** *nm* : literacy — **alfabetizar** {21} *vt* **1** : teach literacy **2** : alphabetize
alfalfa *nf* : alfalfa
alfarería *nf* : pottery
alféizar *nm* : sill, windowsill
alfil *nm* : bishop (in chess)
alfiler *nm* **1** : pin **2** BROCHE : brooch — **alfiletero** *nm* : pincushion
alfombra *nf* : carpet, rug — **alfombrilla** *nf* : small rug, mat
alga *nf* : seaweed
álgebra *nf* : algebra
algo *pron* **1** : something **2** ~ **de** : some, a little — ~ *adv* : somewhat, rather
algodón *nm, pl* **-dones** : cotton
alguacil *nm* : constable, bailiff

alguien *pron* : somebody, someone
alguno, -na *adj* (**algún** *before masculine singular nouns*) **1** : some, any **2** (*in negative constructions*) : not any, not at all **3** **algunas veces** : sometimes — ~ *pron* **1** : one, someone, somebody **2** **algunos, -nas** *pron pl* : some, a few
alhaja *nf* : jewel
alharaca *nf* : fuss
aliado, -da *n* : ally — ~ *adj* : allied — **alianza** *nf* : alliance — **aliarse** {85} *vr* : form an alliance
alias *adv & nm* : alias
alicaído, -da *adj* : depressed
alicates *nmpl* : pliers
aliciente *nm* **1** : incentive **2** : attraction (to a place)
alienar *vt* : alienate — **alienación** *nf, pl* **-ciones** : alienation
aliento *nm* **1** : breath **2** ÁNIMO : encouragement, strength
aligerar *vt* **1** : lighten **2** APRESURAR : hasten, quicken
alimaña *nf* : pest, vermin
alimentar *vt* : feed, nourish — **alimentarse** *vr* ~ **con** : live on — **alimentación** *nf, pl* **-ciones 1** : feeding **2** NUTRICIÓN : nourishment — **alimenticio, -cia** *adj* : nourishing — **alimento** *nm* : food, nourishment
alinear *vt* : align, line up — **alinearse** *vr* ~ **con** : align oneself with — **alineación** *nf, pl* **-ciones 1** : alignment **2** : lineup (in sports)
aliño *nm* : dressing, seasoning — **aliñar** *vt* : season, dress
alisar *vt* : smooth
alistarse *vr* : join up, enlist — **alistamiento** *nm* : enlistment
aliviar *vt* : relieve, soothe — **aliviarse** *vr* : recover, get better — **alivio** *nm* : relief
aljibe *nm* : cistern, tank
allá *adv* **1** : there, over there **2 más** ~ : farther away **3 más** ~ **de** : beyond
allanar *vt* **1** : smooth, level out **2** *Spain* : break into (a house) **3** *Lat* : raid — **allanamiento** *nm* **1** *Spain* : breaking and entering **2** *Lat* : raid
allegado, -da *n* : close friend, relation
allí *adv* : there, over there
alma *nf* : soul
almacén *nm, pl* **-cenes 1** : warehouse **2** *Lat* : shop, store **3 grandes almacenes** : department store — **almacenamiento** *or* **almacenaje** *nm* : storage — **almacenar** *vt* : store
almádena *nf* : sledgehammer
almanaque *nm* : almanac
almeja *nf* : clam
almendra *nf* **1** : almond **2** : kernel (of nuts, fruit, etc.)

almiar *nm* : haystack
almíbar *nm* : syrup
almidón *nm, pl* **-dones** : starch — **almidonar** *vt* : starch
almirante *nm* : admiral
almohada *nf* : pillow — **almohadilla** *nf* : small pillow, pad — **almohadón** *nm, pl* **-dones** : bolster, large cushion
almorranas *nfpl* : hemorrhoids, piles
almorzar {36} *vi* : have lunch — *vt* : have for lunch — **almuerzo** *nm* : lunch
alocado, -da *adj* : crazy, wild
áloe *or* **aloe** *nm* : aloe
alojar *vt* : house, lodge — **alojarse** *vr* : lodge, room — **alojamiento** *nm* : lodging, accommodations *pl*
alondra *nf* : lark
alpaca *nf* : alpaca
alpinismo *nm* : mountain climbing — **alpinista** *nmf* : mountain climber
alpiste *nm* : birdseed
alquilar *vt* : rent, lease — **alquilarse** *vr* : be for rent — **alquiler** *nm* : rent, rental
alquitrán *nm, pl* **-tranes** : tar
alrededor *adv* **1** : around, about **2** ~ **de** : approximately — **alrededor de** *prep phr* : around — **alrededores** *nmpl* : outskirts
alta *nf* : discharge (of a patient)
altanería *nf* : haughtiness — **altanero, -ra** *adj* : haughty
altar *nm* : altar
altavoz *nm, pl* **-voces** : loudspeaker
alterar *vt* **1** : alter, modify **2** PERTURBAR : disturb — **alterarse** *vr* : get upset — **alteración** *nf, pl* **-ciones** **1** : alteration **2** ALBOROTO : disturbance — **altera- do, -da** *adj* : upset
altercado *nm* : altercation, argument
alternar *vi* **1** : alternate **2** ~ **con** : socialize with — *vt* : alternate — **alternarse** *vr* : take turns — **alternativa** *nf* : alternative — **alternativo, -va** *adj* : alternating, alternative — **alterno, -na** *adj* : alternate
Alteza *nf* : Highness
altiplano *nm* : high plateau
altitud *nf* : altitude
altivez *nf, pl* **-veces** : haughtiness — **altivo, -va** *adj* : haughty
alto, -ta *adj* **1** : tall, high **2** RUIDOSO : loud — **alto** *adv* **1** ARRIBA : high **2** : loud, loudly — ~ *nm* **1** ALTURA : height, elevation **2** : stop, halt — ~ *interj* : halt!, stop! — **altoparlante** *nm Lat* : loudspeaker
altruista *adj* : altruistic — **altruismo** *nm* : altruism
altura *nf* **1** : height **2** ALTITUD : altitude **3 a la** ~ **de** : near, up by
alubia *nf* : kidney bean

alucinar *vi* : hallucinate — **alucinación** *nf, pl* **-ciones** : hallucination
alud *nm* : avalanche
aludir *vi* : allude, refer — **aludido, -da** *adj* **darse por** ~ : take it personally
alumbrar *vt* **1** : light, illuminate **2** PARIR : give birth to — **alumbrado** *nm* : (electric) lighting — **alumbramiento** *nm* : childbirth
aluminio *nm* : aluminum
alumno, -na *n* : pupil, student
alusión *nf, pl* **-siones** : allusion
aluvión *nm, pl* **-viones** : flood, barrage
alzar {21} *vt* : lift, raise — **alzarse** *vr* : rise (up) — **alza** *nf* : rise — **alzamiento** *nm* : uprising
ama → **amo**
amabilidad *nf* : kindness — **amable** *adj* : kind, nice
amaestrar *vt* : train
amagar {52} *vt* **1** : show signs of **2** AMENAZAR : threaten — *vi* : be imminent — **amago** *nm* **1** INDICIO : sign **2** AMENAZA : threat
amainar *vi* : abate
amamantar *v* : breast-feed, nurse
amanecer {53} *v impers* : dawn — *vi* : wake up — ~ *nm* : dawn, daybreak
amanerado *adj* : affected, mannered
amansar *vt* **1** : tame **2** APACIGUAR : soothe — **amansarse** *vr* : calm down
amante *adj* ~ **de** : fond of — ~ *nmf* : lover
amañar *vt* : rig, tamper with
amapola *nf* : poppy
amar *vt* : love
amargar {52} *vt* : make bitter — **amargado, -da** *adj* : embittered — **amargo, -ga** *adj* : bitter — **amargo** *nm* : bitterness — **amargura** *nf* : bitterness, grief
amarillo, -lla *adj* : yellow — **amarillo** *nm* : yellow
amarrar *vt* **1** : moor **2** ATAR : tie up
amasar *vt* **1** : knead **2** : amass (a fortune, etc.)
amateur *adj & nmf* : amateur
amatista *nf* : amethyst
ambages *nmpl* **sin** ~ : without hesitation, straight to the point
ámbar *nm* : amber
ambición *nf, pl* **-ciones** : ambition — **ambicionar** *vt* : aspire to — **ambicioso, -sa** *adj* : ambitious
ambiente *nm* **1** AIRE : atmosphere **2** MEDIO : environment, surroundings *pl* — **ambiental** *adj* : environmental
ambigüedad *nf* : ambiguity — **ambiguo, -gua** *adj* : ambiguous
ámbito *nm* : domain, sphere
ambos, -bas *adj & pron* : both
ambulancia *nf* : ambulance

ambulante

ambulante *adj* : traveling, itinerant
ameba *nf* : amoeba
amedrentar *vt* : intimidate
amén *nm* **1** : amen **2** ~ **de** : in addition to
amenazar {21} *vt* : threaten — **amenaza** *nf* : threat, menace
amenizar {21} *vt* : make pleasant, enliven — **ameno, -na** *adj* : pleasant
americano, -na *adj* : American
ameritar *vt Lat* : deserve
ametralladora *nf* : machine gun
amianto *nm* : asbestos
amiba → ameba
amígdala *nf* : tonsil — **amigdalitis** *nf* : tonsilitis
amigo, -ga *adj* : friendly, close — ~ *n* : friend — **amigable** *adj* : friendly
amilanar *vt* : daunt — **amilanarse** *vr* : lose heart
aminorar *vt* : diminish
amistad *nf* : friendship — **amistoso, -sa** *adj* : friendly
amnesia *nf* : amnesia
amnistía *nf* : amnesty
amo, ama *n* **1** : master *m*, mistress *f* **2 ama de casa** : homemaker, housewife **3 ama de llaves** : housekeeper
amodorrado, -da *adj* : drowsy
amolar {19} *vt* **1** : grind, sharpen **2** MOLESTAR : annoy
amoldar *vt* : adapt, adjust — **amoldarse** *vr* ~ **a** : adapt to
amonestar *vt* : admonish, warn — **amonestación** *nf, pl* **-ciones** : admonition, warning
amoníaco *or* **amoniaco** *nm* : ammonia
amontonar *vt* : pile up — **amontonarse** *vr* : pile up (of things), form a crowd (of persons)
amor *nm* : love
amordazar {21} *vt* : gag
amorío *nm* : love affair — **amoroso, -sa** *adj* **1** : loving **2** *Lat* : sweet, lovable
amortado, -da *adj* : black-and-blue
amortiguar {10} *vt* : muffle, soften, tone down — **amortiguador** *nm* : shock absorber
amortizar {21} *vt* : pay off — **amortización** *nf* : repayment
amotinar *vt* : incite (to riot) — **amotinarse** *vr* : riot, rebel
amparar *vt* : shelter, protect — **ampararse** *vr* **1** ~ **de** : take shelter from **2** ~ **en** : have recourse to — **amparo** *nm* : refuge, protection
ampliar {85} *vt* **1** : expand **2** : enlarge (a photograph) — **ampliación** *nf, pl* **-ciones 1** : expansion, enlargement **2** : extension (of a building)

amplificar {72} *vt* : amplify — **amplificador** *nm* : amplifier
amplio, -plia *adj* : broad, wide, ample — **amplitud** *nf* **1** : breadth, extent **2** ESPACIOSIDAD : spaciousness
ampolla *nf* **1** : blister **2** : vial, ampoule — **ampollarse** *vr* : blister
ampuloso, -sa *adj* : pompous
amputar *vt* : amputate — **amputación** *nf, pl* **-ciones** : amputation
amueblar *vt* : furnish (a house, etc.)
amurallar *vt* : wall in
anacardo *nm* : cashew nut
anaconda *nf* : anaconda
anacrónico, -ca *adj* : anachronistic — **anacronismo** *nm* : anachronism
ánade *nmf* : duck
anagrama *nm* : anagram
anales *nmpl* : annals
analfabeto, -ta *adj* & *n* : illiterate — **analfabetismo** *nm* : illiteracy
analgésico *nm* : painkiller, analgesic
analizar {21} *vt* : analyze — **análisis** *nm* : analysis — **analítico, -ca** *adj* : analytical, analytic
analogía *nf* : analogy — **análogo, -ga** *adj* : analogous
ananá *or* **ananás** *nm, pl* **-nás** : pineapple
anaquel *nm* : shelf
anaranjado, -da *adj* : orange-colored
anarquía *nf* : anarchy — **anarquista** *adj* & *nmf* : anarchist
anatomía *nf* : anatomy — **anatómico, -ca** *adj* : anatomic, anatomical
anca *nf* **1** : haunch **2** ~s **de rana** : frogs' legs
ancestral *adj* : ancestral
ancho, -cha *adj* : wide, broad, ample — **ancho** *nm* : width
anchoa *nf* : anchovy
anchura *nf* : width, breadth
anciano, -na *adj* : aged, elderly — ~ *n* : elderly person
ancla *nf* : anchor — **anclar** *v* : anchor
andadas *nfpl* **1** : tracks **2 volver a las** ~ : go back to one's old ways
andadura *nf* : walking, journey
andaluz, -luza *adj* & *n, mpl* **-luces** : Andalusian
andamio *nm* : scaffold
andanada *nf* **1** : volley **2 soltar una** ~ : reprimand
andanzas *nfpl* : adventures
andar {6} *vi* **1** CAMINAR : walk **2** IR : go, travel **3** FUNCIONAR : run, work **4** ~ **en** : rummage around in **5** ~ **por** : be approximately — *vt* : cover, travel — ~ *nm* : gait, walk

andén *nm, pl* **-denes 1 :** (train) platform **2** *Lat* : sidewalk
andino, -na *adj* : Andean
andorrano, -na *adj* : Andorran
andrajos *nmpl* : tatters — **andrajoso, -sa** *adj* : ragged
anécdota *nf* : anecdote
anegar {52} *vt* : flood — **anegarse** *vr* **1** : be flooded **2** AHOGARSE : drown
anemia *nf* : anemia — **anémico, -ca** *adj* : anemic
anestesia *nf* : anesthesia — **anestésico, -ca** *adj* : anesthetic — **anestésico** *nm* : anesthetic
anexar *vt* : annex, attach — **anexo, -xa** *adj* : attached — **anexo** *nm* : annex
anfibio, -bia *adj* : amphibious — **anfibio** *nm* : amphibian
anfiteatro *nm* : amphitheater
anfitrión, -triona *n, mpl* **-triones :** host, hostess *f*
ángel *nm* : angel — **angelical** *adj* : angelic, angelical
angloparlante *adj* : English-speaking
anglosajón, -jona *adj, mpl* **-jones :** Anglo-Saxon
angosto, -ta *adj* : narrow
anguila *nf* : eel
ángulo *nm* **1** : angle **2** ESQUINA : corner — **angular** *adj* : angular — **anguloso, -sa** *adj* : angular
angustiar *vt* **1** : anguish, distress **2** INQUIETAR : worry — **angustiarse** *vr* : get upset — **angustia** *nf* **1** : anguish **2** INQUIETUD : worry — **angustioso, -sa** *adj* **1** : anguished **2** INQUIETANTE : distressing
anhelar *vt* : yearn for, crave — **anhelante** *adj* : yearning, longing — **anhelo** *nm* : longing
anidar *vi* : nest
anillo *nm* : ring
ánima *n* : soul
animación *nf, pl* **-ciones 1** VIVEZA : liveliness **2** BULLICIO : hustle and bustle — **animado, -da** *adj* : cheerful, animated — **animador, -dora** *n* **1** : (television) host **2** : cheerleader
animadversión *nf, pl* **-siones** : animosity
animal *nm* : animal — ~ *nmf* : brute, beast — ~ *adj* : brutish
animar *vt* **1** ALENTAR : encourage **2** ALEGAR : cheer up — **animarse** *vr* **1** : liven up **2** ~ **a** : get up the nerve to
ánimo *nm* **1** : spirit, soul **2** HUMOR : mood, spirits *pl* **3** ALIENTO : encouragement
animosidad *nf* : animosity, ill will
animoso, -sa *adj* : spirited, brave
aniquilar *vt* : annihilate — **aniquilación** *n, pl* **-ciones** : annihilation

anís *nm* : anise
aniversario *nm* : anniversary
ano *nm* : anus
anoche *adv* : last night
anochecer {53} *vi* : get dark — ~ *nm* : dusk, nightfall
anodino, -na *adj* : insipid, dull
anomalía *nf* : anomaly
anonadado, -da *adj* : dumbfounded
anónimo, -ma *adj* : anonymous — **anonimato** *nm* : anonymity
anorexia *nf* : anorexia
anormal *adj* : abnormal — **anormalidad** *nf* : abnormality
anotar *vt* **1** : annotate **2** APUNTAR : jot down — **anotación** *nf, pl* **-ciones** : annotation, note
anquilosarse *vr* **1** : become paralyzed **2** ESTANCARSE : stagnate — **anquilosamiento** *nm* **1** : paralysis **2** ESTANCAMIENTO : stagnation
ansiar {85} *vt* : long for — **ansia** *nf* **1** INQUIETUD : uneasiness **2** ANGUSTIA : anguish **3** ANHELO : longing — **ansiedad** *nf* : anxiety — **ansioso, -sa** *adj* **1** : anxious **2** DESEOSO : eager
antagónico, -ca *adj* : antagonistic — **antagonismo** *nm* : antagonism — **antagonista** *nmf* : antagonist
antaño *adv* : yesteryear, long ago
antártico, -ca *adj* : antarctic
ante¹ *nm* **1** : elk, moose **2** GAMUZA : suede
ante² *prep* **1** : before, in front of **2** : in view of **3** ~ **todo** : above all
anteanoche *adv* : the night before last
anteayer *adv* : the day before yesterday
antebrazo *nm* : forearm
anteceder *vt* : precede — **antecedente** *adj* : previous, prior — ~ *nm* : precedent
antecesor, -sora *n* **1** : ancestor **2** PREDECESOR : predecessor
antedicho, -cha *adj* : aforesaid
antelación *nf, pl* **-ciones 1** : advance notice **2 con** ~ : in advance
antemano *adv* **de** ~ : beforehand
antena *nf* : antenna
antenoche → **anteanoche**
anteojos *nmpl* **1** : glasses, eyeglasses **2** ~ **bifocales** : bifocals
antepasado, -da *n* : ancestor
antepecho *nm* : ledge
antepenúltimo, -ma *adj* : third from last
anteponer {60} *vt* **1** : place before **2** PREFERIR : prefer
anterior *adj* **1** : previous, earlier **2** DELANTERO : front — **anterioridad** *nf* **con** ~ : beforehand, in advance — **anteriormente** *adv* : previously
antes *adv* **1** : before, earlier **2** ANTERIOR-

MENTE : previously **3** PRIMERO : first **4** MEJOR : rather **5** ~ **de** : before, previous to **6** ~ **que** : before
antesala *nf* : waiting room
antiaéreo, -rea *adj* : antiaircraft
antibiótico *nm* : antibiotic
anticipar *vt* **1** : move up (a date, etc.) **2** : pay in advance — **anticiparse** *vr* **1** : be early **2** ADELANTARSE : get ahead — **anticipación** *nf, pl* **-ciones 1** : anticipation **2 con** ~ : in advance — **anticipado, -da** *adj* **1** : advance, early **2 por** ~ : in advance — **anticipo** *nm* **1** : advance (payment) **2** : foretaste
anticoncepción *nf, pl* **-ciones** : contraception — **anticonceptivo, -va** *adj* : contraceptive — **anticonceptivo** *nm* : contraceptive
anticongelante *nm* : antifreeze
anticuado, -da *adj* : antiquated, outdated
anticuario, -ria *n* : antique dealer — **anticuario** *nm* : antique shop
anticuerpo *nm* : antibody
antídoto *nm* : antidote
antier → **anteayer**
antiestético, -ca *adj* : unsightly
antifaz *nm, pl* **-faces** : mask
antífona *nf* : anthem
antigualla *nf* : relic, old thing
antiguo, -gua *adj* **1** : ancient, old **2** ANTERIOR : former **3** ANTICUADO : old-fashioned **4 muebles antiguos** : antique furniture — **antiguamente** *adv* **1** : long ago **2** ANTES : formerly — **antigüedad** *nf* **1** : antiquity **2** : seniority (in the workplace) **3** ~**es** *nfpl* : antiques
antihigiénico, -ca *adj* : unsanitary
antihistamínico *nm* : antihistamine
antiinflamatorio, -ria *adj* : anti-inflammatory
antílope *nm* : antelope
antinatural *adj* : unnatural
antipatía *nf* : aversion, dislike — **antipático, -ca** *adj* : unpleasant
antirreglamentario, -ria *adj* : unlawful
antirrobo, -ba *adj* : antitheft
antisemita *adj* : anti-Semitic — **antisemitismo** *nm* : anti-Semitism
antiséptico, -ca *adj* : antiseptic — **antiséptico** *nm* : antiseptic
antisocial *adj* : antisocial
antítesis *nf* : antithesis
antojarse *vr* **1** APETECER : crave **2** PARECER : seem, appear — **antojadizo, -za** *adj* : capricious — **antojo** *nm* : whim, craving
antología *nf* : anthology
antorcha *nf* : torch
antro *nm* : dive, den
antropófago, -ga *nmf* : cannibal
antropología *nf* : anthropology

anual *adj* : annual, yearly — **anualidad** *nf* : annuity — **anuario** *nm* : yearbook, annual
anudar *vt* : knot — **anudarse** *vr* : tie, knot
anular *vt* : annul, cancel — **anulación** *nf, pl* **-ciones** : annulment, cancellation
anunciar *vt* **1** : announce **2** : advertise (products) — **anunciante** *nmf* : advertiser — **anuncio** *nm* **1** : announcement **2** *or* ~ **publicitario** : advertisement
anzuelo *nm* **1** : fishhook **2 morder el** ~ : take the bait
añadir *vt* : add — **añadidura** *nf* **1** : additive, addition **2 por** ~ : in addition, furthermore
añejo, -ja *adj* : aged, vintage
añicos *nmpl* **hacer(se)** ~ : smash to pieces
añil *adj & nm* : indigo (color)
año *nm* **1** : year **2 Año Nuevo** : New Year
añorar *vt* : long for, miss — **añoranza** *nf* : nostalgia
añoso, -sa *adj* : aged, old
aorta *nf* : aorta
apabullar *vt* : overwhelm
apacentar {55} *vt* : pasture, graze
apachurrar *vt Lat* : crush
apacible *adj* : gentle, mild
apaciguar {10} *vt* : appease, pacify — **apaciguarse** *vr* : calm down
apadrinar *vt* **1** : be a godparent to **2** : sponsor (an artist, etc.)
apagar {52} *vt* **1** : turn or switch off **2** EXTINGUIR : extinguish, put out — **apagarse** *vr* **1** EXTINGUIRSE : go out **2** : die down — **apagado, -da** *adj* **1** : off, out **2** : dull, subdued (of colors, sounds, etc.) — **apagador** *nm Lat* : (light) switch — **apagón** *nm, pl* **-gones** : blackout
apalancar {72} *vt* **1** LEVANTAR : jack up **2** ABRIR : pry open — **apalancamiento** *nm* : leverage
apalear *vt* : beat up, thrash
aparador *nm* **1** : sideboard **2** *Lat* : shop window
aparato *nm* **1** : machine, appliance, apparatus **2** : system (in anatomy) **3** OSTENTACIÓN : ostentation — **aparatoso, -sa** *adj* **1** : ostentatious **2** ESPECTACULAR : spectacular
aparcar {72} *v Spain* : park — **aparcamiento** *nm Spain* **1** : parking **2** : parking lot
aparcero, -ra *n* : sharecropper
aparear *vt* : mate, pair up — **aparearse** *vr* : mate
aparecer {53} *vi* **1** : appear **2** PRESENTARSE : show up — **aparecerse** *vr* : appear
aparejar *vt* **1** : rig (a ship) **2** : harness (an animal) — **aparejado, -da** *adj* **llevar** ~ : entail — **aparejo** *nm* **1** : equipment, gear

2 : harness (for an animal) 3 : rigging (for a ship)
aparentar *vt* 1 : seem 2 FINGIR : feign —
aparente *adj* : apparent, seeming
aparición *nf, pl* **-ciones** 1 : appearance 2 FANTASMA : apparition — **apariencia** *nf* 1 : appearance, look 2 **en ~** : apparently
apartado *nm* 1 : section, paragraph 2 **~ postal** : post office box
apartamento *nm* : apartment
apartar *vt* 1 ALEJAR : move away 2 SEPARAR : set aside, separate — **apartarse** *vr* 1 : move away 2 DESVIARSE : stray — **aparte** *adv* 1 : apart, separately 2 ADEMÁS : besides
apasionar *vt* : excite, fascinate — **apasionarse** *vr* : get excited — **apasionado, -da** *adj* : passionate, excited — **apasionante** *adj* : exciting
apatía *nf* : apathy — **apático, -ca** *adj* : apathetic
apearse *vr* 1 : dismount 2 : get out of or off (a vehicle)
apedrear *vt* : stone
apegarse {52} *vr* **~ a** : become attached to, grow fond of — **apegado, -da** *adj* : devoted — **apego** *nm* : fondness
apelar *vi* 1 : appeal 2 **~ a** : resort to — **apelación** *nf, pl* **-ciones** : appeal
apellido *nm* : last name, surname — **apellidarse** *vr* : have for a last name
apenar *vt* : sadden — **apenarse** *vr* 1 : grieve 2 *Lat* : become embarrassed
apenas *adv* : hardly, scarcely — **~** *conj* : as soon as
apéndice *nm* : appendix — **apendicitis** *nf* : appendicitis
apercibir *vt* 1 : warn 2 *Lat* : notice — **apercibirse** *vr* **~ de** : notice — **apercibimiento** *nm* : warning
aperitivo *nm* 1 : appetizer 2 : aperitif
apero *nm* : tool, implement
apertura *nf* : opening
apesadumbrar *vt* : sadden — **apesadumbrarse** *vr* : be weighed down
apestar *vi* : stink — **apestoso, -sa** *adj* : stinking, foul
apetecer {53} *vt* : crave, long for — **apetecible** *adj* : appealing
apetito *nm* : appetite — **apetitoso, -sa** *adj* : appetizing
ápice *nm* 1 : apex, summit 2 PIZCA : bit, smidgen
apilar *vt* : pile up — **apilarse** *vr* : pile up
apiñar *vt* : pack, cram — **apiñarse** *vr* : crowd together
apio *nm* : celery
apisonadora *nf* : steamroller

aplacar {72} *vt* : appease, placate — **aplacarse** *vr* : calm down
aplanar *vt* : flatten, level
aplastar *vt* : crush — **aplastante** *adj* : overwhelming
aplaudir *v* : applaud — **aplauso** *nm* 1 : applause 2 : acclaim
aplazar {21} *vt* : postpone, defer — **aplazamiento** *nm* : postponement
aplicar {72} *vt* : apply — **aplicarse** *vr* : apply oneself — **aplicable** *adj* : applicable — **aplicación** *nf, pl* **-ciones** : application — **aplicado, -da** *adj* : diligent
aplomo *nm* : aplomb
apocarse {72} *vr* : belittle oneself — **apocado, -da** *adj* : timid — **apocamiento** *nm* : timidity
apodar *vt* : nickname
apoderar *vt* : empower — **apoderarse** *vr* **~ de** : seize — **apoderado, -da** *n* : agent, proxy
apodo *nm* : nickname
apogeo *nm* : peak, height
apología *nf* : defense, apology
apoplegía *nf* : stroke, apoplexy
aporrear *vt* : bang on, beat
aportar *vt* : contribute — **aportación** *nf, pl* **-ciones** : contribution
apostar[1] {19} *v* : bet, wager
apostar[2] *vt* : station, post
apostillar *vt* : annotate — **apostilla** *nf* : note
apóstol *nm* : apostle
apóstrofo *nm* : apostrophe
apostura *nf* : elegance, grace
apoyar *vt* 1 : support 2 INCLINAR : lean, rest — **apoyarse** *vr* **~ en** : lean on, rest on — **apoyo** *nm* : support
apreciar *vt* 1 ESTIMAR : appreciate 2 EVALUAR : appraise — **apreciable** *adj* : considerable — **apreciación** *nf, pl* **-ciones** 1 : appreciation 2 VALORACIÓN : appraisal — **aprecio** *nm* 1 : appraisal 2 ESTIMA : esteem
aprehender *vt* : apprehend — **aprehensión** *nf, pl* **-siones** : apprehension, capture
apremiar *vt* : urge — *vi* : be urgent — **apremiante** *adj* : pressing, urgent — **apremio** *nm* : urgency
aprender *v* : learn — **aprenderse** *vr* : memorize
aprendiz, -diza *n, mpl* **-dices** : apprentice, trainee — **aprendizaje** *nm* : apprenticeship
aprensión *nf, pl* **-siones** : apprehension, dread — **aprensivo, -va** *adj* : apprehensive
apresar *vt* : capture, seize — **apresamiento** *nm* : seizure, capture
aprestar *vt* : make ready — **aprestarse** *vr* : get ready

apresurar *vt* : speed up — **apresurarse** *vr* : hurry — **apresuradamente** *adv* : hurriedly, hastily — **apresurado, -da** *adj* : in a rush
apretar {55} *vt* **1** : press, push (a button) **2** : tighten (a knot, etc.) **3** ESTRECHAR : squeeze — *vi* **1** : press (down) **2** : fit too tightly — **apretón** *nm, pl* -**tones 1** : squeeze **2** ~ **de manos** : handshake — **apretado, -da** *adj* **1** : tight **2** *fam* : tightfisted
aprieto *nm* : predicament, jam
aprisa *adv* : quickly
aprisionar *vt* : imprison
aprobar {19} *vt* **1** : approve of **2** : pass (an exam, etc.) — *vi* : pass — **aprobación** *nf, pl* -**ciones** : approval
apropiarse *vr* ~ **de** : take possession of, appropriate — **apropiación** *nf, pl* -**ciones** : appropriation — **apropiado, -da** *adj* : appropriate
aprovechar *vt* : take advantage of, make good use of — *vi* : be of use — **aprovecharse** *vr* ~ **de** : take advantage of — **aprovechado, -da** *adj* **1** : diligent **2** OPORTUNISTA : opportunistic
aproximar *vt* : bring closer — **aproximarse** *vr* : approach — **aproximación** *nf, pl* -**ciones** : approximation — **aproximadamente** *adv* : approximately — **aproximado, -da** *adj* : approximate
apto, -ta *adj* **1** : suitable **2** CAPAZ : capable — **aptitud** *nf* : aptitude, capability
apuesta *nf* : bet, wager
apuesto, -ta *adj* : elegant, good-looking
apuntalar *vt* : prop up, shore up
apuntar *vt* **1** : aim, point **2** ANOTAR : jot down **3** SEÑALAR : point at **4** : prompt (in theater) — **apuntarse** *vr* **1** : sign up **2** : score, chalk up (a victory, etc.) — **apunte** *nm* : note
apuñalar *vt* : stab
apurar *vt* **1** : hurry, rush **2** AGOTAR : use up **3** PREOCUPAR : trouble — **apurarse** *vr* **1** : worry **2** *Lat* : hurry up — **apuradamente** *adv* : with difficulty — **apurado, -da** *adj* **1** : needy **2** DIFÍCIL : difficult **3** *Lat* : rushed — **apuro** *nm* **1** : predicament, jam **2** *Lat* : hurry
aquejar *vt* : afflict
aquel, aquella *adj, mpl* **aquellos** : that, those
aquél, aquélla *pron, mpl* **aquéllos 1** : that (one), those (ones) **2** : the former
aquello *pron* : that, that matter
aquí *adv* **1** : here **2** AHORA : now **3** por ~ : hereabouts
aquietar *vt* : calm — **aquietarse** *vr* : calm down

ara *nf* **1** : altar **2** en ~s de : for the sake of
árabe *adj* : Arab, Arabic — ~ *nm* : Arabic (language)
arado *nm* : plow
arancel *nm* : tariff
arándano *nm* : blueberry
araña *nf* **1** : spider **2** LÁMPARA : chandelier
arañar *v* : scratch, claw — **arañazo** *nm* : scratch
arar *v* : plow
arbitrar *v* **1** : arbitrate **2** : referee, umpire (in sports) — **arbitraje** *nm* : arbitration — **arbitrario, -ria** *adj* : arbitrary — **arbitrio** *nm* **1** : (free) will **2** JUICIO : judgment — **árbitro, -tra** *n* **1** : arbitrator **2** : referee, umpire (in sports)
árbol *nm* : tree — **arboleda** *nf* : grove
arbusto *nm* : shrub, bush
arca *nf* **1** : ark **2** COFRE : chest
arcada *nf* **1** : arcade **2** ~s *nfpl* : retching
arcaico, -ca *adj* : archaic
arcano, -na *adj* : arcane, secret
arce *nm* : maple tree
archipiélago *nm* : archipelago
archivar *vt* : file — **archivador** *nm* : filing cabinet — **archivo** *nm* **1** : file **2** : archives *pl*
arcilla *nf* : clay
arco *nm* **1** : arch **2** : bow (in sports, music, etc.) **3** : arc (in geometry) **4** ~ **iris** : rainbow
arder *vi* : burn
ardid *nm* : scheme, ruse
ardiente *adj* **1** : burning **2** FOGOSO : ardent
ardilla *nf* **1** : squirrel **2** ~ **listada** : chipmunk
ardor *nm* **1** : burning **2** ENTUSIASMO : passion, ardor
arduo, -dua *adj* : arduous
área *nf* : area
arena *nf* **1** : sand **2** PALESTRA : arena — **arenoso, -sa** *adj* : sandy, gritty
arenque *nm* : herring
arete *nm* *Lat* : earring
argamasa *nf* : mortar
argentino, -na *adj* : Argentinian, Argentine
argolla *nf* : hoop, ring
argot *nm* : slang
argüir {41} *vt* **1** : argue **2** DEMOSTRAR : prove, show — *vi* : argue
argumentar *vt* : argue, contend — **argumentación** *nf, pl* -**ciones** : (line of) argument — **argumento** *nm* **1** : argument, reasoning **2** TRAMA : plot, story line
árido, -da *adj* : dry, arid — **aridez** *nf, pl* -**deces** : aridity
arisco, -ca *adj* : surly
aristocracia *nf* : aristocracy — **aristócrata**

nmf : aristocrat — **aristocrático, -ca** *adj* : aristocratic
aritmética *nf* : arithmetic — **aritmético, -ca** *adj* : arithmetic, arithmetical
armar *vt* **1** : arm **2** MONTAR : assemble — **arma** *nf* **1** : arm, weapon **2** ~ **de fuego** : firearm — **armada** *nf* : navy — **armado, -da** *adj* : armed — **armadura** *nf* **1** : armor **2** ARMAZÓN : framework — **armamento** *nm* : armament, arms *pl*
armario *nm* **1** : (clothes) closet **2** : cupboard, cabinet
armazón *nmf, pl* **-zones** : frame, framework
armisticio *nm* : armistice
armonizar {21} *vt* **1** : harmonize **2** : reconcile (differences, etc.) — *vi* : harmonize, go together — **armonía** *nf* : harmony — **armónica** *nf* : harmonica — **armónico, -ca** *adj* : harmonic — **armonioso, -sa** *adj* : harmonious
arnés *nm, pl* **-neses** : harness
aro *nm* **1** : hoop, ring **2** *Lat* : earring
aroma *nm* : aroma, scent — **aromático, -ca** *adj* : aromatic
arpa *nf* : harp
arpón *nm, pl* **-pones** : harpoon
arquear *vt* : arch, bend — **arquearse** *vr* : bend, bow
arqueología *nf* : archaeology — **arqueológico, -ca** *adj* : archaeological — **arqueólogo, -ga** *n* : archaeologist
arquero, -ra *n* **1** : archer **2** PORTERO : goalkeeper, goalie
arquetipo *nm* : archetype
arquitectura *nf* : architecture — **arquitecto, -ta** *n* : architect — **arquitectónico, -ca** *adj* : architectural
arrabal *nm* **1** : slum **2** ~**es** *nmpl* : outskirts
arracimarse *vr* : cluster together
arraigar {52} *vi* : take root, become established — **arraigarse** *vr* : settle down — **arraigado, -da** *adj* : deeply rooted, well established — **arraigo** *nm* : roots *pl*
arrancar {72} *vt* **1** : pull out, tear off **2** : start (an engine), boot (a computer) — *vi* **1** : start an engine **2** : get going — **arranque** *nm* **1** : starter (of a car) **2** ARREBATO : outburst **3 punto de** ~ : starting point
arrasar *vt* **1** : destroy, devastate **2** LLENAR : fill to the brim
arrastrar *vt* **1** : drag **2** ATRAER : draw, attract — *vi* : hang down, trail — **arrastrarse** *vr* **1** : crawl, creep **2** HUMILLARSE : grovel — **arrastre** *nm* **1** : dragging **2** : trawling (for fish)
arrear *vt* : urge on
arrebatar *vt* **1** : snatch, seize **2** CAUTIVAR : captivate — **arrebatarse** *vr* : get carried away — **arrebatado, -da** *adj* : hotheaded, rash — **arrebato** *nm* : outburst
arreciar *vi* : intensify, worsen
arrecife *nm* : reef
arreglar *vt* **1** COMPONER : fix **2** ORDENAR : tidy up **3** SOLUCIONAR : solve, work out — **arreglarse** *vr* **1** : get dressed (up) **2** **arreglárselas** *fam* : get by, manage — **arreglado, -da** *adj* **1** : fixed, repaired **2** ORDENADO : tidy **3** SOLUCIONADO : settled, sorted out **4** ATAVIADO : smart, dressed-up — **arreglo** *nm* **1** : arrangement **2** REPARACIÓN : repair **3** ACUERDO : agreement
arremangarse {52} *vr* : roll up one's sleeves
arremeter *vi* : attack, charge — **arremetida** *nf* : attack, onslaught
arremolinarse *vr* **1** : crowd around, mill about **2** : swirl (about)
arrendar {55} *vt* : rent, lease — **arrendador, -dora** *n* : landlord, landlady *f* — **arrendamiento** *nm* : rent, rental — **arrendatario, -ria** *n* : tenant, renter
arrepentirse {76} *vr* **1** : regret, be sorry **2** : repent (for one's sins) — **arrepentido, -da** *adj* : repentant — **arrepentimiento** *nm* : regret, repentance
arrestar *vt* : arrest, detain — **arresto** *nm* : arrest
arriar *vt* : lower
arriba *adv* **1** (*indicating position*) : above, overhead **2** (*indicating direction*) : up, upwards **3** : upstairs (of a house) **4** ~ **de** : more than **5 de** ~ **abajo** : from top to bottom
arribar *vi* **1** : arrive **2** : dock, put into port — **arribista** *nmf* : parvenu, upstart — **arribo** *nm* : arrival
arriendo → **arrendimiento**
arriesgar {52} *vt* : risk, venture — **arriesgarse** *vr* : take a chance — **arriesgado, -da** *adj* : risky
arrimar *vt* : bring closer, draw near — **arrimarse** *vr* : approach
arrinconar *vt* **1** : corner, box in **2** ABANDONAR : push aside
arrobar *vt* : entrance — **arrobarse** *vr* : be enraptured — **arrobamiento** *nm* : rapture, ecstasy
arrodillarse *vr* : kneel (down)
arrogancia *nf* : arrogance — **arrogante** *adj* : arrogant
arrojar *vt* **1** : hurl, cast **2** EMITIR : give off, spew out **3** PRODUCIR : yield — **arrojarse** *vr* : throw oneself — **arrojado, -da** *adj* : daring — **arrojo** *nm* : boldness, courage
arrollar *vt* **1** : sweep away **2** DERROTAR : crush, overwhelm **3** : run over (with a vehicle) — **arrollador, -dora** *adj* : overwhelming

arropar *vt* : clothe, cover (up) — **arroparse** *vr* : wrap oneself up

arroyo *nm* **1** RIACHUELO : stream **2** : gutter (in a street)

arroz *nm, pl* **arroces** : rice

arrugar {52} *vt* : wrinkle, crease — **arrugarse** *vr* : get wrinkled — **arruga** *nf* : wrinkle, crease

arruinar *vt* : ruin, wreck — **arruinarse** *vr* **1** : be ruined **2** EMPOBRECERSE : go bankrupt

arrullar *vt* : lull to sleep — *vi* : coo — **arrullo** *nm* **1** : lullaby **2** : cooing (of doves)

arrumbar *vt* : lay aside

arsenal *nm* : arsenal

arsénico *nm* : arsenic

arte *nmf (usually m in singular, f in plural)* **1** : art **2** HABILIDAD : skill **3** ASTUCIA : cunning, cleverness **4** → **bello**

artefacto *nm* : artifact, device

arteria *nf* : artery

artesanía *nm* **1** : craftsmanship **2** : handicrafts *pl* — **artesanal** *adj* : handmade — **artesano, -na** *n* : artisan, craftsman

ártico, -ca *adj* : arctic

articular *vt* : articulate — **articulación** *nf, pl* **-ciones** **1** : articulation, pronunciation **2** COYUNTURA : joint

artículo *nm* **1** : article **2** **~s de primera necesidad** : essentials **3** **~s de tocador** : toiletries

artífice *nmf* : artisan, craftsman

artificial *adj* : artificial

artificio *nm* **1** HABILIDAD : skill **2** APARATO : device **3** ARDID : artifice, ruse — **artificioso, -sa** *adj* : cunning, deceptive

artillería *nf* : artillery

artilugio *nm* : gadget

artimaña *nf* : ruse, trick

artista *nmf* **1** : artist **2** ACTOR : actor, actress *f* — **artístico, -ca** *adj* : artistic

artritis *nms & pl* : arthritis — **artrítico, -ca** *adj* : arthritic

arveja *nf Lat* : pea

arzobispo *nm* : archbishop

as *nm* : ace

asa *nf* : handle

asado, -da *adj* : roasted, grilled — **asado** *nm* : roast — **asador** *nm* : spit — **asaduras** *nfpl* : offal, entrails

asalariado, -da *n* : wage earner — **~** *adj* : salaried

asaltar *vt* **1** : assault **2** ROBAR : mug, rob — **asaltante** *nmf* **1** : assailant **2** ATRACADOR : mugger, robber — **asalto** *nm* **1** : assault **2** ROBO : mugging, robbery

asamblea *nf* : assembly, meeting

asar *vt* : roast, grill — **asarse** *vr fam* : roast, feel the heat

asbesto *nm* : asbestos

ascender {56} *vi* **1** : ascend, rise up **2** : be promoted (in a job) **3** **~ a** : amount to — *vt* : promote — **ascendencia** *nf* : ancestry, descent — **ascendiente** *nmf* : ancestor — **~** *nm* : influence — **ascensión** *nf, pl* **-siones** : ascent — **ascenso** *nm* **1** : ascent, rise **2** : promotion (in a job) — **ascensor** *nm* : elevator

asco *nm* **1** : disgust **2 hacer ~s de** : turn up one's nose at **3 me da ~** : it makes me sick

ascua *nf* **1** : ember **2 estar en ~s** *fam* : be on edge

asear *vt* : clean, tidy up — **asearse** *vr* : get cleaned up — **aseado, -da** *adj* : clean, tidy

asediar *vt* **1** : besiege **2** ACOSAR : harass — **asedio** *nm* **1** : siege **2** ACOSO : harassment

asegurar *vt* **1** : assure **2** FIJAR : secure **3** : insure (a car, house, etc.) — **asegurarse** *vr* : make sure

asemejarse *vr* **1** : be similar **2 ~ a** : look like, resemble

asentar {55} *vt* **1** : set down **2** INSTALAR : set up, establish **3** *Lat* : state — **asentarse** *vr* **1** : settle **2** ESTABLECERSE : settle down — **asentado, -da** *adj* : settled, established

asentir {76} *vi* : assent, agree — **asentimiento** *nm* : assent

aseo *nm* : cleanliness

asequible *adj* : accessible, attainable

aserrar {55} *vt* : saw — **aserradero** *nm* : sawmill — **aserrín** *nm, pl* **-rrines** : sawdust

asesinar *vt* **1** : murder **2** : assassinate — **asesinato** *nm* **1** : murder **2** : assassination — **asesino, -na** *n* **1** : murderer, killer **2** : assassin

asesorar *vt* : advise, counsel — **asesorarse** *vr* **~ de** : consult — **asesor, -sora** *n* : advisor, consultant — **asesoramiento** *nm* : advice, counsel

asestar {55} *vt* **1** : aim (a weapon) **2** : deal (a blow)

aseverar *vt* : assert — **aseveración** *nf, pl* **-ciones** : assertion

asfalto *nm* : asphalt

asfixiar *vt* : asphyxiate, suffocate — **asfixiarse** *vr* : suffocate — **asfixia** *nf* : asphyxiation, suffocation

así *adv* **1** : like this, like that, thus **2 ~ de** : so, that (much) **3 ~ que** : so, therefore **4 ~ que** : as soon as **5 ~ como** : as well as — **~** *adj* : such, like that — **~** *conj* AUNQUE : even though

asiático, -ca *adj* : Asian, Asiatic

asidero *nm* : handle

asiduo, -dua *adj* : frequent, regular

asiento *nm* : seat

asignar *vt* **1** : assign, allocate **2** DESTINAR

: appoint — **asignación** *nf, pl* **-ciones 1**
: assignment **2** SUELDO : salary, pay —
asignatura *nf* : subject, course
asilo *nm* **1** : asylum, home **2** REFUGIO
: refuge, shelter — **asilado, -da** *n* : inmate
asimilar *vt* : assimilate — **asimilarse** *vr* ~
a : resemble
asimismo *adv* **1** : similarly, likewise **2**
TAMBIÉN : as well, also
asir {7} *vt* : seize, grasp — **asirse** *vr* ~ **a**
: cling to
asistir *vi* ~ **a** : attend, be present at — *vt*
: assist — **asistencia** *nf* **1** : attendance **2**
AYUDA : assistance — **asistente** *nmf* **1** : assistant **2 los** ~**s** : those present
asma *nf* : asthma — **asmático, -ca** *adj*
: asthmatic
asno *nm* : ass, donkey
asociar *vt* : associate — **asociarse** *vr* **1**
: form a partnership **2** ~ **a** : join, become
a member of — **asociación** *nf, pl* **-ciones**
: association — **asociado, -da** *adj* : associate, associated — ~ *n* : associate, partner
asolar {19} *vt* : devastate
asomar *vt* : show, stick out — *vi* : appear,
show — **asomarse** *vr* **1** : appear **2** : stick
one's head out (of a window)
asombrar *vt* : amaze, astonish — **asom-
brarse** *vr* : be amazed — **asombro** *nm*
: amazement, astonishment — **asombroso,
-sa** *adj* : amazing, astonishing
asomo *nm* **1** : hint, trace **2 ni por** ~ : by
no means
aspaviento *nm* : exaggerated gestures, fuss
aspecto *nm* **1** : aspect **2** APARIENCIA : appearance, look
áspero, -ra *adj* : rough, harsh — **aspereza**
nf : roughness, harshness
aspersión *nf, pl* **-siones** : sprinkling — **aspersor** *nm* : sprinkler
aspiración *nf, pl* **-ciones 1** : breathing in **2**
ANHELO : aspiration
aspiradora *nf* : vacuum cleaner
aspirar *vi* ~ **a** : aspire to — *vt* : inhale,
breathe in — **aspirante** *nmf* : applicant,
candidate
aspirina *nf* : aspirin
asquear *vt* : sicken, disgust
asquerosidad *nf* : filth, foulness — **asqueroso, -sa** *adj* : disgusting, sickening
asta *nf* **1** : flagpole **2** CUERNO : antler, horn
3 : shaft (of a spear) — **astado, -da** *adj*
: horned
asterisco *nm* : asterisk
asteroide *nm* : asteroid
astigmatismo *nm* : astigmatism
astillar *vt* : splinter — **astilla** *nf* : splinter,
chip
astillero *nm* : shipyard

astral *adj* : astral
astringente *adj & nm* : astringent
astro *nm* **1** : heavenly body **2** : star (of
movies, etc.)
astrología *nf* : astrology
astronauta *nmf* : astronaut — **astronáutica**
nf : astronautics
astronave *nf* : spaceship
astronomía *nf* : astronomy — **astronómico,
-ca** *adj* : astronomical — **astrónomo, -ma**
n : astronomer
astucia *nf* **1** : astuteness **2** ARDID : cunning,
guile — **astuto, -ta** *adj* **1** : astute **2**
TAIMADO : crafty
asueto *nm* : time off, break
asumir *vt* : assume — **asunción** *nf, pl*
-ciones : assumption
asunto *nm* **1** : matter, affair **2** NEGOCIO
: business
asustar *vt* : scare, frighten — **asustarse** *vr*
~ **de** : be frightened of — **asustadizo, -za**
adj : jumpy, skittish — **asustado, -da** *adj*
: frightened, afraid
atacar {72} *v* : attack — **atacante** *nmf* : attacker
atado *nm* : bundle
atadura *nf* : tie, bond
atajar *vt* : block, cut off — *vi* ~ **por** : take a
shortcut through — **atajo** *nm* : shortcut
atañer {79} *vi* ~ **a** : concern, have to do
with
ataque *nm* **1** : attack, assault **2** ACCESO : fit
3 ~ **de nervios** : nervous breakdown
atar *vt* : tie up, tie down — **atarse** *vr* : tie
(up)
atardecer {53} *v impers* : get dark — ~ *nm*
: late afternoon, dusk
atareado, -da *adj* : busy
atascar {72} *vt* **1** : block, clog **2** ESTORBAR
: hinder — **atascarse** *vr* **1** OBSTRUIRSE
: become obstructed **2** : get bogged down
— **atasco** *nm* **1** : blockage **2** EMBOTEL-
LAMIENTO : traffic jam
ataúd *nm* : coffin
ataviar {85} *vt* : dress (up) — **ataviarse** *vr*
: dress up — **atavío** *nm* : attire
atemorizar {21} *vt* : frighten — **atemori-
zarse** *vr* : get scared
atención *nf, pl* **-ciones 1** : attention **2**
prestar ~ : pay attention **3 llamar la** ~
: attract attention — ~ *interj* : attention!,
watch out!
atender {56} *vt* **1** : attend to **2** CUIDAR
: look after **3** : heed (advice, etc.) — *vi* : pay
attention
atenerse {80} *vr* ~ **a** : abide by
atentamente *adv* **1** : attentively **2 le
saluda** ~ : sincerely yours

atentar 18

atentar {55} *vi* ~ contra : make an attempt on — atentado *nm* : attack
atento, -ta *adj* 1 : attentive, mindful 2 CORTÉS : courteous
atenuar {3} *vt* 1 : dim (lights), tone down (colors, etc.) 2 DISMINUIR : lessen — atenuante *nmf* : extenuating circumstances
ateo, atea *adj* : atheistic — ~ *n* : atheist
aterciopelado, -da *adj* : velvety, downy
aterido, -da *adj* : frozen stiff
aterrar {55} *vt* : terrify — aterrador, -dora *adj* : terrifying
aterrizar {21} *vi* : land — aterrizaje *nm* : landing
aterrorizar {21} *vt* : terrify
atesorar *vt* : hoard, amass
atestar {55} *vt* 1 : crowd, pack 2 : testify to (in law) — atestado, -da *adj* : stuffed, packed
atestiguar {10} *vt* : testify to
atiborrar *vt* : stuff, cram — atiborrarse *vr* : stuff oneself
ático *nm* 1 : penthouse 2 DESVÁN : attic
atildado, -da *adj* : smart, neat
atinar *vi* : be on target
atípico, -ca *adj* : atypical
atirantar *vt* : tighten
atisbar *vt* 1 : spy on 2 VISLUMBRAR : catch a glimpse of — atisbo *nm* : sign, hint
atizar {21} *vt* 1 : poke (a fire) 2 : rouse, stir up (passions, etc.) — atizador *nm* : poker
atlántico, -ca *adj* : Atlantic
atlas *nm* : atlas
atleta *nmf* : athlete — atlético, -ca *adj* : athletic — atletismo *nm* : athletics
atmósfera *nf* : atmosphere — atmosférico, -ca *adj* : atmospheric
atolondrado, -da *adj* 1 : scatterbrained 2 ATURDIDO : bewildered, dazed
átomo *nm* : atom — atómico, -ca *adj* : atomic — atomizador *nm* : atomizer
atónito, -ta *adj* : astonished, amazed
atontar *vt* : stun, daze
atorar *vt* : block — atorarse *vr* : get stuck
atormentar *vt* : torment, torture — atormentarse *vr* : torment oneself, agonize — atormentador, -dora *n* : tormenter
atornillar *vt* : screw
atorrante *nmf Lat* : bum, loafer
atosigar {52} *vt* : harass, annoy
atracar {72} *vi* : dock, land — *vt* : hold up, mug — atracarse *vr fam* ~ de : gorge oneself with — atracadero *nm* : dock, pier — atracador, -dora *n* : robber, mugger
atracción *nf, pl* -ciones : attraction
atraco *nm* : holdup, robbery
atractivo, -va *adj* : attractive — atractivo *nm* : attraction, appeal
atraer {81} *vt* : attract

atragantarse *vr* : choke
atrancar {72} *vt* : block, bar — atrancarse *vr* : get blocked, get stuck
atrapar *vt* : trap, capture
atrás *adv* 1 DETRÁS : back, behind 2 ANTES : before, earlier 3 para ~ *or* hacia ~ : backwards
atrasar *vt* 1 : put back (a clock) 2 DEMORAR : delay — *vi* : lose time — atrasarse *vr* : fall behind — atrasado, -da *adj* 1 : late, overdue 2 : backward (of countries, etc.) 3 : slow (of a clock) — atraso *nm* 1 RETRASO : delay 2 : backwardness 3 ~s *nmpl* : arrears
atravesar {55} *vt* 1 CRUZAR : cross 2 TRASPASAR : pierce 3 : lay across (a road, etc.) 4 : go through (a situation) — atravesarse *vr* : be in the way
atrayente *adj* : attractive
atreverse *vr* : dare — atrevido, -da *adj* 1 : bold 2 INSOLENTE : insolent — atrevimiento *nm* 1 : boldness 2 DESCARO : insolence
atribuir {41} *vt* 1 : attribute 2 : confer (powers, etc.) — atribuirse *vr* : take credit for
atribular *vt* : afflict, trouble
atributo *nm* : attribute
atrincherar *vt* : entrench — atrincherarse *vr* : dig oneself in
atrocidad *nf* : atrocity
atronador, -dora *adj* : thunderous
atropellar *vt* 1 : run over 2 : violate, abuse (a person) — atropellarse *vr* : rush — atropellado, -da *adj* : hasty — atropello *nm* : abuse, outrage
atroz *adj, pl* atroces : atrocious
atuendo *nm* : attire
atufar *vt* : vex — atufarse *vr* : get angry
atún *nm, pl* atunes : tuna
aturdir *vt* 1 : stun, shock 2 CONFUNDIR : bewilder — aturdido, -da *adj* : dazed, bewildered
audaz *adj, pl* -daces : bold, daring — audacia *nf* : boldness, audacity
audible *adj* : audible
audición *nf, pl* -ciones 1 : hearing 2 : audition (in theater, etc.)
audiencia *nf* : audience
audífono *nm* 1 : hearing aid 2 ~s *nmpl Lat* : headphones, earphones
audiovisual *adj* : audiovisual
auditar *vt* : audit — auditor, -tora *n* : auditor
auditorio *nm* 1 : auditorium 2 PÚBLICO : audience
auge *nm* 1 : peak 2 : (economic) boom
augurar *vt* : predict, foretell — augurio *nm* : omen
augusto, -ta *adj* : august

aula *nf* : classroom
aullar {8} *vi* : howl — **aullido** *nm* : howl
aumentar *vt* : increase, raise — *vi* : increase, grow — **aumento** *nm* : increase, rise
aun *adv* **1** : even **2** ~ **así** : even so
aún *adv* **1** : still, yet **2 más** ~ : furthermore
aunar {8} *vt* : join, combine — **aunarse** *vr* : unite
aunque *conj* **1** : though, although, even if **2** ~ **sea** : at least
aureola *nf* **1** : halo **2** FAMA : aura
auricular *nm* **1** : telephone receiver **2** ~**es** *nmpl* : headphones
aurora *nf* : dawn
ausentarse *vr* : leave, go away — **ausencia** *nf* : absence — **ausente** *adj* : absent — ~ *nmf* **1** : absentee **2** : missing person (in law)
auspicios *nmpl* : sponsorship, auspices
austero, -ra *adj* : austere — **austeridad** *nf* : austerity
austral *adj* : southern
australiano, -na *adj* : Australian
austriaco *or* **austríaco, -ca** *adj* : Austrian
auténtico, -ca *adj* : authentic, genuine — **autenticidad** *nf* : authenticity
auto *nm* : auto, car
autoayuda *nf* : self-help
autobiografía *nf* : autobiography — **autobiográfico, -ca** *adj* : autobiographical
autobús *nm, pl* **-buses** : bus
autocompasión *nf* : self-pity
autocontrol *nm* : self-control
autocracia *nf* : autocracy
autóctono, -na *adj* : indigenous, native
autodefensa *nf* : self-defense
autodidacta *adj* : self-taught
autodisciplina *nf* : self-discipline
autoestop → **autostop**
autografiar *vt* : autograph — **autógrafo** *nm* : autograph
autómata *nm* : automaton
automático, -ca *adj* : automatic — **automatización** *nf, pl* **-ciones** : automation — **automatizar** {21} *vt* : automate
automotor, -triz *adj, fpl* **-trices** : self-propelled
automóvil *nm* : automobile — **automovilista** *nmf* : motorist — **automovilístico, -ca** *adj* : automobile, car
autonomía *nf* : autonomy — **autónomo, -ma** *adj* : autonomous
autopista *nf* : expressway, highway
autopropulsado, -da *adj* : self-propelled
autopsia *nf* : autopsy
autor, -tora *n* **1** : author **2** : perpetrator (of a crime)
autoridad *nf* : authority — **autoritario, -ria** *adj* : authoritarian

autorizar {21} *vt* : authorize, approve — **autorización** *nf, pl* **-ciones** : authorization — **autorizado, -da** *adj* **1** PERMITIDO : authorized **2** : authoritative
autorretrato *nm* : self-portrait
autoservicio *nm* **1** : self-service restaurant **2** SUPERMERCADO : supermarket
autostop *nm* **1** : hitchhiking **2 hacer** ~ : hitchhike — **autostopista** *nmf* : hitchhiker
autosuficiente *adj* : self-sufficient
auxiliar *vt* : aid, assist — ~ *adj* : auxiliary — ~ *nmf* **1** : assistant, helper **2** ~ **de vuelo** : flight attendant — **auxilio** *nm* **1** : aid, assistance **2 primeros** ~**s** : first aid
avalancha *nf* : avalanche
avalar *vt* : guarantee, endorse — **aval** *nm* : guarantee, endorsement
avanzar {21} *v* : advance, move forward — **avance** *nm* : advance — **avanzado, -da** *adj* : advanced
avaricia *nf* : greed, avarice — **avaricioso, -sa** *adj* : avaricious, greedy — **avaro, -ra** *adj* : miserly — ~ *n* : miser
avasallar *vt* : overpower, subjugate — **avasallador, -dora** *adj* : overwhelming
ave *nf* : bird
avecinarse *vr* : approach
avecindarse *vr* : settle, take up residence
avellana *nf* : hazelnut
avena *nf* **1** : oats *pl* **2** *or* **harina de** ~ : oatmeal
avenida *nf* : avenue
avenir {87} *vt* : reconcile, harmonize — **avenirse** *vr* : agree, come to terms
aventajar *vt* : be ahead of, surpass
aventar {55} *vt* **1** : fan **2** : winnow (grain) **3** *Lat* : throw, toss
aventurar *vt* : venture, risk — **aventurarse** *vr* : take a risk — **aventura** *nf* **1** : adventure **2** RIESGO : risk **3** AMORÍO : love affair — **aventurado, -da** *adj* : risky — **aventurero, -ra** *adj* : adventurous — ~ *n* : adventurer
avergonzar {9} *vt* : shame, embarrass — **avergonzarse** *vr* : be ashamed, be embarrassed
averiar {85} *vt* : damage — **averiarse** *vr* : break down — **avería** *nf* **1** : damage **2** : breakdown (of an automobile) — **averiado, -da** *adj* **1** : damaged, faulty **2** : broken down (of an automobile)
averiguar {10} *vt* **1** : find out **2** INVESTIGAR : investigate — **averiguación** *nf, pl* **-ciones** : investigation, inquiry
aversión *nf, pl* **-siones** : aversion, dislike
avestruz *nm, pl* **-truces** : ostrich
aviación *nf, pl* **-ciones** : aviation — **aviador, -dora** *n* : aviator
aviar {85} *vt* : prepare, make ready

ávido, -da *adj* : eager, avid — **avidez** *nf, pl*
-**deces** : eagerness
avío *nm* 1 : preparation, provision 2 ~s
nmpl : gear, equipment
avión *nm, pl* **aviones** : airplane — **avioneta**
nf : light airplane
avisar *vt* 1 : notify 2 ADVERTIR : warn —
aviso *nm* 1 : notice 2 ADVERTENCIA
: warning 3 *Lat* : advertisement, ad 4 **estar
sobre** ~ : be on the alert
avispa *nf* : wasp — **avispón** *nm, pl* **-pones**
: hornet
avispado, -da *adj fam* : clever, sharp
avistar *vt* : catch sight of
avivar *vt* 1 : enliven, brighten 2 : arouse
(desire, etc.) 3 : intensify (pain)
axila *nf* : underarm, armpit
axioma *nm* : axiom
ay *interj* 1 : oh! 2 : ouch!, ow!
ayer *adv* : yesterday — ~ *nm* : yesteryear,
days gone by
ayote *nm Lat* : pumpkin
ayudar *vt* : help, assist — **ayudarse** *vr* ~
de : make use of — **ayuda** *nf* : help, assistance — **ayudante** *nmf* : helper, assistant
ayunar *vi* : fast — **ayunas** *nfpl* **en** ~ : fast-
ing — **ayuno** *nm* : fast

ayuntamiento *nm* 1 : town hall, city hall
(building) 2 : town or city council
azabache *nm* : jet
azada *nf* : hoe — **azadonar** *vt* : hoe
azafata *nf* : stewardess *f*
azafrán *nm, pl* **-franes** : saffron
azalea *nf* : azalea
azar *nm* 1 : chance 2 **al** ~ : at random —
azaroso, -sa *adj* : hazardous (of a journey,
etc.), eventful (of a life)
azorar *vt* 1 : alarm 2 DESCONCERTAR : embarrass — **azorarse** *vr* : get embarrassed
azotar *vt* : beat, whip — **azote** *nm* 1 LÁTIGO
: whip, lash 2 CALAMIDAD : scourge
azotea *nf* : flat or terraced roof
azteca *adj* : Aztec
azúcar *nmf* : sugar — **azucarado, -da** *adj*
: sugary — **azucarera** *nf* : sugar bowl —
azucarero, -ra *adj* : sugar
azufre *nm* : sulphur
azul *adj & nm* : blue — **azulado, -da** *adj*
: bluish
azulejo *nm* 1 : ceramic tile 2 *Lat* : bluebird
azur *n* : azure, sky blue
azuzar {21} *vt* : incite, urge on

B

b *nf* : b, second letter of the Spanish alphabet
babear *vi* : drool, slobber — **baba** *nf* : saliva,
drool
babel *nmf* : bedlam
babero *nm* : bib
babor *nm* : port (side)
babosa *nf* : slug — **baboso, -sa** *adj* 1
: slimy 2 *Lat fam* : silly
babucha *nf* : slipper
babuino *nm* : baboon
bacalao *nm* : cod
bache *nm* 1 : pothole, rut 2 DIFICULTADES
: bad time
bachiller *nmf* : high school graduate —
bachillerato *nm* : high school diploma
bacon *nm Spain* : bacon
bacteria *nf* : bacterium
bagaje *nm* : baggage, luggage
bagatela *nf* : trinket
bagre *nm* : catfish
bahía *nf* : bay
bailar *v* : dance — **bailarín, -rina** *n, mpl*

-**rines** : dancer — **baile** *nm* 1 : dance 2 FI-
ESTA : dance party, ball
bajar *vt* 1 : bring down, lower 2 DESCENDER
: go down, come down — *vi* : descend, drop
— **bajarse** *vr* ~ **de** : get out of, get off —
baja *nf* 1 : fall, drop 2 CESE : dismissal 3
PERMISO : sick leave 4 : (military) casualty
— **bajada** *nf* 1 : descent, drop 2 PENDIENTE
: slope
bajeza *nf* : lowness, meanness
bajío *nm* : sandbank, shoal
bajo, -ja *adj* 1 : low, lower 2 : short (in
stature) 3 : soft, faint (of sounds) 4 VIL
: base, vile — **bajo** *adv* 1 : low 2 **habla
más** ~ : speak more softly — ~ *nm* 1
: ground floor 2 DOBLADILLO : hem 3
: bass (in music) — ~ *prep* : under, below
— **bajón** *nm, pl* **-jones** : sharp drop, slump
bala *nf* 1 : bullet 2 : bale (of cotton, etc.)
balada *nf* : ballad
balancear *vt* 1 : balance 2 : swing (one's
arms, etc.), rock (a boat) — **balancearse** *vr*
: swing, sway — **balance** *nm* 1 : balance 2

: balance sheet — **balanceo** *nm* : swaying, rocking

balancín *nm, pl* **-cines 1** : seesaw **2** MECE-DORA : rocking chair

balanza *nf* : scales *pl,* balance

balar *vi* : bleat

balaustrada *nf* : balustrade, banister

balazo *nm* **1** DISPARO : shot **2** : bullet wound

balbucear *vi* **1** : stammer, stutter **2** : babble (of a baby) — **balbuceo** *nm* : stammering, muttering, babbling

balcón *nm, pl* **-cones** : balcony

balde *nm* **1** : bucket, pail **2 en ~** : in vain

baldío, -día *adj* **1** : uncultivated **2** INÚTIL : useless — **baldío** *nm* : wasteland

baldosa *nf* : floor tile

balear *vt Lat* : shoot (at) — **baleo** *nm Lat* : shot, shooting

balido *nm* : bleat

balín *nm, pl* **-lines** : pellet

balística *nf* : ballistics — **balístico, -ca** *adj* : ballistic

baliza *nf* **1** : buoy **2** : beacon (for aircraft)

ballena *nf* : whale

ballesta *nf* **1** : crossbow **2** : spring (of an automobile)

ballet *nm* : ballet

balneario *nm* : spa

balompié *nm* : soccer

balón *nm, pl* **-lones** : ball — **baloncesto** *nm* : basketball — **balonvolea** *nm* : volleyball

balsa *nf* **1** : raft **2** ESTANQUE : pond, pool

bálsamo *nm* : balsam, balm — **balsámico, -ca** *adj* : soothing

baluarte *nm* : bulwark, bastion

bambolear *vi* : sway, swing — **bambolearse** *vr* : sway, rock

bambú *nm, pl* **-búes** *or* **-bús** : bamboo

banal *adj* : banal

banana *nf Lat* : banana — **banano** *nm Lat* : banana

banca *nf* **1** : banking **2** BANCO : bench — **bancario, -ria** *adj* : bank, banking — **bancarrota** *nf* : bankruptcy — **banco** *nm* **1** : bank **2** BANCA : stool, bench, pew **3** : school (of fish)

banda *nf* **1** : band, strip **2** : band (in music) **3** PANDILLA : gang **4** : flock (of birds) **5 ~ sonora** : sound track — **bandada** *nf* : flock (of birds), school (of fish)

bandazo *nm* : lurch

bandeja *nf* : tray, platter

bandera *nf* : flag, banner

banderilla *nf* : banderilla

banderín *nm, pl* **-rines** : pennant, small flag

bandido, -da *n* : bandit

bando *nm* **1** : proclamation, edict **2** PAR-TIDO : faction, side

bandolero, -ra *n* : bandit

banjo *nm* : banjo

banquero, -ra *n* : banker

banqueta *nf* **1** : stool, footstool **2** *Lat* : sidewalk

banquete *nm* : banquet

bañar *vt* **1** : bathe, wash **2** SUMERGIR : immerse **3** CUBRIR : coat, cover — **bañarse** *vr* **1** : take a bath **2** : go swimming — **bañera** *nf* : bathtub — **bañista** *nmf* : bather — **baño** *nm* **1** : bath, swim **2** BAÑERA : bathtub **3** **¿donde está el ~?** : where is the bathroom? **4 ~ María** : double boiler

baqueta *nf* **1** : ramrod **2 ~s** *nfpl* : drumsticks

bar *nm* : bar, tavern

barajar *vt* **1** : shuffle (cards) **2** CONSIDERAR : consider — **baraja** *nf* : deck of cards

baranda *nf* : rail, railing — **barandal** *nm* : handrail, banister

barato, -ta *adj* : cheap — **barato** *adv* : cheap, cheaply — **barata** *nf Lat* : sale, bargain — **baratija** *nf* : trinket — **baratillo** *nm* : secondhand store, flea market

barba *nf* **1** : beard, stubble **2** BARBILLA : chin

barbacoa *nf* : barbecue

barbaridad *nf* **1** : barbarity, cruelty **2 ¡qué ~!** : that's outrageous! — **barbarie** *nf* : barbarism, savagery — **bárbaro, -ra** *adj* : barbaric

barbecho *nm* : fallow land

barbero, -ra *n* : barber — **barbería** *nf* : barbershop

barbilla *nf* : chin

barbudo, -da *adj* : bearded

barca *nf* **1** : boat **2 ~ de pasaje** : ferryboat — **barcaza** *nf* : barge — **barco** *nm* : boat, ship

barítono *nm* : baritone

barman *nm* : bartender

barnizar {21} *vt* **1** : varnish **2** : glaze (ceramics) — **barniz** *nm, pl* **-nices 1** : varnish **2** : glaze (on ceramics)

barómetro *nm* : barometer

barón *nm, pl* **-rones** : baron — **baronesa** *nf* : baroness

barquero *nm* : boatman

barquillo *nm* : wafer, cone

barra *nf* **1** : bar, rod, stick **2** : counter (of a bar, etc.)

barraca *nf* **1** : hut, cabin **2** CASETA : booth, stall

barranco *nm or* **barranca** *nf* : ravine, gorge, gully

barredera *nf* : street-sweeping machine

barrenar *vt* : drill — **barrena** *nf* : drill, auger

barrer *v* : sweep

barrera *nf* : barrier

barreta *nf* : crowbar
barriada *nf* : district, quarter
barrica *nf* : cask, keg
barricada *nf* : barricade
barrido *nm* : sweep, sweeping
barriga *nf* : belly
barril *nm* **1** : barrel, keg **2 de ~** : draft
barrio *nm* **1** : neighborhood **2 ~ bajo** : slums *pl*
barro *nm* **1** : mud **2** ARCILLA : clay **3** GRANO : pimple, blackhead — **barroso, -sa** *adj* : muddy
barrote *nm* : bar (on a window)
barrunto *nm* **1** : suspicion **2** INDICIO : sign, indication
bártulos *nmpl* : things, belongings
barullo *nm* : racket, ruckus
basa *nf* : base, pedestal — **basar** *vt* : base — **basarse** *vr* **~ en** : be based on
báscula *nf* : scales *pl*
base *nf* **1** : base **2** FUNDAMENTO : basis, foundation **3 ~ de datos** : database — **básico, -ca** *adj* : basic
basquetbol *or* **básquetbol** *nm Lat* : basketball
bastar *vi* : be enough, suffice — **bastante** *adv* **1** : fairly, rather **2** SUFICIENTE : enough — **~** *adj* : enough, sufficient — **~** *pron* : enough
bastardo, -da *adj & n* : bastard
bastidor *nm* **1** : frame **2** : wing (in theater) **3 entre ~es** : behind the scenes, backstage
bastilla *nf* : hem
bastión *nf, pl* **-tiones** : bastion, stronghold
basto, -ta *adj* : coarse, rough
bastón *nm, pl* **-tones 1** : cane, walking stick **2** : baton (in parades)
basura *nf* : garbage, rubbish — **basurero, -ra** *n* : garbage collector
bata *nf* **1** : bathrobe, housecoat **2** : smock (of a doctor, laboratory worker, etc.)
batallar *vi* : battle, fight — **batalla** *nf* **1** : battle, fight, struggle **2 de ~** : ordinary, everyday — **batallón** *nm, pl* **-llones** : battalion
batata *nf* : yam, sweet potato
batear *v* : bat, hit — **bate** *nm* : baseball bat — **bateador, -dora** *n* : batter, hitter
batería *nf* **1** : battery **2** : drums *pl* **3 ~ de cocina** : kitchen utensils *pl*
batir *vt* **1** : beat, whip **2** DERRIBAR : knock down — **batirse** *vr* : fight — **batido** *nm* : milk shake — **batidor** *nm* : eggbeater, whisk — **batidora** *nf* : electric mixer
batuta *nf* : baton
baúl *nm* : trunk, chest
bautismo *nm* : baptism — **bautismal** *adj* : baptismal — **bautizar** {21} *vt* : baptize — **bautizo** *nm* : baptism, christening

baya *nf* : berry
bayeta *nf* : cleaning cloth
bayoneta *nf* : bayonet
bazar *nm* : bazaar
bazo *nm* : spleen
bazofia *nf fam* : rubbish, hogwash
beato, -ta *adj* : blessed
bebé *nm* : baby
beber *v* : drink — **bebedero** *nm* : watering trough — **bebedor, -dora** *n* : (heavy) drinker — **bebida** *nf* : drink, beverage — **bebido, -da** *adj* : drunk
beca *nf* : grant, scholarship
becerro, -rra *n* : calf
befa *nf* : jeer, taunt
beige *adj & nm* : beige
beisbol *or* **béisbol** *nm* : baseball — **beisbolista** *nmf* : baseball player
beldad *nf* : beauty
belén *nf, pl* **-lenes** : Nativity scene
belga *adj* : Belgian
beliceño, -ña *adj* : Belizean
bélico, -ca *adj* : military, war — **belicoso, -sa** *adj* : warlike
beligerancia *nf* : belligerence — **beligerante** *adj & nmf* : belligerent
belleza *nf* : beauty — **bello, -lla** *adj* **1** : beautiful **2 bellas artes** : fine arts
bellota *nf* : acorn
bemol *adj & nm* : flat (in music)
bendecir {11} *vt* **1** : bless **2 ~ la mesa** : say grace — **bendición** *nf, pl* **-ciones** : benediction, blessing — **bendito, -ta** *adj* **1** : blessed, holy **2** DICHOSO : fortunate **3 ¡bendito sea Dios!** : thank goodness!
benefactor, -tora *n* : benefactor
beneficiar *vt* : benefit, assist — **beneficiarse** *vr* : benefit, profit — **beneficiario, -ria** *n* : beneficiary — **beneficio** *nm* **1** : gain, profit **2** BIEN : benefit — **beneficioso, -sa** *adj* : beneficial — **benéfico, -ca** *adj* : charitable
benemérito, -ta *adj* : worthy
beneplácito *nm* : approval, consent
benévolo, -la *adj* : benevolent, kind — **benevolencia** *nf* : benevolence, kindness
bengala *nf or* **luz de ~** : flare
benigno, -na *adj* **1** : mild **2** : benign (in medicine) — **benignidad** *nf* : mildness, kindness
benjamín, -mina *n, mpl* **-mines** : youngest child
beodo, -da *adj & n* : drunk
berenjena *nf* : eggplant
berrear *vi* **1** : bellow, low **2** : bawl, howl (of a person) — **berrido** *nm* **1** : bellowing **2** : howl, scream (of a person)
berro *nm* : watercress
berza *nf* : cabbage

besar *vt* : kiss — **besarse** *vr* : kiss (each other) — **beso** *nm* : kiss
bestia *nf* : beast, animal — **bestial** *adj* : bestial, brutal — **bestialidad** *nf* : brutality
betabel *nm Lat* : beet
betún *nm, pl* **-tunes** : shoe polish
bianual *adj* : biannual
biberón *nm, pl* **-rones** : baby's bottle
Biblia *nf* : Bible — **bíblico, -ca** *adj* : biblical
bibliografía *nf* : bibliography — **bibliográfico, -ca** *adj* : bibliographic, bibliographical
biblioteca *nf* : library — **bibliotecario, -ria** *n* : librarian
bicarbonato *nm* ~ **de soda** : baking soda
bicentenario *nm* : bicentennial
bíceps *nms & pl* : biceps
bicho *nm* : small animal, bug
bicicleta *nf* : bicycle — **bici** *nf fam* : bike
bicolor *adj* : two-tone
bidón *nm, pl* **-dones** : large can, drum
bien *adv* **1** : well, good **2** CORRECTAMENTE : correctly, right **3** MUY : very, quite **4** DE BUENA GANA : willingly **5** ~ **que** : although **6** **más** ~ : rather — **bien** *adj* **1** : all right, well **2** AGRADABLE : pleasant, nice **3** SATISFACTORIO : satisfactory **4** CORRECTO : correct, right — **bien** *nm* **1** : good **2** ~**es** *nmpl* : property, goods
bienal *adj & nf* : biennial
bienaventurado, -da *adj* : blessed, fortunate
bienestar *nm* : welfare, well-being
bienhechor, -chora *n* : benefactor
bienintencionado, -da *adj* : well-meaning
bienvenido, -da *adj* : welcome — **bienvenida** *nf* **1** : welcome **2 dar la** ~ **a** : welcome (s.o.)
bife *nm Lat* : steak
bifocales *nmpl* : bifocals
bifurcarse {72} *vr* : fork — **bifurcación** *nf, pl* **-ciones** : fork, branch
bigamia *nf* : bigamy
bigote *nm* **1** : mustache **2** ~**s** *nmpl* : whiskers (of an animal)
bikini *nm* : bikini
bilingüe *adj* : bilingual
bilis *nf* : bile
billar *nm* : pool, billiards
billete *nm* **1** : bill, banknote **2** BOLETO : ticket — **billetera** *nf* : billfold, wallet
billón *nm, pl* **-llones** : trillion
bimensual, -suale *adj* : twice a month — **bimestral** *adj* : bimonthly
binario, -ria *adj* : binary
bingo *nm* : bingo
binoculares *nmpl* : binoculars
biodegradable *adj* : biodegradable
biofísica *nf* : biophysics
biografía *nf* : biography — **biográfico, -ca**

adj : biographical — **biógrafo, -fa** *n* : biographer
biología *nf* : biology — **biológico, -ca** *adj* : biological, biologic — **biólogo, -ga** *n* : biologist
biombo *nm* : folding screen
biomecánica *nf* : biomechanics
biopsia *nf* : biopsy
bioquímica *nf* : biochemistry — **bioquímico, -ca** *adj* : biochemical
biotecnología *nf* : biotechnology
bipartidista *adj* : bipartisan
bípedo *nm* : biped
biquini → **bikini**
birlar *vt fam* : swipe, pinch
bis *adv* **1** : twice (in music) **2** : A (in an address) — ~ *nm* : encore
bisabuelo, -la *n* : great-grandfather *m*, great-grandmother *f*
bisagra *nf* : hinge
bisecar {72} *vt* : bisect
biselar *vt* : bevel
bisexual *adj* : bisexual
bisiesto *adj* **año** ~ : leap year
bisnieto, -ta *n* : great-grandson *m*, great-granddaughter *f*
bisonte *nm* : bison, buffalo
bisoño, -ña *n* : novice
bistec *nm* : steak
bisturí *nm* : scalpel
bisutería *nf* : costume jewelry
bit *nm* : bit (unit of information)
bizco, -ca *adj* : cross-eyed
bizcocho *nm* : sponge cake
bizquear *vi* : squint — **bizquera** *nf* : squint
blanco, -ca *adj* : white — **blanco, -ca** *n* : white person — **blanco** *nm* **1** : white **2** DIANA : target, bull's-eye **3** : blank (space) — **blancura** *nf* : whiteness
blandir {1} *vt* : wave, brandish
blando, -da *adj* **1** : soft, tender **2** DÉBIL : weak-willed **3** INDULGENTE : lenient — **blandura** *nf* **1** : softness, tenderness **2** DEBILIDAD : weakness **3** INDULGENCIA : leniency
blanquear *vt* **1** : whiten, bleach **2** : launder (money) — *vi* : turn white — **blanqueador** *nm Lat* : bleach
blasfemar *vi* : blaspheme — **blasfemia** *nf* : blasphemy — **blasfemo, -ma** *adj* : blasphemous
bledo *nm* **no me importa un** ~ *fam* : I couldn't care less
blindaje *nm* : armor, armor plating — **blindado, -da** *adj* : armored
bloc *nm, pl* **blocs** : (writing) pad
bloquear *vt* **1** OBSTRUIR : block, obstruct **2** : blockade — **bloque** *nm* **1** : block **2** : bloc

blusa

(in politics) — **bloqueo** *nm* **1** OBSTRUC-
CIÓN : blockage **2** : blockade
blusa *nf* : blouse — **blusón** *nm, pl* **-sones**
: smock
boato *nm* : showiness
bobina *nf* : bobbin, reel
bobo, -ba *adj* : silly, stupid — ~ *n* : fool,
simpleton
boca *nf* **1** : mouth **2** ENTRADA : entrance **3**
~ **arriba** : faceup **4** ~ **abajo** : facedown,
prone **5** ~ **de riego** : hydrant
bocacalle *nf* : entrance (to a street)
bocado *nm* **1** : bite, mouthful **2** : bit (of a
bridle) — **bocadillo** *nm Spain* : sandwich
bocajarro *nm* **a** ~ : point-blank
bocallave *nf* : keyhole
bocanada *nf* **1** : swallow, swig **2** : puff,
gust (of smoke, wind, etc.)
boceto *nm* : sketch, outline
bochorno *nm* **1** VERGÜENZA : embarrassment **2** : muggy weather — **bochornoso,
-sa** *adj* **1** VERGONZOSO : embarrassing **2**
: muggy, sultry
bocina *nf* **1** : horn **2** : mouthpiece (of a telephone) — **bocinazo** *nm* : honk, toot
boda *nf* : wedding
bodega *nf* **1** : wine cellar **2** : warehouse **3**
: hold (of a ship or airplane) **4** *Lat* : grocery
store
bofetear *vt* : slap — **bofetada** *nf or* **bofetón**
nm : slap (in the face)
boga *nf* : fashion, vogue
bohemio, -mia *adj & n* : bohemian
boicotear *vt* : boycott — **boicot** *nm, pl* **-cots**
: boycott
boina *nf* : beret
bola *nf* **1** : ball **2** *fam* : fib
bolera *nf* : bowling alley
boleta *nf Lat* : ticket — **boletería** *nf Lat*
: ticket office
boletín *nm, pl* **-tines** **1** : bulletin **2** ~ **de
noticias** : news release
boleto *nm* : ticket
boliche *nm* **1** : bowling **2** BOLERA : bowling
alley
bolígrafo *nm* : ballpoint pen
bolillo *nm* : bobbin
boliviano, -na *adj* : Bolivian
bollo *nm* : bun, sweet roll
bolo *nm* **1** : bowling pin **2** ~ **s** *nmpl* : bowling
bolsa *nf* **1** : bag **2** *Lat* : pocketbook, purse
3 la Bolsa : the stock market — **bolsillo** *nm*
: pocket — **bolso** *nm Spain* : pocketbook,
handbag
bomba *nf* **1** : bomb **2** ~ **de gasolina** : gas
pump
bombachos *nmpl* : baggy trousers
bombardear *vt* : bomb, bombard — **bom-**

bardeo *nm* : bombing, bombardment —
bombardero *nm* : bomber (airplane)
bombear *vt* : pump — **bombero, -ra** *n* : firefighter
bombilla *nf* : lightbulb — **bombillo** *nm Lat*
: lightbulb
bombo *nm* **1** : bass drum **2 a** ~**s y platillos**
: with a great fanfare
bombón *nm, pl* **-bones** : candy, chocolate
bonachón, -chona *adj, mpl* **-chones** *fam*
: good-natured
bonanza *nf* **1** : fair weather (at sea) **2** PROS-
PERIDAD : prosperity
bondad *nf* : goodness, kindness — **bondadoso, -sa** *adj* : kind, good
boniato *nm* : sweet potato
bonificación *nf, pl* **-ciones** **1** : bonus, extra
2 DESCUENTO : discount
bonito, -ta *adj* : pretty, lovely
bono *nm* **1** : bond **2** VALE : voucher
boquear *vi* : gasp — **boqueada** *nf* : gasp
boquerón *nm, pl* **-rones** : anchovy
boquete *nm* : gap, opening
boquiabierto, -ta *adj* : open-mouthed,
speechless
boquilla *nf* : mouthpiece (of a musical instrument)
borbollar *vi* : bubble
borbotar *or* **borbotear** *vi* : boil, bubble, gurgle — **borbotón** *nm, pl* **-tones** **1** : spurt **2
salir a borbotones** : gush out
bordar *v* : embroider — **bordado** *nm* : embroidery, needlework
borde *nm* **1** : border, edge **2 al** ~ **de** : on
the verge of — **bordear** *vt* : border — **bor-
dillo** *nm* : curb
bordo *nm* **a** ~ : aboard, on board
borla *nf* **1** : pom-pom, tassel **2** : powder
puff
borracho, -cha *adj & n* : drunk — **bor-
rachera** *nf* : drunkenness
borrar *vt* : erase, blot out — **borrador** *nm* **1**
: rough draft **2** : eraser (for a blackboard)
borrascoso, -sa *adj* : stormy
borrego, -ga *n* : lamb, sheep — **borrego** *nm
Lat* : false rumor, hoax
borrón *nm, pl* **-rrones** **1** : smudge, blot **2**
~ **y cuenta nueva** : let's forget about it —
borroso, -sa *adj* **1** : blurry, smudgy **2** IN-
DISTINTO : vague, hazy
bosque *nm* : woods, forest — **boscoso, -sa**
adj : wooded
bosquejar *vt* : sketch (out) — **bosquejo** *nm*
: outline, sketch
bostezar {21} *vi* : yawn — **bostezo** *nm*
: yawn
bota *nf* : boot
botánica *nf* : botany — **botánico, -ca** *adj*
: botanical

botar *vt* **1** : throw, hurl **2** *Lat* : throw away **3** : launch (a ship) — *vi* : bounce

bote *nm* **1** : small boat **2** *Spain* : can **3** TARRO : jar **4** SALTO : bounce, jump

botella *nf* : bottle

botín *nm, pl* **-tines** **1** : ankle boot **2** DESPOJOS : booty, plunder

botiquín *nm, pl* **-quines** **1** : medicine cabinet **2** : first-aid kit

botón *nm, pl* **-tones** **1** : button **2** YEMA : bud — **botones** *nmfs & pl* : bellhop

botulismo *nm* : botulism

boutique *nf* : boutique

bóveda *nf* : vault

boxear *vi* : box — **boxeador, -dora** *n* : boxer — **boxeo** *nm* : boxing

boya *nf* : buoy — **boyante** *adj* **1** : buoyant **2** PRÓSPERO : prosperous, thriving

bozal *nm* **1** : muzzle **2** : halter (for a horse)

bracear *vi* **1** : wave one's arms **2** NADAR : swim, crawl

bracero, -ra *n* : day laborer

bragas *nf Spain* : panties

bragueta *nf* : fly, pants zipper

braille *adj & nm* : braille

bramante *nm* : twine, string

bramar *vi* **1** : bellow, roar **2** : howl (of the wind) — **bramido** *nm* : bellow, roar

brandy *nm* : brandy

branquia *nf* : gill

brasa *nf* : ember

brasier *nm Lat* : brassiere

brasileño, -ña *adj* : Brazilian

bravata *nf* **1** : boast, bravado **2** AMENAZO : threat

bravo, -va *adj* **1** : fierce, savage **2** : rough (of the sea) **3** *Lat* : angry — ~ *interj* : bravo!, well done! — **bravura** *nf* **1** FEROCIDAD : fierceness **2** VALENTÍA : bravery

braza *nf* **1** : breaststroke **2** : fathom (measurement) — **brazada** *nf* : stroke (in swimming)

brazalete *nm* **1** : bracelet **2** : (cloth) armband

brazo *nm* **1** : arm **2** : branch (of a river, etc.) **3** ~ **derecho** : right-hand man **4** ~**s** *nmpl* : hands, laborers

brea *nf* : tar

brebaje *nm* : concoction

brecha *nf* : breach, gap

brécol *nm* : broccoli

bregar {52} *vi* **1** LUCHAR : struggle **2** TRABAJAR : work hard — **brega** *nf* **andar a la** ~ : struggle

breña *nf or* **breñal** *nm* : scrubland, brush

breve *adj* **1** : brief, short **2 en** ~ : shortly, in short — **brevedad** *nf* : brevity, shortness — **brevemente** *adv* : briefly

brezal *nm* : moor, heath — **brezo** *nm* : heather

bricolaje *or* **bricolage** *nm* : do-it-yourself

brida *nf* : bridle

brigada *nf* **1** : brigade **2** EQUIPO : gang, team, squad

brillar *vi* : shine, sparkle — **brillante** *adj* : brilliant, shiny — ~ *nm* : diamond — **brillantez** *nf* : brilliance — **brillo** *nm* **1** : luster, shine **2** ESPLENDOR : splendor — **brilloso, -sa** *adj* : shiny

brincar {72} *vi* : jump about, frolic — **brinco** *nm* : jump, skip

brindar *vi* : drink a toast — *vt* : offer, provide — **brindarse** *vr* : offer one's assistance — **brindis** *nm* : drink, toast

brío *nm* **1** : force, determination **2** ÁNIMO : spirit, verve — **brioso, -sa** *adj* : spirited, lively

brisa *nf* : breeze

británico, -ca *adj* : British

brizna *nf* **1** : strand, thread **2** : blade (of grass)

brocado *nm* : brocade

brocha *nf* : paintbrush

broche *nm* **1** : fastener, clasp **2** ALFILER : brooch

brocheta *nf* : skewer

brócoli *nm* : broccoli

bromear *vi* : joke, fool around — **broma** *nf* : joke, prank — **bromista** *adj* : fun-loving, joking — ~ *nmf* : joker, prankster

bronca *nf fam* : fight, row

bronce *nm* : bronze — **bronceado, -da** *adj* : suntanned — **bronceado** *nm* : tan — **broncearse** *vr* : get a suntan

bronco, -ca *adj* **1** : harsh, rough **2** : untamed, wild (of a horse)

bronquitis *nf* : bronchitis

broqueta *nf* : skewer

brotar *vi* **1** : bud, sprout **2** : stream, gush (of a river, tears, etc.) **3** : arise (of feelings, etc.) **4** : break out (in medicine) — **brote** *nm* **1** : outbreak **2** : sprout, bud, shoot (of plants)

brujería *nf* : witchcraft — **bruja** *nf* **1** : witch **2** *fam* : old hag — **brujo** *nm* : warlock, sorcerer — **brujo, -ja** *adj* : bewitching

brújula *nf* : compass

bruma *nf* : haze, mist — **brumoso, -sa** *adj* : hazy, misty

bruñir {38} *vt* : burnish, polish

brusco, -ca *adj* **1** SÚBITO : sudden, abrupt **2** TOSCO : brusque, rough — **brusquedad** *nf* : abruptness, brusqueness

brutal *adj* : brutal — **brutalidad** *nf* : brutality

bruto, -ta *adj* **1** : brutish, stupid **2** : crude (of petroleum, etc.), uncut (of diamonds) **3** **peso** ~ : gross weight — ~ *n* : brute

bucal *adj* : oral
bucear *vi* **1** : dive, swim underwater **2** ~ **en** : delve into — **buceo** *nm* : (underwater) diving
bucle *nm* : curl
budín *nm, pl* **-dines** : pudding
budismo *nm* : Buddhism — **budista** *adj & nmf* : Buddhist
buenamente *adv* **1** : easily **2** VOLUNTARIAMENTE : willingly
buenaventura *nf* **1** : good luck **2 decir la** ~ **a uno** : tell s.o.'s fortune
bueno, -na *adj* (**buen** *before masculine singular nouns*) **1** : good **2** AMABLE : kind **3** APROPIADO : appropriate **4** SALUDABLE : well, healthy **5** : nice, fine (of weather) **6 buenos días** : hello, good day **7 buenas noches** : good night **8 buenas tardes** : good afternoon, good evening — **bueno** *interj* : OK!, all right!
buey *nm* : ox, steer
búfalo *nm* : buffalo
bufanda *nf* : scarf
bufar *vi* : snort — **bufido** *nm* : snort
bufet *or* **bufé** *nm* : buffet-style meal
bufete *nm* **1** : law practice **2** MESA : writing desk
bufo, -fa *adj* : comic — **bufón, -fona** *n, mpl* **-fones** : buffoon, jester — **bufonada** *nf* : wisecrack
buhardilla *nf* : attic, garret
búho *nm* : owl
buitre *nm* : vulture
bujía *nf* : spark plug
bulbo *nm* : bulb (of a plant)
bulevar *nm* : boulevard
búlgaro, -ra *adj* : Bulgarian
bulla *nf* : uproar, racket

bulldozer *nm* : bulldozer
bullicio *nm* **1** : uproar **2** AJETREO : hustle and bustle — **bullicioso, -sa** *adj* : noisy, boisterous
bullir {38} *vi* **1** : boil **2** AJETREARSE : bustle, stir
bulto *nm* **1** : package, bundle **2** VOLUMEN : bulk, size **3** FORMA : form, shape **4** PROTUBERANCIA : lump, swelling
bumerán *nm, pl* **-ranes** : boomerang
buñuelo *nm* : fried pastry
buque *nm* : ship
burbujear *vi* : bubble — **burbuja** *nf* : bubble
burdel *nm* : brothel
burdo, -da *adj* : coarse, rough
burgués, -guesa *adj & n, mpl* **-gueses** : bourgeois — **burguesía** *nf* : bourgeoisie
burlar *vt* : trick, deceive — **burlarse** *vr* ~ **de** : make fun of — **burla** *nf* **1** MOFA : mockery, ridicule **2** BROMA : joke, trick
burlesco, -ca *adj* : comic, funny
burlón, -lona *adj, mpl* **-lones** : mocking
burocracia *nf* : bureaucracy — **burócrata** *nmf* : bureaucrat — **burocrático, -ca** *adj* : bureaucratic
burro, -rra *n* **1** : donkey **2** *fam* : dunce — ~ *adj* : stupid — **burro** *nm* **1** : sawhorse **2** *Lat* : stepladder
bus *nm* : bus
buscar {72} *vt* **1** : look for, seek **2 ir a** ~ **a uno** : fetch s.o. — *vi* : search — **busca** *nf* : search — **búsqueda** *nf* : search
busto *nm* : bust (in sculpture)
butaca *nf* **1** : armchair **2** : seat (in a theatre)
butano *nm* : butane
buzo *nm* : diver
buzón *nm, pl* **-zones** : mailbox
byte *nm* : byte

C

c *nf* : c, third letter of the Spanish alphabet
cabal *adj* **1** : exact **2** COMPLETO : complete — **cabales** *nmpl* **no estar en sus** ~ : not be in one's right mind
cabalgar {52} *vi* : ride — **cabalgata** *nf* : cavalcade
caballa *nf* : mackerel
caballería *nf* **1** : cavalry **2** CABALLO : horse, mount — **caballeriza** *nf* : stable
caballero *nm* **1** : gentleman **2** : knight (rank) — **caballerosidad** *nf* : chivalry — **caballeroso, -sa** *adj* : chivalrous

caballete *nm* **1** : ridge (of a roof) **2** : easel (for a canvas) **3** : bridge (of the nose)
caballito *nm* **1** : rocking horse **2** ~s *nmpl* : merry-go-round
caballo *nm* **1** : horse **2** : knight (in chess) **3** ~ **de fuerza** : horsepower
cabaña *nf* : cabin, hut
cabaret *nm, pl* **-rets** : nightclub, cabaret
cabecear *vi* **1** : shake one's head, nod **2** : pitch, lurch (of a boat)
cabecera *nf* **1** : head (of a bed, etc.) **2**

: heading (in a text) **3 médico de ~** : family doctor

cabecilla *nmf* : ringleader

cabello *nm* : hair — **cabelludo, -da** *adj* : hairy

caber {12} *vi* **1** : fit, go (into) **2 no cabe duda** : there's no doubt

cabestro *nm* : halter

cabeza *nf* **1** : head **2 de ~** : head first — **cabezada** *nf* **1** : butt (of the head) **2 dar ~s** : nod off

cabezal *nm* : bolster, headrest

cabida *nf* **1** : room, capacity **2 dar ~ a** : accomodate, find room for

cabina *nf* **1** : booth **2** : cab (of a truck, etc.) **3** : cabin, cockpit (of an airplane)

cabizbajo, -ja *adj* : downcast

cable *nm* : cable

cabo *nm* **1** : end, stub **2** TROZO : bit **3** : corporal (in the military) **4** : cape (in geography) **5 al fin y al ~** : after all **6 llevar a ~** : carry out, do

cabra *nf* : goat

cabriola *nf* **1** : leap, skip **2 hacer ~s** : prance around

cabrito *nm* : kid (goat)

cacahuate *or* **cacahuete** *nm* : peanut

cacao *nm* **1** : cacao (tree) **2** : cocoa (drink)

cacarear *vi* : crow, cackle — *vt fam* : boast about

cacería *nf* : hunt

cacerola *nf* : pan, saucepan

cacharro *nm* **1** *fam* : thing, piece of junk **2** *fam* : jalopy **3 ~s** *nmpl* : pots and pans

cachear *vt* : search, frisk

cachemir *nm or* **cachemira** *nf* : cashmere

cachete *nm Lat* : cheek — **cachetada** *nf Lat* : slap

cacho *nm* **1** *fam* : piece, bit **2** *Lat* : horn

cachorro, -rra *n* **1** : cub **2** PERRITO : puppy

cactus *or* **cacto** *nm* : cactus

cada *adj* : each, every

cadalso *nm* : scaffold

cadáver *nm* : corpse

cadena *nf* **1** : chain **2** : (television) channel **3 ~ de montaje** : assembly line

cadencia *nf* : cadence

cadera *nf* : hip

cadete *nmf* : cadet

caducar {72} *vi* : expire — **caducidad** *nf* : expiration

caer {13} *vi* **1** : fall, drop **2 ~ bien a uno** : be to one's liking **3 dejar ~** : drop **4 me cae bien** : I like her, I like him — **caerse** *vr* : drop, fall (down)

café *nm* **1** : coffee **2** : café — **~** *adj Lat* : brown — **cafetera** *nf* : coffeepot — **cafetería** *nf* : coffee shop, cafeteria — **cafeína** *nf* : caffeine

caída *nf* **1** : fall, drop **2** PENDIENTE : slope

caimán *nm, pl* **-manes** : alligator

caja *nf* **1** : box, case **2** : checkout counter, cashier's desk (in a store) **3 ~ fuerte** : safe **4 ~ registradora** : cash register — **cajero, -ra** *n* **1** : cashier **2** : (bank) teller — **cajetilla** *nf* : pack (of cigarettes) — **cajón** *nm, pl* **-jones 1** : drawer (in furniture) **2** : large box, crate

cajuela *nf Lat* : trunk (of a car)

cal *nf* : lime

cala *nf* : cove

calabaza *nf* **1** : pumpkin, squash, gourd **2 dar ~s a** *fam* : give the brush-off to — **calabacín** *nm, pl* **-cines** *or* **calabacita** *nf Lat* : zucchini

calabozo *nm* **1** : prison **2** CELDA : cell

calamar *nm* : squid

calambre *nm* **1** ESPASMO : cramp **2** : (electric) shock

calamidad *nf* : calamity

calar *vt* **1** : soak (through) **2** PERFORAR : pierce — **calarse** *vr* : get drenched

calavera *nf* : skull

calcar {72} *vt* **1** : trace **2** IMITAR : copy, imitate

calcetín *nm, pl* **-tines** : sock

calcinar *vt* : char

calcio *nm* : calcium

calcomanía *nf* : decal

calcular *vt* : calculate, estimate — **calculador, -dora** *adj* : calculating — **calculadora** *nf* : calculator — **cálculo** *nm* **1** : calculation **2** : calculus (in mathematics and medicine) **3 ~ biliar** : gallstone

caldera *nf* **1** : cauldron **2** : boiler (for heating, etc.) — **caldo** *nm* : broth, stock

calefacción *nf, pl* **-ciones** : heating, heat

calendario *nm* : calendar

calentar {55} *vt* **1** : heat (up), warm (up) — **calentarse** *vr* : get warm, heat up — **calentador** *nm* : heater — **calentura** *nf* : temperature, fever

calibre *nm* **1** : caliber **2** DIÁMETRO : bore, diameter — **calibrar** *vt* : calibrate

calidad *nf* **1** : quality **2 en ~ de** : as, in the capacity of

cálido, -da *adj* : hot, warm

calidoscopio *nm* : kaleidoscope

caliente *adj* **1** : hot **2** ACALORADO : heated, fiery

calificar {72} *vt* **1** : qualify **2** EVALUAR : rate **3** : grade (an exam, etc.) — **calificación** *nf, pl* **-ciones 1** : qualification **2** EVALUACIÓN : rating **3** NOTA : grade — **calificativo, -va** *adj* : qualifying — **calificativo** *nm* : qualifier, epithet

caligrafía *nf* : penmanship

calistenia *nf* : calisthenics

cáliz *nm, pl* **-lices** : chalice
caliza *nf* : limestone
callar *vi* : keep quiet, be silent — *vt* **1** : silence, hush **2** OCULTAR : keep secret — **callarse** *vr* : remain silent — **callado, -da** *adj* : quiet, silent
calle *nf* : street, road — **callejear** *vi* : wander about the streets — **callejero, -ra** *adj* **1** : street **2 perro callejero** : stray dog — **callejón** *nm, pl* **-jones 1** : alley **2 ~ sin salida** : dead-end street
callo *nm* : callus, corn
calma *nf* : calm, quiet — **calmante** *adj* : soothing — **~** *nm* : tranquilizer — **calmar** *vt* : calm, soothe — **calmarse** *vr* : calm down — **calmo, -ma** *adj Lat* : calm — **calmoso, -sa** *adj* **1** : calm **2** LENTO : slow
calor *nm* **1** : heat, warmth **2 tener ~** : be hot — **caloría** *nf* : calorie
calumnia *nf* : slander, libel — **calumniar** *vt* : slander, libel
caluroso, -sa *adj* **1** : hot **2** : warm, enthusiastic (of applause, etc.)
calvo, -va *adj* : bald — **calvicie** *nf* : baldness
calza *nf* : wedge
calzada *nf* : roadway
calzado *nm* : footwear — **calzar** {21} *vt* **1** : wear (shoes) **2** : put shoes on (s.o.)
calzones *nmpl Lat* : panties — **calzoncillos** *nmpl* : underpants, briefs
cama *nf* : bed
camada *nf* : litter, brood
camafeo *nm* : cameo
cámara *nf* **1** : chamber **2** *or* **~ fotográfica** : camera **3** : house (in government)
camarada *nmf* : comrade — **camaradería** *nf* : camaraderie
camarero, -ra *n* **1** : waiter, waitress *f* **2** : steward *m*, stewardess *f* (on a ship, etc.) — **camarera** *nf* : chambermaid *f*
camarón *nm, pl* **-rones** : shrimp
camarote *nm* : cabin, stateroom
cambiar *vt* **1** : change **2** CANJEAR : exchange — *vi* **1** : change **2** : shift gears (of an automobile) — **cambiarse** *vr* **1** : change (clothing) **2** : move (to a new address) — **cambiable** *adj* : changeable — **cambio** *nm* **1** : change **2** CANJE : exchange **3 en ~** : on the other hand
camello *nm* : camel
camilla *nf* : stretcher — **camillero** *nm* : orderly (in a hospital)
caminar *vi* : walk — *vt* : cover (a distance) — **caminata** *nf* : hike
camino *nm* **1** : road, path **2** RUTA : way **3 a medio ~** : halfway (there) **4 ponerse en ~** : set out
camión *nm, pl* **-miones 1** : truck **2** *Lat* : bus — **camionero, -ra** *n* **1** : truck driver **2** *Lat*

: bus driver — **camioneta** *nf* : light truck, van
camisa *nf* **1** : shirt **2 ~ de fuerza** : straitjacket — **camiseta** *nf* : T-shirt, undershirt — **camisón** *nm, pl* **-sones** : nightshirt, nightgown
camorra *nf fam* : fight, trouble
camote *nm Lat* : sweet potato
campamento *nm* : camp
campana *nf* : bell — **campanada** *nf* : stroke (of a bell), peal — **campanario** *nm* : bell tower — **campanilla** *nf* : (small) bell
campaña *nf* **1** : countryside **2** : (military or political) campaign
campeón, -peona *n, mpl* **-peones** : champion — **campeonato** *nm* : championship
campesino, -na *n* : peasant, farm laborer — **campestre** *adj* : rural, rustic
camping *nm* **1** : campsite **2 hacer ~** : go camping
campiña *nf* : countryside
campo *nm* **1** : field **2** CAMPIÑA : countryside, country **3** CAMPAMENTO : camp
camuflaje *nm* : camouflage — **camuflar** *vt* : camouflage
cana *nf* : gray hair
canadiense *adj* : Canadian
canal *nm* **1** : canal **2** MEDIO : channel **3** : (radio or television) channel — **canalizar** {21} *vt* : channel
canalete *nm* : paddle (of a canoe)
canalla *nf* : rabble — **~** *nmf fam* : swine, bastard
canapé *nm* **1** : canapé **2** SOFÁ : sofa, couch
canario *nm* : canary
canasta *nf* : basket — **canasto** *nm* : large basket
cancelar *vt* **1** : cancel **2** : pay off, settle (a debt) — **cancelación** *nf, pl* **-ciones 1** : cancellation **2** : payment in full (of a debt)
cáncer *nm* : cancer — **canceroso, -sa** *adj* : cancerous
cancha *nf* : court, field (for sports)
canciller *nm* : chancellor
canción *nf, pl* **-ciones 1** : song **2 ~ de cuna** : lullaby — **cancionero** *nm* : songbook
candado *nm* : padlock
candela *nf* : candle — **candelabro** *nm* : candelabra — **candelero** *nm* **1** : candlestick **2 estar en el ~** : be in the limelight
candente *adj* : red-hot
candidato, -ta *n* : candidate — **candidatura** *nf* : candidacy
cándido, -da *adj* : naïve — **candidez** *nf* **1** : simplicity **2** INGENUIDAD : naïveté
candil *nm* : oil lamp — **candilejas** *nfpl* : footlights
candor *nm* : naïveté, innocence

canela *nf* : cinnamon
cangrejo *nm* : crab
canguro *nm* : kangaroo
caníbal *nmf* : cannibal — **canibalismo** *nm* : cannibalism
canicas *nfpl* : (game of) marbles
canino, -na *adj* : canine — **canino** *nm* : canine (tooth)
canjear *vt* : exchange — **canje** *nm* : exchange, trade
cano, -na *adj* : gray, gray-haired
canoa *nf* : canoe
canon *nm, pl* **cánones** : canon
canonizar {21} *vt* : canonize
canoso, -sa *adj* : gray, gray-haired
cansar *vt* : tire (out) — *vi* : be tiring — **cansarse** *vr* : get tired — **cansado, -da** *adj* 1 : tired 2 PESADO : tiresome — **cansancio** *nm* : fatigue, weariness
cantalupo *nm* : cantaloupe
cantar *v* : sing — ~ *nm* : song — **cantante** *nmf* : singer
cántaro *nm* 1 : pitcher, jug 2 llover a ~s *fam* : rain cats and dogs
cantera *nf* : quarry (excavation)
cantidad *nf* 1 : quantity, amount 2 una ~ de : lots of
cantimplora *nf* : canteen, water bottle
cantina *nf* 1 : canteen, cafeteria 2 *Lat* : tavern, bar
canto *nm* 1 : singing, song 2 BORDE, LADO : edge 3 de ~ : on end, sideways 4 ~ rodado : boulder — **cantor, -tora** *adj* 1 : singing 2 pájaro ~ : songbird — ~ *n* : singer
caña *nf* 1 : cane, reed 2 ~ de pescar : fishing pole
cáñamo *nm* : hemp
cañería *nf* : pipes, piping — **caño** *nm* 1 : pipe 2 : spout (of a fountain) — **cañón** *nm, pl* **-ñones** 1 : cannon 2 : barrel (of a gun) 3 : canyon (in geography)
caoba *nf* : mahogany
caos *nm* : chaos — **caótico, -ca** *adj* : chaotic
capa *nf* 1 : cape, cloak 2 : coat (of paint, etc.), coating (in cooking) 3 ESTRATO : layer, stratum 4 : (social) class
capacidad *nf* 1 : capacity 2 APTITUD : ability
capacitar *vt* : train, qualify — **capacitación** *nf, pl* **-ciones** : training
caparazón *nm, pl* **-zones** : shell
capataz *nmf, pl* **-taces** : foreman
capaz *adj, pl* **-paces** 1 : capable, able 2 ESPACIOSO : spacious
capellán *nm, pl* **-llanes** : chaplain
capilla *nf* : chapel
capital *adj* 1 : capital 2 PRINCIPAL : chief, principal — ~ *nm* : capital (assets) — ~

nf : capital (city) — **capitalismo** *nm* : capitalism — **capitalista** *adj* & *nmf* : capitalist, capitalistic — **capitalizar** {21} *vt* : capitalize
capitán, -tana *n, mpl* **-tanes** : captain
capitolio *nm* : capitol
capitular *vi* : capitulate, surrender — **capitulación** *nf, pl* **-ciones** : surrender
capítulo *nm* : chapter
capó *nm* : hood (of a car)
capote *nm* : cloak, cape
capricho *nm* : whim, caprice — **caprichoso, -sa** *adj* : whimsical, capricious
cápsula *nf* : capsule
captar *vt* 1 : grasp 2 ATRAER : gain, attract (interest, etc.) 3 : harness (waters)
capturar *vt* : capture, seize — **captura** *nf* : capture, seizure
capucha *nf* : hood (of clothing)
capullo *nm* 1 : cocoon 2 : (flower) bud
caqui *adj* & *nm* : khaki
cara *nf* 1 : face 2 ASPECTO : appearance 3 *fam* : nerve, gall 4 ~ a *or* de ~ a : facing
carabina *nf* : carbine
caracol *nm* 1 : snail 2 *Lat* : conch 3 RIZO : curl
carácter *nm, pl* **-racteres** 1 : character 2 ÍNDOLE : nature — **característica** *nf* : characteristic — **característico, -ca** *adj* : characteristic — **caracterizar** {21} *vt* : characterize
caramba *interj* : oh my!, good grief!
carámbano *nm* : icicle
caramelo *nm* 1 : caramel 2 DULCE : candy
carátula *nf* 1 CARETA : mask 2 : jacket (of a record, etc.) 3 *Lat* : face (of a watch)
caravana *nf* 1 : caravan 2 REMOLQUE : trailer
caray → caramba
carbohidrato *nm* : carbohydrate
carbón *nm, pl* **-bones** 1 : coal 2 : charcoal (for drawing) — **carboncillo** *nm* : charcoal — **carbonero, -ra** *adj* : coal — **carbonizar** {21} *vt* : char — **carbono** *nm* : carbon —
carburador *nm* : carburetor — **carburante** *nm* : fuel
carcajada *nf* : loud laugh, guffaw
cárcel *nf* : jail, prison — **carcelero, -ra** *n* : jailer
carcinógeno *nm* : carcinogen
carcomer *vt* : eat away at — **carcomido, -da** *adj* : worm-eaten
cardenal *nm* 1 : cardinal 2 CONTUSIÓN : bruise
cardíaco *or* cardiaco, -ca *adj* : cardiac, heart
cárdigan *nm, pl* **-gans** : cardigan
cardinal *adj* : cardinal
cardiólogo, -ga *n* : cardiologist

cardo

30

cardo *nm* : thistle
carear *vt* : bring face-to-face
carecer {53} *vi* ∼ **de** : lack — **carencia** *nf* : lack, want — **carente** *adj* ∼ **de** : lacking (in)
carestía *nf* **1** : high cost **2** ESCASEZ : dearth, scarcity
careta *nf* : mask
cargar {52} *vt* **1** : load **2** : charge (a battery, a purchase, etc.) **3** LLEVAR : carry **4** ∼ **de** : burden with — *vi* **1** : load **2** ∼ **con** : pick up, carry away — **carga** *nf* **1** : load **2** CARGAMENTO : freight, cargo **3** RESPONSABILIDAD : burden **4** : charge (in electricity, etc.) — **cargado, -da** *adj* **1** : loaded, burdened **2** PESADO : heavy, stuffy **3** : charged (of a battery) **4** FUERTE : strong, concentrated — **cargamento** *nm* : cargo, load — **cargo** *nm* **1** : charge **2** PUESTO : position, office
cariarse *vr* : decay (of teeth)
caribe *adj* : Caribbean
caricatura *nf* **1** : caricature **2** : (political) cartoon — **caricaturizar** *vt* : caricature
caricia *nf* : caress
caridad *nf* **1** : charity **2** LIMOSNA : alms *pl*
caries *nfs & pl* : cavity (in a tooth)
cariño *nm* : affection, love — **cariñoso, -sa** *adj* : affectionate, loving
carisma *nf* : charisma — **carismático, -ca** *adj* : charismatic
caritativo, -va *adj* : charitable
cariz *nm, pl* **-rices** : appearance, aspect
carmesí *adj & nm* : crimson
carmín *nm, pl* **-mines** *or* ∼ **de labios** : lipstick
carnada *nf* : bait
carnal *adj* **1** : carnal **2 primo** ∼ : first cousin
carnaval *nm* : carnival
carne *nf* **1** : meat **2** : flesh (of persons or fruits) **3** ∼ **de cerdo** : pork **4** ∼ **de gallina** : goose bumps **5** ∼ **de ternera** : veal
carné *nm* → **carnet**
carnero *nm* **1** : ram, sheep **2** : mutton (in cooking)
carnet *nm* **1** ∼ **de conducir** : driver's license **2** ∼ **de identidad** : identification card, ID
carnicería *nf* **1** : butcher shop **2** MATANZA : slaughter — **carnicero, -ra** *n* : butcher
carnívoro, -ra *adj* : carnivorous — **carnívoro** *nm* : carnivore
carnoso, -sa *adj* : fleshy
caro, -ra *adj* **1** : expensive **2** QUERIDO : dear — **caro** *adv* : dearly
carpa *nf* **1** : carp **2** TIENDA : tent
carpeta *nf* : folder

carpintería *nf* : carpentry — **carpintero, -ra** *n* : carpenter
carraspear *vi* : clear one's throat — **carraspera** *nf* **1** : hoarseness **2 tener** ∼ : have a frog in one's throat
carrera *nf* **1** : running, run **2** COMPETICIÓN : race **3** : course (of studies) **4** PROFESIÓN : career, profession
carreta *nf* : cart, wagon
carrete *nm* : reel, spool
carretera *nf* : highway, road
carretilla *nf* : wheelbarrow
carril *nm* **1** : lane (of a road) **2** : rail (for a railroad)
carrillo *nm* : cheek
carrito *nm* : cart, trolley
carrizo *nm* : reed
carro *nm* **1** : wagon, cart **2** *Lat* : automobile, car — **carrocería** *nf* : body (of an automobile)
carroña *nf* : carrion
carroza *nf* **1** : carriage **2** : float (in a parade)
carruaje *nm* : carriage
carrusel *nm* : merry-go-round, carousel
carta *nf* **1** : letter **2** NAIPE : playing card **3** : charter (of an organization, etc.) **4** MENÚ : menu **5** MAPA : map, chart
cartel *nm* : poster, bill — **cartelera** *nf* : billboard
cartera *nf* **1** : briefcase **2** BILLETERA : wallet **3** *Lat* : pocketbook, handbag — **carterista** *nmf* : pickpocket
cartero, -ra *nm* : mail carrier, mailman *m*
cartílago *nm* : cartilage
cartilla *nf* **1** : primer, reader **2** : booklet, record (of a savings account, etc.)
cartón *nm, pl* **-tones 1** : cardboard **2** : carton (of cigarettes, etc.)
cartucho *nm* : cartridge
casa *nf* **1** : house **2** HOGAR : home **3** EMPRESA : company, firm **4** ∼ **flotante** : houseboat
casar *vt* : marry — *vi* : go together, match up — **casarse** *vr* **1** : get married **2** ∼ **con** : marry — **casado, -da** *adj* : married — **casamiento** *nm* **1** : marriage **2** BODA : wedding
cascabel *nm* : small bell
cascada *nf* : waterfall
cascanueces *nms & pl* : nutcracker
cascar {72} *vt* : crack (a shell, etc.) — **cascarse** *vr* : crack, chip — **cáscara** *nf* : skin, peel, shell — **cascarón** *nm, pl* **-rones** : eggshell
casco *nm* **1** : helmet **2** : hull (of a boat) **3** : hoof (of a horse) **4** : fragment (of ceramics, etc.) **5** : center (of a town) **6** ENVASE : empty bottle

caserío nm 1 Spain : country house 2 POBLADO : hamlet
casero, -ra adj 1 : homemade 2 DOMÉSTICO : domestic, household — ~ n : landlord, landlady f
caseta nf : booth, stall
casete → cassette
casi adv 1 : almost, nearly 2 (in negative phrases) : hardly
casilla nf 1 : compartment, pigeonhole 2 CASETA : booth 3 : box (on a form)
casino nm 1 : casino 2 : (social) club
caso nm 1 : case 2 en ~ de : in the event of 3 hacer ~ : pay attention 4 no venir al ~ : be beside the point
caspa nf : dandruff
cassette nmf : cassette
casta nf 1 : lineage, descent 2 : breed (of animals) 3 : caste (in India)
castaña nf : chestnut
castañetear vi : chatter (of teeth)
castaño, -ña adj : chestnut (color)
castañuela nf : castanet
castellano nm : Spanish, Castilian (language)
castidad nf : chastity
castigar {52} vt 1 : punish 2 : penalize (in sports) — castigo nm 1 : punishment 2 : penalty (in sports)
castillo nm : castle
casto, -ta adj : chaste, pure — castizo, -za adj : pure, traditional (in style)
castor nm : beaver
castrar vt : castrate
castrense adj : military
casual adj : chance, accidental — casualidad nf 1 : coincidence 2 por ~ or de ~ : by chance — casualmente adv : by chance
cataclismo nm : cataclysm
catalán, -lana adj, mpl -lanes : Catalan — catalán nm : Catalan (language)
catalizador nm : catalyst
catalogar {52} vt : catalog, classify — catálogo nm : catalog
catapulta nf : catapult
catar vt : taste, sample
catarata nf 1 : waterfall 2 : cataract (in medicine)
catarro nm RESFRIADO : cold
catástrofe nf : catastrophe, disaster — catastrófico, -ca adj : catastrophic, disastrous
catecismo nm : catechism
cátedra nf : chair (at a university)
catedral nf : cathedral
catedrático, -ca n : professor
categoría nf 1 : category 2 RANGO : rank 3 de ~ : first-rate — categórico, -ca adj : categorical

católico, -ca adj & n : Catholic — catolicismo nm : Catholicism
catorce adj & nm : fourteen — catorceavo nm : fourteenth
catre nm : cot
cauce nm 1 : riverbed 2 VÍA : channel, means pl
caucho nm : rubber
caución nf, pl -ciones : security, guarantee
caudal nm 1 : volume of water, flow 2 RIQUEZA : wealth
caudillo nm : leader, commander
causar vt : cause, provoke — causa nf 1 : cause 2 RAZÓN : reason 3 : case (in law) 4 a ~ de : because of
cáustico, -ca adj : caustic
cautela nf : caution — cauteloso, -sa adj : cautious — cautelosamente adv : cautiously, warily
cautivar vt 1 : capture 2 ENCANTAR : captivate — cautiverio nm : captivity — cautivo, -va adj & n : captive
cauto, -ta adj : cautious
cavar v : dig
caverna nf : cavern, cave
cavidad nf : cavity
cavilar vi : ponder
cayado nm : crook, staff
cazar {21} vt 1 : hunt 2 ATRAPAR : catch, bag — vi : go hunting — caza nf 1 : hunt, hunting 2 : game (animals) — cazador, -dora n : hunter
cazo nm 1 : saucepan 2 CUCHARÓN : ladle — cazuela nf : casserole
CD nm : CD, compact disc
cebada nf : barley
cebar vt 1 : bait 2 : feed, fatten (animals) 3 : prime (a firearm, etc.) — cebo nm 1 CARNADA : bait 2 : charge (of a firearm)
cebolla nf : onion — cebolleta nf : scallion, green onion — cebollino nm : chive
cebra nf : zebra
cecear vi : lisp — ceceo nm : lisp
cedazo nm : sieve
ceder vi 1 : yield, give way 2 DISMINUIR : diminish, abate — vt : cede, hand over
cedro nm : cedar
cédula nf : document, certificate
cegar {49} vt 1 : blind 2 TAPAR : block, stop up — vi : be blinded, go blind — ceguera nf : blindness
ceja nf : eyebrow
cejar vi : give in, back down
celada nf : trap, ambush
celador, -dora n : guard, warden
celda nf : cell (of a jail)
celebrar vt 1 : celebrate 2 : hold (a meeting), say (Mass) 3 ALEGRARSE DE : be happy about — celebrarse vr : take place

— **celebración** *nf, pl* **-ciones** : celebration
— **célebre** *adj* : famous, celebrated —
celebridad *nf* : celebrity
celeridad *nf* : swiftness, speed
celeste *adj* **1** : celestial, heavenly **2** *or* **azul**
~ : sky blue — **celestial** *adj* : celestial,
heavenly
celibato *nm* : celibacy — **célibe** *adj* : celibate
celo *nm* **1** : zeal **2 en** ~ : in heat **3** ~**s**
nmpl : jealousy **4 tener** ~**s** : be jealous
celofán *nm, pl* **-fanes** : cellophane
celoso, -sa *adj* **1** : jealous **2** DILIGENTE
: zealous
célula *nf* : cell — **celular** *adj* : cellular
celulosa *nf* : cellulose
cementerio *nm* : cemetery
cemento *nm* **1** : cement **2** ~ **armado** : reinforced concrete
cena *nf* : supper, dinner
cenagal *nm* : bog, quagmire — **cenagoso**
adj : swampy
cenar *vi* : have dinner, have supper — *vt*
: have for dinner or supper
cenicero *nm* : ashtray
cenit *nm* : zenith
ceniza *nf* : ash
censo *nm* : census
censurar *vt* **1** : censor **2** REPROBAR : censure, criticize — **censura** *nf* **1** : censorship
2 REPROBACIÓN : censure, criticism
centavo *nm* **1** : cent **2** : centavo (unit of currency)
centellear *vi* : sparkle, twinkle — **centella**
nf **1** : flash **2** CHISPA : spark — **centelleo**
nm : twinkling, sparkle
centenar *nm* : hundred — **centenario** *nm*
: centennial
centeno *nm* : rye
centésimo, -ma *adj* : hundredth
centígrado *adj* : centigrade, Celsius
centigramo *nm* : centigram
centímetro *nm* : centimeter
centinela *nmf* : sentinel, sentry
central *adj* : central — ~ *nf* : main office,
headquarters — **centralita** *nf* : switchboard
— **centralizar** {21} *vt* : centralize
centrar *vt* : center — **centrarse** *vr* ~ **en**
: focus on — **céntrico, -ca** *adj* : central —
centro *nm* **1** : center **2** : downtown (of a
city) **3** ~ **de mesa** : centerpiece
centroamericano, -na *adj* : Central American
ceñir {67} *vt* **1** : encircle **2** : fit (s.o.) tightly
— **ceñirse** *vr* ~ **a** : limit oneself to —
ceñido, -da *adj* : tight
ceño *nm* **1** : frown **2 fruncir el** ~ : knit
one's brow, frown
cepillo *nm* **1** : brush **2** : (carpenter's) plane

3 ~ **de dientes** : toothbrush — **cepillar** *vt*
1 : brush **2** : plane (wood)
cera *nf* **1** : wax, beeswax **2** : floor wax, furniture wax
cerámica *nf* **1** : ceramics *pl* **2** : (piece of)
pottery
cerca[1] *nf* : fence — **cercado** *nm* : enclosure
cerca[2] *adv* **1** : close, near **2** ~ **de** : near,
close to **3** ~ **de** : nearly, almost — **cercano, -na** *adj* : near, close — **cercanía** *nf* **1**
: proximity **2** ~**s** *nfpl* : outskirts
cercar {72} *vt* **1** : fence in **2** RODEAR : surround
cerciorarse *vr* ~ **de** : make sure of
cerco *nm* **1** : circle, ring **2** ASEDIO : siege **3**
Lat : fence
cerda *nf* : bristle
cerdo *nm* **1** : pig, hog **2** ~ **macho** : boar
cereal *adj* & *nm* : cereal
cerebro *nm* : brain — **cerebral** *adj* : cerebral
ceremonia *nf* : ceremony — **ceremonial** *adj*
: ceremonial — **ceremonioso, -sa** *adj* : ceremonious
cereza *nf* : cherry
cerilla *nf* : match — **cerillo** *nm Lat* : match
cerner {56} *or* **cernir** *vt* : sift — **cernerse** *vr*
1 : hover **2** ~ **sobre** : loom over — **cernidor** *nm* : sieve
cero *nm* : zero
cerrar {55} *vt* **1** : close, shut **2** : turn off (a
faucet, etc.) **3** : bring to an end — *vi* **1**
: close up, lock up **2** : close down (a business, etc.) — **cerrarse** *vr* **1** : close, shut **2**
TERMINAR : come to a close, end — **cerrado, -da** *adj* **1** : closed, shut, locked **2**
: overcast (of weather) **3** : sharp (of a
curve) **4** : thick, broad (of an accent) — **cerradura** *nf* : lock — **cerrajero, -ra** *n* : locksmith
cerro *nm* : hill
cerrojo *nm* : bolt, latch
certamen *nm, pl* **-támenes** : competition,
contest
certero, -ra *adj* : accurate, precise
certeza *nf* : certainty — **certidumbre** *nf*
: certainty
certificar {72} *vt* **1** : certify **2** : register
(mail) — **certificado, -da** *adj* : certified,
registered — **certificado** *nm* : certificate
cervato *nm* : fawn
cerveza *nf* **1** : beer **2** ~ **de barril** : draft
beer — **cervecería** *nf* **1** : brewery **2** BAR
: beer hall, bar
cesar *vi* : cease, stop — *vt* : dismiss, lay off
— **cesación** *nf, pl* **-ciones** : cessation, suspension — **cesante** *adj* **1** : laid off **2** *Lat*
: unemployed — **cesantía** *nf Lat* : unemployment
cesárea *nf* : cesarean (section)

cese *nm* **1** : cessation, stop **2** DESTITUCIÓN : dismissal
césped *nm* : lawn, grass
cesta *nf* : basket — **cesto** *nm* **1** : (large) basket **2** ~ **de basura** : wastebasket
cetro *nm* : scepter
chabacano *nm Lat* : apricot
chabola *nf Spain* : shack, shanty
chacal *nm* : jackal
cháchara *nf fam* : gabbing, chatter
chacra *nf Lat* : (small) farm
chafar *vt fam* : flatten, crush
chal *nm* : shawl
chaleco *nm* : vest
chalet *nm Spain* : house
chalupa *nf* **1** : small boat **2** *Lat* : small stuffed tortilla
chamarra *nf* : jacket
chamba *nf Lat fam* : job
champaña *or* **champán** *nm* : champagne
champiñón *nm, pl* **-ñones** : mushroom
champú *nm, pl* **-pús** *or* **-púes** : shampoo
chamuscar {72} *vt* : scorch
chance *nm Lat* : chance, opportunity
chancho *nm Lat* : pig
chanclos *nmpl* : galoshes
chantaje *nm* : blackmail — **chantajear** *vt* : blackmail
chanza *nf* : joke, jest
chapa *nf* **1** : sheet, plate **2** INSIGNIA : badge — **chapado, -da** *adj* **1** : plated **2 chapado a la antigua** : old-fashioned
chaparrón *nm, pl* **-rrones** : downpour
chapotear *vi* : splash
chapucero, -ra *adj* : shoddy, sloppy — **chapuza** *nf* : botched job
chapuzón *nm, pl* **-zones** : dip, short swim
chaqueta *nf* : jacket
charca *nf* : pond — **charco** *nm* : puddle
charlar *vi* : chat — **charla** *nf* : chat, talk — **charlatán, -tana** *adj, mpl* **-tanes** : talkative — ~ *n* **1** : chatterbox **2** FARSANTE : charlatan
charol *nm* **1** : patent leather **2** BARNIZ : varnish
chasco *nm* **1** : trick, joke **2** DECEPCIÓN : disappointment
chasis *nms & pl* : chassis
chasquear *vt* **1** : click (the tongue), snap (one's fingers) **2** : crack (a whip) — **chasquido** *nm* **1** : click, snap **2** : crack (of a whip)
chatarra *nf* : scrap (metal)
chato, -ta *adj* **1** : pug-nosed **2** APLANADO : flat
chauvinismo *nm* : chauvinism — **chauvinista** *adj* : chauvinist, chauvinistic
chaval, -vala *n fam* : kid, boy *m*, girl *f*

checo, -ca *adj* : Czech — **checo** *nm* : Czech (language)
chef *nm* : chef
cheque *nm* : check — **chequera** *nf* : checkbook
chequear *vt Lat* **1** : check, inspect, verify **2** : check in (baggage) — **chequeo** *nm* **1** : (medical) checkup **2** *Lat* : check, inspection
chica → **chico**
chicano, -na *adj* : Chicano, Mexican-American
chícharo *nm Lat* : pea
chicharrón *nm, pl* **-rrones** : pork rind
chichón *nm, pl* **-chones** : bump
chicle *nm* : chewing gum
chico, -ca *adj* : little, small — ~ *n* : child, boy *m*, girl *f*
chiflar *vt* : whistle at, boo — *vi Lat* : whistle — **chiflado, -da** *adj fam* : crazy, nuts — **chiflido** *nm* : whistling
chile *nm* : chili pepper
chileno, -na *adj* : Chilean
chillar *vi* **1** : shriek, scream **2** CHIRRIAR : screech, squeal — **chillido** *nm* **1** : scream **2** CHIRRIDO : screech, squeal — **chillón, -llona** *adj, mpl* **-llones** : shrill, loud
chimenea *nf* **1** : chimney **2** HOGAR : fireplace
chimpancé *nm* : chimpanzee
chinche *nf* : bedbug
chino, -na *adj* : Chinese — **chino** *nm* : Chinese (language)
chiquillo, -lla *n* : kid, child
chiquito, -ta *adj* : tiny — ~ *n* : little child, tot
chiribita *nf* : spark
chiripa *nf* **1** : fluke **2 de** ~ : by sheer luck
chirivia *nf* : parsnip
chirriar {85} *vi* **1** : squeak, creak **2** : screech (of brakes, etc.) — **chirrido** *nm* **1** : squeak, creak **2** : screech (of brakes)
chisme *nm* : (piece of) gossip — **chismear** *vi* : gossip — **chismoso, -sa** *adj* : gossipy — ~ *n* : gossip
chispear *vi* : spark — **chispa** *nf* : spark
chisporrotear *vi* : crackle, sizzle — **chisporroteo** *nm* : crackle
chiste *nm* : joke, funny story — **chistoso, -sa** *adj* : funny, witty
chivo, -va *n* : kid, young goat
chocar {72} *vi* **1** : crash, collide **2** ENFRENTARSE : clash — **chocante** *adj* **1** : striking, shocking **2** *Lat* : unpleasant, rude
choclo *nm Lat* : ear of corn, corncob
chocolate *nm* : chocolate
chofer *or* **chófer** *nm* **1** : chauffeur **2** CONDUCTOR : driver

choque *nm* **1** : shock **2** : crash, collision (of vehicles) **3** CONFLICTO : clash
chorizo *nm* : chorizo, sausage
chorrear *vi* **1** : drip **2** BROTAR : pour out, gush — **chorro** *nm* **1** : stream, jet **2** HILO : trickle
chovinismo → **chauvinismo**
choza *nf* : hut, shack
chubasco *nm* : downpour, squall
chuchería *nf* **1** : knickknack, trinket **2** DULCE : sweet
chueco, -ca *adj Lat* : crooked
chuleta *nf* : cutlet, chop
chulo, -la *adj fam* : cute, pretty
chupar *vt* **1** : suck **2** ABSORBER : absorb **3** *fam* : guzzle — *vi* : suckle — **chupada** *nf* : suck, sucking — **chupete** *nm* **1** : pacifier **2** *Lat* : lollipop
churro *nm* **1** : fried dough **2** *fam* : botch, mess
chusco, -ca *adj* : funny
chusma *nf* : riffraff, rabble
chutar *vi* : shoot (in soccer)
cianuro *nm* : cyanide
cicatriz *nf, pl* **-trices** : scar — **cicatrizar** {21} *vi* : form a scar, heal
cíclico, -ca *adj* : cyclical
ciclismo *nm* : cycling — **ciclista** *nmf* : cyclist
ciclo *nm* : cycle
ciclón *nm, pl* **-clones** : cyclone
ciego, -ga *adj* : blind — **ciegamente** *adv* : blindly
cielo *nm* **1** : sky **2** : heaven (in religion)
ciempiés *nms & pl* : centipede
cien *adj* : a hundred, hundred — ~ *nm* : one hundred
ciénaga *nf* : swamp, bog
ciencia *nf* **1** : science **2 a** ~ **cierta** : for a fact
cieno *nm* : mire, mud, silt
científico, -ca *adj* : scientific — ~ *n* : scientist
ciento *adj* (*used in compound numbers*) : one hundred — ~ *nm* **1** : hundred, group of a hundred **2 por** ~ : percent
cierre *nm* **1** : closing, closure **2** BROCHE : fastener, clasp
cierto, -ta *adj* **1** : true **2** SEGURO : certain **3 por** ~ : as a matter of fact
ciervo, -va *n* : deer, stag *m,* hind *f*
cifra *nf* **1** : number, figure **2** : sum (of money, etc.) **3** CLAVE : code, cipher — **cifrar** *vt* **1** : write in code **2** ~ **la esperanza en** : pin all one's hopes on
cigarrillo *nm* : cigarrette — **cigarro** *nm* **1** : cigarette **2** PURO : cigar
cigüeña *nf* : stork
cilantro *nm* : cilantro, coriander

cilindro *nm* : cylinder — **cilíndrico, -ca** *adj* : cylindrical
cima *nf* : peak, summit
címbalo *nm* : cymbal
cimbrar *or* **cimbrear** *vt* : shake, rock — **cimbrarse** *or* **cimbrearse** *vr* : sway
cimentar {55} *vt* **1** : lay the foundation of **2** : cement, strengthen (relations, etc.) — **cimientos** *nmpl* : base, foundation(s)
cinc *nm* : zinc
cincel *nm* : chisel — **cincelar** *vt* : chisel
cinco *adj & nm* : five
cincuenta *adj & nm* : fifty — **cincuentavo, -va** *adj* : fiftieth — **cincuentavo** *nm* : fiftieth
cine *nm* : cinema, movies *pl* — **cinematográfico, -ca** *adj* : movie, film
cínico, -ca *adj* : cynical — ~ *n* : cynic — **cinismo** *nm* : cynicism
cinta *nf* **1** : ribbon, band **2** ~ **adhesiva** : adhesive tape **3** ~ **métrica** : tape measure **4** ~ **magnetofónica** : magnetic tape
cinto *nm* : belt, girdle — **cintura** *nf* : waist — **cinturón** *nm, pl* **-rones 1** : belt **2** ~ **de seguridad** : seat belt
ciprés *nm, pl* **-preses** : cypress
circo *nm* : circus
circuito *nm* : circuit
circulación *nf, pl* **-ciones 1** : circulation **2** TRÁFICO : traffic — **circular** *vi* **1** : circulate **2** : drive (a vehicle) — ~ *adj* : circular
círculo *nm* : circle
circuncidar *vt* : circumcise — **circuncisión** *nf, pl* **-siones** : circumcision
circundar *vt* : surround
circunferencia *nf* : circumference
circunscribir {33} *vt* : confine, limit — **circunscribirse** *vr* ~ **a** : limit oneself to — **circunscripción** *nf, pl* **-ciones** : district, constituency
circunspecto, -ta *adj* : circumspect, cautious
circunstancia *nf* : circumstance — **circunstancial** *adj* : chance — **circunstante** *nmf* **1** : bystander **2 los** ~ **s** : those present
circunvalación *nf, pl* **-ciones 1** : encircling **2 carretera de** ~ : bypass
cirio *nm* : candle
ciruela *nf* **1** : plum **2** ~ **pasa** : prune
cirugía *nf* : surgery — **cirujano, -na** *n* : surgeon
cisma *nf* : schism
cisne *nm* : swan
cisterna *nf* : cistern
cita *nf* **1** : appointment, date **2** REFERENCIA : quote, quotation — **citación** *nf, pl* **-ciones** : summons — **citar** *vt* **1** : quote, cite **2** CONVOCAR : make an appointment with **3** : summon (in law) — **citarse** *vr* ~ **con** : arrange to meet

cítrico *nm* : citrus (fruit)
ciudad *nf* : city, town — **ciudadano, -na** *n* 1 : citizen 2 HABITANTE : resident — **ciudadanía** *nf* : citizenship
cívico, -ca *adj* : civic
civil *adj* : civil — ~ *nmf* : civilian — **civilidad** *nf* : civility — **civilización** *nf, pl* **-ciones** : civilization — **civilizar** {21} *vt* : civilize
cizaña *nf* : discord, rift
clamar *vi* : clamor, cry out — **clamor** *nm* : clamor, outcry — **clamoroso, -sa** *adj* : clamorous, loud
clan *nm* : clan
clandestino, -na *adj* : clandestine, secret
clara *nf* : egg white
claraboya *nf* : skylight
claramente *adv* : clearly
clarear *v impers* 1 : dawn 2 ACLARAR : clear up — *vi* : be transparent
claridad *nf* 1 : clarity, clearness 2 LUZ : light
clarificar {72} *vt* : clarify — **clarificación** *nf, pl* **-ciones** : clarification
clarín *nm, pl* **-rines** : bugle
clarinete *nm* : clarinet
clarividente *adj* 1 : clairvoyant 2 PERSPICAZ : perspicacious — **clarividencia** *nf* 1 : clairvoyance 2 PERSPICACIA : farsightedness
claro *adv* 1 : clearly 2 POR SUPUESTO : of course, surely — ~ *nm* 1 : clearing, glade 2 ~ **de luna** : moonlight — **claro, -ra** *adj* 1 : clear, bright 2 : light (of colors) 3 EVIDENTE : clear, evident
clase *nf* 1 : class 2 TIPO : sort, kind
clásico, -ca *adj* : classic, classical — **clásico** *nm* : classic
clasificar {72} *vt* 1 : classify, sort out 2 : rate, rank (a hotel, a team, etc.) — **clasificarse** *vr* : qualify (in competitions) — **clasificación** *nf, pl* **-ciones** 1 : classification 2 : league (in sports)
claudicar {72} *vi* : back down
claustro *nm* : cloister
claustrofobia *nf* : claustrophobia — **claustrofóbico, -ca** *adj* : claustrophobic
cláusula *nf* : clause
clausurar *vt* : close (down) — **clausura** *nf* : closure, closing
clavado *nm Lat* : dive
clavar *vt* 1 : nail, hammer 2 HINCAR : drive in, plunge
clave *nf* 1 CIFRA : code 2 SOLUCIÓN : key 3 : clef (in music) — ~ *adj* : key
clavel *nm* : carnation
clavicémbalo *nm* : harpsichord
clavícula *nf* : collarbone
clavija *nf* 1 : peg, pin 2 : (electric) plug

clavo *nm* 1 : nail 2 : clove (spice)
claxon *nm, pl* **cláxones** : horn (of an automobile)
clemencia *nf* : clemency, mercy — **clemente** *adj* : merciful
clerical *adj* : clerical — **clérigo, -ga** *n* : clergyman, cleric — **clero** *nm* : clergy
cliché *nm* 1 : cliché 2 : negative (of a photograph)
cliente, -ta *n* : customer, client — **clientela** *nf* : clientele, customers *pl*
clima *nm* 1 : climate 2 AMBIENTE : atmosphere — **climático, -ca** *adj* : climatic
climatizar {21} *vt* : air-condition — **climatizado, -da** *adj* : air-conditioned
clímax *nm* : climax
clínica *nf* : clinic — **clínico, -ca** *adj* : clinical
clip *nm, pl* **clips** : (paper) clip
cloaca *nf* : sewer
cloquear *vi* : cluck — **cloqueo** *nm* : cluck, clucking
cloro *nm* : chlorine
clóset *nm Lat, pl* **clósets** : (built-in) closet, cupboard
club *nm* : club
coacción *nf, pl* **-ciones** : coercion — **coaccionar** *vt* : coerce
coagular *v* : clot, coagulate — **coagularse** *vr* : coagulate — **coágulo** *nm* : clot
coalición *nf, pl* **-ciones** : coalition
coartada *nf* : alibi
coartar *vt* : restrict, limit
cobarde *nmf* : coward — ~ *adj* : cowardly — **cobardía** *nf* : cowardice
cobaya *nf* : guinea pig
cobertizo *nm* : shelter, shed
cobertor *nm* : bedspread
cobertura *nf* 1 : cover 2 : coverage (of news, etc.)
cobijar *vt* : shelter — **cobijarse** *vr* : take shelter — **cobija** *nf Lat* : blanket — **cobijo** *nm* : shelter
cobra *nf* : cobra
cobrar *vt* 1 : charge, collect 2 : earn (a salary, etc.) 3 ADQUERIR : acquire, gain 4 : cash (a check) — *vi* : be paid — **cobrador, -dora** *n* 1 : collector 2 : conductor (of a bus, etc.)
cobre *nm* : copper
cobro *nm* : collection (of money), cashing (of a check)
cocaína *nf* : cocaine
cocción *nf, pl* **-ciones** : cooking
cocear *vi* : kick
cocer {14} *vt* 1 : cook 2 HERVIR : boil
coche *nm* 1 : car, automobile 2 : coach (of a train) 3 *or* ~ **de caballos** : carriage 4 ~ **fúnebre** : hearse — **cochecito** *nm* : baby

carriage, stroller — **cochera** *nf* : garage, carport

cochino, -na *n* : pig, hog — ~ *adj fam* : dirty, filthy — **cochinada** *nf fam* : dirty thing — **cochinillo** *nm* : piglet

cocido, -da *adj* **1** : boiled, cooked **2 bien** ~ : well-done — **cocido** *nm* : stew

cociente *nm* : quotient

cocina *nf* **1** : kitchen **2** : (kitchen) stove **3** : (art of) cooking, cuisine — **cocinar** *v* : cook — **cocinero, -ra** *n* : cook, chef

coco *nm* : coconut

cocodrilo *nm* : crocodile

coctel *or* **cóctel** *nm* **1** : cocktail **2** FIESTA : cocktail party

codazo *nm* **1** : nudge **2 dar un** ~ **a** : elbow, nudge

codicia *nf* : greed — **codiciar** *vt* : covet — **codicioso, -sa** *adj* : covetous, greedy

código *nm* **1** : code **2** ~ **postal** : zip code **3** ~ **morse** : Morse code

codo *nm* : elbow

codorniz *nf, pl* **-nices** : quail

coexistir *vi* : coexist

cofre *nm* : chest, coffer

coger {15} *vt* **1** : take (hold of) **2** ATRAPAR : catch **3** : pick up (from the ground) **4** : pick (fruit, etc.) — **cogerse** *vr* : hold on

cohechar *vt* : bribe — **cohecho** *nm* : bribe, bribery

coherencia *nf* : coherence — **coherente** *adj* : coherent — **cohesión** *nf, pl* **-siones** : cohesion

cohete *nm* : rocket

cohibir {62} *vt* **1** : restrict **2** : inhibit (a person) — **cohibirse** *vr* : feel inhibited — **cohibido, -da** *adj* : inhibited, shy

coincidir *vi* **1** : coincide **2** ~ **con** : agree with — **coincidencia** *nf* : coincidence

cojear *vi* **1** : limp **2** : wobble (of furniture, etc.) — **cojera** *nf* : limp

cojín *nm, pl* **-jines** : cushion — **cojinete** *nm* **1** : pad, cushion **2** : bearing (of a machine)

cojo, -ja *adj* **1** : lame **2** : wobbly (of furniture) — ~ *n* : lame person

col *nf* **1** : cabbage **2** ~ **de Bruselas** : Brussels sprout

cola *nf* **1** : tail **2** FILA : line (of people) **3** : end (of a line) **4** PEGAMENTO : glue **5** ~ **de caballo** : ponytail

colaborar *vi* : collaborate — **colaboración** *nf, pl* **-ciones** : collaboration — **colaborador, -dora** *n* **1** : collaborator **2** : contributor (to a periodical)

colada *nf Spain* **1** : laundry **2 hacer la** ~ : do the washing

colador *nm* : colander, strainer

colapso *nm* : collapse

colar {19} *vt* : strain, filter — **colarse** *vr* : sneak in, gate-crash

colcha *nf* : bedspread, quilt — **colchón** *nm, pl* **-chones** : mattress — **colchoneta** *nf* : mat

colear *vi* : wag its tail

colección *nf, pl* **-ciones** : collection — **coleccionar** *vt* : collect — **coleccionista** *nmf* : collector — **colecta** *nf* : collection (of donations)

colectividad *nf* : community — **colectivo, -va** *adj* : collective — **colectivo** *nm* **1** : collective **2** *Lat* : city bus

colector *nm* : sewer

colega *nmf* : colleague

colegio *nm* **1** : school **2** : (professional) college — **colegial, -giala** *n* : schoolboy *m*, schoolgirl *f*

colegir {28} *vt* : gather

cólera *nm* : cholera — ~ *nf* : anger, rage — **colérico, -ca** *adj* **1** : bad-tempered **2** FURIOSO : angry

colesterol *nm* : cholesterol

coleta *nf* : pigtail

colgar {16} *vt* **1** : hang **2** : hang up (a telephone) **3** : hang out (laundry) — *vi* : hang up — **colgante** *adj* : hanging — ~ *nm* : pendant

colibrí *nm* : hummingbird

cólico *nm* : colic

coliflor *nf* : cauliflower

colilla *nf* : (cigarette) butt

colina *nf* : hill

colindar *vi* ~ **con** : be adjacent to — **colindante** *adj* : adjacent

coliseo *nm* : coliseum

colisión *nf, pl* **-siones** : collision — **colisionar** *vi* ~ **contra** : collide with

collar *nm* **1** : necklace **2** : collar (for pets)

colmar *vt* **1** : fill to the brim **2** : fulfill (a wish, etc.) **3** ~ **de** : shower with — **colmado, -da** *adj* : heaping

colmena *nf* : beehive

colmillo *nm* **1** : canine (tooth) **2** : fang (of a dog, etc.), tusk (of an elephant)

colmo *nm* **1** : height, limit **2 ¡eso es el** ~ **!** : that's the last straw!

colocar {72} *vt* **1** PONER : place, put **2** : find a job for — **colocarse** *vr* **1** SITUARSE : position oneself **2** : get a job — **colocación** *nf, pl* **-ciones** **1** : placement, placing **2** EMPLEO : position, job

colombiano, -na *adj* : Colombian

colon *nm* : (intestinal) colon

colonia *nf* **1** : colony **2** PERFUME : cologne **3** *Lat* : residential area — **colonial** *adj* : colonial — **colonizar** {21} *vt* : colonize — **colonización** *nf, pl* **-ciones** : colonization — **colono, -na** *n* : settler, colonist

coloquial *adj* : colloquial — **coloquio** *nm* **1** : talk, discussion **2** CONGRESO : conference
color *nm* : color — **colorado, -da** *adj* : red — **colorear** *vt* : color — **colorete** *nm* : rouge — **colorido** *nm* : colors *pl,* coloring
colosal *adj* : colossal
columna *nf* **1** : column **2** ~ **vertebral** : spine, backbone — **columnista** *nmf* : columnist
columpiar *vt* : push (on a swing) — **columpiarse** *vr* : swing — **columpio** *nm* : swing
coma[1] *nm* : coma
coma[2] *nf* : comma
comadre *nf* **1** : godmother of one's child, mother of one's godchild **2** *fam* : (female) friend — **comadrear** *vi fam* : gossip
comadreja *nf* : weasel
comadrona *nf* : midwife
comandancia *nf* : command headquarters, command — **comandante** *nmf* **1** : commander **2** : major (in the military) — **comando** *nm* **1** : commando **2** *Lat* : command
comarca *nf* : region, area
combar *vt* : bend, curve
combatir *vt* : combat, fight against — *vi* : fight — **combate** *nm* **1** : combat **2** : fight (in boxing) — **combatiente** *nmf* : combatant, fighter
combinar *vt* **1** : combine **2** : put together, match (colors, etc.) — **combinarse** *vr* : get together — **combinación** *nf, pl* **-ciones 1** : combination **2** : connection (in travel)
combustible *nm* : fuel — ~ *adj* : combustible — **combustión** *nf, pl* **-tiones** : combustion
comedia *nf* : comedy
comedido, -da *adj* : moderate
comedor *nm* : dining room
comensal *nmf* : diner, dinner guest
comentar *vt* **1** : comment on, discuss **2** MENCIONAR : mention — **comentario** *nm* **1** : comment, remark **2** ANÁLISIS : commentary — **comentarista** *nmf* : commentator
comenzar {29} *v* : begin, start
comer *vt* **1** : eat **2** *fam* : eat up, eat into — *vi* **1** : eat **2** CENAR : have a meal **3 dar de** ~ : feed — **comerse** *vr* : eat up
comercio *nm* **1** : commerce, trade **2** NEGOCIO : business — **comercial** *adj* : commercial — **comercializar** {21} *vt* : market — **comerciante** *nmf* : merchant, dealer — **comerciar** *vi* : do business, trade
comestible *adj* : edible — **comestibles** *nmpl* : groceries, food
cometa *nm* : comet — ~ *nf* : kite
cometer *vt* **1** : commit **2** ~ **un error** : make a mistake — **cometido** *nm* : assignment, task

comezón *nf, pl* **-zones** : itchiness, itching
comicios *nmpl* : elections
cómico, -ca *adj* : comic, comical — ~ *n* : comic, comedian
comida *nf* **1** ALIMENTO : food **2** *Spain* : lunch **3** *Lat* : dinner **4 tres** ~**s al día** : three meals a day
comienzo *nm* : beginning
comillas *nfpl* : quotation marks
comino *nm* : cumin
comisario, -ria *n* : commissioner — **comisaría** *nf* : police station
comisión *nf, pl* **-siones 1** : commission **2** COMITÉ : committee
comité *nm* : committee
como *conj* **1** : as, since **2 sí** : if — ~ *prep* **1** : like, as **2 así** ~ : as well as — ~ *adv* **1** : as **2** APROXIMADAMENTE : around, about
cómo *adv* **1** : how **2** ~ **no** : by all means **3** ¿~ **te llamas?** : what's your name?
cómoda *nf* : chest of drawers
comodidad *nf* : comfort, convenience
comodín *nm, pl* **-dines** : joker (in playing cards)
cómodo, -da *adj* **1** : comfortable **2** ÚTIL : handy, convenient
comoquiera *adv* **1** : in any way **2** ~ **que** : however
compacto, -ta *adj* : compact
compadecer {53} *vt* : feel sorry for — **compadecerse** *vr* ~ **de** : take pity on
compadre *nm* **1** : godfather of one's child, father of one's godchild **2** *fam* : buddy
compañero, -ra *n* : companion, partner — **compañerismo** *nm* : companionship
compañía *nf* : company
comparar *vt* : compare — **comparable** *adj* : comparable — **comparación** *nf, pl* **-ciones** : comparison — **comparativo, -va** *adj* : comparative
comparecer *vt* : appear (before a court, etc.)
compartimiento *or* **compartimento** *nm* : compartment
compartir *vt* : share
compás *nm, pl* **-pases 1** : compass **2** : rhythm, time (in music)
compasión *nf, pl* **-siones** : compassion, pity — **compasivo, -va** *adj* : compassionate
compatible *adj* : compatible — **compatibilidad** *nf* : compatibility
compatriota *nmf* : compatriot, fellow countryman
compeler *vt* : compel
compendiar *vt* : summarize — **compendio** *nm* : summary
compensar *vt* : compensate for — **compensación** *nf, pl* **-ciones** : compensation
competir {54} *vi* : compete — **competencia** *nf* **1** : competition, rivalry **2** CAPACI-

compilar

DAD : competence — **competente** *adj* : competent — **competición** *nf, pl* **-ciones** : competition — **competidor, -dora** *n* : competitor

compilar *vt* : compile

compinche *nmf fam* : friend, chum

complacer {57} *vt* : please — **complacerse** *vr* ~ **en** : take pleasure in — **complaciente** *adj* : obliging, helpful

complejidad *nf* : complexity — **complejo, -ja** *adj* : complex — **complejo** *nm* : complex

complementar *vt* : complement — **complementario, -ria** *adj* : complementary — **complemento** *nm* **1** : complement **2** : object (in grammar)

completar *vt* : complete — **completo, -ta** *adj* **1** : complete **2** PERFECTO : perfect **3** LLENO : full — **completamente** *adv* : completely

complexión *nf, pl* **-xiones** : constitution, build

complicar {72} *vt* **1** : complicate **2** IMPLICAR : involve — **complicación** *nf, pl* **-ciones** : complication — **complicado, -da** *adj* : complicated, complex

cómplice *nmf* : accomplice — ~ *adj* : conspiratorial, knowing

complot *nm, pl* **-plots** : conspiracy, plot

componer {60} *vt* **1** : make up, compose **2** : compose, write (a song) **3** ARREGLAR : fix, repair — **componerse** *vr* ~ **de** : consist of — **componente** *adj & nm* : component, constituent

comportarse *vr* : behave — **comportamiento** *nm* : behavior

composición *nf, pl* **-ciones** : composition — **compositor, -tora** *n* : composer, songwriter

compostura *nf* **1** : composure **2** REPARACIÓN : repair

comprar *vt* : buy, purchase — **compra** *nf* **1** : purchase **2 ir de ~s** : go shopping — **comprador, -dora** *n* : buyer, shopper

comprender *vt* **1** : comprehend, understand **2** ABARCAR : cover, include — **comprensible** *adj* : understandable — **comprensión** *nf, pl* **-siones** : understanding — **comprensivo, -va** *adj* : understanding

compresa *nf* **1** : compress **2** *or* ~ **higiénica** : sanitary napkin

compresión *nf, pl* **-siones** : compression — **comprimido** *nm* : pill, tablet — **comprimir** *vt* : compress

comprobar {19} *vt* **1** VERIFICAR : check **2** DEMOSTRAR : prove — **comprobación** *nf, pl* **-ciones** : verification, check — **comprobante** *nm* **1** : proof **2** RECIBO : receipt, voucher

comprometer *vt* **1** : compromise **2** ARRIESGAR : jeopardize **3** OBLIGAR : commit, put under obligation — **comprometerse** *vr* **1** : commit oneself **2** ~ **con** : get engaged to — **comprometedor, -dora** *adj* : compromising — **comprometido, -da** *adj* **1** : compromising, awkward **2** : engaged (to be married) — **compromiso** *nm* **1** : obligation, commitment **2** : (marriage) engagement **3** ACUERDO : agreement **4** APURO : awkward situation

compuesto, -ta *adj* **1** : compound **2** ~ **de** : made up of, consisting of — **compuesto** *nm* : compound

compulsivo, -va *adj* : compelling, urgent

computar *vt* : compute, calculate — **computadora** *nf or* **computador** *nm* **1** : computer **2** ~ **portátil** : laptop computer — **cómputo** *nm* : calculation

comulgar {52} *vi* : receive Communion

común *adj, pl* **-munes 1** : common **2** ~ **y corriente** : ordinary **3 por lo** ~ : generally

comuna *nf* : commune — **comunal** *adj* : communal

comunicar {72} *vt* : communicate — **comunicarse** *vr* **1** : communicate **2** ~ **con** : get in touch with — **comunicación** *nf, pl* **-ciones** : communication — **comunicado** *nm* : communiqué — **comunicativo, -va** *adj* : communicative

comunidad *nf* : community

comunión *nf, pl* **-niones** : communion, Communion

comunismo *nm* : Communism — **comunista** *adj & nmf* : Communist

con *prep* **1** : with **2** A PESAR DE : in spite of **3** (*before an infinitive*) : by **4** ~ **(tal) que** : so long as

cóncavo, -va *adj* : concave

concebir {54} *v* : conceive — **concebible** *adj* : conceivable

conceder *vt* **1** : grant, bestow **2** ADMITIR : concede

concejal, -jala *n* : councilman, alderman

concentrar *vt* : concentrate — **concentrarse** *vr* : concentrate — **concentración** *nf, pl* **-ciones** : concentration

concepción *nf, pl* **-ciones** : conception — **concepto** *nm* **1** : concept **2** OPINIÓN : opinion

concernir {17} *vi* ~ **a** : concern — **concerniente** *adj* ~ **a** : concerning

concertar {55} *vt* **1** : arrange, coordinate **2** (*used before an infinitive*) : agree **3** : harmonize (in music) — *vi* : be in harmony

concesión *nf, pl* **-siones 1** : concession **2** : awarding (of prizes, etc.)

concha *nf* : shell

conciencia *nf* **1** : conscience **2** CONO-CIMIENTO : consciousness, awareness —
concientizar {21} *vt Lat* : make aware —
concientizarse *vr Lat* ~ **de** : realize
concienzudo, -da *adj* : conscientious
concierto *nm* **1** : concert **2** : concerto (musical composition)
conciliar *vt* : reconcile — **conciliación** *nf, pl* **-ciones** : reconciliation
concilio *nm* : council
conciso, -sa *adj* : concise
conciudadano, -na *n* : fellow citizen
concluir {41} *vt* : conclude — *vi* : come to an end — **conclusión** *nf, pl* **-siones** : conclusion — **concluyente** *adj* : conclusive
concordar {19} *vi* : agree — *vt* : reconcile — **concordancia** *nf* : agreement — **concordia** *nf* : harmony, concord
concretar *vt* : make concrete, specify — **concretarse** *vr* : become definite, take shape — **concreto, -ta** *adj* **1** : concrete **2** DETERMINADO : specific **3 en** ~ : specifically — **concreto** *nm Lat* : concrete
concurrir *vi* **1** : come together, meet **2** ~ **a** : take part in — **concurrencia** *nf* : audience, turnout — **concurrido, -da** *adj* : busy, crowded
concursar *vi* : compete, participate — **concursante** *nmf* : competitor — **concurso** *nm* **1** : competition **2** CONCURRENCIA : gathering **3** AYUDA : help, cooperation
condado *nm* : county
conde, -desa *n* : count *m*, countess *f*
condenar *vt* **1** : condemn, damn **2** : sentence (a criminal) — **condena** *nf* **1** : condemnation **2** SENTENCIA : sentence — **condenación** *nf, pl* **-ciones** : condemnation, damnation
condensar *vt* : condense — **condensación** *nf, pl* **-ciones** : condensation
condesa *nf* → **conde**
condescender {56} *vi* **1** : acquiesce, agree **2** ~ **a** : condescend to — **condescendiente** *adj* : condescending
condición *nf, pl* **-ciones** **1** : condition, state **2** CALIDAD : capacity, position — **condicional** *adj* : conditional
condimento *nm* : condiment, seasoning
condolerse {47} *vr* : sympathize — **condolencia** *nf* : condolence
condominio *nm* **1** : joint ownership **2** *Lat* : condominium
condón *nm, pl* **-dones** : condom
conducir {61} *vt* **1** DIRIGIR : direct, lead **2** MANEJAR : drive — *vi* **1** : drive **2** ~ **a** : lead to — **conducirse** *vr* : behave
conducta *nf* : behavior, conduct
conducto *nm* : conduit, duct
conductor, -tora *n* : driver

conectar *vt* **1** : connect **2** ENCHUFAR : plug in — *vi* : connect
conejo, -ja *n* : rabbit — **conejera** *nf* : (rabbit) hutch
conexión *nf, pl* **-xiones** : connection — **conexo, -xa** *adj* : connected
confabularse *vr* : conspire, plot
confeccionar *vt* : make (up), prepare — **confección** *nf, pl* **-ciones** **1** : making, preparation **2** : tailoring, dressmaking
confederación *nf, pl* **-ciones** : confederation
conferencia *nf* **1** : lecture **2** REUNIÓN : conference
conferir {76} *vt* : confer, bestow
confesar {55} *v* : confess — **confesarse** *vr* : go to confession — **confesión** *nf, pl* **-siones** **1** : confession **2** CREDO : religion, creed
confeti *nm* : confetti
confiar {85} *vi* : trust — *vt* : entrust — **confiable** *adj* : trustworthy, reliable — **confiado, -da** *adj* **1** : confident **2** CRÉDULO : trusting — **confianza** *nf* **1** : trust **2** : confidence (in oneself)
confidencia *nf* : confidence, secret — **confidencial** *adj* : confidential — **confidencialidad** *nf* : confidentiality — **confidente** *nmf* **1** : confidant, confidante *f* **2** : (police) informer
configuración *nf, pl* **-ciones** : configuration, shape
confín *nm, pl* **-fines** : boundary, limit — **confinar** *vt* **1** : confine **2** DESTERRER : exile
confirmar *vt* : confirm — **confirmación** *nf, pl* **-ciones** : confirmation
confiscar {72} *vt* : confiscate
confitería *nm* : candy store
confitura *nf* : jam
conflagración *nf, pl* **-ciones** **1** : war, conflict **2** INCENDIO : fire
conflicto *nm* : conflict
confluencia *nf* : junction, confluence
conformar *vt* : shape, make up — **conformarse** *vr* **1** RESIGNARSE : resign oneself **2** ~ **con** : content oneself with — **conforme** *adj* **1** : content, satisfied **2** ~ **a** : in accordance with — ~ *conj* : as — **conformidad** *nf* **1** : agreement **2** RESIGNACIÓN : resignation
confortar *vt* : comfort — **confortable** *adj* : comfortable
confrontar *vt* **1** : confront **2** COMPARAR : compare — *vi* : border — **confrontarse** *vr* ~ **con** : face up to — **confrontación** *nf, pl* **-ciones** : confrontation
confundir *vt* : confuse, mix up — **confundirse** *vr* : make a mistake, be confused

— **confusión** *nf, pl* **-siones** : confusion — **confuso, -sa** *adj* **1** : confused **2** INDISTINTO : hazy, indistinct — **congelar** *vt* : freeze — **congelarse** *vr* : freeze — **congelación** *nf, pl* **-ciones** : freezing — **congelado, -da** *adj* : frozen — **congelador** *nm* : freezer
congeniar *vi* : get along
congestión *nf, pl* **-tiones** : congestion — **congestionado, -da** *adj* : congested
congoja *nf* : anguish, grief
congraciarse *vr* : ingratiate oneself
congratular *vt* : congratulate
congregar {52} *vt* : bring together — **congregarse** *vr* : congregate — **congregación** *nf, pl* **-ciones** : congregation, gathering
congreso *nm* : congress — **congresista** *nmf* : member of congress
conjeturar *vt* : guess, conjecture — **conjetura** *nf* : guess, conjecture
conjugar {52} *vt* : conjugate — **conjugación** *nf, pl* **-ciones** : conjugation
conjunción *nf, pl* **-ciones** : conjunction
conjunto, -ta *adj* : joint — **conjunto** *nm* **1** : collection **2** : outfit (of clothing) **3** GRUPO : band **4 en ~** : as a whole
conjurar *vt* : ward off — *vi* : conspire, plot
conllevar *vt* : entail
conmemorar *vt* : commemorate — **conmemoración** *nf, pl* **-ciones** : commemoration — **conmemorativo, -va** *adj* : commemorative
conmigo *pron* : with me
conminar *vt* : threaten
conmiseración *nf, pl* **-ciones** : pity, commiseration
conmocionar *vt* : shock — **conmoción** *nf, pl* **-ciones** **1** : shock, upheaval **2** *or* **~ cerebral** : concussion
conmover {47} *vt* **1** : move, touch **2** SACUDIR : shake (up) — **conmoverse** *vr* : be moved — **conmovedor, -dora** *adj* : moving, touching
conmutador *nm* **1** : (electric) switch **2** *Lat* : switchboard
cono *nm* : cone
conocer {18} *vt* **1** : know **2** : meet (a person), get to know (a city, etc.) **3** RECONOCER : recognize — **conocerse** *vr* **1** : meet, get to know each other **2** : know oneself — **conocedor, -dora** *adj* & *n* : expert — **conocido, -da** *adj* : well-known — **~** *n* : acquaintance — **conocimiento** *nm* **1** : knowledge **2** SENTIDO : consciousness
conque *conj* : so
conquistar *vt* : conquer — **conquista** *nf* : conquest — **conquistador, -dora** *adj* : conquering — **conquistador** *nm* : conqueror

consabido, -da *adj* **1** : well-known **2** HABITUEL : usual
consagrar *vt* **1** : consecrate **2** DEDICAR : devote — **consagración** *nf, pl* **-ciones** : consecration
consciencia *nf* → **conciencia** — **consciente** *adj* : conscious, aware
consecución *nf, pl* **-ciones** : attainment
consecuencia *nf* **1** : consequence **2 en ~** : accordingly — **consecuente** *adj* : consistent
consecutivo, -va *adj* : consecutive
conseguir {75} *vt* **1** : get, obtain **2 ~ hacer algo** : manage to do sth
consejo *nm* **1** : advice, counsel **2** : council (assembly) — **consejero, -ra** *n* : adviser, counselor
consenso *nm* : consensus
consentir {76} *vt* **1** : allow, permit **2** MIMAR : pamper, spoil — *vi* : consent — **consentimiento** *nm* : consent, permission
conserje *nmf* : caretaker, janitor
conservar *vt* **1** : preserve **2** GUARDAR : keep, conserve — **conservarse** *vr* : keep — **conserva** *nf* **1** : preserve(s) **2 ~s** *nfpl* : canned goods — **conservación** *nf, pl* **-ciones** : conservation, preservation — **conservador, -dora** *adj & n* : conservative — **conservatorio** *nm* : conservatory
considerar *vt* **1** : consider **2** RESPETAR : respect — **considerable** *adj* : considerable — **consideración** *nf, pl* **-ciones** **1** : consideration **2** RESPETO : respect — **considerado, -da** *adj* **1** : considerate **2** RESPETADO : respected
consigna *nf* **1** ESLOGAN : slogan **2** ORDEN : orders **3** : checkroom (for baggage)
consigo *pron* : with her, with him, with you, with oneself
consiguiente *adj* **1** : consequent **2 por ~** : consequently
consistir *vi* **~ en 1** : consist of **2** : lie in, consist in — **consistencia** *nf* : consistency — **consistente** *adj* **1** : firm, solid **2 ~ en** : consisting of
consolar {19} *vt* : console, comfort — **consolarse** *vr* : console oneself — **consolación** *nf, pl* **-ciones** : consolation
consolidar *vt* : consolidate — **consolidación** *nf, pl* **-ciones** : consolidation
consomé *nm* : consommé
consonante *adj* : consonant, harmonious — **~** *nf* : consonant
consorcio *nm* : consortium
conspirar *vi* : conspire, plot — **conspiración** *nf, pl* **-ciones** : conspiracy — **conspirador, -dora** *n* : conspirator
constancia *nf* **1** : record, evidence **2** PERSEVERANCIA : perseverance — **constante**

adj : constant — **constantemente** *adv* : constantly, continually

constar *vi* **1** : be evident, be clear **2** ~ **de** : consist of

constatar *vt* **1** : verify **2** AFIRMAR : state, affirm

constelación *nf, pl* **-ciones** : constellation

consternación *nf, pl* **-ciones** : consternation

constipado, -da *adj* **estar** ~ : have a cold — **constipado** *nm* : cold — **constiparse** *vr* : catch a cold

constituir {41} *vt* **1** FORMAR : constitute, form **2** FUNDAR : establish, set up — **constituirse** *vr* ~ **en** : set oneself up as — **constitución** *nf, pl* **-ciones** : constitution — **constitucional** *adj* : constitutional — **constitutivo, -va** *adj* : constituent — **constituyente** *adj* & *nm* : constituent

constreñir {67} *vt* **1** : force, compel **2** RESTRINGIR : restrict, limit

construir {41} *vt* : build, construct — **construcción** *nf, pl* **-ciones** : construction, building — **constructivo, -va** *adj* : constructive — **constructor, -tora** *n* : builder

consuelo *nm* : consolation, comfort

consuetudinario, -ria *adj* : customary

cónsul *nmf* : consul — **consulado** *nm* : consulate

consultar *vt* : consult — **consulta** *nf* : consultation — **consultor, -tora** *n* : consultant — **consultorio** *nm* : office (of a doctor or dentist)

consumar *vt* **1** : consummate, complete **2** : commit (a crime)

consumir *vt* : consume — **consumirse** *vr* : waste away — **consumición** *nf, pl* **-ciones** **1** : consumption **2** : drink (in a restaurant) — **consumido, -da** *adj* : thin, emaciated — **consumidor, -dora** *n* : consumer — **consumo** *nm* : consumption

contabilidad *nf* **1** : accounting, bookkeeping **2** : accountancy (profession) — **contable** *nmf Spain* : accountant, bookkeeper

contactar *vi* ~ **con** : get in touch with, contact — **contacto** *nm* : contact

contado, -da *adj* : numbered, few — **contado** *nm* **al** ~ : (in) cash

contador, -dora *n Lat* : accountant — **contador** *nm* : meter

contagiar *vt* **1** : infect **2** : transmit (a disease) — **contagiarse** *vr* **1** : be contagious **2** : become infected (with a disease) — **contagio** *nm* : contagion, infection — **contagioso, -sa** *adj* : contagious, infectious

contaminar *vt* : contaminate, pollute — **contaminación** *nf, pl* **-ciones** : contamination, pollution

contar {19} *vt* **1** : count **2** NARRAR : tell — *vi* **1** : count **2** ~ **con** : rely on, count on

contemplar *vt* **1** MIRAR : look at, behold **2** CONSIDERAR : contemplate — **contemplación** *nf, pl* **-ciones** : contemplation

contemporáneo, -nea *adj* & *n* : contemporary

contender {56} *vi* : contend, compete — **contendiente** *nmf* : competitor

contener {80} *vt* **1** : contain **2** RESTRINGIR : restrain, hold back — **contenerse** *vr* : restrain oneself — **contenedor** *nm* : container — **contenido, -da** *adj* : restrained — **contenido** *nm* : contents *pl*

contentar *vt* : please, make happy — **contentarse** *vr* ~ **con** : be satisfied with — **contento, -ta** *adj* : glad, happy, contented

contestar *vt* : answer — *vi* : reply, answer back — **contestación** *nf, pl* **-ciones** : answer, reply

contexto *nm* : context

contienda *nf* **1** COMBATE : dispute, fight **2** COMPETICIÓN : contest

contigo *pron* : with you

contiguo, -gua *adj* : adjacent

continente *nm* : continent — **continental** *adj* : continental

contingencia *nf* : contingency — **contingente** *adj* & *nm* : contingent

continuar {3} *v* : continue — **continuación** *nf, pl* **-ciones** **1** : continuation **2 a** ~ : next, then — **continuidad** *nf* : continuity — **continuo, -nua** *adj* **1** : continuous, steady **2** FRECUENTE : continual

contorno *nm* **1** : outline **2** ~**s** *nmpl* : surrounding area

contorsión *nf, pl* **-siones** : contortion

contra *prep* **1** : against **2 en** ~ : against — ~ *nm* **los pros y los** ~**s** : the pros and cons

contraatacar {72} *v* : counterattack — **contraataque** *nm* : counterattack

contrabajo *nm* : double bass

contrabalancear *vt* : counterbalance

contrabandista *nmf* : smuggler — **contrabando** *nm* **1** : smuggling **2** : contraband (goods)

contracción *nf, pl* **-ciones** : contraction

contrachapado *nm* : plywood

contradecir {11} *vt* : contradict — **contradicción** *nf, pl* **-ciones** : contradiction — **contradictorio, -ria** *adj* : contradictory

contraer {81} *vt* **1** : contract **2** ~ **matrimonio** : get married — **contraerse** *vr* : contract, tighten up

contrafuerte *nm* : buttress

contragolpe *nm* : backlash

contralto *nmf* : contralto

contrapartida *nf* : compensation

contrapelo: **a ~** *adv phr* : the wrong way
contrapeso *nm* : counterbalance
contraponer {60} *vt* **1** : counter, oppose **2**
COMPARAR : compare
contraproducente *adj* : counterproductive
contrariar {85} *vt* **1** : oppose **2** MOLESTAR
: vex, annoy — **contrariedad** *nf* **1** : obstacle **2** DISGUSTO : annoyance — **contrario,**
-ria *adj* **1** OPUESTO : opposite **2 al contrario** : on the contrary **3 ser ~ a** : be opposed to
contrarrestar *vt* : counteract
contrasentido *nm* : contradiction (in terms)
contraseña *nf* : password
contrastar *vt* **1** : check, verify **2** RESISTIR
: resist — *vi* : contrast — **contraste** *nm*
: contrast
contratar *vt* **1** : contract for **2** : hire, engage
(workers)
contratiempo *nm* **1** : mishap **2** DIFICULTAD
: setback
contrato *nm* : contract — **contratista** *nmf*
: contractor
contraventana *nf* : shutter
contribuir {41} *vi* **1** : contribute **2** : pay
taxes — **contribución** *nf, pl* **-ciones 1**
: contribution **2** IMPUESTO : tax — **contribuyente** *nmf* **1** : contributor **2** : taxpayer
contrincante *nmf* : opponent
contrito, -ta *adj* : contrite
controlar *vt* **1** : control **2** COMPROBAR
: monitor, check — **control** *nm* **1** : control
2 VERIFICACIÓN : inspection, check — **controlador, -dora** *n* : controller
controversia *nf* : controversy
contundente *adj* **1** : blunt **2** : forceful, convincing (of arguments, etc.)
contusión *nf, pl* **-siones** : bruise
convalecencia *nf* : convalescence — **convaleciente** *adj* & *nmf* : convalescent
convencer {86} *vt* : convince, persuade —
convencerse *vr* : be convinced — **convencimiento** *nm* : conviction, belief
convención *nf, pl* **-ciones** : convention —
convencional *adj* : conventional
convenir {87} *vi* **1** : be suitable, be advisable **2 ~ en** : agree on — **conveniencia** *nf*
1 : convenience **2** : suitability (of an action,
etc.) — **conveniente** *adj* **1** : convenient **2**
ACONSEJABLE : suitable, advisable **3**
PROVECHOSO : useful — **convenio** *nm*
: agreement, pact
convento *nm* : convent, monastery
converger {15} *or* **convergir** *vi* : converge
conversar *vi* : converse, talk — **conversación** *nf, pl* **-ciones** : conversation
conversión *nf, pl* **-siones** : conversion —
converso, -sa *n* : convert
convertir {76} *vt* : convert — **convertirse**

vr **~ en** : turn into — **convertible** *adj* &
nm : convertible
convexo, -xa *adj* : convex
convicción *nf, pl* **-ciones** : conviction —
convicto, -ta *adj* : convicted
convidar *vt* : invite — **convidado, -da** *n*
: guest
convincente *adj* : convincing
convite *nm* **1** : invitation **2** : banquet
convivir *vi* : live together — **convivencia** *nf*
: coexistence, living together
convocar {72} *vt* : convoke, call together
convulsión *nf, pl* **-siones 1** : convulsion **2**
TRASTORNO : upheaval — **convulsivo, -va**
adj : convulsive
conyugal *adj* : conjugal — **cónyuge** *nmf*
: spouse, partner
coñac *nm* : cognac, brandy
cooperar *vi* : cooperate — **cooperación** *nf,*
pl **-ciones** : cooperation — **cooperativa** *nf*
: cooperative, co-op — **cooperativo, -va**
adj : cooperative
coordenada *nf* : coordinate
coordinar *vt* : coordinate — **coordinación**
nf, pl **-ciones** : coordination — **coordinador, -dora** *n* : coordinator
copa *nf* **1** : glass, goblet **2** : cup (in sports)
3 tomar una ~ : have a drink
copia *nf* : copy — **copiar** *vt* : copy
copioso, -sa *adj* : copious, abundant
copla *nf* **1** : (popular) song **2** ESTROFA
: verse, stanza
copo *nm* **1** : flake **2** *or* **~ de nieve** : snowflake
coquetear *vi* : flirt — **coqueteo** *nm* : flirting, flirtation — **coqueto, -ta** *adj* : flirtatious — **~ n** : flirt
coraje *nm* **1** : valor, courage **2** IRA : anger
coral[1] *nm* : coral
coral[2] *adj* : choral — **~** *nf* : choir, chorale
Corán *nm* **el ~** : the Koran
coraza *nf* **1** : armor plating **2** : shell
corazón *nm, pl* **-zones 1** : heart **2** : core (of
fruit) **3 mi ~** : my darling — **corazonada**
nf **1** : hunch **2** IMPULSO : impulse
corbata *nf* : tie, necktie
corchete *nm* **1** : hook and eye, clasp **2**
: square bracket (punctuation mark)
corcho *nm* : cork
cordel *nm* : cord, string
cordero *nm* : lamb
cordial *adj* : cordial — **cordialidad** *nf* : cordiality
cordillera *nf* : mountain range
córdoba *nf* : córdoba (Nicaraguan unit of
currency)
cordón *nm, pl* **-dones 1** : cord **2 ~ policial**
: (police) cordon **3 cordones** *nmpl* : shoelaces

cordura *nf* : sanity
corear *vt* : chant
coreografía *nf* : choreography
cornamenta *nf* : antlers *pl*
corneta *nf* : bugle
coro *nm* **1** : chorus **2** : (church) choir
corona *nf* **1** : crown **2** : wreath, garland (of flowers) — **coronación** *nf, pl* **-ciones** : coronation — **coronar** *vt* : crown
coronel *nm* : colonel
coronilla *nf* **1** : crown (of the head) **2 estar hasta la ~** : be fed up
corporación *nf, pl* **-ciones** : corporation
corporal *adj* : corporal, bodily
corporativo, -va *adj* : corporate
corpulento, -ta *adj* : stout
corral *nm* **1** : farmyard **2** : pen, corral (for animals) **3** *or* **corralito** : playpen
correa *nf* **1** : strap, belt **2** : leash (for a dog, etc.)
corrección *nf, pl* **-ciones** **1** : correction **2** : correctness, propriety (of manners) — **correccional** *nm* : reformatory — **correctivo, -va** *adj* : corrective — **correcto, -ta** *adj* **1** : correct, right **2** CORTÉS : polite
corredizo, -za *adj* : sliding
corredor, -dora *n* **1** : runner, racer **2** AGENTE : agent, broker — **corredor** *nm* : corridor, hallway
corregir {28} *vt* : correct — **corregirse** *vr* : mend one's ways
correlación *nf, pl* **-ciones** : correlation
correo *nm* **1** : mail **2 ~ aéreo** : airmail
correr *vi* **1** : run, race **2** : flow (of a river, etc.) **3** : pass (of time) — *vt* **1** : run **2** RECORRER : travel over, cover **3** : draw (curtains) — **correrse** *vr* **1** : move along **2** : run (of colors)
corresponder *vi* **1** : correspond **2** PERTENECER : belong **3** ENCAJAR : fit **4 ~ a** : reciprocate, repay — **corresponderse** *vr* : write to each other — **correspondencia** *nf* **1** : correspondence **2** : connection (of a train, etc.) — **correspondiente** *adj* : corresponding, respective — **corresponsal** *nmf* : correspondent
corretear *vi* : run about, scamper
corrida *nf* **1** : run **2** *or* **~ de toros** : bullfight — **corrido, -da** *adj* **1** : straight, continuous **2** *fam* : worldly
corriente *adj* **1** : current **2** NORMAL : common, ordinary **3** : running (of water, etc.) — **~** *nf* **1** : current (of water, electricity, etc.), draft (of air) **2** TENDENCIA : tendency, trend — **~** *nm* **al ~ 1** : up-to-date **2** ENTERADO : aware, informed
corrillo *nm* : clique, circle — **corro** *nm* : ring, circle (of people)
corroborar *vt* : corroborate

corroer {69} *vt* **1** : corrode (of metals) **2** : erode, wear away — **corroerse** *vr* : corrode
corromper *vt* **1** : corrupt **2** PUDRIR : rot — **corrompido, -da** *adj* : corrupt
corrosión *nf, pl* **-siones** : corrosion — **corrosivo, -va** *adj* : corrosive
corrupción *nf, pl* **-ciones** **1** : corruption **2** DESCOMPOSICIÓN : decay, rot — **corrupto, -ta** *adj* : corrupt
corsé *nm* : corset
cortar *vt* **1** : cut **2** RECORTAR : cut out **3** QUITAR : cut off — *vi* : cut — **cortarse** *vr* **1** : cut oneself **2** : be cut off (on the telephone) **3** : curdle (of milk) **4 ~ el pelo** : have one's hair cut — **cortada** *nf Lat* : cut — **cortante** *adj* : cutting, sharp
cortauñas *nms & pl* : nail clippers
corte[1] *nm* **1** : cutting **2** ESTILO : cut, style **3 ~ de pelo** : haircut
corte[2] *nf* **1** : court **2 hacer la ~ a** : court, woo — **cortejar** *vt* : court, woo
cortejo *nm* **1** : entourage **2** NOVIAZGO : courtship **3 ~ fúnebre** : funeral procession
cortés *adj* : courteous, polite — **cortesía** *nf* : courtesy, politeness
corteza *nf* **1** : bark **2** : crust (of bread) **3** : rind, peel (of fruit)
cortina *nf* : curtain
corto, -ta *adj* **1** : short **2** ESCASO : scarce **3** *fam* : timid, shy **4 ~ de vista** : nearsighted — **cortocircuito** *nm* : short circuit
corvo, -va *adj* : curved, bent
cosa *nf* **1** : thing **2** ASUNTO : matter, affair **3 ~ de** : about **4 poca ~** : nothing much
cosechar *v* : harvest, reap — **cosecha** *nf* **1** : harvest, crop **2** : vintage (of wine)
coser *v* : sew
cosmético, -ca *adj* : cosmetic — **cosmético** *nm* : cosmetic
cósmico, -ca *adj* : cosmic
cosmopolita *adj* : cosmopolitan
cosmos *nm* : cosmos
cosquillas *nfpl* **1** : tickling **2 hacer ~** : tickle — **cosquilleo** *nm* : tickling sensation, tingle
costa *nf* **1** : coast, shore **2 a toda ~** : at any cost
costado *nm* **1** : side **2 al ~** : alongside
costar {19} *v* : cost
costarricense *or* **costarriqueño, -ña** *adj* : Costa Rican
coste *nm* → **costo** — **costear** *vt* : pay for
costero, -ra *adj* : coastal
costilla *nf* **1** : rib **2** CHULETA : chop, cutlet
costo *nm* : cost, price — **costoso, -sa** *adj* : costly
costra *nf* : scab

costumbre *nf* **1** : custom, habit **2 de ~** : usual
costura *nf* **1** : sewing, dressmaking **2** PUN-TADAS : seam — **costurera** *nf* : dressmaker
cotejar *vt* : compare
cotidiano, -na *adj* : daily
cotizar {21} *vt* : quote, set a price on — **cotización** *nf, pl* **-ciones** : quotation, price — **cotizado, -da** *adj* : in demand
coto *nm* : enclosure, reserve
cotorra *nf* **1** : small parrot **2** *fam* : chatterbox — **cotorrear** *vi fam* : chatter, gab
coyote *nm* : coyote
coyuntura *nf* **1** : joint **2** SITUACIÓN : situation, moment
coz *nm, pl* **coces** : kick (of an animal)
cráneo *nf* : cranium, skull
cráter *nm* : crater
crear *vt* : create — **creación** *nf, pl* **-ciones** : creation — **creativo, -va** *adj* : creative — **creador, -dora** *n* : creator
crecer {53} *vi* **1** : grow **2** AUMENTAR : increase — **crecido, -da** *adj* **1** : full-grown **2** : large (of numbers) — **creciente** *adj* **1** : growing, increasing **2** : crescent (of the moon) — **crecimiento** *nm* **1** : growth **2** AUMENTO : increase
credenciales *nfpl* : credentials
credibilidad *nf* : credibility
crédito *nm* : credit
credo *nm* : creed
crédulo, -la *adj* : credulous, gullible
creer {20} *v* **1** : believe **2** SUPONER : suppose, think — **creerse** *vr* : regard oneself as — **creencia** *nf* : belief — **creíble** *adj* : believable, credible — **creído, -da** *adj fam* : conceited
crema *nf* : cream
cremación *nf, pl* **-ciones** : cremation
cremallera *nf* : zipper
cremoso, -sa *adj* : creamy
crepe *nmf* : crepe, pancake
crepitar *vi* : crackle
crepúsculo *nm* : twilight, dusk
crespo, -pa *adj* : curly, frizzy
crespón *nm, pl* **-pones** : crepe (fabric)
cresta *nf* **1** : crest **2** : comb (of a rooster)
cretino, -na *n* : cretin
creyente *nmf* : believer
criar {85} *vt* **1** : nurse (a baby) **2** EDUCAR : bring up, rear **3** : raise, breed (animals) — **cría** *nf* **1** : breeding, rearing **2** : young animal — **criadero** *nm* : farm, hatchery — **criado, -da** *n* : servant, maid *f* — **criador, -dora** *n* : breeder — **crianza** *nf* : upbringing, rearing
criatura *nf* **1** : creature **2** NIÑO : baby, child
crimen *nm, pl* **crímenes** : crime — **criminal** *adj & nmf* : criminal

críquet *nm* : cricket (game)
crin *nf* : mane
criollo, -lla *adj & n* : Creole
cripta *nf* : crypt
crisantemo *nm* : chrysanthemum
crisis *nf* **1** : crisis **2 ~ nerviosa** : nervous breakdown
crispar *vt* **1** : tense (muscles), clench (one's fist) **2** IRRITAR : irritate, set on edge — **crisparse** *vr* : tense up
cristal *nm* **1** : crystal **2** VIDRIO : glass, piece of glass — **cristalería** *nf* : glassware — **cristalino, -na** *adj* : crystalline — **cristalino** *nm* : lens (of the eye) — **cristalizar** {21} *vi* : crystallize
cristiano, -na *adj & n* : Christian — **cristianismo** *nm* : Christianity — **Cristo** *nm* : Christ
criterio *nm* **1** : criterion **2** JUICIO : judgment, opinion
criticar {72} *vt* : criticize — **crítica** *nf* **1** : criticism **2** RESEÑA : review, critique — **crítico, -ca** *adj* : critical — **~** *n* : critic, reviewer
croar *vi* : croak
cromo *nm* : chromium, chrome
cromosoma *nm* : chromosome
crónica *nf* **1** : chronicle **2** : (news) report
crónico, -ca *adj* : chronic
cronista *nmf* : reporter, newscaster
cronología *nf* : chronology — **cronológico, -ca** *adj* : chronological
cronometrar *vt* : time, clock — **cronómetro** *nm* : chronometer, stopwatch
croqueta *nf* : croquette
croquis *nms & pl* : (rough) sketch
cruce *nm* **1** : crossing **2** : crossroads, intersection **3 ~ peatonal** : crosswalk
crucero *nm* **1** : cruise **2** : cruiser (ship)
crucial *adj* : crucial
crucificar {72} *vt* : crucify — **crucifijo** *nm* : crucifix — **crucifixión** *nf, pl* **-fixiones** : crucifixion
crucigrama *nm* : crossword puzzle
crudo, -da *adj* **1** : harsh, crude **2** : raw (of food) — **crudo** *nm* : crude oil
cruel *adj* : cruel — **crueldad** *nf* : cruelty
crujir *vi* : rustle, creak, crackle, crunch — **crujido** *nm* : rustle, creak, crackle, crunch — **crujiente** *adj* : crunchy, crisp
cruzar {21} *vt* **1** : cross **2** : exchange (words) — **cruzarse** *vr* **1** : intersect **2** : pass each other — **cruz** *nf, pl* **cruces** : cross — **cruzada** *nf* : crusade — **cruzado, -da** *adj* : crossed — **cruzado** *nm* : crusader
cuaderno *nm* : notebook
cuadra *nf* **1** : stable **2** *Lat* : (city) block
cuadrado, -da *adj* : square — **cuadrado** *nm* : square

cuadragésimo, -ma *adj* : fortieth, forty- — ~ *n* : fortieth, forty- (in a series)
cuadrar *vi* **1** : conform, agree **2** : add up, tally (numbers) — *vt* : square — **cuadrarse** *vr* : stand at attention
cuadrilátero *nm* **1** : quadrilateral **2** : ring (in sports)
cuadrilla *nf* : gang, group
cuadro *nm* **1** : square **2** PINTURA : painting **3** DESCRIPCIÓN : picture, description **4** : staff, management (of an organization) **5** CUADRADO : check, square **6** : (baseball) diamond
cuadrúpedo *nm* : quadruped
cuadruple *adj* : quadruple — **cuadruplicar** {72} *vt* : quadruple
cuajar *vi* **1** : curdle **2** COAGULAR : clot, coagulate **3** : set (of pudding, etc.) **4** AFIANZARSE : catch on — *vt* **1** : curdle **2** ~ **de** : fill with
cual *pron* **1 el** ~, **la** ~, **los** ~**es, las** ~**es** : who, whom, which **2 lo** ~ : which **3 cada** ~ : everyone, everybody — ~ *prep* : like, as
cuál *pron* : which (one), what (one) — ~ *adj* : which, what
cualidad *nf* : quality, trait
cualquiera (**cualquier** *before nouns*) *adj, pl* **cualesquiera** : any, whatever — ~ *pron, pl* **cualesquiera** : anyone, whatever
cuán *adv* : how
cuando *conj* **1** : when **2** SI : since, if **3** ~ **más** : at the most **4 de vez en** ~ : from time to time — ~ *prep* : during, at the time of
cuándo *adv* **1** : when **2 ¿desde** ~? : since when?
cuantía *nf* **1** : quantity, extent **2** IMPORTANCIA : importance — **cuantioso, -sa** *adj* : abundant, considerable
cuanto *adv* **1** : as much as **2** ~ **antes** : as soon as possible **3 en** ~ : as soon as **4 en** ~ **a** : as for, as regards — **cuanto, -ta** *adj* : as many, whatever — ~ *pron* **1** : as much as, all that, everything **2 unos cuantos, unas cuantas** : a few
cuánto *adv* : how much, how many — **cuánto, -ta** *adj* : how much, how many — ~ *pron* : how much, how many
cuarenta *adj & nm* **1** : forty — **cuarentavo, -va** *adj* : fortieth — **cuarentavo** *nm* : fortieth
cuarentena *nf* : quarantine
Cuaresma *nf* : Lent
cuartear *vt* : quarter, divide up — **cuartearse** *vr* : crack, split
cuartel *nm* **1** : barracks *pl* **2** ~ **general** : headquarters **3 no dar** ~ : show no mercy

cuarteto *nm* : quartet
cuarto, -ta *adj* : fourth — ~ *n* : fourth (in a series) — **cuarto** *nm* **1** : quarter, fourth **2** HABITACIÓN : room
cuarzo *nm* : quartz
cuatro *adj & nm* : four — **cuatrocientos, -tas** *adj* : four hundred — **cuatrocientos** *nms & pl* : four hundred
cuba *nf* : cask, barrel
cubano, -na *adj* : Cuban
cubeta *nf* **1** : keg, cask **2** *Lat* : pail, bucket
cúbico, -ca *adj* : cubic, cubed — **cubículo** *nm* : cubicle
cubierta *nf* **1** : cover, covering **2** : (automobile) tire **3** : deck (of a ship) — **cubierto** *nm* **1** : cutlery, place setting **2 a** ~ : under cover
cubo *nm* **1** : cube **2** *Spain* : pail, bucket **3** : hub (of a wheel)
cubrecama *nm* : bedspread
cubrir {2} *vt* : cover — **cubrirse** *vr* **1** : cover oneself **2** : cloud over
cucaracha *nf* : cockroach
cuchara *nf* : spoon — **cucharada** *nf* : spoonful — **cucharilla** *or* **cucharita** *nf* : teaspoon — **cucharón** *nm, pl* **-rones** : ladle
cuchichear *vi* : whisper — **cuchicheo** *nm* : whisper
cuchilla *nf* **1** : (kitchen) knife **2** ~ **de afeitar** : razor blade — **cuchillada** *nf* : stab, knife wound — **cuchillo** *nm* : knife
cuclillas *nfpl* **en** ~ : squatting, crouching
cuco *nm* : cuckoo — **cuco, -ca** *adj fam* : pretty, cute
cucurucho *nm* : ice-cream cone
cuello *nm* **1** : neck **2** : collar (of clothing)
cuenca *nf* **1** : river basin **2** : (eye) socket — **cuenco** *nm* **1** : bowl **2** CONCAVIDAD : hollow
cuenta *nf* **1** : calculation, count **2** : (bank) account **3** FACTURA : check, bill **4** : bead (for a necklace, etc.) **5 darse** ~ : realize **6 tener en** ~ : bear in mind
cuento *nm* **1** : story, tale **2** ~ **de hadas** : fairy tale
cuerda *nf* **1** : cord, rope, string **2** ~**s vocales** : vocal cords **3 dar** ~ **a** : wind up
cuerdo, -da *adj* : sane, sensible
cuerno *nm* **1** : horn **2** : antlers *pl* (of a deer)
cuero *nm* **1** : leather, hide **2** ~ **cabelludo** : scalp
cuerpo *nm* **1** : body **2** : corps (in the military, etc.)
cuervo *nm* : crow
cuesta *nf* **1** : slope **2 a** ~**s** : on one's back **3** ~ **abajo** : downhill **4** ~ **arriba** : uphill
cuestión *nf, pl* **-tiones** : matter, affair — **cuestionar** *vt* : question — **cuestionario** *nm* **1** : questionnaire **2** : quiz (in school)

cueva *nf* : cave
cuidar *vt* **1** : take care of, look after **2** : pay attention to (details, etc.) — *vi* **1** ~ **de** : look after **2** ~ **de que** : make sure that — **cuidarse** *vr* : take care of oneself — **cuidado** *nm* **1** : care **2** PREOCUPACIÓN : worry, concern **3 tener** ~ : be careful **4 ¡cuidado!** : watch out!, careful! — **cuidadoso, -sa** *adj* : careful — **cuidadosamente** *adv* : carefully
culata *nf* : butt (of a gun) — **culatazo** *nf* : kick, recoil
culebra *nf* : snake
culinario, -ria *adj* : culinary
culminar *vi* : culminate — **culminación** *nf, pl* **-ciones** : culmination
culo *nm fam* : backside, bottom
culpa *nf* **1** : fault, blame **2** PECADO : sin **3 echar la** ~ **a** : blame **4 tener la** ~ : be at fault — **culpabilidad** *nf* : guilt — **culpable** *adj* : guilty — ~ *nmf* : culprit, guilty party — **culpar** *vt* : blame
cultivar *vt* : cultivate — **cultivo** *nm* **1** : farming, cultivation **2** ~**s** : crops
culto, -ta *adj* : cultured, educated — **culto** *nm* **1** : worship **2** : (religious) cult — **cultura** *nf* : culture — **cultural** *adj* : cultural
cumbre *nf* : summit, top
cumpleaños *nms & pl* : birthday
cumplido, -da *adj* **1** : complete, full **2** CORTÉS : courteous — **cumplido** *nm* : compliment, courtesy
cumplimentar *vt* **1** : congratulate **2** CUMPLIR : carry out — **cumplimiento** *nm* : carrying out, performance
cumplir *vt* **1** : accomplish, carry out **2** : keep (a promise), observe (a law, etc.) **3** : reach (a given age) — *vi* **1** : expire, fall due **2** ~ **con el deber** : do one's duty — **cumplirse** *vr* **1** : expire **2** REALIZARSE : come true
cúmulo *nm* **1** : heap, pile **2** : cumulus (cloud)

cuna *nf* **1** : cradle **2** ORIGEN : birthplace
cundir *vi* **1** PROPAGARSE : spread, propagate **2** : go a long way
cuneta *nf* : ditch (in a road), gutter (in a street)
cuña *nf* : wedge
cuñado, -da *n* : brother-in-law *m*, sister-in-law *f*
cuota *nf* **1** : fee, dues **2** CUPO : quota **3** *Lat* : installment, payment
cupo *nm* **1** : quota, share **2** *Lat* : capacity, room
cupón *nm, pl* **-pones** : coupon
cúpula *nf* : dome, cupola
cura *nf* : cure, treatment — ~ *nm* : priest — **curación** *nf, pl* **-ciones** : healing — **curar** *vt* **1** : cure **2** : dress (a wound) **3** CURTIR : tan (hides) — **curarse** *vr* : get well
curiosear *vi* **1** : snoop, pry **2** : browse (in a store) — *vt* : look over — **curiosidad** *nf* : curiosity — **curioso, -sa** *adj* **1** : curious, inquisitive **2** RARO : unusual, strange
currículum *nm, pl* **-lums** *or* **currículo** *nm* : résumé, curriculum vitae
cursar *vt* **1** : take (a course), study **2** ENVIAR : send, pass on
cursi *adj fam* : affected, pretentious
cursiva *nf* : italics *pl*
curso *nm* **1** : course **2** : (school) year **3 en** ~ : under way **4 en** ~ : current
curtir *vt* **1** : tan **2** : harden (skin, features, etc.) — **curtiduría** *nf* : tannery
curva *nf* **1** : curve, bend **2** ~ **de nivel** : contour — **curvo, -va** *adj* : curved, bent
cúspide *nf* : apex, peak
custodia *nf* : custody — **custodiar** *vt* : guard, look after — **custodio, -dia** *n* : guardian
cutáneo, -nea *adj* : skin
cutícula *nf* : cuticle
cutis *nms & pl* : skin, complexion
cuyo, -ya *adj* **1** : whose, of whom, of which **2 en cuyo caso** : in which case

D

d *nf* : d, fourth letter of the Spanish alphabet

dádiva *nf* : gift, handout — **dadivoso, -sa** *adj* : generous

dado, -da *adj* **1** : given **2 dado que** : provided that, since — **dados** *nmpl* : dice

daga *nf* : dagger

daltónico, -ca *adj* : color-blind

dama *nf* **1** : lady **2 ~s** *nfpl* : checkers

damnificar {72} *vt* : damage, injure

danés, -nesa *adj* : Danish — **danés** *nm* : Danish (language)

danzar {21} *v* : dance — **danza** *nf* : dance, dancing

dañar *vt* : damage, harm — **dañarse** *vr* **1** : be damaged **2** : hurt oneself — **dañino, -na** *adj* : harmful — **daño** *nm* **1** : damage, harm **2 ~s y perjuicios** : damages

dar {22} *vt* **1** : give **2** PRODUCIR : yield, produce **3** : strike (the hour) **4** MOSTRAR : show — *vi* **1 ~ como** : consider, regard as **2 ~ con** : run into, meet **3 ~ contra** : knock against **4 ~ para** : be enough for — **darse** *vr* **1** : happen **2 ~ contra** : bump into **3 ~ por** : consider oneself **4 dárselas de** : pose as

dardo *nm* : dart

dársena *nf* : dock

datar *vt* : date — *vi* **~ de** : date from

dátil *nm* : date (fruit)

dato *nm* **1** : fact **2 ~s** *nmpl* : data

de *prep* **1** : of **2 ~ Managua** : from Managua **3 ~ niño** : as a child **4 ~ noche** : at night **5 las tres ~ la mañana** : three o'clock in the morning **6 más ~ 10** : more than 10

deambular *vi* : wander about, stroll

debajo *adv* **1** : underneath **2 ~ de** : under, underneath **3 por ~** : below, beneath

debatir *vt* : debate — **debatirse** *vr* : struggle — **debate** *nm* : debate

deber *vt* : owe — *v aux* **1** : have to, should **2** (*expressing probability*) : must — **deberse** *vr* **~ a** : be due to — **~** *nm* **1** : duty **2 ~es** *nmpl* : homework — **debido, -da** *adj* **~ a** : due to, owing to

débil *adj* : weak, feeble — **debilidad** *nf* : weakness — **debilitar** *vt* : weaken — **debilitarse** *vr* : get weak — **débilmente** *adv* : weakly, faintly

débito *nm* **1** : debit **2** DEUDA : debt

debutar *vi* : debut — **debut** *nm, pl* **~s** : debut — **debutante** *nf* : debutante *f*

década *nf* : decade

decadencia *nf* : decadence — **decadente** *adj* : decadent

decaer {13} *vi* : decline, weaken

decano, -na *n* : dean

decapitar *vt* : behead

decena *nf* : ten, about ten

decencia *nf* : decency

decenio *nm* : decade

decente *adj* : decent

decepcionar *vt* : disappoint — **decepción** *nf, pl* **-ciones** : disappointment

decibelio *or* **decibel** *nm* : decibel

decidir *vt* : decide, determine — *vi* : decide — **decidirse** *vr* : make up one's mind — **decididamente** *adv* : definitely, decidedly — **decidido, -da** *adj* : determined, resolute

decimal *adj* : decimal

décimo, -ma *adj & n* : tenth

decimoctavo, -va *adj* : eighteenth — **~** *n* : eighteenth (in a series)

decimocuarto, -ta *adj* : fourteenth — **~** *n* : fourteenth (in a series)

decimonoveno, -na *or* **decimonono, -na** *adj* : nineteenth — **~** *n* : nineteenth (in a series)

decimoquinto, -ta *adj* : fifteenth — **~** *n* : fifteenth (in a series)

decimoséptimo, -ma *adj* : seventeenth — **~** *n* : seventeenth (in a series)

decimosexto, -ta *adj* : sixteenth — **~** *n* : sixteenth (in a series)

decimotercero, -ra *adj* : thirteenth — **~** *n* : thirteenth (in a series)

decir {23} *vt* **1** : say **2** CONTAR : tell **3 es ~** : that is to say **4 querer ~** : mean — **decirse** *vr* **1** : tell oneself **2 ¿cómo se dice...en español?** : how do you say...in Spanish? — **~** *nm* : saying, expression

decisión *nf, pl* **-siones** : decision — **decisivo, -va** *adj* : decisive

declarar *vt* : declare — *vi* : testify — **declararse** *vr* **1** : declare oneself **2** : break out (of a fire, an epidemic, etc.) — **declaración** *nf, pl* **-ciones** : statement

declinar *v* : decline

declive *nm* **1** : decline **2** PENDIENTE : slope

decolorar *vt* : bleach — **decolorarse** *vr* : fade

decoración *nf, pl* **-ciones** : decoration — **decorado** *nm* : stage set — **decorar** *vt* : decorate — **decorativo, -va** *adj* : decorative

decoro *nm* : decency, decorum — **decoroso, -sa** *adj* : decent, proper decrecer 48

decrecer {53} *vi* : decrease
decrépito, -ta *adj* : decrepit
decretar *vt* : decree — **decreto** *nm* : decree
dedal *nm* : thimble
dedicar {72} *vt* : dedicate — **dedicarse** *vr*
~ **a** : devote oneself to — **dedicación** *nf*,
pl **-ciones** : dedication — **dedicatoria** *nf*
: dedication, inscription
dedo *nm* 1 : finger 2 ~ **del pie** : toe
deducir {61} *vt* 1 INFERIR : deduce 2 DE-
SCONTAR : deduct — **deducción** *nf*, *pl*
-ciones : deduction
defecar {72} *vi* : defecate
defecto *nm* : defect — **defectuoso, -sa** *adj*
: defective, faulty
defender {56} *vt* : defend — **defenderse** *vr*
: defend oneself — **defensa** *nf* : defense —
defensiva *nf* : defensive — **defensivo, -va**
adj : defensive — **defensor, -sora** *n* 1 : defender 2 *or* **abogado defensor** : defense
counsel
deferencia *nf* : deference — **deferente** *adj*
: deferential
deficiencia *nf* : deficiency — **deficiente** *adj*
: deficient
déficit *nm*, *pl* **-cits** : deficit
definir *vt* : define — **definición** *nf*, *pl*
-ciones : definition — **definitivo, -va** *adj* 1
: definitive 2 **en definitiva** : in short
deformar *vt* 1 : deform 2 : distort (the truth,
etc.) — **deformación** *nf*, *pl* **-ciones** : distortion — **deforme** *adj* : deformed — **deformidad** *nf* : deformity
defraudar *vt* 1 : defraud 2 DECEPCIONAR
: disappoint
degenerar *vi* : degenerate — **degenerado,
-da** *adj* : degenerate
degradar *vt* 1 : degrade 2 : demote (in the
military)
degustar *vt* : taste
dehesa *nf* : pasture
deidad *nf* : deity
dejar *vt* 1 : leave 2 ABANDONAR : abandon
3 PERMITIR : allow — *vi* ~ **de** : quit — **de-
jado, -da** *adj* : slovenly, careless
dejo *nm* 1 : aftertaste 2 : (regional) accent
delantal *nm* : apron
delante *adv* 1 : ahead 2 ~ **de** : in front of
delantera *nf* 1 : front 2 **tomar la** ~ : take
the lead — **delantero, -ra** *adj* : front, forward — ~ *n* : forward (in sports)
delatar *vt* : denounce, inform against
delegar {52} *vt* : delegate — **delegación** *nf*,
pl **-ciones** : delegation — **delegado, -da** *n*
: delegate, representative
deleitar *vt* : delight, please — **deleite** *nm*
: delight
deletrear *vi* : spell (out)
delfín *nm*, *pl* **-fines** : dolphin

delgado, -da *adj* : thin
deliberar *vi* : deliberate — **deliberación** *nf*,
pl **-ciones** : deliberation — **deliberado, -da**
adj : deliberate, intentional
delicadeza *nf* 1 : delicacy, daintiness 2
SUAVIDAD : gentleness 3 TACTO : tact —
delicado, -da *adj* 1 : delicate 2 SENSIBLE
: sensible 3 DISCRETO : tactful
delicia *nf* : delight — **delicioso, -sa** *adj* 1
: delightful 2 RICO : delicious
delictivo, -va *adj* : criminal
delimitar *vt* : define, set the boundaries of
delincuencia *nf* : delinquency, crime —
delincuente *adj* & *nmf* : delinquent, criminal — **delinquir** {24} *vi* : break the law
delirante *adj* : delirious — **delirar** *vi* 1 : be
delirious 2 ~ **por** *fam* : rave about —
delirio *nm* 1 : delirium 2 ~ **de grandeza**
: delusions of grandeur
delito *nm* : crime
delta *nm* : delta
demacrado, -da *adj* : emaciated
demandar *vt* 1 : sue 2 PEDIR : demand 3
Lat : require — **demanda** *nf* 1 : lawsuit 2
PETICIÓN : request 3 **la oferta y la** ~ : supply and demand — **demandante** *nmf*
: plaintiff
demás *adj* : rest of the, other — ~ *pron* 1
lo (la, los, las) ~ : the rest, others 2 **por**
~ : extremely 3 **por lo** ~ : otherwise 4 **y**
~ : and so on
demasiado *adv* 1 : too 2 : too much — ~
adj : too much, too many
demencia *nf* : madness — **demente** *adj* : insane, mad
democracia *nf* : democracy — **demócrata**
nmf : democrat — **democrático, -ca** *adj*
: democratic
demoler {47} *vt* : demolish — **demolición**
nf, *pl* **-ciones** : demolition
demonio *nm* : devil, demon
demorar *v* : delay — **demorarse** *vr* : take a
long time — **demora** *nf* : delay
demostrar {19} *vt* 1 : demonstrate 2
MOSTRAR : show — **demostración** *nf*, *pl*
-ciones : demonstration
demudar *vt* : change, alter
denegar {49} *vt* : deny, refuse — **denegación** *nf*, *pl* **-ciones** : denial, refusal
denigrar *vt* 1 : denigrate 2 INJURIAR : insult
denominador *nm* : denominator
denotar *vt* : denote, show
densidad *nf* : density — **denso, -sa** *adj*
: dense
dental *adj* : dental — **dentado, -da** *adj*
: toothed, notched — **dentadura** *nf* ~ **postiza** : dentures *pl* — **dentífrico** *nm* : toothpaste — **dentista** *nmf* : dentist

dentro *adv* **1** : in, inside **2** ~ **de poco** : soon, shortly **3 por** ~ : inside
denuedo *nm* : courage
denunciar *vt* **1** : denounce **2** : report (a crime) — **denuncia** *nf* **1** : accusation **2** : (police) report
departamento *nm* **1** : department **2** *Lat* : apartment
deponder *vi* **1** : depend **2** ~ **de** : depend on — **dependencia** *nf* **1** : dependence, dependency **2** SUCURSAL : branch office — **dependiente** *adj* : dependent — **dependiente, -ta** *n* : clerk, salesperson
deplorar *vt* : deplore, regret
deponer {60} *vt* : remove from office, depose
deportar *vt* : deport — **deportación** *nf, pl* -**ciones** : deportation
deporte *nm* : sport, sports *pl* — **deportista** *nmf* : sportsman *m*, sportswoman *f* — **deportivo, -va** *adj* **1** : sporty **2 artículos deportivos** : sporting goods
depositar *vt* **1** : put, place **2** : deposit (in a bank, etc.) — **depósito** *nm* **1** : deposit **2** ALMACÉN : warehouse
depravado, -da *adj* : depraved
depreciarse *vr* : depreciate — **depreciación** *nf* : depreciation
depredador *nm* : predator
deprimir *vt* : depress — **deprimirse** *vr* : get depressed — **depresión** *nf, pl* -**siones** : depression
derecha *nf* **1** : right side **2** : right wing (in politics) — **derechista** *adj* : right-wing — **derecho** *nm* **1** : right **2** LEY : law — ~ *adv* : straight — **derecho, -cha** *adj* **1** : right, right-hand **2** VERTICAL : upright **3** RECTO : straight
deriva *nf* **1** : drift **2 a la** ~ : adrift — **derivación** *nf, pl* -**ciones** : derivation — **derivar** *vi* **1** : drift **2** ~ **de** : derive from
derramamiento *nm* ~ **de sangre** : bloodshed
derramar *vt* **1** : spill **2** : shed (tears, blood) — **derramarse** *vr* : overflow — **derrame** *nm* **1** : spilling **2** : discharge, hemorrhage
derrapar *vi* : skid — **derrape** *nm* : skid
derretir {54} *vt* : melt, thaw — **derretirse** *vr* **1** : melt, thaw **2** ~ **por** *fam* : be crazy about
derribar *vt* **1** : demolish **2** : bring down (a plane, a tree, etc.) **3** : overthrow (a government, etc.)
derrocar {72} *vt* : overthrow
derrochar *vt* : waste, squander — **derrochador, -dora** *n* : spendthrift — **derroche** *nm* : extravagance, waste
derrotar *vt* : defeat — **derrota** *nf* : defeat
derruir {41} *vt* : demolish, tear down

derrumbar *vt* : demolish, knock down — **derrumbarse** *vr* : collapse, break down — **derrumbamiento** *nm* : collapse — **derrumbe** *nm* : collapse
desabotonar *vt* : unbutton, undo
desabrido, -da *adj* : bland
desabrochar *vt* : unbutton, undo — **desabrocharse** *vr* : come undone
desacato *nm* **1** : disrespect **2** : contempt (of court) — **desacatar** *vt* : defy, disobey
desacertado, -da *adj* : mistaken, wrong — **desacertar** {55} *vi* : be mistaken — **desacierto** *nm* : mistake, error
desaconsejar *vt* : advise against — **desaconsejable** *adj* : inadvisable
desacreditar *vt* : discredit
desactivar *vt* : deactivate
desacuerdo *nm* : disagreement
desafiar {85} *vt* : defy, challenge — **desafiante** *adj* : defiant
desafilado, -da *adj* : blunt
desafinado, -da *adj* : out-of-tune, off-key
desafío *nm* : challenge, defiance
desafortunado, -da *adj* : unfortunate — **desafortunadamente** *adv* : unfortunately
desagradar *vt* : displease — **desagradable** *adj* : disagreeable, unpleasant
desagradecido, -da *adj* : ungrateful
desagrado *nm* **1** : displeasure **2 con** ~ : reluctantly
desagravio *nm* : amends, reparation
desagregarse {52} *vr* : disintegrate
desaguar {10} *vi* : drain, empty — **desagüe** *nm* **1** : drainage **2** : drain (of a sink, etc.)
desahogar {52} *vt* **1** : relieve **2** : give vent to (anger, etc.) — **desahogarse** *vr* : let off steam, unburden oneself — **desahogado, -da** *adj* **1** : roomy **2** ADINERADO : comfortable, well-off — **desahogo** *nm* **1** : relief **2 con** ~ : comfortably
desahuciar *vt* **1** : deprive of hope **2** DESALOJAR : evict — **desahucio** *nm* : eviction
desaire *vt* : snub, rebuff — **desairar** *vt* : snub, slight
desalentar {55} *vt* : discourage — **desaliento** *nm* : discouragement
desaliñado, -da *adj* : slovenly
desalmado, -da *adj* : heartless, cruel
desalojar *vt* **1** : evacuate **2** DESAHUCIAR : evict
desamparar *vt* : abandon — **desamparo** *nm* : abandonment, desertion
desamueblado, -da *adj* : unfurnished
desangrarse *vr* : lose blood, bleed to death
desanimar *vt* : discourage — **desanimarse** *vr* : get discouraged — **desanimado, -da** *adj* : downhearted, despondent — **desánimo** *nm* : discouragement

desanudar   **50**

desanudar *vt* : untie
desaparecer {53} *vi* : disappear — **desaparecido, -da** *n* : missing person — **desaparición** *nf, pl* **-ciones** : disappearance
desapasionado, -da *adj* : dispassionate
desapego *nm* : indifference
desapercibido, -da *adj* : unnoticed
desaprobar {19} *vt* : disapprove of — **desaprobación** *nf, pl* **-ciones** : disapproval
desaprovechar *vt* : waste
desarmar *vt* **1** : disarm **2** DESMONTAR : dismantle, take apart — **desarme** *nm* : disarmament
desarraigar {52} *vt* : uproot, root out
desarreglar *vt* **1** : mess up **2** : disrupt (plans, etc.) — **desarreglado, -da** *adj* : disorganized — **desarreglo** *nm* : untidiness, disorder
desarrollar *vt* : develop — **desarrollarse** *vr* : take place — **desarrollo** *nm* : development
desarticular *vt* **1** : break up, dismantle **2** : dislocate (a bone)
desaseado, -da *adj* **1** : dirty **2** DESORDENADO : messy
desastre *nm* : disaster — **desastroso, -sa** *adj* : disastrous
desatar *vt* **1** : undo, untie **2** : unleash (passions) — **desatarse** *vr* **1** : come undone **2** DESENCADENARSE : break out, erupt
desatascar {72} *vt* : unclog
desatender {56} *vt* **1** : disregard **2** : neglect (an obligation, etc.) — **desatento, -ta** *adj* : inattentive
desatinado, -da *adj* : foolish, silly
desautorizado, -da *adj* : unauthorized
desavenencia *nf* : disagreement
desayunar *vi* : have breakfast — *vt* : have for breakfast — **desayuno** *nm* : breakfast
desbancar {72} *vt* : oust
desbarajuste *nm* : disorder, confusion
desbaratar *vt* : ruin, destroy — **desbaratarse** *vr* : fall apart
desbocarse {72} *vr* : run away, bolt
desbordar *vt* **1** : overflow **2** : exceed (limits) — **desbordarse** *vr* : overflow — **desbordamiento** *nm* : overflow
descabellado, -da *adj* : crazy
descafeinado, -da *adj* : decaffeinated
descalabrar *vt* : hit on the head — **descalabro** *nm* : misfortune, setback
descalificar {72} *vt* : disqualify — **descalificación** *nf, pl* **-ciones** : disqualification
descalzarse {21} *vr* : take off one's shoes — **descalzo, -za** *adj* : barefoot
descaminar *vt* : mislead, lead astray
descansar *v* : rest — **descanso** *nm* **1** : rest **2** : landing (of a staircase) **3** : intermission (in theater), halftime (in sports)

descapotable *adj* & *nm* : convertible
descarado, -da *adj* : insolent, shameless
descargar {52} *vt* **1** : unload **2** : discharge (a firearm, etc.) — **descarga** *nf* **1** : unloading **2** : discharge (of a firearm, of electricity, etc.) — **descargo** *nm* **1** : unloading **2** : discharge (of a duty, etc.) **3** : defense (in law)
descarnado, -da *adj* : scrawny, gaunt
descaro *nm* : insolence, nerve
descarrilar *vi* : derail — **descarrilarse** *vr* : be derailed
descartar *vt* : reject — **descartarse** *vr* : discard
descascarar *vt* : peel, shell, husk
descender {56} *vt* **1** : go down **2** BAJAR : lower — *vi* **1** : descend **2** ~ **de** : be descended from — **descendencia** *nf* **1** : descendants *pl* **2** LINAJE : lineage, descent — **descendiente** *nmf* : descendant — **descenso** *nm* **1** : descent **2** : drop, fall (in level, in temperature, etc.)
descifrar *vt* : decipher, decode
descolgar {16} *vt* **1** : take down **2** : pick up, answer (the telephone)
descolorarse *vr* : fade — **descolorido, -da** *adj* : faded, discolored
descomponer {60} *vt* : break down — **descomponerse** *vr* **1** : rot, decompose **2** *Lat* : break down — **descompuesto, -ta** *adj Lat* : out of order
descomunal *adj* : enormous
desconcertar {55} *vt* : disconcert, confuse — **desconcertante** *adj* : confusing — **desconcierto** *nm* : confusion, bewilderment
desconectar *vt* : disconnect
desconfiar {85} *vi* ~ **de** : distrust — **desconfiado, -da** *adj* : distrustful — **desconfianza** *nf* : distrust
descongelar *vt* **1** : thaw, defrost **2** : unfreeze (assets)
descongestionante *nm* : decongestant
desconocer {18} *vt* : not know, fail to recognize — **desconocido, -da** *adj* : unknown — ~ *n* : stranger
desconsiderado, -da *adj* : inconsiderate
desconsolar *vt* : distress — **desconsolado, -da** *adj* : heartbroken — **desconsuelo** *nm* : grief, sorrow
descontar {19} *vt* : discount
descontento, -ta *adj* : dissatisfied — **descontento** *nm* : discontent
descontinuar *vt* : discontinue
descorazonado, -da *adj* : discouraged
descorrer *vt* : draw back
descortés *adj, pl* **-teses** : rude — **descortesía** *nf* : discourtesy, rudeness
descoyuntar *vt* : dislocate
descrédito *nm* : discredit

descremado, -da *adj* : nonfat, skim
describir {33} *vt* : describe — **descripción**
nf, pl **-ciones** : description — **descriptivo,**
-va *adj* : descriptive
descubierto, -ta *adj* 1 : exposed, uncovered
2 **al descubierto** : in the open — **descu-**
bierto *nm* : deficit, overdraft
descubrir {2} *vt* 1 : discover 2 REVELAR
: reveal — **descubrimiento** *nm* : discovery
descuento *nm* : discount
descuidar *vt* : neglect — **descuidarse** *vr* 1
: be careless 2 ABANDONARSE : let oneself
go — **descuidado, -da** *adj* 1 : careless,
sloppy 2 DESATENDIDO : neglected — **des-**
cuido *nm* : neglect, carelessness
desde *prep* 1 : from (a place), since (a time)
2 ~ **luego** : of course
desdén *nm* : scorn, disdain — **desdeñar** *vt*
: scorn — **desdeñoso, -sa** *adj* : disdainful
desdicha *nf* 1 : misery 2 DESGRACIA : misfortune — **desdichado, -da** *adj* : unfortunate, unhappy
desear *vt* : wish, want — **deseable** *adj* : desirable
desecar *vt* : dry up
desechar *vt* 1 : throw away 2 RECHAZAR
: reject — **desechable** *adj* : disposable —
desechos *nmpl* : rubbish
desembarazarse {21} *vr* ~ **de** : get rid of
desembarcar {72} *vi* : disembark — *vt* : unload — **desembarcadero** *nm* : jetty, landing pier — **desembarco** *nm* : landing
desembocar {72} *vi* ~ **en** 1 : flow into 2
: lead to (a result) — **desembocadura** *nf* 1
: mouth (of a river) 2 : opening, end (of a
street)
desembolsar *vt* : pay out — **desembolso**
nm : payment, outlay
desembragar *vi* : disengage the clutch
desempacar {72} *v Lat* : unpack
desempate *nm* : tiebreaker
desempeñar *vt* 1 : play (a role) 2 : redeem
(from a pawnshop) — **desempeñarse** *vr*
: get out of debt
desempleo *nm* : unemployment — **desem-**
pleado, -da *adj* : unemployed
desempolvar *vt* : dust
desencadenar *vt* 1 : unchain 2 : trigger,
unleash (protests, crises, etc.) — **desenca-**
denarse *vr* : break loose
desencajar *vt* 1 : dislocate 2 DESCONECTAR
: disconnect
desencanto *nm* : disillusionment
desenchufar *vt* : disconnect, unplug
desenfadado, -da *adj* : carefree, confident
— **desenfado** *nm* : confidence, ease
desenfrenado, -da *adj* : unrestrained — **de-**
senfreno *nm* : abandon, lack of restraint
desenganchar *vt* : unhook

desengañar *vt* : disillusion — **desengaño**
nm : disappointment
desenlace *nm* : ending, outcome
desenmarañar *vt* : disentangle
desenmascarar *vt* : unmask
desenredar *vt* : untangle — **desenredarse**
vr ~ **de** : extricate oneself from
desenrollar *vt* : unroll, unwind
desentenderse {56} *vr* ~ **de** : want nothing to do with
desenterrar {55} *vt* : dig up, disinter
desentonar *vi* 1 : be out of tune 2 : clash
(of colors, etc.)
desenvoltura *nf* : confidence, ease
desenvolver {89} *vt* : unfold, unwrap — **de-**
senvolverse *vr* : unfold, develop
desenvuelto, -ta *adj* : confident, self-
assured
deseo *nm* : desire — **deseoso, -sa** *adj*
: eager, anxious
desequilibrar *vt* : throw off balance — **de-**
sequilibrado, -da *adj* : unbalanced — **de-**
sequilibrio *nm* : imbalance
desertar *vt* : desert — **deserción** *nf, pl*
-ciones : desertion — **desertor, -tora** *n* : deserter
desesperar *vt* : exasperate — *vi* : despair —
desesperarse *vr* : become exasperated —
desesperación *nf, pl* **-ciones** : despera-
tion, despair — **desesperado, -da** *adj*
: desperate, hopeless
desestimar *vt* : reject
desfalcar {72} *vt* : embezzle — **desfalco**
nm : embezzlement
desfallecer {53} *vi* 1 : weaken 2 DESMA-
YARSE : faint
desfavorable *adj* : unfavorable
desfigurar *vt* 1 : disfigure, mar 2 : distort
(the truth)
desfiladero *nm* : mountain pass, gorge
desfilar *vi* : march, parade — **desfile** *nm*
: parade, procession
desfogar {52} *vt* : vent — **desfogarse** *vr*
: let off steam
desgajar *vt* : tear off, break apart — **desga-**
jarse *vr* : come off
desgana *nf* 1 : lack of appetite 2 : lack of
enthusiasm, reluctance
desgarbado, -da *adj* : gawky, ungainly
desgarrar *vt* : tear, rip — **desgarrador,**
-dora *adj* : heartbreaking — **desgarro** *nm*
: tear
desgastar *vt* : wear away, wear down —
desgaste *nm* : deterioration, wear and tear
desgracia *nf* 1 : misfortune 2 **caer en** ~
: fall into disgrace 3 **por** ~ : unfortunately
— **desgraciadamente** *adv* : unfortunately
— **desgraciado, -da** *adj* : unfortunate
deshabitado, -da *adj* : uninhabited

deshacer {40} *vt* **1** : undo **2** DESTRUIR : destroy, ruin **3** DISOLVER : dissolve **4** : break (an agreement), cancel (plans, etc.) — **deshacerse** *vr* **1** : come undone **2** ~ **de** : get rid of **3** ~ **en** : lavish, heap (praise, etc.) —
deshecho, -cha *adj* **1** : undone **2** DESTROZADO : destroyed, ruined
desheredar *vt* : disinherit
deshidratar *vt* : dehydrate
deshielo *nm* : thaw
deshilachar *vt* : unravel — **deshilacharse** *vr* : fray
deshonesto, -ta *adj* : dishonest
deshonrar *vt* : dishonor, disgrace — **deshonra** *nf* : dishonor — **deshonroso, -sa** *adj* : dishonorable
deshuesar *vt* **1** : pit (a fruit) **2** : bone, debone (meat)
desidia *nf* **1** : indolence **2** DESASEO : sloppiness
desierto, -ta *adj* : deserted, uninhabited — **desierto** *nm* : desert
designar *vt* : designate — **designación** *nf, pl* **-ciones** : appointment (to an office, etc.)
designio *nm* : plan
desigual *adj* **1** : unequal **2** DISPAREJO : uneven — **desigualdad** *nf* : inequality
desilusionar *vt* : disappoint, disillusion — **desilusión** *nf, pl* **-siones** : disappointment, disillusionment
desinfectar *vt* : disinfect — **desinfectante** *adj* & *nm* : disinfectant
desinflar *vt* : deflate — **desinflarse** *vr* : deflate, go flat
desinhibido, -da *adj* : uninhibited
desintegrar *vt* : disintegrate — **desintegrarse** *vr* : disintegrate — **desintegración** *nf, pl* **-ciones** : disintegration
desinteresado, -da *adj* : unselfish, generous — **desinterés** *nm* : unselfishness
desistir *vi* ~ **de** : give up
desleal *adj* : disloyal — **deslealtad** *nf* : disloyalty
desleír {66} *vt* : dilute, dissolve
desligar {52} *vt* **1** : untie **2** SEPARAR : separate — **desligarse** *vr* : extricate oneself
desliz *nm, pl* **-lices** : slip, mistake — **deslizar** {21} *vt* : slide, slip — **deslizarse** *vr* : slide, glide
deslucido, -da *adj* : dingy, tarnished
deslumbrar *vt* : dazzle — **deslumbrante** *adj* : dazzling, blinding
deslustrar *vt* : tarnish, dull
desmán *nm, pl* **-manes** : outrage, excess
desmandarse *vr* : get out of hand
desmantelar *vt* : dismantle
desmañado, -da *adj* : clumsy
desmayar *vi* : lose heart — **desmayarse** *vr* : faint — **desmayo** *nm* : faint

desmedido, -da *adj* : excessive
desmejorar *vt* : impair — *vi* : deteriorate
desmemoriado, -da *adj* : forgetful
desmentir {76} *vt* : deny — **desmentido** *nm* : denial
desmenuzar {21} *vt* **1** : crumble **2** EXAMINAR : scrutinize — **desmenuzarse** *vr* : crumble
desmerecer {53} *vt* : be unworthy of — *vi* : decline in value
desmesurado, -da *adj* : excessive
desmigajar *vt* : crumble
desmontar *vt* **1** : dismantle, take apart **2** ALLANAR : level — *vi* : dismount
desmoralizar {21} *vt* : demoralize
desmoronarse *vr* : crumble
desnivel *nm* : unevenness
desnudar *vt* : undress, strip — **desnudarse** *vr* : get undressed — **desnudez** *nf, pl* **-deces** : nudity, nakedness — **desnudo, -da** *adj* : nude, naked — **desnudo** *nm* : nude
desnutrición *nf, pl* **-ciones** : malnutrition
desobedecer {53} *v* : disobey — **desobediencia** *nf* : disobedience — **desobediente** *adj* : disobedient
desocupar *vt* : empty, vacate — **desocupado, -da** *adj* **1** : vacant **2** DESEMPLEADO : unemployed
desodorante *adj* & *nm* : deodorant
desolado, -da *adj* **1** : desolate **2** DESCONSOLADO : devastated, distressed — **desolación** *nf, pl* **-ciones** : desolation
desorden *nm, pl* **desórdenes** : disorder, mess — **desordenado, -da** *adj* : untidy — **desordenadamente** *adv* : in a disorderly way
desorganizar {21} *vt* : disorganize — **desorganización** *nf, pl* **-ciones** : disorganization
desorientar *vt* : disorient, confuse — **desorientarse** *vr* : lose one's way
desovar *vi* : spawn
despachar *vt* **1** : deal with (a task, etc.) **2** ENVIAR : dispatch, send **3** : wait on, serve (customers) — **despacho** *nm* **1** : dispatch, shipment **2** OFICINA : office
despacio *adv* : slowly
desparramar *vt* : spill, scatter, spread
despavorido, -da *adj* : terrified
despecho *nm* **1** : spite **2 a** ~ **de** : despite, in spite of
despectivo, -va *adj* **1** : pejorative **2** DESPRECIATIVO : contemptuous
despedazar {21} *vt* : tear apart
despedir {54} *vt* **1** : see off **2** DESTITUIR : dismiss, fire **3** DESPRENDER : emit — **despedirse** *vr* : say good-bye — **despedida** *nf* : farewell, good-bye
despegar {52} *vt* : detach, unstick — *vi*

: take off — **despegado, -da** *adj* : cold, distant — **despegue** *nm* : takeoff

despeinar *vt* : ruffle (hair) — **despeinado, -da** *adj* : disheveled, unkempt

despejar *vt* : clear, free — *vi* : clear up — **despejado, -da** *adj* **1** : clear, fair **2** LÚCIDO : clear-headed

despellejar *vt* : skin (an animal)

despensa *nf* : pantry, larder

despeñadero *nm* : precipice

desperdiciar *vt* : waste — **desperdicio** *nm* **1** : waste **2** ~**s** *nmpl* : scraps

desperfecto *nm* : flaw, defect

despertar {55} *vi* : awaken, wake up — *vt* : wake, rouse — **despertador** *nm* : alarm clock

despiadado, -da *adj* : pitiless, merciless

despido *nm* : dismissal, layoff

despierto, -ta *adj* : awake

despilfarrar *vt* : squander — **despilfarrador, -dora** *n* : spendthrift — **despilfarro** *nm* : extravagance, wastefulness

despistar *vt* : throw off the track, confuse — **despistarse** *vr* : lose one's way — **despistado, -da** *adj* **1** : absentminded **2** DESORIENTADO : confused — **despiste** *nm* **1** : absentmindedness **2** ERROR : mistake

desplazar {21} *vt* : displace — **desplazarse** *vr* : travel

desplegar {49} *vt* : unfold, spread out — **despliegue** *nm* : display

desplomarse *vr* : collapse

desplumar *vt* **1** : pluck **2** *fam* : fleece

despoblado, -da *adj* : uninhabited, deserted — **despoblado** *nm* : deserted area

despojar *vt* : strip, deprive — **despojos** *nmpl* **1** : plunder **2** RESTOS : remains, scraps

desportillar *vt* : chip — **desportillarse** *vr* : chip — **desportilladura** *nf* : chip, nick

despota *nmf* : despot

despotricar *vi* : rant (and rave)

despreciar *vt* : despise, scorn — **despreciable** *adj* **1** : despicable **2 una cantidad** ~ : a negligible amount — **desprecio** *nm* : disdain, scorn

desprender *vt* **1** : detach, remove **2** EMITIR : give off — **desprenderse** *vr* **1** : come off **2** DEDUCIRSE : be inferred, follow — **desprendimiento** *nm* ~ **de tierras** : landslide

despreocupado, -da *adj* : carefree, unconcerned

desprestigiar *vt* : discredit — **desprestigiarse** *vr* : lose face

desprevenido, -da *adj* : unprepared

desproporcionado, -da : out of proportion

despropósito *nm* : (piece of) nonsense, absurdity

desprovisto, -ta *adj* ~ **de** : lacking in

después *adv* **1** : afterward **2** ENTONCES : then, next **3** ~ **de** : after **4 después (de) que** : after **5** ~ **de todo** : after all

despuntado, -da *adj* : blunt, dull

desquiciar *vt* : drive crazy

desquitarse *vr* **1** : retaliate **2** ~ **con** : take it out on, get back at — **desquite** *nm* : revenge

destacar {72} *vt* : emphasize — *vi* : stand out — **destacado, -da** *adj* : outstanding

destapar *vt* : open, uncover — **destapador** *nm Lat* : bottle opener

destartalado, -da *adj* : dilapidated

destellar *vi* : flash, sparkle — **destello** *nm* : sparkle, twinkle, flash

destemplado, -da *adj* **1** : out of tune **2** MAL : out of sorts **3** : unpleasant (of weather)

desteñir {67} *vt* : fade, bleach — *vi* : run, fade — **desteñirse** *vr* : fade

desterrar {55} *vt* : banish, exile — **desterrado, -da** *n* : exile

destetar *vt* : wean

destiempo *adv* **a** ~ : at the wrong time

destierro *nm* : exile

destilar *vt* : distill — **destilería** *nf* : distillery

destinar *vt* **1** : assign, allocate **2** NOMBRAR : appoint — **destinado, -da** *adj* : destined — **destinatario, -ria** *n* : addressee — **destino** *nm* **1** : destiny **2** RUMBO : destination

destituir {41} *vt* : dismiss — **destitución** *nf, pl* **-ciones** : dismissal

destornillar *vt* : unscrew — **destornillador** *nm* : screwdriver

destreza *nf* : skill, dexterity

destrozar {21} *vt* : destroy, wreck — **destrozos** *nmpl* : damage, destruction

destrucción *nf, pl* **-ciones** : destruction — **destructivo, -va** *adj* : destructive — **destruir** {41} *vt* : destroy

desunir *vt* : split, divide

desusado, -da *adj* **1** : obsolete **2** INSÓLITO : unusual — **desuso** *nm* **caer en** ~ : fall into disuse

desvaído, -da *adj* **1** : pale, washed-out **2** BORROSO : vague, blurred

desvalido, -da *adj* : destitute, needy

desvalijar *vt* : rob

desván *nm, pl* **-vanes** : attic

desvanecer {53} *vt* : make disappear — **desvanecerse** *vr* **1** : vanish **2** DESMAYARSE : faint

desvariar {85} *vi* : be delirious — **desvarío** *nm* : delirium

desvelar *vt* : keep awake — **desvelarse** *vr* : stay awake — **desvelo** *nm* **1** : sleeplessness **2** ~**s** *nmpl* : efforts

desvencijado, -da *adj* : dilapidated, rickety

desventaja *nf* : disadvantage

desventura *nf* : misfortune
desvergonzado, -da *adj* : shameless —
desvergüenza *nf* : shamelessness
desvestir {54} *vt* : undress — **desvestirse**
vr : get undressed
desviación *nf, pl* **-ciones 1** : deviation **2**
: detour (in a road) — **desviar** {85} *vt* : divert, deflect — **desviarse** *vr* **1** : branch off
2 APARTARSE : stray — **desvío** *nm* : diversion, detour
detallar *vt* : detail — **detallado, -da** *adj* : detailed, thorough — **detalle** *nm* **1** : detail **2**
al ~ : retail — **detallista** *adj* : retail — ~
nmf : retailer
detectar *vt* : detect — **detective** *nmf* : detective
detener {80} *vt* **1** : arrest, detain **2** PARAR
: stop **3** RETRASAR : delay — **detenerse** *vr*
1 : stop **2** DEMORARSE : linger — **detención** *nf, pl* **-ciones** : arrest, detention
detergente *nm* : detergent
deteriorar *vt* : damage — **deteriorarse** *vr*
: wear out, deteriorate — **deteriorado, -da**
adj : damaged, worn — **deterioro** *nm* : deterioration, damage
determinar *vt* **1** : determine **2** MOTIVAR
: bring about **3** DECIDIR : decide — **determinarse** *vr* : decide — **determinación** *nf,*
pl **-ciones 1** : determination **2 tomar una**
~ : make a decision — **determinado, -da**
adj **1** : determined **2** ESPECÍFICO : specific
detestar *vt* : detest
detonar *vi* : explode, detonate — **detonación** *nf, pl* **-ciones** : detonation
detrás *adv* **1** : behind **2** ~ **de** : in back of
3 por ~ : from behind
detrimento *nm* **en** ~ **de** : to the detriment
of
deuda *nf* : debt — **deudor, -dora** *n* : debtor
devaluar {3} *vt* : devalue — **devaluarse** *vr*
: depreciate
devastar *vt* : devastate — **devastador, -dora**
adj : devastating
devenir {87} *vi* **1** : come about **2** ~ **en**
: become, turn into
devoción *nf, pl* **-ciones** : devotion
devolución *nf, pl* **-ciones** : return
devolver {89} *vt* **1** RESTITUIR : give back **2**
: refund, pay back — *vi* : vomit — **devolverse** *vr Lat* : return, come back
devorar *vt* : devour
devoto, -ta *adj* : devout — ~ *n* : devotee
día *nm* **1** : day **2** : daytime **3 al** ~ : up-to-
date **4 en pleno** ~ : in broad daylight
diabetes *nf* : diabetes — **diabético, -ca** *adj*
& *n* : diabetic
diablo *nm* : devil — **diablillo** *nm* : imp, rascal — **diablura** *nf* : prank — **diabólico, -ca**
adj : diabolic, diabolical

diafragma *nm* : diaphragm
diagnosticar {72} *vt* : diagnose — **diagnóstico, -ca** *adj* : diagnostic — **diagnóstico** *nm* : diagnosis
diagonal *adj* & *nf* : diagonal
diagrama *nm* : diagram
dial *nm* : dial (of a radio, etc.)
dialecto *nm* : dialect
dialogar {52} *vi* : have a talk — **diálogo** *nm*
: dialogue
diamante *nm* : diamond
diámetro *nm* : diameter
diana *nf* **1** : reveille **2** BLANCO : target,
bull's-eye
diario, -ria *adj* : daily — **diario** *nm* **1** : diary
2 PERIÓDICO : newspaper — **diariamente**
adv : daily
diarrea *nf* : diarrhea
dibujar *vt* **1** : draw **2** DESCRIBIR : portray —
dibujante *nmf* : draftsman *m*, draftswoman
f — **dibujo** *nm* **1** : drawing **2** ~**s anima-**
dos : (animated) cartoons
diccionario *nm* : dictionary
dicha *nf* **1** ALEGRÍA : happiness **2** SUERTE
: good luck — **dicho** *nm* : saying, proverb
— **dichoso, -sa** *adj* **1** : happy **2** AFORTU-
NADO : lucky
diciembre *nm* : December
dictar *vt* **1** : dictate **2** : pronounce (a sentence), deliver (a speech) — **dictado** *nm*
: dictation — **dictador, -dora** *n* : dictator —
dictadura *nf* : dictatorship
diecinueve *adj* & *nm* : nineteen — **diecinueveavo, -va** *adj* : nineteenth
dieciocho *adj* & *nm* : eighteen — **dieciochoavo, -va** *or* **dieciochavo, -va** *adj* : eighteenth
dieciséis *adj* & *nm* : sixteen — **dieciseisavo, -va** *adj* : sixteenth
diecisiete *adj* & *nm* : seventeen — **diecisieteavo, -va** *adj* : seventeenth
diente *nm* **1** : tooth **2** : prong, tine (of a
fork, etc.) **3** ~ **de ajo** : clove of garlic **4** ~
de león : dandelion
diesel *adj* & *nm* : diesel
diestra *nf* : right hand — **diestro, -tra** *adj* **1**
: right **2** HÁBIL : skillful
dieta *nf* : diet — **dietético, -ca** *adj* : dietetic,
dietary
diez *adj* & *nm, pl* **dieces** : ten
difamar *vt* : slander, libel — **difamación** *nf,*
pl **-ciones** : slander, libel
diferencia *nf* : difference — **diferenciar** *vt*
: distinguish between — **diferenciarse** *vr*
: differ — **diferente** *adj* : different
diferir {76} *vt* : postpone — *vi* : differ
difícil *adj* : difficult — **dificultad** *nf* : difficulty — **dificultar** *vt* : hinder, obstruct
difteria *nf* : diphtheria

difundir *vt* **1** : spread (out) **2** : broadcast (television, etc.)
difunto, -ta *adj & n* : deceased
difusión *nf, pl* **-siones** : spreading
digerir {76} *vt* : digest — **digerible** *adj* : digestible — **digestión** *nf, pl* **-tiones** : digestion — **digestivo, -va** *adj* : digestive
dígito *nm* : digit — **digital** *adj* : digital
dignarse *vr* ~ **a** : deign to
dignatario, -ria *n* : dignitary — **dignidad** *nf* : dignity — **digno, -na** *adj* : worthy
digresión *nf, pl* **-ciones** : digression
dilapidar *vt* : waste, squander
dilatar *vt* **1** : expand, dilate **2** PROLONGAR : prolong **3** POSPONER : postpone
dilema *nm* : dilemma
diligencia *nf* **1** : diligence **2** TRÁMITE : procedure, task — **diligente** *adj* : diligent
diluir {41} *vt* : dilute
diluvio *nm* **1** : flood **2** LLUVIA : downpour
dimensión *nf, pl* **-siones** : dimension
diminuto, -ta *adj* : minute, tiny
dimitir *vi* : resign — **dimisión** *nf, pl* **-siones** : resignation
dinámico, -ca *adj* : dynamic
dinamita *nf* : dynamite
dínamo *or* **dinamo** *nmf* : dynamo
dinastía *nf* : dynasty
dineral *nm* : large sum, fortune
dinero *nm* : money
dinosaurio *nm* : dinosaur
diócesis *nfs & pl* : diocese
dios, diosa *n* : god, goddess *f* — **Dios** *nm* : God
diploma *nm* : diploma — **diplomado, -da** *adj* : qualified, trained
diplomacia *nf* : diplomacy — **diplomático, -ca** *adj* : diplomatic — ~ *n* : diplomat
diputación *nf, pl* **-ciones** : delegation — **diputado, -da** *n* : delegate
dique *nm* : dike
dirección *nf, pl* **-ciones** **1** : address **2** SENTIDO : direction **3** GESTIÓN : management **4** : steering (of an automobile) — **direccional** *nf Lat* : turn signal, blinker — **directa** *nf* : high gear — **directiva** *nf* : board of directors — **directivo, -va** *adj* : managerial — ~ *n* : manager, director — **directo, -ta** *adj* **1** : direct **2** DERECHO : straight — **director, -tora** *n* **1** : director, manager **2** : conductor (of an orchestra) — **directorio** *nm* : directory — **directriz** *nf, pl* **-trices** : guideline
dirigencia *nf* : leaders *pl*, leadership — **dirigente** *nmf* : director, leader
dirigible *nm* : dirigible, blimp
dirigir {35} *vt* **1** : direct, lead **2** : address (a letter, etc.) **3** ENCAMINAR : aim **4** : conduct (music) — **dirigirse** *vr* **1** ~ **a** : go towards **2** ~ **a algn** : speak to s.o., write to s.o.

discernir {25} *vt* : discern, distinguish — **discernimiento** *nm* : discernment
disciplinar *vt* : discipline — **disciplina** *nf* : discipline
discípulo, -la *n* : disciple, follower
disco *nm* **1** : disc, disk **2** : discus (in sports) **3** ~ **compacto** : compact disc
discordante *adj* : discordant — **discordia** *nf* : discord
discoteca *nf* : disco, discothèque
discreción *nf, pl* **-ciones** : discretion
discrepancia *nf* **1** : discrepancy **2** DESACUERDO : disagreement — **discrepar** *vi* : differ, disagree
discreto, -ta *adj* : discreet
discriminar *vt* **1** : discriminate against **2** DISTINGUIR : distinguish — **discriminación** *nf, pl* **-ciones** : discrimination
disculpar *vt* : excuse, pardon — **disculparse** *vr* : apologize — **disculpa** *nf* **1** : apology **2** EXCUSA : excuse
discurrir *vi* **1** : pass, go by **2** REFLEXIONAR : ponder, reflect
discurso *nm* : speech, discourse
discutir *vt* **1** : discuss **2** CUESTIONAR : dispute — *vi* : argue — **discusión** *nf, pl* **-siones** **1** : discussion **2** DISPUTA : argument — **discutible** *adj* : debatable
disecar {72} *vt* : dissect — **disección** *nf, pl* **-ciones** : dissection
diseminar *vt* : disseminate, spread
disentería *nf* : dysentery
disentir {76} *vi* ~ **de** : disagree with — **disentimiento** *nm* : disagreement, dissent
diseñar *vt* : design — **diseñador, -dora** *n* : designer — **diseño** *nm* : design
disertación *nf, pl* **-ciones** **1** : lecture **2** : (written) dissertation
disfrazar {21} *vt* : disguise — **disfrazarse** *vr* ~ **de** : disguise oneself as — **disfraz** *nm, pl* **-fraces** **1** : disguise **2** : costume (for a party, etc.)
disfrutar *vt* : enjoy — *vi* : enjoy oneself
disgustar *vt* : upset, annoy — **disgustarse** *vr* **1** : get annoyed **2** ENEMISTARSE : fall out (with s.o.) — **disgusto** *nm* **1** : annoyance, displeasure **2** RIÑA : quarrel
disidente *adj & nmf* : dissident
disimular *vt* : conceal, hide — *vi* : pretend — **disimulo** *nm* : pretense
disipar *vt* **1** : dispel **2** DERROCHAR : squander
diskette *nm* : floppy disk, diskette
dislexia *nf* : dyslexia — **disléxico, -ca** *adj* : dyslexic
dislocar {72} *vt* : dislocate — **dislocarse** *vr* : become dislocated
disminuir {41} *vt* : reduce — *vi* : decrease,

drop — **disminución** *nf, pl* **-ciones** : decrease
disociar *vt* : dissociate
disolver {89} *vt* : dissolve — **disolverse** *vr* : dissolve
disparar *vi* : shoot, fire — *vt* : shoot — **dispararse** *vr* : shoot up, skyrocket
disparatado, -da *adj* : absurd — **disparate** *nm* : nonsense, silly thing
disparejo, -ja *adj* : uneven — **disparidad** *nf* : difference, disparity
disparo *nm* : shot
dispensar *vt* 1 : dispense, distribute 2 DISCULPAR : excuse
dispersar *vt* : disperse, scatter — **dispersarse** *vr* : disperse — **dispersión** *nf, pl* **-siones** : scattering
disponer {60} *vt* 1 : arrange, lay out 2 ORDENAR : decide, stipulate — *vi* ~ **de** : have at one's disposal — **disponerse** *vr* ~ **a** : be ready to — **disponibilidad** *nf* : availability — **disponible** *adj* : available
disposición *nf, pl* **-ciones** 1 : arrangement 2 APTITUD : aptitude 3 : order, provision (in law) 4 **a** ~ **de** : at the disposal of
dispositivo *nm* : device, mechanism
dispuesto, -ta *adj* : prepared, ready
disputar *vi* 1 : argue 2 COMPETIR : compete — *vt* : dispute — **disputa** *nf* : dispute, argument
disquete → **diskette**
distanciar *vt* : space out — **distanciarse** *vr* : grow apart — **distancia** *nf* : distance — **distante** *adj* : distant
distinguir {26} *vt* : distinguish — **distinguirse** *vr* : distinguish oneself, stand out — **distinción** *nf, pl* **-ciones** : distinction — **distintivo, -va** *adj* : distinctive — **distinto, -ta** *adj* 1 : different 2 CLARO : distinct, clear
distorsión *nf, pl* **-siones** : distortion
distraer {81} *vt* 1 : distract 2 DIVERTIR : entertain — **distraerse** *vr* 1 : get distracted 2 ENTRETENERSE : amuse oneself — **distracción** *nf, pl* **-ciones** 1 : amusement 2 DESPISTE : absentmindedness — **distraído, -da** *adj* : distracted, absentminded
distribuir {41} *vt* : distribute — **distribución** *nf, pl* **-ciones** : distribution — **distribuidor, -dora** *n* : distributor
distrito *nm* : district
disturbio *nm* : disturbance
disuadir *vt* : dissuade, discourage — **disuasivo, -va** *adj* : deterrent
diurno, -na *adj* : day, daytime
divagar {52} *vi* : digress
diván *nm, pl* **-vanes** : divan, couch
divergir {35} *vi* 1 : diverge 2 ~ **en** : differ on
diversidad *nf* : diversity

diversificar {72} *vt* : diversify
diversión *nf, pl* **-siones** : fun, entertainment
diverso, -sa *adj* : diverse
divertir {76} *vt* : entertain — **divertirse** *vr* : enjoy oneself, have fun — **divertido, -da** *adj* : entertaining
dividendo *nm* : dividend
dividir *vt* 1 : divide 2 REPARTIR : distribute
divinidad *nf* : divinity — **divino, -na** *adj* : divine
divisa *nf* 1 : currency 2 EMBLEMA : emblem
divisar *vt* : discern, make out
división *nf, pl* **-siones** : division — **divisor** *nm* : denominator
divorciar *vt* : divorce — **divorciarse** *vr* : get a divorce — **divorciado, -da** *n* : divorcé *m*, divorcée *f* — **divorcio** *nm* : divorce
divulgar {52} *vt* 1 : divulge, reveal 2 PROPAGAR : spread, circulate
dizque *adv Lat* : supposedly, apparently
doblar *vt* 1 : double 2 PLEGAR : fold 3 : turn (a corner) 4 : dub (a film) — *vi* : turn — **doblarse** *vr* 1 : double over 2 ~ **a** : give in to — **dobladillo** *nm* : hem — **doble** *adj & nm* : double — ~ *nmf* : stand-in, double — **doblemente** *adv* : doubly — **doblegar** {52} *vt* : force to yield — **doblegarse** *vr* : give in — **doblez** *nm, pl* **-bleces** : fold, crease
doce *adj & nm* : twelve — **doceavo, -va** *adj* : twelfth — **docena** *nf* : dozen
docente *adj* : teaching
dócil *adj* : docile
doctor, -tora *n* : doctor — **doctorado** *nm* : doctorate
doctrina *nf* : doctrine
documentar *vt* : document — **documentación** *nf, pl* **-ciones** : documentation — **documental** *adj & nm* : documentary — **documento** *nm* : document
dogma *nm* : dogma — **dogmático, -ca** *adj* : dogmatic
dólar *nm* : dollar
doler {47} *vi* 1 : hurt 2 **me duelen los pies** : my feet hurt — **dolerse** *vr* ~ **de** : complain about — **dolor** *nm* 1 : pain 2 PENA : grief 3 ~ **de cabeza** : headache 4 ~ **de estómago** : stomachache — **dolorido, -da** 1 : sore 2 AFLIGIDO : hurt — **doloroso, -sa** *adj* : painful
domar *vt* : tame, break in
domesticar {72} *vt* : domesticate, tame — **doméstico, -ca** *adj* : domestic
domicilio *nm* : home, residence
dominar *vt* 1 : dominate, control 2 : master (a subject, a language, etc.) — **dominarse** *vr* : control oneself — **dominación** *nf, pl* **-ciones** : domination — **dominante** *adj* : dominant

domingo *nm* : Sunday — **dominical** *adj*
periódico ~ : Sunday newspaper
dominio *nm* **1** : authority **2** : mastery (of a
subject) **3** TERRITORIO : domain
dominó *nm, pl* **-nós** : dominoes *pl* (game)
don[1] *nm* : courtesy title preceding a man's
first name
don[2] *nm* **1** : gift **2** TALENTO : talent —
donación *nf, pl* **-ciones** : donation — **don-
ador, -dora** *n* : donor
donaire *nm* : grace, charm
donar *vt* : donate — **donante** *nmf* : donor —
donativo *nm* : donation
donde *conj* : where — ~ *prep Lat* : over by
dónde *adv* **1** : where **2** ¿de ~ eres?
: where are you from? **3** ¿por ~? : whereabouts?
dondequiera *adv* **1** : anywhere **2** ~ que
: wherever, everywhere
doña *nf* : courtesy title preceding a woman's
first name
doquier *adv* por ~ : everywhere
dorar *vt* **1** : gild **2** : brown (food) — **dorado, -da** *adj* : gold, golden
dormir {27} *vt* : put to sleep — *vi* : sleep —
dormirse *vr* : fall asleep — **dormido, -da**
adj **1** : asleep **2** ENTUMECIDO : numb —
dormilón, -lona *n* : sleepyhead, late riser —
dormitar *vi* : doze — **dormitorio** *nm* **1**
: bedroom **2** : dormitory (in a college)
dorso *nm* : back
dos *adj & nm* : two — **doscientos, -tas** *adj*
: two hundred — **doscientos** *nms & pl*
: two hundred
dosel *nm* : canopy
dosis *nfs & pl* : dose, dosage
dotar *vt* **1** : provide, equip **2** ~ de : endow
with — **dotación** *nf, pl* **-ciones 1** : endow-
ment, funding **2** PERSONAL : personnel —
dote *nf* **1** : dowry **2** ~s *nfpl* : gift, talent
dragar {52} *vt* : dredge — **draga** *nf* : dredge
dragón *nm, pl* **-gones** : dragon
drama *nm* : drama — **dramático, -ca** *adj*

: dramatic — **dramatizar** {21} *vt* : dramatize — **dramaturgo, -ga** *n* : dramatist, playwright
drástico, -ca *adj* : drastic
drenar *vt* : drain — **drenaje** *nm* : drainage
droga *nf* : drug — **drogadicto, -ta** *n* : drug
addict — **drogar** {52} *vt* : drug — **droga-
rse** *vr* : take drugs — **droguería** *nf* : drugstore
dromedario *nm* : dromedary
dual *adj* : dual
ducha *nf* : shower — **ducharse** *vr* : take a
shower
ducho, -cha *adj* : experienced, skilled
duda *nf* : doubt — **dudar** *vt* : doubt — *vi* ~
en : hesitate to — **dudoso, -sa** *adj* **1**
: doubtful **2** SOSPECHOSO : questionable
duelo *nm* **1** : duel **2** LUTO : mourning
duende *nm* : elf, imp
dueño, -na *n* **1** : owner **2** : landlord, landlady *f*
dulce *adj* **1** : sweet **2** : fresh (of water) **3**
SUAVE : mild, gentle — ~ *nm* : candy,
sweet — **dulzura** *nf* : sweetness
duna *nf* : dune
dúo *nm* : duo, duet
duodécimo, -ma *adj* : twelfth — ~ *n*
: twelfth (in a series)
dúplex *nms & pl* : duplex (apartment)
duplicar {72} *vt* **1** : double **2** : duplicate,
copy (a document, etc.) — **duplicado, -da**
adj : duplicate — **duplicado** *nm* : copy
duqe *nm* : duke — **duquesa** *nf* : duchess
durabilidad *nf* : durability
duración *nf, pl* **-ciones** : duration, length
duradero, -ra *adj* : durable, lasting
durante *prep* **1** : during **2** ~ una hora : for
an hour
durar *vi* : endure, last
durazno *nm Lat* : peach
duro *adv* : hard — **duro, -ra** *adj* **1** : hard **2**
SEVERO : harsh — **dureza** *nf* **1** : hardness **2**
SEVERIDAD : harshness

E

e¹ *nf* : e, fifth letter of the Spanish alphabet
e² *conj* (*used instead of* **y** *before words beginning with i or hi*) : and
ebanista *nmf* : cabinetmaker
ébano *nm* : ebony
ebrio, -bria *adj* : drunk
ebullición *nf, pl* **-ciones** : boiling
echar *vt* **1** : throw, cast **2** EXPULSAR : expel, dismiss **3** : give off, emit (smoke, sparks, etc.) **4** BROTAR : sprout **5** PONER : put (on) **6** ~ **a perder** : spoil, ruin **7** ~ **de menos** : miss — **echarse** *vr* **1** : throw oneself **2** ACOSTARSE : lie down **3** ~ **a** : start (to)
eclesiástico, -ca *adj* : ecclesiastic — ~ *nm* : clergyman
eclipse *nm* : eclipse — **eclipsar** *vi* : eclipse
eco *nm* : echo
ecología *nf* : ecology — **ecológico, -ca** *adj* : ecological — **ecologista** *nmf* : ecologist
economía *nf* **1** : economy **2** : economics (science) — **economico, -ca** *adj* **1** : economic, economical **2** BARATO : inexpensive — **economista** *nmf* : economist — **economizar** {21} *v* : save
ecosistema *nm* : ecosystem
ecuación *nf, pl* **-ciones** : equation
ecuador *nm* : equator
ecuánime *adj* **1** : even-tempered **2** : impartial (in law)
ecuatoriano, -na *adj* : Ecuadorian, Ecuadorean, Ecuadoran
ecuestre *adj* : equestrian
edad *nf* **1** : age **2 Edad Media** : Middle Ages *pl* **3 ¿qué** ~ **tienes?** : how old are you?
edición *nf, pl* **-ciones** **1** : publishing, publication **2** : edition (of a book, etc.)
edicto *nm* : edict
edificar {72} *vt* : build — **edificio** *nm* : building
editar *vt* **1** : publish **2** : edit (a film, a text, etc.) — **editor, -tora** *n* **1** : publisher **2** : editor — **editorial** *adj* : publishing — ~ *nm* : editorial — ~ *nf* : publishing house
edredón *nm, pl* **-dones** : (down) comforter, duvet
educar {72} *vt* **1** : educate **2** CRIAR : bring up, raise **3** : train (the body, the voice, etc.) — **educación** *nf, pl* **-ciones** **1** : education **2** MODALES : (good) manners *pl* — **educado, -da** *adj* : polite — **educador, -dora** *n* : educator — **educativo, -va** *adj* : educational
efectivo, -va *adj* **1** : effective **2** REAL : real

— **efectivo** *nm* : cash — **efectivamente** *adv* **1** : really **2** POR SUPUESTO : yes, indeed — **efecto** *nm* **1** : effect **2 en** ~ : in fact **3** ~**s** *nmpl* : goods, property — **efectuar** {3} *vt* : bring about, carry out
efervescente *adj* : effervescent — **efervescencia** *nf* : effervescence
eficaz *adj, pl* **-caces** **1** : effective **2** EFICIENTE : efficient — **eficacia** *nf* **1** : effectiveness **2** EFICIENCIA : efficiency
eficiente *adj* : efficient — **eficiencia** *nf* : efficiency
efímero, -ra *adj* : ephemeral
efusivo, -va *adj* : effusive
egipcio, -cia *adj* : Egyptian
ego *nm* : ego — **egocéntrico, -ca** *adj* : egocentric — **egoísmo** *nm* : egoism — **egoísta** *adj* : egoistic — ~ *nmf* : egoist
egresar *vi* : graduate — **egresado, -da** *n* : graduate — **egreso** *nm* : graduation, commencement
eje *nm* **1** : axis **2** : axle (of a wheel, etc.)
ejecutar *vt* **1** : execute, put to death **2** REALIZAR : carry out — **ejecución** *nf, pl* **-ciones** : execution
ejecutivo, -va *adj & n* : executive
ejemplar *adj* : exemplary — ~ *nm* **1** : copy, issue **2** EJEMPLO : example — **ejemplificar** {72} *vt* : exemplify — **ejemplo** *nm* **1** : example **2 por** ~ : for example
ejercer {86} *vt* **1** : practice (a profession) **2** : exercise (a right, etc.) — *vi* ~ **de** : practice as, work as — **ejercicio** *nm* **1** : exercise **2** : practice (of a profession, etc.)
ejército *nm* : army
el, la *art, pl* **los, las** : the — **el** *pron* (*referring to masculine nouns*) **1** : the one **2** ~ **que** : he who, whoever, the one that
él *pron* : he, him
elaborar *vt* **1** : manufacture, produce **2** : draw up (a plan, etc.)
elástico, -ca *adj* : elastic — **elástico** *nm* : elastic — **elasticidad** *nf* : elasticity
elección *nf, pl* **-ciones** **1** : election **2** SELECCIÓN : choice — **elector, -tora** *n* : voter — **electorado** *nm* : electorate — **electoral** *adj* : electoral
electricidad *nf* : electricity — **eléctrico, -ca** *adj* : electric, electrical — **electricista** *nmf* : electrician — **electrificar** {72} *vt* : electrify — **electrizar** {21} *vt* : electrify, thrill — **electrocutar** *vt* : electrocute
electrodo *nm* : electrode
electrodoméstico *nm* : electric appliance

electromagnético, -ca *adj* : electromagnetic
electrón *nm, pl* **-trones** : electron — **electrónico, -ca** *adj* : electronic — **electrónica** *nf* : electronics
elefante, -ta *n* : elephant
elegante *adj* : elegant — **elegancia** *nf* : elegance
elegía *nf* : elegy
elegir {28} *vt* **1** : elect **2** ESCOGER : choose, select — **elegible** *adj* : eligible
elemento *nm* : element — **elemental** *adj* **1** : elementary, basic **2** ESENCIAL : fundamental
elenco *nm* : cast (of actors)
elevar *vt* **1** : raise, lift **2** ASCENDER : elevate (in a hierarchy), promote — **elevarse** *vr* : rise — **elevación** *nf, pl* **-ciones** : elevation — **elevador** *nm* **1** : hoist **2** *Lat* : elevator
eliminar *vt* : eliminate — **eliminación** *nf, pl* **-ciones** : elimination
elipse *nf* : ellipse — **elíptico, -ca** *adj* : elliptical, elliptic
elite *or* **élite** *nf* : elite
elixir *or* **elíxir** *nm* : elixir
ella *pron* : she, her — **ello** *pron* : it — **ellos, ellas** *pron pl* **1** : they, them **2 de ellos, de ellas** : theirs .
elocuente *adj* : eloquent — **elocuencia** *nf* : eloquence
elogiar *vt* : praise — **elogio** *nm* : praise
eludir *vt* : avoid, elude
emanar *vi* ~ **de** : emanate from
emancipar *vt* : emancipate — **emanciparse** *vr* : free oneself — **emancipación** *nf, pl* **-ciones** : emancipation
embadurnar *vt* : smear, daub
embajada *nf* : embassy — **embajador, -dora** *n* : ambassador
embalar *vt* : wrap up, pack — **embalaje** *nm* : packing
embaldosar *vt* : pave with tiles
embalsamar *vt* : embalm
embalse *nm* : dam, reservoir
embarazar {21} *vt* **1** : make pregnant **2** IMPEDIR : restrict, hamper — **embarazada** *adj* : pregnant — **embarazo** *nm* **1** : pregnancy **2** IMPEDIMENTO : hindrance, obstacle — **embarazoso, -sa** *adj* : embarrassing
embarcar {72} *vt* : load — **embarcarse** *vr* : embark, board — **embarcación** *nf, pl* **-ciones** : boat, craft — **embarcadero** *nm* : pier, jetty — **embarco** *nm* : embarkation
embargar {52} *vt* **1** : seize, impound **2** : overwhelm (with emotion, etc.) — **embargo** *nm* **1** : embargo **2** : seizure (in law) **3 sin** ~ : nevertheless
embarque *nm* : loading (of goods), boarding (of passengers)

embarrancar {72} *vi* : run aground
embarullarse *vr fam* : get mixed up
embaucar {72} *vt* : trick, swindle — **embaucador, -dora** *n* : swindler
embeber *vt* : absorb — *vi* : shrink — **embeberse** *vr* : become absorbed
embelesar *vt* : enchant, delight — **embelesado, -da** *adj* : spellbound
embellecer {53} *vt* : embellish, beautify
embestir {54} *vt* : attack, charge at — *vi* : charge, attack — **embestida** *nf* **1** : attack **2** : charge (of a bull)
emblema *nm* : emblem
embobar *vt* : amaze, fascinate
embocadura *nf* **1** : mouth (of a river, etc.) **2** : mouthpiece (of an instrument)
émbolo *nm* : piston
embolsarse *vr* : put in one's pocket
emborracharse *vr* : get drunk
emborronar *vt* **1** : smudge, blot **2** GARABATEAR : scribble
emboscar {72} *vt* : ambush — **emboscada** *nf* : ambush
embotar *vt* : dull, blunt
embotellar *vt* : bottle (up) — **embotellamiento** *nm* : traffic jam
embrague *nm* : clutch — **embragar** {52} *vi* : engage the clutch
embriagarse {52} *vr* : get drunk — **embriagado, -da** *adj* : intoxicated, drunk — **embriagador, -dora** *adj* : intoxicating — **embriaguez** *nf* : drunkenness
embrión *nm, pl* **-briones** : embryo
embrollo *nm* : tangle, confusion
embrujar *vt* : bewitch — **embrujo** *nm* : spell, curse
embrutecer *vt* : brutalize
embudo *nm* : funnel
embuste *nm* : lie — **embustero, -ra** *adj* : lying — ~ *n* : liar, cheat
embutir *vt* : stuff — **embutido** *nm* : sausage, cold meat
emergencia *nf* : emergency
emerger {15} *vi* : emerge, appear
emigrar *vi* **1** : emigrate **2** : migrate (of animals) — **emigración** *nf, pl* **-ciones** **1** : emigration **2** : migration (of animals) — **emigrante** *adj & nmf* : emigrant
eminente *adj* : eminent — **eminencia** *nf* : eminence
emitir *vt* **1** : emit **2** EXPRESAR : express (an opinion, etc.) **3** : broadcast (on radio or television) **4** : issue (money, stamps, etc.) — **emisión** *nf, pl* **-siones** **1** : emission **2** : broadcast (on radio or television) **3** : issue (of money, etc.) — **emisora** *nf* : radio station
emoción *nf, pl* **-ciones** : emotion — **emocional** *adj* : emotional — **emocionante** *adj*

1 : moving, touching **2** APASIONANTE : exciting, thrilling — **emocionar** *vt* **1** : move, touch **2** APASIONAR : excite, thrill — **emocionarse** *vr* **1** : be moved **2** APASIONARSE : get excited — **emotivo, -va** *adj* **1** : emotional **2** CONMOVEDOR : moving
empacar {72} *vt Lat* : pack
empachar *vt* : give indigestion to — **empacharse** *vr* : get indigestion — **empacho** *nm* : indigestion
empadronarse *vr* : register to vote
empalagoso, -sa *adj* : excessively sweet, cloying
empalizada *nf* : palisade (fence)
empalmar *vt* : connect, link — *vi* : meet, converge — **empalme** *nm* **1** : connection, link **2** : junction (of a railroad, etc.)
empanada *nf* : pie, turnover — **empanadilla** *nf* : meat or seafood pie
empanar *vt* : bread (in cooking)
empantanar *vt* : flood — **empantanarse** *vr* **1** : become flooded **2** : get bogged down
empañar *vt* **1** : steam (up) **2** : tarnish (one's reputation, etc.) — **empañarse** *vr* : fog up
empapar *vt* : soak — **empaparse** *vr* : get soaking wet
empapelar *vt* : wallpaper
empaquetar *vt* : pack, package
emparedado, -da *adj* : walled in, confined — **emparedado** *nm* : sandwich
emparejar *vt* : match up, pair — **emparejarse** *vr* : pair off
emparentado, -da *adj* : related, kindred
empastar *vt* : fill (a tooth) — **empaste** *nm* : filling
empatar *vi* : result in a draw, be tied — **empate** *nm* : draw, tie
empedernido, -da *adj* : inveterate, hardened
empedrar {55} *vt* : pave (with stones) — **empedrado** *nm* : paving, pavement
empeine *nm* : instep
empeñar *vt* : pawn — **empeñarse** *vr* **1** : insist, persist **2** ENDEUDARSE : go into debt **3** ~ **en** : make an effort to — **empeñado, -da** *adj* **1** : determined, committed **2** ENDEUDADO : in debt — **empeño** *nm* **1** : determination, effort **2 casa de** ~**s** : pawnshop
empeorar *vi* : get worse — *vt* : make worse
empequeñecer {53} *vt* : diminish, make smaller
emperador *nm* : emperor — **emperatriz** *nf, pl* -**trices** : empress
empezar {29} *v* : start, begin
empinar *vt* : raise — **empinarse** *vr* : stand on tiptoe — **empinado, -da** *adj* : steep
empírico, -ca *adj* : empirical
emplasto *nm* : poultice
emplazar {21} *vt* **1** : summon, subpoena **2** SITUAR : place, locate — **emplazamiento**

nm **1** : location, site **2** CITACIÓN : summons, subpoena
emplear *vt* **1** : employ **2** USAR : use — **emplearse** *vr* **1** : get a job **2** USARSE : be used — **empleado, -da** *n* : employee — **empleador, -dora** *n* : employer — **empleo** *nm* **1** : occupation, job **2** USO : use
empobrecer {53} *vt* : impoverish — **empobrecerse** *vr* : become poor
empollar *vi* : brood (eggs) — *vt* : incubate
empolvarse *vr* : powder one's face
empotrar *vt* : fit, build into — **empotrado, -da** *adj* : built-in
emprender *vt* : undertake, begin — **emprendedor, -dora** *adj* : enterprising
empresa *nf* **1** COMPAÑÍA : company, firm **2** TAREA : undertaking — **empresarial** *adj* : business, managerial — **empresario, -ria** *n* **1** : businessman *m*, businesswoman *f* **2** : impresario (in theater), promoter (in sports)
empujar *v* : push — **empuje** *nm* : impetus, drive — **empujón** *nm, pl* -**jones** : push, shove
empuñar *vt* : grasp, take hold of
emular *vt* : emulate
en *prep* **1** : in **2** DENTRO DE : into, inside (of) **3** SOBRE : on **4** ~ **avión** : by plane **5** ~ **casa** : at home
enajenar *vt* : alienate — **enajenación** *nf, pl* -**ciones** : alienation
enagua *nf* : slip, petticoat
enaltecer {53} *vt* : praise, extol
enamorar *vt* : win the love of — **enamorarse** *vr* : fall in love — **enamorado, -da** *adj* : in love — ~ *n* : lover, sweetheart
enano, -na *adj & n* : dwarf
enarbolar *vt* **1** : hoist, raise **2** : brandish (arms, etc.)
enardecer {53} *vt* : stir up, excite
encabezar {21} *vt* **1** : head, lead **2** : put a heading on (an article, a list, etc.) — **encabezamiento** *nm* **1** : heading **2** : headline (in a newspaper)
encabritarse *vr* : rear up
encadenar *vt* **1** : chain, tie (up) **2** ENLAZAR : connect, link
encajar *vt* : fit (together) — *vi* **1** : fit **2** CUADRAR : conform, tally — **encaje** *nm* : lace
encalar *vt* : whitewash
encallar *vi* : run aground
encaminar *vt* : direct, aim — **encaminarse** *vr* ~ **a** : head for — **encaminado, -da** *adj* ~ **a** : aimed at, designed to
encandilar *vt* : dazzle
encanecer {53} *vi* : turn gray
encantar *vt* : enchant, bewitch — *vi* **me encanta esta canción** : I love this song — **encantado, -da** *adj* **1** : delighted **2**

HECHIZADO : bewitched — **encantador, -dora** *adj* : charming, delightful — **encantamiento** *nm* : enchantment, spell — **encanto** *nm* **1** : charm, fascination **2** HECHIZO : spell

encapotarse *vr* : cloud over — **encapotado, -da** *adj* : overcast

encapricharse *vr* ~ **con** : be infatuated with

encapuchado, -da *adj* : hooded

encaramar *vt* : lift up — **encaramarse** *vr* ~ **a** : climb up on

encarar *vt* : face, confront

encarcelar *vt* : imprison — **encarcelamiento** *nm* : imprisonment

encarecer {53} *vt* : increase, raise (price, value, etc.) — **encarecerse** *vr* : become more expensive

encargar {52} *vt* **1** : put in charge of **2** PEDIR : order — **encargarse** *vr* ~ **de** : take charge of — **encargado, -da** *adj* : in charge — ~ *n* : manager, person in charge — **encargo** *nm* **1** : errand **2** TAREA : assignment, task **3** PEDIDO : order

encariñarse *vr* ~ **con** : become fond of

encarnar *vt* : embody — **encarnación** *nf, pl* -**ciones** : embodiment — **encarnado, -da** *adj* **1** : incarnate **2** ROJO : red

encarnizarse {21} *vr* ~ **con** : attack viciously — **encarnizado, -da** *adj* : bitter, bloody

encarrilar *vt* : put on the right track

encasillar *vt* : pigeonhole

encauzar {21} *vt* : channel

encender {56} *vt* **1** : light, set fire to **2** PRENDER : switch on, start **3** AVIVAR : arouse (passions, etc.) — **encenderse** *vr* **1** : get excited **2** RUBORIZARSE : blush — **encendedor** *nm* : lighter — **encendido, -da** *adj* : lit, on — **encendido** *nm* : ignition (switch)

encerar *vt* : wax, polish — **encerado, -da** *adj* : waxed — **encerado** *nm* : blackboard

encerrar {55} *vt* **1** : lock up, shut away **2** CONTENER : contain

encestar *vi* : score (in basketball)

enchilada *nf* : enchilada

enchufar *vt* : plug in, connect — **enchufe** *nm* : plug, socket

encía *nf* : gum (tissue)

encíclica *nf* : encyclical

enciclopedia *nf* : encyclopedia — **enciclopédico, -ca** *adj* : encyclopedic

encierro *nm* **1** : confinement **2** : sit-in (at a university, etc.)

encima *adv* **1** : on top **2** ADEMÁS : as well, besides **3** ~ **de** : on, over, on top of **4** **por** ~ **de** : above, beyond

encinta *adj* : pregnant

enclenque *adj* : weak, sickly

encoger {15} *v* : shrink — **encogerse** *vr* **1** : shrink **2** : cower, cringe **3** ~ **de hombros** : shrug (one's shoulders) — **encogido, -da** *adj* **1** : shrunken **2** TÍMIDO : shy

encolar *vt* : glue, stick

encolerizar {21} *vt* : enrage, infuriate — **encolerizarse** *vr* : get angry

encomendar {55} *vt* : entrust

encomienda *nf* **1** : charge, mission **2** *Lat* : parcel

encono *nm* : rancor, animosity

encontrar {19} *vt* **1** : find **2** : meet, encounter (difficulties, etc.) — **encontrarse** *vr* **1** : meet HALLARSE : find oneself, be — **encontrado, -da** *adj* : contrary, opposing

encorvar *vt* : bend, curve — **encorvarse** *vr* : bend over, stoop

encrespar *vt* **1** : curl **2** IRRITAR : irritate — **encresparse** *vr* **1** : curl one's hair **2** IRRITARSE : get annoyed **3** : become choppy (of the sea)

encrucijada *nf* : crossroads

encuadernar *vt* : bind (a book) — **encuadernación** *nf, pl* -**ciones** : bookbinding

encuadrar *vt* **1** : frame **2** ENCAJAR : fit **3** COMPRENDER : contain, include

encubrir {2} *vt* : conceal, cover (up) — **encubierto, -ta** *adj* : covert — **encubrimiento** *nm* : cover-up

encuentro *nm* : meeting, encounter

encuestar *vt* : poll, take a survey of — **encuesta** *nf* **1** : investigation, inquiry **2** SONDEO : survey — **encuestador, -dora** *n* : pollster

encumbrado, -da *adj* : eminent, distinguished

encurtir *vt* : pickle

endeble *adj* : weak, feeble — **endeblez** *nf* : weakness, frailty

endemoniado, -da *adj* : wicked

enderezar {21} *vt* **1** : straighten (out) **2** : put upright, stand on end

endeudarse *vr* : go into debt — **endeudado, -da** *adj* : indebted, in debt — **endeudamiento** *nm* : debt

endiablado, -da *adj* **1** : wicked, diabolical **2** : complicated, difficult

endibia *or* **endivia** *nf* : endive

endosar *vt* : endorse — **endoso** *nm* : endorsement

endulzar {21} *vt* **1** : sweeten **2** : soften, mellow (a tone, a response, etc.) — **endulzante** *nm* : sweetener

endurecer {53} *vt* : harden — **endurecerse** *vr* : become hardened

enema *nm* : enema

enemigo, -ga *adj* : hostile — ~ *n* : enemy — **enemistad** *nf* : enmity — **enemistar** *vt* : make enemies of — **enemistarse** *vr* ~ **con** : fall out with
energía *nf* : energy — **enérgico, -ca** *adj* : energetic, vigorous, forceful
enero *nm* : January
enervar *vt* **1** : enervate, weaken **2** *fam* : get on one's nerves
enésimo, -ma *adj* **por enésima vez** : for the umpteenth time
enfadar *vt* : annoy, make angry — **enfadarse** *vr* : get annoyed — **enfado** *nm* : anger, annoyance — **enfadoso, -sa** *adj* : annoying
enfatizar {21} *vt* : emphasize — **énfasis** *nms & pl* : emphasis — **enfático, -ca** *adj* : emphatic
enfermar *vt* : make sick — *vi* : get sick — **enfermedad** *nf* : sickness, disease — **enfermería** *nf* : infirmary — **enfermero, -ra** *n* : nurse — **enfermizo, -za** *adj* : sickly — **enfermo, -ma** *adj* : sick — ~ *n* : sick person, patient
enflaquecer {53} *vi* : lose weight
enfocar {72} *vt* **1** : focus (on) **2** : consider (a problem, etc.) — **enfoque** *nm* : focus
enfrascarse {72} *vr* ~ **en** : immerse oneself in, get caught up in
enfrentar *vt* **1** : confront, face **2** : bring face to face — **enfrentarse** *vr* ~ **con** : confront, clash with — **enfrente** *adv* **1** : opposite **2** ~ **de** : in front of
enfriar {85} *vt* : chill, cool — **enfriarse** *vr* **1** : get cold **2** RESFRIARSE : catch a cold — **enfriamiento** *nm* **1** : cooling off **2** CATARRO : cold
enfurecer {53} *vt* : infuriate — **enfurecerse** *vr* : fly into a rage
enfurruñarse *vr fam* : sulk
engalanar *vt* : decorate — **engalanarse** *vr* : dress up
enganchar *vt* : hook, snag, catch — **engancharse** *vr* **1** : get caught **2** ALISTARSE : enlist
engañar *vt* **1** EMBAUCAR : trick, deceive **2** : cheat on, be unfaithful to — **engañarse** *vr* **1** : deceive oneself **2** EQUIVOCARSE : be mistaken — **engaño** *nm* : deception, deceit — **engañoso, -sa** *adj* : deceptive, deceitful
engatusar *vt* : coax, cajole
engendrar *vt* **1** : beget **2** : engender, give rise to (suspicions, etc.)
englobar *vt* : include, embrace
engomar *vt* : glue
engordar *vt* : fatten — *vi* : gain weight
engorroso, -sa *adj* : bothersome
engranar *v* : mesh, engage — **engranaje** *nm* : gears *pl*

engrandecer {53} *vt* **1** : enlarge **2** ENALTECER : exalt
engrapar *vt Lat* : staple — **engrapadora** *nf Lat* : stapler
engrasar *vt* : lubricate, grease — **engrase** *nm* : lubrication
engreído, -da *adj* : conceited
engrosar {19} *vt* : swell — *vi* : gain weight
engrudo *nm* : paste
engullir {38} *vt* : gulp down, gobble up
enhebrar *vt* : thread
enhorabuena *nf* : congratulations *pl*
enigma *nm* : enigma — **enigmático, -ca** *adj* : enigmatic
enjabonar *vt* : soap (up), lather
enjaezar {21} *vt* : harness
enjalbegar {52} *vt* : whitewash
enjambrar *vi* : swarm — **enjambre** *nm* : swarm
enjaular *vt* **1** : cage **2** *fam* : jail
enjuagar {52} *vt* : rinse — **enju-** **ague** *nm* **1** : rinse **2** ~ **bucal** : mouthwash
enjugar {52} *vt* **1** : wipe away (tears) **2** : wipe out (debt)
enjuiciar *vt* **1** : prosecute **2** JUZGAR : try
enjuto, -ta *adj* : gaunt, lean
enlace *nm* **1** : bond, link **2** : junction (of a highway, etc.)
enlatar *vt* : can
enlazar {21} *vt* : join, link — *vi* ~ **con** : link up with
enlistarse *vr Lat* : enlist
enlodar *vt* : cover with mud
enloquecer {53} *vt* : drive crazy — **enloquecerse** *vr* : go crazy
enlosar *vt* : pave, tile
enlutarse *vr* : go into mourning
enmarañar *vt* **1** : tangle **2** COMPLICAR : complicate **3** CONFUNDIR : confuse — **enmarañarse** *vr* **1** : get tangled up **2** CONFUNDIRSE : become confused
enmarcar {72} *vt* : frame
enmascarar *vt* : mask
enmendar {55} *vt* **1** : amend **2** CORREGIR : emend, correct — **enmendarse** *vr* : mend one's ways — **enmienda** *nf* **1** : amendment **2** CORRECCIÓN : correction
enmohecerse {53} *vr* **1** : become moldy **2** OXIDARSE : rust
enmudecer {53} *vt* : silence — *vi* : fall silent
ennegrecer {53} *vt* : blacken
ennoblecer {53} *vt* : ennoble, dignify
enojar *vt* **1** : anger **2** MOLESTAR : annoy — **enojarse** *vr* ~ **con** : get upset with — **enojo** *nm* **1** : anger **2** MOLESTIA : annoyance — **enojoso, -sa** *adj* : annoying
enorgullecer {53} *vt* : make proud — **enorgullecerse** *vr* ~ **de** : pride oneself on
enorme *adj* : enormous — **enormemente**

adv : enormously, extremely — **enormidad**
nf : enormity
enraizar {30} *vi* : take root
enredadera *nf* : climbing plant, vine
enredar *vt* **1** : tangle up, entangle **2** CON-
FUNDIR : confuse **3** IMPLICAR : involve —
enredarse *vr* **1** : become entangled **2** ∼
en : get mixed up in — **enredo** *nm* **1** : tangle **2** EMBROLLO : confusion, mess — **enre-
doso, -sa** *adj* : tangled up, complicated
enrejado *nm* **1** : railing **2** REJILLA : grating,
grille **3** : trellis (for plants)
enrevesado, -da *adj* : complicated
enriquecer {53} *vt* : enrich — **enrique-
cerse** *vr* : get rich
enrojecer {53} *vt* : redden — **enrojecerse**
vr : blush
enrolar *vt* : enlist — **enrolarse** *vr* ∼ **en** : enlist in
enrollar *vt* : roll up, coil
enroscar {72} *vt* **1** : roll up **2** ATORNILLAR
: screw in
ensalada *nf* : salad
ensalzar {21} *vt* : praise
ensamblar *vt* : assemble, fit together
ensanchar *vt* **1** : widen **2** AMPLIAR : expand — **ensanche** *nm* **1** : widening **2**
: (urban) expansion, development
ensangrentado, -da *adj* : bloody, bloodstained
ensañarse *vr* : act cruelly
ensartar *vt* : string, thread
ensayar *vi* : rehearse — *vt* : try out, test —
ensayo *nm* **1** : essay **2** PRUEBA : trial, test
3 : rehearsal (in theater, etc.)
enseguida *adv* : right away, immediately
ensenada *nf* : inlet, cove
enseñar *vt* **1** : teach **2** MOSTRAR : show —
enseñanza *nf* **1** EDUCACIÓN : education **2**
INSTRUCCIÓN : teaching
enseres *nmpl* **1** : equipment **2** ∼ **domésti-
cos** : household goods
ensillar *vt* : saddle (up)
ensimismarse *vr* : lose oneself in thought
ensombrecer {53} *vt* : cast a shadow over,
darken
ensoñación *nf, pl* **-ciones** : fantasy, daydream
ensordecer {53} *vt* : deafen — *vi* : go deaf
— **ensordecedor, -dora** *adj* : deafening
ensortijar *vt* : curl
ensuciar *vt* : soil — **ensuciarse** *vr* : get
dirty
ensueño *nm* : daydream, fantasy
entablar *vt* : initiate, start
entallar *vt* : tailor, fit (clothing) — *vi* : fit
entarimado *nm* : floorboards, flooring
ente *nm* **1** : being **2** ORGANISMO : body, organization

entender {56} *vt* **1** : understand **2** OPINAR
: think, believe — *vi* **1** : understand **2** ∼
de : know about, be good at — **entenderse**
vr **1** : understand each other **2** LLEVARSE
BIEN : get along well — ∼ *nm* **a mi** ∼ : in
my opinion — **entendido, -da** *adj* **1** : understood **2 eso se da por** ∼ : that goes
without saying **3 tener** ∼ : be under the
impression — **entendimiento** *nm* **1** : understanding **2** INTELIGENCIA : intellect
enterar *vt* : inform — **enterarse** *vr* : find
out, learn — **enterado, -da** *adj* : well-in-
formed
entereza *nf* **1** HONRADEZ : integrity **2** FOR-
TALEZA : fortitude **3** FIRMEZA : resolve
enternecer {53} *vt* : move, touch
entero, -ra *adj* **1** : whole **2** TOTAL : absolute, total **3** INTACTO : intact — **entero**
nm : integer, whole number
enterrar {55} *vt* : bury
entibiar *vt* : cool (down) — **entibiarse** *vr*
: become lukewarm
entidad *nf* **1** : entity **2** ORGANIZACIÓN
: body, organization
entierro *nm* **1** : burial **2** : funeral (ceremony)
entomología *nf* : entomology — **entomól-
ogo, -ga** *n* : entomologist
entonar *vt* : sing, intone — *vi* : be in tune
entonces *adv* **1** : then **2 desde** ∼ : since
then
entornado, -da *adj* : half-closed, ajar
entorno *nm* : surroundings *pl*, environment
entorpecer {53} *vt* **1** : hinder, obstruct **2**
: numb, dull (wits, reactions, etc.)
entrada *nf* **1** : entrance, entry **2** BILLETE
: ticket **3** COMIENZO : beginning **4** : inning
(in baseball) **5** ∼**s** *nfpl* : income **6 tener**
∼**s** : have a receding hairline
entraña *nf* **1** : core, heart **2** ∼**s** *nfpl*
VÍSCERAS : entrails, innards — **entrañable**
adj : close, intimate — **entrañar** *vt* : involve
entrar *vi* **1** : enter **2** EMPEZAR : begin — *vt*
: introduce, bring in
entre *prep* **1** : between **2** : among
entreabrir {2} *vt* : leave ajar — **entreabierto, -ta** *adj* : half-open, ajar
entreacto *nm* : intermission
entrecejo *nm* **fruncir el** ∼ : knit one's
brows, frown
entrecortado, -da *adj* : faltering (of the
voice), labored (of breathing)
entrecruzar {21} *vi* : intertwine
entredicho *nm* : doubt, question
entregar {52} *vt* : deliver, hand over — **en-
tregarse** *vr* : surrender — **entrega** *nf* **1**
: delivery **2** DEDICACIÓN : dedication, devotion **3** ∼ **inicial** : down payment

entrelazar {21} *vt* : intertwine — **entrelazarse** *vr* : become intertwined
entremés *nm, pl* -**meses 1** : hors d'oeuvre **2** : short play (in theater)
entremeterse → **entrometerse**
entremezclar *vt* : mix (up)
entrenar *vt* : train, drill — **entrenarse** *vr* : train — **entrenador, -dora** *n* : trainer, coach — **entranamiento** *nm* : training
entrepierna *nf* : crotch
entresacar {72} *vt* : pick out, select
entresuelo *nm* : mezzanine
entretanto *adv* : meanwhile — ~ *nm* **en el** ~ : in the meantime
entretener {80} *vt* **1** : entertain **2** DESPISTAR : distract **3** RETRASAR : delay, hold up — **entretenerse** *vr* **1** : amuse oneself **2** DEMORARSE : dawdle — **entretenido, -da** *adj* : entertaining — **entretenimiento** *nm* **1** : entertainment, amusement **2** PASATIEMPO : pastime
entrever {88} *vt* : catch a glimpse of, make out
entrevistar *vt* : interview — **entrevista** *nf* : interview — **entrevistador, -dora** *n* : interviewer
entristecer {53} *vt* : sadden
entrometerse *vr* : interfere — **entrometido, -da** *adj* : meddling, nosy — *n* : meddler
entroncar {72} *vi* : be related, be connected
entumecer {53} *vt* : make numb — **entumecerse** *vr* : go numb — **entumecido, -da** *adj* **1** : numb **2** : stiff (of muscles, etc.)
enturbiar *vt* : cloud — **enturbiarse** *vr* : become cloudy
entusiasmar *vt* : fill with enthusiasm — **entusiasmarse** *vr* : get excited — **entusiasmo** *nm* : enthusiasm — **entusiasta** *adj* : enthusiastic — ~ *nmf* : enthusiast
enumerar *vt* : enumerate, list — **enumeración** *nf, pl* -**ciones** : enumeration, count
enunciar *vt* : enunciate — **enunciación** *nf, pl* -**ciones** : enunciation
envalentonar *vt* : make bold, encourage — **envalentonarse** *vr* : be brave
envanecerse {53} *vr* : become vain
envasar *vt* **1** : package **2** : bottle, can — **envase** *nm* **1** : packaging **2** RECIPIENTE : container **3** : jar, bottle, can
envejecer {53} *v* : age — **envejecido, -da** *adj* : aged, old — **envejecimiento** *nm* : aging
envenenar *vt* : poison — **envenenamiento** *nm* : poisoning
envergadura *nf* **1** ALCANCE : scope **2** : span (of wings, etc.)
envés *nm, pl* -**veses** : reverse side
enviar {85} *vt* : send — **enviado, -da** *n* : envoy, correspondent

envidiar *vt* : envy — **envidia** *nf* : envy, jealousy — **envidioso, -sa** *adj* : jealous, envious
envilecer {53} *vt* : degrade, debase — **envilecimiento** *nm* : degradation
envío *nm* **1** : sending, shipment **2** : remittance (of funds)
enviudar *vi* : be widowed
envolver {89} *vt* **1** : wrap **2** RODEAR : surround **3** IMPLICAR : involve — **envoltorio** *nm or* **envoltura** *nf* : wrapping, wrapper
enyesar *vt* **1** : plaster **2** ESCAYOLAR : put in a plaster cast
enzima *nf* : enzyme
épico, -ca *adj* : epic — **épica** *nf* : epic
epidemia *nf* : epidemic — **epidémico, -ca** *adj* : epidemic
epilepsia *nf* : epilepsy — **epiléptico, -ca** *adj & n* : epileptic
epílogo *nm* : epilogue
episodio *nm* : episode
epitafio *nm* : epitaph
epíteto *nm* : epithet
época *nf* **1** : epoch, period **2** ESTACIÓN : season
epopeya *nf* : epic poem
equidad *nf* : equity, justice
equilátero, -ra *adj* : equilateral
equilibrar *vt* : balance — **equilibrado, -da** *adj* : well-balanced — **equilibrio** *nm* **1** : balance, equilibrium **2** JUICIO : good sense
equinoccio *nm* : equinox
equipaje *nm* : baggage, luggage
equipar *vt* : equip
equiparar *vt* **1** IGUALAR : make equal **2** COMPARAR : compare — **equiparable** *adj* : comparable
equipo *nm* **1** : equipment **2** : team, crew (in sports, etc.)
equitación *nf, pl* -**ciones** : horseback riding
equitativo, -va *adj* : equitable, fair, just
equivaler {84} *vi* : be equivalent — **equivalencia** *nf* : equivalence — **equivalente** *adj & nm* : equivalent
equivocar {72} *vt* : mistake, confuse — **equivocarse** *vr* : make a mistake — **equivocación** *nf, pl* -**ciones** : error, mistake — **equivocado, -da** *adj* : mistaken, wrong — **equívoco, -ca** *adj* : ambiguous — **equívoco** *nm* : misunderstanding
era *nf* : era
erario *nm* : public treasury, funds *pl*
erección *nf, pl* -**ciones** : erection
erguir {31} *vt* : raise, lift — **erguirse** *vr* : rise (up) — **erguido, -da** *adj* : erect, upright
erigir {35} *vt* : build, erect — **erigirse** *vr* ~ **en** : set oneself up as

erizarse {21} *vr* : bristle, stand on end — **erizado, -da** *adj* : bristly
erizo *nm* **1** : hedgehog **2** ~ **de mar** : sea urchin
ermitaño, -ña *n* : hermit
erosionar *vt* : erode — **erosión** *nf, pl* **-siones** : erosion
erótico, -ca *adj* : erotic
erradicar {72} *vt* : eradicate
errar {32} *vt* : miss — *vi* **1** : be wrong, be mistaken **2** VAGAR : wander — **errado, -da** *adj Lat* : wrong, mistaken
errata *nf* : misprint
errático, -ca *adj* : erratic
error *nm* : error — **erróneo, -nea** *adj* : erroneous, mistaken
eructar *vi* : belch, burp — **eructo** *nm* : belch, burp
erudito, -ta *adj* : erudite, learned
erupción *nf, pl* **-ciones** **1** : eruption **2** SARPULLIDO : rash
esa, ésa → **ese, ése**
esbelto, -ta *adj* : slender, slim
esbozar {21} *vt* : sketch, outline — **esbozo** *nm* : sketch, outline
escabechar *vt* : pickle — **escabeche** *nm* : brine (for pickling)
escabel *nm* : footstool
escabroso, -sa *adj* **1** : rugged, rough **2** ESPINOSO : thorny, difficult **3** ATREVIDO : shocking, risqué
escabullirse {38} *vr* : slip away, escape
escalar *vt* : climb, scale — *vi* : escalate — **escala** *nf* **1** : scale **2** ESCALERA : ladder **3** : stopover (of an airplane, etc.) — **escalada** *nf* : ascent, climb — **escalador, -dora** *n* ALPINISTA : mountain climber
escaldar *vt* : scald
escalera *nf* **1** : stairs *pl*, staircase **2** ESCALA : ladder **3** ~ **mecánica** : escalator
escalfar *vt* : poach
escalinata *nf* : flight of stairs
escalofrío *nm* : shiver, chill — **escalofriante** *adj* : chilling, horrifying
escalonar *vt* **1** : stagger, spread out **2** : terrace (land) — **escalón** *nm, pl* **-lones** : step, rung
escama *nf* **1** : scale (of fish or reptiles) **2** : flake (of skin) — **escamoso, -sa** *adj* : scaly
escamotear *vt* **1** : conceal **2** ~ **algo a algn** : rob s.o. of sth
escandalizar {21} *vt* : scandalize — **escandalizarse** *vr* : be shocked — **escándalo** *nm* **1** : scandal **2** ALBOROTO : scene, commotion — **escandaloso, -sa** *adj* **1** : shocking, scandalous **2** RUIDOSO : noisy
escandinavo, -va *adj* : Scandinavian
escáner *nm* : scanner

escaño *nm* **1** : seat (in a legislative body) **2** BANCO : bench
escapar *vi* : escape, run away — **escaparse** *vr* **1** : escape **2** : leak out (of gas, water, etc.) — **escapada** *nf* : escape
escaparate *nm* : store window
escapatoria *nf* : loophole, way out
escape *nm* **1** : leak (of gas, water, etc.) **2** : exhaust (from a vehicle)
escarabajo *nm* : beetle
escarbar *vt* **1** : dig, scratch, poke **2** ~ **en** : pry into
escarcha *nf* : frost (on a surface)
escarlata *adj* & *nf* : scarlet — **escarlatina** *nf* : scarlet fever
escarmentar {55} *vi* : learn one's lesson — **escarmiento** *nm* : lesson, punishment
escarnecer {53} *vt* : ridicule, mock — **escarnio** *nm* : ridicule, mockery
escarola *nf* : escarole, endive
escarpa *nf* : steep slope — **escarpado, -da** *adj* : steep
escasear *vi* : be scarce — **escasez** *nf, pl* **-seces** : shortage, scarcity — **escaso, -sa** *adj* **1** : scarce **2** ~ **de** : short of
escatimar *vt* : be sparing with, skimp on
escayolar *vt* : put in a plaster cast — **escayola** *nf* **1** : plaster (for casts) **2** : plaster cast
escena *nf* **1** : scene **2** ESCENARIO : stage — **escenario** *nm* **1** : setting, scene **2** ESCENA : stage — **escénico, -ca** *adj* : scenic
escepticismo *nm* : skepticism — **escéptico, -ca** *adj* : skeptical — ~ *n* : skeptic
esclarecer {53} *vt* : shed light on, clarify
esclavo, -va *n* : slave — **esclavitud** *nf* : slavery — **esclavizar** {21} *vt* : enslave
esclerosis *nf* ~ **múltiple** : multiple sclerosis
esclusa *nf* : floodgate, lock (of a canal)
escoba *nf* : broom
escocer {14} *vi* : sting
escocés, -cesa *adj, mpl* **-ceses** **1** : Scottish **2** : tartan, plaid — **escocés** *nm, pl* **-ceses** : Scotch (whiskey)
escoger {15} *vt* : choose — **escogido, -da** *adj* : choice, select
escolar *adj* : school — ~ *nmf* : student, pupil
escolta *nmf* : escort — **escoltar** *vt* : escort, accompany
escombros *nmpl* : ruins, rubble
esconder *vt* : hide, conceal — **esconderse** *vr* : hide — **escondidas** *nfpl* **1** *Lat* : hide-and-seek **2 a** ~ : secretly, in secret — **escondite** *nm* **1** : hiding place **2** : hide-and-seek (game) — **escondrijo** *nm* : hiding place
escopeta *nf* : shotgun
escoplo *nm* : chisel

escoria *nf* **1** : slag **2** : dregs *pl* (of society, etc.)

escorpión *nm, pl* **-piones** : scorpion

escote *nm* **1** : (low) neckline **2 pagar a ~** : go Dutch

escotilla *nf* : hatchway

escribir {33} *v* : write — **escribirse** *vr* **1** : write to one another, correspond **2** : be spelled — **escribiente** *nmf* : clerk — **escrito, -ta** *adj* : written — **escritos** *nmpl* : writings — **escritor, -tora** *n* : writer — **escritorio** *nm* : desk — **escritura** *nf* **1** : handwriting **2** : deed (in law)

escroto *nm* : scrotum

escrúpulo *nm* : scruple — **escrupuloso, -sa** *adj* : scrupulous

escrutar *vt* **1** : scrutinize **2** : count (votes) — **escrutinio** *nm* **1** : scrutiny **2** : count (of votes)

escuadra *nf* **1** : square (instrument) **2** : fleet (of ships), squad (in the military) — **escuadrón** *nm, pl* **-drones** : squadron

escuálido, -da *adj* **1** : skinny **2** SUCIO : squalid

escuchar *vt* **1** : listen to **2** *Lat* : hear — *vi* : listen

escudo *nm* **1** : shield **2** *or* **~ de armas** : coat of arms

escudriñar *vt* : scrutinize, examine

escuela *nf* : school

escueto, -ta *adj* : plain, simple

esculpir *v* : sculpt — **escultor, -tora** *n* : sculptor — **escultura** *nf* : sculpture

escupir *v* : spit

escurrir *vt* **1** : drain **2** : wring out (clothes) — *vi* **1** : drain **2** : drip-dry (of clothes) — **escurrirse** *vr* **1** : drain **2** *fam* : slip away — **escurridizo, -da** *adj* : slippery, evasive — **escurridor** *nm* **1** : dish drainer **2** COLADOR : colander

ese, esa *adj, mpl* **esos** : that, those

ése, ésa *pron, mpl* **ésos** : that one, those ones *pl*

esencia *nf* : essence — **esencial** *adj* : essential

esfera *nf* **1** : sphere **2** : dial (of a watch) — **esférico, -ca** *adj* : spherical

esfinge *nf* : sphinx

esforzar {36} *vt* : strain — **esforzarse** *vr* : make an effort — **esfuerzo** *nm* : effort

esfumarse *vr* : fade away, vanish

esgrimir *vt* **1** : brandish, wield **2** : make use of (an argument, etc.) — **esgrima** *nf* **1** : fencing **2 hacer ~** : fence

esguince *nm* : sprain, strain

eslabonar *vt* : link, connect — **eslabón** *nm, pl* **-bones** : link

eslavo, -va *adj* : Slavic

eslogan *nm, pl* **-lóganes** : slogan

esmaltar *vt* : enamel — **esmalte** *nm* **1** : enamel **2 ~ de uñas** : nail polish

esmerado, -da *adj* : careful

esmeralda *nf* : emerald

esmerarse *vr* : take great care

esmeril *nm* : emery

esmoquin *nm, pl* **-móquines** : tuxedo

esnob *nmf, pl* **esnobs** : snob — **~** *adj* : snobbish

eso *pron* (*neuter*) **1** : that **2 ¡~ es!** : that's it!, that's right! **3 en ~** : at that point, then

esófago *nm* : esophagus

esos, ésos → ese, ése

espabilarse *vr* **1** : wake up **2** DARSE PRISA : get moving — **espabilado, -da** *adj* **1** : awake **2** LISTO : bright, clever

espaciar *vt* : space out, spread out — **espacial** *adj* : space — **espacio** *nm* **1** : space **2 ~ exterior** : outer space — **espacioso, -sa** *adj* : spacious

espada *nf* **1** : sword **2 ~s** *nfpl* : spades (in playing cards)

espagueti *nm* *or* **espaguetis** *nmpl* : spaghetti

espalda *nf* **1** : back **2 ~ s** *nfpl* : shoulders, back

espantar *vt* : scare, frighten — **espantarse** *vr* : become frightened — **espantajo** *nm or* **espantapájaros** *nms & pl* : scarecrow — **espanto** *nm* : fright, fear — **espantoso, -sa** *adj* **1** : frightening, horrific **2** TERRIBLE : awful, terrible

español, -ñola *adj* : Spanish — **español** *nm* : Spanish (language)

esparadrapo *nm* : adhesive bandage

esparcir {83} *vt* : scatter, spread — **esparcirse** *vr* **1** : be scattered, spread out **2** DIVERTIRSE : enjoy oneself

espárrago *nm* : asparagus

espasmo *nm* : spasm — **espasmódico, -ca** *adj* : spasmodic

espátula *nf* : spatula

especia *nf* : spice

especial *adj & nm* : special — **especialidad** *nf* : specialty — **especialista** *nmf* : specialist — **especializarse** {21} *vr* **~ en** : specialize in — **especialmente** *adv* : especially

especie *nf* **1** : species **2** CLASE : type, kind

especificar {72} *vt* : specify — **especificación** *nf, pl* **-ciones** : specification — **específico, -ca** *adj* : specific

espécimen *nm, pl* **especímenes** : specimen

espectáculo *nm* **1** : show, performance **2** VISIÓN : spectacle, view — **espectacular** *adj* : spectacular — **espectador, -dora** *n* : spectator

espectro *nm* **1** : spectrum **2** FANTASMA : ghost

especulación *nf, pl* **-ciones** : speculation
espejo *nm* : mirror — **espejismo** *nm* **1** : mirage **2** ILUSIÓN : illusion
espeluznante *adj* : terrifying, hair- raising
esperar *vt* **1** : wait for **2** CONTAR CON : expect **3** ~ **que** : hope (that) — *vi* : wait — **espera** *nf* : wait — **esperanza** *nf* : hope, expectation — **esperanzado, -da** *adj* : hopeful — **esperanzar** {21} *vt* : give hope to
esperma *nmf* **1** : sperm **2** ~ **de ballena** : blubber
esperpento *nm* : (grotesque) sight, fright
espesar *vt* : thicken — **espesarse** *vr* : thicken — **espeso, -sa** *adj* : thick, heavy — **espesor** *nm* : thickness, density — **espesura** *nf* **1** ESPESOR : thickness **2** : thicket
espetar *vt* : blurt (out)
espiar {85} *vt* : spy on — *vi* : spy — **espía** *nmf* : spy
espiga *nf* : ear (of wheat, etc.)
espina *nf* **1** : thorn **2** : (fish) bone **3** ~ **dorsal** : spine, backbone
espinaca *nf* **1** : spinach (plant) **2** ~**s** *nfpl* : spinach (food)
espinazo *nm* : spine, backbone
espinilla *nf* **1** : shin **2** GRANO : blackhead, pimple
espinoso, -sa *adj* **1** : prickly **2** : bony (of fish) **3** : difficult, thorny (of problems, etc.)
espionaje *nm* : espionage
espiral *adj & nf* : spiral
espirar *v* : breathe out, exhale
espíritu *nm* **1** : spirit **2 Espíritu Santo** : Holy Spirit — **espiritual** *adj* : spiritual — **espiritualidad** *nf* : spirituality
espita *nf* : spigot, faucet
espléndido, -da *adj* **1** : splendid **2** GENEROSO : lavish — **esplendor** *nm* : splendor
espliego *nm* : lavender
espolear *vt* : spur on
espoleta *nf* : fuse
espolvorear *vt* : sprinkle, dust
esponja *nf* **1** : sponge **2 tirar la** ~ : throw in the towel — **esponjoso, -sa** *adj* : spongy
espontaneidad *nf* : spontaneity — **espontáneo, -nea** *adj* : spontaneous
espora *nf* : spore
esporádico, -ca *adj* : sporadic
esposo, -sa *n* : spouse, wife *f*, husband *m* — **esposar** *vt* : handcuff — **esposas** *nfpl* : handcuffs
esprintar *vi* : sprint (in sports) — **esprint** *nm* : sprint
espuela *nf* : spur
espumar *vt* : skim — **espuma** *nf* **1** : foam, froth **2** : (soap) lather **3** : head (on beer) — **espumoso, -sa** *adj* **1** : foamy, frothy **2** : sparkling (of wine)

esqueleto *nm* : skeleton
esquema *nf* : outline, sketch
esquí *nm* **1** : ski **2** : skiing (sport) **3** ~ **acuático** : waterskiing — **esquiador, -dora** *n* : skier — **esquiar** {85} *vi* : ski
esquilar *vt* : shear
esquimal *adj* : Eskimo
esquina *nf* : corner
esquirol *nm* : strikebreaker, scab
esquivar *vt* **1** : evade, dodge (a blow) **2** EVITAR : avoid — **esquivo, -va** *adj* : shy, elusive
esquizofrenia *nf* : schizophrenia — **esquizofrénico, -ca** *adj & n* : schizophrenic
esta, ésta → **este[1], éste**
estable *adj* : stable — **estabilidad** *nf* : stability — **estabilizar** {21} *vt* : stabilize
establecer {53} *vt* : establish — **establecerse** *vr* : establish oneself, settle — **establecimiento** *nm* : establishment
establo *nm* : stable
estaca *nf* : stake — **estacada** *nf* **1** : (picket) fence **2 dejar en la** ~ : leave in a lurch
estación *nf, pl* **-ciones 1** : season **2** ~ **de servicio** : gas station — **estacionar** *v* : park — **estacionamiento** *nm* : parking — **estacionario, -ria** *adj* : stationary
estadía *nf Lat* : stay
estadio *nm* **1** : stadium **2** FASE : phase, stage
estadista *nmf* : statesman
estadística *nf* : statistics — **estadístico, -ca** *adj* : statistical
estado *nm* **1** : state **2** ~ **civil** : marital status
estadounidense *adj & nmf* : American (from the United States)
estafar *vt* : swindle, defraud — **estafa** *nf* : swindle, fraud — **estafador, -dora** *n* : cheat, swindler
estallar *vi* **1** : explode **2** : break out (of war, an epidemic, etc.) **3** ~ **en llamas** : burst into flames — **estallido** *nm* **1** : explosion **2** : report (of a gun) **3** : outbreak (of war, etc.)
estampar *vt* : stamp, print — **estampa** *nf* **1** : print, illustration **2** ASPECTO : appearance — **estampado, -da** *adj* : printed
estampida *nf* : stampede
estampilla *nf* : stamp
estancarse {72} *vr* **1** : stagnate **2** : come to a halt — **estancado, -da** *adj* : stagnant
estancia *nf* **1** : stay **2** HABITACIÓN : (large) room **3** *Lat* : (cattle) ranch
estanco, -ca *adj* : watertight
estándar *adj & nm* : standard — **estandarizar** {21} *vt* : standardize
estandarte *nm* : standard, banner
estanque *nm* **1** : pool, pond **2** : reservoir (for irrigation)

estante *nm* : shelf — **estantería** *nf* : shelves *pl*, bookcase
estaño *nm* : tin
estar {34} *v aux* : be — *vi* **1** : be **2** : be at home **3** QUEDARSE : stay, remain **4** ¿cómo **estás?** : how are you? **5** ~ **a** : cost **6** ~ **bien (mal)** : be well (sick) **7** ~ **para** : be in the mood for **8** ~ **por** : be in favor of **9** ~ **por** : be about to — **estarse** *vr* : stay, remain
estarcir {83} *vt* : stencil
estárter *nm* : choke (of an automobile)
estatal *adj* : state, national
estático, -ca *adj* **1** : static **2** INMÓVIL : unmoving, still — **estática** *nf* : static
estatua *nf* : statue
estatura *nf* : height
estatus *nm* : status, prestige
estatuto *nm* : statute — **estatutario, -ria** *adj* : statutory
este[1], **esta** *adj, mpl* **estos** : this, these
este[2] *adj* : eastern, east — **este** *nm* **1** : east **2** : east wind **3 el Este** : the Orient
éste, ésta *pron, mpl* **éstos 1** : this one, these ones *pl* **2** : the latter
estela *nf* **1** : wake (of a ship) **2** : trail (of smoke, etc.)
estera *nf* : mat
estéreo *adj & nm* : stereo — **estereofónico, -ca** *adj* : stereophonic
estereotipo *nm* : stereotype
estéril *adj* **1** : sterile **2** : infertile — **esterilidad** *nf* **1** : sterility **2** : infertility — **esterilizar** {21} *vt* : sterilize
estética *nf* : aesthetics — **estético, -ca** *adj* : aesthetic
estiércol *nm* : dung, manure
estigma *nm* : stigma — **estigmatizar** {21} *vt* : stigmatize
estilarse {21} *vr* : be in fashion
estilo *nm* **1** : style **2** MANERA : fashion, manner — **estilista** *nmf* : stylist
estima *nf* : esteem, regard — **estimación** *nf, pl* -**ciones 1** : esteem **2** VALORACIÓN : estimate — **estimado, -da** *adj* **Estimado señor** : Dear Sir — **estimar** *vt* **1** : esteem, respect **2** VALORAR : value, estimate **3** CONSIDERAR : consider
estimular *vt* **1** : stimulate **2** ALENTAR : encourage — **estimulante** *adj* : stimulating — ~ *nm* : stimulant — **estímulo** *nm* : stimulus
estío *nm* : summertime
estipular *vt* : stipulate
estirar *vt* : stretch (out), extend — **estirado, -da** *adj* **1** : stretched, extended **2** ALTANERO : stuck-up, haughty — **estiramiento** *nm* ~ **facial** : face-lift — **estirón** *nm, pl* -**rones** : pull, tug
estirpe *nf* : lineage, stock

estival *adj* : summer
esto *pron (neuter)* **1** : this **2 en** ~ : at this point **3 por** ~ : for this reason
estofa *nf* **1** : class, quality **2 de baja** ~ : low-class
estofar *vt* : stew — **estofado** *nm* : stew
estoicismo *nm* : stoicism — **estoico, -ca** *adj* : stoic, stoical — ~ *n* : stoic
estómago *nm* : stomach — **estomacal** *adj* : stomach
estorbar *vt* : obstruct — *vi* : get in the way — **estorbo** *nm* **1** : obstacle **2** MOLESTIA : nuisance
estornino *nm* : starling
estornudar *vi* : sneeze — **estornudo** *nm* : sneeze
estos, éstos → **este, éste**
estrabismo *nm* : squint
estrado *nm* : platform, stage
estrafalario, -ria *adj* : eccentric, bizarre
estragar {52} *vt* : devastate — **estragos** *nmpl* **1** : ravages **2 hacer** ~ **en** *or* **causar** ~ **entre** : wreak havoc with
estragón *nm* : tarragon
estrangular *vt* : strangle — **estrangulación** *nf* : strangulation
estratagema *nf* : stratagem
estrategia *nf* : strategy — **estratégico, -ca** *adj* : strategic
estrato *nm* : stratum
estratosfera *nf* : stratosphere
estrechar *vt* **1** : narrow **2** : strengthen (a bond) **3** ABRAZAR : embrace **4** ~ **la mano a uno** : shake s.o.'s hand — **estrecharse** *vr* : narrow — **estrechez** *nf, pl* -**checes 1** : narrowness **2 estrecheces** *nfpl* : financial problems — **estrecho, -cha** *adj* **1** : tight, narrow **2** ÍNTIMO : close — **estrecho** *nm* : strait
estrella *nf* **1** : star **2** DESTINO : destiny **3** ~ **de mar** : starfish — **estrellado, -da** *adj* **1** : starry **2** : star-shaped
estrellar *v* : crash — **estrellarse** *vr* ~ **contre** : smash into
estremecer {53} *vt* : cause to shudder — *vi* : tremble, shake — **estremecerse** *vr* : shudder, shiver (with emotion) — **estremecimiento** *nm* : shaking, shivering
estrenar *vt* **1** : use for the first time **2** : premiere, open (a film, etc.) — **estrenarse** *vr* : make one's debut — **estreno** *nm* : debut, premiere
estreñirse {67} *vr* : be constipated — **estreñimiento** *nm* : constipation
estrépito *nm* : clamor, din — **estrepitoso, -sa** *adj* : noisy, clamorous
estrés *nm, pl* **estreses** : stress — **estresante** *adj* : stressful — **estresar** *vt* : stress (out)

estría *nf* : groove
estribaciones *nfpl* : foothills
estribar *vi* ~ **en** : stem from, lie in
estribillo *nm* : refrain, chorus
estribo *nm* **1** : stirrup **2** : running board (of a vehicle) **3** CONTRAFUERTE : buttress **4 perder los** ~**s** : lose one's temper
estribor *nm* : starboard
estricto, -ta *adj* : strict
estridente *adj* : strident, shrill
estrofa *nf* : stanza, verse
estropajo *nm* : scouring pad
estropear *vt* **1** : ruin, spoil **2** DAÑAR : damage — **estropearse** *vr* **1** : go bad **2** AVERIARSE : break down — **estropicio** *nm* : damage, havoc
estructura *nf* : structure — **estructural** *adj* : structural
estruendo *nm* : din, roar — **estruendoso, -sa** *adj* : thunderous
estrujar *vt* : squeeze
estuario *nm* : estuary
estuche *nm* : kit, case
estuco *nm* : stucco
estudiar *v* : study — **estudiante** *nmf* : student — **estudiantil** *adj* : student — **estudio** *nm* **1** : study **2** OFICINA : studio, office **3** ~**s** *nmpl* : studies, education — **estudioso, -sa** *adj* : studious
estufa *nf* : stove, heater
estupefaciente *adj* & *nm* : narcotic — **estupefacto, -ta** *adj* : astonished
estupendo, -da *adj* : stupendous, marvelous
estúpido, -da *adj* : stupid — **estupidez** *nf*, *pl* **-deces** : stupidity
estupor *nm* **1** : stupor **2** ASOMBRO : amazement
etapa *nf* : stage, phase
etcétera : et cetera, and so on
éter *nm* : ether
etéreo, -rea *adj* : ethereal
eterno, -na *adj* : eternal — **eternidad** *nf* : eternity — **eternizarse** {21} *vr* : take forever
ética *nf* : ethics — **ético, -ca** *adj* : ethical
etimología *nf* : etymology
etíope *adj* : Ethiopian
etiqueta *nf* **1** : tag, label **2** PROTOCOLO : etiquette **3 de** ~ : formal, dressy — **etiquetar** *vt* : label
étnico, -ca *adj* : ethnic
eucalipto *nm* : eucalyptus
Eucaristía *nf* : Eucharist, communion
eufemismo *nm* : euphemism — **eufemístico, -ca** *adj* : euphemistic
euforia *nf* : euphoria — **eufórico, -ca** *adj* : euphoric
europeo, -pea *adj* : European
eutanasia *nf* : euthanasia

evacuar *vt* : evacuate, vacate — *vi* : have a bowel movement — **evacuación** *nf*, *pl* **-ciones** : evacuation
evadir *vt* : evade, avoid — **evadirse** *vr* : escape
evaluar {3} *vt* : evaluate — **evaluación** *nf*, *pl* **-ciones** : evaluation
evangelio *nm* : gospel — **evangélico, -ca** *adj* : evangelical — **evangelismo** *nm* : evangelism
evaporar *vt* : evaporate — **evaporarse** *vr* : evaporate, disappear — **evaporación** *nf*, *pl* **-ciones** : evaporation
evasión *nf*, *pl* **-siones 1** : evasion **2** FUGA : escape — **evasiva** *nf* : excuse, pretext — **evasivo, -va** *adj* : evasive
evento *nm* : event
eventual *adj* **1** : temporary **2** POSIBLE : possible — **eventualidad** *nf* : possibility, eventuality
evidencia *nf* **1** : evidence, proof **2 poner en** ~ : demonstrate — **evidenciar** *vt* : demonstrate, show — **evidente** *adj* : evident — **evidentemente** *adj* : evidently, apparently
evitar *vt* **1** : avoid **2** IMPEDIR : prevent — **evitable** *adj* : avoidable
evocar {72} *vt* : evoke
evolución *nf*, *pl* **-ciones** : evolution — **evolucionar** *vi* : evolve
exacerbar *vt* **1** : exacerbate **2** IRRITAR : irritate
exacto, -ta *adj* : precise, exact — **exactamente** *adv* : exactly — **exactitud** *nf* : precision, accuracy
exagerar *v* : exaggerate — **exageración** *nf*, *pl* **-ciones** : exaggeration — **exagerado, -da** *adj* : exaggerated
exaltar *vt* **1** : exalt, extol **2** EXCITAR : excite, arouse — **exaltarse** *vr* : get worked-up — **exaltado, -da** *adj* : worked up, hotheaded
examen *nm*, *pl* **exámenes 1** : examination, test **2** ANÁLISIS : investigation — **examinar** *vt* **1** : examine **2** ESTUDIAR : study, inspect — **examinarse** *vr* : take an exam
exánime *adj* : lifeless
exasperar *vt* : exasperate, irritate — **exasperación** *nf*, *pl* **-ciones** : exasperation
excavar *v* : excavate — **excavación** *nf*, *pl* **-ciones** : excavation
exceder *vt* : exceed, surpass — **excederse** *vr* : go too far — **excedente** *adj* & *nm* : surplus, excess
excelente *adj* : excellent — **excelencia** *nf* **1** : excellence **2 Su Excelencia** : His/Her Excellency
excéntrico, -ca *adj* & *n* : eccentric — **excentricidad** *nf* : eccentricity

excepción *nf, pl* **-ciones** : exception — **excepcional** *adj* : exceptional
excepto *prep* : except (for) — **exceptuar** {3} *vt* : exclude, except
exceso *nm* 1 : excess 2 ~ **de velocidad** : speeding — **excesivo, -va** *adj* : excessive
excitar *vt* : excite, arouse — **excitarse** *vr* : get excited — **excitable** *adj* : excitable — **excitación** *nf, pl* **-ciones** : excitement, agitation, arousal — **excitante** *adj* : exciting
exclamar *v* : exclaim — **exclamación** *nf, pl* **-ciones** : exclamation
excluir {41} *vt* : exclude — **exclusión** *nf, pl* **-siones** : exclusion — **exclusivo, -va** *adj* : exclusive
excomulgar {52} *vt* : excommunicate — **excomunión** *nf, pl* **-niones** : excommunication
excremento *nm* : excrement
exculpar *vt* : exonerate
excursión *nf, pl* **-siones** : excursion — **excursionista** *nmf* 1 : tourist, sightseer 2 : hiker
excusar *vt* 1 : excuse 2 EXIMIR : exempt — **excusarse** *vr* : apologize — **excusa** *nf* 1 : excuse 2 DISCULPA : apology
exento, -ta *adj* : exempt
exequias *nfpl* : funeral rites
exhalar *vt* 1 : exhale 2 : give off (an odor, etc.)
exhaustivo, -va *adj* : exhaustive — **exhausto, -ta** *adj* : exhausted, worn-out
exhibir *vt* : exhibit, show — **exhibición** *nf, pl* **-ciones** : exhibition
exhortar *vt* : exhort, admonish
exigir {35} *vt* : demand, require — **exigencia** *nf* : demand, requirement — **exigente** *adj* : demanding
exiguo, -gua *adj* : meager
exiliar *vt* : exile — **exiliarse** *vr* : go into exile — **exiliado, -da** *adj* : exiled, in exile — ~ *n* : exile — **exilio** *nm* : exile
eximir *vt* : exempt
existir *vi* : exist — **existencia** *nf* 1 : existence 2 ~s *nfpl* MERCANCÍA : goods, stock — **existente** *adj* : existing
éxito *nm* 1 : success, hit 2 **tener** ~ : be successful — **exitoso, -sa** *adj Lat* : successful
éxodo *nm* : exodus
exorbitante *adj* : exorbitant
exorcizar {21} *vt* : exorcize — **exorcismo** *nm* : exorcism
exótico, -ca *adj* : exotic
expandir *vt* : expand — **expandirse** *vr* : spread — **expansión** *nf, pl* **-siones** : expansion — **expansivo, -va** *adj* : expansive
expatriarse {85} *vr* 1 : emigrate 2 EXIL-

IARSE : go into exile — **expatriado, -da** *adj* & *n* : expatriate
expectativa *nf* 1 : expectation, hope 2 ~s *nfpl* : prospects
expedición *nf, pl* **-ciones** : expedition
expediente *nm* 1 : expedient 2 DOCUMENTOS : file, record 3 INVESTIGACIÓN : inquiry, proceedings
expedir {54} *vt* 1 : issue 2 ENVIAR : dispatch — **expedito, -ta** *adj* : free, clear
expeler *vt* : expel, eject
expendedor, -dora *n* : dealer, seller
expensas *nfpl* 1 : expenses 2 a ~ **de** : at the expense of
experiencia *nf* : experience
experimentar *vi* : experiment — *vt* 1 : experiment with, test out 2 SENTIR : experience, feel — **experimentado, -da** *adj* : experienced — **experimental** *adj* : experimental — **experimento** *nm* : experiment
experto, -ta *adj* & *n* : expert
expiar {85} *vt* : atone for
expirar *vi* 1 : expire 2 MORIR : die
explayar *vt* : extend — **explayarse** *vr* 1 : spread out 2 HABLAR : speak at length
explicar {72} *vt* : explain — **explicarse** *vr* : understand — **explicación** *nf, pl* **-ciones** : explanation — **explicativo, -va** *adj* : explanatory
explícito, -ta *adj* : explicit
explorar *vt* : explore — **exploración** *nf, pl* **-ciones** : exploration — **explorador, -dora** *n* : explorer, scout — **exploratorio, -ria** *adj* : exploratory
explosión *nf, pl* **-siones** 1 : explosion 2 : outburst (of anger, laughter, etc.) — **explosivo, -va** *adj* : explosive — **explosivo** *nm* : explosive
explotar *vt* 1 : exploit 2 : operate, run (a factory, etc.), work (a mine) — *vi* : explode — **explotación** *nf, pl* **-ciones** 1 : exploitation 2 : running (of a business), working (of a mine)
exponer {60} *vt* 1 : expose 2 : explain, set out (ideas, theories, etc.) 3 EXHIBIR : exhibit, display — *vi* : exhibit — **exponerse** *vr* ~ **a** : expose oneself to
exportar *vt* : export — **exportaciones** *nfpl* : exports — **exportador, -dora** *n* : exporter
exposición *nf, pl* **-ciones** 1 : exposure 2 : exhibition (of objects, art, etc.) 3 : exposition, setting out (of ideas, etc.) — **expositor, -tora** *n* 1 : exhibitor 2 : exponent (of a theory, etc.)
exprés *nms* & *pl* 1 : express (train) 2 *or* **café** ~ : espresso
expresamente *adv* : expressly, on purpose
expresar *vt* : express — **expresarse** *vr* : express oneself — **expresión** *nf, pl* **-siones**

: expression — **expresivo, -va** *adj* **1** : expressive **2** CARIÑOSO : affectionate
expreso, -sa *adj* : express — **expreso** *nm* : express train, express
exprimir *vt* **1** : squeeze **2** EXPLOTAR : exploit — **exprimidor** *nm* : squeezer, juicer
expuesto, -ta *adj* **1** : exposed **2** PELIGROSO : risky, dangerous
expulsar *vt* : expel, eject — **expulsión** *nf, pl* **-siones** : expulsion
exquisito, -ta *adj* **1** : exquisite **2** RICO : delicious — **exquisitez** *nf* **1** : exquisiteness **2** : delicacy, special dish
éxtasis *nms & pl* : ecstasy — **extático, -ta** *adj* : ecstatic
extender {56} *vt* **1** : spread out **2** : draw up (a document), write out (a check) — **extenderse** *vr* **1** : extend, spread **2** DURAR : last — **extendido, -da** *adj* **1** : widespread **2** : outstretched (of arms, wings, etc.)
extensamente *adv* : extensively
extensión *nf, pl* **-siones** **1** : extension **2** AMPLITUD : expanse **3** ALCANCE : range, extent — **extenso, -sa** *adj* : extensive
extenuar {3} *vt* : exhaust, tire out
exterior *adj* **1** : exterior, external **2** EXTRANJERO : foreign — **~** *nm* **1** : outside **2 en el ~** : abroad — **exteriorizar** {21} *vt* : show, reveal — **exteriormente** *adv* : outwardly, externally
exterminar *vt* : exterminate — **exterminación** *nf, pl* **-ciones** : extermination — **exterminio** *nm* : extermination
externo, -na *adj* : external
extinguir {26} *vt* **1** : extinguish (a fire) **2** : put an end to, wipe out — **extinguirse** *vr* **1** : go out (of fire, light, etc.) **2** : become extinct — **extinción** *nf, pl* **-ciones** : extinction — **extinguidor** *nm Lat* : fire extinguisher — **extinto, -ta** *adj* : extinct — **extintor** *nm* : fire extinguisher
extirpar *vt* : remove, eradicate

extorsión *nf, pl* **-siones** **1** : extortion **2** MOLESTIA : trouble
extra *adv* : extra — **~** *adj* **1** ADICIONAL : additional **2** : top-quality — **~** *nmf* : extra (in movies) — **~** *nm* : extra (expense)
extraditar *vt* : extradite
extraer {81} *vt* : extract — **extracción** *nf, pl* **-ciones** : extraction — **extracto** *nm* **1** : extract **2** RESUMEN : abstract, summary
extranjero, -ra *adj* : foreign — **~** *n* : foreigner — **extranjero** *nm* : foreign countries *pl*
extrañar *vt* : miss (someone) — **extrañarse** *vr* : be surprised — **extrañeza** *nf* : surprise — **extraño, -ña** *adj* **1** : foreign **2** RARO : strange, odd — **~** *n* : stranger
extraoficial *adj* : unofficial
extraordinario, -ria *adj* : extraordinary
extrasensorial *adj* : extrasensory
extraterrestre *adj & nmf* : extraterrestrial
extravagante *adj* : extravagant, outrageous — **extravagancia** *nf* : extravagance, outlandishness
extraviar {85} *vt* : lose, misplace — **extraviarse** *vr* : get lost — **extravío** *nm* : loss
extremar *vt* : carry to extremes — **extremarse** *vr* : do one's utmost — **extremadamente** *adv* : extremely — **extremado, -da** *adj* : extreme — **extremidad** *nf* **1** : tip, end **2 ~es** *nfpl* : extremities — **extremista** *adj & nmf* : extremist — **extremo, -ma** *adj* **1** : extreme **2 en caso ~** : as a last resort — **extremo** *nm* **1** : end **2 en ~** : in the extreme, extremely **3 en ultimo ~** : as a last resort
extrovertido -da *adj* : extroverted — **~** *n* : extrovert
exuberante *adj* : exuberant — **exuberancia** *nf* : exuberance
exudar *vt* : exude
eyacular *vi* : ejaculate — **eyaculación** *nf, pl* **-ciones** : ejaculation

F

f *nf* : f, sixth letter of the Spanish alphabet
fabricar {72} *vt* **1** : manufacture **2** CON-
STRUIR : build, construct **3** INVENTAR : fabricate — **fábrica** *nf* : factory — **fabricación**
nf, *pl* **-ciones** : manufacture — **fabricante**
nmf : manufacturer
fábula *nf* **1** : fable **2** MENTIRA : story, lie
fabuloso, -sa *adj* : fabulous
facción *nf*, *pl* **-ciones 1** : faction **2** ~es
nfpl RASGOS : features
faceta *nf* : facet
facha *nf* : appearance, look
fachada *nf* : façade
facial *adj* : facial
fácil *adj* **1** : easy **2** PROBABLE : likely —
facilemente *adv* : easily, readily — **facilidad** *nf* **1** : facility, ease **2** ~es *nfpl* : facilities, services — **facilitar** *vt* **1** : facilitate **2**
PROPORCIONAR : provide, supply
facsímil *or* **facsímile** *nm* **1** COPIA : facsimile, copy **2** : fax
factible *adj* : feasible
factor *nm* : factor
factoría *nf* : factory
factura *nf* **1** : bill, invoice **2** HECHURA
: making, manufacture — **facturar** *vt* **1**
: bill for **2** : check in (baggage, etc.)
facultad *nf* **1** : faculty, ability **2** AUTORIDAD
: authority **3** : school (of a university) —
facultativo, -va *adj* : optional
faena *nf* **1** : task, job **2** ~s **domésticas**
: housework
fagot *nm* : bassoon
faisán *nm*, *pl* **-sanes** : pheasant
faja *nf* **1** : sash **2** : girdle, corset **3** : strip (of
land)
fajo *nm* : bundle, sheaf
falda *nf* **1** : skirt **2** : side, slope (of a mountain)
falible *adj* : fallible
fálico, -ca *adj* : phallic
fallar *vi* : fail, go wrong — *vt* **1** : pronounce
judgment on **2** ERRAR : miss — **falla** *nf* **1**
: flaw, defect **2** : (geological) fault
fallecer {53} *vi* : pass away, die — **fallecimiento** *nm* : demise, death
fallido, -da *adj* : failed, unsuccessful
fallo *nm* **1** : error **2** SENTENCIA : sentence,
verdict
falo *nm* : phallus, penis
falsear *vt* : falsify, distort — **falsedad** *nf* **1**
: falseness **2** MENTIRA : falsehood, lie —
falsificación *nf*, *pl* **-ciones** : forgery, fake
— **falsificador, -dora** *n* : forger — **falsi-**

ficar {72} *vt* **1** : counterfeit, forge **2**
ALTERAR : falsify — **falso, -sa** *adj* **1** : false,
untrue **2** FALSIFICADO : counterfeit, forged
falta *nf* **1** CARENCIA : lack **2** DEFECTO : defect, fault, error **3** AUSENCIA : absence **4**
: offense, misdemeanor (in law) **5** : foul (in
sports) **6 hacer** ~ : be lacking, be needed
7 sin ~ : without fail — **faltar** *vi* **1** : be
lacking, be needed **2** : be missing **3**
QUEDAR : remain, be left **4 ¡no faltaba
más!** : don't mention it! — **falto, -ta** *adj* ~
de : lacking (in)
fama *nf* **1** : fame **2** REPUTACIÓN : reputation
famélico, -ca *adj* : starving
familia *nf* : family — **familiar** *adj* **1** : famil-
ial, family **2** CONOCIDO : familiar **3** : informal (of language, etc.) — ~ *nmf* : relation,
relative — **familiaridad** *nf* : familiarity —
familiarizarse {21} *vr* ~ **con** : familiarize
oneself with
famoso, -sa *adj* : famous
fanático, -ca *adj* : fanatic, fanatical — ~ *n*
: fanatic — **fanatismo** *nm* : fanaticism
fanfarria *nf* : fanfare
fanfarrón, -rrona *adj*, *mpl* **-rrones** *fam*
: boastful — ~ *n fam* : braggart — **fanfar-
ronear** *vi* : boast, brag
fango *nm* : mud, mire — **fangoso, -sa** *adj*
: muddy
fantasear *vi* : fantasize, daydream — **fantasía** *nf* **1** : fantasy **2** IMAGINACIÓN : imagination
fantasma *nm* : ghost, phantom — **fantasmal**
adj : ghostly
fantástico, -ca *adj* : fantastic
fardo *nm* : bundle
farfullar *v* : jabber, gabble
farmacéutico, -ca *adj* : pharmaceutical —
~ *n* : pharmacist — **farmacia** *nf* : drugstore, pharmacy
faro *nm* **1** : lighthouse **2** : headlight (of an
automobile) — **farol** *nm* **1** LINTERNA
: lantern **2** FAROLA : streetlight — **farola** *nf*
1 : lamppost **2** FAROL : streetlight
farsa *nf* : farce — **farsante** *nmf* : charlatan,
fraud
fascículo *nm* : installment, part (of a publication)
fascinar *vt* : fascinate — **fascinación** *nf*, *pl*
-ciones : fascination — **fascinante** *adj*
: fascinating
fascismo *nm* : fascism — **fascista** *adj* &
nmf : fascist
fase *nf* : phase

fastidiar *vt* : annoy, bother — *vi* : be annoying or bothersome — **fastidio** *nm* : annoyance — **fastidioso, -sa** *adj* : annoying, bothersome
fatal *adj* **1** : fateful **2** MORTAL : fatal **3** *fam* : awful, terrible — **fatalidad** *nf* **1** : fate, destiny **2** DESGRACIA : misfortune
fatídico, -ca *adj* : fateful, momentous
fatiga *nf* : fatigue — **fatigado, -da** *adj* : weary, tired — **fatigar** {52} *vt* : tire — **fatigarse** *vr* : get tired — **fatigoso, -sa** *adj* : fatiguing, tiring
fatuo, -tua *adj* **1** : fatuous **2** PRESUMIDO : conceited
fauna *nf* : fauna
favor *nm* **1** : favor **2 a ～ de** : in favor of **3 por ～** : please — **favorable** *adj* **1** : favorable **2 ser ～ a** : be in favor of — **favorecedor, -dora** *adj* : flattering — **favorecer** {53} *vt* **1** AYUDAR : favor **2** : look well on, suit — **favoritismo** *nm* : favoritism — **favorito, -ta** *adj* & *n* : favorite
fax *nm* : fax — **faxear** *vt* : fax
faz *nf, pl* **faces** : face, countenance
fe *nf* **1** : faith **2 dar ～ de** : bear witness to **3 de buena ～** : in good faith
fealdad *nf* : ugliness
febrero *nm* : February
febril *adj* : feverish
fecha *nf* **1** : date **2 ～ de caducidad** *or* **～ de vencimiento** : expiration date **3 ～ límite** : deadline — **fechar** *vt* : date, put a date on
fechoría *nf* : misdeed
fécula *nf* : starch (in food)
fecundar *vt* **1** : fertilize (an egg) **2** : make fertile — **fecundo, -da** *adj* : fertile
federación *nf, pl* **-ciones** : federation — **federal** *adj* : federal
felicidad *nf* **1** : happiness **2 ¡～es!** : best wishes!, congratulations!, happy birthday! — **felicitación** *nf, pl* **-ciones** : congratulation — **felicitar** *vt* : congratulate — **felicitarse** *vr* **～ de** : be glad about
feligrés, -gresa *n, mpl* **-greses** : parishioner
felino, -na *adj* & *n* : feline
feliz *adj, pl* **-lices** **1** : happy **2** AFORTUNADO : fortunate **3 Feliz Navidad** : Merry Christmas
felpa *nf* **1** : plush **2** : terry cloth (for towels, etc.)
felpudo *nm* : doormat
femenino, -na *adj* **1** : feminine **2** : female (in biology) — **femenino** *nm* : feminine (in grammar) — **femineidad** *nf* : femininity — **feminismo** *nm* : feminism — **feminista** *adj* & *nmf* : feminist
fenómeno *nm* : phenomenon — **fenomenal**

adj **1** : phenomenal **2** *fam* : fantastic, terrific
feo, fea *adj* **1** : ugly **2** DESAGRADABLE : unpleasant, nasty
féretro *nm* : coffin
feria *nf* **1** : fair, market **2** FIESTA : festival, holiday **3** *Lat fam* : small change — **feriado, -da** *adj* **día feriado** : public holiday
fermentar *v* : ferment — **fermentación** *nf, pl* **-ciones** : fermentation — **fermento** *nm* : ferment
feroz *adj, pl* **-roces** : ferocious, fierce — **ferocidad** *nf* : ferocity, fierceness
férreo, -rrea *adj* **1** : iron **2 vía férrea** : railroad track
ferretería *nf* : hardware store
ferrocarril *nm* : railroad, railway — **ferroviario, -ria** *adj* : rail, railroad
ferry *nm, pl* **ferrys** : ferry
fértil *adj* : fertile, fruitful — **fertilidad** *nf* : fertility — **fertilizante** *nm* : fertilizer — **fertilizar** *vt* : fertilize
fervor *nm* : fervor, zeal — **ferviente** *adj* : fervent
festejar *vt* **1** : celebrate **2** AGASAJAR : entertain, wine and dine — **festejo** *nm* : celebration, festivity
festín *nm, pl* **-tines** : banquet, feast
festival *nm* : festival — **festividad** *nf* : festivity — **festivo, -va** *adj* **1** : festive **2 día festivo** : holiday
fetiche *nm* : fetish
fétido, -da *adj* : foul-smelling, fetid
feto *nm* : fetus — **fetal** *adj* : fetal
feudal *adj* : feudal
fiable *adj* : reliable — **fiabilidad** *nf* : reliability
fiado, -da *adj* : on credit — **fiador, -dora** *n* : bondsman, guarantor
fiambres *nfpl* : cold cuts
fianza *nf* **1** : bail, bond **2 dar ～** : pay a deposit
fiar {85} *vt* **1** : guarantee **2** : sell on credit — *vi* **ser de ～** : be trustworthy — **fiarse** *vr* **～ de** : place trust in
fiasco *nm* : fiasco
fibra *nf* **1** : fiber **2 ～ de vidrio** : fiberglass
ficción *nf, pl* **-ciones** : fiction
ficha *nf* **1** : token **2** TARJETA : index card **3** : counter, chip (in games) — **fichar** *vt* : file, index — **fichero** *nm* **1** : card file **2** : filing cabinet
ficticio, -cia *adj* : fictitious
fidedigno, -na *adj* : reliable, trustworthy
fidelidad *nf* : fidelity, faithfulness
fideo *nm* : noodle
fiebre *nf* **1** : fever **2 ～ del heno** : hay fever **3 ～ palúdica** : malaria
fiel *adj* **1** : faithful, loyal **2** PRECISO : accu-

fieltro

rate, reliable — ~ *nm* **1** : pointer (of a scale) **2 los ~es** : the faithful — **fielmente** *adv* : faithfully
fieltro *nm* : felt
fiero, -ra *adj* : fierce, ferocious — **fiera** *nf* : wild animal, beast
fierro *nm Lat* : iron (bar)
fiesta *nf* **1** : party **2** DIA FESTIVO : holiday, feast day
figura *nf* **1** : figure **2** FORMA : shape, form — **figurar** *vi* **1** : figure (in), be included (among) **2** DESTACAR : stand out — *vt* : represent — **figurarse** *vr* : imagine
fijar *vt* **1** : fasten, affix **2** CONCRETAR : set, fix — **fijarse** *vr* **1** : settle **2 ~ en** : notice, pay attention to — **fijo, -ja** *adj* **1** : fixed, firm **2** PERMANENTE : permanent
fila *nf* **1** : line, filc, row **2 ponerse en ~** : line up
filantropía *nf* : philanthropy — **filantrópico, -ca** *adj* : philanthropic — **filántropo, -pa** *n* : philanthropist
filatelia *nf* : philately, stamp collecting
filete *nm* : fillet
filial *adj* : filial — ~ *nf* : affiliate, subsidiary
filigrana *nf* **1** : filigree **2** : watermark (on paper)
filipino, -na *adj* : Filipino
filmar *vt* : film, shoot — **filme** *or* **film** *nm* : film, movie
filo *nm* **1** : edge **2 dar ~ a** : sharpen
filón *nm, pl* **-lones 1** : vein (of minerals) **2** *fam* : gold mine
filoso, -sa *adj Lat* : sharp
filosofía *nf* : philosophy — **filosófico, -ca** *adj* : philosophical — **filósofo, -fa** *n* : philosopher
filtrar *v* : filter — **filtrarse** *vr* : leak out, seep through — **filtro** *nm* : filter
fin *nm* **1** : end **2** OBJETIVO : purpose, aim **3 en ~** : well, in short **4 ~ de semana** : weekend **5 por ~** : finally, at last
final *adj* : final — ~ *nm* : end, conclusion — ~ *nf* : final (in sports) — **finalidad** *nf* : purpose, aim — **finalista** *nmf* : finalist — **finalizar** {21} *v* : finish, end — **finalmente** *adv* : finally
financiar *vt* : finance, fund — **financiero, -ra** *adj* : financial — ~ *n* : financier — **finanzas** *nfpl* : finance
finca *nf* **1** : farm, ranch **2** *Lat* : country house
fingir {35} *v* : feign, pretend — **fingido, -da** *adj* : false, feigned
finito, -ta *adj* : finite
finlandés, -desa *adj* : Finnish
fino, -na *adj* **1** : fine **2** DELGADO : slender **3** REFINADO : refined **4** AGUDO : sharp, keen

— **finura** *nf* **1** : fineness **2** REFINAMIENTO : refinement
firma *nf* **1** : signature **2** : (act of) signing **3** EMPRESA : firm, company
firmamento *nm* : firmament, sky
firmar *v* : sign
firme *adj* **1** : firm, resolute **2** ESTABLE : steady, stable — **firmeza** *nf* **1** : strength, resolve **2** ESTABILIDAD : firmness, stability
fiscal *adj* : fiscal — ~ *nmf* : district attorney — **fisco** *nm* : (national) treasury
fisgar {52} *vt* : pry into — *vi* : pry — **fisgón, -gona** *n, mpl* **-gones** : snoop, busybody
física *nf* : physics — **físico, -ca** *adj* : physical — ~ *n* : physicist — **físico** *nm* : physique
fisiología *nf* : physiology — **fisiológico, -ca** *adj* : physiological — **fisiólogo, -ga** *n* : physiologist
fisioterapia *nf* : physical therapy — **fisioterapeuta** *nmf* : physical therapist
fisonomía *nf* : features *pl*, appearance
fisura *nf* : fissure
fláccido, -da *or* **flácido, -da** *adj* : flaccid, flabby
flaco, -ca *adj* **1** : thin, skinny **2** DÉBIL : weak
flagrante *adj* : flagrant
flamante *adj* **1** : bright, brilliant **2** NUEVO : brand-new
flamenco, -ca *adj* **1** : flamenco (of music or dance) **2** : Flemish — **flamenco** *nm* **1** : flamingo **2** : flamenco (music or dance)
flaquear *vi* : weaken, flag — **flaqueza** *nf* **1** : thinness **2** DEBILIDAD : weakness
flash *nm* : flash
flatulencia *nf* : flatulence
flauta *nf* **1** : flute **2 ~ dulce** : recorder — **flautín** *nm, pl* **-tines** : piccolo — **flautista** *nmf* : flutist
flecha *nf* : arrow
fleco *nm* **1** : fringe **2** *Lat* : bangs *pl*
flema *nf* : phlegm — **flemático, -ca** *adj* : phlegmatic
flequillo *nm* : bangs *pl*
fletar *vt* **1** : charter, rent **2** *Lat* : transport — **flete** *nm* **1** : charter **2** : shipping (charges) **3** *Lat* : transport, freight
flexible *adj* : flexible — **flexibilidad** *nf* : flexibility
flirtear *vi* : flirt
flojo, -ja *adj* **1** SUELTO : loose, slack **2** DÉBIL : weak **3** PEREZOSO : lazy — **flojera** *nf fam* : lethargy
flor *nf* : flower — **flora** *nf* : flora — **floral** *adj* : floral — **floreado, -da** *adj* : flowered — **florear** *vi Lat* : flower, bloom — **florecer** {53} *vi* **1** : bloom, blossom **2** PROSPERAR : flourish — **floreciente** *adj* : flourishing — **florero** *nm* : vase — **florido, -da** *adj* : flow-

ery — **florista** *nmf* : florist — **floritura** *nf*
: frill, flourish
flota *nf* : fleet
flotar *vi* : float — **flotador** *nm* 1 : float 2
: life preserver (for a swimmer) — **flotante**
adj : floating, buoyant — **flote: a** ~ *adv*
phr : afloat
flotilla *nf* : flotilla, fleet
fluctuar {3} *vi* : fluctuate — **fluctuación** *nf*,
pl -**ciones** : fluctuation
fluir {41} *vi* : flow — **fluidez** *nf* 1 : fluidity
2 : fluency (of language, etc.) — **fluido, -da**
adj 1 : fluid 2 : fluent (of language) — **fluido** *nm* : fluid — **flujo** *nm* : flow
fluorescente *adj* : fluorescent
fluoruro *nm* : fluoride
fluvial *adj* : river
fobia *nf* : phobia
foca *nf* : seal (animal)
foco *nm* 1 : focus 2 : spotlight, floodlight
(in theater, etc.) 3 *Lat* : lightbulb
fofo, -fa *adj* : flabby
fogata *nf* : bonfire
fogón *nm, pl* -**gones** : burner
fogoso, -sa *adj* : ardent
folklore *nm* : folklore — **folklórico, -ca** *adj*
: folk, traditional
follaje *nm* : foliage
folleto *nm* : pamphlet, leaflet
fomentar *vt* : promote, encourage — **fomento** *nm* : promotion, encouragement
fonda *nf* : boarding house
fondear *vt* : sound out, examine — *vi* : anchor
fondillos *nmpl* : seat (of pants, etc.)
fondo *nm* 1 : bottom 2 : rear, back, end 3
PROFUNDIDAD : depth 4 : background (of a
painting, etc.) 5 *Lat* : slip, petticoat 6 ~**s**
nmpl : funds, resources 7 **a** ~ : thoroughly, in depth 8 **en el** ~ : deep down
fonético, -ca *adj* : phonetic — **fonética** *nf*
: phonetics
fontanería *nf Spain* : plumbing —
fontanero, -ra *n Spain* : plumber
footing *nm* 1 : jogging 2 **hacer** ~ : jog
forajido, -da *n* : bandit, outlaw
foráneo, -nea *adj* : foreign, strange
forastero, -ra *n* : stranger, outsider
forcejear *vi* : struggle — **forcejeo** *nm*
: struggle
forense *adj* : forensic
forja *nf* : forge — **forjar** *vt* 1 : forge 2
CREAR, FORMAR : build up, create
forma *nf* 1 : form, shape 2 MANERA : manner, way 3 **en** ~ : fit, healthy 4 ~**s** *nfpl*
: appearances, conventions — **formación**
nf, pl -**ciones** 1 : formation 2 EDUCACIÓN
: training
formal *adj* 1 : formal 2 SERIO : serious 3 FI-

ABLE : dependable, reliable — **formalidad**
nf 1 : formality 2 SERIEDAD : seriousness
3 FIABILIDAD : reliability
formar *vt* 1 : form, shape 2 CONSTITUIR
: constitute 3 EDUCAR : train, educate —
formarse *vr* 1 DESARROLLARSE : develop,
take shape 2 EDUCARSE : be educated
formato *nm* : format
formidable *adj* 1 : tremendous 2 *fam* : fantastic, terrific
fórmula *nf* : formula
formular *vt* 1 : formulate, draw up 2
: make, lodge (a complaint, etc.)
formulario *nm* : form
fornido, -da *adj* : well-built, burly
foro *nm* : forum
forraje *nm* : forage, fodder — **forrajear** *vi*
: forage
forrar *vt* 1 : line (a garment) 2 : cover (a
book) — **forro** *nm* 1 : lining 2 CUBIERTA
: book cover
fortalecer {53} *vt* : strengthen — **fortaleza**
nf 1 : fortress 2 FUERZA : strength 3
: (moral) fortitude
fortificar {72} *vt* : fortify — **fortificación** *nf,
pl* -**ciones** : fortification
fortuito, -ta *adj* : fortuitous, chance
fortuna *nf* 1 SUERTE : fortune, luck 2
RIQUEZA : wealth, fortune 3 **por** ~ : fortunately
forzar {36} *vt* 1 : force 2 : strain (one's
eyes) — **forzosamente** *adv* : necessarily —
forzoso, -sa *adj* : necessary, inevitable
fosa *nf* 1 : pit, ditch 2 TUMBA : grave 3 ~**s**
nasales : nostrils
fósforo *nm* 1 : phosphorus 2 CERILLA
: match — **fosforescente** *adj* : phosphores-
cent
fósil *nm* : fossil
foso *nm* 1 : ditch 2 : pit (of a theater) 3
: moat (of a castle)
foto *nf* : photo
fotocopia *nf* : photocopy — **fotocopiadora**
nf : photocopier — **fotocopiar** *vt* : photocopy
fotogénico, -ca *adj* : photogenic
fotografía *nf* 1 : photography 2 : photograph, picture — **fotografiar** {85} *vt* : photograph — **fotográfico, -ca** *adj* : photographic — **fotógrafo, -fa** *n* : photographer
fotosíntesis *nf* : photosynthesis
fracasar *vi* : fail — **fracaso** *nm* : failure
fracción *nf, pl* -**ciones** 1 : fraction 2 : faction (in politics) — **fraccionamiento** *nm*
Lat : housing development
fractura *nf* : fracture — **fracturarse** *vr*
: fracture, break (a bone)
fragancia *nf* : fragrance, scent — **fragante**
adj : fragrant

fragata *nf* : frigate
frágil *adj* **1** : fragile **2** DÉBIL : frail, delicate — **fragilidad** *nf* **1** : fragility **2** DEBILIDAD : frailty
fragmento *nm* : fragment
fragor *nm* : clamor, din
fragoso, -sa *adj* : rough, rugged
fragua *nf* : forge — **fraguar** {10} *vt* **1** : forge **2** IDEAR : concoct — *vi* : harden, solidify
fraile *nm* : friar, monk
frambuesa *nf* : raspberry
francés, -cesa *adj, mpl* **-ceses** : French — **francés** *nm* : French (language)
franco, -ca *adj* **1** : frank, candid **2** : free (in commerce) — **franco** *nm* : franc
francotirador, -dora *n* : sniper
francla *nf* : flannel
franja *nf* **1** : stripe, band **2** FLECO : fringe
franquear *vt* **1** : clear (a path, etc.) **2** : cross over (a doorstep, etc.) **3** : pay postage on (mail) — **franqueo** *nm* : postage
franqueza *nf* : frankness
frasco *nm* : small bottle, vial, flask
frase *nf* **1** : phrase **2** ORACIÓN : sentence
fraternal *adj* : brotherly, fraternal — **fraternidad** *nf* : brotherhood, fraternity — **fraternizar** {21} *vi* : fraternize — **fraterno, -na** *adj* : brotherly, fraternal
fraude *nm* : fraud — **fraudulento, -ta** *adj* : fraudulent
fray *nm* (*used in titles*) : brother, friar
frazada *nf Lat* : blanket
frecuencia *nf* **1** : frequency **2 con ~** : often, frequently — **frecuentar** *vt* : frequent, haunt — **frecuente** *adj* : frequent
fregadero *nm* : kitchen sink
fregar {49} *vt* **1** : scrub, wash **2** *Lat fam* : annoy — *vi Lat fam* : be a pest
freír {37} *vt* : fry
fregona *nf Spain* : mop
frenar *vt* **1** : brake **2** RESTRINGIR : curb, check
frenesí *nm* : frenzy — **frenético, -ca** *adj* : frantic, frenzied
freno *nm* **1** : brake **2** : bit (of a bridle) **3** CONTROL : check, restraint
frente *nm* **1** : front **2** : facade (of a building) **3 al ~ de** : at the head of **4 ~ a** : opposite **5 de ~** : (facing) forward **6 hacer ~ a** : face up to, brave — **~** *nf* : forehead
fresa *nf* : strawberry
fresco, -ca *adj* **1** : fresh **2** FRÍO : cool **3** *fam* : insolent, nervy — **fresco** *nm* **1** : fresh air **2** FRESCOR : coolness **3** : fresco (art or painting) — **frescor** *nm* : coolness, cool air — **frescura** *nf* **1** : freshness **2** FRÍO : coolness **3** *fam* : nerve, insolence
fresno *nm* : ash (tree)

frialdad *nf* **1** : coldness **2** INDIFERENCIA : indifference
fricción *nf, pl* **-ciones 1** : friction **2** MASAJE : rubbing, massage — **friccionar** *vt* : rub
frigidez *nf* : frigidity
frigorífico *nm Spain* : refrigerator
frijol *nm Lat* : bean
frío, fría *adj* **1** : cold **2** INDIFERENTE : cool, indifferent — **frío** *nm* **1** : cold **2** INDIFERENCIA : coldness, indifference **3 hacer ~** : be cold (outside) **4 tener ~** : be cold, feel cold
frito, -ta *adj* **1** : fried **2** *fam* : fed up
frívolo, -la *adj* : frivolous — **frivolidad** *nf* : frivolity
fronda *nf* **1** : frond **2** *or* **~s** *nfpl* : foliage — **frondoso, -sa** *adj* : leafy
frontera *nf* : border, frontier — **fronterizo, -za** *adj* : border, on the border — **frontero, -ra** *adj* : facing, opposite
frotar *vt* : rub — **frotarse** *vr* **~ las manos** : rub one's hands
fructífero, -ra *adj* : fruitful
frugal *adj* : frugal, thrifty — **frugalidad** *adj* : frugality
fruncir {83} *vt* **1** : gather (in pleats) **2 ~ el ceño** : frown **3 ~ la boca** : purse one's lips
frustrar *vt* : frustrate — **frustrarse** *vr* : fail — **frustración** *nf, pl* **-ciones** : frustration — **frustrado, -da** *adj* **1** : frustrated **2** FRACASADO : failed, unsuccessful — **frustrante** *adj* : frustrating
fruta *nf* : fruit — **frutilla** *nf Lat* : strawberry — **fruto** *nm* **1** : fruit **2** RESULTADO : result, consequence
fucsia *adj & nm* : fuchsia
fuego *nm* **1** : fire **2** : flame, burner (on a stove) **3 ~s artificiales** *nmpl* : fireworks **4 ¿tienes fuego?** : have you got a light?
fuelle *nm* : bellows
fuente *nf* **1** : fountain **2** MANANTIAL : spring **3** ORIGEN : source **4** PLATO : platter, serving dish
fuera *adv* **1** : outside, out **2** : abroad, away **3 ~ de** : outside of, beyond **4 ~ de** : aside from, in addition to
fuerte *adj* **1** : strong **2** : bright (of colors), loud (of sounds) **3** EXTREMO : intense **4** DURO : hard — **~** *adv* **1** : strongly, hard **2** : loudly **3** MUCHO : abundantly, a lot — **~** *nm* **1** : fort **2** ESPECIALIDAD : strong point
fuerza *nf* **1** : strength **2** VIOLENCIA : force **3** PODER : power, might **4 ~s armadas** *nfpl* : armed forces **5 a ~ de** : by dint of **6 a la ~** : necessarily
fuga *nf* **1** : flight, escape **2** : fugue (in music) **3** ESCAPE : leak — **fugarse** {52} *vr* : flee, run away — **fugaz** *adj, pl* **-gaces** : fleeting — **fugitivo, -va** *adj & n* : fugitive

fulano, -na *n* : so-and-so, what's-his-name, what's-her-name
fulgor *nm* : brilliance, splendor
fulminar *vt* **1** : strike with lightning **2** : strike down (with an illness, etc.) — **fulminante** *adj* : devastating
fumar *v* : smoke — **fumarse** *vr* **1** : smoke **2** *fam* : squander — **fumador, -dora** *n* : smoker
funámbulo, -la *n* : tightrope walker
función *nf, pl* **-ciones 1** : function **2** TRABAJOS : duties *pl* **3** : performance, show (in theater) — **funcional** *adj* : functional — **funcionamiento** *nm* **1** : functioning **2 en** ~ : in operation — **funcionar** *vi* **1** : function, run, work **2 no funciona** : out of order — **funcionario, -ria** *n* : civil servant, official
funda *nf* **1** : cover, sheath **2** *or* ~ **de almohada** : pillowcase
fundar *vt* **1** ESTABLECER : found, establish **2** BASAR : base — **fundarse** *vr* ~ **en** : be based on — **fundación** *nf, pl* **-ciones** : foundation — **fundador, -dora** *n* : founder — **fundamental** *adj* : fundamental, basic — **fundamentalmente** *adv* : basically — **fundamentar** *vt* **1** : lay the foundations for **2** BASAR : base — **fundamento** *nm* **1** : foundation **2** ~**s** *nmpl* : fundamentals
fundir *vt* **1** : melt down, smelt **2** FUSIONAR : fuse, merge — **fundirse** *vr* **1** : blend,

merge **2** DERRETIRSE : melt **3** : burn out (of a lightbulb) — **fundición** *nf, pl* **-ciones 1** : smelting **2** : foundry
fúnebre *adj* **1** : funeral **2** LÚGUBRE : gloomy
funeral *adj* : funeral, funerary — ~ *nm* **1** : funeral **2** ~**es** *nmpl* EXEQUIAS : funeral (rites) — **funeraria** *nf* : funeral home
funesto, ta *adj* : terrible, disastrous
funglr {35} *vi Lat* : act, function
furgón *nm, pl* **-gones 1** : van, truck **2** : freight car (of a train) **3** ~ **de cola** : caboose — **furgoneta** *nf* : van
furia *nf* **1** CÓLERA : fury, rage **2** VIOLENCIA : violence — **furibundo, -da** *adj* : furious — **furioso, -sa** *adj* **1** : furious, irate **2** INTENSO : intense, violent — **furor** *nm* : fury
furtivo, -va *adj* : furtive
furúnculo *nm* : boil
fuselaje *nm* : fuselage
fusible *nm* : fuse
fusil *nm* : rifle — **fusilar** *vt* : shoot (by firing squad)
fusión *nf, pl* **-siones 1** : fusion **2** UNIÓN : union, merger — **fusionar** *vt* **1** : fuse **2** UNIR : merge — **fusionarse** *vr* : merge
futbol *or* **fútbol** *nm* **1** : soccer **2** ~ **americano** : football — **futbolista** *nmf* : soccer player, football player
fútil *adj* : trifling, trivial
futuro, -ra *adj* : future — **futuro** *nm* : future

G

g *nf* : g, seventh letter of the Spanish alphabet
gabán *nm, pl* **-banes** : topcoat, overcoat
gabardina *nf* **1** : trench coat, raincoat **2** : gabardine (fabric)
gabinete *nm* **1** : cabinet (in government) **2** : (professional) office
gacela *nf* : gazelle
gaceta *nf* : gazette
gachas *nfpl* : porridge
gacho, -cha *adj* : drooping
gaélico, -ca *adj* : Gaelic
gafas *nfpl* **1** : eyeglasses **2** ~ **de sol** : sunglasses
gaita *nf* : bagpipes *pl*
gajo *nm* : segment (of fruit)
gala *nf* **1** : gala **2 de** ~ : formal **3 hacer** ~ **de** : display, show off **4** ~**s** *nfpl* : finery
galáctico, -ca *adj* : galactic

galán *nm, pl* **-lanes 1** : leading man (in theater) **2** *fam* : boyfriend
galante *adj* : gallant — **galantear** *vt* : court, woo — **galantería** *nf* **1** : gallantry **2** CUMPLIDO : compliment
galápago *nm* : (aquatic) turtle
galardón *nm, pl* **-dones** : reward
galaxia *nf* : galaxy
galera *nf* : galley
galería *nf* **1** : corridor **2** : gallery, balcony (in a theater)
galés, -lesa *adj, mpl* **-leses** : Welsh
galgo *nm* : greyhound
galimatías *nms & pl* : gibberish
gallardía *nf* **1** : bravery **2** ELEGANCIA : elegance — **gallardo, -da** *adj* **1** : brave **2** APUESTO : elegant, good-looking
gallego, -ga *adj* : Galician

galleta *nf* **1** : (sweet) cookie **2** : (salted) cracker
gallina *nf* **1** : hen **2** ～ **de Guinea** : guinea fowl — **gallinero** *nm* : henhouse, (chicken) coop — **gallo** *nm* : rooster, cock
galón *nm, pl* **-lones 1** : gallon **2** : stripe (military insignia)
galopar *vi* : gallop — **galope** *nm* : gallop
galvanizar {21} *vt* : galvanize
gama *nf* **1** : range, spectrum **2** : scale (in music)
gamba *nf* : large shrimp, prawn
gamuza *nf* **1** : chamois (animal) **2** : chamois (leather), suede
gana *nf* **1** : desire, wish **2** APETITO : appetite **3 de buena** ～ : willingly, heartily **4 de mala** ～ : unwillingly **5 no me da la** ～ : I don't feel like it **6 tener** ～**s de** : feel like, be in the mood for
ganado *nm* **1** : cattle *pl*, livestock **2** ～ **ovino** : sheep *pl* **3** ～ **porcino** : swine *pl* — **ganadería** *nf* **1** : cattle raising **2** GANADO : livestock
ganador, -dora *adj* : winning — ～ *n* : winner
ganancia *nf* : profit
ganar *vt* **1** : earn **2** : win (in games, etc.) **3** CONSEGUIR : gain **4** ADQUERIR : get, obtain **5** ～ **a algn** : win over s.o., beat s.o. — *vi* : win — **ganarse** *vr* **1** : win, gain **2** ～ **la vida** : make a living
gancho *nm* **1** : hook **2** HORQUILLA : hairpin **3** *Lat* : (clothes) hanger
gandul, -dula *adj* & *n fam* : good-for-nothing — **gandul** *nm Lat* : pigeon pea
ganga *nf* : bargain
gangrena *nf* : gangrene
gángster *nmf* : gangster
ganso, -sa *n* : goose, gander *m* — **gansada** *nf* : silly thing, nonsense
gañir {38} *vi* : yelp — **gañido** *nm* : yelp
garabatear *v* : scribble — **garabato** *nm* : scribble
garaje *nm* : garage
garantizar {21} *vt* : guarantee — **garante** *nmf* : guarantor — **garantía** *nf* **1** : guarantee, warranty **2** FIANZA : surety
garapiñar *vt* : candy (fruits, etc.)
garbanzo *nm* : chickpea, garbanzo
garbo *nm* : grace, elegance — **garboso, -sa** *adj* : graceful, elegant
gardenia *nf* : gardenia
garfio *nm* : hook, gaff
garganta *nf* **1** : throat **2** CUELLO : neck **3** DESFILADERO : ravine, gorge — **gargantilla** *nf* : necklace
gárgara *nf* **1** : gargling, gargle **2 hacer** ～**s** : gargle
gárgola *nf* : gargoyle

garita *nf* **1** : sentry box **2** CABAÑA : cabin, hut
garito *nm* : gambling den
garra *nf* **1** : claw, talon **2** *fam* : hand, paw
garrafa *nf* : decanter, carafe — **garrafón** *nm, pl* **-fones** : large decanter or bottle
garrapata *nf* : tick
garrocha *nf* **1** : lance, pike **2** *Lat* : pole (in sports)
garrote *nm* : club, cudgel
garúa *nf Lat* : drizzle
garza *nf* : heron
gas *nm* **1** : gas **2** ～ **lacrimógeno** : tear gas
gasa *nf* : gauze
gaseosa *nf* : soda, soft drink
gasolina *nf* : gasoline, gas — **gasoil** *or* **gasóleo** *nm* : diesel fuel — **gasolinera** *nf* : gas station, service station
gastar *vt* **1** : spend **2** CONSUMIR : consume, use up **3** DESPERDICIAR : squander, waste — **gastarse** *vr* **1** : spend **2** DETERIORARSE : wear out — **gastado, -da** *adj* **1** : spent **2** : worn-out (of clothing, etc.) — **gastador, -dora** *n* : spendthrift — **gasto** *nm* **1** : expense, expenditure **2** ～**s generales** : overhead
gástrico, -ca *adj* : gastric
gastronomía *nf* : gastronomy — **gastrónomo, -ma** *n* : gourmet
gatas: a ～ *adv phr* : on all fours
gatear *vi* : crawl, creep
gatillo *nm* : trigger — **gatillero** *nm Mex* : gunman
gato, -ta *n* : cat — **gatito, -ta** *n* : kitten — **gato** *nm* : jack (for an automobile)
gaucho *nm* : gaucho
gaveta *nf* : drawer
gavilla *nf* **1** : sheaf **2** PANDILLA : gang
gaviota *nf* : gull, seagull
gay *adj* : gay (homosexual)
gaza *nf* : loop
gazpacho *nm* : gazpacho
géiser *nm* : geyser
gelatina *nf* : gelatin
gema *nf* : gem
gemelo, -la *adj* & *n* : twin — **gemelo** *nm* **1** : cuff link **2** ～**s** *nmpl* : binoculars
gemir {54} *vi* : moan, groan, whine — **gemido** *nm* : moan, groan, whine
gen *or* **gene** *nm* : gene
genealogía *nf* : genealogy — **genealógico, -ca** *adj* : genealogical
generación *nf, pl* **-ciones** : generation
generador *nm* : generator
general *adj* **1** : general **2 en** ～ *or* **por lo** ～ : in general, generally — ～ *nmf* : general — **generalidad** *nf* **1** : generalization **2** MAYORÍA : majority — **generalizar** {21} *vi* : generalize — *vt* : spread (out) — **gener-**

alizarse *vr* : become widespread — **generalmente** *adv* : usually, generally
generar *vt* : generate
género *nm* **1** : kind, sort **2** : gender (in grammar) **3** ~ **humano** : human race — **genérico, -ca** *adj* : generic
generoso, -sa *adj* **1** : generous, unselfish **2** : ample (in quantity) — **generosidad** *nf* : generosity
génesis *nfs & pl* : genesis
genética *nf* : genetics — **genético, -ca** *adj* : genetic
genial *adj* **1** : brilliant **2** ESTUPENDO : great, terrific
genio *nm* **1** : genius **2** CARÁCTER : temper, disposition **3** : genie (in mythology)
genital *adj* : genital — **genitales** *nmpl* : genitals
genocidio *nm* : genocide
gente *nf* **1** : people **2** *fam* : relatives *pl,* folks *pl* **3 ser buena** ~ : be nice, be kind
gentil *adj* **1** AMABLE : kind **2** : gentile (in religion) — **gentileza** *nf* : kindness, courtesy
gentío *nm* : crowd, mob
gentuza *nf* : riffraff, rabble
genuflexión *nf, pl* **-xiones** : genuflection
genuino, -na *adj* : genuine
geografía *nf* : geography — **geográfico, -ca** *adj* : geographic, geographical
geología *nf* : geology — **geológico, -ca** *adj* : geologic, geological
geometría *nf* : geometry — **geométrico, -ca** *adj* : geometric, geometrical
geranio *nm* : geranium
gerencia *nf* : management — **gerente** *nmf* : manager
geriatría *nf* : geriatrics — **geriátrico, -ca** *adj* : geriatric
germen *nm, pl* **gérmenes** : germ
germinar *vi* : germinate, sprout
gestación *nf, pl* **-ciones** : gestation
gesticular *vi* : gesticulate, gesture — **gesticulación** *nf, pl* **-ciones** : gesticulation
gestión *nf, pl* **-tiones 1** : procedure, step **2** ADMINISTRACIÓN : management — **gestionar** *vt* **1** : negotiate, work towards **2** ADMINISTRAR : manage, handle
gesto *nm* **1** : gesture **2** : (facial) expression **3** MUECA : grimace
gigante *adj & nm* : giant — **gigantesco, -ca** *adj* : gigantic
gimnasia *nf* : gymnastics — **gimnasio** *nm* : gymnasium, gym — **gimnasta** *nmf* : gymnast
gimotear *vi* : whine, whimper
ginebra *nf* : gin
ginecología *nf* : gynecology — **ginecólogo, -ga** *n* : gynecologist

gira *nf* : tour
girar *vi* : turn (around), revolve — *vt* **1** : turn, twist, rotate **2** : draft (checks) **3** : transfer (funds)
girasol *nm* : sunflower
giratorio, -ria *adj* : revolving
giro *nm* **1** : turn, rotation **2** LOCUCIÓN : expression **3** ~ **bancario** : bank draft **4** ~ **postal** : money order
giroscopio *nm* : gyroscope
gis *nm* *Lat* : chalk
gitano, -na *adj & n* : Gypsy
glaciar *nm* : glacier — **glacial** *adj* : glacial, icy
gladiador *nm* : gladiator
glándula *nf* : gland
glasear *vt* : glaze, ice (cake, etc.) — **glaseado** *nm* : icing
glicerina *nf* : glycerin
globo *nm* **1** : globe **2** : balloon **3** ~ **ocular** : eyeball — **global** *adj* **1** : global **2** TOTAL : total, overall
glóbulo *nm* : blood cell, corpuscle
gloria *nf* : glory
glorieta *nf* **1** : bower, arbor **2** *Spain* : rotary, traffic circle
glorificar {72} *vt* : glorify
glorioso, -sa *adj* : glorious
glosario *nm* : glossary
glotón, -tona *adj, mpl* **-tones** : gluttonous — ~ *n* : glutton — **glotonería** *nf* : gluttony
glucosa *nf* : glucose
gnomo *nm* : gnome
gobernar {55} *v* **1** : govern, rule **2** DIRIGIR : direct, manage **3** : steer (a boat, etc.) — **gobernación** *nf, pl* **-ciones** : governing, government — **gobernador, -dora** *n* : governor — **gobernante** *adj* : ruling, governing — ~ *n* : ruler, leader — **gobierno** *nm* : government
goce *nm* : enjoyment
gol *nm* : goal (in sports)
golf *nm* : golf — **golfista** *nmf* : golfer
golfo *nm* : gulf
golondrina *nf* **1** : swallow **2** ~ **de mar** : tern
golosina *nf* : sweet, candy — **goloso, -sa** *adj* : fond of sweets
golpe *nm* **1** : blow **2** PUÑETAZO : punch **3** : knock (on a door, etc.) **4 de** ~ : suddenly **5 de un** ~ : all at once **6** ~ **de estado** : coup d'etat — **golpear** *vt* **1** : hit, punch **2** : slam, bang (a door, etc.) — *vi* : knock (at a door)
goma *nf* **1** CAUCHO : rubber **2** PEGAMENTO : glue **3** *or* ~ **elástica** : rubber band **4** ~ **de mascar** : chewing gum **5** ~ **de borrar** : eraser
gong *nm* : gong

gordo   **80**

gordo, -da *adj* **1** : fat, plump **2** GRUESO
: thick **3** : fatty (of meat) **4** *fam* : big, serious — **~** *n* : fat person — **gorda** *nf Lat*
: thick corn tortilla — **gordo** *nm* **1** GRASA
: fat **2** : jackpot (in a lottery) — **gordura** *nf*
: fatness, flab
gorgotear *vi* : gurgle, bubble
gorila *nm* : gorilla
gorjear *vi* **1** : chirp, tweet **2** : gurgle (of a
baby) — **gorjeo** *nm* : chirping
gorra *nf* **1** : cap, bonnet **2 de ~** *fam* : for
free
gorrear *vt fam* : bum, scrounge
gorrión *nm, pl* **-rriones** : sparrow
gorro *nm* **1** : cap, bonnet **2 de ~** *fam* : for
free
gota *nf* **1** : drop **2** : gout (in medicine) —
gotear *vi* : drip, leak — **goteo** *nm* : drip,
dripping — **gotera** *nf* : leak
gótico, -ca *adj* : Gothic
gozar {21} *vi* **1** : enjoy oneself **2 ~ de**
algo : enjoy sth
gozne *nm* : hinge
gozo *nm* **1** : joy **2** PLACER : enjoyment,
pleasure — **gozoso, -sa** *adj* : joyful, glad
grabar *vt* **1** : engrave **2** : record, tape —
grabación *nf, pl* **-ciones** : recording —
grabado *nm* : engraving — **grabadora** *nf*
: tape recorder
gracia *nf* **1** : grace **2** FAVOR : favor, kindness
3 HUMOR : humor, wit **4 ~s** *nfpl* : thanks
5 ¡(muchas) ~s! : thank you (very much)!
— **gracioso, -sa** *adj* : funny, amusing
grada *nf* **1** : step, stair **2** : row (in a theater,
etc.) **3 ~s** *nfpl* : bleachers, grandstand —
gradación *nf, pl* **-ciones** : gradation, scale
— **gradería** *nf* : rows *pl*, stands *pl* — **grado**
nm **1** : degree **2** : grade (in school) **3 de**
buen ~ : willingly
graduar {3} *vt* **1** : regulate, adjust **2** MAR-
CAR : calibrate **3** : confer a degree on (in
education) — **graduarse** *vr* : graduate
(from a school) — **graduación** *nf, pl*
-ciones 1 : graduation **2** : alcohol content,
proof — **graduado, -da** *n* : graduate —
gradual *adj* : gradual — **gradualmente** *adv*
: little by little, gradually
gráfico, -ca *adj* : graphic — **gráfica** *nf*
: graph — **gráfico** *nm* **1** : graph **2** : graphic
(in computers)
gragea *nf* : pill, tablet
grajo *nm* : rook (bird)
gramática *nf* : grammar — **gramatical** *adj*
: grammatical
gramo *nm* : gram
gran → **grande**
grana *nf* : scarlet
granada *nf* **1** : pomegranate **2** : grenade (in
the military)

granate *nm* : garnet
grande *adj* (**gran** *before singular nouns*) **1**
: large, big **2** ALTO : tall **3** : great (in quality, intensity, etc.) **4** *Lat* : grown-up —
grandeza *nf* **1** : greatness **2** NOBLEZA : nobility — **grandiosidad** *nf* : grandeur —
grandioso, -sa *adj* : grand, magnificent
granel: a ~ *adv phr* **1** : in bulk **2** : in abundance
granero *nm* : barn, granary
granito *nm* : granite
granizar {21} *v impers* : hail — **granizada** *nf*
: hailstorm — **granizado** *nm* : iced drink —
granizo *nm* : hail
granja *nf* : farm — **granjero, -ra** *n* : farmer
grano *nm* **1** : grain **2** SEMILLA : seed **3**
: (coffee) bean **4** BARRO : pimple
granuja *nmf* : rascal
grapa *nf* : staple — **grapadora** *nf* : stapler —
grapar *vt* : staple
grasa *nf* **1** : grease **2** : fat (in cooking, etc.)
— **grasiento, -ta** *adj* : greasy, oily — **graso,**
-sa *adj* : fatty, greasy, oily — **grasoso, -sa**
adj Lat : greasy, oily
gratificar {72} *vt* **1** : give a tip or bonus to **2**
SATISFACER : gratify, satisfy — **gratifi-**
cación *nf, pl* **-ciones 1** : bonus, tip, reward
2 SATISFACCIÓN : gratification
gratis *adv & adj* : free
gratitud *nf* : gratitude
grato, -ta *adj* : pleasant, agreeable
gratuito, -ta *adj* **1** : gratuitous, unwarranted
2 GRATIS : free
grava *nf* : gravel
gravar *vt* **1** : tax **2** CARGAR : burden —
gravamen *nm, pl* **-vámenes 1** : burden,
obligation **2** IMPUESTO : tax
grave *adj* **1** : grave, serious **2** : deep, low
(of a voice, etc.) — **gravedad** *nf* : gravity
gravilla *nf* : gravel
gravitar *vi* **1** : gravitate **2 ~ sobre** : weigh
on — **gravitación** *nf, pl* **-ciones** : gravita-
tion
gravoso, -sa *adj* : costly, burdensome
graznar *vi* : caw, quack, honk — **graznido**
nm : caw, quack, honk
gregario, -ria *adj* : gregarious
gremio *nm* : guild, (trade) union
greñas *nfpl* : shaggy hair, mop
griego, -ga *adj* : Greek — **griego** *nm*
: Greek (language)
grieta *nf* : crack, crevice
grifo *nm Spain* : faucet, tap
grillete *nm* : shackle
grillo *nm* **1** : cricket **2 ~s** *nmpl* : fetters,
shackles
grima *nf* **dar ~** : annoy, irritate
gringo, -ga *adj & n Lat fam* : Yankee, gringo
gripe *nf or* **gripa** *nf Lat* : flu, influenza

gris *adj & nm* : gray
gritar *v* : shout, scream, cry — **grito** *nm* **1** : shout, scream, cry **2 dar ~s** : shout
grosella *nf* : currant
grosería *nf* **1** : vulgar remark **2** DES-CORTESÍA : rudeness — **grosero, -ra** *adj* **1** : coarse, vulgar **2** DESCORTÉS : rude
grosor *nm* : thickness
grotesco, -ca *adj* : grotesque, hideous
grúa *nf* : crane, derrick
grueso, -sa *adj* **1** : thick **2** CORPULENTO : stout, heavy — **gruesa** *nf* : gross — **grueso** *nm* **1** GROSOR : thickness **2** : main body, mass **3 en ~** : wholesale
grulla *nf* : crane (bird)
grumo *nm* : lump, clot — **grumoso, -sa** *adj* : lumpy
gruñir {38} *vi* **1** : growl, grunt **2** *fam* : grumble — **gruñido** *nm* **1** : growl, grunt **2** *fam* : grumble — **gruñón, -ñona** *adj, mpl* **-ñones** *fam* : grumpy, grouchy — **~** *n fam* : grouch
grupa *nf* : rump, hindquarters *pl*
grupo *nm* : group
gruta *nf* : grotto
guacamayo *nm or* **guacamaya** *nf Lat* : macaw
guacamole *nm* : guacamole
guadaña *nf* : scythe
guagua *nf Lat* **1** : baby **2** AUTOBÚS : bus
guajalote, -ta *or* **guajolote, -ta** *n Lat* : turkey
guante *nm* : glove
guapo, -pa *adj* : handsome, good-looking
guaraní *nm* : Guarani (language of Paraguay)
guarda *nmf* **1** : keeper, custodian **2** GUARDIÁN : security guard — **guardabarros** *nms & pl* : fender — **guardabosque** *nmf* : forest ranger — **guardacostas** *nmfs & pl* : coast guard vessel — **guardaespaldas** *nmfs & pl* : bodyguard — **guardameta** *nmf* : goalkeeper — **guardapolvo** *nm* : overalls *pl* — **guardar** *vt* **1** : keep **2** PROTEGER : guard, protect **3** RESERVAR : save — **guardarse** *vr* **~ de 1** : refrain from **2** : guard against — **guardarropa** *nm* **1** : cloakroom, checkroom **2** ARMARIO : wardrobe
guardería *nf* : nursery, day-care center
guardia *nf* **1** : guard, vigilence **2** TURNO : duty, watch — **~** *nmf* **1** : guard **2** *or* **~ municipal** : police officer — **guardián, -diana** *n, mpl* **-dianes 1** : guardian, keeper **2** GUARDA : security guard

guarecer {53} *vt* : shelter, protect — **guarecerse** *vr* : take shelter
guarida *nf* **1** : den, lair (of animals) **2** : hideout (of persons)
guarnecer {53} *vt* **1** : adorn, garnish **2** : garrison (an area) — **guarnición** *nf, pl* **-ciones 1** : garnish, trimming **2** : (military) garrison
guasa *nf fam* **1** : joke **2 de ~** : in jest — **guasón, -sona** *adj, mpl* **-sones** *fam* : joking, witty — **~** *n fam* : joker
guatemalteco, -ca *adj* : Guatemalan
guayaba *nf* : guava
gubernamental *or* **gubernativo, -va** *adj* : governmental
guepardo *nm* : cheetah
güero, -ra *adj Lat* : blond, fair
guerra *nf* **1** : war, warfare **2** LUCHA : conflict, struggle — **guerrear** *vi* : wage war — **guerrero, -ra** *adj* **1** : war, fighting **2** BELI-COSO : warlike — **~** *n* : warrior — **guerrilla** *nf* : guerrilla warfare — **guerrillero, -ra** *adj & n* : guerrilla
gueto *nm* : ghetto
guiar {85} *vt* **1** : guide, lead **2** ACONSEJAR : advise — **guiarse** *vr* : be guided by, go by — **guía** *nf* **1** : guidebook **2** ORIENTACIÓN : guidance — **~** *nmf* : guide, leader
guijarro *nm* : pebble
guillotina *nf* : guillotine
guinda *nf* : morello (cherry)
guiñar *vi* : wink — **guiño** *nm* : wink
guión *nm, pl* **guiones 1** : script, screenplay **2** : hyphen, dash (in punctuation) — **guionista** *nmf* : scriptwriter, screenwriter
guirnalda *nf* : garland
guisa *nf* **1** : manner, fashion **2 a ~ de** : by way of **3 de tal ~** : in such a way
guisado *nm* : stew
guisante *nm* : pea
guisar *vt* : cook — **guiso** *nm* : stew, casserole
guitarra *nf* : guitar — **guitarrista** *nmf* : guitarist
gula *nf* : gluttony
gusano *nm* **1** : worm **2** : maggot (larva)
gustar *vt* **1** : taste **2** *Lat* : like — *vi* **1** : be pleasing **2 como guste** : as you like **3 me gustan los dulces** : I like sweets — **gusto** *nm* **1** : taste **2** PLACER : pleasure, liking **3 a ~** : comfortable, at ease **4 al ~** : to taste **5 mucho ~** : pleased to meet you — **gustoso, -sa** *adj* **1** : tasty **2** AGRADABLE : pleasant **3 hacer algo ~** : do sth willingly
gutural *adj* : guttural

H

h *nf* : h, eighth letter of the Spanish alphabet
haba *nf* : broad bean
habanero, -ra *adj* : Havanan — **habano** *nm* : Havana cigar
haber {39} *v aux* **1** : have, has **2** ~ **de** : must — *v impers* **1 hay** : there is, there are **2 hay que** : it is necessary (to) **3 ¿qué hay?** *or* **¿qué hubo?** : how's it going? — ~ *nm* **1** : assets *pl* **2** : credit side (in accounting) **3** ~**es** *nmpl* : income, earnings
habichuela *nf* **1** : bean **2** ~ **verde** : string bean
hábil *adj* **1** : able, skillful **2** LISTO : clever **3 horas** ~**es** : business hours — **habilidad** *nf* : ability, skill
habilitar *vt* **1** : equip, furnish **2** AUTORIZAR : authorize
habitar *vt* : inhabit — *vi* : reside, dwell — **habitable** *adj* : habitable, inhabitable — **habitación** *nf, pl* -**ciones** **1** : room, bedroom **2** MORADA : dwelling, abode **3** : habitat (in biology) — **habitante** *nmf* : inhabitant, resident — **hábitat** *nm* : habitat
hábito *nm* : habit — **habitual** *adj* : habitual, usual — **habituar** {3} *vt* : accustom, habituate — **habituarse** *vr* ~ **a** : get used to
hablar *vi* **1** : speak, talk **2** ~ **de** : mention, talk about **3** ~ **con** : talk to, speak with — *vt* **1** : speak (a language) **2** DISCUTIR : discuss — **hablarse** *vr* **1** : speak to each other **2 se habla inglés** : English spoken — **habla** *nf* **1** : speech **2** IDIOMA : language, dialect **3 de** ~ **inglesa** : English-speaking — **hablador, -dora** *adj* : talkative — ~ *n* : chatterbox — **habladuría** *nf* **1** : rumor **2** ~**s** *nfpl* : gossip — **hablante** *nmf* : speaker
hacedor, -dora *n* : creator, maker
hacendado, -da *n* : landowner, rancher
hacer {40} *vt* **1** : do, perform **2** CONSTRUIR, CREAR : make **3** OBLIGAR : force, oblige — *vi* : act — *v impers* **1** ~ **calor/viento** : be hot/be windy **2** ~ **falta** : be necessary **3 hace mucho tiempo** : a long time ago **4 no lo hace** : it doesn't matter — **hacerse** *vr* **1** VOLVERSE : become **2** : pretend (to be) **3** ~ **a** : get used to **4 se hace tarde** : it's getting late
hacha *nf* **1** : hatchet, ax **2** ANTORCHA : torch
hachís *nm* : hashish
hacia *prep* **1** : toward, towards **2** CERCA DE : near, around, about **3** ~ **abajo** : downward **4** ~ **adelante** : forward
hacienda *nf* **1** : estate, ranch **2** BIENES : property **3** *Lat* : livestock **4 Hacienda** : department of revenue

hacinar *vt* : stack
hada *nf* : fairy
hado *nm* : fate
halagar {52} *vt* : flatter — **halagador, -dora** *adj* : flattering — **halago** *nm* : flattery — **halagüeño, -ña** *adj* **1** : flattering **2** PROMETEDOR : promising
halcón *nm, pl* -**cones** : hawk, falcon
halibut *nm, pl* -**buts** : halibut
hálito *nm* : breath
hallar *vt* **1** : find **2** DESCUBRIR : discover, find out — **hallarse** *vr* : be, find oneself — **hallazgo** *nm* : discovery, find
halo *nm* : halo
hamaca *nf* : hammock
hambre *nf* **1** : hunger **2** INANICIÓN : starvation, famine **3 tener** ~ : be hungry — **hambriento, -ta** *adj* : hungry, starving — **hambruna** *nf* : famine
hamburguesa *nf* : hamburger
hampa *nf* : underworld — **hampón, -pona** *n, mpl* -**pones** : criminal, thug
hámster *nm* : hamster
hándicap *nm* : handicap (in sports)
hangar *nm* : hangar
haragán, -gana *adj, mpl* -**ganes** : lazy, idle — ~ *n* : slacker, idler — **haraganear** : be lazy, loaf
harapiento, -ta *adj* : ragged, in rags — **harapos** *nmpl* : rags, tatters
harina *nf* : flour
hartar *vt* **1** : glut, satiate **2** FASTIDIAR : annoy — **hartarse** *vr* **1** : gorge oneself **2** CANSARSE : get fed up — **harto, -ta** *adj* **1** : full, satiated **2** CANSADO : tired, fed up — **harto** *adv* : extremely, very — **hartura** *nf* **1** : surfeit **2** ABUNDANCIA : abundance, plenty
hasta *prep* **1** : until, up until (in time) **2** : as far as, up to (in space) **3 ¡**~ **luego!** : see you later! **4** ~ **que** : until — ~ *adv* : even
hastiar {85} *vt* **1** : make weary, bore **2** ASQUEAR : sicken — **hastiarse** *vr* ~ **de** : get tired of — **hastío** *nm* **1** : weariness, tedium **2** REPUGNANCIA : disgust
hato *nm* **1** : flock, herd **2** : bundle (of possessions)
haya *nf* : beech
haz *nm, pl* **haces** **1** : bundle, sheaf **2** : beam (of light)
hazaña *nf* : feat, exploit
hazmerreír *nm fam* : laughingstock
he {39} *v impers* ~ **aquí** : here is, here are, behold

hebilla *nf* : buckle
hebra *nf* : strand, thread
hebreo, -brea *adj* : Hebrew — **hebreo** *nm*
: Hebrew (language)
hecatombe *nm* : disaster
hechizo *nm* **1** : spell **2** ENCANTO : charm,
fascination — **hechicería** *nf* : sorcery,
witchcraft — **hechicero, -ra** *n* : sorcerer,
sorceress *f* — **hechizar** {21} *vt* **1** : bewitch
2 CAUTIVAR : charm
hecho, -cha *adj* **1** : made, done **2** : ready-
to-wear (of clothing) **3** ~ **y derecho** : full-
fledged, mature — **hecho** *nm* **1** : fact **2**
SUCESO : event **3** ACTO : act, deed **4 de** ~
: in fact — **hechura** *nf* **1** : making, creation
2 FORMA : shape, form **3** : build (of the
body) **4** ARTESANÍA : workmanship
heder {56} *vi* : stink, reek — **hediondez** *nf,*
pl **-deces** : stench — **hediondo, -da** *adj*
: stinking — **hedor** *nm* : stench
helar {55} *v* : freeze — **helarse** *vr* : freeze
up, freeze over — **helado, -da** *adj* **1** : freezing cold **2** CONGELADO : frozen — **helada**
nf : frost — **heladería** *nf* : ice-cream parlor
— **helado** *nm* : ice cream — **heladora** *nf*
: freezer
helecho *nm* : fern
hélice *nf* **1** : propeller **2** ESPIRAL : spiral,
helix
helicóptero *nm* : helicopter
helio *nm* : helium
hembra *nf* **1** : female **2** MUJER : woman
hemisferio *nm* : hemisphere
hemorragia *nf* **1** : hemorrhage **2** ~ **nasal**
: nosebleed
hemorroides *nfpl* : hemorrhoids, piles
henchir {54} *vt* : stuff, fill
hender {56} *vt* : cleave, split — **hendidura**
nf : crevice, fissure
henequén *nm, pl* **-quenes** : sisal
heno *nm* : hay
hepatitis *nf* : hepatitis
heraldo *nm* : herald
herbolario, -ria *n* : herbalist
heredar *vt* : inherit — **heredad** *nm* : rural
property, estate — **heredero, -ra** *n* : heir,
heiress *f* — **hereditario, -ria** *adj* : hereditary
hereje *nmf* : heretic — **herejía** *nf* : heresy
herencia *nf* **1** : inheritance **2** : heredity (in
biology)
herir {76} *vt* **1** : injure, wound **2** : hurt (feelings, pride, etc.) — **herida** *nf* : injury, wound
— **herido, -da** *adj* **1** : injured, wounded **2**
: hurt (of feelings, pride, etc.) — ~ *n* : injured person, casualty
hermano, -na *n* : brother *m*, sister *f* — **hermanastro, -tra** *n* : half brother *m*, half sister
f — **hermandad** *nf* : brotherhood
hermético, -ca *adj* : hermetic, watertight

hermoso, -sa *adj* : beautiful, lovely — **her-
mosura** *nf* : beauty
hernia *nf* : hernia
héroe *nm* : hero — **heroico, -ca** *adj* : heroic
— **heroína** *nf* **1** : heroine **2** : heroin (narcotic) — **heroísmo** *nm* : heroism
herradura *nf* : horseshoe
herramienta *nf* : tool
herrero, -ra *n* : blacksmith
herrumbre *nf* : rust
hervir {76} *v* : boil — **hervidero** *nm* **1**
: mass, swarm **2** : hotbed (of intrigue, etc.)
— **hervidor** *nm* : kettle — **hervor** *nm* **1**
: boiling **2** ENTUSIASMO : fervor, ardor
heterogéneo, -nea *adj* : heterogeneous
heterosexual *adj* & *nmf* : heterosexual
hexágono *nm* : hexagon — **hexagonal** *adj*
: hexagonal
hez *nf, pl* **heces** : dregs *pl,* scum
hiato *nm* : hiatus
hibernar *vi* : hibernate — **hibernación** *nf, pl*
-ciones : hibernation
híbrido, -da *adj* : hybrid — **híbrido** *nm* : hybrid
hidalgo, -ga *n* : nobleman *m*, noblewoman *f*
hidratante *adj* : moisturizing
hidrato *nm* ~ **de carbono** : carbohydrate
hidráulico, -ca *adj* : hydraulic
hidroavión *nm, pl* **-aviones** : seaplane
hidroeléctrico, -ca *adj* : hydroelectric
hidrofobia *nf* : rabies
hidrógeno *nm* : hydrogen
hidroplano *nm* : hydroplane
hiedra *nf* **1** : ivy **2** ~ **venenosa** : poison ivy
hiel *nm* **1** : bile **2** AMARGURA : bitterness
hielo *nm* **1** : ice **2** FRIALDAD : coldness **3**
romper el ~ : break the ice
hiena *nf* : hyena
hierba *nf* **1** : herb **2** CÉSPED : grass **3 mala**
~ : weed — **hierbabuena** *nf* : mint
hierro *nm* **1** : iron **2** ~ **fundido** : cast iron
hígado *nm* : liver
higiene *nf* : hygiene — **higiénico, -ca** *adj*
: hygienic
higo *nm* : fig
hijo, -ja *n* **1** : son *m*, daughter *f* **2 hijos** *nmpl*
: children, offspring — **hijastro, -tra** *n*
: stepson *m*, stepdaughter *f*
hilar *v* **1** : spin **2** ~ **delgado** : split hairs —
hilado *nm* : yarn, thread
hilaridad *nf* : hilarity
hilera *nf* : file, row
hilo *nm* **1** : thread **2** LINO : linen **3** ALAM-
BRE : wire **4** : trickle (of water, etc.) **5** ~
dental : dental floss
hilvanar *vt* **1** : baste, tack **2** : put together
(ideas, etc.)
himno *nm* **1** : hymn **2** ~ **nacional** : national anthem

hincapié

hincapié *nm* **hacer ∼ en** : emphasize, stress
hincar {72} *vt* : drive in, plunge — **hincarse**
vr **∼ de rodillas** : kneel (down)
hinchar *vt Spain* : inflate, blow up — **hincharse** *vr* **1** : swell (up) **2** *Spain fam* : stuff
oneself — **hinchado, -da** *adj* **1** : swollen **2**
POMPOSO : pompous — **hinchazón** *nf, pl*
-zones : swelling
hindú *adj & nmf* : Hindu — **hinduismo** *nm*
: Hinduism
hinojo *nm* : fennel
hiperactivo, -va *adj* : hyperactive
hipersensible *adj* : oversensitive
hipertensión *nf, pl* **-siones** : hypertension,
high blood pressure
hípico, -ca *adj* : equestrian, horse
hipil → **huipil**
hipnosis *nfs & pl* : hypnosis — **hipnótico,
-ca** *adj* : hypnotic — **hipnotismo** *nm* : hypnotism — **hipnotizador, -dora** *n* : hypnotist
— **hipnotizar** {21} *vt* : hypnotize
hipo *nm* **1** : hiccup, hiccups *pl* **2 tener ∼**
: have hiccups
hipocondríaco, -ca *adj* : hypochondriacal
— **∼** *n* : hypochondriac
hipocresía *nf* : hypocrisy — **hipócrita** *adj*
: hypocritical — **∼** *nmf* : hypocrite
hipodérmico, -ca *adj* : hypodermic
hipódromo *nm* : racetrack
hipopótamo *nm* : hippopotamus
hipoteca *nf* : mortgage — **hipotecar** {72} *vt*
: mortgage
hipótesis *nfs & pl* : hypothesis — **hipotético, -ca** *adj* : hypothetical
hiriente *adj* : hurtful, offensive
hirsuto, -ta *adj* **1** : hairy **2** : bristly, wiry (of
hair)
hirviente *adj* : boiling
hispano, -na *or* **hispánico, -ca** *adj & adj*
: Hispanic — **hispanoamericano, -na** *adj*
: Latin-American — **∼** *n* : Latin American
— **hispanohablante** *or* **hispanoparlante**
adj : Spanish-speaking
histeria *nf* : hysteria — **histérico, -ca** *adj*
: hysterical — **histerismo** *nm* : hysteria
historia *nf* **1** : history **2** CUENTO : story —
historiador, -dora *n* : historian — **historial**
nm : record, background — **histórico, -ca**
adj **1** : historical **2** IMPORTANTE : historic,
important — **historieta** *nf* : comic strip
hito *nm* : milestone, landmark
hocico *nm* : snout, muzzle
hockey *nm* : hockey
hogar *nm* **1** : home **2** CHIMENEA : hearth,
fireplace — **hogareño, -ña** *adj* **1** : homeloving **2** DOMÉSTICO : home, domestic
hoguera *nf* : bonfire
hoja *nf* **1** : leaf **2** : sheet (of paper) **3 ∼ de
afeitar** : razor blade — **hojalata** *nf* : tinplate

84

— **hojaldre** *nm* : puff pastry — **hojear** *vt*
: leaf through — **hojuela** *nf Lat* : flake
hola *interj* : hello!, hi!
holandés, -desa *adj, mpl* **-deses** : Dutch
holgado, -da *adj* **1** : loose, baggy **2** : comfortable (of an economic situation, a victory, etc.) — **holgazán, -zana** *adj, mpl*
-zanes : lazy — **∼** *n* : slacker, idler — **holgazanear** *vi* : laze about, loaf — **holgura** *nf*
1 : looseness **2** BIENESTAR : comfort, ease
hollín *nm, pl* **-llines** : soot
holocausto *nm* : holocaust
hombre *nm* **1** : man **2 el ∼** : mankind **3
∼ de estado** : statesman **4 ∼ de negocios** : businessman
hombrera *nf* **1** : shoulder pad **2** : epaulet
(of a uniform)
hombría *nf* : manliness
hombro *nm* : shoulder
hombruno, -na *adj* : mannish
homenaje *nm* **1** : homage **2 rendir ∼ a**
: pay tribute to
homeopatía *nf* : homeopathy
homicidio *nm* : homicide, murder — **homicida** *adj* : homicidal, murderous — **∼** *nmf*
: murderer
homogéneo, -nea *adj* : homogeneous
homólogo, -ga *adj* : equivalent — **∼** *n*
: counterpart
homosexual *adj & nmf* : homosexual — **homosexualidad** *nf* : homosexuality
hondo, -da *adj* : deep — **hondo** *adv* : deeply
— **hondonada** *nf* : hollow — **hondura** *nf*
: depth
hondureño, -ña *adj* : Honduran
honesto, -ta *adj* : decent, honorable — **honestidad** *nf* : honesty, integrity
hongo *nm* **1** : mushroom **2** : fungus (in
botany and medicine)
honor *nm* : honor — **honorable** *adj* : honorable — **honorario, -ria** *adj* : honorary —
honorarios *nmpl* : payment, fee — **honra** *nf*
: honor — **honradez** *nf, pl* **-deces** : honesty,
integrity — **honrado, -da** *adj* : honest, upright — **honrar** *vt* : honor — **honrarse** *vr* : be
honored — **honroso, -sa** *adj* : honorable
hora *nf* **1** : hour **2** : (specific) time **3** CITA
: appointment **4 a la última ∼** : at the last
minute **5 ∼ punta** : rush hour **6 media ∼**
: half an hour **7 ¿qué ∼ es?** : what time is
it? **8 ∼s de oficina** : office hours **9 ∼s
extraordinarias** : overtime
horario *nm* : schedule, timetable
horca *nf* **1** : gallows *pl* **2** : pitchfork (in
agriculture)
horcajadas: a ∼ *adv phr* : astride
horda *nf* : horde
horizonte *nm* : horizon — **horizontal** *adj*
: horizontal

horma *nf* **1** : form, mold, last **2** : shoe tree
hormiga *nf* : ant
hormigón *nm, pl* **-gones** : concrete
hormigueo *nm* : tingling, pins and needles
hormiguero *nm* **1** : anthill **2** : swarm (of people)
hormona *nf* : hormone
horno *nm* **1** : oven (for cooking) **2** : small furnace, kiln — **hornada** *nf* : batch — **hornear** *vt* : bake — **hornillo** *nf* : portable stove
horóscopo *nm* : horoscope
horquilla *nf* **1** : hairpin, bobby pin **2** HORCA : pitchfork
horrendo, -da *adj* : horrendous, awful — **horrible** *adj* : horrible — **horripilante** *adj* : horrifying — **horror** *nm* **1** : horror, dread **2** ATROCIDAD : atrocity — **horrorizar** {21} *vt* : horrify, terrify — **horrorizarse** *vr* : be horrified — **horroroso, -sa** *adj* : horrifying, dreadful
hortaliza *nf* : (garden) vegetable — **hortelano, -na** *n* : truck farmer — **horticultura** *nf* : horticulture
hosco, -ca *adj* : sullen, gloomy
hospedar *vt* : put up, lodge — **hospedarse** *vr* : stay, lodge — **hospedaje** *nm* : lodging
hospital *nm* : hospital — **hospitalario, -ria** *adj* : hospitable — **hospitalidad** *nf* : hospitality — **hospitalizar** {21} *vt* : hospitalize
hostería *nf* : small hotel, inn
hostia *nf* : host (in religion)
hostigar {52} *vt* **1** : whip **2** ACOSAR : harass, pester
hostil *adj* : hostile — **hostilidad** *nf* : hostility
hotel *nm* : hotel — **hotelero, -ra** *adj* : hotel — ~ *n* : hotel manager, hotelier
hoy *adv* **1** : today **2 de ~ en adelante** : from now on **3 ~ (en) día** : nowadays **4 ~ mismo** : this very day
hoyo *nm* : hole — **hoyuelo** *nm* : dimple
hoz *nf, pl* **hoces** : sickle
huarache *nm* : huarache (sandal)
hueco, -ca *adj* **1** : hollow, empty **2** ESPONJOSO : soft, spongy **3** RESONANTE : resonant — **hueco** *nm* **1** : hollow, cavity **2** : recess (in a wall, etc.) **3 ~ de escalera** : stairwell
huelga *nf* **1** : strike **2 declararse en ~** : go on strike — **huelguista** *nmf* : striker
huella *nf* **1** : footprint **2** VESTIGIO : track, mark **3 ~ digital** *or* **~ dactilar** : fingerprint
huérfano, -na *n* : orphan — ~ *adj* : orphaned
huerta *nf* : truck farm — **huerto** *nm* **1** : vegetable garden **2** : (fruit) orchard
hueso *nm* **1** : bone **2** : pit, stone (of a fruit)

huésped, -peda *n* : guest — **huésped** *nm* : host (organism)
huesudo, -da *adj* : bony
huevo *nm* **1** : egg **2 ~s estrellados** : fried eggs **3 ~s revueltos** : scrambled eggs — **hueva** *nf* : roe
huida *nf* : flight, escape — **huidizo, -za** *adj* **1** : shy **2** FUGAZ : fleeting
huipil *nm* *Lat* : traditional embroidered blouse or dress
huir {41} *vi* **1** : escape, flee **2 ~ de** : shun, avoid
hule *nm* **1** : oilcloth **2** *Lat* : rubber
humano, -na *adj* **1** : human **2** COMPASIVO : humane — **humano** *nm* : human (being) — **humanidad** *nf* **1** : humanity, mankind **2** BENEVOLENCIA : humaneness **3 ~es** *nfpl* : humanities — **humanismo** *nm* : humanism — **humanista** *nmf* : humanist — **humanitario, -ria** *adj & n* : humanitarian
humear *vi* : smoke, steam — **humareda** *nf* : cloud of smoke
humedad *nf* **1** : dampness **2** : humidity (in meteorology) — **humedecer** {53} *vt* : moisten, dampen — **humedecerse** *vr* : become moist — **húmedo, -da** *adj* **1** : moist, damp **2** : humid (in meteorology)
humildad *nf* : humility — **humilde** *adj* : humble — **humillación** *nf, pl* **-ciones** : humiliation — **humillante** *adj* : humiliating — **humillar** *vt* : humiliate — **humillarse** *vr* : humble oneself
humo *nm* **1** : smoke, steam, fumes **2 ~s** *nmpl* : airs, conceit
humor *nm* **1** : mood, temper **2** GRACIA : humor **3 de buen ~** : in a good mood — **humorismo** *nm* : humor, wit — **humorista** *nmf* : humorist, comedian — **humorístico, -ca** *adj* : humorous
hundir *vt* **1** : sink **2** : destroy, ruin (a building, plans, etc.) — **hundirse** *vr* **1** : sink **2** DERRUMBARSE : collapse — **hundido, -da** *adj* : sunken — **hundimiento** *nm* **1** : sinking **2** DERRUMBE : collapse
húngaro, -ra *adj* : Hungarian
huracán *nm, pl* **-canes** : hurricane
huraño, -ña *adj* : unsociable
hurgar {52} *vi* **~ en** : rummage around in
hurón *nm, pl* **-rones** : ferret
hurra *interj* : hurrah!, hooray!
hurtadillas: a ~ *adv phr* : stealthily, on the sly
hurtar *vt* : steal — **hurto** *nm* **1** ROBO : theft **2** : stolen property
husmear *vt* : sniff out, pry into — *vi* : nose around
huy *interj* : ow!, ouch!

I

i *nf* : i, ninth letter of the Spanish alphabet
ibérico, -ca *adj* : Iberian — **ibero, -ra** *or*
  íbero, -ra *adj* : Iberian
iceberg *nm, pl* **-bergs** : iceberg
icono *nm* : icon
ictericia *nf* : jaundice
ida *nf* **1** : outward journey **2** ~ **y vuelta**
  : round-trip **3** ~**s y venidas** : comings and
  goings
idea *nf* **1** : idea **2** OPINIÓN : opinion
ideal *adj & nm* : ideal — **idealismo** *nm* : ide-
  alism — **idealista** *adj* : idealistic — ~ *nmf*
  : idealist — **idealizar** {21} *vt* : idealize
idear *vt* : devise, think up
ídem *nm* : the same, ditto
identidad *nf* : identity — **idéntico, -ca** *adj*
  : identical — **identificar** {72} *vt* : identify
  — **identificarse** *vr* **1** : identify oneself **2**
  ~ **con** : identify with — **identificación** *nf,*
  pl **-ciones** : identification
ideología *nf* : ideology — **ideológico, -ca**
  adj : ideological
idílico, -ca *adj* : idyllic
idioma *nm* : language — **idiomático, -ca** *adj*
  : idiomatic
idiosincrasia *nf* : idiosyncrasy — **idiosin-**
  crásico, -ca *adj* : idiosyncratic
idiota *adj* : idiotic — ~ *nmf* : idiot — **id-**
  iotez *nf* : idiocy
ídolo *nm* : idol — **idolatrar** *vt* : idolize —
  idolatría *nf* : idolatry
idóneo, -nea *adj* : suitable, fitting — **idonei-**
  dad *nf* : fitness, suitability
iglesia *nf* : church
iglú *nm* : igloo
ignición *nf, pl* **-ciones** : ignition
ignífugo, -ga *adj* : fire-resistant, fireproof
ignorar *vt* **1** : ignore **2** DESCONOCER : be
  unaware of — **ignorancia** *nf* : ignorance —
  ignorante *adj* : ignorant — ~ *nmf* : ignorant person
igual *adv* **1** : in the same way **2 por** ~
  : equally — ~ *adj* **1** : equal **2** IDÉNTICO
  : the same **3** LISO : smooth, even **4** SEME-
  JANTE : similar — ~ *nmf* : equal, peer —
  igualar *vt* **1** : make equal **2** : be equal to **3**
  NIVELAR : level (off) — **igualdad** *nf* **1**
  : equality **2** UNIFORMIDAD : uniformity —
  igualmente *adv* : likewise
iguana *nf* : iguana
ijada *nf* : flank
ilegal *adj* : illegal
ilegible *adj* : illegible

ilegítimo, -ma *adj* : illegitimate — **ilegitimi-**
  dad *nf* : illegitimacy
ileso, -sa *adj* : unharmed
ilícito, -ta *adj* : illicit
ilimitado, -da *adj* : unlimited
ilógico, -ca *adj* : illogical
iluminar *vt* : illuminate — **iluminarse** *vr*
  : light up — **iluminación** *nf, pl* **-ciones 1**
  : illumination **2** ALUMBRADO : lighting
ilusionar *vt* : excite — **ilusionarse** *vr* : get
  one's hopes up — **ilusión** *nf, pl* **-siones 1**
  : illusion **2** ESPERANZA : hope — **ilusion-**
  ado, -da *adj* : excited
iluso -sa *adj* : naïve, gullible — ~ *n*
  : dreamer, visionary — **ilusorio, -ria** *adj*
  : illusory
ilustrar *vt* **1** : illustrate **2** ACLARAR : explain
  — **ilustración** *nf, pl* **-ciones 1** : illustration
  2 SABER : learning **3 la Ilustración** : the
  Enlightenment — **ilustrado, -da** *adj* **1** : il-
  lustrated **2** ERUDITO : learned —
  ilustrador, -dora *n* : illustrator
ilustre *adj* : illustrious
imagen *nf, pl* **imágenes** : image, picture
imaginar *vt* : imagine — **imaginarse** *vr*
  : imagine — **imaginación** *nf, pl* **-ciones**
  : imagination — **imaginario, -ria** *adj*
  : imaginary — **imaginativo, -va** *adj* : imaginative
imán *nm, pl* **imanes** : magnet — **imantar** *vt*
  : magnetize
imbécil *adj* : stupid, idiotic — ~ *nmf* : idiot
imborrable *adj* : indelible
imbuir {41} *vt* ~ **de** : imbue with
imitar *vt* **1** COPIAR : imitate, copy **2** : impersonate — **imitación** *nf, pl* **-ciones 1** COPIA
  : imitation, copy **2** : impersonation — **imi-**
  tador, -dora *n* : impersonator
impaciencia *nf* : impatience — **impacientar**
  vt : make impatient, exasperate —**impa-**
  cientarse *vr* : grow impatient — **impa-**
  ciente *adj* : impatient
impacto *nm* : impact
impar *adj* : odd — ~ *nm* : odd number
imparcial *adj* : impartial — **imparcialidad**
  nf : impartiality
impartir *vt* : impart, give
impasible *adj* : impassive
impasse *nm* : impasse
impávido, -da *adj* : fearless
impecable *adj* : impeccable, spotless
impedir {54} *vt* **1** : prevent **2** DIFICULTAR
  : impede, hinder — **impedido, -da** *adj* : dis-

abled — **impedimento** *nm* : obstacle, impediment
impeler *vt* : drive, propel
impenetrable *adj* : impenetrable
impenitente *adj* : unrepentant
impensable *adj* : unthinkable — **impensado, -da** *adj* : unexpected
imperar *vi* 1 : reign, rule 2 PREDOMINAR : prevail — **imperante** *adj* : prevailing
imperativo, -va *adj* : imperative — **Imperativo** *nm* : imperative
imperceptible *adj* : imperceptible
imperdible *nm* : safety pin
imperdonable *adj* : unforgivable
imperfección *nf, pl* **-ciones** : imperfection — **imperfecto, -ta** *adj* : imperfect — **imperfecto** *nm* : imperfect (tense)
imperial *adj* : imperial — **imperialismo** *nm* : imperialism — **imperialista** *adj & nmf* : imperialist
impericia *nf* : lack of skill
imperio *nm* 1 : empire 2 DOMINIO : rule — **imperioso, -sa** *adj* 1 : imperious 2 URGENTE : pressing, urgent
impermeable *adj* 1 : waterproof 2 ~ a : impervious to — ~ *nm* : raincoat
impersonal *adj* : impersonal
impertinente *adj* : impertinent — **impertinencia** *nf* : impertinence
ímpetu *nm* 1 : impetus 2 ENERGÍA : energy, vigor 3 VIOLENCIA : force — **impetuoso, -sa** *adj* : impetuous — **impetuosidad** *nf* : impetuosity
impío, -pía *adj* : impious, ungodly
implacable *adj* : implacable
implantar *vt* 1 : implant 2 ESTABLECER : establish, introduce
implemento *nm Lat* : implement, tool
implicar {72} *vt* 1 : involve, implicate 2 SIGNIFICAR : imply — **implicación** *nf, pl* **-ciones** : implication
implícito, -ta *adj* : implicit
implorar *vt* : implore
imponer {60} *vt* 1 : impose 2 : command (respect, etc.) — *vi* : be imposing — **imponerse** *vr* 1 : assert oneself, command respect 2 PREVALECER : prevail — **imponente** *adj* : imposing, impressive — **imponible** *adj* : taxable
impopular *adj* : unpopular — **impopularidad** *nf* : unpopularity
importación *nf, pl* **-ciones** 1 : importation 2 **importaciones** *nfpl* : imports — **importado, -da** *adj* : imported — **importador, -dora** *adj* : importing — ~ *n* : importer
importancia *nf* : importance — **importante** *adj* : important — **importar** *vi* 1 : matter, be important 2 **no me importa** : I don't care

— *vt* 1 : import 2 ASCENDER A : amount to, cost
importe *nm* 1 : price 2 CANTIDAD : sum, amount
importunar *vt* : bother — **importuno, -na** *adj* 1 : inopportune 2 MOLESTO : bothersome
imposible *adj* : impossible — **imposibilidad** *nf* : impossibility
imposición *nf, pl* **-ciones** 1 : imposition 2 IMPUESTO : tax
impostor, -tora *n* : impostor
impotente *adj* : powerless, impotent — **impotencia** *nf* : impotence
impracticable *adj* 1 : impracticable 2 INTRANSITABLE : impassable
impreciso, -sa *adj* : vague, imprecise — **imprecisión** *nf, pl* **-siones** 1 : vagueness 2 ERROR : inaccuracy
impredecible *adj* : unpredictable
impregnar *vt* : impregnate
imprenta *nf* 1 : printing 2 : printing shop, press
imprescindible *adj* : essential, indispensable
impresión *nf, pl* **-siones** 1 : impression 2 IMPRENTA : printing — **impresionable** *adj* : impressionable — **impresionante** *adj* : impressive — **impresionar** *vt* 1 : impress 2 CONMOVER : affect, move — *vi* : make an impression — **impresionarse** *vr* 1 : be impressed 2 CONMOVERSE : be affected
impreso, -sa *adj* : printed — **impreso** *nm* 1 FORMULARIO : form 2 **~s** *nmpl* : printed matter — **impresor, -sora** *n* : printer — **impresora** *nf* : (computer) printer
imprevisible *adj* : unforeseeable — **imprevisto, -ta** *adj* : unexpected, unforeseen
imprimir {42} *vt* 1 : print 2 DAR : impart, give
improbable *adj* : improbable — **improbabilidad** *nf* : improbability
improcedente *adj* : inappropriate
improductivo, -va *adj* : unproductive
improperio *nm* : insult
impropio, -pia *adj* 1 : inappropriate 2 INCORRECTO : incorrect
improvisar *v* : improvise — **improvisado, -da** *adj* : improvised, impromptu — **improvisación** *nf, pl* **-ciones** : improvisation — **improviso: de ~** *adv phr* : suddenly
imprudente *adj* : imprudent, rash — **imprudencia** *nf* : imprudence, carelessness
impúdico, -ca *adj* : shameless, indecent
impuesto *nm* 1 : tax 2 **~ sobre la renta** : income tax
impugnar *vt* : challenge, contest
impulsar *vt* : propel, drive — **impulsividad**

nf : impulsiveness — **impulsivo, -va** *adj* : impulsive — **impulso** *nm* **1** : drive, thrust **2** MOTIVACIÓN : impulse
impune *adj* : unpunished — **impunidad** *nf* : impunity
impuro, -ra *adj* : impure — **impureza** *nf* : impurity
imputar *vt* : impute, attribute
inacabable *adj* : interminable, endless
inaccesible *adj* : inaccessible
inaceptable *adj* : unacceptable
inactivo, -va *adj* : inactive — **inactividad** *nf* : inactivity
inadaptado, -da *adj* : maladjusted — ～ *n* : misfit
inadecuado, -da *adj* **1** : inadequate **2** INAPROPIADO : inappropriate
inadmisible *adj* : inadmissible
inadvertido, -da *adj* **1** : unnoticed **2** DISTRAÍDO : distracted — **inadvertencia** *nf* : oversight
inagotable *adj* : inexhaustible
inaguantable *adj* : unbearable
inalámbrico, -ca *adj* : wireless, cordless
inalcanzable *adj* : unreachable, unattainable
inalterable *adj* **1** : unchangeable **2** : impassive (of character) **3** : fast (of colors)
inanición *nf, pl* **-ciones** : starvation, famine
inanimado, -da *adj* : inanimate
inaplicable *adj* : inapplicable
inapreciable *adj* : imperceptible
inapropiado, -da *adj* : inappropriate
inarticulado, -da *adj* : inarticulate
inasequible *adj* : unattainable
inaudito, -ta *adj* : unheard-of, unprecedented
inaugurar *vt* : inaugurate — **inauguración** *nf, pl* **-ciones** : inauguration — **inaugural** *adj* : inaugural
inca *adj* : Inca, Incan
incalculable *adj* : incalculable
incandescencia *nf* : incandescence — **incandescente** *adj* : incandescent
incansable *adj* : tireless
incapacitar *vt* : incapacitate, disable — **incapacidad** *nf* : incapacity, inability — **incapaz** *adj, pl* **-paces** : incapable
incautar *vt* : confiscate, seize
incendiar *vt* : set fire to, burn (down) — **incendiarse** *vr* : catch fire — **incendiario, -ria** *adj* : incendiary — ～ *n* : arsonist — **incendio** *nm* **1** : fire **2** ～ **premeditado** : arson
incentivo *nm* : incentive
incertidumbre *nf* : uncertainty
incesante *adj* : incessant
incesto *nm* : incest — **incestuoso, -sa** *adj* : incestuous
incidencia *nf* **1** : impact **2** SUCESO : inci-

dent — **incidental** *adj* : incidental — **incidente** *nm* : incident
incidir *vi* ～ **en 1** : fall into (a habit, mistake, etc.) **2** INFLUIR EN : affect, influence
incienso *nm* : incense
incierto, -ta *adj* : uncertain
incinerar *vt* **1** : incinerate **2** : cremate (a corpse) — **incineración** *nf, pl* **-ciones 1** : incineration **2** : cremation (of a corpse) — **incinerador** *nm* : incinerator
incipiente *adj* : incipient
incisión *nf, pl* **-siones** : incision
incisivo, -va *adj* : incisive — **incisivo** *nm* : incisor
incitar *vt* : incite, rouse
incivilizado, -da *adj* : uncivilized
inclinar *vt* : tilt, lean — **inclinarse** *vr* **1** : lean (over) **2** ～ **a** : be inclined to — **inclinación** *nf, pl* **-ciones 1** : inclination **2** LADEAR : incline, tilt
incluir {41} *vt* **1** : include **2** ADJUNTAR : enclose — **inclusión** *nf, pl* **-siones** : inclusion — **inclusive** *adv* : up to and including — **inclusivo, -va** *adj* : inclusive — **incluso** *adv* : even, in fact — **incluso, -sa** *adj* : enclosed
incógnito, -ta *adj* **1** : unknown **2 de** ～ : incognito
incoherente *adj* : incoherent — **incoherencia** *nf* : incoherence
incoloro, -ra *adj* : colorless
incombustible *adj* : fireproof
incomible *adj* : inedible
incomodar *vt* **1** : inconvenience **2** ENFADAR : bother, annoy — **incomodarse** *vr* **1** : take the trouble **2** ENFADARSE : get annoyed — **incomodidad** *nf* : discomfort — **incómodo, -da** *adj* **1** : uncomfortable **2** INCONVENIENTE : inconvenient, awkward
incomparable *adj* : incomparable
incompatible *adj* : incompatible — **incompatibilidad** *nf* : incompatibility
incompetente *adj* : incompetent — **incompetencia** *nf* : incompetence
incompleto, -ta *adj* : incomplete
incomprendido, -da *adj* : misunderstood — **incomprensible** *adj* : incomprehensible — **incomprensión** *nf, pl* **-siones** : lack of understanding
incomunicado, -da *adj* **1** : isolated **2** : in solitary confinement
inconcebible *adj* : inconceivable
inconcluso, -sa *adj* : unfinished
incondicional *adj* : unconditional
inconformista *adj & nmf* : nonconformist
inconfundible *adj* : unmistakable
incongruente *adj* : incongruous
inconmensurable *adj* : vast, immeasurable
inconsciente *adj* **1** : unconscious, unaware **2** IRREFLEXIVO : reckless — ～ *nm* **el** ～

: the unconscious — **inconsciencia** *nf* 1
: unconsciousness 2 INSENSATEZ : thoughtlessness
inconsecuente *adj* : inconsistent — **inconsecuencia** *nf* : inconsistency
inconsiderado, -da *adj* : inconsiderate
inconsistente *adj* 1 : flimsy 2 : watery (of
a sauce, etc.) 3 : inconsistent (of an argument) — **inconsistenoia** *nf* : inconsistency
inconsolable *adj* : inconsolable
inconstante *adj* : changeable, unreliable —
inconstancia *nf* : inconstancy
inconstitucional *adj* : unconstitutional
incontable *adj* : countless
incontenible *adj* : irrepressible
incontestable *adj* : indisputable
incontinente *adj* : incontinent — **inconti-
nencia** *nf* : incontinence
inconveniente *adj* 1 : inconvenient 2 IN-
APROPIADO : inappropriate — ~ *nm* : obstacle, problem — **inconveniencia** *nf* 1 : inconvenience 2 : tactless remark
Incorporar *vt* 1 AGREGAR : incorporate, add
2 : mix (in cooking) — **incorporarse** *vr* 1
: sit up 2 ~ **a** : join — **incorporación** *nf,
pl* **-ciones** : incorporation
incorrecto, -ta *adj* 1 : incorrect 2 DES-
CORTÉS : impolite
incorregible *adj* : incorrigible
incrédulo, -la *adj* : incredulous — **incredulidad** *nf* : incredulity, disbelief
increíble *adj* : incredible, unbelievable
incrementar *vt* : increase — **incremento** *nm*
: increase
incriminar *vt* 1 : incriminate 2 ACUSAR : accuse
incrustar *vt* : set, inlay — **incrustarse** *vr*
: become embedded
incubar *vt* : incubate — **incubadora** *nf* : incubator
incuestionable *adj* : unquestionable
inculcar {72} *vt* : instill
inculpar *vt* : accuse, charge
inculto, -ta *adj* 1 : uneducated 2 : uncultivated (of land)
incumplimiento *nm* 1 : noncompliance 2
~ **de contrato** : breach of contract
incurable *adj* : incurable
incurrir *vi* ~ **en** 1 : incur (expenses, etc.) 2
: fall into, commit (crimes)
incursión *nf, pl* **-siones** : raid
indagar {52} *vt* : investigate — **indagación**
nf, pl **-ciones** : investigation
indebido, -da *adj* : undue
indecente *adj* : indecent, obscene — **indecencia** *nf* : indecency, obscenity
indecible *adj* : inexpressible
indecisión *nf, pl* **-siones** : indecision — **in-**

deciso, -sa *adj* 1 : undecided 2 IRRESO-
LUTO : indecisive
indefenso, -sa *adj* : defenseless, helpless
indefinido, -da *adj* : indefinite — **indefinidamente** *adv* : indefinitely
indeleble *adj* : indelible
indemnizar {21} *vt* : indemnify, compensate
— **indemnización** *nf, pl* **-ciones** : compensation
Independiente *adj* : independent — **independencia** *nf* : independence — **indepen-
dizarse** {21} *vr* : become independent
indescifrable *adj* : indecipherable
indescriptible *adj* : indescribable
indeseable *adj* : undesirable
indestructible *adj* : indestructible
indeterminado, -da *adj* : indeterminate
indicar {72} *vt* 1 : indicate 2 MOSTRAR
: show — **indicación** *nf, pl* **-ciones** 1
: sign, indication 2 **indicaciones** *nfpl* : directions — **indicador** *nm* 1 : sign, signal 2
: gauge, dial, meter — **indicativo, -va** *adj*
: indicative — **indicativo** *nm* : indicative
(mood)
índice *nm* 1 : indication 2 : index (of a
book, etc.) 3 : index finger 4 ~ **de natalidad** : birth rate
indicio *nm* : indication, sign
indiferente *adj* 1 : indifferent 2 **me es** ~
: it doesn't matter to me — **indiferencia** *nf*
: indifference
indígena *adj* : indigenous, native — ~ *nmf*
: native
indigente *adj & nmf* : indigent — **indigen-
cia** *nf* : poverty
indigestión *nf, pl* **-tiones** : indigestion —
indigesto, -ta *adj* : indigestible
indignar *vt* : outrage, infuriate — **indig-
narse** *vr* : become indignant — **indignación** *nf, pl* **-ciones** : indignation — **indignado, -da** *adj* : indignant — **indignidad**
nf : indignity — **indigno, -na** *adj* : unworthy
indio, -dia *adj* 1 : American Indian 2 : Indian (from India)
indirecta *nf* 1 : hint 2 **lanzar una** ~ : drop
a hint — **indirecto, -ta** *adj* : indirect
indisciplina *nf* : lack of discipline — **indisciplinado, -da** *adj* : undisciplined
indiscreto, -ta *adj* : indiscreet — **indiscreción** *nf, pl* **-ciones** 1 : indiscretion 2 : tactless remark
indiscriminado, -da *adj* : indiscriminate
indiscutible *adj* : indisputable
indispensable *adj* : indispensable
indisponer {60} *vt* 1 : upset, make ill 2 EN-
EMISTAR : set against, set at odds — **in-
disponerse** *vr* 1 : become ill 2 ~ **con**
: fall out with — **indisposición** *nf, pl*

-ciones : indisposition, illness — **indispuesto, -ta** adj : unwell, indisposed
indistinto, -ta adj : indistinct
individual adj : individual — **individualidad** nf : individuality — **individualizar** {21} vt : individualize — **individuo** nm : individual
indivisible adj : indivisible
índole nf 1 : nature, character 2 TIPO : type, kind
indolente adj : indolent, lazy — **indolencia** nf : indolence, laziness
indoloro, -ra adj : painless
indómito, -ta adj : indomitable
indonesio, -sia adj : Indonesian
inducir {61} vt 1 : induce 2 DEDUCIR : infer
indudable adj : beyond doubt — **indudablemente** adv : undoubtedly
indulgente adj : indulgent — **indulgencia** nf : indulgence
indultar vt : pardon, reprieve — **indulto** nm : pardon, reprieve
industria nf : industry — **industrial** adj : industrial — ~ nmf : industrialist, manufacturer — **industrialización** nf, pl **-ciones** : industrialization — **industrializar** {21} vt : industrialize — **industrioso, -sa** adj : industrious
inédito, -ta adj : unpublished
inefable adj : inexpressible
ineficaz adj, pl **-caces** 1 : ineffective 2 INEFICIENTE : inefficient
ineficiente adj : inefficient — **ineficiencia** nf : inefficiency
inelegible adj : ineligible
ineludible adj : unavoidable, inescapable
inepto, -ta adj : inept — **ineptitud** nf : ineptitude
inequívoco, -ca adj : unequivocal
inercia nf : inertia
inerme adj : unarmed, defenseless
inerte adj : inert
inesperado, -da adj : unexpected
inestable adj : unstable — **inestabilidad** nf : instability
inevitable adj : inevitable
inexacto, -ta adj 1 : inexact 2 INCORRECTO : incorrect, wrong
inexistente adj : nonexistent
inexorable adj : inexorable
inexperiencia nf : inexperience — **inexperto, -ta** adj : inexperienced, unskilled
inexplicable adj : inexplicable
infalible adj : infallible
infame adj 1 : infamous, vile 2 fam : horrible — **infamia** nf : infamy, disgrace
infancia nf : infancy — **infanta** nf : infanta, princess — **infante** nm 1 : infante, prince 2 : infantryman (in the military) — **infantería**

nf : infantry — **infantil** adj 1 : child's, children's 2 INMADURO : childish
infarto nm : heart attack
infatigable adj : tireless
infectar vt : infect — **infectarse** vr : become infected — **infección** nf, pl **-ciones** : infection — **infeccioso, -sa** adj : infectious — **infecto, -ta** adj 1 : infected 2 : foul, sickening
infecundo, -da adj : infertile
infeliz adj, pl **-lices** : unhappy — **infelicidad** nf : unhappiness
inferior adj & nmf : inferior — **inferioridad** nf : inferiority
inferir {76} vt 1 DEDUCIR : infer 2 : cause (harm or injury)
infernal adj : infernal, hellish
infestar vt : infest
infiel adj : unfaithful — **infidelidad** nf : infidelity
infierno nm 1 : hell 2 **el quinto** ~ fam : the middle of nowhere
infiltrar vt : infiltrate — **infiltrarse** vr : infiltrate
infinidad nf 1 : infinity 2 **una** ~ **de** : countless — **infinitivo** nm : infinitive — **infinito, -ta** adj : infinite — **infinito** nm : infinity
inflación nf, pl **-ciones** : inflation — **inflacionario, -ria** or **inflacionista** adj : inflationary
inflamar vt : inflame — **inflamable** adj : flammable, inflammable — **inflamación** nf, pl **-ciones** : inflammation — **inflamatorio, -ria** adj : inflammatory
inflar vt 1 : inflate 2 EXAGERAR : exaggerate — **inflarse** vr ~ **de** : swell (up) with
inflexible adj : inflexible — **inflexión** nf, pl **-xiones** : inflection
infligir {35} vt : inflict
influencia nf : influence — **influenciar** → **influir**
influenza nf : influenza
influir {41} vt : influence — vi ~ **en** or ~ **sobre** : have an influence on — **influjo** nm : influence — **influyente** adj : influential
información nf, pl **-ciones** 1 : information 2 NOTICIAS : news 3 : directory assistance (on the telephone)
informal adj 1 : informal 2 IRRESPONSABLE : unreliable
informar v 1 : inform — **informarse** vr : get information, find out — **informante** nmf : informant — **informática** nf : information technology — **informativo, -va** adj : informative — **informatizar** {21} vt : computerize
informe adj : shapeless — ~ nm 1 : report 2 ~**s** nmpl : information, data 3 ~**s** nmpl : references (for employment)

infortunado, -da *adj* : unfortunate — **infortunio** *nm* : misfortune
infracción *nf, pl* **-ciones** : violation, infraction
infraestructura *nf* : infrastructure
infrahumano, -na *adj* : subhuman
infranqueable *adj* **1** : impassable **2** INSUPERABLE : insurmountable
infrarrojo, -ja *adj* : infrared
infrecuente *adj* : infrequent
infringir {35} *vt* : infringe
infructuoso, -sa *adj* : fruitless
infundado, -da *adj* : unfounded, baseless
infundir *vt* : instill, infuse — **infusión** *nf, pl* **-siones** : infusion
ingeniar *vt* : invent, think up
ingeniería *nf* : engineering — **ingeniero, -ra** *n* : engineer
ingenio *nm* **1** : ingenuity **2** AGUDEZA : wit **3** MÁQUINA : device, apparatus **4** ~ **azucarero** *Lat* : sugar refinery — **ingenioso, -sa** *adj* **1** : ingenious **2** AGUDO : clever, witty — **ingeniosamente** *adv* : cleverly
ingenuidad *nf* : naïveté, ingenuousness — **ingenuo, -nua** *adj* : naive
ingerir {76} *vt* : ingest, consume
ingle *nf* : groin
inglés, -glesa *adj, mpl* **-gleses** : English — **inglés** *nm* : English (language)
ingrato, -ta *adj* **1** : ungrateful **2 un trabajo ingrato** : a thankless task — **ingratitud** *nf* : ingratitude
ingrediente *nm* : ingredient
ingresar *vt* : deposit — *vi* ~ **en** : enter, be admitted into, join — **ingreso** *nm* **1** : entrance, entry **2** : admission (into a hospital, etc.) **3** ~**s** *nmpl* : income, earnings
inhábil *adj* **1** : unskillful, clumsy **2** ~ **para** : unsuited for — **inhabilidad** *nf* : unskillfulness
inhabitable *adj* : uninhabitable — **inhabitado, -da** *adj* : uninhabited
inhalar *vt* : inhale — **inhalación** *nf* : inhalation
inherente *adj* : inherent
inhibir *vt* : inhibit — **inhibición** *nf, pl* **-ciones** : inhibition
inhóspito, -ta *adj* : inhospitable
inhumano, -na *adj* : inhuman, inhumane — **inhumanidad** *nf* : inhumanity
iniciar *vt* : initiate, begin — **iniciación** *nf, pl* **-ciones** **1** : initiation **2** COMIENZO : beginning — **inicial** *adj* & *nf* : initial — **iniciativa** *nf* : initiative — **inicio** *nm* : start, beginning
inigualado, -da *adj* : unequaled
ininterrumpido, -da *adj* : uninterrupted
injerirse {76} *vr* : interfere — **injerencia** *nf* : interference
injertar *vt* : graft — **injerto** *nm* : graft

injuriar *vt* : insult — **injuria** *nf* : insult — **injurioso, -sa** *adj* : insulting, abusive
injusticia *nf* : injustice, unfairness — **injusto, -ta** *adj* : unfair, unjust
inmaculado, -da *adj* : immaculate
inmaduro, -ra *adj* **1** : immature **2** : unripe (of fruit) — **inmadurez** *nf* : immaturity
inmediaciones *nfpl* : surrounding area
inmediato, -ta *adj* **1** : immediate **2** CONTIGUO : adjoining **3 de** ~ : immediately, right away **4** ~ **a** : next to, close to — **inmediatamente** *adv* : immediately
inmejorable *adj* : excellent
inmenso, -sa *adj* : immense, vast — **inmensidad** *nf* : immensity
inmerecido, -da *adj* : undeserved
inmersión *nf, pl* **-siones** : immersion
inmigrar *vi* : immigrate — **inmigración** *nf, pl* **-ciones** : immigration — **inmigrante** *adj* & *nmf* : immigrant
inminente *adj* : imminent, impending — **inminencia** *nf* : imminence
inmiscuirse {41} *vr* : interfere
inmobiliario, -ria *adj* : real estate, property
inmodesto, -ta *adj* : immodest
inmoral *adj* : immoral — **inmoralidad** *nf* : immorality
inmortal *adj* & *nmf* : immortal — **inmortalidad** *nf* : immortality
inmóvil *adj* : motionless, still — **inmovilizar** {21} *vt* : immobilize
inmueble *nm* : building, property
inmundicia *nf* : filth, trash — **inmundo, -da** *adj* : dirty, filthy
inmunizar {21} *vt* : immunize — **inmune** *adj* : immune — **inmunidad** *nf* : immunity — **inmunización** *nf, pl* **-ciones** : immunization
inmutable *adj* : unchangeable
innato, -ta *adj* : innate
innecesario, -ria *adj* : unnecessary, needless
innegable *adj* : undeniable
innoble *adj* : ignoble
innovar *vt* : introduce — *vi* : innovate — **innovación** *nf, pl* **-ciones** : innovation — **innovador, -dora** *adj* : innovative — ~ *n* : innovator
innumerable *adj* : innumerable
inocencia *nf* : innocence — **inocente** *adj* & *nmf* : innocent — **inocentón, -tona** *adj, mpl* **-tones** : naive — ~ *n* : simpleton, dupe
inocular *vt* : inoculate — **inoculación** *nf, pl* **-ciones** : inoculation
inocuo, -cua *adj* : innocuous
inodoro, -ra *adj* : odorless — **inodoro** *nm* : toilet
inofensivo, -va *adj* : inoffensive, harmless
inolvidable *adj* : unforgettable
inoperable *adj* : inoperable

inoperante

inoperante *adj* : ineffective
inopinado, -da *adj* : unexpected
inoportuno, -na *adj* : untimely, inopportune
inorgánico, -ca *adj* : inorganic
inoxidable *adj* 1 : rustproof 2 **acero** ~ : stainless steel
inquebrantable *adj* : unwavering
inquietar *vt* : disturb, worry — **inquietarse** *vr* : worry — **inquietante** *adj* : disturbing, worrisome — **inquieto, -ta** *adj* : anxious, worried — **inquietud** *nf* : anxiety, worry
inquilino, -na *n* : tenant
inquirir {4} *vi* : make inquiries — *vt* : investigate
insaciable *adj* : insatiable
insalubre *adj* : unhealthy
insatisfecho, -cha *adj* 1 : unsatisfied 2 DESCONTENTO : dissatisfied
inscribir {33} *vt* 1 : enroll, register 2 GRABAR : inscribe, engrave — **inscribirse** *vr* : register — **inscripción** *nf, pl* -ciones 1 : inscription 2 REGISTRO : registration
insecto *nm* : insect — **insecticida** *nm* : insecticide
inseguro, -ra *adj* 1 : insecure 2 PELIGROSO : unsafe 3 DUDOSO : uncertain — **inseguridad** *nf* 1 : insecurity 2 PELIGRO : lack of safety 3 DUDA : uncertainty
inseminar *vt* : inseminate — **inseminación** *nf, pl* -ciones : insemination
insensato, -ta *adj* : senseless, foolish — **insensatez** *nf* : foolishness, thoughtlessness
insensible *adj* 1 : insensitive, unfeeling 2 : numb (in medicine) 3 IMPERCEPTIBLE : imperceptible — **insensibilidad** *nf* : insensitivity
inseparable *adj* : inseparable
insertar *vt* : insert
insidia *nf* : snare, trap — **insidioso, -sa** *adj* : insidious
insigne *adj* : noted, famous
insignia *nf* 1 : insignia, badge 2 BANDERA : flag
insignificante *adj* : insignificant, negligible
insincero, -ra *adj* : insincere
insinuar {3} *vt* : insinuate — **insinuarse** *vr* ~ **en** : worm one's way into — **insinuación** *nf, pl* -ciones : insinuation — **insinuante** *adj* : insinuating, suggestive
insípido, -da *adj* : insipid
insistir *v* : insist — **insistencia** *nf* : insistence — **insistente** *adj* : insistent
insociable *adj* : unsociable
insolación *nf, pl* -ciones : sunstroke
insolencia *nf* : insolence — **insolente** *adj* : insolent
insólito, -ta *adj* : rare, unusual
insoluble *adj* : insoluble

insolvencia *nf* : insolvency, bankruptcy — **insolvente** *adj* : insolvent, bankrupt
insomnio *nm* : insomnia — **insomne** *nmf* : insomniac
insondable *adj* : unfathomable
insonorizado, -da *adj* : soundproof
insoportable *adj* : unbearable
insospechado, -da *adj* : unexpected
insostenible *adj* : untenable
inspeccionar *vt* : inspect — **inspección** *nf, pl* -ciones : inspection — **inspector, -tora** *n* : inspector
inspirar *vt* : inspire — *vi* : inhale — **inspirarse** *vr* : be inspired — **inspiración** *nf, pl* -ciones 1 : inspiration 2 RESPIRACIÓN : inhalation — **inspirador, -dora** *adj* : inspirational
instalar *vt* : install — **instalarse** *vr* : settle — **instalación** *nf, pl* -ciones : installation
instancia *nf* 1 : request 2 **en última** ~ : ultimately, as a last resort
instantáneo, -nea *adj* : instantaneous, instant — **instantánea** *nf* : snapshot — **instante** *nm* 1 : instant 2 **a cada** ~ : frequently, all the time 3 **al** ~ : immediately
instar *vt* : urge, press
instaurar *vt* : establish — **instauración** *nf, pl* -ciones : establishment
instigar {52} *vt* : incite, instigate — **instigador, -dora** *n* : instigator
instinto *nm* : instinct — **instintivo, -va** *adj* : instinctive
institución *nf, pl* -ciones : institution — **institucional** *adj* : institutional — **institucionalizar** {21} *vt* : institutionalize — **instituir** {41} *vt* : institute, establish — **instituto** *nm* : institute — **institutriz** *nf, pl* -trices : governess
instruir {41} *vt* : instruct — **instrucción** *nf, pl* -ciones 1 : instruction 2 **instrucciones** *nfpl* : instructions, directions — **instructivo, -va** *adj* : instructive — **instructor, -tora** *n* : instructor
instrumento *nm* : instrument — **instrumental** *adj* : instrumental
insubordinarse *vr* : rebel — **insubordinado, -da** *adj* : insubordinate — **insubordinación** *nf, pl* -ciones : insubordination
insuficiente *adj* : insufficient, inadequate — **insuficiencia** *nf* 1 : insufficiency, inadequacy 2 ~ **cardíaca** : heart failure
insufrible *adj* : insufferable
insular *adj* : insular, island
insulina *nf* : insulin
insulso, -sa *adj* 1 : insipid, bland 2 SOSO : dull
insultar *vt* : insult — **insultante** *adj* : insulting — **insulto** *nm* : insult
insuperable *adj* : insurmountable

insurgente *adj & nmf* : insurgent
insurrección *nf, pl* **-ciones** : insurrection, uprising
intachable *adj* : irreproachable
intacto, -ta *adj* : intact
intangible *adj* : intangible
integrar *vt* : integrate — **integrarse** *vr* : become integrated — **integración** *nf, pl* **-ciones** : integration — **integral** *adj* **1** : integral **2** pan ~ : whole grain bread — **íntegro, -gra** *adj* **1** : honest, upright **2** ENTERO : whole, complete — **integridad** *nf* **1** RECTITUD : integrity **2** TOTALIDAD : wholeness
intelecto *nm* : intellect — **intelectual** *adj & nmf* : intellectual
inteligencia *nf* : intelligence — **inteligente** *adj* : intelligent — **inteligible** *adj* : intelligible
intemperie *nf* **a la** ~ : in the open air, outside
intempestivo, -va *adj* : untimely, inopportune
intención *nf, pl* **-ciones** : intention, intent — **intencionado, -da** *adj* **1** : intended **2 bien** ~ : well-meaning **3 mal** ~ : malicious — **intencional** *adj* : intentional
intensidad *nf* : intensity — **intensificar** {72} *vt* : intensify — **intensificarse** *vr* : intensify — **intensivo, -va** *adj* : intensive — **intenso, -sa** *adj* : intense
intentar *vt* : attempt, try — **intento** *nm* **1** : intention **2** TENTATIVA : attempt
interactuar {3} *vi* : interact — **interacción** *nf, pl* **-ciones** : interaction — **interactivo, -va** *adj* : interactive
intercalar *vt* : insert, intersperse
intercambio *nm* : exchange — **intercambiable** *adj* : interchangeable — **intercambiar** *vt* : exchange, trade
interceder *vi* : intercede
interceptar *vt* : intercept — **intercepción** *nf, pl* **-ciones** : interception
intercesión *nf, pl* **-siones** : intercession
interés *nm, pl* **-reses** : interest — **interesado, -da** *adj* **1** : interested **2** EGOISTA : selfish — **interesante** *adj* : interesting — **interesar** *vt* : interest — *vi* : be of interest — **interesarse** *vr* : take an interest
interfaz *nf, pl* **-faces** : interface
interferir {76} *vi* : interfere — *vt* : interfere with — **interferencia** *nf* : interference
interino, -na *adj* : temporary, interim — **interiormente** *adv* : inwardly
interior *adj* : interior, inner — ~ *nm* : interior, inside — **interiormente** *adv* : inwardly
interjección *nf, pl* **-ciones** : interjection
interlocutor, -tora *n* : speaker
intermediario, -ria *adj & n* : intermediary

intermedio, -dia *adj* : intermediate — **intermedio** *nm* : intermission
interminable *adj* : interminable, endless
intermisión *nf, pl* **-siones** : intermission, pause
intermitente *adj* : intermittent — ~ *nm* : blinker, turn signal
internacional *adj* : international
internar *vt* : commit, confine — **internarse** *vr* : penetrate — **internado** *nm* : boarding school — **interno, -na** *adj* : internal — ~ *n* **1** : boarder **2** : inmate (in a jail, etc.)
interponer {60} *vt* : interpose — **interponerse** *vr* : intervene
interpretar *vt* **1** : interpret **2** : play, perform (in theater, etc.) — **interpretación** *nf, pl* **-ciones** : interpretation — **intérprete** *nmf* **1** TRADUCTOR : interpreter **2** : performer (of music)
interrogar {52} *vt* : interrogate, question — **interrogación** *nf, pl* **-ciones** **1** : interrogation **2 signo de** ~ : question mark — **interrogativo, -va** *adj* : interrogative — **interrogatorio** *nm* : interrogation, questioning
interrumpir *v* : interrupt — **interrupción** *nf, pl* **-ciones** : interruption — **interruptor** *nm* : (electrical) switch
intersección *nf, pl* **-ciones** : intersection
intervalo *nm* : interval
intervenir {87} *vi* **1** : take part **2** MEDIAR : intervene — *vt* **1** : tap (a telephone) **2** INSPECCIONAR : audit **3** OPERAR : operate on — **intervención** *nf, pl* **-ciones** **1** : intervention **2** : audit (in business) **3** *or* ~ **quirúrgica** : operation — **interventor, -tora** *n* : inspector, auditor
intestino *nm* : intestine — **intestinal** *adj* : intestinal
intimar *vi* ~ **con** : become friendly with — **intimidad** *nf* **1** : private life **2** AMISTAD : intimacy
intimidar *vt* : intimidate
íntimo, -ma *adj* **1** : intimate, close **2** PRIVADO : private
intolerable *adj* : intolerable — **intolerancia** *nf* : intolerance — **intolerante** *adj* : intolerant
intoxicar {72} *vt* : poison — **intoxicación** *nf, pl* **-ciones** : poisoning
intranquilizar {21} *vt* : make uneasy — **intranquilizarse** *vr* : be anxious — **intranquilidad** *nf* : uneasiness, anxiety — **intranquilo, -la** *adj* : uneasy, worried
intransigente *adj* : unyielding, intransigent
intransitable *adj* : impassable
intransitivo, -va *adj* : intransitive
intrascendente *adj* : unimportant, insignificant
intravenoso, -sa *adj* : intravenous

intrépido

intrépido, -da *adj* : intrepid, fearless
intrigar {52} *v* : intrigue — **intriga** *nf* : intrigue — **intrigante** *adj* : intriguing
intrincado, -da *adj* : intricate, involved
intrínseco, -ca *adj* : intrinsic — **intrínsecamente** *adv* : intrinsically, inherently
introducción *nf, pl* **-ciones** : introduction — **introducir** {61} *vt* **1** : introduce **2** METER : insert — **introducirse** *vr* ~ **en** : penetrate, get into — **introductorio, -ria** *adj* : introductory
intromisión *nf, pl* **-siones** : interference
introvertido, -da *adj* : introverted — ~ *n* : introvert
intrusión *nf, pl* **-siones** : intrusion — **intruso, -sa** *adj* : intrusive — ~ *n* : intruder
intuir {41} *vt* : sense — **intuición** *nf, pl* **-ciones** : intuition — **intuitivo, -va** *adj* : intuitive
inundar *vt* : flood — **inundarse** *vr* ~ **de** : be inundated with — **inundación** *nf, pl* **-ciones** : flood
inusitado, -da *adj* : unusual, uncommon
inútil *adj* **1** : useless **2** INVÁLIDO : disabled — **inutilidad** *nf* : uselessness — **inutilizar** {21} *vt* **1** : make useless **2** INCAPACITAR : disable
invadir *vt* : invade
invalidez *nf, pl* **-deces 1** : invalidity **2** : disability (in medicine) — **inválido, -da** *adj & n* : invalid
invalorable *adj Lat* : invaluable
invariable *adj* : invariable
invasión *nf, pl* **-siones** : invasion — **invasor, -sora** *adj* : invading — ~ *n* : invader
invencible *adj* : invincible
inventar *vt* **1** : invent **2** : fabricate, make up (a word, an excuse, etc.) — **invención** *nf, pl* **-ciones 1** : invention **2** MENTIRA : lie, fabrication
inventario *nm* : inventory
inventiva *nf* : inventiveness — **inventivo, -va** *adj* : inventive — **inventor, -tora** *n* : inventor
invernadero *nm* : greenhouse
invernal *adj* : winter
inverosímil *adj* : unlikely
inversión *nf, pl* **-siones 1** : inversion, reversal **2** : investment (of money, time, etc.)
inverso, -sa *adj* **1** : inverse **2** CONTRARIO : opposite **3 a la inversa** : the other way around, inversely
inversor, -sora *n* : investor
invertebrado, -da *adj* : invertebrate — **invertebrado** *nm* : invertebrate
invertir {76} *vt* **1** : invert, reverse **2** : invest (money, time, etc.) — *vi* : make an investment
investidura *nf* : investiture
investigar {52} *vt* **1** : investigate **2** ESTU-

94

DIAR : research — *vi* ~ **sobre** : do research into — **investigación** *nf, pl* **-ciones 1** : investigation **2** ESTUDIO : research — **investigador, -dora** *n* : investigator, researcher
investir {54} *vt* : invest
inveterado, -da *adj* : deep-seated, inveterate
invicto, -ta *adj* : undefeated
invierno *nm* : winter
invisible *adj* : invisible — **invisibilidad** *nf* : invisibility
invitar *vt* : invite — **invitación** *nf, pl* **-ciones** : invitation — **invitado, -da** *n* : guest
invocar {72} *vt* : invoke — **invocación** *nf, pl* **-ciones** : invocation
involuntario, -ria *adj* : involuntary
invulnerable *adj* : invulnerable
inyectar *vt* : inject — **inyección** *nf, pl* **-ciones** : injection, shot — **inyectado, -da** *adj* **ojos inyectados** : bloodshot eyes
ion *nm* : ion — **ionizar** {21} *vt* : ionize
ir {43} *vi* **1** : go **2** FUNCIONAR : work, function **3** CONVENIR : suit **4** ¿cómo te va? : how are you? **5** ~ **con prisa** : be in a hurry **6** ~ **por** : follow, go along **7 vamos** : let's go — *v aux* **1** ~ **a** : be going to, be about to **2** ~ **caminando** : take a walk **3 vamos a ver** : we shall see — **irse** *vr* : go away, be gone
ira *nf* : rage, anger — **iracundo, -da** *adj* : irate, angry
iraní *adj* : Iranian
iraquí *adj* : Iraqi
iris *nms & pl* **1** : iris (of the eye) **2 arco** ~ : rainbow
irlandés, -desa *adj, mpl* **-deses** : Irish
ironía *nf* : irony — **irónico, -ca** *adj* : ironic, ironical
irracional *adj* : irrational
irradiar *vt* : radiate, irradiate
irrazonable *adj* : unreasonable
irreal *adj* : unreal
irreconciliable *adj* : irreconcilable
irreconocible *adj* : unrecognizable
irrecuperable *adj* : irretrievable
irreductible *adj* : unyielding
irreemplazable *adj* : irreplaceable
irreflexivo, -va *adj* : rash, unthinking
irrefutable *adj* : irrefutable
irregular *adj* : irregular — **irregularidad** *nf* : irregularity
irrelevante *adj* : irrelevant
irreparable *adj* : irreparable
irreprimible *adj* : irrepressible
irreprochable *adj* : irreproachable
irresistible *adj* : irresistible
irresoluto, -ta *adj* : indecisive, irresolute
irrespetuoso, -sa *adj* : disrespectful
irresponsable *adj* : irresponsible — **irresponsabilidad** *nf* : irresponsibility

irreverente *adj* : irreverent
irreversible *adj* : irreversible
irrevocable *adj* : irrevocable
irrigar {52} *vt* : irrigate — **irrigación** *nf, pl* -**ciones** : irrigation
irrisorio, -ria *adj* : laughable, ridiculous
irritar *vt* : irritate — **irritarse** *vr* : get annoyed — **irritable** *adj* : irritable — **irritación** *nf, pl* -**ciones** : irritation — **irritante** *adj* : irritating
irrompible *adj* : unbreakable
irrumpir *vi* ~ **en** : burst into

isla *nf* : island
islámico, -ca *adj* : Islamic, Muslim
islandés, -desa *adj, mpl* -**deses** : Icelandic
isleño, -ña *n* : islander
israelí *adj* : Israeli
istmo *nm* : isthmus
italiano, -na *adj* : Italian — **italiano** *nm* : Italian (language)
itinerario *nm* : itinerary
izar {21} *vt* : hoist, raise
izquierda *nf* : left — **izquierdista** *adj & nmf* : leftist — **izquierdo, -da** *adj* : left

J

j *nf* : j, tenth letter of the Spanish alphabet
jabalí *nm, pl* -**líes** : wild boar
jabalina *nf* : javelin
jabón *nm, pl* -**bones** : soap — **jabonar** *vt* : soap (up) — **jabonera** *nf* : soap dish — **jabonoso, -sa** *adj* : soapy
jaca *nf* : pony
jacinto *nm* : hyacinth
jactarse *vr* : boast, brag — **jactancia** *nf* : boastfulness, bragging — **jactancioso, -sa** *adj* : boastful
jadear *vi* : pant, gasp — **jadeante** *adj* : panting, breathless — **jadeo** *nm* : gasp, panting
jaez *nm, pl* **jaeces** **1** : harness **2 jaeces** *nmpl* : trappings
jaguar *nm* : jaguar
jaiba *nf Lat* : crab
jalapeño *nm Lat* : jalapeño pepper
jalar *v Lat* : pull, tug
jalea *nf* : jelly
jaleo *nm fam* **1** : uproar, racket **2 armar un** ~ : raise a ruckus
jalón *nm, pl* -**lones** *Lat* : pull, tug
jamaicano, -na *or* **jamaiquino, -na** *adj* : Jamaican
jamás *adv* **1** : never **2 para siempre** ~ : for ever and ever
jamelgo *nm* : nag (horse)
jamón *nm, pl* -**mones** **1** : ham **2** ~ **serrano** : cured ham
Januká *nmf* : Hanukkah
japonés, -nesa *adj, mpl* -**neses** : Japanese — **japonés** *nm* : Japanese (language)
jaque *nm* **1** : check (in chess) **2** ~ **mate** : checkmate
jaqueca *nf* : headache, migraine
jarabe *nm* : syrup
jardín *nm, pl* -**dines** **1** : garden **2** ~ **infan-**
til *or* ~ **de niños** *Lat* : kindergarten — **jardinería** *nf* : gardening — **jardinero, -ra** *n* : gardener
jarra *nf* : pitcher, jug — **jarro** *nm* : pitcher — **jarrón** *nm, pl* -**rrones** : vase
jaula *nf* : cage
jauría *nf* : pack of hounds
jazmín *nm, pl* -**mines** : jasmine
jazz *nm* : jazz
jeans *nmpl* : jeans
jefe, -fa *n* **1** : chief, leader **2** PATRÓN : boss **3** ~ **de cocina** : chef — **jefatura** *nf* **1** : leadership **2** SEDE : headquarters
jengibre *nm* : ginger
jeque *nm* : sheikh, sheik
jerarquía *nf* **1** : hierarchy **2** RANGO : rank — **jerárquico, -ca** *adj* : hierarchical
jerez *nm, pl* -**reces** : sherry
jerga *nf* **1** : coarse cloth **2** ARGOT : jargon, slang
jerigonza *nf* **1** : jargon **2** GALIMATÍAS : gibberish
jeringa *or* **jeringuilla** *nf* : syringe — **jeringar** {52} *vt fam* : annoy, pester
jeroglífico *nm* : hieroglyphic
jersey *nm, pl* -**seys** : jersey
jesuita *adj & nm* : Jesuit
Jesús *nm* : Jesus
jilguero *nm* : goldfinch
jinete *nmf* : horseman, horsewoman *f,* rider
jirafa *nf* : giraffe
jirón *nm, pl* -**rones** : shred, tatter
jitomate *nm Lat* : tomato
jockey *nmf, pl* -**keys** : jockey
jocoso, -sa *adj* : humorous, jocular
jofaina *nf* : washbowl
jolgorio *nm* : merrymaking
jornada *nf* **1** : day's journey **2** : working

day — **jornal** *nm* : day's pay — **jornalero,
-ra** *n* : day laborer
joroba *nf* : hump — **jorobado, -da** *adj*
: hunchbacked, humpbacked — ~ *n*
: hunchback — **jorobar** *vt fam* : annoy
jota *nf* **1** : iota, jot **2 no veo ni** ~ : I can't
see a thing
joven *adj, pl* **jóvenes** : young — ~ *nmf*
: young man *m*, young woman *f*, youth
jovial *adj* : jovial, cheerful
joya *nf* : jewel — **joyería** *nf* : jewelry store —
joyero, -ra *n* : jeweler — **joyero** *nm* : jewelry box
juanete *nm* : bunion
jubilación *nf, pl* **-ciones** : retirement — **jubilado, -da** *adj* : retired — ~ *nmf* : retiree
— **jubilar** *vt* : retire, pension off — **jubilarse** *vr* : retire — **jubileo** *nm* : jubilee
júbilo *nm* : joy, jubilation — **jubiloso, -sa**
adj : joyous, jubilant
judaísmo *nm* : Judaism
judía *nf* **1** : bean **2** *or* ~ **verde** : green
bean, string bean
judicial *adj* : judicial
judío, -día *adj* : Jewish — ~ *n* : Jew
judo *nm* : judo
juego *nm* **1** : game **2** : playing (of children,
etc.) **3** *or* ~**s de azar** : gambling **4** CON-
JUNTO : set **5 estar en** ~ : be at stake **6
fuera de** ~ : offside (in sports) **7 hacer** ~
: go together, match **8** ~ **de manos** : con-
juring trick **9 poner en** ~ : bring into play
juerga *nf fam* : spree, binge
jueves *nms & pl* : Thursday
juez *nmf, pl* **jueces 1** : judge **2** ÁRBITRO
: umpire, referee
jugar {44} *vi* **1** : play **2** : gamble (in a
casino, etc.) **3** APOSTAR : bet **4** ~ **(al) tenis**
: play tennis — *vt* : play — **jugarse** *vr* : risk,
gamble (away) — **jugada** *nf* **1** : play, move
2 TRETA : (dirty) trick — **jugador, -dora** *n*
1 : player **2** : gambler
juglar *nm* : minstrel

jugo *nm* **1** : juice **2** SUSTANCIA : substance,
essence — **jugoso, -sa** *adj* **1** : juicy **2** SUS-
TANCIAL : substantial, important
juguete *nm* : toy — **juguetear** *vi* : play —
juguetería *nf* : toy store — **juguetón, -tona**
adj, mpl **-tones** : playful
juicio *nm* **1** : judgment **2** RAZÓN : reason,
sense **3 a mi** ~ : in my opinion —
juicioso, -sa *adj* : wise, sensible
julio *nm* : July
junco *nm* : reed, rush
jungla *nf* : jungle
junio *nm* : June
juntar *vt* **1** UNIR : join, unite **2** REUNIR : collect — **juntarse** *vr* **1** : join (together) **2** RE-
UNIRSE : meet, get together — **junta** *nf* **1**
: board, committee **2** REUNIÓN : meeting **3**
: (political) junta **4** : joint, gasket — **junto,
-ta** *adj* **1** : joined **2** PRÓXIMO : close, adjacent **3** (*used adverbially*) : together **4** ~ **a**
: next to **5** ~ **con** : together with — **juntura** *nf* : joint
Júpiter *nm* : Jupiter
jurar *v* **1** : swear **2** ~ **en falso** : commit
perjury — **jurado** *nm* **1** : jury **2** : juror,
member of a jury — **juramento** *nm* : oath
jurídico, -ca *adj* : legal
jurisdicción *nf, pl* **-ciones** : jurisdiction
jurisprudencia *nf* : jurisprudence
justamente *adv* **1** : fairly, justly **2** PRECISA-
MENTE : precisely, exactly
justicia *nf* : justice, fairness
justificar {72} *vt* **1** : justify **2** DISCULPAR
: excuse, vindicate — **justificación** *nf, pl*
-ciones : justification
justo, -ta *adj* **1** : just, fair **2** EXACTO : exact
3 APRETADO : tight — **justo** *adv* **1** : just, exactly **2** ~ **a tiempo** : just in time
juvenil *adj* : youthful — **juventud** *nf* **1**
: youth **2** JÓVENES : young people
juzgar {52} *vt* **1** : try (a case in court) **2** ES-
TIMAR : judge, consider **3 a** ~ **por** : judging by — **juzgado** *nm* : court, tribunal

K

k *nf* : k, eleventh letter of the Spanish alphabet
kaki → **caqui**
karate *or* **kárate** *nm* : karate
kilo *nm* : kilo — **kilogramo** *nm* : kilogram

kilómetro *nm* : kilometer — **kilometraje** *nm*
: distance in kilometers, mileage — **kilo-
métrico, -ca** *adj fam* : end- less
kilovatio *nm* : kilowatt
kiosco *nm* → **quiosco**

L

l *nf* : l, twelfth letter of the Spanish alphabet
la *pron* **1** : her, it **2** (*formal*) : you **3** ~ que
: the one who — ~ *art* → **el**
laberinto *nm* : labyrinth, maze
labia *nf fam* : gift of gab
labio *nm* : lip
labor *nf* **1** : work, labor **2** TAREA : task **3**
~es domésticas : housework — **laborable**
adj día ~ : business day — **laborar** *vi*
: work — **laboratorio** *nm* : laboratory, lab
— **laborioso, -sa** *adj* : laborious
labrar *vt* **1** : cultivate, till **2** : work (metals),
carve (stone, wood) **3** CAUSAR : cause,
bring about — **labrado, -da** *adj* **1** : culti-
vated, tilled **2** : carved, wrought —
labrador, -dora *n* : farmer — **labranza** *nf*
: farming
laca *nf* **1** : lacquer **2** : hair spray
lacayo *nm* : lackey
lacerar *vt* : lacerate
lacio, -cia *adj* **1** : limp **2** : straight (of hair)
lacónico, -ca *adj* : laconic
lacra *nf* : scar
lacrar *vt* : seal — **lacre** *nm* : sealing wax
lacrimógeno, -na *adj* gas lacrimógeno
: tear gas — **lacrimoso, -sa** *adj* : tearful
lácteo, -tea *adj* **1** : dairy **2** Vía Láctea
: Milky Way
ladear *vt* : tilt — **ladearse** *vr* : lean
ladera *nf* : slope, hillside
ladino, -na *adj* : crafty
lado *nm* **1** : side **2** al ~ : next door, nearby
3 al ~ de : beside, next to **4** de ~ : sideways **5** por otro ~ : on the other hand **6**
por todos ~s : everywhere, all around
ladrar *vi* : bark — **ladrido** *nm* : bark
ladrillo *nm* : brick
ladrón, -drona *n, mpl* **-drones** : thief
lagarto *nm* : lizard — **lagartija** *nf* : (small)
lizard
lago *nm* : lake
lágrima *nf* : tear
laguna *nf* **1** : lagoon **2** VACÍO : gap
laico, -ca *adj* : lay, secular — ~ *n* : layman
m, layperson
lamentar *vt* **1** : regret, be sorry about **2** lo
lamento : I'm sorry — **lamentarse** *vr*
: lament — **lamentable** *adj* **1** : deplorable
2 TRISTE : sad, pitiful — **lamento** *nm*
: lament, moan
lamer *vt* **1** : lick **2** : lap (against) — **lamida**
nf : lick
lámina *nf* **1** PLANCHA : sheet **2** DIBUJO
: plate, illustration — **laminar** *vt* : laminate

lámpara *nf* : lamp
lampiño, -ña *adj* : beardless, hairless
lana *nf* **1** : wool **2** de ~ : woolen
lance *nm* **1** : event, incident **2** : throw (of
dice, etc.) **3** RIÑA : quarrel
lanceta *nf* : lancet
lancha *nf* **1** : boat, launch **2** ~ motora
: motorboat
langosta *nf* **1** : lobster **2** : locust (insect) —
langostino *nm* : prawn, crayfish
languidecer {53} *vi* : languish — **languidez**
nf, pl **-deces** : languor — **lánguido, -da** *adj*
: languid, listless
lanilla *nf* : nap (of fabric)
lanudo, -da *adj* : woolly
lanza *nf* : spear, lance
lanzar {21} *vt* **1** : throw **2** : shoot (a glance),
give (a sigh, etc.) **3** : launch (a missile, a
project) — **lanzarse** *vr* : throw oneself —
lanzamiento *nm* : throwing, launching
lapicero *nm* : (mechanical) pencil
lápida *nf* : tombstone
lapidar *vt* : stone
lápiz *nm, pl* **-pices 1** : pencil **2** ~ de
labios : lipstick
lapso *nm* : lapse (of time) — **lapsus** *nms &
pl* : lapse, slip (of the tongue)
largar {52} *vt* **1** AFLOJAR : loosen, slacken
2 *fam* : give — **largarse** *vr fam* : go away,
beat it — **largo, -ga** *adj* **1** : long **2** a la
larga : in the long run **3** a lo largo : lengthwise **4** a lo largo de : along — **largo** *nm*
: length — **largometraje** *nm* : feature film
— **largueza** *nf* : generosity
laringe *nf* : larynx — **laringitis** *nfs & pl*
: laryngitis
larva *nf* : larva
las → **el**
lascivo, -va *adj* : lascivious, lewd
láser *nm* : laser
lastimar *vt* : hurt — **lastimarse** *vr* : hurt oneself — **lástima** *nf* **1** : pity **2** dar ~ : be pitiful **3** me dan ~ : I feel sorry for them **4**
¡qué ~! : what a shame! — **lastimero, -ra**
adj : pitiful, wretched — **lastimoso, -sa** *adj*
: pitiful, terrible
lastre *nm* : ballast
lata *nf* **1** : tinplate **2** : (tin) can **3** *fam* : nuisance, bore **4** dar (la) lata a *fam* : bother,
annoy
latente *adj* : latent
lateral *adj* : side, lateral
latido *nm* **1** : beat, throb **2** ~ del corazón
: heartbeat

98

latifundio *nm* : large estate
látigo *nm* : whip — **latigazo** *nm* : lash
latín *nm* : Latin (language)
latino, -na *adj* **1** : Latin **2** : Latin-American — ~ *n* : Latin American — **latinoamericano, -na** *adj* : Latin-American — ~ *n* : Latin American
latir *vi* : beat, throb
latitud *nf* : latitude
latón *nm, pl* **-tones** : brass
latoso, -sa *adj fam* : annoying
laúd *nm* : lute
laudable *adj* : laudable
laureado, -da *adj* : prize-winning
laurel *nm* **1** : laurel **2** : bay leaf (in cooking)
lava *nf* : lava
lavar *vt* : wash — **lavarse** *vr* **1** : wash oneself **2** ~ **las manos** : wash one's hands — **lavable** *adj* : washable — **lavabo** *nm* **1** : sink **2** RETRETE : lavatory, toilet — **lavadero** *nm* : laundry room — **lavado** *nm* : wash, washing — **lavadora** *nf* : washing machine — **lavamanos** *nms & pl* : washbowl — **lavandería** *nf* : laundry (service) — **lavaplatos** *nms & pl* **1** : dishwasher **2** *Lat* : kitchen sink — **lavativa** *nf* : enema — **lavatorio** *nm* : lavatory, washroom — **lavavajillas** *nms & pl* : dishwasher
laxante *adj & nm* : laxative — **laxo, -xa** *adj* : loose
lazo *nm* **1** VÍNCULO : link, bond **2** LAZADA : bow **3** : lasso, lariat — **lazada** *nf* : bow, loop
le *pron* **1** : (to) her, (to) him, (to) it **2** *(formal)* : (to) you **3** *(as direct object)* : him, you
leal *adj* : loyal, faithful — **lealtad** *nf* : loyalty, allegiance
lebrel *nm* : hound
lección *nf, pl* **-ciones** **1** : lesson **2** : lecture (in a classroom)
leche *nf* **1** : milk **2** ~ **descremada** *or* ~ **desnatada** : skim milk **3** ~ **en polvo** : powdered milk — **lechera** *nf* : milk jug — **lechería** *nf* : dairy store — **lechero, -ra** *adj* : dairy — ~ *n* : milkman *m*, milk dealer
lecho *nm* : bed
lechón, -chona *n, mpl* **-chones** : suckling pig
lechoso, -sa *adj* : milky
lechuga *nf* : lettuce
lechuza *nf* : owl
lector, -tora *n* : reader — **lectura** *nf* **1** : reading **2** ESCRITOS : reading matter
leer {20} *v* : read
legación *nf, pl* **-ciones** : legation
legado *nm* **1** : legacy **2** ENVIADO : legate, emissary
legajo *nm* : dossier, file

legal *adj* : legal — **legalidad** *nf* : legality — **legalizar** {21} *vt* : legalize — **legalización** *nf, pl* **-ciones** : legalization
legar {52} *vt* : bequeath
legendario, -ria *adj* : legendary
legible *adj* : legible
legión *nf, pl* **-giones** : legion — **legionario, -ria** *n* : legionnaire
legislar *vi* : legislate — **legislación** *nf, pl* **-ciones** : legislation — **legislador, -dora** *n* : legislator — **legislatura** *nf* : legislature
legítimo, -ma *adj* **1** : legitimate **2** GENUINO : authentic — **legitimidad** *nf* : legitimacy
lego, -ga *adj* **1** : secular, lay **2** IGNORANTE : ignorant — ~ *n* : layman *m*, layperson
legua *nf* : league
legumbre *nf* : vegetable
leído, -da *adj* : well-read
lejano, -na *adj* : distant, far away — **lejanía** *nf* : distance
lejía *nf* : bleach
lejos *adv* **1** : far (away) **2 a lo** ~ : in the distance **3 de** ~ *or* **desde** ~ : from afar **4** ~ **de** : far from
lelo, -la *adj* : silly, stupid
lema *nm* : motto
lencería *nf* **1** : linen **2** : (women's) lingerie
lengua *nf* **1** : tongue **2** IDIOMA : language **3 morderse la** ~ : hold one's tongue
lenguado *nm* : sole, flounder
lenguaje *nm* : language
lengüeta *nf* **1** : tongue (of a shoe) **2** : reed (of a musical instrument)
lengüetada *nf* **beber a** ~**s** : lap (up)
lente *nmf* **1** : lens **2** ~**s** *nmpl* : eyeglasses **3** ~**s de contacto** : contact lenses
lenteja *nf* : lentil — **lentejuela** *nf* : sequin
lento, -ta *adj* : slow — **lento** *adv* : slowly — **lentitud** *nf* : slowness
leña *nf* : firewood — **leñador, -dora** *n* : lumberjack, woodcutter — **leño** *nm* : log
león, -ona *n, mpl* **leones** : lion, lioness *f*
leopardo *nm* : leopard
leotardo *nm* : leotard, tights *pl*
lepra *nf* : leprosy — **leproso, -sa** *n* : leper
lerdo, -da *adj* **1** TORPE : clumsy **2** TONTO : slow-witted
les *pron* **1** : (to) them, (to) you **2** *(as direct object)* : them, you
lesbiano, -na *adj* : lesbian — **lesbiana** *nf* : lesbian — **lesbianismo** *nm* : lesbianism
lesión *nf, pl* **-siones** : lesion, wound — **lesionado, -da** *adj* : injured, wounded — **lesionar** *vt* **1** : injure, wound **2** DAÑAR : damage
letal *adj* : lethal
letanía *nf* : litany
letárgico, -ca *adj* : lethargic — **letargo** *nm* : lethargy

letra *nf* **1** : letter **2** ESCRITURA : handwriting **3** : lyrics *pl* (of a song) **4** ~ **de cambio** : bill of exchange **5** ~**s** *nfpl* : arts — **letrado, -da** *adj* : learned — **letrero** *nm* : sign, notice

letrina *nf* : latrine

leucemia *nf* : leukemia

levadizo, -za *adj* **puente levadizo** : drawbridge

levadura *nf* **1** : yeast **2** ~ **en polvo** : baking powder

levantar *vt* **1** : lift, raise **2** RECOGER : pick up **3** CONSTRUIR : erect, put up **4** ENCENDER : rouse, stir up **5** ~ **la mesa** *Lat* : clear the table — **levantarse** *vr* **1** : rise, stand up **2** : get out of bed **3** SUBLEVARSE : rise up — **levantamiento** *nm* **1** : raising, lifting **2** SUBLEVACIÓN : uprising

levante *nm* **1** : east **2** : east wind

levar *vt* ~ **anclas** : weigh anchor

leve *adj* **1** : light, slight **2** : minor, trivial (of wounds, sins, etc.) — **levedad** *nf* : lightness — **levemente** *adv* : lightly, slightly

léxico *nm* : vocabulary, lexicon

ley *nf* **1** : law **2 de (buena)** ~ : genuine, pure (of metals)

leyenda *nf* **1** : legend **2** : caption (of an illustration, etc.)

liar {85} *vt* **1** : bind, tie (up) **2** : roll (a cigarette) **3** CONFUNDIR : confuse, muddle — **liarse** *vr* : get mixed up

libanés, -nesa *adj, mpl* **-neses** : Lebanese

libelo *nm* **1** : libel **2** : petition (in court)

libélula *nf* : dragonfly

liberación *nf, pl* **-ciones** : liberation, deliverance

liberal *adj & nmf* : liberal — **liberalidad** *nf* : generosity, liberality

liberar *vt* : liberate, free — **libertad** *nf* **1** : freedom, liberty **2** ~ **bajo fianza** : bail **3** ~ **condicional** : parole **4 en** ~ : free — **libertar** *vt* : set free

libertinaje *nm* : licentiousness — **libertino, -na** *n* : libertine

libido *nf* : libido

libio, -bia *adj* : Libyan

libra *nf* **1** : pound **2** ~ **esterlina** : pound sterling

librar *vt* **1** : free, save **2** : wage, fight (a battle) **3** : draw, issue (a check, etc.) — **librarse** *vr* ~ **de** : free oneself from, get rid of

libre *adj* **1** : free **2** : unoccupied (of space), spare (of time) **3 al aire** ~ : in the open air **4** ~ **de impuestos** : tax-free

librea *nf* : livery

libro *nm* **1** : book **2** ~ **de bolsillo** : paperback — **librería** *nf* : bookstore — **librero, -ra** *n* : bookseller — **librero** *nm Lat* : bookcase — **libreta** *nf* : notebook

licencia *nf* **1** : license, permit **2** PERMISO : permission **3** : (military) leave — **licenciado, -da** *n* **1** : graduate **2** *Lat* : lawyer — **licenciar** *vt* : dismiss, discharge — **licenciarse** *vr* : graduate — **licenciatura** *nf* : degree

licencioso, -sa *adj* : licentious

liceo *nm* : high school

licitar *vt* : bid for

lícito, -ta *adj* **1** : lawful, legal **2** JUSTO : just, fair

licor *nm* **1** : liquor **2** : liqueur — **licorera** *nf* : decanter

licuadora *nf* : blender — **licuado** *nm* : milk shake — **licuar** {3} *vt* : liquefy

lid *nf* **1** : fight **2 en buena** ~ : fair and square

líder *adj* : leading — ~ *nmf* : leader — **liderato** *or* **liderazgo** *nm* : leadership

lidia *nf* : bullfight — **lidiar** *v* : fight

liebre *nf* : hare

lienzo *nm* **1** : cotton or linen cloth **2** : canvas (for a painting) **3** PARED : wall

liga *nf* **1** : league **2** *Lat* : rubber band **3** : garter (for stockings) — **ligadura** *nf* **1** ATADURA : tie, bond **2** : ligature (in medicine or music) — **ligamento** *nm* : ligament — **ligar** {52} *vt* : bind, tie (up)

ligero, -ra *adj* **1** : light, lightweight **2** LEVE : slight **3** ÁGIL : agile **4** FRÍVOLO : lighthearted, superficial — **ligeramente** *adv* : lightly, slightly — **ligereza** *nf* **1** : lightness **2** : flippancy (of character), thoughtlessness (of actions) **3** AGILIDAD : agility

lija *nf* : sandpaper — **lijar** *vt* : sand

lila *nf* : lilac

lima *nf* **1** : file **2** : lime (fruit) **3** ~ **para uñas** : nail file — **limar** *vt* : file

limbo *nm* : limbo

limitar *vt* : limit — *vi* ~ **con** : border on — **limitación** *nf, pl* **-ciones** : limitation, limit — **límite** *nm* **1** : limit **2** CONFÍN : boundary, border **3** ~ **de velocidad** : speed limit **4 fecha** ~ : deadline — **limítrofe** *adj* : bordering

limo *nm* : slime, mud

limón *nm, pl* **-mones 1** : lemon **2** ~ **verde** *Lat* : lime — **limonada** *nf* : lemonade

limosna *nf* **1** : alms **2 pedir** ~ : beg — **limosnero, -ra** *n* : beggar

limpiabotas *nmfs & pl* : bootblack

limpiaparabrisas *nms & pl* : windshield wiper

limpiar *vt* **1** : clean, wipe (away) **2** ~ **en seco** : dry-clean — **limpieza** *nf* **1** : cleanliness **2** : (act of) cleaning — **limpio** *adv* : cleanly, fairly — **limpio, -pia** *adj* **1** : clean, neat **2** HONRADO : honest **3** NETO : net, clear

limusina *nf* : limousine

linaje

linaje *nm* : lineage, ancestry
linaza *nf* : linseed
lince *nm* : lynx
linchar *vt* : lynch
lindar *vi* ~ **con** : border on — **lindante** *adj* : bordering — **linde** *nmf or* **lindero** *nm* : boundary
lindo, -da *adj* **1** : pretty, lovely **2 de lo lindo** *fam* : a lot
línea *nf* **1** : line **2** ~ **de conducta** : course of action **3 en** ~ : on-line **4 guardar la** ~ : watch one's figure — **lineal** *adj* : linear
lingote *nm* : ingot
lingüista *nmf* : linguist — **lingüística** *nf* : linguistics — **lingüístico, -ca** *adj* : linguistic
linimento *nm* : liniment
lino *nm* **1** : flax (plant) **2** : linen (fabric)
linóleo *nm* : linoleum
linterna *nf* **1** FAROL : lantern **2** : flashlight
lío *nm* **1** : bundle **2** *fam* : mess, trouble **3** *fam* : (love) affair
liofilizar {21} *vt* : freeze-dry
liquen *nm* : lichen
liquidar *vt* **1** : liquefy **2** : liquidate (merchandise, etc.) **3** : settle, pay off (a debt, etc.) — **liquidación** *nf, pl* **-ciones 1** : liquidation **2** REBAJA : clearance sale — **líquido, -da** *adj* **1** : liquid **2** NETO : net — **líquido** *nm* : liquid
lira *nf* : lyre
lírico, -ca *adj* : lyric, lyrical — **lírica** *nf* : lyric poetry
lirio *nm* : iris
lisiado, -da *adj* : disabled — ~ *n* : disabled person — **lisiar** *vt* : disable, cripple
liso, -sa *adj* **1** : smooth **2** PLANO : flat **3** SENCILLO : plain **4 pelo** ~ : straight hair
lisonjear *vt* : flatter — **lisonja** *nf* : flattery
lista *nf* **1** : stripe **2** ENUMERACIÓN : list **3** : menu (in a restaurant) — **listado, -da** *adj* : striped
listo, -ta *adj* **1** : clever, smart **2** PREPARADO : ready
listón *nm, pl* **-tones 1** : ribbon **2** : strip (of wood)
lisura *nf* : smoothness
litera *nf* : bunk bed, berth
literal *adj* : literal
literatura *nf* : literature — **literario, -ria** *adj* : literary
litigar {52} *vi* : litigate — **litigio** *nm* **1** : litigation **2 en** ~ : in dispute
litografía *nf* **1** : lithography **2** : lithograph (picture)
litoral *adj* : coastal — ~ *nm* : shore, seaboard
litro *nm* : liter

liturgia *nf* : liturgy — **litúrgico, -ca** *adj* : liturgical
liviano, -na *adj* **1** LIGERO : light **2** INCONSTANTE : fickle
lívido, -da *adj* : livid
llaga *nf* : sore, wound
llama *nf* **1** : flame **2** : llama (animal)
llamar *vt* **1** : call **2** : call up (on the telephone) — *vi* **1** : phone, call **2** : knock, ring (at the door) — **llamarse** *vr* **1** : be called **2 ¿cómo te llamas?** : what's your name? — **llamada** *nf* : call — **llamado, -da** *adj* : named, called — **llamamiento** *nm* : call, appeal
llamarada *nf* **1** : blaze **2** : flushing (of the face)
llamativo, -va *adj* : flashy, showy
llamear *vi* : flame, blaze
llano, -na *adj* **1** : flat **2** : straightforward (of a person, a message, etc.) **3** SENCILLO : plain, simple — **llano** *nm* : plain — **llaneza** *nf* : simplicity
llanta *nf* **1** : rim (of a wheel) **2** *Lat* : tire
llanto *nm* : crying, weeping
llanura *nf* : plain
llave *nf* **1** : key **2** *Lat* : faucet **3** INTERRUPTOR : switch **4 cerrar con** ~ : lock **5** ~ **inglesa** : monkey wrench — **llavero** *nm* : key chain
llegar {52} *vi* **1** : arrive, come **2** ALCANZAR : reach **3** BASTAR : be enough **4** ~ **a** : manage to **5** ~ **a ser** : become — **llegada** *nf* : arrival
llenar *vt* : fill (up), fill in — **lleno, -na** *adj* **1** : full **2 de lleno** : completely — **lleno** *nm* : full house
llevar *vt* **1** : take, carry **2** CONDUCIR : lead **3** : wear (clothing, etc.) **4** TENER : have **5 llevo una hora aquí** : I've been here for an hour — **llevarse** *vr* **1** : take (away) **2** ~ **bien** : get along well — **llevadero, -ra** *adj* : bearable
llorar *vi* : cry, weep — **lloriquear** *vi* : whimper, whine — **lloro** *nm* : crying — **llorón, -rona** *n, mpl* **-rones** : crybaby, whiner — **lloroso, -sa** *adj* : tearful
llover {47} *v impers* : rain — **llovizna** *nf* : drizzle — **lloviznar** *v impers* : drizzle
lluvia *nf* : rain — **lluvioso, -sa** *adj* : rainy
lo *pron* **1** : him, it **2** (*formal, masculine*) : you **3** ~ **que** : what, that which — ~ *art* **1** : the **2** ~ **mejor** : the best (part) **3 sé** ~ **bueno que eres** : I know how good you are
loa *nf* : praise — **loable** *adj* : praiseworthy — **loar** *vt* : praise
lobo, -ba *n* : wolf
lóbrego, -ga *adj* : gloomy
lóbulo *nm* : lobe

local *adj* : local — ~ *nm* : premises *pl* — **localidad** *nf* : town, locality — **localizar** {21} *vt* **1** : localize **2** ENCONTRAR : locate — **localizarse** *vr* : be located
loción *nf, pl* **-ciones** : lotion
loco, -ca *adj* **1** : crazy, insane **2 a lo loco** : wildly, recklessly **3 volverse** ~ : go mad — ~ *n* **1** : crazy person, lunatic **2 hacerse el loco** : act the fool
locomoción *nf, pl* **-ciones** : locomotion — **locomotora** *nf* : engine, locomotive
locuaz *adj, pl* **-cuaces** : talkative, loquacious
locución *nf, pl* **-ciones** : expression, phrase
locura *nf* **1** : insanity, madness **2** INSENSATEZ : crazy act, folly
locutor, -tora *n* : announcer
locutorio *nm* : phone booth
lodo *nm* : mud — **lodazal** *nm* : quagmire
logaritmo *nm* : logarithm
lógica *nf* : logic — **lógico, -ca** *adj* : logical — **logística** *nf* : logistics *pl*
logotipo *nm* : logo
lograr *vt* **1** : achieve, attain **2** CONSEGUIR : get, obtain **3** ~ **hacer** : manage to do — **logro** *nm* : achievement, success
loma *nf* : hill, hillock
lombriz *nf, pl* **-brices** : worm
lomo *nm* **1** : back (of an animal) **2** : spine (of a book) **3** ~ **de cerdo** : pork loin
lona *nf* : canvas
loncha *nf* : slice (of bacon, etc.)
lonche *nm Lat* : lunch — **lonchería** *nf Lat* : luncheonette
longaniza *nf* : sausage
longevidad *nf* : longevity — **longevo, -va** *adj* : long-lived
longitud *nf* **1** : longitude **2** LARGO : length
lonja → **loncha**
loro *nm* : parrot
los, las *pron* **1** : them **2** : you **3 los que, las que** : those who, the ones who — **los** *art* → **el**
losa *nf* **1** : flagstone **2** *or* ~ **sepulcral** : tombstone
lote *nm* **1** : batch, lot **2** *Lat* : plot of land
lotería *nf* : lottery
loto *nm* : lotus
loza *nf* : crockery, earthenware
lozano, -na *adj* **1** : healthy-looking, vigorous **2** : luxuriant (of plants) — **lozanía** *nf*

1 : (youthful) vigor **2** : luxuriance (of plants)
lubricar {72} *vt* : lubricate — **lubricante** *adj* : lubricating — ~ *nm* : lubricant
lucero *nm* : bright star
luchar *vi* **1** : fight, struggle **2** : wrestle (in sports) — **lucha** *nf* **1** : struggle, fight **2** : wrestling (sport) — **luchador, -dora** *n* : fighter, wrestler
lucidez *nf, pl* **-deces** : lucidity — **lúcido, -da** *adj* : lucid
lucido, -da *adj* : magnificent, splendid
luciérnaga *nf* : firefly, glowworm
lucir {45} *vi* **1** : shine **2** *Lat* : appear, seem — *vt* **1** : wear, sport **2** OSTENTAR : show off — **lucirse** *vr* **1** : shine, excel **2** PRESUMIR : show off — **lucimiento** *nm* **1** : brilliance **2** ÉXITO : brilliant performance, success
lucrativo, -va *adj* : lucrative — **lucro** *nm* : profit
luego *adv* **1** : then **2** : later (on) **3 desde** ~ : of course **4 ¡hasta** ~! : see you later! **5** ~ **que** : as soon as — ~ *conj* : therefore
lugar *nm* **1** : place — ESPACIO : space, room **3 dar** ~ **a** : give rise to **4 en** ~ **de** : instead of **5 tener** ~ : take place
lugarteniente *nmf* : deputy
lúgubre *adj* : gloomy
lujo *nm* **1** : luxury **2 de** ~ : deluxe — **lujoso, -sa** *adj* : luxurious
lujuria *nf* : lust
lumbre *nf* **1** : fire **2 poner en la** ~ : put on the stove
luminoso, -sa *adj* : shining, luminous
luna *nf* **1** : moon **2** : (window) glass **3** ESPEJO : mirror **4** ~ **de miel** : honeymoon — **lunar** *adj* : lunar — ~ *nm* : mole, beauty spot
lunes *nms & pl* : Monday
lupa *nf* : magnifying glass
lúpulo *nm* : hops
lustrar *vt* : shine, polish — **lustre** *nm* **1** BRILLO : luster, shine **2** ESPLENDOR : glory — **lustroso, -sa** *adj* : lustrous, shiny
luto *nm* **1** : mourning **2 estar de** ~ : be in mourning
luxación *nf, pl* **-ciones** : dislocation
luz *nf, pl* **luces 1** : light **2** : lighting (in a room, etc.) **3** *fam* : electricity **4 a la** ~ **de** : in light of **5 dar a** ~ : give birth **6 sacar a la** ~ : bring to light

M

m *nf* : m, 13th letter of the Spanish alphabet
macabro, -bra *adj* : macabre
macarrón *nm, pl* **-rrones 1** : macaroon **2**
  macarrones *nmpl* : macaroni
maceta *nf* : flowerpot
machacar {72} *vt* : crush, grind — *vi* ~
  sobre : go on about — **machacón, -cona**
  adj, mpl **-cones** : tiresome, boring
machete *nm* : machete — **machetear** *vt*
  : hack with a machete
macho *adj* **1** : male **2** *fam* : macho — ~
  nm **1** : male **2** *fam* : he-man — **machista**
  nm : male chauvinist
machucar {72} *vt* **1** : beat, crush **2** : bruise
  (fruit)
macizo, -za *adj* : solid — **macizo** *nm* ~ **de**
  flores : flower bed
mácula *nf* : stain
madeja *nf* : skein, hank
madera *nf* **1** : wood **2** : lumber (for construction) **3** ~ **dura** : hardwood —
  madero *nm* : piece of lumber, plank
madre *nf* **1** : mother **2** ~ **política** : mother-
  in-law — **madrastra** *nf* : stepmother
madreselva *nf* : honeysuckle
madriguera *nf* : burrow, den
madrileño, -ña *adj* : of or from Madrid
madrina *nf* **1** : godmother **2** : bridesmaid
  (at a wedding)
madrugada *nf* : dawn, daybreak — **madrugador, -dora** *n* : early riser
madurar *v* **1** : mature **2** : ripen (of fruit) —
  madurez *nf, pl* **-reces 1** : maturity **2**
  : ripeness (of fruit) — **maduro, -ra** *adj* **1**
  : mature **2** : ripe (of fruit)
maestría *nf* : mastery, skill — **maestro, -tra**
  adj : masterly, skilled — ~ *n* **1** : teacher
  (in grammar school) **2** EXPERTO : expert,
  master
Mafia *nf* : Mafia
magia *nf* : magic — **mágico, -ca** *adj*
  : magic, magical
magisterio *nm* : teachers *pl*, teaching profession
magistrado, -da *n* : magistrate, judge
magistral *adj* **1** : masterful **2** : magisterial
  (of an attitude, etc.)
magnánimo, -ma *adj* : magnanimous —
  magnanimidad *nf* : magnanimity
magnate *nmf* : magnate, tycoon
magnesia *nf* : magnesia — **magnesio** *nm*
  : magnesium
magnético, -ca *adj* : magnetic — **magnet-**

ismo *nm* : magnetism — **magnetizar** {21}
  vt : magnetize
magnetófono *nm* : tape recorder
magnificencia *nf* : magnificence — **magnífico, -ca** *adj* : magnificent
magnitud *nf* : magnitude
magnolia *nf* : magnolia
mago, -ga *n* **1** : magician **2 los Reyes
  Magos** : the Magi
magro, -gra *adj* **1** : lean **2** MEZQUINO
  : poor, meager
magullar *vt* : bruise — **magulladura** *nf*
  : bruise
mahometano, -na *adj* : Islamic, Muslim —
  ~ *n* : Muslim
maicena *nf* : cornstarch
maíz *nm* : corn
maja *nf* : pestle
majadero, -ra *adj* : foolish, silly — ~ *n*
  : fool
majar *vt* : crush
majestad *nf* **1** : majesty **2 Su Majestad**
  : His/Her Majesty — **majestuoso, -sa** *adj*
  : majestic
majo, -ja *adj* **1** : nice **2** GUAPO : good-looking
mal *adv* **1** : badly, poorly **2** INCORRECTA-
  MENTE : incorrectly **3** DIFÍCILMENTE : with
  difficulty, hardly **4 de** ~ **en peor** : from
  bad to worse **5 menos** ~ : it's just as well
  — ~ *nm* **1** : evil **2** DAÑO : harm, damage
  3 ENFERMEDAD : illness — ~ *adj* → **malo**
malabarismo *nm* : juggling — **malabarista**
  nmf : juggler
malacostumbrar *vt* : spoil, pamper — **mala-
  costumbrado, -da** *adj* : spoiled
malaria *nf* : malaria
malasio, -sia *adj* : Malaysian
malaventura *nf* : misfortune — **malaven-
  turado, -da** *adj* : unfortunate
malayo, -ya *adj* : Malay, Malayan
malcriado, -da *adj* : bad-mannered, spoiled
maldad *nf* **1** : evil **2** : evil deed
maldecir {11} *vt* : curse, damn — *vi* **1**
  : curse, swear **2** ~ **de** : speak ill of —
  maldición *nf, pl* **-ciones** : curse —
  maldito, -ta *adj fam* : damned
maleable *adj* : malleable
maleante *nmf* : crook
malecón *nm, pl* **-cones** : jetty
maleducado, -da *adj* : rude
maleficio *nm* : curse — **maléfico, -ca** *adj*
  : evil, harmful
malentendido *nm* : misunderstanding

malestar *nm* **1** : discomfort **2** INQUIETUD : uneasiness

maleta *nf* **1** : suitcase **2 hacer la ~** : pack one's bags — **maletero, -ra** *n* : porter — **maletero** *nm* : trunk (of an automobile) — **maletín** *nm, pl* **-tines 1** PORTAFOLIO : briefcase **2** : overnight bag

malévolo, -la *adj* : malevolent — **malevolencia** *nf* : malevolence

maleza *nf* **1** : underbrush **2** MALAS HIERBAS : weeds *pl*

malgastar *vt* : waste, squander

malhablado, -da *adj* : foul-mouthed

malhechor, -chora *n* : criminal, delinquent

malhumorado, -da *adj* : bad-tempered, cross

malicia *nf* : malice — **malicioso, -sa** *adj* : malicious

maligno, -na *adj* **1** : malignant **2** PERNICIOSO : harmful, evil

malla *nf* **1** : mesh **2 ~s** *nfpl* : tights

malo, -la *adj* (**mal** *before masculine singular nouns*) **1** : bad **2** : poor (in quality) **3** ENFERMO : unwell **4 estar de malas** : be in a bad mood — **~** *n* : villain, bad guy (in movies, etc.)

malograr *vt* : waste — **malograrse** *vr* **1** FRACASAR : fail **2** : die young — **malogro** *nm* : failure

maloliente *adj* : smelly

malpensado, -da *adj* : malicious, nasty

malsano, -na *adj* : unhealthy

malsonante *adj* : rude

malta *nf* : malt

maltratar *vt* : mistreat

maltrecho, -cha *adj* : battered

malvado, -da *adj* : evil, wicked

malvavisco *nm* : marshmallow

malversar *vt* : embezzle — **malversación** *nf, pl* **-ciones** : embezzlement

mama *nf* : teat (of an animal), breast (of a woman)

mamá *nf fam* : mom, mama

mamar *vi* **1** : suckle **2 dar de ~ a** : breastfeed — *vt* **1** : suckle, nurse **2** : learn from childhood, grow up with — **mamario, -ria** *adj* : mammary

mamarracho *nm fam* : mess, sight

mambo *nm* : mambo

mamífero, -ra *adj* : mammalian — **mamífero** *nm* : mammal

mamografía *nf* : mammogram

mampara *nf* : screen, room divider

mampostería *nf* : masonry

manada *nf* **1** : flock, herd, pack **2 en ~** : in droves

manar *vi* **1** : flow **2 ~ en** : be rich in — **manantial** *nm* **1** : spring **2** ORIGEN : source

manchar *vt* **1** : stain, spot, mark **2** : tarnish

(a reputation, etc.) — **mancharse** *vr* : get dirty — **mancha** *nf* : stain

mancillar *vt* : sully, stain

manco, -ca *adj* : one-armed, one-handed

mancomunar *vt* : combine, join — **mancomunarse** *vr* : unite — **mancomunidad** *nf* : union

mandar *vt* **1** : command, order **2** ENVIAR : send **3** *Lat* : hurl, throw — *vi* **1** : be in charge **2 ¿mande?** *Lat* : yes?, pardon? — **mandadero, -ra** *nm* : messenger — **mandado** *nm* : errand — **mandamiento** *nm* **1** : order, warrant **2** : commandment (in religion)

mandarina *nf* : mandarin orange, tangerine

mandato *nm* **1** : term of office **2** ORDEN : mandate — **mandatario, -ria** *n* **1** : leader (in politics) **2** : agent (in law)

mandíbula *nf* : jaw, jawbone

mandil *nm* : apron

mando *nm* **1** : command, leadership **2 al ~ de** : in charge of **3 ~ a distancia** : remote control

mandolina *nf* : mandolin

mandón, -dona *adj, mpl* **-dones** : bossy

manecilla *nf* : hand (of a clock), pointer

manejar *vt* **1** : handle, operate **2** : manage (a business, etc.) **3** : manipulate (a person) **4** *Lat* : drive (a car) — **manejarse** *vr* **1** : manage, get by **2** *Lat* : behave — **manejo** *nm* **1** : handling, use **2** : management (of a business, etc.)

manera *nf* **1** : way, manner **2 de ~ que** : so that **3 de ninguna ~** : by no means **4 de todas ~s** : anyway

manga *nf* **1** : sleeve **2** MANGUERA : hose

mango *nm* **1** : hilt, handle **2** : mango (fruit)

mangonear *vt fam* : boss around — *vi* **1** : be bossy **2** HOLGAZANEAR : loaf, fool around

manguera *nf* : hose

maní *nm, pl* **-níes** *Lat* : peanut

manía *nf* **1** : mania, obsession **2** MODA PASAJERA : craze, fad **3** ANTIPATÍA : dislike — **maníaco, -ca** *adj* : maniacal — **~** *n* : maniac

maniatar *vt* : tie the hands of

maniático, -ca *adj* : obsessive, fussy — **~** *n* : fussy person, fanatic

manicomio *nm* : insane asylum

manicura *nf* : manicure — **manicuro, -ra** *n* : manicurist

manido, -da *adj* : stale, hackneyed

manifestar {55} *vt* **1** : demonstrate, show **2** DECLARAR : express, declare — **manifestarse** *vr* **1** : become evident **2** : demonstrate (in politics) — **manifestación** *nf, pl* **-ciones 1** : manifestation, sign **2** : demonstration (in politics) — **manifestante** *nmf* : protester, demonstrator — **manifiesto, -ta**

manija

adj : manifest, evident — **manifiesto** *nm*
: manifesto
manija *nf* : handle
manillar *nm* : handlebars *pl*
maniobra *nf* : maneuver — **maniobrar** *v*
: maneuver
manipular *vt* **1** : manipulate **2** MANEJAR
: handle — **manipulación** *nf, pl* **-ciones**
: manipulation
maniquí *nmf, pl* **-quíes** : mannequin, model
— ~ *nm* : mannequin, dummy
manirroto, -ta *adj* : extravagant — ~ *n*
: spendthrift
manivela *nf* : crank
manjar *nm* : delicacy, special dish
mano *nf* **1** : hand **2** : coat (of paint, etc.) **3**
a ~ *or* **a la** ~ : at hand, nearby **4 dar la**
~ : shake hands **5 de segunda** ~ : secondhand **6** ~ **de obra** : labor, manpower
manojo *nm* : bunch
manopla *nf* : mitten
manosear *vt* **1** : handle excessively **2** : fondle (a person)
manotazo *nm* : slap
mansalva: a ~ *adv phr* : at close range,
without risk
mansarda *nf* : attic
mansedumbre *nf* **1** : gentleness **2** : tame-
ness (of an animal)
mansión *nf, pl* **-siones** : mansion
manso, -sa *adj* **1** : gentle **2** : tame (of an
animal)
manta *nf* **1** : blanket **2** *Lat* : poncho
manteca *nf*: lard, fat — **mantecoso, -sa** *adj*
: greasy
mantel *nm* : tablecloth — **mantelería** *nf*
: table linen
mantener {80} *vt* **1** : support **2** CONSERVAR
: preserve **3** : keep up, maintain (relations,
correspondence, etc.) **4** AFIRMAR : affirm
— **mantenerse** *vr* **1** : support oneself **2** ~
firme : hold one's ground — **mantenimiento** *nm* **1** : maintenance **2** SUSTENTO
: sustenance
mantequilla *nf* : butter — **mantequera** *nf*
: churn — **mantequería** *nf*: dairy
mantilla *nf*: mantilla
manto *nm* : cloak
mantón *nm, pl* **-tones** : shawl
manual *adj* : manual — ~ *nm* : manual,
handbook
manubrio *nm* **1** : handle, crank **2** *Lat* : handlebars *pl*
manufactura *nf* **1** : manufacture **2** FÁBRICA
: factory
manuscrito *nm* : manuscript — **manuscrito, -ta** *adj* : handwritten
manutención *nf, pl* **-ciones** : maintenance
manzana *nf* **1** : apple **2** : (city) block —

manzanar *nm* : apple orchard — **manzano**
nm : apple tree
maña *nf* **1** : skill **2** ASTUCIA : cunning, guile
mañana *adv* : tomorrow — ~ *nm* **el** ~
: the future — ~ *nf*: morning
mañoso, -sa *adj* **1** : skillful **2** *Lat* : finicky
mapa *nm* : map — **mapamundi** *nm* : map of
the world
mapache *nm* : raccoon
maqueta *nf* : model, mock-up
maquillaje *nm* : makeup — **maquillarse** *vr*
: put on makeup
máquina *nf* **1** : machine **2** LOCOMOTORA
: locomotive **3 a toda** ~ : at full speed **4**
~ **de escribir** : typewriter — **maquinación**
nf, pl **-ciones** : machination — **maquinal**
adj : mechanical — **maquinaria** *nf* **1** : machinery **2** : mechanism, works *pl* (of a
watch, etc.) — **maquinilla** *nf* : small machine — **maquinista** *nmf* **1** : machinist **2**
: (railroad) engineer
mar *nmf* **1** : sea **2 alta** ~ : high seas *pl*
maraca *nf*: maraca
maraña *nf* **1** : thicket **2** ENREDO : tangle,
mess
maratón *nm, pl* **-tones** : marathon
maravilla *nf* **1** : wonder, marvel **2** : marigold
(flower) — **maravillar** *vt* : astonish — **maravillarse** *vr* : be amazed — **maravilloso,
-sa** *adj* : marvelous
marca *nf* **1** : mark **2** : brand (on livestock)
3 *or* ~ **de fábrica** : trademark **4** : record (in
sports) — **marcado, -da** *adj* : marked —
marcador *nm* **1** : scoreboard **2** *Lat*
: marker, felt-tipped pen
marcapasos *nms & pl* : pacemaker
marcar {72} *vt* **1** : mark **2** : brand (livestock) **3** INDICAR : indicate, show **4** : dial
(a telephone, etc.) **5** : score (in sports) — *vi*
1 : score **2** : dial (on the telephone, etc.)
marchar *vi* **1** : go **2** CAMINAR : walk **3** FUN-
CIONAR : work, run — **marcharse** *vr* : leave,
go — **marcha** *nf* **1** : march **2** PASO : pace,
speed **3** : gear (of an automobile) **4 poner
en** ~ : put in motion
marchitarse *vr* : wither, wilt — **marchito,
-ta** *adj* : withered
marcial *adj* : martial, military
marco *nm* **1** : frame **2** : goalposts *pl* (in
sports) **3** ENTORNO : setting, framework
marea *nf*: tide — **marear** *vt* **1** : make nauseous or dizzy **2** CONFUNDIR : confuse —
marearse *vr* **1** : become nauseated or dizzy
2 CONFUNDIRSE : get confused — **mareado,
-da** *adj* **1** : sick, nauseous **2** ATURDIDO
: dazed, dizzy
maremoto *nm* : tidal wave
mareo *nm* **1** : nausea, seasickness **2** VÉR-
TIGO : dizziness

marfil *nm* : ivory
margarina *nf* : margarine
margarita *nf* : daisy
margen *nm, pl* **márgenes 1** : edge, border **2** : margin (of a page, etc.) — **marginado, -da** *adj* **1** : alienated **2 clases marginadas** : underclass — ~ *n* : outcast — **marginal** *adj* : marginal — **marginar** *vt* : ostracize, exclude
mariachi *nm* : mariachi musician or band
maridaje *nm* : marriage, union — **marido** *nm* : husband
marihuana *or* **mariguana** *or* **marijuana** *nf* : marijuana
marimba *nf* : marimba
marina *nf* **1** : coast **2** *or* ~ **de guerra** : navy, fleet
marinada *nf* : marinade — **marinar** *vt* : marinate
marinero, -ra *adj* **1** : sea, marine **2** : seaworthy (of a ship) — **marinero** *nm* : sailor — **marino, -na** *adj* : marine — **marino** *nm* : seaman, sailor
marioneta *nf* : puppet, marionette
mariposa *nf* **1** : butterfly **2** ~ **nocturna** : moth
mariquita *nf* : ladybug
marisco *nm* **1** : shellfish **2** ~**s** *nmpl* : seafood
marisma *nf* : salt marsh
marítimo, -ma *adj* : maritime, shipping
mármol *nm* : marble
marmota *nf* ~ **de América** : groundhog
marquesina *nf* : marquee, (glass) canopy
marrano, -na *n* **1** : pig, hog **2** *fam* : slob
marrar *vt* : miss (a target) — *vi* : fail
marrón *adj & nm, pl* **-rrones** : brown
marroquí *adj* : Moroccan
marsopa *nf* : porpoise
marsupial *nm* : marsupial
Marte *nm* : Mars
martes *nms & pl* : Tuesday
martillo *nm* **1** : hammer **2** ~ **neumático** : jackhammer — **martillar** *or* **martillear** *v* : hammer
mártir *nmf* : martyr — **martirio** *nm* : martyrdom — **martirizar** {21} *vt* **1** : martyr **2** ATORMENTAR : torment
marxismo *nm* : Marxism — **marxista** *adj & nmf* : Marxist
marzo *nm* : March
mas *conj* : but
más *adv* **1** : more **2 el/la/lo** ~ : (the) most **3** (*in negative constructions*) : (any) longer **4 ¡qué día** ~ **bonito!** : what a beautiful day! — ~ *adj* **1** : more **2** : most **3 ¿quién** ~? : who else? — ~ *prep* : plus — ~ *pron* **1** **a lo** ~ : at most **2 de** ~ : extra, spare **3**

~ **o menos** : more or less **4 ¿tienes** ~? : do you have more?
masa *nf* **1** : mass, volume **2** : dough (in cooking) **3** ~**s** *nfpl* : people, masses
masacre *nf* : massacre
masaje *nm* : massage — **masajear** *vt* : massage
mascar {72} *v* : chew
máscara *nf* : mask — **mascarada** *nf* : masquerade — **mascarilla** *nf* : mask (in medecine, etc.)
mascota *nf* : mascot
masculino, -na *adj* **1** : masculine, male **2** VARONIL : manly **3** : masculine (in grammar) — **masculinidad** *nf* : masculinity
mascullar *v* : mumble
masilla *nf* : putty
masivo, -va *adj* : mass, large-scale
masón *nm, pl* **-sones** : Mason, Freemason — **masónico, -ca** *adj* : Masonic
masoquismo *nm* : masochism — **masoquista** *adj* : masochistic — ~ *nmf* : masochist
masticar {72} *v* : chew
mástil *nm* **1** : mast **2** ASTA : flagpole **3** : neck (of a stringed instrument)
mastín *nm, pl* **-tines** : mastiff
masturbarse *vr* : masturbate — **masturbación** *nf, pl* **-ciones** : masturbation
mata *nf* : bush, shrub
matadero *nm* : slaughterhouse
matador *nm* : matador, bullfighter
matamoscas *nms & pl* : flyswatter
matar *vt* **1** : kill **2** : slaughter (animals) — **matarse** *vr* **1** : be killed **2** SUICIDARSE : commit suicide — **matanza** *nf* : slaughter, killing
matasanos *nms & pl fam* : quack
matasellos *nms & pl* : postmark
mate *adj* : matte, dull — ~ *nm* **1** : maté **2 jaque** ~ : checkmate
matemáticas *nfpl* : mathematics — **matemático, -ca** *adj* : mathematical — ~ *n* : mathematician
materia *nf* **1** ASUNTO : matter **2** MATERIAL : material — **material** *adj* **1** : material **2** : material **2** EQUIPO : equipment, gear — **materialismo** *nm* : materialism — **materialista** *adj* : materialistic — **materializar** {21} *vt* : bring to fruition — **materializarse** *vr* : materialize — **materialmente** *adv* : absolutely
maternal *adj* : maternal — **maternidad** *nf* **1** : motherhood **2** : maternity hospital — **materno, -na** *adj* **1** : maternal **2 lengua materna** : mother tongue
matinal *adj* : morning
matinée *or* **matiné** *nf* : matinee

matiz *nm, pl* **-tices 1** : nuance **2** : hue, shade (of colors) — **matizar** {21} *vt* **1** : blend (colors) **2** : qualify (a statement, etc.) **3** ~ **de** : tinge with

matón *nm, pl* **-tones 1** : bully **2** CRIMINAL : gangster, hoodlum

matorral *nm* : thicket

matraca *nf* **1** : rattle, noisemaker **2 dar la** ~ **a** : pester

matriarcado *nm* : matriarchy

matrícula *nf* **1** : list, roll, register **2** INSCRIPCIÓN : registration **3** : license plate (of an automobile) — **matricular** *vt* : register — **matricularse** *vr* : register, matriculate

matrimonio *nm* **1** : marriage **2** PAREJA : (married) couple — **matrimonial** *adj* : marital

matriz *nf, pl* **-trices 1** : matrix **2** : uterus, womb (in anatomy)

matrona *nf* : matron

matutino, -na *adj* : morning

maullar {8} *vi* : meow — **maullido** *nm* : meow

maxilar *nm* : jaw, jawbone

máxima *nf* : maxim

máxime *adv* : especially

máximo, -ma *adj* : maximum, highest — **máximo** *nm* **1** : maximum **2 al** ~ : to the full

maya *adj*: Mayan

mayo *nm* : May

mayonesa *nf* : mayonnaise

mayor *adj* **1** (*comparative of* **grande**) : bigger, larger, greater, older **2** (*superlative of* **grande**) : biggest, largest, greatest, oldest **3 al por** ~ : wholesale **4** ~ **de edad** : of (legal) age — ~ *nmf* **1** : major (in the military) **2** ADULTO : adult **3** ~**es** *nmfpl* : grown-ups — **mayoral** *nm* : foreman

mayordomo *nm* : butler

mayoreo *nm Lat* : wholesale

mayoría *nf* : majority

mayorista *adj* : wholesale — ~ *nmf* : wholesaler

mayormente *adv* : primarily

mayúscula *nf* : capital letter — **mayúsculo, -la** *adj* **1** : capital, uppercase **2 un fallo mayúsculo** : a terrible mistake

maza *nf* : mace (weapon)

mazapán *nm, pl* **-panes** : marzipan

mazmorra *nf* : dungeon

mazo *nm* **1** : mallet **2** MAJA : pestle

mazorca *nf* ~ **de maíz** : corncob

me *pron* **1** (*direct object*) : me **2** (*indirect object*) : to me, for me, from me **3** (*reflexive*) : myself, to myself, for myself, from myself

mecánica *nf* : mechanics — **mecánico, -ca** *adj* : mechanical — ~ *n* : mechanic

mecanismo *nm* : mechanism — **mecanización** *nf, pl* **-ciones** : mechanization — **mecanizar** {21} *vt* : mechanize

mecanografiar {85} *vt* : type — **mecanografía** *nf* : typing — **mecanógrafo, -fa** *n* : typist

mecate *nm Lat* : rope

mecedora *nf* : rocking chair

mecenas *nmfs & pl* : patron, sponsor — **mecenazgo** *nm* : patronage, sponsorship

mecer {86} *vt* **1** : rock **2** : push (on a swing) — **mecerse** *vr* : rock, swing

mecha *nf* **1** : fuse (of a bomb, etc.) **2** : wick (of a candle)

mechero *nm* **1** : burner **2** *Spain* : cigarette lighter

mechón *nm, pl* **-chones** : lock (of hair)

medalla *nf* : medal — **medallón** *nm, pl* **-llones** **1** : medallion **2** : locket (jewelry)

media *nf* **1** : average **2** ~**s** *nfpl* : stockings **3 a** ~**s** : by halves, halfway

mediación *nf, pl* **-ciones** : mediation

mediado, -da *adj* **1** : half full, half empty, half over **2** : halfway through — **mediados** *nmpl* **a** ~ **de** : halfway through, in the middle of

mediador, -dora *n* : mediator

medialuna *nf* **1** : crescent **2** : croissant (pastry)

medianamente *adv* : fairly

medianero, -ra *adj* **pared medianera** : dividing wall

mediano, -na *adj* **1** : medium, average **2** MEDIOCRE : mediocre

medianoche *nf* : midnight

mediante *prep* : through, by means of

mediar *vi* **1** : be in the middle **2** INTERVENIR : mediate **3** ~ **entre** : be between

medicación *nf, pl* **-ciones** : medication — **medicamento** *nm* : medicine — **medicar** {72} *vt* : medicate — **medicarse** *vr* : take medicine — **medicina** *nf* : medicine — **medicinal** *adj* : medicinal

medición *nf, pl* **-ciones** : measurement

médico, -ca *adj* : medical — ~ *n* : doctor, physician

medida *nf* **1** : measurement, measure **2** MODERACIÓN : moderation **3** GRADO : extent, degree **4 tomar** ~**s** : take steps — **medidor** *nm Lat* : meter, gauge

medieval *adj* : medieval

medio, -dia *adj* **1** : half **2** MEDIANO : average **3 una media hora** : half an hour **4 la clase media** : the middle class — **medio** *adv* : half — ~ *nm* **1** : half **2** MANERA : means *pl*, way **3 en** ~ **de** : in the middle of **4** ~ **ambiente** : environment **5** ~**s** *nmpl* : means, resources

mediocre *adj* : mediocre, average — **mediocridad** *nf* : mediocrity
mediodía *nm* : noon, midday
medioevo *nm* : Middle Ages
medir {54} *vt* **1** : measure **2** CONSIDERAR : weigh, consider — **medirse** *vr* : be moderate
meditar *vi* : meditate, contemplate — *vt* **1** : think over, consider **2** PLANEAR : plan, work out — **meditación** *nf, pl* **-ciones** : meditation
mediterráneo, -nea *adj* : Mediterranean
medrar *vt* : flourish, thrive
medroso, -sa *adj* : fearful
médula *nf* **1** : marrow **2** ~ **espinal** : spinal cord
medusa *nf* : jellyfish
megabyte *nm* : megabyte
megáfono *nm* : megaphone
mejicano → **mexicano**
mejilla *nf* : cheek
mejillón *nm, pl* **-llones** : mussel
mejor *adv* **1** (*comparative*) : better **2** (*superlative*) : best **3 a lo** ~ : maybe, perhaps — ~ *adj* **1** (*comparative of* **bueno** *or* **bien**) : better **2** (*superlative of* **bueno** *or* **bien**) : best **3 lo** ~ : the best thing **4 tanto** ~ : so much the better — **mejora** *nf* : improvement
mejorana *nf* : marjoram
mejorar *vt* : improve — *vi* : improve, get better
mejunje *nm* : concoction, brew
melancolía *nf* : melancholy — **melancólico, -ca** *adj* : melancholic, melancholy
melaza *nf* : molasses
melena *nf* **1** : long hair **2** : mane (of a lion)
melindroso, -sa *adj* **1** : affected **2** *Lat* : finicky
mella *nf* : chip, nick — **mellado, -da** *adj* : chipped, jagged
mellizo, -za *adj & n* : twin
melocotón *nm, pl* **-tones** : peach
melodía *nf* : melody — **melódico, -ca** *adj* : melodic
melodrama *nm* : melodrama — **melodramático, -ca** *adj* : melodramatic
melón *nm, pl* **-lones** : melon
meloso, -sa *adj* **1** : sweet, honeyed **2** EMPALAGOSO : cloying
membrana *nf* : membrane
membrete *nm* : letterhead, heading
membrillo *nm* : quince
membrudo, -da *adj* : muscular, burly
memorable *adj* : memorable
memorándum *or* **memorando** *nm, pl* **-dums** *or* **-dos** **1** : memorandum **2** AGENDA : notebook
memoria *nf* **1** : memory **2** RECUERDO : re-

membrance **3** INFORME : report **4 de** ~ : by heart **5** ~**s** *nfpl* : memoirs — **memorizar** {21} *vt* : memorize
mena *nf* : ore
menaje *nm* : household goods *pl*, furnishings *pl*
mencionar *vt* : mention, refer to — **mención** *nf, pl* **-ciones** : mention
mendaz *adj, pl* **-daces** : lying
mendigar {52} *vi* : beg — *vt* : beg for — **mendicidad** *nf* : begging — **mendigo, -ga** *n* : beggar
mendrugo *nm* : crust (of bread)
menear *vt* **1** : move, shake **2** : sway (one's hips) **3** : wag (a tail) — **menearse** *vr* **1** : sway, shake, move **2** *fam* : hurry up
menester *nm* **ser** ~ : be necessary — **menesteroso, -sa** *adj* : needy
menguar *vt* : diminish, lessen — *vi* **1** : decline, decrease **2** : wane (of the moon) — **mengua** *nf* : decrease, decline
menopausia *nf* : menopause
menor *adj* **1** (*comparative of* **pequeño**) : smaller, lesser, younger **2** (*superlative of* **pequeño**) : smallest, least, youngest **3** : minor (in music) **4 al por** ~ : retail — ~ *nmf* : minor, juvenile
menos *adv* **1** (*comparative*) : less **2** (*superlative*) : least **3** ~ **de** : fewer than — ~ *adj* **1** (*comparative*) : less, fewer **2** (*superlative*) : least, fewest — ~ *prep* **1** : minus **2** EXCEPTO : except — ~ *pron* **1** : less, fewer **2 al** ~ *or* **por lo** ~ : at least **3 a** ~ **que** : unless — **menoscabar** *vt* **1** : lessen **2** ESTROPEAR : harm, damage — **menospreciar** *vt* **1** DESPRECIAR : scorn **2** SUBESTIMAR : undervalue — **menosprecio** *nm* : contempt
mensaje *nm* : message — **mensajero, -ra** *n* : messenger
menso, -sa *adj Lat fam* : foolish, stupid
menstruar {3} *vi* : menstruate — **menstruación** *nf* : menstruation
mensual *adj* : monthly — **mensualidad** *nf* **1** : monthly payment **2** : monthly salary
mensurable *adj* : measurable
menta *nf* **1** : mint, peppermint **2** ~ **verde** : spearmint
mental *adj* : mental — **mentalidad** *nf* : mentality
mentar {55} *vt* : mention, name
mente *nf* : mind
mentir {76} *vi* : lie — **mentira** *nf* : lie — **mentirilla** *nf* : fib — **mentiroso, -sa** *adj* : lying — ~ *n* : liar
mentís *nms & pl* : denial
mentol *nm* : menthol
mentón *nm, pl* **-tones** : chin
menú *nm, pl* **-nús** : menu

menudear *vi* : occur frequently — **menudeo** *nm Lat* : retail, retailing
menudillos *nmpl* : giblets
menudo, -da *adj* **1** : small, insignificant **2 a ~** : often
meñique *nm or* **dedo ~** : little finger, pinkie
meollo *nm* **1** : marrow **2** ESENCIA : essence, core
mercado *nm* **1** : market **2 ~ de valores** : stock market — **mercadería** *nf* : merchandise, goods *pl*
mercancía *nf* : merchandise, goods *pl* — **mercante** *nmf* : merchant, dealer — **mercantil** *adj* : commercial
mercenario, -ria *adj & n* : mercenary
mercería *nf* : notions store
mercurio *nm* : mercury
Mercurio *nm* : Mercury (planet)
merecer {53} *vt* : deserve — *vi* : be worthy — **merecedor, -dora** *adj* : deserving, worthy — **merecido** *nm* **recibir su ~** : get one's just deserts
merendar {55} *vi* : have an afternoon snack — *vt* : have as an afternoon snack — **merendero** *nm* **1** : snack bar **2** : picnic area
merengue *nm* **1** : meringue **2** : merengue (dance)
meridiano, -na *adj* **1** : midday **2** CLARO : crystal-clear — **meridiano** *nm* : meridian — **meridional** *adj* : southern
merienda *nf* : afternoon snack, tea
mérito *nm* : merit, worth — **meritorio, -ria** *adj* : deserving — **~** *n* : intern, trainee
mermar *vi* : decrease — *vt* : reduce, cut down — **merma** *nf* : decrease
mermelada *nf* : marmalade, jam
mero, -ra *adj* **1** : mere, simple **2** *Lat fam* (*used as an intensifier*) : very, real — **mero** *adv Lat fam* **1** : nearly, almost **2 aquí ~** : right here
merodear *vi* **1** : maraud **2 ~ por** : prowl about (a place)
mes *nm* : month
mesa *nf* **1** : table **2** COMITÉ : committee, board
mesarse *vr* **~ los cabellos** : tear one's hair
meseta *nf* : plateau
Mesías *nm* : Messiah
mesilla *nf* : small table
mesón *nm, pl* **-sones** : inn — **mesonero, -ra** *nm* : innkeeper
mestizo, -za *adj* **1** : of mixed ancestry **2** HÍBRIDO : hybrid — **~** *n* : person of mixed ancestry
mesura *nf* : moderation — **mesurado, -da** *adj* : moderate, restrained
meta *nf* : goal, objective
metabolismo *nm* : metabolism

metafísica *nf* : metaphysics — **metafísico, -ca** *adj* : metaphysical
metáfora *nf* : metaphor — **metafórico, -ca** *adj* : metaphoric, metaphorical
metal *nm* **1** : metal **2** : brass section (in an orchestra) — **metálico, -ca** *adj* : metallic, metal — **metalurgia** *nf* : metallurgy
metamorfosis *nfs & pl* : metamorphosis
metano *nm* : methane
metedura *nf* **~ de pata** *fam* : blunder
meteoro *nm* : meteor — **meteórico, -ca** *adj* : meteoric — **meteorito** *nm* : meteorite — **meteorología** *nf* : meteorology — **meteorólogo, -ga** *adj* : meteorological, meteorologic — **~** *n* : meteorologist
meter *vt* **1** : put (in) **2** : place (in a job, etc.) **3** ENREDAR : involve **4** CAUSAR : make, cause **5** : spread (a rumor) **6** *Lat* : strike (a blow) — **meterse** *vr* **1** : get in, enter **2 ~ en** : get involved in, meddle in **3 ~ con** *fam* : pick a fight with
meticuloso, -sa *adj* : meticulous
método *nm* : method — **metódico, -ca** *adj* : methodical — **metodología** *nf* : methodology
metomentodo *nmf fam* : busybody
metralla *nf* : shrapnel — **metralleta** *nf* : submachine gun
métrico, -ca *adj* : metric, metrical
metro *nm* **1** : meter **2** : subway (train)
metrópoli *nf or* **metrópolis** *nfs & pl* : metropolis — **metropolitano, -na** *adj* : metropolitan
mexicano, -na *adj* : Mexican — **mexicoamericano, -na** *adj* : Mexican-American
mezcla *nf* **1** : mixture **2** ARGAMASA : mortar — **mezclar** *vt* **1** : mix, blend **2** CONFUNDIR : mix up, muddle **3** INVOLUCRAR : involve — **mezclarse** *vr* **1** : get mixed up **2** : mingle (socially) — **mezcolanza** *nf* : mixture
mezclilla *nf Lat* : denim
mezquino, -na *adj* **1** : mean, petty **2** ESCASO : meager — **mezquindad** *nf* : meanness, stinginess
mezquita *nf* : mosque
mezquite *nm* : mesquite
mi *adj* : my
mí *pron* **1** : me **2** *or* **~ mismo, ~ misma** : myself **3 a ~ no me importa** : it doesn't matter to me
miajas → **migajas**
miau *nm* : meow
mica *nf* : mica
mico *nm* : (long-tailed) monkey
microbio *nm* : microbe, germ — **microbiología** *nf* : microbiology
microbús *nm, pl* **-buses** : minibus
microcosmos *nms & pl* : microcosm

microfilm *nm, pl* **-films** : microfilm
micrófono *nm* : microphone
microondas *nms & pl* : microwave (oven)
microorganismo *nm* : microorganism
microscopio *nm* : microscope — **microscópico, -ca** *adj* : microscopic
miedo *nm* **1** : fear **2 dar** ~ : be frightening — **miedoso, -sa** *adj* : fearful
miel *nf* : honey
miembro *nm* **1** : member **2** EXTREMIDAD : limb, extremity
mientras *adv or* ~ **tanto** : meanwhile, in the meantime — ~ *conj* **1** : while, as **2** ~ **que** : while, whereas **3** ~ **viva** : as long as I live
miércoles *nms & pl* : Wednesday
mies *nf* : (ripe) corn, grain
miga *nf* : crumb — **migajas** *nfpl* **1** : breadcrumbs **2** SOBRAS : leftovers
migración *nf, pl* **-ciones** : migration
migraña *nf* : migraine
migrar *vi* : migrate
mijo *nm* : millet
mil *adj & nm* : thousand
milagro *nm* : miracle — **milagroso, -sa** *adj* : miraculous
milenio *nm* : millennium
milésimo, -ma *adj* : thousandth
milicia *nf* **1** : militia **2** : military (service)
miligramo *nm* : milligram
mililitro *nm* : milliliter
milímetro *nm* : millimeter
militante *adj & nmf* : militant
militar *adj* : military — ~ *nmf* : soldier — **militarizar** {21} *vt* : militarize
milla *nf* : mile
millar *nm* : thousand
millón *nm, pl* **-llones 1** : million **2 mil millones** : billion — **millonario, -ria** *n* : millionaire — **millonésimo, -ma** *adj* : millionth
mimar *vt* : pamper, spoil
mimbre *nm* : wicker
mímica *nf* **1** : mime, sign language **2** IMITACIÓN : mimicry
mimo *nm* : pampering — ~ *nmf* : mime
mina *nf* **1** : mine **2** : lead (for pencils) — **minar** *vt* **1** : mine **2** DEBILITAR : undermine
mineral *adj* : mineral — ~ *nm* **1** : mineral **2** : ore (of a metal)
minería *nf* : mining — **minero, -ra** *adj* : mining — ~ *n* : miner
miniatura *nf* : miniature
minifalda *nf* : miniskirt
minifundio *nm* : small farm
minimizar {21} *vt* : minimize
mínimo, -ma *adj* **1** : minimum **2** MINÚSCULO : minute **3 en lo más** ~ : in the slightest — **mínimo** *nm* : minimum

minino, -na *n fam* : pussycat
ministerio *nm* : ministry — **ministro, -tra** *n* **1** : minister, secretary **2 primer ministro** : prime minister
minoría *nf* : minority
minorista *adj* : retail — ~ *nmf* : retailer
minoritario, -ria *adj* : minority
minucia *nf* : trifle, small detail — **minucioso, -sa** *adj* **1** : detailed **2** METICULOSO : thorough
minué *nm* : minuet
minúsculo, -la *adj* : minuscule, tiny
minusvalía *nf* : handicap, disability — **minusválido, -da** *adj* : disabled
minuta *nf* **1** : bill, fee **2** BORRADOR : rough draft
minuto *nm* : minute — **minutero** *nm* : minute hand
mío, mía *adj* **1** : mine **2 una amiga mía** : a friend of mine — ~ *pron* **el mío, la mía** : mine, my own
miope *adj* : nearsighted
mirar *vt* **1** : look at **2** OBSERVAR : watch **3** CONSIDERAR : consider — *vi* **1** : look **2** ~ **a** : face, overlook **3** ~ **por** : look after — **mirarse** *vr* **1** : look at oneself **2** : look at each other — **mira** *nf* **1** : sight (of a firearm or instrument) **2** INTENCIÓN : aim, objective — **mirada** *nf* : look — **mirado, -da** *adj* **1** : careful **2** CONSIDERADO : considerate **3 bien** ~ : well thought of — **mirador** *nm* **1** BALCÓN : balcony **2** : lookout, vantage point — **miramiento** *nm* : consideration
mirlo *nm* : blackbird
misa *nf* : Mass
miscelánea *nf* : miscellany
miserable *adj* **1** : poor **2** LASTIMOSO : miserable, wretched — **miseria** *nf* **1** : poverty **2** DESGRACIA : misfortune, misery
misericordia *nf* : mercy — **misericordioso, -sa** *adj* : merciful
mísero, -ra *adj* : wretched, miserable
misil *nm* : missile
misión *nf, pl* **-siones** : mission — **misionero, -ra** *adj & n* : missionary
mismo *adv* (*used for emphasis*) : right, exactly — **mismo, -ma** *adj* **1** : same **2** (*used for emphasis*) : very **3** : -self **4 por lo** ~ : for that reason
misoginia *nf* : misogyny — **misógino** *nm* : misogynist
misterio *nm* : mystery — **misterioso, -sa** *adj* : mysterious
mística *nf* : mysticism — **místico, -ca** *adj* : mystic, mystical — ~ *n* : mystic
mitad *nf* **1** : half **2** MEDIO : middle
mítico, -ca *adj* : mythical, mythic
mitigar {52} *vt* : mitigate
mitin *nm, pl* **mítines** : (political) meeting

mito *nm* : myth — **mitología** *nm* : mythology — **mitológico, -ca** *adj* : mythological
mixto, -ta *adj* **1** : mixed, joint **2** : coeducational (of a school)
mnemónico, -ca *adj* : mnemonic
mobiliario *nm* : furniture
mocasín *nm, pl* **-sines** : moccasin
mochila *nf* : backpack, knapsack
moción *nf, pl* **-ciones** : motion
moco *nm* **1** : mucus **2 limpiarse los** ~**s** : wipe one's nose — **mocoso, -sa** *n fam* : kid, brat
moda *nf* **1** : fashion, style **2 a la** ~ *or de* ~ : in style, fashionable **3** ~ **pasajera** : fad — **modal** *adj* : modal — **modales** *nmpl* : manners — **modalidad** *nf* : type, kind
modelar *vt* : model, mold — **modelo** *adj* : model — ~ *nm* : model, pattern — ~ *nmf* : model, mannequin
módem *or* **modem** [ˈmoðem] *nm* : modem
moderar *vt* **1** : moderate **2** : reduce (speed, etc.) **3** PRESIDIR : chair (a meeting) — **moderarse** *vr* : restrain oneself — **moderación** *nf, pl* **-ciones** : moderation — **moderado, -da** *adj & n* : moderate — **moderador, -dora** *n* : moderator, chairperson
moderno, -na *adj* : modern — **modernismo** *nm* : modernism — **modernizar** {21} *vt* : modernize
modesto, -ta *adj* : modest — **modestia** *nf* : modesty
modificar {72} *vt* : modify, alter — **modificación** *nf, pl* **-ciones** : alteration
modismo *nm* : idiom
modista *nmf* **1** : dressmaker **2** : (fashion) designer
modo *nm* **1** : way, manner **2** : mood (in grammar) **3** : mode (in music) **4 a** ~ **de** : by way of **5 de** ~ **que** : so (that) **6 de todos** ~**s** : in any case, anyway
modorra *nf* : drowsiness
modular *vt* : modulate — **modulación** *nf, pl* **-ciones** : modulation
módulo *nm* : module, unit
mofa *nf* : ridicule, mockery — **mofarse** *vr* ~ **de** : make fun of
mofeta *nf* : skunk
moflete *nm fam* : fat cheek — **mofletudo, -da** *adj fam* : fat-cheeked, chubby
mohín *nm, pl* **-hines** : grimace — **mohino, -na** *adj* : sulky
moho *nm* **1** : mold, mildew **2** ÓXIDO : rust — **mohoso, -sa** *adj* **1** : moldy **2** OXIDADO : rusty
moisés *nm, pl* **-seses** : bassinet, cradle
mojar *vt* **1** : wet, moisten **2** : dunk (food) — **mojarse** *vr* : get wet — **mojado, -da** *adj* : wet, damp

mojigato, -ta *adj* : prudish — ~ *n* : prude
mojón *nm, pl* **-jones** : boundary stone, marker
molar *nm* : molar
moldear *vt* : mold, shape — **molde** *nm* : mold, form — **moldura** *nf* : molding
mole[1] *nf* : mass, bulk
mole[2] *nm* **1** : Mexican chili sauce **2** : meat served with mole
molécula *nf* : molecule — **molecular** *adj* : molecular
moler {47} *vt* : grind, crush
molestar *vt* **1** : annoy, bother **2 no** ~ : do not disturb — *vi* : be a nuisance — **molestarse** *vr* **1** : bother **2** OFENDERSE : take offense — **molestia** *nf* **1** : annoyance, nuisance **2** MALESTAR : discomfort — **molesto, -ta** *adj* **1** : annoyed **2** FASTIDIOSO : annoying **3** INCÓMODO : in discomfort — **molestoso, -sa** *adj* : bothersome, annoying
molido, -da *adj* **1** : ground (of meat, etc.) **2** *fam* : worn out, exhausted
molino *nm* **1** : mill **2** ~ **de viento** : windmill — **molinero, -ra** *n* : miller — **molinillo** *nm* : grinder, mill
mollera *nf* **1** : crown (of the head) **2** *fam* : brains *pl*
molusco *nm* : mollusk
momento *nm* **1** : moment, instant **2** : (period of) time **3** : momentum (in physics) **4 de** ~ : for the moment **5 de un** ~ **a otro** : any time now — **momentáneamente** *adv* : momentarily — **momentáneo, -nea** *adj* **1** : momentary **2** PASAJERO : temporary
momia *nf* : mummy
monaguillo *nm* : altar boy
monarca *nmf* : monarch — **monarquía** *nf* : monarchy — **monástico, -ca** *adj* : monastic
monasterio *nm* : monastery — **monástico, -ca** *adj* : monastic
mondadientes *nms & pl* : toothpick
mondar *vt* : peel
mondongo *nm* : innards *pl*, guts *pl*
moneda *nf* **1** : coin **2** : currency (of a country) — **monedero** *nm* : change purse
monetario, -ria *adj* : monetary
monitor *nm* : monitor
monja *nf* : nun — **monje** *nm* : monk
mono, -na *n* : monkey — ~ *adj fam* : lovely, cute
monogamia *nf* : monogamy — **monógamo -ma** *adj* : monogamous
monografía *nf* : monograph
monograma *nm* : monogram
monolingüe *adj* : monolingual
monólogo *nm* : monologue
monopatín *nm, pl* **-tines** : scooter, skateboard

monopolio *nm* : monopoly — **monopolizar**
{21} *vt* : monopolize
monosílabo *nm* : monosyllable — **mono-
silábico, -ca** *adj* : monosyllabic
monoteísmo *nm* : monotheism — **mono-
teísta** *adj* : monotheistic
monotonía *nf* : monotony — **monótono,
-na** *adj* : monotonous
monóxido *nm* ~ **de carbono** : carbon
monoxide
monstruo *nm* : monster — **monstruosidad**
nf : monstrosity — **monstruoso, -sa** *adj*
: monstrous
monta *nf* : importance, value
montaje *nm* **1** : assembly **2** : staging (in
theater), editing (of films)
montaña *nf* **1** : mountain **2** ~ **rusa** : roller
coaster — **montañero, -ra** *n* : mountain
climber — **montañoso, -sa** *adj* : mountainous
montar *vt* **1** : mount **2** ESTABLECER : establish **3** ENSAMBLAR : assemble, put together
4 : stage (a performance) **5** : cock (a gun)
— *vi* **1** ~ **a caballo** : ride horseback **2** ~
en bicicleta : get on a bicycle
monte *nm* **1** : mountain **2** BOSQUE : wood-
land **3** *or* ~ **bajo** : scrubland **4** ~ **de
piedad** : pawnshop
montés *adj, pl* **-teses** : wild (of animals or
plants)
montículo *nm* : mound, hillock
montón *nm, pl* **-tones** **1** : heap, pile **2 un**
~ **de** *fam* : lots of
montura *nf* **1** : mount (horse) **2** SILLA : saddle **3** : frame (of glasses)
monumento *nm* : monument — **monumental** *adj fam* : monumental, huge
monzón *nm, pl* **-zones** : monsoon
moño *nm* **1** : bun (of hair) **2** *Lat* : bow
(knot)
mora *nf* **1** : mulberry **2** ZARZAMORA
: blackberry
morada *nf* : residence, dwelling
morado, -da *adj* : purple — **morado** *nm*
: purple
moral *adj* : moral — ~ *nf* **1** : ethics, morals
pl **2** ÁNIMO : morale — **moraleja** *nf* : moral
(of a story) — **moralidad** *nf* : morality —
moralista *adj* : moralistic — ~ *nmf*
: moralist
morar *vi* : live, reside
morboso, -sa *adj* : morbid
mordaz *adj* : caustic, scathing — **mordaci-
dad** *nf* : bite, sharpness
mordaza *nf* : gag
morder {47} *v* : bite — **mordedura** *nf* : bite
(of an animal)
mordisquear *vt* : nibble (on) — **mordisco**
nm : nibble, bite

moreno, -na *adj* **1** : dark-haired, brunette **2**
: dark-skinned — ~ *n* **1** : brunette **2**
: dark-skinned person
moretón *nm, pl* **-tones** : bruise
morfina *nf* : morphine
morir {46} *vi* **1** : die **2** APAGARSE : die out,
go out — **morirse** *vr* **1** ~ **de** : die of **2** ~
por : be dying for — **moribundo, -da** *adj*
: dying
moro, -ra *adj* : Moorish — ~ *n* : Moor
moroso, -sa *adj* : delinquent, in arrears —
morosidad *nf* : delinquency (in payment)
morral *nm* : backpack
morriña *nf* : homesickness
morro *nm* : snout
morsa *nf* : walrus
morse *nm* : Morse code
mortaja *nf* : shroud
mortal *adj* **1** : mortal **2** : deadly (of a
wound, an enemy, etc.) — ~ *nmf* : mortal
— **mortalidad** *nf* : mortality — **mortandad**
nf : death toll
mortero *nm* : mortar
mortífero, -ra *adj* : deadly, lethal
mortificar {72} *vt* **1** : mortify **2** ATORMEN-
TAR : torment — **mortificarse** *vr* : be distressed
mosaico *nm* : mosaic
mosca *nf* : fly
moscada *adj* → **nuez**
mosquearse *vr fam* **1** : become suspicious
2 ENFADARSE : get annoyed
mosquito *nm* : mosquito — **mosquitero** *nm*
1 : (window) screen **2** : mosquito net
mostachón *nm, pl* **-chones** : macaroon
mostaza *nf* : mustard
mostrador *nm* : counter (in a store)
mostrar {19} *vt* : show — **mostrarse** *vr*
: show oneself, appear
mota *nf* : spot, speck — **moteado, -da** *adj*
: speckled, spotted
mote *nm* : nickname
motel *nm* : motel
motín *nm, pl* **-tines** **1** : riot, uprising **2**
: mutiny (of troops)
motivo *nm* **1** : motive, cause **2** : motif (in
art, music, etc.) — **motivación** *nf, pl*
-ciones : motivation — **motivar** *vt* **1** : cause
2 IMPULSAR : motivate
moto *nf* : motorcycle, motorbike — **motocicleta** *nf* : motorcycle — **motociclista** *nmf*
: motorcyclist
motor, -triz *or* **-tora** *adj* : motor — **motor**
nm : motor, engine — **motorista** *nmf* **1**
: motorcyclist **2** *Lat* : motorist
mover {47} *vt* **1** : move, shift **2** : shake (the
head) **3** PROVOCAR : provoke — **moverse**
vr **1** : move (over) **2** APRESURARSE : get a

move on — **movedizo, -za** *adj* : movable, shifting — **movible** *adj* : movable

móvil *adj* : mobile — ~ *nm* **1** MOTIVO : motive **2** : mobile — **movilidad** *nf* : mobility — **movilizar** {21} *vt* : mobilize

movimiento *nm* **1** : movement, motion **2** ~ **sindicalista** : labor movement

mozo, -za *adj* : young — ~ *n* **1** : young man *m*, young woman *f* **2** *Lat* : waiter *m*, waitress *f*

muchacho, -cha *n* : kid, boy *m*, girl *f*

muchedumbre *nf* : crowd

mucho *adv* **1** : very much, a lot **2** : long, a long time — **mucho, -cha** *adj* **1** : a lot of, many, much **2 muchas veces** : often — ~ *pron* : a lot, many, much

mucosidad *nf* : mucus

muda *nf* **1** : molting (of animals) **2** : change (of clothing) — **mudanza** *nf* **1** : change **2** TRASLADO : move, change of residence — **mudar** *v* **1** : molt, shed **2** CAMBIAR : change — **mudarse** *vr* **1** : change (one's clothes) **2** TRASLADARSE : move (one's residence)

mudo, -da *adj* **1** : mute **2** SILENCIOSO : silent

mueble *nm* **1** : piece of furniture **2** ~s *nmpl* : furniture, furnishings

mueca *nf* **1** : grimace, face **2 hacer** ~s : makes faces

muela *nf* **1** : tooth, molar **2** ~ **de juicio** : wisdom tooth

muelle *adj* : soft — ~ *nm* **1** : wharf, jetty **2** RESORTE : spring

muérdago *nm* : mistletoe

muerte *nf* : death — **muerto, -ta** *adj* **1** : dead **2** : dull (of colors, etc.) — ~ *nm* : dead person, deceased

muesca *nf* : nick, notch

muestra *nf* **1** : sample **2** SEÑAL : sign, show

mugir {35} *vi* : moo, bellow — **mugido** *nm* : mooing, bellowing

mugre *nf* : grime, filth — **mugriento, -ta** *adj* : filthy, grimy

muguete *nm* : lily of the valley

mujer *nf* **1** : woman **2** ESPOSA : wife **3** ~ **de negocios** : businesswoman

mulato, -ta *adj & n* : mulatto

muleta *nf* **1** : crutch **2** APOYO : prop, support

mullido, -da *adj* : soft, spongy

mulo, -la *n* : mule

multa *nf* : fine — **multar** *vt* : fine

multicolor *adj* : multicolored

multicultural *adj* : multicultural

multimedia *adj* : multimedia

multinacional *adj* : multinational

multiplicar {72} *v* : multiply — **multiplicarse** *vr* : multiply, reproduce — **múltiple** *adj* : multiple — **multiplicación** *nf, pl* **-ciones** : multiplication — **múltiplo** *nm* : multiple

multitud *nf* : crowd, multitude

mundo *nm* **1** : world **2 todo el** ~ : everyone, everybody — **mundanal** *adj* : worldly — **mundano, -na** *adj* **1** : worldly, earthly **2 la vida mundana** : high society — **mundial** *adj* : world, worldwide

municiones *nfpl* : ammunition

municipal *adj* : municipal — **municipio** *nm* **1** : municipality **2** AYUNTAMIENTO : town council

muñeca *nf* **1** : doll **2** : wrist (in anatomy) — **muñeco** *nm* **1** : boy doll **2** MANIQUÍ : dummy, puppet

muñón *nm, pl* **-ñones** : stump (of an arm or leg)

mural *adj & nm* : mural — **muralla** *nf* : wall, rampart

murciélago *nm* : bat (animal)

murmullo *nm* **1** : murmur, murmuring **2** : rustling (of leaves, etc.)

murmurar *vi* **1** : murmur, whisper **2** CRITICAR : gossip

muro *nm* : wall

musa *nf* : muse

musaraña *nf* : shrew

músculo *nm* : muscle — **muscular** *adj* : muscular — **musculatura** *nf* : muscles *pl* — **musculoso, -sa** *adj* : muscular

muselina *nf* : muslin

museo *nm* : museum

musgo *nm* : moss — **musgoso, -sa** *adj* : mossy

música *nf* : music — **musical** *adj* : musical — **músico, -ca** *adj* : musical — ~ *n* : musician

musitar *vt* : mumble

muslo *nm* : thigh

musulmán, -mana *adj & n, mpl* **-manes** : Muslim

mutar *v* : mutate — **mutación** *nf, pl* **-ciones** : mutation — **mutante** *adj & nmf* : mutant

mutilar *vt* : mutilate — **mutilación** *nf, pl* **-ciones** : mutilation

mutuo, -tua *adj* : mutual

muy *adv* **1** : very, quite **2** DEMASIADO : too

N

n *nf* : n, 14th letter of the Spanish alphabet
nabo *nm* : turnip
nácar *nm* : mother-of-pearl
nacer {48} *vi* **1** : be born **2** : hatch (of an egg), sprout (of a plant) **3** SURGIR : arise, spring up — **nacido, -da** *adj* & *n* **recién** ∼ : newborn — **naciente** *adj* **1** : new, growing **2** : rising (of the sun) — **nacimiento** *nm* **1** : birth **2** : source (of a river) **3** ORIGEN : beginning **4** BELÉN : Nativity scene
nación *nf, pl* **-ciones** : nation, country — **nacional** *adj* : national — ∼ *nmf* : national, citizen — **nacionalidad** *nf* : nationality — **nacionalismo** *nm* : nationalism — **nacionalista** *adj* & *nmf* : nationalist — **nacionalizar** {21} *vt* **1** : nationalize **2** : naturalize (as a citizen) — **nacionalizarse** *vr* : become naturalized
nada *pron* **1** : nothing **2 de** ∼ : you're welcome **3** ∼ **más** : nothing else, nothing more — ∼ *adv* : not at all — ∼ *nf* **la** ∼ : nothingness
nadar *v* : swim — **nadador, -dora** *n* : swimmer
nadería *nf* : small thing, trifle
nadie *pron* : nobody, no one
nado: a ∼ *adv phr* : swimming
nafta *nf Lat* : gasoline
naipe *nm* : playing card
nalgas *nfpl* : buttocks, bottom
nana *nf* : lullaby
naranja *adj* & *nm* : orange (color) — ∼ *nf* : orange (fruit) — **naranjal** *nm* : orange grove — **naranjo** *nm* : orange tree
narciso *nm* : narcissus, daffodil
narcótico, -ca *adj* : narcotic — **narcótico** *nm* : narcotic — **narcotizar** {21} *vt* : drug — **narcotraficante** *nmf* : drug trafficker — **narcotráfico** *nm* : drug trafficking
nariz *nf, pl* **-rices 1** : nose **2** OLFATO : sense of smell **3 narices** *nfpl* : nostrils
narrar *vt* : narrate, tell — **narración** *nf, pl* **-ciones** : narration — **narrador, -dora** *n* : narrator — **narrativa** *nf* : narrative, storytelling
nasal *adj* : nasal
nata *nf Spain* : cream
natación *nf, pl* **-ciones** : swimming
natal *adj* : native, birth — **natalicio** *nm* : birthday — **natalidad** *nf* : birthrate
natillas *nfpl* : custard
natividad *nf* : birth, nativity
nativo, -va *adj* & *n* : native
natural *adj* **1** : natural **2** NORMAL : normal

3 ∼ **de** : native of, from — ∼ *nm* **1** : temperament **2** NATIVO : native — **naturaleza** *nf* : nature — **naturalidad** *nf* : naturalness — **naturalista** *adj* : naturalistic — **naturalización** *nf, pl* **-ciones** : naturalization — **naturalizar** {21} *vt* : naturalize — **naturalizarse** *vr* : become naturalized — **naturalmente** *adv* **1** : naturally **2** POR SUPUESTO : of course
naufragar {52} *vi* **1** : be shipwrecked **2** FRACASAR : fail — **naufragio** *nm* : shipwreck — **náufrago, -ga** *adj* : shipwrecked — ∼ *n* : castaway
náusea *nf* **1** : nausea **2 dar** ∼**s** : nauseate **3** ∼**s matutinas** : morning sickness — **nauseabundo, -da** *adj* : nauseating
náutico, -ca *adj* : nautical
navaja *nf* : pocketknife, penknife
naval *adj* : naval
nave *nf* **1** : ship **2** : nave (of a church) **3** ∼ **espacial** : spaceship
navegar {52} *v* **1** : navigate, sail — **navegable** *adj* : navigable — **navegación** *nf, pl* **-ciones** : navigation — **navegante** *adj* : sailing, seafaring — ∼ *nmf* : navigator
Navidad *nf* **1** : Christmas **2 feliz** ∼ : Merry Christmas — **navideño, -ña** *adj* : Christmas
naviero, -ra *adj* : shipping
nazi *adj* & *nmf* : Nazi — **nazismo** *nm* : Nazism
neblina *nf* : mist
nebuloso, -sa *adj* **1** : hazy, misty, foggy **2** VAGO : vague, nebulous
necedad *nf* **1** : stupidity **2 decir** ∼**es** : talk nonsense
necesario, -ria *adj* : necessary — **necesariamente** *adv* : necessarily — **necesidad** *nf* **1** : need, necessity **2** POBREZA : poverty **3** ∼**es** *nfpl* : hardships — **necesitado, -da** *adj* : needy — **necesitar** *vt* : need — *vi* ∼ **de** : have need of
necio, -cia *adj* : silly, dumb
necrología *nf* : obituary
néctar *nm* : nectar
nectarina *nf* : nectarine
neerlandés, -desa *adj, mpl* **-deses** : Dutch — **neerlandés** *nm* : Dutch (language)
nefasto, -ta *adj* **1** : ill-fated **2 fam** : terrible, awful
negar {49} *vt* **1** : deny **2** REHUSAR : refuse **3** : disown (a person) — **negarse** *vr* : refuse — **negación** *nf, pl* **-ciones 1** : denial **2** : negative (in grammar) — **negativa** *nf* **1** : denial **2** RECHAZO : refusal — **negativo,**

-va *adj* : negative — **negativo** *nm* : negative (of a photograph)
negligente *adj* : negligent — **negligencia** *nf* : negligence
negociar *vt* : negotiate — *vi* : deal, do business — **negociable** *adj* : negotiable — **negociación** *nf, pl* **-ciones** : negotiation — **negociante** *nmf* : businessman *m*, businesswoman *f* — **negocio** *nm* **1** : business **2** TRANSACCIÓN : deal **3** ~**s** : business, commerce
negro, -gra *adj* : black, dark — ~ *n* : dark-skinned person — **negro** *nm* : black (color) — **negrura** *nf* : blackness — **negruzco, -ca** *adj* : blackish
nene, -na *n fam* : baby, small child
nenúfar *nm* : water lily
neón *nm* : neon
neoyorquino, -na *adj* : of or from New York
nepotismo *nm* : nepotism
Neptuno *nm* : Neptune
nervio *nm* **1** : nerve **2** : sinew (in meat) **3** VIGOR : vigor, energy **4 tener** ~**s** : be nervous — **nerviosismo** *nf* : nervousness — **nervioso, -sa** *adj* **1** : nervous, anxious **2 sistema nervioso** : nervous system
nervudo, -da *adj* : sinewy
neto, -ta *adj* **1** : clear, distinct **2** : net (of weight, salaries, etc.)
neumático *nm* : tire
neumonía *nf* : pneumonia
neurología *nf* : neurology — **neurológico, -ca** *adj* : neurological, neurologic — **neurólogo, -ga** *n* : neurologist
neurosis *nfs & pl* : neurosis — **neurótico, -ca** *adj & n* : neurotic
neutral *adj* : neutral — **neutralidad** *nf* : neutrality — **neutralizar** {21} *vt* : neutralize — **neutro, -tra** *adj* **1** : neutral **2** : neuter (in biology and grammar)
neutrón *nm, pl* **-trones** : neutron
nevar {55} *v impers* : snow — **nevada** *nf* : snowfall — **nevado, -da** *adj* **1** : snow-covered, snowy **2** : snow-white — **nevasca** *nf* : snowstorm
nevera *nf* : refrigerator
nevisca *nf* : light snowfall, flurry
nexo *nm* : link, connection
ni *conj* **1** : neither, nor **2** ~ **que** : as if **3** ~ **siquiera** : not even
nicaragüense *adj* : Nicaraguan
nicho *nm* : niche
nicotina *nf* : nicotine
nidada *nf* : brood (of chicks, etc.)
nido *nm* **1** : nest **2** GUARIDA : hiding place, den
niebla *nf* : fog, mist
nieto, -ta *n* **1** : grandson *m*, granddaughter *f* **2 nietos** *nmpl* : grandchildren

nieve *nf* : snow
nigeriano, -na *adj* : Nigerian
nilón *or* **nilon** *nm, pl* **-lones** : nylon
nimio, -mia *adj* : insignificant, trivial — **nimiedad** *nf* **1** : trifle **2** INSIGNIFICANCIA : triviality
ninfa *nf* : nymph
ninguno, -na (**ningún** *before masculine singular nouns*) *adj* : no, not any — ~ *pron* **1** : neither, none **2** : no one, nobody
niña *nf* **1** : pupil (of the eye) **2 la** ~ **de los ojos** : the apple of one's eye
niño, -ña *n* : child, boy *m*, girl *f* — ~ *adj* **1** : young **2** INFANTIL : immature, childish — **niñero, -ra** *n* : baby-sitter, nanny — **niñez** *nf, pl* **-ñeces** : childhood
nipón, -pona *adj* : Japanese
níquel *nm* : nickel
nítido, -da *adj* : clear, sharp — **nitidez** *nf, pl* **-deces** : clarity, sharpness
nitrato *nm* : nitrate
nitrógeno *nm* : nitrogen
nivel *nm* **1** : level, height **2** ~ **de vida** : standard of living — **nivelar** *vt* : level (out)
no *adv* **1** : not **2** (*in answer to a question*) : no **3 ¡como** ~**!** : of course! **4** ~ **bien** : as soon as **5** ~ **fumador** : non-smoker — ~ *nm* : no
noble *adj & nmf* : noble — **nobleza** *nf* : nobility
noche *nf* **1** : night, evening **2 buenas** ~**s** : good evening, good night **3 de** ~ *or* **por la** ~ : at night **4 hacerse de** ~ : get dark — **Nochebuena** *nf* : Christmas Eve — **nochecita** *nf* : dusk — **Nochevieja** *nf* : New Year's Eve
noción *nf, pl* **-ciones** **1** : notion, concept **2 nociones** *nfpl* : rudiments
nocivo, -va *adj* : harmful, noxious
nocturno, -na *adj* **1** : night **2** : nocturnal (of animals, etc.) — **nocturno** *nm* : nocturne
nogal *nm* **1** : walnut tree **2** ~ **americano** : hickory
nómada *nmf* : nomad — ~ *adj* : nomadic
nomás *adv Lat* : only, just
nombrar *vt* **1** : appoint **2** CITAR : mention — **nombrado, -da** *adj* : famous, well-known — **nombramiento** *nm* : appointment, nomination — **nombre** *nm* **1** : name **2** SUSTANTIVO : noun **3** FAMA : fame, renown **4** ~ **de pila** : first name
nómina *nf* : payroll
nominal *adj* : nominal
nominar *vt* : nominate — **nominación** *nf, pl* **-ciones** : nomination
nomo *nm* : gnome
non *adj* : odd, not even — ~ *nm* : odd number
nonagésimo, -ma *adj & n* : ninetieth

nopal *nm* : nopal, prickly pear
nordeste *or* **noreste** *adj* **1** : northeastern **2** : northeasterly (of wind, etc.) — ⁓ *nm* : northeast
nórdico, -ca *adj* : Scandinavian
noreste → **nordeste**
noria *nf* **1** : waterwheel **2** : Ferris wheel (at a fair, etc.)
norma *nf* : rule, norm, standard — **normal** *adj* **1** : normal **2 escuela** ⁓ : teacher-training college — **normalidad** *nf* : normality — **normalizar** {21} *vt* **1** : normalize **2** ESTANDARIZAR : standardize — **normalizarse** *vr* : return to normal — **normalmente** *adv* : ordinarily, generally
noroeste *adj* **1** : northwestern **2** : northwesterly (of wind, etc.) — ⁓ *nm* : northwest
norte *adj* : north, northern — ⁓ *nm* **1** : north **2** : north wind
norteamericano, -na *adj* : North American
norteño, -ña *adj* : northern
noruego, -ga *adj* : Norwegian — **noruego** *nm* : Norwegian (language)
nos *pron* **1** (*direct object*) : us **2** (*indirect object*) : to us, for us, from us **3** (*reflexive*) : ourselves **4** : each other, one another
nosotros, -tras *pron* **1** (*subject*) : we **2** (*object*) : us **3** *or* ⁓ **mismos** : ourselves
nostalgia *nf* **1** : nostalgia **2 sentir** ⁓ **por** : be homesick for — **nostálgico, -ca** *adj* : nostalgic
nota *nf* **1** : note **2** : grade, mark (in school) **3** CUENTA : bill, check — **notable** *adj* : noteworthy, notable — **notar** *vt* : notice — **notarse** *vr* : be evident, seem
notario, -ria *n* : notary (public)
noticia *nf* **1** : news item, piece of news **2** ⁓**s** *nfpl* : news — **noticiario** *nm* : newscast — **noticiero** *nm Lat* : newscast
notificar {72} *vt* : notify — **notificación** *nf, pl* **-ciones** : notification
notorio, -ria *adj* **1** : obvious **2** CONOCIDO : well-known — **notoriedad** *nf* : fame, notoriety
novato, -ta *adj* : inexperienced — ⁓ *n* : beginner, novice
novecientos, -tas *adj* : nine hundred — **novecientos** *nms & pl* : nine hundred
novedad *nf* **1** : newness, innovation **2** NOTICIAS : news **3** ⁓**es** : novelties, latest news — **novedoso, -sa** *adj* : original, novel
novela *nf* **1** : novel **2** : soap opera (on television) — **novelesco, -ca** *adj* **1** : fictional **2** FANTÁSTICO : fabulous — **novelista** *nmf* : novelist
noveno, -na *adj* : ninth — **noveno** *nm* : ninth
noventa *adj & nm* : ninety — **noventavo,**

-va *adj* : ninetieth — **noventavo** *nm* : ninetieth
novia → **novio**
noviazgo *nm* : engagement
novicio, -cia *n* : novice
noviembre *nm* : November
novillo, -lla *n* : young bull *m*, heifer *f*
novio, -via *n* **1** : boyfriend *m*, girlfriend *f* **2** PROMETIDO : fiancé *m*, fiancée *f* **3** : bridegroom *m*, bride *f* (at a wedding)
novocaína *nf* : novocaine
nube *nf* : cloud — **nubarrón** *nm, pl* **-rrones** : storm cloud — **nublado, -da** *adj* **1** : cloudy **2** ENTURBIADO : clouded, dim — **nublado** *nm* : storm cloud — **nublar** *vt* **1** : cloud **2** OSCURECER : obscure — **nublarse** *vr* : get cloudy — **nuboso, -sa** *adj* : cloudy
nuca *nf* : nape, back of the neck
núcleo *nm* **1** : nucleus **2** CENTRO : center, core — **nuclear** *adj* : nuclear
nudillo *nm* : knuckle
nudismo *nm* : nudism — **nudista** *adj & nmf* : nudist
nudo *nm* **1** : knot **2** : crux, heart (of a problem, etc.) — **nudoso, -sa** *adj* : knotty, gnarled
nuera *nf* : daughter-in-law
nuestro, -tra *adj* : our — ⁓ *pron* (*with definite article*) : ours, our own
nuevamente *adv* : again, anew
nueve *adj & nm* : nine
nuevo, -va *adj* **1** : new **2 de nuevo** : again, once more
nuez *nf, pl* **nueces 1** : nut **2** *or* ⁓ **de nogal** : walnut **3** ⁓ **de Adán** : Adam's apple **4** ⁓ **moscada** : nutmeg
nulo, -la *adj* **1** *or* ⁓ **y sin efecto** : null and void **2** INCAPAZ : useless, inept — **nulidad** *nf* **1** : nullity **2 es una** ⁓ *fam* : he's a total loss
numerar *vt* : number — **numeración** *nf, pl* **-ciones 1** : numbering **2** NÚMEROS : numbers *pl*, numerals *pl* — **numeral** *adj* : numeral — **número** *nm* **1** : number, numeral **2** : issue (of a publication) **3 sin** ⁓ : countless — **numérico, -ca** *adj* : numerical — **numeroso, -sa** *adj* : numerous
nunca *adv* **1** : never, ever **2** ⁓ **más** : never again **3** ⁓ **jamás** : never ever
nupcial *adj* : nuptial, wedding — **nupcias** *nfpl* : nuptials, wedding
nutria *nf* : otter
nutrir *vt* **1** ALIMENTAR : feed, nourish **2** FOMENTAR : fuel, foster — **nutrición** *nf, pl* **-ciones** : nutrition — **nutrido, -da** *adj* **1** : nourished **2** ABUNDANTE : considerable, abundant — **nutriente** *nm* : nutrient — **nutritivo, -va** *adj* : nourishing, nutritious

O

o¹ *nf* : o, 16th letter of the Spanish alphabet

o² *conj* (**u** *before words beginning with o- or ho-*) **1** : or, either **2** ~ **sea** : in other words

oasis *nms & pl* : oasis

obcecar {72} *vt* : blind (by emotions) — **obcecarse** *vr* : become stubborn

obedecer {53} *vt* : obey — *vi* **1** : obey **2** ~ **a** : respond to **3** ~ **a** : be due to — **obediencia** *nf* : obedience — **obediente** *adj* : obedient

obertura *nf* : overture

obeso, -sa *adj* : obese — **obesidad** *nf* : obesity

obispo *nm* : bishop

objetar *v* : object — **objeción** *nf, pl* **-ciones** : objection

objeto *nm* : object — **objetivo, -va** *adj* : objective — **objetivo** *nm* **1** : objective, goal **2** : lens (in photography, etc.)

objetor, -tora *n* ~ **de conciencia** : conscientious objector

oblicuo, -cua *adj* : oblique

obligar {52} *vt* : require, oblige — **obligarse** *vr* : commit oneself (to do something) — **obligación** *nf, pl* **-ciones** : obligation — **obligado, -da** *adj* **1** : obliged **2** FORZOSO : obligatory — **obligatorio, -ria** *adj* : mandatory

oblongo, -ga *adj* : oblong

oboe *nm* : oboe — ~ *nmf* : oboist

obra *nf* **1** : work, deed **2** : work (of art, literature, etc.) **3** CONSTRUCCIÓN : construction work **4** ~ **maestra** : masterpiece **5** ~**s públicas** : public works — **obrar** *vt* : work, produce — *vi* : act, behave — **obrero, -ra** *adj* **la clase obrera** : the working class — ~ *n* : worker, laborer

obsceno, -na *adj* : obscene — **obscenidad** *nf* : obscenity

obsequiar *vt* : give, present — **obsequio** *nm* : gift, present

observar *vt* **1** : observe, watch **2** ADVERTIR : notice **3** ACATAR : observe, obey **4** COMENTAR : remark — **observación** *nf, pl* **-ciones** : observation — **observador, -dora** *adj* : observant — ~ *n* : observer — **observancia** *nf* : observance — **observatorio** *nm* : observatory

obsesionar *vt* : obsess — **obsesionarse** *vr* : be obsessed — **obsesión** *nf, pl* **-siones** : obsession — **obsesivo, -va** *adj* : obsessive — **obseso, -sa** *adj* : obsessed

obsoleto, -ta *adj* : obsolete

obstaculizar {21} *vt* : hinder — **obstáculo** *nm* : obstacle

obstante: **no** ~ *conj phr* : nevertheless, however — ~ *prep phr* : in spite of, despite

obstar {21} *vi* ~ **a** *or* ~ **para** : stop, prevent

obstetricia *nf* : obstetrics — **obstetra** *nmf* : obstetrician

obstinarse *vr* : be stubborn — **obstinado, -da** *adj* **1** : obstinate, stubborn **2** TENAZ : persistent

obstruir {41} *vt* : obstruct — **obstrucción** *nf, pl* **-ciones** : obstruction

obtener {80} *vt* : obtain, get

obtuso, -sa *adj* : obtuse

obviar *vt* : get around, avoid

obvio, -via *adj* : obvious — **obviamente** *adv* : obviously, clearly

oca *nf* : goose

ocasión *nf, pl* **-siones** **1** : occasion **2** OPORTUNIDAD : opportunity **3** GANGA : bargain — **ocasional** *adj* **1** : occasional **2** ACCIDENTAL : accidental, chance — **ocasionar** *vt* : cause

ocaso *nm* **1** : sunset **2** DECADENCIA : decline

occidente *nm* **1** : west **2 el Occidente** : the West — **occidental** *adj* : western, Western

océano *nm* : ocean — **oceanografía** *nf* : oceanography

ochenta *adj & nm* : eighty

ocho *adj & nm* : eight — **ochocientos, -tas** *adj* : eight hundred — **ochocientos** *nms & pl* : eight hundred

ocio *nm* **1** : free time, leisure **2** INACTIVIDAD : idleness — **ociosidad** *nf* : idleness, inactivity — **ocioso, -sa** *adj* **1** : idle, inactive **2** INÚTIL : useless

ocre *adj & nm* : ocher

octágono *nm* : octagon — **octagonal** *adj* : octagonal

octava *nf* : octave

octavo, -va *adj & n* : eighth

octeto *nm* : byte

octogésimo, -ma *adj & n* : eightieth

octubre *nm* : October

ocular *adj* : ocular, eye — **oculista** *nmf* : ophthalmologist

ocultar *vt* : conceal, hide — **ocultarse** *vr* : hide — **oculto, -ta** *adj* : hidden, occult

ocupar *vt* **1** : occupy **2** : hold (a position, etc.) **3** : provide work for — **ocuparse** *vr* **1** ~ **de** : concern oneself with **2** ~ **de** : take care of (children, etc.) — **ocupación** *nf, pl*

-ciones 1 : occupation 2 EMPLEO : job —
ocupado, -da adj 1 : busy 2 : occupied (of
a place) 3 señal de occupado : busy signal — ocupante nmf : occupant
ocurrir vi : occur, happen — ocurrirse vr ~
a : occur to — occurrencia nf 1 : occurrence, event 2 SALIDA : witty remark, quip
oda nf : ode
odiar vt : hate — odio nm : hatred —
odioso, -sa adj : hateful
odisea nf : odyssey
odontología nf : dentistry, dental surgery —
odontólogo, -ga n : dentist, dental surgeon
oeste adj : west, western — ~ nm 1 : west
2 el Oeste : the West
ofender v : offend — ofenderse vr : take offense — ofensa nf : offense, insult — ofensiva nf : offensive — ofensivo, -va adj : offensive
oferta nf 1 : offer 2 de ~ : on sale 3 ~ y
demanda : supply and demand
oficial adj : official — ~ nmf 1 : skilled
worker 2 : officer (in the military)
oficina nf : office — oficinista nmf : office
worker
oficio nm : trade, profession — oficioso, -sa
adj : unofficial
ofrecer {53} vt 1 : offer 2 : provide, present
(an opportunity, etc.) — ofrecerse vr : volunteer — ofrecimiento nm : offer
ofrenda nf : offering
oftalmología nf : ophthalmology — of-
talmólogo, -ga n : ophthalmologist
ofuscar {72} vt 1 : blind, dazzle 2 CON-
FUNDIR : confuse — ofuscarse vr ~ con
: be blinded by — ofuscación nf, pl
-ciones 1 : blindness 2 CONFUSIÓN : confusion
ogro nm : ogre
oír {50} vi : hear — vt 1 : hear 2 ESCUCHAR
: listen to 3 ¡oiga! or ¡oye! : excuse me!,
listen! — oídas: de ~ adv phr : by hearsay
— oído nm 1 : ear 2 : (sense of) hearing 3
duro de ~ : hard of hearing
ojal nm : buttonhole
ojalá interj : I hope so!, if only!
ojear vt : eye, look at — ojeada nf : glimpse,
glance
ojeriza nf 1 : ill will 2 tener ~ a : have a
grudge against
ojo nm 1 : eye 2 PERSPICACIA : shrewdness
3 : span (of a bridge) 4 ¡~! : look out!, pay
attention!
ola nf : wave — oleada nf : wave, surge —
oleaje nm : swell (of the sea)
olé interj : bravo!
oleada nf : wave, swell — oleaje nm : waves
pl, surf

óleo nm 1 : oil 2 CUADRO : oil painting —
oleoducto nm : oil pipeline
oler {51} vt : smell — vi 1 : smell 2 ~ a
: smell of — olerse vr fam : have a hunch
about
olfatear vt 1 : sniff 2 OLER : sense, sniff out
— olfato nm 1 : sense of smell 2 PERSPI-
CACIA : nose, instinct
Olimpiada or Olimpíada nf : Olympics pl,
Olympic Games pl — olímpico, -ca adj
: Olympic
oliva nf : olive — olivo nm : olive tree
olla nf 1 : pot 2 ~ podrida : (Spanish)
stew
olmo nm : elm
olor nm : smell — oloroso, -sa adj : fragrant
olvidar vt 1 : forget 2 DEJAR : leave (behind)
— olvidarse vr : forget — olvidadizo, -za
adj : forgetful — olvido nm 1 : forgetful-
ness 2 DESCUIDO : oversight
ombligo nm : navel
omelette nmf Lat : omelet
ominoso, -sa adj : ominous
omitir vt : omit — omisión nf, pl -siones
: omission
ómnibus nm, pl -bus or -buses : bus
omnipotente adj : omnipotent
omóplato or omoplato nm : shoulder blade
once adj & nm : eleven — onceavo, -va adj
& n : eleventh
onda nf : wave — ondear vi : ripple — on-
dulación nf, pl -ciones : undulation — ondulado, -da adj : wavy — ondular vt
: wave (hair) — vi : undulate, ripple
ónice nmf or ónix nm : onyx
onza nf : ounce
opaco, -ca adj 1 : opaque 2 DESLUSTRADO
: dull
ópalo nm : opal
opción nf, pl -ciones : option — opcional
adj : optional
ópera nf : opera
operar vt 1 : operate on 2 Lat : operate, run
(a machine) — vi 1 : operate 2 NEGOCIAR
: deal, do business — operarse vr 1 : have
an operation 2 OCURRIR : take place — op-
eración nf, pl -ciones 1 : operation 2
TRANSACCIÓN : transaction, deal — operacional adj : operational — operador, -dora
n 1 : operator 2 : cameraman (for television, etc.)
opereta nf : operetta
opinar vt : think — vi : express an opinion —
opinión nf, pl -niones : opinion
opio nm : opium
oponer {60} vt 1 : raise, put forward (arguments, etc.) 2 ~ resistencia : put up a
fight — oponerse vr ~ a : oppose, be
against — oponente nmf : opponent

oporto *nm* : port (wine)
oportunidad *nf* : opportunity — **oportunista** *nmf* : opportunist — **oportuno, -na** *adj* **1** : opportune, timely **2** APROPIADO : suitable
opositor, -tora *n* **1** : opponent **2** : candidate (for a position) — **oposición** *nf, pl* **-ciones** : opposition
oprimir *vt* **1** : press, squeeze **2** TIRANIZAR : oppress — **opresión** *nf, pl* **-siones 1** : oppression **2** ~ **de pecho** : tightness in the chest — **opresivo, -va** *adj* : oppressive — **opresor, -sora** *n* : oppressor
optar *vi* **1** ~ **a** : apply for **2** ~ **por** : choose, opt for
óptica *nf* **1** : optics **2** : optician's (shop) — **óptico, -ca** *adj* : optical — ~ *n* : optician
optimismo *nm* : optimism — **optimista** *adj* : optimistic — ~ *nmf* : optimist
optometría *nf* : optometry — **optometrista** *nmf* : optometrist
opuesto *adj* **1** : opposite **2** CONTRADICTO-RIO : opposed, conflicting
opulencia *nf* : opulence — **opulento, -ta** *adj* : opulent
oración *nf, pl* **-ciones 1** : prayer **2** FRASE : sentence, clause
oráculo *nm* : oracle
orador, -dora *n* : speaker
oral *adj* : oral
orar *vi* : pray
órbita *nf* **1** : orbit (in astronomy) **2** : eye socket — **orbitar** *vi* : orbit
orden *nm, pl* **órdenes 1** : order **2** ~ **del día** : agenda (at a meeting) **3** ~ **público** : law and order — ~ *nf, pl* **órdenes 1** : order (of food) **2** ~ **religiosa** : religious order **3** ~ **de compra** : purchase order
ordenador *nm Spain* : computer
ordenar *vt* **1** : order, command **2** AR-REGLAR : put in order **3** : ordain (a priest) — **ordenanza** *nf* : orderly (in the armed forces) — ~ *nf* : ordinance, regulation
ordeñar *vt* : milk
ordinal *adj & nm* : ordinal
ordinario, -ria *adj* **1** : ordinary **2** GROSERO : common, vulgar
orear *vt* : air
orégano *nm* : oregano
oreja *nf* : ear
orfanato *or* **orfelinato** *nm* : orphanage
orfebre *nmf* : goldsmith, silversmith
orgánico, -ca *adj* : organic
organigrama *nm* : flowchart
organismo *nm* **1** : organism **2** ORGANI-ZACIÓN : agency, organization
organista *nmf* : organist
organizar {21} *vt* : organize — **organizarse** *vr* : get organized — **organización** *nf, pl*

-ciones : organization — **organizador, -dora** *n* : organizer
órgano *nm* : organ
orgasmo *nm* : orgasm
orgía *nf* : orgy
orgullo *nm* : pride — **orgulloso, -sa** *adj* : proud
orientación *nf, pl* **-ciones 1** : orientation **2** DIRECCIÓN : direction **3** CONSEJO : guidance
oriental *adj* **1** : eastern **2** : oriental — ~ *nmf* : Oriental
orientar *vt* **1** : orient, position **2** GUIAR : guide, direct — **orientarse** *vr* **1** : orient oneself **2** ~ **hacia** : turn towards
oriente *nm* **1** : east, East **2 el Oriente** : the Orient
orificio *nm* : orifice, opening
origen *nm, pl* **orígenes** : origin — **original** *adj & nm* : original — **originalidad** *nf* : originality — **originar** *vt* : give rise to — **originarse** *vr* : originate, arise — **originario, -ria** *adj* ~ **de** : native of
orilla *nf* **1** : border, edge **2** : bank (of a river), shore (of the sea)
orinar *vi* : urinate — **orina** *nf* : urine
oriol *nm* : oriole
oriundo, -da *adj* ~ **de** : native of
orla *nf* : border
ornamental *adj* : ornamental — **ornamento** *nm* : ornament
ornar *vt* : adorn
ornitología *nf* : ornithology
oro *nm* : gold
orquesta *nf* : orchestra — **orquestar** *vt* : orchestrate
orquídea *nf* : orchid
ortiga *nf* : nettle
ortodoxia *nf* : orthodoxy — **ortodoxo, -xa** *adj* : orthodox
ortografía *nf* : spelling
ortopedia *nf* : orthopedics — **ortopédico, -ca** *adj* : orthopedic
oruga *nf* : caterpillar
orzuelo *nm* : sty (in the eye)
os *pron pl Spain* **1** (*direct or indirect object*) : you, to you **2** (*reflexive*) : yourselves, to yourselves **3** : each other, to each other
osado, -da *adj* : bold, daring — **osadía** *nf* **1** : boldness, daring **2** DESCARO : audacity, nerve
osamenta *nf* : skeleton
osar *vi* : dare
oscilar *vi* **1** : swing, sway **2** FLUCTUAR : fluctuate — **oscilación** *nf, pl* **-ciones 1** : swinging **2** FLUCTUACIÓN : fluctuation
oscuro, -ra *adj* **1** : dark **2** : obscure (of ideas, persons, etc.) **3 a oscuras** : in the dark — **oscurecer** {53} *vt* **1** : darken **2** : confuse,

cloud (the mind) **3 al ~** : at nightfall — *v impers* : get dark — **oscurecerse** *vr* : grow dark — **oscuridad** *nf* **1** : darkness **2** : obscurity (of ideas, persons, etc.)

óseo, ósea *adj* : skeletal, bony

oso, osa *n* **1** : bear **2 ~ de peluche** *or* **~ de felpa** : teddy bear

ostensible *adj* : evident, obvious

ostentar *vt* **1** : flaunt, display **2** POSEER : have, hold — **ostentación** *nf, pl* -ciones : ostentation — **ostentoso, -sa** *adj* : ostentatious, showy

osteopatía *n* : osteopathy — **osteópata** *nmf* : osteopath

osteoporosis *nf* : osteoporosis

ostra *nf* : oyster

ostracismo *nm* : ostracism

otear *vt* : scan, survey

otoño *nm* : autumn, fall — **otoñal** *adj* : autumn, fall

otorgar {52} *vt* **1** : grant, award **2** : draw up (a legal document)

otro, otra *adj* **1** : another, other **2 otra vez** : again — **~** *pron* **1** : another (one), other (one) **2 los otros, las otras** : the others, the rest

ovación *nf, pl* **-ciones** : ovation

óvalo *nm* : oval — **oval** *or* **ovalado, -da** *adj* : oval

ovario *nm* : ovary

oveja *nf* **1** : sheep, ewe **2 ~ negra** : black sheep

overol *Lat* : overalls *pl*

ovillo *nm* **1** : ball (of yarn) **2 hacerse un ~** : curl up (into a ball)

ovni *or* **OVNI** *nm* (*objeto volador no identificado*) : UFO

ovular *vi* : ovulate — **ovulación** *nf, pl* -ciones : ovulation

oxidar *vi* : rust — **oxidarse** *vr* : get rusty — **oxidación** *nf, pl* **-ciones** : rusting — **oxidado, -da** *adj* : rusty — **óxido** *nm* : rust

oxígeno *nm* : oxygen

oye → **oír**

oyente *nmf* **1** : listener **2** : auditor (student)

ozono *nm* : ozone

P

p *nf* : p, 17th letter of the Spanish alphabet

pabellón *nm, pl* **-llones 1** : pavilion **2** : block, building (in a hospital complex, etc.) **3** : summerhouse (in a garden, etc.) **4** BANDERA : flag

pabilo *nm* : wick

pacer {48} *v* : graze

paces → **paz**

paciencia *nf* : patience — **paciente** *adj* & *nmf* : patient

pacificar {72} *vt* : pacify, calm — **pacificarse** *vr* : calm down — **pacífico, -ca** *adj* : peaceful, pacific — **pacifismo** *nm* : pacifism — **pacifista** *adj* & *nmf* : pacifist

pacotilla *nf* **de ~** : second-rate, trashy

pacto *nm* : pact, agreement — **pactar** *vt* : agree on — *vi* : come to an agreement

padecer {53} *vt* : suffer, endure — *vi* **~ de** : suffer from — **padecimiento** *nm* : suffering

padre *nm* **1** : father **2 ~s** *nmpl* : parents — **~** *adj* *Lat* *fam* : great, fantastic — **padrastro** *nm* : stepfather — **padrino** *nm* **1** : godfather **2** : best man (at a wedding)

padrón *nm, pl* **-drones** : register, roll

paella *nf* : paella

paga *nf* : pay, wages *pl* — **pagadero, -ra** *adj* : payable

pagano, -na *adj* & *n* : pagan, heathen

pagar {52} *vt* : pay, pay for — *vi* : pay — **pagaré** *nm* : IOU

página *nf* : page

pago *nm* : payment

país *nm* **1** : country, nation **2** REGIÓN : region, land — **paisaje** *nm* : scenery, landscape — **paisano, -na** *n* : compatriot

paja *nf* **1** : straw **2** *fam* : nonsense

pájaro *nm* **1** : bird **2 ~ carpintero** : woodpecker — **pajarera** *nf* : aviary

pajita *nf* : (drinking) straw

pala *nf* **1** : shovel, spade **2** : blade (of an oar or a rotor) **3** : paddle, racket (in sports)

palabra *nf* **1** : word **2** HABLA : speech **3 tener la ~** : have the floor — **palabrota** *nf* : swearword

palacio *nm* **1** : palace, mansion **2 ~ de justicia** : courthouse

paladar *nm* : palate — **paladear** *vt* : savor

palanca *nf* **1** : lever, crowbar **2** *fam* : leverage, influence **3 ~ de cambio** *or* **~ de velocidades** : gearshift

palangana *nf* : washbowl

palco *nm* : box (in a theater)
palestino, -na *adj* : Palestinian
paleta *nf* 1 : small shovel, trowel 2 : palette (in art) 3 : paddle (in sports, etc.)
paletilla *nf* : shoulder blade
paliar *vt* : alleviate, ease — paliativo, -va *adj* : palliative
pálido, -da *adj* : pale — palidecer {53} *vi* : turn pale — palidez *nf, pl* -deces : paleness, pallor
palillo *nm* 1 : small stick 2 *or* ~ de dientes : toothpick
paliza *nf* : beating
palma *nf* 1 : palm (of the hand) 2 : palm (tree or leaf) 3 batir ~s : clap, applaud — palmada *nf* 1 : pat, slap 2 ~s *nfpl* : clapping
palmera *nf* : palm tree
palmo *nm* 1 : span, small amount 2 ~ a ~ : bit by bit
palmotear *vi* : applaud — palmoteo *nm* : clapping, applause
palo *nm* 1 : stick 2 MANGO : shaft, handle 3 MÁSTIL : mast 4 POSTE : pole 5 GOLPE : blow 6 : suit (of cards)
paloma *nf* : pigeon, dove — palomilla *nf* : moth — palomitas *nfpl* : popcorn
palpar *vt* : feel, touch — palpable *adj* : palpable
palpitar *vi* : palpitate, throb — palpitación *nf, pl* -ciones : palpitation
palta *nf Lat* : avocado
paludismo *nm* : malaria
pampa *nf* : pampa
pan *nm* 1 : bread 2 : loaf (of bread, etc.) 3 ~ tostado : toast
pana *nf* : corduroy
panacea *nf* : panacea
panadería *nf* : bakery, bread shop — panadero, -ra *n* : baker
panal *nm* : honeycomb
panameño, -ña *adj* : Panamanian
pancarta *nf* : placard, banner
pancito *nm Lat* : (bread) roll
páncreas *nms & pl* : pancreas
panda *nmf* : panda
pandemonio *nm* : pandemonium
pandero *nm* : tambourine — pandereta *nf* : (small) tambourine
pandilla *nf* : gang
panecillo *nm Spain* : (bread) roll
panel *nm* : panel
panfleto *nm* : pamphlet
pánico *nm* : panic
panorama *nm* : panorama — panorámico, -ca *adj* : panoramic
panqueque *nm Lat* : pancake
pantaletas *nfpl Lat* : panties
pantalla *nf* 1 : screen 2 : lampshade

pantalón *nm, pl* -lones 1 *or* pantalones *nmpl* : pants *pl*, trousers *pl* 2 pantalones vaqueros : jeans
pantano *nm* 1 : swamp, marsh 2 EMBALSE : reservoir — pantanoso, -sa *adj* : marshy, swampy
pantera *nf* : panther
pantimedias *nfpl Lat* : panty hose
pantomima *nf* : pantomime
pantorrilla *nf* : calf (of the leg)
pantufla *nf* : slipper
panza *nf* : belly, paunch — panzón, -zona *adj, mpl* -zones : potbellied
pañal *nm* : diaper
paño *nm* 1 : cloth 2 TRAPO : rag, dust cloth 3 ~ de cocina : dishcloth 4 ~ higiénico : sanitary napkin 5 ~s menores : underwear
pañuelo *nm* 1 : handkerchief 2 : scarf, kerchief
papa[1] *nm* : pope
papa[2] *nf Lat* 1 : potato 2 ~s fritas : potato chips, french fries
papá *nm fam* 1 : dad, pop 2 ~s *nmpl* : parents, folks
papada *nf* : double chin
papagayo *nm* : parrot
papal *adj* : papal
papalote *nm Lat* : kite
papanatas *nmfs & pl fam* : simpleton
papaya *nf* : papaya
papel *nm* 1 : paper, sheet of paper 2 : role, part (in theater, etc.) 3 ~ de aluminio : aluminum foil 4 ~ higiénico *or* ~ de baño : toilet paper 5 ~ de lija : sandpaper 6 ~ pintado : wallpaper — papeleo *nm* : paperwork, red tape — papelera *nf* : wastebasket — papelería *nf* : stationery store — papeleta *nf* 1 : ticket, slip 2 : ballot (paper)
paperas *nfpl* : mumps
papilla *nf* 1 : baby food, pap 2 hacer ~ : smash to bits
paquete *nm* 1 : package, parcel 2 : pack (of cigarettes, etc.)
paquistaní *adj* : Pakistani
par *nm* 1 : pair, couple 2 : par (in golf) 3 NOBLE : peer 4 abierto de ~ en ~ : wide open 5 sin ~ : without equal — ~ *adj* : even (in number) — ~ *nf* 1 : par 2 a la ~ que : at the same time as
para *prep* 1 : for 2 HACIA : towards 3 : (in order) to 4 : around, by (a time) 5 ~ adelante : forwards 6 ~ atrás : backwards 7 ~ que : so (that), in order that
parabienes *nmpl* : congratulations
parábola *nf* : parable
parabrisas *nms & pl* : windshield
paracaídas *nms & pl* : parachute — para-

caidista *nmf* 1 : parachutist 2 : paratrooper (in the military)
parachoques *nms & pl* : bumper
parada *nf* 1 : stop 2 : (act of) stopping 3 DESFILE : parade — paradero *nm* 1 : whereabouts 2 *Lat* : bus stop — parado, -da *adj* 1 : idle, stopped 2 *Lat* : standing (up) 3 bien (mal) parado : in good (bad) shape
paradoja *nf* : paradox
parafernalia *nf* : paraphernalia
parafina *nf* : paraffin
parafrasear *vt* : paraphrase — paráfrasis *nfs & pl* : paraphrase
paraguas *nms & pl* : umbrella
paraguayo, -ya *adj* : Paraguayan
paraíso *nm* : paradise
paralelo, -la *adj* : parallel — paralelo *nm* : parallel — paralelismo *nm* : similarity
parálisis *nfs & pl* : paralysis — paralítico, -ca *adj* : paralytic — paralizar {21} *vt* : paralyze
parámetro *nm* : parameter
páramo *nm* : barren plateau
parangón *nm, pl* -gones 1 : comparison 2 sin ~ : matchless
paraninfo *nm* : auditorium, hall
paranoia *nf* : paranoia — paranoico, -ca *adj & n* : paranoid
parapeto *nm* : parapet, rampart
parapléjico, -ca *adj & n* : paraplegic
parar *vt* 1 : stop 2 *Lat* : stand, prop — *vi* 1 : stop 2 ir a ~ : end up, wind up — pararse *vr* 1 : stop 2 *Lat* : stand up
pararrayos *nms & pl* : lightning rod
parásito, -ta *adj* : parasitic — parásito *nm* : parasite
parasol *nm* : parasol
parcela *nf* : parcel, tract (of land) — parcelar *vt* : parcel (up)
parche *nm* : patch
parcial *adj* 1 : partial 2 a tiempo ~ : part-time — parcialidad *nf* : partiality, bias
parco, -ca *adj* : sparing, frugal
pardo, -da *adj* : brownish grey
parear *vt* : pair (up)
parecer {53} *vi* 1 : seem, look 2 ASEMEJARSE A : look like, seem like 3 me parece que : I think that, in my opinion 4 ¿qué te parece? : what do you think? 5 según parece : apparently — parecerse *vr* ~ a : resemble — ~ *nm* 1 : opinion 2 ASPECTO : appearance 3 al ~ : apparently — parecido, -da *adj* 1 : similar 2 bien parecido : good-looking — parecido *nm* : resemblance, similarity
pared *nf* : wall
parejo, -ja *adj* 1 : even, smooth 2 SEMEJANTE : similar — pareja *nf* 1 : couple, pair

2 : partner (person)
parentela *nf* : relatives *pl*, kin — parentesco *nm* : relationship, kinship
paréntesis *nms & pl* 1 : parenthesis 2 DIGRESIÓN : digression 3 entre ~ : by the way
paria *nmf* : outcast
paridad *nf* : equality
pariente *nmf* : relative, relation
parir *vi* : give birth, have a baby — *vt* : give birth to
parking *nm* : parking lot
parlamentar *vi* : discuss — parlamentario, -ria *adj* : parliamentary — ~ *n* : member of parliament — parlamento *nm* : parliament
parlanchín, -china *adj, mpl* -chines : talkative, chatty — ~ *n* : chatterbox
parlotear *vi fam* : chatter — parloteo *nm fam* : chatter
paro *nm* 1 : stoppage, shutdown 2 DESEMPLEO : unemployment 3 *Lat* : strike 4 ~ cardíaco : cardiac arrest
parodia *nf* : parody — parodiar *vt* : parody
párpado *nm* : eyelid — parpadear *vi* 1 : blink 2 : flicker (of light), twinkle (of stars) — parpadeo *nm* 1 : blink 2 : flicker (of light), twinkling (of stars)
parque *nm* 1 : park 2 ~ de atracciones : amusement park
parqué *nm* : parquet
parquear *vt Lat* : park
parquedad *nf* : frugality, moderation
parquímetro *nm* : parking meter
parra *nf* : grapevine
párrafo *nm* : paragraph
parranda *nf fam* : party, spree
parrilla *nf* 1 : broiler, grill 2 : grate (of a chimney, etc.) — parrillada *nf* : barbecue
párroco *nm* : parish priest — parroquia *nf* 1 : parish 2 : parish church — parroquial *adj* : parochial — parroquiano, -na *nm* 1 : parishioner 2 CLIENTE : customer
parsimonia *nf* 1 : calm, FRUGALIDAD : thrift — parsimonioso, -sa *adj* 1 : calm, unhurried 2 FRUGAL : thrifty
parte *nf* 1 : part 2 PORCIÓN : share 3 LADO : side 4 : party (in negotiations, etc.) 5 de ~ de : on behalf of 6 ¿de ~ de quién? : who is speaking? 7 en alguna ~ : somewhere 8 en todas ~s : everywhere 9 tomar ~ : take part — ~ *nm* 1 : report 2 ~ meteorológico : weather forecast
partero, -ra *n* : midwife
partición *nf, pl* -ciones : division, sharing
participar *vi* 1 : participate, take part 2 ~ en : have a share in — *vt* : notify — participación *nf, pl* -ciones 1 : participation 2 : share, interest (in a fund, etc.) 3 NOTICIA : notice — participante *adj* : participating

participio   **122**

— ~ *nmf* : participant — **partícipe** *nmf*
: participant
participio *nm* : participle
partícula *nf* : particle
particular *adj* **1** : particular **2** PRIVADO
: private — ~ *nm* **1** : matter **2** PERSONA
: individual — **particularidad** *nf* : peculiarity — **particularizar** {21} *vt* : distinguish,
characterize — *vi* : go into details
partir *vt* **1** : split, divide **2** ROMPER : break,
crack **3** REPARTIR : share (out) — *vi* **1** : depart **2** ~ **de** : start from **3 a** ~ **de** : as of,
from — **partirse** *vr* **1** : split (open) **2** RA-
JARSE : crack — **partida** *nf* **1** : departure **2**
: entry, item (in a register, etc.) **3** JUEGO
: game **4** : group (of persons) **5 mala** ~
: dirty trick **6** ~ **de nacimiento** : birth certificate — **partidario, -ria** *n* : follower, supporter — **partido** *nm* **1** : (political) party **2**
: game, match (in sports) **3** PARTIDARIOS
: following **4 sacar** ~ **de** : make the most
of
partitura *nf* : (musical) score
parto *nm* **1** : childbirth **2 estar de** ~ : be
in labor
parvulario *nm* : nursery school
pasa *nf* **1** : raisin **2** ~ **de Corinto** : currant
pasable *adj* : passable
pasada *nf* **1** : pass, wipe, coat (of paint, etc.)
2 de ~ : in passing **3 mala** ~ : dirty trick
— **pasadizo** *nm* : corridor — **pasado, -da**
adj **1** : past **2** PODRIDO : bad, spoiled **3**
ANTICUADO : out-of-date **4 el año pasado**
: last year — **pasado** *nm* : past
pasador *nm* **1** CERROJO : bolt **2** : barrette
(for the hair)
pasaje *nm* **1** : passage **2** BILLETE : ticket,
fare **3** PASILLO : passageway **4** PASAJEROS
: passengers *pl* — **pasajero, -ra** *adj* : passing — ~ *n* : passenger
pasamanos *nms & pl* : handrail, banister
pasaporte *nm* : passport
pasar *vi* **1** : pass, go (by) **2** ENTRAR : come
in **3** SUCEDER : happen **4** TERMINARSE : be
over, end **5** ~ **de** : exceed **6 ¿qué pasa?**
: what's the matter? — *vt* **1** : pass **2**
: spend (time) **3** CRUZAR : cross **4** TOL-
ERAR : tolerate **5** SUFRIR : go through, suffer **6** : show (a movie, etc.) **7 pasarlo bien**
: have a good time **8** ~ **por alto** : overlook, omit — **pasarse** *vr* **1** : pass, go away
2 ESTROPEARSE : spoil, go bad **3** OLVI-
DARSE : slip one's mind **4** EXCEDERSE : go
too far
pasarela *nf* **1** : footbridge **2** : gangway (on
a ship)
pasatiempo *nm* : pastime, hobby
Pascua *nf* **1** : Easter (Christian feast) **2**

: Passover (Jewish feast) **3** NAVIDAD
: Christmas
pase *nm* : pass
pasear *vi* : take a walk, go for a ride — *vt* **1**
: take for a walk **2** EXHIBIR : parade, show
off — **pasearse** *vr* : go for a walk, go for a
ride — **paseo** *nm* **1** : walk, ride **2** *Lat* : outing
pasillo *nm* : passage, corridor
pasión *nf*, *pl* **-siones** : passion
pasivo, -va *adj* : passive — **pasivo** *nm* : liabilities *pl*
pasmar *vt* : astonish, amaze — **pasmarse** *vr*
: be astonished — **pasmado, -da** *adj*
: stunned, flabbergasted — **pasmo** *nm* : astonishment — **pasmoso, -sa** *adj* : astonishing
paso¹, -sa *adj* : dried (of fruit)
paso² *nm* **1** : step **2** HUELLA : footprint **3**
RITMO : pace **4** CRUCE : crossing **5** PASAJE
: passage, way through **6** : (mountain) pass
7 de ~ : in passing
pasta *nf* **1** : paste **2** MASA : dough **3** *or* ~**s**
: pasta **4** ~ **de dientes** *or* ~ **dentífrica**
: toothpaste
pastar *v* : graze
pastel *nm* **1** : cake **2** EMPANADA : pie **3**
: pastel (crayon) — **pastelería** *nf* : pastry
shop
pasteurizar {21} *vt* : pasteurize
pastilla *nf* **1** : pill, tablet **2** : bar (of chocolate, soap, etc.) **3** ~ **para la tos** : lozenge,
cough drop
pasto *nm* **1** : pasture **2** *Lat* : grass, lawn —
pastor, -tora *n* **1** : shepherd **2** : pastor (in
religion) — **pastoral** *adj* : pastoral
pata *nf* **1** : paw, leg (of an animal) **2** : foot,
leg (of furniture) **3 meter la** ~ *fam* : put
one's foot in it — **patada** *nf* **1** : kick **2**
: stamp (of the foot) — **patalear** *vi* **1** : kick
2 : stamp (one's feet)
patata *nf Spain* : potato
patear *vt* : kick — *vi* **1** : kick **2** : stamp
(one's feet)
patentar *vt* : patent — **patente** *adj* : obvious,
patent — ~ *nf* : patent
paternal *adj* : fatherly, paternal — **paternidad** *nf* **1** : fatherhood **2** : paternity (in
law) — **paterno, -na** *adj* : paternal
patético, -ca *adj* : pathetic, moving
patillas *nfpl* : sideburns
patinar *vi* **1** : skate **2** RESBALAR : slip, slide
— **patín** *nm*, *pl* **-tines** : skate — **patinador,
-dora** *n* : skater — **patinaje** *nm* : skating —
patinazo *nm* **1** : skid **2** *fam* : blunder —
patinete *nm* : scooter
patio *nm* **1** : courtyard, patio **2** *or* ~ **de
recreo** : playground

pato, -ta *n* **1** : duck **2 pagar el pato** *fam* : take the blame — **patito, -ta** *n* : duckling
patología *nf* : pathology — **patológico, -ca** *adj* : pathological
patraña *nf* : hoax
patria *nf* : native land
patriarca *nm* : patriarch
patrimonio *nm* **1** : inheritance **2** : (historical or cultural) heritage
patriota *adj* : patriotic — ~ *nmf* : patriot — **patriótico, -ca** *adj* : patriotic — **patriotismo** *nm* : patriotism
patrocinador, -dora *n* : sponsor — **patrocinar** *vt* : sponsor — **patrocinio** *nm* : sponsorship
patrón, -trona *n, mpl* **-trones 1** : patron **2** JEFE : boss **3** : landlord, landlady *f* (of a boarding house, etc.) — **patrón** *nm, pl* **-trones** : pattern (in sewing) — **patronato** *nm* **1** : patronage **2** FUNDACIÓN : foundation, trust
patrulla *nf* **1** : patrol **2** : (police) cruiser — **patrullar** *v* : patrol
paulatino, -na *adj* : gradual
pausa *nf* : pause, break — **pausado, -da** *adj* : slow, deliberate
pauta *nf* : guideline
pavimento *nm* : pavement — **pavimentar** *vt* : pave
pavo, -va *n* **1** : turkey **2 pavo real** : peacock
pavonearse *vr* : strut, swagger
pavor *nm* : dread, terror — **pavoroso, -sa** *adj* : terrifying
payaso, -sa *n* : clown — **payasada** *nf* : antic, buffoonery — **payasear** *vi Lat fam* : clown (around)
paz *nf, pl* **paces 1** : peace **2 dejar en** ~ : leave alone **3 hacer las paces** : make up, reconcile
peaje *nm* : toll
peatón *nm, pl* **-tones** : pedestrian
peca *nf* : freckle
pecado *nm* : sin — **pecador, -dora** *adj* : sinful — ~ *n* : sinner — **pecaminoso, -sa** *adj* : sinful — **pecar** {72} *vi* : sin
pecera *nf* : fishbowl, fish tank
pecho *nm* **1** : chest **2** MAMA : breast **3** CORAZÓN : heart, courage **4 dar el** ~ : breast-feed **5 tomar a** ~ : take to heart — **pechuga** *nf* : breast (of fowl)
pecoso, -sa *adj* : freckled
pectoral *adj* : pectoral
peculiar *adj* **1** : particular **2** RARO : peculiar, odd — **peculiaridad** *nf* : peculiarity
pedagogía *nf* : education, pedagogy — **pedagogo, -ga** *n* : educator, teacher
pedal *nm* : pedal — **pedalear** *vi* : pedal
pedante *adj* : pedantic, pompous

pedazo *nm* **1** : piece, bit **2 hacerse** ~**s** : fall to pieces
pedernal *nm* : flint
pedestal *nm* : pedestal
pediatra *nmf* : pediatrician
pedigrí *nm* : pedigree
pedir {54} *vt* **1** : ask for, request **2** : order (food, merchandise, etc.) — *vi* **1** : ask **2** ~ **prestado** : borrow — **pedido** *nm* **1** : order **2 hacer un** ~ : place an order
pedregoso, -sa *adj* : rocky, stony
pedrería *nf* : precious stones *pl*
pegar {52} *vt* **1** : stick, glue, paste **2** : sew on (a button, etc.) **3** JUNTAR : bring together **4** GOLPEAR : hit, strike **5** PROPINAR : deal (a blow, etc.) **6** : transmit (an illness) **7** ~ **un grito** : let out a scream — *vi* **1** : adhere, stick **2** GOLPEAR : hit — **pegarse** *vr* **1** : hit oneself, hit each other **2** ADHERIRSE : stick, adhere **3** CONTAGIARSE : be transmitted — **pegadizo, -za** *adj* **1** : catchy **2** CONTAGIOSO : contagious — **pegajoso, -sa** *adj* **1** : sticky **2** *Lat* : catchy — **pegamento** *nm* : glue
peinar *vt* : comb — **peinarse** *vr* : comb one's hair — **peinado** *nm* : hairstyle, hairdo — **peine** *nm* : comb — **peineta** *nf* : ornamental comb
pelado, -da *adj* **1** : shorn, hairless **2** : peeled (of fruit, etc.) **3** *fam* : bare **4** *fam* : broke, penniless
pelaje *nm* : coat (of an animal), fur
pelar *vt* **1** : cut the hair of (a person) **2** MONDAR : peel (fruit) **3** : pluck (a chicken, etc.), skin (an animal) — **pelarse** *vr* **1** : peel **2** *fam* : get a haircut
peldaño *nm* **1** : step (of stairs) **2** : rung (of a ladder)
pelear *vi* **1** : fight **2** DISCUTIR : quarrel — **pelearse** *vr* : have a fight — **pelea** *nf* **1** : fight **2** DISCUSIÓN : quarrel
peletería *nf* : fur shop
peliagudo, -da *adj* : tricky, difficult
pelícano *nm* : pelican
película *nf* : movie, film
peligro *nm* **1** : danger **2** RIESGO : risk — **peligroso, -sa** *adj* : dangerous
pelirrojo, -ja *adj* : red-haired — ~ *n* : redhead
pellejo *nm* : skin, hide
pellizcar {72} *vt* : pinch — **pellizco** *nm* : pinch
pelo *nm* **1** : hair **2** : coat, fur (of an animal) **3** : pile, nap (of fabric) **4 con** ~**s y señales** : in great detail **5 no tener** ~ **en la lengua** *fam* : not to mince words **6 tomar el** ~ **a algn** *fam* : pull someone's leg — **pelón, -lona** *adj fam, mpl* **-lones** : bald
pelota *nf* : ball

pelotón *nm, pl* **-tones** : squad, detachment
peltre *nm* : pewter
peluca *nf* : wig
peluche *nm* **1** : plush **2 oso de** ~ : teddy
bear
peludo, -da *adj* : hairy, furry
peluquería *nf* : hairdresser's, barber shop —
peluquero, -ra *n* : barber, hairdresser
pelusa *nf* : fuzz, lint
pelvis *nfs & pl* : pelvis
pena *nf* **1** : penalty **2** TRISTEZA : sorrow **3**
DOLOR : suffering, pain **4** *Lat* : embarrassment **5 a duras** ~**s** : with great difficulty
6 ¡qué ~**!** : what a shame! **7 valer la** ~
: be worthwhile
penacho *nm* **1** : crest, tuft **2** : plume (ornament)
penal *adj* : penal — ~ *nm* : prison, penitentiary — **penalidad** *nf* **1** : hardship **2**
: penalty (in law) — **penalizar** {21} *vt* : penalize
penalty *nm* : penalty (in sports)
penar *vt* : punish — *vi* : suffer
pendenciero, -ra *adj* : quarrelsome
pender *vi* : hang — **pendiente** *adj* **1** : pending **2 estar** ~ **de** : be watching out for —
~ *nf* : slope — ~ *nm Spain* : earring
pendón *nm, pl* **-dones** : banner
péndulo *nm* : pendulum
pene *nm* : penis
penetrar *vi* **1** : penetrate **2** ~ **en** : go into
— *vt* **1** : penetrate **2** : pierce (one's heart,
etc.) **3** ENTENDER : fathom, grasp — **penetración** *nf, pl* **-ciones** **1** : penetration **2**
PERSPICACIA : insight — **penetrante** *adj* **1**
: penetrating **2** : sharp (of odors, etc.),
piercing (of sounds) **3** : deep (of a wound,
etc.)
penicilina *nf* : penicillin
península *nf* : peninsula — **peninsular** *adj*
: peninsular
penitencia *nf* **1** : penitence **2** CASTIGO
: penance — **penitenciaría** *nf* : penitentiary
— **penitente** *adj & nmf* : penitent
penoso, -sa *adj* **1** : painful, distressing **2**
TRABAJOSO : difficult **3** *Lat* : shy
pensar {55} *vi* **1** : think **2** ~ **en** : think
about — *vt* **1** : think **2** CONSIDERAR : think
about **3** ~ **hacer algo** : intend to do sth —
pensador, -dora *n* : thinker — **pensamiento** *nm* **1** : thought **2** : pansy
(flower) — **pensativo, -va** *adj* : pensive,
thoughtful
pensión *nf, pl* **-siones** **1** : boarding house **2**
: (retirement) pension **3** ~ **alimenticia** : alimony — **pensionista** *nmf* **1** : lodger **2** JU-
BILADO : retiree
pentágono *nm* : pentagon
pentagrama *nm* : staff (in music)

penúltimo, -ma *adj* : next to last, penulti-
mate
penumbra *nf* : half-light
penuria *nf* : dearth, shortage
peña *nf* : rock, crag — **peñasco** *nm* : crag,
large rock — **peñón** *nm, pl* **-ñones** : craggy
rock
peón *nm, pl* **peones** **1** : laborer, peon **2**
: pawn (in chess)
peonía *nf* : peony
peor *adv* **1** (*comparative of* **mal**) : worse **2**
(*superlative of* **mal**) : worst — ~ *adj* **1**
(*comparative of* **malo**) : worse **2** (*superlative of* **malo**) : worst
pepino *nm* : cucumber — **pepinillo** *nm*
: pickle, gherkin
pepita *nf* **1** : seed, pip **2** : nugget (of gold,
etc.)
pequeño, -ña *adj* : small, little — **pequeñez**
nf, pl **-ñeces** **1** : smallness **2** NIMIEDAD
: trifle
pera *nf* : pear — **peral** *nm* : pear tree
percance *nm* : mishap, setback
percatarse *vr* ~ **de** : notice
percepción *nf, pl* **-ciones** : perception —
perceptible *adj* : perceptible
percha *nf* **1** : perch (for birds) **2** : (coat)
hanger **3** : coatrack (on a wall)
percibir *vt* **1** : perceive **2** : receive (a salary,
etc.)
percusión *nf, pl* **-siones** : percussion
perder {56} *vt* **1** : lose **2** : miss (an opportunity, etc.) **3** DESPERDICIAR : waste (time)
— *vi* : lose — **perderse** *vr* **1** : get lost **2** DE-
SAPARECER : disappear **3** DESPERDICIARSE
: be wasted — **perdedor, -dora** *n* : loser —
pérdida *nf* **1** : loss **2** ESCAPE : leak **3** ~
de tiempo : waste of time — **perdido, -da**
adj **1** : lost **2 un caso perdido** *fam* : a
hopeless case
perdigón *nm, pl* **-gones** : shot, pellet
perdiz *nf, pl* **-dices** : partridge
perdón *nm, pl* **-dones** : forgiveness, pardon
— **perdón** *interj* : sorry! — **perdonar** *vt* **1**
DISCULPAR : forgive **2** : pardon (in law)
perdurar *vi* : last, endure — **perdurable** *adj*
: lasting
perecer {53} *vi* : perish, die — **perecedero,
-ra** *adj* : perishable
peregrinación *nf, pl* **-ciones** *or* **peregrinaje**
nm : pilgrimage — **peregrino, -na** *adj* **1**
: migratory **2** RARO : unusual, odd — ~ *n*
: pilgrim
perejil *nm* : parsley
perenne *adj & nm* : perennial
pereza *nf* : laziness — **perezoso, -sa** *adj*
: lazy
perfección *nf, pl* **-ciones** : perfection —
perfeccionar *vt* **1** : perfect **2** MEJORAR

: improve — **perfeccionista** *nmf* : perfectionist — **perfecto, -ta** *adj* : perfect
perfidia *nf* : treachery — **pérfido, -da** *adj* : treacherous
perfil *nm* **1** : profile **2** CONTORNO : outline **3** ~es *nmpl* RASGOS : features — **perfilar** *vt* : outline — **perfilarse** *vr* **1** : be outlined **2** CONCRETARSE : take shape
perforar *vt* **1** : perforate **2** : drill, bore (a hole) — **perforación** *nf, pl* -**ciones** : perforation — **perforadora** *nf* : (paper) punch
perfume *nm* : perfume, scent — **perfumar** *vt* : perfume — **perfumarse** *vr* : put perfume on
pergamino *nm* : parchment
pericia *nf* : skill
periferia *nf* : periphery, outskirts (of a city, etc.) — **periférico, -ca** *adj* : peripheral
perilla *nf* **1** : goatee **2** *Lat* : knob **3 venir de** ~**s** *fam* : come in handy
perímetro *nm* : perimeter
periódico, -ca *adj* : periodic — **periódico** *nm* : newspaper — **periodismo** *nm* : journalism — **periodista** *nmf* : journalist
período *or* **periodo** *nm* : period
periquito *nm* : parakeet
periscopio *nm* : periscope
perito, -ta *adj & n* : expert
perjudicar {72} *vt* : harm, damage — **perjudicial** *adj* : harmful — **perjuicio** *nm* **1** : harm, damage **2 en** ~ **de** : to the detriment of
perjurar *vi* : perjure oneself — **perjurio** *nm* : perjury
perla *nf* **1** : pearl **2 de** ~**s** *fam* : great, just fine
permanecer {53} *vi* : remain — **permanencia** *nf* **1** : permanence **2** : stay, staying (in a place) — **permanente** *adj* : permanent — ~ *nf* : permanent (wave)
permeable *adj* : permeable
permitir *vt* **1** : permit, allow **2 ¿me permite?** : may I? — **permitirse** *vr* : allow oneself — **permisible** *adj* : permissible, allowable — **permisivo, -va** *adj* : permissive — **permiso** *nm* **1** : permission **2** : permit, license (document) **3** : leave (in the military) **4 con** ~ : excuse me
permuta *nf* : exchange
pernicioso, -sa *adj* : pernicious, destructive
pero *conj* : but — ~ *nm* **1** : fault **2** REPARO : objection
perorar *vi* : make a speech — **perorata** *nf* : (long-winded) speech
perpendicular *adj & nf* : perpendicular
perpetrar *vt* : perpetrate
perpetuar {3} *vt* : perpetuate — **perpetuo, -tua** *adj* : perpetual

perplejo, -ja *adj* : perplexed — **perplejidad** *nf* : perplexity
perro, -rra *n* **1** : dog, bitch *f* **2 perro caliente** : hot dog — **perrera** *nf* : kennel
perseguir {75} *vt* **1** : pursue, chase **2** ACOSAR : persecute — **persecución** *nf, pl* -**ciones** **1** : pursuit, chase **2** ACOSO : persecution
perseverar *vi* : persevere — **perseverancia** *nf* : perseverance
persiana *nf* : (venetian) blind
persistir *vi* : persist — **persistencia** *nf* : persistence — **persistente** *adj* : persistent
persona *nf* : person — **personaje** *nm* **1** : character (in literature, etc.) **2** : important person, celebrity — **personal** *adj* : personal — ~ *nm* : personnel, staff — **personalidad** *nf* : personality — **personificar** {72} *vi* : personify
perspectiva *nf* **1** : perspective **2** VISTA : view **3** POSIBILIDAD : prospect, outlook
perspicacia *nf* : shrewdness, insight — **perspicaz** *adj, pl* -**caces** : shrewd, discerning
persuadir *vt* : persuade — **persuadirse** *vr* : become convinced — **persuasión** *nf, pl* -**siones** : persuasion — **persuasivo, -va** *adj* : persuasive
pertenecer {53} *vi* ~ **a** : belong to — **perteneciente** *adj* ~ **a** : belonging to — **pertenencia** *nf* **1** : ownership **2** ~**s** *nfpl* : belongings
pertinaz *adj, pl* -**naces** **1** OBSTINADO : obstinate **2** PERSISTENTE : persistent
pertinente *adj* : pertinent, relevant — **pertinencia** *nf* : relevance
perturbar *vt* : disturb — **perturbación** *nf, pl* -**ciones** : disturbance
peruano, -na *adj* : Peruvian
pervertir {76} *vt* : pervert — **perversión** *nf, pl* -**siones** : perversion — **perverso, -sa** *adj* : perverse — **pervertido, -da** *adj* : perverted, depraved — ~ *n* : pervert
pesa *nf* **1** : weight **2** ~**s** : weights (in sports) — **pesadez** *nf, pl* -**deces** **1** : heaviness **2** *fam* : tediousness, drag
pesadilla *nf* : nightmare
pesado, -da *adj* **1** : heavy **2** LENTO : sluggish **3** MOLESTO : annoying **4** ABURRIDO : tedious **5** DURO : tough, difficult — ~ *n fam* : bore, pest — **pesadumbre** *nf* : grief, sorrow
pésame *nm* : condolences *pl*
pesar *vt* : weigh — *vi* **1** : weigh, be heavy **2** INFLUIR : carry weight **3 pese a** : despite — ~ *nm* **1** : sorrow, grief **2** REMORDIMIENTO : remorse **3 a** ~ **de** : in spite of
pescado *nm* : fish — **pesca** *nf* **1** : fishing **2** PECES : fish *pl*, catch **3 ir de** ~ : go fishing

— **pescadería** *nf* : fish market — **pescador, -dora** *n, mpl* **-dores** : fisherman —
pescar {72} *vt* **1** : fish for **2** *fam* : catch (a cold, etc.) **3** *fam* : catch hold of, nab — *vi* : fish
pescuezo *nm* : neck (of an animal)
pese a → **pesar**
pesebre *nm* : manger
pesero *nm Lat* : minibus
peseta *nf* : peseta
pesimismo *nm* : pessimism — **pesimista** *adj* : pessimistic — ~ *nmf* : pessimist
pésimo, -ma *adj* : awful
peso *nm* **1** : weight **2** CARGA : burden **3** : peso (currency) **4** ~ **pesado** : heavyweight
pesquero, -ra *adj* : fishing
pesquisa *nf* : inquiry
pestaña *nf* : eyelash — **pestañear** *vi* : blink — **pestañeo** *nm* : blink
peste *nm* **1** : plague **2** *fam* : stench, stink **3** *Lat fam* : cold, bug — **pesticida** *nm* : pesticide — **pestilencia** *nf* **1** : stench **2** PLAGA : pestilence
pestillo *nm* : bolt, latch
petaca *nf Lat* : suitcase
pétalo *nm* : petal
petardo *nm* : firecracker
petición *nf, pl* **-ciones** : petition, request
petirrojo *nm* : robin
petrificar {72} *vt* : petrify
petróleo *nm* : oil, petroleum — **petrolero, -ra** *adj* : oil — **petrolero** *nm* : oil tanker
petulante *adj* : insolent, arrogant
peyorativo, -va *adj* : pejorative
pez *nm, pl* **peces** **1** : fish **2** ~ **de colores** : goldfish **3** ~ **espada** : swordfish **4** ~ **gordo** *fam* : big shot
pezón *nm, pl* **-zones** : nipple
pezuña *nf* : hoof
piadoso, -sa *adj* **1** : compassionate **2** DEVOTO : pious, devout
piano *nm* : piano — **pianista** *nmf* : pianist, piano player
piar {85} *vi* : chirp, tweet
pibe, -ba *n Lat fam* : kid, child
pica *nf* **1** : pike, lance **2** : spade (in playing cards)
picado, -da *adj* **1** : perforated **2** : minced, chopped (of meat, etc.) **3** : decayed (of teeth) **4** : choppy (of the sea) **5** *fam* : annoyed — **picada** *nf* **1** : bite, sting **2** *Lat* : sharp descent — **picadillo** *nm* : minced meat — **picadura** *nf* **1** : sting, bite **2** : (moth) hole
picante *adj* : hot, spicy
picaporte *nm* **1** : door handle **2** ALDABA : door knocker **3** PESTILLO : latch
picar {72} *vt* **1** : sting, bite **2** : peck at, nib-

ble on (food) **3** PERFORAR : prick, puncture **4** TRITURAR : chop, mince — *vi* **1** : bite, take the bait **2** ESCOCER : sting, itch **3** COMER : nibble **4** : be spicy (of food) — **picarse** *vr* **1** : get a cavity **2** ENFADARSE : take offense
picardía *nf* **1** : craftiness **2** TRAVESURA : prank — **picaresco, -ca** *adj* **1** : picaresque **2** TRAVIESO : roguish — **pícaro, -ra** *adj* **1** : mischievous **2** MALICIOSO : villainous — ~ *n* : rascal, scoundrel
picazón *nf, pl* **-zones** : itch
pichón, -chona *n, mpl* **-chones** : (young) pigeon
picnic *nm, pl* **-nics** : picnic
pico *nm* **1** : beak **2** CIMA : peak **3** PUNTA : (sharp) point **4** : pick, pickax (tool) **5 las siete y** ~ : a little after seven — **picotazo** *nm* : peck — **picotear** *vt* : peck — *vi fam* : nibble, pick — **picudo, -da** *adj* : pointy
pie *nm* **1** : foot (in anatomy) **2** : base, bottom, stem **3 al** ~ **de la letra** : word for word **4 dar** ~ **a** : give rise to **5 de** ~ : standing (up) **6 de** ~**s a cabeza** : from top to bottom
piedad *nf* **1** : pity, mercy **2** DEVOCIÓN : piety
piedra *nf* **1** : stone **2** : flint (of a lighter) **3** GRANIZO : hailstone **4** ~ **angular** : cornerstone **5** → **pómez**
piel *nf* **1** : skin **2** CUERO : leather **3** PELO : fur, pelt
pienso *nm* : feed, fodder
pierna *nf* : leg
pieza *nf* **1** : piece, part **2** *or* ~ **de teatro** : play **3** HABITACIÓN : room
pigmento *nm* : pigment — **pigmentación** *nf, pl* **-ciones** : pigmentation
pigmeo, -mea *adj* : pygmy
pijama *nm* : pajamas *pl*
pila *nf* **1** : battery **2** MONTÓN : pile **3** FREGADERO : sink **4** : basin (of a fountain, etc.)
pilar *nm* : pillar
píldora *nf* : pill
pillar *vt* **1** : catch **2** : get (a joke, etc.) — **pillaje** *nm* : pillage — **pillo, -lla** *adj* : crafty — ~ *n* : rascal, scoundrel
piloto *nmf* : pilot — **pilotar** *vt* : pilot
pimienta *nf* : pepper (condiment) — **pimiento** *nm* : pepper (fruit) — **pimentero** *nm* : pepper shaker — **pimentón** *nm, pl* **-tones** **1** : paprika **2** : cayenne pepper
pináculo *nm* : pinnacle
pincel *nm* : paintbrush
pinchar *vt* **1** : pierce, prick **2** : puncture (a tire, etc.) **3** INCITAR : goad — **pinchazo** *nm* **1** : prick **2** : puncture (of a tire, etc.)
pingüino *nm* : penguin
pino *nm* : pine (tree)

pintar *v* : paint — **pintarse** *vr* : put on makeup — **pinta** *nf* **1** : spot **2** : pint (measure) **3** *fam* : appearance — **pintada** *nf* : graffiti — **pinto, -ta** *adj* : speckled, spotted — **pintor, -tora** *n, mpl* **-tores** : painter — **pintoresco, -ca** *adj* : picturesque, quaint — **pintura** *nf* **1** : paint **2** CUADRO : painting
pinza *nf* **1** : clothespin **2** : claw, pincer (of a crab, etc.) **3** ~s *nfpl* : tweezers
pinzón *nm, pl* **-zones** : finch
piña *nf* **1** : pine cone **2** ANANÁS : pineapple
piñata *nf* : piñata
piñón *nm, pl* **-ñones** : pine nut
pío¹, pía *adj* **1** : pious **2** : piebald (of a horse)
pío² *nm* : peep, chirp
piojo *nm* : louse
pionero, -ra *n* : pioneer
pipa *nf* **1** : pipe (for smoking) **2** *Spain* : seed, pip
pique *nm* **1** : grudge **2** RIVALIDAD : rivalry **3 irse a** ~ : sink, founder
piqueta *nf* : pickax
piquete *nm* : picket (line) — **piquetear** *v* : picket
piragua *nf* : canoe
pirámide *nf* : pyramid
piraña *nf* : piranha
pirata *adj* : bootleg, pirated — ~ *nmf* : pirate — **piratear** *vt* **1** : bootleg, pirate **2** : hack into (a computer)
piropo *nm* : (flirtatious) compliment
pirueta *nf* : pirouette
pirulí *nm* : (cone-shaped) lollipop
pisada *nf* **1** : footstep **2** HUELLA : footprint
pisapapeles *nms & pl* : paperweight
pisar *vt* **1** : step on **2** HUMILLAR : walk all over, abuse — *vi* : step, tread
piscina *nf* **1** : swimming pool **2** : (fish) pond
piso *nm* **1** : floor, story **2** *Lat* : floor (of a room) **3** *Spain* : apartment
pisotear *vt* : trample (on)
pista *nf* **1** : trail, track **2** INDICIO : clue **3** ~ **de aterrizaje** : runway, airstrip **4** ~ **de baile** : dance floor **5** ~ **de hielo** : ice-skating rink
pistacho *nm* : pistachio
pistola *nf* **1** : pistol, gun **2** PULVERIZADOR : spray gun — **pistolera** *nf* : holster — **pistolero** *nm* : gunman
pistón *nm, pl* **-tones** : piston
pito *nm* **1** SILBATO : whistle **2** CLAXON : horn — **pitar** *vi* **1** : blow a whistle **2** : beep, honk (of a horn) — *vt* : whistle at — **pitido** *nm* **1** : whistle, whistling **2** : beep (of a horn) — **pitillo** *nm fam* : cigarette
pitón *nm, pl* **-tones** *nm* : python
pitorro *nm* : spout

pivote *nm* : pivot
piyama *nmf Lat* : pajamas *pl*
pizarra *nf* **1** : slate **2** ENCERADO : blackboard — **pizarrón** *nm, pl* **-rrones** *Lat* : blackboard
pizca *nf* **1** : pinch (of salt) **2** ÁPICE : speck, tiny bit **3** *Lat* : harvest
pizza *nf* : pizza — **pizzería** *nf* : pizzeria
placa *nf* **1** : sheet, plate **2** INSCRIPCIÓN : plaque **3** : (police) badge
placenta *nf* : placenta
placer {57} *vt* : please — ~ *nm* : pleasure — **placentero, -ra** *adj* : pleasant, agreeable
plácido, -da *adj* : placid, calm
plaga *nf* **1** : plague **2** CALAMIDAD : disaster — **plagar** {52} *vt* : plague, infest
plagiar *vt* : plagiarize — **plagio** *nm* : plagiarism
plan *nm* **1** : plan **2 en** ~ **de** : as **3 no te pongas en ese** ~ *fam* : don't be that way
plana *nf* **1** : page **2 en primera** ~ : on the front page
plancha *nf* **1** : iron (for ironing) **2** : grill (for cooking) **3** LÁMINA : sheet, plate — **planchar** *v* : iron — **planchado** *nm* : ironing
planear *vt* : plan — *vi* : glide — **planeador** *nm* : glider
planeta *nm* : planet
planicie *nf* : plain
planificar {72} *vt* : plan — **planificación** *nf, pl* **-ciones** : planning
planilla *nf Lat* : list, roster
plano, -na *adj* : flat — **plano** *nm* **1** : map, plan **2** : plane (surface) **3** NIVEL : level **4 de** ~ : flatly, outright **5 primer** ~ : foreground, close-up (in photography)
planta *nf* **1** : plant **2** PISO : floor, story **3** : sole (of the foot) — **plantación** *nf, pl* **-ciones** : plantation **2** : (action of) planting — **plantar** *vt* **1** : plant **2** *fam* : deal, land — **plantarse** *vr* : stand firm
plantear *vt* **1** : expound, set forth **2** : raise (a question) **3** CAUSAR : create, pose (a problem) — **plantearse** *vr* : think about, consider
plantel *nm* **1** : staff, team **2** *Lat* : educational institution
plantilla *nf* **1** : insole **2** PATRÓN : pattern, template **3** : staff (of a business, etc.)
plasma *nm* : plasma
plástico, -ca *adj* : plastic — **plástico** *nm* : plastic
plata *nf* **1** : silver **2** *Lat fam* : money **3** ~ **de ley** : sterling silver
plataforma *nf* **1** : platform **2** ~ **petrolífera** : oil rig **3** ~ **de lanzamiento** : launching pad
plátano *nm* **1** : banana **2** : plantain

platea *nf* : orchestra, pit (in a theater)
plateado, -da *adj* 1 : silver, silvery (color)
2 : silver-plated
platicar {72} *vi* : talk, chat — plática *nf*
. : chat, conversation
platija *nf* : flatfish, flounder
platillo *nm* 1 : saucer 2 CÍMBALO : cymbal
3 *Lat* : dish, course
platino *nm* : platinum
plato *nm* 1 : plate, dish 2 : course (of a
meal) 3 ~ principal : entrée
platónico, -ca *adj* : platonic
playa *nf* 1 : beach, seashore 2 ~ de estacionamiento *Lat* : parking lot
plaza *nf* 1 : square, plaza 2 : seat (in transportation) 3 PUESTO : post, position 4 MER-
CADO : market, marketplace 5 ~ de toros
. : bullring
plazo *nm* 1 : period, term 2 PAGO : installment 3 a largo ~ : long-term
plazoleta *or* plazuela *nf* : small square
pleamar *nf* : high tide
plebe *nf* : common people — plebeyo, -ya
adj & nm : plebeian
plegar {49} *vt* : fold, bend — plegarse *vr* 1
. : give in, yield 2 : jackknife (of a truck) —
plegable *or* plegadizo, -za *adj* : folding,
collapsible
plegaria *nf* : prayer
pleito *nm* 1 : lawsuit 2 *Lat* : dispute, fight
plenilunio *nm* : full moon
pleno, -na *adj* 1 : full, complete 2 en plena
forma : in top form 3 en pleno día : in
broad daylight — plenitud *nf* : fullness,
abundance
pleuresía *nf* : pleurisy
pliego *nm* : sheet (of paper) — pliegue *nm*
1 : crease, fold 2 : pleat (in fabric)
plisar *vt* : pleat
plomería *nf Lat* : plumbing — plomero, -ra
n Lat : plumber
plomo *nm* 1 : lead 2 FUSIBLE : fuse
pluma *nf* 1 : feather 2 : (fountain) pen —
plumaje *nm* : plumage — plumero *nm*
. : feather duster — plumilla *nf* : nib —
plumón *nm, pl* -mones : down
plural *adj & nm* : plural — pluralidad *nf*
. : plurality
pluriempleo *nm* hacer ~ : have more than
one job
plus *nm* : bonus
plusvalía *nf* : appreciation, capital gain
plutocracia *nf* : plutocracy
Plutón *nm* : Pluto
plutonio *nm* : plutonium
pluvial *adj* : rain
poblar {19} *vt* 1 : settle, colonize 2
HABITAR : inhabit — poblarse *vr* : become
crowded — población *nf, pl* -ciones 1

: city, town, village 2 HABITANTES : population — poblado, -da *adj* 1 : populated 2
: thick, bushy (of a beard, eyebrows, etc.) —
poblado *nm* : village
pobre *adj* 1 : poor 2 ¡~ de mí! : poor me!
— ~ *nmf* 1 : poor person 2 los ~s : the
poor 3 ¡pobre! : poor thing! — pobreza *nf*
: poverty
pocilga *nf* : pigsty
poción *nf, pl* -ciones *or* pócima *nf* : potion
poco, -ca *adj* 1 : little, not much, (a) few 2
pocas veces : rarely — ~ *pron* 1 : little,
few 2 hace poco : not long ago 3 poco a
poco : bit by bit, gradually 4 por poco
: nearly, just about 5 un poco : a little, a bit
— poco *adv* : little, not much
podar *vt* : prune
poder {58} *v aux* 1 : be able to, can 2 (*expressing possibility*) : might, may 3 (*expressing permission*) : can, may 4 ¿cómo
puede ser? : how can it be? 5 ¿puedo
pasar? : may I come in? — *vi* 1 : be possible 2 ~ con : cope with, manage 3 no
puedo más : I've had enough — ~ *nm* 1
: power 2 POSESIÓN : possession — poderío
nm : power — poderoso, -sa *adj* : powerful
podólogo, -ga *n* : chiropodist
podrido, -da *adj* : rotten
poema *nm* : poem — poesía *nf* 1 : poetry 2
POEMA : poem — poeta *nmf* : poet —
poético, -ca *adj* : poetic
póker *nm* → póquer
polaco, -ca *adj* : Polish
polar *adj* : polar — polarizar {21} *vt* : polarize
polea *nf* : pulley
polémica *nf* : controversy — polémico, -ca
adj : controversial — polemizar *vt* : argue
polen *nm, pl* pólenes : pollen
policía *nf* : police — ~ *nmf* : police officer,
policeman *m*, policewoman *f* — policíaco,
-ca *adj* 1 : police 2 novela policíaca : detective story
poliéster *nm* : polyester
poligamia *nf* : polygamy — polígamo, -ma
n : polygamist
polígono *nm* : polygon
polilla *nf* : moth
polio *or* poliomielitis *nf* : polio, poliomyelitis
politécnico, -ca *adj* : polytechnic
política *nf* 1 : politics 2 POSTURA : policy
— político, -ca *adj* 1 : political 2 hermano político : brother-in-law — ~ *n*
: politician
póliza *nf or* ~ de seguros : insurance policy
polizón *nm, pl* -zones : stowaway
pollo, -lla *n* 1 : chicken, chick 2 : chicken

(for cooking) — **pollera** *nf Lat* : skirt —
pollería *nf* : poultry shop — **pollito, -ta** *n*
: chick
polo *nm* **1** : pole **2** : polo (sport) **3** ~
norte : North Pole
poltrona *nf* : easy chair
polución *nf, pl* **-ciones** : pollution
polvo *nm* **1** : powder **2** SUCIEDAD : dust **3**
~**s** *nmpl* : face powder **4 hacer** ~ *fam*
: crush, shatter — **polvareda** *nf* : cloud of
dust — **polvera** *nf* : compact (for powder)
— **pólvora** *nf* : gunpowder — **polvoriento,
-ta** *adj* : dusty
pomada *nf* : ointment
pomelo *nm* : grapefruit
pómez *nm or* **piedra** ~ *nf* : pumice
pomo *nm* : knob, doorknob
pompa *nf* **1** : (soap) bubble **2** ESPLENDOR
: pomp **3** ~**s fúnebres** : funeral — **pomposo, -sa** *adj* **1** : pompous **2** ESPLÉNDIDO
: splendid
pómulo *nm* : cheekbone
ponchar *vt Lat* : puncture — **ponchadura** *nf*
Lat : puncture
ponche *nm* : punch (drink)
poncho *nm* : poncho
ponderar *vt* **1** : consider **2** ALABAR : speak
highly of
poner {60} *vt* **1** : put **2** AGREGAR : add **3**
CONTRIBUIR : contribute **4** SUPONER : suppose **5** DISPONER : arrange, set out **6** : give
(a name), call **7** ENCENDER : turn on **8** ES-
TABLECER : set up, establish **9** : lay (eggs)
— *vi* : lay eggs — **ponerse** *vr* **1** : move
(into a position) **2** : put on (clothing, etc.) **3**
: set (of the sun) **4** ~ **furioso** : become
angry
poniente *nm* **1** OCCIDENTE : west **2** : west
wind
pontífice *nm* : pontiff
pontón *nm, pl* **-tones** : pontoon
ponzoña *nf* : poison, venom
popa *nf* **1** : stern **2 a** ~ : astern
popelín *nm, pl* **-lines** : poplin
popote *nm Lat* : (drinking) straw
populacho *nm* : rabble, masses *pl*
popular *adj* **1** : popular **2** : colloquial (of
language) — **popularidad** *nf* : popularity —
popularizar {21} *vt* : popularize — **popu-
loso, -sa** *adj* : populous
póquer *nm* : poker (card game)
por *prep* **1** : for **2** (*indicating an approximate time*) : around, during **3** (*indicating
an approximate place*) : around, about **4** A
TRAVÉS DE : through, along **5** A CAUSA DE
: because of **6** (*indicating rate or ratio*)
: per **7** *or* ~ **medio de** : by means of **8**
: times (in mathematics) **9** SEGÚN : as for,
according to **10 estar** ~ : be about to **11**

~ **ciento** : percent **12** ~ **favor** : please
13 ~ **lo tanto** : therefore **14 ¿por qué?**
: why?
porcelana *nf* : porcelain, china
porcentaje *nm* : percentage
porción *nf, pl* **-ciones** : portion, piece
pordiosero, -ra *n* : beggar
porfiar {85} *vi* : insist — **porfiado, -da** *adj*
: obstinate, persistent
pormenor *nm* : detail
pornografía *nf* : pornography — **pornográfico, -ca** *adj* : pornographic
poro *nm* : pore — **poroso, -sa** *adj* : porous
poroto *nm Lat* : bean
porque *conj* **1** : because **2** *or* **por que** : in
order that — **porqué** *nm* : reason
porquería *nf* **1** SUCIEDAD : filth **2** : shoddy
thing, junk
porra *nf* : nightstick, club — **porrazo** *nm*
: blow, whack
portaaviones *nms & pl* : aircraft carrier
portada *nf* **1** : facade **2** : title page (of a
book), cover (of a magazine)
portador, -dora *n* : bearer
portaequipajes *nms & pl* : luggage rack
portafolio *or* **portafolios** *nm, pl* **-lios 1**
: portfolio **2** MALETÍN : briefcase
portal *nm* **1** : doorway **2** VESTÍBULO : hall,
vestibule
portamonedas *nms & pl* : purse
portar *vt* : carry, bear — **portarse** *vr* : behave
portátil *adj* : portable
portaviones *nm* → **portaaviones**
portavoz *nmf, pl* **-voces** : spokesperson,
spokesman *m*, spokeswoman *f*
portazo *nm* **dar un** ~ : slam the door
porte *nm* **1** : transport, freight **2** ASPECTO
: bearing, appearance **3** ~ **pagado**
: postage paid
portento *nm* : marvel, wonder — **porten-
toso, -sa** *adj* : marvelous
porteño, -ña *adj* : of or from Buenos Aires
portería *nf* **1** : superintendent's office **2**
: goal, goalposts *pl* (in sports) — **portero,
-ra** *n* **1** : goalkeeper, goalie **2** CONSERJE
: janitor, superintendent
portezuela *nf* : door (of an automobile)
pórtico *nm* : portico
portilla *nf* : porthole
portugués, -guesa *adj, mpl* **-gueses** : Portuguese — **portugués** *nm* : Portuguese
(language)
porvenir *nm* : future
pos: en ~ **de** *adv phr* : in pursuit of
posada *nf* : inn
posaderas *nfpl fam* : backside, bottom
posar *vi* : pose — *vt* : place, lay — **posarse**
vr : settle, rest

posavasos *nms & pl* : coaster
posdata *nf* : postscript
pose *nf* : pose
poseer {20} *vt* : possess, own — **poseedor,**
-dora *n* : possessor, owner — **poseído, -da**
adj : possessed — **posesión** *nf, pl* **-siones**
: possession — **posesionarse** *vr* ~ **de**
: take possession of, take over — **posesivo,**
-va *adj* : possessive
posguerra *nf* : postwar period
posibilidad *nf* : possibility — **posibilitar** *vt*
: make possible — **posible** *adj* **1** : possible
2 de ser ~ : if possible
posición *nf, pl* **-ciones** : position — **posi-**
cionar *vt* : position — **posicionarse** *vr*
: take a stand
positivo, -va *adj* : positive
poso *nm* : sediment, (coffee) grounds
posponer {60} *vt* **1** : postpone **2** RELEGAR
: put behind, subordinate
postal *adj* : postal — ~ *nf* : postcard
postdata → **posdata**
poste *nm* : post, pole
póster *nm, pl* **-ters** : poster
postergar {52} *vt* **1** : pass over **2** APLAZAR
: postpone
posteridad *nf* : posterity — **posterior** *adj* **1**
: later, subsequent **2** TRASERO : back, rear
— **posteriormente** *adv* : subsequently,
later
postigo *nm* **1** : small door **2** CONTRAVEN-
TANA : shutter
postizo, -za *adj* : artificial, false
postrarse *vr* : prostrate oneself —
postrado, -da *adj* : prostrate
postre *nm* : dessert
postular *vt* **1** : advance, propose **2** *Lat*
: nominate — **postulado** *nm* : postulate
póstumo, -ma *adj* : posthumous
postura *nf* : position, stance
potable *adj* : drinkable, potable
potaje *nm* : thick vegetable soup
potasio *nm* : potassium
pote *nm* : jar
potencia *nf* : power — **potencial** *adj & nm*
: potential — **potente** *adj* : powerful
potro, -tra *n* : colt *m*, filly *f* — **potro** *nm*
: horse (in gymnastics)
pozo *nm* **1** : well **2** : shaft (in a mine)
práctica *nf* **1** : practice **2 en la** ~ : in practice — **practicable** *adj* : practicable, feasible — **practicante** *adj* : practicing — ~
nmf : practitioner — **practicar** {72} *vt* **1**
: practice **2** REALIZAR : perform, carry out
— *vi* : practice — **práctico, -ca** *adj* : practical
pradera *nf* : grassland, prairie — **prado** *nm*
: meadow
pragmático, -ca *adj* : pragmatic

preámbulo *nm* : preamble
precario, -ria *adj* : precarious
precaución *nf, pl* **-ciones 1** : precaution **2**
PRUDENCIA : caution, care **3 con** ~ : cautiously
precaver *vt* : guard against — **precavido,**
-da *adj* : prudent, cautious
preceder *v* : precede — **precedencia** *nf*
: precedence, priority — **precedente** *adj*
: preceding, previous — ~ *nm* : precedent
precepto *nm* : precept
preciado, -da *adj* : prized, valuable — **pre-**
ciarse *vr* ~ **de** : pride oneself on, boast
about
precinto *nm* : seal
precio *nm* : price, cost — **preciosidad** *nf* **1**
VALOR : value **2** : beautiful thing — **pre-**
cioso, -sa *adj* **1** HERMOSO : beautiful **2**
VALIOSO : precious
precipicio *nm* : precipice
precipitar *vt* **1** : hasten, speed up **2** ARROJAR
: hurl — **precipitarse** *vr* **1** APRESURARSE
: rush **2** : act rashly **3** ARROJARSE : throw
oneself — **precipitación** *nf, pl* **-ciones 1**
: precipitation **2** PRISA : haste — **precipi-**
tadamente *adv* : in a rush, hastily — **pre-**
cipitado, -da *adj* : hasty
preciso, -sa *adj* **1** : precise **2** NECESARIO
: necessary — **precisamente** *adv* : precisely, exactly — **precisar** *vt* **1** : specify,
determine **2** NECESITAR : require — **pre-**
cisión *nf, pl* **-siones 1** : precision **2**
NECESIDAD : necessity
preconcebido *adj* : preconceived
precoz *adj, pl* **-coces 1** : early **2** : precocious (of children)
precursor, -sora *n* : forerunner
predecesor, -sora *n* : predecessor
predecir {11} *vt* : foretell, predict
predestinado, -da *adj* : predestined
predeterminar *vt* : predetermine
prédica *nf* : sermon
predicado *nm* : predicate
predicar {72} *v* : preach — **predicador,**
-dora *n* : preacher
predicción *nf, pl* **-ciones 1** : prediction **2**
PRONÓSTICO : forecast
predilección *nf, pl* **-ciones** : preference —
predilecto, -ta *adj* : favorite
predisponer {60} *vt* : predispose — **predis-**
posición *nf, pl* **-ciones** : predisposition
predominar *vi* : predominate — **predomi-**
nante *adj* : predominant, prevailing — **pre-**
dominio *nm* : predominance
preeminente *adj* : preeminent
prefabricado, -da *adj* : prefabricated
prefacio *nm* : preface
preferir {76} *vt* : prefer — **preferencia** *nf* **1**
: preference **2 de** ~ : preferably — **prefer-**

ente adj : preferential — **preferible** adj : preferable — **preferido, -da** adj : favorite
prefijo nm **1** : prefix **2** Spain : area code
pregonar vt : proclaim, announce
pregunta nf **1** : question **2 hacer** ~**s** : ask questions — **preguntar** v : ask — **preguntarse** vr : wonder
prehistórico, -ca adj : prehistoric
prejuicio nm : prejudice
preliminar adj & nm : preliminary
preludio nm : prelude
prematrimonial adj : premarital
prematuro, -ra adj : premature
premeditar vt : premeditate — **premeditación** nf, pl -**ciones** : premeditation
premenstrual adj : premenstrual
premio nm **1** : prize **2** RECOMPENSA : reward **3** ~ **gordo** : jackpot — **premiado, -da** adj : prizewinning — **premiar** vt **1** : award a prize to **2** RECOMPENSAR : reward
premisa nf : premise
premonición nf, pl -**ciones** : premonition
premura nf : haste, urgency
prenatal adj : prenatal
prenda nf **1** : piece of clothing **2** GARANTÍA : pledge **3** : forfeit (in a game) — **prendar** vt : captivate — **prendarse** vr ~ **de** : fall in love with
prender vt **1** SUJETAR : pin, fasten **2** APRESAR : capture **3** : light (a match, etc.) **4** Lat : turn on (a light, etc.) — vi **1** : take root **2** ARDER : catch, burn (of fire) — **prenderse** vr : catch fire — **prendedor** nm Lat : brooch, pin
prensa nf : press — **prensar** vt : press
preñado, -da adj **1** : pregnant **2** ~ **de** : filled with
preocupar vt : worry — **preocuparse** vr **1** : worry **2** ~ **de** : take care of — **preocupación** nf, pl -**ciones** : worry
preparar vt : prepare — **prepararse** vr : get ready — **preparación** nf, pl -**ciones** : preparation — **preparado, -da** adj : prepared, ready — **preparado** nm : preparation — **preparativo, -va** adj : preparatory, preliminary — **preparativos** nmpl : preparations — **preparatorio, -ria** adj : preparatory
preposición nf, pl -**ciones** : preposition
prepotente adj : arrogant, domineering
prerrogativa nf : prerogative
presa nf **1** : catch, prey **2** DIQUE : dam **3 hacer** ~ **en** : seize
presagiar vt : presage, forebode — **presagio** nm **1** : omen **2** PREMONICIÓN : premonition
presbítero nm : presbyter, priest
prescindir vi ~ **de 1** : do without **2** OMITIR : dispense with

prescribir {33} vt : prescribe — **prescripción** nf, pl -**ciones** : prescription
presencia nf **1** : presence **2** ASPECTO : appearance — **presenciar** vt : be present at, witness
presentar vt **1** : present **2** OFRECER : offer, give **3** MOSTRAR : show **4** : introduce (persons) — **presentarse** vr **1** : show up **2** : arise, come up (of a problem, etc.) **3** : introduce oneself — **presentación** nf, pl -**ciones 1** : presentation **2** : introduction (of persons) **3** ASPECTO : appearance — **presentador, -dora** n : presenter, host (of a television program, etc.)
presente adj **1** : present **2 tener** ~ : keep in mind — ~ nm **1** : present **2 entre los** ~**s** : among those present
presentir {76} vt : have a presentiment of — **presentimiento** nm : premonition
preservar vt : preserve, protect — **preservación** nf, pl -**ciones** : preservation — **preservativo** nm : condom
presidente, -ta n **1** : president **2** : chair, chairperson (of a meeting) — **presidencia** nf **1** : presidency **2** : chairmanship (of a meeting) — **presidencial** adj : presidential
presidio nm : prison — **presidiario, -ria** n : convict
presidir vt **1** : preside over, chair **2** PREDOMINAR : dominate
presión nf, pl -**siones 1** : pressure **2** ~ **arterial** : blood pressure **3 hacer** ~ : press — **presionar** vt **1** : press **2** COACCIONAR : put pressure on
preso, -sa adj : imprisoned — ~ n : prisoner
prestar vt **1** : lend, loan **2** : give (aid) **3** ~ **atención** : pay attention — **prestado, -da** adj **1** : borrowed, on loan **2 pedir** ~ : borrow — **prestamista** nmf : moneylender — **préstamo** nm : loan
prestidigitación nf, pl -**ciones** : sleight of hand — **prestidigitador, -dora** n : magician
prestigio nm : prestige — **prestigioso, -sa** adj : prestigious
presto, -ta adj : prompt, ready — **presto** adv : promptly, right away
presumir vt : presume — vi : boast, show off — **presumido, -da** adj : conceited, vain — **presunción** nf, pl -**ciones 1** : presumption **2** VANIDAD : vanity — **presunto, -ta** adj : presumed, alleged — **presuntuoso, -sa** adj : conceited
presuponer {60} vt : presuppose — **presupuesto** nm **1** : budget, estimate **2** SUPUESTO : assumption
presuroso, -sa adj : hasty, quick
pretender vt **1** : try to **2** AFIRMAR : claim **3** CORTEJAR : court, woo **4** ~ **que** : expect

— **pretencioso, -sa** *adj* : pretentious — **pretendido** *adj* : supposed — **pretendiente** *nmf* **1** : candidate **2** : pretender (to a throne) — ~ *nm* : suitor — **pretensión** *nf, pl* **-siones 1** INTENCIÓN : intention, aspiration **2** : claim (to a throne, etc.) **3 pretensiones** *nfpl* : pretensions

pretérito *nm* : past (in grammar)

pretexto *nm* : pretext, excuse

prevalecer {53} *vi* : prevail — **prevaleciente** *adj* : prevailing, prevalent

prevenir {87} *vt* **1** : prevent **2** AVISAR : warn — **prevenirse** {87} *vr* ~ **contra** *or* ~ **de** : take precautions against — **prevención** *nf, pl* **-ciones 1** : prevention **2** PRECAUCIÓN : precaution **3** PREJUICIO : prejudice — **prevenido, -da** *adj* **1** : prepared, ready **2** PRECAVIDO : cautious — **preventivo, -va** *adj* : preventive

prever {88} *vt* **1** : foresee **2** PLANEAR : plan

previo, -via *adj* : previous, prior

previsible *adj* : foreseeable — **previsión** *nf, pl* **-siones 1** : foresight **2** PREDICCIÓN : prediction, forecast — **previsor, -sora** *adj* : farsighted, prudent

prieto, -ta *adj* **1** CEÑIDO : tight **2** *Lat fam* : dark-skinned

prima *nf* **1** : bonus **2** : (insurance) premium **3** → **primo**

primario, -ria *adj* **1** : primary **2 escuela primaria** : elementary school

primate *nm* : primate

primavera *nf* **1** : spring (season) **2** : primrose (flower) — **primaveral** *adj* : spring

primero, -ra *adj* (**primer** *before masculine singular nouns*) **1** : first **2** MEJOR : top, leading **3** PRINCIPAL : main, basic **4 de primera** : first-rate — ~ *n* : first (person or thing) — **primero** *adv* **1** : first **2** MÁS BIEN : rather, sooner

primitivo, -va *adj* : primitive

primo, -ma *n* : cousin

primogénito, -ta *adj* & *n* : firstborn

primor *nm* : beautiful thing

primordial *adj* : basic, fundamental

primoroso, -sa *adj* **1** : exquisite, fine **2** HÁBIL : skillful

princesa *nf* : princess

principado *nm* : principality

principal *adj* : main, principal

príncipe *nm* : prince

principio *nm* **1** : principle **2** COMIENZO : beginning, start **3** ORIGEN : origin **4 al** ~ : at first **5 a** ~**s de** : at the beginning of — **principiante** *nmf* : beginner

pringar {52} *vt* : spatter (with grease) — **pringoso, -sa** *adj* : greasy

prioridad *nf* : priority

prisa *nf* **1** : hurry, rush **2 a** ~ *or* **de** ~ : quickly **3 a toda** ~ : as fast as possible **4 darse** ~ : hurry **5 tener** ~ : be in a hurry

prisión *nf, pl* **-siones 1** : prison **2** ENCARCELAMIENTO : imprisonment — **prisionero, -ra** *n* : prisoner

prisma *nm* : prism — **prismáticos** *nmpl* : binoculars

privar *vt* **1** : deprive **2** PROHIBIR : forbid **3** *Lat* : knock out — **privarse** *vr* : deprive oneself — **privación** *nf, pl* **-ciones** : deprivation — **privado, -da** *adj* : private — **privativo, -va** *adj* : exclusive

privilegio *nm* : privilege — **privilegiado, -da** *adj* : privileged

pro *prep* : for, in favor of — ~ *nm* **1** : pro, advantage **2 en** ~ **de** : for, in support of **3 los pros y los contras** : the pros and cons

proa *nf* : bow, prow

probabilidad *nf* : probability — **probable** *adj* : probable, likely — **probablemente** *adv* : probably

probar {19} *vt* **1** : try, test **2** : try on (clothing) **3** DEMOSTRAR : prove **4** DEGUSTAR : taste — *vi* : try — **probarse** *vr* : try on (clothing) — **probeta** *nf* : test tube

problema *nm* : problem — **problemático, -ca** *adj* : problematic

proceder *vi* **1** : proceed, act **2** : be appropriate **3** ~ **de** : come from — **procedencia** *nf* : origin — **procedente** *adj* ~ **de** : coming from, originating in — **procedimiento** *nm* **1** : procedure, method **2** : proceedings *pl* (in law)

procesar *vt* **1** : prosecute **2** : process (data) — **procesador** *nm* ~ **de textos** : word processor — **procesamiento** *nm* : processing — **procesión** *nf, pl* **-siones** : procession — **proceso** *nm* **1** : process **2** : trial, proceedings *pl* (in law)

proclamar *vt* : proclaim — **proclama** *nf* : proclamation — **proclamación** *nf, pl* **-ciones** : proclamation

procrear *vi* : procreate — **procreación** *nf, pl* **-ciones** : procreation

procurar *vt* **1** : try, endeavor **2** CONSEGUIR : obtain, procure — **procurador, -dora** *n* : attorney

prodigar {52} *vt* : lavish — **prodigio** *nm* : wonder, prodigy — **prodigioso, -sa** *adj* : prodigious

pródigo, -ga *adj* : extravagant, prodigal

producir {61} *vt* **1** : produce **2** CAUSAR : cause **3** : yield, bear (interest, fruit, etc.) — **producirse** *vr* : take place — **producción** *nf, pl* **-ciones** : production — **productividad** *nf* : productivity — **productivo, -va** *adj* : productive — **producto** *nm* : product — **productor, -tora** *n* : producer

proeza *nf* : exploit

profanar *vt* : profane, desecrate — **profanación** *nf, pl* **-ciones** : desecration — **profano, -na** *adj* : profane
profecía *nf* : prophecy
proferir {76} *vt* **1** : utter **2** : hurl (insults)
profesar *vt* **1** : profess **2** : practice (a profession, etc.) — **profesión** *nf, pl* **-siones** : profession — **profesional** *adj & nmf* : professional — **profesor, -sora** *n* **1** : teacher **2** : professor (at a university, etc.) — **profesorado** *nm* **1** : teaching profession **2** PROFESORES : faculty
profeta *nm* : prophet — **profético, -ca** *adj* : prophetic — **profetisa** *nf* : (female) prophet — **profetizar** {21} *vt* : prophesy
prófugo, -ga *adj & n* : fugitive
profundo, -da *adj* **1** HONDO : deep **2** : profound (of thoughts, etc.) — **profundamente** *adv* : deeply, profoundly — **profundidad** *nf* : depth — **profundizar** {21} *vt* : study in depth
profuso, -sa *adj* : profuse — **profusión** *nf, pl* **-siones** : profusion
progenie *nf* : progeny, offspring
programa *nm* **1** : program **2** : curriculum (in education) — **programación** *nf, pl* **-ciones** : programming — **programador, -dora** *n* : programmer — **programar** *vt* **1** : schedule **2** : program (a computer, etc.)
progreso *nm* : progress — **progresar** *vi* : (make) progress — **progresión** *nf, pl* **-ciones** : progression — **progresista** *adj & nmf* : progressive — **progresivo, -va** *adj* : progressive, gradual
prohibir {62} *vt* : prohibit, forbid — **prohibición** *nf, pl* **-ciones** : ban, prohibition — **prohibido, -da** *adj* : forbidden — **prohibitivo, -va** *adj* : prohibitive
prójimo *nm* : neighbor, fellow man
prole *nf* : offspring
proletariado *nm* : proletariat — **proletario, -ria** *adj & n* : proletarian
proliferar *vi* : proliferate — **proliferación** *nf, pl* **-ciones** : proliferation — **prolífico, -ca** *adj* : prolific
prolijo, -ja *adj* : wordy, long-winded
prólogo *nm* : prologue, foreword
prolongar {52} *vt* **1** : prolong **2** ALARGAR : lengthen — **prolongarse** *vr* : last, continue — **prolongación** *nf, pl* **-ciones** : extension
promedio *nm* : average
promesa *nf* : promise — **prometedor, -dora** *adj* : promising, hopeful — **prometer** *vt* : promise — *vi* : show promise — **prometerse** *vr* : get engaged — **prometido, -da** *adj* : engaged — *~ n* : fiancé *m*, fiancée *f*
prominente *adj* : prominent — **prominencia** *nf* : prominence

promiscuo, -cua *adj* : promiscuous — **promiscuidad** *nf* : promiscuity
promocionar *vt* : promote — **promoción** *nf, pl* **-ciones** : promotion
promontorio *nm* : promontory
promover {47} *vt* **1** : promote **2** CAUSAR : cause — **promotor, -tora** *n* : promoter
promulgar {52} *vt* **1** : proclaim **2** : enact (a law)
pronombre *nm* : pronoun
pronosticar {72} *vt* : predict, forecast — **pronóstico** *nm* **1** : prediction, forecast **2** : (medical) prognosis
pronto, -ta *adj* **1** : quick, prompt **2** PREPARADO : ready — **pronto** *adv* **1** : soon **2** RAPIDAMENTE : quickly, promptly **3 de ~** : suddenly **4 por lo ~** : for the time being **5 tan ~ como** : as soon as
pronunciar *vt* **1** : pronounce **2** : give, deliver (a speech) — **pronunciarse** *vr* **1** : declare oneself **2** SUBLEVARSE : revolt — **pronunciación** *nf, pl* **-ciones** : pronunciation
propagación *nf, pl* **-ciones** : propagation
propaganda *nf* **1** : propaganda **2** PUBLICIDAD : advertising
propagar {52} *vt* : propagate, spread — **propagarse** *vr* : propagate
propano *nm* : propane
propasarse *vr* : go too far
propensión *nf, pl* **-siones** : inclination, propensity — **propenso, -sa** *adj* : prone, inclined
propiamente *adv* : exactly
propicio, -cia *adj* : favorable, propitious
propiedad *nf* **1** : property **2** PERTINENCIA : ownership, possession — **propietario, -ria** *n* : owner, proprietor
propina *nf* : tip
propinar *vt* : give, deal (a blow, etc.)
propio, -pia *adj* **1** : own **2** APROPIADO : proper, appropriate **3** CARACTERÍSTICO : characteristic, typical **4** MISMO : himself, herself, oneself
proponer {60} *vt* **1** : propose **2** : nominate (a person) — **proponerse** *vr* : propose, intend
proporción *nf, pl* **-ciones** : proportion — **proporcionado, -da** *adj* : proportionate — **proporcional** *adj* : proportional — **proporcionar** *vt* **1** : provide **2** AJUSTAR : adapt, proportion
proposición *nf, pl* **-ciones** : proposal, proposition
propósito *nm* **1** : purpose, intention **2 a ~** : incidentally, by the way **3 a ~** : on purpose, intentionally
propuesta *nf* **1** : proposal **2** : offer (of employment, etc.)
propulsar *vt* **1** : propel, drive **2** PROMOVER

: promote — **propulsión** *nf, pl* **-siones**
: propulsion
prorrogar {52} *vt* **1** : extend **2** APLAZAR
: postpone — **prórroga** *nf* **1** : extension, de-
ferment **2** : overtime (in sports)
prorrumpir *vi* : burst forth, break out
prosa *nf* : prose
proscribir {33} *vt* **1** : prohibit, ban **2**
DESTERRAR : exile — **proscripción** *nf, pl*
-ciones 1 : ban **2** DESTIERRO : banishment
— **proscrito, -ta** *adj* : banned — ~ *n*
: exile, outlaw
proseguir {75} *v* : continue — **prosecu-
ción** *nf, pl* **-ciones** : continuation
prospección *nf, pl* **-ciones** : prospecting,
exploration
prospecto *nm* : prospectus
prosperar *vi* : prosper, thrive — **prosperidad** *nf* : prosperity — **próspero, -ra** *adj*
: prosperous, fluorishing
prostituir {41} *vt* : prostitute — **prostitución** *nf, pl* **-ciones** : prostitution — **prostituta** *nf* : prostitute
protagonista *nmf* : protagonist — **protagonizar** *vt* : star in
proteger {15} *vt* : protect — **protegerse** *vr*
: protect oneself — **protección** *nf, pl*
-ciones : protection — **protector, -tora** *adj*
: protective — ~ *n* : protector — **protegido, -da** *n* : protégé
proteína *nf* : protein
protestar *v* : protest — **protesta** *nf* : protest
— **protestante** *adj & nmf* : Protestant
protocolo *nm* : protocol
prototipo *nm* : prototype
protuberancia *nf* : protuberance — **protu-
berante** *adj* : protuberant
provecho *nm* **1** : benefit, advantage **2 ¡buen
~!** : enjoy your meal! — **provechoso, -sa**
adj : profitable, beneficial
proveer {63} *vt* : provide, supply — **proveedor, -dora** *n* : supplier
provenir {87} *vi* **~ de** : come from
proverbio *nm* : proverb — **proverbial** *adj*
: proverbial
providencia *nf* **1** : providence **2** PRECAU-
CIÓN : precaution — **providencial** *adj*
: providential
provincia *nf* : province — **provincial** *adj*
: provincial — **provinciano, -na** *adj*
: provincial, parochial
provisión *nf, pl* **-siones** : provision — **provisional** *adj* : provisional
provocar {72} *vt* **1** : provoke, cause **2** IRRI-
TAR : irritate — **provocación** *nf, pl* **-ciones**
: provocation — **provocativo, -va** *adj*
: provocative
próximo, -ma *adj* **1** CERCANO : near **2**
SIGUIENTE : next — **próximamente** *adv*

: shortly, soon — **proximidad** *nf* **1** : proximity **2** ~**es** *nfpl* : vicinity
proyectar *vt* **1** : plan **2** LANZAR : throw, hurl
3 : cast (light) **4** : show (a film) — **proyec-
ción** *nf, pl* **-ciones** : projection — **proyectil**
nm : missile — **proyecto** *nm* : plan, project
— **proyector** *nm* : projector
prudencia *nf* : prudence, care — **prudente**
adj : prudent, sensible
prueba *nf* **1** : proof, evidence **2** : test (in education, medicine, etc.) **3** : event (in sports)
4 a ~ **de agua** : waterproof
psicoanálisis *nm* : psychoanalysis — **psicoanalista** *nmf* : psychoanalyst — **psicoanalizar** {21} *vt* : psychoanalyze
psicología *nf* : psychology — **psicológico,
-ca** *adj* : psychological — **psicólogo, -ga** *n*
: psychologist
psicópata *nmf* : psychopath
psicosis *nfs & pl* : psychosis
psicoterapia *nf* : psychotherapy — **psi-
coterapeuta** *nmf* : psychotherapist
psicótico, -ca *adj & n* : psychotic
psiquiatría *nf* : psychiatry — **psiquiatra**
nmf : psychiatrist — **psiquiátrico, -ca** *adj*
: psychiatric
psíquico, -ca *adj* : psychic
púa *nf* **1** : sharp point **2** : tooth (of a comb)
3 : thorn (of a plant), quill (of a porcupine,
etc.) **4** : (guitar) pick
pubertad *nf* : puberty
publicar {72} *vt* **1** : publish **2** DIVULGAR
: divulge, disclose — **publicación** *nf, pl*
-ciones : publication
publicidad *nf* **1** : publicity **2** : advertising
(in marketing) — **publicista** *nmf* : publicist
— **publicitar** *vt* **1** : publicize **2** : advertise
(a product, etc.) — **publicitario, -ria** *adj*
: advertising
público, -ca *adj* : public — **público** *nm* **1**
: public **2** : audience (of theater, etc.), spec-
tators *pl* (of sports)
puchero *nm* **1** : (cooking) pot **2** GUISADO
: stew **3 hacer ~s** : pout
púdico, -ca *adj* : modest
pudiente *adj* : wealthy
pudín *nm, pl* **-dines** : pudding
pudor *nm* : modesty — **pudoroso, -sa** *adj*
: modest
pudrir {59} *vt* **1** : rot **2** *fam* : annoy — **pudrirse** *vr* : rot
pueblo *nm* **1** : town, village **2** NACIÓN
: people, nation
puente *nm* **1** : bridge **2 hacer** ~ : have a
long weekend **3** ~ **levadizo** : drawbridge
puerco, -ca *n* **1** : pig **2 puerco espín** : porcupine — ~ *adj* : dirty, filthy
pueril *adj* : childish
puerro *nm* : leek

puerta *nf* **1** : door, gate **2 a ~ cerrada** : behind closed doors
puerto *nm* **1** : port **2** : (mountain) pass **3** REFUGIO : haven
puertorriqueño, -ña *adj* : Puerto Rican
pues *conj* **1** : since, because **2** POR LO TANTO : so, therefore **3** (*used interjectionally*) : well, then
puesta *nf* **1 ~ a punto** : tune-up **2 ~ de sol** : sunset **3 ~ en marcha** : starting up —
puesto, -ta *adj* **1** : put, set **2** VESTIDO : dressed — **puesto** *nm* **1** : place **2** EMPLEO : position, job **3** : stand, stall (in a market) **4 ~ avanzado** : outpost — **~ que** *conj* : since, given that
púgil *nm* : boxer
pugnar *vi* : fight — **pugna** *nf* : fight, battle
pulcro, -cra *adj* : tidy, neat
pulga *nf* **1** : flea **2 tener malas ~s** : have a bad temper
pulgada *nf* : inch — **pulgar** *nm* **1** : thumb **2** : big toe
pulir *vt* **1** : polish **2** REFINAR : touch up, perfect
pulla *nf* : cutting remark, gibe
pulmón *nm, pl* **-mones** : lung — **pulmonar** *adj* : pulmonary — **pulmonía** *nf* : pneumonia
pulpa *nf* : pulp
pulpería *nf Lat* : grocery store
púlpito *nm* : pulpit
pulpo *nm* : octopus
pulsar *vt* **1** : press (a button), strike (a key) **2** : play (music) — **pulsación** *nf, pl* **-ciones 1** : beat, throb **2** : keystroke (on a typewriter, etc.)
pulsera *nf* : bracelet
pulso *nm* **1** : pulse **2** : steadiness (of hand)
pulular *vi* : swarm
pulverizar {21} *vt* **1** : pulverize, crush **2** : spray (a liquid) — **pulverizador** *nm* : atomizer, spray
puma *nf* : puma
punitivo, -va *adj* : punitive
punta *nf* **1** : tip, end **2** : point (of a needle, etc.) **3 ~ del dedo** : fingertip **4 sacar ~ a** : sharpen
puntada *nf* **1** : stitch **2 ~s** *nfpl* : seam
puntal *nm* : prop, support
puntapié *nm* : kick
puntear *vt* : pluck (a guitar)

puntería *nf* : aim, marksmanship
puntiagudo, -da *adj* : sharp, pointed
puntilla *nf* **1** : lace edging **2 de ~s** : on tiptoe
punto *nm* **1** : dot, point **2** : period (in punctuation) **3** ASUNTO : item, question **4** LUGAR : spot, place **5** MOMENTO : moment **6** : point (in a score) **7** PUNTADA : stitch **8 a las dos en ~** : at two o'clock sharp **9 dos ~s** : colon **10 hasta cierto ~** : up to a point **11 ~ de partida** : starting point **12 ~ muerto** : deadlock **13 ~ y coma** : semicolon
puntuación *nf, pl* **-ciones 1** : punctuation **2** : scoring, score (in sports)
puntual *adj* **1** : prompt, punctual **2** EXACTO : accurate, detailed — **puntualidad** *nf* **1** : punctuality **2** EXACTITUD : accuracy
puntuar {3} *vt* : punctuate — *vi* : score (in sports)
punzar {21} *vt* : prick, puncture — **punzada** *nf* **1** PINCHAZO : prick **2** : sharp pain — **punzante** *adj* **1** : sharp **2** MORDAZ : biting, caustic
puñado *nm* **1** : handful **2 a ~s** : by the handful
puñal *nm* : dagger — **puñalada** *nf* : stab
puño *nm* **1** : fist **2** : cuff (of a shirt) **3** : handle, hilt (of a sword, etc.) — **puñetazo** *nm* : punch (with the fist)
pupila *nf* : pupil (of the eye)
pupitre *nm* : desk
puré *nm* **1** : purée **2 ~ de papas** *or* **~ de patatas** *Spain* : mashed potatoes
pureza *nf* : purity
purga *nf* : purge — **purgar** {52} *vt* : purge — **purgatorio** *nm* : purgatory
purificar {72} *vt* : purify — **purificación** *nf, pl* **-ciones** : purification
puritano, -na *adj* : puritanical — **~** *n* : puritan
puro, -ra *adj* **1** : pure **2** SIMPLE : plain, simple **3** *Lat fam* : only, just — **puro** *nm* : cigar
púrpura *nf* : purple — **purpúreo, -rea** *adj* : purple
pus *nm* : pus
pusilánime *adj* : cowardly
puta *nf* : whore
putrefacción *nf, pl* **-ciones** : putrefaction, rot — **pútrido, -da** *adj* : putrid, rotten

Q

q *nf* : q, 18th letter of the Spanish alphabet

que *conj* **1** : that **2** (*in comparisons*) : than **3** (*introducing a reason or cause*) : so that, or else **4 es ~** : the thing is that **5 yo ~ tú** : if I were you — **~** *pron* **1** (*referring to persons*) : who, whom **2** (*referring to things*) : that, which **3 el** (**la, lo, las, los**) **~** : he (she, it, they) who, whoever, the one(s) that

qué *adv* **1** : how, what **2 ¡~ lindo!** : how lovely! — **~** *adj* : what, which — **~** *pron* **1** : what **2 ¿~ crees?** : what do you think?

quebrar {55} *vt* : break — *vi* : go bankrupt — **quebrarse** *vr* : break — **quebrada** *nf* : ravine, gorge — **quebradizo, -za** *adj* : breakable, fragile — **quebrado, -da** *adj* **1** : bankrupt **2** : rough, uneven (of land, etc.) **3** ROTO : broken — **quebrado** *nm* : fraction — **quebradura** *nf* : crack, fissure — **quebrantar** *vt* **1** : break **2** DEBILITAR : weaken — **quebranto** *nm* **1** : harm, damage **2** AFLICCIÓN : grief, pain

queda *nf* → **toque**

quedar *vi* **1** PERMANECER : remain, stay **2** ESTAR : be **3** FALTAR : be left **4** : fit, look (of clothing, etc.) **5 no queda lejos** : it's not far **6 ~ en** : agree to, agree on — **quedarse** *vr* **1** : stay **2 ~ con** : keep

quedo, -da *adj* : quiet, still — **quedo** *adv* : softly, quietly

quehacer *nm* **1** : task **2 ~es** *nmpl* : chores

queja *nf* : complaint — **quejarse** *vr* **1** : complain **2** GEMIR : moan, groan — **quejido** *nm* : moan, whimper — **quejoso, -sa** *adj* : complaining, whining

quemar *vt* **1** : burn **2** MALGASTAR : squander — *vi* : burn — **quemarse** *vr* **1** : burn oneself **2** : burn (up) **3** : get sunburned — **quemado, -da** *adj* **1** : burned **2** AGOTADO : burned-out **3 estar ~** : be fed up — **quemador** *nm* : burner — **quemadura** *nf* : burn — **quemarropa: a ~** *adj & adv phr* : point-blank

querella *nf* **1** : dispute, quarrel **2** : charge (in law)

querer {64} *vt* **1** : want **2** AMAR : love **3 ~ decir** : mean **4 ¿quieres pasarme la leche?** : please pass the milk **5 sin ~** : unintentionally — *vi* — *nm* : love — **querido, -da** *adj* : dear, beloved — **~** *n* **1** : darling **2** AMANTE : lover

queroseno *nm* : kerosene

querubín *nm, pl* **-bines** : cherub

queso *nm* : cheese — **quesadilla** *nf Lat* : quesadilla

quicio *nm* **1 estar fuera de ~** : be beside oneself **2 sacar de ~** : drive crazy

quiebra *nf* **1** : break **2** BANCARROTA : bankruptcy

quien *pron, pl* **quienes** **1** (*subject*) : who **2** (*object*) : whom **3** (*indefinite*) : whoever, anyone, some people

quién *pron, pl* **quiénes** **1** (*subject*) : who **2** (*object*) : whom **3 ¿de ~ es este lápiz?** : whose pencil is this?

quienquiera *pron, pl* **quienesquiera** : whoever, whomever

quieto, -ta *adj* **1** : calm, quiet **2** INMÓVIL : still — **quietud** *nf* : stillness

quijada *nf* : jaw, jawbone (of an animal)

quilate *nm* : carat, karat

quilla *nf* : keel

quimera *nf* : illusion — **quimérico, -ca** *adj* : fanciful

química *nf* : chemistry — **químico, -ca** *adj* : chemical — **~** *n* : chemist

quince *adj & nm* : fifteen — **quinceañero, -ra** *n* : fifteen-year-old, teenager — **quincena** *nf* : two-week period, fortnight — **quincenal** *adj* : semimonthly, twice a month

quincuagésimo, -ma *adj & n* : fiftieth

quinientos, -tas *adj* : five hundred — **quinientos** *nms & pl* : five hundred

quinina *nf* : quinine

quinqué *nm* : oil lamp

quinta *nf* : country house, villa

quintaesencia *nf* : quintessence

quinteto *nm* : quintet

quinto, -ta *adj & n* : fifth — **quinto** *nm* : fifth

quiosco *nm* : kiosk, newsstand

quiropráctico, -ca *n* : chiropractor

quirúrgico, -ca *adj* : surgical

quisquilloso, -sa *adj* : fastidious, fussy

quiste *nm* : cyst

quitar *vt* **1** : remove, take away **2** : take off (clothes) **3** : get rid of, relieve (pain, etc.) — **quitarse** *vr* **1** : withdraw, leave **2** : take off (one's clothes) **3 ~ de** : give up (a habit) **4 ~ de encima** : get rid of — **quitaesmalte** *nm* : nail-polish remover — **quitamanchas** *nms & pl* : stain remover — **quitanieves** *nm* : snowplow — **quitasol** *nm* : parasol

quizá *or* **quizás** *adv* : maybe, perhaps

R

r *nf* : r, 19th letter of the Spanish alphabet
rábano *nm* **1** : radish **2 ~ picante** : horse-radish
rabí *nmf, pl* **-bíes** : rabbi
rabia *nf* **1** : rage, anger **2** : rabies (disease) — **rabiar** *vi* **1** : be furious **2** : be in great pain **3 ~ por** : be dying for — **rabioso, -sa** *adj* **1** : enraged, furious **2** : rabid, having rabies
rabino, -na *n* : rabbi
rabo *nm* **1** : tail **2 el ~ del ojo** : the corner of one's eye
racha *nf* **1** : gust of wind **2** SERIE : series, string — **racheado, -da** *adj* : gusty
racial *adj* : racial
racimo *nm* : bunch, cluster
raciocinio *nm* : reason, reasoning
ración *nf, pl* **-ciones** **1** : share, ration **2** : helping (of food)
racional *adj* : rational — **racionalizar** {21} *vt* : rationalize
racionar *vt* : ration — **racionamiento** *nm* : rationing
racismo *nm* : racism — **racista** *adj & nmf* : racist
radar *nm* : radar
radiación *nf, pl* **-ciones** : radiation
radiactivo, -va *adj* : radioactive — **radiactividad** *nf* : radioactivity
radiador *nm* : radiator
radiante *adj* : radiant
radical *adj & nmf* : radical
radicar {72} *vi* **~ en** : lie in, be rooted in
radio *nm* **1** : radius **2** : spoke (of a wheel) **3** : radium (element) — **~** *nmf* : radio
radioactivo, -va *adj* : radioactive — **radioactividad** *nf* : radioactivity
radiodifusión *nf, pl* **-siones** : broadcasting — **radioemisora** *nf* : radio station — **radioescucha** *nmf* : listener — **radiofónico, -ca** *adj* : radio
radiografía *nf* : X ray — **radiografiar** {85} *vt* : x-ray
radiología *nf* : radiology — **radiólogo, -ga** *n* : radiologist
raer {65} *vt* : scrape off
ráfaga *nf* **1** : gust (of wind) **2** : flash (of light)
raído, -da *adj* : worn, shabby
raíz *nf, pl* **raíces** **1** : root **2** ORIGEN : origin, source **3 echar raíces** : take root
raja *nf* **1** : crack, slit **2** RODAJA : slice — **rajar** *vt* : crack, split — **rajarse** *vr* **1** : crack, split open **2** *fam* : back out

rajatabla: a ~ *adv phr* : strictly, to the letter
ralea *nf* : sort, kind
ralentí *nm* : neutral (gear)
rallar *vt* : grate — **rallador** *nm* : grater
rama *nf* : branch — **ramaje** *nm* : branches *pl* — **ramal** *nm* : branch (of a railroad, etc.) — **ramificarse** {72} *vr* : branch (off) — **ramillete** *nm* **1** : bouquet **2** GRUPO : cluster, bunch — **ramo** *nm* **1** : branch **2** RAMILLETE : bouquet
rampa *nf* : ramp, incline
rana *nf* **1** : frog **2 ~ toro** : bullfrog
rancho *nm* : ranch, farm — **ranchero, -ra** *n* : rancher, farmer
rancio, -cia *adj* **1** : rancid **2** : aged (of wine)
rango *nm* **1** : rank **2** : (social) standing
ranúnculo *nm* : buttercup
ranura *nf* : groove, slot
rapar *vt* **1** : shave **2** : crop (hair)
rapaz *adj, pl* **-paces** : rapacious, predatory
rápido, -da *adj* : rapid, quick — **rápidamente** *adv* : rapidly, fast — **rapidez** *nf* : speed — **rápido** *adv* : quickly, fast — **~** *nm* **1** : express train **2 ~s** *nmpl* : rapids
rapiña *nf* **1** : plunder **2 ave de ~** : bird of prey
rapsodia *nf* : rhapsody
raptar *vt* : kidnap — **rapto** *nm* : kidnapping — **raptor, -tora** *n* : kidnapper
raqueta *nf* : racket (in sports)
raro, -ra *adj* **1** : rare **2** EXTRAÑO : odd, strange — **raramente** *adv* : rarely, infrequently — **rareza** *nf* : rarity
ras *nm* **a ~ de** : level with
rascacielos *nms & pl* : skyscraper
rascar {72} *vt* **1** : scratch **2** RASPAR : scrape — **rascarse** *vr* : scratch oneself
rasgar {52} *vt* : rip, tear — **rasgarse** *vr* : rip
rasgo *nm* **1** : stroke (of a pen) **2** CARACTERÍSTICA : trait, characteristic **3 ~s** *nmpl* FACCIONES : features
rasguear *vt* : strum
rasguñar *vt* : scratch — **rasguño** *nm* : scratch
raso, -sa *adj* **1** : level, flat **2** : low (of a flight) **3 soldado raso** : private (in the army) — **raso** *nm* : satin
raspar *vt* **1** : scrape **2** LIMAR : file down, smooth — *vi* : be rough — **raspadura** *nf* **1** : scratch **2 ~s** *nfpl* : scrapings
rastra *nf* **1** : rake **2 a ~s** : unwillingly — **rastrear** *vt* : track, trace — **rastrero, -ra** *adj* **1** : creeping **2** DESPRECIABLE : despicable

— **rastrillar** *vt* : rake — **rastrillo** *nm* : rake
— **rastro** *nm* **1** : trail, track **2** SEÑAL : sign
rasurar *vt Lat* : shave — **rasurarse** *vr Lat*
: shave
rata *nf* : rat
ratear *vt* : steal — **ratero, -ra** *n* : thief
ratificar {72} *vt* : ratify — **ratificación** *nf, pl*
-ciones : ratification
rato *nm* **1** : while **2 al poco** ~ : shortly
after **3 pasar el** ~ : pass the time
ratón *nm, pl* -tones : mouse — **ratonera** *nf*
: mousetrap
raudal *nm* **1** : torrent **2 a** ~es : in abundance — **raudo, -da** *adj* : swift
raya *nf* **1** : line **2** LISTA : stripe **3** : part (in
the hair) — **rayar** *vt* : scratch — *vi* **1 al** ~
el día : at daybreak **2** ~ **en** : border on —
rayarse *vr* : get scratched
rayo *nm* **1** : ray, beam **2** : bolt of lightning
3 ~s **X** : X rays
rayón *nm* : rayon
raza *nf* **1** : (human) race **2** : breed (of animals) **3 de** ~ : thoroughbred, pedigreed
razón *nf, pl* -zones **1** : reason **2 dar** ~ : inform **3 en** ~ **de** : because of **4 tener** ~
: be right — **razonable** *adj* : reasonable —
razonamiento *nm* : reasoning — **razonar** *v*
: reason, think
reacción *nf, pl* -ciones : reaction — **reaccionar** *vi* : react — **reaccionario, -ria** *adj &
n* : reactionary
reacio, -cia *adj* : resistant, stubborn
reactivar *vt* : reactivate, revive
reactor *nm* **1** : jet (airplane) **2** ~ **nuclear**
: nuclear reactor
reajustar *vt* : readjust — **reajuste** *nm* : read-
justment
real *adj* **1** : royal **2** VERDADERO : real, true
realce *nm* **1** : relief **2 dar** ~ : highlight
realeza *nf* : royalty
realidad *nf* **1** : reality **2 en** ~ : actually, in
fact
realismo *nm* : realism — **realista** *adj* : realistic — ~ *nmf* : realist
realizar {21} *vt* **1** : carry out **2** : achieve
(a goal) **3** : produce (a film or play) **4** : realize (a profit) — **realizarse** *vr* **1** : fulfill
oneself **2** : come true (of a dream, etc.) —
realización *nf, pl* -ciones : execution, realization
realmente *adv* : really, actually
realzar {21} *vt* : highlight, enhance
reanimar *vt* : revive
reanudar *vt* : resume, renew — **reanudarse**
vr : resume
reaparecer {53} *vi* : reappear — **reapari-
ción** *nf, pl* -ciones : reappearance
reavivar *vt* : revive
rebajar *vt* **1** : lower, reduce **2** HUMILLAR

: humiliate — **rebajarse** *vr* **1** : humble oneself **2** ~ **a** : stoop to — **rebaja** *nf* **1** : reduction **2** DESCUENTO : discount **3** ~s *nfpl*
: sales
rebanada *nf* : slice
rebaño *nm* **1** : herd **2** : flock (of sheep)
rebasar *vt* : surpass, exceed
rebatir *vt* : refute
rebelarse *vr* : rebel — **rebelde** *adj* : rebellious — ~ *nmf* : rebel — **rebeldía** *nf* : re-
belliousness — **rebelión** *nf, pl* -liones : rebellion
reblandecer *vt* : soften
rebobinar *vt* : rewind
rebosar *vi* **1** : overflow **2** ~ **de** : be bursting with — *vt* : overflow with
rebotar *vi* : bounce, rebound — **rebote** *nm*
1 : bounce **2 de** ~ : on the rebound
rebozar {21} *vt* : coat in batter
rebuscado, -da *adj* : pretentious
rebuznar *vi* : bray
recabar *vt* **1** : obtain, collect **2** ~ **fondos**
: raise money
recado *nm* **1** MENSAJE : message **2** *Spain*
: errand
recaer {13} *vi* **1** : relapse **2** ~ **sobre** : fall
on — **recaída** *nf* : relapse
recalcar {72} *vt* : emphasize, stress
recalcitrante *adj* : recalcitrant
recalentar {55} *vt* **1** : overheat **2** : reheat,
warm up (food) — **recalentarse** *vr* : overheat
recámara *nf* **1** : chamber (of a firearm) **2**
Lat : bedroom
recambio *nm* **1** : spare part **2** : refill (for a
pen, etc.)
recapitular *vt* : recapitulate, sum up — **reca-
pitulación** *nf, pl* -ciones : recapitulation
recargar {52} *vt* **1** : overload **2** : recharge
(a battery), reload (a firearm, etc.) — **recargado, -da** *adj* : overly elaborate — **recargo**
nm : surcharge
recato *nm* : modesty — **recatado, -da** *adj*
: modest, demure
recaudar *vt* : collect — **recaudación** *nf, pl*
-ciones : collection — **recaudador, -dora**
n ~ **de impuestos** : tax collector
recelar *vt* : distrust, fear — **recelo** *nm* : distrust, suspicion — **receloso, -sa** *adj* : distrustful, suspicious
recepción *nf, pl* -ciones : reception — **recepcionista** *nmf* : receptionist
receptáculo *nm* : receptacle
receptivo, -va *adj* : receptive — **receptor,
-tora** *n* : recipient — **receptor** *nm* : receiver
(of a radio, etc.)
recesión *nf, pl* -siones : recession
receso *nm Lat* : recess, adjournment

receta *nf* **1** : recipe **2** : prescription (in medicine)
rechazar {21} *vt* **1** : reject, refuse **2** REPELER : repel **3** : reflect (light) — **rechazo** *nm* : rejection
rechinar *vi* **1** : squeak, creak **2** : grind, gnash (one's teeth)
rechoncho, -cha *adj fam* : chubby
recibir *vt* **1** : receive **2** ACOGER : welcome — *vi* : receive visitors — **recibidor** *nm* : vestibule, entrance hall — **recibimiento** *nm* : reception, welcome — **recibo** *nm* : receipt
reciclar *vt* **1** : recycle **2** : retrain (workers) — **reciclaje** *nm* : recycling
recién *adv* **1** : newly, recently **2** ~ **casados** : newlyweds — **reciente** *adj* : recent — **recientemente** *adv* : recently
recinto *nm* **1** : enclosure **2** ÁREA : area, site
recio, -cia *adj* : tough, strong
recipiente *nm* : container, receptacle — ~ *nmf* : recipient
recíproco, -ca *adj* : reciprocal, mutual
recitar *vt* : recite — **recital** *nm* : recital
reclamar *vt* : demand, ask for — *vi* : complain — **reclamación** *nf, pl* -**ciones** **1** : claim, demand **2** QUEJA : complaint — **reclamo** *nm* **1** : lure (in hunting) **2** *Lat* : inducement, attraction
reclinar *vt* : rest, lean — **reclinarse** *vr* : recline, lean back
recluir {41} *vt* : confine, lock up — **recluirse** *vr* : shut oneself away — **reclusión** *nf, pl* -**siones** : imprisonment — **recluso, -sa** *n* : prisoner
recluta *nmf* : recruit — **reclutamiento** *nm* : recruitment — **reclutar** *vt* : recruit, enlist
recobrar *vt* : recover, regain — **recobrarse** *vr* ~ **de** : recover from
recodo *nm* : bend
recoger {15} *vt* **1** : collect, gather **2** COGER : pick up **3** LIMPIAR, ORDENAR : clean up, tidy (up) — **recogerse** *vr* : retire, withdraw — **recogedor** *nm* : dustpan — **recogido, -da** *adj* : quiet, secluded
recolección *nf, pl* -**ciones** **1** : collection **2** COSECHA : harvest
recomendar {55} *vt* : recommend — **recomendación** *nf, pl* -**ciones** : recommendation
recompensar *vt* : reward — **recompensa** *nf* : reward
reconciliar *vt* : reconcile — **reconciliarse** *vr* : be reconciled — **reconciliación** *nf, pl* -**ciones** : reconciliation
recóndito, -ta *adj* : hidden
reconfortar *vt* : comfort
reconocer {18} *vt* **1** : recognize **2** ADMITIR : admit **3** EXAMINAR : examine — **recono-**

cible *adj* : recognizable — **reconocido, -da** *adj* **1** : recognized, accepted **2** AGRADECIDO : grateful — **reconocimiento** *nm* **1** : recognition **2** AGRADECIMIENTO : gratitude **3** : (medical) examination
reconsiderar *vt* : reconsider
reconstruir {41} *vt* : reconstruct — **reconstrucción** *nf, pl* -**ciones** : reconstruction
recopilar *vt* **1** RECOGER : collect, gather **2** : compile — **recopilación** *nf, pl* -**ciones** : collection, compilation
récord *nm, pl* -**cords** : record
recordar {19} *vt* **1** ACORDARSE DE : remember **2** : remind — *vi* : remember — **recordatorio** *nm* : reminder
recorrer *vt* **1** : travel through **2** : cover (a distance) — **recorrido** *nm* **1** : journey, trip **2** TRAYECTO : route, course
recortar *vt* **1** : reduce **2** CORTAR : cut (out) **3** : trim (hair) — **recortarse** *vr* : stand out — **recorte** *nm* **1** : cut, cutting **2** ~**s de periódicos** : newspaper clippings
recostar {19} *vt* : lean, rest — **recostarse** *vr* : lie down
recoveco *nm* **1** : bend **2** RINCÓN : nook, corner
recrear *vt* **1** : recreate **2** ENTRETENER : entertain — **recrearse** *vr* : to enjoy oneself — **recreativo, -va** *adj* : recreational — **recreo** *nm* **1** : recreation, amusement **2** : recess, break (at school)
recriminar *vt* : reproach
recrudecer {53} *vi* : worsen — **recrudecerse** *vr* : intensify, get worse
rectángulo *nm* : rectangle — **rectangular** *adj* : rectangular
rectificar {72} *vt* **1** : rectify, correct **2** AJUSTAR : straighten (out) — **rectitud** *nf* **1** : straightness **2** : (moral) rectitude — **recto, -ta** *adj* **1** : straight **2** ÍNTEGRO : upright, honorable — **recto** *nm* : rectum
rector, -tora *adj* : governing, managing — ~ *n* : rector — **rectoría** *nf* : rectory
recubrir {2} *vt* : cover, coat
recuento *nm* : count, recount
recuerdo *nm* **1** : memory **2** : souvenir, remembrance (of a journey, etc.) **3** ~**s** *nmpl* SALUDOS : regards
recuperar *vt* **1** : recover, retrieve **2** ~ **el tiempo perdido** : make up for lost time — **recuperarse** *vr* ~ **de** : recover from — **recuperación** *nf, pl* -**ciones** **1** : recovery **2** ~ **de datos** : data retrieval
recurrir *vi* ~ **a** : turn to (a person), resort to (force, etc.) — **recurso** *nm* **1** : recourse, resort **2** : appeal (in law) **3** ~**s** *nmpl* : resources
red *nf* **1** : net **2** SISTEMA : network, system **3 la Red** : the Internet

redactar *vt* : write (up), draft — **redacción** *nf, pl* **-ciones 1** : writing, drafting **2** : editing (of a newspaper, etc.) — **redactor, -tora** *n* : editor

redada *nf* **1** : (police) raid **2** : catch (in fishing)

redescubrir {2} *vt* : rediscover

redención *nf, pl* **-ciones** : redemption — **redentor, -tora** *adj* : redeeming

redil *nm* : fold, pen

rédito *nm* : interest, yield

redoblar *vt* : redouble

redomado, -da *adj* : out-and-out

redondear *vt* **1** : make round **2** : round off (a number, etc.) — **redonda** *nf* **1** : whole note (in music) **2 a la** ～ : in the surrounding area — **redondel** *nm* **1** : ring, circle **2** : bullring — **redondo, -da** *adj* **1** : round **2** PERFECTO : excellent

reducir {61} *vt* : reduce — **reducirse** *vr* ～ **a** : come down to, amount to — **reducción** *nf, pl* **-ciones** : reduction — **reducido, -da** *adj* **1** : reduced, limited **2** PEQUEÑO : small

redundante *adj* : redundant — **redundancia** *nf* : reduncancy

reedición *nf, pl* **-ciones** : reprint

reembolsar *vt* : refund, reimburse, repay — **reembolso** *nm* : refund, reimbursement

reemplazar {21} *vt* : replace — **reemplazo** *nm* : replacement

reencarnación *nf, pl* **-ciones** : reincarnation

reencuentro *nm* : reunion

reestructurar *vt* : restructure

refaccionar *vt Lat* : repair, renovate — **refacciones** *nfpl Lat* : repairs, renovations

referir {76} *vt* **1** : tell **2** REMITIR : refer — **referirse** *vr* ～ **a** : refer to — **referencia** *nf* **1** : reference **2 hacer** ～ **a** : refer to — **referéndum** *nm, pl* **-dums** : referendum — **referente** *adj* ～ **a** : concerning

refinar *vt* : refine — **refinado, -da** *adj* : refined — **refinamiento** *nm* : refinement — **refinería** *nf* : refinery

reflector *nm* **1** : reflector **2** : spotlight, searchlight, floodlight

reflejar *vt* : reflect — **reflejarse** *vr* : be reflected — **reflejo** *nm* **1** : reflection **2** : (physical) reflex **3** ～**s** *nmpl* : highlights (in hair)

reflexionar *vi* : reflect, think — **reflexión** *nf, pl* **-xiones** : reflection, thought — **reflexivo, -va** *adj* **1** : reflective, thoughtful **2** : reflexive (in grammar)

reflujo *nm* : ebb (tide)

reforma *nf* **1** : reform **2** ～**s** *nfpl* : renovations — **reformador, -dora** *n* : reformer — **reformar** *vt* **1** : reform **2** : renovate, repair (a house, etc.) — **reformarse** *vr* : mend

one's ways — **reformatorio** *nm* : reformatory

reforzar {36} *vt* : reinforce

refrán *nm, pl* **-franes** : proverb, saying

refregar {49} *vt* : scrub

refrenar *vt* **1** : rein in (a horse) **2** CONTENER : restrain — **refrenarse** *vr* : restrain oneself

refrendar *vt* : approve, endorse

refrescar {72} *vt* **1** : refresh, cool **2** : brush up on (knowledge) — *vi* : turn cooler — **refrescante** *adj* : refreshing — **refresco** *nm* : soft drink

refriega *nf* : scuffle, skirmish

refrigerar *vt* **1** : refrigerate **2** CLIMATIZAR : air-condition — **refrigeración** *nf, pl* **-ciones 1** : refrigeration **2** AIRE ACONDICIONADO : air-conditioning — **refrigerador** *nmf Lat* : refrigerator — **refrigerio** *nm* : refreshments *pl*

refrito, -ta *adj* : refried — **refrito** *nm* : rehash

refuerzo *nm* : reinforcement

refugiar *vt* : shelter — **refugiarse** *vr* : take refuge — **refugiado, -da** *n* : refugee — **refugio** *nm* : refuge, shelter

refulgir {35} *vi* : shine brightly

refunfuñar *vi* : grumble, groan

refutar *vt* : refute

regadera *nf* **1** : watering can **2** *Lat* : shower head, shower

regalar *vt* : give (as a gift) — **regalarse** *vr* ～ **con** : treat oneself to

regaliz *nm, pl* **-lices** : licorice

regalo *nm* **1** : gift, present **2** PLACER : pleasure, delight

regañadientes: a ～ *adv phr* : reluctantly, unwillingly

regañar *vt* : scold — *vi* **1** QUEJARSE : grumble **2** *Spain* : quarrel — **regañon, -ñona** *adj, mpl* **-ñones** *fam* : grumpy, irritable

regar {49} *vt* **1** : irrigate, water **2** ESPARCIR : scatter

regatear *vt* **1** : haggle over **2** ESCATIMAR : skimp on — *vi* : bargain, haggle

regazo *nm* : lap (of a person)

regenerar *vt* : regenerate

regentar *vt* : run, manage

régimen *nm, pl* **regímenes 1** : regime **2** DIETA : diet **3** ～ **de vida** : lifestyle

regimiento *nm* : regiment

regio, -gia *adj* : royal, regal

región *nf, pl* **-giones** : region, area — **regional** *adj* : regional

regir {28} *vt* **1** : rule **2** ADMINISTRAR : manage, run **3** DETERMINAR : govern, determine — *vi* : apply, be in force — **regirse** *vr* ～ **por** : be guided by

registrar *vt* **1** : register **2** GRABAR : record, tape **3** : search (a house, etc.), frisk (a person) — **registrarse** *vr* **1** : register **2** : be recorded (of temperatures, etc.) — **registrador, -dora** *adj* **caja registradora** : cash register — ~ *n* : registrar — **registro** *nm* **1** : registration **2** : register (book) **3** : registry (office) **4** : range (of a voice, etc.) **5** INSPECCIÓN : search

regla *nf* **1** : rule, regulation **2** : ruler (for measuring) **3** MENSTRUACIÓN : period — **reglamentación** *nf, pl* **-clones 1** : regulation **2** REGLAS : rules *pl* — **reglamentar** *vt* : regulate — **reglamentario, -ria** *adj* : regulation, official — **reglamento** *nm* : regulations *pl*, rules *pl*

regocijar *vt* : gladden, delight — **regocijarse** *vr* : rejoice — **regocijo** *nm* : delight, rejoicing

regodearse *vr* : be delighted — **regodeo** *nm* : delight

regordete *adj fam* : chubby

regresar *vi* : return, come back, go back — *vt Lat* : give back — **regresión** *nf, pl* **-siones** : regression — **regresivo, -va** *adj* : regressive — **regreso** *nm* **1** : return **2 estar de** ~ : be back, be home again

reguero *nm* **1** : irrigation ditch **2** SEÑAL : trail, trace **3 correr como un** ~ **de pólvora** : spread like wildfire

regular *adj* **1** : regular **2** MEDIANO : medium, average **3 por lo** ~ : in general — ~ *vt* : regulate, control — **regulación** *nf, pl* **-ciones** : regulation, control — **regularidad** *nf* : regularity — **regularizar** {21} *vt* : normalize, make regular

rehabilitar *vt* **1** : rehabilitate **2** : reinstate (s.o. in a position) **3** : renovate (a building, etc.) — **rehabilitación** *nf* **1** : rehabilitation **2** : reinstatement (in a position) **3** : renovation (of a building, etc.)

rehacer {40} *vt* **1** : redo **2** REPARAR : repair — **rehacerse** *vr* **1** : recover **2** ~ **de** : get over

rehén *nm, pl* **-henes** : hostage

rehuir {41} *vt* : avoid, shun

rehusar {8} *v* : refuse

reimprimir *vt* : reprint — **reimpresión** *nf, pl* **-siones** : reprinting, reprint

reina *nf* : queen — **reinado** *nm* : reign — **reinante** *adj* : reigning — **reinar** *vi* **1** : reign **2** PREVALECER : prevail

reincidir *vi* : backslide, relapse

reino *nm* : kingdom, realm

reintegrar *vt* **1** : reinstate **2** : refund (money), reimburse (expenses, etc.) — **reintegrarse** *vr* ~ **a** : return to — **reintegro** *nm* : reimbursement

reír {66} *vi* : laugh — *vt* : laugh at — **reírse** *vr* : laugh

reiterar *vt* : repeat, reiterate

reivindicar {72} *vt* **1** : claim **2** RESTAURAR : restore

reja *nf* : grille, grating — **rejilla** *nf* : grille, grate, screen

rejuvenecer {53} *vt* : rejuvenate — **rejuvenecerse** *vr* : be rejuvenated

relación *nf, pl* **-ciones 1** : relation, connection **2** COMUNICACIÓN : relationship, relations *pl* **3** RELATO : account **4** LISTA : list **5 con** ~ **a** *or* **en** ~ **a** : in relation to — **relacionar** *vt* : relate, connect — **relacionarse** *vr* ~ **con** : be connected to, interact with

relajar *vt* : relax — **relajarse** *vr* : relax — **relajación** *nf, pl* **-ciones** : relaxation — **relajado, -da** *adj* **1** : relaxed **2** : dissolute, lax (in behavior)

relamerse *vr* : smack one's lips, lick its chops

relámpago *nm* : flash of lightning — **relampaguear** *vi* : flash

relatar *vt* : relate, tell

relativo, -va *adj* **1** : relative **2 en lo relativo a** : with regard to — **relatividad** *nf* : relativity

relato *nm* **1** : account, report **2** CUENTO : story, tale

releer {20} *vt* : reread

relegar {52} *vt* : relegate

relevante *adj* : outstanding, important

relevar *vt* **1** : relieve, take over from **2** ~ **de** : exempt from — **relevo** *nm* **1** : relief, replacement **2 carrera de** ~**s** : relay race

relieve *nm* **1** : relief (in art, etc.) **2** IMPORTANCIA : prominence, importance **3 poner en** ~ : emphasize

religión *nf, pl* **-giones** : religion — **religioso, -sa** *adj* : religious — ~ *n* : monk *m*, nun *f*

relinchar *vi* : neigh, whinny — **relincho** *nm* : neigh, whinny

reliquia *nf* **1** : relic **2** ~ **de familia** : family heirloom

rellenar *vt* **1** : refill **2** : stuff, fill (in cooking) — **relleno, -na** *adj* : stuffed, filled — **relleno** *nm* : stuffing, filling

reloj *nm* **1** : clock **2** *or* ~ **de pulsera** : wristwatch **3** ~ **de arena** : hourglass **4 como un** ~ : like clockwork

relucir {45} *vi* **1** : glitter, shine **2 sacar a** ~ : bring up, mention — **reluciente** *adj* : brilliant, shining

relumbrar *vi* : shine brightly

remachar *vt* **1** : rivet **2** RECALCAR : stress, drive home — **remache** *nm* : rivet

remanente *nm* : remainder, surplus

remanso *nm* : pool

remar *vi* : row

rematar *vt* **1** : conclude, finish up **2** MATAR : finish off **3** LIQUIDAR : sell off cheaply **4**

remedar

Lat : auction — *vi* **1** : shoot (in sports) **2** TERMINAR : end — **rematado, -da** *adj* : utter, complete — **remate** *nm* **1** : shot (in sports) **2** FIN : end

remedar *vt* : imitate, mimic

remediar *vt* **1** : remedy, repair **2** : solve (a problem) **3** EVITAR : avoid — **remedio** *nm* **1** : remedy, cure **2** SOLUCIÓN : solution **3** **sin ~** : hopeless

rememorar *vi* : recall

remendar {55} *vt* : mend

remesa *nf* **1** : remittance **2** : shipment (of merchandise)

remezón *nm, pl* **-zones** *Lat* : mild earthquake, tremor

remiendo *nm* : mend, patch

remilgado, -da *adj* **1** : prudish **2** AFECTADO : affected — **remilgo** *nm* : primness, affectation

reminiscencia *nf* : reminiscence

remisión *nf, pl* **-siones** : remission

remiso, -sa *adj* **1** : reluctant **2** NEGLIGENTE : remiss

remitir *vt* **1** : send, remit **2 ~ a** : refer to, direct to — *vi* : subside, let up — **remite** *nm* : return address — **remitente** *nmf* : sender (of a letter, etc.)

remo *nm* : paddle, oar

remodelar *vt* **1** : remodel **2** : restructure (an organization)

remojar *vt* : soak, steep — **remojo** *nm* **poner en ~** : soak

remolacha *nf* : beet

remolcar {72} *vt* : tow, tug — **remolcador** *nm* : tugboat

remolino *nm* **1** : whirlwind, whirlpool **2** : crowd (of people) **3** : cowlick (of hair)

remolque *nm* **1** : towing, tow **2** : trailer (vehicle)

remontar *vt* **1** : overcome **2** SUBIR : go up — **remontarse** *vr* **1** : soar **2 ~ a** : date from, go back to

rémora *nf* : hindrance

remorder {47} *vt* : trouble, worry — **remordimiento** *nm* : remorse

remoto, -ta *adj* : remote — **remotamente** *adv* : remotely, slightly

remover {47} *vt* **1** : stir **2** : move around, turn over (earth, embers, etc.) **3** REAVIVIR : bring up again **4** DESPEDIR : fire, dismiss

remunerar *vt* : remunerate

renacer {48} *vi* : be reborn, revive — **renacimiento** *nm* **1** : rebirth, revival **2 el Renacimiento** : the Renaissance

renacuajo *nm* : tadpole, pollywog

rencilla *nf* : quarrel

renco, -ca *adj Lat* : lame

rencor *nm* **1** : rancor, hostility **2 guardar**

~ : hold a grudge — **rencoroso, -sa** *adj* : resentful

rendición *nf, pl* **-ciones** : surrender — **rendido, -da** *adj* **1** : submissive **2** AGOTADO : exhausted

rendija *nf* : crack, split

rendir {54} *vt* **1** : render, give **2** PRODUCIR : yield, produce **3** CANSAR : exhaust — *vi* : make progress, go a long way — **rendirse** *vr* : surrender, give up — **rendimiento** *nm* **1** : performance **2** : yield, return (in finance, etc.)

renegar {49} *vt* : deny — *vi* **1** QUEJARSE : grumble **2 ~ de** ABJURAR : renounce, disown — **renegado, -da** *n* : renegade

renglón *nm, pl* **-glones** **1** : line (of writing) **2** *Lat* : line (of products)

reno *nm* : reindeer

renombre *nm* : renown — **renombrado, -da** *adj* : famous, renowned

renovar {19} *vt* **1** : renew, restore **2** : renovate (a building, etc.) — **renovación** *nf, pl* **-ciones** **1** : renewal **2** : renovation (of a building, etc.)

renquear *vi* : limp, hobble

rentar *vt* **1** : produce, yield **2** *Lat* : rent — **renta** *nf* **1** : income **2** ALQUILER : rent **3** **impuesto sobre la ~** : income tax — **rentable** *adj* : profitable

renunciar *vi* **1** : resign **2 ~ a** : renounce, relinquish — **renuncia** *nf* **1** : renunciation **2** DIMISIÓN : resignation

reñir {67} *vi* **~ con** : argue with, fall out with — *vt* **1** : scold **2** DISPUTAR : fight — **reñido, -da** *adj* **1** : hard-fought **2 ~ con** : on bad terms with

reo, rea *n* **1** : accused, defendant **2** CULPABLE : culprit

reojo *nm* **de ~** : out of the corner of one's eye

reorganizar {21} *vt* : reorganize

repantigarse {52} *vr* : sprawl out

reparar *vt* **1** : repair, fix **2** : make amends for (an offense, etc.) — *vi* **1 ~ en** ADVERTIR : take notice of **2 ~ en** CONSIDERAR : consider — **reparación** *nf, pl* **-ciones** **1** : reparation, amends **2** ARREGLO : repair — **reparo** *nm* **1** : reservation, objection **2 poner ~ a** : object to

repartir *vt* **1** : allocate **2** DISTRIBUIR : distribute **3** ESPARCIR : spread — **repartición** *nf, pl* **-ciones** : distribution — **repartidor, -dora** *n* : delivery person, distributor — **reparto** *nm* **1** : allocation **2** DISTRIBUCIÓN : delivery **3** : cast (of characters)

repasar *vt* **1** : review, go over **2** ZURCIR : mend — **repaso** *nm* **1** : review **2** : mending (of clothes)

repeler *vt* **1** : repel **2** REPUGNAR : disgust —
repelente *adj* : repellent, repulsive
repente *nm* **1** : fit, outburst **2 de** ~ : suddenly — **repentino, -na** *adj* : sudden
repercutir *vi* **1** : reverberate **2** ~ **en** : have repercussions on — **repercusión** *nf, pl* **-siones** : repercussion
repertorio *nm* : repertoire
repetir {54} *vt* **1** : repeat **2** : have a second helping of (food) — **repetirse** *vr* **1** : repeat oneself **2** : recur (of an event, etc.) —
repetición *nf, pl* **-ciones 1** : repetition **2** : rerun, repeat (of a program, etc.) —
repetido, -da *adj* **1** : repeated **2 repetidas veces** : repeatedly, time and again —
repetitivo, -va *adj* : repetitive, repetitious
repicar {72} *vt* : ring — *vi* : ring out, peal —
repique *nm* : ringing, pealing
repisa *nf* **1** : shelf, ledge **2** ~ **de ventana** : windowsill
replegar {49} *vt* : fold — **replegarse** *vr* : retreat, withdraw
repleto, -ta *adj* **1** : replete, full **2** ~ **de** : packed with
replicar {72} *vt* : reply, retort — *vi* : answer back — **réplica** *nf* **1** RESPUESTA : reply **2** COPIA : replica, reproduction
repliegue *nm* **1** : fold **2** : (military) withdrawal
repollo *nm* : cabbage
reponer {60} *vt* **1** : replace **2** REPLICAR : reply — **reponerse** *vr* : recover
reportar *vt* **1** : yield, bring **2** *Lat* : report —
reportaje *nm* : article, (news) report — **reporte** *nm Lat* : report — **reportero, -ra** *n* : reporter
reposar *vi* **1** DESCANSAR : rest **2** : stand, settle (of liquids, dough, etc.) — **reposado, -da** *adj* : calm, relaxed — **reposición** *nf, pl* **-ciones 1** : replacement **2** : rerun, repeat (of a program, etc.) — **reposo** *nm* : rest
repostar *vi* **1** : stock up on **2** : refuel (an airplane, etc.) — *vi* : fill up, refuel
reprender *vt* : reprimand, scold — **reprensible** *adj* : reprehensible
represalia *nf* **1** : reprisal **2 tomar** ~**s** : retaliate
represar *vt* : dam
representar *vt* **1** : represent **2** : perform (a play, etc.) **3** APARENTAR : look, appear as — **representación** *nf, pl* **-ciones 1** : representation **2** : performance (of a play, etc.) **3 en** ~ **de** : on behalf of — **representante** *nmf* **1** : representative **2** ACTOR : performer — **representativo, -va** *adj* : representative
represión *nf, pl* **-siones** : repression
reprimenda *nf* : reprimand
reprimir *vt* **1** : repress **2** : suppress (a rebellion, etc.)

reprobar {19} *vt* **1** : reprove, condemn **2** *Lat* : fail (an exam, etc.)
reprochar *vt* : reproach — **reprocharse** *vr* : reproach oneself — **reproche** *nm* : reproach
reproducir {61} *vt* : reproduce — **reproducirse** *vr* **1** : breed, reproduce **2** : recur (of an event, etc.) — **reproducción** *nf, pl* **-ciones** : reproduction — **reproductor, -tora** *adj* : reproductive
reptil *nm* : reptile
república *nf* : republic — **republicano, -na** *adj & n* : republican
repudiar *vt* : repudiate
repuesto *nm* : spare (auto) part
repugnar *vt* : disgust — **repugnancia** *nf* : disgust — **repugnante** *adj* : disgusting
repujar *vt* : emboss
repulsivo, -va *adj* : repulsive
reputar *vt* : consider, deem — **reputación** *nf, pl* **-ciones** : reputation
requerir {76} *vt* **1** : require **2** : summon, send for (a person)
requesón *nm, pl* **-sones** : cottage cheese
réquiem *nm* : requiem
requisito *nm* **1** : requirement **2** ~ **previo** : prerequisite
res *nf* **1** : beast, animal **2** *Lat or* **carne de** ~ : beef
resabio *nm* **1** VICIO : bad habit, vice **2** DEJO : aftertaste
resaca *nf* **1** : undertow **2 tener** ~ : have a hangover
resaltar *vi* **1** : stand out **2 hacer** ~ : bring out, highlight — *vt* : emphasize
resarcir {83} *vt* : compensate, repay — **resarcirse** *vr* ~ **de** : make up for
resbalar *vi* **1** : slip, slide **2** : skid (of an automobile) — **resbalarse** *vr* : slip, skid — **resbaladizo, -za** *adj* : slippery — **resbalón** *nm, pl* **-lones** : slip — **resbaloso, -sa** *adj Lat* : slippery
rescatar *vt* **1** : rescue, ransom **2** RECUPERAR : recover, get back — **rescate** *nm* **1** : rescue **2** : ransom (money) **3** RECUPERACIÓN : recovery
rescindir *vt* : cancel — **rescisión** *nf, pl* **-siones** : cancellation
rescoldo *nm* : embers *pl*
resecar {72} *vt* : dry (out) — **resecarse** *vr* : dry up — **reseco, -ca** *adj* : dry, dried-up
resentirse {76} *vr* **1** : suffer, be weakened **2** OFENDERSE : be offended **3** ~ **de** : feel the effects of — **resentido, -da** *adj* : resentful — **resentimiento** *nm* : resentment
reseñar *vt* **1** : review **2** DESCRIBIR : describe — **reseña** *nf* **1** : review, report **2** DESCRIPCIÓN : description
reservar *vt* **1** : reserve **2** GUARDAR : keep,

save — **reservarse** *vr* **1** : save oneself **2** : keep for oneself — **reserva** *nf* **1** : reservation **2** PROVISIÓN : reserve **3 de** ~ : spare, in reserve — **reservación** *nf, pl* **-ciones** : reservation — **reservado, -da** *adj* **1** : reserved **2** : confidential (of a document, etc.)

resfriar {85} *vt* : cool — **resfriarse** *vr* **1** : cool off **2** CONSTIPARSE : catch a cold — **resfriado** *nm* CATARRO : cold — **resfrío** *nm* Lat : cold

resguardar *vt* : protect — **resguardarse** *vr* : protect oneself — **resguardo** *nm* **1** : protection **2** RECIBO : receipt

residir *vi* **1** : reside, live **2** ~ **en** : lie in — **residencia** *nf* **1** : residence **2** *or* ~ **universitaria** : dormitory — **residencial** *adj* : residential — **residente** *adj & nmf* : resident

residuo *nm* **1** : residue **2** ~**s** *nmpl* : waste — **residual** *adj* : residual

resignar *vt* : resign — **resignarse** *vr* ~ **a** : resign oneself to — **resignación** *nf, pl* **-ciones** : resignation

resina *nf* **1** : resin **2** ~ **epoxídica** : epoxy

resistir *vt* **1** AGUANTAR : stand, bear **2** : withstand (temptation, etc.) — *vi* : resist — **resistirse** *vr* ~ **a** : be resistant to — **resistencia** *nf* **1** : resistance **2** AGUANTE : endurance, stamina — **resistente** *adj* : resistant, strong, tough

resma *nf* : ream

resollar {19} *vi* : breathe heavily, pant

resolver {89} *vt* **1** : resolve **2** DECIDIR : decide — **resolverse** *vr* : make up one's mind — **resolución** *nf, pl* **-ciones** **1** : resolution **2** DECISIÓN : decision **3** FIRMEZA : determination, resolve

resonar {19} *vi* : resound — **resonancia** *nf* **1** : resonance **2** CONSECUENCIAS : impact, repercussions *pl* — **resonante** *adj* : resonant, resounding

resoplar *vi* **1** : puff, pant **2** : snort (with annoyance)

resorte *nm* **1** MUELLE : spring **2 tocar** ~**s** : pull strings

respaldar *vt* : back, endorse — **respaldarse** *vr* : lean back — **respaldo** *nm* **1** : back (of a chair, etc.) **2** APOYO : support, backing

respectar *vt* : concern, relate to — **respectivo, -va** *adj* : respective — **respecto** *nm* **1 al** ~ : in this respect **2** ~ **a** : in regard to, concerning

respetar *vt* : respect — **respetable** *adj* : respectable — **respeto** *nm* **1** : respect **2 presentar sus** ~**s** : pay one's respects — **respetuoso, -sa** *adj* : respectful

respingo *nm* : start, jump

respirar *v* : breathe — **respiración** *nf, pl* **-ciones** : respiration, breathing — **respira-**

torio, -ria *adj* : respiratory — **respiro** *nm* **1** : breath **2** DESCANSO : respite, break

resplandecer {53} *vi* : shine — **resplandeciente** *adj* : shining, gleaming — **resplandor** *nm* **1** : brilliance, gleam **2** : flash (of lightning, etc.)

responder *vt* : answer, reply — *vi* **1** : answer **2** REPLICAR : answer back **3** ~ **a** : respond to **4** ~ **de** : answer for (something)

responsable *adj* : responsible — **responsabilidad** *nf* : responsibility

respuesta *nf* **1** : answer, reply **2** REACCIÓN : response

resquebrajar *vt* : split, crack — **resquebrajarse** *vr* : crack

resquicio *nm* **1** : crack, crevice **2** VESTIGIO : trace, glimmer

resta *nf* : subtraction

restablecer {53} *vt* : reestablish, restore — **restablecerse** *vr* : recover — **restablecimiento** *nm* : restoration, recovery

restallar *vi* : crack, crackle

restar *vt* **1** : deduct, subtract **2** DISMINUIR : minimize — *vi* : be left — **restante** *adj* **1** : remaining **2 lo** ~ : the rest

restauración *nf, pl* **-ciones** : restoration

restaurante *nm* : restaurant

restaurar *vt* : restore

restituir {41} *vt* : return, restore — **restitución** *nf, pl* **-ciones** : restitution

resto *nm* **1** : rest, remainder **2** ~**s** *nmpl* : leftovers **3** *or* ~**s mortales** : mortal remains

restregar {49} *vt* : rub, scrub — **restregarse** *vr* : rub

restringir {35} *vt* : restrict, limit — **restricción** *nf, pl* **-ciones** : restriction, limitation — **restrictivo, -va** *adj* : restrictive

resucitar *vt* : resuscitate, revive — *vi* : come back to life

resuelto, -ta *adj* : determined, resolved

resuello *nm* : heavy breathing, panting

resultar *vi* **1** : succeed, work out **2** SALIR : turn out (to be) **3** ~ **de** : be the result of **4** ~ **en** : result in — **resultado** *nm* : result, outcome

resumir *v* : summarize, sum up — **resumen** *nm, pl* **-súmenes** **1** : summary **2 en** ~ : in short

resurgir {35} *vi* : reappear, revive — **resurgimiento** *nm* : resurgence — **resurrección** *nf, pl* **-ciones** : resurrection

retahíla *nf* : string, series

retal *nm* : remnant

retardar *vt* **1** RETRASAR : delay **2** POSPONER : postpone

retazo *nm* **1** : remnant, scrap **2** : fragment (of a text, etc.)

retener {80} *vt* **1** : retain, keep **2** : withhold (funds, etc.) **3** DETENER : detain — **retención** *nf, pl* **-ciones 1** : retention **2** : deduction, withholding (of funds)

reticente *adj* : reluctant — **reticencia** *nf* : reluctance

retina *nf* : retina

retintín *nm, pl* **-tines 1** : tinkling, jingle **2** **con** ~ : sarcastically

retirar *vt* **1** : remove, take away **2** : withdraw (funds, statements, etc.) — **retirarse** *vr* **1** : retreat, withdraw **2** JUBILARSE : retire — **retirada** *nf* **1** : withdrawal **2 batirse en** ~ : beat a retreat — **retirado, -da** *adj* **1** : remote, secluded **2** JUBILADO : retired — **retiro** *nm* **1** : retreat **2** JUBILACIÓN : retirement **3** *Lat* : withdrawal

reto *nm* : challenge, dare

retocar {72} *vt* : touch up

retoño *nm* : sprout, shoot

retoque *nm* **1** : retouching **2 el último** ~ : the finishing touch

retorcer {14} *vt* **1** : twist, contort **2** : wring out (clothes, etc.) — **retorcerse** *vr* **1** : get twisted up **2** : squirm, writhe (in pain) — **retorcijón** *nm, pl* **-jones** : cramp, spasm — **retorcimiento** *nm* : twisting, wringing out

retórica *nf* : rhetoric — **retórico, -ca** *adj* : rhetorical

retornar *v* : return — **retorno** *nm* : return

retozar {21} *vi* : frolic, romp — **retozón, -zona** *adj* : playful, frisky

retractarse *vr* **1** : withdraw, back down **2** ~ **de** : take back, retract

retraer {81} *vt* : retract — **retraerse** *vr* : withdraw — **retraído, -da** *adj* : withdrawn, shy

retrasar *vt* **1** : delay, hold up **2** APLAZAR : postpone **3** : set back (a clock) — **retrasarse** *vr* **1** : be late **2** : fall behind (in work, etc.) — **retrasado, -da** *adj* **1** : retarded **2** : in arrears (of payments) **3** : backward (of a country) **4** : slow (of a clock) — **retraso** *nm* **1** : delay **2** SUBDESARROLLO : backwardness **3** ~ **mental** : mental retardation

retratar *vt* **1** : portray **2** FOTOGRAFIAR : photograph **3** DIBUJAR : paint a portrait of — **retrato** *nm* **1** : portrayal **2** DIBUJO : portrait **3** FOTOGRAFÍA : photograph

retrete *nm* : restroom, toilet

retribuir {41} *vt* **1** : pay **2** RECOMPENSAR : reward — **retribución** *nf, pl* **-ciones 1** : payment **2** RECOMPENSA : reward

retroactivo, -va *adj* : retroactive

retroceder *vi* **1** : go back, turn back **2** CEDER : back down — **retroceso** *nm* **1** : backward movement **2** : backing down

retrógrado, -da *adj & nmf* : reactionary

retrospectiva *nf* : hindsight — **retrospectivo, -va** *adj* : retrospective

retrovisor *nm* : rearview mirror

retumbar *vi* : resound, reverberate, rumble

reumatismo *nm* : rheumatism

reunir {68} *vt* **1** : unite, join **2** TENER : have, possess **3** RECOGER : gather, collect — **reunirse** *vr* : meet, gather — **reunión** *nf, pl* **-niones 1** : meeting **2** : (social) gathering, reunion

revalidar *vt* : confirm, ratify

revancha *nf* **1** : revenge **2** : rematch (in sports)

revelar *vt* **1** : reveal, disclose **2** : develop (film) — **revelación** *nf, pl* **-ciones** : revelation — **revelado** *nm* : developing (of film) — **revelador, -dora** *adj* : revealing

reventar {55} *v* : burst, blow up — **reventarse** *vr* : burst — **reventón** *nm, pl* **-tones** : blowout, flat tire

reverberar *vi* : reverberate — **reverberación** *nf, pl* **-ciones** : reverberation

reverenciar *vt* : revere — **reverencia** *nf* **1** : bow, curtsy **2** VENERACIÓN : reverence — **reverendo, -da** *adj & nmf* : reverend — **reverente** *adj* : reverent

reversa *nf Lat* : reverse (gear)

reverso *nm* **1** : back, reverse **2 el** ~ **de la medalla** : the complete opposite — **reversible** *adj* : reversible

revertir {76} *vi* **1** : revert **2** ~ **en** : result in

revés *nm, pl* **-veses 1** : back, wrong side **2** CONTRATIEMPO : setback **3** BOFETADA : slap **4** : backhand (in sports) **5 al** ~ : the other way around, upside down, inside out

revestir {54} *vt* **1** : coat, cover **2** ASUMIR : take on, assume — **revestimiento** *nm* : covering, coating

revisar *vt* **1** : examine, inspect **2** : check over, overhaul (machinery, etc.) **3** MODIFICAR : revise — **revisión** *nf, pl* **-siones 1** : revision **2** INSPECCIÓN : inspection, check — **revisor, -sora** *n* : inspector

revistar *vt* : review, inspect (troops, etc.) — **revista** *nf* **1** : magazine, journal **2** : revue (in theater) **3 pasar** ~ : review, inspect

revivir *vi* : revive, come alive again — *vt* : relive

revocar {72} *vt* : revoke

revolcar {82} *vt* : knock over, knock down — **revolcarse** *vr* : roll around

revolotear *vi* : flutter, flit — **revoloteo** *nm* : fluttering, flitting

revoltijo *nm* : mess, jumble

revoltoso, -sa *adj* : rebellious

revolución *nf, pl* **-ciones** : revolution — **revolucionar** *vt* : revolutionize — **revolucionario, -ria** *adj & n* : revolutionary

revolver {89} *vt* **1** : mix, stir **2** : upset (one's

stomach) **3** DESORGANIZAR : mess up — **re-volverse** *vr* **1** : toss and turn **2** VOLVERSE : turn around
revólver *nm* : revolver
revuelo *nm* : commotion
revuelta *nf* : uprising, revolt — **revuelto, -ta** *adj* **1** : choppy, rough **2** DESORDENADO : messed up **3 huevos revueltos** : scrambled eggs
rey *nm* : king
reyerta *nf* : brawl, fight
rezagarse {52} *vr* : fall behind, lag
rezar {21} *vi* **1** : pray **2** DECIR : say — *vt* : say, recite — **rezo** *nm* : prayer
rezongar {52} *vi* : gripe, grumble
rezumar *v* : ooze
ría *nf* : estuary
riachuelo *nm* : brook, stream
riada *nf* : flood
ribera *nf* : bank, shore
ribetear *vt* : border, trim — **ribete** *nm* **1** : border, trim **2** : embellishment
rico, -ca *adj* **1** : rich, wealthy **2** ABUNDANTE : abundant **3** SABROSO : rich, tasty — ~ *n* : rich person
ridiculizar {21} *vt* : ridicule — **ridículo, -la** *adj* : ridiculous — **ridículo** *nm* **1 hacer el** ~ : make a fool of oneself **2 poner en** ~ : ridicule
riego *nm* : irrigation
riel *nm* : rail
rienda *nf* **1** : rein **2 dar** ~ **suelta a** : give free rein to
riesgo *nm* : risk
rifa *nf* : raffle — **rifar** *vt* : raffle (off) — **rifarse** *vr fam* : fight over
rifle *nm* : rifle
rígido, -da *adj* **1** : rigid, stiff **2** SEVERO : harsh, strict — **rigidez** *nf, pl* **-deces 1** : rigidity, stiffness **2** SEVERIDAD : harshness, strictness
rigor *nm* **1** : rigor, harshness **2** EXACTITUD : precision **3 de** ~ : essential, obligatory — **riguroso, -sa** *adj* : rigorous
rima *nf* **1** : rhyme **2** ~**s** *nfpl* : verse, poetry — **rimar** *vi* : rhyme
rimbombante *adj* : showy, pompous
rímel *nm* : mascara
rincón *nm, pl* **-cones** : corner, nook
rinoceronte *nm* : rhinoceros
riña *nf* **1** : fight, brawl **2** DISPUTA : dispute, quarrel
riñón *nm, pl* **-ñones** : kidney
río *nm* **1** : river **2** TORRENTE : torrent, stream
riqueza *nf* **1** : wealth **2** ABUNDANCIA : richness **3** ~**s naturales** : natural resources
risa *nf* **1** : laughter, laugh **2 dar** ~ **a algn** : make s.o. laugh **3 morirse de la** ~ *fam* : die laughing

risco *nm* : crag, cliff
risible *adj* : laughable
ristra *nf* : string, series
risueño, -ña *adj* : cheerful, smiling
ritmo *nm* **1** : rhythm **2** VELOCIDAD : pace, speed — **rítmico, -ca** *adj* : rhythmical
rito *nm* : rite, ritual — **ritual** *adj & nm* : ritual
rival *adj & nmf* : rival — **rivalidad** *nf* : rivalry, competition — **rivalizar** {21} *vi* ~ **con** : rival, compete with
rizar {21} *vt* **1** : curl **2** : ripple (a surface) — **rizarse** *vr* : curl **2** : choppy (of water) — **rizo** *nm* **1** : curl **2** : ripple (in water) **3** : loop (in aviation)
róbalo *nm* : bass (fish)
robar *vt* **1** : steal **2** : burglarize (a house, etc.) **3** SECUESTRAR : kidnap — **robo** *nm* : robbery, theft
roble *nm* : oak
robot *nm, pl* **-bots** : robot — **robótica** *nf* : robotics
robustecer {53} *vt* : make stronger, strengthen — **robusto, -ta** *adj* : robust, sturdy
roca *nf* : rock, boulder
roce *nm* **1** : rubbing, chafing **2** RASGUÑO : graze, scratch **3 tener un** ~ **con** : have a brush with
rociar {85} *vt* : spray, sprinkle — **rocío** *nm* : dew
rocoso, -sa *adj* : rocky
rodaja *nf* : slice
rodar {19} *vi* **1** : roll, roll down, roll along **2** GIRAR : turn, go around **3** : travel (of a vehicle) **4** : film (of movies, etc.) — *vt* **1** : film, shoot **2** : break in (a vehicle) — **rodaje** *nm* **1** : filming, shooting **2** : breaking in (of a vehicle)
rodear *vt* **1** : surround, encircle **2** *Lat* : round up (cattle) — **rodearse** *vr* ~ **de** : surround oneself with — **rodeo** *nm* **1** : rodeo, roundup **2** DESVÍO : detour **3 andar con** ~**s** : beat around the bush
rodilla *nf* : knee
rodillo *nm* **1** : roller **2** : rolling pin (for pastry)
roer {69} *vt* **1** : gnaw **2** ATORMENTAR : eat away at, torment — **roedor** *nm* : rodent
rogar {16} *vt* : beg, request — *vi* : pray
rojo, -ja *adj* **1** : red **2 ponerse** ~ : blush — **rojo** *nm* : red — **rojez** *nf* : redness — **rojizo, -za** *adj* : reddish
rollizo, -za *adj* : plump, chubby
rollo *nm* **1** : roll, coil **2** *fam* : boring speech, lecture
romance *nm* **1** : romance **2** : Romance (language)
romano, -na *adj & n* : Roman

romántico, -ca *adj* : romantic — **romanticismo** *nm* : romanticism
romería *nf* : pilgrimage, procession
romero *nm* : rosemary
romo, -ma *adj* : blunt, dull
rompecabezas *nms & pl* : puzzle
romper {70} *vt* **1** : break **2** RASGAR : rip, tear **3** : break off (relations), break (a contract) — *vi* **1** : break (of the day, waves, etc.) **2** ~ **a** : begin to, burst out with **3** ~ **con** : break off with — **romperse** *vr* : break
ron *nm* : rum
roncar {72} *vi* : snore — **ronco, -ca** *adj* : hoarse
ronda *nf* **1** : rounds *pl*, patrol **2** : round (of drinks, etc.) — **rondar** *vt* **1** : patrol **2** : hang around (a place) **3** : be approximately (an age, a number, etc.) — *vi* **1** : be on patrol **2** MERODEAR : prowl about
ronquera *nf* : hoarseness
ronquido *nm* : snore
ronronear *vi* : purr — **ronroneo** *nm* : purr, purring
ronzar {21} *vt* : munch, crunch
roña *nf* **1** : mange **2** SUCIEDAD : dirt, filth — **roñoso, -sa** *adj* **1** : mangy **2** SUCIO : dirty **3** *fam* : stingy
ropa *nf* **1** : clothes *pl*, clothing **2** ~ **interior** : underwear — **ropaje** *nm* : robes *pl*, regalia — **ropero** *nm* : wardrobe, closet
rosa *nf* : rose (flower) — ~ *adj* : rose-colored — ~ *nm* : rose (color) — **rosado, -da** *adj* **1** : pink **2** **vino rosado** : rosé — **rosado** *nm* : pink (color) — **rosal** *nm* : rosebush
rosario *nm* : rosary
rosbif *nm* : roast beef
rosca *nf* **1** : thread (of a screw) **2** ESPIRAL : ring, coil
roseta *nf* : rosette
rosquilla *nf* : doughnut
rostro *nm* : face
rotación *nf*, *pl* **-ciones** : rotation — **rotativo, -va** *adj* : rotary, revolving
roto, -ta *adj* : broken, torn
rotonda *nf* : traffic circle, rotary
rótula *nf* : kneecap
rótulo *nm* **1** : heading, title **2** ETIQUETA : label, sign
rotundo, -da *adj* : categorical, absolute
rotura *nf* : break, tear, fracture
rozar {21} *vt* **1** : graze, touch lightly **2** APROXIMARSE DE : touch on, border on — *vi*

: scrape, rub — **rozarse** *vr* **1** : rub, chafe **2** ~ **con** *fam* : rub elbows with — **rozadura** *nf* : scratch
rubí *nm*, *pl* **rubíes** : ruby
rubicundo, -da *adj* : ruddy
rubio, -bia *adj & n* : blond
rubor *nm* : flush, blush — **ruborizarse** {21} *vr* : blush
rúbrica *nf* **1** : flourish (in writing) **2** TÍTULO : title, heading
rudeza *nf* : roughness, coarseness
rudimentos *nmpl* : rudiments, basics — **rudimentario, -ria** *adj* : rudimentary
rudo, -da *adj* **1** : rough, harsh **2** GROSERO : coarse, unpolished
rueda *nf* **1** : wheel **2** CORRO : circle, ring **3** RODAJA : (round) slice **4** **ir sobre** ~**s** : go smoothly — **ruedo** *nm* : bullring
ruego *nm* : request
rugir {35} *vi* : roar — **rugido** *nm* : roar
rugoso, -sa *adj* **1** : rough **2** ARRUGADO : wrinkled
ruibarbo *nm* : rhubarb
ruido *nm* : noise — **ruidoso, -sa** *adj* : loud, noisy
ruina *nf* **1** : ruin, destruction **2** COLAPSO : collapse **3** ~**s** *nfpl* : ruins, remains — **ruinoso, -sa** *adj* : run-down, dilapidated
ruiseñor *nm* : nightingale
ruleta *nf* : roulette
rulo *nm* : curler, roller
rumano, -na *adj* : Romanian, Rumanian
rumba *nf* : rumba
rumbo *nm* **1** : direction, course **2** ESPLENDIDEZ : lavishness **3** **con** ~ **a** : bound for, heading for **4** **perder el** ~ : go off course
rumiar *vt* : mull over — *vi* : chew the cud — **rumiante** *adj & nm* : ruminant
rumor *nm* **1** : rumor **2** MURMULLO : murmur — **rumorearse** *or* **rumorarse** *vr* : be rumored — **rumoroso, -sa** *adj* : murmuring, babbling
ruptura *nf* **1** : break, rupture **2** : breach (of a contract) **3** : breaking off (of relations)
rural *adj* : rural
ruso, -sa *adj* : Russian — **ruso** *nm* : Russian (language)
rústico, -ca *adj* **1** : rural, rustic **2** **en rústica** : in paperback
ruta *nf* : route
rutina *nf* : routine — **rutinario, -ria** *adj* : routine

S

s *nf* : s, 20th letter of the Spanish alphabet
sábado *nm* : Saturday
sábana *nf* : sheet
sabandija *nf* : bug
saber {71} *vt* **1** : know **2** SER CAPAZ DE : know how to, be able to **3** ENTERARSE : learn, find out **4 a ~** : namely — *vi* **1** : taste **2 ~ de** : know about — **~** *nm* : knowledge — **sabelotodo** *nmf fam* : know-it-all — **sabido, -da** *adj* : well-known — **sabiduría** *nf* **1** : wisdom **2** CONOCIMIENTO : learning, knowledge — **sabiendas: a ~** *adv phr* : knowingly — **sabio, -bia** *adj* **1** : learned **2** PRUDENTE : wise, sensible
sabor *nm* : flavor, taste — **saborear** *vt* : savor
sabotaje *nm* : sabotage — **saboteador, -dora** *n* : saboteur — **sabotear** *vt* : sabotage
sabroso, -sa *adj* : delicious, tasty
sabueso *nm* **1** : bloodhound **2** *fam* : sleuth
sacacorchos *nms & pl* : corkscrew
sacapuntas *nms & pl* : pencil sharpener
sacar {72} *vt* **1** : take out **2** OBTENER : get, obtain **3** EXTRAER : extract, withdraw **4** : bring out (a book, a product, etc.) **5** : take (photos), make (copies) **6** QUITAR : remove **7 ~ adelante** : bring up (children), carry out (a project, etc.) **8 ~ la lengua** : stick out one's tongue — *vi* : serve (in sports)
sacarina *nf* : saccharin
sacerdote, -tisa *n* : priest *m*, priestess *f* — **sacerdocio** *nm* : priesthood — **sacerdotal** *adj* : priestly
saciar *vt* : satisfy
saco *nm* **1** : bag, sack **2** : sac (in anatomy) **3** *Lat* : jacket
sacramento *nm* : sacrament — **sacramental** *adj* : sacramental
sacrificar {72} *vt* : sacrifice — **sacrificarse** *vr* : sacrifice oneself — **sacrificio** *nm* : sacrifice
sacrilegio *nm* : sacrilege — **sacrílego, -ga** *adj* : sacrilegious
sacro, -cra *adj* : sacred — **sacrosanto, -ta** *adj* : sacrosanct
sacudir *vt* **1** : shake **2** GOLPEAR : beat **3** CONMOVER : shake up, shock — **sacudirse** *vr* : shake off — **sacudida** *nf* **1** : shaking **2** : jolt (of a train, etc.), tremor (of an earthquake) **3** : (emotional) shock
sádico, -ca *adj* : sadistic — **~** *n* : sadist — **sadismo** *nm* : sadism
saeta *nf* : arrow

safari *nm* : safari
sagaz *adj, pl* **-gaces** : shrewd, sagacious — **sagacidad** *nf* : shrewdness
sagrado, -da *adj* : sacred, holy
sal *nf* : salt
sala *nf* **1** : room, hall **2** : living room (of a house) **3 ~ de espera** : waiting room
salar *vt* : salt — **salado, -da** *adj* **1** : salty **2** GRACIOSO : witty **3 agua salada** : salt water
salario *nm* : salary, wage
salchicha *nf* : sausage — **salchichón** *nf, pl* **-chones** : salami-like cold cut
saldar *vt* **1** : settle, pay off **2** VENDER : sell off — **saldo** *nm* **1** : balance (of an account) **2 ~s** *nmpl* : remainders, sale items
salero *nm* : saltshaker
salir {73} *vi* **1** : go out, come out **2** PARTIR : leave **3** APARECER : appear **4** RESULTAR : turn out **5** : rise (of the sun) **6 ~ adelante** : get by **7 ~ con** : go out with, date **8 ~ de** : come from — **salirse** *vr* **1** : leave **2** ESCAPARSE : leak out, escape **3** SOLTARSE : come off **4 ~ con la suya** : get one's own way — **salida** *nf* **1** : exit **2** : (action of) leaving, departure **3** SOLUCIÓN : way out **4** : leak (of gas, liquid, etc.) **5** OCURRENCIA : witty remark **6 ~ de emergencia** : emergency exit **7 ~ del sol** : sunrise — **saliente** *adj* **1** : departing, outgoing **2** DESTACADO : outstanding
saliva *nf* : saliva
salmo *nm* : psalm
salmón *nm, pl* **-mones** : salmon
salmuera *nf* : brine
salón *nm, pl* **-lones** **1** : lounge, sitting room **2 ~ de belleza** : beauty salon **3 ~ de clase** : classroom
salpicar {72} *vt* **1** : splash, spatter **2 ~ de** : pepper with — **salpicadera** *nf Lat* : fender — **salpicadura** *nf* : splash
salsa *nf* **1** : sauce **2** : (meat) gravy **3** : salsa (music)
saltamontes *nms & pl* : grasshopper
saltar *vi* **1** : jump, leap **2** REBOTAR : bounce **3** : come off (of a button, etc.) **4** ROMPERSE : shatter **5** ESTALLAR : explode, blow up — *vt* : jump (over) **2** OMITIR : skip, miss — **saltarse** *vr* **2** OMITIR : skip, miss
saltear *vt* : sauté
saltimbanqui *nmf* : acrobat
salto *nm* **1** : jump, leap **2** : dive (into water) **3 ~ de agua** : waterfall — **saltón, -tona** *adj, mpl* **-tones** : bulging, protruding

salud *nf* **1** : health **2** ¡salud! : here's to your
health! **3** ¡salud! *Lat* : bless you! (when
someone sneezes) — **saludable** *adj*
: healthy
saludar *vt* **1** : greet, say hello to **2** : salute
(in the military) — **saludo** *nm* **1** : greeting
2 : (military) salute **3** ～s : best wishes, regards
salva *nf* ～ **de aplausos** : round of applause
salvación *nf, pl* -**ciones** : salvation
salvado *nm* : bran
salvador, -dora *n* : savior, rescuer
salvadoreño, -ña *adj* : (El) Salvadoran
salvaguardar *vt* : safeguard
salvaje *adj* **1** : wild **2** PRIMITIVO : savage,
primitive — ～ *nmf* : savage
salvar *vt* **1** : save, rescue **2** RECORRER
: cover, travel **3** SUPERAR : overcome — **sal-
varse** *vr* : save oneself — **salvavidas** *nms &
pl* **1** : life preserver **2** bote ～ : lifeboat
salvia *nf* : sage (plant)
salvo, -va *adj* : safe — **salvo** *prep* **1** : except
(for), save **2** ～ **que** : unless
samba *nf* : samba
San → **santo**
sanar *vt* : heal, cure — *vi* : recover — **sanatorio** *nm* **1** : sanatorium **2** HOSPITAL
: clinic, hospital
sanción *nf, pl* -**ciones** : sanction — **sancionar** *vt* : sanction
sandalia *nf* : sandal
sándalo *nm* : sandalwood
sandía *nf* : watermelon
sandwich [ˌsandwitʃ, ˌsaŋgwitʃ] *nm, pl*
-**wiches** [-dwitʃes, -gwi-] : sandwich
saneamiento *nm* : sanitation
sangrar *vt* **1** : bleed **2** : indent (a paragraph)
— *vi* : bleed — **sangrante** *adj* : bleeding —
sangre *nf* **1** : blood **2 a** ～ **fría** : in cold
blood — **sangriento, -ta** *adj* : bloody
sanguijuela *nf* : leech
sanguinario, -ria *adj* : bloodthirsty — **sanguíneo, -nea** *adj* : blood
sano, -na *adj* **1** : healthy **2** : (morally)
wholesome **3** ENTERO : intact **4 sano y
salvo** : safe and sound — **sanidad** *nf* **1**
: health **2** : public health, sanitation — **sanitario, -ria** *adj* : sanitary, health — **sanitario**
nm Lat : toilet
santiamén *nm* **en un** ～ : in no time at all
santo, -ta *adj* **1** : holy **2 Santo, Santa** (San
*before masculine names except those begin-
ning with D or T*) : Saint — ～ *n* : saint —
santo *nm* **1** : saint's day **2** *Lat* : birthday —
santidad *nf* : holiness, sanctity — **san-
tiguarse** {10} *vr* : cross oneself — **santuario** *nm* : sanctuary
saña *nf* **1** : fury **2** BRUTALIDAD : vicious-
ness

sapo *nm* : toad
saque *nm* : serve (in tennis, etc.), throw-in
(in soccer)
saquear *vt* : sack, loot — **saqueador, -dora**
n : looter — **saqueo** *nm* : sacking, looting
sarampión *nm* : measles *pl*
sarape, -tra *nm Lat* : serape
sarcasmo *nm* : sarcasm — **sarcástico, -ca**
adj : sarcastic
sardina *nf* : sardine
sardónico, -ca *adj* : sardonic
sargento *nmf* : sergeant
sarpullido *nm* : rash
sartén *nmf, pl* -**tenes** : frying pan
sastre, -tra *n* : tailor — **sastrería** *nf* **1** : tailoring **2** : tailor's shop
Satanás *nm* : Satan — **satánico, -ca** *adj*
: satanic
satélite *nm* : satellite
sátira *nf* : satire — **satírico, -ca** *adj* : satirical
satisfacer {74} *vt* **1** : satisfy **2** CUMPLIR
: fulfill, meet **3** PAGAR : pay — **satisfac-
erse** *vr* **1** : be satisfied **2** VENGARSE : take
revenge — **satisfacción** *nf, pl* -**ciones**
: satisfaction — **satisfactorio, -ria** *adj*
: satisfactory — **satisfecho, -cha** *adj* : satisfied
saturar *vt* : saturate — **saturación** *nf, pl*
-**ciones** : saturation
Saturno *nm* : Saturn
sauce *nm* : willow
sauna *nmf* : sauna
savia *nf* : sap
saxofón *nm, pl* -**fones** : saxophone
sazón *nf, pl* -**zones** **1** : seasoning **2**
MADUREZ : ripeness **3 a la** ～ : at that time,
then **4 en** ～ : ripe, in season — **sazonar** *vt*
: season
se *pron* **1** (*reflexive*) : himself, herself, itself, oneself, yourself, yourselves, themselves **2** (*indirect object*) : (to) him, (to)
her, (to) you, (to) them **3** : each other, one
another **4** ～ **dice que** : it is said that **5** ～
habla inglés : English spoken
sebo *nm* **1** : fat **2** : tallow (for candles, etc.)
3 : suet (for cooking)
secar {72} *v* : dry — **secarse** *vr* : dry (up)
— **secador** *nm* : hair dryer — **secadora** *nf*
: (clothes) dryer
sección *nf, pl* -**ciones** : section
seco, -ca *adj* **1** : dry **2** : dried (of fruits,
etc.) **3** TAJANTE : sharp, brusque **4** *fam*
: thin, skinny **5 a secas** : simply, just **6 en
seco** : suddenly
secretar *vt* : secrete — **secreción** *nf, pl*
-**ciones** : secretion
secretario, -ria *n* : secretary — **secretaría** *nf*
: secretariat

secreto, -ta *adj* : secret — **secreto** *nm* **1** : secret **2 en ~** : in confidence

secta *nf* : sect

sector *nm* : sector

secuaz *nmf, pl* **-cuaces** : follower, henchman

secuela *nf* : consequence

secuencia *nf* : sequence

secuestrar *vt* **1** : kidnap **2** : hijack (an airplane, etc.) **3** EMBARGAR : confiscate, seize — **secuestrador, -dora** *n* **1** : kidnapper **2** : hijacker (of an airplane, etc.) — **secuestro** *nm* **1** : kidnapping **2** : hijacking (of an airplane, etc.) **3** : seizure (of goods)

secular *adj* : secular

secundar *vt* : support, second — **secundario, -ria** *adj* : secondary

sed *nf* **1** : thirst **2 tener ~** : be thirsty

seda *nf* : silk

sedal *nm* : fishing line

sedar *vt* : sedate — **sedante** *adj & nm* : sedative

sede *nf* **1** : seat, headquarters **2 Santa Sede** : Holy See

sedentario, -ria *adj* : sedentary

sedición *nf, pl* **-ciones** : sedition — **sedicioso, -sa** *adj* : seditious

sediento, -ta *adj* : thirsty

sedimento *nm* : sediment

sedoso, -sa *adj* : silky, silken

seducir {61} *vt* **1** : seduce **2** ATRAER : captivate, charm — **seducción** *nf, pl* **-ciones** : seduction — **seductor, -tora** *adj* **1** : seductive **2** ENCANTADOR : charming — **~** *n* : seducer

segar {49} *vt* : reap — **segador, -dora** *n* : reaper, harvester

seglar *adj* : lay, secular — **~** *nm* : layperson, layman *m*, laywoman *f*

segmento *nm* : segment

segregar {52} *vt* : segregate — **segregación** *nf, pl* **-ciones** : segregation

seguir {75} *vt* : follow — *vi* : go on, continue — **seguida: en ~** *adv phr* : right away — **seguido** *adv* **1** : straight (ahead) **2** *Lat* : often — **seguido, -da** *adj* **1** : continuous **2** CONSECUTIVO : consecutive — **seguidor, -dora** *n* : follower

según *prep* : according to — **~** *adv* : it depends — **~** *conj* : as, just as

segundo, -da *adj* : second — **~** *n* : second (one) — **segundo** *nm* : second (unit of time)

seguro, -ra *adj* **1** : safe **2** FIRME : secure **3** CIERTO : sure, certain **4** FIABLE : reliable — **seguramente** *adv* : for sure, surely — **seguridad** *nf* **1** : safety **2** GARANTÍA : security **3** CERTEZA : certainty **4** CONFIANZA : confidence — **seguro** *adv* : certainly — **~** *nm* **1** : insurance **2** : safety (device)

seis *adj & nm* : six — **seiscientos, -tas** *adj* : six hundred — **seiscientos** *nms & pl* : six hundred

seísmo *nm* : earthquake

selección *nf, pl* **-ciones** : selection — **seleccionar** *vt* : select, choose — **selectivo, -va** *adj* : selective — **selecto, -ta** *adj* : choice, select

sellar *vt* **1** : seal **2** TIMBRAR : stamp — **sello** *nm* **1** : seal **2** TIMBRE : stamp **3** *or* **~** distintivo : hallmark

selva *nf* **1** : jungle **2** BOSQUE : forest

semáforo *nm* : traffic light

semana *nf* : week — **semanal** *adj* : weekly — **semanario** *nm* : weekly

semántica *nf* : semantics — **semántico, -ca** *adj* : semantic

semblante *nm* **1** : countenance, face **2** APARIENCIA : look

sembrar {55} *vt* **1** : sow **2 ~ de** : strew with

semejar *vi* : resemble — **semejarse** *vr* : look alike — **semejante** *adj* **1** : similar **2** TAL : such — **~** *nm* : fellowman — **semejanza** *nf* : similarity

semen *nm* : semen — **semental** *nm* **1** : stud **2 caballo ~** : stallion

semestre *nm* : semester

semiconductor *nm* : semiconductor

semifinal *nf* : semifinal

semilla *nf* : seed — **semillero** *nm* **1** : nursery (for plants) **2** HERVIDERO : hotbed, breeding ground

seminario *nm* **1** : seminary **2** CURSO : seminar, course

sémola *nf* : semolina

senado *nm* : senate — **senador, -dora** *n* : senator

sencillo, -lla *adj* **1** : simple **2** ÚNICO : single — **sencillez** *nf* : simplicity

senda *nf or* **sendero** *nm* : path, way

sendos, -das *adj pl* : each, both

senil *adj* : senile

seno *nm* **1** : breast, bosom **2** : sinus (in anatomy) **3 ~ materno** : womb

sensación *nf, pl* **-ciones** : feeling, sensation — **sensacional** *adj* : sensational — **sensacionalista** *adj* : sensationalistic, lurid

sensato, -ta *adj* : sensible — **sensatez** *nf* : good sense

sensible *adj* **1** : sensitive **2** APRECIABLE : considerable, significant — **sensibilidad** *nf* : sensitivity — **sensitivo, -va** *or* **sensorial** *adj* : sense, sensory

sensual *adj* : sensual, sensuous — **sensualidad** *nf* : sensuality

sentar {55} *vt* **1** : seat, sit **2** ESTABLECER : establish, set — *vi* **1** : suit **2 ~ bien a** : agree with (of food or drink) — **sentarse**

vr : sit (down) — **sentado, -da** *adj* **1** : sitting, seated **2 dar por sentado** : take for granted

sentencia *nf* **1** FALLO : sentence, judgment **2** MÁXIMA : saying — **sentenciar** *vt* : sentence

sentido, -da *adj* **1** : heartfelt, sincere **2** SENSIBLE : touchy, sensitive — **sentido** *nm* **1** : sense **2** CONOCIMIENTO : consciousness **3** DIRECCIÓN : direction **4 doble ~** : double entendre **5 ~ común** : common sense **6 ~ del humor** : sense of humor **7 ~ único** : one-way

sentimiento *nm* **1** : feeling, emotion **2** PESAR : regret — **sentimental** *adj* : sentimental — **sentimentalismo** *nm* : sentimentality

sentir {76} *vt* **1** : feel **2** OÍR : hear **3** LAMENTAR : be sorry for **4 lo siento** : I'm sorry — *vi* : feel — **sentirse** *vr* : feel

seña *nf* **1** : sign **2 ~s** *nfpl* DIRECCIÓN : address **3 ~s particulares** : distinguishing marks

señal *nf* **1** : signal **2** AVISO, INDICIO : sign **3** DEPÓSITO : deposit **4 dar ~es de** : show signs of **5 en ~ de** : as a token of — **señalado, -da** *adj* : notable — **señalar** *vt* **1** INDICAR : indicate, point out **2** MARCAR : mark **3** FIJAR : fix, set — **señalarse** *vr* : distinguish oneself

señor, -ñora *n* **1** : gentleman *m*, man *m*, lady *f*, woman *f* **2** : Sir *m*, Madam *f* **3** : Mr. *m*, Mrs. *f* **4 señora** : wife *f* **5 el Señor** : the Lord — **señorial** *adj* : stately — **señorita** *nf* **1** : young lady, young woman **2** : Miss

señuelo *nm* **1** : decoy **2** TRAMPA : bait, lure

separar *vt* **1** : separate **2** QUITAR : detach, remove **3** APARTAR : move away **4** DESTITUIR : dismiss — **separarse** *vr* **1** APARTARSE : separate **2** : part company — **separación** *nf, pl* **-ciones** : separation — **separado, -da** *adj* **1** : separate **2** : separated (of persons) **3 por separado** : separately

septentrional *adj* : northern

séptico, -ca *adj* : septic

septiembre *nm* : September

séptimo, -ma *adj* : seventh — **~** *n* : seventh

sepulcro *nm* : tomb, sepulchre — **sepultar** *vt* : bury — **sepultura** *nf* **1** : burial **2** TUMBA : grave

sequedad *nf* : dryness — **sequía** *nf* : drought

séquito *nm* : retinue, entourage

ser {77} *vi* **1** : be **2 a no ~ que** : unless **3 ¿cuánto es?** : how much is it? **4 es más** : what's more **5 ~ de** : belong to **6 ~ de** : come from **7 son las diez** : it's ten o'-clock — **~** *nm* **1** ENTE : being **2 ~ humano** : human being

serbio, -bia *adj* : Serb, Serbian

serenar *vt* : calm — **serenarse** *vr* : calm down — **serenata** *nf* : serenade — **serenidad** *nf* : serenity — **sereno, -na** *adj* **1** : serene, calm **2** : fair, clear (of weather) — **sereno** *nm* : night watchman

serie *nf* **1** : series **2 fabricación en ~** : mass production **3 fuera de ~** : extraordinary — **serial** *nm* : serial

serio, -ria *adj* **1** : serious **2** RESPONSABLE : reliable **3 en serio** : seriously — **seriedad** *nf* : seriousness

sermón *nm, pl* **-mones** : sermon — **sermonear** *vt* : lecture, reprimand

serpentear *vi* : twist, wind — **serpiente** *nf* **1** : serpent, snake **2 ~ de cascabel** : rattlesnake

serrado, -da *adj* : serrated

serrano, -na *adj* **1** : mountain **2 jamón serrano** : cured ham

serrar {55} *vt* : saw — **serrín** *nm, pl* **-rrines** : sawdust — **serrucho** *nm* : saw, handsaw

servicio *nm* **1** : service **2 ~s** *nmpl* : restroom — **servicial** *adj* : obliging, helpful — **servidor, -dora** *n* **1** : servant **2 su seguro servidor** : yours truly — **servidumbre** *nf* **1** : servitude **2** CRIADOS : help, servants *pl* — **servil** *adj* : servile

servilleta *nf* : napkin

servir {54} *vt* : serve — *vi* **1** : work, function **2** VALER : be of use — **servirse** *vr* **1** : help oneself **2 sírvase sentarse** : please have a seat

sesenta *adj & nm* : sixty

sesgo *nm* : bias, slant

sesión *nf, pl* **-siones** **1** : session **2** : showing (of a film), performance (of a play)

seso *nm* : brain — **sesudo, -da** *adj* **1** : sensible **2** *fam* : brainy

seta *nf* : mushroom

setecientos, -tas *adj* : seven hundred — **setecientos** *nms & pl* : seven hundred

setenta *adj & nm* : seventy

setiembre *nm* → **septiembre**

seto *nm* **1** : fence **2 ~ vivo** : hedge

seudónimo *nm* : pseudonym

severo, -ra *adj* **1** : harsh, severe **2** : strict (of a teacher, etc.) — **severidad** *nf* : severity

sexagésimo, -ma *adj & n* : sixtieth

sexo *nm* : sex — **sexismo** *nm* : sexism — **sexista** *adj & nmf* : sexist

sexteto *nm* : sextet

sexto, -ta *adj & n* : sixth

sexual *adj* : sexual — **sexualidad** *nf* : sexuality

sexy *adj, pl* **sexy** *or* **sexys** : sexy

si *conj* **1** : if **2** (*in indirect questions*) : whether **3** ~ **bien** : although **4** ~ **no** : otherwise, or else

sí[1] *adv* **1** : yes **2 creo que** ~ : I think so **3 porque** ~ *fam* : (just) because — ~ *nm* : consent

sí[2] *pron* **1 de por** ~ *or* **en** ~ : by itself, in itself, per se **2 fuera de** ~ : beside oneself **3 para** ~ **(mismo)** : to himself, to herself, for himself, for herself **4 entre** ~ : among themselves

sico- → **psico-**

SIDA *or* **sida** *nm* : AIDS

siderurgia *nf* : iron and steel industry

sidra *nf* : (hard) cider

siega *nf* **1** : harvesting **2** : harvest (time)

siembra *nf* **1** : sowing **2** : sowing season

siempre *adv* **1** : always **2** *Lat* : still **3 para** ~ : forever, for good **4** ~ **que** : whenever, every time **5** ~ **que** *or* ~ **y cuando** : provided that

sien *nf* : temple

sierra *nf* **1** : saw **2** CORDILLERA : mountain range **3 la** ~ : the mountains *pl*

siervo, -va *n* : slave

siesta *nf* : nap, siesta

siete *adj* & *nm* : seven

sífilis *nf* : syphilis

sifón *nm, pl* **-fones** : siphon

sigilo *nm* : secrecy

sigla *nf* : acronym, abbreviation

siglo *nm* **1** : century **2 hace** ~s : for ages

significar {72} *vt* **1** : mean, signify **2** EXPRESAR : express — **significación** *nf, pl* **-ciones 1** : significance, importance **2** : meaning (of a word, etc.) — **significado, -da** *adj* : well-known — **significado** *nm* : meaning — **significativo, -va** *adj* : significant

signo *nm* **1** : sign **2** ~ **de admiración** : exclamation point **3** ~ **de interrogación** : question mark

siguiente *adj* : next, following

sílaba *nf* : syllable

silbar *v* **1** : whistle **2** ABUCHEAR : hiss, boo — **silbato** *nm* : whistle — **silbido** *nm* **1** : whistle, whistling **2** ABUCHEO : hiss, booing

silenciar *vt* : silence — **silenciador** *nm* : muffler — **silencio** *nm* : silence — **silencioso, -sa** *adj* : silent, quiet

silicio *nm* : silicon

silla *nf* **1** : chair **2** *or* ~ **de montar** : saddle **3** ~ **de ruedas** : wheelchair — **sillón** *nm, pl* **-llones** : armchair, easy chair

silo *nm* : silo

silueta *nf* **1** : silhouette **2** CONTORNO : outline, shape

silvestre *adj* : wild

silvicultura *nf* : forestry

símbolo *nm* : symbol — **simbólico, -ca** *adj* : symbolic — **simbolismo** *nm* : symbolism — **simbolizar** {21} *vt* : symbolize

simetría *nf* : symmetry — **simétrico, -ca** *adj* : symmetrical, symmetric

simiente *nf* : seed

símil *nm* **1** : simile **2** COMPARACIÓN : comparison — **similar** *adj* : similar, alike

simio *nm* : ape

simpatía *nf* **1** : liking, affection **2** AMABILIDAD : friendliness — **simpático, -ca** *adj* **1** : nice, likeable **2** AMABLE : pleasant, kind — **simpatizante** *nmf* : sympathizer — **simpatizar** {21} *vi* **1** : get along, hit it off **2** ~ **con** : sympathize with

simple *adj* **1** SENCILLO : simple **2** MERO : pure, sheer **3** TONTO : simpleminded — ~ *n* : fool, simpleton — **simpleza** *nf* **1** : simpleness **2** TONTERÍA : silly thing — **simplicidad** *nf* : simplicity — **simplificar** {72} *vt* : simplify

simposio *or* **simposium** *nm* : symposium

simular *vt* **1** : simulate **2** FINGIR : feign — **simulacro** *nm* : simulation, drill

simultáneo, -nea *adj* : simultaneous

sin *prep* **1** : without **2** ~ **que** : without

sinagoga *nf* : synagogue

sincero, -ra *adj* : sincere — **sinceramente** *adv* : sincerely — **sinceridad** *nf* : sincerity

síncopa *nf* : syncopation

sincronizar {21} *vt* : synchronize

sindicato *nm* : (labor) union — **sindical** *adj* : union, labor

síndrome *nm* : syndrome

sinfín *nm* **1** : endless number **2 un** ~ **de** : no end of

sinfonía *nf* : symphony — **sinfónico, -ca** *adj* : symphonic

singular *adj* **1** : exceptional, outstanding **2** PECULIAR : peculiar **3** : singular (in grammar) — ~ *nm* : singular — **singularizar** {21} *vt* : single out — **singularizarse** *vr* : stand out

siniestro, -tra *adj* **1** : sinister **2** IZQUIERDO : left — **siniestro** *nm* : disaster

sinnúmero *nm* → **sinfín**

sino *conj* **1** : but, rather **2** EXCEPTO : except, save

sinónimo, -ma *adj* : synonymous — **sinónimo** *nm* : synonym

sinopsis *nfs* & *pl* : synopsis

sinrazón *nf, pl* **-zones** : wrong

sintaxis *nfs* & *pl* : syntax

síntesis *nfs* & *pl* : synthesis — **sintético, -ca** *adj* : synthetic — **sintetizar** {21} *vt* **1** : synthesize **2** RESUMIR : summarize

síntoma *nm* : symptom — **sintomático, -ca** *adj* : symptomatic

sintonía *nf* **1** : tuning in (of a radio) **2 en** ~ **con** : in tune with — **sintonizar** {21} *vt* : tune (in) to
sinuoso, -sa *adj* : winding
sinvergüenza *nmf* : scoundrel
sionismo *nm* : Zionism
siquiera *adv* **1** : at least **2 ni** ~ : not even — ~ *conj* : even if
sirena *nf* **1** : mermaid **2** : siren (of an ambulance, etc.)
sirio, -ria *adj* : Syrian
sirviente, -ta *n* : servant, maid *f*
sisear *vi* : hiss — **siseo** *nm* : hiss
sismo *nm* : earthquake — **sísmico, -ca** *adj* : seismic
sistema *nm* **1** : system **2 por** ~ : systematically — **sistemático, -ca** *adj* : systematic
sitiar *vt* : besiege
sitio *nm* **1** : place, site **2** ESPACIO : room, space **3** CERCO : siege **4 en cualquier** ~ : anywhere
situar {3} *vt* : situate, place — **situarse** *vr* **1** : be located **2** ESTABLECERSE : get oneself established — **situación** *nf, pl* **-ciones** : situation, position — **situado, -da** *adj* : situated, placed
slip *nm* : briefs *pl*, underpants *pl*
smoking *nm* : tuxedo
so *prep* : under
sobaco *nm* : armpit
sobar *vt* **1** : finger, handle **2** : knead (dough) — **sobado, -da** *adj* : worn, shabby
soberanía *nf* : sovereignty — **soberano, -na** *adj & n* : sovereign
soberbia *nf* : pride, arrogance — **soberbio, -bia** *adj* : proud, arrogant
sobornar *vt* : bribe — **soborno** *nm* **1** : bribe **2** : (action of) bribery
sobrar *vi* **1** : be more than enough **2** RESTAR : be left over — **sobra** *nf* **1** : surplus **2 de** ~ : to spare **3** ~**s** *nfpl* : leftovers — **sobrado, -da** *adj* : more than enough — **sobrante** *adj* : remaining
sobre[1] *nm* : envelope
sobre[2] *prep* **1** : on, on top of **2** POR ENCIMA DE : over, above **3** ACERCA DE : about **4** ~ **todo** : especially, above all
sobrecama *nmf Lat* : bedspread
sobrecargar {52} *vt* : overload, overburden
sobrecoger {15} *vt* : startle — **sobrecogerse** *vr* : be startled
sobrecubierta *nf* : dust jacket
sobredosis *nfs & pl* : overdose
sobreentender {56} *vt* : infer, understand — **sobreentenderse** *vr* : be understood
sobreestimar *vt* : overestimate
sobregiro *nm* : overdraft
sobrellevar *vt* : endure, bear
sobremesa *nf de* ~ : after-dinner

sobrenatural *adj* : supernatural
sobrenombre *nm* : nickname
sobrentender → **sobreentender**
sobrepasar *vt* : exceed
sobreponer {60} *vt* **1** : superimpose **2** ANTEPONER : put before — **sobreponerse** *vr* ~ **a** : overcome
sobresalir {73} *vi* **1** : protrude **2** DESTACARSE : stand out — **sobresaliente** *adj* : outstanding
sobresaltar *vt* : startle — **sobresaltarse** *vr* : start, jump up — **sobresalto** *nm* : fright
sobrestimar → **sobreestimar**
sobretodo *nm* : overcoat
sobrevenir {87} *vi* : happen, ensue
sobrevivencia *nf* → **supervivencia**
sobreviviente *adj & nmf* → **superviviente**
sobrevivir *vi* : survive — *vt* : outlive
sobrevolar {19} *vt* : fly over
sobriedad *nf* **1** : sobriety **2** MODERACIÓN : restraint
sobrino, -na *n* : nephew *m*, niece *f*
sobrio, -bria *adj* : sober
sooarrón, -rrona *adj, mpl* **-rrones** : sarcastic
socavar *vt* : undermine
sociable *adj* : sociable — **social** *adj* : social — **socialismo** *nm* : socialism — **socialista** *adj & nmf* : socialist — **sociedad** *nf* **1** : society **2** EMPRESA : company **3** ~ **anónima** : incorporated company — **socio, -cia** *n* **1** : partner **2** MIEMBRO : member — **sociología** *nf* : sociology — **sociólogo, -ga** *n* : sociologist
socorrer *vt* : help — **socorrista** *nmf* : lifeguard — **socorro** *nm* : help
soda *nf* : soda (water)
sodio *nf* : sodium
sofá *nm* : couch, sofa
sofisticación *nf, pl* **-ciones** : sophistication — **sofisticado, -da** *adj* : sophisticated
sofocar {72} *vt* **1** : suffocate, smother **2** : put out (a fire), stifle (a rebellion, etc.) — **sofocarse** *vr* **1** : suffocate **2** *fam* : get upset — **sofocante** *adj* : suffocating, stifling
sofreír {66} *vt* : sauté
soga *nf* : rope
soja *nf* → **soya**
sojuzgar *vt* : subdue, subjugate
sol *nm* **1** : sun **2 hacer** ~ : be sunny
solamente *adv* : only, just
solapa *nf* **1** : lapel (of a jacket) **2** : flap (of an envelope) — **solapado, -da** *adj* : secret, underhanded
solar[1] *adj* : solar, sun
solar[2] *nm* : lot, site
solariego, -ga *adj* : ancestral
solaz *nm, pl* **-laces** **1** : solace **2** DESCANSO : relaxation — **solazarse** {21} *vr* : relax

soldado

soldado *nm* **1** : soldier **2** ~ **raso** : private
soldar {19} *vt* : weld, solder — **soldador** *nm* : soldering iron — **soldador, -dora** *n* : welder
soleado, -da *adj* : sunny
soledad *nf* : loneliness, solitude
solemne *adj* : solemn — **solemnidad** *nf* : solemnity
soler {78} *vi* **1** : be in the habit of **2 suele llegar tarde** : he usually arrives late
solicitar *vt* **1** : request, solicit **2** : apply for (a job, etc.) — **solicitante** *nmf* : applicant — **solícito, -ta** *adj* : solicitous, obliging — **solicitud** *nf* **1** : concern **2** PETICIÓN : request **3** : application (for a job, etc.)
solidaridad *nf* : solidarity
sólido, -da *adj* **1** : solid **2** : sound (of an argument, etc.) — **sólido** *nm* : solid — **solidez** *nf* : solidity — **solidificar** {72} *vt* : solidify — **solidificarse** *vr* : solidify, harden
soliloquio *nm* : soliloquy
solista *nmf* : soloist
solitario, -ria *adj* **1** : solitary **2** AISLADO : lonely, deserted — ~ *n* : recluse — **solitaria** *nf* : tapeworm — **solitario** *nm* : solitaire
sollozar {21} *vi* : sob — **sollozo** *nm* : sob
solo, -la *adj* **1** : alone **2** AISLADO : lonely **3 a solas** : alone, by oneself — **solo** *nm* : solo
sólo *adv* : just, only
solomillo *nm* : sirloin
solsticio *nm* : solstice
soltar {19} *vt* **1** : release **2** DEJAR CAER : let go of, drop **3** DESATAR : unfasten, undo — **soltarse** *vr* **1** : break free **2** DESATARSE : come undone
soltero, -ra *adj* : single, unmarried — ~ *n* **1** : bachelor *m*, single woman *f* **2 apellido de soltera** : maiden name
soltura *nf* **1** : looseness **2** : fluency (in language) **3** AGILIDAD : agility, ease
soluble *adj* : soluble
solución *nf*, *pl* **-ciones** : solution — **solucionar** *vt* : solve, resolve
solventar *vt* **1** : settle, pay **2** RESOLVER : resolve — **solvente** *adj & nm* : solvent
sombra *nf* **1** : shadow **2** : shade (of a tree, etc.) **3** ~**s** *nfpl* : darkness, shadows — **sombreado, -da** *adj* : shady
sombrero *nm* : hat
sombrilla *nf* : parasol, umbrella
sombrío, -bría *adj* : dark, somber, gloomy
somero, -ra *adj* : superficial
someter *vt* **1** : subjugate **2** SUBORDINAR : subordinate **3** : subject (to treatment, etc.) **4** PRESENTAR : submit, present — **someterse** *vr* **1** : submit, yield **2** ~ **a** : undergo
somnífero, -ra *adj* : soporific — **somnífero**

nm : sleeping pill — **somnoliento, -ta** *adj* : drowsy, sleepy
somos → **ser**
son¹ → **ser**
son² *nm* **1** : sound **2 en** ~ **de** : as, in the manner of
sonajero *nm* : (baby's) rattle
sonámbulo, -la *n* : sleepwalker
sonar {19} *vi* **1** : sound **2** : ring (as a bell) **3** : look or sound familiar **4** ~ **a** : sound like — **sonarse** *vr or* ~ **las narices** : blow one's nose
sonata *nf* : sonata
sondear *vt* **1** : sound, probe **2** : survey, sound out (opinions, etc.) — **sondeo** *nm* **1** : sounding, probing **2** ENCUESTA : survey, poll
soneto *nm* : sonnet
sónico, -ca *adj* : sonic
sonido *nm* : sound
sonoro, -ra *adj* **1** : resonant, sonorous **2** RUIDOSO : loud
sonreír {66} *vi* : smile — **sonreírse** *vr* : smile — **sonriente** *adj* : smiling — **sonrisa** *nf* : smile
sonrojar *vt* : cause to blush — **sonrojarse** *vr* : blush — **sonrojo** *nm* : blush
sonrosado, -da *adj* : rosy, pink
sonsacar {72} *vt* : wheedle (out)
soñar {19} *v* **1** : dream **2** ~ **con** : dream about **3** ~ **despierto** : daydream — **soñador, -dora** *adj* : dreamy — ~ *n* : dreamer — **soñoliento, -ta** *adj* : sleepy, drowsy
sopa *nf* : soup
sopesar *vt* : weigh, consider
soplar *vi* : blow — *vt* : blow out, blow off, blow up — **soplete** *nm* : blowtorch — **soplo** *nm* : puff, gust
soplón, -plona *n*, *pl* **-plones** *fam* : sneak
sopor *nm* : drowsiness — **soporífero, -ra** *adj* : soporific
soportar *vt* **1** SOSTENER : support **2** AGUANTAR : bear — **soporte** *nm* : support
soprano *nmf* : soprano
sor *nf* : Sister (in religion)
sorber *vt* **1** : sip **2** ABSORBER : absorb **3** CHUPAR : suck up — **sorbete** *nm* : sherbet — **sorbo** *nm* **1** : sip, swallow **2 beber a** ~**s** : sip
sordera *nf* : deafness
sórdido, -da *adj* : sordid, squalid
sordo, -da *adj* **1** : deaf **2** : muted (of a sound) — **sordomudo, -da** *n* : deaf-mute
sorna *nf* : sarcasm
sorprender *vt* : surprise — **sorprenderse** *vr* : be surprised — **sorprendente** *adj* : surprising — **sorpresa** *nf* : surprise
sortear *vt* **1** : raffle off, draw lots for **2**

ESQUIVAR : dodge — **sorteo** *nm* : drawing, raffle
sortija *nf* **1** : ring **2** : ringlet (of hair)
sortilegio *nm* **1** HECHIZO : spell **2** HECHI-CERÍA : sorcery
sosegar {49} *vt* : calm, pacify — **sosegarse** *vr* : calm down — **sosegado, -da** *adj* : calm, tranquil — **sosiego** *nm* : calm
soslayo: de ~ *adv phr* : obliquely, sideways
soso, -sa *adj* **1** : insipid, tasteless **2** ABURRIDO : dull
sospechar *vt* : suspect — **sospecha** *nf* : suspicion — **sospechoso, -sa** *adj* : suspicious — ~ *n* : suspect
sostener {80} *vt* **1** : support **2** SUJETAR : hold **3** MANTENER : sustain, maintain — **sostenerse** *vr* **1** : stand (up) **2** CONTINUAR : remain **3** SUSTENTARSE : support oneself — **sostén** *nm, pl* **-tenes 1** APOYO : support **2** SUSTENTO : sustenance **3** : brassiere, bra — **sostenido, -da** *adj* **1** : sustained **2** : sharp (in music) — **sostenido** *nm* : sharp
sótano *nm* : basement
soterrar {55} *vt* **1** : bury **2** ESCONDER : hide
soto *nm* : grove
soviético, -ca *adj* : Soviet
soy → **ser**
soya *nf* : soy
Sr. *nm* : Mr. — **Sra.** *nf* : Mrs., Ms. — **Srta.** *or* **Srita.** *nf* : Miss, Ms.
su *adj* **1** : his, her, its, their, one's **2** (*formal*) : your
suave *adj* **1** : soft **2** LISO : smooth **3** APACIBLE : gentle, mild — **suavidad** *nf* **1** : softness, smoothness **2** APACIBILIDAD : mildness, gentleness — **suavizar** {21} *vt* : soften, smooth
subalimentado, -da *adj* : undernourished, underfed
subalterno, -na *adj* **1** SUBORDINADO : subordinate **2** SECUNDARIO : secondary — ~ *n* : subordinate
subarrendar {55} *vt* : sublet
subasta *nf* : auction — **subastar** *vt* : auction (off)
subcampeón, -peona *n, mpl* **-peones** : runner-up
subcomité *nm* : subcommittee
subconsciente *adj & nm* : subconscious
subdesarrollado, -da *adj* : underdeveloped
subdirector, -tora *n* : assistant manager
súbdito, -ta *n* : subject
subdividir *vt* : subdivide — **subdivisión** *nf, pl* **-siones** : subdivision
subestimar *vt* : underestimate
subir *vt* **1** : climb, go up **2** LLEVAR : bring up, take up **3** AUMENTAR : raise — *vi* **1** : go up, come up **2** ~ **a** : get in (a car), get

on (a bus, etc.) — **subirse** *vr* **1** : climb (up) **2** ~ **a** : get in (a car), get on (a bus, etc.) **3** ~ **a la cabeza** : go to one's head — **subida** *nf* **1** : ascent, climb **2** AUMENTO : rise **3** PENDIENTE : slope — **subido, -da** *adj* **1** : bright, strong **2** ~ **de tono** : risqué
súbito, -ta *adj* **1** : sudden **2 de súbito** : all of a sudden, suddenly
subjetivo, -va *adj* : subjective
subjuntivo, -va *adj* : subjunctive — **subjuntivo** *nm* : subjunctive (case)
sublevar *vt* : stir up, incite to rebellion — **sublevarse** *vr* : rebel — **sublevación** *nf, pl* **-ciones** : uprising, rebellion
sublime *adj* : sublime
submarino, -na *adj* : underwater — **submarino** *nm* : submarine — **submarinismo** *nm* : scuba diving
subordinar *vt* : subordinate — **subordinado, -da** *adj & n* : subordinate
subproducto *nm* : by-product
subrayar *vt* **1** : underline **2** ENFATIZAR : emphasize, stress
subrepticio, -cia *adj* : surreptitious
subsanar *vt* **1** : rectify, correct **2** : make up for (a deficiency), overcome (an obstacle)
subscribir → **suscribir**
subsidio *nm* : subsidy, benefit
subsiguiente *adj* : subsequent
subsistir *vi* **1** : live, subsist **2** SOBREVIVIR : survive — **subsistencia** *nf* : subsistence
substancia *nf* → **sustancia**
subterfugio *nm* : subterfuge
subterráneo, -nea *adj* : underground, subterranean — **subterráneo** *nm* : underground passage
subtítulo *nm* : subtitle
suburbio *nm* **1** : suburb **2** : slum (outside a city) — **suburbano, -na** *adj* : suburban
subvencionar *vt* : subsidize — **subvención** *nf, pl* **-ciones** : subsidy, grant
subvertir {76} *vt* : subvert — **subversión** *nf, pl* **-siones** : subversion — **subversivo, -va** *adj & n* : subversive
subyacente *adj* : underlying
subyugar {52} *vt* : subjugate, subdue
succión *nf, pl* **-ciones** : suction — **succionar** *vt* : suck up, draw in
sucedáneo *nm* : substitute
suceder *vi* **1** : happen, occur **2** ~ **a** : follow **3 suceda lo que suceda** : come what may — **sucesión** *nf, pl* **-siones** : succession — **sucesivo, -va** *adj* : successive — **suceso** *nm* **1** : event **2** INCIDENTE : incident — **sucesor, -sora** *n* : successor
suciedad *nf* **1** : dirtiness **2** MUGRE : dirt, filth
sucinto, -ta *adj* : succinct, concise
sucio, -cia *adj* : dirty, filthy

suculento, -ta *adj* : succulent
sucumbir *vi* : succumb
sucursal *nf* : branch (of a business)
sudadera *nf* : sweatshirt — **sudado, -da** *adj*
: sweaty
sudafricano, -na *adj* : South African
sudamericano, -na *adj* : South American
sudar *vi* : sweat
sudeste → **sureste**
sudoeste → **suroeste**
sudor *nm* : sweat — **sudoroso, -sa** *adj*
: sweaty
sueco, -ca *adj* : Swedish — **sueco** *nm*
: Swedish (language)
suegro, -gra *n* **1** : father-in-law *m,* mother-
in-law *f* **2 suegros** *nmpl* : in-laws
suela *nf* : sole (of a shoe)
sueldo *nm* : salary, wage
suelo *nm* **1** : ground **2** : floor (in a house) **3**
TIERRA : soil, land
suelto, -ta *adj* : loose, free — **suelto** *nm*
: loose change
sueño *nm* **1** : dream **2 coger el** ~ : get to
sleep **3 tener** ~ : be sleepy
suero *nm* **1** : whey **2** : serum (in medicine)
suerte *nf* **1** : luck, fortune **2** AZAR : chance
3 DESTINO : fate **4** CLASE : sort, kind **5 por**
~ : luckily **6 tener** ~ : be lucky
suéter *nm* : sweater
suficiencia *nf* **1** CAPACIDAD : competence,
proficiency **2** PRESUNCIÓN : smugness —
suficiente *adj* **1** : enough, sufficient **2**
PRESUNTUOSO : smug — **suficientemente**
adv : enough
sufijo *nm* : suffix
sufragio *nm* : suffrage, vote
sufrir *vt* **1** : suffer **2** SOPORTAR : bear, stand
— *vi* : suffer — **sufrido, -da** *adj* **1** : long-
suffering **2** : sturdy, serviceable (of clothing) — **sufrimiento** *nm* : suffering
sugerir {76} *vt* : suggest — **sugerencia** *nf*
: suggestion — **sugestión** *nf, pl* -**tiones**
: suggestion — **sugestionable** *adj* : impressionable — **sugestionar** *vt* : influence
— **sugestivo, -va** *adj* **1** : suggestive **2** ES-
TIMULANTE : interesting, stimulating
suicidio *nm* : suicide — **suicida** *adj* : suicidal — *nmf* : suicide (victim) — **suicidarse** *vr* : commit suicide
suite *nf* : suite
suizo, -za *adj* : Swiss
sujetar *vt* **1** : hold (on to) **2** FIJAR : fasten **3**
DOMINAR : subdue — **sujetarse** *vr* **1** ~ **a**
: hold on to, cling to **2** ~ **a** : abide by —
sujeción *nf, pl* -**ciones** **1** : fastening **2**
DOMINACIÓN : subjection — **sujetador** *nm*
Spain : brassiere, bra — **sujetapapeles**
nms & pl : paper clip — **sujeto, -ta** *adj* **1**

: fastened **2** ~ **a** : subject to — **sujeto** *nm*
1 : individual **2** : subject (in grammar)
sulfuro *nm* : sulfur — **sulfúrico, -ca** *adj*
: sulfuric
sultán *nm, pl* -**tanes** : sultan
suma *nf* **1** : sum, total **2** : addition (in mathematics) **3 en** ~ : in short — **sumamente**
adv : extremely — **sumar** *vt* **1** : add (up) **2**
TOTALIZAR : add up to, total — *vi* : add up —
sumarse *vr* ~ **a** : join
sumario, -ria *adj* : concise — **sumario** *nm* **1**
: summary **2** : indictment (in law)
sumergir {35} *vt* : submerge, plunge —
sumergirse *vr* : be submerged — **sumergi-
ble** *adj* : waterproof (of a watch, etc.)
sumidero *nm* : drain
suministrar *vt* : supply, provide — **suministro** *nm* : supply, provision
sumir *vt* : plunge, immerse — **sumirse** *vr*
~ **en** : sink into
sumisión *nf, pl* -**siones** : submission —
sumiso, -sa *adj* : submissive
sumo, -ma *adj* **1** : highest, supreme **2 de
suma importancia** : of great importance
suntuoso, -sa *adj* : sumptuous, lavish
super *or* **súper** *nm fam* : supermarket
superabundancia *nf* : overabundance
superar *vt* **1** : surpass, outdo **2** VENCER
: overcome — **superarse** *vr* : improve oneself
superávit *nm* : surplus
superestructura *nf* : superstructure
superficie *nf* **1** : surface **2** ÁREA : area —
superficial *adj* : superficial
superfluo, -flua *adj* : superfluous
superintendente *nmf* : supervisor, superintendent
superior *adj* **1** : superior **2** : upper (of a
floor, etc.) **3** ~ **a** : above, higher than —
~ *nm* : superior — **superioridad** *nf* : superiority
superlativo, -va *adj* : superlative — **superlativo** *nm* : superlative
supermercado *nm* : supermarket
superpoblado, -da *adj* : overpopulated
supersónico, -ca *adj* : supersonic
superstición *nf, pl* -**ciones** : superstition —
supersticioso, -sa *adj* : superstitious
supervisar *vt* : supervise, oversee — **supervisión** *nf, pl* -**siones** : supervision — **supervisor, -sora** *n* : supervisor
supervivencia *nf* : survival — **superviviente** *adj* : surviving — ~ *nmf* : survivor
suplantar *vt* : supplant, replace
suplemento *nm* : supplement — **suplementario, -ria** *adj* : supplementary
suplente *adj & nmf* : substitute

suplicar {72} *vt* : beg, entreat — **súplica** *nf* : plea, entreaty
suplicio *nm* : ordeal, torture
suplir *vt* **1** : make up for **2** REEMPLAZAR : replace
supo, etc. → **saber**
suponer {60} *vt* **1** : suppose, assume **2** SIGNIFICAR : mean **3** IMPLICAR : involve, entail — **suposición** *nf, pl* -**ciones** : supposition
supositorio *nm* : suppository
supremo, -ma *adj* : supreme — **supremacía** *nf* : supremacy
suprimir *vt* **1** : suppress, eliminate **2** : delete (text) — **supresión** *nf, pl* -**siones** **1** : suppression, elimination **2** : deletion (of text)
supuesto, -ta *adj* **1** : supposed, alleged **2 por supuesto** : of course — **supuesto** *nm* : assumption — **supuestamente** *adv* : allegedly
sur *nm* **1** : south, South **2** : south wind **3 del** ~ : south, southerly
surafricano, -na → **sudafricano**
suramericano, -na → **sudamericano**
surcar {72} *vt* **1** : plow (earth) **2** : cut through (air, water, etc.) — **surco** *nm* : groove, furrow, rut
sureño, -ña *adj* : southern, Southern — ~ *n* : Southerner
sureste *adj* **1** : southeast, southeastern **2** : southeasterly (of wind, etc.) — ~ *nm* : southeast, Southeast
surf *or* **surfing** *nm* : surfing
surgir {35} *vi* **1** : arise **2** APARECER : appear — **surgimiento** *nm* : rise, emergence
suroeste *adj* **1** : southwest, southwestern **2** : southwesterly (of wind, etc.) — ~ *nm* : southwest, Southwest
surtir *vt* **1** : supply, provide **2** ~ **efecto** : have an effect — **surtirse** *vr* ~ **de** : stock up on — **surtido, -da** *adj* **1** : assorted, varied **2** : stocked (with merchandise) — **surtido** *nm* : assortment, selection — **surtidor** *nm* : gas pump
susceptible *adj* **1** : susceptible, sensitive **2** ~ **de** : capable of — **susceptibilidad** *nf* : sensitivity

suscitar *vt* : provoke, arouse
suscribir {33} *vt* **1** : sign (a formal document) **2** RATIFICAR : endorse — **suscribirse** *vr* ~ **a** : subscribe to — **suscripción** *nf, pl* -**ciones** : subscription — **suscriptor, -tora** *n* : subscriber
susodicho, -cha *adj* : aforementioned
suspender *vt* **1** : suspend **2** COLGAR : hang **3** *Spain* : fail (an exam, etc.) — **suspensión** *nf, pl* -**siones** : suspension — **suspenso** *nm* **1** *Spain* : failure (in an exam, etc.) **2** *Lat* : suspense
suspicaz *adj, pl* -**caces** : suspicious
suspirar *vi* : sigh — **suspiro** *nm* : sigh
sustancia *nf* **1** : substance **2 sin** ~ : shallow, lacking substance — **sustancial** *adj* : substantial, significant — **sustancioso, -sa** *adj* : substantial, solid
sustantivo *nm* : noun
sustentar *vt* **1** : support **2** ALIMENTAR : sustain, nourish **3** MANTENER : maintain — **sustentarse** *vr* : support oneself — **sustentación** *nf, pl* -**ciones** : support — **sustento** *nm* **1** : means of support, livelihood **2** ALIMENTO : sustenance
sustituir {41} *vt* : replace, substitute — **sustitución** *nf, pl* -**ciones** : replacement, substitution — **sustituto, -ta** *n* : substitute
susto *nm* : fright, scare
sustraer {81} *vt* **1** : remove, take away **2** : subtract (in mathematics) — **sustraerse** *vr* ~ **a** : avoid, evade — **sustracción** *nf, pl* -**ciones** : subtraction
susurrar *vi* **1** : whisper **2** : murmur (of water) **3** : rustle (of leaves, etc.) — *vt* : whisper — **susurro** *nm* **1** : whisper **2** : murmur (of water) **3** : rustle, rustling (of leaves, etc.)
sutil *adj* **1** : delicate, fine **2** : subtle (of fragrances, differences, etc.) — **sutileza** *nf* : subtlety
sutura *nf* : suture
suyo, -ya *adj* **1** : his, her, its, one's, theirs **2** (*formal*) : yours **3 un primo suyo** : a cousin of his/hers — ~ *pron* **1** : his, hers, its (own), one's own, theirs **2** (*formal*) : yours
switch *nm Lat* : switch

T

t *nf* : t, 21st letter of the Spanish alphabet
taba *nf* : anklebone
tabaco *nm* : tobacco — **tabacalero, -ra** *adj* : tobacco
tábano *nm* : horsefly
taberna *nf* : tavern
tabicar {72} *vt* : wall up — **tabique** *nm* : thin wall, partition
tabla *nf* **1** : board, plank **2** LISTA : table, list **3** ∼ **de planchar** : ironing board **4** ∼**s** *nfpl* : stage, boards *pl* — **tablado** *nm* **1** : flooring **2** PLATAFORMA : platform **3** : (theater) stage — **tablero** *nm* **1** : bulletin board **2** : board (in games) **3** PIZARRA : blackboard **4** ∼ **de instrumentos** : dashboard, instrument panel
tableta *nf* **1** : tablet, pill **2** : bar (of chocolate)
tablilla *nf* : slat — **tablón** *nm, pl* **-lones 1** : plank, beam **2** ∼ **de anuncios** : bulletin board
tabú *adj* : taboo — **tabú** *nm, pl* **-búes** or **-bús** : taboo
tabular *vt* : tabulate
taburete *nm* : stool
tacaño, -na *adj* : stingy, miserly
tacha *nf* **1** : flaw, defect **2 sin** ∼ : flawless
tachar *vt* **1** : cross out, delete **2** ∼ **de** : accuse of, label as
tachón *nm, pl* **-chones** : stud, hobnail — **tachuela** *nf* : tack, hobnail
tácito, -ta *adj* : tacit
taciturno, -na *adj* : taciturn
taco *nm* **1** : stopper, plug **2** *Lat* : heel (of a shoe) **3** : cue (in billiards) **4** : taco (in cooking)
tacón *nm, pl* **-cones 1** : heel (of a shoe) **2 de** ∼ **alto** : high-heeled
táctica *nf* : tactic, tactics *pl* — **táctico, -ca** *adj* : tactical
tacto *nm* **1** : (sense of) touch, feel **2** DELICADEZA : tact
tafetán *nm, pl* **-tanes** : taffeta
tailandés, -desa *adj* : Thai
taimado, -da *adj* : crafty, sly
tajar *vt* : cut, slice — **tajada** *nf* **1** : slice **2 sacar** ∼ *fam* : get one's share — **tajante** *adj* : categorical — **tajo** *nm* **1** : cut, gash **2** ESCARPA : steep cliff
tal *adv* **1** : so, in such a way **2 con** ∼ **que** : provided that, as long as **3 ¿qué** ∼**?** : how are you?, how's it going? — ∼ *adj* **1** : such, such a **2** ∼ **vez** : maybe, perhaps — ∼ *pron* **1** : such a one, such a thing **2** ∼ **para cual** : two of a kind

taladrar *vt* : drill — **taladro** *nm* : drill
talante *nm* **1** HUMOR : mood **2** VOLUNTAD : willingness
talar *vt* : cut down, fell
talco *nm* : talcum powder
talego *nm* : sack
talento *nm* : talent — **talentoso, -sa** *adj* : talented
talismán *nm, pl* **-manes** : talisman, charm
talla *nf* **1** : sculpture, carving **2** ESTATURA : height **3** : size (in clothing) — **tallar** *vt* **1** : sculpt, carve **2** : measure (someone's height)
tallarín *nf, pl* **-rines** : noodle
talle *nm* **1** : waist, waistline **2** FIGURA : figure **3** : measurements *pl* (of clothing)
taller *nm* **1** : workshop **2** : studio (of an artist)
tallo *nm* : stalk, stem
talón *nm, pl* **-lones 1** : heel (of the foot) **2** : stub (of a check) — **talonario** *nm* : checkbook
taltuza *nf* : gopher
tamal *nm* : tamale
tamaño, -ña *adj* : such a, such a big — **tamaño** *nm* **1** : size **2 de** ∼ **natural** : life-size
tambalearse *vr* **1** : teeter, wobble **2** : stagger, totter (of persons)
también *adv* : too, as well, also
tambor *nm* : drum — **tamborilear** *vi* : drum
tamiz *nm* : sieve — **tamizar** {21} *vt* : sift
tampoco *adv* : neither, not either
tampón *nm, pl* **-pones 1** : tampon **2** : ink pad (for stamping)
tan *adv* **1** : so, so very **2** ∼ **pronto como** : as soon as **3** ∼ **sólo** : only, merely
tanda *nf* **1** TURNO : turn, shift **2** GRUPO : batch, lot, series
tangente *nf* : tangent
tangible *adj* : tangible
tango *nm* : tango
tanque *nm* : tank
tantear *vt* **1** : feel, grope **2** SOPESAR : size up, weigh — *vi* : feel one's way — **tanteador** *nm* : scoreboard — **tanteo** *nm* **1** : weighing, sizing up **2** PUNTUACIÓN : scoring (in sports)
tanto *adv* **1** : so much **2** (*in expressions of time*) : so long — ∼ *nm* **1** : certain amount **2** : goal, point (in sports) **3 un** ∼ : somewhat, rather — **tanto, -ta** *adj* **1** : so much, so many **2** (*in comparisons*) : as much, as many **3** *fam* : however many — ∼ *pron* **1**

: so much, so many **2 entre ~** : meanwhile
3 por lo ~ : therefore
tañer {79} *vt* **1** : ring (a bell) **2** : play (a musical instrument)
tapa *nf* **1** : cover, top, lid **2** *Spain* : snack
tapacubos *nms & pl* : hubcap
tapar *vt* **1** : cover, put a lid on **2** OCULTAR : block out **3** ENCUBRIR : cover up — **tapadera** *nf* **1** : cover, lid **2** : front (to hide a deception)
tapete *nm* **1** : small rug, mat **2** : cover (for a table)
tapia *nf* : (adobe) wall, garden wall — **tapiar** *vt* **1** : wall in **2** : block off (a door, etc.)
tapicería *nf* **1** : upholstery **2** TAPIZ : tapestry — **tapicero, -ra** *n* : upholsterer
tapioca *nf* : tapioca
tapiz *nm, pl* **-pices** : tapestry — **tapizar** {21} *vt* : upholster
tapón *nm, pl* **-pones** **1** : cork **2** : cap (for a bottle, etc.) **3** : plug, stopper (for a sink)
tapujo *nm* **sin ~s** : openly, outright
taquigrafía *nf* : stenography, shorthand — **taquígrafo, -fa** *n* : stenographer
taquilla *nf* **1** : box office **2** RECAUDACIÓN : earnings *pl*, take — **taquillero, -ra** *adj* **un éxito taquillero** : a box-office hit
tarántula *nf* : tarantula
tararear *vt* : hum
tardar *vi* **1** : take a long time, be late **2 a más ~** : at the latest — *vt* : take (time) — **tardanza** *nf* : lateness, delay — **tarde** *adv* **1** : late **2 ~ o temprano** : sooner or later — **~** *nf* **1** : afternoon, evening **2 ¡buenas ~s!** : good afternoon!, good evening! **3 en la ~** *or* **por la ~** : in the afternoon, in the evening — **tardío, -día** *adj* : late, tardy — **tardo, -da** *adj* : slow
tarea *nf* **1** : task, job **2** : homework (in education)
tarifa *nf* **1** : fare, rate **2** LISTA : price list **3** ARANCEL : duty, tariff
tarima *nf* : platform, stage
tarjeta *nf* **1** : card **2 ~ de crédito** : credit card **3 ~ postal** : postcard
tarro *nm* : jar, pot
tarta *nf* **1** : cake **2** TORTA : tart
tartamudear *vi* : stammer, stutter — **tartamudeo** *nm* : stutter, stammer
tartán *nm, pl* **-tanes** : tartan, plaid
tártaro *nm* : tartar
tarugo *nm* **1** : block (of wood) **2** *fam* : blockhead, dunce
tasa *nf* **1** : rate **2** IMPUESTO : tax **3** VALORACIÓN : appraisal — **tasación** *nf, pl* **-ciones** : appraisal — **tasar** *vt* **1** : set the price of **2** VALORAR : appraise, value
tasca *nf* : cheap bar, dive

tatuar {3} *vt* : tattoo — **tatuaje** *nm* : tattoo, tattooing
taurino, -na *adj* : bull, bullfighting — **tauromaquia** *nf* : (art of) bullfighting
taxi *nm, pl* **taxis** : taxi, taxicab — **taxista** *nmf* : taxi driver
taza *nf* **1** : cup **2** : (toilet) bowl — **tazón** *nm, pl* **-zones** : bowl
te *pron* **1** (*direct object*) : you **2** (*indirect object*) : for you, to you, from you **3** (*reflexive*) : yourself, for yourself, to yourself, from yourself
té *nm* : tea
teatro *nm* : theater — **teatral** *adj* : theatrical
techo *nm* **1** : roof **2** : ceiling (of a room) **3** LÍMITE : upper limit, ceiling — **techumbre** *nf* : roofing
tecla *nf* : key (of a musical instrument or a machine) — **teclado** *nm* : keyboard — **teclear** *vt* : type in, enter
técnica *nf* **1** : technique, skill **2** TECNOLOGÍA : technology — **técnico, -ca** *adj* : technical — **~** *n* : technician
tecnología *nf* : technology — **tecnológico, -ca** *adj* : technological
tecolote *nm Lat* : owl
tedio *nm* : boredom — **tedioso, -sa** *adj* : tedious, boring
teja *nf* : tile — **tejado** *nm* : roof
tejer *v* **1** : knit, crochet **2** : weave (on a loom)
tejido *nm* **1** : fabric, cloth **2** : tissue (of the body)
tejón *nm, pl* **-jones** : badger
tela *nf* **1** : fabric, material **2 ~ de araña** : spiderweb — **telar** *nm* : loom — **telaraña** *nf* : spiderweb, cobweb
tele *nf fam* : TV, television
telecomunicación *nf, pl* **-ciones** : telecommunication
teledifusión *nf, pl* **-siones** : television broadcasting
teledirigido, -da *adj* : remote-controlled
telefonear *v* : telephone, call — **telefónico, -ca** *adj* : telephone — **telefonista** *nmf* : telephone operator — **teléfono** *nm* **1** : telephone **2 llamar por ~** : make a phone call
telegrafiar {85} *v* : telegraph — **telegráfico, -ca** *adj* : telegraphic — **telégrafo** *nm* : telegaph
telegrama *nm* : telegram
telenovela *nf* : soap opera
telepatía *nf* : telepathy — **telepático, -ca** *adj* : telepathic
telescopio *nm* : telescope — **telescópico, -ca** *adj* : telescopic
telespectador, -dora *n* : (television) viewer
telesquí *nm, pl* **-squís** : ski lift

televidente *nmf* : (television) viewer
televisión *nf, pl* **-siones** : television, TV —
televisar *vt* : televise — **televisor** *nm* : television set
telón *nm, pl* **-lones** 1 : curtain (in theater) 2 ~ **de fondo** : backdrop, background
tema *nm* : theme
temblar {55} *vi* 1 : tremble, shiver 2 : shake (of a building, the ground, etc.) —
temblor *nm* 1 : shaking, trembling 2 *or* ~ **de tierra** : tremor, earthquake — **tembloroso, -sa** *adj* : trembling, shaky
temer *vt* : fear, dread — *vi* : be afraid —
temerario, -ria *adj* : reckless — **temeridad** *nf* 1 : recklessness 2 : rash act — **temeroso, -sa** *adj* : fearful — **temor** *nm* : fear, dread
temperamento *nm* : temperament — **temperamental** *adj* : temperamental
temperatura *nf* : temperature
tempestad *nf* : storm — **tempestuoso, -sa** *adj* : stormy
templar *vt* 1 : temper (steel) 2 : moderate (temperature) 3 : tune (a musical instrument) — **templarse** *vr* : warm up, cool down — **templado, -da** *adj* 1 : temperate, mild 2 TIBIO : lukewarm 3 VALIENTE : courageous — **templanza** *nf* 1 : moderation 2 : mildness (of weather)
templo *nm* : temple, synagogue
tempo *nm* : tempo
temporada *nf* 1 : season, time 2 PERÍODO : period, spell — **temporal** *adj* 1 : temporal 2 PROVISIONAL : temporary — ~ *nm* : storm — **temporero, -ra** *n* : temporary or seasonal worker
temporizador *nm* : timer
temprano, -na *adj* : early — **temprano** *adv* : early
tenaz *adj, pl* **-naces** : tenacious — **tenaza** *nf or* **tenazas** *nfpl* 1 : pliers 2 : tongs (for the fireplace, etc.) 3 : claw (of a crustacean)
tendedero *nm* : clothesline
tendencia *nf* : tendency, trend
tender {56} *vt* 1 : spread out, stretch out 2 : hang out (clothes) 3 : lay (cables, etc.) 4 : set (a trap) — *vi* ~ **a** : have a tendency towards — **tenderse** *vr* : stretch out, lie down
tendero, -ra *n* : shopkeeper
tendido *nm* 1 : laying (of cables, etc.) 2 : seats *pl*, stand (at a bullfight)
tendón *nm, pl* **-dones** : tendon
tenebroso, -sa *adj* 1 : gloomy, dark 2 SINIESTRO : sinister
tenedor, -dora *n* 1 : holder 2 ~ **de libros** : bookkeeper — **tenedor** *nm* : table fork — **teneduría** *nf* ~ **de libros** : bookkeeping
tener {80} *vt* 1 : have, possess 2 SUJETAR : hold 3 TOMAR : take 4 ~ **frío (hambre,**

etc.) : be cold (hungry, etc.) 5 ~ ... **años** : be ... years old 6 ~ **por** : think, consider — *v aux* 1 ~ **que** : have to, ought to 2 **tenía pensado escribirte** : I've been thinking of writing to you — **tenerse** *vr* 1 : stand up 2 ~ **por** : consider oneself
tenería *nf* : tannery
tengo → **tener**
tenia *nf* : tapeworm
teniente *nmf* : lieutenant
tenis *nms & pl* 1 : tennis 2 ~ *nmpl* : sneakers — **tenista** *nmf* : tennis player
tenor *nm* 1 : tenor 2 : tone, sense (in style)
tensar *vt* 1 : tense, make taut 2 : draw (a bow) — **tensarse** *vr* : become tense — **tensión** *nf, pl* **-siones** 1 : tension 2 ~ **arterial** : blood pressure — **tenso, -sa** *adj* : tense
tentación *nf, pl* **-ciones** : temptation
tentáculo *nm* : tentacle
tentar {55} *vt* 1 : feel, touch 2 ATRAER : tempt — **tentador, -dora** *adj* : tempting
tentativa *nf* : attempt
tentempié *nm fam* : snack
tenue *adj* 1 : tenuous 2 : faint, weak (of sounds) 3 : light, fine (of thread, rain, etc.)
teñir {67} *vt* 1 : dye 2 ~ **de** : tinge with
teología *nf* : theology — **teólogo, -ga** *n* : theologian
teorema *nm* : theorem
teoría *nf* : theory — **teórico, -ca** *adj* : theoretical
tequila *nm* : tequila
terapia *nf* 1 : therapy 2 ~ **ocupacional** : occupational therapy — **terapeuta** *nmf* : therapist — **terapéutico, -ca** *adj* : therapeutic
tercermundista *adj* : third-world
tercero, -ra *adj* (**tercer** *before masculine singular nouns*) 1 : third 2 **el Tercer Mundo** : the Third World — ~ *n* : third (in a series)
terciar *vt* : sling (sth over one's shoulders), tilt (a hat) — *vi* 1 : intervene 2 ~ **en** : take part in
tercio *nm* : third
terciopelo *nm* : velvet
terco, -ca *adj* : obstinate, stubborn
tergiversar *vt* : distort, twist
termal *adj* : thermal, hot — **termas** *nfpl* : hot springs
terminar *vt* : conclude, finish — *vi* 1 : finish 2 ACABARSE : come to an end — **terminarse** *vr* 1 : run out 2 ACABARSE : come to an end — **terminación** *nf, pl* **-ciones** : termination, conclusion — **terminal** *adj* : terminal, final — ~ *nm* (*in some regions f*) : (electric or electronic) terminal — ~ *nf* (*in some regions m*) : terminal, station —

término *nm* **1** : end **2** PLAZO : period, term **3** ∼ **medio** : happy medium **4** ∼s *nmpl* : terms — **terminología** *nf* : terminology
termita *nf* : termite
termo *nm* : thermos
termómetro *nm* : thermometer
termóstato *nm* : thermostat
ternero, -ra *n* : calf — **ternera** *nf* : veal
ternura *nf* : tenderness
terquedad *nf* : obstinacy, stubbornness
terracota *nf* : terra-cotta
terraplén *nm, pl* **-plenes** : embankment
terráqueo, -quea *adj* : earth, terrestrial
terrateniente *nmf* : landowner
terraza *nf* **1** : terrace **2** BALCÓN : balcony
terremoto *nm* : earthquake
terreno *nm* **1** : terrain **2** SUELO : earth, ground **3** SOLAR : plot, tract of land — **terreno, -na** *adj* : earthly — **terrestre** *adj* : terrestrial
terrible *adj* : terrible
terrier *nmf* : terrier
territorio *nm* : territory — **territorial** *adj* : territorial
terrón *nm, pl* **-rones 1** : clod (of earth) **2** ∼ **de azúcar** : lump of sugar
terror *nm* : terror — **terrorífico, -ca** *adj* : terrifying — **terrorismo** *nm* : terrorism — **terrorista** *adj & nmf* : terrorist
terroso, -sa *adj* : earthy
terso, -sa *adj* **1** : smooth **2** : polished, flowing (of a style) — **tersura** *nf* : smoothness
tertulia *nf* : gathering, group
tesis *nfs & pl* : thesis
tesón *nm* : persistence, tenacity
tesoro *nm* **1** : treasure **2** : thesaurus (book) **3 el Tesoro** : the Treasury — **tesorero, -ra** *n* : treasurer
testaferro *nm* : figurehead
testamento *nm* : testament, will — **testamentario, -ria** *n* : executor, executrix *f* — **testar** *vi* : draw up a will
testarudo, -da *adj* : stubborn
testículo *nm* : testicle
testificar {72} *v* : testify — **testigo** *nmf* **1** : witness **2** ∼ **ocular** : eyewitness — **testimoniar** *vi* : testify — **testimonio** *nm* : testimony
tétano *or* **tétanos** *nm* : tetanus
tetera *nf* : teapot
tetilla *nf* **1** : teat, nipple (of a man) **2** : nipple (of a baby bottle) — **tetina** *nf* : nipple (of a baby bottle)
tétrico, -ca *adj* : somber, gloomy
textil *adj & nm* : textile
texto *nm* : text — **textual** *adj* **1** : textual **2** EXACTO : literal, exact
textura *nf* : texture
tez *nf, pl* **teces** : complexion

ti *pron* **1** : you **2** ∼ **mismo,** ∼ **misma** : yourself
tía → **tío**
tianguis *nms & pl Lat* : open-air market
tibio, -bia *adj* : lukewarm
tiburón *nm, pl* **-rones** : shark
tic *nm* : tic
tiempo *nm* **1** : time **2** ÉPOCA : age, period **3** : weather (in meteorology) **4** : halftime (in sports) **5** : tempo (in music) **6** : tense (in grammar)
tienda *nf* **1** : store, shop **2** *or* ∼ **de campaña** : tent
tiene → **tener**
tienta *nf* **andar a** ∼s : feel one's way, grope around
tierno, -na *adj* **1** : tender, fresh, young **2** CARIÑOSO : affectionate
tierra *nf* **1** : land **2** SUELO : ground, earth **3** *or* ∼ **natal** : native land **4 la Tierra** : the Earth **5 por** ∼ : overland **6** ∼ **adentro** : inland
tieso, -sa *adj* **1** : stiff, rigid **2** ERGUIDO : erect **3** ENGREÍDO : haughty
tiesto *nm* : flowerpot
tifoideo, -dea *adj* **fiebre tifoidea** : typhoid fever
tifón *nm, pl* **-fones** : typhoon
tifus *nm* : typhus
tigre, -gresa *n* **1** : tiger, tigress *f* **2** *Lat* : jaguar
tijera *nf or* **tijeras** *nfpl* : scissors — **tijeretada** *nf* : cut, snip
tildar *vt* ∼ **de** : brand as, call
tilde *nf* **1** : tilde **2** ACENTO : accent mark
tilo *nm* : linden (tree)
timar *vt* : swindle, cheat
timbre *nm* **1** : bell **2** : tone, timbre (of a voice, etc.) **3** SELLO : seal, stamp **4** *Lat* : postage stamp — **timbrar** *vt* : stamp
tímido, -da *adj* : timid, shy — **timidez** *nf* : timidity, shyness
timo *nm fam* : swindle, hoax
timón *nm, pl* **-mones 1** : rudder **2 coger el** ∼ : take the helm, take charge
tímpano *nm* **1** : eardrum **2** ∼s *nmpl* : timpani, kettledrums
tina *nf* **1** : vat **2** BAÑERA : bathtub
tinieblas *nfpl* **1** : darkness **2 estar en** ∼ **sobre** : be in the dark about
tino *nm* **1** : good judgment, sense **2** TACTO : tact
tinta *nf* **1** : ink **2 saberlo de buena** ∼ : have it on good authority — **tinte** *nm* **1** : dye, coloring **2** MATIZ : overtone — **tintero** *nm* : inkwell
tintinear *vi* : jingle, tinkle, clink — **tintineo** *nm* : jingle, tinkle, clink

tinto, -ta *adj* **1** : dyed, stained **2** : red (of wine)
tintorería *nf* : dry cleaner (service)
tintura *nf* **1** : dye, tint **2** ~ **de yodo** : tincture of iodine
tiña *nf* : ringworm
tío, tía *n* : uncle *m*, aunt *f*
tiovivo *nm* : merry-go-round
típico, -ca *adj* : typical
tiple *nm* : soprano
tipo *nm* **1** : type, kind **2** FIGURA : figure (of a woman), build (of a man) **3** : rate (of interest, etc.) **4** : (printing) type, typeface — **tipo, -pa** *n fam* : guy *m*, gal *f*
tipografía *nf* : typography, printing — **tipográfico, -ca** *adj* : typographical — **tipógrafo, -fa** *n* : printer
tique *or* **tíquet** *nm* : ticket — **tiquete** *nm Lat* : ticket
tira *nf* **1** : strip, strap **2** ~ **cómica** : comic strip
tirabuzón *nf, pl* **-zones** **1** : corkscrew **2** RIZO : curl, coil
tirada *nf* **1** : throw **2** DISTANCIA : distance **3** IMPRESIÓN : printing, issue — **tirador** *nm* : handle, knob — **tirador, -dora** *n* : marksman *m*, markswoman *f*
tiranía *nf* : tyranny — **tiránico, -ca** *adj* : tyrannical — **tiranizar** {21} *vt* : tyrannize — **tirano, -na** *adj* : tyrannical — ~ *n* : tyrant
tirante *adj* **1** : taut, tight **2** : tense (of a situation, etc.) — ~ *nm* **1** : (shoulder) strap **2** ~**s** *nmpl* : suspenders
tirar *vt* **1** : throw **2** DESECHAR : throw away **3** DERRIBAR : knock down **4** DISPARAR : shoot, fire **5** IMPRIMIR : print — *vi* **1** : pull **2** DISPARAR : shoot **3** ATRAER : attract **4** *fam* : get by, manage **5** ~ **a** : tend towards — **tirarse** *vr* **1** : throw oneself **2** *fam* : spend (time)
tiritar *vi* : shiver
tiro *nm* **1** : shot, gunshot **2** : shot, kick (in sports) **3** : team (of horses, etc.) **4 a** ~ : within range
tiroides *nmf* : thyroid (gland)
tirón *nm, pl* **-rones** **1** : pull, yank **2 de un** ~ : in one go
tirotear *vt* : shoot at — **tiroteo** *nm* : shooting
tisis *nfs & pl* : tuberculosis
títere *nm* : puppet
titilar *vi* : flicker
titiritero, -ra *n* **1** : puppeteer **2** ACRÓBATA : acrobat
titubear *vi* **1** : hesitate **2** BALBUCEAR : stutter, stammer — **titubeante** *adj* : hesitant, faltering — **titubeo** *nm* : hesitation
titular *vt* : title, call — **titularse** *vr* **1** : be called, be titled **2** LICENCIARSE : receive a

degree — ~ *adj* : titular, official — ~ *nm* : headline — ~ *nmf* : holder, incumbent —
título *nm* **1** : title **2** : degree, qualification (in education)
tiza *nf* : chalk
tiznar *vt* : blacken (with soot, etc.) — **tizne** *nm* : soot
toalla *nf* : towel — **toallero** *nm* : towel rack
tobillo *nm* : ankle
tobogán *nm, pl* **-ganes** **1** : toboggan, sled **2** : slide (in a playground, etc.)
tocadiscos *nms & pl* : record player
tocado, -da *adj fam* : touched, not all there — **tocado** *nm* : headgear, headdress
tocador *nm* : dressing table
tocar {72} *vt* **1** : touch, feel **2** MENCIONAR : touch on, refer to **3** : play (a musical instrument) — *vi* **1** : knock, ring **2** ~ **en** : touch on, border on
tocayo, -ya *n* : namesake
tocino *nm* **1** : bacon **2** : salt pork (for cooking) — **tocineta** *nf Lat* : bacon
tocólogo, -ga *n* : obstetrician
tocón *nm, pl* **-cones** : stump (of a tree)
todavía *adv* **1** AÚN : still **2** (in comparisons) : even **3** ~ **no** : not yet
todo, -da *adj* **1** : all **2** CADA, CUALQUIER : every, each **3 a toda velocidad** : at top speed **4 todo el mundo** : everyone, everybody — ~ *pron* **1** : everything, all **2 todos, -das** *pl* : everybody, everyone, all — **todo** *nm* : whole — **todopoderoso, -sa** *adj* : almighty, all-powerful
toga *nf* **1** : toga **2** : gown, robe (of a judge, etc.)
toldo *nm* : awning, canopy
tolerar *vt* : tolerate — **tolerancia** *nf* : tolerance — **tolerante** *adj* : tolerant
toma *nf* **1** : capture **2** DOSIS : dose **3** : take (in film) **4** ~ **de corriente** : wall socket, outlet **5** ~ **y daca** : give-and-take — **tomar** *vt* **1** : take **2** : have (food or drink) **3** CAPTURAR : capture, seize **4** ~ **el sol** : sunbathe **5** ~ **tierra** : land — *vi* : drink (alcohol) — **tomarse** *vr* **1** : take (time, etc.) **2** : drink, eat, have (food, drink)
tomate *nm* : tomato
tomillo *nm* : thyme
tomo *nm* : volume
ton *nm* **sin** ~ **ni son** : without rhyme or reason
tonada *nf* : tune
tonel *nm* : barrel, cask
tonelada *nf* : ton — **tonelaje** *nm* : tonnage
tónica *nf* **1** : tonic (water) **2** TENDENCIA : trend, tone — **tónico, -ca** *adj* : tonic — **tónico** *nm* : tonic (in medicine)
tono *nm* **1** : tone **2** : shade (of colors) **3** : key (in music)

tontería *nf* **1** : silly thing or remark **2** ESTU-
PIDEZ : foolishness **3 decir ~s** : talk nonsense — **tonto, -ta** *adj* **1** : stupid, silly **2 a
tontas y a locas** : haphazardly — **~** *n*
: fool, idiot
topacio *nm* : topaz
toparse *vr* **~ con** : run into, come across
tope *nm* **1** : limit, end **2** *or* **~ de puerta**
: doorstop **3** *Lat* : bump — **~** *adj* : maximum
tópico, -ca *adj* **1** : topical, external **2** MANI-
DO : trite — **tópico** *nm* : cliché
topo *nm* : mole (animal)
toque *nm* **1** : (light) touch **2** : ringing, peal
(of a bell) **3 ~ de queda** : curfew **4 ~ de
diana** : reveille — **toquetear** *vt* : finger,
handle
tórax *nms & pl* : thorax
torbellino *nm* : whirlwind
torcer {14} *vt* **1** : twist, bend **2** : turn (a corner) **3** : wring (out) — *vi* : turn — **torcerse**
vr **1** : twist, sprain **2** FRUSTRARSE : go
wrong **3** DESVIARSE : go astray — **torcedura** *nf* **1** : twisting **2** ESGUINCE : sprain —
torcido, -da *adj* : twisted, crooked
tordo, -da *adj* : dappled — **tordo** *nm* : thrush
(bird)
torear *vt* **1** : fight (bulls) **2** ELUDIR : dodge,
sidestep — *vi* : fight bulls — **toreo** *nm*
: bullfighting — **torero, -ra** *n* : bullfighter
tormenta *nf* : storm — **tormento** *nm* **1** : torture **2** ANGUSTIA : torment, anguish — **tormentoso, -sa** *adj* : stormy
tornado *nm* : tornado
tornar *vt* CONVERTIR : render, turn — *vi* : go
back, return — **tornarse** *vr* : become, turn
into
torneo *nm* : tournament
tornillo *nm* : screw
torniquete *nm* **1** : turnstile **2** : tourniquet
(in medicine)
torno *nm* **1** : winch **2** : (carpenter's) lathe **3
~ de alfarero** : (potter's) wheel **4 ~ de
banco** : vise **5 en ~ a** : around, about
toro *nm* **1** : bull **2 ~s** *nmpl* : bullfight
toronja *nf* : grapefruit
torpe *adj* **1** : clumsy, awkward **2** ESTÚPIDO
: stupid, dull
torpedear *vt* : torpedo — **torpedo** *nm* : torpedo
torpeza *nf* **1** : clumsiness, awkwardness **2**
ESTUPIDEZ : slowness, stupidity
torre *nf* **1** : tower **2** : turret (on a ship, etc.)
3 : rook, castle (in chess)
torrente *nm* **1** : torrent **2 ~ sanguíneo**
: bloodstream — **torrencial** *adj* : torrential
tórrido, -da *adj* : torrid
torsión *nf, pl* **-siones** : twisting
torta *nf* **1** : torte, cake **2** *Lat* : sandwich

tortazo *nm fam* : blow, wallop
tortícolis *nfs & pl* : stiff neck
tortilla *nf* **1** : tortilla **2** *or* **~ de huevo**
: omelet
tórtola *nf* : turtledove
tortuga *nf* **1** : turtle, tortoise **2 ~ de agua
dulce** : terrapin
tortuoso, -sa *adj* : tortuous, winding
tortura *nf* : torture — **torturar** *vt* : torture
tos *nf* **1** : cough **2 ~ ferina** : whooping
cough
tosco, -ca *adj* : rough, coarse
toser *vi* : cough
tosquedad *nf* : coarseness
tostar {19} *vt* **1** : toast **2** BRONCEAR : tan —
tostarse *vr* : get a tan — **tostada** *nf* **1**
: piece of toast **2** *Lat* : tostada — **tostador**
nm : toaster
tostón *nm, pl* **-tones** *Lat* : fried plantain
chip
total *adj & nm* : total — **~** *adv* : so, after all
— **totalidad** *nf* : whole — **totalitario, -ria**
adj & n : totalitarian — **totalitarismo** *nm*
: totalitarianism — **totalizar** {21} *vt* : total,
add up to
tóxico, -ca *adj* : toxic, poisonous — **tóxico**
nm : poison — **toxicomanía** *nf* : drug addiction — **toxicómano, -na** *n* : drug addict
— **toxina** *nf* : toxin
tozudo, -da *adj* : stubborn
traba *nf* : obstacle, hindrance
trabajar *vi* **1** : work **2** : act, perform (in theater, etc.) — *vt* **1** : work (metal) **2** : knead
(dough) **3** MEJORAR : work on, work at —
trabajador, -dora *adj* : hard-working — **~**
n : worker — **trabajo** *nm* **1** : work **2** EM-
PLEO : job **3** TAREA : task **4** ESFUERZO : effort **5 costar ~** : be difficult **6 ~ en
equipo** : teamwork **7 ~s** *nmpl* : hardships, difficulties — **trabajoso, -sa** *adj*
: hard, laborious
trabalenguas *nms & pl* : tongue twister
trabar *vt* **1** : join, connect **2** OBSTACULIZAR
: impede **3** : strike up (a conversation, etc.)
4 : thicken (sauces) — **trabarse** *vr* **1** : jam
2 ENREDARSE : become entangled **3 se le
traba la lengua** : he gets tongue-tied
trabucar {72} *vt* : mix up
tracción *nf* : traction
tractor *nm* : tractor
tradición *nf, pl* **-ciones** : tradition — **tradicional** *adj* : traditional
traducir {61} *vt* : translate — **traducción** *nf,
pl* **-ciones** : translation — **traductor, -tora**
n : translator
traer {81} *vt* **1** : bring **2** CAUSAR : cause,
bring about **3** CONTENER : carry, have **4** LL-
EVAR : wear — **traerse** *vr* **1** : bring along **2**
traérselas : be difficult

traficar

traficar {72} *vi* ~ **en** : traffic in — **traficante** *nmf* : dealer, trafficker — **tráfico** *nm* **1** : trade (of merchandise) **2** : traffic (of vehicles)

tragaluz *nf, pl* **-luces** : skylight

tragar {52} *vt* **1** : swallow **2** *fam* : put up with — *vi* : swallow — **tragarse** *vr* **1** : swallow **2** ABSORBER : absorb, swallow up

tragedia *nf* : tragedy — **trágico, -ca** *adj* : tragic

trago *nm* **1** : swallow, swig **2** *fam* : drink, liquor — **tragón, -gona** *adj fam* : greedy — ~ *nmf fam* : glutton

traicionar *vt* : betray — **traición** *nf, pl* **-ciones 1** : betrayal **2** : treason (in law) — **traidor, -dora** *adj* : traitorous, treacherous — ~ *n* : traitor

trailer *nm* : trailer

traje *nm* **1** : dress, costume **2** : (man's) suit **3** ~ **de baño** : bathing suit

trajinar *vi fam* : rush around — **trajín** *nm, pl* **-jines** *fam* : hustle and bustle

trama *nf* **1** : plot **2** : weave, weft (of fabric) — **tramar** *vt* **1** : plot, plan **2** : weave (fabric)

tramitar *vt* : negotiate — **trámite** *nm* : procedure, step

tramo *nm* **1** : stretch, section **2** : flight (of stairs)

trampa *nf* **1** : trap **2 hacer** ~**s** : cheat — **trampear** *vt* : cheat

trampilla *nf* : trapdoor

trampolín *nm, pl* **-lines 1** : diving board **2** : trampoline (in a gymnasium, etc.)

tramposo, -sa *adj* : crooked, cheating — ~ *n* : cheat, swindler

tranca *nf* **1** : cudgel, club **2** : bar (for a door or window)

trance *nm* **1** : critical juncture **2** : (hypnotic) trance **3 en** ~ **de** : in the process of

tranquilo, -la *adj* : calm, tranquil — **tranquilidad** *nf* : tranquility, peace — **tranquilizante** *nm* : tranquilizer — **tranquilizar** {21} *vt* : calm, soothe — **tranquilizarse** *vr* : calm down

trans- *see also* **tras-**

transacción *nf, pl* **-ciones** : transaction

transatlántico, -ca *adj* : transatlantic — **transatlántico** *nm* : ocean liner

transbordador *nm* **1** : ferry **2** ~ **espacial** : space shuttle — **transbordar** *vt* : transfer — *vi* : change (of trains, etc.) — **transbordo** *nm* **hacer** ~ : change (trains, etc.)

transcribir {33} *vt* : transcribe — **transcripción** *nf, pl* **-ciones** : transcription

transcurrir *vi* : elapse, pass — **transcurso** *nm* : course, progression

transeúnte *nmf* : passerby

transferir {76} *vt* : transfer — **transferencia** *nf* : transfer, transference

---

164

transformar *vt* **1** : transform, change **2** CONVERTIR : convert — **transformarse** *vr* : be transformed — **transformación** *nf, pl* **-ciones** : transformation — **transformador** *nm* : transformer

transfusión *nf, pl* **-siones** : transfusion

transgredir {1} *vt* : transgress — **transgresión** *nf* : transgression

transición *nf, pl* **-ciones** : transition

transido, -da *adj* : overcome, stricken

transigir {35} *vi* : give in, compromise

transistor *nm* : transistor

transitar *vi* : go, travel — **transitable** *adj* : passable

transitivo, -va *adj* : transitive

tránsito *nm* **1** : transit **2** TRÁFICO : traffic **3** **hora de máximo** ~ : rush hour — **transitorio, -ria** *adj* : transitory

transmitir *vt* **1** : transmit **2** : broadcast (radio, TV, etc.) **3** CEDER : pass on — **transmisión** *nf, pl* **-siones 1** : broadcast **2** TRANSFERENCIA : transfer **3** : transmission (of an automobile) — **transmisor** *nm* : transmitter

transparentarse *vr* : be transparent — **transparente** *adj* : transparent

transpirar *vi* : perspire, sweat — **transpiración** *nf, pl* **-ciones** : perspiration, sweat

transponer {60} *vt* : transpose, move — **transponerse** *vr* **1** : set (of the sun, etc.) **2** DORMITAR : doze off

transportar *vt* : transport, carry — **transportarse** *vr* : get carried away — **transporte** *nm* : transport, transportation

transversal *adj* **corte** ~ : cross section

tranvía *nm* : streetcar, trolley

trapear *vt Lat* : mop

trapecio *nm* : trapeze

trapisonda *nf* : scheme, plot

trapo *nm* **1** : cloth, rag **2** ~**s** *nmpl fam* : clothes

tráquea *nf* : trachea, windpipe

traquetear *vi* : rattle around, shake — **traqueteo** *nm* : rattling

tras *prep* **1** DESPUÉS DE : after **2** DÉTRAS DE : behind

tras- *see also* **trans-**

trascender {56} *vi* **1** : leak out, become known **2** EXTENDERSE : spread **3** ~ **de** : transcend — **trascendencia** *nf* : importance — **trascendental** *adj* **1** : transcendental **2** IMPORTANTE : important

trasegar *vt* : move around

trasero, -ra *adj* : rear, back — **trasero** *nm* : buttocks *pl*

trasfondo *nm* **1** : background **2** : undercurrent (of suspicion, etc.)

trasladar *vt* **1** : transfer, move **2** POSPONER : postpone — **trasladarse** *vr* : move, relocate — **traslado** *nm* **1** : transfer, move **2** COPIA : copy

traslapar *vt* : overlap — **traslaparse** *vr* : overlap

traslucirse {45} *vr* **1** : be translucent **2** REVELARSE : be revealed — **traslúcido, -da** : translucent

trasnochar *vi* : stay up all night

traspasar *vt* **1** : pierce, go through **2** EXCEDER : go beyond **3** ATRAVESAR : cross, go across **4** : transfer (a business, etc.) — **traspaso** *nm* : transfer, sale

traspié *nm* **1** : stumble, trip **2** ERROR : blunder

trasplantar *vt* : transplant — **trasplante** *nm* : transplant

trasquilar *vt* : shear

traste *nm* **1** : fret (on a guitar, etc.) **2** *Lat* : (kitchen) utensil **3 dar al ~ con** : ruin **4 irse al ~** : fall through

trastos *nmpl fam* : pieces of junk, stuff

trastornar *vt* **1** : disturb, disrupt **2** VOLVER LOCO : drive crazy — **trastornarse** *vr* : go crazy — **trastornado, -da** *adj* : disturbed, deranged — **trastorno** *nm* **1** : disturbance, disruption **2** : (medical or psychological) disorder

trastrocar *vt* : change, switch around

tratable *adj* : friendly, sociable

tratar *vi* **1 ~ con** : deal with **2 ~ de** : try to **3 ~ de** *or* **~ sobre** : be about, concern **4 ~ en** : deal in — *vt* **1** : treat **2** MANEJAR : deal with, handle — **tratarse** *vr* **~ de** : be about, concern — **tratado** *nm* **1** : treatise **2** CONVENIO : treaty — **tratamiento** *nm* : treatment — **trato** *nm* **1** : treatment **2** ACUERDO : deal, agreement **3 ~s** *nmpl* : dealings

trauma *nm* : trauma — **traumático, -ca** *adj* : traumatic

través *nm* **1 a ~ de** : across, through **2 de ~** : sideways

travesaño *nm* : crosspiece

travesía *nf* : voyage, crossing (of the sea)

travesura *nf* **1** : prank **2 ~s** *nfpl* : mischief — **travieso, -sa** *adj* : mischievous, naughty

trayecto *nm* **1** : trajectory, path **2** VIAJE : journey **3** RUTA : route — **trayectoria** *nf* : path, trajectory

traza *nf* **1** : design, plan **2** ASPECTO : appearance — **trazado** *nm* **1** : outline, sketch **2** DISEÑO : plan, layout — **trazar** {21} *vt* **1** : trace, outline **2** : draw up (a plan, etc.) — **trazo** *nm* : stroke, line

trébol *nm* **1** : clover, shamrock **2 ~es** *nmpl* : clubs (in playing cards)

trece *adj* & *nm* : thirteen — **treceavo, -va** *adj* : thirteenth — **treceavo** *nm* : thirteenth (fraction)

trecho *nm* **1** : stretch, period **2** DISTANCIA : distance **3 de ~ a ~** : at intervals

tregua *nf* **1** : truce **2 sin ~** : without respite

treinta *adj* & *nm* : thirty — **treintavo, -va** *adj* : thirtieth — **treintavo** *nm* : thirtieth (fraction)

tremendo, -da *adj* : tremendous, enormous

trementina *nf* : turpentine

trémulo, -la *adj* : trembling, flickering

tren *nm* **1** : train **2 ~ de aterrizaje** : landing gear

trenza *nf* : braid, pigtail — **trenzar** {21} *vt* : braid — **trenzarse** *vr Lat* : get involved

trepar *vi* **1** : climb **2** : creep, spread (of a plant) — **treparse** *vr* : climb (up) — **trepador, -dora** *adj* : climbing — **trepadora** *nf* **1** : climbing plant **2** *fam* : social climber

trepidar *vi* : shake, vibrate

tres *adj* & *nm* : three — **trescientos, -tas** *adj* : three hundred — **trescientos** *nms* & *pl* : three hundred

treta *nf* : trick

triángulo *nm* : triangle — **triangular** *adj* : triangular

tribu *nf* : tribe — **tribal** *adj* : tribal

tribulación *nf, pl* **-ciones** : tribulation

tribuna *nf* **1** : dais, platform **2** : grandstand, bleachers *pl* (in a stadium)

tribunal *nm* : court, tribunal

tributar *vt* : pay, render — *vi* : pay taxes — **tributo** *nm* **1** : tribute **2** IMPUESTO : tax

triciclo *nm* : tricycle

tricolor *adj* : tricolored

tridimensional *adj* : three-dimensional

trigésimo, -ma *adj* & *n* : thirtieth

trigo *nm* : wheat

trigonometría *nf* : trigonometry

trillado, -da *adj* : trite

trillar *vt* : thresh — **trilladora** *nf* : threshing machine

trillizo, -za *n* : triplet

trilogía *nf* : trilogy

trimestral *adj* : quarterly

trinar *vi* : warble

trinchar *vt* : carve

trinchera *nf* **1** : trench, ditch **2** IMPERMEABLE : trench coat

trineo *nm* : sled, sleigh

trinidad *nf* : trinity

trino *nm* : trill, warble

trío *nm* : trio

tripa *nf* **1** : gut, intestine **2 ~s** *nfpl fam* : belly, tummy

triple *adj* & *nm* : triple — **triplicar** {72} *vt* : triple

trípode *nm* : tripod

tripular *vt* : man — **tripulación** *nf, pl* **-ciones** : crew — **tripulante** *nmf* : crew member

tris *nm* **estar en un ~ de** : be within an inch of
triste *adj* **1** : sad **2** SOMBRÍO : dismal, gloomy **3** MISERABLE : sorry, miserable — **tristeza** *nf* : sadness, grief
tritón *nm, pl* **-tones** : newt
triturar *vt* : crush, grind
triunfar *vi* : triumph, win — **triunfal** *adj* : triumphal — **triunfante** *adj* : triumphant — **triunfo** *nm* : triumph, victory
trivial *adj* : trivial
triza *nf* **1** : shred, bit **2 hacer ~s** : smash to pieces
trocar {82} *vt* **1** CONVERTIR : change **2** INTERCAMBIAR : exchange
trocha *nf* : path, trail
trofeo *nm* : trophy
trombón *nm, pl* **-bones 1** : trombone **2** : trombonist (musician)
trombosis *nf* : thrombosis
trompa *nf* **1** : trunk (of an elephant), snout **2** : horn (musical instrument) **3** : tube (in anatomy)
trompeta *nf* : trumpet — **trompetista** *nmf* : trumpet player
trompo *nm* : top (toy)
tronada *nf* : thunderstorm — **tronar** {19} *vi* : thunder, rage — *vt Lat fam* : shoot — *v impers* : thunder
tronchar *vt* **1** : snap **2** TRUNCAR : cut short
tronco *nm* **1** : trunk (of a tree) **2** : torso (of a person) **3 dormir como un ~** : sleep like a log
trono *nm* : throne
tropa *nf* : troops *pl*, soldiers *pl*
tropel *nm* : mob
tropezar {29} *vi* **1** : trip, stumble **2 ~ con** : come up against, run into — **tropezón** *nm, pl* **-zones 1** : stumble **2** EQUIVOCACIÓN : mistake, slip
trópico *nm* : tropic — **tropical** *adj* : tropical
tropiezo *nm* **1** CONTRATIEMPO : snag, setback **2** EQUIVOCACIÓN : mistake, slip
trotar *vi* **1** : trot **2** *fam* : rush about — **trote** *nm* **1** : trot **2** *fam* : rush, bustle **3 al ~** : at a trot, quickly
trozo *nm* : piece, bit, chunk
trucha *nf* : trout
truco *nm* **1** : knack **2** ARDID : trick
trueno *nm* : thunder
trueque *nm* : barter, exchange
trufa *nf* : truffle
truncar {72} *vt* **1** : cut short **2** : thwart, spoil (plans, etc.)
tu *adj* : your
tú *pron* : you

tuba *nf* : tuba
tuberculosis *nf* : tuberculosis
tubo *nm* **1** : tube, pipe **2 ~ de escape** : exhaust pipe (of a vehicle) **3 ~ de desagüe** : drainpipe — **tubería** *nf* : pipes *pl*, tubing
tuerca *nf* : nut (for a screw)
tuerto, -ta *adj* : one-eyed, blind in one eye
tuétano *nm* : marrow
tufo *nm* **1** : vapor **2** *fam* : stench, stink
tugurio *nm* : hovel
tulipán *nm, pl* **-panes** : tulip
tullido, -da *adj* : crippled, paralyzed
tumba *nf* : tomb, grave
tumbar *vt* : knock down, knock over — **tumbarse** *vr* : lie down — **tumbo** *nm* **dar ~s** : jolt, bump around
tumor *nm* : tumor
tumulto *nm* **1** : commotion, tumult **2** MOTÍN : riot — **tumultuoso, -sa** *adj* : tumultuous
tuna *nf* : prickly pear
túnel *nm* : tunnel
túnica *nf* : tunic
tupé *nm* : toupee
tupido, -da *adj* : dense, thick
turba *nf* **1** : peat **2** MUCHEDUMBRE : mob, throng
turbación *nf, pl* **-ciones 1** : disturbance **2** CONFUSIÓN : confusion
turbante *nm* : turban
turbar *vt* **1** : disturb, upset **2** CONFUNDIR : confuse, bewilder
turbina *nf* : turbine
turbio, -bia *adj* **1** : cloudy, murky **2** : blurred (of vision, etc.) — **turbión** *nm, pl* **-biones** : squall
turbulencia *nf* : turbulence — **turbulento, -ta** *adj* : turbulent
turco, -ca *adj* : Turkish — **turco** *nm* : Turkish (language)
turista *nmf* : tourist — **turismo** *nm* : tourism, tourist industry — **turístico, -ca** *adj* : tourist, travel
turnarse *vr* : take turns, alternate — **turno** *nm* **1** : turn **2 ~ de noche** : night shift
turquesa *nf* : turquoise
turrón *nm, pl* **-rrones** : nougat
tutear *vt* : address as *tú*
tutela *nf* **1** : guardianship (in law) **2 bajo la ~ de** : under the protection of
tuteo *nm* : addressing as *tú*
tutor, -tora *n* **1** : guardian **2** : tutor (in education)
tuyo, -ya *adj* : yours, of yours — **~** *pron* **1 el tuyo, la tuya, lo tuyo, los tuyos, las tuyas** : yours **2 los tuyos** : your family, your friends

U

u¹ *nf* : u, 22d letter of the Spanish alphabet
u² *conj* (*used before words beginning with o- or ho-*) : or
uapití *nm* : American elk, wapiti
ubicar {72} *vt Lat* **1** COLOCAR : place, position **2** LOCALIZAR : find — **ubicarse** *vr* : be located
ubre *nf* : udder
Ud., Uds. → **usted**
ufanarse *vr* ~ **de** : boast about — **ufano, -na** *adj* **1** : proud **2** ENGREÍDO : self-satisfied
ujier *nm* : usher
úlcera *nf* : ulcer
ulterior *adj* : later, subsequent — **ulteriormente** *adv* : subsequently
últimamente *adv* : lately, recently
ultimar *vt* **1** : complete, finish **2** *Lat* : kill — **ultimátum** *nm, pl* **-tums** : ultimatum
último, -ma *adj* **1** : last **2** : latest, most recent (in time) **3** : farthest (in space) **4 por último** : finally
ultrajar *vt* : outrage, insult — **ultraje** *nm* : outrage, insult
ultramar *nm* **de** ~ *or* **en** ~ : overseas — **ultramarino, -na** *adj* : overseas — **ultramarinos** *nmpl* **tienda de** ~ : grocery store
ultranza: a ~ *adv phr* : to the extreme — **a** ~ *adj phr* : out-and-out, complete
ultrasonido *nm* : ultrasound
ultravioleta *adj* : ultraviolet
ulular *vi* **1** : hoot (of an owl) **2** : howl (of a wolf, the wind, etc.) — **ululato** *nm* : hoot (of an owl)
umbilical *adj* : umbilical
umbral *nm* : threshold
un, una *art, mpl* **unos 1** : a, an **2 unos** *or* **unas** *pl* : some, a few **3 unos** *or* **unas** *pl* : about, approximately — **un** *adj* → **uno**
unánime *adj* : unanimous — **unanimidad** *nf* : unanimity
uncir {83} *vt* : yoke
undécimo, -ma *adj & n* : eleventh
ungir {35} *vt* : anoint — **ungüento** *nm* : ointment
único, -ca *adj* **1** : only, sole **2** EXCEPCIONAL : unique — ~ *n* : only one — **únicamente** *adv* : only
unicornio *nm* : unicorn
unidad *nf* **1** : unit **2** ARMONÍA : unity — **unido, -da** *adj* **1** : united **2** : close (of friends, etc.)
unificar {72} *vt* : unify — **unificación** *nf, pl* **-ciones** : unification

uniformar *vt* **1** : standardize **2** : put into uniform — **uniformado, -da** *adj* : uniformed — **uniforme** *adj & nm* : uniform — **uniformidad** *nf* : uniformity
unilateral *adj* : unilateral
unir *vt* **1** : unite, join **2** COMBINAR : combine, mix together — **unirse** *vr* **1** : join together **2** ~ **a** : join — **unión** *nf, pl* **uniones 1** : union **2** JUNTURA : joint, coupling
unísono *nm* **al** ~ : in unison
unitario, -ria *adj* : unitary
universal *adj* : universal
universidad *nf* : university, college — **universitario, -ria** *adj* : university, college
universo *nm* : universe
uno, una (**un** *before masculine singular nouns*) *adj* : one — ~ *pron* **1** : one **2 unos, unas** *pl* : some **3 uno(s) a otro(s)** : one another, each other **4 uno y otro** : both — **uno** *nm* : one (number)
untar *vt* **1** : smear, grease **2** *fam* : bribe — **untuoso, -sa** *adj* : greasy, sticky
uña *nf* **1** : nail, fingernail **2** : claw (of a cat, etc.), hoof (of a horse, etc.)
uranio *nm* : uranium
Urano *nm* : Uranus
urbano, -na *adj* : urban, city — **urbanidad** *nf* : politeness, courtesy — **urbanización** *nf, pl* **-ciones** : housing development — **urbanizar** *vt* : develop, urbanize — **urbe** *nf* : large city
urdir *vt* **1** : warp **2** PLANEAR : plot — **urdimbre** *nf* : warp (of a fabric)
urgir {35} *v impers* : be urgent, be pressing — **urgencia** *nf* **1** : urgency **2** EMERGENCIA : emergency — **urgente** *adj* : urgent
urinario, -ria *adj* : urinary — **urinario** *nm* : urinal (place)
urna *nf* **1** : urn **2** : ballot box (for voting)
urraca *nf* : magpie
uruguayo, -ya *adj* : Uruguayan
usar *vt* **1** : use **2** LLEVAR : wear — **usarse 1** EMPLEARSE : be used **2** : be worn, be in fashion — **usado, -da** *adj* **1** : used **2** GASTADO : worn, worn-out — **usanza** *nf* : custom, usage — **uso** *nm* **1** : use **2** DESGASTE : wear and tear **3** USANZA : custom, usage
usted *pron* **1** (*used in formal address; often written as* **Ud.** *or* **Vd.**) : you **2** ~**es** *pl* (*often written as* **Uds.** *or* **Vds.**) : you (all)
usual *adj* : usual
usuario, -ria *n* : user
usura *nf* : usury — **usurero, -ra** *n* : usurer

usurpar *vt* : usurp
utensilio *nm* : utensil, tool
útero *nm* : uterus, womb
utilizar {21} *vt* : use, utilize — **útil** *adj* : useful — **útiles** *nmpl* : implements, tools —

utilidad *nf* : utility, usefulness — **utilitario, -ria** *adj* : utilitarian — **utilización** *nf, pl* **-ciones** : utilization, use
uva *nf* : grape

V

v *nf* : v, 23d letter of the Spanish alphabet
va → **ir**
vaca *nf* : cow
vacaciones *nfpl* **1** : vacation **2 estar de** ～ : be on vacation **3 irse de** ～ : go on vacation
vacante *adj* : vacant — ～ *nf* : vacancy
vaciar {85} *vt* **1** : empty (out) **2** AHUECAR : hollow out **3** : cast, mold (a statue, etc.)
vacilar *vi* **1** : hesitate, waver **2** : flicker (of light) **3** TAMBALEARSE : be unsteady, wobble **4** *fam* : joke, fool around — **vacilación** *nf, pl* **-ciones** : hesitation — **vacilante** *adj* **1** : hesitant **2** OSCILANTE : unsteady
vacío, -cía *adj* : empty — **vacío** *nm* **1** : void **2** : vacuum (in physics) **3** HUECO : space, gap
vacuna *nf* : vaccine — **vacunación** *nf, pl* **-ciones** : vaccination — **vacunar** *vt* : vaccinate
vacuno, -na *adj* : bovine
vadear *vt* : ford — **vado** *nm* : ford
vagabundear *vi* : wander — **vagabundo, -da** *adj* **1** : vagrant **2** : stray (of a dog, etc.) — ～ *n* : hobo, bum — **vagancia** *nf* **1** : vagrancy **2** PEREZA : laziness, idleness — **vagar** {52} *vi* : roam, wander
vagina *nf* : vagina
vago, -ga *adj* **1** : vague **2** PEREZOSO : lazy, idle — ～ *n* : idler, loafer
vagón *nm, pl* **-gones** : car (of a train)
vahído *nm* : dizzy spell
vaho *nm* **1** : breath **2** VAPOR : vapor, steam
vaina *nf* **1** : sheath, scabbard **2** : pod (in botany) **3** *Lat fam* : bother, pain
vainilla *nf* : vanilla
vaivén *nm, pl* **-venes 1** : swinging, swaying **2** : coming and going (of people, etc.) **3 vaivenes** *nmpl* : ups and downs
vajilla *nf* : dishes *pl*
vale *nm* **1** : voucher **2** PAGARÉ : IOU — **valedero, -ra** *adj* : valid
valentía *nf* : courage, bravery
valer {84} *vt* **1** : be worth **2** COSTAR : cost **3** GANAR : gain, earn **4** EQUIVALER A : be

equal to — *vi* **1** : have value, cost **2** SER VÁLIDO : be valid, count **3** SERVIR : be of use **4 hacerse** ～ : assert oneself **5 más vale** : it's better — **valerse** *vr* **1** ～ **de** : take advantage of **2** ～ **solo** *or* ～ **por sí mismo** : look after oneself
valeroso, -sa *adj* : courageous
valga, etc. → **valer**
valía *nf* : worth
validar *vt* : validate — **validez** *nf* : validity — **válido, -da** *adj* : valid
valiente *adj* **1** : brave **2** (*used ironically*) : fine, great
valija *nf* : case, valise
valioso, -sa *adj* : valuable
valla *nf* **1** : fence **2** : hurdle (in sports) — **vallar** *vt* : put a fence around
valle *nm* : valley
valor *nm* **1** : value, worth **2** VALENTÍA : courage, valor **3 objetos de** ～ : valuables **4 sin** ～ : worthless **5** ～**es** *nmpl* : values, principles **6** ～**es** *nmpl* : securities, bonds — **valoración** *nf, pl* **-ciones** : valuation — **valorar** *vt* : evaluate, assess
vals *nm* : waltz
válvula *nf* : valve
vamos → **ir**
vampiro *nm* : vampire
van → **ir**
vanagloriarse *vr* : boast, brag
vándalo *nm* : vandal — **vandalismo** : vandalism
vanguardia *nf* **1** : vanguard **2** : avant-garde (in art, music, etc.) **3 a la** ～ : at/in the forefront
vanidad *nf* : vanity — **vanidoso, -sa** *adj* : vain, conceited
vano, -na *adj* **1** INÚTIL : vain, useless **2** SUPERFICIAL : empty, hollow **3 en vano** : in vain
vapor *nm* **1** : steam, vapor **2 al** ～ : steamed — **vaporizador** *nm* : vaporizer — **vaporizar** {21} *vt* : vaporize
vaquero, -ra *n* : cowboy *m*, cowgirl *f* — **vaqueros** *nmpl* : jeans

vara *nf* **1** : stick, rod **2** : staff (of office)
varado, -da *adj* : stranded
variar {85} *vt* **1** : vary **2** CAMBIAR : change, alter — *vi* : vary, change — **variable** *adj* & *nf* : variable — **variación** *nf, pl* **-ciones** : variation — **variado, -da** *adj* : varied — **variante** *nf* : variant
varicela *nf* : chicken pox
varicoso, -sa *adj* : varicose
variedad *nf* : variety
varilla *nf* : rod, stick
vario, -ria *adj* **1** : varied **2** ~s *pl* : several
varita *nf* : wand
variz *nf, pl* **-rices** *or* **várices** : varicose vein
varón *nm, pl* **-rones 1** : man, male **2** NIÑO : boy — **varonil** *adj* : manly
vas → **ir**
vasco, -ca *adj* : Basque — **vasco** *nm* : Basque (language)
vasija *nf* : container, vessel
vaso *nm* **1** : glass **2** : vessel (in anatomy)
vástago *nm* **1** : offspring, descendent **2** BROTE : shoot **3** VARILLA : rod
vasto, -ta *adj* : vast
vaticinar *vt* : prophesy, predict — **vaticinio** *nm* : prophecy
vatio *nm* : watt
vaya, etc. → **ir**
Vd., Vds. → **usted**
ve, etc. → **ir, ver**
vecinal *adj* : local
vecino, -na *n* **1** : neighbor **2** HABITANTE : resident, inhabitant — ~ *adj* : neighboring — **vecindad** *nf* : neighborhood, vicinity — **vecindario** *nm* **1** : neighborhood **2** VECINOS : community, residents *pl*
vedar *vt* : prohibit — **veda** *nf* **1** : prohibition, ban **2** : closed season (for hunting and fishing) — **vedado** *nm* : preserve (for game, etc.)
vega *nf* : fertile lowland
vegetal *nm* : vegetable, plant — ~ *adj* : vegetable — **vegetación** *nf, pl* **-ciones** : vegetation — **vegetar** *vi* : vegetate — **vegetariano, -na** *adj* & *n* : vegetarian
vehemente *adj* : vehement
vehículo *nm* : vehicle
veinte *adj* & *nm* : twenty — **veinteavo, -va** *adj* : twentieth — **veinteavo** *nm* : twentieth — **veintena** *nf* : group of twenty, score
vejar *vt* : mistreat, humiliate — **vejación** *nf, pl* **-ciones** : humiliation
vejez *nf* : old age
vejiga *nf* **1** : bladder **2** AMPOLLA : blister
vela *nf* **1** : candle **2** : sail (of a ship) **3** VIGILIA : vigil **4 pasar la noche en** ~ : have a sleepless night
velada *nf* : evening (party)
velar *vt* **1** : hold a wake over **2** CUIDAR : watch over **3** : blur (a photograph) **4** OCULTAR : veil, mask — *vi* **1** : stay awake **2** ~ **por** : watch over — **velado, -da** *adj* **1** : veiled, hidden **2** : blurred (of a photograph)
velero *nm* : sailing ship
veleta *nf* : weather vane
vello *nm* **1** : body hair **2** PELUSA : down, fuzz — **vellón** *nm, pl* **-llones** : fleece — **velloso, -sa** *adj* : downy, fluffy — **velludo, -da** *adj* : hairy
velo *nm* : veil
veloz *adj, pl* **-loces** : fast, quick — **velocidad** *nf* **1** : speed, velocity **2** MARCHA : gear (of an automobile) — **velocímetro** *nm* : speedometer
vena *nf* **1** : vein **2** : grain (of wood) **3** DISPOSICIÓN : mood **4 tener** ~ **de** : have a talent for
venado *nm* **1** : deer **2** : venison (in cooking)
vencer {86} *vt* **1** : beat, defeat **2** SUPERAR : overcome — *vi* **1** : win **2** CADUCAR : expire — **vencerse** *vr* : collapse, give way — **vencedor, -dora** *adj* : winning — ~ *n* : winner — **vencido, -da** *adj* **1** : beaten, defeated **2** CADUCADO : expired **3** : due, payable (in finance) **4 darse por** ~ : give up — **vencimiento** *nm* **1** : expiration **2** : maturity (of a loan)
venda *nf* : bandage — **vendaje** *nm* : bandage, dressing — **vendar** *vt* : bandage **2** ~ **los ojos** : blindfold
vendaval *nm* : gale
vender *vt* : sell — **venderse** *vr* **1** : be sold **2 se vende** : for sale — **vendedor, -dora** *n* **1** : seller **2** : salesman *m*, saleswoman *f* (in a store)
vendimia *nf* : grape harvest
vendrá, etc. → **venir**
veneno *nm* **1** : poison **2** : venom (of a snake, etc.) — **venenoso, -sa** *adj* : poisonous
venerar *vt* : venerate, revere — **venerable** *adj* : venerable — **veneración** *nf, pl* **-ciones** : veneration, reverence
venéreo, -rea *adj* : venereal
venezolano, -na *adj* : Venezuelan
venga → **venir**
vengar {52} *vt* : avenge — **vengarse** *vr* : get even, take revenge — **venganza** *nf* : vengeance, revenge — **vengativo, -va** *adj* : vindictive, vengeful
venia *nf* **1** : permission **2** : pardon (in law)
venial *adj* : venial, petty
venir {87} *vi* **1** : come **2** LLEGAR : arrive **3** HALLARSE : be, appear **4** QUEDAR : fit **5 que viene** : coming, next **6** ~ **a ser** : turn out to be **7** ~ **bien** : be suitable — **venirse** *vr* **1** : come **2** ~ **abajo** : fall apart, col-

venta

lapse — **venida** *nf* **1** : arrival, coming **2** REGRESO : return — **venidero, -ra** *adj* : coming
venta *nf* **1** : sale, selling **2 en** ~ : for sale
ventaja *nf* : advantage — **ventajoso, -sa** *adj* : advantageous
ventana *nf* **1** : window **2** ~ **de la nariz** : nostril — **ventanilla** *nf* **1** : window (of a vehicle or airplane) **2** : ticket window, box office (of a theater, etc.)
ventilar *vt* : ventilate, air (out) — **ventilación** *nf, pl* **-ciones** : ventilation — **ventilador** *nm* : fan, ventilator
ventisca *nf* : blizzard — **ventisquero** *nm* : snowdrift
ventoso, -sa *adj* : windy — **ventosidad** *nf* : wind, flatulence
ventrílocuo, -cua *n* : ventriloquist
ventura *nf* **1** : fortune, luck **2** SATISFACCIÓN : happiness **3 a la** ~ : at random — **venturoso, -sa** *adj* : fortunate, happy
ver {88} *vt* **1** : see **2** : watch (television, etc.) — *vi* **1** : see **2 a** ~ *or* **vamos a** ~ : let's see **3 no tener nada que** ~ **con** : have nothing to do with **4 ya veremos** : we'll see — **verse** *vr* **1** : see oneself **2** HALLARSE : find oneself **3** ENCONTRARSE : see each other, meet
vera *nf* **1** : side, edge **2** : bank (of a river)
veracidad *nf* : truthfulness
verano *nm* : summer — **veraneante** *nmf* : summer vacationer — **veranear** *vi* : spend the summer — **veraniego, -ga** *adj* : summer
veras *nfpl* **de** ~ : really
veraz *adj, pl* **-races** : truthful
verbal *adj* : verbal
verbena *nf* : festival, fair
verbo *nm* : verb — **verboso, -sa** *adj* : verbose
verdad *nf* **1** : truth **2 de** ~ : really, truly **3** ¿**verdad?** : right?, isn't that so? — **verdaderamente** *adv* : really, truly — **verdadero, -dera** *adj* : true, real
verde *adj* **1** : green **2** : dirty, risqué (of a joke, etc.) — ~ *nm* : green — **verdor** *nm* : greenness
verdugo *nm* **1** : executioner, hangman **2** : cruel person, tyrant
verdura *nf* : vegetable(s), green(s)
vereda *nf* **1** : path, trail **2** *Lat* : sidewalk
veredicto *nm* : verdict
vergüenza *nf* **1** : shame **2** TIMIDEZ : bashfulness, shyness — **vergonzoso, -sa** *adj* **1** : shameful **2** TÍMIDO : bashful, shy
verídico, -ca *adj* : true, truthful
verificar {72} *vt* **1** : verify, confirm **2** EXAMINAR : test, check out — **verificarse** *vr* **1** : take place **2** : come true (of a prophecy,

etc.) — **verificación** *nf, pl* **-ciones** : verification
verja *nf* **1** : (iron) gate **2** : rails *pl* (of a fence) **3** ENREJADO : grating, grille
vermut *nm, pl* **-muts** : vermouth
vernáculo, -la *adj* : vernacular
verosímil *adj* **1** : probable, likely **2** CREÍBLE : credible
verraco *nm* : boar
verruga *nf* : wart
versar *vi* ~ **sobre** : deal with, be about — **versado, -da** *adj* ~ **en** : versed in
versátil *adj* **1** : versatile **2** VOLUBLE : fickle
versión *nf, pl* **-siones 1** : version **2** TRADUCCIÓN : translation
verso *nm* **1** : poem, verse **2** : line (of poetry)
vértebra *nf* : vertebra
verter {56} *vt* **1** : pour (out) **2** DERRAMAR : spill **3** TIRAR : dump — *vi* : flow — **vertedero** *nm* **1** : dump, landfill **2** DESAGÜE : drain, outlet
vertical *adj & nf* : vertical
vértice *nm* : vertex, apex
vertiente *nf* : slope
vértigo *nm* : vertigo, dizziness — **vertiginoso, -sa** *adj* : dizzy
vesícula *nf* **1** : blister **2** ~ **biliar** : gallbladder
vestíbulo *nm* : vestibule, hall, foyer
vestido *nm* **1** : dress **2** ROPA : clothing, clothes *pl*
vestigio *nm* : vestige, trace
vestir {54} *vt* **1** : dress, clothe **2** LLEVAR : wear — *vi* : dress — **vestirse** *vr* : get dressed — **vestimenta** *nf* : clothing — **vestuario** *nm* **1** : wardrobe, clothes *pl* **2** : dressing room (in a theater), locker room (in sports)
veta *nf* **1** : vein, seam **2** : grain (of wood)
vetar *vt* : veto
veteado, -da *adj* : streaked, veined
veterano, -na *adj & n* : veteran
veterinaria *nf* : veterinary medicine — **veterinario, -ria** *adj* : veterinary — ~ *n* : veterinarian
veto *nm* : veto
vetusto, -ta *adj* : ancient
vez *nf, pl* **veces 1** : time **2** TURNO : turn **3 a la** ~ : at the same time **4 a veces** : sometimes **5 de una** ~ : all at once **6 de una** ~ **para siempre** : once and for all **7 de** ~ **en cuando** : from time to time **8 dos veces** : twice **9 en** ~ **de** : instead of **10 una** ~ : once
vía *nf* **1** : way, road, route **2** MEDIO : means **3** : track, line (of a railroad) **4** : (anatomical) tract **5 en** ~ **de** : in the process of — ~ *prep* : via

viable *adj* : viable, feasible — **viabilidad** *nf*
: viability
viaducto *nm* : viaduct
viajar *vi* : travel — **viajante** *nmf* : traveling
salesperson — **viaje** *nm* : trip, journey — **viajero, -ra** *adj* : traveling — ~ *n* 1 : traveler
2 PASAJERO : passenger
vial *adj* : road, traffic
víbora *nf* : viper
vibrar *vi* : vibrate — **vibración** *nf, pl*
-ciones : vibration — **vibrante** *adj* : vibrant
vicario, -ria *n* : vicar
vicepresidente, -ta *n* : vice president
viceversa *adv* : vice versa
vicio *nm* 1 : vice 2 MALA COSTUMBRE : bad
habit 3 DEFECTO : defect — **viciado, -da**
adj 1 : corrupt 2 : stuffy, stale (of air, etc.)
— **viciar** *vt* 1 : corrupt 2 ESTROPEAR
: spoil, pollute — **vicioso, -sa** *adj* : depraved, corrupt
vicisitud *nf* : vicissitude
víctima *nf* : victim
victoria *nf* : victory — **victorioso, -sa** *adj*
: victorious
vid *nf* : vine, grapevine
vida *nf* 1 : life 2 DURACIÓN : lifetime 3 de
por ~ : for life 4 estar con ~ : be alive
video *or* **vídeo** *nm* 1 : video 2 : VCR,
videocassette recorder
vidrio *nm* : glass — **vidriado** *nm* : glaze —
vidriar *vt* : glaze — **vidriera** *nf* 1 : stained-
glass window 2 : glass door 3 *Lat* : shopwindow — **vidrioso, -sa** *adj* 1 : delicate (of
a subject, etc.) 2 **ojos vidriosos** : glassy
eyes
vieira *nf* : scallop
viejo, -ja *adj* : old — ~ *n* 1 : old man *m*, old
woman *f* 2 **hacerse** ~ : get old
viene, etc. → **venir**
viento *nm* : wind
vientre *nm* 1 : abdomen, belly 2 MATRIZ
: womb 3 INTESTINO : bowels *pl*
viernes *nms & pl* 1 : Friday 2 **Viernes
Santo** : Good Friday
vietnamita *adj & nm* : Vietnamese
viga *nf* : beam, girder
vigencia *nf* 1 : validity 2 **entrar en** ~ : go
into effect — **vigente** *adj* : valid, in force
vigésimo, -ma *adj & n* : twentieth
vigía *nmf* : lookout
vigilar *vt* : look after, watch over — *vi* : keep
watch — **vigilancia** *nf* 1 : vigilance 2 **bajo**
~ : under surveillance — **vigilante** *adj*
: vigilant — ~ *nmf* : watchman, guard —
vigilia *nf* 1 : wakefulness 2 : vigil (in religion)
vigor *nm* 1 : vigor 2 **entrar en** ~ : go into
effect — **vigorizante** *adj* : invigorating —
vigoroso, -sa *adj* : vigorous

VIH *nm* : HIV
vil *adj* : vile, despicable — **vileza** *nf* 1 : vile-
ness 2 : despicable act — **vilipendiar** *vt*
: revile
villa *nf* 1 : town, village 2 : villa (house)
villancico *nm* : (Christmas) carol
villano, -na *n* : villain
vilo *nm* **en** ~ : suspended, in the air
vinagre *nm* : vinegar — **vinagrera** *nf* : cruet
— **vinagreta** *nf* : vinaigrette
vincular *vt* : tie, link — **vínculo** *nm* : link,
tie, bond
vindicar *vt* 1 : vindicate 2 VENGAR : avenge
vino¹, etc. → **venir**
vino² *nm* : wine
viña *nf or* **viñedo** *nm* : vineyard
vio, etc. → **ver**
viola *nf* : viola
violar *vt* 1 : violate (a law, etc.) 2 : rape (a
person) — **violación** *nf, pl* **-ciones** 1 : violation, offense 2 : rape (of a person)
violencia *nf* : violence, force — **violentar** *vt*
1 : force 2 : break into (a house, etc.) — **vi-
olentarse** *vr* 1 : force oneself 2 AVERGON-
ZARSE : be embarrassed — **violento, -ta** *adj*
1 : violent 2 INCÓMODO : awkward, embarrassing
violeta *adj & nm* : violet (color) — ~ *nf*
: violet (flower)
violín *nm, pl* **-lines** : violin — **violinista** *nmf*
: violinist — **violoncelista** *or* **violonche-
lista** *nmf* : cellist — **violoncelo** *or* **vio-
lonchelo** *nm* : cello, violoncello
virar *vi* : turn, change direction — **viraje** *nm*
1 : turn, swerve 2 CAMBIO : change
virgen *adj & nmf, pl* **vírgenes** : virgin —
virginal *adj* : virginal — **virginidad** *nf* : virginity
viril *adj* : virile — **virilidad** *nf* : virility
virtual *adj* : virtual
virtud *nf* 1 : virtue 2 **en** ~ **de** : by virtue of
— **virtuoso, -sa** *adj* : virtuous — ~ *n* : virtuoso
viruela *nf* 1 : smallpox 2 **picado de** ~**s**
: pockmarked
virulento, -ta *adj* : virulent
virus *nms & pl* : virus
visa *nf Lat* : visa — **visado** *nm Spain* : visa
vísceras *nfpl* : entrails — **visceral** *adj* : visceral
viscoso, -sa *adj* : viscous — **viscosidad** *nf*
: viscosity
visera *nf* : visor
visible *adj* : visible — **visibilidad** *nf* : visibility
visión *nf, pl* **-siones** 1 : eyesight 2 APARI-
CIÓN : vision, illusion 3 PUNTO DE VISTA
: view, perspective — **visionario, -ria** *adj &
n* : visionary

visitar vt : visit — **visita** nf 1 : visit 2 **tener** ~ : have company — **visitante** adj : visiting — ~ nmf : visitor
vislumbrar vt : make out, discern — **vislumbre** nf 1 : glimpse, sign 2 RESPLANDOR : glimmer, gleam
viso nm 1 : sheen 2 **tener** ~s **de** : seem, show signs of
visón nm, pl **-sones** : mink
víspera nf : eve, day before
vista nf 1 : vision, eyesight 2 MIRADA : look, gaze 3 PANORAMA : view, vista 4 : hearing (in court) 5 **a primera** ~ or **a simple** ~ : at first sight 6 **hacer la** ~ **gorda** : turn a blind eye 7 **perder de** ~ : lose sight of — **vistazo** nm 1 : glance 2 **echar un** ~ : have a look
visto, -ta adj 1 : clear, obvious 2 COMÚN : commonly seen 3 **estar bien** ~ : be approved of 4 **estar mal** ~ : be frowned upon 5 **nunca** ~ : unheard-of 6 **por lo visto** : apparently 7 **visto que** : since, given that — **visto** nm ~ **bueno** : approval — ~ pp → **ver**
vistoso, -sa adj : colorful, bright
visual adj : visual — **visualizar** {21} vt : visualize
vital adj : vital — **vitalicio, -cia** adj : life, for life — **vitalidad** nf : vitality
vitamina nf : vitamin
viticultor, -tora n : winegrower — **viticultura** nf : wine growing
vitorear vt : cheer, acclaim
vítreo, -trea adj : glassy
vitrina nf 1 : showcase, display case 2 Lat : shopwindow
vituperar vt : censure — **vituperio** nm : censure
viudo, -da n : widower m, widow f — ~ adj : widowed — **viudez** nf : widowerhood, widowhood
viva nm dar ~s : cheer
vivacidad nf : vivacity, liveliness
vivamente adv 1 : vividly 2 PROFUNDAMENTE : deeply, acutely
vivaz adj, pl **-vaces** 1 : lively, vivacious 2 AGUDO : vivid, sharp
víveres nmpl : provisions, supplies
vivero nm 1 : nursery (for plants) 2 : (fish) hatchery, (oyster) bed
viveza nf 1 : liveliness 2 : vividness (of colors, descriptions, etc.) 3 ASTUCIA : sharpness (of mind) — **vívido, -da** adj : vivid
vividor, -dora n : freeloader
vivienda nf 1 : housing 2 MORADA : dwelling
viviente adj : living
vivificar {72} vt : enliven
vivir vi 1 : live, be alive 2 ~ **de** : live on —

vt : experience, live (through) — ~ nm 1 : life, lifestyle 2 **de mal** ~ : disreputable — **vivo, -va** adj 1 : alive 2 INTENSO : intense, bright 3 ANIMADO : lively 4 ASTUTO : sharp, quick 5 **en vivo** : live
vocablo nm : word — **vocabulario** nm : vocabulary
vocación nf, pl **-ciones** : vocation — **vocacional** adj : vocational
vocal adj : vocal — ~ nmf : member (of a committee, etc.) — ~ nf : vowel — **vocalista** nmf : singer, vocalist
vocear v : shout — **vocerío** nm : shouting
vociferar vi : shout
vodka nmf : vodka
volar {19} vi 1 : fly 2 : blow away (of papers, etc.) 3 fam : disappear 4 **irse volando** : rush off — vt : blow up — **volador, -dora** adj : flying — **volandas: en** ~ adv phr : in the air — **volante** adj : flying — ~ nm 1 : steering wheel 2 : shuttlecock (in badminton) 3 : flounce (of fabric) 4 Lat : flier, circular
volátil adj : volatile
volcán nm, pl **-canes** : volcano — **volcánico, -ca** adj : volcanic
volcar {82} vt 1 : upset, knock over 2 VACIAR : empty out — vi : overturn — **volcarse** vr 1 : overturn, tip over 2 ~ **en** : throw oneself into
voleibol nm : volleyball
voltaje nm : voltage
voltear vt : turn over, turn upside down — **voltearse** vr Lat : turn (around) — **voltereta** nf : somersault
voltio nm : volt
voluble adj : fickle
volumen nm, pl **-lúmenes** : volume — **voluminoso, -sa** adj : voluminous
voluntad nf 1 : will 2 DESEO : wish 3 INTENCIÓN : intention 4 **a** ~ : at will 5 **buena** ~ : goodwill 6 **mala** ~ : ill will 7 **fuerza de** ~ : willpower — **voluntario, -ria** adj : voluntary — ~ n : volunteer — **voluntarioso, -sa** adj 1 : willing 2 TERCO : stubborn, willful
voluptuoso, -sa adj : voluptuous
volver {89} vi 1 : return, come or go back 2 ~ **a** : return to, do again 3 ~ **en sí** : come to — vt 1 : turn, turn over, turn inside out 2 CONVERTIR EN : turn (into) 3 ~ **loco** : drive crazy — **volverse** vr 1 : turn (around) 2 HACERSE : become
vomitar vi : vomit — vt 1 : vomit 2 : spew (out) — **vómito** nm 1 : (action of) vomiting 2 : vomit
voraz adj, pl **-races** : voracious
vos pron Lat : you
vosotros, -tras pron Spain : you, yourselves

votar *vi* : vote — *vt* : vote for — **votación** *nf,*
  pl **-ciones** : vote, voting — **votante** *nmf*
  : voter — **voto** *nm* **1** : vote **2** : vow (in religion)
voy → **ir**
voz *nf, pl* **voces 1** : voice **2** GRITO : shout,
  yell **3** VOCABLO : word, term **4** RUMOR
  : rumor **5 dar voces** : shout **6 en ~ alta**
  : loudly **7 en ~ baja** : softly
vuelco *nm* : upset, overturning
vuelo *nm* **1** : flight **2** : (action of) flying **3**
  : flare (of clothing) **4 al ~** : on the wing
vuelta *nf* **1** : turn **2** REVOLUCIÓN : circle, revolution **3** CURVA : bend, curve **4** REGRESO
  : return **5** : round, lap (in sports) **6** PASEO
  : walk, drive, ride **7** REVÉS : back, other side
  8 *Spain* : change **9 dar ~s** : spin **10 estar**
  de ~ : be back — **vuelto** *nm Lat* : change
vuestro, -tra *adj Spain* : your, of yours — **~**
  pron Spain (with definite article) : yours
vulgar *adj* **1** : vulgar **2** CORRIENTE : common — **vulgaridad** *nf* **1** : vulgarity **2** BA-
  NALIDAD : banality — **vulgo** *nm* **el ~** : the
  masses, common people
vulnerable *adj* : vulnerable — **vulnerabili-**
  dad *nf* : vulnerability

WXYZ

w *nf* : w, 24th letter of the Spanish alphabet
wáter *nm Spain* : toilet
whisky *nm, pl* **-skys** *or* **-skies** : whiskey
x *nf* : x, 25th letter of the Spanish alphabet
xenofobia *nf* : xenophobia
xilófono *nm* : xylophone
y[1] *nf* : y, 26th letter of the Spanish alphabet
y[2] *conj* : and
ya *adv* **1** : already **2** AHORA : (right) now **3**
  MÁS TARDE : later, soon **4 ~ no** : no longer
  5 ~ que : now that, since, inasmuch as
yacer {90} *vi* : lie (on or in the ground) —
  yacimiento *nm* : bed, deposit
yanqui *adj & nmf* : Yankee
yate *nm* : yacht
yegua *nf* : mare
yelmo *nm* : helmet
yema *nf* **1** : bud, shoot **2** : yolk (of an egg)
  3 *or* **~ del dedo** : fingertip
yerba *nf* **1** *or* **~ mate** : maté **2** → **hierba**
yermo, -ma *adj* : barren, deserted — **yermo**
  nm : wasteland
yerno *nm* : son-in-law
yerro *nm* : blunder, mistake
yerto, -ta *adj* : stiff
yesca *nf* : tinder
yeso *nm* **1** : gypsum **2** : plaster (for art,
  construction)
yo *pron* **1** (*subject*) : I **2** (*object*) : me **3 soy**
  ~ : it is I, it's me — **~** *nm* : ego, self
yodo *nm* : iodine
yoga *nm* : yoga
yogurt *or* **yogur** *nm* : yogurt
yuca *nf* : yucca
yugo *nm* : yoke (of oxen)
yugoslavo, -va *adj* : Yugoslavian
yugular *adj* : jugular

yunque *nm* : anvil
yunta *nf* : yoke
yuxtaponer {60} *vt* : juxtapose — **yuxta-**
  posición *nf, pl* **-ciones** : juxtaposition
z *nf* : z, 27th letter of the Spanish alphabet
zacate *nm Lat* : grass
zafar *vt Lat* : loosen, untie — **zafarse** *vr* **1**
  : come undone **2** : get free of (an obligation, etc.)
zafio, -fia *adj* : coarse
zafiro *nm* : sapphire
zaga *nf* **a la ~** *or* **en ~** : behind, in the rear
zaguán *nm, pl* **-guanes** : (entrance) hall
zaherir {76} *vt* : hurt (s.o.'s feelings)
zaino, -na *adj* : chestnut (color)
zalamería *nf* : flattery — **zalamero, -ra** *adj*
  : flattering — **~** *n* : flatterer
zambullirse {38} *vr* : dive, plunge — **zam-**
  bullida *nf* : dive, plunge
zanahoria *nf* : carrot
zancada *nf* : stride, step — **zancadilla** *nf* **1**
  : trip, stumble **2 hacer una ~ a algn** : trip
  s.o. up
zancos *nmpl* : stilts
zancudo *nm Lat* : mosquito
zángano, -na *n fam* : lazy person, slacker —
  zángano *nm* : drone (bee)
zanja *nf* : ditch, trench — **zanjar** *vt* : settle,
  resolve
zapallo *nm Lat* : pumpkin — **zapallito** *nm*
  Lat : zucchini
zapapico *nm* : pickax
zapato *nm* : shoe — **zapatería** *nf* : shoe store
  — **zapatero, -ra** *n* : shoemaker, cobbler —
  zapatilla *nf* **1** : slipper **2** : sneaker (for
  sports, etc.)
zar *nm* : czar

zarandear *vt* **1** : sift **2** SACUDIR : shake
zarcillo *nm* : earring
zarpa *nf* : paw
zarpar *vi* : set sail, raise anchor
zarza *nf* : bramble — **zarzamora** *nf* : blackberry
zigzag *nm, pl* **-zags** *or* **-zagues** : zigzag —
  zigzaguear *vi* : zigzag
zinc *nm* : zinc
zíper *nm Lat* : zipper
zircón *nm, pl* **-cones** : zircon
zócalo *nm* **1** : base (of a column, etc.) **2**
  : baseboard (of a wall) **3** *Lat* : main square,
  plaza
zodíaco *nm* : zodiac
zona *nf* : zone, area
zoo *nm* : zoo — **zoología** *nf* : zoology — **zo-**

ológico, -ca *adj* : zoological — **zoológico**
  nm : zoo — **zoólogo, -ga** *n* : zoologist
zopilote *nm Lat* : buzzard
zoquete *nmf fam* : oaf, blockhead
zorrillo *nm Lat* : skunk
zorro, -rra *n* : fox, vixen *f* — ~ *adj* : foxy,
  sly
zozobra *nf* : anxiety, worry — **zozobrar** *vi*
  : capsize
zueco *nm* : clog (shoe)
zumbar *vi* : buzz — *vt fam* : hit, beat —
  zumbido *nm* : buzzing
zumo *nf* : juice
zurcir {83} *vt* : darn, mend
zurdo, -da *adj* : left-handed — ~ *n* : left-
  handed person — **zurda** *nf* : left hand
zutano, -na → fulano

English-Spanish Dictionary

A

a[1] *n, pl* **a's** *or* **as** : a *f*, primera letra del alfabeto inglés

a[2] *art* (**an** *before vowel or silent h*) **1** : un *m*, una *f* **2** PER : por, a la, al

aback *adv* **be taken** ～ : quedarse desconcertado

abacus *n, pl* **abaci** *or* **abacuses** : ábaco *m*

abandon *vt* **1** DESERT : abandonar **2** GIVE UP : renunciar a — ～ *n* : desenfreno *m* — **abandonment** *n* : abandono *m*

abashed *adj* : avergonzado

abate *vi* **abated; abating** : amainar, disminuir

abattoir *n* : matadero *m*

abbey *n, pl* **-beys** : abadía *f* — **abbot** *n* : abad *m*

abbreviate *vt* **-ated; -ating** : abreviar — **abbreviation** *n* : abreviatura *f*, abreviación *f*

abdicate *v* **-cated; -cating** : abdicar — **abdication** *n* : abdicación *f*

abdomen *n* : abdomen *m*, vientre *m* — **abdominal** *adj* : abdominal

abduct *vt* : secuestrar — **abduction** *n* : secuestro *m*

aberration *n* : aberración *f*

abet *vt* **abetted; abetting** *or* **aid and** ～ : ser cómplice de

abeyance *n* : desuso *m*

abhor *vt* **-horred; -horring** : aborrecer

abide *v* **abode** *or* **abided; abiding** *vt* : soportar, tolerar — *vi* **1** DWELL : morar **2** ～ **by** : atenerse a

ability *n, pl* **-ties** **1** CAPABILITY : aptitud *f*, capacidad *f* **2** SKILL : habilidad *f*

abject *adj* : miserable, desdichado

ablaze *adj* : en llamas

able *adj* **abler; ablest** **1** CAPABLE : capaz, hábil **2** COMPETENT : competente

abnormal *adj* : anormal — **abnormality** *n, pl* **-ties** : anormalidad *f*

aboard *adv* : a bordo — ～ *prep* : a bordo de

abode *n* : morada *f*, domicilio *m*

abolish *vt* : abolir, suprimir — **abolition** *n* : abolición *f*

abominable *adj* : abominable, aborrecible — **abomination** *n* : abominación *f*

aborigine *n* : aborigen *mf*

abort *vt* : abortar — **abortion** *n* : aborto *m* — **abortive** *adj* UNSUCCESSFUL : malogrado

abound *vi* ～ **in** : abundar en

about *adv* **1** APPROXIMATELY : aproximadamente, más o menos **2** AROUND : alrededor **3 be** ～ **to** : estar a punto de **4 be up and** ～ : estar levantado — ～ *prep* **1** AROUND : alrededor de **2** CONCERNING : acerca de, sobre

above *adv* : arriba — ～ *prep* **1** : encima de **2** ～ **all** : sobre todo — **aboveboard** *adj* : honrado

abrasive *adj* **1** : abrasivo **2** BRUSQUE : brusco, mordaz

abreast *adv* **1** : al lado **2 keep** ～ **of** : mantenerse al corriente de

abridge *vt* **abridged; abridging** : abreviar

abroad *adv* **1** : en el extranjero **2** WIDELY : por todas partes **3 go** ～ : ir al extranjero

abrupt *adj* **1** SUDDEN : repentino **2** BRUSQUE : brusco

abscess *n* : absceso *m*

absence *n* **1** : ausencia *f* **2** LACK : falta *f*, carencia *f* — **absent** *adj* : ausente — **absentee** *n* : ausente *mf* — **absentminded** *adj* : distraído, despistado

absolute *adj* : absoluto — **absolutely** *adv* : absolutamente

absolve *vt* **-solved; -solving** : absolver

absorb *vt* : absorber — **absorbent** *adj* : absorbente — **absorption** *n* : absorción *f*

abstain *vi* ～ **from** : abstenerse de — **abstinence** *n* : abstinencia *f*

abstract *adj* : abstracto — ～ *vt* : extraer — ～ *n* : resumen *m* — **abstraction** *n* : abstracción *f*

absurd *adj* : absurdo — **absurdity** *n, pl* **-ties** : absurdo *m*

abundant *adj* : abundante — **abundance** *n* : abundancia *f*

abuse *vt* **abused; abusing** **1** MISUSE : abusar de **2** MISTREAT : maltratar **3** REVILE : insultar — ～ *n* **1** : abuso *m* **2** INSULTS : insultos *mpl* — **abusive** *adj* : injurioso

abut *vi* **abutted; abutting** ～ **on** : colindar con

abyss *n* : abismo *m* — **abysmal** *adj* : atroz, pésimo

academy *n, pl* **-mies** : academia *f* — **academic** *adj* **1** : académico **2** THEORETICAL : teórico

accelerate *v* **-ated; -ating** : acelerar — **acceleration** *n* : aceleración *f*

accent *vt* : acentuar — ～ *n* : acento *m* — **accentuate** *vt* **-ated; -ating** : acentuar, subrayar

accept *vt* : aceptar — **acceptable** *adj* : aceptable — **acceptance** *n* **1** : aceptación *f* **2** APPROVAL : aprobación *f*

access *n* : acceso *m* — **accessible** *adj* : accesible, asequible

accessory *n, pl* **-ries** **1** : accesorio *m* **2** ACCOMPLICE : cómplice *mf*

accident *n* **1** MISHAP : accidente *m* **2** CHANCE : casualidad *f* — **accidental** *adj* : accidental — **accidentally** *adv* **1** BY CHANCE : por casualidad **2** UNINTENTIONALLY : sin querer

acclaim *vt* : aclamar — ~ *n* : aclamación *f*

acclimatize *vt* **-tized; -tizing** : aclimatar

accommodate *vt* **-dated; -dating** **1** ADAPT : acomodar, adaptar **2** SATISFY : complacer, satisfacer **3** HOLD : tener cabida para — **accomodation** *n* **1** : adaptación *f* **2** ~s *npl* LODGING : alojamiento *m*

accompany *vt* **-nied; -nying** : acompañar

accomplice *n* : cómplice *mf*

accomplish *vt* : realizar, llevar a cabo — **accomplishment** *n* **1** COMPLETION : realización *f* **2** ACHIEVEMENT : logro *m*, éxito *m*

accord *n* **1** AGREEMENT : acuerdo *m* **2** **of one's own** ~ : voluntariamente — **accordance** *n* **in** ~ **with** : conforme a, de acuerdo con — **accordingly** *adv* : en consecuencia — **according to** *prep* : según

accordion *n* : acordeón *m*

accost *vt* : abordar

account *n* **1** : cuenta *f* **2** REPORT : relato *m*, informe *m* **3** WORTH : importancia *f* **4** **on** ~ **of** : a causa de, debido a **5** **on no** ~ : de ninguna manera — ~ *vi* ~ **for** : dar cuenta de, explicar — **accountable** *adj* : responsable — **accountant** *n* : contador *m*, -dora *f* Lat; contable *mf* Spain — **accounting** *n* : contabilidad *f*

accrue *vi* **-crued; -cruing** : acumularse

accumulate *v* **-lated; -lating** *vt* : acumular — *vi* : acumularse — **accumulation** *n* : acumulación *f*

accurate *adj* : exacto, preciso — **accuracy** *n* : exactitud *f*, precisión *f*

accuse *vt* **-cused; -cusing** : acusar — **accusation** *n* : acusación *f*

accustomed *adj* **1** : acostumbrado **2** **become** ~ **to** : acostumbrarse a

ace *n* : as *m*

ache *vi* **ached; aching** : doler — ~ *n* : dolor *m*

achieve *vt* **achieved; achieving** : lograr, realizar — **achievement** *n* : logro *m*, éxito *m*

acid *adj* : ácido — ~ *n* : ácido *m*

acknowledge *vt* **-edged; -edging** **1** ADMIT : admitir **2** RECOGNIZE : reconocer **3** ~ **receipt of** : acusar recibo de — **acknowledgment** *n* **1** : reconocimiento *m* **2** THANKS : agradecimiento *m* **3** ~ **of receipt** : acuse *m* de recibo

acne *n* : acné *m*

acorn *n* : bellota *f*

acoustic *or* **acoustical** *adj* : acústico — **acoustics** *ns & pl* : acústica *f*

acquaint *vt* **1** ~ **s.o. with** : poner a algn al corriente de **2** **be** ~**ed with** : conocer a (una persona), saber (un hecho) — **acquaintance** *n* **1** : conocimiento *m* **2** : conocido *m*, -da *f* (persona)

acquire *vt* **-quired; -quiring** : adquirir — **acquisition** *n* : adquisición *f*

acquit *vt* **-quitted; -quitting** : absolver

acre *n* : acre *m* — **acreage** *n* : superficie *f* en acres

acrid *adj* : acre

acrobat *n* : acróbata *mf* — **acrobatic** *adj* : acrobático

acronym *n* : siglas *fpl*

across *adv* **1** : de un lado a otro **2** CROSSWISE : a través **3** **go** ~ : atravesar — ~ *prep* **1** : a través de **2** ~ **the street** : al otro lado de la calle

acrylic *n* : acrílico *m*

act *vi* **1** : actuar **2** PRETEND : fingir **3** FUNCTION : funcionar **4** ~ **as** : servir de — *vt* : interpretar (un papel) — ~ *n* **1** ACTION : acto *m*, acción *f* **2** DECREE : ley *f* **3** : acto *m* (en una obra de teatro), número *m* (en un espectáculo) — **acting** *adj* : interino

action *n* **1** : acción *f* **2** LAWSUIT : demanda *f* **3** **take** ~ : tomar medidas

activate *vt* **-vated; -vating** : activar

active *adj* **1** : activo **2** LIVELY : enérgico **3** ~ **volcano** : volcán *m* en actividad — **activity** *n, pl* **-ties** : actividad *f*

actor *n* : actor *m* — **actress** *n* : actriz *f*

actual *adj* : real, verdadero — **actually** *adv* : realmente, en realidad

acupuncture *n* : acupuntura *f*

acute *adj* **acuter; acutest** **1** : agudo **2** PERCEPTIVE : perspicaz

ad → **advertisement**

adamant *adj* : inflexible

adapt *vt* : adaptar — *vi* : adaptarse — **adaptable** *adj* : adaptable — **adaptation** *n* : adaptación *f* — **adapter** *n* : adaptador *m*

add *vt* **1** : añadir **2** *or* ~ **up** : sumar — *vi* : sumar

addict *n* **1** : adicto *m*, -ta *f* **2** *or* **drug** ~ : drogadicto *m*, -ta *f*; toxicómano *m*, -na *f* — **addiction** *n* : dependencia *f*

addition *n* **1** : suma *f* (en matemáticas) **2** ADDING : adición *f* **3** **in** ~ : además — **additional** *adj* : adicional — **additive** *n* : aditivo *m*

address *vt* **1** : dirigirse a (una persona) **2** : ponerle la dirección a (una carta) **3** : tratar (un asunto) — ~ *n* **1** : dirección *f*, domicilio *m* **2** SPEECH : discurso *m*

adept *adj* : experto, hábil

adequate *adj* : adecuado, suficiente
adhere *vi* **-hered; -hering 1** STICK : adherirse **2** ~ **to** : observar — **adherence** *n* **1** : adhesión *f* **2** : observancia *f* (de una ley, etc.) — **adhesive** *adj* : adhesivo — ~ *n* : adhesivo *m*
adjacent *adj* : adyacente, contiguo
adjective *n* : adjetivo *m*
adjoining *adj* : contiguo, vecino
adjourn *vt* : aplazar, suspender — *vi* : suspenderse
adjust *vt* : ajustar, arreglar — *vi* : adaptarse — **adjustable** *adj* : ajustable — **adjustment** *n* : ajuste *m* (a una máquina, etc.), adaptación *f* (de una persona)
ad-lib *v* **-libbed; -libbing** : improvisar
administer *vt* : administrar — **administration** *n* : administración *f* — **administrative** *adj* : administrativo — **administrator** *n* : administrador *m*, -dora *f*
admirable *adj* : admirable
admiral *n* : almirante *m*
admire *vt* **-mired; -miring** : admirar — **admiration** *n* : admiración *f* — **admirer** *n* : admirador *m*, -dora *f*
admit *vt* **-mitted; -mitting 1** : admitir, dejar entrar **2** ACKNOWLEDGE : reconocer — **admission** *n* **1** ADMITTANCE : entrada *f*, admisión *f* **2** ACKNOWLEDGMENT : reconocimiento *m* — **admittance** *n* : admisión *f*, entrada *f*
admonish *vt* : amonestar, reprender
ado *n* **1** : alboroto *m*, bulla *f* **2 without further** ~ : sin más (preámbulos)
adolescent *n* : adolescente *mf* — **adolescence** *n* : adolescencia *f*
adopt *vt* : adoptar — **adoption** *n* : adopción *f*
adore *vt* **adored; adoring 1** : adorar **2** LIKE, LOVE : encantarle (algo a uno) — **adorable** *adj* : adorable — **adoration** *n* : adoración *f*
adorn *vt* : adornar — **adornment** *n* : adorno *m*
adrift *adj* & *adv* : a la deriva
adroit *adj* : diestro, hábil
adult *adj* : adulto — ~ *n* : adulto *m*, -ta *f*
adultery *n*, *pl* **-teries** : adulterio *m*
advance *v* **-vanced; -vancing** *vt* : adelantar — *vi* : avanzar, adelantarse — ~ *n* **1** : avance *m* **2** PROGRESS : adelanto *m* **3 in** ~ : por adelantado — **advancement** *n* : adelanto *m*, progreso *m*
advantage *n* **1** : ventaja *f* **2 take** ~ **of** : aprovecharse de — **advantageous** *adj* : ventajoso
advent *n* **1** ARRIVAL : llegada *f* **2 Advent** : Adviento *m*
adventure *n* : aventura *f* — **adventurous** *adj* **1** : intrépido **2** RISKY : arriesgado

adverb *n* : adverbio *m*
adversary *n*, *pl* **-saries** : adversario *m*, -ria *f*
adverse *adj* : adverso, desfavorable — **adversity** *n*, *pl* **-ties** : adversidad *f*
advertise *v* **-tised; -tising** *vt* : anunciar — *vi* : hacer publicidad — **advertisement** *n* : anuncio *m* — **advertiser** *n* : anunciante *mf* — **advertising** *n* : publicidad *f*
advice *n* : consejo *m*
advise *vt* **-vised; -vising 1** COUNSEL : aconsejar, asesorar **2** RECOMMEND : recomendar **3** INFORM : informar — **advisable** *adj* : aconsejable — **adviser** *n* : consejero *m*, -ra *f*; asesor *m*, -sora *f* — **advisory** *adj* : consultivo
advocate *vt* **-cated; -cating** : recomendar — ~ *n* : defensor *m*, -sora *f*
aerial *adj* : aéreo — ~ *n* : antena *f*
aerobics *ns* & *pl* : aeróbic *m*
aerodynamic *adj* : aerodinámico
aerosol *n* : aerosol *m*
aesthetic *adj* : estético
afar *adv* : lejos
affable *adj* : afable
affair *n* **1** : asunto *m*, cuestión *f* **2** *or* **love** ~ : amorío *m*, aventura *f*
affect *vt* **1** : afectar **2** FEIGN : fingir — **affection** *n* : afecto *m*, cariño *m* — **affectionate** *adj* : afectuoso, cariñoso
affinity *n*, *pl* **-ties** : afinidad *f*
affirm *vt* : afirmar — **affirmative** *adj* : afirmativo
affix *vt* : fijar, pegar
afflict *vt* : afligir — **affliction** *n* : aflicción *f*
affluent *adj* : próspero, adinerado
afford *vt* **1** : tener los recursos para, permitirse (el lujo de) **2** PROVIDE : brindar
affront *n* : afrenta *f*
afloat *adv* & *adj* : a flote
afoot *adj* : en marcha
afraid *adj* **1 be** ~ : tener miedo **2 I'm** ~ **not** : me temo que no
African *adj* : africano
after *adv* **1** AFTERWARD : después **2** BEHIND : detrás, atrás — ~ *conj* : después de (que) — ~ *prep* **1** : después de **2** ~ **all** : después de todo **3 it's ten** ~ **five** : son las cinco y diez
aftereffect *n* : efecto *m* secundario
aftermath *n* : consecuencias *fpl*
afternoon *n* : tarde *f*
afterward *or* **afterwards** *adv* : después, más tarde
again *adv* **1** : otra vez, de nuevo **2** ~ **and** ~ : una y otra vez **3 then** ~ : por otra parte
against *prep* : contra, en contra de
age *n* **1** : edad *f* **2** ERA : era *f*, época *f* **3 be of** ~ : ser mayor de edad **4 for** ~**s** : hace

siglos **5 old** ⁓ : vejez *f* — ⁓ *vi* **aged;**
aging : envejecer — **aged** *adj* **1** OLD : anciano, viejo **2 children** ⁓ **10 to 17** : niños de 10 a 17 años
agency *n, pl* **-cies** : agencia *f*
agenda *n* : orden *m* del día
agent *n* : agente *mf*, representante *mf*
aggravate *vt* **-vated; -vating 1** WORSEN : agravar, empeorar **2** ANNOY : irritar
aggregate *adj* : total, global — ⁓ *n* : total *m*
aggression *n* : agresión *f* — **aggressive** *adj* : agresivo — **aggressor** *n* : agresor *m*, -sora *f*
aghast *adj* : horrorizado
agile *adj* : ágil — **agility** *n, pl* **-ties** : agilidad *f*
agitate *v* **-tated; -tating** *vt* **1** SHAKE : agitar **2** TROUBLE : inquietar — **agitation** *n* : agitación *f*, inquietud *f*
agnostic *n* : agnóstico *m*, -ca *f*
ago *adv* **1** : hace **2 long** ⁓ : hace mucho tiempo
agony *n, pl* **-nies 1** PAIN : dolor *m* **2** ANGUISH : angustia *f* — **agonize** *vi* **-nized; -nizing** : atormentarse — **agonizing** *adj* : angustioso
agree *v* **agreed; agreeing** *vt* **1** : acordar **2** ⁓ **that** : estar de acuerdo de que — *vi* **1** : estar de acuerdo **2** CORRESPOND : concordar **3** ⁓ **to** : acceder a **4 this climate** ⁓**s with me** : este clima me sienta bien — **agreeable** *adj* **1** PLEASING : agradable **2** WILLING : dispuesto — **agreement** *n* : acuerdo *m*
agriculture *n* : agricultura *f* — **agricultural** *adj* : agrícola
aground *adv* **run** ⁓ : encallar
ahead *adv* **1** IN FRONT : delante, adelante **2** BEFOREHAND : por adelantado **3** LEADING : a la delantera **4 get** ⁓ : adelantar — **ahead of** *prep* **1** : delante de, antes de **2 get** ⁓ **of** : adelantarse a
aid *vt* : ayudar — ⁓ *n* : ayuda *f*, asistencia *f*
AIDS *n* : SIDA *m*, sida *m*
ail *vi* : estar enfermo — **ailment** *n* : enfermedad *f*
aim *vt* : apuntar (un arma), dirigir (una observación) — *vi* **1** : apuntar **2** ASPIRE : aspirar — ⁓ *n* **1** : puntería *f* **2** GOAL : propósito *m*, objetivo *m* — **aimless** *adj* : sin objetivo
air *vt or* ⁓ **out** : airear **2** EXPRESS : expresar **3** BROADCAST : emitir — ⁓ *n* **1** : aire *m* **2 be on the** ⁓ : estar en el aire — **air–conditioning** *n* : aire *m* acondicionado — **air conditioned** *n* : climatizado — **aircraft** *ns & pl* **1** : avión *m*, aeronave *f* **2** ⁓ **carrier** : portaaviones *m* — **air force** *n*

: fuerza *f* aérea — **airline** *n* : aerolínea *f*, línea *f* aérea — **airliner** *n* : avión *m* de pasajeros — **airmail** *n* : correo *m* aéreo — **airplane** *n* : avión *m* — **airport** *n* : aeropuerto *m* — **airstrip** *n* : pista *f* de aterrizaje — **airtight** *adj* : hermético — **airy** *adj* **airier; -est** : aireado, bien ventilado
aisle *n* **1** : pasillo *m* **2** : nave *f* lateral (de una iglesia)
ajar *adj* : entreabierto
akin *adj* ⁓ **to** : semejante a
alarm *n* **1** : alarma *f* **2** ANXIETY : inquietud *f* — *vt* : alarmar, asustar — **alarm clock** *n* : despertador *m*
alas *interj* : ¡ay!
album *n* : álbum *m*
alcohol *n* : alcohol *m* — **alcoholic** *adj* : alcohólico — ⁓ *n* : alcohólico *m*, -ca *f* — **alcoholism** *n* : alcoholismo *m*
alcove *n* : nicho *m*, hueco *m*
ale *n* : cerveza *f*
alert *adj* **1** WATCHFUL : alerta, atento **2** LIVELY : vivo — ⁓ *n* : alerta *f* — ⁓ *vt* : alertar, poner sobre aviso
alfalfa *n* : alfalfa *f*
alga *n, pl* **-gae** : alga *f*
algebra *n* : álgebra *f*
alias *adv* : alias — ⁓ *n* : alias *m*
alibi *n* : coartada *f*
alien *adj* : extranjero — ⁓ *n* **1** FOREIGNER : extranjero *m*, -ra *f* **2** EXTRATERRESTRIAL : extraterrestre *mf*
alienate *vt* **-ated; -ating** : enajenar — **alienation** *n* : enajenación *f*
alight *vi* **1** LAND : posarse **2** ⁓ **from** : apearse de
align *vt* : alinear — **alignment** *n* : alineación *f*
alike *adv* : igual, del mismo modo — ⁓ *adj* : parecido
alimony *n, pl* **-nies** : pensión *f* alimenticia
alive *adj* **1** LIVING : vivo, viviente **2** LIVELY : animado, activo
all *adv* **1** COMPLETELY : todo, completamente **2** ⁓ **the better** : tanto mejor **3** ⁓ **the more** : aún más, todavía más — ⁓ *adj* : todo — ⁓ *pron* **1** : todo, -da **2** ⁓ **in** ⁓ : en general **3 not at** ⁓ : de ninguna manera — **all–around** *adj* VERSATILE : completo
allay *vt* **1** ALLEVIATE : aliviar **2** CALM : aquietar
allege *vt* **-leged; -leging** : alegar — **allegation** *n* : alegato *m*, acusación *f* — **alleged** *adj* : presunto — **allegedly** *adv* : supuestamente
allegiance *n* : lealtad *f*
allegory *n, pl* **-ries** : alegoría *f* — **allegorical** *adj* : alegórico

allergy *n, pl* **-gies** : alergia *f* — **allergic** *adj* : alérgico
alleviate *vt* **-ated; -ating** : aliviar
alley *n, pl* **-leys** : callejón *m*
alliance *n* : alianza *f*
alligator *n* : caimán *m*
allocate *vt* **-cated; -cating** : asignar — **allocation** *n* : asignación *f*, reparto *m*
allot *vt* **-lotted; -lotting** : asignar — **allotment** *n* : reparto *m*, asignación *f*
allow *vt* **1** PERMIT : permitir **2** GRANT : dar, conceder **3** ADMIT : admitir **4** CONCEDE : reconocer — *vi* ~ **for** : tener en cuenta — **allowance** *n* **1** : pensión *f*, subsidio *m* **2** **make** ~**s for** : tener en cuenta, disculpar
alloy *n* : aleación *f*
all right *adv* **1** YES : sí, de acuerdo **2** WELL : bien **3** DEFINITELY : bien, sin duda — ~ *adj* : bien, bueno
allude *vi* **-luded; -luding** : aludir
allure *vt* **-lured; -luring** : atraer — **alluring** *adj* : atrayente, seductor
allusion *n* : alusión *f*
ally *vi* **-lied; -lying** ~ **oneself with** : aliarse con — ~ *n* : aliado *m*, -da *f*
almanac *n* : almanaque *m*
almighty *adj* : omnipotente, todopoderoso
almond *n* : almendra *f*
almost *adv* : casi
alms *ns & pl* : limosna *f*
alone *adv* : sólo, solamente, únicamente — ~ *adj* : solo
along *adv* **1** FORWARD : adelante **2** ~ **with** : con, junto con **3 all** ~ : desde el principio — ~ *prep* : por, a lo largo de — **alongside** *adv* : al costado — ~ *or* ~ **of** *prep* : al lado de
aloof *adj* : distante, reservado
aloud *adv* : en voz alta
alphabet *n* : alfabeto *m* — **alphabetical** *or* **alphabetic** *adj* : alfabético
already *adv* : ya
also *adv* : también, además
altar *n* : altar *m*
alter *vt* : alterar, modificar — **alteration** *n* : alteración *f*, modificación *f*
alternate *adj* : alterno — ~ *v* **-nated; -nating** : alternar — **alternating current** *n* : corriente *f* alterna — **alternative** *adj* : alternativo — ~ *n* : alternativa *f*
although *conj* : aunque
altitude *n* : altitud *f*
altogether *adv* **1** COMPLETELY : completamente, del todo **2** ON THE WHOLE : en suma, en general
aluminum *n* : aluminio *m*
always *adv* **1** : siempre **2** FOREVER : para siempre
am → **be**

amass *vt* : amasar, acumular
amateur *adj* : amateur — ~ *n* : amateur *mf*; aficionado *m*, -da *f*
amaze *vt* **amazed; amazing** : asombrar — **amazement** *n* : asombro *m* — **amazing** *adj* : asombroso
ambassador *n* : embajador *m*, -dora *f*
amber *n* : ámbar *m*
ambiguous *adj* : ambiguo — **ambiguity** *n*, *pl* **-tles** : ambigüedad *f*
ambition *n* : ambición *f* — **ambitious** *adj* : ambicioso
ambivalence *n* : ambivalencia *f* — **ambivalent** *adj* : ambivalente
amble *vi or* ~ **along** : andar sin prisa
ambulance *n* : ambulancia *f*
ambush *vt* : emboscar — ~ *n* : emboscada *f*
amen *interj* : amén
amenable *adj* ~ **to** : receptivo a
amend *vt* : enmendar — **amendment** *n* : enmienda *f* — **amends** *ns & pl* **make** ~ **for** : reparar
amenities *npl* : servicios *mpl*, comodidades *fpl*
American *adj* : americano
amethyst *n* : amatista *f*
amiable *adj* : amable, agradable
amicable *adj* : amigable, amistoso
amid *or* **amidst** *prep* : en medio de, entre
amiss *adv* **1** : mal **2 take sth** ~ : tomar algo a mal — ~ *adj* **1** WRONG : malo **2 something is** ~ : algo anda mal
ammonia *n* : amoníaco *m*
ammunition *n* : municiones *fpl*
amnesia *n* : amnesia *f*
amnesty *n, pl* **-ties** : amnistía *f*
among *prep* : entre
amorous *adj* : amoroso
amount *vi* **1** ~ **to** : equivaler a **2** ~ **to** TOTAL : sumar, ascender a — ~ *n* : cantidad *f*
amphibian *n* : anfibio *m* — **amphibious** *adj* : anfibio
amphitheater *n* : anfiteatro *m*
ample *adj* **-pler; -plest 1** SPACIOUS : amplio, extenso **2** ABUNDANT : abundante
amplify *vt* **-fied; -fying** : amplificar — **amplifier** *n* : amplificador *m*
amputate *vt* **-tated; -tating** : amputar — **amputation** *n* : amputación *f*
amuse *vt* **amused; amusing 1** : hacer reír, divertir **2** ENTERTAIN : entretener — **amusement** *n* : diversión *f* — **amusing** *adj* : divertido
an → **a²**
analogy *n, pl* **-gies** : analogía *f* — **analogous** *adj* : análogo
analysis *n, pl* **-yses** : análisis *m* — **analytic**

or **analytical** *adj* : analítico — **analyze** *vt* -**lyzed; -lyzing** : analizar
anarchy *n* : anarquía *f*
anatomy *n, pl* -**mies** : anatomía *f* — **anatomic** *or* **anatomical** *adj* : anatómico
ancestor *n* : antepasado *m*, -da *f* — **ancestral** *adj* : ancestral — **ancestry** *n* **1** DESCENT : linaje *m*, abolengo *m* **2** ANCESTORS : antepasados *mpl*, -das *fpl*
anchor *n* **1** : ancla *f* **2** : presentador *m*, -dora *f* (en televisión) — ⁓ *vt* **1** : anclar **2** FASTEN : sujetar — *vi* : anclar
anchovy *n, pl* -**vies** *or* -**vy** : anchoa *f*
ancient *adj* : antiguo, viejo
and *conj* **1** : y (e *before words beginning with i- or hi-*) **2 come** ⁓ **see** : ven a ver **3 more** ⁓ **more** : cada vez más **4 try** ⁓ **finish it soon** : trata de terminarlo pronto
anecdote *n* : anécdota *f*
anemia *n* : anemia *f* — **anemic** *adj* : anémico
anesthesia *n* : anestesia *f* — **anesthetic** *adj* : anestésico — ⁓ *n* : anestésico *m*
anew *adv* : de nuevo, nuevamente
angel *n* : ángel *m* — **angelic** *or* **angelical** *adj* : angélico
anger *vt* : enojar, enfadar — ⁓ *n* : ira *f*, enojo *m*, enfado *m*
angle *n* **1** : ángulo *m* **2** POINT OF VIEW : perspectiva *f*, punto *m* de vista — **angler** *n* : pescador *m*, -dora *f*
Anglo–Saxon *adj* : anglosajón
angry *adj* -**grier; -est** : enojado, enfadado
anguish *n* : angustia *f*
angular *adj* **1** : angular **2** ⁓ **features** : rasgos *mpl* angulosos
animal *n* : animal *m*
animate *adj* : animado — ⁓ *vt* -**mated; -mating** : animar — **animated** *adj* **1** : animado **2** ⁓ **cartoon** : dibujos *mpl* animados — **animation** *n* : animación *f*
animosity *n, pl* -**ties** : animosidad *f*
anise *n* : anís *m*
ankle *n* : tobillo *m*
annals *npl* : anales *mpl*
annex *vt* : anexar — ⁓ *n* : anexo *m*
annihilate *vt* -**lated; -lating** : aniquilar — **annihilation** *n* : aniquilación *f*
anniversary *n, pl* -**ries** : aniversario *m*
annotate *vt* -**tated; -tating** : anotar — **annotation** *n* : anotación *f*
announce *vt* -**nounced; -nouncing** : anunciar — **announcement** *n* : anuncio *m* — **announcer** *n* : locutor *m*, -tora *f*
annoy *vt* : fastidiar, molestar — **annoyance** *n* : fastidio *m*, molestia *f* — **annoying** *adj* : molesto, fastidioso
annual *adj* : anual — ⁓ *n* : anuario *m*
annuity *n, pl* -**ties** : anualidad *f*

annul *vt* **annulled; annulling** : anular — **annulment** *n* : anulación *f*
anoint *vt* : ungir
anomaly *n, pl* -**lies** : anomalía *f*
anonymous *adj* : anónimo — **anonymity** *n* : anonimato *m*
another *adj* **1** : otro **2 in** ⁓ **minute** : en un minuto más — ⁓ *pron* : otro, otra
answer *n* **1** REPLY : respuesta *f*, contestación *f* **2** SOLUTION : solución *f* — ⁓ *vt* **1** : contestar a, responder a **2** ⁓ **the door** : abrir la puerta — *vi* : contestar, responder
ant *n* : hormiga *f*
antagonize *vt* -**nized; -nizing** : provocar la enemistad de — **antagonism** *n* : antagonismo *m*
antarctic *adj* : antártico
antelope *n, pl* -**lope** *or* -**lopes** : antílope *m*
antenna *n, pl* -**nae** *or* -**nas** : antena *f*
anthem *n* : himno *m*
anthology *n, pl* -**gies** : antología *f*
anthropology *n* : antropología *f*
antibiotic *adj* : antibiótico — ⁓ *n* : antibiótico *m*
antibody *n, pl* -**bodies** : anticuerpo *m*
anticipate *vt* -**pated; -pating 1** FORESEE : anticipar, prever **2** EXPECT : esperar — **anticipation** *n* : anticipación *f*, expectación *f*
antics *npl* : payasadas *fpl*
antidote *n* : antídoto *m*
antifreeze *n* : anticongelante *m*
antipathy *n, pl* -**thies** : antipatía *f*
antiquated *adj* : anticuado
antique *adj* : antiguo — ⁓ *n* : antigüedad *f* — **antiquity** *n, pl* -**ties** : antigüedad *f*
anti–Semitic *adj* : antisemita
antiseptic *adj* : antiséptico — ⁓ *n* : antiséptico *m*
antisocial *adj* **1** : antisocial **2** UNSOCIABLE : poco sociable
antithesis *n, pl* -**eses** : antítesis *f*
antlers *npl* : cornamenta *f*
antonym *n* : antónimo *m*
anus *n* : ano *m*
anvil *n* : yunque *m*
anxiety *n, pl* -**eties 1** APPREHENSION : inquietud *f*, ansiedad *f* **2** EAGERNESS : anhelo *m* — **anxious** *adj* **1** WORRIED : inquieto, preocupado **2** EAGER : ansioso — **anxiously** *adv* : con ansiedad
any *adj* **1** SOMEWHAT : algo, un poco **2 it's not** ⁓ **good** : no sirve para nada **3 we can't wait** ⁓ **longer** : no podemos esperar más — ⁓ *adj* **1** : alguno **2** (*in negative constructions*) : ningún **3** WHATEVER : cualquier **4 in** ⁓ **case** : en todo caso — ⁓ *pron* **1** : alguno, -na **2** : ninguno, -na **3 do you want** ⁓ **more rice?** : ¿quieres más arroz?

anybody → **anyone**
anyhow *adv* **1** : de todas formas **2** HAPHAZ-
ARDLY : de cualquier modo
anymore *adv* **not** ~ : ya no
anyone *pron* **1** SOMEONE : alguien **2** WHO-
EVER : quienquiera **3 I don't see** ~ : no
veo a nadie
anyplace → **anywhere**
anything *pron* **1** SOMETHING : algo, alguna
cosa **2** (*in negative constructions*) : nada **3**
WHATEVER : cualquier cosa, lo que sea
anytime *adv* : en cualquier momento
anyway → **anyhow**
anywhere *adv* **1** : en cualquier parte, dondequiera **2** (*used in questions*) : en algún
sitio **3 I can't find it** ~ : no lo encuentro
por ninguna parte
apart *adv* **1** : aparte **2** ~ **from** : excepto,
aparte de **3 fall** ~ : deshacerse, hacerse
pedazos **4 live** ~ : vivir separados **5 take**
~ : desmontar, desmantelar
apartment *n* : apartamento *m*
apathy *n* : apatía *f* — **apathetic** *adj* : apático,
indiferente
ape *n* : simio *m*
aperture *n* : abertura *f*
apex *n, pl* **apexes** *or* **apices** : ápice *m*, cumbre *f*
apiece *adv* : cada uno
aplomb *n* : aplomo *m*
apology *n, pl* **-gies** : disculpa *f* — **apolo-
getic** *adj* : lleno de disculpas — **apologize**
vi **-gized; -gizing** : disculparse, pedir
perdón
apostle *n* : apóstol *m*
apostrophe *n* : apóstrofo *m*
appall *vt* : horrorizar — **appalling** *adj* : horroroso
apparatus *n, pl* **-tuses** *or* **-tus** : aparato *m*
apparel *n* : ropa *f*
apparent *adj* **1** OBVIOUS : claro, evidente **2**
SEEMING : aparente — **apparently** *adv* : al
parecer, por lo visto
apparition *n* : aparición *f*
appeal *vi* **1** ~ **for** : solicitar **2** ~ **to**
: apelar a (la bondad de algn, etc.) **3** ~ **to**
ATTRACT : atraer a — ~ *n* **1** : apelación *f*
(en derecho) **2** REQUEST : llamamiento *m* **3**
ATTRACTION : atractivo *m* — **appealing** *adj*
: atractivo
appear *vi* **1** : aparecer **2** : comparecer (ante
un tribunal), actuar (en el teatro) **3** SEEM
: parecer — **appearance** *n* **1** : aparición *f* **2**
LOOK : apariencia *f*, aspecto *m*
appease *vt* **-peased; -peasing** : apaciguar,
aplacar
appendix *n, pl* **-dixes** *or* **-dices** : apéndice
m — **appendicitis** *n* : apendicitis *f*

appetite *n* : apetito *m* — **appetizer** *n* : aperitivo *m* — **appetizing** *adj* : apetitoso
applaud *v* : aplaudir — **applause** *n*
: aplauso *m*
apple *n* : manzana *f*
appliance *n* : aparato *m*
apply *v* **-plied; -plying** *vt* **1** : aplicar **2** ~
oneself : aplicarse — *vi* **1** : aplicarse **2** ~
for : solicitar, pedir — **applicable** *adj*
: aplicable — **applicant** *n* : solicitante *mf*;
candidato *m*, -ta *f* — **application** *n* **1** : aplicación *f* **2** : solicitud *f* (para un empleo, etc.)
appoint *vt* **1** NAME : nombrar **2** FIX, SET
: fijar, señalar — **appointment** *n* **1** AP-
POINTING : nombramiento *m* **2** ENGAGE-
MENT : cita *f*
apportion *vt* : distribuir, repartir
appraise *vt* **-praised; -praising** : evaluar,
valorar — **appraisal** *n* : evaluación *f*
appreciate *v* **-ated; -ating** *vt* **1** VALUE
: apreciar **2** UNDERSTAND : darse cuenta de
3 I ~ **your help** : te agradezco tu ayuda —
vi : aumentar en valor — **appreciation** *n* **1**
GRATITUDE : agradecimiento *m* **2** VALUING
: apreciación *f*, valoración *f* — **appreciative**
adj **1** : apreciativo **2** GRATEFUL : agradecido
apprehend *vt* **1** ARREST : aprehender, detener **2** DREAD : temer **3** COMPREHEND
: comprender — **apprehension** *n* **1** AR-
REST : detención *f*, aprehensión *f* **2** ANXI-
ETY : aprensión *f*, temor *m* — **apprehensive** *adj* : aprensivo, inquieto
apprentice *n* : aprendiz *m*, -diza *f*
approach *vt* **1** NEAR : acercarse a **2** : dirigirse a (algn), abordar (un problema, etc.)
— *vi* : acercarse — ~ *n* **1** NEARING : acer-
camiento *m* **2** POSITION : enfoque *m* **3** AC-
CESS : acceso *m* — **approachable** *adj* : accesible, asequible
appropriate *vt* **-ated; -ating** : apropiarse de
— ~ *adj* : apropiado
approve *vt* **-proved; -proving** : aprobar —
approval *n* : aprobación *f*
approximate *adj* : aproximado — ~ *vt*
-mated; -mating : aproximarse a — **approximately** *adv* : aproximadamente
apricot *n* : albaricoque *m*, chabacano *m* *Lat*
April *n* : abril *m*
apron *n* : delantal *m*
apropos *adv* : a propósito
apt *adj* **1** FITTING : apto, apropiado **2** LI-
ABLE : propenso — **aptitude** *n* : aptitud *f*
aquarium *n, pl* **-iums** *or* **-ia** : acuario *m*
aquatic *adj* : acuático
aqueduct *n* : acueducto *m*
Arab *adj* : árabe — **Arabic** *adj* : árabe — ~
n : árabe *m* (idioma)
arbitrary *adj* : arbitrario

arbitrate v -**trated**; -**trating** : arbitrar — **arbitration** n : arbitraje m
arc n : arco m
arcade n **1** : arcada f **2 shopping** ~ : galería f comercial
arch n : arco m — ~ vt : arquear — vi : arquearse
archaeology or **archeology** n : arqueología f — **archaeological** adj : arque- ológico — **archaeologist** n : arqueólogo m, -ga f
archaic adj : arcaico
archbishop n : arzobispo m
archery n : tiro m al arco
archipelago n, pl -**goes** or -**gos** : archipiélago m
architecture n : arquitectura f — **architect** n : arquitecto m, -ta f — **architectural** adj : arquitectónico
archives npl : archivo m
archway n : arco m (de entrada)
arctic adj : ártico
ardent adj : ardiente, fervoroso — **ardor** n : ardor m, fervor m
arduous adj : arduo
are → **be**
area n **1** REGION : área f, zona f **2** FIELD : campo m **3** ~ **code** : código m de la zona Lat, prefijo m Spain
arena n : arena f, ruedo m
aren't (contraction of **are not**) → **be**
Argentine or **Argentinean** or **Argentinian** adj : argentino
argue v -**gued**; -**guing** vi **1** QUARREL : discutir **2** ~ **against** : argumentar contra — vt : argumentar, sostener — **argument** n **1** QUARREL : disputa f, discusión f **2** REASONING : argumentos mpl
arid adj : árido — **aridity** n : aridez f
arise vi **arose**; **arisen**; **arising 1** : levantarse **2** ~ **from** : surgir de
aristocracy n, pl -**cies** : aristocracia f — **aristocrat** n : aristócrata mf — **aristocratic** adj : aristocrático
arithmetic n : aritmética f
ark n : arca f
arm n **1** : brazo m **2** WEAPON : arma f — ~ vt : armar — **armament** n : armamento m — **armchair** n : sillón m — **armed** adj **1** ~ **forces** : fuerzas fpl armadas **2** ~ **robbery** : robo m a mano armada
armistice n : armisticio m
armor or Brit **armour** n : armadura f — **armored** or Brit **armoured** adj : blindado, acorazado — **armory** or Brit **armoury** n : arsenal m
armpit n : axila f, sobaco m
army n, pl -**mies** : ejército m
aroma n : aroma m — **aromatic** adj : aromático

around adv **1** : de circunferencia **2** NEARBY : por ahí **3** APPROXIMATELY : más o menos, aproximadamente **4 all** ~ : por todos lados, todo alrededor **5 turn** ~ : voltearse — ~ prep **1** SURROUNDING : alrededor de **2** THROUGHOUT : por **3** NEAR : cerca de **4** ~ **the corner** : a la vuelta de la esquina
arouse vt **aroused**; **arousing 1** AWAKE : despertar **2** EXCITE : excitar
arrange vt -**ranged**; -**ranging** : arreglar, poner en orden — **arrangement** n **1** ORDER : arreglo m **2** ~**s** npl : preparativos mpl
array n : selección f, surtido m
arrears npl **1** : atrasos mpl **2 be in** ~ : estar atrasado en pagos
arrest vt : detener — ~ n **1** : arresto m, detención f **2 under** ~ : detenido
arrive vi -**rived**; -**riving** : llegar — **arrival** n : llegada f
arrogance n : arrogancia f — **arrogant** adj : arrogante
arrow n : flecha f
arsenal n : arsenal m
arsenic n : arsénico m
arson n : incendio m premeditado
art n **1** : arte m **2** ~**s** npl : letras fpl (en educación) **3 fine** ~**s** : bellas artes fpl
artefact Brit → **artifact**
artery n, pl -**teries** : arteria f
artful adj : astuto, taimado
arthritis n, pl -**tides** : artritis f — **arthritic** adj : artrítico
artichoke n : alcachofa f
article n : artículo m
articulate vt -**lated**; -**lating** : articular — adj **be** ~ : expresarse bien
artifact or Brit **artefact** n : artefacto m
artificial adj : artificial
artillery n, pl -**leries** : artillería f
artisan n : artesano m, -na f
artist n : artista mf — **artistic** adj : artístico
as adv **1** : tan, tanto **2** ~ **much** : tanto como **3** ~ **tall** ~ : tan alto como **4** ~ **well** : también — ~ conj **1** WHILE : mientras **2** (referring to manner) : como **3** SINCE : ya que **4** THOUGH : por más que — ~ prep **1** : de **2** LIKE : como — ~ pron : que
asbestos n : asbesto m, amianto m
ascend vi : ascender, subir — vt : subir (a) — **ascent** n : ascensión f, subida f
ascertain vt : averiguar, determinar
ascribe vt -**cribed**; -**cribing** : atribuir
as for prep : en cuanto a
ash[1] n : ceniza f
ash[2] n : fresno m (árbol)
ashamed adj : avergonzado, apenado Lat
ashore adv **1** : en tierra **2 go** ~ : desembarcar

ashtray *n* : cenicero *m*
Asian *adj* : asiático
aside *adv* **1** : a un lado **2** APART : aparte **3** set ~ : guardar — **aside from** *prep* **1** BE- SIDES : además de **2** EXCEPT : aparte de, menos
as if *conj* : como si
ask *vt* **1** : preguntar **2** REQUEST : pedir **3** IN- VITE : invitar — *vi* : preguntar
askance *adv* **look** ~ : mirar de soslayo
askew *adj* : torcido, ladeado
asleep *adj* **1** : dormido **2 fall** ~ : dormirse, quedarse dormido
as of *prep* : desde, a partir de
asparagus *n* : espárrago *m*
aspect *n* : aspecto *m*
asphalt *n* : asfalto *m*
asphyxiate *v* **-ated; -ating** *vt* : asfixiar — **asphyxiation** *n* : asfixia *f*
aspire *vi* **-pired; -piring** : aspirar — **aspiration** *n* : aspiración *f*
aspirin *n, pl* **aspirin** *or* **aspirins** : aspirina *f*
ass *n* **1** : asno *m* **2** IDIOT : imbécil *mf*, idiota *mf*
assail *vt* : atacar, asaltar — **assailant** *n* : asaltante *mf*, atacante *mf*
assassin *n* : asesino *m*, -na *f* — **assassinate** *vt* **-nated; -nating** : asesinar — **assassination** *n* : asesinato *m*
assault *n* **1** : ataque *m*, asalto *m* **2** : agresión *f* (contra algn) — ~ *vt* : atacar, asaltar
assemble *v* **-bled; -bling** *vt* **1** GATHER : reunir, juntar **2** CONSTRUCT : montar — *vi* : reunirse — **assembly** *n, pl* **-blies 1** MEET- ING : reunión *f*, asamblea *f* **2** CONSTRUCT- ING : montaje *m*
assent *vi* : asentir, consentir — ~ *n* : asentimiento *m*
assert *vt* **1** : afirmar **2** ~ **oneself** : hacerse valer — **assertion** *n* : afirmación *f* — **assertive** *adj* : firme, enérgico
assess *vt* : evaluar, valorar — **assessment** *n* : evaluación *f*, valoración *f*
asset *n* **1** : ventaja *f*, recurso *m* **2** ~**s** *npl* : bienes *mpl*, activo *m*
assiduous *adj* : asiduo
assign *vt* **1** APPOINT : designar, nombrar **2** ALLOT : asignar — **assignment** *n* **1** TASK : misión *f* **2** HOMEWORK : tarea *f* **3** ASSIGN- ING : asignación *f*
assimilate *vt* **-lated; -lating** : asimilar
assist *vt* : ayudar — **assistance** *n* : ayuda *f* — **assistant** *n* : ayudante *mf*
associate *v* **-ated; -ating** *vt* : asociar — *vi* : asociarse — ~ *n* : asociado *m*, -da *f*; socio *m*, -cia *f* — **association** *n* : asociación *f*
as soon as *conj* : tan pronto como
assorted *adj* : surtido — **assortment** *n* : surtido *m*, variedad *f*

assume *vt* **-sumed; -suming 1** SUPPOSE : suponer **2** UNDERTAKE : asumir **3** TAKE ON : adquirir, tomar — **assumption** *n* : suposición *f*
assure *vt* **-sured; -suring** : asegurar — **assurance** *n* **1** CERTAINTY : certeza *f*, garantía *f* **2** CONFIDENCE : confianza *f*, seguridad *f* (de sí mismo)
asterisk *n* : asterisco *m*
asthma *n* : asma *m*
as though → **as if**
as to *prep* : sobre, acerca de
astonish *vt* : asombrar — **astonishing** *adj* : asombroso — **astonishment** *n* : asombro *m*
astound *vt* : asombrar, pasmar — **astounding** *adj* : asombroso, pasmoso
astray *adv* **1 go** ~ : extraviarse **2 lead** ~ : llevar por mal camino
astrology *n* : astrología *f*
astronaut *n* : astronauta *mf*
astronomy *n, pl* **-mies** : astronomía *f* — **astronomer** *n* : astrónomo *m*, -ma *f* — **astronomical** *adj* : astronómico
astute *adj* : astuto, sagaz — **astuteness** *n* : astucia *f*
as well as *conj* : tanto como — ~ *prep* : además de, aparte de
asylum *n* **1** : asilo *m* **2 insane** ~ : manicomio *m*
at *prep* **1** : a **2** ~ **home** : en casa **3** ~ **night** : en la noche, por la noche **4** ~ **two o'clock** : a las dos **5 be angry** ~ : estar enojado con **6 laugh** ~ : reírse de — **at all** *adv* **not** ~ : en absoluto, nada
ate → **eat**
atheist *n* : ateo *m*, atea *f* — **atheism** *n* : ateísmo *m*
athlete *n* : atleta *mf* — **athletic** *adj* : atlético — **athletics** *ns* & *pl* : atletismo *m*
atlas *n* : atlas *m*
atmosphere *n* **1** : atmósfera *f* **2** AMBIENCE : ambiente *m* — **atmospheric** *adj* : atmosférico
atom *n* : átomo *m* — **atomic** *adj* : atómico
atomizer *n* : atomizador *m*
atone *vi* **atoned; atoning** ~ **for** : expiar
atrocity *n, pl* **-ties** : atrocidad *f* — **atrocious** *adj* : atroz
atrophy *vi* **-phied; -phying** : atrofiarse
attach *vt* **1** : sujetar, atar **2** : adjuntar (un documento, etc.) **3** ~ **importance to** : atribuir importancia a **4 become** ~**ed to s.o.** : encariñarse con algn — **attachment** *n* **1** ACCESSORY : accesorio *m* **2** FONDNESS : cariño *m*
attack *v* : atacar — ~ *n* : ataque *m* — **attacker** *n* : agresor *m*, -sora *f*

attain *vt* : lograr, alcanzar — **attainment** *n*
: logro *m*
attempt *vt* : intentar — ~ *n* : intento *m*
attend *vt* : asistir a — vi **1** : asistir **2** ~ **to**
: ocuparse de — **attendance** *n* **1** : asistencia *f* **2** TURNOUT : concurrencia *f* — **attendant** *n* : encargado *m*, -da *f;* asistente *mf*
attention *n* **1** : atención *f* **2 pay** ~ : prestar
atención, hacer caso — **attentive** *adj*
: atento
attest *vt* : atestiguar
attic *n* : desván *m*
attire *n* : atavío *m*
attitude *n* **1** : actitud *f* **2** POSTURE : postura *f*
attorney *n*, *pl* **-neys** : abogado *m*, -da *f*
attract *vt* : atraer — **attraction** *n* **1** : atracción *f* **2** APPEAL : atractivo *m* — **attractive**
adj : atractivo, atrayente
attribute *n* : atributo *m* — ~ *vt* **-tributed;
-tributing** : atribuir, imputar
auburn *adj* : castaño rojizo
auction *n* : subasta *f* — ~ *vt or* ~ **off** : subastar
audacious *adj* : audaz — **audacity** *n, pl*
-ties : audacia *f*, atrevimiento *m*
audible *adj* : audible
audience *n* **1** INTERVIEW : audiencia *f* **2**
PUBLIC : público *m*
audiovisual *adj* : audiovisual
audition *n* : audición *f*
auditor *n* **1** : auditor *m*, -tora *f* (de finanzas)
2 STUDENT : oyente *mf*
auditorium *n, pl* **-riums** *or* **-ria** : auditorio *m*
augment *vt* : aumentar
augur *vi* ~ **well** : ser de buen agüero
August *n* : agosto *m*
aunt *n* : tía *f*
aura *n* : aura *f*
auspices *npl* : auspicios *mpl*
auspicious *adj* : propicio, prometedor
austere *adj* : austero — **austerity** *n, pl* **-ties**
: austeridad *f*
Australian *adj* : australiano
authentic *adj* : auténtico
author *n* : autor *m*, -tora *f*
authority *n, pl* **-ties** : autoridad *f* — **authoritarian** *adj* : autoritario — **authoritative** *adj*
1 RELIABLE : autorizado **2** DICTATORIAL
: autoritario — **authorization** *n* : autorización *f* — **authorize** *vt* **-rized; -rizing**
: autorizar
autobiography *n, pl* **-phies** : autobiografía *f*
— **autobiographical** *adj* : autobiográfico
autograph *n* : autógrafo *m* — ~ *vt* : autografiar
automatic *adj* : automático — **automate** *vt*
-mated; -mating : automatizar — **automation** *n* : automatización *f*
automobile *n* : automóvil *m*

autonomy *n, pl* **-mies** : autonomía *f* — **autonomous** *adj* : autónomo
autopsy *n, pl* **-sies** : autopsia *f*
autumn *n* : otoño *m*
auxiliary *adj* : auxiliar — ~ *n, pl* **-ries**
: auxiliar *mf*
avail *vt* ~ **oneself of** : aprovecharse de —
~ *n* **to no** ~ : en vano — **available** *adj*
: disponible — **availability** *n, pl* **-ties**
: disponibilidad *f*
avalanche *n* : avalancha *f*
avarice *n* : avaricia *f*
avenge *vt* **avenged; avenging** : vengar
avenue *n* **1** : avenida *f* **2** MEANS : vía *f*
average *n* : promedio *m* — ~ *adj* **1** MEAN
: medio **2** ORDINARY : regular, ordinario —
~ *vt* **-aged; -aging** **1** : hacer un promedio
de **2** *or* ~ **out** : calcular el promedio de
averse *adj* **be** ~ **to** : sentir aversión por —
aversion *n* : aversión *f*
avert *vt* **1** AVOID : evitar, prevenir **2** ~
one's eyes : apartar los ojos
aviation *n* : aviación *f* — **aviator** *n* : aviador
m, -dora *f*
avid *adj* : ávido — **avidly** *adv* : con avidez
avocado *n, pl* **-dos** : aguacate *m*
avoid *vt* : evitar — **avoidable** *adj* : evitable
await *vt* : esperar
awake *v* **awoke; awoken** *or* **awaked; awak-
ing** : despertar — ~ *adj* : despierto —
awaken *v* → **awake**
award *vt* **1** : otorgar, conceder (un premio,
etc.) **2** : adjudicar (daños y perjuicios) —
~ *n* **1** PRIZE : premio *m* **2** : adjudicación *f*
aware *adj* **be** ~ **of** : estar consciente de —
awareness *n* : conciencia *f*
away *adv* **1** (*referring to distance*) : de aquí,
de distancia **2 far** ~ : lejos **3 give** ~ : regalar **4 go** ~ : irse **5 right** ~ : en seguida
6 take ~ : quitar — ~ *adj* **1** ABSENT
: ausente **2** ~ **game** : partido *m* fuera de
casa
awe *n* : temor *m* reverencial — **awesome**
adj : imponente, formidable
awful *adj* **1** : terrible, espantoso **2 an** ~ **lot**
: muchísimo — **awfully** *adv* : terriblemente
awhile *adv* : un rato
awkward *adj* **1** CLUMSY : torpe **2** EMBAR-
RASSING : embarazoso, delicado **3** DIFFI-
CULT : difícil — **awkwardly** *adv* **1** : con dificultad **2** CLUMSILY : de manera torpe
awning *n* : toldo *m*
awry *adj* **1** ASKEW : torcido **2 go** ~ : salir
mal
ax *or* **axe** *n* : hacha *f*
axiom *n* : axioma *m*
axis *n, pl* **axes** : eje *m*
axle *n* : eje *m*

B

b *n*, *pl* **b's** *or* **bs** : b, segunda letra del alfabeto inglés

babble *vi* **-bled; -bling 1** : balbucear **2** MURMUR ; murmurar — ∼ *n* : balbuceo *m* (de bebé), murmullo *m* (de voces, de un arroyo)

baboon *n* : babuino *m*

baby *n*, *pl* **-bies** : bebé *m;* niño *m*, -ña *f* — **baby** *vt* **-bied; -bying** : mimar, consentir — **babyish** *adj* : infantil — **baby–sit** *vi* **-sat; -sitting** : cuidar a los niños

bachelor *n* **1** : soltero *m* **2** GRADUATE : licenciado *m*, -da *f*

back *n* **1** : espalda *f* **2** REVERSE : reverso *m*, dorso *m*, revés *m* **3** REAR : fondo *m*, parte *f* trasera **4** : defensa *mf* (en deportes) — ∼ *adv* **1** : atrás **2 be** ∼ : estar de vuelta **3 go** ∼ : volver **4 two years** ∼ : hace dos años — ∼ *adj* **1** REAR : de atrás, trasero **2** OVERDUE : atrasado — ∼ *vt* **1** SUPPORT : apoyar **2** *or* ∼ **up** : darle marcha atrás a (un vehículo) — *vi* **1** ∼ **down** : volverse atrás **2** ∼ **up** : retroceder — **backache** *n* : dolor *m* de espalda — **backbone** *n* : columna *f* vertebral — **backfire** *vi* **-fired; -firing** : petardear — **background** *n* **1** : fondo *m* (de un cuadro, etc.), antecedentes *mpl* (de una situación) **2** EXPERIENCE : formación *f* — **backhand** *adv* : de revés, con el revés — **backhanded** *adj* : indirecto — **backing** *n* : apoyo *m*, respaldo *m* — **backlash** *n* : reacción *f* violenta — **backlog** *n* : atrasos *mpl* — **backpack** *n* : mochila *f* — **backstage** *adv* & *adj* : entre bastidores — **backtrack** *vi* : dar marcha atrás — **backup** *n* **1** SUPPORT : respaldo *m*, apoyo *m* **2** : copia *f* de seguridad (para computadoras) — **backward** *or* **backwards** *adv* **1** : hacia atrás **2 do it** ∼ : hacerlo al revés **3 fall** ∼ : caer de espaldas **4 bend over** ∼**s** : hacer todo lo posible — **backward** *adj* **1** : hacia atrás **2** RETARDED : retrasado **3** SHY : tímido **4** UNDERDEVELOPED : atrasado

bacon *n* : tocino *m*, tocineta *f Lat*, bacon *m Spain*

bacteria : bacterias *fpl*

bad *adj* **worse; worst 1** : malo **2** ROTTEN : podrido **3** SEVERE : grave **4 from** ∼ **to worse** : de mal en peor **5 too** ∼**!** : ¡qué lástima! — ∼ *adv* → **badly**

badge *n* : insignia *f*, chapa *f*

badger *n* : tejón *m* — ∼ *vt* : acosar

badly *adv* **1** : mal **2** SEVERELY : gravemente **3 want** ∼ : desear mucho

baffle *vi* **-fled; -fling** : desconcertar

bag *n* **1** : bolsa *f*, saco *m* **2** HANDBAG : bolso *m*, cartera *f Lat* **3** SUITCASE : maleta *f* — ∼ *vt* **bagged; bagging** : ensacar, poner en una bolsa

baggage *n* : equipaje *m*

baggy *adj* **-gier; -est** : holgado

bail *n* : fianza *f* — ∼ *vt* **1** : achicar (agua de un bote) **2** ∼ **out** RELEASE : poner en libertad bajo fianza **3** ∼ **out** EXTRICATE : sacar de apuros

bailiff *n* : alguacil *mf*

bait *vt* **1** : cebar **2** HARASS : acosar — ∼ *n* : cebo *m*, carnada *f*

bake *v* **baked; baking** *vt* : cocer al horno — *vi* : cocerse (al horno) — **baker** *n* : panadero *m*, -ra *f* — **bakery** *n*, *pl* **-ries** : panadería *f*

balance *n* **1** SCALES : balanza *f* **2** COUNTERBALANCE : contrapeso *m* **3** EQUILIBRIUM : equilibrio *m* **4** REMAINDER : resto *m* **5** *or* **bank** ∼ : saldo *m* — ∼ *v* **-anced; -ancing** *vt* **1** : hacer el balance de (una cuenta) **2** EQUALIZE : equilibrar **3** WEIGH : sopesar — *vi* **1** : sostenerse en equilibrio **2** : cuadrar (dícese de una cuenta)

balcony *n*, *pl* **-nies 1** : balcón *m* **2** : galería *f* (de un teatro)

bald *adj* **1** : calvo **2** WORN : pelado **3 the** ∼ **truth** : la pura verdad

bale *n* : bala *f*, fardo *m*

baleful *adj* : siniestro

balk *vi* ∼ **at** : resistarse a

ball *n* **1** : pelota *f*, bola *f*, balón *m* **2** DANCE : baile *m* **3** ∼ **of string** : ovillo *m* de cuerda

ballad *n* : balada *f*

ballast *n* : lastre *m*

ball bearing *n* : cojinete *m* de bola

ballerina *n* : bailarina *f*

ballet *n* : ballet *m*

ballistic *adj* : balístico

balloon *n* : globo *m*

ballot *n* **1** : papeleta *f* (de voto) **2** VOTING : votación *f*

ballpoint pen *n* : bolígrafo *m*

ballroom *n* : sala *f* de baile

balm *n* : bálsamo *m* — **balmy** *adj* **balmier; -est** : templado, agradable

baloney *n* NONSENSE : tonterías *fpl*

bamboo *n* : bambú *m*

bamboozle *vt* **-zled; -zling** : engañar, embaucar

ban *vt* **banned; banning** : prohibir — ∼ *n* : prohibición *f*

banal *adj* : banal

banana *n* : plátano *m*, banana *f Lat,* banano *m Lat*

band *n* **1** STRIP : banda *f* **2** GROUP : banda *f,* grupo *m,* conjunto *m* — ~ *vi* ~ **together** : unirse, juntarse

bandage *n* : vendaje *m,* venda *f* — ~ *vt* **-daged; -daging** : vendar

bandit *n* : bandido *m,* -da *f*

bandy *vt* **-died; -dying** ~ **about** : circular, repetir

bang *vt* **1** STRIKE : golpear **2** SLAM : cerrar de un golpe — *vi* **1** SLAM : cerrarse de un golpe **2** ~ **on** : golpear — ~ *n* **1** BLOW : golpe *m* **2** NOISE : estrépito *m* **3** SLAM : portazo *m*

bangle *n* : brazalete *m,* pulsera *f*

bangs *npl* : flequillo *m*

banish *vt* : desterrar

banister *n* : pasamanos *m,* barandal *m*

bank *n* **1** : banco *m* **2** : orilla *f,* ribera *f* (de un río) **3** EMBANKMENT : terraplén *m* — ~ *vt* : depositar — *vi* **1** : ladearse (dícese de un avión) **2** : tener una cuenta (en un banco) **3** ~ **on** : contar con — **banker** *n* : banquero *m,* -ra *f* — **banking** *n* : banca *f*

bankrupt *adj* : en bancarrota, en quiebra — **bankruptcy** *n, pl* **-cies** : quiebra *f,* bancarrota *f*

banner *n* : bandera *f,* pancarta *f*

banquet *n* : banquete *m*

banter *n* : bromas *fpl* — ~ *vi* : hacer bromas

baptize *vt* **-tized; -tizing** : bautizar — **baptism** *n* : bautismo *m*

bar *n* **1** : barra *f* **2** BARRIER : barrera *f,* obstáculo *m* **3** COUNTER : mostrador *m,* barra *f* **4** TAVERN : bar *m* **5 behind** ~**s** : entre rejas **6** ~ **of soap** : pastilla *f* de jabón — ~ *vt* **barred; barring 1** OBSTRUCT : obstruir, bloquear **2** EXCLUDE : excluir **3** PROHIBIT : prohibir — ~ *prep* **1** : excepto **2** ~ **none** : sin excepción

barbarian *n* : bárbaro *m,* -ra *f*

barbecue *vt* **-cued; -cuing** : asar a la parrilla — ~ *n* : barbacoa *f*

barbed wire *n* : alambre *m* de púas

barber *n* : barbero *m,* -ra *f*

bare *adj* **1** : desnudo **2** EMPTY : vacío **3** MINIMUM : mero, esencial — **barefaced** *adj* : descarado — **barefoot** *or* **barefooted** *adv & adj* : descalzo — **barely** *adv* : apenas, por poco

bargain *n* **1** AGREEMENT : acuerdo *m* **2** BUY : ganga *f* — ~ *vi* **1** : regatear, negociar **2** ~ **for** : contar con

barge *n* : barcaza *f* — ~ *vi* **barged; barging** ~ **in** : entrometerse, interrumpir

baritone *n* : barítono *m*

bark[1] *vi* : ladrar — ~ *n* : ladrido *m* (de un perro)

bark[2] *n* : corteza *f* (de un árbol)

barley *n* : cebada *f*

barn *n* : granero *m* — **barnyard** *n* : corral *m*

barometer *n* : barómetro *m*

baron *n* : barón *m* — **baroness** *n* : baronesa *f*

barracks *ns & pl* : cuartel *m*

barrage *n* **1** : descarga *f* (de artillería) **2** : aluvión *m* (de preguntas, etc.)

barrel *n* **1** : barril *m,* tonel *m* **2** : cañón *m* (de un arma de fuego)

barren *adj* : estéril

barricade *vt* **-caded; -cading** : cerrar con barricadas — ~ *n* : barricada *f*

barrier *n* : barrera *f*

barring *prep* : salvo

barrio *n* : barrio *m*

bartender *n* : camarero *m,* -ra *f*

barter *vt* : cambiar, trocar — ~ *n* : trueque *m*

base *n, pl* **bases** : base *f* — ~ *vt* **based; basing** : basar, fundamentar — ~ *adj* **baser; basest** : vil

baseball *n* : beisbol *m,* béisbol *m*

basement *n* : sótano *m*

bash *vt* : golpear violentamente — ~ *n* **1** BLOW : golpe *m* **2** PARTY : fiesta *f*

bashful *adj* : tímido, vergonzoso

basic *adj* : básico, fundamental — **basically** *adv* : fundamentalmente

basil *n* : albahaca *f*

basin *n* **1** WASHBOWL : palangana *f,* lavabo *m* **2** : cuenca *f* (de un río)

basis *n, pl* **bases** : base *f*

bask *vi* ~ **in the sun** : tostarse al sol

basket *n* : cesta *f,* cesto *m* — **basketball** *n* : baloncesto *m,* basquetbol *m Lat*

bass[1] *n, pl* **bass** *or* **basses** : róbalo *m* (pesca)

bass[2] *n* : bajo *m* (tono, voz, instrumento)

bassoon *n* : fagot *m*

bastard *n* : bastardo *m,* -da *f*

baste *vt* **basted; basting 1** STITCH : hilvanar **2** : bañar (carne)

bat[1] *n* : murciélago *m* (animal)

bat[2] *n* : bate *m* — ~ *vt* **batted; batting** : batear

batch *n* : hornada *f* (de pasteles, etc.), lote *m* (de mercancías), montón *m* (de trabajo), grupo *m* (de personas)

bath *n, pl* **baths 1** : baño *m* **2** BATHROOM : baño *m,* cuarto *m* de baño **3 take a** ~ : bañarse — **bathe** *v* **bathed; bathing** *vt* : bañar, lavar — *vi* : bañarse — **bathrobe** *n* : bata *f* (de baño) — **bathroom** *n* : baño *m,* cuarto *m* de baño — **bathtub** *n* : bañera *f,* tina *f* (de baño)

baton *n* : batuta *f*
battalion *n* : batallón *m*
batter *vt* **1** BEAT : golpear **2** MISTREAT
: maltratar — ~ *n* **1** : masa *f* para rebozar
2 HITTER : bateador *m*, -dora *f*
battery *n*, *pl* **-teries** : batería *f*, pila *f* (de
electricidad)
battle *n* **1** : batalla *f* **2** STRUGGLE : lucha *f* —
~ *vi* **-tled; -tling** : luchar — **battlefield** *n*
: campo *m* de batalla — **battleship** *n* : acorazado *m*
bawl *vi* : llorar a gritos
bay[1] *n* INLET : bahía *f*
bay[2] *n or* ~ **leaf** : laurel *m*
bay[3] *vi* : aullar — ~ *n* : aullido *m*
bayonet *n* : bayoneta *f*
bay window *n* : ventana *f* en saliente
bazaar *n* **1** : bazar *m* **2** SALE : venta *f* benéfica
be *v* **was , were; been; being; am , is , are**
vi **1** : ser **2** (*expressing location*) : estar **3**
(*expressing existence*) : ser, existir **4** (*expressing a state of being*) : estar, tener — *v*
impers **1** (*indicating time*) : ser **2** (*indicating a condition*) : hacer, estar — *v aux* **1**
(*expressing occurrence*) : ser **2** (*expressing
possibility*) : poderse **3** (*expressing obligation*) : deber **4** (*expressing progression*)
: estar
beach *n* : playa *f*
beacon *n* : faro *m*
bead *n* **1** : cuenta *f* **2** DROP : gota *f* **3** ~**s**
npl NECKLACE : collar *m*
beak *n* : pico *m*
beam *n* **1** : viga *f* (de madera, etc.) **2** RAY
: rayo *m* — ~ *vi* SHINE : brillar — *vt*
BROADCAST : transmitir, emitir
bean *n* **1** : habichuela *f*, frijol *m* **2 coffee**
~ : grano *m* **3 string** ~ : judía *f*
bear[1] *n*, *pl* **bears** *or* **bear** : oso *m*, osa *f*
bear[2] *v* **bore; borne; bearing** *vt* **1** CARRY
: portar **2** ENDURE : soportar — *vi* ~
right/left : doble a la derecha/a la izquierda
— **bearable** *adj* : soportable
beard *n* : barba *f*
bearer *n* : portador *m*, -dora *f*
bearing *n* **1** MANNER : comportamiento *m* **2**
SIGNIFICANCE : relacíon *f*, importancia *f* **3**
get one's ~**s** : orientarse
beast *n* : bestia *f*
beat *v* **beat; beaten** *or* **beat; beating** *vt* **1**
HIT : golpear **2** : batir (huevos, etc.) **3** DE-
FEAT : derrotar — *vi* : latir (dícese del
corazón) — ~ *n* **1** : golpe *m* **2** : latido *m*
(del corazón) **3** RHYTHM : ritmo *m*, tiempo
m — **beating** *n* **1** : paliza *f* **2** DEFEAT : derrota *f*
beauty *n*, *pl* **-ties** : belleza *f* — **beautiful** *adj*
: hermoso, lindo — **beautifully** *adv* WON-

DERFULLY : maravillosamente — **beautify**
vt **-fied; -fying** : embellecer
beaver *n* : castor *m*
because *conj* : porque — **because of** *prep*
: por, a causa de, debido a
beckon *vt* : llamar, hacer señas a — *vi*
: hacer una seña
become *v* **-came; -come; -coming** *vi* : hacerse, ponerse — *vt* SUIT : favorecer — **becoming** *adj* **1** SUITABLE : apropiado **2**
FLATTERING : favorecedor
bed *n* **1** : cama *f* **2** : cauce *m* (de un río),
fondo *m* (del mar) **3** : macizo *m* (de flores)
4 go to ~ : irse a la cama — **bedclothes**
npl : ropa *f* de cama
bedlam *n* : confusión *f*, caos *m*
bedraggled *adj* : desaliñado, sucio
bedridden *adj* : postrado en cama
bedroom *n* : dormitorio *m*, recámara *f* Lat
bedspread *n* : colcha *f*
bedtime *n* : hora *f* de acostarse
bee *n* : abeja *f*
beech *n*, *pl* **beeches** *or* **beech** : haya *f*
beef *n* : carne *f* de vaca, carne *f* de res Lat —
beefsteak *n* : bistec *m*
beehive *n* : colmena *f*
beeline *n* **make a** ~ **for** : irse derecho a
beep *n* : pitido *m* — ~ *v* : pitar
beer *n* : cerveza *f*
beet *n* : remolacha *f*
beetle *n* : escarabajo *m*
before *adv* **1** : antes **2 the month** ~ : el
mes anterior — ~ *prep* **1** (*in space*) : delante de, ante **2** (*in time*) : antes de — ~
conj : antes de que — **beforehand** *adv*
: antes
befriend *vt* : hacerse amigo de
beg *v* **begged; begging** *vt* **1** : pedir, mendigar **2** ENTREAT : suplicar — *vi* : mendigar,
pedir limosna — **beggar** *n* : mendigo *m*, -ga
f
begin *v* **-gan; -gun; -ginning** : empezar,
comenzar — **beginner** *n* : principiante *mf*
— **beginning** *n* : principio *m*, comienzo *m*
begrudge *vt* **-grudged; -grudging** **1** : dar
de mala gana **2** ENVY : envidiar
behalf *n* **on** ~ **of** : de parte de, en nombre
de
behave *vi* **-haved; -having** : comportarse,
portarse — **behavior** *n* : comportamiento
m, conducta *f*
behind *adv* **1** : detrás **2 fall** ~ : atrasarse
— ~ *prep* **1** : atrás de, detrás de **2 be** ~
schedule : ir retrasado **3 her friends are**
~ **her** : tiene el apoyo de sus amigos
behold *vt* **-held; -holding** : contemplar
beige *adj & nm* : beige
being *n* **1** : ser *m* **2 come into** ~ : nacer
belated *adj* : tardío

belch *vi* : eructar — ‿ *n* : eructo *m*
Belgian *adj* : belga
belie *vt* **-lied; -lying** : contradecir, desmentir
belief *n* **1** TRUST : confianza *f* **2** CONVICTION : creencia *f*, convicción *f* **3** FAITH : fe *f* — **believable** *adj* : creíble — **believe** *v* **-lieved; -lieving** : creer — **believer** *n* : creyente *mf*
belittle *vt* **-littled; -littling** : menospreciar
Belizean *adj* : beliceño *m*, -ña *f*
bell *n* **1** : campana *f* **2** : timbre *m* (de teléfono, de la puerta, etc.)
belligerent *adj* : beligerante
bellow *vi* : bramar, mugir — *vt or* ‿ **out** : gritar
bellows *ns & pl* : fuelle *m*
belly *n*, *pl* **-lies** : vientre *m*
belong *vi* **1** ‿ **to** : pertenecer a, ser propiedad de **2** ‿ **to** : ser miembro de (un club, etc.) **3** **where does it** ‿ : ¿dónde va? — **belongings** *npl* : pertenencias *fpl*, efectos *mpl* personales
beloved *adj* : querido, amado — ‿ *n* : querido *m*, -da *f*
below *adv* : abajo — ‿ *prep* **1** : abajo de, debajo de **2** ‿ **average** : por debajo del promedio **3** ‿ **zero** : bajo cero
belt *n* **1** : cinturón *m* **2** BAND, STRAP : cinta *f*, correa *f* **3** AREA : frente *m*, zona *f* — ‿ *vt* **1** : ceñir con un cinturón **2** THRASH : darle una paliza a
bench *n* **1** : banco *m* **2** WORKBENCH : mesa *f* de trabajo **3** COURT : tribunal *m*
bend *v* **bent; bending** *vt* : doblar, torcer — *vi* **1** : torcerse **2** ‿ **over** : inclinarse — ‿ *n* : curva *f*, ángulo *m*
beneath *adv* : abajo, debajo — ‿ *prep* : bajo, debajo de
benediction *n* : bendición *f*
benefactor *n* : benefactor *m*, -tora *f*
benefit *n* **1** ADVANTAGE : ventaja *f*, provecho *m* **2** AID : asistencia *f*, beneficio *m* — ‿ *vt* : beneficiar — *vi* : beneficiarse — **beneficial** *adj* : beneficioso — **beneficiary** *n*, *pl* **-ries** : beneficiario *m*, -ria *f*
benevolent *adj* : benévolo
benign *adj* **1** KIND : benévolo, amable **2** : benigno (en medicina)
bent *adj* **1** : encorvado **2** **be** ‿ **on** : estar empeñado en — ‿ *n* : aptitud *f*, inclinación *f*
bequeath *vt* : legar — **bequest** *n* : legado *m*
berate *vt* **-rated; -rating** : reprender, regañar
bereaved *adj* : desconsolado, a luto
beret *n* : boina *f*
berry *n*, *pl* **-ries** : baya *f*
berserk *adj* **1** : enloquecido **2** **go** ‿ : volverse loco

berth *n* **1** MOORING : atracadero *m* **2** BUNK : litera *f*
beseech *vt* **-sought** *or* **-seeched; -seeching** : suplicar, implorar
beset *vt* **-set; -setting** **1** HARASS : acosar **2** SURROUND : rodear
beside *prep* **1** : al lado de, junto a **2** **be** ‿ **oneself** : estar fuera de sí — **besides** *adv* : además — ‿ *prep* **1** : además de **2** EXCEPT : excepto
besiege *vt* **-sieged; -sieging** : asediar
best *adj* (*superlative of* **good**) : mejor — ‿ *adv* (*superlative of* **well**) : mejor — ‿ *n* **1** **at** ‿ : a lo más **2** **do one's** ‿ : hacer todo lo posible **3** **the** ‿ : lo mejor — **best man** *n* : padrino *m* (de boda)
bestow *vt* : otorgar, conceder
bet *n* : apuesta *f* — ‿ *v* **bet; betting** *vt* : apostar — *vi* ‿ **on sth** : apostarle a algo
betray *vt* : traicionar — **betrayal** *n* : traición *f*
better *adj* (*comparative of* **good**) **1** : mejor **2** **get** ‿ : mejorar — ‿ *adv* (*comparative of* **well**) **1** : mejor **2** **all the** ‿ : tanto mejor — ‿ *n* **1** **the** ‿ : el mejor, la mejor **2** **get the** ‿ **of** : vencer a — ‿ *vt* **1** IMPROVE : mejorar **2** SURPASS : superar
between *prep* : entre — ‿ *adv or* **in** ‿ : en medio
beverage *n* : bebida *f*
beware *vi* ‿ **of** : tener cuidado con
bewilder *vt* : desconcertar — **bewilderment** *n* : desconcierto *m*
bewitch *vt* : hechizar, encantar
beyond *adv* : más allá, más lejos (en el espacio), más adelante (en el tiempo) — ‿ *prep* : más allá de
bias *n* **1** PREJUDICE : prejuicio *m* **2** TENDENCY : inclinación *f*, tendencia *f* — **biased** *adj* : parcial
bib *n* : babero *m* (para niños)
Bible *n* : Biblia *f* — **biblical** *adj* : bíblico
bibliography *n*, *pl* **-phies** : bibliografía *f*
bicarbonate of soda *n* : bicarbonato *m* de soda
biceps *ns & pl* : bíceps *m*
bicker *vi* : reñir
bicycle *n* : bicicleta *f* — ‿ *vi* **-cled; -cling** : ir en bicicleta
bid *vt* **bade** *or* **bid; bidden** *or* **bid; bidding** **1** OFFER : ofrecer **2** ‿ **farewell** : decir adios — ‿ *n* **1** OFFER : oferta *f* **2** ATTEMPT : intento *m*, tentativa *f*
bide *vt* **bode** *or* **bided; bided; biding** ‿ **one's time** : esperar el momento oportuno
bifocals *npl* : anteojos *mpl* bifocales
big *adj* **bigger; biggest** : grande
bigamy *n* : bigamía *f*

bigot *n* : intolerante *mf* — **bigotry** *n, pl* -**tries** : intolerancia *f,* fanatismo *m*
bike *n* **1** BICYCLE : bici *f fam* **2** MOTORCY-CLE : moto *f*
bikini *n* : bikini *m*
bile *n* : bilis *f*
bilingual *adj* : bilingüe
bill *n* **1** BEAK : pico *m* **2** INVOICE : cuenta *f,* factura *f* **3** BANKNOTE : billete *m* **4** LAW : proyecto *m* de ley, ley *f* — ~ *vt* : pasarle la cuenta a — **billboard** *n* : cartelera *f* — **billfold** *n* : billetera *f,* cartera *f*
billiards *n* : billar *m*
billion *n, pl* **billions** *or* **billion** : mil millones *mpl*
billow *vi* : ondular, hincharse
billy goat *n* : macho *m* cabrío
bin *n* : cubo *m,* cajón *m*
binary *adj* : binario *m*
bind *vt* **bound; binding 1** TIE : atar **2** OBLIGATE : obligar **3** UNITE : unir **4** BANDAGE : vendar **5** : encuadernar (un libro) — **binder** *n* FOLDER : carpeta *f* — **binding** *n* : encuadernación *f* (de libros)
binge *n* : juerga *f fam*
bingo *n, pl* **-gos** : bingo *m*
binoculars *npl* : binoculares *mpl,* gemelos *mpl*
biochemistry *n* : bioquímica *f*
biography *n, pl* **-phies** : biografía *f* — **biographer** *n* : biógrafo *m,* -fa *f* — **biographical** *adj* : biográfico
biology *n* : biología *f* — **biological** *adj* : biológico — **biologist** *n* : biólogo *m,* -ga *f*
birch *n* : abedul *m*
bird *n* : pájaro *m* (pequeño), ave *f* (grande)
birth *n* **1** : nacimiento *m,* parto *m* **2 give** ~ **to** : dar a luz a — **birthday** *n* : cumpleaños *m* — **birthmark** *n* : mancha *f* de nacimiento — **birthplace** *n* : lugar *m* de nacimiento — **birthrate** *n* : índice *m* de natalidad
biscuit *n* : bizcocho *m*
bisect *vt* : bisecar
bisexual *adj* : bisexual
bishop *n* : obispo *m*
bison *ns & pl* : bisonte *m*
bit[1] *n* : bocado *m* (de una brida)
bit[2] **1** : trozo *m,* pedazo *m* **2** : bit *m* (de información) **3 a** ~ : un poco
bitch *n* : perra *f* — ~ *vi* COMPLAIN : quejarse, reclamar
bite *v* **bit; bitten; biting** *vt* **1** : morder **2** STING : picar — *vi* : morder — *n* **1** : picadura *f* (de un insecto), mordedura *f* (de un animal) **2** SNACK : bocado *m* — **biting** *adj* **1** PENETRATING : cortante, penetrante **2** CAUSTIC : mordaz
bitter *adj* **1** : amargo **2 it's** ~ **cold** : hace

un frío glacial **3 to the** ~ **end** : hasta el final — **bitterness** *n* : amargura *f*
bizarre *adj* : extraño
black *adj* : negro — ~ *n* **1** : negro *m* (color) **2** : negro *m,* -gra *f* (persona) — **black-and-blue** *adj* : amoratado — **blackberry** *n, pl* **-ries** : mora *f* — **blackbird** *n* : mirlo *m* — **blackboard** *n* : pizarra *f,* pizarrón *m Lat* — **blacken** *vt* : ennegrecer — **blackmail** *n* : chantaje *m* — ~ *vt* : chantajear — **black market** *n* : mercado *m* negro — **blackout** *n* **1** : apagón *m* (de poder eléctrico) **2** FAINT : desmayo *m* — **blacksmith** *n* : herrero *m* — **blacktop** *n* : asfalto *m*
bladder *n* : vejiga *f*
blade *n* **1** : hoja *f* (de un cuchillo), cuchilla *f* (de un patín) **2** : pala *f* (de un remo, una hélice, etc.) **3** ~ **of grass** : brizna *f* (de hierba)
blame *vt* **blamed; blaming** : culpar, echar la culpa a — ~ *n* : culpa *f* — **blameless** *adj* : inocente
bland *adj* : soso, insulso
blank *adj* **1** : en blanco (dícese de un papel), liso (dícese de una pared) **2** EMPTY : vacío — ~ *n* : espacio *m* en blanco
blanket *n* **1** : manta *f,* cobija *f Lat* **2** ~ **of snow** : manto *m* de nieve — ~ *vt* : cubrir
blare *vi* **blared; blaring** : resonar
blasphemy *n, pl* **-mies** : blasfemia *f*
blast *n* **1** GUST : ráfaga *f* **2** EXPLOSION : explosión *f* **3** : toque *m* (de trompeta, etc.) — ~ *vt* BLOW UP : volar — **blast-off** *n* : despegue *m*
blatant *adj* : descarado
blaze *n* **1** FIRE : fuego *m* **2** BRIGHTNESS : resplandor *m,* brillantez *f* **3** ~ **of anger** : arranque *m* de cólera — ~ *v* **blazed; blazing** *vi* : arder, brillar — *vt* ~ **a trail** : abrir un camino
blazer *n* : chaqueta *f* deportiva
bleach *vt* : blanquear, decolorar — ~ *n* : lejía *f,* blanqueador *m Lat*
bleachers *ns & pl* : gradas *fpl*
bleak *adj* **1** DESOLATE : desolado **2** GLOOMY : triste, sombrío
bleary-eyed *adj* : con los ojos nublados
bleat *vi* : balar — ~ *n* : balido *m*
bleed *v* **bled; bleeding** : sangrar
blemish *vt* : manchar, marcar — ~ *n* : mancha *f,* marca *f*
blend *vt* : mezclar, combinar — ~ *n* : mezcla *f,* combinación *f* — **blender** *n* : licuadora *f*
bless *vt* **blessed; blessing** : bendecir — **blessed** *or* **blest** *adj* : bendito — **blessing** *n* : bendición *f*
blew → **blow**
blind *adj* : ciego — ~ *vt* **1** : cegar, dejar

ciego **2** DAZZLE : deslumbrar — ~ *n* **1** : persiana *f* (para una ventana) **2 the** ~ : los ciegos — **blindfold** *vt* : vendar los ojos — ~ *n* : venda *f* (para los ojos) — **blindly** *adv* : ciegamente — **blindness** *n* : ceguera *f*
blink *vi* **1** : parpadear **2** FLICKER : brillar intermitentemente — ~ *n* : parpadeo *m* — **blinker** *n* : intermitente *m*, direccional *f Lat*
bliss *n* : dicha *f*, felicidad *f* (absoluta) — **blissful** *adj* : feliz
blister *n* : ampolla *f* — ~ *vi* : ampollarse
blitz *n* : bombardeo *m* aéreo
blizzard *n* : ventisca *f* (de nieve)
bloated *adj* : hinchado
blob *n* **1** DROP : gota *f* **2** SPOT : mancha *f*
block *n* **1** : bloque *m* **2** OBSTRUCTION : obstrucción *f* **3** : manzana *f*, cuadra *f Lat* (de edificios) **4** *or* **building** ~ : cubo *m* de construcción — ~ *vt* : obstruir, bloquear — **blockade** *n* : bloqueo *m* — **blockage** *n* : obstrucción *f*
blond *or* **blonde** *adj* : rubio — ~ *n* : rubio *m*, -bia *f*
blood *n* : sangre *f* — **bloodhound** *n* : sabueso *m* — **blood pressure** *n* : tensión *f* (arterial) — **bloodshed** *n* : derramamiento *m* de sangre — **bloodshot** *adj* : inyectado de sangre — **bloodstained** *adj* : manchado de sangre — **bloodstream** *n* : sangre *f*, torrente *m* sanguíneo — **bloody** *adj* **bloodier; -est** : ensangrentado, sangriento
bloom *n* **1** : flor *f* **2 in full** ~ : en plena floración — ~ *vi* : florecer
blossom *n* : flor *f* — ~ *vi* : florecer
blot *n* **1** : borrón *m* (de tinta, etc.) **2** BLEMISH : mancha *f* — ~ *vt* **blotted; blotting 1** : emborronar **2** DRY : secar
blotch *n* : mancha *f*, borrón *m* — **blotchy** *adj* **blotchier; -est** : lleno de manchas
blouse *n* : blusa *f*
blow *v* **blew; blown; blowing** *vi* **1** : soplar **2** SOUND : sonar **3** *or* ~ **out** : fundirse (dícese de un fusible eléctrico), reventarse (dícese de una llanta) — *vt* **1** : soplar **2** SOUND : tocar, sonar **3** BUNGLE : echar a perder — ~ *n* : golpe *m* — **blowout** *n* : reventón *m* — **blow up** *vi* : estallar, hacer explosión — *vt* **1** EXPLODE : volar **2** INFLATE : inflar
blubber *n* : esperma *f* de ballena
bludgeon *vt* : aporrear
blue *adj* **bluer; bluest 1** : azul **2** MELANCHOLY : triste — ~ *n* : azul *m* — **blueberry** *n*, *pl* **-ries** : arándano *m* — **bluebird** *n* : azulejo *m* — **blue cheese** *n* : queso *m* azul — **blueprint** *n* PLAN : proyecto *m* — **blues** *npl* **1** SADNESS : tristeza *f* **2** : blues *m* (en música)
bluff *vi* : hacer un farol — ~ *n* : farol *m*

blunder *vi* : meter la pata *fam* — ~ *n* : metedura *f* de pata *fam*
blunt *adj* **1** DULL : desafilado **2** DIRECT : directo, franco
blur *n* : imágen *f* borrosa — ~ *vt* **blurred; blurring** : hacer borroso
blurb *n* : nota *f* publicitaria
blurt *vt or* ~ **out** : espetar
blush *n* : rubor *m* — ~ *vi* : ruborizarse
blustery *adj* : borrascoso, tempestuoso
boar *n* : cerdo *m* macho
board *n* **1** PLANK : tabla *f*, tablón *m* **2** COMMITTEE : junta *f*, consejo *m* **3** : tablero *m* (de juegos) **4 room and** ~ : comida y alojamiento — ~ *vt* **1** : subir a bordo de (una nave, un avión, etc.), subir a (un tren) **2** LODGE : hospedar **3** ~ **up** : cerrar con tablas — **boarder** *n* : huésped *mf*
boast *n* : jactancia *f* — ~ *vi* : alardear, jactarse — **boastful** *adj* : jactancioso
boat *n* : barco *m* (grande), barca *f* (pequeña)
bob *vi* **bobbed; bobbing** *or* ~ **up and down** : subir y bajar
bobbin *n* : bobina *f*, carrete *m*
bobby pin *n* : horquilla *f*
body *n*, *pl* **bodies 1** : cuerpo *m* **2** CORPSE : cadáver *m* **3** : carrocería (de un automóvil, etc.) **4** COLLECTION : conjunto *m* **5** ~ **of water** : masa *f* de agua — **bodily** *adj* : corporal — **bodyguard** *n* : guardaespaldas *mf*
bog *n* : ciénaga *f* — ~ *vt* **bogged; bogging** *or* ~ **down** : empantanarse
bogus *adj* : falso
boil *v* : hervir — **boiler** *n* : caldera *f*
bold *adj* **1** DARING : audaz **2** IMPUDENT : descarado — **boldness** *n* : audacia *f*
Bolivian *adj* : boliviano *m*, -na *f*
bologna *n* : salchicha *f* ahumada
bolster *vt* **-stered; -stering** *or* ~ **up** : reforzar
bolt *n* **1** LOCK : cerrojo *m* **2** SCREW : tornillo *m* **3** ~ **of lightning** : relámpago *m*, rayo *m* — ~ *vt* **1** FASTEN : atornillar **2** LOCK : echar el cerrojo a — *vi* FLEE : salir corriendo
bomb *n* : bomba *f* — ~ *vt* : bombardear — **bombard** *vt* : bombardear — **bombardment** *n* : bombardeo *m* — **bomber** *n* : bombardero *m*
bond *n* **1** TIE : vínculo *m*, lazo *m* **2** SURETY : fianza *f* **3** : bono *m* (en finanzas) — ~ *vi* STICK : adherirse
bondage *n* : esclavitud *f*
bone *n* : hueso *m* — ~ *vt* **boned; boning** : deshuesar
bonfire *n* : hoguera *f*
bonus *n* **1** PAY : prima *f* **2** BENEFIT : beneficio *m* adicional

bony *adj* **bonier; -est 1 :** huesudo **2 :** lleno de espinas (dícese de pescados)
boo *n, pl* **boos :** abucheo *m* — ~ *vt* : abuchear
book *n* **1 :** libro *m* **2** NOTEBOOK : libreta *f*, cuaderno *m* — ~ *vt* : reservar — **bookcase** *n* : estantería *f* — **bookkeeping** *n* : teneduría *f* de libros, contabilidad *f* — **booklet** *n* : folleto *m* — **bookmark** *n* : marcador *m* de libros — **bookseller** *n* : librero *m*, -ra *f* — **bookshelf** *n, pl* **-shelves** : estante *m* — **bookstore** *n* : librería *f*
boom *vi* **1 :** tronar, resonar **2** PROSPER : estar en auge, prosperar — ~ *n* **1 :** bramido *m*, estruendo *m* **2 :** auge *m* (económico)
boon *n* : ayuda *f*, beneficio *m*
boost *vt* **1** LIFT : levantar **2** INCREASE : aumentar — ~ *n* **1** INCREASE : aumento *m* **2** ENCOURAGEMENT : estímulo *m*
boot *n* : bota *f*, botín *m* — ~ *vt* **1 :** dar una patada a **2** *or* ~ **up** : cargar (un ordenador)
booth *n, pl* **booths** : cabina *f* (de teléfono, de votar), caseta *f* (de información)
booty *n, pl* **-ties** : botín *m*
booze *n* : trago *m*, bebida *f* (alcohólica)
border *n* **1** EDGE : borde *m*, orilla *f* **2** TRIM : ribete *m* **3** FRONTIER : frontera *f*
bore[1] *vt* **bored; boring** DRILL : taladrar
bore[2] *vt* TIRE : aburrir — ~ *n* : pesado *m*, -da *fam f* (persona), lata *f fam* (cosa, situación) — **boredom** *n* : aburrimiento *m* — **boring** *adj* : aburrido, pesado
born *adj* **1 :** nacido **2 be** ~ : nacer
borough *n* : distrito *m* municipal
borrow *vt* **:** pedir prestado, tomar prestado
Bosnian *adj* : bosnio *m*, -nia *f*
bosom *n* BREAST : pecho *m*, seno *m* — ~ *adj* ~ **friend** : amigo *m* íntimo
boss *n* : jefe *m*, -fa *f*; patrón *m*, -trona *f* — ~ *vt* SUPERVISE : dirigir — **bossy** *adj* **bossier; -est :** autoritario
botany *n* : botánica *f* — **botanical** *adj* : botánico
botch *vt* : hacer una chapuza de, estropear
both *adj* : ambos, los dos, las dos — ~ *pron* : ambos *m*, -bas *f*; los dos, las dos
bother *vt* **1** TROUBLE : preocupar **2** PESTER : molestar, fastidiar — *vi* ~ **to** : molestarse en — ~ *n* : molestia *f*
bottle *n* **1 :** botella *f*, frasco *m* **2** *or* **baby** ~ : biberón *m* — ~ *vt* **bottled; bottling** : embotellar — **bottleneck** *n* : embotellamiento *m*
bottom *n* **1 :** fondo *m* (de una caja, del mar, etc.), pie *m* (de una escalera, una montaña, etc.), final *m* (de una lista) **2** BUTTOCKS : nalgas *fpl*, trasero *m* — ~ *adj* : más bajo, inferior, de abajo — **bottomless** *adj* : sin fondo

bough *n* : rama *f*
bought → **buy**
bouillon *n* : caldo *m*
boulder *n* : canto *m* rodado
boulevard *n* : bulevar *m*
bounce *v* **bounced; bouncing** *vt* : hacer rebotar — *vi* : rebotar — ~ *n* : rebote *m*
bound[1] *adj* **be** ~ **for** : ir rumbo a
bound[2] *adj* **1** OBLIGED : obligado **2** DETERMINED : decidido **3 be** ~ **to** : tener que
bound[3] *n* **out of** ~**s** : (en) zona prohibida — **boundary** *n, pl* **-aries** : límite *m* — **boundless** *adj* : sin límites
bouquet *n* : ramo *m*
bourgeois *adj* : burgués
bout *n* **1 :** combate *m* (en deportes) **2 :** ataque *m* (de una enfermedad) **3 :** período *m* (de actividad)
bow[1] *vi* : inclinarse — *vt* ~ **one's head** : inclinar la cabeza — ~ *n* : reverencia *f*, inclinación *f*
bow[2] *n* **1 :** arco *m* **2 tie a** ~ : hacer un lazo
bow[3] *n* : proa *f* (de un barco)
bowels *npl* **1 :** intestinos *mpl* **2** DEPTHS : entrañas *fpl*
bowl[1] *n* : tazón *m*, cuenco *m*
bowl[2] *vi* : jugar a los bolos — **bowling** *n* : bolos *mpl*
box[1] *vi* FIGHT : boxear — **boxer** *n* : boxeador *m*, -dora *f* — **boxing** *n* : boxeo *m*
box[2] *n* **1 :** caja *f*, cajón *m* **2 :** palco *m* (en el teatro) — ~ *vt* : empaquetar — **box office** *n* : taquilla *f*, boletería *f Lat*
boy *n* : niño *m*, chico *m*
boycott *vt* : boicotear — ~ *n* : boicot *m*
boyfriend *n* : novio *m*
bra → **brassiere**
brace *n* **1** SUPPORT : abrazadera *f* **2** ~**s** *npl* : aparatos *mpl* (para dientes) — ~ *vi* ~ **oneself for** : prepararse para
bracelet *n* : brazalete *m*
bracket *n* **1** SUPPORT : soporte *m* **2 :** corchete *m* (marca de puntuación) **3** CATEGORY : categoría *f* — ~ *vt* **1 :** poner entre corchetes **2** CATEGORIZE : catalogar
brag *vi* **bragged; bragging** : jactarse
braid *vt* : trenzar — ~ *n* : trenza *f*
braille *n* : braille *m*
brain *n* **1 :** cerebro *m* **2** ~**s** *npl* : inteligencia *f* — **brainstorm** *n* : idea *f* genial — **brainwash** *vt* : lavar el cerebro — **brainy** *adj* **brainier; -est** : inteligente, listo
brake *n* : freno *m* — ~ *v* **braked; braking** : frenar
bramble *n* : zarza *f*
bran *n* : salvado *m*
branch *n* **1 :** rama *f* (de una planta) **2** DIVISION : ramal *m* (de un camino, etc.), sucursal *f* (de una empresa), agencia *f* (del gob-

ierno) — ~ *vi or* ~ **off** : ramificarse, bifurcarse

brand *n* **1** : marca *f* (de ganado) **2** *or* ~ **name** : marca *f* de fábrica — ~ *vt* **1** : marcar (ganado) **2** LABEL : tachar, tildar

brandish *vt* : blandir

brand–new *adj* : flamante

brandy *n, pl* **-dies** : brandy *m*, coñac *m*

brass *n* **1** : latón *m* **2** : metales *mpl* (de una orquesta)

brassiere *n* : sostén *m*, brasier *m Lat*

brat *n* : mocoso *m*, -sa *f fam*

bravado *n, pl* **-does** *or* **-dos** : bravuconadas *fpl*

brave *adj* **braver; bravest** : valiente, valeroso — ~ *vt* **braved; braving** : afrontar, hacer frente a — ~ *n* : guerrero *m* indio — **bravery** *n* : valor *m*, valentía *f*

brawl *n* : pelea *f*, reyerta *f*

brawn *n* : músculos *mpl* — **brawny** *adj* **brawnier; -est** : musculoso

bray *vi* : rebuznar

brazen *adj* : descarado

Brazilian *adj* : brasileño *m*, -ña *f*

breach *n* **1** VIOLATION : infracción *f*, violación *f* **2** GAP : brecha *f*

bread *n* **1** : pan *m* **2** ~ **crumbs** : migajas *fpl*

breadth *n* : anchura *f*

break *v* **broke; broken; breaking** *vt* **1** : romper, quebrar **2** VIOLATE : infringir, violar **3** INTERRUPT : interrumpir **4** SURPASS : batir (un récord, etc.) **5** ~ **a habit** : quitarse una costumbre **6** ~ **the news** : dar la noticia — *vi* **1** : romperse, quebrarse **2** ~ **away** : escapar **3** ~ **down** : estropearse (dícese de una máquina), fallar (dícese de un sistema, etc.) **4** ~ **into** : entrar en **5** ~ **off** : interrumpirse **6** ~ **out of** : escaparse de **7** ~ **up** SEPARATE : separarse — ~ *n* **1** : ruptura *f*, fractura *f* **2** GAP : interrupción *f*, claro *m* (entre las nubes) **3** **lucky** ~ : golpe *m* de suerte **4 take a** ~ : tomar(se) un descanso — **breakable** *adj* : quebradizo, frágil — **breakdown** *n* **1** : avería *f* (de máquinas), interrupción *f* (de comunicaciones), fracaso *m* (de negociaciones) **2** *or* **nervous** ~ : crisis *f* nerviosa

breakfast *n* : desayuno *m*

breast *n* **1** : seno *m* (de una mujer) **2** CHEST : pecho *m* — **breast–feed** *vt* **-fed; -feeding** : amamantar

breath *n* : aliento *m*, respiración *f* — **breathe** *v* **breathed; breathing** : respirar — **breathless** *adj* : sin aliento, jadeante — **breathtaking** *adj* : impresionante

breed *v* **bred; breeding** *vt* **1** : criar (animales) **2** ENGENDER : engendrar, producir

— *vi* : reproducirse — ~ *n* **1** : raza *f* **2** CLASS : clase *f*, tipo *m*

breeze *n* : brisa *f* — **breezy** *adj* **breezier; -est 1** WINDY : ventoso **2** NONCHALANT : despreocupado

brevity *n, pl* **-ties** : brevedad *f*

brew *vt* : hacer (cerveza, etc.), preparar (té) — *vi* **1** : fabricar cerveza **2** : amenazar (dícese de una tormenta) — **brewery** *n, pl* **-eries** : cervecería *f*

bribe *n* : soborno *m* — ~ *vt* **bribed; bribing** : sobornar — **bribery** *n, pl* **-eries** : soborno *m*

brick *n* : ladrillo *m* — **bricklayer** *n* : albañil *mf*

bride *n* : novia *f* — **bridal** *adj* : nupcial, de novia — **bridegroom** *n* : novio *m* — **bridesmaid** *n* : dama *f* de honor

bridge *n* **1** : puente *m* **2** : caballete *m* (de la nariz) **3** : bridge *m* (juego de naipes) — ~ *vt* **bridged; bridging 1** : tender un puente sobre **2** ~ **the gap** : salvar las diferencias

bridle *n* : brida *f* — ~ *vt* **-dled; -dling** : embridar

brief *adj* : breve — ~ *n* **1** : resumen *m*, sumario *m* **2** ~**s** *npl* UNDERPANTS : calzoncillos *mpl* — ~ *vt* : dar órdenes a, instruir — **briefcase** *n* : portafolio *m*, maletín *m* — **briefly** *adv* : brevemente

bright *adj* **1** : brillante, claro **2** CHEERFUL : alegre, animado **3** INTELLIGENT : listo, inteligente — **brighten** *vi* **1** : hacerse más brillante **2** *or* ~ **up** : animarse, alegrarse — *vt* **1** ILLUMINATE : iluminar **2** ENLIVEN : alegrar, animar

brilliant *adj* : brillante — **brilliance** *n* **1** BRIGHTNESS : resplandor *m*, brillantez *f* **2** INTELLIGENCE : inteligencia *f*

brim *n* **1** : borde *m* (de una taza, etc.) **2** : ala *f* (de un sombrero) — ~ *vi* **brimmed; brimming** *or* ~ **over** : desbordarse, rebosar

brine *n* : salmuera *f*

bring *vt* **brought; bringing 1** : traer **2** ~ **about** : ocasionar **3** ~ **around** PERSUADE : convencer **4** ~ **back** : devolver **5** ~ **down** : derribar **6** ~ **on** CAUSE : provocar **7** ~ **out** : sacar **8** ~ **to an end** : terminar (con) **9** ~ **up** REAR : criar **10** ~ **up** MENTION : sacar

brink *n* : borde *m*

brisk *adj* **1** FAST : rápido **2** LIVELY : enérgico

bristle *n* : cerda *f* (de un animal), pelo *m* (de una planta) — ~ *vi* **-tled; -tling** : erizarse

British *adj* : británico

brittle *adj* **-tler; -tlest** : frágil, quebradizo

broach *vt* : abordar

broad *adj* **1** WIDE : ancho **2** GENERAL : general **3 in** ~ **daylight** : en pleno día

broadcast vt -cast; -casting : emitir — ～ n : emisión f
broaden vt : ampliar, ensanchar — vi : ensancharse — **broadly** adv : en general — **broad–minded** adj : de miras amplias, tolerante
broccoli n : brócoli m, brécol m
brochure n : folleto m
broil vt : asar a la parrilla
broke → **break** — ～ adj : pelado fam — **broken** adj : roto, quebrado — **brokenhearted** adj : desconsolado, con el corazón destrozado
broker n : corredor m, -dora f
bronchitis n : bronquitis f
bronze n : bronce m
brooch n : broche m
brood n : nidada f (de pájaros), camada f (de mamíferos) — ～ vi **1** INCUBATE : empollar **2** ～ **about** : dar vueltas a, pensar demasiado en
brook n : arroyo m
broom n : escoba f — **broomstick** n : palo m de escoba
broth n, pl **broths** : caldo m
brothel n : burdel m
brother n : hermano m — **brotherhood** n : fraternidad f — **brother–in–law** n, pl **brothers–in–law**: cuñado m — **brotherly** adj : fraternal
brought → **bring**
brow n **1** EYEBROW : ceja f **2** FOREHEAD : frente f **3** : cima f (de una colina)
brown adj : marrón, castaño (dícese del pelo), moreno (dícese de la piel) — ～ n : marrón m — ～ vt : dorar (en cocinar)
browse vi **browsed; browsing** : mirar, echar un vistazo
bruise vt **bruised; bruising 1** : contusionar, magullar (a una persona) **2** : machucar (frutas) — ～ n : cardenal m, magulladura f
brunch n : brunch m
brunet or **brunette** adj : moreno — ～ n : moreno m, -na f
brunt n **bear the** ～ **of** : aguantar el mayor impacto de
brush n **1** : cepillo m, pincel m (de artista), brocha f (de pintor) **2** UNDERBRUSH : maleza f — ～ vt **1** : cepillar **2** GRAZE : rozar **3** ～ **aside** : rechazar **4** ～ **off** DISREGARD : hacer caso omiso de — vi ～ **up on** : repasar — **brush–off** n **give the** ～ **to** : dar calabazas a
brusque adj : brusco
brutal adj : brutal — **brutality** n, pl -ties : brutalidad f
brute adj : bruto — ～ n : bestia f; bruto m, -ta f

bubble n : burbuja f — ～ vi -bled; -bling : burbujear
buck n, pl **buck** or **bucks 1** : animal m macho, ciervo m (macho) **2** DOLLAR : dólar m — ～ vi **1** : corcovear (dícese de un caballo) **2** ～ **up** : animarse, levantar el ánimo — vt OPPOSE : oponerse a, ir en contra de
bucket n : cubo m
buckle n : hebilla f — ～ v -led; -ling vt **1** FASTEN : abrochar **2** BEND : combar, torcer — vi **1** : combarse, torcerse **2** : doblarse (dícese de las rodillas)
bud n **1** : brote m **2** or **flower** ～ : capullo m — ～ vi **budded; budding** : brotar, hacer brotes
Buddhism n : budismo m — **Buddhist** adj : budista — ～ n : budista mf
buddy n, pl -**dies** : compañero m, -ra f
budge vi **budged; budging 1** MOVE : moverse **2** YIELD : ceder
budget n : presupuesto m — ～ vi : presupuestar — **budgetary** adj : presupuestario
buff n **1** : beige m, color m de ante **2** ENTHUSIAST : aficionado m, -da f — ～ adj : beige — ～ vt POLISH : pulir
buffalo n, pl -**lo** or -**loes** : búfalo m
buffet n **1** : bufé m (comida) **2** SIDEBOARD : aparador m
bug n **1** INSECT : bicho m, insecto m **2** FLAW : defecto m **3** GERM : microbio m **4** MICROPHONE : micrófono m (oculto) — ～ vt **bugged; bugging 1** PESTER : fastidiar, molestar **2** : ocultar micrófonos en (una habitación, etc.)
buggy n, pl -**gies 1** CARRIAGE : calesa f **2** or **baby** ～ : cochecito m (para niños)
bugle n : clarín m, corneta f
build v **built; building** vt **1** : construir **2** DEVELOP : desarrollar — vi **1** or ～ **up** INTENSIFY : aumentar, intensificar **2** or ～ **up** ACCUMULATE : acumularse — ～ n PHYSIQUE : físico m, complexión f — **builder** n : constructor m, -tora f — **building** n **1** STRUCTURE : edificio m **2** CONSTRUCTION : construcción f — **built–in** adj : empotrado
bulb n **1** : bulbo m (de una planta) **2** LIGHTBULB : bombilla f
bulge vi **bulged; bulging** : sobresalir — ～ n : bulto m, protuberancia f
bulk n **1** VOLUME : volumen m, bulto m **2 in** ～ : en grandes cantidades — **bulky** adj **bulkier; -est** : voluminoso
bull n **1** : toro m **2** MALE : macho m
bulldog n : buldog m
bulldozer n : bulldozer m
bullet n : bala f
bulletin n : boletín m — **bulletin board** n : tablón m de anuncios

bulletproof *adj* : a prueba de balas

bullfight *n* : corrida *f* (de toros) — **bullfighter** *n* : torero *m*, -ra *f;* matador *m*

bullion *n* : oro *m* en lingotes, plata *f* en lingotes

bull's–eye *n, pl* **bull's–eyes** : diana *f*

bully *n, pl* **-lies** : matón *m* — ~ *vt* **-lied; -lying** : intimidar

bum *n* : vagabundo *m*, -da *f*

bumblebee *n* : abejorro *m*

bump *n* **1** BULGE : bulto *m*, protuberancia *f* **2** IMPACT : golpe *m* **3** JOLT : sacudida *f* — ~ *vt* : chocar contra — *vi* ~ **into** MEET : encontrarse con — **bumper** *n* : parachoques *mpl* — ~ *adj* : extraordinario, récord — **bumpy** *adj* **bumpier; -est 1** : desigual, lleno de baches (dícese de un camino) **2 a** ~ **flight** : un vuelo agitado

bun *n* : bollo *m*

bunch *n* : grupo *m* (de personas), racimo *m* (de frutas, etc.), ramo *m* (de flores), manojo *m* (de llaves) — ~ *vi or* ~ **up** : amontarse, agruparse

bundle *n* **1** : lío *m*, bulto *m*, atado *m*, haz *m* (de palos) **2** PARCEL : paquete *m* **3** ~ **of nerves** : manojo *m* de nervios — ~ *vt* **-dled; -dling** *or* ~ **up** : liar, atar

bungalow *n* : casa *f* de un solo piso

bungle *vt* **-gled; -gling** : echar a perder

bunion *n* : juanete *m*

bunk *n or* **bunk bed** : litera *f*

bunny *n, pl* **-nies** : conejo *m*, -ja *f*

buoy *n* : boya *f* — ~ *vt or* ~ **up** HEARTEN : animar, levantar el ánimo a — **buoyant** *adj* **1** : boyante, flotante **2** LIGHTHEARTED : alegre, optimista

burden *n* : carga *f* — ~ *vt* ~ **s.o. with** : cargar a algn con — **burdensome** *adj* : oneroso

bureau *n* **1** : cómoda *f* (mueble) **2** : departamento *m* (del gobierno) **3** AGENCY : agencia *f* — **bureaucracy** *n, pl* **-cies** : burocracia *f* — **bureaucrat** *n* : burócrata *mf* — **bureaucratic** *adj* : burocrático

burglar *n* : ladrón *m*, -drona *f* — **burglarize** *vt* **-ized; -izing** : robar — **burglary** *n, pl* **-glaries** : robo *m*

burgundy *n, pl* **-dies** : borgoña *m*, vino *m* de Borgoña

burial *n* : entierro *m*

burly *adj* **-lier; -liest** : fornido

burn *v* **burned** *or* **burnt; burning** *vt* **1** : quemar **2** *or* ~ **down** : incendiar **3** ~ **up** : consumir — *vi* **1** : arder (dícese de un fuego), quemarse (dícese de la comida, etc.) **2** : estar encendido (dícese de una luz) **3** ~ **out** : apagarse — ~ *n* : quemadura *f* — **burner** *n* : quemador *m*

burnish *vt* : pulir

burp *vi* : eructar — ~ *n* : eructo *m*

burro *n, pl* **-os** : burro *m*

burrow *n* : madriguera *f* — ~ *vi* **1** : cavar **2** ~ **into** : hurgar en

bursar *n* : tesorero *m*, -ra *f*

burst *v* **burst** *or* **bursted; bursting** *vi* : reventarse — *vt* : reventar — ~ *n* **1** EXPLOSION : estallido *m*, explosión *f* **2** OUTBURST : arranque *m*, arrebato *m* **3** ~ **of laughter** : carcajada *f*

bury *vt* **buried; burying 1** INTER : enterrar **2** HIDE : esconder

bus *n, pl* **buses** *or* **busses** : autobús *m*, bus *m* — ~ *v* **bused** *or* **bussed; busing** *or* **bussing** *vt* : transportar en autobús — *vi* : viajar en autobús

bush *n* SHRUB : arbusto *m*, mata *f*

bushel *n* : medida *f* de áridos igual a 35.24 litros

bushy *adj* **bushier; -est** : poblado, espeso

busily *adv* : afanosamente

business *n* **1** COMMERCE : negocios *mpl*, comercio *m* **2** COMPANY : empresa *f*, negocio *m* **3 it's none of your** ~ : no es asunto tuyo — **businessman** *n, pl* **-men** : empresario *m*, hombre *m* de negocios — **businesswoman** *n, pl* **-women** : empresaria *f*, mujer *f* de negocios

bust¹ *vt* BREAK : romper

bust² *n* **1** : busto *m* (en la escultura) **2** BREASTS : pecho *m*, senos *mpl*

bustle *vi* **-tled; -tling** *or* ~ **about** : ir y venir, ajetrearse — ~ *n or* **hustle and** ~ : bullicio *m*, ajetreo *m*

busy *adj* **busier; -est 1** : ocupado **2** BUSTLING : concurrido

but *conj* **1** : pero **2 not one** ~ **two** : no uno sino dos — ~ *prep* : excepto, menos

butcher *n* : carnicero *m*, -ra *f* — ~ *vt* **1** : matar **2** BOTCH : hacer una carnicería de

butler *n* : mayordomo *m*

butt *vt* : embestir (con los cuernos), darle un cabezazo a — *vi* ~ **in** : interrumpir — ~ *n* **1** BUTTING : embestida *f* (de cuernos) **2** TARGET : blanco *m* **3** : extremo *m*, culata *f* (de un rifle), colilla *f* (de un cigarillo)

butter *n* : mantequilla *f* — ~ *vt* : untar con mantequilla

buttercup *n* : ranúnculo *m*

butterfly *n, pl* **-flies** : mariposa *f*

buttocks *npl* : nalgas *fpl*

button *n* : botón *m* — ~ *vt* : abotonar — *vi or* ~ **up** : abotonarse — **buttonhole** *n* : ojal *m* — ~ *vt* **-holed; -holing** : acorralar

buy *vt* **bought; buying** : comprar — ~ *n* : compra *f* — **buyer** *n* : comprador *m*, -dora *f*

buzz *vi* : zumbar — ~ *n* : zumbido *m*

buzzard *n* : buitre *m*

buzzer *n* : timbre *m*
by *prep* **1** NEAR : cerca de **2** VIA : por **3** PAST : por, por delante de **4** DURING : de, durante **5** (*in expressions of time*) : para **6** (*indicating cause or agent*) : por, de, a —
~ *adv* **1** ~ **and** ~ : poco después **2** ~ **and large** : en general **3 go** ~ : pasar **4 stop** ~ : pasar por casa

bygone *adj* : pasado — ~ *n* **let** ~**s be** ~**s** : lo pasado, pasado está
bypass *n* : carretera *f* de circunvalación — ~ *vt* : evitar
by-product *n* : subproducto *m*
bystander *n* : espectador *m*, -dora *f*
byte *n* : byte *m*, octeto *m*
byword *n* **be a** ~ **for** : estar sinónimo de

C

c *n*, *pl* **c's** *or* **cs** : c, tercera letra del alfabeto inglés
cab *n* **1** : taxi *m* **2** : cabina *f* (de un camión, etc.)
cabbage *n* : col *f*, repollo *m*
cabin *n* **1** : cabaña *f* **2** : cabina *f* (de un avión, etc.), camarote *m* (de un barco)
cabinet *n* **1** CUPBOARD : armario *m* **2** : gabinete *m* (del gobierno) **3** *or* **medicine** ~ : botiquín *m*
cable *n* : cable *m* — **cable television** *n* : televisión *f* por cable
cackle *vi* **-led; -ling 1** CLUCK : cacarear **2** LAUGH : reírse a carcajadas
cactus *n*, *pl* **cacti** *or* **-tuses** : cactus *m*
cadence *n* : cadencia *f*, ritmo *m*
cadet *n* : cadete *mf*
café *n* **1** : café *m*, cafetería *f* — **cafeteria** *n* : restaurante *m* autoservicio, cantina *f*
caffeine *n* : cafeína *f*
cage *n* : jaula *f* — ~ *vt* **caged; caging** : enjaular
cajole *vt* **-joled; -joling** : engatusar
cake *n* **1** : pastel *m*, torta *f* **2** : pastilla *f* (de jabón) **3 take the** ~ : ser el colmo — **caked** *adj* ~ **with** : cubierto de
calamity *n*, *pl* **-ties** : calamidad *f*
calcium *n* : calcio *m*
calculate *v* **-lated; -lating** : calcular — **calculating** *adj* : calculador — **calculation** *n* : cálculo *m* — **calculator** *n* : calculadora *f*
calendar *n* : calendario *m*
calf¹ *n*, *pl* **calves 1** : becerro *m*, -rra *f*; ternero *m*, -ra *f* (de vacunos) **2** : cría *f* (de otros mamíferos)
calf² *n*, *pl* **calves** : pantorrilla *f* (de la pierna)
caliber *or* **calibre** *n* : calibre *m*
call *vi* **1** : llamar **2** VISIT : pasar, hacer (una) visita **3** ~ **for** : requerir — *vt* **1** : llamar **2** ~ **off** : cancelar — ~ *n* **1** : llamada *f* **2** SHOUT : grito *m* **3** VISIT : visita *f* **4** DEMAND : petición *f* — **calling** *n* : vocación *f*

callous *adj* : insensible, cruel
calm *n* : calma *f*, tranquilidad *f* — ~ *vt* : calmar — *vi* *or* ~ **down** : calmarse — ~ *adj* : tranquilo, en calma — **calmly** *adv* : con calma
calorie *n* : caloría *f*
came → **come**
camel *n* : camello *m*
camera *n* : cámara *f*
camouflage *n* : camuflaje *m* — ~ *vt* **-flaged; -flaging** : camuflar
camp *n* **1** : campamento *m* **2** FACTION : bando *m* — ~ *vi* : acampar, ir de camping
campaign *n* : campaña *f* — ~ *vi* : hacer (una) campaña
camping *n* : camping *m*
campus *n* : ciudad *f* universitaria
can¹ *v aux, past* **could**; *present s & pl* **can 1** (*expressing possibility or permission*) : poder **2** (*expressing knowledge or ability*) : saber **3 that cannot be!** : ¡no puede ser!
can² *n* : lata *f* — ~ *vt* **canned; canning** : enlatar
Canadian *adj* : canadiense
canal *n* : canal *m*
canary *n*, *pl* **-naries** : canario *m*
cancel *vt* **-celed** *or* **-celled; -celing** *or* **-celling** : cancelar — **cancellation** *n* : cancelación *f*
cancer *n* : cáncer *m* — **cancerous** *adj* : canceroso
candelabra *n*, *pl* **-bra** *or* **-bras** : candelabro *m*
candid *adj* : franco
candidate *n* : candidato *m*, -ta *f* — **candidacy** *n*, *pl* **-cies** : candidatura *f*
candle *n* : vela *f* — **candlestick** *n* : candelero *m*
candor *or Brit* **candour** *n* : franqueza *f*
candy *n*, *pl* **-dies** : dulce *m*, caramelo *m*
cane *n* **1** : bastón *m* (para andar), vara *f* (para castigar) **2** REED : caña *f*, mimbre *m*

canine   198

— ~ *vt* **caned; caning 1** : tapizar con mimbre **2** FLOG : azotar
canine *n or* ~ **tooth** : colmillo *m*, diente *m* canino — ~ *adj* : canino
canister *n* : lata *f*, bote *m* Spain
cannibal *n* : caníbal *mf*
cannon *n*, *pl* **-nons** *or* **-non** : cañón *m*
cannot (can not) → **can**[1]
canny *adj* **cannier; -est** : astuto
canoe *n* : canoa *f*, piragua *f* — ~ *vt* **-noed; -noeing** : ir en canoa
canon *n* : canon *m* — **canonize** *vt* **-ized; -izing** : canonizar
can opener *n* : abrelatas *m*
canopy *n*, *pl* **-pies** : dosel *m*
can't (*contraction of* **can not**) → **can**[1]
cantaloupe *n* : melón *m*, cantalupo *m*
cantankerous *adj* : irritable, irascible
canteen *n* **1** FLASK : cantimplora *f* **2** CAFETERIA : cantina *f*
canter *vi* : ir a medio galope — ~ *n* : medio galope *m*
canvas *n* **1** : lona *f* (tela) **2** : lienzo *m* (de pintar)
canvass *vt* **1** : solicitar votos de, hacer campaña entre **2** POLL : sondear — ~ *n* **1** : solicitación *f* (de votos) **2** POLL : sondeo *m*
canyon *n* : cañón *m*
cap *n* **1** : gorra *f*, gorro *m* **2** TOP : tapa *f*, tapón *m* (de botellas) **3** LIMIT : tope *m* — ~ *vt* **capped; capping 1** COVER : tapar, cubrir **2** OUTDO : superar
capable *adj* : capaz, competente — **capability** *n*, *pl* **-ties** : capacidad *f*
capacity *n*, *pl* **-ties 1** : capacidad *f* **2** ROLE : calidad *f*
cape[1] *n* : cabo *m* (en geografía)
cape[2] *n* CLOAK : capa *f*
caper[1] *n* : alcaparra *f*
caper[2] *n* PRANK : broma *f*, travesura *f*
capital *adj* **1** : capital **2** : mayúsculo (dícese de las letras) — ~ *n* **1** *or* ~ **city** : capital *f* **2** WEALTH : capital *m* **3** *or* ~ **letter** : mayúscula *f* — **capitalism** *n* : capitalismo *m* — **capitalist** *or* **capitalistic** *adj* : capitalista — **capitalize** *vt* **-ized; -izing 1** FINANCE : capitalizar **2** : escribir con mayúscula — *vi* ~ **on** : sacar partido de
capitol *n* : capitolio *m*
capitulate *vi* **-lated; -lating** : capitular
capsize *v* **-sized; -sizing** *vt* : hacer volcar — *vi* : zozobrar, volcar(se)
capsule *n* : cápsula *f*
captain *n* : capitán *m*, -tana *f*
caption *n* **1** : leyenda *f* (al pie de una ilustración) **2** SUBTITLE : subtítulo *m*
captivate *vt* **-vated; -vating** : cautivar, encantar

captive *adj* : cautivo — ~ *n* : cautivo *m*, -va *f* — **captivity** *n* : cautiverio *m*
capture *n* : captura *f*, apresamiento *m* — ~ *vt* **-tured; -turing 1** SEIZE : capturar, apresar **2** ~ **one's interest** : captar el interés de uno
car *n* **1** : automóvil *m*, coche *m*, carro *m* Lat **2** *or* **railroad** ~ : vagón *m*
carafe *n* : garrafa *f*
caramel *n* : caramelo *m*, azúcar *f* quemada
carat *n* : quilate *m*
caravan *n* : caravana *f*
carbohydrate *n* : carbohidrato *m*, hidrato *m* de carbono
carbon *n* : carbono *m* — **carbon copy** *n* : copia *f*, duplicado *m*
carburetor *n* : carburador *m*
carcass *n* : cuerpo *m* (de un animal muerto)
card *n* **1** : tarjeta *f* **2** *or* **playing** ~ : carta *f*, naipe *m* — **cardboard** *n* : cartón *m*
cardiac *adj* : cardíaco
cardigan *n* : cárdigan *m*
cardinal *n* : cardenal *m* — ~ *adj* : cardinal, fundamental
care *n* **1** : cuidado *m* **2** WORRY : preocupación **3 take** ~ **of** : cuidar (de) — ~ *vi* **cared; caring 1** : preocuparse, inquietarse **2** ~ **for** TEND : cuidar (de), atender **3** ~ **for** LIKE : querer **4 I don't** ~ : no me importa
career *n* : carrera *f* — ~ *vi* : ir a toda velocidad
carefree *adj* : despreocupado
careful *adj* : cuidadoso — **carefully** *adv* : con cuidado, cuidadosamente — **careless** *adj* : descuidado — **carelessness** *n* : descuido *m*
caress *n* : caricia *f* — ~ *vt* : acariciar
cargo *n*, *pl* **-goes** *or* **-gos** : cargamento *m*, carga *f*
caricature *n* : caricatura *f* — ~ *vt* **-tured; -turing** : caricaturizar
caring *adj* : solícito, afectuoso
carnage *n* : matanza *f*, carnicería *f*
carnal *adj* : carnal
carnation *n* : clavel *m*
carnival *n* : carnaval *m*
carol *n* : villancico *m*
carp *vi* ~ **at** : quejarse de
carpenter *n* : carpintero *m*, -ra *f* — **carpentry** *n* : carpintería *f*
carpet *n* : alfombra *f*
carriage *n* **1** : transporte *m* (de mercancías) **2** BEARING : porte *m* **3** *or* **baby** ~ : cochecito *m* **4** *or* **horse-drawn** ~ : carruaje *m*, coche *m*
carrier *n* **1** : transportista *mf*, empresa *f* de transportes **2** : portador *m*, -dora *f* (de una enfermedad)

carrot n : zanahoria f
carry v -**ried; -rying** vt **1** : llevar **2** TRANS-
PORT : transportar **3** STOCK : vender **4** EN-
TAIL : acarrear, implicar **5** ~ **oneself**
: portarse — vi : oírse (dícese de sonidos) —
carry away vt **get carried away** : exaltarse,
entusiasmarse — **carry on** vt CONDUCT : realizar — vi **1** : portarse inapropiadamente
2 CONTINUE : seguir, continuar — **carry out**
vt **1** PERFORM : llevar a cabo, realizar **2**
FULFILL : cumplir
cart n : carreta f, carro m — ~ vt or ~
around : acarrear
cartilage n : cartílago m
carton n : caja f (de cartón)
cartoon n **1** : caricatura f **2** COMIC STRIP
: historieta f **3** or **animated** ~ : dibujos
mpl animados
cartridge n : cartucho m
carve vt **carved; carving 1** : tallar, esculpir
2 : trinchar (carne)
case n **1** : caso m **2** BOX : caja f **3 in any** ~
: en todo caso **4 in** ~ **of** : en caso de **5 just
in** ~ : por si acaso
cash n : efectivo m, dinero m en efectivo —
~ vt : convertir en efectivo, cobrar
cashew n : anacardo m
cashier n : cajero m, -ra f
cashmere n : cachemira f
cash register n : caja f registradora
casino n, pl -**nos** : casino m
cask n : barril m
casket n : ataúd m
casserole n **1** or ~ **dish** : cazuela f **2**
: guiso m (comida)
cassette n : cassette mf
cast vt **cast; casting 1** THROW : arrojar,
lanzar **2** : depositar (un voto) **3** : repartir
(papeles dramáticos) **4** MOLD : fundir — ~
n **1** : elenco m, reparto m (de actores) **2** or
plaster ~ : molde m de yeso, escayola f
castanets npl : castañuelas fpl
castaway n : náufrago m, -ga f
cast iron n : hierro m fundido
castle n **1** : castillo m **2** : torre f (en ajedrez)
castrate vt -**trated; -trating** : castrar
casual adj **1** CHANCE : casual, fortuito **2** IN-
DIFFERENT : despreocupado **3** INFORMAL
: informal — **casually** adv **1** : de manera
despreocupada **2** INFORMALLY : informal-
mente
casualty n, pl -**ties 1** : accidente m **2** VIC-
TIM : víctima f; herido m, -da f **3 casual-
ties** npl : bajas fpl (militares)
cat n : gato m, -ta f
catalog or **catalogue** n : catálogo m — ~
vt -**loged** or -**logued; -loging** or -**loguing**
: catalogar
catapult n : catapulta f

cataract n : catarata f
catastrophe n : catástrofe f — **catastrophic**
adj : catastrófico
catch v **caught; catching** vt **1** CAPTURE,
TRAP : capturar, atrapar **2** SURPRISE : sorprender **3** GRASP : agarrar, captar **4** SNAG
: enganchar **5** : tomar (un tren, etc.) **6** ~ **a
cold** : resfriarse — vi **1** SNAG : engancharse
2 ~ **fire** : prender fuego — **catching** adj
: contagioso — **catchy** adj **catchier; -est**
: pegadizo, pegajoso Lat
category n, pl -**ries** : categoría f — **categorical** adj : categórico
cater vi **1** : proveer comida **2** ~ **to** : atender a — **caterer** n : proveedor m, -dora f de
comida
caterpillar n : oruga f
catfish n : bagre m
cathedral n : catedral f
catholic adj **1** : universal **2 Catholic**
: católico — **catholicism** n : catolicismo m
cattle npl : ganado m (vacuno)
caught → **catch**
cauldron n : caldera f
cauliflower n : coliflor f
cause n **1** : causa f **2** REASON : motivo m —
~ vt **caused; causing** : causar
caustic adj : cáustico
caution n **1** WARNING : advertencia f **2**
CARE : precaución f, cautela f — ~ vt : advertir — **cautious** adj : cauteloso, precavido — **cautiously** adv : con precaución
cavalier adj : arrogante, desdeñoso
cavalry n, pl -**ries** : caballería f
cave n : cueva f — ~ vi **caved; caving** or
~ **in** : hundirse
cavern n : caverna f
cavity n, pl -**ties 1** : cavidad f **2** : caries f
(dental)
cavort vi : brincar
CD n : CD m, disco m compacto
cease v **ceased; ceasing** vt : dejar de — vi
: cesar — **cease-fire** n : alto m el fuego —
ceaseless adj : incesante
cedar n : cedro m
ceiling n : techo m
celebrate v -**brated; -brating** vt : celebrar —
vi : divertirse — **celebrated** adj : célebre —
celebration n **1** : celebración f **2** FESTIV-
ITY : fiesta f — **celebrity** n, pl -**ties** : celebridad f
celery n, pl -**eries** : apio m
cell n **1** : célula f **2** : celda f (en una cárcel,
etc.)
cellar n **1** BASEMENT : sótano m **2** : bodega
f (de vinos)
cello n, pl -**los** : violoncelo m
cellular adj : celular
cement n : cemento m — ~ vt : cementar

cemetery *n, pl* **-teries** : cementerio *m*
censor *vt* : censurar — **censorship** *n* : censura *f* — **censure** *n* : censura *f* — ~ *vt*
-**sured; -suring** : censurar, criticar
census *n* : censo *m*
cent *n* : centavo *m*
centennial *n* : centenario *m*
center *or Brit* **centre** *n* : centro *m* — ~ *v*
centered *or Brit* **centred; centering** *or*
Brit **centring** *vt* : centrar — *vi* ~ **on** : centrarse en
centigrade *adj* : centígrado
centimeter *n* : centímetro *m*
centipede *n* : ciempiés *m*
central *adj* **1** : central **2 a** ~ **location** : un lugar céntrico — **centralize** *vt* -**ized; -izing**
: centralizar
centre → **center**
century *n, pl* -**ries** : siglo *m*
ceramics *npl* : cerámica *f*
cereal *n* : cereal *m*
ceremony *n, pl* -**nies** : ceremonia *f* — **ceremonial** *adj* : ceremonial
certain *adj* **1** : cierto **2 be** ~ **of** : estar seguro de **3 for** ~ : seguro, con toda seguridad **4 make** ~ **of** : asegurarse de — **certainly** *adv* : desde luego, por supuesto —
certainty *n, pl* -**ties** : certeza *f*, seguridad *f*
certify *vt* -**fied; -fying** : certificar — **certificate** *n* : certificado *m*, partida *f*, acta *f*
chafe *v* **chafed; chafing** *vi* : rozarse — *vt*
: rozar
chain *n* **1** : cadena *f* **2** ~ **of events** : serie *f* de acontecimientos — ~ *vt* : encadenar
chair *n* **1** : silla *f* **2** : cátedra *f* (en una universidad) — ~ *vt* : presidir — **chairman** *n*,
pl -**men** : presidente *m* — **chairperson** *n*
: presidente *m*, -ta *f*
chalk *n* : tiza *f*, gis *m Lat*
challenge *vt* -**lenged; -lenging 1** DISPUTE
: disputar, poner en duda **2** DARE : desafiar
— ~ *n* : reto *m*, desafío *m* — **challenging**
adj : estimulante
chamber *n* : cámara *f* — **chambermaid** *n*
: camarera *f*
champagne *n* : champaña *m*, champán *m*
champion *n* : campeón *m*, -peona *f* — ~ *vt*
: defender — **championship** *n* : campeonato *m*
chance *n* **1** LUCK : azar *m*, suerte *f* **2** OPPORTUNITY : oportunidad *f* **3** LIKELIHOOD
: probabilidad *f* **4 by** ~ : por casualidad **5**
take a ~ : arriesgarse — ~ *vt* **chanced;**
chancing RISK : arriesgar — ~ *adj* : fortuito
chandelier *n* : araña *f* (de luces)
change *v* **changed; changing** *vt* **1** : cambiar **2** SWITCH : cambiar de — *vi* **1** : cambiar **2** *or* ~ **clothes** : cambiarse (de ropa)

— ~ *n* : cambio *m* — **changeable** *adj*
: cambiable
channel *n* **1** : canal *m* **2** : cauce *m* (de un río)
3 MEANS : vía *f*, medio *m*
chant *v* : cantar — ~ *n* : canto *m*
chaos *n* : caos *m* — **chaotic** *adj* : caótico
chap[1] *vi* **chapped; chapping** : agrietarse
chap[2] *n* : tipo *m fam*
chapel *n* : capilla *f*
chaperon *or* **chaperone** *n* : acompañante
mf
chaplain *n* : capellán *m*
chapter *n* : capítulo *m*
char *vt* **charred; charring** : carbonizar
character *n* **1** : carácter *m* **2** : personaje *m*
(en una novela, etc.) — **characteristic** *adj*
: característico — ~ *n* : característica *f* —
characterize *vt* -**ized; -izing** : caracterizar
charcoal *n* : carbón *m*
charge *n* **1** : carga *f* (eléctrica) **2** COST : precio *m* **3** BURDEN : carga *f*, peso *m* **4** ACCUSATION : cargo *m*, acusación *f* **5 in** ~ **of**
: encargado de **6 take** ~ **of** : hacerse cargo
de — ~ *v* **charged; charging** *vt* **1** : cargar
2 ENTRUST : encargar **3** COMMAND : ordenar, mandar **4** ACCUSE : acusar — *vi* **1**
: cargar **2** ~ **too much** : cobrar demasiado
charisma *n* : carisma *m* — **charismatic** *adj*
: carismático
charity *n, pl* -**ties 1** : organización *f* benéfica **2** GOODWILL : caridad *f*
charlatan *n* : charlatán *m*, -tana *f*
charm *n* **1** : encanto *m* **2** SPELL : hechizo *m*
— ~ *vt* : encantar, cautivar — **charming**
adj : encantador
chart *n* **1** MAP : carta *f* **2** DIAGRAM : gráfico
m, tabla *f* — ~ *vt* : trazar un mapa de
charter *n* : carta *f* — ~ *vt* : alquilar, fletar
chase *n* : persecución *f* — ~ *vt* **chased;**
chasing 1 PURSUE : perseguir **2** *or* ~
away : ahuyentar
chasm *n* : abismo *m*
chaste *adj* **chaster; -est** : casto — **chastity**
n : castidad *f*
chat *vi* **chatted; chatting** : charlar — ~ *n*
: charla *f* — **chatter** *vi* **1** : parlotear *fam* **2**
: castañetear (dícese de los dientes) — ~ *n*
: parloteo *m*, cháchara *f* — **chatterbox** *n*
: parlanchín *m*, -china *f* — **chatty** *adj* **chattier; chattiest 1** : parlanchín **2** INFORMAL
: familiar
chauffeur *n* : chofer *mf*
chauvinist *or* **chauvinistic** *adj* : chauvinista, patriotero
cheap *adj* **1** INEXPENSIVE : barato **2**
SHODDY : de baja calidad — ~ *adv* : barato
— **cheapen** *vt* : rebajar — **cheaply** *adv*
: barato, a precio bajo
cheat *vt* : defraudar, estafar — *vi* **1** : hacer

trampa(s) **2** ~ **on s.o.** : engañar a algn —
~ *or* **cheater** *n* : tramposo *m*, -sa *f*
check *n* **1** RESTRAINT : freno *m* **2** INSPEC-
TION : inspección *f*, comprobación *f* **3**
DRAFT : cheque *m* **4** BILL : cuenta *f* **5**
: jaque *m* (en ajedrez) **6** : tela *f* a cuadros —
~ *vt* **1** RESTRAIN : frenar, contener **2** IN-
SPECT : revisar **3** VERIFY : comprobar **4**
: dar jaque (en ajedrez) **5** ~ **in** : enregis-
trarse (en un hotel) **6** ~ **out** : irse (de un
hotel) **7** ~ **out** VERIFY : verificar, comprobar
checkers *n* : damas *fpl*
checkmate *n* : jaque *m* mate
checkpoint *n* : puesto *m* de control
checkup *n* : chequeo *m*, examen *m* médico
cheek *n* : mejilla *f*
cheer *n* **1** CHEERFULNESS : alegría *f* **2** AP-
PLAUSE : aclamación *f* **3** ~**s!** : ¡salud! —
~ *vt* **1** GLADDEN : alegrar **2** APPLAUD,
SHOUT : aclamar, aplaudir — **cheerful** *adj*
: alegre
cheese *n* : queso *m*
cheetah *n* : guepardo *m*
chef *n* : chef *m*
chemical *adj* : químico — ~ *n* : sustancia *f*
química — **chemist** *n* : químico *m*, -ca *f* —
chemistry *n*, *pl* **-tries** : química *f*
cheque *Brit* → **check**
cherish *vt* **1** : querer, apreciar **2** HARBOR
: abrigar (un recuerdo, una esperanza, etc.)
cherry *n*, *pl* **-ries** : cereza *f*
chess *n* : ajedrez *m*
chest *n* **1** BOX : cofre *m* **2** : pecho *m* (del
cuerpo) **3** *or* ~ **of drawers** : cómoda *f*
chestnut *n* : castaña *f*
chew *vt* : masticar, mascar — **chewing gum**
n : chicle *m*
chic *adj* : elegante
chick *n* : polluelo *m*, -la *f* — **chicken** *n*
: pollo *m* — **chicken pox** *n* : varicela *f*
chicory *n*, *pl* **-ries** **1** : endivia *f* (para ensal-
adas) **2** : achicoria *f* (aditivo de café)
chief *adj* : principal — ~ *n* : jefe *m*, -fa *f* —
chiefly *adv* : principalmente
child *n*, *pl* **children** **1** : niño *m*, -ña *f* **2** OFF-
SPRING : hijo *m*, -ja *f* — **childbirth** *n* : parto
m — **childhood** *n* : infancia *f*, niñez *f* —
childish *adj* : infantil — **childlike** *adj* : infantil, inocente — **childproof** *adj* : a prueba
de niños
Chilean *adj* : chileno
chili *or* **chile** *or* **chilli** *n*, *pl* **chilies** *or* **chiles**
or **chillies** **1** *or* ~ **pepper** : chile *m* **2**
: chile *m* con carne
chill *n* **1** CHILLINESS : frío *m* **2** **catch a** ~
: resfriarse **3** **there's a** ~ **in the air** : hace
fresco — ~ *adj* : frío — ~ *v* : enfriar —
chilly *adj* **chillier; -est** : fresco, frío

chime *vi* **chimed; chiming** : repicar, sonar
— ~ *n* : carillón *m*
chimney *n*, *pl* **-neys** : chimenea *f*
chimpanzee *n* : chimpancé *m*
chin *n* : barbilla *f*
china *n* : porcelana *f*, loza *f*
Chinese *adj* : chino — ~ *n* : chino *m* (idioma)
chink *n* : grieta *f*
chip *n* **1** : astilla *f* (de madera o vidrio), lasca
f (de piedra) **2** : ficha *f* (de póker, etc.) **3**
NICK : desportilladura *f* **4** *or* **computer** ~
: chip *m* **5** → **potato chips** — ~ *v*
chipped; chipping *vt* : desportillar — *vi* **1**
: desportillarse **2** ~ **in** : contribuir
chipmunk *n* : ardilla *f* listada
chiropodist *n* : podólogo *m*, -ga *f*
chiropractor *n* : quiropráctico *m*, -ca *f*
chirp *vi* : piar, gorjear
chisel *n* : cincel *m* (para piedras, etc.), for-
món *m*, escoplo *m* (para madera) — ~ *vt*
-eled *or* **-elled; -eling** *or* **-elling** : cincelar,
tallar
chit *n* : nota *f*
chitchat *n* : cháchara *f* fam
chivalrous *adj* : caballeroso — **chivalry** *n*,
pl **-ries** : caballerosidad *f*
chive *n* : cebollino *m*
chlorine *n* : cloro *m*
chock–full *adj* : repleto, atestado
chocolate *n* : chocolate *m*
choice *n* **1** : elección *f*, selección *f* **2** PREF-
ERENCE : preferencia *f* — ~ *adj* **choicer;**
-est : selecto
choir *n* : coro *m*
choke *v* **choked; choking** *vt* **1** : asfixiar, estrangular **2** BLOCK : atascar — *vi* : asfixiarse, atragantarse (con comida) — ~ *n* : estárter *m* (de un motor)
choose *v* **chose; chosen; choosing** *vt* **1**
SELECT : escoger, elegir **2** DECIDE : decidir
— *vi* : escoger — **choosy** *or* **choosey** *adj*
choosier; -est : exigente
chop *vt* **chopped; chopping** **1** : cortar,
picar (carne, etc.) **2** ~ **down** : talar — ~
n : chuleta *f* (de cerdo, etc.) — **choppy** *adj*
-pier; -est : picado, agitado
chopsticks *npl* : palillos *mpl*
chord *n* : acorde *m* (en música)
chore *n* **1** : tarea *f* **2** **household** ~**s** : faenas *fpl* domésticas
choreography *n*, *pl* **-phies** : coreografía *f*
chortle *vi* **-tled; -tling** : reírse (con satisfacción o júbilo)
chorus *n* **1** : coro *m* (grupo de personas) **2**
REFRAIN : estribillo *m*
chose, chosen → **choose**
christen *vt* : bautizar — **christening** *n* : bautizo *m*

Christian *n* : cristiano *m*, -na *f* — ～ *adj* : cristiano — **Christianity** *n* : cristianismo *m*
Christmas *n* : Navidad *f*
chrome *n* : cromo *m*
chronic *adj* : crónico
chronicle *n* : crónica *f*
chronology *n, pl* **-gies** : cronología *f* — **chronological** *adj* : cronológico
chrysanthemum *n* : crisantemo *m*
chubby *adj* **-bier; -est** : regordete *fam*, rechoncho *fam*
chuck *vt* : tirar, arrojar
chuckle *vi* **-led; -ling** : reírse (entre dientes) — ～ *n* : risa *f* ahogada
chum *n* : amigo *m*, -ga *f;* compinche *mf fam* — **chummy** *adj* **-mier; -est** : muy amigable
chunk *n* : trozo *m*, pedazo *m*
church *n* : iglesia *f*
churn *n* : mantequera *f* — ～ *vt* **1** : agitar **2** ～ **out** : producir en grandes cantidades
chute *n* **1** : vertedor *m* **2** SLIDE : tobogán *m*
cider *n* : sidra *f*
cigar *n* : puro *m* — **cigarette** *n* : cigarrillo *m*, cigarro *m*
cinch *n* **it's a** ～ : es pan comido
cinema *n* : cine *m*
cinnamon *n* : canela *f*
cipher *n* **1** ZERO : cero *m* **2** CODE : cifra *f*
circa *prep* : hacia
circle *n* : círculo *m* — ～ *v* **-cled; -cling** *vt* **1** : dar vueltas alrededor de **2** : trazar un círculo alrededor de (un número, etc.) — *vi* : dar vueltas
circuit *n* : circuito *m* — **circuitous** *adj* : tortuoso
circular *adj* : circular — ～ *n* LEAFLET : circular *f*
circulate *v* **-lated; -lating** *vt* : hacer circular — *vi* : circular — **circulation** *n* **1** : circulación *f* **2** : tirada *f* (de una publicación)
circumcise *vt* **-cised; -cising** : circuncidar — **circumcision** *n* : circuncisión *f*
circumference *n* : circunferencia *f*
circumspect *adj* : circunspecto, prudente
circumstance *n* **1** : circunstancia *f* **2 under no** ～**s** : bajo ningún concepto
circus *n* : circo *m*
cistern *n* : cisterna *f*
cite *vt* **cited; citing** : citar — **citation** *n* : citación *f*
citizen *n* : ciudadano *m*, -na *f* — **citizenship** *n* : ciudadanía *f*
citrus *n, pl* **-rus** *or* **-ruses** *or* ～ **fruit** : cítrico *m*
city *n, pl* **cities** : ciudad *f*
civic *adj* : cívico — **civics** *ns & pl* : civismo *m*
civil *adj* : civil — **civilian** *n* : civil *mf* — **civility** *n, pl* **-ties** : cortesía *f* — **civilization** *n*

: civilización *f* — **civilize** *vt* **-lized; -lizing** : civilizar
clad *adj* ～ **in** : vestido de
claim *vt* **1** DEMAND : reclamar **2** MAINTAIN : afirmar, sostener **3** ～ **responsibility** : atribuirse la responsabilidad — ～ *n* **1** DEMAND : demanda *f*, reclamación *f* **2** ASSERTION : afirmación *f*
clam *n* : almeja *f*
clamber *vi* : trepar (con torpeza)
clammy *adj* **-mier; -est** : húmedo y algo frío
clamor *n* : clamor *m* — ～ *vi* : clamar
clamp *n* : abrazadera *f* — ～ *vt* : sujetar con abrazaderas — *vi* ～ **down on** : reprimir
clan *n* : clan *m*
clandestine *adj* : clandestino
clang *n* : ruido *m* metálico
clap *v* **clapped; clapping** *vt* **1** : aplaudir **2** ～ **one's hands** : dar palmadas — *vi* : aplaudir — ～ *n* : palmada *f*
clarify *vt* **-fied; -fying** : aclarar — **clarification** *n* : clarificación *f*
clarinet *n* : clarinete *m*
clarity *n* : claridad *f*
clash *vi* **1** : chocar, enfrentarse **2** CONFLICT : estar en conflicto — ～ *n* **1** CRASH : choque *m* **2** CONFLICT : conflicto *m*
clasp *n* : broche *m*, cierre *m* — ～ *vt* **1** : abrazar (a una persona), agarrar (una cosa) **2** FASTEN : abrochar
class *n* : clase *f*
classic *or* **classical** *adj* : clásico — **classic** *n* : clásico *m*
classify *vt* **-fied; -fying** : clasificar — **classification** *n* : clasificación *f* — **classified** *adj* RESTRICTED : secreto
classmate *n* : compañero *m*, -ra *f* de clase
classroom *n* : aula *f*, salón *m* de clase
clatter *vi* : hacer ruido — ～ *n* : estrépito *m*
clause *n* : cláusula *f*
claustrophobia *n* : claustrofobia *f*
claw *n* : garra *f*, uña *f* (de un gato), pinza *f* (de un crustáceo) — ～ *v* : arañar
clay *n* : arcilla *f*
clean *adj* **1** : limpio **2** UNADULTERATED : puro **3** SPOTLESS : impecable — ～ *vt* : limpiar — ～ *adv* : limpio — **cleaner** *n* **1** : limpiador *m*, -dora *f* **2** DRY CLEANER : tintorería *f* — **cleanliness** *n* : limpieza *f* — **cleanse** *vt* **cleansed; cleansing** : limpiar, purificar
clear *adj* **1** : claro **2** TRANSPARENT : transparente **3** UNOBSTRUCTED : despejado, libre — ～ *vt* **1** : despejar (una superficie), desatascar (un tubo, etc.) **2** EXONERATE : absolver **3** : saltar por encima de (un obstáculo) **4** ～ **the table** : levantar la mesa **5** ～ **up** RESOLVE : aclarar, resolver — *vi* **1** ～ **up** BRIGHTEN : despejarse (dícese del

tiempo, etc.) **2 ~ up** VANISH : desaparecer (dícese de una infección, etc.) — **~** *adv* **1 make oneself ~** : explicarse **2 stand ~** ! : ¡aléjate! — **clearance** *n* **1** SPACE : espacio *m* (libre) **2** AUTHORIZATION : autorización *f* **3 ~ sale** : liquidación *f* — **clearing** *n* : claro *m* — **clearly** *adv* **1** DISTINCTLY : claramente **2** OBVIOUSLY : obviamente

cleaver *n* : cuchillo *m* de carnicero

clef *n* : clave *f*

cleft *n* : hendidura *f*, grieta *f*

clement *adj* : clemente — **clemency** *n* : clemencia *f*

clench *vt* : apretar

clergy *n, pl* **-gies** : clero *m* — **clergyman** *n, pl* **-men** : clérigo *m* — **clerical** *adj* **1** : clerical **2 ~ work** : trabajo *m* de oficina

clerk *n* **1** : oficinista *mf*; empleado *m*, -da *f* de oficina **2** SALESPERSON : dependiente *m*, -ta *f*

clever *adj* **1** SKILLFUL : ingenioso, hábil **2** SMART : listo, inteligente — **cleverly** *adv* : ingeniosamente — **cleverness** *n* **1** SKILL : ingenio *m* **2** INTELLIGENCE : inteligencia *f*

cliché *n* : cliché *m*

click *vt* : chasquear — *vi* **1** : chasquear **2** GET ALONG : llevarse bien — **~** *n* : chasquido *m*

client *n* : cliente *m*, -ta *f* — **clientele** *n* : clientela *f*

cliff *n* : acantilado *m*

climate *n* : clima *m*

climax *n* : clímax *m*, punto *m* culminante

climb *vt* : escalar, subir a, trepar a — *vi* **1** RISE : subir **2** *or* **~ up** : subirse, treparse — **~** *n* : subida *f*

clinch *vt* : cerrar (un acuerdo, etc.)

cling *vi* **clung; clinging** : adherirse, pegarse

clinic *n* : clínica *f* — **clinical** *adj* : clínico

clink *vi* : tintinear

clip *vt* **clipped; clipping 1** CUT : cortar, recortar **2** FASTEN : sujetar (con un clip) — **~** *n* **1** FASTENER : clip *m* **2 at a good ~** : a buen trote **3 → paper clip** — **clippers** *npl* **1** : maquinilla *f* para cortar el pelo **2** *or* **nail ~** : cortauñas *m*

cloak *n* : capa *f*

clock *n* **1** : reloj *m* (de pared) **2 around the ~** : las veinticuatro horas — **clockwise** *adv & adj* : en el sentido de las agujas del reloj — **clockwork** *n* **1** : mecanismo *m* de relojería **2 like ~** : con precisión

clog *n* : zueco *m* — **~** *v* **clogged; clogging** *vt* : atascar, obstruir — *vi or* **~ up** : atascarse

cloister *n* : claustro *m*

close[1] *v* **closed; closing** *vt* : cerrar — *vi* **1** : cerrarse **2** TERMINATE : terminar **3 ~ in** : acercarse — **~** *n* : final *m*

close[2] *adj* **closer; closest 1** NEAR : cercano, próximo **2** INTIMATE : íntimo **3** STRICT : estricto **4** STUFFY : sofocante **5 a ~ game** : un juego reñido — **~** *adv* : cerca, de cerca — **closely** *adv* : cerca, de cerca — **closeness** *n* **1** NEARNESS : cercanía *f* **2** INTIMACY : intimidad *f*

closet *n* : armario *m*, clóset *m Lat*

closure *n* : cierre *m*

clot *n* : coágulo *m* — **~** *v* **clotted; clotting** *vt* : coagular, cuajar — *vi* : coagularse

cloth *n, pl* **cloths 1** FABRIC : tela *f* **2** RAG : trapo *m*

clothe *vt* **clothed** *or* **clad; clothing** : vestir — **clothes** *npl* **1** : ropa *f* **2 put on one's ~** : vestirse — **clothespin** *n* : pinza *f* (para la ropa) — **clothing** *n* : ropa *f*

cloud *n* : nube *f* — **~** *vt* : nublar — *vi or* **~ over** : nublarse — **cloudy** *adj* **cloudier; -est** : nublado

clout *n* **1** BLOW : golpe *m*, tortazo *m fam* **2** INFLUENCE : influencia *f*

clove *n* **1** : clavo *m* **2** : diente *m* (de ajo)

clover *n* : trébol *m*

clown *n* : payaso *m*, -sa *f* — **~** *or* **~ around** *vi* : payasear

cloying *adj* : empalagoso

club *n* **1** : garrote *m*, porra *f* **2** ASSOCIATION : club *m* **3 ~s** *mpl* : tréboles *mpl* (en los naipes) — **~** *vt* **clubbed; clubbing** : aporrear

cluck *vi* : cloquear

clue *n* **1** : pista *f*, indicio *m* **2 I haven't got a ~** : no tengo la menor idea

clump *n* : grupo *m* (de arbustos)

clumsy *adj* **-sier; -est** : torpe — **clumsiness** *n* : torpeza *f*

cluster *n* : grupo *m*, racimo *m* (de uvas, etc.) — **~** *vi* : agruparse

clutch *vt* : agarrar, asir — *vi* **~ at** : tratar de agarrarse de — **~** *n* : embrague *m*, clutch *m Lat* (de un automóvil)

clutter *vt* : llenar desordenadamente — **~** *n* : desorden *m*, revoltijo *m*

coach *n* **1** CARRIAGE : carruaje *m*, carroza *f* **2** : vagón *m* de pasajeros (de un tren) **3** BUS : autobús *m* **4** : pasaje *m* aéreo de segunda clase **5** TRAINER : entrenador *m*, -dora *f* — *vt* : entrenar (a un atleta), dar clases particulares a (un alumno)

coagulate *v* **-lated; -lating** *vt* : coagular — *vi* : coagularse

coal *n* : carbón *m*

coalition *n* : coalición *f*

coarse *adj* **coarser; -est 1** : tosco, basto **2** CRUDE, VULGAR : grosero, ordinario — **coarseness** *n* : aspereza *f*, tosquedad *f*

coast *n* : costa *f* — **~** *vi* : ir en punto muerto (dícese de un automóvil), deslizarse (dícese de una bicicleta) — **coastal** *adj* : costero

coaster n : posavasos m
coast guard n : guardacostas mpl
coastline n : litoral m
coat n **1** : abrigo m **2** : pelaje m (de un animal) **3** : mano f (de pintura) — ~ vt : cubrir, revestir — **coating** n : capa f —
coat of arms : escudo m de armas
coax vt : engatusar
cob → **corncob**
cobblestone n : adoquín m
cobweb n : telaraña f
cocaine n : cocaína f
cock n **1** ROOSTER : gallo m **2** FAUCET : grifo m **3** : martillo m (de un arma de fuego) — ~ vt **1** : amartillar (un arma de fuego) **2** ~ **one's head** : ladear la cabeza — **cockeyed** adj **1** ASKEW : ladeado **2** ABSURD : absurdo
cockpit n : cabina f
cockroach n : cucaracha f
cocktail n : coctel m, cóctel m
cocky adj cockier; -est : engreído, arrogante
cocoa n **1** : cacao m **2** : chocolate m (bebida)
coconut n : coco m
cocoon n : capullo m
cod ns & pl : bacalao m
coddle vt -dled; -dling : mimar
code n : código m
coeducational adj : mixto
coerce vt -erced; -ercing : coaccionar, forzar — **coercion** n : coacción f
coffee n : café m — **coffeepot** n : cafetera f
coffer n : cofre m
coffin n : ataúd m, féretro m
cog n : diente m (de una rueda)
cogent adj : convincente, persuasivo
cognac n : coñac m
cogwheel n : rueda f dentada
coherent adj : coherente
coil vt : enrollar — vi : enrollarse — ~ n **1** ROLL : rollo m **2** : tirabuzón m (de pelo), espiral f (de humo)
coin n : moneda f — ~ vt : acuñar
coincide vi -cided; -ciding : coincidir — **coincidence** n : coincidencia f, casualidad f — **coincidental** adj : casual, fortuito
coke n : coque m (combustible)
colander n : colador m
cold adj **1** : frío **2** be ~ : tener frío **3** it's ~ today : hace frío hoy — ~ n **1** : frío m **2** : resfriado m (en medicina) **3** catch a ~ : resfriarse
coleslaw n : ensalada f de col
colic n : cólico m
collaborate vi -rated; -rating : colaborar — **collaboration** n : colaboración f — **collaborator** n : colaborador m, -dora f

collapse vi -lapsed; -lapsing **1** : derrumbarse, hundirse **2** : sufrir un colapso (físico o mental) — ~ n **1** FALL : derrumbamiento m **2** BREAKDOWN : colapso m — **collapsible** adj : plegable
collar n : cuello m (de camisa, etc.), collar m (para animales) — **collarbone** n : clavícula f
colleague n : colega mf
collect vt **1** GATHER : reunir **2** : coleccionar, juntar (timbres, etc.) **3** : recaudar (fondos, etc.) — vi **1** ACCUMULATE : acumularse, juntarse **2** CONGREGATE : congregarse, reunirse — ~ adv **call** ~ : llamar a cobro revertido, llamar por cobrar Lat — **collection** n **1** : colección f **2** : colecta f (de contribuciones) — **collective** adj : colectivo — **collector** n **1** : coleccionista mf **2** : cobrador m, -dora f (de deudas)
college n **1** : instituto m (a nivel universitario) **2** : colegio m (electoral, etc.)
collide vi -lided; -liding : chocar, colisionar — **collision** n : choque m, colisión f
colloquial adj : coloquial, familiar
cologne n : colonia f
Colombian adj : colombiano
colon[1] n, pl **colons** or **cola** : colon m (en anatomía)
colon[2] n, pl **colons** : dos puntos mpl (signo de puntuación)
colonel n : coronel m
colony n, pl -nies : colonia f — **colonial** adj : colonial — **colonize** vt -nized; -nizing : colonizar
color or Brit **colour** n : color m — ~ vt : colorear, pintar — vi BLUSH : sonrojarse — **color-blind** or Brit **colour-blind** adj : daltónico — **colored** or Brit **coloured** adj : de color — **colorful** or Brit **colourful** adj **1** : de vivos colores **2** PICTURESQUE : pintoresco — **colorless** or Brit **colourless** adj : incoloro
colossal adj : colosal
colt n : potro m
column n : columna f — **columnist** n : columnista mf
coma n : coma m
comb n **1** : peine m **2** : cresta f (de un gallo) — ~ vt : peinar
combat n : combate m — ~ vt -bated or -batted; -bating or -batting : combatir — **combatant** n : combatiente mf
combine v -bined; -bining vt : combinar — vi : combinarse — ~ n HARVESTER : cosechadora f — **combination** n : combinación f
combustion n : combustión f
come vi came; come; coming **1** : venir **2** ARRIVE : llegar **3** ~ **about** : suceder **4** ~

back : regresar, volver **5** ~ **from** : venir de, provenir de **6** ~ **in** : entrar **7** ~ **out** : salir **8** ~ **to** REVIVE : volver en sí **9** ~ **on!** : ¡ándale! **10** ~ **up** OCCUR : surgir **11** **how** ~**?** : ¿por qué? — **comeback** n **1** RE-TURN : retorno m **2** RETORT : réplica f
comedy n, pl **-dies** : comedia f — **comedian** n : cómico m, -ca f
comet n : cometa m
comfort vt : consolar — ~ n **1** : comodidad f **2** SOLACE : consuelo m — **comfortable** adj : cómodo
comic or **comical** adj : cómico — ~ n **1** COMEDIAN : cómico m, -ca f **2** or ~ **book** : revista f de historietas, cómic m — **comic strip** n : tira f cómica, historieta f
coming adj : próximo, que viene
comma n : coma f
command vt **1** ORDER : ordenar, mandar **2** : estar al mando de (un barco, etc.) **3** ~ **respect** : inspirar (el) respeto — vi : dar órdenes — ~ n **1** ORDER : orden f **2** LEADERSHIP : mando m **3** MASTERY : maestría f, dominio m — **commander** n : comandante mf — **commandment** n : mandamiento m
commemorate vt **-rated; -rating** : conmemorar — **commemoration** n : conmemoración f
commence v **-menced; -mencing** : comenzar, empezar — **commencement** n **1** BEGINNING : comienzo m **2** GRADUATION : ceremonia f de graduación
commend vt **1** ENTRUST : encomendar **2** PRAISE : alabar — **commendable** adj : loable
comment n : comentario m, observación f — ~ vi : hacer comentarios — **commentary** n, pl **-taries** : comentario m — **commentator** n : comentarista mf
commerce n : comercio m — **commercial** adj : comercial — ~ n : anuncio m, aviso m Lat — **commercialize** vt **-ized; -izing** : comercializar
commiserate vi **-ated; -ating** : compadecerse
commission n : comisión f — ~ vt : encargar (una obra de arte) — **commissioner** n : comisario m, -ria f
commit vt **-mitted; -mitting** **1** ENTRUST : confiar **2** : cometer (un crimen) **3** : internar (a algn en un hospital) **4** ~ **oneself** : comprometerse **5** ~ **to memory** : aprender de memoria — **commitment** n : compromiso m
committee n : comité m, comisión f
commodity n, pl **-ties** : artículo m de comercio, producto m
common adj **1** : común **2** ORDINARY : ordinario, común y corriente — ~ n **in** ~ : en

común — **commonly** adv : comúnmente — **commonplace** adj : común, banal — **common sense** n : sentido m común
commotion n : alboroto m, jaleo m
commune[1] n : comuna f — **communal** adj : comunal
commune[2] vi **-muned; -muning** ~ **with** : comunicarse con
communicate v **-cated; -cating** vt : comunicar — vi : comunicarse — **communicable** adj : transmisible — **communication** n : comunicación f — **communicative** adj : comunicativo
communion n : comunión f
Communism n : comunismo m — **Communist** adj : comunista — ~ n : comunista mf
community n, pl **-ties** : comunidad f
commute v **-muted; -muting** vt : conmutar, reducir (una sentencia) — vi : viajar de la residencia al trabajo
compact adj : compacto — ~ n **1** or ~ **car** : auto m compacto **2** or **powder** ~ : polvera f — **compact disc** n : disco m compacto
companion n : compañero m, -ra f — **companionship** n : compañerismo m
company n, pl **-nies** **1** : compañía f **2** GUESTS : visita f
compare v **-pared; -paring** vt : comparar — vi ~ **with** : poderse comparar con — **comparable** adj : comparable — **comparative** adj : comparativo, relativo — **comparison** n : comparación f
compartment n : compartimento m
compass n **1** : compás m **2** **points of the** ~ : puntos mpl cardinales
compassion n : compasión f — **compassionate** adj : compasivo
compatible adj : compatible, afín — **compatibility** n : compatibilidad f
compel vt **-pelled; -pelling** : obligar — **compelling** adj : convincente
compensate v **-sated; -sating** vi ~ **for** : compensar — vt : indemnizar, compensar — **compensation** n : compensación f, indemnización f
compete vi **-peted; -peting** : competir — **competent** adj : competente — **competition** n **1** : competencia f **2** CONTEST : concurso m — **competitor** n : competidor m, -dora f
compile vt **-piled; -piling** : compilar, recopilar
complacency n : satisfacción f consigo mismo — **complacent** adj : satisfecho de sí mismo
complain vi : quejarse — **complaint** n **1** : queja f **2** AILMENT : enfermedad f
complement n : complemento m — ~ vt

: complementar — **complementary** *adj* : complementario

complete *adj* **-pleter; -est** **1** WHOLE : completo, entero **2** FINISHED : terminado **3** TOTAL : total — ~ *vt* **-pleted; -pleting** : completar — **completion** *n* : conclusión *f*

complex *adj* : complejo — ~ *n* : complejo *m*

complexion *n* : cutis *m*, tez *f*

complexity *n, pl* **-ties** : complejidad *f*

compliance *n* **1** : acatamiento *m* **2 in** ~ **with** : conforme a — **compliant** *adj* : sumiso

complicate *vt* **-cated; -cating** : complicar — **complicated** *adj* : complicado — **complication** *n* : complicación *f*

compliment *n* **1** : cumplido *m* **2** ~**s** *npl* : saludos *mpl* — ~ *vt* : felicitar — **complimentary** *adj* **1** FLATTERING : halagador, halagueño **2** FREE : de cortesía, gratis

comply *vi* **-plied; -plying** ~ **with** : cumplir, obedecer

component *n* : componente *m*

compose *vt* **-posed; -posing** **1** : componer **2** ~ **oneself** : serenarse — **composer** *n* : compositor *m*, -tora *f* — **composition** *n* **1** : composición *f* **2** ESSAY : ensayo *m* — **composure** *n* : calma *f*

compound[1] *vt* **1** COMPOSE : componer **2** : agravar (un problema, etc.) — ~ *adj* : compuesto — ~ *n* : compuesto *m*

compound[2] *n* ENCLOSURE : recinto *m*

comprehend *vt* : comprender — **comprehension** *n* : comprensión *f* — **comprehensive** *adj* **1** INCLUSIVE : inclusivo **2** BROAD : amplio

compress *vt* : comprimir — **compression** *n* : compresión *f*

comprise *vt* **-prised; -prising** : comprender

compromise *n* : acuerdo *m*, arreglo *m* — ~ *v* **-mised; -mising** *vi* : llegar a un acuerdo — *vt* : comprometer

compulsion *n* **1** COERCION : coacción *f* **2** URGE : impulso *m* — **compulsive** *adj* : compulsivo — **compulsory** *adj* : obligatorio

compute *vt* **-puted; -puting** : computar — **computer** *n* : computadora *f,* computador *m*, ordenador *m* Spain — **computerize** *vt* **-ized; -izing** : informatizar

comrade *n* : camarada *mf*

con *vt* **conned; conning** : estafar — ~ *n* **1** SWINDLE : estafa *f* **2 the pros and** ~**s** : los pros y los contras

concave *adj* : cóncavo

conceal *vt* : ocultar

concede *vt* **-ceded; -ceding** : conceder, admitir

conceit *n* : vanidad *f* — **conceited** *adj* : engreído

conceive *v* **-ceived; -ceiving** *vt* : concebir — *vi* ~ **of** : concebir — **conceivable** *adj* : concebible

concentrate *v* **-trated; -trating** *vt* : concentrar — *vi* : concentrarse — **concentration** *n* : concentración *f*

concept *n* : concepto *m* — **conception** *n* : concepción *f*

concern *vt* **1** : concernir **2** ~ **oneself about** : preocuparse por — ~ *n* **1** AFFAIR : asunto *m* **2** WORRY : preocupación *f* **3** BUSINESS : negocio *m* — **concerned** *adj* **1** ANXIOUS : ansioso **2 as far as I'm** ~ : en cuanto a mí — **concerning** *prep* : con respecto a

concert *n* : concierto *m* — **concerted** *adj* : concertado

concession *n* : concesión *f*

concise *adj* : conciso

conclude *v* **-cluded; -cluding** : concluir — **conclusion** *n* : conclusión *f* — **conclusive** *adj* : concluyente

concoct *vt* **1** PREPARE : confeccionar **2** DEVISE : inventarse, tramar — **concoction** *n* : mezcla *f,* brebaje *m*

concourse *n* : vestíbulo *m*, salón *m*

concrete *adj* : concreto — ~ *n* : hormigón *m*, concreto *m* Lat

concur *vi* **concurred; concurring** AGREE : estar de acuerdo

concussion *n* : conmoción *f* cerebral

condemn *vt* : condenar — **condemnation** *n* : condenación *f*

condense *v* **-densed; -densing** *vt* : condensar — *vi* : condensarse — **condensation** *n* : condensación *f*

condescending *adj* : condescendiente

condiment *n* : condimento *m*

condition *n* **1** : condición *f* **2 in good** ~ : en buen estado — **conditional** *adj* : condicional

condolences *npl* : pésame *m*

condom *n* : condón *m*

condominium *n, pl* **-ums** : condominio *m* Lat

condone *vt* **-doned; -doning** : aprobar

conducive *adj* : propicio, favorable

conduct *n* : conducta *f* — ~ *vt* **1** DIRECT, GUIDE : conducir, dirigir **2** CARRY OUT : llevar a cabo **3** ~ **oneself** : conducirse, comportarse — **conductor** *n* : revisor *m*, -sora *f* (en un tren); cobrador *m*, -dora *f* (en un autobús); director *m*, -tora *f* (de una orquesta)

cone *n* **1** : cono *m* **2** *or* **ice– cream** ~ : cucurucho *m*, barquillo *m* Lat

confection *n* : dulce *m*

confederation *n* : confederación *f*

confer *v* **-ferred; -ferring** *vt* : conferir, otorgar — *vi* ~ **with** : consultar — **conference** *n* : conferencia *f*

confess *vt* : confesar — *vi* **1** : confesarse **2** ~ **to** : confesar, admitir — **confession** *n* : confesión *f*

confetti *n* : confeti *m*

confide *v* **-fided; -fiding** : confiar — **confidence** *n* **1** TRUST : confianza *f* **2** SELF-ASSURANCE : confianza *f* en sí mismo **3** SECRET : confidencia *f* — **confident** *adj* **1** SURE : seguro **2** SELF-ASSURED : confiado, seguro de sí mismo — **confidential** *adj* : confidencial

confine *vt* **-fined; -fining 1** LIMIT : confinar, limitar **2** IMPRISON : encerrar — **confines** *npl* : confines *mpl*

confirm *vt* : confirmar — **confirmation** *n* : confirmación *f* — **confirmed** *adj* : inveterado

confiscate *vt* **-cated; -cating** : confiscar

conflict *n* : conflicto *m* — ~ *vi* : estar en conflicto, oponerse

conform *vi* **1** COMPLY : ajustarse **2** ~ **with** : corresponder a — **conformity** *n, pl* **-ties** : conformidad *f*

confound *vt* : confundir, desconcertar

confront *vt* : afrontar, encarar — **confrontation** *n* : confrontación *f*

confuse *vt* **-fused; -fusing** : confundir — **confusing** *adj* : confuso, desconcertante — **confusion** *n* : confusión *f*, desconcierto *m*

congeal *vi* : coagularse

congenial *adj* : agradable

congested *adj* : congestionado — **congestion** *n* : congestión *f*

congratulate *vt* **-lated; -lating** : felicitar — **congratulations** *npl* : felicitaciones *fpl*

congregate *vi* **-gated; -gating** : congregarse — **congregation** *n* : feligreses *mpl* (en religión)

congress *n* : congreso *m* — **congressional** *adj* : del congreso — **congressman** *n, pl* **-men** : congresista *mf*

conjecture *n* : conjetura *f*, presunción *f* — ~ *v* **-tured; -turing** *vt* : conjeturar — *vi* : hacer conjeturas

conjugal *adj* : conyugal

conjugate *vt* **-gated; -gating** : conjugar — **conjugation** *n* : conjugación *f*

conjunction *n* **1** : conjunción *f* **2 in** ~ **with** : en combinación con

conjure *v* **-jured; -juring** *vi* : hacer juegos de manos — ~ *vt or* ~ **up** : evocar

connect *vi* : conectarse — *vt* **1** JOIN : conectar, juntar **2** ASSOCIATE : asociar — **connection** *n* **1** : conexión *f* **2** : enlace *m* (con un tren, etc.) **3** ~**s** *npl* : relaciones *fpl* (personas)

connoisseur *n* : conocedor *m*, -dora *f*

connote *vt* **-noted; -noting** : connotar, implicar

conquer *vt* : conquistar — **conqueror** *n* : conquistador *m*, -dora *f* — **conquest** *n* : conquista *f*

conscience *n* : conciencia *f* — **conscientious** *adj* : concienzudo

conscious *adj* **1** AWARE : consciente **2** INTENTIONAL : intencional — **consciously** *adv* : deliberadamente — **consciousness** *n* **1** AWARENESS : conciencia *f* **2 lose** ~ : perder el conocimiento

consecrate *vt* **-crated; -crating** : consagrar — **consecration** *n* : consagración *f*

consecutive *adj* : consecutivo, sucesivo

consensus *n* : consenso *m*

consent *vi* : consentir — ~ *n* : consentimiento *m*

consequence *n* **1** : consecuencia *f* **2 of no** ~ : sin importancia — **consequent** *adj* : consiguiente — **consequently** *adv* : por consiguiente

conserve *vt* **-served; -serving** : conservar, preservar — **conservation** *n* : conservación *f* — **conservative** *adj* **1** : conservador **2** CAUTIOUS : moderado, prudente — ~ *n* : conservador *m*, -dora *f* — **conservatory** *n, pl* **-ries** : conservatorio *m*

consider *vt* **1** : considerar **2 all things considered** : teniéndolo todo en cuenta — **considerable** *adj* : considerable — **considerate** *adj* : considerado — **consideration** *n* **1** : consideración *f* **2 take into** ~ : tener en cuenta — **considering** *prep* : teniendo en cuenta

consign *vt* **1** : relegar **2** SEND : enviar — **consignment** *n* : envío *m*

consist *vi* **1** ~ **in** : consistir en **2** ~ **of** : constar de, componerse de — **consistency** *n, pl* **-cies 1** TEXTURE : consistencia *f* **2** COHERENCE : coherencia *f* **3** UNIFORMITY : regularidad *f* — **consistent** *adj* **1** UNCHANGING : constante, regular **2** ~ **with** : consecuente con

console *vt* **-soled; -soling** : consolar — **consolation** *n* **1** : consuelo *m* **2** ~ **prize** : premio *m* de consolación

consolidate *vt* **-dated; -dating** : consolidar — **consolidation** *n* : consolidación *f*

consonant *n* : consonante *f*

conspicuous *adj* **1** OBVIOUS : visible, evidente **2** STRIKING : llamativo — **conspicuously** *adv* : de manera llama- tiva

conspire *vi* **-spired; -spiring** : conspirar — **conspiracy** *n, pl* **-cies** : conspiración *f*

constant *adj* : constante — **constantly** *adv* : constantemente

constellation *n* : constelación *f*

constipated *adj* : estreñido — **constipation** *n* : estreñimiento *m*
constituent *n* **1** COMPONENT : componente *m* **2** VOTER : elector *m*, -tora *f*; votante *mf*
constitute *vt* **-tuted; -tuting** : constituir — **constitution** *n* : constitución *f* — **constitutional** *adj* : constitucional
constraint *n* : restricción *f*, limitación *f*
construct *vt* : construir — **construction** *n* : construcción *f* — **constructive** *adj* : constructivo
construe *vt* **-strued; -struing** : interpretar
consul *n* : cónsul *mf* — **consulate** *n* : consulado *m*
consult *v* : consultar — **consultant** *n* : asesor *m*, -sora *f*; consultor *m*, -tora *f* — **consultation** *n* : consulta *f*
consume *vt* **-sumed; -suming** : consumir — **consumer** *n* : consumidor *m*, -dora *f* — **consumption** *n* : consumo *m*
contact *n* : contacto *m* — ~ *vt* : ponerse en contacto con — **contact lens** *n* : lente *mf* (de contacto)
contagious *adj* : contagioso
contain *vt* **1** : contener **2** ~ **oneself** : contenerse — **container** *n* : recipiente *m*, envase *m*
contaminate *vt* **-nated; -nating** : contaminar — **contamination** *n* : contaminación *f*
contemplate *v* **-plated; -plating** *vt* **1** : contemplar **2** CONSIDER : considerar, pensar en — *vi* : reflexionar — **contemplation** *n* : contemplación *f*
contemporary *adj* : contemporáneo — ~ *n, pl* **-raries** : contemporáneo *m*, -nea *f*
contempt *n* : desprecio *m* — **contemptible** *adj* : despreciable — **contemptuous** *adj* : desdeñoso
contend *vi* **1** COMPETE : contender, competir **2** ~ **with** : enfrentarse a — *vt* : sostener, afirmar — **contender** *n* : contendiente *mf*
content[1] *n* **1** : contenido *m* **2 table of** ~**s** : índice *m* de materias
content[2] *adj* : contento — ~ *vt* ~ **oneself with** : contentarse con — **contented** *adj* : satisfecho, contento
contention *n* **1** DISPUTE : disputa *f* **2** OPINION : argumento *m*, opinión *f*
contentment *n* : satisfacción *f*
contest *vt* : disputar — ~ *n* **1** STRUGGLE : contienda *f* **2** COMPETITION : concurso *m*, competencia *f* — **contestant** *n* : concursante *mf*, contendiente *mf*
context *n* : contexto *m*
continent *n* : continente *m* — **continental** *adj* : continental
contingency *n, pl* **-cies** : contingencia *f*
continue *v* **-tinued; -tinuing** : continuar — **continual** *adj* : continuo, constante — **con-**tinuation *n* : continuación *f* — **continuity** *n, pl* **-ties** : continuidad *f* — **continuous** *adj* : continuo
contort *vt* : retorcer — **contortion** *n* : contorsión *f*
contour *n* **1** : contorno *m* **2** *or* ~ **line** : curva *f* de nivel
contraband *n* : contrabando *m*
contraception *n* : anticoncepción *f* — **contraceptive** *adj* : anticonceptivo — ~ *n* : anticonceptivo *m*
contract *n* : contrato *m* — ~ *vt* : contraer — *vi* : contraerse — **contraction** *n* : contracción *f* — **contractor** *n* : contratista *mf*
contradiction *n* : contradicción *f* — **contradict** *vt* : contradecir — **contradictory** *adj* : contradictorio
contraption *n* : artilugio *m*, artefacto *m*
contrary *n, pl* **-traries** **1** : contrario **2 on the** ~ : al contrario — ~ *adj* **1** : contrario, opuesto **2** ~ **to** : en contra de
contrast *v* : contrastar — ~ *n* : contraste *m*
contribute *v* **-uted; -uting** : contribuir — **contribution** *n* : contribución *f* — **contributor** *n* **1** : contribuyente *mf* **2** : colaborador *m*, -dora *f* (en periodismo)
contrite *adj* : arrepentido
contrive *vt* **-trived; -triving** **1** DEVISE : idear **2** ~ **to do sth** : lograr hacer algo
control *vt* **-trolled; -trolling** : controlar — ~ *n* **1** : control *m* **2** ~**s** *npl* : mandos *mpl*
controversy *n, pl* **-sies** : controversia *f* — **controversial** *adj* : polémico
convalescence *n* : convalecencia *f* — **convalescent** *adj* : convaleciente — ~ *n* : convaleciente *mf*
convene *v* **-vened; -vening** *vt* : convocar — *vi* : reunirse
convenience *n* : conveniencia *f*, comodidad *f* — **convenient** *adj* : conveniente
convent *n* : convento *m*
convention *n* : convención *f* — **conventional** *adj* : convencional
converge *vi* **-verged; -verging** : converger, convergir
converse[1] *vi* **-versed; -versing** : conversar — **conversation** *n* : conversación *f* — **conversational** *adj* : familiar
converse[2] *adj* : contrario, opuesto — **conversely** *adv* : a la inversa
conversion *n* : conversión *f* — **convert** *vt* : convertir — *vi* : convertirse — **convertible** *adj* : convertible — ~ *n* : descapotable *m*, convertible *m* *Lat*
convex *adj* : convexo
convey *vt* **1** TRANSPORT : llevar, transportar **2** TRANSMIT : comunicar
convict *vt* : declarar culpable a — ~ *n* : presidiario *m*, -ria *f* — **conviction** *n* **1** : con-

dena *f* (de un acusado) **2** BELIEF : convicción *f*
convince *vt* **-vinced; -vincing** : convencer — **convincing** *adj* : convincente
convoke *vt* **-voked; -voking** : convocar
convoluted *adj* : complicado
convulsion *n* : convulsión *f* — **convulsive** *adj* : convulsivo
cook *n* : cocinero *m*, -ra *f* — ∼ *vi* : cocinar, guisar — *vt* : preparar (comida) — **cookbook** *n* : libro *m* de cocina
cookie *or* **cooky** *n*, *pl* **-ies** : galleta *f* (dulce)
cooking *n* : cocina *f*
cool *adj* **1** : fresco **2** CALM : tranquilo **3** UNFRIENDLY : frío — ∼ *vt* : enfriar — *vi* : enfriarse — ∼ *n* **1** : fresco *m* **2** COMPOSURE : calma *f* — **cooler** *n* : nevera *f* portátil — **coolness** *n* : frescura *f*
coop *n* : gallinero *m* — ∼ *vt or* ∼ **up** : encerrar
cooperate *vi* **-ated; -ating** : cooperar — **cooperation** *n* : cooperación *f* — **cooperative** *adj* : cooperativo
coordinate *v* **-nated; -nating** *vt* : coordinar — **coordination** *n* : coordinación *f*
cop *n* **1** : poli *mf fam* **2 the** ∼**s** : la poli *fam*
cope *vi* **coped; coping 1** : arreglárselas **2** ∼ **with** : hacer frente a, poder con
copier *n* : fotocopiadora *f*
copious *adj* : copioso
copper *n* : cobre *m*
copy *n*, *pl* **copies 1** : copia *f* **2** : ejemplar *m* (de un libro), número *m* (de una revista) — ∼ *vt* **copied; copying 1** DUPLICATE : hacer una copia de **2** IMITATE : copiar — **copyright** *n* : derechos *mpl* de autor
coral *n* : coral *m*
cord *n* **1** : cuerda *f* **2** *or* **electric** ∼ : cable *m* (eléctrico)
cordial *adj* : cordial
corduroy *n* : pana *f*
core *n* **1** : corazón *m* (de una fruta) **2** CENTER : núcleo *m*, centro *m*
cork *n* : corcho *m* — **corkscrew** *n* : sacacorchos *m*
corn *n* **1** : grano *m* **2** *or* **Indian** ∼ : maíz *m* **3** : callo *m* (del pie) — **corncob** *n* : mazorca *f*
corner *n* : ángulo *m*, rincón *m* (en una habitación), esquina *f* (de una intersección) — ∼ *vt* **1** TRAP : acorralar **2** MONOPOLIZE : acaparar (un mercado) — **cornerstone** *n* : piedra *f* angular
cornmeal *n* : harina *f* de maíz — **cornstarch** *n* : maicena *f*
corny *adj* : cursi, sentimental
coronary *n*, *pl* **-naries** : trombosis *f* coronaria
coronation *n* : coronación *f*

corporal *n* : cabo *m*
corporation *n* : sociedad *f* anónima, compañía *f* — **corporate** *adj* : corporativo
corps *n*, *pl* **corps** : cuerpo *m*
corpse *n* : cadáver *m*
corpulent *adj* : obeso, gordo
corpuscle *n* : glóbulo *m*
corral *n* : corral *m* — ∼ *vt* **-ralled; -ralling** : acorralar
correct *vt* : corregir — ∼ *adj* : correcto — **correction** *n* : corrección *f*
correlation *n* : correlación *f*
correspond *vi* **1** WRITE : corresponderse **2** ∼ **to** : corresponder a — **correspondence** *n* : correspondencia *f*
corridor *n* : pasillo *m*
corroborate *vt* **-rated; -rating** : corroborar
corrode *v* **-roded; -roding** *vt* : corroer — *vi* : corroerse — **corrosion** *n* : corrosión *f* — **corrosive** *adj* : corrosivo
corrugated *adj* : ondulado
corrupt *vt* : corromper — ∼ *adj* : corrupto, corrompido — **corruption** *n* : corrupción *f*
corset *n* : corsé *m*
cosmetic *n* : cosmético *m* — ∼ *adj* : cosmético
cosmic *adj* : cósmico
cosmopolitan *adj* : cosmopolita
cosmos *n* : cosmos *m*
cost *n* : costo *m*, coste *m* — ∼ *vi* **cost; costing 1** : costar **2 how much does it** ∼**?** : ¿cuánto cuesta?, ¿cuánto vale?
Costa Rican *adj* : costarricense
costly *adj* : costoso
costume *n* **1** OUTFIT : traje *m* **2** DISGUISE : disfraz *m*
cot *n* : catre *m*
cottage *n* **1** : casita *f* (de campo) — **cottage cheese** *n* : requesón *m*
cotton *n* : algodón *m*
couch *n* : sofá *m*
cough *vi* : toser — ∼ *n* : tos *f*
could → **can**[1]
council *n* **1** : concejo *m* **2** *or* **city** ∼ : ayuntamiento *m* — **councillor** *or* **councilor** *n* : concejal *m*, -jala *f*
counsel *n* **1** ADVICE : consejo *m* **2** LAWYER : abogado *m*, -da *f* — ∼ *vt* **-seled** *or* **-selled; -seling** *or* **-selling** : aconsejar — **counselor** *or* **counsellor** *n* : consejero *m*, -ra *f*
count[1] *vt* : contar — *vi* **1** : contar **2** ∼ **on** : contar con **3 that doesn't** ∼ : eso no vale — ∼ *n* **1** : recuento *m* **2 keep** ∼ **of** : llevar la cuenta de
count[2] *n* : conde *m* (noble)
counter[1] *n* **1** : mostrador *m* (de un negocio) **2** TOKEN : ficha *f* (de un juego)
counter[2] *vt* : oponerse a — *vi* : contraatacar

countess

— ~ *adv* ~ **to** : contrario a — **counteract** *vt* : contrarrestar — **counterattack** *n* : contraataque *m* — **counterbalance** *n* : con- trapeso *m* — **counterclockwise** *adv & adj* : en sentido opuesto a las agujas del reloj — **counterfeit** *vt* : falsificar — ~ *adj* : falsificado — ~ *n* : falsificación *f* — **counterpart** *n* : homólogo *m* (de una persona), equivalente *m* (de una cosa) — **counterproductive** *adj* : contraproducente
countess *n* : condesa *f*
countless *adj* : incontable, innumerable
country *n, pl* -**tries** **1** NATION : país *m* **2** COUNTRYSIDE : campo *m* — ~ *adj* : campestre, rural — **countryman** *n, pl* -**men** *or* **fellow** ~ : compatriota *mf* — **countryside** *n* : campo *m*, campiña *f*
county *n, pl* -**ties** : condado *m*
coup *n, pl* **coups** *or* ~ **d'etat** : golpe *m* (de estado)
couple *n* **1** : pareja *f* (de personas) **2 a** ~ **of** : un par de — ~ *vt* -**pled; -pling** : acoplar, unir
coupon *n* : cupón *m*
courage *n* : valor *m* — **courageous** *adj* : valiente
courier *n* : mensajero *m*, -ra *f*
course *n* **1** : curso *m* **2** : plato *m* (de una cena) **3** *or* **golf** ~ : campo *m* de golf **4 in the** ~ **of** : en el transcurso de **5 of** ~ : desde luego, por supuesto
court *n* **1** : corte *f* (de un rey, etc.) **2** : cancha *f*, pista *f* (en deportes) **3** TRIBUNAL : corte *f*, tribunal *m* — ~ *vt* : cortejar
courteous *adj* : cortés — **courtesy** *n, pl* -**sies** : cortesía *f*
courthouse *n* : palacio *m* de justicia, juzgado *m* — **courtroom** *n* : sala *f* (de un tribunal)
courtship *n* : cortejo *m*, noviazgo *m*
courtyard *n* : patio *m*
cousin *n* : primo *m*, -ma *f*
cove *n* : ensenada *f*, cala *f*
covenant *n* : pacto *m*, convenio *m*
cover *vt* **1** : cubrir **2** *or* ~ **up** : encubrir, ocultar **3** TREAT : tratar — ~ *n* **1** : cubierta *f* **2** SHELTER : abrigo *m*, refugio *m* **3** LID : tapa *f* **4** : cubierta *f* (de un libro), portada *f* (de una revista) **5** ~**s** *npl* BEDCLOTHES : mantas *fpl*, cobijas *fpl Lat* **6 take** ~ : ponerse a cubierto **7 under** ~ **of** : al amparo de — **coverage** *n* : cobertura *f* — **covert** *adj* : encubierto — **cover-up** *n* : encubrimiento *m*
covet *vt* : codiciar — **covetous** *adj* : codicioso
cow *n* : vaca *f* — ~ *vt* : intimidar, acobardar
coward *n* : cobarde *mf* — **cowardice** *n* : cobardía *f* — **cowardly** *adj* : cobarde

cowboy *n* : vaquero *m*
cower *vi* : encogerse (de miedo)
coy *adj* : tímido y coqueto
coyote *n, pl* **coyotes** *or* **coyote** : coyote *m*
cozy *adj* -**zier; -est** : acogedor
crab *n* : cangrejo *m*, jaiba *f Lat*
crack *vt* **1** SPLIT : rajar, partir **2** : cascar (nueces, huevos) **3** : chasquear (un látigo, etc.) **4** ~ **down on** : tomar medidas enérgicas contra — *vi* **1** SPLIT : rajarse, agrietarse **2** : chasquear (dícese de un látigo) **3** ~ **up** : sufrir una crisis nerviosa — ~ *n* **1** CRACKING : chasquido *m*, crujido *m* **2** CREVICE : raja *f*, grieta *f* **3 have a** ~ **at** : intentar
cracker *n* : galleta *f* (de soda, etc.)
crackle *vi* -**led; -ling** : crepitar, chisporrotear — ~ *n* : crujido *m*, chisporroteo *m*
cradle *n* : cuna *f* — ~ *vt* -**dled; -dling** : acunar
craft *n* **1** TRADE : oficio *m* **2** CUNNING : astucia *f* **3** → **craftsmanship 4** *pl usually* **craft** BOAT : embarcación *f* — **craftsman** *n, pl* -**men** : artesano *m*, -na *f* — **craftsmanship** *n* : artesanía *f*, destreza *f* — **crafty** *adj* **craftier; -est** : astuto, taimado
crag *n* : peñasco *m*
cram *v* **crammed; cramming** *vt* **1** STUFF : embutir **2** ~ **with** : atiborrar de — *vi* : estudiar a última hora
cramp *n* **1** : calambre *m*, espasmo *m* (de los músculos) **2** ~**s** *npl* : retorcijones *mpl*
cranberry *n, pl* -**berries** : arándano *m* (rojo y agrio)
crane *n* **1** : grulla *f* (ave) **2** : grúa *f* (máquina) — ~ *vt* **craned; craning** : estirar (el cuello)
crank *n* **1** : manivela *f* **2** ECCENTRIC : excéntrico *m*, -ca *f* — **cranky** *adj* **crankier; -est** : malhumorado
crash *vi* **1** : caerse con estrépito **2** COLLIDE : estrellarse, chocar — *vt* : estrellar — ~ *n* **1** DIN : estrépito *m* **2** COLLISION : choque *m*
crass *adj* : burdo, grosero
crate *n* : cajón *m* (de madera)
crater *n* : cráter *m*
crave *vt* **craved; craving** : ansiar — **craving** *n* : ansia *f*
crawl *vi* **1** : arrastrarse, gatear (dícese de un bebé) — ~ *n* **at a** ~ : a paso lento
crayon *n* : lápiz *m* de cera
craze *n* : moda *f* pasajera, manía *f*
crazy *adj* -**zier; -est 1** : loco **2 go** ~ : volverse loco — **craziness** *n* : locura *f*
creak *vi* : chirriar, crujir — ~ *n* : chirrido *m*, crujido *m*
cream *n* : crema *f*, nata *f Spain* — **cream cheese** *n* : queso *m* crema — **creamy** *adj* **creamier; -est** : cremoso

crease *n* : pliegue *m*, raya *f* (del pantalón) — ~ *vt* **creased; creasing** : plegar, poner una raya en (el pantalón)
create *vt* **-ated; -ating** : crear — **creation** *n* : creación *f* — **creative** *adj* : creativo — **creator** *n* : creador *m*, -dora *f*
creature *n* : criatura *f*, animal *m*
credence *n* **lend** ~ **to** : dar crédito a
credentials *npl* : credenciales *fpl*
credible *adj* : creíble — **credibility** *n* : credibilidad *f*
credit *n* **1** : crédito *m* **2** RECOGNITION : reconocimiento *m* **3** **be a** ~ **to** : ser el orgullo de — ~ *vt* **1** BELIEVE : creer **2** : abonar (en una cuenta) **3** ~ **s.o. with sth** : atribuir algo a algn — **credit card** *n* : tarjeta *f* de crédito
credulous *adj* : crédulo
creed *n* : credo *m*
creek *n* : arroyo *m*, riachuelo *m*
creep *vi* **crept; creeping 1** CRAWL : arrastrarse **2** SLINK : ir a hurtadillas — ~ *n* **1** CRAWL : paso *m* lento **2 the** ~**s** : escalofríos *mpl* — **creeping** *adj* ~ **plant** : planta *f* trepadora
cremate *vt* **-mated; -mating** : incinerar
crescent *n* : media luna *f*
cress *n* : berro *m*
crest *n* : cresta *f* — **crestfallen** *adj* : alicaído
crevice *n* : grieta *f*
crew *n* **1** : tripulación *f* (de una nave) **2** TEAM : equipo *m*
crib *n* : cuna *f* (de un bebé)
cricket *n* **1** : grillo *m* (insecto) **2** : críquet *m* (juego)
crime *n* : crimen *m* — **criminal** *adj* : criminal — ~ *n* : criminal *mf*
crimp *vt* : rizar
crimson *n* : carmesí *m*
cringe *vi* **cringed; cringing** : encogerse
crinkle *vt* **-kled; -kling** : arrugar
cripple *vt* **-pled; -pling 1** DISABLE : lisiar, dejar inválido **2** INCAPACITATE : inutilizar, paralizar
crisis *n, pl* **crises** : crisis *f*
crisp *adj* **1** CRUNCHY : crujiente **2** : frío y vigorizante (dícese del aire) — **crispy** *adj* **crispier; -est** : crujiente
crisscross *vt* : entrecruzar
criterion *n, pl* **-ria** : criterio *m*
critic *n* : crítico *m*, -ca *f* — **critical** *adj* : crítico — **criticism** *n* : crítica *f* — **criticize** *vt* **-cized; -cizing** : criticar
croak *vi* : croar
crock *n* : vasija *f* de barro — **crockery** *n* : vajilla *f*, loza *f*
crocodile *n* : cocodrilo *m*
crony *n, pl* **-nies** : amigote *m fam*
crook *n* **1** STAFF : cayado *m* **2** THIEF : ratero

m, -ra *f*; ladrón *m*, -drona *f* **3** BEND : pliegue *m* — **crooked** *adj* **1** BENT : torcido, chueco *Lat* **2** DISHONEST : deshonesto
crop *n* **1** WHIP : fusta *f* **2** HARVEST : cosecha *f* **3** : cultivo *m* (de maíz, tabaco, etc.) — ~ *v* **cropped; cropping** *vt* TRIM : recortar, cortar — *vi* ~ **up** : surgir
cross *n* **1** : cruz *f* **2** HYBRID : cruce *m* — ~ *vt* **1** : cruzar, atravesar **2** CROSSBREED : cruzar **3** *or* ~ **out** : tachar — ~ *adj* **1** : que atraviesa **2** ANGRY : enojado — **crossbreed** *vt* **-bred; -breeding** : cruzar — **cross–examine** *vt* : interrogar — **cross–eyed** *adj* : bizco — **cross fire** *n* : fuego *m* cruzado — **crossing** *n* **1** INTERSECTION : cruce *m*, paso *m* **2** VOYAGE : travesía *f* (del mar) — **cross–reference** *n* : referencia *f* — **crossroads** *n* : cruce *m* — **cross section** *n* **1** : corte *m* transversal **2** SAMPLE : muestra *f* representativa — **crosswalk** *n* : cruce *m* peatonal, paso *m* de peatones — **crossword puzzle** *n* : crucigrama *m*
crotch *n* : entrepierna *f*
crouch *vi* : agacharse
crouton *n* : crutón *m*
crow *n* : cuervo *m* — ~ *vi* **crowed** *or Brit* **crew; crowing** : cacarear
crowbar *n* : palanca *f*
crowd *vi* : amontonarse — *vt* : atestar, llenar — ~ *n* : multitud *f*, muchedumbre *f*
crown *n* **1** : corona *f* **2** : cima *f* (de una colina) — ~ *vt* : coronar
crucial *adj* : crucial
crucify *vt* **-fied; -fying** : crucificar — **crucifix** *n* : crucifijo *m* — **crucifixion** *n* : crucifixión *f*
crude *adj* **cruder; -est 1** RAW : crudo **2** VULGAR : grosero **3** ROUGH : tosco, rudo
cruel *adj* **-eler** *or* **-eller; -elest** *or* **-ellest** : cruel — **cruelty** *n, pl* **-ties** : crueldad *f*
cruet *n* : vinagrera *f*
cruise *vi* **cruised; cruising 1** : hacer un crucero **2** : ir a velocidad de crucero — ~ *n* : crucero *m* — **cruiser** *n* **1** WARSHIP : crucero *m* **2** : patrulla *f* (de policía)
crumb *n* : miga *f*, migaja *f*
crumble *v* **-bled; -bling** *vt* : desmenuzar — *vi* : desmenuzarse, desmoronarse
crumple *vt* **-pled; -pling** : arrugar
crunch *vt* : ronzar (con los dientes), hacer crujir (con los pies, etc.) — **crunchy** *adj* **crunchier; -est** : crujiente
crusade *n* : cruzada *f*
crush *vt* : aplastar, apachurrar *Lat* — ~ *n* **have a** ~ **on** : estar chiflado por
crust *n* : corteza *f*
crutch *n* : muleta *f*
crux *n* : quid *m*

cry *vi* **cried; crying 1** SHOUT : gritar **2** WEEP : llorar — ∿ *n, pl* **cries** : grito *m*
crypt *n* : cripta *f*
crystal *n* : cristal *m*
cub *n* : cachorro *m,* -rra *f*
Cuban *adj* : cubano
cube *n* : cubo *m* — **cubic** *adj* : cúbico
cubicle *n* : cubículo *m*
cuckoo *n* : cuco *m,* cuclillo *m*
cucumber *n* : pepino *m*
cuddle *v* **-dled; -dling** *vi* : acurrucarse, abrazarse — *vt* : abrazar
cudgel *n* : porra *f* — ∿ *vt* **-geled** *or* **-gelled; -geling** *or* **-gelling** : aporrear
cue[1] *n* SIGNAL : señal *f*
cue[2] *n* : taco *m* (de billar)
cuff[1] **1** : puño *m* (de una camisa) **2** ∿s *npl* → **handcuffs**
cuff[2] *vt* : bofetear — ∿ *n* SLAP : bofetada *f*
cuisine *n* : cocina *f*
culinary *adj* : culinario
cull *vt* : seleccionar, entresacar
culminate *vi* **-nated; -nating** : culminar — **culmination** *n* : culminación *f*
culprit *n* : culpable *mf*
cult *n* : culto *m*
cultivate *vt* **-vated; -vating** : cultivar — **cultivation** *n* : cultivo *m*
culture *n* **1** : cultura *f* **2** : cultivo *m* (en biología) — **cultural** *adj* : cultural — **cultured** *adj* : culto
cumbersome *adj* : torpe (y pesado), difícil de manejar
cumulative *adj* : acumulativo
cunning *adj* : astuto, taimado — ∿ *n* : astucia *f*
cup *n* **1** : taza *f* **2** TROPHY : copa *f*
cupboard *n* : alacena *f,* armario *m*
curator *n* : conservador *m,* -dora *f;* director *m,* -tora *f*
curb *n* **1** RESTRAINT : freno *m* **2** : borde *m* de la acera — ∿ *vt* : refrenar
curdle *v* **-dled; -dling** *vi* : cuajarse — *vt* : cuajar
cure *n* : cura *f,* remedio *m* — ∿ *vt* **cured; curing** : curar
curfew *n* : toque *m* de queda
curious *adj* : curioso — **curio** *n, pl* **-rios** : curiosidad *f* — **curiosity** *n, pl* **-ties** : curiosidad *f*
curl *vt* **1** : rizar **2** COIL : enrollar, enroscar — *vi* **1** : rizarse **2** ∿ **up** : acurrucarse — ∿ *n* : rizo *m* — **curler** *n* : rulo *m* — **curly** *adj* **curlier; -est** : rizado

currant *n* **1** : grosella *f* (fruta) **2** RAISIN : pasa *f* de Corinto
currency *n, pl* **-cies 1** MONEY : moneda *f* **2** **gain** ∿ : ganar aceptación
current *adj* **1** PRESENT : actual **2** PREVALENT : corriente — ∿ *n* : corriente *f*
curriculum *n, pl* **-la** : plan *m* de estudios
curry *n, pl* **-ries** : curry *m*
curse *n* : maldición *f* — ∿ *v* **cursed; cursing** : maldecir
cursor *n* : cursor *m*
cursory *adj* : superficial
curt *adj* : corto, seco
curtail *vt* : acortar
curtain *n* : cortina *f* (de una ventana), telón *m* (en un teatro)
curtsy *vi* **-sied** *or* **-seyed; -sying** *or* **-seying** : hacer una reverencia — ∿ *n* : reverencia *f*
curve *v* **curved; curving** *vi* : hacer una curva — *vt* : encorvar — ∿ *n* : curva *f*
cushion *n* : cojín *m* — ∿ *vt* : amortiguar
custard *n* : natillas *fpl*
custody *n, pl* **-dies 1** : custodia *f* **2 be in** ∿ : estar detenido — **custodian** *n* : custodio *m,* -dia *f;* guardián, -diana *f*
custom *n* : costumbre *f* — **customary** *adj* : habitual, acostumbrado — **customer** *n* : cliente *m,* -ta *f* — **customs** *npl* : aduana *f*
cut *v* **cut; cutting** *vt* **1** : cortar **2** REDUCE : reducir, rebajar **3** ∿ **oneself** : cortarse **4** ∿ **up** : cortar en pedazos — *vi* **1** : cortar **2** ∿ **in** : interrumpir — ∿ *n* **1** : corte *m* **2** REDUCTION : rebaja *f,* reducción *f*
cute *adj* **cuter; -est** : mono *fam,* lindo
cutlery *n* : cubiertos *mpl*
cutlet *n* : chuleta *f*
cutting *adj* : cortante, mordaz
cyanide *n* : cianuro *m*
cycle *n* **1** : ciclo *m* **2** BICYCLE : bicicleta *f* — ∿ *vi* **-cled; -cling** : ir en bicicleta — **cyclic** *or* **cyclical** *adj* : cíclico — **cyclist** *n* : ciclista *mf*
cyclone *n* : ciclón *m*
cylinder *n* : cilindro *m* — **cylindrical** *adj* : cilíndrico
cymbal *n* : platillo *m,* címbalo *m*
cynic *n* : cínico *m,* -ca *f* — **cynical** *adj* : cínico — **cynicism** *n* : cinismo *m*
cypress *n* : ciprés *m*
cyst *n* : quiste *m*
czar *n* : zar *m*
Czech *adj* : checo — ∿ *n* : checo *m* (idioma)

D

d *n, pl* **d's** *or* **ds** : d *f*, cuarta letra del alfabeto inglés

dab *n* : toque *m* — ~ *vt* **dabbed; dabbing** : dar toques ligeros a, aplicar suavemente

dabble *vi* **-bled; -bling** ~ **in** : interesarse superficialmente en — **dabbler** *n* : aficionado *m*, -da *f*

dad *n* : papá *m fam* — **daddy** *n, pl* **-dies** : papá *m fam*

daffodil *n* : narciso *m*

dagger *n* : daga *f*, puñal *m*

daily *adj* : diario — ~ *adv* : diariamente

dainty *adj* **-tier; -est** : delicado

dairy *n, pl* **-ies 1** : lechería *f* (tienda) **2** *or* ~ **farm** : granja *f* lechera

daisy *n, pl* **-sies** : margarita *f*

dam *n* : presa *f* — ~ *vt* **dammed; damming** : represar

damage *n* **1** : daño *m*, perjuicio *m* **2** ~**s** *npl* : daños y perjuicios *mpl* — ~ *vt* **-aged; -aging** : dañar

damn *vt* **1** CONDEMN : condenar **2** CURSE : maldecir — ~ *n* **not give a** ~ : no importarse un comino *fam* — ~ *or* **damned** *adj* : maldito *fam*

damp *adj* : húmedo — **dampen** *vt* **1** MOISTEN : humedecer **2** DISCOURAGE : desalentar, desanimar — **dampness** *n* : humedad *f*

dance *v* **danced; dancing** : bailar — ~ *n* : baile *m* — **dancer** *n* : bailarín *m*, -rina *f*

dandelion *n* : diente *m* de león

dandruff *n* : caspa *f*

dandy *adj* **-dier; -est** : de primera, excelente

danger *n* : peligro *m* — **dangerous** *adj* : peligroso

dangle *v* **-gled; -gling** *vi* HANG : colgar, pender — *vt* : hacer oscilar

Danish *adj* : danés — ~ *n* : danés *m* (idioma)

dank *adj* : frío y húmedo

dare *v* **dared; daring** *vt* : desafiar — *vi* : osar — ~ *n* : desafío *m* — **daredevil** *n* : persona *f* temeraria — **daring** *adj* : atrevido, audaz — ~ *n* : audacia *f*

dark *adj* **1** : oscuro **2** : moreno (dícese del pelo o de la piel) **3** GLOOMY : sombrío **4** **get** ~ : hacerse de noche — **darken** *vt* : oscurecer — *vi* : oscurecerse — **darkness** *n* : oscuridad *f*

darling *n* BELOVED : querido *m*, -da *f* — ~ *adj* : querido

darn *vt* : zurcir — ~ *adj* : maldito *fam*

dart *n* **1** : dardo *m* **2** ~**s** *npl* : juego *m* de dardos — ~ *vi* : precipitarse

dash *vt* **1** SMASH : romper **2** HURL : lanzar **3** ~ **off** : hacer (algo) rápidamente — *vi* : lanzarse, irse corriendo — ~ *n* **1** : guión *m* largo (signo de puntuación) **2** PINCH : poquito *m*, pizca *f* **3** RACE : carrera *f* — **dashboard** *n* : tablero *m* de instrumentos — **dashing** *adj* : gallardo, apuesto

data *ns & pl* : datos *mpl* — **database** *n* : base *f* de datos

date¹ *n* : dátil *m* (fruta)

date² *n* **1** : fecha *f* **2** APPOINTMENT : cita *f* — ~ *v* **dated; dating** *vt* **1** : fechar (una carta, etc.) **2** : salir con (algn) — *vi* ~ **from** : datar de — **dated** *adj* : pasado de moda

daub *vt* : embadurnar

daughter *n* : hija *f* — **daughter–in–law** *n, pl* **daughters–in–law** : nuera *f*

daunt *vt* : intimidar

dawdle *vi* **-dled; -dling** : entretenerse, perder tiempo

dawn *vi* **1** : amanecer **2 it** ~**ed on him that** : cayó en la cuenta de que — ~ *n* : amanecer *m*

day *n* **1** : día *m* **2** *or* **working** ~ : jornada *f* **3 the** ~ **before** : el día anterior **4 the** ~ **before yesterday** : anteayer **5 the** ~ **after** : el día siguiente **6 the** ~ **after tomorrow** : pasada mañana — **daybreak** *n* : amanecer *m* — **daydream** *n* : ensueño *m* — ~ *vi* : soñar despierto — **daylight** *n* : luz *f* del día — **daytime** *n* : día *m*

daze *vt* **dazed; dazing** : aturdir — ~ *n* **in a** ~ : aturdido

dazzle *vt* **-zled; -zling** : deslumbrar

dead *adj* **1** LIFELESS : muerto **2** NUMB : entumecido — ~ *n* **1 in the** ~ **of night** : en plena noche **2 the** ~ : los muertos — ~ *adv* ABSOLUTELY : absolutamente — **deaden** *vt* **1** : atenuar (dolores) **2** MUFFLE : amortiguar — **dead end** *n* : callejón *m* sin salida — **deadline** *n* : fecha *f* límite — **deadlock** *n* : punto *m* muerto — **deadly** *adj* **-lier; -est 1** : mortal, letal **2** ACCURATE : certero, preciso

deaf *adj* : sordo — **deafen** *vt* : ensordecer — **deafness** *n* : sordera *f*

deal *n* **1** TRANSACTION : trato *m*, transacción *f* **2** : reparto *m* (de naipes) **3 a good** ~ : mucho — ~ *v* **dealt; dealing 1** : dar **2** : repartir, dar (naipes) **3** ~ **a blow** : asestar un golpe — *vi* **1** : dar, repartir (en juegos de naipes) **2** ~ **in** : comerciar en **3** ~ **with** CONCERN : tratar de **4** ~ **with s.o.** : tratar con algn — **dealer** *n* : comerciante *mf* — **dealings** *npl* : trato *m*, relaciones *fpl*

dean *n* : decano *m*, -na *f*

dear *adj* : querido — ∼ *n* : querido *m*, -da *f* — **dearly** *adv* 1 : mucho 2 pay ∼ : pagar caro

death *n* : muerte *f*

debar *vt* : excluir

debate *n* : debate *m*, discusión *f* — ∼ *vt* -**bated; -bating** : debatir, discutir

debit *vt* : adeudar, cargar — ∼ *n* : débito *m*, debe *m*

debris *n*, *pl* -**bris** : escombros *mpl*

debt *n* : deuda *f* — **debtor** *n* : deudor *m*, -dora *f*

debunk *vt* : desmentir

debut *n* : debut *m* — ∼ *vi* : debutar

decade *n* : década *f*

decadence *n* : decadencia *f* — **decadent** *adj* : decadente

decal *n* : calcomanía *f*

decanter *n* : licorera *f*

decapitate *vt* -**tated; -tating** : decapitar

decay *vi* 1 DECOMPOSE : descomponerse 2 DETERIORATE : deteriorarse 3 : cariarse (dícese de los dientes) — ∼ *n* 1 : descomposición *f* 2 : deterioro *m* (de un edificio, etc.) 3 : caries *f* (de los dientes)

deceased *adj* : difunto — ∼ *n* **the** ∼ : el difunto, la difunta

deceive *vt* -**ceived; -ceiving** : engañar — **deceit** *n* : engaño *m* — **deceitful** *adj* : engañoso

December *n* : diciembre *m*

decent *adj* 1 : decente 2 KIND : bueno, amable — **decency** *n*, *pl* -**cies** : decencia *f*

deception *n* : engaño *m* — **deceptive** *adj* : engañoso

decide *v* -**cided; -ciding** *vt* : decidir — *vi* : decidirse — **decided** *adj* 1 UNQUESTIONABLE : indudable 2 RESOLUTE : decidido — **decidedly** *adv* 1 DEFINITELY : decididamente 2 RESOLUTELY : con decisión

decimal *adj* : decimal — ∼ *n* : número *m* decimal — **decimal point** *n* : coma *f* decimal

decipher *vt* : descifrar

decision *n* : decisión *f* — **decisive** *adj* 1 RESOLUTE : decidido 2 CONCLUSIVE : decisivo

deck *n* 1 : cubierta *f* (de un barco) 2 *or* ∼ **of cards** : baraja *f* (de naipes) 3 TERRACE : entarimado *m*

declare *vt* -**clared; -claring** : declarar — **declaration** *n* : declaración *f*

decline *v* -**clined; -clining** *vt* REFUSE : declinar, rehusar — *vi* DECREASE : disminuir — ∼ *n* 1 DETERIORATION : decadencia *f*, deterioro *m* 2 DECREASE : disminución *f*

decode *vt* -**coded; -coding** : descodificar

decompose *vt* -**posed; -posing** : descomponer — *vi* : descomponerse

decongestant *n* : descongestionante *m*

decorate *vt* -**rated; -rating** : decorar — **decor** *or* **décor** *n* : decoración *f* — **decoration** *n* : decoración *f* — **decorator** *n* : decorador *m*, -dora *f*

decoy *n* : señuelo *m*

decrease *v* -**creased; -creasing** : disminuir — ∼ *n* : disminución *f*

decree *n* : decreto *m* — ∼ *vt* -**creed; -creeing** : decretar

decrepit *adj* 1 FEEBLE : decrépito 2 DILAPIDATED : ruinoso

dedicate *vt* -**cated; -cating** 1 : dedicar 2 ∼ **oneself to** : consagrarse a — **dedication** *n* 1 DEVOTION : dedicación *f* 2 INSCRIPTION : dedicatoria *f*

deduce *vt* -**duced; -ducing** : deducir — **deduct** *vt* : deducir — **deduction** *n* : deducción *f*

deed *n* : acción *f*, hecho *m*

deem *vt* : considerar, juzgar

deep *adj* : hondo, profundo — ∼ *adv* 1 DEEPLY : profundamente 2 ∼ **down** : en el fondo 3 **dig** ∼ : cavar hondo — **deepen** *vt* : ahondar — *vi* : hacerse más profundo — **deeply** *adv* : hondo, profundamente

deer *ns* & *pl* : ciervo *m*

deface *vt* -**faced; -facing** : desfigurar

default *n* **by** ∼ : en rebeldía — ∼ *vi* 1 ∼ **on** : no pagar (una deuda) 2 : no presentarse (en deportes)

defeat *vt* 1 BEAT : vencer, derrotar 2 FRUSTRATE : frustrar — ∼ *n* : derrota *f*

defect *n* : defecto *m* — ∼ *vi* : desertar — **defective** *adj* : defectuoso

defend *vt* : defender — **defendant** *n* : acusado *m*, -da *f* — **defense** *or Brit* **defence** *n* : defensa *f* — **defenseless** *or Brit* **defenceless** *adj* : indefenso — **defensive** *adj* : defensivo — ∼ *n* **on the** ∼ : a la defensiva

defer *v* -**ferred; -ferring** *vt* : diferir, aplazar — *vi* ∼ **to** : deferir a — **deference** *n* : deferencia *f* — **deferential** *adj* : deferente

defiance *n* 1 : desafío *m* 2 **in** ∼ **of** : a despecho de — **defiant** *adj* : desafiante

deficiency *n*, *pl* -**cies** : deficiencia *f* — **deficient** *adj* : deficiente

deficit *n* : déficit *m*

defile *vt* -**filed; -filing** 1 DIRTY : ensuciar 2 DESECRATE : profanar

define *vt* -**fined; -fining** : definir — **definite** *adj* 1 : definido 2 CERTAIN : seguro, incuestionable — **definition** *n* : definición *f* — **definitive** *adj* : definitivo

deflate *v* -**flated; -flating** *vt* : desinflar (una llanta, etc.) — *vi* : desinflarse

deflect *vt* : desviar — *vi* : desviarse
deform *vt* : deformar — **deformity** *n, pl* **-ties**
: deformidad *f*
defraud *vt* : defraudar
defrost *vt* : descongelar — *vi* : descongelarse
deft *adj* : hábil, diestro
defy *vt* **-fied; -fying 1** CHALLENGE : desafiar
2 RESIST : resistir
degenerate *vi* : degenerar — ~ *adj* : degenerado
degrade *vt* **-graded; -grading** : degradar — **degrading** *adj* : degradante
degree *n* **1** : grado *m* **2** *or* **academic** ~ : título *m*
dehydrate *vt* **-drated; -drating** : deshidratar
deign *vi* ~ **to** : dignarse (a)
deity *n, pl* **-ties** : deidad *f*
dejected *adj* : abatido — **dejection** *n* : abatimiento *m*
delay *n* : retraso *m* — ~ *vt* **1** POSTPONE : aplazar **2** HOLD UP : retrasar — *vi* : demorar
delectable *adj* : delicioso
delegate *n* : delegado *m*, **-da** *f* — ~ *v* **-gated; -gating** : delegar — **delegation** *n* : delegación *f*
delete *vt* **-leted; -leting** : borrar
deliberate *v* **-ated; -ating** *vt* : deliberar sobre — *vi* : deliberar — ~ *adj* : deliberado — **deliberately** *adv* INTENTIONALLY : a propósito — **deliberation** *n* : deliberación *f*
delicacy *n, pl* **-cies 1** : delicadeza *f* **2** FOOD : manjar *m*, exquisitez *f* — **delicate** *adj* : delicado
delicatessen *n* : charcutería *f*
delicious *adj* : delicioso
delight *n* : placer *m*, deleite *m* — ~ *vt* : deleitar, encantar — *vi* ~ **in** : deleitarse con — **delightful** *adj* : delicioso, encantador
delinquent *adj* : delincuente — ~ *n* : delincuente *mf*
delirious *adj* : delirante — **delirium** *n* : delirio *m*
deliver *vt* **1** DISTRIBUTE : entregar, repartir **2** FREE : liberar **3** : asistir en el parto de (un niño) **4** : pronunciar (un discurso, etc.) **5** DEAL : asestar (un golpe, etc.) — **delivery** *n, pl* **-eries 1** DISTRIBUTION : entrega *f*, reparto *m* **2** LIBERATION : liberación *f* **3** CHILDBIRTH : parto *m*, alumbramiento *m*
delude *vt* **-luded; -luding 1** : engañar **2** ~ **oneself** : engañarse
deluge *n* : diluvio *m*
delusion *n* : ilusión *f*
deluxe *adj* : de lujo
delve *vi* **delved; delving 1** : escarbar **2** ~ **into** PROBE : investigar
demand *n* **1** REQUEST : petición *f* **2** CLAIM

: reclamación *f*, exigencia *f* **3** → **supply** — ~ *vt* : exigir — **demanding** *adj* : exigente
demean *vt* ~ **oneself** : rebajarse
demeanor *n* : comportamiento *m*
demented *adj* : demente, loco
demise *n* : fallecimiento *m*
democracy *n, pl* **-cies** : democracia *f* — **democrat** *n* : demócrata *mf* — **democratic** *adj* : democrático
demolish *vt* : demoler — **demolition** *n* : demolición *f*
demon *n* : demonio *m*
demonstrate *v* **-strated; -strating** *vt* : demostrar — *vi* RALLY : manifestarse — **demonstration** *n* **1** : demostración *f* **2** RALLY : manifestación *f*
demoralize *vt* **-ized; -izing** : desmoralizar
demote *vt* **-moted; -moting** : bajar de categoría
demure *adj* : recatado
den *n* LAIR : guarida *f*
denial *n* **1** : negación *f*, rechazo *m* **2** REFUSAL : denegación *f*
denim *n* : tela *f* vaquera, mezclilla *f Lat*
denomination *n* **1** : confesión *f* (religiosa) **2** : valor *m* (de una moneda)
denounce *vt* **-nounced; -nouncing** : denunciar
dense *adj* **denser; -est 1** THICK : denso **2** STUPID : estúpido — **density** *n, pl* **-ties** : densidad *f*
dent *vt* : abollar — ~ *n* : abolladura *f*
dental *adj* : dental — **dental floss** *n* : hilo *m* dental — **dentist** *n* : dentista *mf* — **dentures** *npl* : dentadura *f* postiza
deny *vt* **-nied; -nying 1** : negar **2** REFUSE : denegar
deodorant *n* : desodorante *m*
depart *vi* **1** : salir **2** ~ **from** : apartarse de (la verdad, etc.)
department *n* : sección *f* (de una tienda, etc.), departamento *m* (de una empresa, etc.), ministerio *m* (del gobierno) — **department store** *n* : grandes almacenes *mpl*
departure *n* **1** : salida *f* **2** DEVIATION : desviación *f*
depend *vi* **1** ~ **on** : depender de **2** ~ **on** s.o. : contar con algn **3 that** ~**s** : eso depende — **dependable** *adj* : digno de confianza — **dependence** *n* : dependencia *f* — **dependent** *adj* : dependiente
depict *vt* **1** PORTRAY : representar **2** DESCRIBE : describir
deplete *vt* **-pleted; -pleting** : agotar, reducir
deplore *vt* **-plored; -ploring** : deplorar, lamentar — **deplorable** *adj* : lamentable
deploy *vt* : desplegar

deport *vt* : deportar, expulsar (de un país) —
deportation *n* : deportación *f*
depose *vt* -posed; -posing : deponer
deposit *vt* -ited; -iting : depositar — ~ *n* 1
: depósito *m* 2 DOWN PAYMENT : entrega *f*
inicial
depot *n* 1 WAREHOUSE : almacén *m*, depósito *m* 2 STATION : terminal *mf*
depreciate *vi* -ated; -ating : depreciarse —
depreciation *n* : depreciación *f*
depress *vt* 1 : deprimir 2 PRESS : apretar —
depressed *adj* : abatido, deprimido — **de-
pressing** *adj* : deprimente — **depression** *n*
: depresión *f*
deprive *vt* -prived; -priving : privar
depth *n*, *pl* **depths** 1 : profundidad *f* 2 **in
the ~s of night** : en lo más profundo de la
noche
deputy *n*, *pl* -ties : suplente *mf*; sustituto *m*,
-ta *f*
derail *vt* : hacer descarrilar
deranged *adj* : trastornado
derelict *adj* : abandonado
deride *vt* -rided; -riding : burlarse de — **de-
rision** *n* : mofa *f*
derive *vi* -rived; -riving : derivar — **derivation** *n* : derivación *f*
derogatory *adj* : despectivo
descend *v* : descender, bajar — **descendant** *n* : descendiente *mf* — **descent** *n* 1
: descenso *m* 2 LINEAGE : descendencia *f*
describe *vt* -scribed; -scribing : describir
— **description** *n* : descripción *f* — **descriptive** *adj* : descriptivo
desecrate *vt* -crated; -crating : profanar
desert *n* : desierto *m* — ~ *adj* ~ **island**
: isla *f* desierta — ~ *vt* : abandonar — *vi*
: desertar — **deserter** *n* : desertor *m*, -tora *f*
deserve *vt* -served; -serving : merecer
design *vt* 1 DEVISE : diseñar 2 PLAN
: proyectar — ~ *n* 1 : diseño *m* 2 PLAN
: plan *m*, proyecto *m*
designate *vt* -nated; -nating : nombrar, designar
designer *n* : diseñador *m*, -dora *f*
desire *vt* -sired; -siring : desear — ~ *n*
: deseo *m* — **desirable** *adj* : deseable
desk *n* : escritorio *m*, pupitre *m* (en la escuela)
desolate *adj* : desolado
despair *vi* : desesperar — ~ *n* : desesperación *f*
desperate *adj* : desesperado — **despera-
tion** *n* : desesperación *f*
despise *vt* -spised; -spising : despreciar —
despicable *adj* : despreciable
despite *prep* : a pesar de
despondent *adj* : desanimado
dessert *n* : postre *m*

destination *n* : destino *m* — **destined** *adj* 1
: destinado 2 ~ **for** : con destino a — **destiny** *n*, *pl* -nies : destino *m*
destitute *adj* : indigente
destroy *vt* : destruir — **destruction** *n* : destrucción *f* — **destructive** *adj* : destructivo
detach *vt* : separar — **detached** *adj* 1 : separado 2 IMPARTIAL : objetivo
detail *n* 1 : detalle *m* 2 **go into** ~ : entrar
en detalles — ~ *vt* : detallar — **detailed**
adj : detallado
detain *vt* 1 : detener (un prisionero) 2
DELAY : entretener
detect *vt* : detectar — **detection** *n* : detec-
ción *f*, descubrimiento *m* — **detective** *n*
: detective *mf*
detention *n* : detención *m*
deter *vt* -terred; -terring : disuadir
detergent *n* : detergente *m*
deteriorate *vi* -rated; -rating : deteriorarse
— **deterioration** *n* : deterioro *m*
determine *vt* -mined; -mining : determinar
— **determined** *adj* RESOLUTE : decidido —
determination *n* : determinación *f*
deterrent *n* : medida *f* disuasiva
detest *vt* : detestar — **detestable** *adj*
: odioso
detonate *v* -nated; -nating *vt* : hacer detonar — *vi* EXPLODE : detonar, estallar —
detonation *n* : detonación *f*
detour *n* 1 : desviación *f* 2 **make a** ~ : dar
un rodeo — ~ *vi* : desviarse
detract *vi* ~ **from** : aminorar, restar importancia a
detrimental *adj* : perjudicial
devalue *vt* -ued; -uing : devaluar
devastate *vt* -tated; -tating : devastar —
devastating *adj* : devastador — **devasta-
tion** *n* : devastación *f*
develop *vt* 1 : desarrollar 2 ~ **an illness**
: contraer una enfermedad — *vi* 1 GROW
: desarrollarse 2 HAPPEN : aparecer — **development** *n* : desarrollo *m*
deviate *v* -ated; -ating *vi* : desviarse — **deviation** *n* : desviación *f*
device *n* : dispositivo *m*, mecanismo *m*
devil *n* : diablo *m*, demonio *m* — **devilish**
adj : diabólico
devious *adj* 1 CRAFTY : taimado 2 WIND-
ING : tortuoso
devise *vt* -vised; -vising : idear, concebir
devoid *adj* ~ **of** : desprovisto de
devote *vt* -voted; -voting : consagrar,
dedicar — **devoted** *adj* : leal — **devotee** *n*
: devoto *m*, -ta *f* — **devotion** *n* 1 : devoción
f, dedicación *f* 2 : oración *f* (en religión)
devour *vt* : devorar
devout *adj* : devoto
dew *n* : rocío *m*

dexterity *n, pl* **-ties** : destreza *f*
diabetes *n* : diabetes *f* — **diabetic** *adj* : diabético — ~ *n* : diabético *m*, -ca *f*
diabolic *or* **diabolical** *adj* : diabólico
diagnosis *n, pl* **-noses** : diagnóstico *m* — **diagnose** *vt* **-nosed; -nosing** : diagnosticar — **diagnostic** *adj* : diagnóstico
diagonal *adj* : diagonal, en diagonal — ~ *n* : diagonal *f*
diagram *n* : diagrama *m*
dial *n* : esfera *f* (de un reloj), dial *m* (de un radio, etc.) — ~ *v* **dialed** *or* **dialled; dialing** *or* **dialling** : marcar
dialect *n* : dialecto *m*
dialogue *n* : diálogo *m*
diameter *n* : diámetro *m*
diamond *n* **1** : diamante *m* **2** : rombo *m* (forma) **3** *or* **baseball** ~ : cuadro *m*, diamante *m*
diaper *n* : pañal *m*
diaphragm *n* : diafragma *m*
diarrhea *n* : diarrea *f*
diary *n, pl* **-ries**: diario *m*
dice *ns & pl* : dados *mpl* (juego)
dictate *vt* **-tated; -tating** : dictar — **dictation** *n* : dictado *m* — **dictator** *n* : dictador *m*, -dora *f* — **dictatorship** *n* : dictadura *f*
dictionary *n, pl* **-naries** : diccionario *m*
did → **do**
die[1] *vi* **died; dying 1** : morir **2** ~ **down** : amainar, disminuir **3** ~ **out** : extinguirse **4 be dying for** : morirse por
die[2] *n* **1** *pl* **dice** : dado *m* (para jugar) **2** *pl* **dies** MOLD : molde *m*
diesel *n* : diesel *m*
diet *n* **1** FOOD : alimentación *f* **2 go on a** ~ : ponerse a régimen — ~ *vi* : estar a régimen
differ *vi* **-ferred; -ferring 1** : diferir, ser distinto **2** DISAGREE : no estar de acuerdo — **difference** *n* : diferencia *f* — **different** *adj* : distinto, diferente — **differentiate** *v* **-ated; -ating** *vt* : diferenciar — *vi* : distinguir — **differently** *adv* : de otra manera
difficult *adj* : difícil — **difficulty** *n, pl* **-ties** : dificultad *f*
diffident *adj* : tímido, que falta confianza
dig *v* **dug; digging** *vt* **1** : cavar **2** ~ **up** : desenterrar — *vi* : cavar — ~ *n* **1** GIBE : pulla *f* **2** EXCAVATION : excavación *f*
digest *n* : resumen *m* — ~ *vt* **1** : digerir **2** SUMMARIZE : resumir — **digestible** *adj* : digerible — **digestion** *n* : digestión *f* — **digestive** *adj* : digestivo
digit *n* **1** NUMERAL : dígito *m*, número *m* **2** FINGER, TOE : dedo *m* — **digital** *adj* : digital
dignity *n, pl* **-ties** : dignidad *f* — **dignified** *adj* : digno, decoroso

digress *vi* : desviarse del tema, divagar — **digression** *n* : digresión *f*
dike *n* : dique *m*
dilapidated *adj* : ruinoso
dilate *v* **-lated; -lating** *vt* : dilatar — *vi* : dilatarse
dilemma *n* : dilema *m*
diligence *n* : diligencia *f* — **diligent** *adj* : diligente
dilute *vt* **-luted; -luting** : diluir
dim *v* **dimmed; dimming** *vt* : atenuar — *vi* : irse atenuando — ~ *adj* **dimmer; dimmest 1** DARK : oscuro **2** FAINT : débil, tenue
dime *n* : moneda *f* de diez centavos
dimension *n* : dimensión *f*
diminish *v* : disminuir
diminutive *adj* : diminuto
dimple *n* : hoyuelo *m*
din *n* : estrépito *m*
dine *vi* **dined; dining** : cenar — **diner** *n* **1** : comensal *mf* (persona) **2** : cafetería *f* (restaurante)
dingy *adj* **-gier; -est** : sucio, deslucido
dinner *n* : cena *f*, comida *f*
dinosaur *n* : dinosaurio *m*
dint *n* **by** ~ **of** : a fuerza de
dip *v* **dipped; dipping** *vt* : mojar — *vi* : bajar, descender — ~ *n* **1** DROP : descenso *m*, caída *f* **2** SWIM : chapuzón *m* **3** SAUCE : salsa *f*
diploma *n, pl* **-mas** : diploma *m*
diplomacy *n* : diplomacia *f* — **diplomat** *n* : diplomático *m*, -ca *f* — **diplomatic** *adj* : diplomático
dire *adj* **direr; direst 1** : grave, terrible **2** EXTREME : extremo
direct *vt* **1** : dirigir **2** ORDER : mandar — ~ *adj* **1** STRAIGHT : directo **2** FRANK : franco — ~ *adv* : directamente — **direct current** *n* : corriente *f* continua — **direction** *n* **1** : dirección *f* **2 ask** ~**s** : pedir indicaciones — **directly** *adv* **1** STRAIGHT : directamente **2** IMMEDIATELY : en seguida — **director** *n* **1** : director *m*, -tora *f* **2 board of** ~**s** : directorio *m* — **directory** *n, pl* **-ries** : guía *f* (telefónica)
dirt *n* **1** : suciedad *f* **2** SOIL : tierra *f* — **dirty** *adj* **dirtier; -est 1** : sucio **2** INDECENT : obsceno, cochino *fam*
disability *n, pl* **-ties** : minusvalía *f*, invalidez *f* — **disable** *vt* **-abled; -abling** : incapacitar — **disabled** *adj* : minusválido
disadvantage *n* : desventaja *f*
disagree *vi* **1** : no estar de acuerdo (con algn) **2** CONFLICT : no coincidir — **disagreeable** *adj* : desagradable — **disagreement** *n* **1** : desacuerdo *m* **2** ARGUMENT : discusión *f*

disappear *vi* : desaparecer — **disappearance** *n* : desaparición *f*
disappoint *vt* : decepcionar, desilusionar — **disappointment** *n* : decepción *f*, desilusión *f*
disapprove *vi* -proved; -proving ~ of : desaprobar — **disapproval** *n* : desaprobación *f*
disarm *vt* : desarmar — **disarmament** *n* : desarme *m*
disarray *n* : desorden *m*
disaster *n* : desastre *m* — **disastrous** *adj* : desastroso
disbelief *n* : incredulidad *f*
disc → **disk**
discard *vt* : desechar, deshacerse de
discern *vt* : percibir, discernir — **discernible** *adj* : perceptible
discharge *vt* -charged; -charging **1** UNLOAD : descargar **2** RELEASE : liberar, poner en libertad **3** DISMISS : despedir **4** CARRY OUT : cumplir con (una obligación) — ~ *n* **1** : descarga *f* (de electricidad), emisión *f* (de humo, etc.) **2** DISMISSAL : despido *m* **3** RELEASE : alta *f* (de un paciente), puesta *f* en libertad (de un preso) **4** : supuración *f* (en medicina)
disciple *n* : discípulo *m*, -la *f*
discipline *n* **1** : disciplina *f* **2** PUNISHMENT : castigo *m* — ~ *vt* -plined; -plining **1** CONTROL : disciplinar **2** PUNISH : castigar
disclaim *vt* : negar
disclose *vt* -closed; -closing : revelar — **disclosure** *n* : revelación *f*
discomfort *n* **1** : incomodidad *f* **2** PAIN : malestar *m* **3** UNEASINESS : inquietud *f*
disconcert *vt* : desconcertar
disconnect *vt* : desconectar
disconsolate *adj* : desconsolado
discontented *adj* : descontento
discontinue *vt* -ued; -uing : suspender, descontinuar
discount *n* : descuento *m*, rebaja *f* — ~ *vt* **1** : descontar (precios) **2** DISREGARD : descartar
discourage *vt* -aged; -aging : desalentar, desanimar — **discouragement** *n* : desánimo *m*, desaliento *m*
discover *vt* : descubrir — **discovery** *n*, *pl* -ries : descubrimiento *m*
discredit *vt* : desacreditar — ~ *n* : descrédito *m*
discreet *adj* : discreto
discrepancy *n*, *pl* -cies : discrepancia *f*
discretion *n* : discreción *f*
discriminate *vi* -nated; -nating **1** ~ against : discriminar **2** ~ between : distinguir entre — **discrimination** *n* **1** PREJUDICE : discriminación *f* **2** DISCERNMENT : discernimiento *m*

discuss *vt* : hablar de, discutir — **discussion** *n* : discusión *f*
disdain *n* : desdén *m* — ~ *vt* : desdeñar
disease *n* : enfermedad *f* — **diseased** *adj* : enfermo
disembark *vi* : desembarcar
disengage *vt* -gaged; -gaging **1** RELEASE : soltar **2** ~ the clutch : desembragar
disentangle *vt* -gled; -gling : desenredar
disfavor *n* : desaprobación *f*
disfigure *vt* -ured; -uring : desfigurar
disgrace *vt* -graced; -gracing : deshonrar — ~ *n* **1** DISHONOR : deshonra *f* **2** SHAME : vergüenza *f* — **disgraceful** *adj* : vergonzoso, deshonroso
disgruntled *adj* : descontento
disguise *vt* -guised; -guising : disfrazar — ~ *n* : disfraz *m*
disgust *n* : asco *m*, repugnancia *f* — ~ *vt* : asquear — **disgusting** *adj* : asqueroso
dish *n* **1** : plato *m* **2** *or* **serving** ~ : fuente *f* **3 wash the** ~es : lavar los platos — ~ *vt or* ~ **up** : servir — **dishcloth** *n* : paño *m* de cocina (para secar), trapo *m* de fregar (para lavar)
dishearten *vt* : desanimar
disheveled *or* **dishevelled** *adj* : desaliñado, despeinado (dícese del pelo)
dishonest *adj* : deshonesto — **dishonesty** *n*, *pl* -ties : falta *f* de honradez
dishonor *n* : deshonra *f* — ~ *vt* : deshonrar — **dishonorable** *adj* : deshonroso
dishwasher *n* : lavaplatos *m*, lavavajillas *m*
disillusion *vt* : desilusionar — **disillusionment** *n* : desilusión *f*
disinfect *vt* : desinfectar — **disinfectant** *n* : desinfectante *m*
disintegrate *vi* -grated; -grating : desintegrarse
disinterested *adj* : desinteresado
disk *or* **disc** *n* : disco *m*
dislike *n* : aversión *f*, antipatía *f* — ~ *vt* -liked; -liking **1** : tener aversión a **2 I** ~ **dancing** : no me gusta bailar
dislocate *vt* -cated; -cating : dislocar
dislodge *vt* -lodged; -lodging : sacar, desalojar
disloyal *adj* : desleal — **disloyalty** *n*, *pl* -ties : deslealtad *f*
dismal *adj* : sombrío, deprimente
dismantle *vt* -tled; -tling : desmontar, desarmar
dismay *vt* : consternar — ~ *n* : consternación *f*
dismiss *vt* **1** DISCHARGE : despedir, destituir **2** REJECT : descartar, rechazar — **dismissal** *n* **1** : despido *m* (de un empleado), destitución *f* (de un funcionario) **2** REJECTION : rechazo *m*

dismount *vi* : desmontar
disobey *v* : desobedecer — **disobedience** *n* : desobediencia *f* — **disobedient** *adj* : desobediente
disorder *n* **1** : desorden *m* **2** AILMENT : afección *f*, problema *m* — **disorderly** *adj* : desordenado
disorganize *vt* -nized; -nizing : desorganizar
disown *vt* : renegar de
dispassionate *adj* : desapasionado
dispatch *vt* : despachar, enviar
dispel *vt* -pelled; -pelling : disipar
dispensation *n* EXEMPTION : exención *m*, dispensa *f*
dispense *v* -pensed; -pensing *vt* : repartir, distribuir — *vi* ~ **with** : prescindir de
disperse *v* -persed; -persing *vt* : dispersar — *vi* : dispersarse
displace *vt* -placed; -placing **1** : desplazar **2** REPLACE : reemplazar
display *vt* **1** EXHIBIT : exponer, exhibir **2** ~ **anger** : manifestar la ira — ~ *n* : muestra *f*, exposición *f*
displease *vt* -pleased; -pleasing : desagradar — **displeasure** *n* : desagrado *m*
dispose *v* -posed; -posing *vt* : disponer — *vi* ~ **of** : deshacerse de — **disposable** *adj* : desechable — **disposal** *n* **1** REMOVAL : eliminación *f* **2** **have at one's** ~ : tener a su disposición — **disposition** *n* **1** ARRANGEMENT : disposición *f* **2** TEMPERAMENT : temperamento *m*, carácter *m*
disprove *vt* -proved; -proving : refutar
dispute *v* -puted; -putting *vt* QUESTION : cuestionar — *vi* ARGUE : discutir — ~ *n* : disputa *f*, conflicto *m*
disqualification *n* : descalificación *f* — **disqualify** *vt* -fied; -fying : descalificar
disregard *vt* : ignorar, hacer caso omiso de — ~ *n* : indiferencia *f*
disrepair *n* : mal estado *m*
disreputable *adj* : de mala fama
disrespect *n* : falta *f* de respeto — **disrespectful** *adj* : irrespetuoso
disrupt *vt* : trastornar, perturbar — **disruption** *n* : trastorno *m*
dissatisfaction *n* : descontento *m* — **dissatisfied** *adj* : descontento
dissect *vt* : disecar
disseminate *vt* -nated; -nating : diseminar, difundir
dissent *vi* : disentir — ~ *n* : disentimiento *m*
dissertation THESIS : tesis *f*
disservice *n* **do a** ~ **to** : no hacer justicia a
dissident *n* : disidente *mf*
dissimilar *adj* : distinto

dissipate *vt* -pated; -pating **1** DISPEL : disipar **2** SQUANDER : desperdiciar
dissolve *v* -solved; -solving *vt* : disolver — *vi* : disolverse
dissuade *vt* -suaded; -suading : disuadir
distance *n* **1** : distancia *f* **2 in the** ~ : a lo lejos — **distant** *adj* : distante
distaste *n* : desagrado *m* — **distasteful** *adj* : desagradable
distend *vt* : dilatar — *vi* : dilatarse
distill *or Brit* **distil** *vt* -tilled; -tilling : destilar
distinct *adj* **1** DIFFERENT : distinto **2** CLEAR : claro — **distinction** *n* : distinción *f* — **distinctive** *adj* : distintivo
distinguish *vt* : distinguir — **distinguished** *adj* : distinguido
distort *vt* : deformar, distorsionar — **distortion** *n* : deformación *f*
distract *vt* : distraer — **distraction** *n* : distracción *f*
distraught *adj* : muy afligido
distress *n* **1** : angustia *f*, aflicción *f* **2 in** ~ : en peligro — ~ *vt* : afligir — **distressing** *adj* : penoso
distribute *vt* -uted; -uting : distribuir, repartir — **distribution** *n* : distribución *f* — **distributor** *n* : distribuidor *m*, -dora *f*
district *n* **1** REGION : región *f*, zona *f*, barrio *m* (de una ciudad) **2** : distrito *m* (zona política)
distrust *n* : desconfianza *f* — ~ *vt* : desconfiar de
disturb *vt* **1** BOTHER : molestar, perturbar **2** WORRY : inquietar — **disturbance** *n* **1** COMMOTION : alboroto *m*, disturbio *m* **2** INTERRUPTION : interrupción *f*
disuse *n* **fall into** ~ : caer en desuso
ditch *n* : zanja *f*, cuneta *f* — ~ *vt* DISCARD : deshacerse de, botar
ditto *n*, *pl* -tos **1** : ídem *m* **2** ~ **marks** : comillas *fpl*
dive *vi* **dived** *or* **dove; dived; diving 1** : zambullirse, tirarse al agua **2** DESCEND : bajar en picada (dícese de un avión, etc.) — ~ *n* **1** : zambullida *f*, clavado *m Lat* **2** DESCENT : descenso *m* en picada — **diver** *n* : saltador *m*, -dora *f*
diverge *vi* -verged; -verging : divergir
diverse *adj* : diverso — **diversify** *v* -fied; -fying *vt* : diversificar — *vi* : diversificarse
diversion *n* **1** : desviación *f* **2** AMUSEMENT : diversión *f*, distracción *f*
diversity *n*, *pl* -ties : diversidad *f*
divert *vt* **1** : desviar **2** DISTRACT : distraer **3** AMUSE : divertir
divide *v* -vided; -viding *vt* : dividir — *vi* : dividirse
dividend *n* : dividendo *m*

divine *adj* -viner; -est : divino — **divinity** *n*, *pl* -ties : divinidad *f*
division *n* : división *f*
divorce *n* : divorcio *m* — ~ *v* -vorced; -vorcing *vt* : divorciar — *vi* : divorciarse — **divorcée** *n* : divorciada *f*
divulge *vt* -vulged; -vulging : revelar, divulgar
dizzy *adj* **dizzier; -est 1** : mareado **2 a** ~ **speed** : una velocidad vertiginosa — **dizziness** *n* : mareo *m*, vértigo *m*
DNA *n* : AND *m*
do *v* **did; done; doing; does** *vt* **1** : hacer **2** PREPARE : preparar — *vi* **1** BEHAVE : hacer **2** FARE : estar, ir, andar **3** SUFFICE : ser suficiente **4** ~ **away with** : abolir, eliminar **5 how are you doing?** : ¿cómo estás? — *v aux* **1** (*used in interrogative sentences*) **do you know her?** : ¿la conoces? **2** (*used in negative statements*) **I don't know** : yo no se **3** (*used as a substitute verb to avoid repetition*) **do you speak English? yes, I do** : ¿habla inglés? sí
dock *n* : muelle *m* — ~ *vt* : descontar dinero de (un sueldo) — *vi* ANCHOR : fondear, atracar
doctor *n* **1** : doctor *m*, -tora *f* (en derecho, etc.) **2** PHYSICIAN : médico *m*, -ca; doctor *m*, -tora *f* — ~ *vt* ALTER : alterar, falsificar
doctrine *n* : doctrina *f*
document *n* : documento *m* — ~ *vt* : documentar — **documentary** *n*, *pl* -ries : documental *m*
dodge *n* : artimaña *f*, truco *m* — ~ *v* **dodged; dodging** *vt* : esquivar, eludir — *vi* : echarse a un lado
doe *n*, *pl* **does** *or* **doe** : gama *f*, cierva *f*
does → **do**
dog *n* : perro *m*, -rra *f* — ~ *vt* **dogged; dogging** : perseguir — **dogged** *adj* : tenaz
dogma *n* : dogma *m* — **dogmatic** *adj* : dogmático
doily *n*, *pl* -lies : tapete *m*
doings *npl* : actividades *fpl*
doldrums *npl* **be in the** ~ : estar abatido
dole *n* : subsidio *m* de desempleo — ~ *vt* **doled; doling** *or* ~ **out** : repartir
doleful *adj* : triste, lúgubre
doll *n* : muñeco *m*, -ca *f*
dollar *n* : dólar *m*
dolphin *n* : delfín *m*
domain *n* **1** TERRITORY : dominio *m* **2** FIELD : campo *m*, esfera *f*
dome *n* : cúpula *f*
domestic *adj* **1** : doméstico **2** INTERNAL : nacional — ~ *n* SERVANT : empleado *m* doméstico, empleada *f* doméstica — **domesticate** *vt* -cated; -cating : domesticar
domination *n* : dominación *f* — **dominant**

adj : dominante — **dominate** *v* -nated; -nating : dominar — **domineer** *vi* : dominar, tiranizar
dominos *n* : dominó *m* (juego)
donate *vt* -nated; -nating : donar, hacer un donativo de — **donation** *n* : donativo *m*
done → **do** — ~ *adj* **1** FINISHED : terminado, hecho **2** COOKED : cocido
donkey *n*, *pl* -keys : burro *m*
donor *n* : donante *mf*
don't (*contraction of* **do** not) → **do**
doodle *v* -dled; -dling : garabatear — ~ *n* : garabato *m*
doom *n* : perdición *f*, fatalidad *f* — ~ *vt* : condenar
door *n* **1** : puerta *f* **2** ENTRANCE : entrada *f* — **doorbell** *n* : timbre *m* — **doorknob** *n* : pomo *m* — **doorman** *n*, *pl* -men : portero *m* — **doormat** *n* : felpudo *m* — **doorstep** *n* : umbral *m* — **doorway** *n* : entrada *f*, portal *m*
dope *n* **1** DRUG : droga *f* **2** IDIOT : idiota *mf* — ~ *vt* **doped; doping** : drogar
dormant *adj* : inactivo, latente
dormitory *n*, *pl* -ries : dormitorio *m*
dose *n* : dosis *f* — **dosage** *n* : dosis *f*
dot *n* **1** : punto *m* **2 on the** ~ : en punto
dote *vi* **doted; doting** ~ **on** : adorar
double *adj* : doble — ~ *v* -bled; -bling *vt* : doblar — *vi* : doblarse — ~ *adv* : (el) doble — ~ *n* : doble *mf* — **double bass** *n* : contrabajo *m* — **double-cross** *vt* : traicionar — **doubly** *adv* : doblemente
doubt *vt* **1** : dudar **2** DISTRUST : desconfiar de, dudar de — ~ *n* : duda *f* — **doubtful** *adj* : dudoso — **doubtless** *adv* : sin duda
dough *n* : masa *f* — **doughnut** *n* : rosquilla *f*, dona *f* Lat
douse *vt* **doused; dousing 1** DRENCH : empapar, mojar **2** EXTINGUISH : apagar
dove¹ → **dive**
dove² *n* : paloma *f*
dowdy *adj* **dowdier; -est** : poco elegante
down *adv* **1** DOWNWARD : hacia abajo **2 come/go** ~ : bajar **3** ~ **here** : aquí abajo **4 fall** ~ : caer **5 lie** ~ : acostarse **6 sit** ~ : sentarse — ~ *prep* **1** ALONG : a lo largo de **2** THROUGH : a través de **3** ~ **the hill** : cuesta abajo — ~ *adj* **1** DESCENDING : de bajada **2** DOWNCAST : abatido — ~ *n* : plumón *m* — **downcast** *adj* : triste, abatido — **downfall** *n* : ruina *f* — **downhearted** *adj* : desanimado — **downhill** *adv* & *adj* : cuesta abajo — **down payment** *n* : entrega *f* inicial — **downpour** *n* : chaparrón *m* — **downright** *adv* : absolutamente — ~ *adj* : absoluto, categórico — **downstairs** *adv* : abajo — ~ *adj* : de abajo — **downstream** *adv* : río abajo — **down–**

to–earth *adj* : realista — **downtown** *n*
: centro *m* (de la ciudad) — ~ *adv* : al centro, en el centro — ~ *adj* : del centro —
downward *or* **downwards** *adv* & *adj*
: hacia abajo
dowry *n, pl* **-ries** : dote *f*
doze *vi* **dozed; dozing** : dormitar
dozen *n, pl* **dozens** *or* **dozen** : docena *f*
drab *adj* **drabber; drabbest** : monótono,
apagado
draft *n* **1** : corriente *f* de aire **2** *or* **rough** ~
: borrador *m* **3** : conscripción *f* (militar) **4**
or ~ **beer** : cerveza *f* de barril — ~ *vt* **1**
SKETCH : hacer el borrador de **2** CONSCRIPT
: reclutar — **drafty** *adj* **draftier; -est** : con
corrientes de aire
drag *v* **dragged; dragging** *vt* **1** : arrastrar **2**
DREDGE : dragar — *vi* : arrastrar(se) — ~ *n*
1 RESISTANCE : resistencia *f* (aerodinámica)
2 BORE : pesadez *f*, plomo *m fam*
dragon *n* : dragón *m* — **dragonfly** *n, pl*
-flies : libélula *f*
drain *vt* **1** EMPTY : vaciar, drenar **2** EX-
HAUST : agotar — *vi* **1** : escurrir(se) (se dice
de los platos) **2** *or* ~ **away** : desaparecer
poco a poco — ~ *n* **1** : desagüe *m* **2**
SEWER : alcantarilla *f* **3** DEPLETION : agotamiento *m* — **drainage** *n* : drenaje *m* —
drainpipe *n* : tubo *m* de desagüe
drama *n* : drama *m* — **dramatic** *adj*
: dramático — **dramatist** *n* : dramaturgo *m*,
-ga *f* — **dramatize** *vt* **-tized; -tizing**
: dramatizar
drank → **drink**
drape *vt* **draped; draping 1** COVER : cubrir
(con tela) **2** HANG : drapear —**drapes** *npl*
CURTAINS : cortinas *fpl*
drastic *adj* : drástico
draught → **draft**
draw *v* **drew** ; **drawn** ; **drawing** *vt* **1** PULL
: tirar de **2** ATTRACT : atraer **3** SKETCH
: dibujar, trazar **4** : sacar (una espada, etc.)
5 ~ **a conclusion** : llegar a una conclusión
6 ~ **up** DRAFT : redactar — *vi* **1** SKETCH
: dibujar **2** ~ **near** : acercarse — ~ *n* **1**
DRAWING : sorteo *m* **2** TIE : empate *m* **3** AT-
TRACTION : atracción *f* — **drawback** *n*
: desventaja *f* — **drawer** *n* : gaveta *f*, cajón
m (en un mueble) — **drawing** *n* **1** LOTTERY
: sorteo *m* **2** SKETCH : dibujo *m*
drawl *n* : habla *f* lenta y con vocales prolon-
gadas
dread *vt* : temer — ~ *n* : pavor *m*, temor *m*
— **dreadful** *adj* : espantoso, terrible
dream *n* : sueño *m* — ~ *v* **dreamed** *or*
dreamt; dreaming *vi* : soñar — *vt* **1** : soñar
2 ~ **up** : idear — **dreamer** *n* : soñador *m*,
-dora *f* — **dreamy** *adj* **dreamier; -est**
: soñador

dreary *adj* **-rier; -est** : sombrío, deprimente
dredge *vt* **dredged; dredging** : dragar —
~ *n* : draga *f*
dregs *npl* : heces *fpl*
drench *vt* : empapar
dress *vt* **1** : vestir **2** : preparar (pollo o
pescado), aliñar (ensalada) — *vi* **1** : vestirse
2 ~ **up** : ponerse elegante — ~ *n* **1**
CLOTHING : ropa *f* **2** : vestido *m* (de mujer)
— **dresser** *n* : cómoda *f* con espejo
dressing *n* **1** : aliño *m* (de ensalada), relleno *m* (de pollo) **2** BANDAGE : vendaje *m*
— **dressmaker** *n* : modista *mf* — **dressy**
adj **dressier; -est** : elegante
drew → **draw**
dribble *vi* **-bled; -bling 1** DRIP : gotear **2**
DROOL : babear **3** : driblar (en basquetbol)
— ~ *n* **1** TRICKLE : goteo *m*, hilo *m* **2**
DROOL : baba *f*
drier, driest → **dry**
drift *n* **1** MOVEMENT : movimiento *m* **2**
HEAP : montón *m* (de arena, etc.), ventisquero *m* (de nieve) **3** MEANING : sentido *m*
— ~ *vi* **1** : ir a la deriva **2** ACCUMULATE
: amontonarse
drill *n* **1** : taladro *m* **2** : ejercicio *m* (en educación), simulacro *m* (de incendio, etc.) —
~ *vt* **1** : perforar, taladrar **2** TRAIN : instruir por repetición — *vi* ~ **for** : perforar
en busca de
drink *v* **drank; drunk** *or* **drank; drinking**
: beber — ~ *n* : bebida *f*
drip *vi* **dripped; dripping** : gotear — ~ *n* **1**
DROP : gota *f* **2** DRIPPING : goteo *m*
drive *v* **drove; driven; driving** *vt* **1** : manejar **2** IMPEL : impulsar **3** ~ **crazy** : volver
loco **4** ~ **s.o. to (do sth)** : llevar a algn a
(hacer algo) — *vi* : manejar, conducir — ~
n **1** : paseo *m* (en coche) **2** CAMPAIGN
: campaña *f* **3** VIGOR : energía *f* **4** NEED
: instinto *m*
drivel *n* : tonterías *fpl*
driver *n* : conductor *m*, -tora *f*; chofer *m*
driveway *n* : camino *m* de entrada
drizzle *n* : llovizna *f* — ~ *vi* **-zled; -zling**
: lloviznar
drone *n* **1** BEE : zángano *m* **2** HUM
: zumbido *m* — ~ *vi* **droned; droning 1**
BUZZ : zumbar **2** *or* ~ **on** : hablar con monotonía
drool *vi* : babear — ~ *n* : baba *f*
droop *vi* : inclinarse (dícese de la cabeza),
encorvarse (dícese de los escombros), marchitarse (dícese de las flores)
drop *n* **1** : gota *f* (de líquido) **2** DECLINE,
FALL : caída *f* — ~ *v* **dropped; dropping**
vt **1** : dejar caer **2** LOWER : bajar **3** ABAN-
DON : abandonar, dejar **4** ~ **off** LEAVE

: dejar — *vi* 1 FALL : caer(se) 2 DECREASE : bajar, descender 3 ~ **by** *or* ~ **in** : pasar

drought *n* : sequía *f*

drove → **drive**

droves *n* **in** ~ : en manada

drown *vt* : ahogar — *vi* : ahogarse

drowsy *adj* **drowsier; -est** : somnoliento

drudgery *n, pl* **-eries** : trabajo *m* pesado

drug *n* 1 MEDICATION : medicamento *m* 2 NARCOTIC : droga *f*, estupefaciente *m* — ~ *vt* **drugged; drugging** : drogar — **drugstore** *n* : farmacia *f*

drum *n* 1 : tambor *m* 2 *or* **oil** ~ : bidón *m* (de petróleo) — ~ *v* **drummed; drumming** *vi* : tocar el tambor — *vt* : tamborilear con (los dedos, etc.) — **drumstick** *n* 1 : palillo *m* (de tambor) 2 : muslo *m* (de pollo)

drunk → **drink** — ~ *adj* : borracho — ~ *or* **drunkard** *n* : borracho *m*, -cha *f* — **drunken** *adj* : borracho, ebrio

dry *adj* **drier; driest** : seco — ~ *v* **dried; drying** *vt* : secar — *vi* : secarse — **dry–clean** *vt* : limpiar en seco — **dry cleaner** *n* : tintorería *f* (servicio) — **dry cleaning** *n* : limpieza *f* en seco — **dryer** *n* : secadora *f* — **dryness** *n* : sequedad *f*, aridez *f*

dual *adj* : doble

dub *vt* **dubbed; dubbing** 1 CALL : apodar 2 : doblar (una película)

dubious *adj* 1 UNCERTAIN : dudoso 2 QUESTIONABLE : sospechoso

duchess *n* : duquesa *f*

duck *n, pl* **duck** *or* **ducks** : pato *m*, -ta *f* — ~ *vt* 1 LOWER : agachar, bajar 2 EVADE : eludir, esquivar — *vi* : agacharse — **duckling** *n* : patito *m*, -ta *f*

duct *n* : conducto *m*

due *adj* 1 PAYABLE : pagadero 2 APPROPRIATE : debido, apropiado 3 EXPECTED : esperado 4 ~ **to** : debido a — ~ *n* 1 **give s.o. their** ~ : hacer justicia a algn 2 ~ **s** *npl* : cuota *f* — ~ *adv* ~ **east** : justo al este

duel *n* : duelo *m*

duet *n* : dúo *m*

dug → **dig**

duke *n* : duque *m*

dull *adj* 1 STUPID : torpe 2 BLUNT : desafilado 3 BORING : aburrido 4 LACKLUSTER : apagado — ~ *vt* : entorpecer (los sentidos), aliviar (el dolor)

dumb *adj* 1 MUTE : mudo 2 STUPID : estúpido

dumbfound *or* **dumfound** *vt* : dejar sin habla

dummy *n, pl* **-mies** 1 SHAM : imitación *f* 2 MANNEQUIN : maniquí *m* 3 IDIOT : tonto *m*, -ta *f*

dump *vt* : descargar, verter — ~ *n* 1 : vertedero *m*, tiradero *m* *Lat* 2 **down in the** ~**s** : triste, deprimido

dumpling *n* : bola *f* de masa hervida

dumpy *adj* **dumpier; -est** : regordete

dunce *n* : burro *m*, -rra *f* *fam*

dune *n* : duna *f*

dung *n* 1 : excrementos *mpl* 2 MANURE : estiércol *m*

dungarees *npl* JEANS : vaqueros *mpl*, jeans *mpl*

dungeon *n* : calabozo *m*

dunk *vt* : mojar

duo *n, pl* **duos** : dúo *m*

dupe *vt* **duped; duping** : engañar — ~ *n* : inocentón *m*, -tona *f*

duplex *n* : casa *f* de dos viviendas, dúplex *m*

duplicate *adj* : duplicado — ~ *vt* **-cated; -cating** : duplicar, hacer copias de — ~ *n* : duplicado *m*, copia *f*

durable *adj* : duradero

duration *n* : duración *f*

duress *n* : coacción *f*

during *prep* : durante

dusk *n* : anochecer *m*, crepúsculo *m*

dust *n* : polvo *m* — ~ *vt* 1 : quitar el polvo a 2 SPRINKLE : espolvorear — **dustpan** *n* : recogedor *m* — **dusty** *adj* **dustier; -est** : polvoriento

Dutch *adj* : holandés — ~ *n* 1 : holandés *m* (idioma) 2 **the** ~ : los holandeses

duty *n, pl* **-ties** 1 OBLIGATION : deber *m* 2 TAX : impuesto *m* 3 **on** ~ : de servicio — **dutiful** *adj* : obediente

dwarf *n, pl* **dwarfs** *or* **dwarves** : enano *m*, -na *f* — ~ *vt* : hacer parecer pequeño

dwell *vi* **dwelled** *or* **dwelt; dwelling** 1 RESIDE : morar, vivir 2 ~ **on** : pensar demasiado en — **dweller** *n* : habitante *mf* — **dwelling** *n* : morada *f*, vivienda *f*

dwindle *vi* **-dled; -dling** : disminuir

dye *n* : tinte *m* — ~ *vt* **dyed; dyeing** : teñir

dying → **die**[1]

dynamic *adj* : dinámico

dynamite *n* : dinamita *f*

dynamo *n, pl* **-mos** : dínamo *m*

dynasty *n, pl* **-ties** : dinastía *f*

dysentery *n, pl* **-teries** : disentería *f*

E

e *n*, *pl* **e's** *or* **es** : e *f*, quinta letra del alfabeto inglés
each *adj* : cada — ~ *pron* **1** : cada uno *m*, cada una *f* **2** ~ **other** : el uno al otro **3** **they hate** ~ **other** : se odian — ~ *adv* : cada uno, por persona
eager *adj* **1** ENTHUSIASTIC : entusiasta **2** IMPATIENT : impaciente — **eagerness** *n* : entusiasmo *m*, impaciencia *f*
eagle *n* : águila *f*
ear *n* **1** : oreja *f* **2** ~ **of corn** : mazorca *f*, choclo *m Lat* — **eardrum** *n* : tímpano *m*
earl *n* : conde *m*
earlobe *n* : lóbulo *m* de la oreja
early *adv* **earlier; -est 1** : temprano **2 as** ~ **as possible** : lo más pronto posible **3 ten minutes** ~ : diez minutos de adelanto — ~ *adj* **earlier; -est 1** FIRST : primero **2** ANCIENT : primitivo, antiguo **3 an** ~ **death** : una muerte prematura **4 be** ~ : llegar temprano **5 in the** ~ **spring** : a principios de la primavera
earmark *vt* : destinar
earn *vt* **1** : ganar **2** DESERVE : merecer
earnest *adj* : serio — ~ *n* **in** ~ : en serio
earnings *npl* **1** WAGES : ingresos *mpl* **2** PROFITS : ganancias *fpl*
earphone *n* : audífono *m*
earring *n* : pendiente *m*, arete *m Lat*
earshot *n* **within** ~ : al alcance del oído
earth *n* : tierra *f* — **earthenware** *n* : loza *f* — **earthly** *adj* : terrenal — **earthquake** *n* : terremoto *m* — **earthworm** *n* : lombriz *f* (de tierra) — **earthy** *adj* **earthier; -est 1** : terroso **2** COARSE, CRUDE : grosero
ease *n* **1** FACILITY : facilidad *f* **2** COMFORT : comodidad *f* **3 feel at** ~ : sentir cómodo — ~ *v* **eased; easing** *vt* **1** ALLEVIATE : aliviar, calmar **2** FACILITATE : facilitar — *vi* **1** : calmarse **2** ~ **up** : disminuir
easel *n* : caballete *m*
easily *adv* **1** : fácilmente, con facilidad **2** UNQUESTIONABLY : con mucho, de lejos *Lat*
east *adv* : al este — ~ *adj* : este, del este — ~ *n* **1** : este *m* **2 the East** : el Oriente
Easter *n* : Pascua *f*
easterly *adv & adj* : del este
eastern *adj* **1** : del este **2 Eastern** : oriental, del este
easy *adj* **easier; -est 1** : fácil **2** RELAXED : relajado — **easygoing** *adj* : tolerante, relajado
eat *v* **ate; eaten; eating** *vt* : comer — *vi* **1** : comer **2** ~ **into** CORRODE : corroer **3** ~

into DEPLETE : comerse — **eatable** *adj* : comestible
eaves *npl* : alero *m* — **eavesdrop** *vi* **-dropped; -dropping** : escuchar a escondidas
ebb *n* : reflujo *m* — ~ *vi* **1** : bajar (dícese de la marea) **2** DECLINE : decaer
ebony *n*, *pl* **-nies** : ébano *m*
eccentric *adj* : excéntrico — ~ *n* : ecéntrico *m*, -ca *f* — **eccentricity** *n*, *pl* **-ties** : excentricidad *f*
echo *n*, *pl* **echoes** : eco *m* — ~ *v* **echoed; echoing** *vt* : repetir — *vi* : hacer eco, resonar
eclipse *n* : eclipse *m* — ~ *vt* **eclipsed; eclipsing** : eclipsar
ecology *n*, *pl* **-gies** : ecología *f* — **ecological** *adj* : ecológico
economy *n*, *pl* **-mies** : economía *f* — **economic** *or* **economical** *adj* : económico — **economics** *n* : economía *f* — **economist** *n* : economista *mf* — **economize** *v* **-mized; -mizing** : economizar
ecstasy *n*, *pl* **-sies** : éxtasis *m* — **ecstatic** *adj* : extático
Ecuadoran *or* **Ecuadorean** *or* **Ecuadorian** *adj* : ecuatoriano
edge *n* **1** BORDER : borde *m* **2** : filo *m* (de un cuchillo) **3** ADVANTAGE : ventaja *f* — ~ *v* **edged; edging** *vt* **1** : bordear, ribetear — *vi* : avanzar poco a poco — **edgewise** *adv* : de lado — **edgy** *adj* **edgier; -est** : nervioso
edible *adj* : comestible
edit *vt* **1** : editar, redactar, corregir **2** ~ **out** : suprimir, cortar — **edition** *n* : edición *f* — **editor** *n* : director *m*, -tora *f* (de un periódico); redactor *m*, -tora *f* (de un libro) — **editorial** *n* : editorial *m*
educate *vt* **-cated; -cating 1** TEACH : educar, instruir **2** INFORM : informar — **education** *n* : educación *f* — **educational** *adj* **1** : educativo, instructivo **2** TEACHING : docente — **educator** *n* : educador *m*, -dora *f*
eel *n* : anguila *f*
eerie *adj* **-rier; -est** : extraño e inquietante, misterioso
effect *n* **1** : efecto *m* **2 go into** ~ : entrar en vigor — ~ *vt* : efectuar, llevar a cabo — **effective** *adj* **1** : eficaz **2** ACTUAL : efectivo, vigente — **effectiveness** *n* : eficacia *f*
effeminate *adj* : afeminado
effervescent *adj* : efervescente
efficient *adj* : eficiente — **efficiency** *n*, *pl* **-cies** : eficiencia *f*

effort **224**

effort *n* **1** : esfuerzo *m* **2** it's not worth the ~ : no vale la pena — **effortless** *adj* : fácil, sin esfuerzo

egg *n* : huevo *m* — ~ *vt* ~ **on** : incitar — **eggplant** *n* : berenjena *f* — **eggshell** *n* : cascarón *m*

ego *n, pl* **egos 1** SELF : ego *m*, yo *m* **2** SELF-ESTEEM : amor *m* propio — **egotism** *n* : egotismo *m* — **egotist** *n* : egotista *mf* — **egotistic** *or* **egotistical** *adj* : egotista

eiderdown *n* **1** DOWN : plumón *m* **2** COMFORTER : edredón *m*

eight *n* : ocho *m* — ~ *adj* : ocho — **eight hundred** *n* : ochocientos *m*

eighteen *n* : dieciocho *m* — ~ *adj* : dieciocho — **eighteenth** *adj* : decimoctavo — ~ *n* **1** : decimoctavo *m*, -va *f* (en una serie) **2** : dieciochoavo *m*, dieciochoava parte *f*

eighth *n* **1** : octavo *m*, -va *f* (en una serie) **2** : octavo *m*, octava parte *f* — ~ *adj* : octavo

eighty *n, pl* **eighties** : ochenta *m* — ~ *adj* : ochenta

either *adj* **1** : cualquiera (de los dos) **2** (*in negative constructions*) : ninguno (de los dos) **3** EACH : cada — ~ *pron* **1** : cualquiera *mf* (de los dos) **2** (*in negative constructions*) : ninguno *m*, -na *f* (de los dos) **3** *or* ~ **one** : algún *m*, alguna *f* — ~ *conj* **1** : o **2** (*in negative constructions*) : ni

eject *vt* : expulsar, expeler

eke *vt* **eked; eking** *or* ~ **out** : ganar a duras penas

elaborate *adj* **1** DETAILED : detallado **2** COMPLEX : complicado — ~ *v* **-rated; -rating** *vt* : elaborar — *vi* : entrar en detalles

elapse *vi* **elapsed; elapsing** : transcurrir

elastic *adj* : elástico — ~ *n* **1** : elástico *m* **2** RUBBER BAND : goma *f* (elástica) — **elasticity** *n, pl* **-ties** : elasticidad *f*

elated *adj* : regocijado

elbow *n* : codo *m*

elder *adj* : mayor — ~ *n* **1** : mayor *mf* **2** : anciano *m*, -na *f* (de un tribu, etc.) — **elderly** *adj* : mayor, anciano

elect *vt* : elegir — ~ *adj* : electo — **election** *n* : elección *f* — **electoral** *adj* : electoral — **electorate** *n* : electorado *m*

electricity *n, pl* **-ties** : electricidad *f* — **electric** *or* **electrical** *adj* : eléctrico — **electrician** *n* : electricista *mf* — **electrify** *vt* **-fied; -fying** : electrificar — **electrocute** *vt* **-cuted; -cuting** : electrocutar

electron *n* : electrón *m* — **electronic** *adj* : electrónico — **electronic mail** *n* : correo *m* electrónico — **electronics** *n* : electrónica *f*

elegant *adj* : elegante — **elegance** *n* : elegancia *f*

element *n* **1** : elemento *m* **2** ~**s** *npl* BASICS : elementos *mpl*, rudimentos *mpl* — **elementary** *adj* : elemental — **elementary school** *n* : escuela *f* primaria

elephant *n* : elefante *m*, -ta *f*

elevate *vt* **-vated; -vating** : elevar — **elevator** *n* : ascensor *m*

eleven *n* : once *m* — ~ *adj* : once — **eleventh** *adj* : undécimo — ~ *n* **1** : undécimo *m*, -ma *f* (en una serie) **2** : onceavo *m*, onceava parte *f*

elf *n, pl* **elves** : duende *m*

elicit *vt* : provocar

eligible *adj* : elegible

eliminate *vt* **-nated; -nating** : eliminar — **elimination** *n* : eliminación *f*

elite *n* : elite *f*

elk *n* : alce *m* (de Europa), uapití *m* (de América)

elliptical *or* **elliptic** *adj* : elíptico

elm *n* : olmo *m*

elongate *vt* **-gated; -gating** : alargar

elope *vi* **eloped; eloping** : fugarse — **elopement** *n* : fuga *f*

eloquence *n* : elocuencia *f* — **eloquent** *adj* : elocuente

else *adv* **1** how ~ ? : ¿de qué otro modo? **2** where ~ ? : ¿en qué otro sitio? **3 or** ~ : si no, de lo contrario — ~ *adj* **1** everyone ~ : todos los demás **2** nobody ~ : ningún otro, nadie más **3** nothing ~ : nada más **4** what ~ ? : ¿qué más? — **elsewhere** *adv* : en otra parte

elude *vt* **eluded; eluding** : eludir, esquivar — **elusive** *adj* : esquivo

elves → **elf**

emaciated *adj* : escuálido, demacrado

E-mail → **electronic mail**

emanate *vi* **-nated; -nating** : emanar

emancipate *vt* **-pated; -pating** : emancipar — **emancipation** *n* : emancipación *f*

embalm *vt* : embalsamar

embankment *n* : terraplén *m*, dique *m* (de un río)

embargo *n, pl* **-goes** : embargo *m*

embark *vt* : embarcar — *vi* **1** : embarcarse **2** ~ **upon** : emprender — **embarkation** *n* : embarque *m*, embarco *m*

embarrass *vt* : avergonzar — **embarrassing** *adj* : embarazoso — **embarrassment** *n* : vergüenza *f*

embassy *n, pl* **-sies** : embajada *f*

embed *vt* **-bedded; -bedding** : incrustar, enterrar

embellish *vt* : adornar, embellecer — **embellishment** *n* : adorno *m*

embers *npl* : ascuas *fpl*

embezzle *vt* **-zled; -zling** : desfalcar, malversar — **embezzlement** *n* : desfalco *m*, malversación *f*

emblem *n* : emblema *m*

embody *vt* **-bodied; -bodying** : encarnar, personificar
emboss *vt* : repujar, grabar en relieve
embrace *v* **-braced; -bracing** *vt* : abrazar — *vi* : abrazarse — ~ *n* : abrazo *m*
embroider *vt* : bordar — **embroidery** *n, pl* **-deries** : bordado *m*
embryo *n, pl* **embryos** : embrión *m*
emerald *n* : esmeralda *f*
emerge *vi* **emerged; emerging** : salir, aparecer — **emergence** *n* : aparición *f*
emergency *n, pl* **-cies** 1 : emergencia *f* 2 ~ **exit** : salida *f* de emergencia 3 ~ **room** : sala *f* de urgencias, sala *f* de guardia
emery *n, pl* **-eries** 1 : esmeril *m* 2 ~ **board** : lima *f* de uñas
emigrant *n* : emigrante *mf* — **emigrate** *vi* **-grated; -grating** : emigrar — **emigration** *n* : emigración *f*
eminence *n* : eminencia *f* — **eminent** *adj* : eminente
emission *n* : emisión *f* — **emit** *vt* **emitted; emitting** : emitir
emotion *n* : emoción *f* — **emotional** *adj* 1 : emocional 2 MOVING : emotivo
emperor *n* : emperador *m*
emphasis *n, pl* **-phases** : énfasis *m* — **emphasize** *vt* **-sized; -sizing** : subrayar, hacer hincapié en — **emphatic** *adj* : enérgico, categórico
empire *n* : imperio *m*
employ *vt* : emplear — **employee** *n* : empleado *m*, -da *f* — **employer** *n* : patrón *m*, -trona *f*; empleador *m*, -dora *f* — **employment** *n* : trabajo *m*, empleo *m*
empower *vt* : autorizar
empress *n* : emperatriz *f*
empty *adj* **emptier; -est** 1 : vacío 2 MEANINGLESS : vano — ~ *v* **-tied; -tying** *vt* : vaciar — *vi* : vaciarse — **emptiness** *n* : vacío *m*
emulate *vt* **-lated; -lating** : emular
enable *vt* **-abled; -abling** : hacer posible, permitar
enact *vt* 1 : promulgar (un ley o un decreto) 2 PERFORM : representar
enamel *n* : esmalte *m*
encampment *n* : campamento *m*
encase *vt* **-cased; -casing** : encerrar, revestir
enchant *vt* : encantar — **enchanting** *adj* : encantador — **enchantment** *n* : encanto *m*
encircle *vt* **-cled; -cling** : rodear
enclose *vt* **-closed; -closing** 1 SURROUND : encerrar, cercar 2 INCLUDE : adjuntar (a una carta) — **enclosure** *n* 1 AREA : recinto *m* 2 : anexo *m* (con una carta)
encompass *vt* 1 ENCIRCLE : cercar 2 INCLUDE : abarcar

encore *n* : bis *m*
encounter *vt* : encontrar — ~ *n* : encuentro *m*
encourage *vt* **-aged; -aging** 1 : animar, alentar 2 FOSTER : promover, fomentar — **encouragement** *n* 1 : aliento *m* 2 PROMOTION : fomento *m*
encroach *vi* ~ **on** : invadir, usurpar, quitar (el tiempo)
encyclopedia *n* : enciclopedia *f*
end *n* 1 : fin 2 EXTREMITY : extremo *m*, punta *f* 3 **come to an** ~ : llegar a su fin 4 **in the** ~ : por fin — ~ *vt* : terminar, poner fin a — *vi* : terminar(se)
endanger *vt* : poner en peligro
endearing *adj* : simpático
endeavor *or Brit* **endeavour** *vt* ~ **to** : esforzarse por — ~ *n* : esfuerzo *m*
ending *n* : final *m*, desenlace *m*
endive *n* : endibia *f*, endivia *f*
endless *adj* 1 INTERMINABLE : interminable 2 INNUMERABLE : innumerable 3 ~ **possibilities** : posibilidades *fpl* infinitas
endorse *vt* **-dorsed; -dorsing** 1 SIGN : endosar 2 APPROVE : aprobar — **endorsement** *n* APPROVAL : aprobación *f*
endow *vt* : dotar
endure *v* **-dured; -during** *vt* : soportar, aguantar — *vi* LAST : durar — **endurance** *n* : resistencia *f*
enemy *n, pl* **-mies** : enemigo *m*, -ga *f*
energy *n, pl* **-gies** : energía *f* — **energetic** *adj* : enérgico
enforce *vt* **-forced; -forcing** 1 : hacer cumplir (un ley, etc.) 2 IMPOSE : imponer — **enforced** *adj* : forzoso — **enforcement** *n* : imposición *f* del cumplimiento
engage *v* **-gaged; -gaging** *vt* 1 : captar, atraer (la atención, etc.) 2 ~ **the clutch** : embragar — *vi* ~ **in** : dedicarse a, meterse en — **engagement** *n* 1 APPOINTMENT : cita *f*, hora *f* 2 BETROTHAL : compromiso *m* — **engaging** *adj* : atractivo
engine *n* 1 : motor *m* 2 LOCOMOTIVE : locomotora *f* — **engineer** *n* 1 : ingeniero *m*, -ra *f* 2 : maquinista *mf* (de locomotoras) — ~ *vt* 1 CONSTRUCT : construir 2 CONTRIVE : tramar — **engineering** *n* : ingeniería *f*
English *adj* : inglés — ~ *n* : inglés *m* (idioma) — **Englishman** *n* : inglés *m* — **Englishwoman** *n* : inglesa *f*
engrave *vt* **-graved; -graving** : grabar — **engraving** *n* : grabado *m*
engross *vt* : absorber
engulf *vt* : envolver
enhance *vt* **-hanced; -hancing** : aumentar, mejorar
enjoy *vt* 1 : disfrutar, gozar de 2 ~ **one-**

enlarge

self : divertirse — **enjoyable** adj : agradable — **enjoyment** n : placer m

enlarge v **-larged; -larging** vt : agrandar, ampliar — vi **1** : agrandarse **2** ~ **upon** : extenderse sobre — **enlargement** n : ampliación f

enlighten vt : aclarar, iluminar

enlist vt **1** ENROLL : alistar **2** OBTAIN : conseguir — vi : alistarse

enliven vt : animar

enmity n, pl **-ties** : enemistad f

enormous adj : enorme

enough adj : bastante, suficiente — ~ adv : bastante — ~ pron **1** : (lo) suficiente, (lo) bastante **2 it's not** ~ : no basta **3 I've had** ~ ! : ¡estoy harto!

enquire , enquiry → inquire, inquiry

enrage vt **-raged; -raging** : enfurecer

enrich vt : enriquecer

enroll or **enrol** v **-rolled; -rolling** vt : matricular, inscribir — vi : matricularse, inscribirse

ensemble n : conjunto m

ensign n **1** FLAG : enseña f **2** : alférez mf (de fragata)

enslave vt **-slaved; -slaving** : esclavizar

ensue vi **-sued; -suing** : seguir, resultar

ensure vt **-sured; -suring** : asegurar

entail vt : suponer, conllevar

entangle vt **-gled; -gling** : enredar — **entanglement** n : enredo m

enter vt **1** : entrar en **2** RECORD : inscribir — vi **1** : entrar **2** ~ **into** : firmar (un acuerdo), entablar (negociaciones, etc.)

enterprise n **1** : empresa f **2** INITIATIVE : iniciativa f — **enterprising** adj : emprendedor

entertain vt **1** AMUSE : entretener, divertir **2** CONSIDER : considerar **3** ~ **guests** : recibir invitados — **entertainment** n : entretenimiento m, diversión f

enthrall or **enthral** vt **-thralled; -thralling** : cautivar, embelesar

enthusiasm n : entusiasmo m — **enthusiast** n : entusiasta mf — **enthusiastic** adj : entusiasta

entice vt **-ticed; -ticing** : atraer, tentar

entire adj : entero, completo — **entirely** adv : completamente — **entirety** n, pl **-ties** : totalidad f

entitle vt **-tled; -tling 1** NAME : titular **2** AUTHORIZE : dar derecho a — **entitlement** n : derecho m

entity n, pl **-ties** : entidad f

entrails npl : entrañas fpl, vísceras fpl

entrance[1] vt **-tranced; -trancing** : encantar, fascinar

entrance[2] n : entrada f — **entrant** n : participante mf

entreat vt : suplicar

entrée or **entree** n : plato m principal

entrepreneur n : empresario m, -ria f

entrust vt : confiar

entry n, pl **-tries 1** ENTRANCE : entrada f **2** NOTATION : entrada f, anotación f

enumerate vt **-ated; -ating** : enumerar

enunciate vt **-ated; -ating 1** STATE : enunciar **2** PRONOUNCE : articular

envelop vt : envolver — **envelope** n : sobre m

envious adj : envidioso — **enviously** adv : con envidia

environment n : medio m ambiente — **environmental** adj : ambiental — **environmentalist** n : ecologista mf

envision vt : prever, imaginar

envoy n : enviado m, -da f

envy n, pl **envies** : envidia f — ~ vt **-vied; -vying** : envidiar

enzyme n : enzima f

epic adj : épico — ~ n : epopeya f

epidemic n : epidemia f — ~ adj : epidémico

epilepsy n, pl **-sies** : epilepsia f — **epileptic** adj : epiléptico — ~ n : epiléptico m, -ca f

episode n : episodio m

epitaph n : epitafio m

epitome n : personificación f — **epitomize** vt **-mized; -mizing** : ser la personificación de, personificar

epoch n : época f

equal adj **1** SAME : igual **2 be** ~ **to** : estar a la altura de (una tarea, etc.) — ~ n : igual mf — ~ vt **equaled** or **equalled; equaling** or **equalling 1** : igualar **2** : ser igual a (en matemáticas) — **equality** n, pl **-ties** : igualdad f — **equalize** vt **-ized; -izing** : igualar — **equally** adv **1** : igualmente **2** ~ **important** : igual de importante

equate vt **equated; equating** : ~ **with** : equiparar con — **equation** n : ecuación f

equator n : ecuador m

equilibrium n, pl **-riums** or **-ria** : equilibrio m

equinox n : equinoccio m

equip vt **equipped; equipping** : equipar — **equipment** n : equipo m

equity n, pl **-ties 1** FAIRNESS : equidad f **2** **equities** npl STOCKS : acciones fpl ordinarias

equivalent adj : equivalente — ~ n : equivalente m

era n : era f, época f

eradicate vt **-cated; -cating** : erradicar

erase vt **erased; erasing** : borrar — **eraser** n : goma f de borrar, borrador m

erect adj : erguido — ~ vt : erigir, levantar

— **erection** n **1** BUILDING : construcción f **2** : erección f (en fisiología)
erode vt **eroded; eroding** : erosionar (el suelo), corroer (metales) — **erosion** n : erosión f, corrosión f
erotic adj : erótico
err vi : equivocarse, errar
errand n : mandado m, recado m Spain
erratic adj : errático, irregular
error n : error m — **erroneous** adj : erróneo
erupt vi **1** : hacer erupción (dícese de un volcán) **2** : estallar (dícese de la cólera, violencia, etc.) — **eruption** n : erupción f
escalate vi -lated; -lating : intensificarse
escalator n : escalera f mecánica
escapade n : aventura f
escape v -caped; -caping vt : escapar a, evitar — vi : escaparse, fugarse — ~ n **1** : fuga f **2** ~ **from reality** : evasión f de la realidad — **escapee** n : fugitivo m, -va f
escort n **1** GUARD : escolta f **2** COMPANION : acompañante mf — ~ vt **1** : escoltar **2** ACCOMPANY : acompañar
Eskimo adj : esquimal
especially adv : especialmente
espionage n : espionaje m
espresso n, pl -sos : café m exprés
essay n : ensayo m (literario), composición f (académica)
essence n : esencia f — **essential** adj : esencial — ~ n **1** : elemento m esencial **2** **the ~s** : lo indispensable
establish vt : establecer — **establishment** n : establecimiento m
estate n **1** POSSESSIONS : bienes mpl **2** LAND, PROPERTY : finca f
esteem n : estima f — ~ vt : estimar
esthetic → **aesthetic**
estimate vt -mated; -mating : calcular, estimar — ~ n **1** : cálculo m (aproximado) **2** or ~ **of costs** : presupuesto m — **estimation** n **1** JUDGMENT : juicio m **2** ESTEEM : estima f
estuary n, pl -aries : estuario m, ría f
eternal adj : eterno — **eternity** n, pl -ties : eternidad f
ether n : éter m
ethical adj : ético — **ethics** ns & pl : ética f, moralidad f
ethnic adj : étnico
etiquette n : etiqueta f
Eucharist n : Eucaristía f
eulogy n, pl -gies : elogio m, panegírico m
euphemism n : eufemismo m
euphoria n : euforia f
European adj : europeo
evacuate vt -ated; -ating : evacuar — **evacuation** n : evacuación f
evade vt evaded; evading : evadir, eludir

evaluate vt -ated; -ating : evaluar
evaporate vi -rated; -rating : evaporarse
evasion n : evasión f — **evasive** adj : evasivo
eve n : víspera f
even adj **1** REGULAR, STEADY : regular, constante **2** LEVEL : plano, llano **3** SMOOTH : liso **4** EQUAL : igual **5** ~ **number** : número m par **6 get** ~ **with** : desquitarse con — ~ adv **1** : hasta, incluso **2** ~ **better** : aún mejor, todavía mejor **3** ~ **if** : aunque **4** ~ **so** : aun así — ~ vt : igualar — vi or **out** : nivelarse
evening n : tarde f, noche f
event n **1** : acontecimiento m, suceso m **2** : prueba f (en deportes) **3 in the** ~ **of** : en caso de — **eventful** adj : lleno de incidentes
eventual adj : final — **eventuality** n, pl -ties : eventualidad f — **eventually** adv : al fin, finalmente
ever adv **1** ALWAYS : siempre **2** ~ **since** : desde entonces **3 hardly** ~ : casi nunca **4 have you** ~ **done it?** : ¿lo has hecho alguna vez?
evergreen n : planta f de hoja perenne
everlasting adj : eterno
every adj **1** EACH : cada **2** ~ **month** : todos los meses **3** ~ **other day** : cada dos días — **everybody** pron : todos mpl, -das fpl; todo el mundo — **everyday** adj : cotidiano, de todos los días — **everyone** → **everybody** — **everything** pron : todo — **everywhere** adv : en todas partes, por todas partes
evict vt : desahuciar, desalojar — **eviction** n : desahucio m
evidence n **1** PROOF : pruebas fpl **2** TESTIMONY : testimonio m, declaración f — **evident** adj : evidente — **evidently** adv **1** OBVIOUSLY : obviamente **2** APPARENTLY : evidentemente, al parecer
evil adj eviler or eviller; evilest or evillest : malvado, malo — ~ n : mal m, maldad f
evoke vt evoked; evoking : evocar
evolution n : evolución f, desarrollo m — **evolve** vi evolved; evolving : evolucionar, desarrollarse
exact adj : exacto, preciso — ~ vt : exigir — **exacting** adj : exigente — **exactly** adv : exactamente
exaggerate v -ated; -ating : exagerar — **exaggeration** n : exageración f
examine vt -ined; -ining **1** : examinar **2** INSPECT : revisar **3** QUESTION : interrogar — **exam** n : examen m — **examination** n : examen m
example n : ejemplo m
exasperate vt -ated; -ating : exasperar — **exasperation** n : exasperación f

excavate *vt* -vated; -vating : excavar — **excavation** *n* : excavación *f*
exceed *vt* : exceder, sobrepasar — **exceedingly** *adv* : extremadamente
excel *v* -celled; -celling *vi* : sobresalir — *vt* SURPASS : superar — **excellence** *n* : excelencia *f* — **excellent** *adj* : excelente
except *prep or* ~ **for** : excepto, menos, salvo — ~ *vt* : exceptuar — **exception** *n* : excepción *f* — **exceptional** *adj* : excepcional
excerpt *n* : extracto *m*
excess *n* : exceso *m* — ~ *adj* : excesivo, de sobra — **excessive** *adj* : excesivo
exchange *n* **1** : intercambio *m* **2** : cambio *m* (en finanzas) — ~ *vt* -changed; -changing : cambiar, intercambiar
excise *n* ~ **tax** : impuesto *m* interno, impuesto *m* sobre el consumo
excite *vt* -cited; -citing : excitar, emocionar — **excited** *adj* : excitado, entusiasmado — **excitement** *n* : entusiasmo *m*, emoción *f*
exclaim *v* : exclamar — **exclamation** *n* : exclamación *f* — **exclamation point** *n* : signo *m* de admiración
exclude *vt* -cluded; -cluding : excluir — **excluding** *prep* : excepto, con excepción de — **exclusion** *n* : exclusión *f* — **exclusive** *adj* : exclusivo
excrement *n* : excremento *m*
excruciating *adj* : insoportable, atroz
excursion *n* : excursión *f*
excuse *vt* -cused; -cusing **1** : perdonar **2** ~ **me** : perdóne, perdón — ~ *n* : excusa *f*
execute *vt* -cuted; -cuting : ejecutar — **execution** *n* : ejecución *f* — **executioner** *n* : verdugo *m*
executive *adj* : ejecutivo — ~ *n* **1** MANAGER : ejecutivo *m*, -va *f* **2** *or* ~ **branch** : poder *m* ejecutivo
exemplify *vt* -fied; -fying : ejemplificar — **exemplary** *adj* : ejemplar
exempt *adj* : exento — ~ *vt* : dispensar — **exemption** *n* : exención *f*
exercise *n* : ejercicio *m* — ~ *v* -cised; -cising *vt* USE : ejercer, hacer uso de — *vi* : hacer ejercicio
exert *vt* **1** : ejercer **2** ~ **oneself** : esforzarse — **exertion** *n* : esfuerzo *m*
exhale *v* -haled; -haling : exhalar
exhaust *vt* : agotar — ~ *n* **1** *or* ~ **fumes** : gases *mpl* de escape **2** *or* ~ **pipe** : tubo *m* de escape — **exhaustion** *n* : agotamiento *m* — **exhaustive** *adj* : exhaustivo
exhibit *vt* **1** DISPLAY : exponer **2** SHOW : mostrar — ~ *n* **1** : objeto *m* expuesto **2** EXHIBITION : exposición *f* — **exhibition** *n* : exposición *f*

exhilarate *vt* -rated; -rating : alegrar — **exhilaration** *n* : regocijo *m*
exile *n* **1** : exilio *m* **2** OUTCAST : exiliado *m*, -da *f* — ~ *vt* **exiled; exiling** : exiliar
exist *vi* : existir — **existence** *n* : existencia *f* — **existing** *adj* : existente
exit *n* : salida *f* — ~ *vi* : salir
exodus *n* : éxodo *m*
exonerate *vt* -ated; -ating : exonerar, disculpar
exorbitant *adj* : exorbitante, excesivo
exotic *adj* : exótico
expand *vt* **1** : ampliar, extender **2** : dilatar (metales, etc.) — *vi* **1** : ampliarse, extenderse **2** : dilatarse (dícese de metales, etc.) — **expanse** *n* : extensión *f* — **expansion** *n* : expansión *f*
expatriate *n* : expatriado *m*, -da *f* — ~ *adj* : expatriado
expect *vt* **1** : esperar **2** REQUIRE : contar con — *vi* **be expecting** : estar embarazada — **expectancy** *n*, *pl* -cies : esperanza *f* — **expectant** *adj* **1** : expectante **2** ~ **mother** : futura madre *f* — **expectation** *n* : esperanza *f*
expedient *adj* : conveniente — ~ *n* : expediente *m*, recurso *m*
expedition *n* : expedición *f*
expel *vt* -pelled; -pelling : expulsar (a una persona), expeler (humo, etc.)
expend *vt* : gastar — **expendable** *adj* : prescindible — **expenditure** *n* : gasto *m* — **expense** *n* **1** : gasto *m* **2** ~s *npl* : gastos *mpl*, expensas *fpl* **3 at the** ~ **of** : a expensas de — **expensive** *adj* : caro
experience *n* : experiencia *f* — ~ *vt* -enced; -encing : experimentar — **experienced** *adj* : experimentado — **experiment** *n* : experimento *m* — ~ *vi* : experimentar — **experimental** *adj* : experimental
expert *adj* : experto — ~ *n* : experto *m*, -ta *f* — **expertise** *n* : pericia *f*, competencia *f*
expire *vi* -pired; -piring **1** : caducar, vencer **2** DIE : expirar, morir — **expiration** *n* : vencimiento *m*, caducidad *f*
explain *vt* : explicar — **explanation** *n* : explicación *f* — **explanatory** *adj* : explicativo
explicit *adj* : explícito
explode *v* -ploded; -ploding *vt* : hacer explotar — *vi* : explotar, estallar
exploit *n* : hazaña *f*, proeza *f* — ~ *vt* : explotar — **exploitation** *n* : explotación *f*
exploration *n* : exploración *f* — **explore** *vt* -plored; -ploring : explorar — **explorer** *n* : explorador *m*, -dora *f*
explosion *n* : explosión *f* — **explosive** *adj* : explosivo — ~ *n* : explosivo *m*
export *vt* : exportar — ~ *n* : exportación *f*
expose *vt* -posed; -posing **1** : exponer **2**

REVEAL : descubrir, revelar — **exposed** *adj*
: expuesto, al descubierto — **exposure** *n*
: exposición *f*
express *adj* **1** SPECIFIC : expreso, específico
2 FAST : expreso, rápido — ∼ *adv* : por
correo urgente — ∼ *n or* ∼ **train** : expreso
m — ∼ *vt* : expresar — **expression** *n* : expresión *f* — **expressive** *adj* : expresivo —
expressly *adv* : expresamente — **expressway** *n* : autopista *f*
expulsion *n* : expulsión *f*
exquisite *adj* : exquisito
extend *vt* **1** STRETCH : extender **2**
LENGTHEN : prolongar **3** ENLARGE : ampliar **4** ∼ **one's hand** : tender la mano —
vi : extenderse — **extension** *n* **1** : extensión *f* **2** LENGTHENING : prolongación *f* **3**
ANNEX : ampliación *f*, anexo *m* **4** ∼ **cord**
: alargador *m* — **extensive** *adj* : extenso —
extent *n* **1** SIZE : extensión *f* **2** DEGREE : alcance *m*, grado *m* **3 to a certain** ∼ : hasta
cierto punto
extenuating *adj* ∼ **circumstances** : circunstancias *fpl* atenuantes
exterior *adj* : exterior — ∼ *n* : exterior *m*
exterminate *vt* **-nated; -nating** : exterminar
— **extermination** *n* : exterminación *f*
external *adj* : externo — **externally** *adv* : exteriormente
extinct *adj* : extinto — **extinction** *n* : extinción *f*
extinguish *vt* : extinguir, apagar — **extinguisher** *n* : extintor *m*
extol *vt* **-tolled; -tolling** : ensalzar, alabar
extort *vt* : arrancar (algo a algn) por la fuerza
— **extortion** *n* : extorsión *f*

extra *adj* : suplementario, de más — ∼ *n*
: extra *m* — ∼ *adv* **1** : extra, más **2** ∼
special : super especial
extract *vt* : extraer, sacar — ∼ *n* : extracto
m — **extraction** *n* : extracción *f*
extracurricular *adj* : extracurricular
extradite *vt* **-dited; -diting** : extraditar
extraordinary *adj* : extraordinario
extraterrestrial *adj* : extraterrestre — ∼ *n*
: extraterrestre *mf*
extravagant *adj* **1** WASTEFUL : despilfarrador, derrochador **2** EXAGGERATED : extravagante, exagerado — **extravagance** *n* **1**
WASTEFULNESS : derroche *m*, despilfarro *m*
2 LUXURY : lujo *m* **3** EXAGGERATION : extravagancia *f*
extreme *adj* : extremo — ∼ *n* : extremo *m*
— **extremely** *adv* : extremadamente — **extremity** *n*, *pl* **-ties** : extremidad *f*
extricate *vt* **-cated; -cating** : librar, (lograr)
sacar
extrovert *n* : extrovertido *m*, **-da** *f* — **extroverted** *adj* : extrovertido
exuberant *adj* **1** JOYOUS : eufórico **2** LUSH
: exuberante — **exuberance** *n* **1** JOYOUS-
NESS : euforia *f* **2** VIGOR : exuberancia *f*
exult *vi* : exultar
eye *n* **1** : ojo *m* **2** VISION : visión *f*, vista *f* **3**
GLANCE : mirada *f* — ∼ *vt* **eyed; eyeing** *or*
eying : mirar — **eyeball** *n* : globo *m* ocular
— **eyebrow** *n* : ceja *f* — **eyeglasses** *npl*
: anteojos *mpl*, lentes *mpl* — **eyelash** *n*
: pestaña *f* — **eyelid** *n* : párpado *m* — **eyesight** *n* : vista *f*, visión *f* — **eyesore** *n*
: monstruosidad *f* — **eyewitness** *n* : testigo
mf ocular

F

f *n*, *pl* **f's** *or* **fs** : f, sexta letra del alfabeto inglés
fable *n* : fábula *f*
fabric *n* : tela *f*, tejido *m*
fabulous *adj* : fabuloso
facade *n* : fachada *f*
face *n* **1** : cara *f*, rostro *m* (de una persona) **2**
APPEARANCE : fisonomía *f*, aspecto *m* **3**
: cara *f* (de una moneda), fachada *f* (de un
edificio) **4** ∼ **value** : valor *m* nominal **5 in
the** ∼ **of** : en medio de, ante **6 lose** ∼
: desprestigiarse **7 make** ∼**s** : hacer muecas — ∼ **faced; facing** *vt* **1** : estar frente a

2 CONFRONT : enfrentarse a **3** OVERLOOK
: dar a — *vi* ∼ **to the north** : mirar hacia el
norte — **facedown** *adv* : boca abajo —
faceless *adj* : anónimo — **face-lift** *n* : estiramiento *m* facial
facet *n* : faceta *f*
face-to-face *adv* & *adj* : cara a cara
facial *adj* : de la cara, facial — ∼ *n*
: limpieza *f* de cutis
facetious *adj* : gracioso, burlón
facility *n*, *pl* **-ties 1** EASE : facilidad *f* **2**
CENTER : centro *m* **3 facilities** *npl* : comodidades *fpl*, servicios *mpl*

facsimile *n* : facsímile *m*, facsímil *m*
fact *n* **1** : hecho *m* **2 in** ~ : en realidad, de hecho
faction *n* : facción *m*, bando *m*
factor *n* : factor *m*
factory *n*, *pl* **-ries** : fábrica *f*
factual *adj* : basado en hechos
faculty *n*, *pl* **-ties** : facultad *f*
fad *n* : moda *f* pasajera, manía *f*
fade *v* **faded; fading** *vi* **1** WITHER : marchitarse **2** DISCOLOR : desteñirse, decolorarse **3** DIM : apagarse **4** VANISH : desvanecerse — *vt* : desteñir
fail *vi* **1** : fracasar (dícese de una empresa, un matrimonio, etc.) **2** BREAK DOWN : fallar **3** ~ **in** : faltar a, no cumplir con **4** FLUNK : suspender *Spain*, ser reprobado *Lat* **5** ~ **to do sth** : no hacer algo — *vt* **1** DISAPPOINT : fallar **2** FLUNK : suspender *Spain*, reprobar *Lat* — ~ *n* **without** ~ : sin falta — **failing** *n* : defecto *m* — **failure** *n* **1** : fracaso *m* **2** BREAKDOWN : falla *f*
faint *adj* **1** WEAK : débil **2** INDISTINCT : tenue, indistinto **3 feel** ~ : estar mareado — ~ *vi* : desmayarse — ~ *n* : desmayo *m* — **fainthearted** *adj* : cobarde, pusilánime — **faintly** *adv* **1** WEAKLY : débilmente **2** SLIGHTLY : ligeramente, levemente
fair[1] *n* : feria *f*
fair[2] *adj* **1** BEAUTIFUL : bello, hermoso **2** : bueno (dícese del tiempo) **3** JUST : justo **4** : rubio (dícese del pelo), blanco (dícese de la tez) **5** ADEQUATE : adecuado — ~ *adv* **play** ~ : jugar limpio — **fairly** *adv* **1** JUSTLY : justamente **2** QUITE : bastante — **fairness** *n* : justicia *f*
fairy *n*, *pl* **fairies 1** : hada *f* **2** ~ **tale** : cuento *m* de hadas
faith *n*, *pl* **faiths** : fe *f* — **faithful** *adj* : fiel — **faithfully** *adv* : fielmente — **faithfulness** *n* : fidelidad *f*
fake *v* **faked; faking** *vt* **1** FALSIFY : falsificar, falsear **2** FEIGN : fingir — *vi* PRETEND : fingir — ~ *adj* : falso — ~ *n* **1** IMITATION : falsificación *f* **2** IMPOSTOR : impostor *m*, -tora *f*
falcon *n* : halcón *m*
fall *vi* **fell; fallen; falling 1** : caer, bajar (dícese de los precios), descender (dícese de la temperatura) **2** ~ **asleep** : dormirse **3** ~ **back** : retirarse **4** ~ **back on** : recurrir a **5** ~ **down** : caerse **6** ~ **in love** : enamorarse **7** ~ **out** QUARREL : pelearse **8** ~ **through** : fracasar — ~ *n* **1** : caída *f*, bajada *f* (de precios), descenso *m* (de temperatura) **2** AUTUMN : otoño *m* **3** ~**s** *npl* WATERFALL : cascada *f*, catarata *f*
fallacy *n*, *pl* **-cies** : concepto *m* erróneo
fallible *adj* : falible

fallow *adj* **lie** ~ : estar en barbecho
false *adj* **falser; falsest 1** : falso **2** ~ **alarm** : falsa alarma *f* **3** ~ **teeth** : dentadura *f* postiza — **falsehood** *n* : mentira — **falseness** *n* : falsedad *f* — **falsify** *vt* **-fied; fying** : falsificar, falsear
falter *vi* **-tered; -tering 1** STUMBLE : tambalearse **2** WAVER : vacilar
fame *n* : fama *f*
familiar *adj* **1** : familiar **2 be** ~ **with** : estar familiarizado con — **familiarity** *n*, *pl* **-ties** : familiaridad *f* — **familiarize** *vt* **-ized; -izing** ~ **oneself** : familiarizarse
family *n*, *pl* **-lies** : familia *f*
famine *n* : hambre *f*, hambruna *f*
famished *adj* : famélico
famous *adj* : famoso
fan *n* **1** : ventilador *m*, abanico *m* **2** : aficionado *m*, -da *f* (a un pasatiempo); admirador *m*, -dora *f* (de una persona) — ~ *vt* **fanned; fanning** : abanicar (a una persona), avivar (un fuego)
fanatic *or* **fanatical** *adj* : fanático — ~ *n* : fanático *m*, -ca *f* — **fanaticism** *n* : fanatismo *m*
fancy *vt* **-cied; -cying 1** IMAGINE : imaginarse **2** DESIRE : apetecerle (algo a uno) — ~ *adj* **-cier; -est 1** ELABORATE : elaborado **2** LUXURIOUS : lujoso, elegante — ~ *n*, *pl* **-cies 1** WHIM : capricho *m* **2** IMAGINATION : imaginación *f* **3 take a** ~ **to** : aficionarse a (una cosa), tomar cariño a (una persona) — **fanciful** *adj* **1** CAPRICIOUS : caprichoso **2** IMAGINATIVE : imaginativo
fanfare *n* : fanfarria *f*
fang *n* : colmillo *m* (de un animal), diente *m* (de una serpiente)
fantasy *n*, *pl* **-sies** : fantasía *f* — **fantasize** *vi* **-sized; -sizing** : fantasear — **fantastic** *adj* : fantástico
far *adv* **farther** *or* **further; farthest** *or* **furthest 1** : lejos **2** MUCH : muy, mucho **3 as** ~ **as** : hasta (un lugar), con respecto a (un tema) **4 by** ~ : con mucho **5** ~ **and wide** : por todas partes **6** ~ **away** : a lo lejos **7** ~ **from it!** : ¡todo lo contrario! **8 so** ~ : hasta ahora, todavía — ~ *adj* **farther** *or* **further; farthest** *or* **furthest** REMOTE : lejano **2** EXTREME : extremo — **faraway** *adj* : remoto, lejano
farce *n* : farsa *f*
fare *vi* **fared; faring** : irle a uno — ~ *n* **1** : precio *m* del pasaje **2** FOOD : comida *f*
farewell *n* : despedida *f* — ~ *adj* : de despedida
far-fetched *adj* : improbable, exagerado
farm *n* : granja *f*, hacienda *f* — ~ *vt* : cultivar (la tierra), criar (animales) — *vi* : ser agricultor — **farmer** *n* : agricultor *m*, -tora *f*;

granjero *m*, -jera — **farmhand** *n* : peón *m*
— **farmhouse** *n* : granja *f*, casa *f* de hacienda — **farming** *n* : agricultura *f*, cultivo *m* (de plantas), crianza *f* (de animales) —
farmyard *n* : corral *m*
far–off *adj* : lejano
far–reaching *adj* : de gran alcance
farsighted *adj* **1** : hipermétrope **2** PRUDENT : previsor
farther *adv* **1** : más lejos **2** MORE : más — *adj* : más lejano — **farthest** *adv* **1** : lo más lejos **2** MOST : más — *adj* : más lejano
fascinate *vt* **-nated; -nating** : fascinar — **fascination** *n* : fascinación *f*
fascism *n* : fascismo *m* — **fascist** *adj* : fascista — ~ *n* : fascista *mf*
fashion *n* **1** MANNER : manera *f* **2** STYLE : moda *f* **3 out of** ~ : pasada de moda — **fashionable** *adj* : de moda
fast¹ *vi* : ayunar — ~ *n* : ayuno *m*
fast² *adj* **1** SWIFT : rápido **2** SECURE : firme, seguro **3** : adelantado (dícese de un reloj) **4** ~ **friends** : amigos *mpl* leales — ~ *adv* **1** SECURELY : firmemente **2** SWIFTLY : rápidamente **3** ~ **asleep** : profundamente dormido
fasten *vt* : sujetar (papeles, etc.), abrochar (una blusa, etc.), cerrar (una maleta, etc.) — *vi* : abrocharse, cerrar — **fastener** *n* : cierre *m*
fat *adj* **fatter; fattest 1** : gordo **2** THICK : grueso — ~ *n* : grasa *f*
fatal *adj* **1** : mortal **2** FATEFUL : fatal, fatídico — **fatality** *n*, *pl* **-ties** : víctima *f* mortal
fate *n* **1** : destino *m* **2** LOT : suerte *f* — **fateful** *adj* : fatídico
father *n* : padre *m* — ~ *vt* : engendrar — **fatherhood** *n* : paternidad *f* — **father–in–law** *n*, *pl* **fathers–in–law** : suegro *m* — **fatherly** *adj* : paternal
fathom *vt* : comprender
fatigue *n* : fatiga *f* — ~ *vt* **-tigued; -tiguing** : fatigar
fatten *vt* : engordar — **fattening** *adj* : que engorda
fatty *adj* **fattier; -est** : graso
faucet *n* : llave *f Lat*, grifo *m Spain*
fault *n* **1** FLAW : defecto *m* **2** RESPONSIBILITY : culpa *f* **3** : falla *f* (geológica) — *vt* : encontrar defectos a — **faultless** *adj* : impecable — **faulty** *adj* **faultier; -est** : defectuoso
fauna *n* : fauna *f*
favor *or Brit* **favour** *n* **1** : favor *m* **2 in** ~ **of** : a favor de — ~ *vt* **1** : favorecer **2** SUPPORT : estar a favor de **3** PREFER : preferir — **favorable** *or Brit* **favourable** *adj* : favorable — **favorite** *or Brit* **favourite** : favorito *m*,

-ta *f* — ~ *adj* : favorito — **favoritism** *or Brit* **favouritism** *n* : favoritismo *m*
fawn¹ *vi* ~ **over** : adular
fawn² *n* : cervato *m*
fax *n* : fax *m* — ~ *vt* : faxear, enviar por fax
fear *v* : temer — ~ *n* **1** : miedo *m*, temor *m* **2 for** ~ **of** : por temor a — **fearful** *adj* **1** FRIGHTENING : espantoso **2** AFRAID : temeroso
feasible *adj* : viable, factible
feast *n* **1** BANQUET : banquete *m*, festín *m* **2** FESTIVAL : fiesta *f* — ~ *vi* **1** : banquetear **2** ~ **upon** : darse un festín de
feat *n* : hazaña *f*
feather *n* : pluma *f*
feature *n* **1** : rasgo *m* (de la cara) **2** CHARACTERISTIC : característica *f* **3** : artículo *m* (en un periódico) **4** ~ **film** : largometraje *m* — ~ *v* **-tured; -turing** *vt* **1** PRESENT : presentar **2** EMPHASIZE : destacar — *vi* : figurar
February *n* : febrero *m*
feces *npl* : excremento *mpl*
federal *adj* : federal — **federation** *n* : federación *f*
fed up *adj* : harto
fee *n* **1** : honorarios *mpl* **2 entrance** ~ : entrada *f*
feeble *adj* **-bler; -blest 1** : débil **2 a** ~ **excuse** : una pobre excusa
feed *v* **fed; feeding** *vt* **1** : dar de comer a, alimentar **2** SUPPLY : alimentar — *vi* : comer, alimentarse — ~ *n* : pienso *m*
feel *v* **felt; feeling** *vt* **1** : sentir (una sensación, etc.) **2** TOUCH : tocar, palpar **3** BELIEVE : creer — *vi* **1** : sentirse (bien, cansado, etc.) **2** SEEM : parecer **3** ~ **hot/thirsty** : tener calor/sed **4** ~ **like doing** : tener ganas de hacer — ~ *n* **1** : tacto *m*, sensación *f* — **feeling** *n* **1** SENSATION : sensación *f* **2** EMOTION : sentimiento *m* **3** OPINION : opinión *f* **4 hurt s.o.'s** ~**s** : herir los sentimientos de algn
feet → **foot**
feign *vt* : fingir
feline *adj* : felino — ~ *n* : felino *m*, -na *f*
fell¹ → **fall**
fell² *vt* : talar (un árbol)
fellow *n* **1** COMPANION : compañero *m*, -ra *f* **2** MEMBER : socio *m*, -cia *f* **3** MAN : tipo *m* — **fellowship** *n* **1** : compañerismo *m* **2** ASSOCIATION : fraternidad *f* **3** GRANT : beca *f*
felon *n* : criminal *mf* — **felony** *n*, *pl* **-nies** : delito *m* grave
felt¹ → **feel**
felt² *n* : fieltro *m*
female *adj* : femenino — ~ *n* **1** : hembra *f* (animal) **2** WOMAN : mujer *f*
feminine *adj* : femenino — **femininity** *n* : femineidad *f* — **feminism** *n* : feminismo *m*

fence

— **feminist** *adj* : feminista — ~ *n* : feminista *mf*
fence *n* : cerca *f*, valla *f*, cerco *m Lat* — ~ *v*
fenced; fencing *vt or* ~ **in** : vallar, cercar — *vi* : hacer esgrima — **fencing** *n* : esgrima *m* (deporte)
fend *vt* ~ **off** : rechazar (un enemigo), eludir (una pregunta) — *vi* ~ **for oneself** : valerse por sí mismo
fender *n* : guardabarros *mpl*
fennel *n* : hinojo *m*
ferment *v* : fermentar — **fermentation** *n* : fermentación *f*
fern *n* : helecho *m*
ferocious *adj* : feroz — **ferocity** *n* : ferocidad *f*
ferret *n* : hurón *m* — ~ *vt* ~ **out** : descubrir
Ferris wheel *n* : noria *f*
ferry *vt* -**ried; -rying** : transportar — ~ *n, pl* -**ries** : ferry *m*
fertile *adj* : fértil — **fertility** *n* : fertilidad *f* — **fertilize** *vt* -**ized; -izing** : fecundar (un huevo), abonar (el suelo) — **fertilizer** *n* : fertilizante *m*, abono *m*
fervent *adj* : ferviente — **fervor** *or Brit* **fervour** *n* : fervor *m*
fester *vi* : enconarse
festival *n* **1** : fiesta *f* **2 film** ~ : festival *m* de cine — **festive** *adj* : festivo — **festivity** *n, pl* -**ties** : festividad *f*
fetch *vt* **1** : ir a buscar **2** : venderse por (un precio)
fête *n* : fiesta *f*
fetid *adj* : fétido
fetish *n* : fetiche *m*
fetters *npl* : grillos *mpl* — **fetter** *vt* : encadenar
fetus *n* : feto *m*
feud *n* : enemistad *f* (entre familiares) — ~ *vi* : pelear
feudal *adj* : feudal — **feudalism** *n* : feudalismo *m*
fever *n* : fiebre *f* — **feverish** *adj* : febril
few *adj* **1** : pocos **2 a** ~ **times** : varias veces — ~ *pron* **1** : pocos **2 a** ~ : algunos, unos cuantos **3 quite a** ~ : muchos — **fewer** *adj & pron* : menos
fiancé, fiancée *n* : prometido *m*, -da *f*; novio *m*, -via *f*
fiasco *n, pl* -**coes** : fiasco *m*
fib *n* : mentirilla *f* — ~ *vi* **fibbed; fibbing** : decir mentirillas
fiber *or* **fibre** *n* : fibra *f* — **fiberglass** *n* : fibra *f* de vidrio — **fibrous** *adj* : fibroso
fickle *adj* : inconstante
fiction *n* : ficción *f* — **fictional** *or* **fictitious** *adj* : ficticio
fiddle *n* : violín *m* — ~ *vi* -**dled; -dling 1** : tocar el violín **2** ~ **with** : juguetear con

fidelity *n, pl* -**ties** : fidelidad *f*
fidget *vi* **1** : estarse inquieto, moverse **2** ~ **with** : juguetear con — **fidgety** *adj* : inquieto, nervioso
field *n* : campo *m* — ~ *vt* : interceptar (una pelota), sortear (una pregunta) — **field glasses** *n* : binoculares *mpl*, gemelos *mpl* — **field trip** *n* : viaje *m* de estudio
fiend *n* **1** : demonio *m* **2 FANATIC** : fanático *m*, -ca *f* — **fiendish** *adj* : diabólico
fierce *adj* **fiercer; -est 1** : feroz **2 INTENSE** : fuerte (dícese del viento), acalorado (dícese de un debate) — **fierceness** *n* : ferocidad *f*
fiery *adj* **fierier; -est 1 BURNING** : llameante **2 SPIRITED** : ardiente, fogoso — **fieriness** *n* : pasión *f*, ardor *m*
fifteen *n* : quince *m* — ~ *adj* : quince — **fifteenth** *adj* : decimoquinto — ~ *n* **1** : decimoquinto *m*, -ta *f* (en una serie) **2** : quinceavo *m* (en matemáticas)
fifth *n* **1** : quinto *m*, -ta *f* (en una serie) **2** : quinto *m* (en matemáticas) — ~ *adj* : quinto
fiftieth *adj* : quincuagésimo — ~ *n* **1** : quincuagésimo *m*, -ma *f* (en una serie) **2** : cincuentavo *m* (en matemáticas)
fifty *n, pl* -**ties** : cincuenta *m* — ~ *adj* : cincuenta — **fifty-fifty** *adv* : a medias, mitad y mitad — ~ *adj* **a** ~ **chance** : un cincuenta por ciento de posibilidades
fig *n* : higo *m*
fight *v* **fought; fighting** *vi* **1 BATTLE** : luchar **2 QUARREL** : pelear **3** ~ **back** : defenderse — *vt* : luchar contra — ~ *n* **1 STRUGGLE** : lucha *f* **2 QUARREL** : pelea *f* — **fighter** *n* **1** : luchador *m*, -dora *f* **2** *or* ~ **plane** : avión *m* de caza
figment *n* ~ **of the imagination** : producto *m* de la imaginación
figurative *adj* : figurado
figure *n* **1 NUMBER** : número *m*, cifra *f* **2 PERSON, SHAPE** : figura *f* **3** ~ **of speech** : figura *f* retórica **4 watch one's** ~ : cuidar la línea — ~ *v* -**ured; -uring** *vt* : calcular — *vi* **1** : figurar **2 that** ~**s!** : ¡no me extraña! — **figurehead** *n* : testaferro *m* — **figure out** *vt* **1 UNDERSTAND** : entender **2 RESOLVE** : resolver
file¹ *n* : lima *f* (instrumento) — ~ *vt* **filed; filing** : limar
file² *vt* **filed; filing 1** : archivar (documentos) **2** ~ **charges** : presentar cargos — ~ *n* : archivo *m*
file³ *n* **LINE** : fila *f* — ~ *vi* ~ **in/out** : entrar/salir en fila
fill *vt* **1** : llenar, rellenar **2** : cumplir con (un requisito) **3** : tapar (un agujero), empastar (un diente) — *vi* **1** ~ **in for** : reemplazar **2**

or ~ **up** : llenarse — ~ *n* **1 eat one's** ~ : comer lo suficiente **2 have one's** ~ **of** : estar harto de

fillet *n* : filete *m*

filling *n* **1** : relleno *m* **2** : empaste *m* (de dientes) **3** ~ **station** → **service station**

filly *n, pl* **-lies** : potra *f*

film *n* : película *f* — ~ *vt* : filmar

filter *n* : filtro *m* — ~ *vt* : filtrar

filth *n* : mugre *f* — **filthy** *adj* **filthier; -est 1** : mugriento **2** OBSCENE : obsceno

fin *n* : aleta *f*

final *adj* **1** LAST : último **2** DEFINITIVE : definitivo **3** ULTIMATE : final — ~ *n* **1** : final *f* (en deportes) **2** ~**s** *npl* : exámenes *mpl* finales — **finalist** *n* : finalista *mf* — **finalize** *vt* **-ized; -izing** : finalizar — **finally** *adv* : finalmente

finance *n* **1** : finanzas *fpl* **2** ~**s** *npl* : recursos *mpl* financieros — ~ *vt* **-nanced; -nancing** : financiar — **financial** *adj* : financiero — **financially** *adv* : económicamente

find *vt* **found; finding 1** LOCATE : encontrar **2** REALIZE : darse cuenta de **3** ~ **guilty** : declarar culpable **4** *or* ~ **out** : descubrir — *vi* ~ **out** : enterarse — ~ *n* : hallazgo *m* — **finding** *n* **1** FIND : hallazgo *m* **2** ~**s** *npl* : conclusiones *fpl*

fine¹ *n* : multa *f* — ~ *vt* **fined; fining** : multar

fine² *adj* **finer; -est 1** DELICATE : fino **2** EXCELLENT : excelente **3** SUBTLE : sutil **4** : bueno (dícese del tiempo) **5** ~ **print** : letra *f* menuda **6 it's** ~ **with me** : me parece bien — ~ *adv* OK : bien — **fine arts** *npl* : bellas artes *fpl* — **finely** *adv* **1** EXCELLENTLY : excelentemente **2** PRECISELY : con precisión **3** MINUTELY : fino, menudo

finger *n* : dedo *m* — ~ *vt* : tocar, toquetear — **fingernail** *n* : uña *f* — **fingerprint** *n* : huella *f* digital — **fingertip** *n* : punta *f* del dedo

finicky *adj* : maniático, mañoso *Lat*

finish *v* : acabar, terminar — ~ *n* **1** END : fin *m*, final *m* **2** *or* ~ **line** : meta *f* **3** SURFACE : acabado *m*

finite *adj* : finito

fir *n* : abeto *m*

fire *n* **1** : fuego *m* **2** CONFLAGRATION : incendio *m* **3 catch** ~ : incendiarse (dícese de bosques, etc.), prenderse (dícese de fósforos, etc.) **4 on** ~ : en llamas **5 open** ~ **on** : abrir fuego sobre — ~ *vt* **fired; firing 1** DISMISS : despedir **2** SHOOT : disparar — *vi* : disparar — **fire alarm** *n* : alarma *f* contra incendios — **firearm** *n* : arma *f* de fuego — **firecracker** *n* : petardo *m* — **fire engine** *n* : carro *m* de bomberos *Lat*, coche *m* de

bomberos *Spain* — **fire escape** *n* : escalera *f* de incendios — **fire extinguisher** *n* : extintor *m* (de incendios) — **firefighter** *n* : bombero *m*, -ra *f* — **firefly** *n, pl* **-flies** : luciérnaga *f* — **firehouse** → **fire station** — **fireman** *n, pl* **-men** → **firefighter** — **fireplace** *n* : hogar *m*, chimenea *f* — **fireproof** *adj* : ignífugo — **fireside** *n* : hogar *m* — **fire station** *n* : estación *f* de bomberos *Lat*, parque *m* de bomberos *Spain* —— **firewood** *n* : leña *f* — **fireworks** *npl* : fuegos *mpl* artificiales

firm¹ *n* : empresa *f*

firm² *adj* : firme — **firmly** *adv* : firmemente — **firmness** *n* : firmeza *f*

first *adj* **1** : primero **2 at** ~ **sight** : a primera vista **3 for the** ~ **time** : por primera vez — ~ *adv* **1** : primero **2** ~ **and foremost** : ante todo **3** ~ **of all** : en primer lugar — ~ *n* **1** : primero *m*, -ra *f* **2 at** ~ : al principio — **first aid** *n* : primeros auxilios *mpl* — **first–class** *adv* : en primera — ~ *adj* : de primera *f* — **firsthand** *adv* : directamente — ~ *adj* : de primera mano — **firstly** *adv* : en primer lugar — **first name** *n* : nombre *m* de pila — **first–rate** *adj* → **first–class**

fiscal *adj* : fiscal

fish *n, pl* **fish** *or* **fishes** : pez *m* (vivo), pescado *m* (para comer) — ~ *vi* **1** : pescar **2** ~ **for** SEEK : buscar **3 go** ~**ing** : ir de pesca — **fisherman** *n, pl* **-men** : pescador *m*, -dora *f* — **fishhook** *n* : anzuelo *m* — **fishing** *n* : pesca *f* — **fishing pole** *n* : caña *f* de pescar — **fish market** *n* : pescadería *f* — **fishy** *adj* **fishier; -est 1** : a pescado (dícese de sabores, etc.) **2** SUSPICIOUS : sospechoso

fist *n* : puño *m*

fit¹ *n* **1** : ataque *m* **2 he had a** ~ : le dio un ataque

fit² *adj* **fitter; fittest 1** SUITABLE : apropiado **2** HEALTHY : en forma **3 be** ~ **for** : ser apto para — ~ *v* **fitted; fitting** *vt* **1** : encajar en (un hueco, etc.) **2** *(relating to clothing)* : quedar bien a **3** SUIT : ser apropiado para **4** MATCH : coincidir con **5** *or* ~ **out** : equipar — *vi* **1** : caber (en una caja, etc.), encajar (en un hueco, etc.) **2** *or* ~ **in** BELONG : encajar **3 this dress doesn't** ~ : este vestido no me queda bien — ~ *n* **it's a good fit** : me queda bien — **fitful** *adj* : irregular — **fitness** *n* **1** HEALTH : salud *f* **2** SUITABILITY : idoneidad *f* — **fitting** *adj* : apropiado

five *n* : cinco *m* — ~ *adj* : cinco — **five hundred** *n* : quinientos *m* — ~ *adj* : quinientos

fix *vt* **1** ATTACH : fijar, sujetar **2** REPAIR : ar-

reglar **3** PREPARE : preparar — ~ *n*
PREDICAMENT : aprieto *m*, apuro *m* — **fixed**
adj : fijo — **fixture** *n* : instalación *f*
fizz *vi* : burbujear — ~ *n* : efervescencia *f*
fizzle *vi* **-zled; -zling** *or* ~ **out** : quedar en
nada
flabbergasted *adj* : estupefacto, pasmado
flabby *adj* **-bier; -est** : fofo
flaccid *adj* : fláccido
flag[1] *vi* WEAKEN : flaquear
flag[2] *n* : bandera *f* — ~ *vt* **flagged; flag-**
ging *or* ~ **down** : hacer señales de parada
a — **flagpole** *n* : asta *f*
flagrant *adj* : flagrante
flair *n* : don *m*, facilidad *f*
flake *n* : copo *m* (de nieve), escama *f* (de pintura, de la piel) — ~ *vi* **flaked; flaking**
: pelarse
flamboyant *adj* : extravagante
flame *n* **1** : llama *f* **2 burst into** ~**s** : estallar en llamas **3 go up in** ~**s** : incendiarse
flamingo *n*, *pl* **-gos** : flamenco *m*
flammable *adj* : inflamable
flank *n* : ijado *m* (de un animal), flanco *m*
(militar) — ~ *vt* : flanquear
flannel *n* : franela *f*
flap *n* : solapa *f* (de un sobre, un libro, etc.),
tapa *f* (de un recipiente) — ~ *v* **flapped;**
flapping *vi* : agitarse — *vt* : batir, agitar
flapjack → **pancake**
flare *vi* **flared; flaring 1** ~ **up** BLAZE
: llamear **2** ~ **up** EXPLODE, ERUPT : estallar, explotar — ~ *n* **1** BLAZE : llamarada *f*
2 SIGNAL : (luz *f* de) bengala *f*
flash *vi* **1** : brillar, destellar **2** ~ **past**
: pasar como un rayo — *vt* **1** : dirigir (una
luz) **2** SHOW : mostrar **3** ~ **a smile** : sonreír — ~ *n* **1** : destello *m* **2** ~ **of light-**
ning : relámpago *m* **3 in a** ~ : de repente
— **flashlight** *n* : linterna *f* — **flashy** *adj*
flashier; -est : ostentoso
flask *n* : frasco *m*
flat *adj* **flatter; flattest 1** LEVEL : plano,
llano **2** DOWNRIGHT : categórico **3** FIXED
: fijo **4** MONOTONOUS : monótono **5** : bemol
(en la música) **6** ~ **tire** : neumático *m*
desinflado — ~ *n* **1** : bemol *m* (en la
música) **2** *Brit* APARTMENT : apartamento
m, departamento *m* *Lat* **3** PUNCTURE : pinchazo *m* — ~ *adv* **1** ~ **broke** : pelado **2 in**
one hour ~ : en una hora justa — **flatly** *adv*
: categóricamente — **flat–out** *adj* **1**
: frenético **2** DOWNRIGHT : categórico —
flatten *vt* **1** LEVEL : aplanar, allanar **2**
KNOCK DOWN : arrasar
flatter *vt* **1** : halagar **2** BECOME : favorecer
— **flatterer** *n* : adulador *m*, -dora *f* — **flatter-**
ing *adj* **1** : halagador **2** BECOMING : favorecedor — **flattery** *n*, *pl* **-ries** : halagos *mpl*

flaunt *vt* : hacer alarde de
flavor *or Brit* **flavour** *n* : gusto *m*, sabor *m* —
~ *vt* : sazonar — **flavorful** *or Brit* **flavour-**
ful *adj* : sabroso — **flavoring** *or Brit*
flavouring *n* : condimento *m*, sazón *f*
flaw *n* : defecto *m* — **flawless** *adj* : perfecto
flax *n* : lino *m*
flea *n* : pulga *f*
fleck *n* **1** PARTICLE : mota *f* **2** SPOT : pinta *f*
flee *v* **fled; fleeing** *vi* : huir — *vt* : huir de
fleece *n* : vellón *m* — ~ *vt* **fleeced; fleec-**
ing 1 SHEAR : esquilar **2** DEFRAUD : desplumar
fleet *n* : flota *f*
fleeting *adj* : fugaz
Flemish *adj* : flamenco
flesh *n* **1** : carne *f* **2** PULP : pulpa *f* **3 in the**
~ : en persona — **fleshy** *adj* **fleshier; -est**
1 : gordo **2** PULPY : carnoso
flew → **fly**
flex *vt* : flexionar — **flexibility** *n*, *pl* **-ties**
: flexibilidad *f* — **flexible** *adj* : flexible
flick *n* : golpecito *m* — ~ *vt* : dar un
golpecito a — *vi* ~ **through** : hojear
flicker *vi* : parpadear — ~ *n* **1** : parpadeo *m*
2 a ~ **of hope** : un rayo de esperanza
flier *n* **1** AVIATOR : aviador *m*, -dora *f* **2** *or*
flyer LEAFLET : folleto *m*, volante *m* *Lat*
flight[1] *n* **1** : vuelo *m* **2** TRAJECTORY : trayectoria *f* **3** ~ **of stairs** : tramo *m*
flight[2] *n* ESCAPE : huida *f*
flimsy *adj* **flimsier; -est 1** LIGHT : ligero **2**
SHAKY : poco sólido **3 a** ~ **excuse** : una
excusa floja
flinch *vi* ~ **from** : encogerse ante
fling *vt* **flung; flinging 1** : arrojar **2** ~
open : abrir de un golpe — ~ *n* **1** AFFAIR
: aventura *f* **2 have a** ~ **at** : intentar
flint *n* : pedernal *m*
flip *v* **flipped; flipping** *vt* **1** *or* ~ **over** : dar
la vuelta a **2** ~ **a coin** : echarlo a cara o
cruz — *vi* **1** *or* ~ **over** : volcarse **2** ~
through : hojear — ~ *n* SOMERSAULT
: voltereta *f*
flippant *adj* : ligero, frívolo
flipper *n* : aleta *f*
flirt *vi* : coquetear — ~ *n* : coqueto *m*, -ta *f*
— **flirtatious** *adj* : coqueto
flit *vi* **flitted; flitting** : revolotear
float *n* **1** : flotador *m* **2** : carroza *f* (en un
desfile) — ~ *vi* : flotar — *vt* : hacer flotar
flock *n* : rebaño *m* (de ovejas), bandada *f* (de
pájaros) — ~ *vi* : congregarse
flog *vt* **flogged; flogging** : azotar
flood *n* **1** : inundación *f* **2** : torrente *m* (de
palabras, de lágrimas, etc.) — ~ *vt* : inun-
dar — **floodlight** *n* : foco *m*
floor *n* **1** : suelo *m*, piso *m* *Lat* **2** STORY
: piso *m* **3 dance** ~ : pista *f* de baile **4**

ground ~ : planta *f* baja — ~ *vt* **1** KNOCK DOWN : derribar **2** NONPLUS : desconcertar — **floorboard** *n* : tabla *f* del suelo
flop *vi* **flopped; flopping 1** FLAP : agitarse **2** COLLAPSE : dejarse caer **3** FAIL : fracasar — ~ *n* FAILURE : fracaso *m* — **floppy** *adj* **-pier; -est** : flojo, flexible — **floppy disk** *n* : diskette *m*, disquete *m*
flora *n* : flora *f* — **floral** *adj* : floral — **florid** *adj* **1** FLOWERY : florido **2** RUDDY : rojizo — **florist** *n* : florista *mf*
floss *n* → **dental floss**
flounder[1] *n, pl* **flounder** *or* **flounders** : platija *f*
flounder[2] *vi* **1** *or* ~ **about** : resbalarse, revolcarse **2** : titubear (en un discurso)
flour *n* : harina *f*
flourish *vi* : florecer — *vt* BRANDISH : blandir — ~ *n* : floritura *f* — **flourishing** *adj* : floreciente
flout *vt* : desacatar, burlarse de
flow *vi* : fluir, correr — ~ *n* **1** : flujo *m*, circulación *f* **2** : corriente *f* (de información, etc.)
flower *n* : flor *f* — ~ *vi* : florecer — **flowered** *adj* : floreado — **flowerpot** *n* : maceta *f* — **flowery** *adj* : florido
flown → **fly**
flu *n* : gripe *f*
fluctuate *vi* **-ated; -ating** : fluctuar — **fluctuation** *n* : fluctuación *f*
fluency *n* : fluidez *f* — **fluent** *adj* **1** : fluido **2 be** ~ **in** : hablar con fluidez — **fluently** *adv* : con fluidez
fluff *n* : pelusa *f* — **fluffy** *adj* **fluffier; -est** : de pelusa, velloso
fluid *adj* : fluido — ~ *n* : fluido *m*
flung → **fling**
flunk *vt* : reprobar *Lat*, suspender *Spain* — *vi* : ser reprobado *Lat*, suspender *Spain*
fluorescence *n* : fluorescencia *f* — **fluorescent** *adj* : fluorescente
flurry *n, pl* **-ries 1** GUST : ráfaga *f* **2** *or* **snow** ~ : nevisca *f* **3** ~ **of questions** : aluvión *m* de preguntas
flush *vi* BLUSH : ruborizarse, sonrojarse — *vt* ~ **the toilet** : tirar de la cadena, jalarle a la cadena *Lat* — ~ *n* BLUSH : rubor *m*, sonrojo *m* — ~ *adj* ~ **with** : a nivel con, a ras de — ~ *adv* : al mismo nivel, a ras
fluster *vt* : poner nervioso
flute *n* : flauta *f*
flutter *vi* **1** FLIT : revolotear **2** WAVE : ondear **3** *or* ~ **about** : ir y venir — ~ *n* **1** : revoloteo *m* (de alas) **2** STIR : revuelo *m*
flux *n* **be in a state of** ~ : cambiar continuamente
fly[1] *v* **flew; flown; flying** *vi* **1** : volar **2** TRAVEL : ir en avión **3** WAVE : ondear **4**

RUSH : correr **5** ~ **by** : pasar volando — *vt* **1** PILOT : pilotar **2** : hacer volar (una cometa), enarbolar (una bandera) — ~ *n, pl* **flies** : braqueta *f* (de un pantalón)
fly[2] *n, pl* **flies** : mosca *f* (insecto)
flyer → **flier**
flying saucer *n* : platillo *m* volador *Lat*, platillo *m* volante *Spain*
flyswatter *n* : matamoscas *m*
foal *n* : potro *m*, -tra *f*
foam *n* : espuma *f* — ~ *vi* : hacer espuma — **foamy** *adj* **foamier; -est** : espumoso
focus *n, pl* **-ci 1** : foco *m* **2 be in** ~ : estar enfocado **3** ~ **of attention** : centro *m* de atención — ~ *v* **-cused** *or* **-cussed; -cusing** *or* **-cussing** *vt* **1** : enfocar **2** : centrar (la atención, etc.) — *vi* ~ **on** : enfocar (con los ojos), concentrarse en (con la mente)
fodder *n* : forraje *m*
foe *n* : enemigo *m*, -ga *f*
fog *n* : niebla *f* — ~ *v* **fogged; fogging** *vt* : empañar — *vi or* ~ **up** : empañarse — **foggy** *adj* **foggier; -est** : nebuloso — **foghorn** *n* : sirena *f* de niebla
foil[1] *vt* : frustrar
foil[2] *n or* **aluminum** ~ : papel *m* de aluminio
fold[1] *n* **1** : redil *m* (para ovejas) **2 return to the** ~ : volver al redil
fold[2] *vt* **1** : doblar, plegar **2** ~ **one's arms** : cruzar los brazos — *vi* **1** *or* ~ **up** : doblarse, plegarse **2** FAIL : fracasar — ~ *n* : pliegue *m* — **folder** *n* : carpeta *f*
foliage *n* : follaje *m*
folk *n, pl* **folk** *or* **folks 1** : gente *f* **2** ~**s** *npl* PARENTS : padres *mpl* — ~ *adj* **1** : popular **2** ~ **dance** : danza *f* folklórica — **folklore** *n* : folklore *m*
follow *vt* **1** : seguir **2** UNDERSTAND : entender **3** ~ **up** : seguir — *vi* **1** : seguir **2** UNDERSTAND : entender **3** ~ **up on** : seguir con — **follower** *n* : seguidor *m*, -dora *f* — **following** *adj* : siguiente — ~ *n* : seguidores *mpl* — ~ *prep* : después de
folly *n, pl* **-lies** : locura *f*
fond *adj* **1** : cariñoso **2 be** ~ **of sth** : ser aficionado a algo **3 be** ~ **of s.o.** : tener cariño a algn
fondle *vt* **-dled; -dling** : acariciar
fondness *n* **1** LOVE : cariño *m* **2** LIKING : afición *f*
food *n* : comida *f*, alimento *m* — **foodstuffs** *npl* : comestibles *mpl*
fool *n* **1** : idiota *mf* **2** JESTER : bufón *m*, -fona *f* — ~ *vi* **1** JOKE : bromear **2** ~ **around** : perder el tiempo — *vt* TRICK : engañar — **foolhardy** *adj* : temerario — **foolish** *adj* : tonto — **foolishness** *n* : tontería *f* — **foolproof** *adj* : infalible

foot *n, pl* **feet** : pie *m* — **footage** *n* : secuencias *fpl* (cinemáticas) — **football** *n* : fútbol *m* americano — **footbridge** *n* : pasarela *f*, puente *m* peatonal — **foothills** *npl* : estribaciones *fpl* — **foothold** *n* : punto *m* de apoyo — **footing** *n* **1** BALANCE : equilibrio *m* **2 on equal** ~ : en igualdad — **footlights** *npl* : candilejas *fpl* — **footnote** *n* : nota *f* al pie de la página — **footpath** *n* : sendero *m* — **footprint** *n* : huella *f* — **footstep** *n* : paso *m* — **footstool** *n* : escabel *m* — **footwear** *n* : calzado *m*

for *prep* (*indicating purpose, etc.*) : para **2** (*indicating motivation, etc.*) : por **3** (*indicating duration*) : durante **4 we walked** ~ **3 miles** : andamos 3 millas **5** AS FOR : con respecto a — ~ *conj* : puesto que, porque

forage *n* : forraje *m* — ~ *vi* **-aged; -aging 1** : forrajear **2** ~ **for** : buscar

foray *n* : incursión *f*

forbid *vt* **-bade** *or* **-bad; -bidden; -bidding** : prohibir — **forbidding** *adj* : intimidante, severo

force *n* **1** : fuerza *f* **2 by** ~ : por la fuerza **3 in** ~ : en vigor, en vigencia **4 armed** ~**s** : fuerzas *fpl* armadas — ~ *vt* **forced; forcing 1** : forzar **2** OBLIGATE : obligar — **forced** *adj* : forzado, forzoso — **forceful** *adj* : fuerte, enérgico

forceps *ns & pl* : fórceps *m*

forcibly *adv* : por la fuerza

ford *n* : vado *m* — ~ *vt* : vadear

fore *n* **come to the** ~ : empezar a destacarse

forearm *n* : antebrazo *m*

foreboding *n* : premonición *f*, presentimiento *m*

forecast *vt* **-cast; -casting** : predecir, pronosticar — ~ *n* : predicción *f*, pronóstico *m*

forefathers *n* : antepasados *mpl*

forefinger *n* : índice *m*, dedo *m* índice

forefront *n* **at/in the** ~ : a la vanguardia

forego → **forgo**

foregone *adj* ~ **conclusion** : resultado *m* inevitable

foreground *n* : primer plano *m*

forehead *n* : frente *f*

foreign *adj* **1** : extranjero **2** ~ **trade** : comercio *m* exterior — **foreigner** *n* : extranjero *m*, -ra *f*

foreman *n, pl* **-men** : capataz *mf*

foremost *adj* : principal — ~ *adv* **first and** ~ : ante todo

forensic *adj* : forense

forerunner *n* : precursor *m*, -sora *f*

foresee *vt* **-saw; -seen; -seeing** : prever — **foreseeable** *adj* : previsible

foreshadow *vt* : presagiar

foresight *n* : previsión *f*

forest *n* : bosque *m* — **forestry** *n* : silvicultura *f*

foretaste *n* : anticipo *m*

foretell *vt* **-told; -telling** : predecir

forethought *n* : reflexión *f* previa

forever *adv* **1** ETERNALLY : para siempre **2** CONTINUALLY : siempre, constantemente

forewarn *vt* : advertir, prevenir

foreword *n* : prólogo *m*

forfeit *n* **1** PENALTY : pena *f* **2** : prenda *f* (en un juego) — ~ *vt* : perder

forge *n* : forja *f* — ~ *v* **forged; forging 1** : forjar (metal, etc.) **2** COUNTERFEIT : falsificar — *vi* ~ **ahead** : avanzar, seguir adelante — **forger** *n* : falsificador *m*, -dora *f* — **forgery** *n, pl* **-eries** : falsificación *f*

forget *v* **-got; -gotten** *or* **-got; -getting** *vt* : olvidar, olvidarse de — *vi* **1** : olvidarse **2 I forgot** : se me olvidó — **forgetful** *adj* : olvidadizo

forgive *vt* **-gave; -given; -giving** : perdonar — **forgiveness** *n* : perdón *m*

forgo *or* **forego** *vt* **-went; -gone; -going** : privarse de, renunciar a

fork *n* **1** : tenedor *m* **2** PITCHFORK : horca *f* **3** : bifurcación *f* (de un camino, etc.) — *vi* : ramificarse, bifurcarse — *vt* ~ **over** : desembolsar

forlorn *adj* : triste

form *n* **1** : forma *f* **2** DOCUMENT : formulario *m* **3** KIND : tipo *m* — ~ *vt* **1** : formar **2** ~ **a habit** : adquirir un hábito — *vi* : formarse

formal *adj* : formal — ~ *n* **1** BALL : baile *m* (formal) **2** *or* ~ **dress** : traje *m* de etiqueta — **formality** *n, pl* **-ties** : formalidad *f*

format *n* : formato *m* — ~ *vt* **-matted; -matting** : formatear

formation *n* **1** : formación *f* **2** SHAPE : forma *f*

former *adj* **1** PREVIOUS : antiguo, anterior **2** : primero (de dos) — **formerly** *adv* : anteriormente, antes

formidable *adj* : formidable

formula *n, pl* **-las** *or* **-lae 1** : fórmula *f* **2** *or* **baby** ~ : preparado *m* para biberón

forsake *vt* **-sook; -saken; -saking** : abandonar

fort *n* : fuerte *m*

forth *adv* **1 and so** ~ : etcétera **2 back and** ~ → **back 3 from this day** ~ : de hoy en adelante — **forthcoming** *adj* **1** COMING : próximo **2** OPEN : comunicativo — **forthright** *adj* : directo, franco

fortieth *adj* : cuadragésimo — ~ *n* **1** : cuadragésimo *m*, -ma *f* (en una serie) **2** : cuarentavo *m*, cuarentava parte *f*

fortify *vt* **-fied; -fying** : fortificar — **fortification** *n* : fortificación *f*
fortitude *n* : fortaleza *f*
fortnight *n* : quince días *mpl*, quincena *f*
fortress *n* : fortaleza *f*
fortunate *adj* : afortunado — **fortunately** *adv* : afortunadamente — **fortune** *n* : fortuna *f* — **fortune–teller** *n* : adivino *m*, -na *f*
forty *n*, *pl* **forties** : cuarenta *m* — ~ *adj* : cuarenta
forum *n*, *pl* **-rums** : foro *m*
forward *adj* **1** : hacia adelante (en dirección), delantero (en posición) **2** BRASH : descarado — ~ *adv* **1** : (hacia) adelante **2 from this day** ~ : de aquí en adelante — ~ *vt* : remitir, enviar — ~ *n* : delantero *m*, -ra *f* (en deportes) — **forwards** *adv* → **forward**
fossil *n* : fósil *m*
foster *adj* : adoptivo — ~ *vt* : promover, fomentar
fought → **fight**
foul *adj* **1** REPULSIVE : asqueroso **2** ~ **language** : palabrotas *fpl* **3** ~ **play** : actos *mpl* criminales **4** ~ **weather** : mal tiempo *m* — ~ *n* : falta *f* (en deportes) — ~ *vi* : cometer faltas (en deportes) — ~ *vt* : ensuciar
found¹ → **find**
found² *vt* : fundar, establecer — **foundation** *n* **1** fundación *f* **2** BASIS : fundamento *m* **3** : cimientos *mpl* (de un edificio)
founder¹ *n* : fundador *m*, -dora *f*
founder² *vi* SINK : hundirse
fountain *n* : fuente *f*
four *n* : cuatro *m* — ~ *adj* : cuatro — **fourfold** *adj* : cuádruple — **four hundred** *adj* : cuatrocientos — ~ *n* : cuatrocientos *m*
fourteen *n* : catorce *m* — ~ *adj* : catorce — **fourteenth** *adj* : decimocuarto — ~ *n* **1** : decimocuarto *m*, -ta *f* (en una serie) **2** : catorceavo *m*, catorceava parte *f*
fourth *n* **1** : cuarto *m*, -ta *f* (en una serie) **2** : cuarto *m*, cuarta parte *f* — ~ *adj* : cuarto
fowl *n*, *pl* **fowl** *or* **fowls** : ave *f*
fox *n*, *pl* **foxes** : zorro *m*, -ra *f* — ~ *vt* TRICK : engañar — **foxy** *adj* **foxier; -est** SHREWD : astuto
foyer *n* : vestíbulo *m*
fraction *n* : fracción *f*
fracture *n* : fractura *f* — ~ *vt* **-tured; -turing** : fracturar
fragile *adj* : frágil
fragment *n* : fragmento *m*
fragrant *adj* : fragante — **fragrance** *n* : fragancia *f*, aroma *m*
frail *adj* : débil, delicado
frame *vt* **framed; framing 1** ENCLOSE : enmarcar **2** COMPOSE, DRAFT : formular **3** INCRIMINATE : incriminar — ~ *n* **1** : ar-

mazón *mf* (de un edificio, etc.) **2** : marco *m* (de un cuadro, una puerta, etc.) **3** *or* ~**s** *npl* : montura *f* (para anteojos) **4** ~ **of mind** : estado *m* de ánimo — **framework** *n* : armazón *f*
franc *n* : franco *m*
frank *adj* : franco — **frankly** *adv* : francamente — **frankness** *n* : franqueza *f*
frantic *adj* : frenético
fraternal *adj* : fraterno, fraternal — **fraternity** *n*, *pl* **-ties** : fraternidad *f* — **fraternize** *vi* **-nized; -nizing** : confraternizar
fraud *n* **1** DECEIT : fraude *m* **2** IMPOSTOR : impostor *m*, -tora *f* — **fraudulent** *adj* : fraudulento
fraught *adj* ~ **with** : lleno de, cargado de
fray¹ *n* **1 join the** ~ : salir a la palestra **2 return to the** ~ : volver a la carga
fray² *vt* : crispar (los nervios) — *vi* : deshilacharse
freak *n* **1** ODDITY : fenómeno *m* **2** ENTHUSIAST : entusiasta *mf* — **freakish** *adj* : anormal
freckle *n* : peca *f*
free *adj* **freer; freest 1** : libre **2** *or* ~ **of charge** : gratuito, gratis **3** LOOSE : suelto — ~ *vt* **freed; freeing 1** : liberar, poner en libertad **2** RELEASE, UNFASTEN : soltar, desatar — ~ *adv* *or* **for** ~ : gratis — **freedom** *n* : libertad *f* — **freelance** *adj* : por cuenta propia — **freely** *adv* **1** : libremente **2** LAVISHLY : con generosidad — **freeway** *n* : autopista *f* — **free will** *n* **1** : libre albedrío *m* **2 of one's own** ~ : por su propia voluntad
freeze *v* **froze; frozen; freezing** *vi* **1** : congelarse, helarse **2** STOP : quedarse inmóvil — ~ *vt* : helar (agua, etc.), congelar (alimentos, precios, etc.) — **freeze–dry** *vt* **-dried; -drying** : liofilizar — **freezer** *n* : congelador *m* — **freezing** *adj* **1** CHILLY : helado **2 it's freezing!** : ¡hace un frío espantoso!
freight *n* **1** SHIPPING : porte *m*, flete *m* *Lat* **2** CARGO : carga *f*
French *adj* : francés — ~ *n* **1** : francés *m* (idioma) **2 the** ~ *npl* : los franceses — **Frenchman** *n* : francés *m* — **Frenchwoman** *n* : francesa *f* — **french fries** *npl* : papas *fpl* fritas
frenetic *adj* : frenético
frenzy *n*, *pl* **-zies** : frenesí *m* — **frenzied** *adj* : frenético
frequent *vt* : frecuentar — ~ *adj* : frecuente — **frequency** *n*, *pl* **-cies** : frecuencia *f* — **frequently** *adv* : a menudo, frecuentemente
fresco *n*, *pl* **-coes** : fresco *m*
fresh *adj* **1** : fresco **2** IMPUDENT : descarado **3** CLEAN : limpio **4** NEW : nuevo **5** ~ **water** : agua *m* dulce — **freshen** *vt* : refres-

car — *vi* ~ **up** : arreglarse — **freshly** *adv* : recién — **freshman** *n, pl* **-men** : estudiante *mf* de primer año — **freshness** *n* : frescura *f*
fret *vi* **fretted; fretting** : preocuparse — **fretful** *adj* : nervioso, irritable
friar *n* : fraile *m*
friction *n* : fricción *f*
Friday *n* : viernes *m*
friend *n* : amigo *m*, -ga *f* — **friendliness** *n* : simpatía *f* — **friendly** *adj* **-lier; -est** : simpático, amable — **friendship** *n* : amistad *f*
frigate *n* : fragata *f*
fright *n* : miedo *m*, susto *m* — **frighten** *vt* : asustar, espantar — **frightened** *adj* **1** : asustado, temeroso **2 be** ~ **of** : tener miedo de — **frightening** *adj* : espantoso — **frightful** *adj* : espantoso, terrible
frigid *adj* : frío, glacial
frill *n* **1** RUFFLE : volante *m* **2** LUXURY : lujo *m*
fringe *n* **1** : fleco *m* **2** EDGE : periferia *f*, margen *m* **3** ~ **benefits** : incentivos *mpl*, extras *mpl*
frisk *vt* SEARCH : cachear, registrar — **frisky** *adj* **friskier; -est** : retozón, juguetón
fritter *n* : buñuelo *m* — ~ *vt or* ~ **away** : malgastar (dinero), desperdiciar (tiempo)
frivolous *adj* : frívolo — **frivolity** *n, pl* **-ties** : frivolidad *f*
frizzy *adj* **frizzier; -est** : rizado, crespo
fro *adv* **to and** ~ → **to**
frock *n* : vestido *m*
frog *n* **1** : rana *f* **2 have a** ~ **in one's throat** : tener carraspera
frolic *vi* **-icked; -icking** : retozar
from *prep* **1** : de **2** (*indicating a starting point*) : desde **3** (*indicating a cause*) : de, por **4** ~ **now on** : a partir de ahora
front *n* **1** : parte *f* delantera **2** : delantera *f* (de un vestido, etc.), fachada *f* (de un edificio), frente *m* (militar) **3 cold** ~ : frente *m* frío **4 in** ~ **of** : delante de, adelante de *Lat* — ~ *vi or* ~ **on** : dar a, estar orientado a — ~ *adj* **1** : delantero, de adelante **2 the** ~ **row** : la primera fila
frontier *n* : frontera *f*
frost *n* **1** : helada *f* **2** : escarcha *f* (en una superficie) — ~ *vt* ICE : bañar (pasteles) — **frostbite** *n* : congelación *f* — **frosting** *n* ICING : baño *m* — **frosty** *adj* **frostier; -est** **1** : cubierto de escarcha **2** CHILLY : helado, frío
froth *n, pl* **froths** : espuma *f* — **frothy** *adj* **frothier; -est** : espumoso
frown *vi* **1** : fruncir el ceño, fruncir el entrecejo **2** ~ **at** : mirar con ceño **3** ~ **upon** : desaprobar — ~ *n* : ceño *m* (fruncido)
froze, frozen → **freeze**

frugal *adj* : frugal
fruit *n* **1** : fruta *f* **2** PRODUCT, RESULT : fruto *m* — **fruitcake** *n* : pastel *m* de frutas — **fruitful** *adj* : fructífero — **fruition** *n* **come to** ~ : realizarse — **fruitless** *adj* : infructuoso — **fruity** *adj* **fruitier; -est** : (con sabor) a fruta
frustrate *vt* **-trated; -trating** : frustrar — **frustrating** *adj* : frustrante — **frustration** *n* : frustración *f*
fry *vt* **fried; frying** : freír — ~ *n, pl* **fries 1 small** ~ : gente *f* de poca monta **2 fries** *npl* → **french fries** — **frying pan** *n* : sartén *mf*
fudge *n* : dulce *m* blando de chocolate y leche
fuel *n* : combustible *m* — ~ *vt* **-eled** *or* **-elled; -eling** *or* **-elling 1** : alimentar (un horno), abastecer de combustible (un avión) **2** STIMULATE : estimular
fugitive *n* : fugitivo *m*, -va *f*
fulfill *or* **fulfil** *vt* **-filled; -filling 1** : cumplir con (una obligación), desarrollar (potencial) **2** FILL, MEET : cumplir — **fulfillment** *n* **1** ACCOMPLISHMENT : cumplimiento *m* **2** SATISFACTION : satisfacción *f*
full *adj* **1** FILLED : lleno **2** COMPLETE : completo, detallado **3** : redondo (dícese de la cara), amplio (dícese de ropa) **4 at** ~ **speed** : a toda velocidad **5 in** ~ **bloom** : en plena flor — ~ *adv* **1** DIRECTLY : de lleno **2 know** ~ **well** : saber muy bien — ~ *n* **1 pay in** ~ : pagar en su totalidad **2 to the** ~ : al máximo — **full–fledged** *adj* : hecho y derecho — **fully** *adv* **1** COMPLETELY : completamente **2** AT LEAST : al menos, por lo menos
fumble *vi* **-bled; -bling 1** RUMMAGE : hurgar **2** ~ **with** : manejar con torpeza
fume *vi* **fumed; fuming 1** SMOKE : echar humo, humear **2** RAGE : estar furioso — **fumes** *npl* : gases *mpl*
fumigate *vt* **-gated; -gating** : fumigar
fun *n* **1** AMUSEMENT : diversión *f* **2 have** ~ : divertirse **3 make** ~ **of** : reírse de, burlarse de — ~ *adj* : divertido
function *n* **1** : función *f* **2** GATHERING : recepción *f*, reunión *f* social — ~ *vi* : funcionar — **functional** *adj* : funcional
fund *n* **1** : fondo *m* **2** ~**s** *npl* RESOURCES : fondos *mpl* — ~ *vt* : financiar
fundamental *adj* : fundamental — **fundamentals** *npl* : fundamentos *mpl*
funeral *adj* : funeral, fúnebre — ~ *n* : funeral *m*, funerales *mpl* — **funeral home** *or* **funeral parlor** *n* : funeraria *f*
fungus *n, pl* **fungi** : hongo *m*
funnel *n* **1** : embudo *m* **2** SMOKESTACK : chimenea *f*

funny *adj* **funnier; -est 1 :** divertido, gracioso **2** STRANGE : extraño, raro — **funnies** *npl* : tiras *fpl* cómicas
fur *n* **1 :** pelaje *m*, pelo *m* (de un animal) **2** *or* ~ **coat :** (prenda *f* de) piel *f* — ~ *adj* : de piel
furious *adj* : furioso
furnace *n* : horno *m*
furnish *vt* **1** SUPPLY : proveer **2 :** amueblar (una casa, etc.) — **furnishings** *npl* : muebles *mpl*, mobiliario *m* — **furniture** *n* : muebles *mpl*, mobiliario *m*
furrow *n* : surco *m*
furry *adj* **furrier; -est :** peludo (dícese de un animal), de peluche (dícese de un juguete, etc.)
further *adv* **1** FARTHER : más lejos **2** MOREOVER : además **3** MORE : más — ~ *vt* : promover, fomentar — ~ *adj* **1** FARTHER : más lejano **2** ADDITIONAL : adicional, más **3 until** ~ **notice :** hasta nuevo aviso — **furthermore** *adv* : además — **furthest** → **farthest**
fumble *vi* **-bled; -bling 1** RUMMAGE : hurgar **2** ~ **with :** manejar con torpeza
fume *vi* **fumed; fuming 1** SMOKE : echar humo, humear **2** RAGE : estar furioso — **fumes** *npl* : gases *mpl*
fumigate *vt* **-gated; -gating :** fumigar
fun *n* **1** AMUSEMENT : diversión *f* **2 have** ~ : divertirse **3 make** ~ **of :** reírse de, burlarse de — ~ *adj* : divertido
function *n* **1 :** función *f* **2** GATHERING : recepción *f*, reunión *f* social — ~ *vi* : funcionar — **functional** *adj* : funcional
fund *n* **1 :** fondo *m* **2** ~**s** *npl* RESOURCES : fondos *mpl* — ~ *vt* : financiar
fundamental *adj* : fundamental — **fundamentals** *npl* : fundamentos *mpl*
funeral *adj* : funeral, fúnebre — ~ *n* : funeral *m*, funerales *mpl* — **funeral home** *or* **funeral parlor** *n* : funeraria *f*
fungus *n, pl* **fungi :** hongo *m*
funnel *n* **1 :** embudo *m* **2** SMOKESTACK : chimenea *f*

funny *adj* **funnier; -est 1 :** divertido, gracioso **2** STRANGE : extraño, raro — **funnies** *npl* : tiras *fpl* cómicas
fur *n* **1 :** pelaje *m*, pelo *m* (de un animal) **2** *or* ~ **coat :** (prenda *f* de) piel *f* — ~ *adj* : de piel
furious *adj* : furioso
furnace *n* : horno *m*
furnish *vt* **1** SUPPLY : proveer **2 :** amueblar (una casa, etc.) — **furnishings** *npl* : muebles *mpl*, mobiliario *m* — **furniture** *n* : muebles *mpl*, mobiliario *m*
furrow *n* : surco *m*
furry *adj* **furrier; -est :** peludo (dícese de un animal), de peluche (dícese de un juguete, etc.)
further *adv* **1** FARTHER : más lejos **2** MOREOVER : además **3** MORE : más — ~ *vt* : promover, fomentar — ~ *adj* **1** FARTHER : más lejano **2** ADDITIONAL : adicional, más **3 until** ~ **notice :** hasta nuevo aviso — **furthermore** *adv* : además — **furthest** → **farthest**
furtive *adj* : furtivo
fury *n, pl* **-ries :** furia *f*
fuse[1] *or* **fuze** *n* : mecha *f* (de una bomba, etc.)
fuse[2] *v* **fused; fusing** *vt* **1** MELT : fundir **2** UNITE : fusionar — *vi* : fundirse, fusionarse — ~ *n* **1 :** fusible *m* **2 blow a** ~ : fundir un fusible — **fusion** *n* : fusión *f*
fuss *n* **1 :** jaleo *m*, alboroto *m* **2 make a** ~ : armar un escándalo — ~ *vi* **1** WORRY : preocuparse **2** COMPLAIN : quejarse — **fussy** *adj* **fussier; -est 1** IRRITABLE : irritable **2** ELABORATE : recargado **3** FINICKY : quisquilloso
futile *adj* : inútil, vano — **futility** *n, pl* **-ties :** inutilidad *f*
future *adj* : futuro — ~ *n* : futuro *m*
fuze → **fuse**[1]
fuzz *n* : pelusa *f* — **fuzzy** *adj* **fuzzier; -est 1** FURRY : con pelusa, peludo **2** BLURRY : borroso **3** VAGUE : confuso

G

g *n, pl* **g's** *or* **gs** : g *f*, séptima letra del alfabeto inglés
gab *vi* **gabbed; gabbing** : charlar, cotorrear *fam* — ～ *n* CHATTER : charla *f*
gable *n* : aguilón *m*
gadget *n* : artilugio *m*
gag *v* **gagged; gagging** *vt* : amordazar — *vi* CHOKE : atragantarse — ～ *n* **1** : mordaza *f* **2** JOKE : chiste *m*
gage → **gauge**
gaiety *n, pl* **-eties** : alegría *f* — **gaily** *adv* : alegremente
gain *n* **1** PROFIT : ganancia *f* **2** INCREASE : aumento *m* — *vt* **1** OBTAIN : ganar, adquirir **2** ～ **weight** : aumentar de peso — *vi* **1** PROFIT : beneficiarse **2** : adelantar(se) (dícese de un reloj) — **gainful** *adj* : lucrativo
gait *n* : modo *m* de andar
gala *n* : fiesta *f*
galaxy *n, pl* **-axies** : galaxia *f*
gale *n* **1** : vendaval *f* **2** ～**s of laughter** : carcajadas *fpl*
gall *n* **have the** ～ **to** : tener el descaro de
gallant *adj* **1** BRAVE : valiente **2** CHIVALROUS : galante
gallbladder *n* : vesícula *f* biliar
gallery *n, pl* **-leries** : galería *f*
gallon *n* : galón *m*
gallop *vi* : galopar — ～ *n* : galope *m*
gallows *n, pl* **-lows** *or* **-lowses** : horca *f*
gallstone *n* : cálculo *m* biliar
galore *adj* : en abundancia
galoshes *n* : galochas *fpl*, chanclos *mpl*
galvanize *vt* **-nized; -nizing** : galvanizar
gamble *v* **-bled; -bling** *vi* : jugar — *vt* : jugarse — ～ *n* **1** BET : apuesta *f* **2** RISK : riesga *f* — **gambler** *n* : jugador *m*, -dora *f*
game *n* **1** : juego *m* **2** MATCH : partido *m* **3** *or* ～ **animals** : caza *f* — ～ *adj* READY : listo, dispuesto
gamut *n* : gama *f*
gang *n* : banda *f*, pandilla *f* — ～ *vi* ～ **up on** : unirse contra
gangplank *n* : pasarela *f*
gangrene *n* : gangrena *f*
gangster *n* : gángster *mf*
gangway *n* → **gangplank**
gap *n* **1** OPENING : espacio *m* **2** INTERVAL : intervalo *m* **3** DISPARITY : brecha *f*, distancia *f* **4** DEFICIENCY : laguna *f*
gape *vi* **gaped; gaping 1** OPEN : estar abierto **2** STARE : mirar boquiabierto
garage *n* : garaje *m* — ～ *vt* **-raged; -raging** : dejar en un garaje

garb *n* : vestido *m*
garbage *n* : basura *f* — **garbage can** *n* : cubo *m* de la basura
garble *vt* **-bled; -bling** : tergiversar — **garbled** *adj* : confuso, incomprensible
garden *n* : jardín *m* — ～ *vi* : trabajar en el jardín — **gardener** *n* : jardinero *m*, -ra *f* — **gardening** *n* : jardinería *f*
gargle *vi* **-gled; -gling** : hacer gárgaras
garish *adj* : chillón
garland *n* : guirnalda *f*
garlic *n* : ajo *m*
garment *n* : prenda *f*
garnish *vt* : guarnecer — ～ *n* : adorno *m*, guarnición *f*
garret *n* : buhardilla *f*
garrison *n* : guarnición *f*
garrulous *adj* : charlatán, parlanchín
garter *n* : liga *f*
gas *n, pl* **gases 1** : gas *m* **2** GASOLINE : gasolina *f* — ～ *v* **gassed; gassing** *vt* : asfixiar con gas — *vi* ～ **up** : llenar el tanque con gasolina
gash *n* : tajo *m* — ～ *vt* : hacer un tajo en, cortar
gasket *n* : junta *f*
gasoline *n* : gasolina *f*
gasp *vi* **1** : dar un grito ahogado **2** PANT : jadear — ～ *n* : grito *m* ahogado
gas station *n* : gasolinera *f*
gastric *adj* : gástrico
gastronomy *n* : gastronomía *f*
gate *n* **1** DOOR : puerta *f* **2** BARRIER : barrera *f* — **gateway** *n* : puerta *f*
gather *vt* **1** ASSEMBLE : reunir **2** COLLECT : recoger **3** CONCLUDE : deducir **4** : fruncir (una tela) **5** ～ **speed** : acelerar — *vi* : reunirse (dícese de personas), acumularse (dícese de cosas) — **gathering** *n* : reunión *f*
gaudy *adj* **gaudier; -est** : chillón, llamativo
gauge *n* **1** INDICATOR : indicador *m* **2** CALIBER : calibre *m* — ～ *vt* **gauged; gauging 1** MEASURE : medir **2** ESTIMATE : calcular, evaluar
gaunt *adj* : demacrado, descarnado
gauze *n* : gasa *f*
gave → **give**
gawky *adj* **gawkier; -est** : desgarbado
gay *adj* **1** : alegre **2** HOMOSEXUAL : gay, homosexual
gaze *vi* **gazed; gazing** : mirar (fijamente) — ～ *n* : mirada *f*
gazelle *n* : gacela *f*
gazette *n* : gaceta *f*

gear n **1** EQUIPMENT : equipo m **2** POSSES-SIONS : efectos mpl personales **3** : marcha f (de un vehículo) **4** or ∼ **wheel** : rueda f dentada — ∼ vt : orientar, adaptar — vi ∼ **up** : prepararse — **gearshift** n : palanca f de cambio, palanca f de velocidades Lat

geese → **goose**

gelatin n : gelatina f

gem n : gema f, piedra f preciosa — **gemstone** n : piedra f preciosa

gender n **1** SEX : sexo m **2** : género m (en la gramática)

gene n : gen m, gene m

genealogy n, pl **-gies** : genealogía f

general adj : general — ∼ n **1** : general mf (militar) **2** in ∼ : en general, por lo general — **generalize** v **-ized; -izing** : generalizar — **generally** adv : generalmente, en general — **general practitioner** n : médico m, -ca f de cabecera

generate vt **-ated; -ating** : generar — **generation** n : generación f — **generator** n : generador m

generous adj **1** : generoso **2** AMPLE : abundante — **generosity** n, pl **-ties** : generosidad f

genetic adj : genético — **genetics** n : genética f

genial adj : afable, simpático

genital adj : genital — **genitals** npl : genitales mpl

genius n : genio m

genocide n : genocidio m

genteel adj : refinado

gentle adj **-tler; -tlest 1** MILD : suave, dulce **2** LIGHT : ligero **3** a ∼ **hint** : una indirecta discreta — **gentleman** n, pl **-men 1** MAN : caballero m, señor m **2** a perfect ∼ : un perfecto caballero — **gentleness** n : delicadeza f, ternura f

genuine adj **1** AUTHENTIC : verdadero, auténtico **2** SINCERE : sincero

geography n, pl **-phies** : geografía f — **geographic** or **geographical** adj : geográfico

geology n : geología f — **geologic** or **geological** adj : geológico

geometry n, pl **-tries** : geometría f — **geometric** or **geometrical** adj : geométrico

geranium n : geranio m

geriatric adj : geriátrico — **geriatrics** n : geriatría f

germ n **1** : germen m **2** MICROBE : microbio m

German adj : alemán — ∼ n : alemán m (idioma)

germinate v **-nated; -nating** vi : germinar — vt : hacer germinar

gestation n : gestación f

gesture n : gesto m — ∼ vi **-tured; -turing 1** : hacer gestos **2** ∼ **to** : hacer señas a

get v **got; got** or **gotten; getting** vt **1** OBTAIN : conseguir, obtener **2** RECEIVE : recibir **3** EARN : ganar **4** FETCH : traer **5** CATCH : coger, agarrar Lat **6** UNDERSTAND : entender **7** PREPARE : preparar **8** ∼ **one's hair cut** : cortarse el pelo **9** ∼ **s.o. to do sth** : lograr que uno haga algo **10** **have got** : tener **11** **have got to** : tener que — vi **1** BECOME : ponerse, hacerse **2** GO, MOVE : ir **3** PROGRESS : avanzar **4** ∼ **ahead** : progresar **5** ∼ **at** MEAN : querer decir **6** ∼ **away** : escaparse **7** ∼ **away with** : salir impune de **8** ∼ **back at** : desquitarse con **9** ∼ **by** : arreglárselas **10** ∼ **home** : llegar a casa **11** ∼ **out** : salir **12** ∼ **over** : reponerse de, consolarse de **13** ∼ **together** : reunirse **14** ∼ **up** : levantarse — **getaway** n : fuga f, huida f — **get–together** n : reunión f

geyser n : géiser m

ghastly adj **-lier; -est** : horrible, espantoso

ghetto n, pl **-tos** or **-toes** : gueto m

ghost n : fantasma f, espectro m — **ghostly** adv : fantasmal

giant n : gigante m, -ta f — ∼ adj : gigantesco

gibberish n : galimatías m, jerigonza f

gibe vi **gibed; gibing** ∼ **at** : mofarse de — ∼ n : pulla f, mofa f

giblets npl : menudillos mpl

giddy adj **-dier; -est** : mareado, vertiginoso — **giddiness** n : vértigo m

gift n **1** PRESENT : regalo m **2** TALENT : don m — **gifted** adj : talentoso, de talento

gigantic adj : gigantesco

giggle vi **-gled; -gling** : reírse tontamente — ∼ n : risa f tonta

gild vt **gilded** or **gilt; gilding** : dorar

gill n : agalla f, branquia f

gilt adj : dorado

gimmick n : truco m, ardid m

gin n : ginebra f

ginger n : jengibre m — **ginger ale** n : refresco m de jengibre — **gingerbread** n : pan m de jengibre — **gingerly** adv : con cuidado, cautelosamente

giraffe n : jirafa f

girder n : viga f

girdle n CORSET : faja f

girl n **1** : niña f, muchacha f, chica f — **girlfriend** n : novia f, amiga f

girth n : circunferencia f

gist n **get the** ∼ **of** : comprender lo esencial de

give v **gave; given; giving** vt **1** : dar **2** INDICATE : señalar **3** PRESENT : presentar **4** ∼ **away** : regalar **5** ∼ **back** : devolver **6**

~ out : repartir **7** ~ **up smoking** : dejar de fumar — *vi* **1** YIELD : ceder **2** COLLAPSE : romperse **3** ~ **out** : agotarse **4** ~ **up** : rendirse — ~ *n* : elasticidad *f* — **given** *adj* **1** SPECIFIED : determinado **2** INCLINED : dado, inclinado — **given name** *n* : nombre *m* de pila

glacier *n* : glaciar *m*

glad *adj* **gladder; gladdest 1** : alegre, contento **2 be** ~ : alegrarse **3** ~ **to meet you!** : ¡mucho gusto! — **gladden** *vt* : alegrar — **gladly** *adv* : con mucho gusto — **gladness** *n* : alegría *f*, gozo *m*

glade *n* : claro *m*

glamor *or* **glamour** *n* : atractivo *m*, encanto *m* — **glamorous** *adj* : atractivo

glance *vi* **glanced; glancing 1** ~ **at** : mirar, dar un vistazo a **2** ~ **off** : rebotar en — ~ *n* : mirada *f*, vistazo *m*

gland *n* : glándula *f*

glare *vi* **glared; glaring 1** : brillar, relumbrar **2** ~ **at** : lanzar una mirada feroz a — ~ *n* **1** : luz *f* deslumbrante **2** STARE : mirada *f* feroz — **glaring** *adj* **1** BRIGHT : deslumbrante **2** FLAGRANT : flagrante

glass *n* **1** : vidrio *m*, cristal *m* **2 a** ~ **of milk** : un vaso de leche **3** ~**es** *npl* SPECTACLES : anteojos *mpl*, lentes *fpl* — ~ *adj* : de vidrio — **glassware** *n* : cristalería *f* — **glassy** *adj* **glassier; -est 1** : vítreo **2** ~ **eyes** : ojos *mpl* vidriosos

glaze *vt* **glazed; glazing 1** : poner vidrios a (una ventana, etc.) **2** : vidriar (cerámica) **3** ICE : glasear — ~ *n* **1** : vidriado *m*, barniz *m* (de cerámica) **2** ICING : glaseado *m*

gleam *n* **1** : destello *m* **2 a** ~ **of hope** : un rayo de esperanza — ~ *vi* : destellar, relucir

glee *n* : alegría *f* — **gleeful** *adj* : lleno de alegría

glib *adj* **glibber; glibbest 1** : de mucha labia **2 a** ~ **reply** : una respuesta simplista — **glibly** *adv* : con mucha labia

glide *vi* **glided; gliding** : deslizarse (en una superficie), planear (en el aire) — **glider** *n* : planeador *m*

glimmer *vi* : brillar con luz trémula — ~ *n* : luz *f* trémula, luz *f* tenue

glimpse *vt* **glimpsed; glimpsing** : vislumbrar — ~ *n* : vislumbre *f*

glint *vi* : destellar — ~ *n* : destello *m*

glisten *vi* : brillar

glitter *vi* : relucir, brillar

gloat *vi* ~ **over** : regodearse con

globe *n* : globo *m* — **global** *adj* : global, mundial

gloom *n* **1** DARKNESS : oscuridad *f* **2** SADNESS : tristeza *f* — **gloomy** *adj* **gloomier; -est 1** DARK : sombrío, tenebroso **2** DIS-

MAL : deprimente, lúgubre **3** PESSIMISTIC : pesimista

glory *n*, *pl* **-ries** : gloria *f* — **glorify** *vt* **-fied; -fying** : glorificar — **glorious** *adj* : glorioso, espléndido

gloss *n* : lustre *m*, brillo *m* — ~ *vt* ~ **over** : minimizar (la importancia de algo)

glossary *n*, *pl* **-ries** : glosario *m*

glossy *adj* **glossier; -est** : lustroso, brillante

glove *n* : guante *m*

glow *vi* **1** : brillar, resplandecer **2** ~ **with health** : rebosar de salud — ~ *n* : resplandor *m*, brillo *m*

glue *n* : pegamento *m*, cola *f* — ~ *vt* **glued; gluing** *or* **glueing** : pegar

glum *adj* **glummer; glummest** : sombrío, triste

glut *n* : superabundancia *f*, exceso *m*

glutton *n* : glotón *m*, -tona *f* — **gluttonous** *adj* : glotón — **gluttony** *n*, *pl* **-tonies** : glotonería *f*

gnarled *adj* : nudoso

gnash *vt* ~ **one's teeth** : hacer rechinar los dientes

gnat *n* : jején *m*

gnaw *vt* : roer

go *v* **went; gone; going; goes** *vi* **1** : ir **2** LEAVE : irse, salir **3** EXTEND : ir, extenderse **4** SELL : venderse **5** FUNCTION : funcionar, marchar **6** DISAPPEAR : desaparecer **7** ~ **back on one's word** : faltar a su palabra **8** ~ **crazy** : volverse loco **9** ~ **for** LIKE : gustar **10** ~ **off** EXPLODE : estallar **11** ~ **with** MATCH : armonizar con **12** ~ **without** : pasar sin — *v aux* **be going to** : ir a — ~ *n*, *pl* **goes 1 be on the** ~ : no parar **2 have a** ~ **at** : intentar

goad *vt* : aguijonear (un animal), incitar (a una persona)

goal *n* **1** AIM : meta *m*, objetivo *m* **2** : gol *m* (en deportes) — **goalkeeper** *or* **goalie** *n* : portero *m*, -ra *f*; arquero *m*, -ra *f*

goat *n* : cabra *f*

goatee *n* : barbita *f* de chivo

gobble *vt* **-bled; -bling** *or* ~ **up** : engullir

goblet *n* : copa *f*

goblin *n* : duende *m*

god *n* **1** : dios *m* **2 God** : Dios *m* — **goddess** *n* : diosa *f* — **godchild** *n*, *pl* **-children** : ahijado *m*, -da *f* — **godfather** *n* : padrino *m* — **godmother** *n* : madrina *f* — **godparents** *npl* : padrinos *mpl* — **godsend** *n* : bendición *f* (del cielo)

goes → **go**

goggles *npl* : gafas *fpl* (protectoras), anteojos *mpl*

goings–on *npl* : sucesos *mpl*

gold *n* : oro *m* — **golden** *adj* **1** : (hecho) de oro **2** : dorado, de color oro — **goldfish** *n*

: pez *m* de colores — **goldsmith** *n* : orfebre *mf*

golf *n* : golf *m* — ~ *vi* : jugar (al) golf — **golf ball** *n* : pelota *f* de golf — **golf course** *n* : campo *m* de golf — **golfer** *n* : golfista *mf*

gone *adj* **1** : ido, pasado **2** DEAD : muerto **3** LOST : desaparecido

good *adj* **better; best 1** : bueno **2** KIND : amable **3** ~ **afternoon (evening)** : buenas tardes **4 be** ~ **at** : tener facilidad para **5 feel** ~ : sentirse bien **6** ~ **for a cold** : beneficioso para los resfriados **7 have a** ~ **time** : divertirse **8** ~ **morning** : buenos días **9** ~ **night** : buenas noches — ~ *n* **1** : bien *m* **2** GOODNESS : bondad *f* **3** ~**s** *npl* PROPERTY : bienes *mpl* **4** ~**s** *npl* WARES : mercancías *fpl*, mercaderías *fpl* **5 for** ~ : para siempre — ~ *adv* : bien — **good–bye** *or* **good–by** *n* : adiós *m* — **Good Friday** *n* : Viernes *m* Santo — **good–looking** *adj* : bello, guapo — **goodness** *n* **1** : bondad *f* **2 thank** ~**!** : ¡gracias a Dios!, ¡menos mal! — **goodwill** *n* : buena voluntad *f* — **goody** *n, pl* **goodies** : golosina *f*

gooey *adj* **gooier; gooiest** : pegajoso

goof *n* : pifia *f fam* — ~ *vi* **1** *or* ~ **up** : cometer un error **2** ~ **around** : hacer tonterías

goose *n, pl* **geese** : ganso *m*, -sa *f*; oca *f* — **goose bumps** *or* **goose pimples** *npl* : carne *f* de gallina

gopher *n* : taltuza *f*

gore[1] *n* BLOOD : sangre *f*

gore[2] *vt* **gored; goring** : cornear

gorge *n* RAVINE : cañon *m* — ~ *vt* **gorged; gorging** ~ **oneself** : hartarse

gorgeous *adj* : magnífico, espléndido

gorilla *n* : gorila *m*

gory *adj* **gorier; -est** : sangriento

gospel *n* **1** : evangelio *m* **2 the Gospel** : el Evangelio

gossip *n* **1** : chismoso *m*, -sa *f* (persona) **2** RUMOR : chisme *m* — ~ *vi* : chismear, contar chismes — **gossipy** *adj* : chismoso

got → **get**

Gothic *adj* : gótico

gotten → **get**

gourmet *n* : gastrónomo *m*, -ma *f*

gout *n* : gota *f*

govern *v* : gobernar — **governess** *n* : institutriz *f* — **government** *n* : gobierno *m* — **governor** *n* : gobernador *m*, -dora *f*

gown *n* **1** : vestido *m* **2** : toga *f* (de magistrados, etc.)

grab *v* **grabbed; grabbing** *vt* : agarrar, arrebatar

grace *n* **1** : gracia *f* **2 say** ~ : bendecir la mesa — ~ *vt* **graced; gracing 1** HONOR

: honrar **2** ADORN : adornar — **graceful** *adj* : lleno de gracia, grácil — **gracious** *adj* : cortés, gentil

grade *n* **1** QUALITY : calidad *f* **2** RANK : grado *m*, rango *m* (militar) **3** YEAR : grado *m*, año *m* (a la escuela) **4** MARK : nota *f* **5** SLOPE : cuesta *f* — ~ *vt* **graded; grading 1** CLASSIFY : clasificar **2** MARK : calificar (exámenes, etc.) — **grade school** → **elementary school**

gradual *adj* : gradual — **gradually** *adv* : gradualmente, poco a poco

graduate *n* : licenciado *m*, -da *f* (de la universidad), bachiller *mf* (de la escuela secondaria) — ~ *v* **-ated; -ating** *vi* : graduarse, licenciarse — *vt* CALIBRATE : graduar — **graduation** *n* : graduación *f*

graffiti *npl* : graffiti *mpl*

graft *n* : injerto *m* — ~ *vt* : injertar

grain *n* **1** : grano *m* **2** CEREALS : cereales *mpl* **3** : veta *f*, vena *f* (de madera)

gram *n* : gramo *m*

grammar *n* : gramática *f* — **grammar school** → **elementary school**

grand *adj* **1** : magnífico, espléndido **2** FABULOUS, GREAT : fabuloso, estupendo — **grandchild** *n, pl* **-children** : nieto *m*, -ta *f* — **granddaughter** *n* : nieta *f* — **grandeur** *n* : grandiosidad *f* — **grandfather** *n* : abuelo *m* — **grandiose** *adj* : grandioso — **grandmother** *n* : abuela *f* — **grandparents** *npl* : abuelos *mpl* — **grandson** *n* : nieto *m* — **grandstand** *n* : tribuna *f*

granite *n* : granito *m*

grant *vt* **1** : conceder **2** ADMIT : reconocer, admitir **3 take for granted** : dar (algo) por sentado — ~ *n* **1** SUBSIDY : subvención *f* **2** SCHOLARSHIP : beca *f*

grape *n* : uva *f*

grapefruit *n* : toronja *f*, pomelo *m*

grapevine *n* **1** : vid *f*, parra *f* **2 I heard it through the** ~ : me lo dijo un pajarito *fam*

graph *n* : gráfica *f*, gráfico *m* — **graphic** *adj* : gráfico

grapple *vi* **-pled; -pling** ~ **with** : forcejear con (una persona), luchar con (un problema)

grasp *vt* **1** : agarrar **2** UNDERSTAND : comprender, captar — ~ *n* **1** : agarre *m* **2** UNDERSTANDING : comprensión *f* **3** REACH : alcance *m*

grass *n* **1** : hierba *f* (planta) **2** LAWN : césped *m*, pasto *m* *Lat* — **grasshopper** *n* : saltamontes *m* — **grassy** *adj* **grassier; -est** : cubierto de hierba

grate[1] *v* **grated; -ing** *vt* **1** : rallar (en cocina) **2** ~ **one's teeth** : hacer rechinar los dientes — *vi* RASP : chirriar

grate[2] *n* GRATING : reja *f*, rejilla *f*

grateful *adj* : agradecido — **gratefully** *adv*
: con agradecimiento — **gratefulness** *n*
: gratitud *f,* agradecimiento *m*
grater *n* : rallador *m*
gratify *vt* -**fied; -fying** 1 PLEASE : complacer
2 SATISFY : satisfacer
grating *n* : reja *f,* rejilla *f*
gratitude *n* : gratitud *f*
gratuitous *adj* : gratuito
grave¹ *n* : tumba *f,* sepultura *f*
grave² *adj* **graver; -est** : grave
gravel *n* : grava *f,* gravilla *f*
gravestone *n* : lápida *f* — **graveyard** *n* : cementerio *m*
gravity *n, pl* -**ties** : gravedad *f*
gravy *n, pl* -**vies** : salsa *f* (preparada con jugo de carne)
gray *adj* 1 : gris 2 ∼ **hair** : pelo *m* canoso — ∼ *n* : gris *m* — ∼ *vi or* **turn** ∼ : encanecer, ponerse gris
graze¹ *vi* **grazed; grazing** : pastar, pacer
graze² *vt* 1 TOUCH : rozar 2 SCRATCH : rasguñarse
grease *n* : grasa *f* — ∼ *vt* **greased; greasing** : engrasar — **greasy** *adj* **greasier; -est** 1 : grasiento 2 OILY : graso, grasoso
great *adj* 1 : grande 2 FANTASTIC : estupendo, fabuloso — **great–grandchild** *n, pl* -**children** : bisnieto *m,* -ta *f* — **great–grandfather** *n* : bisabuelo *m* — **great–grandmother** *n* : bisabuela *f* — **greatly** *adv* 1 MUCH : mucho 2 VERY : muy — **greatness** *n* : grandeza *f*
greed *n* 1 : codicia *f,* avaricia *f* 2 GLUTTONY : glotonería *f* — **greedily** *adv* : con avaricia — **greedy** *adj* **greedier; -est** 1 : codicioso, avaro 2 GLUTTONOUS : glotón
Greek *adj* : griego — ∼ *n* : griego *m* (idioma)
green *adj* 1 : verde 2 INEXPERIENCED : novato — ∼ *n* 1 : verde *m* (color) 2 ∼s *npl* : verduras *fpl* — **greenery** *n, pl* -**eries** : vegetación *f* — **greenhouse** *n* : invernadero *m*
greet *vt* 1 : saludar 2 WELCOME : recibir — **greeting** *n* 1 : saludo *m* 2 ∼s *npl* REGARDS : saludos *mpl,* recuerdos *mpl*
gregarious *adj* : sociable
grenade *n* : granada *f*
grew → **grow**
grey → **gray**
greyhound *n* : galgo *m*
grid *n* 1 GRATING : rejilla *f* 2 NETWORK : red *f* 3 : cuadriculado *m* (de un mapa)
griddle *n* : plancha *f*
grief *n* : dolor *m,* pesar *m* — **grievance** *n* : queja *f* — **grieve** *v* **grieved; grieving** *vt* : entristecer — *vi* ∼ **for** : llorar (a), lamentar — **grievous** *adj* : grave, doloroso
grill *vt* 1 : asar a la parrilla 2 INTERROGATE

: interrogar — ∼ *n* : parrilla *f* (para cocinar) — **grille** *or* **grill** GRATING *n* : reja *f,* rejilla *f*
grim *adj* **grimmer; grimmest** 1 STERN : severo 2 GLOOMY : sombrío
grimace *n* : mueca *f* — ∼ *vi* -**maced; -macing** : hacer muecas
grime *n* : mugre *f,* suciedad *f* — **grimy** *adj* **grimier; -est** : mugriento, sucio
grin *vi* **grinned; grinning** : sonreír (abiertamente) — ∼ *n* : sonrisa *f* (abierta)
grind *v* **ground; grinding** *vt* 1 : moler (el café, etc.) 2 SHARPEN : afilar 3 ∼ **one's teeth** : rechinar los dientes — *vi* : rechinar — ∼ *n* **the daily** ∼ : la rutina diaria — **grinder** *n* : molinillo *m*
grip *vt* **gripped; gripping** 1 : agarrar, asir 2 INTEREST : captar el interés de — ∼ *n* 1 GRASP : agarre *m* 2 CONTROL : control *m,* dominio *m* 3 HANDLE : empuñadura *f* 4 **come to** ∼**s with** : llegar a entender de
gripe *vi* **griped; griping** : quejarse — ∼ *n* : queja *f*
grisly *adj* -**lier; -est** : espeluznante, horrible
gristle *n* : cartílago *m*
grit *n* 1 : arena *f,* grava *f* 2 GUTS : agallas *fpl fam* 3 ∼**s** *npl* : sémola *f* de maíz — ∼ *vt* **gritted; gritting** ∼ **one's teeth** : acorazarse
groan *vi* : gemir — ∼ *n* : gemido *m*
grocery *n, pl* -**ceries** 1 *or* ∼ **store** : tienda *f* de comestibles, tienda *f* de abarrotes *Lat* 2 **groceries** *npl* : comestibles *mpl,* abarrotes *mpl Lat* — **grocer** *n* : tendero *m,* -ra *f*
groggy *adj* -**gier; -est** : atontado, grogui *fam*
groin *n* : ingle *f*
groom *n* BRIDEGROOM : novio *m* — ∼ *vt* 1 : almohazar (un animal) 2 PREPARE : preparar
groove *n* : ranura *f,* surco *m*
grope *vi* **groped; groping** 1 : andar a tientas 2 ∼ **for:** buscar a tientas
gross *adj* 1 SERIOUS : grave 2 OBESE : obeso 3 TOTAL : bruto 4 VULGAR : grosero, basto — ∼ *n* 1 *or* ∼ **income** : ingresos *mpl* brutos 2 *pl* ∼ : gruesa *f* (12 docenas) — **grossly** *adv* 1 EXTREMELY : enormemente 2 CRUDELY : groseramente
grotesque *adj* : grotesco
grouch *n* : gruñón *m,* -ñona *f fam* — **grouchy** *adj* **grouchier; -est** : gruñon *fam*
ground¹ → **grind**
ground² *n* 1 : suelo *m,* tierra *f* 2 *or* ∼**s** LAND : terreno *m* 3 ∼**s** REASON : razón *f,* motivos *mpl* 4 ∼**s** DREGS : pozo *m* (de café) — ∼ *vt* 1 BASE : fundar, basar 2 : conectar a tierra (un aparato eléctrico) 3 : restringir (un avión o un piloto) a la tierra — **groundhog** *n* : marmota *f* (de América)

— **groundless** *adj* : infundado — **groundwork** *n* : trabajo *m* preparatorio
group *n* : grupo *m* — ~ *vt* : agrupar — *vi or* ~ **together** : agruparse
grove *n* : arboleda *f*
grovel *vi* **-eled** *or* **-elled; -eling** *or* **-elling** : arrastrarse, humillarse
grow *v* **grew; grown; growing** *vi* **1** : crecer **2** INCREASE : aumentar **3** BECOME : volverse, ponerse **4** ~ **dark** : oscurecerse **5** ~ **up** : hacerse mayor — *vt* **1** CULTIVATE : cultivar **2** : dejarse crecer (el pelo, etc.) — **grower** *n* : cultivador *m*, -dora *f*
growl *vi* : gruñir — ~ *n* : gruñido *m*
grown–up *adj* : mayor — ~ *n* : persona *f* mayor
growth *n* **1** : crecimiento *m* **2** INCREASE : aumento *m* **3** DEVELOPMENT : desarrollo *m* **4** TUMOR : tumor *m*
grub *n* **1** LARVA : larva *f* **2** FOOD : comida *f*
grubby *adj* **grubbier; -est** : mugriento, sucio
grudge *vt* **grudged; grudging** : dar de mala gana — ~ *n* **hold a** ~ : guardar rencor
grueling *or* **gruelling** *adj* : extenuante, agotador
gruesome *adj* : horripilante
gruff *adj* **1** BRUSQUE : brusco **2** HOARSE : bronco
grumble *vi* **-bled; -bling** : refunfuñar, rezongar
grumpy *adj* **grumpier; -est** : malhumorado, gruñón *fam*
grunt *vi* : gruñir — ~ *n* : gruñido *m*
guarantee *n* : garantía *f* — ~ *vt* **-teed; -teeing** : garantizar
guard *n* **1** : guardia *f* **2** PRECAUTION : protección *f* — ~ *vt* : proteger, vigilar — *vi* ~ **against** : protegerse contra — **guardian** *n* **1** : tutor *m*, -tora *f* (de niños) **2** PROTECTOR : guardián *m*, -diana *f*
guava *n* : guayaba *f*
guerrilla *or* **guerilla** *n* **1** : guerrillero *m*, -ra *f* **2** ~ **warfare** : guerra *f* de guerrillas
guess *vt* **1** : adivinar **2** SUPPOSE : suponer, creer — *vi* ~ **at** : adivinar — ~ *n* : conjetura *f*, suposición *f*
guest *n* **1** : invitado *m*, -da *f* **2** : huésped *mf* (a un hotel)
guide *n* : guía *mf* (persona), guía *f* (libro, etc.) — ~ *vt* **guided; guiding** : guiar — **guidance** *n* : orientación *f* — **guidebook** *n* : guía *f* — **guideline** *n* : pauta *f*, directriz *f*
guild *n* : gremio *m*

guile *n* : astucia *f*
guilt *n* : culpa *f*, culpabilidad *f* — **guilty** *adj* **guiltier; -est** : culpable
guinea pig *n* : conejillo *m* de Indias, cobaya *f*
guise *n* : apariencia *f*
guitar *n* : guitarra *f*
gulf *n* **1** : golfo *m* **2** ABYSS : abismo *m*
gull *n* : gaviota *f*
gullet *n* **1** THROAT : garganta *f* **2** ESOPHAGUS : esófago *m*
gullible *adj* : crédulo
gully *n, pl* **-lies** : barranco *m*
gulp *vt or* ~ **down** : tragarse, engullir — *vi* : tragar saliva — ~ *n* : trago *m*
gum¹ *n* : encía *f* (de la boca)
gum² *n* **1** : resina *f* (de plantas) **2** CHEWING GUM : goma *f* de mascar, chicle *m*
gumption *n* : iniciativa *f*, agallas *fpl fam*
gun *n* **1** FIREARM : arma *f* de fuego **2** *or* **spray** ~ : pistola *f* **3** → **cannon, pistol, revolver, rifle** — ~ *vt* **gunned; gunning 1** *or* ~ **down** : matar a tiros, asesinar **2** ~ **the engine** : acelerar (el motor) — **gunboat** *n* : cañonero *m* — **gunfire** *n* : disparos *mpl* — **gunman** *n, pl* **-men** : pistolero *m*, gatillero *m Lat* — **gunpowder** *n* : pólvora *f* — **gunshot** *n* : disparo *m*, tiro *m*
gurgle *vi* **-gled; -gling 1** : borbotar, gorgotear **2** : gorjear (dícese de un niño)
gush *vi* **1** SPOUT : salir a chorros **2** ~ **with praise** : deshacerse en elogios
gust *n* : ráfaga *f*
gusto *n, pl* **gustoes** : entusiasmo *m*
gusty *adj* **gustier; -est** : racheado, ventoso
gut *n* **1** : intestino *m* **2** ~**s** *npl* INNARDS : tripas *fpl* **3** ~**s** *npl* COURAGE : agallas *fpl fam* — ~ *vt* **gutted; gutting 1** EVISCERATE : destripar (un pollo, etc.), limpiar (un pescado) **2** : destruir el interior de (un edificio)
gutter *n* : canaleta *f* (de un techo), cuneta *f* (de una calle)
guy *n* : tipo *m fam*
guzzle *vt* **-zled; -zling** : chupar *fam*, tragar
gym *or* **gymnasium** *n, pl* **-siums** *or* **-sia** : gimnasio *m* — **gymnast** *n* : gimnasta *mf* — **gymnastics** *ns & pl* : gimnasia *f*
gynecology *n* : ginecología *f* — **gynecologist** *n* : ginecólogo *m*, -ga *f*
gyp *vt* **gypped; gypping** : estafar, timar
Gypsy *n, pl* **-sies** : gitano *m*, -na *f*
gyrate *vi* **-rated; -rating** : girar

H

h *n, pl* **h's** *or* **hs** : h *f*, octava letra del alfabeto inglés

habit *n* **1** CUSTOM : hábito *m*, costumbre *f* **2** : hábito *m* (religioso)

habitat *n* : hábitat *m*

habitual *adj* **1** CUSTOMARY : habitual **2** INVETERATE : empedernido

hack¹ *n* **1** : caballo *m* de alquiler **2** *or* ~ **writer** : escritorzuelo *m*, -la *f*

hack² *vt* : cortar — *vi* *or* ~ **into** : piratear (un sistema informático)

hackneyed *adj* : manido, trillado

hacksaw *n* : sierra *f* para metales

had → **have**

haddock *ns & pl* : eglefino *m*

hadn't (*contraction of* **had not**) → **have**

hag *n* : bruja *f*

haggard *adj* : demacrado

haggle *vi* **-gled; -gling** : regatear

hail¹ *vt* **1** GREET : saludar **2** : llamar (un taxi)

hail² *n* : granizo *m* (en meteorología) — ~ *vi* : granizar — **hailstone** *n* : piedra *f* de granizo

hair *n* **1** : pelo *m*, cabello *m* **2** : vello *m* (en las piernas, etc.) — **hairbrush** *n* : cepillo *m* (para el pelo) — **haircut** *n* **1** : corte *m* de pelo **2 get a** ~ : cortarse el pelo — **hairdo** *n, pl* **-dos** : peinado *m* — **hairdresser** *n* : peluquero *m*, -ra *f* — **hairless** *adj* : sin pelo, calvo — **hairpin** *n* : horquilla *f* — **hair-raising** *adj* : espeluznante — **hairstyle** → **hairdo** — **hair spray** *n* : laca *f* (para el pelo) — **hairy** *adj* **hairier; -est** : peludo, velludo

hale *adj* : saludable, robusto

half *n, pl* **halves 1** : mitad *f* **2** *or* **halftime** : tiempo *m* (en deportes) **3 in** ~ : por la mitad — ~ *adj* **1** : medio **2** ~ **an hour** : una media hora — ~ *adv* : medio — **half brother** *n* : medio hermano *m*, hermanastro *m* — **halfhearted** *adj* : sin ánimo, poco entusiasta — **half sister** *n* : media hermana *f*, hermanastra *f* — **halfway** *adv* : a medio camino — ~ *adj* : medio

halibut *ns & pl* : halibut *m*

hall *n* **1** HALLWAY : corredor *m*, pasillo *m* **2** AUDITORIUM : sala *f* **3** LOBBY : vestíbulo *m* **4** DORMITORY : residencia *f* universitaria

hallmark *n* : sello *m* (distintivo)

Halloween *n* : víspera *f* de Todos los Santos

hallucination *n* : alucinación *f*

hallway *n* **1** ENTRANCE : entrada *f* **2** CORRIDOR : corredor *m*, pasillo *m*

halo *n, pl* **-los** *or* **-loes** : aureola *f*, halo *m*

halt *n* **1 call a** ~ **to** : poner fin a **2 come to a** ~ : pararse — ~ *vi* : pararse — *vt* : parar

halve *vt* **halved; halving 1** DIVIDE : partir por la mitad **2** REDUCE : reducir a la mitad — **halves** → **half**

ham *n* : jamón *m*

hamburger *or* **hamburg** *n* **1** : carne *f* molida **2** *or* ~ **patty** : hamburguesa *f*

hammer *n* : martillo *m* — ~ *v* : martillar, martillear

hammock *n* : hamaca *f*

hamper¹ *vt* : obstaculizar, dificultar

hamper² *n* : cesto *m*, canasta *f* (para ropa sucia)

hamster *n* : hámster *m*

hand *n* **1** : mano *f* **2** : manecilla *f*, aguja *f* (de un reloj, etc.) **3** HANDWRITING : letra *f*, escritura *f* **4** WORKER : obrero *m*, -ra *f* **5 by** ~ : a mano **6 lend a** ~ : echar una mano **7 on** ~ : a mano, disponible **8 on the other** ~ : por otro lado — ~ *vt* **1** : pasar, dar **2** ~ **out** : distribuir **3** ~ **over** : entregar — **handbag** *n* : cartera *f* Lat, bolso *m* Spain — **handbook** *n* : manual *m* — **handcuffs** *npl* : esposas *fpl* — **handful** *n* : puñado *m* — **handgun** *n* : pistola *f*, revólver *m*

handicap *n* **1** : minusvalía *f* (física) **2** : hándicap *m* (en deportes) — ~ *vt* **-capped; -capping 1** : asignar un handicap a (en deportes) **2** HAMPER : obstaculizar — **handicapped** *adj* : minusválido

handicrafts *npl* : artesanía(s) *f(pl)*

handiwork *n* : trabajo *m* (manual)

handkerchief *n, pl* **-chiefs** : pañuelo *m*

handle *n* : asa *f* (de una taza, etc.), mango *m* (de un utensilio), pomo *m* (de una puerta), tirador *m* (de un cajón) — ~ *vt* **-dled; -dling 1** TOUCH : tocar **2** MANAGE : tratar, manejar — **handlebars** *npl* : manillar *m*, manubrio *m* Lat

handmade *adj* : hecho a mano

handout *n* **1** ALMS : dádiva *f*, limosna *f* **2** LEAFLET : folleto *m*

handrail *n* : pasamanos *m*

handshake *n* : apretón *m* de manos

handsome *adj* **-somer; -est 1** ATTRACTIVE : apuesto, guapo **2** GENEROUS : generoso **3** SIZABLE : considerable

handwriting *n* : letra *f*, escritura *f* — **handwritten** *adj* : escrito a mano

handy *adj* **handier; -est 1** NEARBY : a mano **2** USEFUL : práctico, útil **3** DEFT : habili-

doso — **handyman** *n, pl* **-men** : hombre *m* habilidoso
hang *v* **hung; hanging** *vt* **1** : colgar **2** (*past tense often* **hanged**) EXECUTE : ahorcar **3** ∼ **one's head** : bajar la cabeza — *vi* **1** : colgar, pender **2** : caer (dícese de la ropa, etc.) **3** ∼ **up on s.o.** : colgar a algn — ∼ *n* **1** DRAPE : caída *f* **2 get the** ∼ **of** : agarrar la onda de
hangar *n* : hangar *m*
hanger *n* : percha *f*, gancho *m* (para ropa) *Lat*
hangover *n* : resaca *f*
hanker *vi* ∼ **for** : tener ansias de — **hankering** *n* : ansia *f*, anhelo *m*
haphazard *adj* : casual, fortuito
happen *vi* **1** : pasar, suceder, ocurrir **2** ∼ **to do sth** : hacer algo por casualidad **3 it so happens that...** : da la casualidad de que... — **happening** *n* : suceso *m*, acontecimiento *m*
happy *adj* **-pier; -est 1** : feliz **2 be** ∼ : alegrarse **3 be** ∼ **with** : estar contento con **4 be** ∼ **to do sth** : hacer algo con mucho gusto — **happily** *adv* : alegremente — **happiness** *n* : felicidad *f* — **happy-go-lucky** *adj* : despreocupado
harass *vt* : acosar — **harassment** *n* : acoso *m*
harbor *or Brit* **harbour** *n* : puerto *m* — *vt* **1** SHELTER : albergar **2** ∼ **a grudge against** : guardar rencor a
hard *adj* **1** : duro **2** DIFFICULT : difícil **3 be a** ∼ **worker** : ser muy trabajador **4** ∼ **liquor** : bebidas *fpl* fuertes **5** ∼ **water** : agua *f* dura — ∼ *adv* **1** FORCEFULLY : fuerte **2 work** ∼ : trabajar duro **3 take sth** ∼ : tomarse algo muy mal — **harden** *vt* : endurecer — **hardheaded** *adj* : testarudo, terco — **hard-hearted** *adj* : duro de corazón — **hardly** *adv* **1** : apenas **2** ∼ **ever** : casi nunca — **hardness** *n* **1** : dureza *f* **2** DIFFICULTY : dificultad *f* — **hardship** *n* : dificultad *f* — **hardware** *n* **1** : ferretería *f* **2** : hardware *m* (en informática) — **hardworking** *adj* : trabajador
hardy *adj* **-dier; -est** : fuerte (dícese de personas), resistente (dícese de las plantas)
hare *n, pl* **hare** *or* **hares** : liebre *f*
harm *n* : daño *m* — ∼ *vt* : hacer daño a (una persona), dañar (una cosa), perjudicar (la reputación de algn, etc.) — **harmful** *adj* : perjudicial — **harmless** *adj* : inofensivo
harmonica *n* : armónica *f*
harmony *n, pl* **-nies** : armonía *f* — **harmonious** *adj* : armonioso — **harmonize** *v* **-nized; -nizing** : armonizar
harness *n* : arnés *m* — ∼ *vt* **1** : enjaezar **2** UTILIZE : utilizar

harp *n* : arpa *m* — ∼ *vi* ∼ **on** : insistir sobre
harpoon *n* : arpón *m*
harpsichord *n* : clavicémbalo *m*
harsh *adj* **1** ROUGH : áspero **2** SEVERE : duro, severo **3** : fuerte (dícese de una luz), discordante (dícese de sonidos) — **harshness** *n* : severidad *f*
harvest *n* : cosecha *f* — ∼ *v* : cosechar
has → **have**
hash *vt* **1** CHOP : picar **2** ∼ **over** DISCUSS : discutir — ∼ *n* : picadillo *m* (comida)
hasn't (*contraction of* **has not**) → **has**
hassle *n* : problemas *mpl*, lío *m* — ∼ *vt* **-sled; -sling** : fastidiar
haste *n* **1** : prisa *f*, apuro *m Lat* **2 make** ∼ : darse prisa, apurarse *Lat* — **hasten** *vt* : acelerar — *vi* : apresurarse, apurarse *Lat* — **hasty** *adj* **hastier; -est** : precipitado
hat *n* : sombrero *m*
hatch *n* : escotilla *f* — ∼ *vt* **1** : empollar (huevos) **2** CONCOCT : tramar — *vi* : salir del cascarón
hatchet *n* : hacha *f*
hate *n* : odio *m* — ∼ *vt* **hated; hating** : odiar, aborrecer — **hateful** *adj* : odioso, aborrecible — **hatred** *n* : odio *m*
haughty *adj* **-tier; -est** : altanero, altivo
haul *vt* : arrastrar, jalar *Lat* — ∼ *n* **1** CATCH : redada *f* (de peces) **2** LOOT : botín *m* **3 a long** ∼ : un trayecto largo
haunch *n* : cadera *f* (de una persona), anca *f* (de un animal)
haunt *vt* **1** : frecuentar, rondar **2** TROUBLE : inquietar — ∼ *n* : sitio *m* predilecto — **haunted** *adj* : embrujado
have *v* **had; having; has** *vt* **1** : tener **2** CONSUME : comer, tomar **3** ALLOW : permitir **4** : dar (una fiesta, etc.), convocar (una reunión) **5** ∼ **one's hair cut** : cortarse el pelo **6** ∼ **sth done** : mandar hacer algo — *v aux* **1** : haber **2** ∼ **just done sth** : acabar de hacer algo **4 you've finished, haven't you?** : has terminado, ¿no?
haven *n* : refugio *m*
havoc *n* : estragos *mpl*
hawk[1] *n* : halcón *m*
hawk[2] *vt* : pregonar (mercancías)
hay *n* : heno *m* — **hay fever** *n* : fiebre *f* del heno — **haystack** *n* : almiar *m* — **haywire** *adj* **go** ∼ : estropearse
hazard *n* : peligro *m*, riesgo *m* — ∼ *vt* : arriesgar, aventurar — **hazardous** *adj* : arriesgado, peligroso
haze *n* : bruma *f*, neblina *f*
hazel *n* : color *m* avellana — **hazelnut** *n* : avellana *f*
hazy *adj* **hazier; -est** : nebuloso
he *pron* : él

head

head *n* **1** : cabeza *f* **2** END, TOP : cabeza *f* (de un clavo, etc.), cabecera *f* (de una mesa) **3** LEADER : jefe *m*, -fa *f* **4 be out of one's ~** : estar loco **5 come to a ~** : llegar a un punto crítico **6 ~s or tails** : cara o cruz **7 per ~** : por cabeza — **~** *adj* MAIN : principal — **~** *vt* : encabezar — *vi* : dirigirse — **headache** *n* : dolor *m* de cabeza — **headband** *n* : cinta *f* del pelo — **headdress** *n* : tocado *m* — **headfirst** *adv* : de cabeza — **heading** *n* : encabezamiento *m*, título *m* — **headland** *n* : cabo *m* — **headlight** *n* : faro *m* — **headline** *n* : titular *m* — **headlong** *adv* **1** HEADFIRST : de cabeza **2** HASTILY : precipitadamente — **headmaster** *n* : director *m* — **headmistress** *n* : directora *f* — **head–on** *adv* & *adj* : de frente — **headphones** *npl* : auriculares *mpl*, audífonos *mpl Lat* — **headquarters** *ns* & *pl* : oficina *f* central (de una compañía), cuartel *m* general (de los militares) — **head start** *n* : ventaja *f* — **headstrong** *adj* : testarudo, obstinado — **headwaiter** *n* : jefe *m*, -fa *f* de comedor — **headway** *n* **1** : progreso *m* **2 make ~** : avanzar — **heady** *adj* **headier; -est** : embriagador
heal *vt* : curar — *vi* : cicatrizar
health *n* : salud *f* — **healthy** *adj* **healthier; -est** : sano, saludable
heap *n* : montón *m* — **~** *vt* : amontonar
hear *v* **heard; hearing** *vt* : oír — *vi* **1** : oír **2 ~ about** : enterarse de **3 ~ from** : tener noticias de — **hearing** *n* **1** : oído *m* **2** : vista *f* (en un tribunal) — **hearing aid** *n* : audífono *m* — **hearsay** *n* : rumores *mpl*
hearse *n* : coche *m* fúnebre
heart *n* **1** : corazón *m* **2 at ~** : en el fondo **3 by ~** : de memoria **4 lose ~** : descorazonarse **5 take ~** : animarse — **heartache** *n* : pena *f*, dolor *m* — **heart attack** *n* : infarto *m*, ataque *m* al corazón — **heartbeat** *n* : latido *m* (del corazón) — **heartbreak** *n* : congoja *f*, angustia *f* — **heartbroken** *adj* : desconsolado — **heartburn** *n* : acidez *f* estomacal
hearth *n* : hogar *m*
heartily *adv* : de buena gana
heartless *adj* : de mal corazón, cruel
hearty *adj* **heartier; -est 1** : cordial, caluroso **2** : abundante (dícese de una comida)
heat *vt* : calentar — *vi or* **~ up** : calentarse — **~** *n* **1** : calor *m* **2** HEATING : calefacción *f* — **heated** *adj* : acalorado — **heater** *n* : calentador *m*
heath *n* : brezal *m*
heathen *adj* : pagano — **~** *n*, *pl* **-thens** *or* **-then** : pagano *m*, -na *f*
heather *n* : brezo *m*

heave *v* **heaved** *or* **hove; heaving** *vt* **1** LIFT : levantar (con esfuerzo) **2** HURL : lanzar, tirar **3 ~ a sigh** : suspirar — **~** *vi or* **~ up** : levantarse
heaven *n* : cielo *m* — **heavenly** *adj* **1** : celestial **2 ~ body** : cuerpo *m* celeste
heavy *adj* **heavier; -est 1** : pesado **2** INTENSE : fuerte **3 ~ sigh** : suspiro *m* profundo **4 ~ traffic** : tráfico *m* denso — **heavily** *adv* **1** : pesadamente **2** EXCESSIVELY : mucho — **heaviness** *n* : peso *m*, pesadez *f* — **heavyweight** *n* : peso *m* pesado
Hebrew *adj* : hebreo — **~** *n* : hebreo *m* (idioma)
heckle *vt* **-led; -ling** : interrumpir (a un orador) con preguntas molestas
hectic *adj* : agitado, ajetreado
he'd (*contraction of* **he had** *or* **he would**) → **have, would**
hedge *n* : seto *m* vivo — **~** *v* **hedged; hedging** *vt* **~ one's bets** : cubrirse — *vi* : contestar con evasivas — **hedgehog** *n* : erizo *m*
heed *vt* : prestar atención a, hacer caso de — **~** *n* **take ~** : tener cuidado — **heedless** *adj* **be ~ of** : hacer caso omiso de
heel *n* : talón *m* (del pie), tacón *m* (de un zapato)
hefty *adj* **heftier; -est** : robusto y pesado
heifer *n* : novilla *f*
height *n* **1** : estatura *f* (de una persona), altura *f* (de un objeto) **2** PEAK : cumbre *f* **3 the ~ of folly** : el colmo de la locura **4 what is your ~ ?** : ¿cuánto mides? — **heighten** *vt* : aumentar, intensificar
heir *n* : heredero *m*, -ra *f* — **heiress** *n* : heredera *f* — **heirloom** *n* : reliquia *f* de familia
held → **hold**
helicopter *n* : helicóptero *m*
hell *n* : infierno *m* — **hellish** *adj* : infernal
he'll (*contraction of* **he shall** *or* **he will**) → **shall, will**
hello *interj* : ¡hola!
helm *n* : timón *m*
helmet *n* : casco *m*
help *vt* **1** : ayudar **2 ~ oneself** : servirse **3 I can't ~ it** : no lo puedo remediar — **~** *n* **1** : ayuda *f* **2** STAFF : personal *m* **3 help!** : ¡socorro!, ¡auxilio! — **helper** *n* : ayudante *mf* — **helpful** *adj* **1** OBLIGING : servicial, amable **2** USEFUL : útil — **helping** *n* : porción *f* — **helpless** *adj* **1** POWERLESS : incapaz **2** DEFENSELESS : indefenso
hem *n* : dobladillo *m* — **~** *vt* **hemmed; hemming ~ in** : encerrar
hemisphere *n* : hemisferio *m*
hemorrhage *n* : hemorragia *f*

hemorrhoids *npl* : hemorroides *fpl*, almorranas *fpl*
hemp *n* : cáñamo *m*
hen *n* : gallina *f*
hence *adv* **1** : de aquí, de ahí **2** THEREFORE : por lo tanto **3 ten years** ~ : de aquí a 10 años — **henceforth** *adv* : de ahora en adelante
henpeck *vt* : dominar (al marido)
hepatitis *n, pl* **-titides** : hepatitis *f*
her *adj* : su, sus — ~ *pron* **1** (*used as direct object*) : la **2** (*used as indirect object*) : le, se **3** (*used as object of a preposition*) : ella
herald *vt* : anunciar
herb *n* : hierba *f*
herd *n* : manada *f* — ~ *vt* : conducir (en manada) — *vi or* ~ **together** : reunir
here *adv* **1** : aquí, acá **2** ~ **you are!** : ¡toma! — **hereabouts** *or* **hereabout** *adv* : por aquí (cerca) — **hereafter** *adv* : en el futuro — **hereby** *adv* : por este medio
hereditary *adj* : hereditario — **heredity** *n* : herencia *f*
heresy *n, pl* **-sies** : herejía *f*
herewith *adv* : adjunto
heritage *n* **1** : herencia *f* **2** : patrimonio *m* (nacional)
hermit *n* : ermitaño *m*, -ña *f*
hernia *n, pl* **-nias** *or* **-niae** : hernia *f*
hero *n, pl* **-roes** : héroe *m* — **heroic** *adj* : heroico — **heroine** *n* : heroína *f* — **heroism** *n* : heroísmo *m*
heron *n* : garza *f*
herring *n, pl* **-ring** *or* **-rings** : arenque *m*
hers *pron* **1** : (el) suyo, (la) suya, (los) suyos, (las) suyas **2 some friends of** ~ : unos amigos suyos, unos amigos de ella — **herself** *pron* **1** (*used reflexively*) : se **2** (*used emphatically*) : ella misma
he's (*contraction of* **he is** *or* **he has**) → **be**, **have**
hesitant *adj* : titubeante, vacilante — **hesitate** *vi* **-tated; -tating** : vacilar, titubear — **hesitation** *n* : vacilación *f*, titubeo *m*
heterosexual *adj* : heterosexual — ~ *n* : heterosexual *mf*
hexagon *n* : hexágono *m*
hey *interj* : ¡eh!, ¡oye!
heyday *n* : auge *m*, apogeo *m*
hi *interj* : ¡hola!
hibernate *vi* **-nated; -nating** : hibernar
hiccup *n* **have the** ~**s** : tener hipo — ~ *vi* **-cuped; -cuping** : tener hipo
hide[1] *n* : piel *f*, cuero *m*
hide[2] *v* **hid; hidden** *or* **hid; hiding** *vt* **1** : esconder **2** : ocultar (motivos, etc.) — *vi* : esconderse — **hide-and-seek** *n* : escondite *m*, escondidas *fpl Lat*
hideous *adj* : horrible, espantoso

hideout *n* : escondite *m*, guarida *f*
hierarchy *n, pl* **-chies** : jerarquía *f* — **hierarchical** *adj* : jerárquico
high *adj* **1** : alto **2** INTOXICATED : borracho, drogado **3 a** ~ **voice** : una voz aguda **4 it's two feet** ~ : tiene dos pies de alto **5** ~ **winds** : fuertes vientos *mpl* — ~ *adv* : alto — ~ *n* : récord *m*, máximo *m* — **higher** *adj* **1** : superior **2** ~ **education** : enseñanza *f* superior — **highlight** *n* : punto *m* culminante — **highly** *adv* **1** VERY : muy, sumamente **2 think** ~ **of** : tener en mucho a — **Highness** *n* **His/Her** ~ : Su Alteza *f* — **high school** *n* : escuela *f* superior, escuela *f* secundaria — **high-strung** *adj* : nervioso, excitable — **highway** *n* : carretera *f*
hijack *vt* : secuestrar — **hijacker** *n* : secuestrador *m*, -dora *f* — **hijacking** *n* : secuestro *m*
hike *v* **hiked; hiking** *vi* : ir de caminata — *vt or* ~ **up** RAISE : subir — ~ *n* : caminata *f*, excursión *f* — **hiker** *n* : excursionista *mf*
hilarious *adj* : muy divertido — **hilarity** *n* : hilaridad *f*
hill *n* **1** : colina *f*, cerro *m* **2** SLOPE : cuesta *f* — **hillside** *n* : ladera *f*, cuesta *f* — **hilly** *adj* **hillier; -est** : accidentado
hilt *n* : puño *m*
him *pron* **1** (*used as direct object*) : lo **2** (*used as indirect object*) : le, se **3** (*used as object of a preposition*) : él — **himself** *pron* **1** (*used reflexively*) : se **2** (*used emphatically*) : él mismo
hind *adj* : trasero, posterior
hinder *vt* : dificultar, estorbar — **hindrance** *n* : obstáculo *m*
hindsight *n* **in** ~ : en retrospectiva
Hindu *adj* : hindú
hinge *n* : bisagra *f*, gozne *m* — ~ *vi* **hinged; hinging** ~ **on** : depender de
hint *n* **1** : indirecta *f* **2** TIP : consejo *m* **3** TRACE : asomo *m*, toque *m* — ~ *vt* : dar a entender — *vi* ~ **at** : insinuar
hip *n* : cadera *f*
hippopotamus *n, pl* **-muses** *or* **-mi** : hipopótamo *m*
hire *n* **1** : alquiler *m* **2 for** ~ : se alquila — ~ *vt* **hired; hiring 1** EMPLOY : contratar, emplear **2** RENT : alquilar
his *adj* : su, sus, de él — ~ *pron* **1** : (el) suyo, (la) suya, (los) suyos, (las) suyas **2 some friends of** ~ : unos amigos suyos, unos amigos de él
Hispanic *adj* : hispano, hispánico
hiss *vi* : silbar — *n* : silbido *m*
history *n, pl* **-ries 1** : historia *f* **2** BACKGROUND : historial *m* — **historian** *n* : historiador *m*, -dora *f* — **historic** *or* **historical** *adj* : histórico

hit

250

hit *v* hit; hitting *vt* **1** : golpear, pegar **2** : dar (con un proyectil) **3** AFFECT : afectar **4** REACH : alcanzar **5 the car ~ a tree** : el coche chocó contra un árbol — *vi* : pegar — **~** *n* **1** : golpe *m* **2** SUCCESS : éxito *m*

hitch *vt* **1** ATTACH : enganchar **2** *or* **~ up** RAISE : subirse **3 ~ a ride** : hacer autostop — **~** *n* PROBLEM : problema *m* — **hitchhike** *vi* -hiked; -hiking : hacer autostop —

hitchhiker *n* : autostopista *mf*

hitherto *adv* : hasta ahora

HIV *n* : VIH *m*, virus *m* del sida

hive *n* : colmena *f*

hives *ns & pl* : urticaria *f*

hoard *n* : tesoro *m* (de dinero), reserva *f* (de provisiones) — **~** *vt* : acumular

hoarse *adj* hoarser; -est : ronco

hoax *n* : engaño *m*

hobble *vi* -bled; -bling : cojear

hobby *n*, *pl* -bies : pasatiempo *m*

hobo *n*, *pl* -boes : vagabundo *m*, -da *f*

hockey *n* : hockey *m*

hoe *n* : azada *f* — **~** *vt* hoed; hoeing : azadonar

hog *n* : cerdo *m* — **~** *vt* hogged; hogging MONOPOLIZE : acaparar

hoist *vt* **1** : izar (una vela, etc.) **2** LIFT : levantar — **~** *n* : grúa *f*

hold[1] *n* : bodega *f* (en un barco o un avión)

hold[2] *v* held; holding *vt* **1** GRIP : agarrar **2** POSSESS : tener **3** SUPPORT : sostener **4** : celebrar (una reunión, etc.), mantener (una conversación) **5** CONTAIN : contener **6** CONSIDER : considerar **7** *or* **~ back** : detener **8 ~ hands** : agarrarse de la mano **9 ~ up** ROB : atracar **10 ~ up** DELAY : retrasar — *vi* **1** LAST : durar, continuar **2** APPLY : ser válido — **~** *n* **1** GRIP : agarre *m* **2 get ~ of** : conseguir **3 get ~ of oneself** : controlarse — **holder** *n* : tenedor *m*, -dora *f* —

holdup *n* **1** ROBBERY : atraco *m* **2** DELAY : retraso *m*, demora *f*

hole *n* : agujero *m*, hoyo *m*

holiday *n* **1** : día *m* feriado, fiesta *f* **2** *Brit* VACATION : vacaciones *fpl*

holiness *n* : santidad *f*

holler *vi* : gritar — **~** *n* : grito *m*

hollow *n* **1** : hueco *m* **2** VALLEY : hondonada *f* — **~** *adj* -lower; -est **1** : hueco **2** FALSE : vacío, falso — **~** *vt or* **~ out** : ahuecar

holly *n*, *pl* -lies : acebo *m*

holocaust *n* : holocausto *m*

holster *n* : pistolera *f*

holy *adj* -lier; -est : santo, sagrado

homage *n* : homenaje *m*

home *n* **1** : casa *f* **2** FAMILY : hogar *m* **3** INSTITUTION : residencia *f*, asilo *m* **4 at ~ and abroad** : dentro y fuera del país — **~** *adv* **go ~** : ir a casa — **homeland** *n* : patria

f — **homeless** *adj* : sin hogar — **homely** *adj* -lier; -est **1** DOMESTIC : casero **2** UGLY : feo — **homemade** *adj* : casero, hecho en casa — **homemaker** *n* : ama *f* de casa — **home run** *n* : jonrón *m* — **homesick** *adj* **be ~** : echar de menos a la familia — **homeward** *adj* : de vuelta, de regreso — **homework** *n* : tarea *f*, deberes *mpl* — **homey** *adj* **homier; -est** : hogareño, acogedor

homicide *n* : homicidio *m*

homogeneous *adj* : homogéneo

homosexual *adj* : homosexual — **~** *n* : homosexual *mf* — **homosexuality** *n* : homosexualidad *f*

honest *adj* **1** : honrado **2** FRANK : sincero — **honestly** *adv* : sinceramente — **honesty** *n*, *pl* -ties : honradez *f*

honey *n*, *pl* -eys : miel *f* — **honeycomb** *n* : panal *m* — **honeymoon** *n* : luna *f* de miel

honk *vi* : tocar la bocina — **~** *n* : bocinazo *m*

honor *or Brit* **honour** *n* : honor *m* — **~** *vt* **1** : honrar **2** : aceptar (un cheque, etc.), cumplir con (una promesa) — **honorable** *or Brit* **honourable** *adj* : honorable, honroso — **honorary** *adj* : honorario

hood *n* **1** : capucha *f* (de un abrigo, etc.) **2** : capó *m* (de un automóvil)

hoodlum *n* : matón *m*

hoodwink *vt* : engañar

hoof *n*, *pl* **hooves** *or* **hoofs** : pezuña *f* (de una vaca, etc.), casco *m* (de un caballo)

hook *n* **1** : gancho *m* **2** *or* **~ and eye** : corchete *m* **3** → fishhook **4 off the ~** : descolgado — **~** *vt* : enganchar — *vi* : engancharse

hoop *n* : aro *m*

hooray → hurrah

hoot *vi* **1** : ulular (dícese de un búho) **2 ~ with laughter** : reírse a carcajadas — **~** *n* **1** : ululato *m* (de un búho) **2 I don't give a ~** : me importa un comino

hop[1] *vi* hopped; hopping : saltar a la pata coja — **~** *n* : salto *m* a la pata coja

hop[2] *n* **~s** : lúpulo *m* (planta)

hope *v* hoped; hoping *vi* : esperar — *vt* : esperar que — **~** *n* : esperanza *f* — **hopeful** *adj* : esperanzado — **hopefully** *adv* **1** : con esperanza **2 ~ it will help** : se espera que ayude — **hopeless** *adj* : desesperado — **hopelessly** *adv* : desesperadamente

horde *n* : horda *f*

horizon *n* : horizonte *m* — **horizontal** *adj* : horizontal

hormone *n* : hormona *f*

horn *n* **1** : cuerno *m* (de un animal) **2** : trompa *f* (instrumento musical) **3** : bocina *f*, claxon *m* (de un vehículo)

hornet *n* : avispón *m*

horoscope n : horóscopo m

horror n : horror m — **horrendous** adj : horrendo — **horrible** adj : horrible — **horrid** adj : horroroso, horrible — **horrify** vt -fied; -fying : horrorizar

hors d'oeuvre n, pl **hors d'oeuvres** : entremés m

horse n : caballo m — **horseback** n on ~ : a caballo — **horsefly** n, pl -flies : tábano m — **horseman** n, pl -men : jinete m — **horseplay** n : payasadas fpl — **horsepower** n : caballo m de fuerza — **horseradish** n : rábano m picante — **horseshoe** n : herradura f — **horsewoman** n, pl -women : jinete f

horticulture n : horticultura f

hose n 1 pl **hoses** : manguera f, manga f 2 **hose** pl STOCKINGS : medias fpl — ~ vt **hosed; hosing** : regar (con manguera) — **hosiery** n : calcetería f

hospice n : hospicio m

hospital n : hospital m — **hospitable** adj : hospitalario — **hospitality** n, pl -ties : hospitalidad f — **hospitalize** vt -ized; -izing : hospitalizar

host[1] n a ~ of : toda una serie de

host[2] n 1 : anfitrión m, -triona f 2 : presentador m, -dora f (de televisión, etc.) — ~ vt : presentar (un programa de televisión, etc.)

host[3] n EUCHARIST : hostia f, Eucaristía f

hostage n : rehén m

hostel n or **youth** ~ : albergue m juvenil

hostess n : anfitriona f

hostile adj : hostil — **hostility** n, pl -ties : hostilidad f

hot adj **hotter; hottest** 1 : caliente, caluroso (dícese del tiempo), cálido (dícese del clima) 2 SPICY : picante 3 feel ~ : tener calor 4 **have a** ~ **temper** : tener mal genio 5 ~ **news** : noticias fpl de última hora 6 **it's** ~ **today** : hace calor

hot dog n : perro m caliente

hotel n : hotel m

hotheaded adj : exaltado

hound n : perro m (de caza) — ~ vt : acosar, perseguir

hour n : hora f — **hourglass** n : reloj m de arena — **hourly** adv & adj : cada hora, por hora

house n, pl **houses** 1 : casa f 2 : cámara f (del gobierno) 3 **publishing** ~ : editorial f — ~ vt **housed; housing** : albergar — **houseboat** n : casa f flotante — **housefly** n, pl -flies : mosca f común — **household** adj 1 : doméstico 2 ~ **name** : nombre m muy conocido — ~ n : casa f — **housekeeper** n : ama f de llaves — **housekeeping** n : gobierno m de la casa — **housewarming** n : fiesta f de estreno de una casa

— **housewife** n, pl -wives : ama f de casa — **housework** n : faenas fpl domésticas —

housing n 1 : viviendas fpl 2 CASE : caja f protectora

hove → **heave**

hovel n : casucha f, tugurio m

hover vi 1 : cernerse 2 ~ **about** : rondar

how adv 1 : cómo 2 (used in exclamations) : qué 3 ~ **are you?** : ¿cómo está Ud.? 4 ~ **come** : por qué 5 ~ **much** : cuánto 6 ~ **do you do?** : mucho gusto 7 ~ **old are you?** : ¿cuántos años tienes? — ~ conj : como

however conj 1 : de cualquier manera que 2 ~ **you like** : como quieras — ~ adv 1 NEVERTHELESS : sin embargo, no obstante 2 ~ **difficult it is** : por díficil que sea 3 ~ **hard I try** : por más que me esfuerce

howl vi : aullar — ~ n : aullido m

hub n 1 CENTER : centro m 2 : cubo m (de una rueda)

hubbub n : alboroto m, jaleo m

hubcap n : tapacubos m

huddle vi -dled; -dling or ~ **together** : apiñarse

hue n : color m, tono m

huff n be in a ~ : estar enojado

hug vt **hugged; hugging** : abrazar — ~ n : abrazo m

huge adj **huger; hugest** : inmenso, enorme

hull n : casco m (de un barco, etc.)

hum v **hummed; humming** vi 1 : tararear 2 BUZZ : zumbar — vt : tararear (una melodía) — ~ n : zumbido m

human adj : humano — ~ n : (ser m) humano m — **humane** adj : humano, humanitario — **humanitarian** adj : humanitario — **humanity** n, pl -ties : humanidad f

humble vt -bled; -bling 1 : humillar 2 ~ **oneself** : humillarse — ~ adj -bler; -blest : humilde

humdrum adj : monótono, rutinario

humid adj : húmedo — **humidity** n, pl -ties : humedad f

humiliate vt -ated; -ating : humillar — **humiliating** adj : humillante — **humiliation** n : humillación f — **humility** n : humildad f

humor or Brit **humour** n : humor m — ~ vt : seguir la corriente a, complacer — **humorous** adj : humorístico, cómico

hump n : joroba f

hunch vi or ~ **over** : encorvarse — ~ n : presentimiento m

hundred adj : cien, ciento — ~ n, pl -dreds or -dred : ciento m — **hundredth** adj : centésimo — ~ n 1 : centésimo m, -ma f (en una serie) 2 : centésimo m (en matemáticas)

hung → **hang**

Hungarian *adj* : húngaro — ～ *n* : húngaro *m* (idioma)

hunger *n* : hambre *m* — ～ *vi* **1** : tener hambre **2** ～ **for** : ansiar, anhelar — **hungry** *adj* **-grier; -est 1** : hambriento **2 be** ～ : tener hambre

hunk *n* : pedazo *m* (grande)

hunt *vt* **1** : cazar **2** ～ **for** : buscar — ～ *n* **1** : caza *f*, cacería *f* **2** SEARCH : búsqueda *f*, busca *f* — **hunter** *n* : cazador *m*, -dora *f* — **hunting** *n or* **1** : caza *f* **2 go** ～ : ir de caza

hurdle *n* **1** : valla *f* (en deportes) **2** OBSTACLE : obstáculo *m*

hurl *vt* : lanzar, arrojar

hurrah *interj* : ¡hurra!

hurricane *n* : huracán *m*

hurry *n* : prisa *f*, apuro *f* Lat — *v* **-ried; -rying** *vi* : darse prisa, apurarse Lat — *vt* : apurar, dar prisa a — **hurried** *adj* : apresurado — **hurriedly** *adv* : apresuradamente, de prisa

hurt *v* **hurt; hurting** *vt* **1** INJURE : hacer daño a, lastimar **2** OFFEND : ofender, herir — *vi* **1** : doler **2 my foot** ～**s** : me duele el pie — ～ *n* **1** INJURY : herida *f* **2** DISTRESS : dolor *m*, pena *f* — **hurtful** *adj* : hiriente, doloroso

hurtle *vi* **-tled; -tling** : lanzarse, precipitarse

husband *n* : esposo *m*, marido *m*

hush *vt* : hacer callar, acallar — ～ *n* : silencio *m*

husk *n* : cáscara *f*

husky[1] *adj* **-kier; -est** HOARSE : ronco

husky[2] *n*, *pl* **-kies** : perro *m*, -rra *f* esquimal

husky[3] *adj* BURLY : fornido

hustle *v* **-tled; -tling** *vt* : dar prisa a, apurar Lat — *vi* : darse prisa, apurarse Lat — ～ *n* ～ **and bustle** : ajetreo *m*, bullicio *m*

hut *n* : cabaña *f*

hutch *n or* **rabbit** ～ : conejera *f*

hyacinth *n* : jacinto *m*

hybrid *n* : híbrido *m* — ～ *adj* : híbrido

hydrant *n or* **fire** ～ : boca *f* de incendios

hydraulic *adj* : hidráulico

hydroelectric *adj* : hidroeléctrico

hydrogen *n* : hidrógeno *m*

hyena *n* : hiena *f*

hygiene *n* : higiene *f* — **hygienic** *adj* : higiénico

hymn *n* : himno *m*

hyperactive *adj* : hiperactivo

hyphen *n* : guión *m*

hypnosis *n*, *pl* **-noses** : hipnosis *f* — **hypnotic** *adj* : hipnótico — **hypnotism** *n* : hipnotismo *m* — **hypnotize** *vt* **-tized; -tizing** : hipnotizar

hypochondriac *n* : hipocondríaco *m*, -ca *f*

hypocrisy *n*, *pl* **-sies** : hipocresía *f* — **hypocrite** *n* : hipócrita *mf* — **hypocritical** *adj* : hipócrita

hypothesis *n*, *pl* **-eses** : hipótesis *f* — **hypothetical** *adj* : hipotético

hysteria *n* : histeria *f*, histerismo *m* — **hysterical** *adj* : histérico

I

i *n*, *pl* **i's** *or* **is** : i *f*, novena letra del alfabeto inglés

I *pron* : yo

ice *n* : hielo *m* — ～ *v* **iced; icing** *vt* **1** FREEZE : congelar **2** CHILL : enfriar **3** : bañar (pasteles, etc.) — ～ *vi or* ～ **up** : helarse, congelarse — **iceberg** *n* : iceberg *m* — **icebox** → **refrigerator** — **ice–cold** *adj* : helado — **ice cream** *n* : helado *m* — **ice cube** *n* : cubito *m* de hielo — **ice–skate** *vi* **-skated; -skating** : patinar — **ice skate** *n* : patín *m* de cuchilla — **icicle** *n* : carámbano *m* — **icing** *n* : baño *m*

icon *n* : icono *m*

icy *adj* **icier; -est 1** : cubierto de hielo (dícese de pavimento, etc.) **2** FREEZING : helado

I'd (*contraction of* **I should** *or* **I would**) → **should, would**

idea *n* : idea *f*

ideal *adj* : ideal — ～ *n* : ideal *m* — **idealist** *n* : idealista *mf* — **idealistic** *adj* : idealista — **idealize** *vt* **-ized; -izing** : idealizar

identity *n*, *pl* **-ties** : identidad *f* — **identical** *adj* : idéntico — **identify** *v* **-fied; -fying** *vt* : identificar — *vi* ～ **with** : identificarse con — **identification** *n* **1** : identificación *f* **2** ～ **card** : carnet *m*, carné *m*

ideology *n*, *pl* **-gies** : ideología *f* — **ideological** *adj* : ideológico

idiocy *n*, *pl* **-cies** : idiotez *f*

idiom *n* EXPRESSION : modismo *m* — **idiomatic** *adj* : idiomático

idiosyncrasy *n*, *pl* **-sies** : idiosincrasia *f*

idiot n : idiota mf — **idiotic** adj : idiota
idle adj **idler; idlest 1** LAZY : haragán, holgazán **2** INACTIVE : parado (dícese de una máquina) **3** UNEMPLOYED : desocupado **4** VAIN : frívolo, vano **5 out of** ~ **curiosity** : por pura curiosidad — ~ v **idled; idling** vi : andar al ralentí (dícese de un motor) — vt ~ **away the hours** : pasar el rato — **idleness** n : ociosidad f
idol n : ídolo m — **idolize** vt **-ized; -izing** : idolatrar
idyllic adj : idílico
if conj **1** : si **2** THOUGH : aunque, si bien **3** ~ **so** : si es así
igloo n, pl **-loos** : iglú m
ignite v **-nited; -niting** vt : encender — vi : encenderse — **ignition** n **1** : ignición f **2** or ~ **switch** : encendido m
ignore vt **-nored; -noring** : ignorar, no hacer caso de — **ignorance** n : ignorancia f — **ignorant** adj **1** : ignorante **2 be** ~ **of** : desconocer, ignorar
ilk n : tipo m, clase f
ill adj **worse; worst 1** SICK : enfermo **2** BAD : malo — adv **worse; worst** : mal — **ill–advised** adj : imprudente — **ill at ease** adj : incómodo
I'll (contraction of **I shall** or **I will**) → **shall, will**
illegal adj : ilegal
illegible adj : ilegible
illegitimate adj : ilegítimo — **illegitimacy** n : ilegitimidad f
illicit adj : ilícito
illiterate adj : analfabeto — **illiteracy** n, pl **-cies** : analfabetismo m
ill–mannered adj : descortés, maleducado
ill–natured adj : de mal genio
illness n : enfermedad f
illogical adj : ilógico
ill–treat vt : maltratar
illuminate vt **-nated; -nating** : iluminar — **illumination** n : iluminación f
illusion n : ilusión f — **illusory** adj : ilusorio
illustrate v **-trated; -trating** : ilustrar — **illustration** n **1** : ilustración f **2** EXAMPLE : ejemplo m — **illustrative** adj : ilustrativo
illustrious adj : ilustre, glorioso
ill will n : animadversión f, mala voluntad f
I'm (contraction of **I am**) → **be**
image n : imagen f — **imaginary** adj : imaginario — **imagination** n : imaginación f — **imaginative** adj : imaginativo — **imagine** vt **-ined; -ining** : imaginar(se)
imbalance n : desequilibrio m
imbecile n : imbécil mf
imbue vt **-bued; -buing** : imbuir
imitation n : imitación f — ~ adj : de imitación, artificial — **imitate** vt **-tated; -tat-**

ing : imitar, remedar — **imitator** n : imitador m, -dora f
immaculate adj : inmaculado
immaterial adj : irrelevante, sin importancia
immature adj : inmaduro — **immaturity** n, pl **-ties** : inmadurez f
immediate adj : inmediato — **immediately** adv : inmediatamente
immense adj : inmenso — **immensity** n, pl **-ties** : inmensidad f
immerse vt **-mersed; -mersing** : sumergir — **immersion** n : inmersión f
immigrate vi **-grated; -grating** : inmigrar — **immigrant** n : inmigrante mf — **immigration** n : inmigración f
imminent adj : inminente — **imminence** n : inminencia f
immobile adj : inmóvil — **immobilize** vt **-lized; -lizing** : inmovilizar
immoral adj : inmoral — **immorality** n, pl **-ties** : inmoralidad f
immortal adj : inmortal — ~ n : inmortal mf — **immortality** n : inmortalidad f
immune adj : inmune — **immunity** n, pl **-ties** : inmunidad f — **immunization** n : inmunización f — **immunize** vt **-nized; -nizing** : inmunizar
imp n RASCAL : diablillo m
impact n : impacto m
impair vt : dañar, perjudicar
impart vt : impartir (información), conferir (una calidad, etc.)
impartial adj : imparcial — **impartiality** n, pl **-ties** : imparcialidad f
impassable adj : intransitable
impasse n : impasse m
impassioned adj : apasionado
impassive adj : impasible
impatience n : impaciencia f — **impatient** adj : impaciente — **impatiently** adv : con impaciencia
impeccable adj : impecable
impede vt **-peded; -peding** : dificultar — **impediment** n : impedimento m, obstáculo m
impel vt **-pelled; -pelling** : impeler
impending adj : inminente
impenetrable adj : impenetrable
imperative adj **1** COMMANDING : imperativo **2** NECESSARY : imprescindible — ~ n : imperativo m
imperceptible adj : imperceptible
imperfection n : imperfección f — **imperfect** adj : imperfecto — ~ n or ~ **tense** : imperfecto m
imperial adj : imperial — **imperialism** n : imperialismo m — **imperious** adj : imperioso
impersonal adj : impersonal

impersonate *vt* -ated; -ating : hacerse pasar por, imitar — **impersonation** *n* : imitación *f* — **impersonator** *n* : imitador *m*, -dora *f*
impertinent *adj* : impertinente — **impertinence** *n* : impertinencia *f*
impervious *adj* ∼ **to** : impermeable a
impetuous *adj* : impetuoso, impulsivo
impetus *n* : ímpetu *m*, impulso *m*
impinge *vi* -pinged; -pinging ∼ **on** : afectara, incidir en
impish *adj* : pícaro, travieso
implant *vt* : implantar
implausible *adj* : inverosímil
implement *n* : instrumento *m*, implemento *m* Lat — ∼ *vt* : poner en práctica
implicate *vt* -cated; -cating : implicar — **implication** *n* **1** INVOLVEMENT : implicación *f* **2** CONSEQUENCE : consecuencia *f* **3 by** ∼ : de forma indirecta
implicit *adj* **1** : implícito **2** UNQUESTIONING : absoluto, incondicional
implore *vt* -plored; -ploring : implorar, suplicar
imply *vt* -plied; -plying **1** HINT : insinuar **2** ENTAIL : implicar
impolite *adj* : descortés, maleducado
import *vt* : importar (mercancías) — **important** *adj* : importante — **importance** *n* : importancia *f* — **importation** *n* : importación *f* — **importer** *n* : importador *m*, -dora *f*
impose *v* -posed; -posing *vt* : imponer — *vi* ∼ **on** : importunar, molestar — **imposing** *adj* : imponente — **imposition** *n* **1** ENFORCEMENT : imposición *f* **2 be an** ∼ **on** : molestar
impossible *adj* : imposible — **impossibility** *n*, *pl* -ties : imposibilidad *f*
impostor *or* **imposter** *n* : impostor *m*, -tora *f*
impotent *adj* : impotente — **impotence** *n* : impotencia *f*
impound *vt* : incautar, embargar
impoverished *adj* : empobrecido
impracticable *adj* : impracticable
impractical *adj* : poco práctico
imprecise *adj* : impreciso — **imprecision** *n* : imprecisión *f*
impregnable *adj* : impenetrable
impregnate *vt* -nated; -nating **1** : impregnar **2** FERTILIZE : fecundar
impress *vt* **1** : causar una buena impresión a **2** AFFECT : impresionar **3** ∼ **sth on s.o.** : recalcar algo a algn — *vi* : impresionar — **impression** *n* : impresión *f* — **impressionable** *adj* : impresionable — **impressive** *adj* : impresionante
imprint *vt* : imprimir — ∼ *n* MARK : impresión *f*, huella *f*
imprison *vt* : encarcelar — **imprisonment** *n* : encarcelamiento *m*

improbable *adj* : improbable — **improbability** *n*, *pl* -ties : improbabilidad *f*
impromptu *adj* : improvisado
improper *adj* **1** UNSEEMLY : indecoroso **2** INCORRECT : impropio — **impropriety** *n*, *pl* -eties : inconveniencia *f*
improve *v* -proved; -proving : mejorar — **improvement** *n* : mejora *f*
improvise *v* -vised; -vising : improvisar — **improvisation** *n* : improvisación *f*
impudent *adj* : insolente — **impudence** *n* : insolencia *f*
impulse *n* **1** : impulso *m* **2 on** ∼ : sin reflexionar — **impulsive** *adj* : impulsivo — **impulsiveness** *n* : impulsividad *f*
impunity *n* **1** : impunidad *f* **2 with** ∼ : impunemente
impure *adj* : impuro — **impurity** *n*, *pl* -ties : impureza *f*
in *prep* **1** : en **2** DURING : por, en Lat **3** WITHIN : dentro de **4 dressed** ∼ **red** : vestido de rojo **5** ∼ **the rain** : bajo la lluvia **6** ∼ **the sun** : al sol **7** ∼ **this way** : de esta manera **8 the best** ∼ **the world** : el mejor del mundo **9 written** ∼ **ink/French** : escrito con tinta/en francés — *adv* **1** INSIDE : dentro, adentro **2 be** ∼ : estar (en casa) **3 be** ∼ **on** : participar en **4 come in!** : ¡entre!, ¡pase! **5 he's** ∼ **for a shock** : se va a llevar un shock — ∼ *adj* : de moda
inability *n*, *pl* -ties : incapacidad *f*
inaccessible *adj* : inaccesible
inaccurate *n* : inexacto
inactive *n* : inactivo — **inactivity** *n*, *pl* -ties : inactividad *f*
inadequate *adj* : insuficiente
inadvertently *adv* : sin querer
inadvisable *adj* : desaconsejable
inane *adj* **inaner**; -est : estúpido, tonto
inanimate *adj* : inanimado
inapplicable *adj* : inaplicable
inappropriate *adj* : impropio, inoportuno
inarticulate *adj* : incapaz de expresarse
inasmuch as *conj* : ya que, puesto que
inattentive *adj* : poco atento
inaudible *adj* : inaudible
inaugural *adj* **1** : inaugural **2** ∼ **address** : discurso *m* de investidura — **inaugurate** *vt* -rated; -rating **1** : investir (a un presidente, etc.) **2** BEGIN : inaugurar — **inauguration** *n* : investidura *f* (de una persona), inauguración *f* (de un edificio, etc.)
inborn *adj* : innato
inbred *adj* INNATE : innato
incalculable *adj* : incalculable
incapable *adj* : incapaz — **incapacitate** *vt* -tated; -tating : incapacitar — **incapacity** *n*, *pl* -ties : incapacidad *f*
incarcerate *vt* -ated; -ating : encarcelar

incarnate *adj* : encarnado — **incarnation** *n* : encarnación *f*

incendiary *adj* : incendiario

incense¹ *n* : incienso *m*

incense² *vt* **-censed; -censing** : indignar, enfurecer

incentive *n* : incentivo *m*

inception *n* : comienzo *m*, principio *m*

incessant *adj* : incesante

incest *n* : incesto *m* — **incestuous** *adj* : incestuoso

inch *n* : pulgada *f* — ~ *v* : avanzar poco a poco

incident *n* : incidente *m* — **incidence** *n* : índice *m* (de crímenes, etc.) — **incidental** *adj* **1** MINOR : incidental **2** CHANCE : casual — **incidentally** *adv* : a propósito

incinerate *vt* **-ated; -ating** : incinerar — **incinerator** *n* : incinerador *m*

incision *n* : incisión *f*

incite *vt* **-cited; -citing** : incitar, instigar

incline *v* **-clined; -clining** *vt* **1** BEND : inclinar **2 be ~ed to** : inclinarse a, tender a — ~ *vi* : inclinarse — ~ *n* : pendiente *f* — **inclination** *n* **1** : inclinación *f* **2** DESIRE : deseo *m*, ganas *fpl*

include *vt* **-cluded; -cluding** : incluir — **inclusion** *n* : inclusión *f* — **inclusive** *adj* : inclusivo

incognito *adv* & *adj* : de incógnito

incoherent *adj* : incoherente — **incoherence** *n* : incoherencia *f*

income *n* : ingresos *mpl* — **income tax** *n* : impuesto *m* sobre la renta

incomparable *adj* : incomparable

incompatible *adj* : incompatible

incompetent *adj* : incompetente — **incompetence** *n* : incompetencia *f*

incomplete *adj* : incompleto

incomprehensible *adj* : incomprensible

inconceivable *adj* : inconcebible

inconclusive *adj* : no concluyente

incongruous *adj* : incongruente

inconsiderate *adj* : desconsiderado

inconsistent *adj* **1** : inconsecuente **2 be ~ with** : no concordar con — **inconsistency** *n*, *pl* **-cies** : inconsecuencia *f*

inconspicuous *adj* : que no llama la atención

inconvenient *adj* : incómodo, inconveniente — **inconvenience** *n* **1** BOTHER : incomodidad *f*, molestia *f* **2** DRAWBACK : inconveniente *m* — ~ *vt* **-nienced; -niencing** *vt* : importunar, molestar

incorporate *vt* **-rated; -rating** : incorporar

incorrect *adj* : incorrecto

increase *n* : aumento *m* — ~ *v* **-creased; -creasing** : aumentar — **increasingly** *adv* : cada vez más

incredible *adj* : increíble

incredulous *adj* : incrédulo

incriminate *vt* **-nated; -nating** : incriminar

incubator *n* : incubadora *f*

incumbent *n* : titular *mf*

incur *vt* **incurred; incurring** : provocar (al enojo, etc.), incurrir en (gastos)

incurable *adj* : incurable

indebted *adj* **1** : endeudado **2 be ~ to s.o.** : estar en deuda con algn

indecent *adj* : indecente — **indecency** *n*, *pl* **-cies** : indecencia *f*

indecisive *adj* : indeciso

indeed *adv* **1** TRULY : verdaderamente, sin duda **2** IN FACT : en efecto **3** ~? : ¿de veras?

indefinite *adj* **1** : indefinido **2** VAGUE : impreciso — **indefinitely** *adv* : indefinidamente

indelible *adj* : indeleble

indent *vt* : sangrar (un párrafo) — **indentation** *n* DENT, NOTCH : mella *f*

independent *adj* : independiente — **independence** *n* : independencia *f*

indescribable *adj* : indescriptible

indestructible *adj* : indestructible

index *n*, *pl* **-dexes** *or* **-dices** : índice *m* — ~ *vt* : incluir en un índice — **index finger** *n* : dedo *m* índice

Indian *adj* : indio *m*, -dia *f*

indication *n* : indicio *m*, señal *f* — **indicate** *vt* **-cated; -cating** : indicar — **indicative** *adj* : indicativo — **indicator** *n* : indicador *m*

indict *vt* : acusar (de un crimen) — **indictment** *n* : acusación *f*

indifferent *adj* **1** : indiferente **2** MEDIOCRE : mediocre — **indifference** *n* : indiferencia *f*

indigenous *adj* : indígena

indigestion *n* : indigestión *f* — **indigestible** *adj* : indigesto

indignation *n* : indignación *f* — **indignant** *adj* : indignado — **indignity** *n*, *pl* **-ties** : indignidad *f*

indigo *n*, *pl* **-gos** *or* **-goes** : añil *m*

indirect *adj* : indirecto

indiscreet *adj* : indiscreto — **indiscretion** *n* : indiscreción *f*

indiscriminate *adj* : indiscriminado

indispensable *adj* : indispensable, imprescindible

indisputable *adj* : indiscutible

indistinct *adj* : indistinto

individual *adj* **1** : individual **2** PARTICULAR : particular — ~ *n* : individuo *m* — **individuality** *n*, *pl* **-ties** : individualidad *f* — **individually** *adv* : individualmente

indoctrinate *vt* **-nated; -nating** : adoctrinar — **indoctrination** *n* : adoctrinamiento *m*

indoor *adj* **1** : (de) interior **2** ~ **plant** : planta *f* de interior **3** ~ **pool** : piscina *f* cubierta **4** ~ **sports** : deportes *mpl* bajo techo — **indoors** *adv* : adentro, dentro
induce *vt* **-duced; -ducing 1** : inducir **2** CAUSE : provocar — **inducement** *n* : incentivo *m*
indulge *v* **-dulged; -dulging** *vt* **1** GRATIFY : satisfacer **2** PAMPER : consentir — *vi* ~ **in** : permitirse — **indulgence** *n* **1** : indulgencia *f* **2** SATISFYING : satisfacción *f* — **indulgent** *adj* : indulgente
industry *n, pl* **-tries 1** : industria *f* **2** DILIGENCE : diligencia *f* — **industrial** *adj* : industrial — **industrialize** *vt* **-ized; -izing** : industrializar — **industrious** *adj* : diligente, trabajador
inebriated *adj* : ebrio, embriagado
inedible *adj* : no comestible
ineffective *adj* **1** : ineficaz **2** INCOMPETENT : incompetente — **ineffectual** *adj* : inútil, ineficaz
inefficient *adj* **1** : ineficiente **2** INCOMPETENT : incompetente — **inefficiency** *n, pl* **-cies** : ineficiencia *f*
ineligible *adj* : inelegible
inept *adj* **1** : inepto **2** ~ **at** : incapaz para
inequality *n, pl* **-ties** : desigualdad *f*
inert *adj* : inerte — **inertia** *n* : inercia *f*
inescapable *adj* : ineludible
inevitable *adj* : inevitable — **inevitably** *adv* : inevitablemente
inexcusable *adj* : inexcusable
inexpensive *adj* : barato, económico
inexperienced *adj* : inexperto
inexplicable *adj* : inexplicable
infallible *adj* : infalible
infamous *adj* : infame
infancy *n, pl* **-cies** : infancia *f* — **infant** *n* : bebé *m;* niño *m,* -ña *f* — **infantile** *adj* : infantil
infantry *n, pl* **-tries** : infantería *f*
infatuated *adj* be ~ **with** : estar encaprichado con — **infatuation** *n* : encaprichamiento *m*
infect *vt* : infectar — **infection** *n* : infección *f* — **infectious** *adj* : contagioso
infer *vt* **inferred; inferring** : deducir, inferir — **inference** *n* : deducción *f*
inferior *adj* : inferior — *n* : inferior *mf* — **inferiority** *n, pl* **-ties** : inferioridad *f*
infernal *adj* : infernal — **inferno** *n, pl* **-nos** : infierno *m*
infertile *adj* : estéril — **infertility** *n* : esterilidad *f*
infest *vt* : infestar
infidelity *n, pl* **-ties** : infidelidad *f*
infiltrate *v* **-trated; -trating** *vt* : infiltrar — *vi* : infiltrarse

infinite *adj* : infinito
infinitive *n* : infinitivo *m*
infinity *n, pl* **-ties 1** : infinito *m* **2 an** ~ **of** : una infinidad de
infirm *adj* : enfermizo, endeble — **infirmary** *n, pl* **-ries** : enfermería *f* — **infirmity** *n, pl* **-ties 1** FRAILTY : endeblez *f* **2** AILMENT : enfermedad *f*
inflame *vt* **-flamed; -flaming** : inflamar — **inflammable** *adj* : inflamable — **inflammation** *n* : inflamación *f* — **inflammatory** *adj* : inflamatorio
inflate *vt* **-flated; -flating** : inflar — **inflation** *n* : inflación *f* — **inflationary** *adj* : inflacionario, inflacionista
inflexible *adj* : inflexible
inflict *vt* : infligir
influence *n* **1** : influencia *f* **2 under the** ~ : embriagado — ~ *vt* **-enced; -encing** : influir en, influenciar — **influential** *adj* : influyente
influenza *n* : gripe *f,* influenza *f*
influx *n* : afluencia *f*
inform *vt* **1** : informar **2 keep me** ~**ed** : manténme al corriente — *vi* ~ **on** : delatar, denunciar
informal *adj* **1** : informal **2** : familiar (dícese del lenguaje) — **informality** *n, pl* **-ties** : falta *f* de ceremonia — **informally** *adv* : de manera informal
information *n* : información *f* — **informative** *adj* : informativo — **informer** *n* : informante *mf*
infrared *adj* : infrarrojo
infrastructure *n* : infraestructura *f*
infrequent *adj* : infrequente — **infrequently** *adv* : raramente
infringe *v* **-fringed; -fringing** *vt* : infringir — *vi* ~ **on** : violar — **infringement** *n* : violación *f*
infuriate *vt* **-ated; -ating** : enfurecer, poner furioso — **infuriating** *adj* : exasperante
infuse *vt* **-fused; -fusing** : infundir — **infusion** *n* : infusión *f*
ingenious *adj* : ingenioso — **ingenuity** *n, pl* **-ities** : ingenio
ingenuous *adj* : ingenuo
ingest *vt* : ingerir
ingot *n* : lingote *m*
ingrained *adj* : arraigado
ingratiate *vt* **-ated; -ating** ~ **oneself with** : congraciarse con
ingratitude *n* : ingratitud *f*
ingredient *n* : ingrediente *m*
ingrown *adj* ~ **nail** : uña *f* encarnada
inhabit *vt* : habitar — **inhabitant** *n* : habitante *mf*
inhale *v* **-haled; -haling** *vt* : inhalar, aspirar — *vi* : inspirar

inherent *adj* : inherente — **inherently** *adv* : intrínsecamente

inherit *vt* : heredar — **inheritance** *n* : herencia *f*

inhibit *vt* IMPEDE : inhibir — **inhibition** *n* : inhibición *f*

inhuman *adj* : inhumano — **inhumane** *adj* : inhumano — **inhumanity** *n, pl* **-ties** : inhumanidad *f*

initial *adj* : inicial — *n* : inicial *f* — *vt* **-tialed** *or* **-tialled; -tialing** *or* **-tialling** : poner las iniciales a

initiate *vt* **-ated; -ating** 1 BEGIN : iniciar 2 ~ **s.o. into sth** : iniciar a algn en algo — **initiation** *n* : iniciación *f* — **initiative** *n* : iniciativa *f*

inject *vt* : inyectar — **injection** *n* : inyección *f*

injure *vt* **-jured; -juring** 1 : herir 2 ~ **oneself** : hacerse daño — **injurious** *adj* : perjudicial — **injury** *n, pl* **-ries** 1 : herida *f* 2 HARM : perjuicio *m*

injustice *n* : injusticia *f*

ink *n* : tinta *f* — **inkwell** *n* : tintero *m*

inland *adj* : interior — ~ *adv* : hacia el interior, tierra adentro

in–laws *npl* : suegros *mpl*

inlet *n* : ensenada *f*, cala *f*

inmate *n* 1 PATIENT : paciente *mf* 2 PRISONER : preso *m*, -sa *f*

inn *n* : posada *f*, hostería *f*

innards *npl* : entrañas *fpl*, tripas *fpl fam*

innate *adj* : innato

inner *adj* : interior, interno — **innermost** *adj* : más íntimo, más profundo

inning *n* : entrada *f*

innocent *adj* : inocente — ~ *n* : inocente *mf* — **innocence** *n* : inocencia *f*

innocuous *adj* : inocuo

innovate *vi* **-vated; -vating** : innovar — **innovation** *n* : innovación *f* — **innovative** *adj* : innovador — **innovator** *n* : innovador *m*, -dora *f*

innuendo *n, pl* **-dos** *or* **-does** : insinuación *f*, indirecta *f*

innumerable *adj* : innumerable

inoculate *vt* **-lated; -lating** : inocular — **inoculation** *n* : inoculación *f*

inoffensive *adj* : inofensivo

inpatient *n* : paciente *mf* hospitalizado

input *n* 1 : contribución *f* 2 : entrada *f* (de datos) — ~ *vt* **-putted** *or* **-put; -putting** : entrar (datos, etc.)

inquire *v* **-quired; -quiring** *vt* : preguntar — *vi* 1 ~ **about** : informarse sobre 2 ~ **into** : investigar — **inquiry** *n, pl* **-ries** 1 QUESTION : pregunta *f* 2 INVESTIGATION : investigación *f* — **inquisition** *n* : inquisición *f* — **inquisitive** *adj* : curioso

insane *adj* : loco — **insanity** *n, pl* **-ties** : locura *f*

insatiable *adj* : insaciable

inscribe *vt* **-scribed; -scribing** : inscribir — **inscription** *n* : inscripción *f*

inscrutable *adj* : inescrutable

insect *n* : insecto *m* — **insecticide** *n* : insecticida *m*

insecure *adj* : inseguro, poco seguro — **insecurity** *n, pl* **-ties** : inseguridad *f*

insensitive *adj* : insensible — **insensitivity** *n, pl* **-ties** : insensibilidad *f*

inseparable *adj* : inseparable

insert *vt* : insertar (texto), introducir (una moneda, etc.)

inside *n* 1 : interior *m* 2 ~ **out** : al revés — *adv* : dentro, adentro — ~ *adj* : interior — ~ *prep* 1 *or* ~ **of** : dentro de 2 ~ **an hour** : en menos de una hora

insidious *adj* : insidioso

insight *n* : perspicacia *f*

insignia *or* **insigne** *n, pl* **-nia** *or* **-nias** : insignia *f*, enseña *f*

insignificant *adj* : insignificante

insincere *adj* : insincero

insinuate *vt* **-ated; -ating** : insinuar — **insinuation** *n* : insinuación *f*

insipid *adj* : insípido

insist *v* : insistir — **insistent** *adj* : insistente

insofar as *conj* : en la medida en que

insole *n* : plantilla *f*

insolent *adj* : insolente — **insolence** *n* : insolencia *f*

insolvent *adj* : insolvente

insomnia *n* : insomnio *m*

inspect *vt* : inspeccionar, revisar — **inspection** *n* : inspección *f* — **inspector** *n* : inspector *m*, -tora *f*

inspire *vt* **-spired; -spiring** : inspirar — **inspiration** *n* : inspiración *f* — **inspirational** *adj* : inspirador

instability *n, pl* **-ties** : inestabilidad *f*

install *vt* **-stalled; -stalling** : instalar — **installation** *n* : instalación *f* — **installment** *n* 1 PAYMENT : plazo *m*, cuota *f* 2 : entrega *f* (de una publicación o telenovela)

instance *n* 1 : ejemplo *m* 2 **for** ~ : por ejemplo 3 **in this** ~ : en este caso

instant *n* : instante *m* — ~ *adj* 1 IMMEDIATE : inmediato 2 ~ **coffee** : café *m* instantáneo — **instantaneous** *adj* : instantáneo — **instantly** *adv* : al instante, instantáneamente

instead *adv* 1 : en cambio 2 **I went** ~ : fui en su lugar — **instead of** *prep* : en vez de, en lugar de

instep *n* : empeine *m*

instigate *vt* **-gated; -gating** : instigar a —

instigation *n* : instigación *f* — **instigator** *n* : instigador *m*, -dora *f*
instill *or Brit* **instil** *vt* **-stilled; -stilling** : inculcar, infundir
instinct *n* : instinto *m* — **instinctive** *or* **instinctual** *adj* : instintivo
institute *vt* **-tuted; -tuting** 1 : instituir 2 INITIATE : iniciar — ~ *n* : instituto *m* — **institution** *n* : institución *f*
instruct *vt* 1 : instruir 2 COMMAND : mandar — **instruction** *n* : instrucción *f* — **instructor** *n* : instructor *m*, -tora *f*
instrument *n* : instrumento *m* — **instrumental** *adj* 1 : instrumental 2 be ~ in : jugar un papel fundamental en
insubordinate *adj* : insubordinado — **insubordination** *n* : insubordinación *f*
insufferable *adj* : insoportable
insufficient *adj* : insuficiente
insular *adj* 1 : insular 2 NARROW-MINDED : estrecho de miras
insulate *vt* **-lated; -lating** : aislar — **insulation** *n* : aislamiento *m*
insulin *n* : insulina *f*
insult *vt* : insultar — ~ *n* : insulto *m* — **insulting** *adj* : insultante, ofensivo
insure *vt* **-sured; -suring** : asegurar — **insurance** *n* : seguro *m*
insurmountable *adj* : insuperable
intact *adj* : intacto
intake *n* : consumo *m* (de alimentos), entrada *f* (de aire, etc.)
intangible *adj* : intangible
integral *adj* : integral
integrate *v* **-grated; -grating** *vt* : integrar — *vi* : integrarse
integrity *n* : integridad *f*
intellect *n* : intelecto *m* — **intellectual** *adj* : intelectual — ~ *n* : intelectual *mf* — **intelligence** *n* : inteligencia *f* — **intelligent** *adj* : inteligente — **intelligible** *adj* : inteligible
intend *vt* 1 be ~ed for : ser para 2 ~ to do : pensar hacer, tener la intención de hacer — **intended** *adj* : intencionado, deliberado
intense *adj* : intenso — **intensely** *adv* : sumamente, profundamente — **intensify** *v* **-fied; -fying** *vt* : intensificar — *vi* : intensificarse — **intensity** *n, pl* **-ties** : intensidad *f* — **intensive** *adj* : intensivo
intent *n* : intención *f* — ~ *adj* 1 : atento, concentrado 2 ~ on doing : resuelto a hacer — **intention** *n* : intención *f* — **intentional** *adj* : intencional, deliberado — **intently** *adv* : atentamente, fijamente
interact *vi* 1 : interactuar 2 ~ with : relacionarse con — **interaction** *n* : interacción *f* — **interactive** *adj* : interactivo
intercede *vi* **-ceded; -ceding** : interceder

intercept *vt* : interceptar
interchange *vt* **-changed; -changing** : intercambiar — ~ *n* 1 : intercambio *m* 2 JUNCTION : enlace *m* — **interchangeable** *adj* : intercambiable
intercourse *n* : relaciones *fpl* (sexuales)
interest *n* : interés *m* — ~ *vt* : interesar — **interested** *adj* : interesado — **interesting** *adj* : interesante
interface *n* : interfaz *mf* (de una computadora)
interfere *vi* **-fered; -fering** 1 ~ in : entrometerse en, interferir en 2 ~ with DISRUPT : afectar (una actividad, etc.) — **interference** *n* 1 : interferencia *f* 2 : intromisión *f* (en el radio, etc.)
interim *n* 1 : interín *m* 2 in the ~ : mientras tanto — ~ *adj* : interino, provisional
interior *adj* : interior — ~ *n* : interior *m*
interjection *n* : interjección *f*
interlock *vt* : engranar
interloper *n* : intruso *m*, -sa *f*
interlude *n* 1 : intervalo *m* 2 : interludio *m* (en música, etc.)
intermediate *adj* : intermedio — **intermediary** *n, pl* **-aries** : intermediario *m*, -ria *f*
interminable *adj* : interminable
intermission *n* : intervalo *m*, intermedio *m*
intermittent *adj* : intermitente
intern[1] *vt* : confinar
intern[2] *vi* : hacer las prácticas — ~ *n* : interno *m*, -na *f*
internal *adj* : interno
international *adj* : internacional
interpret *vt* : interpretar — **interpretation** *n* : interpretación *f* — **interpreter** *n* : intérprete *mf*
interrogate *vt* **-gated; -gating** : interrogar — **interrogation** *n* QUESTIONING : interrogatorio *m* — **interrogative** *adj* : interrogativo
interrupt *v* : interrumpir — **interruption** *n* : interrupción *f*
intersect *vt* : cruzar (dícese de calles), cortar (dícese de líneas) — *vi* : cruzarse, cortarse — **intersection** *n* : cruce *m*, intersección *f*
intersperse *vt* **-spersed; -spersing** : intercalar
interstate *n or* ~ **highway** : carretera *f* interestatal
intertwine *vi* **-twined; -twining** : entrelazarse
interval *n* : intervalo *m*
intervene *vi* **-vened; -vening** 1 : intervenir 2 ELAPSE : transcurrir, pasar — **intervention** *n* : intervención *f*
interview *n* : entrevista *f* — ~ *vt* : entrevistar — **interviewer** *n* : entrevistador *m*, -dora *f*

intestine n : intestino m — **intestinal** adj : intestinal

intimate[1] vt -mated; -mating : insinuar, dar a entender

intimate[2] adj : íntimo — **intimacy** n, pl -cies : intimidad f

intimidate vt -dated; -dating : intimidar — **intimidation** n : intimidación f

into prep 1 : en, a 2 **bump** ~ : darse contra 3 (used in mathematics) 3 ~ 12 : 12 dividido por 3

intolerable adj : intolerable — **intolerance** n : intolerancia f — **intolerant** adj : intolerante

intoxicate vt -cated; -cating : embriagar — **intoxicated** adj 1 : embriagado 2 ~ **with** : ebrio de

intransitive adj : intransitivo

intravenous adj : intravenoso

intrepid adj : intrépido

intricate adj : complicado, intrincado — **intricacy** n, pl -cies : complejidad f

intrigue n : intriga f — ~ v -trigued; -triguing : intrigar — **intriguing** adj : intrigante

intrinsic adj : intrínseco

introduce vt -duced; -ducing 1 : introducir 2 : presentar (a una persona) — **introduction** n 1 : introducción f 2 : presentación f (de una persona) — **introductory** adj : introductorio

introvert n : introvertido m, -da f — **introverted** adj : introvertido

intrude vi -truded; -truding 1 : entrometerse 2 ~ **on** s.o. : molestar a algn — **intruder** n : intruso m, -sa f — **intrusion** n : intrusión f — **intrusive** adj : intruso

intuition n : intuición f — **intuitive** adj : intuitivo

inundate vt -dated; -dating : inundar

invade vt -vaded; -vading : invadir

invalid[1] adj : inválido

invalid[2] n : inválido m, -da f

invaluable adj : inestimable, invalorable Lat

invariable adj : invariable

invasion n : invasión f

invent vt : inventar — **invention** n : invención f — **inventive** adj : inventivo — **inventor** n : inventor m, -tora f

inventory n, pl -ries : inventario m

invert vt : invertir

invertebrate adj : invertebrado — ~ n : invertebrado m

invest vt : invertir

investigate v -gated; -gating : investigar — **investigation** n : investigación f — **investigator** n : investigador m, -dora f

investment n : inversión f — **investor** n : inversor m, -sora f

inveterate adj : inveterado

invigorating adj : vigorizante

invincible adj : invencible

invisible adj : invisible

invitation n : invitación f — **invite** vt -vited; -viting 1 : invitar 2 SEEK : buscar (problemas, etc.) — **inviting** adj : atrayente

invoice n : factura f

invoke vt -voked; -voking : invocar

involuntary adj : involuntario

involve vt -volved; -volving 1 CONCERN : concernir, afectar 2 ENTAIL : suponer — **involved** adj 1 COMPLEX : complicado 2 CONCERNED : afectado — **involvement** n : participación f

invulnerable adj : invulnerable

inward adj INNER : interior, interno — ~ or **inwards** adv : hacia adentro, hacia el interior

iodine n : yodo m, tintura f de yodo

ion n : ion m

iota n : pizca f, ápice m

IOU n : pagaré m, vale m

Iranian adj : iraní

Iraqi adj : iraquí

ire n : ira f — **irate** adj : furioso

iris n, pl **irises** or **irides** 1 : iris m (del ojo) 2 : lirio m (planta)

Irish adj : irlandés

irksome adj : irritante, fastidioso

iron n 1 : hierro m, fierro m Lat (metal) 2 : plancha f (para la ropa) — ~ v : planchar

ironic or **ironical** adj : irónico

ironing board n : tabla f (de planchar)

irony n, pl -nies : ironía f

irrational adj : irracional

irreconcilable adj : irreconciliable

irrefutable adj : irrefutable

irregular adj : irregular — **irregularity** n, pl -ties : irregularidad f

irrelevant adj : irrelevante

irreparable adj : irreparable

irreplaceable adj : irreemplazable

irresistible adj : irresistible

irresolute adj : irresoluto

irrespective of prep : sin tener en cuenta

irresponsible adj : irresponsable — **irresponsibility** n, pl -ties : irresponsabilidad f

irreverent adj : irreverente

irreversible adj : irreversible, irrevocable

irrigate vt -gated; -gating : irrigar, regar — **irrigation** n : irrigación f, riego m

irritate vt -tated; -tating : irritar — **irritable** adj : irritable — **irritably** adv : con irritación — **irritating** adj : irritante — **irritation** n : irritación f

is → be

Islam n : el Islam — **Islamic** adj : islámico

island n : isla f — **isle** n : isla f

isolate *vt* -lated; -lating : aislar — **isolation** *n* : aislamiento *m*

Israeli *adj* : israelí

issue *n* **1** MATTER : asunto *m,* cuestión *f* **2** : número *m* (de una revista, etc.) **3 make an ~ of** : insistir demasiado sobre **4 take ~ with** : disentir de — **~** *v* -sued; -suing *vi* **~ from** : surgir de — *vt* **1** : emitir (sellos, etc.), distribuir (provisiones, etc.) **2** PUBLISH : publicar

isthmus *n* : istmo *m*

it *pron* **1** (*as subject*) : él, ella **2** (*as indirect object*) : le, se **3** (*as direct object*) : lo, la **4** (*as object of a preposition*) : él, ella **5 it's raining** : está lloviendo **6 it's 8 o'clock** : son las ocho **7 it's hot out** : hace calor **8 ~ is necessary** : es necesario **9 who is ~?** : ¿quién es? **10 it's me** : soy yo

Italian *adj* : italiano — **~** *n* : italiano *m* (idioma)

italics *n* : cursiva *f*

itch *vi* **1** : picar **2 be ~ing to** : morirse por — **~** *n* : picazón *f* — **itchy** *adj* **itchier; -est** : que pica

it'd (*contraction of* it had *or* it would) → **have, would**

item *n* **1** : artículo *m* **2** : punto *m* (en una agenda) **3 ~ of clothing** : prenda *f* de vestir **4 news ~** : noticia *f* — **itemize** *vt* -ized; -izing : detallar, enumerar

itinerant *adj* : ambulante

itinerary *n, pl* -aries : itinerario *m*

it'll (*contraction of* it shall *or* it will) → **shall, will**

its *adj* : su, sus

it's (*contraction of* it is *or* it has) → **be, have**

itself *pron* **1** (*used reflexively*) : se **2** (*used for emphasis*) : (él) mismo, (ella) misma, sí (mismo) **3 by ~** : solo

I've (*contraction of* I have) → **have**

ivory *n, pl* -ries : marfil *m*

ivy *n, pl* **ivies** : hiedra *f*

J

j *n, pl* **j's** *or* **js** : j *f,* décima letra del alfabeto inglés

jab *vt* **jabbed; jabbing 1** PIERCE : pinchar **2** POKE : golpear (con la punta de algo) — **~** *n* **1** PRICK : pinchazo *m* **2** POKE : golpe *m* abrupto

jabber *vi* : farfullar

jack *n* **1** : gato *m* (mecanismo) **2** : sota *f* (de naipes) — **~** *vt or* **~ up 1** : levantar (con un gato) **2** INCREASE : subir

jackal *n* : chacal *m*

jackass *n* : asno *m,* burro *m*

jacket *n* **1** : chaqueta *f* **2** : sobrecubierta *f* (de un libro), carátula *f* (de un disco)

jackhammer *n* : martillo *m* neumático

jackknife *n* : navaja *f* — **~** *vi* -knifed; -knifing : plegarse (dícese de un camión)

jack–o'–lantern *n* : linterna *f* hecha de una calabaza

jackpot *n* : premio *m* gordo

jaded *adj* **1** TIRED : agotado **2** BORED : hastiado

jagged *adj* : dentado

jail *n* : cárcel *f* — **~** *vt* : encarcelar — **jailer** *or* **jailor** *n* : carcelero *m,* -ra *f*

jalapeño *n* : jalapeño *m Lat*

jam¹ *v* **jammed; jamming** *vt* **1** CRAM : apiñar, embutir **2** BLOCK : atascar, atorar — *vi* : atascarse, atrancarse — **~** *n* **1** *or* **traffic ~** : embotellamiento *m* (de tráfico) **2** FIX : lío *m,* aprieto *m*

jam² *n* PRESERVES : mermelada *f*

jangle *v* -gled; -gling *vi* : hacer un ruido metálico — *vt* : hacer sonar — **~** *n* : ruido *m* metálico

janitor *n* : portero *m,* -ra *f;* conserje *mf*

January *n* : enero *m*

Japanese *adj* : japonés — **~** *n* : japonés *m* (idioma)

jar¹ *v* **jarred; jarring** *vi* **1** GRATE : chirriar **2** CLASH : desentonar **3 ~ on** IRRITATE : crispar, enervar (a algn) — *vt* JOLT : sacudir — **~** *n* : sacudida *f*

jar² *n* : tarro *m*

jargon *n* : jerga *f*

jaundice *n* : ictericia *f*

jaunt *n* : excursión *f*

jaunty *adj* -tier; -est : garboso, desenvuelto

jaw *n* : mandíbula *f* (de una persona), quijada *f* (de un animal) — **jawbone** *n* : mandíbula *f,* quijada *f*

jay *n* : arrendajo *m*

jazz *n* : jazz *m* — **~** *vt or* **~ up** : animar, alegrar — **jazzy** *adj* **jazzier; -est** FLASHY : llamativo

jealous *adj* : celoso — **jealousy** *n* : celos *mpl*, envidia *f*
jeans *npl* : jeans *mpl*, vaqueros *mpl*
jeer *vt* **1** BOO : abuchear **2** MOCK : mofarse de — *vi* **~ at** : mofarse de — **~** *n* : mofa *f*
jell *vi* : cuajar
jelly *n*, *pl* **-lies** : jalea *f* — **jellyfish** *n* : medusa *f*
jeopardy *n* : peligro *m*, riesgo *m* — **jeopardize** *vt* **-dized; -dizing** : arriesgar, poner en peligro
jerk *n* **1** JOLT : sacudida *f* brusca **2** FOOL : idiota *mf* — **~** *vt* : sacudir — *vi* JOLT : dar sacudidas
jersey *n*, *pl* **-seys** : jersey *m*
jest *n* : broma *f* — **~** *vi* : bromear — **jester** *n* : bufón *m*
Jesus *n* : Jesús *m*
jet *n* **1** STREAM : chorro *m* **2** *or* **~ airplane** : avión *m* a reacción, reactor *m* — **jet–propelled** *adj* : a reacción
jettison *vt* **1** : echar al mar **2** DISCARD : deshacerse de
jetty *n*, *pl* **-ties** : desembarcadero *m*, muelle *m*
jewel *n* **1** : joya *f* **2** GEM : piedra *f* preciosa — **jeweler** *or* **jeweller** *n* : joyero *m*, -ra *f* — **jewelry** *n* : joyas *fpl*, alhajas *fpl*
Jewish *adj* : judío
jibe *vi* **jibed; jibing** AGREE : concordar
jiffy *n*, *pl* **-fies** : santiamén *m*, segundo *m*
jig *n* : giga *f*
jiggle *vt* **-gled; -gling** : sacudir, zarandear — **~** *n* : sacudida *f*
jigsaw *n* **1** : sierra *f* de vaivén **2** *or* **~ puzzle** : rompecabezas *m*
jilt *vt* : dejar plantado
jingle *v* **-gled; -gling** *vi* : tintinear — *vt* : hacer sonar — **~** *n* TINKLE : tintineo *m*
jinx *n* CURSE : maldición *f*
jitters *npl* **have the ~** : estar nervioso — **jittery** *adj* : nervioso
job *n* **1** EMPLOYMENT : empleo *m*, trabajo *m* **2** TASK : trabajo *m*
jockey *n*, *pl* **-eys** : jockey *mf*
jog *v* **jogged; jogging** *vt* **~ s.o.'s memory** : refrescar la memoria a algn — *vi* : hacer footing — **jogging** *n* : footing *m*
join *vt* **1** UNITE : unir, juntar **2** MEET : reunirse con **3** : hacerse socio de (una organización, etc.) — *vi* **1** *or* **~ together** : unirse **2** : hacerse socio (de una organización, etc.)
joint *n* **1** : articulación *f* (en anatomía) **2** JUNCTURE : juntura *f*, unión *f* — **~** *adj* : conjunto — **jointly** *adv* : conjuntamente
joke *n* : chiste *m*, broma *f* — **~** *vi* **joked; joking** : bromear — **joker** *n* **1** : bromista *mf* **2** : comodín *m* (en los naipes)
jolly *adj* **-lier; -est** : alegre, jovial

jolt *vt* : sacudir — **~** *n* **1** : sacudida *f* brusca **2** SHOCK : golpe *m* (emocional)
jostle *v* **-tled; -tling** *vt* : empujar, dar empujones — *vi* : empujarse
jot *vt* **jotted; jotting** *or* **~ down** : anotar, apuntar
journal *n* **1** DIARY : diario *m* **2** PERIODICAL : revista *f* — **journalism** *n* : periodismo *m* — **journalist** *n* : periodista *mf*
journey *n*, *pl* **-neys** : viaje *m* — **~** *vi* **-neyed; -neying** : viajar
jovial *adj* : jovial
joy *n* : alegría *f* — **joyful** *adj* : alegre, feliz — **joyous** *adj* : jubiloso, alegre
jubilant *adj* : jubiloso — **jubilee** *n* : aniversario *m* especial
Judaism *n* : judaísmo *m*
judge *vt* **judged; judging** : juzgar — **~** *n* : juez *mf* — **judgment** *or* **judgement** *n* **1** RULING : fallo *m*, sentencia *f* **2** VIEW : juicio *m*
judicial *adj* : judicial — **judicious** *adj* : juicioso
jug *n* : jarra *f*
juggle *vi* **-gled; -gling** : hacer juegos malabares — **juggler** *n* : malabarista *mf*
jugular vein *n* : vena *f* yugular
juice *n* : jugo *m* — **juicy** *adj* **juicier; -est** : jugoso
jukebox *n* : máquina *f* de discos
July *n* : julio *m*
jumble *vt* **-bled; -bling** : mezclar — **~** *n* : revoltijo *m*
jumbo *adj* : gigante
jump *vi* **1** LEAP : saltar **2** START : sobresaltarse **3** RISE : subir de un golpe **4 ~ at** : no dejar escapar (una oportunidad, etc.) — *vt* : saltar — **~** *n* **1** LEAP : salto *m* **2** INCREASE : aumento *m* — **jumper** *n* **1** : saltador *m*, -dora *f* (en deportes) **2** : jumper *m* (vestido) — **jumpy** *adj* **jumpier; -est** : nervioso
junction *n* **1** JOINING : unión *f* **2** : cruce *m* (de calles), empalme *m* (de un ferrocarril) — **juncture** *n* : coyuntura *f*
June *n* : junio *m*
jungle *n* : selva *f*
junior *adj* **1** YOUNGER : más joven **2** SUBORDINATE : subalterno — **~** *n* **1** : persona *f* de menor edad **2** SUBORDINATE : subalterno *m*, -na *f* **3** : estudiante *mf* de penúltimo año
junk *n* : trastos *mpl* (viejos) — **~** *vt* : echar a la basura
junta *n* : junta *f* (militar)
jurisdiction *n* : jurisdicción *f*
jury *n*, *pl* **-ries** : jurado *m* — **juror** *n* : jurado *mf*

just *adj* : justo — ~ *adv* **1** BARELY : apenas **2** EXACTLY : exactamente **3** ONLY : sólo, solamente **4** ~ **now** : ahora mismo **5 she has** ~ **left** : acaba de salir **6 we were** ~ **leaving** : justo íbamos a salir

justice *n* **1** : justicia *f* **2** JUDGE : juez *mf*

justify *vt* **-fied; -fying** : justificar — **justification** *n* : justificación *f*

jut *vi* **jutted; jutting** *or* ~ **out** : sobresalir

juvenile *adj* **1** YOUNG : juvenil **2** CHILDISH : infantil — ~ *n* : menor *mf*

juxtapose *vt* **-posed; -posing** : yuxtaponer

K

k *n, pl* **k's** *or* **ks** : k *f*, undécima letra del alfabeto inglés

kaleidoscope *n* : calidoscopio *m*

kangaroo *n, pl* **-roos** : canguro *m*

karat *n* : quilate *m*

karate *n* : karate *m*

keel *n* : quilla *f* — ~ *vi or* ~ **over** : volcarse (dícese de un barco), desplomarse (dícese de una persona)

keen *adj* **1** SHARP : afilado **2** PENETRATING : cortante, penetrante **3** ENTHUSIASTIC : entusiasta **4** ~ **eyesight** : visión *f* aguda

keep *v* **kept; keeping** *vt* **1** : guardar **2** : cumplir (una promesa), acudir a (una cita) **3** DETAIN : hacer quedar, detener **4** PREVENT : impedir **5** ~ **up** : mantener — *vi* **1** REMAIN : mantenerse **2** LAST : conservarse **3** *or* ~ **on** CONTINUE : no dejar — ~ *n* **1 earn one's** ~ : ganarse el pan **2 for** ~**s** : para siempre — **keeper** *n* : guarda *mf* — **keeping** *n* **1** CARE : cuidado *m* **2 in** ~ **with** : de acuerdo con — **keepsake** *n* : recuerdo *m*

keg *n* : barril *m*

kennel *n* : caseta *f* para perros, perrera *f*

kept → **keep**

kerchief *n* : pañuelo *m*

kernel *n* **1** : almendra *f* **2** CORE : meollo *m*

kerosene *or* **kerosine** *n* : queroseno *m*

ketchup *n* : salsa *f* de tomate

kettle *n* : hervidor *m*, tetera *f* (para hervir)

key *n* **1** : llave *f* **2** : tecla *f* (de un piano o una máquina) — ~ *vt* **be keyed up** : estar nervioso — ~ *adj* : clave — **keyboard** *n* : teclado *m* — **keyhole** *n* : ojo *m* (de la cerradura) — **keynote** *n* : tónica *f* — **key ring** *n* : llavero *m*

khaki *adj* : caqui

kick *vt* **1** : dar una patada a **2** ~ **out** : echar a patadas — *vi* **1** : dar patadas (dícese de una persona), cocear (dícese de un animal) **2** RECOIL : dar un culatazo — ~ *n* **1** : patada *f*, coz *f* (de un animal) **2** RECOIL : culatazo *m* **3** PLEASURE, THRILL : placer *m*

kid *n* **1** GOAT : chivo *m*, -va *f*; cabrito *m* **2** CHILD : niño *m*, -ña *f* — ~ *v* **kidded; kidding** *vi or* ~ **around** : bromear — *vt* TEASE : tomar el pelo a — **kidnap** *vt* **-napped** *or* **-naped; -napping** *or* **-naping** : secuestrar, raptar

kidney *n, pl* **-neys** : riñón *m*

kidney bean *n* : frijol *m*

kill *vt* **1** : matar **2** DESTROY : acabar con **3** ~ **time** : matar el tiempo — ~ *n* **1** KILLING : matanza *f* **2** PREY : presa *f* — **killer** *n* : asesino *m*, -na *f* — **killing** *n* **1** : matanza *f* **2** MURDER : asesinato *m*

kiln *n* : horno *m*

kilo *n, pl* **-los** : kilo *m* — **kilogram** *n* : kilogramo *m* — **kilometer** *n* : kilómetro *m* — **kilowatt** *n* : kilovatio *m*

kin *n* : parientes *mpl*

kind *n* **1** : tipo *m*, clase *f* — ~ *adj* : amable

kindergarten *n* : jardín *m* infantil, jardín *m* de niños *Lat*

kindhearted *adj* : de buen corazón

kindle *vt* **-dled; -dling 1** : encender (un fuego) **2** AROUSE : despertar

kindly *adj* **-lier; -est** : bondadoso, amable — ~ *adv* **1** : amablemente **2 take** ~ **to** : aceptar de buena gana **3 we** ~ **ask you not smoke** : les rogamos que no fumen — **kindness** *n* : bondad *f* — **kind of** *adv* SOMEWHAT : un tanto, algo

kindred *adj* **1** : emparentado **2** ~ **spirit** : alma *f* gemela

king *n* : rey *m* — **kingdom** *n* : reino *m*

kink *n* **1** TWIST : vuelta *f*, curva *f* **2** FLAW : problema *m*

kinship *n* : parentesco *m*

kiss *vt* : besar — *vi* : besarse — ~ *n* : beso *m*

kit *n* **1** : juego *m*, kit *m* **2 first-aid** ~ : botiquín *m* **3 tool** ~ : caja *f* de herramientas

kitchen *n* : cocina *f*

kite *n* : cometa *f*, papalote *m Lat*

kitten *n* : gatito *m*, -ta *f* — **kitty** *n, pl* **-ties** FUND : fondo *m* común

knack *n* : maña *f*, facilidad *f*
knapsack *n* : mochila *f*
knead *vt* **1** : amasar, sobar **2** MASSAGE : masajear
knee *n* : rodilla *f* — **kneecap** *n* : rótula *f*
kneel *vi* **knelt** *or* **kneeled; kneeling** : arrodillarse
knew → **know**
knickknack *n* : chuchería *f*
knife *n*, *pl* **knives** : cuchillo *m* — ~ *vt* **knifed; knifing** : acuchillar
knight *n* **1** : caballero *m* **2** : caballo *m* (en ajedrez) — **knighthood** *n* : título *m* de Sir
knit *v* **knit** *or* **knitted; knitting** *v* : tejer — ~ *n* : prenda *f* tejida
knob *n* : tirador *m*, botón *m*, perilla *f Lat*
knock *vt* **1** : golpear **2** CRITICIZE : criticar **3** ~ **down** : derribar, echar al suelo — *vi* **1** : dar un golpe, llamar (a la puerta) **2** COL-LIDE : darse, chocar — ~ *n* : golpe *m*, llamada *f* (a la puerta)
knot *n* : nudo *m* — ~ *vt* **knotted; knotting** : anudar — **knotty** *adj* **-tier; -est 1** : nudoso **2** : enredado (dícese de un problema)
know *v* **knew; known; knowing** *vt* **1** : saber **2** : conocer (a una persona, un lugar) **3** ~ **how to** : saber — *vi* : saber — **knowing** *adj* : cómplice — **knowingly** *adv* **1** : de manera cómplice **2** DELIBERATELY : a sabiendas — **know–it–all** *n* : sabelotodo *mf fam* — **knowledge** *n* **1** : conocimiento *m* **2** LEARNING : conocimientos *mpl*, saber *m* — **knowledgeable** *adj* : informado, entendido
knuckle *n* : nudillo *m*
Koran *n* **the Koran** : el Corán *m*
Korean *adj* : coreano *m*, -na *f* — ~ *n* : coreano *m* (idioma)
kosher *adj* : aprobado por la ley judía

L

l *n*, *pl* **l's** *or* **ls** : l *f*, duodécima letra del alfabeto inglés
lab → **laboratory**
label *n* **1** TAG : etiqueta *f* **2** BRAND : marca *f* — ~ *vt* **-beled** *or* **-belled; -beling** *or* **-belling** : etiquetar
labor *n* **1** : trabajo *m* **2** WORKERS : mano *f* de obra **3 in** ~ : de parto — ~ *vi* **1** : trabajar **2** STRUGGLE : avanzar penosamente — *vt* BELABOR : insistir en (un punto)
laboratory *n*, *pl* **-ries** : laboratorio *m*
laborer *n* : trabajador *m*, -dora *f*
laborious *adj* : laborioso
lace *n* **1** : encaje *m* **2** SHOELACE : cordón *m* (de zapatos), agujeta *f Lat* — ~ *vt* **laced; lacing 1** TIE : atar **2 be laced with** : echar licor a (una bebida, etc.)
lacerate *vt* **-ated; -ating** : lacerar
lack *vt* : carecer de, no tener — *vi* **be lacking** : faltar — ~ *n* : falta *f*, carencia *f*
lackadaisical *adj* : apático, indolente
lackluster *adj* : sin brillo, apagado
laconic *adj* : lacónico
lacquer *n* : laca *f*
lacrosse *n* : lacrosse *f*
lacy *adj* **lacier; -est** : como de encaje
lad *n* : muchacho *m*, niño *m*
ladder *n* : escalera *f*
laden *adj* : cargado
ladle *n* : cucharón *m* — ~ *vt* **-dled; -dling** : servir con cucharón
lady *n*, *pl* **-dies** : señora *f*, dama *f* — **ladybug** *n* : mariquita *f* — **ladylike** *adj* : elegante, como señora
lag *n* **1** DELAY : retraso *m* **2** INTERVAL : intervalo *m* — ~ *vi* **lagged; lagging** : quedarse atrás, rezagarse
lager *n* : cerveza *f* rubia
lagoon *n* : laguna *f*
laid *pp* → **lay¹**
lain *pp* → **lie¹**
lair *n* : guarida *f*
lake *n* : lago *m*
lamb *n* : cordero *m*
lame *adj* **lamer; lamest 1** : cojo, renco **2 a** ~ **excuse** : una excusa poco convincente
lament *vt* **1** MOURN : llorar **2** DEPLORE : lamentar — ~ *n* : lamento *m* — **lamentable** *adj* : lamentable
laminate *vt* **-nated; -nating** : laminar
lamp *n* : lámpara *f* — **lamppost** *n* : farol *m* — **lampshade** *n* : pantalla *f*
lance *n* : lanza *f* — ~ *vt* **lanced; lancing** : abrir con lanceta (en medicina)
land *n* **1** : tierra *f* **2** COUNTRY : país *m* **3 or plot of** ~ : terreno *m* — ~ *vt* **1** : desembarcar (pasajeros de un barco), hacer aterrizar (un avión) **2** CATCH : sacar (un pez) del agua **3** SECURE : conseguir (empleo, etc.) — *vi* **1** : aterrizar (dícese de un avión) **2** FALL : caer — **landing** *n* **1** : aterrizaje *m* (de aviones) **2** : desembarco *m* (de barcos)

3 : descanso *m* (de una escalera) — **land-lady** *n*, *pl* **-dies** : casera *f* — **landlord** *n* : casero *m* — **landmark** *n* **1** : punto *m* de referencia **2** MONUMENT : monumento *m* histórico — **landowner** *n* : hacendado *m*, -da *f*; terrateniente *mf* — **landscape** *n* : paisaje *m* — ~ *vt* **-scaped; -scaping** : ajardinar — **landslide** *n* **1** : desprendimiento *m* de tierras **2** *or* ~ **victory** : victoria *f* arrolladora

lane *n* **1** : carril *m* (de una carretera) **2** PATH, ROAD : camino *m*

language *n* **1** : idioma *m*, lengua *f* **2** SPEECH : lenguaje *m*

languid *adj* : lánguido — **languish** *vi* : languidecer

lanky *adj* **lankier; -est** : delgado, larguirucho *fam*

lantern *n* : linterna *f*

lap *n* **1** : regazo *m* (de una persona) **2** : vuelta *f* (en deportes) — ~ *v* **lapped; lapping** *vt or* ~ **up** : beber a lengüetadas — *vi* ~ **against** : lamer

lapel *n* : solapa *f*

lapse *n* **1** : lapsus *m*, falla *f* (de memoria, etc.) **2** INTERVAL : lapso *m*, intervalo *m* — ~ *vi* **lapsed; lapsing 1** EXPIRE : caducar **2** ELAPSE : transcurrir, pasar **3** ~ **into** : caer en

laptop *adj* : portátil

larceny *n*, *pl* **-nies** : robo *m*

lard *n* : manteca *f* de cerdo

large *adj* **larger; largest 1** : grande **2 at** ~ : en libertad **3 by and** ~ : por lo general — **largely** *adv* : en gran parte

lark *n* **1** : alondra *f* (pájaro) **2 for a** ~ : por divertirse

larva *n*, *pl* **-vae** : larva *f*

larynx *n*, *pl* **-rynges** *or* **-ynxes** : laringe *f* — **laryngitis** *n* : laringitis *f*

lasagna *n* : lasaña *f*

laser *n* : láser *m*

lash *vt* **1** WHIP : azotar **2** BIND : amarrar — *vi* ~ **out at** : arremeter contra — ~ *n* **1** BLOW : latigazo *m* (con un látigo) **2** EYELASH : pestaña *f*

lass *or* **lassie** *n* : muchacha *f*, chica *f*

lasso *n*, *pl* **-sos** *or* **-soes** : lazo *m*

last *vi* : durar — ~ *n* **1** : último *m*, -ma *f* **2 at** ~ : por fin, finalmente — ~ *adv* **1** : por última vez, en último lugar **2 arrive** ~ : llegar el último — ~ *adj* **1** : último **2** ~ **year** : el año pasado — **lastly** *adv* : por último, finalmente

latch *n* : picaporte *m*, pestillo *m*

late *adj* **later; latest 1** : tarde **2** : avanzado (dícese de la hora) **3** DECEASED : difunto **4** RECENT : reciente — ~ *adv* **later; latest** : tarde — **lately** *adv* : recientemente, últi-

mamente — **lateness** *n* **1** : retraso *m* **2** : lo avanzado (de la hora)

latent *adj* : latente

lateral *adj* : lateral

latest *n* **at the** ~ : a más tardar

lathe *n* : torno *m*

lather *n* : espuma *f* — ~ *vt* : enjabonar — *vi* : hacer espuma

Latin–American *adj* : latinoamericano

latitude *n* : latitud *f*

latter *adj* **1** : último **2** SECOND : segundo — ~ *pron* **the** ~ : éste, ésta, éstos *pl*, éstas *pl*

lattice *n* : enrejado *m*

laugh *vi* : reír(se) — ~ *n* : risa *f* — **laughable** *adj* : risible, ridículo — **laughter** *n* : risa *f*, risas *fpl*

launch *vt* : lanzar — ~ *n* : lanzamiento *m*

launder *vt* **1** : lavar y planchar (ropa) **2** : blanquear, lavar (dinero) — **laundry** *n*, *pl* **-dries 1** : ropa *f* sucia **2** : lavandería *f* (servicio) **3 do the** ~ : lavar la ropa

lava *n* : lava *f*

lavatory *n*, *pl* **-ries** BATHROOM : baño *m*, cuarto *m* de baño

lavender *n* : lavanda *f*

lavish *adj* **1** EXTRAVAGANT : pródigo **2** ABUNDANT : abundante **3** LUXURIOUS : lujoso — ~ *vt* : prodigar

law *n* **1** : ley *f* **2** : derecho *m* (profesión, etc.) **3 practice** ~ : ejercer la abogacía — **lawful** *adj* : legal, legítimo

lawn *n* : césped *m* — **lawn mower** *n* : cortadora *f* de césped

lawsuit *n* : pleito *m*

lawyer *n* : abogado *m*, -da *f*

lax *adj* : poco estricto, relajado

laxative *n* : laxante *m*

lay[1] *vt* **laid; laying 1** PLACE, PUT : poner, colocar **2** ~ **eggs** : poner huevos **3** ~ **off** : despedir (un empleado) **4** ~ **out** PRESENT : presentar, exponer **5** ~ **out** DESIGN : diseñar (el trazado de)

lay[2] *pp* → **lie**[1]

lay[3] *adj* **1** SECULAR : laico **2** NONPROFESSIONAL : lego, profano

layer *n* : capa *f*

layman *n*, *pl* **-men** : lego *m*, laico *m* (en religión)

layout *n* ARRANGEMENT : disposición *f*

lazy *adj* **-zier; -est** : perezoso — **laziness** *n* : pereza *f*

lead[1] *vt* **led; leading 1** GUIDE : conducir **2** DIRECT : dirigir **3** HEAD : encabezar, ir al frente de — *vi* : llevar, conducir (a algo) — ~ *n* **1** : delantera *f* **2 follow s.o.'s** ~ : seguir el ejemplo de algn

lead[2] *n* **1** : plomo *m* (metal) **2** GRAPHITE : mina *f* — **leaden** *adj* **1** : de plomo **2** HEAVY : pesado

leader *n* : jefe *m*, -fa *f* — **leadership** *n* : mando *m*, dirección *f*

leaf *n*, *pl* **leaves** 1 : hoja *f* 2 **turn over a new** ~ : hacer borrón y cuenta nueva — ~ *vi* ~ **through** : hojear (un libro, etc.) — **leaflet** *n* : folleto *m*

league *n* 1 : liga *f* 2 **be in** ~ **with** : estar confabulado con

leak *vt* 1 : dejar escapar (un líquido o un gas) 2 : filtrar (información) — *vi* 1 : gotear, escaparse (dícese de un líquido o un gas) 2 : filtrarse (dícese de información) — ~ *n* 1 : agujero *m* (de un cubo, etc.), gotera *f* (de un techo) 2 : fuga *f*, escape *m* (de un líquido o un gas) 3 : filtración *f* (de información) — **leaky** *adj* **leakier; -est** : que hace agua

lean[1] *v* **leaned** *or Brit* **leant; leaning** *vi* 1 BEND : inclinarse 2 ~ **against** : apoyarse contra — *vt* : apoyar

lean[2] *adj* 1 THIN : delgado 2 : sin grasa (dícese de la carne)

leaning *n* : inclinación *f*

leanness *n* : delgadez *f* (de una persona), lo magro (de la carne)

leap *vi* **leapt** *or* **leaped; leaping** : saltar, brincar — ~ *n* : salto *m*, brinco *m* — **leap year** *n* : año *m* bisiesto

learn *v* **learned; learning** : aprender — **learned** *adj* : sabio, erudito — **learner** *n* : principiante *mf*, estudiante *mf* — **learning** *n* : erudición *f*, saber *m*

lease *n* : contrato *m* de arrendamiento — ~ *vt* **leased; leasing** : arrendar

leash *n* : correa *f*

least *adj* 1 : menor 2 SLIGHTEST : más mínimo — ~ *n* 1 **at** ~ : por lo menos 2 **the** ~ : lo menos 3 **to say the** ~ : por no decir más — ~ *adv* : menos

leather *n* : cuero *m*

leave *v* **left; leaving** *vt* 1 : dejar 2 : salir(se) de (un lugar) 3 ~ **out** : omitir — *vi* DEPART : irse — ~ *n* 1 *or* ~ **of absence** : permiso *m*, licencia *f* 2 **take one's** ~ : despedirse

leaves → **leaf**

lecture *n* 1 TALK : conferencia *f* 2 REPRIMAND : sermón *m*, reprimenda *f* — ~ *v* **-tured; -turing** *vt* : sermonear — *vi* : dar clase, dar una conferencia

led *pp* → **lead**[1]

ledge *n* : antepecho *m* (de una ventana), saliente *m* (de una montaña)

leech *n* : sanguijuela *f*

leek *n* : puerro *m*

leer *vi* : lanzar una mirada lasciva — ~ *n* : mirada *f* lasciva

leery *adj* : receloso

leeway *n* : libertad *f* de acción, margen *m*

left[1] → **leave**

left[2] *adj* : izquierdo — ~ *adv* : a la izquierda — ~ *n* : izquierda *f* — **left-handed** *adj* : zurdo

leftovers *npl* : restos *mpl*, sobras *fpl*

leg *n* 1 : pierna *f* (de una persona, de ropa), pata *f* (de un animal, de muebles) 2 : etapa *f* (de un viaje)

legacy *n*, *pl* **-cies** : legado *m*

legal *adj* 1 LAWFUL : legítimo, legal 2 JUDICIAL : legal, jurídico — **legality** *n*, *pl* **-ties** : legalidad *f* — **legalize** *vt* **-ized; -izing** : legalizar

legend *n* : leyenda *f* — **legendary** *adj* : lengendario

legible *adj* : legible

legion *n* : legión *f*

legislate *vi* **-lated; -lating** : legislar — **legislation** *n* : legislación *f* — **legislative** *adj* : legislativo, legislador — **legislature** *n* : asamblea *f* legislativa

legitimate *adj* : legítimo — **legitimacy** *n* : legitimidad *f*

leisure *n* 1 : ocio *m*, tiempo *m* libre 2 **at your** ~ : cuando te venga bien — **leisurely** *adj & adv* : lento, sin prisas

lemon *n* : limón *m* — **lemonade** *n* : limonada *f*

lend *vt* **lent; lending** : prestar

length *n* 1 : largo *m* 2 DURATION : duración *f* 3 **at** ~ FINALLY : por fin 4 **at** ~ : EXTENSIVELY : extensamente 5 **go to any** ~**s** : hacer todo lo posible — **lengthen** — *vt* 1 : alargar 2 PROLONG : prolongar — *vi* : alargarse — **lengthways** *or* **lengthwise** *adv* : a lo largo — **lengthy** *adj* **lengthier; -est** : largo

lenient *adj* : indulgente — **leniency** *n*, *pl* **-cies** : indulgencia *f*

lens *n* 1 : cristalino *m* (del ojo) 2 : lente *mf* (de un instrumento) 3 → **contact lens**

Lent *n* : Cuaresma *f*

lentil *n* : lenteja *f*

leopard *n* : leopardo *m*

leotard *n* : leotardo *m*, malla *f*

lesbian *n* : lesbiana *f*

less *adv* (*comparative of* **little**) : menos — ~ *adj* (*comparative of* **little**) : menos — ~ *pron* : menos — ~ *prep* MINUS : menos — **lessen** *v* : disminuir — **lesser** *adj* : menor

lesson *n* 1 CLASS : clase *f*, curso *m* 2 **learn one's** ~ : aprender la lección

lest *conj* ~ **we forget** : para que no olvidemos

let *vt* **let; letting** 1 ALLOW : dejar, permitir 2 RENT : alquilar 3 ~**'s go!** : ¡vamos!, ¡vámonos! 4 ~ **down** DISAPPOINT : fallar 5 ~ **in** : dejar entrar 6 ~ **off** FORGIVE : perdonar 7 ~ **up** ABATE : amainar, disminuir

letdown *n* : chasco *m*, decepción *f*

lethal *adj* : letal

lethargic *adj* : letárgico
let's (*contraction of* **let us**) → **let**
letter *n* **1** : carta *f* **2** : letra *f* (del alfabeto)
lettuce *n* : lechuga *f*
letup *n* : pausa *f*, descanso *m*
leukemia *n* : leucemia *f*
level *n* **1** : nivel *m* **2 be on the** ~ : ser honrado — ~ *vt* **-eled** *or* **-elled; -eling** *or* **-elling 1** : nivelar **2** AIM : apuntar **3** RAZE : arrasar — ~ *adj* **1** FLAT : llano, plano **2** : nivel (de altura) — **levelheaded** *adj* : sensato, equilibrado
lever *n* : palanca *f* — **leverage** *n* **1** : apalancamiento *m* (en física) **2** INFLUENCE : influencia *f*
levity *n* : ligereza *f*
levy *n*, *pl* **levies** : impuesto *m* — ~ *vt* **levied; levying** : imponer, exigir (un impuesto)
lewd *adj* : lascivo
lexicon *n*, *pl* **-ica** *or* **-icons** : léxico *m*, lexicón *m*
liable *adj* **1** : responsable **2** LIKELY : probable **3** SUSCEPTIBLE : propenso — **liability** *n*, *pl* **-ties 1** RESPONSIBILITY : responsabilidad *f* **2** DRAWBACK : desventaja *f* **3 liabilities** *npl* DEBTS : deudas *fpl*, pasivo *m*
liaison *n* **1** : enlace *m* **2** AFFAIR : amorío *m*
liar *n* : mentiroso *m*, -sa *f*
libel *n* : libelo *m*, difamación *f* — ~ *vt* **-beled** *or* **-belled; -beling** *or* **-belling** : difamar
liberal *adj* : liberal — ~ *n* : liberal *mf*
liberate *vt* **-ated; -ating** : liberar — **liberation** *n* : liberación *f*
liberty *n*, *pl* **-ties** : libertad *f*
library *n*, *pl* **-braries** : biblioteca *f* — **librarian** *n* : bibliotecario *m*, -ria *f*
lice → **louse**
license *or* **licence** *n* **1** PERMIT : licencia *f* **2** FREEDOM : libertad *f* **3** AUTHORIZATION : permiso *m* — ~ *vt* **licensed; licensing** : autorizar
lick *vt* **1** : lamer **2** DEFEAT : dar una paliza a *fam* — ~ *n* : lamida *f*
licorice *n* : regaliz *m*
lid *n* **1** : tapa *f* **2** EYELID : párpado *m*
lie[1] *vi* **lay; lain; lying 1** *or* ~ **down** : acostarse, echarse **2** BE : estar, encontrarse
lie[2] *vi* **lied; lying** : mentir — ~ *n* : mentira *f*
lieutenant *n* : teniente *mf*
life *n*, *pl* **lives** : vida *f* — **lifeboat** *n* : bote *m* salvavidas — **lifeguard** *n* : socorrista *mf* — **lifeless** *adj* : sin vida — **lifelike** *adj* : natural, realista — **lifelong** *adj* : de toda la vida — **life preserver** *n* : salvavidas *m* — **lifestyle** *n* : estilo *m* de vida — **lifetime** *n* : vida *f*
lift *vt* **1** RAISE : levantar **2** STEAL : robar —

vi **1** CLEAR UP : despejarse **2** *or* ~ **off** : despegar (dícese de un avión, etc.) — ~ *n* **1** LIFTING : levantamiento *m* **2 give s.o. a** ~ : llevar en coche a algn — **liftoff** *n* : despegue *m*
light[1] *n* **1** : luz *f* **2** LAMP : lámpara *f* **3** HEADLIGHT : faro *m* **4 do you have a** ~? : ¿tienes fuego? — ~ *adj* **1** BRIGHT : bien iluminado **2** : claro (dícese de los colores), rubio (dícese del pelo) — ~ *v* **lit** *or* **lighted; lighting** *vt* **1** : encender (un fuego) **2** ILLUMINATE : iluminar — *vi* *or* ~ **up** : iluminarse — **lightbulb** *n* : bombilla *f*, bombillo *m* *Lat* — **lighten** *vt* BRIGHTEN : iluminar — **lighter** *n* : encendedor *m* — **lighthouse** *n* : faro *m* — **lighting** *n* : alumbrado *m* — **lightning** *n* : relámpago *m*, rayo *m* — **light–year** *n* : año *m* luz
light[2] *adj* : ligero — **lighten** *vt* : aligerar — **lightly** *adv* **1** : suavemente **2 let off** ~ : tratar con indulgencia — **lightness** *n* : ligereza *f* — **lightweight** *adj* : ligero
like[1] *v* **liked; liking** *vt* **1** : gustarle (a uno) **2** WANT : querer — *vi* **if you** ~ : si quieres — **likes** *npl* : preferencias *fpl*, gustos *mpl* — **likable** *or* **likeable** *adj* : simpático
like[2] *adj* SIMILAR : parecido — ~ *prep* : como — ~ *conj* **1** AS : como **2** AS IF : como si — **likelihood** *n* : probabilidad *f* — **likely** *adj* **-lier; -est** : probable — **liken** *vt* : comparar — **likeness** *n* : semejanza *f*, parecido *m* — **likewise** *adv* **1** : lo mismo **2** ALSO : también
liking *n* : afición *f* (por una cosa), simpatía *f* (por una persona)
lilac *n* : lila *f*
lily *n*, *pl* **lilies** : lirio *m*, azucena *f* — **lily of the valley** *n* : lirio *m* de los valles
lima bean *n* : frijol *m* de media luna
limb *n* **1** : miembro *m* (en anatomía) **2** : rama *f* (de un árbol)
limber *vi* *or* ~ **up** : calentarse, hacer ejercicios preliminares — ~ *adj* : ágil
limbo *n*, *pl* **-bos** : limbo *m*
lime *n* : lima *f*, limón *m* verde *Lat*
limelight *n* **be in the** ~ : estar en el candelero
limerick *n* : poema *m* jocoso de cinco versos
limestone *n* : (piedra *f*) caliza *f*
limit *n* : límite *m* — ~ *vt* : limitar, restringir — **limitation** *n* : limitación *f*, restricción *f* — **limited** *adj* : limitado
limousine *n* : limusina *f*
limp[1] *vi* : cojear — ~ *n* : cojera *f*
limp[2] *adj* : flojo, fláccido
line *n* **1** : línea *f* **2** ROPE : cuerda *f* **3** ROW : fila *f* **4** QUEUE : cola *f* **5** WRINKLE : arruga *f* **6 drop a** ~ : mándar unas líneas — ~ *v* **lined; lining** *vt* **1** : forrar (un vestido, etc.),

lodge

cubrir (las paredes, etc.) **2** MARK : rayar, trazar líneas en **3** BORDER : bordear — *vi* **~ up** : ponerse in fila, hacer cola
lineage *n* : linaje *m*
linear *adj* : lineal
linen *n* : lino *m*
liner *n* **1** LINING : forro *m* **2** SHIP : buque *m*, transatlántico *m*
lineup *n* **1** *or* **police ~** : fila *f* de sospechosos **2** : alineación *f* (en deportes)
linger *vi* **1** : quedarse, entretenerse **2** PERSIST : persistir
lingerie *n* : ropa *f* íntima femenina, lencería *f*
lingo *n*, *pl* **-goes** JARGON : jerga *f*
linguistics *n* : lingüística *f* — **linguist** *n* : lingüista *mf* — **linguistic** *adj* : lingüístico
lining *n* : forro *m*
link *n* **1** : eslabón *m* (de una cadena) **2** BOND : lazo *m* **3** CONNECTION : conexión *f* — **~** *vt* : enlazar, conectar — *vi* **~ up** : unirse, conectar
linoleum *n* : linóleo *m*
lint *n* : pelusa *f*
lion *n* : león *m* — **lioness** *n* : leona *f*
lip *n* **1** : labio *m* **2** EDGE : borde *m* — **lipstick** *n* : lápiz *m* de labios
liqueur *n* : licor *m*
liquid *adj* : líquido — **~** *n* : líquido *m* — **liquidate** *vt* **-dated; -dating** : liquidar — **liquidation** *n* : liquidación *f*
liquor *n* : bebidas *fpl* alcohólicas
lisp *vi* : cecear — **~** *n* : ceceo *m*
list[1] *n* : lista *f* — **~** *vt* **1** ENUMERATE : hacer una lista de, enumerar **2** INCLUDE : incluir (en una lista)
list[2] *vi* : escorar (dícese de un barco)
listen *vi* **1** : escuchar **2 ~ to** HEED : hacer caso de **3 ~ to reason** : atender a razones — **listener** *n* : oyente *mf*
listless *adj* : apático
lit *pp* → **light**
litany *n*, *pl* **-nies** : letanía *f*
liter *n* : litro *m*
literacy *n* : alfabetismo *m*
literal *adj* : literal — **literally** *adv* : literalmente, al pie de la letra
literate *adj* : alfabetizado
literature *n* : literatura *f* — **literary** *adj* : literario
lithe *adj* : ágil y grácil
litigation *n* : litigio *m*
litre → **liter**
litter *n* **1** RUBBISH : basura *f* **2** : camada *f* (de animales) **3** *or* **kitty ~** : arena *f* higiénica — **~** *vt* : tirar basura en, ensuciar — *vi* : tirar basura
little *adj* **littler** *or* **less** *or* **lesser; littlest** *or* **least 1** SMALL : pequeño **2 a ~** SOME : un poco de **3 he speaks ~ English** : habla

poco inglés — **~** *adv* **less; least** : poco — **~** *pron* **1** : poco *m*, **-ca** *f* **2 ~ by ~** : poco a poco
liturgy *n*, *pl* **-gies** : liturgia *f* — **liturgical** *adj* : litúrgico
live *vi* **lived; living 1** : vivir **2** RESIDE : residir **3 ~ on** : vivir de — *vt* : vivir, llevar (una vida) — **~** *adj* **1** : vivo **2** : con corriente (dícese de cables eléctricos) **3** : en vivo, en directo (dícese de programas de televisión, etc.) — **livelihood** *n* : sustento *m*, medio *m* de vida — **lively** *adj* **-lier; -est** : animado, alegre — **liven** *vt or* **~ up** : animar — *vi* : animarse
liver *n* : hígado *m*
livestock *n* : ganado *m*
livid *adj* **1** : lívido **2** ENRAGED : furioso
living *adj* : vivo — **~** *n* **make a ~** : ganarse la vida — **living room** *n* : living *m*, sala *f* (de estar)
lizard *n* : lagarto *m*
llama *n* : llama *f*
load *n* **1** CARGO : carga *f* **2** BURDEN : carga *f*, peso *m* **3 ~s of** : un montón de — **~** *vt* : cargar
loaf[1] *n*, *pl* **loaves** : pan *m*, barra *f* (de pan)
loaf[2] *vi* : holgazanear — **loafer** *n* **1** : holgazán *m*, -zana *f* **2** : mocasín *m* (zapato)
loan *n* : préstamo *m* — **~** *vt* : prestar
loathe *vt* **loathed; loathing** : odiar — **loathsome** *adj* : odioso
lobby *n*, *pl* **-bies 1** : vestíbulo *m* **2** *or* **political ~** : grupo *m* de presión, lobby *m* — **~** *v* **-bied; -bying** *vt* : ejercer presión sobre
lobe *n* : lóbulo *m*
lobster *n* : langosta *f*
local *adj* : local — **~** *n* **the ~s** : los vecinos del lugar — **locale** *n* : escenario *m* — **locality** *n*, *pl* **-ties** : localidad *f*
locate *vt* **-cated; -cating 1** SITUATE : situar, ubicar **2** FIND : localizar — **location** *n* : situación *f*, lugar *m*
lock[1] *n* : mechón *m* (de pelo)
lock[2] *n* **1** : cerradura *f* (de una puerta, etc.) **2** : esclusa *f* (de un canal) — **~** *vt* **1** : cerrar (con llave) **2** *or* **~ up** CONFINE : encerrar — *vi* **1** : cerrarse con llave **2** : bloquearse (dícese de una rueda, etc.) — **locker** *n* : armario *m* — **locket** *n* : medallón *m* — **locksmith** *n* : cerrajero *m*, -ra *f*
locomotive *n* : locomotora *f*
locust *n* : langosta *f*, chapulín *m* *Lat*
lodge *v* **lodged; lodging** *vt* **1** HOUSE : hospedar, alojar **2** FILE : presentar — *vi* : hospedarse, alojarse — **~** *n* : pabellón *m* — **lodger** *n* : huésped *m*, -peda *f* — **lodging** *n* **1** : alojamiento *m* **2 ~s** *npl* : habitaciones *fpl*

loft *n* **1** : desván *m* (en una casa) **2** HAYLOFT
: pajar *m* — **lofty** *adj* **loftier; -est 1** : noble,
elevado **2** HAUGHTY : altanero
log *n* **1** : tronco *m*, leño *m* **2** RECORD : diario
m — ∼ *vi* **logged; logging 1** : talar (árboles) **2** RECORD : registrar, anotar **3** ∼
on : entrar (en el sistema) **4** ∼ **off** : salir
(del sistema) — **logger** *n* : leñador *m*, -dora
f
logic *n* : lógica *f* — **logical** *adj* : lógico — **logistics** *ns & pl* : logística *f*
logo *n, pl* **logos** : logotipo *m*
loin *n* : lomo *m*
loiter *vi* : vagar, holgazanear
lollipop *or* **lollypop** *n* : pirulí *m*, chupete *m*
Lat
lone *adj* : solitario — **loneliness** *n* : soledad
f — **lonely** *adj* **-lier; -est** : solitario, solo —
loner *n* : solitario *m*, -ria *f* — **lonesome** *adj*
: solo, solitario
long¹ *adj* **longer; longest** : largo — ∼ *adv*
1 : mucho tiempo **2 all day** ∼ : todo el día
3 as ∼ **as** : mientras **4 no** ∼**er** : ya no **5
so** ∼**!** : ¡hasta luego!, ¡adiós! — ∼ *n* **1
before** ∼ : dentro de poco **2 the** ∼ **and
the short** : lo esencial
long² *vi* ∼ **for** : anhelar, desear
longevity *n* : longevidad *f*
longing *n* : ansia *f*, anhelo *m*
longitude *n* : longitud *f*
look *vi* **1** : mirar **2** SEEM : parecer **3** ∼
after : cuidar (de) **4** ∼ **for** EXPECT : esperar **5** ∼ **for** SEEK : buscar **6** ∼ **into** : investigar **7** ∼ **out** : tener cuidado **8** ∼
over EXAMINE : revisar **9** ∼ **up to** : respetar — *vt* : mirar — ∼ *n* **1** : mirada *f* **2**
APPEARANCE : aspecto *m*, aire *m* — **lookout**
n **1** : puesto *m* de observación **2** WATCH-
MAN : vigía *mf* **3 be on the** ∼ **for** : estar al
acecho de
loom¹ *n* : telar *m*
loom² *vi* **1** APPEAR : aparecer, surgir **2** AP-
PROACH : ser inminente
loop *n* : lazada *f*, lazo *m* — ∼ *vt* : hacer
lazadas con — **loophole** *n* : escapatoria *f*
loose *adj* **looser; -est 1** MOVABLE : flojo,
suelto **2** SLACK : flojo **3** ROOMY : holgado
4 APPROXIMATE : libre, aproximado **5** FREE
: suelto **6** IMMORAL : relajado — **loosely**
adv **1** : sin apretar **2** ROUGHLY : aproximadamente — **loosen** *vt* : aflojar
loot *n* : botín *m* — ∼ *vt* : saquear, robar —
looter *n* : saqueador *m*, -dora *f* — **looting** *n*
: saqueo *m*
lop *vt* **lopped; lopping** : cortar, podar
lopsided *adj* : torcido, chueco *Lat*
lord *n* **1** : señor *m*, noble *m* **2 the Lord** : el
Señor
lore *n* : saber *m* popular, tradición *f*

lose *v* **lost; losing** *vt* **1** : perder **2** ∼ **one's
way** : perderse **3** ∼ **time** : atrasarse
(dícese de un reloj) — *vi* : perder — **loser** *n*
: perdedor *m*, -dora *f* — **loss** *n* **1** : pérdida *f*
2 DEFEAT : derrota *f* **3 be at a** ∼ **for words**
: no encontrar palabras — **lost** *adj* **1** : perdido **2 get** ∼ : perderse
lot *n* **1** FATE : suerte *f* **2** PLOT : solar *m* **3 a**
∼ **of** *or* ∼**s of** : mucho, un montón de
lotion *n* : loción *f*
lottery *n, pl* **-teries** : lotería *f*
loud *adj* **1** : alto, fuerte **2** NOISY : ruidoso **3**
FLASHY : llamativo — ∼ *adv* **1** : fuerte **2
out** ∼ : en voz alta — **loudly** *adv* : en voz
alta — **loudspeaker** *n* : altavoz *m*
lounge *vi* **lounged; lounging 1** : repantigarse **2** *or* ∼ **about** : holgazanear — ∼ *n*
: salón *m*
louse *n, pl* **lice** : piojo *m* — **lousy** *adj*
lousier; -est 1 : piojoso **2** BAD : pésimo,
muy malo
love *n* **1** : amor *m* **2 fall in** ∼ : enamorarse
— ∼ *v* **loved; loving** : querer, amar — **lovable** *adj* : adorable, amoroso *Lat* — **lovely**
adj **-lier; -est** : lindo, precioso — **lover** *n*
: amante *mf* — **loving** *adj* : cariñoso
low *adj* **lower; -est 1** : bajo **2** SCARCE : escaso **3** DEPRESSED : deprimido — ∼ *adv* **1**
: bajo **2 turn the lights down** ∼ : bajar las
luces — ∼ *n* **1** : punto *m* bajo **2** *or* ∼
gear : primera velocidad *f* — **lower** *adj* : inferior, más bajo — ∼ *vt* : bajar — **lowly** *adj*
-lier; -est : humilde
loyal *adj* : leal, fiel — **loyalty** *n, pl* **-ties**
: lealtad *f*
lozenge *n* : pastilla *f*
lubricate *vt* **-cated; -cating** : lubricar — **lubricant** *n* : lubricante *m* — **lubrication** *n*
: lubricación *f*
lucid *adj* : lúcido — **lucidity** *n* : lucidez *f*
luck *n* **1** : suerte *f* **2 good** ∼**!** : ¡buena
suerte! — **luckily** *adv* : afortunadamente —
lucky *adj* **luckier; -est 1** : afortunado **2** ∼
charm : amuleto *m* (de la suerte)
lucrative *adj* : lucrativo
ludicrous *adj* : ridículo, absurdo
lug *vt* **lugged; lugging** : arrastrar
luggage *n* : equipaje *m*
lukewarm *adj* : tibio
lull *vt* **1** CALM : calmar **2** ∼ **to sleep**
: adormecer — ∼ *n* : período *m* de calma,
pausa *f*
lullaby *n, pl* **-bies** : canción *f* de cuna, nana *f*
lumber *n* : madera *f* — **lumberjack** *n*
: leñador *m*, -dora *f*
luminous *adj* : luminoso
lump *n* **1** CHUNK, PIECE : pedazo *m*, trozo *m*
2 SWELLING : bulto *m* **3** : grumo *m* (en un
líquido) — ∼ *vt* *or* ∼ **together** : juntar,

agrupar — **lumpy** *adj* **lumpier; -est** : grumoso (dícese de una salsa), lleno de bultos (dícese de un colchón)
lunacy *n, pl* **-cies** : locura *f*
lunar *adj* : lunar
lunatic *n* : loco *m*, -ca *f*
lunch *n* : almuerzo *m*, comida *f* — ∼ *vi* : almorzar, comer — **luncheon** *n* : comida *f*, almuerzo *m*
lung *n* : pulmón *m*
lunge *vi* **lunged; lunging 1** : lanzarse **2** ∼ **at** : arremeter contre
lurch¹ *vi* **1** STAGGER : tambalearse **2** : dar bandazos (dícese de un vehículo)
lurch² *n* **leave in a** ∼ : dejar en la estacada
lure *n* **1** BAIT : señuelo *m* **2** ATTRACTION : atractivo *m* — ∼ *vt* **lured; luring** : atraer
lurid *adj* **1** GRUESOME : espeluznante **2**

SENSATIONAL : sensacionalista **3** GAUDY : chillón
lurk *vi* : estar al acecho
luscious *adj* : delicioso, exquisito
lush *adj* : exuberante, suntuoso
lust *n* **1** : lujuria *f* **2** CRAVING : ansia *f*, anhelo *m* — ∼ *vi* ∼ **after** : desear (a una persona), codiciar (riquezas, etc.)
luster *or* **lustre** *n* : lustre *m*
lusty *adj* **lustier; -est** : fuerte, vigoroso
luxurious *adj* : lujoso — **luxury** *n, pl* **-ries** : lujo *m*
lye *n* : lejía *f*
lying → **lie**
lynch *vt* : linchar
lynx *n* : lince *m*
lyric *or* **lyrical** *adj* : lírico — **lyrics** *npl* : letra *f* (de una canción)

M

m *n, pl* **m's** *or* **ms** : m *f*, decimotercera letra del alfabeto inglés
ma'am → **madam**
macabre *adj* : macabro
macaroni *n* : macarrones *mpl*
mace *n* **1** : maza *f* (arma o símbolo) **2** : macis *f* (especia)
machete *n* : machete *m*
machine *n* : máquina *f* — **machinery** *n, pl* **-eries 1** : maquinaria *f* **2** WORKS : mecanismo *m* — **machine gun** *n* : ametralladora *f*
mad *adj* **madder; maddest 1** INSANE : loco **2** FOOLISH : insensato **3** ANGRY : furioso
madam *n, pl* **mesdames** : señora *f*
madden *vt* : enfurecer
made → **make**
madly *adv* : como un loco, locamente — **madman** *n, pl* **-men** : loco *m* — **madness** *n* : locura *f*
Mafia *n* : Mafia *f*
magazine *n* **1** PERIODICAL : revista *f* **2** : recámara *f* (de un arma de fuego)
maggot *n* : gusano *m*
magic *n* : magia *f* — ∼ *or* **magical** *adj* : mágico — **magician** *n* : mago *m*, -ga *f*
magistrate *n* : magistrado *m*, -da *f*
magnanimous *adj* : magnánimo
magnate *n* : magnate *mf*
magnet *n* : imán *m* — **magnetic** *adj* : magnético — **magnetism** *n* : magnetismo *m* — **magnetize** *vt* **-tized; -tizing** : magnetizar

magnificent *adj* : magnífico — **magnificence** *n* : magnificencia *f*
magnify *vt* **-fied; -fying 1** ENLARGE : ampliar **2** EXAGGERATE : exagerar — **magnifying glass** *n* : lupa *f*
magnitude *n* : magnitud *f*
magnolia *n* : magnolia *f*
mahogany *n, pl* **-nies** : caoba *f*
maid *n* : sirvienta *f*, criada *f*, muchacha *f* — **maiden** *adj* FIRST : inaugural — **maiden name** *n* : nombre *m* de soltera
mail *n* **1** : correo *m* **2** LETTERS : correspondencia *f* — ∼ *vt* : enviar por correo — **mailbox** *n* : buzón *m* — **mailman** *n, pl* **-men** : cartero *m*
maim *vt* : mutilar
main *n* : tubería *f* principal (de agua o gas), cable *m* principal (de un circuito) — ∼ *adj* : principal — **mainframe** *n* : computadora *f* central — **mainland** *n* : continente *m* — **mainly** *adv* : principalmente — **mainstay** *n* : sostén *m* (principal) — **mainstream** *n* : corriente *f* principal — ∼ *adj* : dominante, convencional
maintain *vt* : mantener — **maintenance** *n* : mantenimiento *m*
maize *n* : maíz *m*
majestic *adj* : majestuoso — **majesty** *n, pl* **-ties** : majestad *f*
major *adj* **1** : muy importante, principal **2** : mayor (en música) — ∼ *n* **1** : mayor *mf*, comandante *mf* (en las fuerzas armadas) **2**

: especialidad *f* (universitaria) — ~ *vi* -joring : especializarse — **majority** *n, pl* -ties : mayoría *f*
make *v* made; making *vt* 1 : hacer 2 MANUFACTURE : fabricar 3 CONSTITUTE : constituir 4 PREPARE : preparar 5 RENDER : poner 6 COMPEL : obligar 7 ~ a decision : tomar una decisión 8 ~ a living : ganar la vida — *vi* 1 ~ do : arreglárselas 2 ~ for : dirigirse a 3 ~ good SUCCEED : tener éxito — ~ *n* BRAND : marca *f* — **make–believe** *n* : fantasía *f* — ~ *adj* : imaginario — **make out** *vt* 1 : hacer (un cheque, etc.) 2 DISCERN : distinguir 3 UNDERSTAND : comprender — *vi* **how did you ~?** : ¿qué tal te fue? — **maker** *n* MANUFACTURER : fabricante *mf* — **makeshift** *adj* : improvisado — **makeup** *n* 1 COMPOSITION : composición *f* 2 COSMETICS : maquillaje *m* — **make up** *vt* 1 PREPARE : preparar 2 INVENT : inventar 3 CONSTITUTE : formar — *vi* RECONCILE : hacer las paces
maladjusted *adj* : inadaptado
malaria *n* : malaria *f*, paludismo *m*
male *n* : macho *m* (de animales o plantas), varón *m* (de personas) — ~ *adj* 1 : macho 2 MASCULINE : masculino
malevolent *adj* : malévolo
malfunction *vi* : funcionar mal — ~ *n* : mal funcionamiento *m*
malice *n* : mala intención *f*, rencor *m* — **malicious** *adj* : malicioso
malign *adj* : maligno — ~ *vt* : calumniar
malignant *adj* : maligno
mall *n or* **shopping ~** : centro *m* comercial
malleable *adj* : maleable
mallet *n* : mazo *m*
malnutrition *n* : desnutrición *f*
malpractice *n* : mala práctica *f*, negligencia *f*
malt *n* : malta *f*
mama *or* **mamma** *n* : mamá *f*
mammal *n* : mamífero *m*
mammogram *n* : mamografía *f*
mammoth *adj* : gigantesco
man *n, pl* **men** : hombre *m* — ~ *vt* **manned; manning** : tripular (un barco o avión), encargarse de (un servicio)
manage *v* -aged; -aging *vt* 1 HANDLE : manejar 2 DIRECT : administrar, dirigir — *vi* COPE : arreglárselas — **manageable** *adj* : manejable — **management** *n* : dirección *f* — **manager** *n* : director *m*, -tora *f*; gerente *mf* — **managerial** *adj* : directivo
mandarin *n or* ~ **orange** : mandarina *f*
mandate *n* : mandato *m* — **mandatory** *adj* : obligatorio
mane *n* : crin *f* (de un caballo), melena *f* (de un león)

maneuver *n* : maniobra *f* — ~ *v* -vered; -vering : maniobrar
mangle *vt* -gled; -gling : destrozar
mango *n, pl* -goes : mango *m*
mangy *adj* mangier; -est : sarnoso
manhandle *vi* -dled; -dling : maltratar
manhole *n* : boca *f* de alcantarilla
manhood *n* 1 : madurez *f* (de un hombre) 2 VIRILITY : virilidad *f*
mania *n* : manía *f* — **maniac** *n* : maníaco *m*, -ca *f*
manicure *n* : manicura *f* — ~ *vt* -cured; -curing : hacer la manicura a
manifest *adj* : manifiesto, patente — ~ *vt* : manifestar — **manifesto** *n, pl* -tos *or* -toes : manifiesto *m*
manipulate *vt* -lated; -lating : manipular — **manipulation** *n* : manipulación *f*
mankind *n* : género *m* humano, humanidad *f*
manly *adj* -lier; -est : viril — **manliness** *n* : virilidad *f*
man–made *adj* : artificial
mannequin *n* : maniquí *m*
manner *n* 1 : manera *f* 2 KIND : clase *f* 3 ~s *npl* ETIQUETTE : modales *mpl*, educación *f* — **mannerism** *n* : peculiaridad *f* (de una persona)
manoeuvre *Brit* → **maneuver**
manor *n* : casa *f* solariega
manpower *n* : mano *f* de obra
mansion *n* : mansión *f*
manslaughter *n* : homicidio *m* sin premeditación
mantel *or* **mantelpiece** *n* : repisa *f* de la chimenea
manual *adj* : manual — ~ *n* : manual *m*
manufacture *n* : fabricación *f* — ~ *vt* -tured; -turing : fabricar — **manufacturer** *n* : fabricante *mf*
manure *n* : estiércol *m*
manuscript *n* : manuscrito *m*
many *adj* **more; most** 1 : muchos 2 **as ~** : tantos 3 **how ~** : cuántos 4 **too ~** : demasiados — ~ *pron* : muchos *pl*, -chas *pl*
map *n* : mapa *m* — ~ *vt* **mapped; mapping** 1 : trazar el mapa de 2 *or* ~ **out** : planear, proyectar
maple *n* : arce *m*
mar *vt* **marred; marring** : estropear
marathon *n* : maratón *m*
marble *n* 1 : mármol *m* 2 ~s *npl* : canicas *fpl* (para jugar)
march *n* : marcha *f* — ~ *vi* : marchar, desfilar
March *n* : marzo *m*
mare *n* : yegua *f*
margarine *n* : margarina *f*
margin *n* : margen *m* — **marginal** *adj* : marginal

marigold *n* : caléndula *f*
marijuana *n* : marihuana *f*
marinate *vt* **-nated; -nating** : marinar
marine *adj* : marino — ~ *n* : soldado *m* de
marina
marionette *n* : marioneta *f*
marital *adj* **1** : matrimonial **2** ~ **status**
: estado *m* civil
maritime *adj* : marítimo
mark *n* **1** : marca *f* **2** STAIN : mancha *f* **3** IM
PRINT : huella *f* **4** TARGET : blanco *m* **5**
GRADE : nota *f* — ~ *vt* **1** : marcar **2** STAIN
: manchar **3** POINT OUT : señalar **4** : calificar (un examen, etc.) **5** COMMEMORATE
: conmemorar **6** CARACTERIZE : caracterizar **7** ~ **off** : delimitar — **marked** *adj*
: marcado, notable — **markedly** *adv* : notablemente — **marker** *n* : marcador *m*
market *n* : mercado *m* — ~ *vt* : vender,
comercializar — **marketable** *adj* : vendible
— **marketplace** *n* : mercado *m*
marksman *n, pl* **-men** : tirador *m* — **marksmanship** *n* : puntería *f*
marmalade *n* : mermelada *f*
maroon[1] *vt* : abandonar, aislar
maroon[2] *n* : rojo *m* oscuro
marquee *n* CANOPY : marquesina *f*
marriage *n* **1** : matrimonio *m* **2** WEDDING
: casamiento *m*, boda *f* — **married** *adj* **1**
: casado **2 get** ~ : casarse
marrow *n* : médula *f*, tuétano *m*
marry *v* **-ried; -rying** *vt* **1** : casar **2** WED
: casarse con — *vi* : casarse
Mars *n* : Marte *m*
marsh *n* **1** : pantano *m* **2** *or* **salt** ~
: marisma *f*
marshal *n* : mariscal *m* (en el ejército); jefe
m, -fa *f* (de policía, de bomberos, etc.) — ~
vt **-shaled** *or* **-shalled; -shaling** *or*
-shalling : poner en orden (los pensamien-
tos, etc.), reunir (las tropas)
marshmallow *n* : malvavisco *m*
marshy *adj* **marshier; -est** : pantanoso
mart *n* : mercado *m*
martial *adj* : marcial
martyr *n* : mártir *mf* — ~ *vt* : martirizar
marvel *n* : maravilla *f* — ~ *vi* **-veled** *or*
-velled; -veling *or* **-velling** : maravillarse
— **marvelous** *or* **marvellous** *adj* : maravilloso
mascara *n* : rímel *m*
mascot *n* : mascota *f*
masculine *adj* : masculino — **masculinity** *n*
: masculinidad *f*
mash *vt* **1** CRUSH : aplastar, majar **2** PUREE
: hacer puré de — **mashed potatoes** *npl*
: puré *m* de patatas, puré *m* de papas *Lat*
mask *n* : máscara *f* — ~ *vt* : enmascarar
masochism *n* : masoquismo *m* — **maso-**

chist *n* : masoquista *mf* — **masochistic** *adj*
: masoquista
mason *n* : albañil *mf* — **masonry** *n, pl* **-ries**
: albañilería *f*
masquerade *n* : mascarada *f* — ~ *vi* **-aded;
-ading** ~ **as** : disfrazarse de, hacerse pasar
por
mass *n* **1** : masa *f* **2** MULTITUDE : cantidad *f*
3 the ~ **es** : las masas
Mass *n* : misa *f*
massacre *n* : masacre *f* — ~ *vt* **-cred;
-cring** : masacrar
massage *n* : masaje *m* — ~ *vt* **-saged;
-saging** : dar masaje a, masajear —
masseur *n* : masajista *m* — **masseuse** *n*
: masajista *f*
massive *adj* **1** BULKY, SOLID : macizo **2**
HUGE : enorme, masivo
mast *n* : mástil *m*
master *n* **1** : amo *m*, señor *m* (de la casa) **2**
EXPERT : maestro *m*, -tra *f* **3** ~ **'s degree**
: maestría *f* — ~ *vt* : dominar — **masterful**
adj : magistral — **masterpiece** *n* : obra *f*
maestra — **mastery** *n* : maestría *f*
masturbate *v* **-bated; -bating** *vi* : masturbarse — **masturbation** *n* : masturbación *f*
mat *n* **1** DOORMAT : felpudo *m* **2** RUG : estera *f*
matador *n* : matador *m*
match *n* **1** EQUAL : igual *mf* **2** : fósforo *m*,
cerilla *f* (para encender) **3** GAME : partido
m, combate *m* (en boxeo) **4 be a good** ~
: hacer buena pareja — ~ *vt* **1** *or* ~ **up**
: emparejar **2** EQUAL : igualar **3** : combinar
con, hacer juego con (ropa, colores, etc.) —
vi : concordar, coincidir
mate *n* **1** COMPANION : compañero *m*, -ra *f*;
amigo *m*, -ga *f* **2** : macho *m*, hembra *f* (de
animales) — ~ *vi* **mated; mating**
: aparearse
material *adj* **1** : material **2** IMPORTANT : importante — ~ *n* **1** : material *m* **2** CLOTH
: tela *f*, tejido *m* — **materialistic** *adj* : materialista — **materialize** *vi* **-ized; -izing**
: aparecer
maternal *adj* : maternal — **maternity** *n, pl*
-ties : maternidad *f* — ~ *adj* **1** : de maternidad **2** ~ **clothes** : ropa *f* de futura mamá
math → **mathematics**
mathematics *ns & pl* : matemáticas *fpl* —
mathematical *adj* : matemático — **mathematician** *n* : matemático *m*, -ca *f*
matinee *or* **matinée** *n* : matiné(e) *f*, fonción
f de tarde
matrimony *n* : matrimonio *m* — **matrimonial** *adj* : matrimonial
matrix *n, pl* **-trices** *or* **-trixes** : matriz *f*
matte *adj* : mate
matter *n* **1** SUBSTANCE : materia *f* **2** QUES-

TION : asunto *m*, cuestión *f* **3 as a** ～ **of fact** : en efecto, en realidad **4 for that** ～ : de hecho **5 to make** ～**s worse** : para colmo de males **6 what's the** ～**?** : ¿qué pasa? — ～ *vi* : importar

mattress *n* : colchón *m*

mature *adj* **-turer; -est** : maduro — ～ *vi* **-tured; -turing** : madurar — **maturity** *n* : madurez *f*

maul *vt* : maltratar, aporrear

mauve *n* : malva *m*

maxim *n* : máxima *f*

maximum *n, pl* **-ma** *or* **-mums** : máximo *m* — ～ *adj* : máximo — **maximize** *vt* **-mized; -mizing** : llevar al máximo

may *v aux, past* **might;** *present s & pl* **may 1** : poder **2 come what** ～ : pase lo que pase **3 it** ～ **happen** : puede pasar **4** ～ **the best man win** : que gane el mejor

May *n* : mayo *m*

maybe *adv* : quizás, tal vez

mayhem *n* : alboroto *m*

mayonnaise *n* : mayonesa *f*

mayor *n* : alcalde *m*, -desa *f*

maze *n* : laberinto *m*

me *pron* **1** : me **2 for** ～ : para mí **3 give it to** ～**!** : ¡dámelo! **4 it's** ～ : soy yo **5 with** ～ : conmigo

meadow *n* : prado *m*, pradera *f*

meager *or* **meagre** *adj* : escaso

meal *n* **1** : comida *f* **2** : harina *f* (de maíz, etc.) — **mealtime** *n* : hora *f* de comer

mean[1] *vt* **meant; meaning 1** SIGNIFY : querer decir **2** INTEND : querer, tener la intención de **3 be meant for** : estar destinado a **4 he didn't** ～ **it** : no lo dijo en serio

mean[2] *adj* **1** UNKIND : malo **2** STINGY : mezquino, tacaño **3** HUMBLE : humilde

mean[3] *adj* AVERAGE : medio — ～ *n* : promedio *m*

meander *vi* **-dered; -dering 1** WIND : serpentear **2** WANDER : vagar

meaning *n* : significado *m*, sentido *m* — **meaningful** *adj* : significativo — **meaningless** *adj* : sin sentido

meanness *n* **1** UNKINDNESS : maldad *f* **2** STINGINESS : mezquindad *f*

means *n* **1** : medio *m* **2 by all** ～ : por supuesto **3 by** ～ **of** : por medio de **4 by no** ～ : de ninguna manera

meantime *n* **1** : interín *m* **2 in the** ～ : mientras tanto — ～ *adv* → **meanwhile**

meanwhile *adv* : mientras tanto — ～ *n* → **meantime**

measles *npl* : sarampión *m*

measly *adj* **-slier; -est** : miserable, mísero

measure *n* : medida *f* — ～ *v* **-sured; -suring** : medir — **measurable** *adj* : mensura-

ble — **measurement** *n* : medida *f* — **measure up** *vi* ～ **to** : estar a la altura de

meat *n* : carne *f* — **meatball** *n* : albóndiga *f* — **meaty** *adj* **meatier; -est 1** : carnoso **2** SUBSTANTIAL : sustancioso

mechanic *n* : mecánico *m*, -ca *f* — **mechanical** *adj* : mecánico — **mechanics** *ns & pl* **1** : mecánica *f* **2** WORKINGS : mecanismo *m* — **mechanism** *n* : mecanismo *m* — **mechanize** *vt* **-nized; -nizing** : mecanizar

medal *n* : medalla *f* — **medallion** *n* : medallón *m*

meddle *vi* **-dled; -dling** : entrometerse

media *or* **mass** ～ *npl* : medios *mpl* de comunicación

median *adj* : medio

mediate *vi* **-ated; -ating** : mediar — **mediation** *n* : mediación *f* — **mediator** *n* : mediador *m*, -dora *f*

medical *adj* : médico — **medicated** *adj* : medicinal — **medication** *n* : medicamento *m* — **medicinal** *adj* : medicinal — **medicine** *n* **1** : medicina *f* **2** MEDICATION : medicina *f*, medicamento *m*

medieval *or* **mediaeval** *adj* : medieval

mediocre *adj* : mediocre — **mediocrity** *n, pl* **-ties** : mediocridad *f*

meditate *vi* **-tated; -tating** : meditar — **meditation** *n* : meditación *f*

medium *n, pl* **-diums** *or* **-dia 1** MEANS : medio *m* **2** MEAN : punto *m* medio, término *m* medio **3** → **media** — ～ *adj* : mediano

medley *n, pl* **-leys 1** : mezcla *f* **2** : popurrí *m* (de canciones)

meek *adj* : dócil

meet *v* **met; meeting** *vt* **1** ENCOUNTER : encontrarse con **2** SATISFY : satisfacer **3 pleased to** ～ **you** : encantado de conocerlo — *vi* **1** : encontrarse **2** ASSEMBLE : reunirse **3** BE INTRODUCED : conocerse — ～ *n* : encuentro *m* — **meeting** *n* : reunión *f*

megabyte *n* : megabyte *m*

megaphone *n* : megáfono *m*

melancholy *n, pl* **-cholies** : melancolía *f* — ～ *adj* : melancólico, triste

mellow *adj* **1** : suave, dulce **2** CALM : apacible **3** : maduro (dícese de frutas), añejo (dícese de vinos) — ～ *vt* : suavizar, endulzar — *vi* : suavizarse

melody *n, pl* **-dies** : melodía *f*

melon *n* : melón *m*

melt *vi* : derretirse, fundirse — *vt* : derretir

member *n* : miembro *m* — **membership** *n* **1** : calidad *f* de miembro **2** MEMBERS : miembros *mpl*

membrane *n* : membrana *f*

memory *n, pl* **-ries 1** : memoria *f* **2** RECOLLECTION : recuerdo *m* — **memento** *n, pl* **-tos**

or **-toes** : recuerdo *m* — **memo** *n, pl* **memos**
or **memorandum** *n, pl* **-dums** *or* **-da** : memorándum *m* — **memoirs** *npl* : memorias *fpl* — **memorable** *adj* : memorable — **memorial** *adj* : conmemorativo — **~** *n* : monumento *m* (conmemorativo) — **memorize** *vt* **-rized; -rizing** : aprender de memoria
men → **man**
menace *n* : amenaza *f* — **~** *vt* **-aced; -acing** : amenazar — **menacing** *adj* : amenazador
mend *vt* **1** : reparar, arreglar **2** DARN : zurcir — *vi* HEAL : curarse
menial *adj* : servil, bajo
meningitis *n, pl* **-gitides** : meningitis *f*
menopause *n* : menopausia *f*
menstruate *vi* **-ated; -ating** : menstruar — **menstruation** *n* : menstruación *f*
mental *adj* : mental — **mentality** *n, pl* **-ties** : mentalidad *f*
mention *n* : mención *f* — **mention** *vt* **1** : mencionar **2 don't ~ it!** : ¡de nada!, ¡no hay de qué!
menu *n* : menú *m*
meow *n* : maullido *m*, miau *m* — **~** *vi* : maullar
mercenary *n, pl* **-naries** : mercenario *m*, -ria *f* — **~** *adj* : mercenario
merchant *n* : comerciante *mf* — **merchandise** *n* : mercancía *f*, mercadería *f*
merciful *adj* : misericordioso, compasivo — **merciless** *adj* : despiadado
mercury *n, pl* **-ries** : mercurio *m*
Mercury *n* : Mercurio *m*
mercy *n, pl* **-cies** **1** : misericordia *f*, compasión *f* **2 at the ~ of** : a merced de
mere *adj, superlative* **merest** : mero, simple — **merely** *adv* : simplemente
merge *v* **merged; merging** *vi* : unirse, fusionarse (dícese de las compañías), confluir (dícese de los ríos, las calles, etc.) — *vt* : unir, fusionar, combinar — **merger** *n* : unión *f*, fusión *f*
merit *n* : mérito *m* — **~** *vt* : merecer
mermaid *n* : sirena *f*
merry *adj* **-rier; -est** : alegre — **merry-go-round** *n* : tiovivo *m*
mesa *n* : mesa *f*
mesh *n* : malla *f*
mesmerize *vt* **-ized; -izing** : hipnotizar
mess *n* **1** : desorden *m* **2** MUDDLE : lío *m* **3** : rancho *m* (militar) — **~** *vt* **1** *or* **~ up** SOIL : ensuciar **2 ~ up** DISARRANGE : desordenar **3 ~ up** BUNGLE : echar a perder — *vi* **1 ~ around** PUTTER : entretenerse **2 ~ with** PROVOKE : meterse con
message *n* : mensaje *m* — **messenger** *n* : mensajero *m*, -ra *f*
messy *adj* **messier; -est** : desordenado, sucio

met → **meet**
metabolism *n* : metabolismo *m*
metal *n* : metal *m* — **metallic** *adj* : metálico
metamorphosis *n, pl* **-phoses** : metamorfosis *f*
metaphor *n* : metáfora *f*
meteor *n* : meteoro *m* — **meteorological** *adj* : meteorológico — **meteorologist** *n* : meteorólogo *m*, -ga *f* — **meteorology** *n* : meteorología *f*
meter *or Brit* **metre** *n* **1** : metro *m* **2** : contador *m* (de electricidad, etc.)
method *n* : método *m* — **methodical** *adj* : metódico
meticulous *adj* : meticuloso
metric *or* **metrical** *adj* : métrico
metropolis *n* : metrópoli *f* — **metropolitan** *adj* : metropolitano
Mexican *adj* : mexicano
mice → **mouse**
microbe *n* : microbio *m*
microfilm *n* : microfilm *m*
microphone *n* : micrófono *m*
microscope *n* : microscopio *m* — **microscopic** *adj* : microscópico
microwave *n or* **~ oven** : microondas *m*
mid *adj* **1 ~ morning** : a media mañana **2 in ~-August** : a mediados de agosto **3 she is in her mid thirties** : tiene alrededor de 35 años — **midair** *n* **in ~** : en el aire —
midday *n* : mediodía *m*
middle *adj* : de en medio, del medio — **~** *n* **1** : medio *m*, centro *m* **2 in the ~ of** : en medio de (un espacio), a mitad de (una actividad) **3 in the ~ of the month** : a mediados del mes — **middle–aged** *adj* : de mediana edad — **Middle Ages** *npl* : Edad *f* Media — **middle class** *n* : clase *f* media — **middleman** *n, pl* **-men** : intermediario *m*, -ria *f*
midget *n* : enano *m*, -na *f*
midnight *n* : medianoche *f*
midriff *n* : diafragma *m*
midst *n* **1 in the ~ of** : en medio de **2 in our ~** : entre nosotros
midsummer *n* : pleno verano *m*
midway *adv* : a mitad de camino, a medio camino
midwife *n, pl* **-wives** : comadrona *f*
midwinter *n* : pleno invierno *m*
miff *vt* : ofender
might[1] (*used to express permission or possibility or as a polite alternative to* **may**) → **may**
might[2] *n* : fuerza *f*, poder *m* — **mighty** *adj* **mightier; -est 1** : fuerte, poderoso **2** GREAT : enorme — **~** *adv* : muy
migraine *n* : jaqueca *f*, migraña *f*

migrate *vi* **-grated; -grating** : emigrar —
migrant *n* : trabajador *m*, -dora *f* ambulante
mild *adj* **1** GENTLE : suave **2** LIGHT : leve **3**
a ~ **climate** : una clima templada
mildew *n* : moho *m*
mildly *adv* : ligeramente, suavemente —
mildness *n* : apacibilidad *f* (de personas),
suavedad *f* (de sabores, etc.)
mile *n* : milla *f* — **mileage** *n* : distancia *f*
recorrida (en millas), kilometraje *m* —
milestone *n* : hito *m*
military *adj* : militar — ~ *n* **the** ~ : las
fuerzas armadas — **militant** *adj* : militante
— ~ *n* : militante *mf* — **militia** *n* : milicia
f
milk *n* : leche *f* — ~ *vt* **1** : ordeñar (una
vaca, etc.) **2** EXPLOIT : explotar — **milky**
adj **milkier; -est** : lechoso — **Milky Way** *n*
the ~ : la Vía Láctea
mill *n* **1** : molino *m* **2** FACTORY : fábrica *f* **3**
GRINDER : molinillo *m* — ~ *vt* : moler — *vi*
or ~ **about** : arremolinarse
millennium *n, pl* **-nia** *or* **-niums** : milenio *m*
miller *n* : molinero *m*, -ra *f*
milligram *n* : miligramo *m* — **millimeter** *or*
Brit **millimetre** *n* : milímetro *m*
million *n, pl* **millions** *or* **million** **1** : millón
m **2** a ~ **people** : un millón de personas —
~ *adj* a ~ : un millón de — **millionaire** *n*
: millonario *m*, -ria *f* — **millionth** *adj* : millonésimo
mime *n* **1** : mimo *mf* **2** PANTOMIME : pantomima *f* — ~ *v* **mimed; miming** *vt* : imitar — *vi* : hacer la mímica — **mimic** *vt*
-icked; -icking : imitar, remedar — ~ *n*
: imitador *m*, -dora *f* — **mimicry** *n, pl* **-ries**
: imitación *f*
mince *v* **minced; mincing** *vt* **1** : picar,
moler **2 not to** ~ **one's words** : no tener
pelos en la lengua
mind *n* **1** : mente *f* **2** INTELLECT : capacidad
f intelectual **3** OPINION : opinión *f* **4** REA-
SON : razón *f* **5 have a** ~ **to** : tener intención de — ~ *vt* **1** TEND : cuidar **2** OBEY
: obedecer **3** WATCH : tener cuidado con **4 I**
don't ~ **the heat** : no me molesta el calor
— *vi* **1** OBEY : obedecer **2 I don't** ~ : no
me importa, me es igual — **mindful** *adj*
: atento — **mindless** *adj* **1** SENSELESS : estúpido, sin sentido **2** DULL : aburrido
mine¹ *pron* **1** : (el) mío, (la) mía, (los) míos,
(las) mías **2 a friend of** ~ : un amigo mío
mine² *n* : mina *f* — ~ *vt* **mined; mining** **1**
: extraer (oro, etc.) **2** : minar (con artefactos
explosivos) — **minefield** *n* : campo *m* de
minas — **miner** *n* : minero *m*, -ra *f*
mineral *n* : mineral *m*
mingle *v* **-gled; -gling** *vt* : mezclar — *vi* **1**
: mezclarse **2** : circular (a una fiesta, etc.)

miniature *n* : miniatura *f* — ~ *adj* : en
miniatura
minimal *adj* : mínimo — **minimize** *vt*
-mized; -mizing : minimizar — **minimum**
adj : mínimo — ~ *n, pl* **-ma** *or* **-mums**
: mínimo *m*
mining *n* : minería *f*
minister *n* **1** : pastor *m*, -tora *f* (de una iglesia) **2** : ministro *m*, -tra *f* (en política) — ~
vi ~ **to** : cuidar (de), atender a — **ministe-**
rial *adj* : ministerial — **ministry** *n, pl* **-tries**
: ministerio *m*
mink *n, pl* **mink** *or* **minks** : visón *m*
minnow *n, pl* **-nows** : pececillo *m* de agua
dulce
minor *adj* **1** : menor **2** INSIGNIFICANT : sin
importancia — ~ *n* **1** : menor *mf* (de edad)
2 : asignatura *f* secundaria (de estudios) —
minority *n, pl* **-ties** : minoría *f*
mint¹ *n* **1** : menta *f* (planta) **2** : pastilla *f* de
menta (dulce)
mint² *n* **1 the U.S. Mint** : la casa de la moneda de los EE.UU. **2 be worth a** ~ : valer
un dineral — ~ *vt* : acuñar — ~ *adj* **in** ~
condition : como nuevo
minus *prep* **1** : menos **2** WITHOUT : sin —
~ *n or* ~ **sign** : signo *m* de menos
minuscule *adj* : minúsculo
minute¹ *n* **1** : minuto *m* **2** MOMENT : momento *m* **3** ~**s** *npl* : actas *fpl* (de una reunión)
minute² *adj* **-nuter; -est** **1** TINY : diminuto,
minúsculo **2** DETAILED : minucioso
miracle *n* : milagro *m* — **miraculous** *adj*
: milagroso
mirage *n* : espejismo *m*
mire *n* : lodo *m*, fango *m*
mirror *n* : espejo *m* — ~ *vt* : reflejar
mirth *n* : alegría *f*, risas *fpl*
misapprehension *n* : malentendido *m*
misbehave *vi* **-haved; -having** : portarse
mal — **misbehavior** *n* : mala conducta *f*
miscalculate *v* **-lated; -lating** : calcular mal
miscarriage *n* **1** : aborto *m* **2** ~ **of justice**
: error *m* judicial
miscellaneous *adj* : diverso, vario
mischief *n* : travesuras *fpl* — **mischievous**
adj : travieso
misconception *n* : concepto *m* erróneo
misconduct *n* : mala conducta *f*
misdeed *n* : fechoría *f*
misdemeanor *n* : delito *m* menor
miser *n* : avaro *m*, -ra *f*; tacaño *m*, -ña *f*
miserable *adj* **1** UNHAPPY : triste **2**
WRETCHED : miserable **3** ~ **weather**
: tiempo *m* malo
miserly *adj* : mezquino
misery *n, pl* **-eries** **1** : sufrimiento *m* **2**
WRETCHEDNESS : miseria *f*

misfire *vi* -fired; -firing : fallar
misfit *n* : inadaptado *m*, -da *f*
misfortune *n* : desgracia *f*
misgiving *n* : duda *f*
misguided *adj* : descaminado, equivocado
mishap *n* : contratiempo *m*
misinform *vt* : informar mal
misinterpret *vt* : interpretar mal
misjudge *vt* -judged; -judging : juzgar mal
mislay *vt* -laid; -laying : extraviar, perder
mislead *vt* -led; -leading : engañar — misleading *adj* : engañoso
misnomer *n* : nombre *m* inapropiado
misplace *vt* -placed; -placing : extraviar, perder
misprint *n* : errata *f*, error *m* de imprenta
miss *vt* 1 : errar, faltar 2 OVERLOOK : pasar por alto 3 : perder (una oportunidad, un vuelo, etc.) 4 AVOID : evitar 5 OMIT : saltarse 6 I ~ you : te echo de menos — ~ *n* 1 : fallo *m* (de un tiro, etc.) 2 FAILURE : fracaso *m*
Miss *n* : señorita *f*
missile *n* 1 : misil *m* 2 PROJECTILE : proyectil *m*
missing *adj* : perdido, desaparecido
mission *n* : misión *f* — missionary *n*, *pl* -aries : misionero *m*, -ra *f*
misspell *vt* : escribir mal
mist *n* : neblina *f*, bruma *f*
mistake *vt* mistook; mistaken; -taking 1 MISINTERPRET : entender mal 2 CONFUSE : confundir — ~ *n* 1 : error *m* 2 make a ~ : equivocarse — mistaken *adj* : equivocado
mister *n* : señor *m*
mistletoe *n* : muérdago *m*
mistreat *vt* : maltratar
mistress *n* 1 : dueña *f*, señora *f* (de una casa) 2 LOVER : amante *f*
mistrust *n* : desconfianza *f* — ~ *vt* : desconfiar de
misty *adj* mistier; -est : neblinoso, nebuloso
misunderstand *vt* -stood; -standing : entender mal — misunderstanding *n* : malentendido *m*
misuse *vt* -used; -using 1 : emplear mal 2 MISTREAT : maltratar — ~ *n* : mal empleo *m*, abuso *m*
mitigate *vt* -gated; -gating : mitigar
mitt *n* : manopla *f*, guante *m* (de béisbol) — mitten *n* : manopla *f*, mitón *m*
mix *vt* 1 : mezclar 2 ~ up : confundir — *vi* : mezclarse — ~ *n* : mezcla *f* — mixture *n* : mezcla *f* — mix–up *n* : confusión *f*, lío *m* fam
moan *n* : gemido *m* — ~ *vi* : gemir
mob *n* : muchedumbre *f* — ~ *vt* mobbed; mobbing : acosar
mobile *adj* : móvil — ~ *n* : móvil *m* — mo-

bile home *n* : caravana *f* — mobility *n* : movilidad *f* — mobilize *vt* -lized; -lizing : movilizar
moccasin *n* : mocasín *m*
mock *vt* : burlarse de, mofarse de — ~ *adj* : falso — mockery *n*, *pl* -eries : burla *f* — mock–up *n* : maqueta *f*
mode *n* 1 : modo *m* 2 FASHION : moda *f*
model *n* 1 : modelo *m* 2 MOCK-UP : maqueta *f* 3 : modelo *mf* (persona) — ~ *v* -eled *or* -elled; -eling *or* -elling *vt* 1 SHAPE : modelar 2 WEAR : lucir — *vi* : trabajar de modelo — ~ *adj* : modelo
modem *n* : módem *m*
moderate *adj* : moderado — ~ *n* : moderado *m*, -da *f* — ~ *v* -ated; -ating *vt* : moderar — *vi* : moderarse — moderation *n* : moderación *f* — moderator *n* : moderador *m*, -dora *f*
modern *adj* : moderno — modernize *vt* -ized; -izing : modernizar
modest *adj* : modesto — modesty *n* : modestia *f*
modify *vt* -fied; -fying : modificar
moist *adj* : húmedo — moisten *vt* : humedecer — moisture *n* : humedad *f* — moisturizer *n* : crema *f* hidratante
molar *n* : muela *f*
molasses *n* : melaza *f*
mold[1] *n* FORM : molde *m* — ~ *vt* : moldear, formar
mold[2] *n* FUNGUS : moho *m* — moldy *adj* moldier; -est : mohoso
mole[1] *n* : lunar *m* (en la piel)
mole[2] *n* : topo *m* (animal)
molecule *n* : molécula *f*
molest *vt* 1 HARASS : importunar 2 : abusar (sexualmente)
molten *adj* : fundido
mom *n* : mamá *f*
moment *n* : momento *m* — momentarily *adv* 1 : momentáneamente 2 SOON : dentro de poco, pronto — momentary *adj* : momentáneo
momentous *adj* : muy importante
momentum *n*, *pl* -ta *or* -tums 1 : momento *m* (en física) 2 IMPETUS : ímpetu *m*
monarch *n* : monarca *mf* — monarchy *n*, *pl* -chies : monarquía *f*
monastery *n*, *pl* -teries : monasterio *m*
Monday *n* : lunes *m*
money *n*, *pl* -eys *or* -ies : dinero *m* — monetary *adj* : monetario — money order *n* : giro *m* postal
mongrel *n* : perro *m* mestizo
monitor *n* : monitor *m* (de una computadora, etc.) — ~ *vt* : controlar
monk *n* : monje *m*

monkey *n, pl* **-keys** : mono *m*, -na *f* — **monkey wrench** *n* : llave *f* inglesa
monogram *n* : monograma *m*
monologue *n* : monólogo *m*
monopoly *n, pl* **-lies** : monopolio *m* — **monopolize** *vt* **-lized; -lizing** : monopolizar
monotonous *adj* : monótono — **monotony** *n* : monotonía *f*
monster *n* : monstruo *m* — **monstrosity** *n, pl* **-ties** : monstruosidad *f* — **monstrous** *adj* **1** : monstruoso **2** HUGE : gigantesco
month *n* : mes *m* — **monthly** *adv* : mensualmente — ~ *adj* : mensual
monument *n* : monumento *m* — **monumental** *adj* : monumental
moo *vi* : mugir — ~ *n* : mugido *m*
mood *n* : humor *m* — **moody** *adj* **moodier; -est 1** GLOOMY : melancólico, deprimido **2** IRRITABLE : malhumorado **3** TEMPERAMENTAL : de humor variable
moon *n* : luna *f* — **moonlight** *n* : luz *f* de la luna
moor[1] *n* : brezal *m*, páramo *m*
moor[2] *vt* : amarrar — **mooring** *n* DOCK : atracadero *m*
moose *ns & pl* : alce *m*
moot *adj* : discutible
mop *n* **1** : trapeador *m Lat*, fregona *f Spain* **2** *or* ~ **of hair** : pelambrera *f* — ~ *vt* **mopped; mopping** : trapear *Lat*, pasar la fregona a *Spain*
mope *vi* **moped; moping** : andar deprimido
moped *n* : ciclomotor *m*
moral *adj* : moral — ~ *n* **1** : moraleja *f* (de un cuento, etc.) **2** ~**s** *npl* : moral *f*, moralidad *f* — **morale** *n* : moral *f* — **morality** *n, pl* **-ties** : moralidad *f*
morbid *adj* : morboso
more *adj* : más — ~ *adv* **1** : más **2** ~ **and** ~ : cada vez más **3** ~ **or less** : más o menos **4 once** ~ : una vez más — ~ *n* : más *m* — ~ *pron* : más — **moreover** *adv* : además
morgue *n* : depósito *m* de cadáveres
morning *n* **1** : mañana *f* **2 good** ~**!** : ¡buenos días! **3 in the** ~ : por la mañana
moron *n* : estúpido *m*, -da *f;* imbécil *mf*
morose *adj* : malhumorado
morphine *n* : morfina *f*
morsel *n* **1** BITE : bocado *m* **2** FRAGMENT : pedazo *m*
mortal *adj* : mortal — ~ *n* : mortal *mf* — **mortality** *n* : mortalidad *f*
mortar *n* : mortero *m*
mortgage *n* : hipoteca *f* — ~ *vt* **-gaged; -gaging** : hipotecar
mortify *vt* **-fied; -fying 1** : mortificar **2** HUMILIATE : avergonzar
mosaic *n* : mosaico *m*

Moslem → **Muslim**
mosque *n* : mezquita *f*
mosquito *n, pl* **-toes** : mosquito *m*, zancudo *m Lat*
moss *n* : musgo *m*
most *adj* **1** : la mayoría de, la mayor parte de **2 (the)** ~ : más — ~ *adv* : más — ~ *n* : más *m*, máximo *m* — ~ *pron* : la mayoría, la mayor parte — **mostly** *adv* **1** MAINLY : en su mayor parte, principalmente **2** USUALLY : normalmente
motel *n* : motel *m*
moth *n* : palomilla *f*, polilla *f*
mother *n* : madre *f* — ~ *vt* **1** : cuidar de **2** SPOIL : mimar — **motherhood** *n* : maternidad *f* — **mother-in-law** *n, pl* **mothers-in-law** : suegra *f* — **motherly** *adj* : maternal — **mother-of-pearl** *n* : nácar *m*
motif *n* : motivo *m*
motion *n* **1** : movimiento *m* **2** PROPOSAL : moción *f* **3 set in** ~ : poner en marcha — ~ *vi* — **to s.o.** : hacer una señal a algn — **motionless** *adj* : inmóvil — **motion picture** *n* : película *f*
motive *n* : motivo *m* — **motivate** *vt* **-vated; -vating** : motivar — **motivation** *n* : motivación *f*
motor *n* : motor *m* — **motorbike** *n* : motocicleta *f* (pequeña), moto *f* — **motorboat** *n* : lancha *f* motora — **motorcycle** *n* : motocicleta *f* — **motorcyclist** *n* : motociclista *mf* — **motorist** *n* : automovilista *mf*, motorista *mf Lat*
motto *n, pl* **-toes** : lema *m*
mould → **mold**
mound *n* **1** PILE : montón *m* **2** HILL : montículo *m*
mount[1] *n* **1** HORSE : montura *f* **2** SUPPORT : soporte *m* — ~ *vt* : montar (un caballo, etc.), subir (una escalera) — *vi* INCREASE : aumentar
mount[2] *n* HILL : monte *m* — **mountain** *n* : montaña *f* — **mountainous** *adj* : montañoso
mourn *vt* : llorar (por) — *vi* : lamentarse — **mourner** *n* : doliente *mf* — **mournful** *adj* : triste — **mourning** *n* : luto *m*
mouse *n, pl* **mice** : ratón *m* — **mousetrap** *n* : ratonera *f*
moustache → **mustache**
mouth *n* : boca *f* (de una persona o un animal), desembocadura *f* (de un río) — **mouthful** *n* : bocado *m* — **mouthpiece** *n* : boquilla *f* (de un instrumento musical)
move *v* **moved; moving** *vi* **1** GO : ir **2** RELOCATE : mudarse **3** STIR : moverse **4** ACT : tomar medidas — *vt* **1** : mover **2** AFFECT : conmover **3** TRANSPORT : transportar,

trasladar **4** PROPOSE : proponer — ～ *n* **1** MOVEMENT : movimiento *m* **2** RELOCATION : mudanza *f* **3** STEP : medida *f* — **movable** *or* **moveable** *adj* : movible, móvil — **movement** *n* : movimiento *m*
movie *n* **1** : película *f* **2** ～**s** *npl* : cine *m*
mow *vt* **mowed; mowed** *or* **mown ; mowing** : cortar (la hierba) — **mower** → **lawn mower**
Mr. *n, pl* **Messrs.** : señor *m*
Mrs. *n, pl* **Mesdames** : señora *f*
Ms. *n* : señora *f*, señorita *f*
much *adj* **more; most** : mucho — ～ *adv* **more; most** **1** : mucho **2 as** ～ **as** : tanto como **3 how** ～**?** : ¿cuánto? **4 too** ～ : demasiado — ～ *pron* : mucho, -cha
muck *n* **1** DIRT : mugre *f*, suciedad *f* **2** MANURE : estiércol *m*
mucus *n* : mucosidad *f*
mud *n* : barro *m*, lodo *m*
muddle *v* **-dled; -dling** *vt* **1** CONFUSE : confundir **2** JUMBLE : desordenar — *vi* ～ **through** : arreglárselas — ～ *n* : confusión *f*, lío *m fam*
muddy *adj* **-dier; -est** : fangoso, lleno de barro
muffin *n* : mollete *m*
muffle *vt* **-fled; -fling** : amortiguar (un sonido) — **muffler** *n* **1** SCARF : bufanda *f* **2** : silenciador *m*, mofle *m Lat* (de un automóvil)
mug *n* CUP : tazón *m* — ～ *vt* : asaltar, atracar — **mugger** *n* : atracador *m*, -dora *f*
muggy *adj* **-gier; -est** : bochornoso
mule *n* : mula *f*
mull *vt or* ～ **over** : reflexionar sobre
multicolored *adj* : multicolor
multimedia *adj* : multimedia
multinational *adj* : multinacional
multiple *adj* : múltiple — ～ *n* : múltiplo *m* — **multiplication** *n* : multiplicación *f* — **multiply** *v* **-plied; -plying** *vt* : multiplicar — *vi* : multiplicarse
multitude *n* : multitud *f*
mum *adj* **keep** ～ : guardar silencio
mumble *v* **-bled; -bling** *vt* : mascullar — *vi* : hablar entre dientes
mummy *n, pl* **-mies** : momia *f*
mumps *ns & pl* : paperas *fpl*
munch *v* : mascar, masticar
mundane *adj* : rutinario, ordinario
municipal *adj* : municipal — **municipality** *n, pl* **-ties** : municipio *m*
munitions *npl* : municiónes *fpl*
mural *n* : mural *m*
murder *n* : asesinato *m*, homicidio *m* — ～ *vt* : asesinar, matar — *vi* : matar — **murderer** *n* : asesino *m*, -na *f*; homicida *mf* — **murderous** *adj* : asesino, homicida

murky *adj* **-kier; -est** : turbio, oscuro
murmur *n* : murmullo *m* — **murmur** *v* : murmurar
muscle *n* : músculo *m* — ～ *vi* **-cled; -cling** *or* ～ **in** : meterse por la fuerza en — **muscular** *adj* **1** : muscular **2** STRONG : musculoso
muse¹ *n* : musa *f*
muse² *vi* **mused; musing** : meditar
museum *n* : museo *m*
mushroom *n* **1** : hongo *m*, seta *f* **2** : champiñón *m* (en la cocina) — *vi* GROW : crecer rápidamente, multiplicarse
mushy *adj* **mushier; -est 1** SOFT : blando **2** MAWKISH : sensiblero
music *n* : música *f* — **musical** *adj* : musical — ～ *n* : comedia *f* musical — **musician** *n* : músico *m*, -ca *f*
Muslim *adj* : musulmán — ～ *n* : musulmán *m*, -mana *f*
muslin *n* : muselina *f*
mussel *n* : mejillón *m*
must *v aux* **1** : deber, tener que **2 you** ～ **come** : tienes que venir **3 you** ～ **be tired** : debes (de) estar cansado — ～ *n* : necesidad *f*
mustache *n* : bigote *m*, bigotes *mpl*
mustang *n* : mustang *m*
mustard *n* : mostaza *f*
muster *vt* **1** : reunir **2** *or* ～ **up** : armarse de, cobrar (valor, fuerzas, etc.)
musty *adj* **mustier; -est** : que huele a cerrado
mute *adj* **muter; mutest** : mudo — ～ *n* : mudo *m*, -da *f*
mutilate *vt* **-lated; -lating** : mutilar
mutiny *n, pl* **-nies** : motín *m* — ～ *vi* **-nied; -nying** : amotinarse
mutter *vi* : murmurar
mutton *n* : carne *f* de carnero
mutual *adj* **1** : mutuo **2** COMMON : común — **mutually** *adv* : mutuamente
muzzle *n* **1** SNOUT : hocico *m* **2** : bozal *m* (para un perro, etc.) **3** : boca *f* (de un arma de fuego) — ～ *vt* **-zled; -zling** : poner un bozal a (un animal)
my *adj* : mi
myopia *n* : miopía *f* — **myopic** *adj* : miope
myself *pron* **1** (*reflexive*) : me **2** (*emphatic*) : yo mismo **3 by** ～ : solo
mystery *n, pl* **-teries** : misterio *m* — **mysterious** *adj* : misterioso
mystic *adj or* **mystical** : místico
mystify *vt* **-fied; -fying** : dejar perplejo, confundir
mystique *n* : aura *f* de misterio
myth *n* : mito *m* — **mythical** *adj* : mítico

N

n *n*, *pl* **n's** *or* **ns** : n *f*, decimocuarta letra del alfabeto inglés

nab *vt* **nabbed; nabbing 1** ARREST : pescar *fam* **2** GRAB : agarrar

nag *v* **nagged; nagging** *vi* COMPLAIN : quejarse — *vt* **1** ANNOY : fastidiar, dar la lata a **2** SCOLD : regañar — **nagging** *adj* : persistente

nail *n* **1** : clavo *m* **2** : uña *f* (de un dedo) — ∼ *vt or* ∼ **down** : clavar — **nail file** *n* : lima *f* de uñas

naive *or* **naïve** *adj* **-iver; -est** : ingenuo — **naïveté** *n* : ingenuidad *f*

naked *adj* **1** : desnudo **2 the** ∼ **truth** : la pura verdad **3 to the** ∼ **eye** : a simple vista

name *n* **1** : nombre *m* **2** REPUTATION : fama *f* **3 what is your** ∼? : ¿cómo se llama? **4** → **first name, surname** — ∼ *vt* **named; naming 1** : poner nombre a **2** APPOINT : nombrar **3** ∼ **a price** : fijar un precio — **nameless** *adj* : anónimo — **namely** *adv* : a saber — **namesake** *n* : tocayo *m*, -ya *f*

nap[1] *vi* **napped; napping** : echarse una siesta — ∼ *n* : siesta *f*

nap[2] *n* : pelo *m* (de una tela)

nape *n or* ∼ **of the neck** : nuca *f*

napkin *n* **1** : servilleta *f* **2** → **sanitary napkin**

narcotic *n* : narcótico *m*, estupefaciente *m*

narrate *vt* **-rated; -rating** : narrar — **narration** *n* : narración *f* — **narrative** *n* : narración *f* — **narrator** *n* : narrador *m*, -dora *f*

narrow *adj* **1** : estrecho, angosto **2** RESTRICTED : limitado — ∼ *vi* : estrecharse — *vt* **1** : estrechar **2** *or* ∼ **down** : limitar — **narrowly** *adv* : por poco — **narrow-minded** *adj* : de miras estrechas

nasal *adj* : nasal

nasty *adj* **-tier; -est 1** MEAN : malo, cruel **2** UNPLEASANT : desagradable **3** REPUGNANT : asqueroso — **nastiness** *n* : maldad *f*

nation *n* : nación *f* — **national** *adj* : nacional — **nationalism** *n* : nacionalismo *m* — **nationality** *n*, *pl* **-ties** : nacionalidad *f* — **nationalize** *vt* **-ized; -izing** : nacionalizar — **nationwide** *adj* : por todo el país

native *adj* **1** : natal (dícese de un país, etc.) **2** INNATE : innato **3** ∼ **language** : lengua *f* materna — ∼ *n* **1** : nativo *m*, -va *f* **2 be a** ∼ **of** : ser natural de — **Native American** : indio *m* americano, india *f* americana — **nativity** *n*, *pl* **-ties the Nativity** : la Navidad

nature *n* **1** : naturaleza *f* **2** KIND : índole *f*,

clase *f* **3** DISPOSITION : carácter *m*, natural *m* — **natural** *adj* : natural — **naturalize** *vt* **-ized; -izing** : naturalizar — **naturally** *adv* : naturalmente

naught *n* **1** NOTHING : nada *f* **2** ZERO : cero *m*

naughty *adj* **-tier; -est 1** : travieso, pícaro **2** RISQUÉ : picante

nausea *n* : náuseas *fpl* — **nauseating** *adj* : nauseabundo — **nauseous** *adj* **1 feel** ∼ : sentir náuseas **2** SICKENING : nauseabundo

nautical *adj* : náutico

naval *adj* : naval

nave *n* : nave *f* (de una iglesia)

navel *n* : ombligo *m*

navigate *v* **-gated; -gating** *vi* : navegar — *vt* **1** : gobernar (un barco), pilotar (un avión) **2** : navegar por (un río, etc.) — **navigable** *adj* : navegable — **navigation** *n* : navegación *f* — **navigator** *n* : navegante *mf*

navy *n*, *pl* **-vies 1** : marina *f* de guerra **2** *or* ∼ **blue** : azul *m* marino

near *adv* : cerca — ∼ *prep* : cerca de — ∼ *adj* : cercano, próximo — ∼ *vt* : acercarse a — **nearby** *adv* : cerca — ∼ *adj* : cercano — **nearly** *adv* : casi — **nearsighted** *adj* : miope, corto de vista

neat *adj* **1** TIDY : muy arreglado **2** CLEVER : hábil, ingenioso — **neatly** *adv* **1** : ordenadamente **2** CLEVERLY : hábilmente — **neatness** *n* : pulcritud *f*, orden *m*

nebulous *adj* : nebuloso

necessary *adj* : necesario — **necessarily** *adv* : necesariamente — **necessitate** *vt* **-tated; -tating** : exigir, requerir — **necessity** *n*, *pl* **-ties 1** : necesidad *f* **2** **necessities** *npl* : cosas *fpl* indispensables

neck *n* **1** : cuello *m* (de una persona o una botella), pescuezo *m* (de un animal) **2** COLLAR : cuello *m* — **necklace** *n* : collar *m* — **necktie** *n* : corbata *f*

nectar *n* : néctar *m*

nectarine *n* : nectarina *f*

need *n* **1** : necesidad *f* **2 if** ∼ **be** : si hace falta — ∼ *vt* **1** : necesitar, exigir **2** ∼ **to** : tener que — *v aux* : tener que

needle *n* : aguja *f* — ∼ *vt* **-dled; -dling** : pinchar

needless *adj* **1** : innecesario **2** ∼ **to say** : de más está decir

needlework *n* : bordado *m*

needn't (*contraction of* **need not**) → **need**

needy needier; -est *adj* : necesitado

negative *adj* : negativo — ~ *n* **1** : negación *f* (en gramática) **2** : negativo *m* (en fotografía)
neglect *vt* : descuidar — ~ *n* : descuido *m*, abandono *m*
negligee *n* : negligé *m*
negligence *n* : negligencia *f*, descuido *m* —
negligent *adj* : negligente, descuidado
negligible *adj* : insignificante
negotiate *v* -ated; -ating : negociar — negotiable *adj* : negociable — negotiation *n* : negociación *f* — negotiator *n* : negociador *m*, -dora *f*
Negro *n*, *pl* -groes *sometimes considered offensive* : negro *m*, -gra *f*
neigh *vi* : relinchar — ~ *n* : relincho *m*
neighbor *or Brit* neighbour *n* : vecino *m*, -na *f* — neighborhood *or Brit* neighbourhood *n* **1** : barrio *m*, vecindario *m* **2 in the** ~ **of** : alrededor de — neighborly *or Brit* neighbourly *adv* : amable
neither *conj* **1** ~...nor : ni...ni **2** ~ am/do I : yo tampoco — ~ *pron* : ninguno, -na — ~ *adj* : ninguno (de los dos)
neon *n* : neón *m*
nephew *n* : sobrino *m*
Neptune *n* : Neptuno *m*
nerve *n* **1** : nervio *m* **2** COURAGE : coraje *m* **3** GALL : descaro *m* **4** ~s *npl* JITTERS : nervios *mpl* — nervous *adj* : nervioso — nervousness *n* : nerviosismo *m* — nervy *adj* nervier; -est : descarado
nest *n* : nido *m* — ~ *vi* : anidar
nestle *vi* -tled; -tling : acurrucarse
net¹ *n* : red *f* — ~ *vt* netted; netting : pescar, atrapar (con una red)
net² *adj* : neto — ~ *vt* netted; netting YIELD : producir neto
nettle *n* : ortiga *f*
network *n* : red *f*
neurology *n* : neurología *f*
neurosis *n*, *pl* -roses : neurosis *f* — neurotic *adj* : neurótico
neuter *adj* : neutro — ~ *vt* : castrar
neutral *n* : punto *m* muerto (de un automóvil) — ~ *adj* **1** : neutral **2** : neutro (en electrotecnia o química) — neutrality *n* : neutralidad *f* — neutralize *vt* -ized; -izing : neutralizar
neutron *n* : neutrón *m*
never *adv* **1** : nunca, jamás **2** NOT : no **3** ~ again : nunca más **4** ~ mind : no importa — nevermore *adv* : nunca jamás — nevertheless *adv* : sin embargo, no obstante
new *adj* : nuevo — newborn *adj* : recién nacido — newcomer *n* : recién llegado *m*, -da *f* — newly *adv* : recién, recientemente — newlywed *n* : recién casado *m*, -da *f* — news *n* : noticias *fpl* — newscast *n*

: noticiario *m*, noticiero *m* Lat — newscaster *n* : presentador *m*, -dora *f* (de un noticiario) — newsletter *n* : boletín *m* informativo — newspaper *n* : periódico *m*, diario *m* — newsstand *n* : puesto *m* de periódicos
newt *n* : tritón *m*
New Year's Day *n* : día *m* del Año Nuevo
next *adj* **1** : próximo **2** FOLLOWING : siguiente — ~ *adv* **1** : la próxima vez **2** AFTERWARD : después, luego **3** NOW : ahora — next-door *adj* : de al lado — next to *adv* ALMOST : casi — ~ *prep* BESIDE : al lado de
nib *n* : plumilla *f*
nibble *vt* -bled; -bling : mordisquear
Nicaraguan *adj* : nicaragüense
nice *adj* nicer; nicest **1** PLEASANT : agradable, bueno **2** KIND : amable — nicely *adv* **1** WELL : bien **2** KINDLY : amablemente — niceness *n* : amabilidad *f* — niceties *npl* : detalles *mpl*, sutilezas *fpl*
niche *n* **1** : nicho *m* **2 find one's** ~ : hacerse su hueco
nick *n* **1** : corte *m* pequeño, muesca *f* **2 in the** ~ **of time** : justo a tiempo — ~ *vt* : hacer una muesca en
nickel *n* **1** : níquel *m* (metal) **2** : moneda *f* de cinco centavos
nickname *n* : apodo *m*, sobrenombre *m* — ~ *vt* -named; -naming : apodar
nicotine *n* : nicotina *f*
niece *n* : sobrina *f*
niggling *adj* **1** PETTY : insignificante **2** PERSISTENT : constante
night *n* **1** : noche *f* **2 at** ~ : de noche **3 last** ~ : anoche **4 tomorrow** ~ : mañana por la noche — nightclub *n* : club *m* nocturno — nightfall *n* : anochecer *m* — nightgown *n* : camisón *m* (de noche) — nightly *adj* : de todas las noches — ~ *adv* : cada noche — nightmare *n* : pesadilla *f* — nighttime *n* : noche *f*
nil *n* NOTHING : nada *f*
nimble *adj* -bler; -blest : ágil
nine *adj* : nueve — ~ *n* : nueve *m* — nine hundred *adj* : novecientos — ~ *n* : novecientos *m* — nineteen *adj* : diecinueve — ~ *n* : diecinueve *m* — nineteenth *adj* : decimonoveno, decimonono — ~ *n* **1** : decimonoveno *m*, -na *f*; decimonono *m*, -na *f* (en una serie) — diecinueveavo *m* (en matemáticas) — ninetieth *adj* : nonagésimo — ~ *n* **1** : nonagésimo *m*, -ma *f* (en una serie) **2** : noventavo *m* (en matemáticas) — ninety *adj* : noventa — ~ *n*, *pl* -ties : noventa *m* — ninth *adj* : noveno — ~ *n* **1** : noveno *m*, -na *f* (en una serie) **2** : noveno *m* (en matemáticas)

nip *vt* **nipped; nipping 1** PINCH : pellizcar **2** BITE : mordisquear **3** ~ **in the bud** : cortar de raíz — ~ *n* **1** PINCH : pellizco *m* **2** NIBBLE : mordisco *m*

nipple *n* **1** : pezón *m* (de una mujer) **2** : tetilla *f* (de un hombre o un biberón)

nitrogen *n* : nitrógen *m*

nitwit *n* : idiota *mf*

no *adv* : no — ~ *adj* **1** : ninguno **2 I have** ~ **money** : no tengo dinero **3 it's** ~ **trouble** : no es ningún problema **4** ~ **smoking** : prohibido fumar — ~ *n, pl* **noes** *or* **nos** : no *m*

noble *adj* **-bler; -blest** : noble — ~ *n* : noble *mf* — **nobility** *n* : nobleza *f*

nobody *pron* : nadie

nocturnal *adj* : nocturno

nod *v* **nodded; nodding** *vi* **1** *or* ~ **yes** : asentir con la cabeza **2** ~ **off** : dormirse — *vt* ~ **one's head** : asentir con la cabeza — ~ *n* : señal *m* con la cabeza

noes → **no**

noise *n* : ruido *m* — **noisily** *adv* : ruidosamente — **noisy** *adj* **noisier; -est** : ruidoso

nomad *n* : nómada *mf* — **nomadic** *adj* : nómada

nominal *adj* : nominal

nominate *vt* **-nated; -nating 1** : proponer, postular *Lat* **2** APPOINT : nombrar — **nomination** *n* **1** : propuesta *f*, postulación *f Lat* **2** APPOINTMENT : nombramiento *m*

nonalcoholic *adj* : no alcohólico

nonchalant *adj* : despreocupado

noncommissioned officer *n* : suboficial *mf*

noncommittal *adj* : evasivo

nondescript *adj* : anodino, soso

none *pron* **1** : ninguno, ninguna **2 there are** ~ **left** : no hay más — ~ *adv* **1 be** ~ **the worse** : no sufrir daño alguno **2** ~ **too happy** : nada contento **3** ~ **too soon** : a buena hora

nonentity *n, pl* **-ties** : persona *f* insignificante

nonetheless *adv* : sin embargo, no obstante

nonexistent *adj* : inexistente

nonfat *adj* : sin grasa

nonfiction *n* : no ficción *f*

nonprofit *adj* : sin fines lucrativos

nonsense *n* : tonterías *fpl*, disparates *mpl* — **nonsensical** *adj* : absurdo

nonsmoker *n* : no fumador *m*, -dora *f*

nonstop *adj* : directo — ~ *adv* : sin parar

noodle *n* : fideo *m*

nook *n* : rincón *m*

noon *n* : mediodía *m*

no one *pron* : nadie

noose *n* **1** : dogal *m*, soga *f* **2** LASSO : lazo *m*

nor *conj* **1 neither...**~ : ni...ni **2** ~ **I** : yo tampoco

norm *n* **1** : norma *f* **2 the** ~ : lo normal — **normal** *adj* : normal — **normality** *n* : normalidad *f* — **normally** *adv* : normalmente

north *adv* : al norte — ~ *adj* : norte, del norte — ~ *n* **1** : norte *m* **2 the North** : el Norte — **North American** *adj* : norteamericano — **northeast** *adv* : hacia el nordeste — ~ *adj* : nordeste, del nordeste — ~ *n* : nordeste *m*, noreste *m* — **northeastern** *adj* : nordeste, del nordeste — **northerly** *adj* : del norte — **northern** *adj* : del norte, norteño — **northwest** *adv* : hacia el noroeste — ~ *adj* : noroeste, del noroeste — ~ *n* : noroeste *m* — **northwestern** *adj* : noroeste, del noroeste

Norwegian *adj* : noruego

nose *n* **1** : nariz *f* (de una persona), hocico *m* (de un animal) **2 blow one's** ~ : sonarse las narices — ~ *vi* **nosed; nosing** *or* ~ **around** : meter las narices — **nosebleed** *n* : hemorragia *f* nasal — **nosedive** *n* : descenso *m* en picada

nostalgia *n* : nostalgia *f* — **nostalgic** *adj* : nostálgico

nostril *n* : ventana *f* de la nariz

nosy *or* **nosey** *adj* **nosier; -est** : entrometido

not *adv* **1** : no **2 he's** ~ **tired** : no esta cansado **3 I hope** ~ : espero que no **4** ~ **... anything** : no...nada

notable *adj* : notable — ~ *n* : personaje *m* — **notably** *adv* : notablemente

notary public *n, pl* **notaries public** *or* **notary publics** : notario *m*, -ria *f*

notation *n* : anotación *f*

notch *n* : muesca *f*, corte *m* — ~ *vt* : hacer un corte en

note *vt* **noted; noting 1** NOTICE : observar, notar **2** RECORD : anotar — ~ *n* **1** : nota *f* **2 of** ~ : destacado **3 take** ~ **of** : prestar atención a **4 take** ~**s** : apuntar — **notebook** *n* : libreta *f*, cuaderno *m* — **noted** *adj* : renombrado, célebre — **noteworthy** *adj* : notable

nothing *pron* **1** : nada **2 be** ~ **but** : no ser más que **3 for** ~ FREE : gratis — ~ *n* **1** ZERO : zero *m* **2** TRIFLE : nimiedad *f*

notice *n* **1** SIGN : letrero *m*, aviso *m* **2 at a moment's** ~ : sin previo aviso **3 be given one's** ~ : ser despedido **4 take** ~ **of** : prestar atención a — ~ *vt* **-ticed; -ticing** : notar — **noticeable** *adj* : perceptible, evidente

notify *vt* **-fied; -fying** : notificar, avisar — **notification** *n* : notificación *f*, aviso *m*

notion *n* **1** : noción *f*, idea *f* **2** ~**s** *npl* : artículos *mpl* de mercería

notorious *adj* : de mala fama — **notoriety** *n* : mala fama *f*, notoriedad *f*

notwithstanding *prep* : a pesar de, no obstante — ∼ *adv* : sin embargo — ∼ *conj* : a pesar de que

nougat *n* : turrón *m*

nought → **naught**

noun *n* : nombre *m*, sustantivo *m*

nourish *vt* : nutrir — **nourishing** *adj* : nutritivo — **nourishment** *n* : alimento *m*

novel *adj* : original, novedoso — ∼ *n* : novela *f* — **novelist** *n* : novelista *mf* — **novelty** *n, pl* **-ties** : novedad *f*

November *n* : noviembre *m*

novice *n* : novato *m*, -ta *f*; principiante *mf*

now *adv* **1** : ahora **2** THEN : entonces **3 from** ∼ **on** : de ahora en adelante **4** ∼ **and then** : de vez en cuando **5 right** ∼ : ahora mismo — ∼ *conj or* ∼ **that** : ahora que, ya que — ∼ *n* **1 a year from** ∼ : dentro de un año **2 by** ∼ : ya **3 until** ∼ : hasta ahora — **nowadays** *adv* : hoy en día

nowhere *adv* **1** (*indicating location*) : por ninguna parte, por ningún lado **2** (*indicating motion*) : a ninguna parte, a ningún lado **3 I'm** ∼ **near finished** : aún me falta mucho para terminar **4 it's** ∼ **near here** : queda bastante lejos de aquí — ∼ *n* : ninguna parte *f*

nozzle *n* : boca *f* (de una manguera, etc.)

nuance *n* : matiz *m*

nucleus *n, pl* **-clei** : núcleo *m* — **nuclear** *adj* : nuclear

nude *adj* **nuder; nudest** : desnudo — ∼ *n* : desnudo *m*

nudge *vt* **nudged; nudging** : dar un codazo a — ∼ *n* : toque *m* (con el codo)

nudity *n* : desnudez *f*

nugget *n* : pepita *f* (de oro, etc.)

nuisance *n* **1** ANNOYANCE : fastidio *m*, molestia *f* **2** PEST : pesado *m*, -da *f fam*

null *adj* ∼ **and void** : nulo y sin efecto

numb *adj* **1** : entumecido, dormido **2** ∼ **with fear** : paralizado de miedo — ∼ *vt* : entumecer, adormecer

number *n* **1** : número *m* **2 a** ∼ **of** : varios — ∼ *vt* **1** : numerar **2** INCLUDE : contar, incluir **3** TOTAL : ascender a

numeral *n* : número *m* — **numeric** *or* **numerical** *adj* : numérico — **numerous** *adj* : numeroso

nun *n* : monja *f*

nuptial *adj* : nupcial

nurse *n* **1** : enfermero *m*, -ra *f* **2** → **nursemaid** — ∼ *vt* **nursed; nursing 1** : cuidar (de), atender **2** SUCKLE : amamantar — **nursemaid** *n* : niñera *f* — **nursery** *n, pl* **-eries 1** : cuarto *m* de los niños **2** *or* **day** ∼ : guardería *f* **3** : vivero *m* (de plantas) — **nursing home** *n* : asilo *m* de ancianos

nurture *vt* **-tured; -turing 1** NOURISH : nutrir **2** EDUCATE : criar, educar **3** FOSTER : alimentar

nut *n* **1** : nuez *f* **2** LUNATIC : loco *m*, -ca *f* **3** ENTHUSIAST : fanático *m*, -ca *f* **4** ∼**s and bolts** : tuercas y tornillos — **nutcracker** *n* : cascanueces *m*

nutmeg *n* : nuez *f* moscada

nutrient *n* : nutriente *m*

nutrition *n* : nutrición *f* — **nutritional** *adj* : nutritivo — **nutritious** *adj* : nutritivo

nuts *adj* : loco

nutshell *n* **1** : cáscara *f* de nuez **2 in a** ∼ : en pocas palabras

nutty *adj* **-tier; -tiest** : loco

nuzzle *v* **-zled; -zling** *vi* : acurrucarse — *vt* : acariciar con el hocico

nylon *n* **1** : nilón *m* **2** ∼**s** *npl* : medias *fpl* de nilón

nymph *n* : ninfa *f*

O

o *n, pl* **o's** *or* **os 1** : o *f*, decimoquinta letra del alfabeto inglés **2** ZERO : cero *m*

O → **oh**

oaf *n* : zoquete *m*

oak *n, pl* **oaks** *or* **oak** : roble *m*

oar *n* : remo *m*

oasis *n, pl* **oases** : oasis *m*

oath *n, pl* **oaths 1** : juramento *m* **2** SWEARWORD : palabrota *f*

oats *npl* : avena *f* — **oatmeal** *n* : harina *f* de avena

obedient *adj* : obediente — **obedience** *n* : obediencia *f*

obese *adj* : obeso — **obesity** *n* : obesidad *f*

obey *v* **obeyed; obeying** : obedecer

obituary *n, pl* **-aries** : obituario *m*

object *n* **1** : objeto *m* **2** AIM : objetivo *m* **3** : complemento *m* (en gramática) — ∼ *vt* : objetar — *vi* ∼ **to** : oponerse a — **objection** *n* : objeción *f* — **objectionable** *adj* : desagradable — **objective** *adj* : objetivo — ∼ *n* : objetivo *m*

oblige *vt* **obliged; obliging 1** : obligar **2 be much ~d** : estar muy agradecido **3 ~ s.o.** : hacer un favor a algn — **obligation** *n* : obligación *f* — **obligatory** *adj* : obligatorio — **obliging** *adj* : atento, servicial

oblique *adj* **1** SLANTING : oblicuo **2** INDIRECT : indirecto

obliterate *vt* **-ated; -ating 1** ERASE : borrar **2** DESTROY : arrasar

oblivion *n* : olvido *m* — **oblivious** *adj* : inconsciente

oblong *adj* : oblongo — **~** *n* : rectángulo *m*

obnoxious *adj* : odioso

oboe *n* : oboe *m*

obscene *adj* : obsceno — **obscenity** *n, pl* **-ties** : obscenidad *f*

obscurity *n, pl* **-ties** : oscuridad *f* — **obscure** *adj* : oscuro — **~** *vt* **-scured; -scuring 1** DARKEN : oscurecer **2** HIDE : ocultar

observe *v* **-served; -serving** *vt* : observar — *vi* WATCH : mirar — **observance** *n* **1** : observancia *f* **2 religious ~s** : prácticas *fpl* religiosas — **observant** *adj* : observador — **observation** *n* : observación *f* — **observatory** *n, pl* **-ries** : observatorio *m*

obsess *vt* : obsesionar — **obsession** *n* : obsesión *f* — **obsessive** *adj* : obsesivo

obsolete *adj* : obsoleto, desusado

obstacle *n* : obstáculo *m*

obstetrics *n* : obstetricia *f*

obstinate *adj* : obstinado

obstruct *vt* **1** BLOCK : obstruir **2** HINDER : obstaculizar — **obstruction** *n* : obstrucción *f*

obtain *vt* : obtener, conseguir — **obtainable** *adj* : asequible

obtrusive *adj* : entrometido (dícese de las personas), demasiado prominente (dícese de las cosas)

obtuse *adj* : obtuso

obvious *adj* : obvio, evidente — **obviously** *adv* **1** CLEARLY : obviamente **2** OF COURSE : claro, por supuesto

occasion *n* **1** : ocasión *f* **2 on ~** : de vez en cuando — **~** *vt* : ocasionar — **occasional** *adj* : poco frecuente, ocasional — **occasionally** *adv* : de vez en cuando

occult *adj* : oculto

occupy *vt* **-pied; -pying 1** : ocupar **2 ~ oneself** : entretenerse — **occupancy** *n, pl* **-cies** : ocupación *f* — **occupant** *n* : ocupante *mf* — **occupation** *n* : ocupación *f* — **occupational** *adj* : profesional

occur *vi* **occurred; occurring 1** : ocurrir **2** APPEAR : encontrarse **3 ~ to s.o.** : ocurrirse a algn — **occurrence** *n* **1** EVENT : acontecimiento *m*, suceso *m* **2** INCIDENCE : incidencia *f*

ocean *n* : océano *m*

ocher *or* **ochre** *n* : ocre *m*

o'clock *adv* **1 at 6 ~** : a las seis **2 it's one ~** : es la una **3 it's ten ~** : son las diez

octagon *n* : octágono *m* — **octagonal** *adj* : octagonal

octave *n* : octava *f*

October *n* : octubre *m*

octopus *n, pl* **-puses** *or* **-pi** : pulpo *m*

oculist *n* : oculista *mf*

odd *adj* **1** STRANGE : extraño, raro **2** : sin pareja (dícese de un calcetín, etc.) **3 forty ~ years** : cuarenta y tantos años **4 ~ jobs** : algunos trabajos *mpl* **5 ~ number** : número *m* impar — **oddity** *n, pl* **-ties** : rareza *f* — **oddly** *adv* : de manera extraña — **odds** *npl* **1** CHANCES : probabilidades *fpl* **2 at ~** : en desacuerdo **3 five to one ~** : cinco contra uno (en apuestas) — **odds and ends** *npl* : cosas *fpl* sueltas

ode *n* : oda *f*

odious *adj* : odioso

odor *or Brit* **odour** *n* : olor *m* — **odorless** *or Brit* **odourless** *adj* : inodoro

of *prep* **1** : de **2 five minutes ~ ten** : las diez menos cinco **3 the eighth ~ April** : el ocho de abril

off *adv* **1 be ~** LEAVE : irse **2 cut ~** : cortar **3 day ~** : día *m* de descanso **4 fall ~** : caerse **5 doze ~** : dormirse **6 far ~** : lejos **7 ~ and on** : de vez en cuando **8 shut ~** : apagar **9 ten miles ~** : a diez millas de aquí — **~** *prep* **1** : de **2 be ~ duty** : estar libre **3 ~ center** : descentrado — **~** *adj* **1** CANCELED : cancelado **2** OUT : apagado **3 an ~ chance** : una posibilidad remota

offend *vt* : ofender — **offender** *n* : delincuente *mf* — **offense** *or* **offence** *n* **1** AFFRONT : afrenta *f* **2** ASSAULT : ataque *m* **3** : ofensiva *f* (en deportes) **4** CRIME : delito *m* **5 take ~** : ofenderse — **offensive** *adj* : ofensivo — **~** *n* : ofensiva *f*

offer *vt* : ofrecer — **~** *n* : oferta *f* — **offering** *n* : ofrenda *f*

offhand *adv* : de improviso, en este momento — **~** *adj* : improvisado

office *n* **1** : oficina *f* **2** POSITION : cargo *m* **3 run for ~** : presentarse como candidato — **officer** *n* **1** : oficial *mf* **2 or police ~** : agente *mf* (de policía) — **official** *n* : funcionario *m*, -ria *f* — **~** *adj* : oficial

offing *n* **in the ~** : en perspectiva

offset *vt* **-set; -setting** : compensar

offshore *adv* : a una distancia de la costa

offspring *ns & pl* **-spring** : prole *f*, progenie *f*

often *adv* **1** : muchas veces, a menudo, con frecuencia **2 every so ~** : de vez en cuando

ogle *vt* **ogled; ogling** : comerse con los ojos

ogre *n* : ogro *m*
oh *interj* **1** : ¡oh!, ¡ah! **2** ～ **no!** : ¡ay no! **3**
  ～ **really?** : ¿de veras?
oil *n* **1** : aceite *m* **2** PETROLEUM : petróleo *m*
  3 *or* ～ **painting** : óleo *m* — ～ *vt* : lubricar
  — **oilskin** *n* : hule *m* — **oily** *adj* **oilier; -est**
  : aceitoso, grasiento
ointment *n* : ungüento *m*, pomada *f*
OK *or* **okay** *adv* **1** : muy bien **2** ～! : ¡de
  acuerdo!, ¡bueno! — ～ *adj* **1** ALL RIGHT
  : bien **2** **it's** ～ **with me** : por mí no hay
  problema — ～ *n* : visto *m* bueno — ～ *vt*
  OK'd *or* **okayed; OK'ing** *or* **okaying** : dar
  el visto bueno a
okra *n* : quingombó *m*
old *adj* **1** : viejo **2** FORMER : antiguo **3** any
  ～ : cualquier **4 be ten years** ～ : tener
  diez años (de edad) **5** ～ **age** : vejez *f* **6** ～
  man : anciano *m* **7** ～ **woman** : anciana *f*
  — ～ *n* **the** ～ : los viejos, los ancianos —
  old-fashioned *adj* : anticuado
olive *n* **1** : aceituna *f* (fruta) **2** *or* ～ **green**
  : verde *m* oliva
Olympic *adj* : olímpico — **Olympics** *npl* **the**
  ～ : las Olimpiadas, las Olimpíadas
omelet *or* **omelette** *n* : omelette *mf Lat*, tortilla *f* francesa *Spain*
omen *n* : agüero *m* — **ominous** *adj* : ominoso, de mal agüero
omit *vt* **omitted; omitting** : omitir — **omission** *n* : omisión *f*
omnipotent *adj* : omnipotente
on *prep* **1** : en **2** ABOUT : sobre **3** ～ **foot**
  : a pie **4** ～ **Monday** : el lunes **5** ～ **the**
  right : a la derecha **6** ～ **vacation** : de vacaciones **7 talk** ～ **the phone** : hablar por
  teléfono — ～ *adv* **1 and so** ～ : etcétera
  2 from that moment ～ : a partir de ese
  momento **3 keep** ～ : seguir **4 later** ～
  : más tarde **5** ～ **and** ～ : sin parar **6 put**
  ～ : ponerse (ropa), poner (música, etc.) **7**
  turn ～ : encender (una luz, etc.), abrir (una
  llave) — ～ *adj* **1** : encendido (dícese de
  luces, etc.), abierto (dícese de llaves) **2 be**
  ～ **to** : estar enterado de
once *adv* **1** : una vez **2** FORMERLY : antes —
  ～ *n* **1 at** ～ **TOGETHER** : al mismo tiempo
  2 at ～ IMMEDIATELY : inmediatamente —
  ～ *conj* : una vez que
oncoming *adj* : que viene
one *adj* **1** : un, uno **2** ONLY : único **3** *or* ～
  and the same : el mismo — ～ *n* **1** : uno
  m (número) **2** ～ **by** ～ : uno a uno — ～
  pron **1** : uno, una **2** ～ **another** : el uno al
  otro **3** ～ **never knows** : nunca se sabe **4**
  that ～ : aquél, aquella **5 which** ～?
  : ¿cuál? — **oneself** *pron* **1** (*used reflexively*) : se **2** (*used after prepositions*) : sí
  mismo, sí misma **3** (*used emphatically*)

: uno mismo, una misma **4 by** ～ : solo —
one-sided *adj* **1** UNEQUAL : desigual **2** BI-
  ASED : parcial — **one-way** *adj* **1** : de sentido único (dícese de una calle) **2** ～ **ticket**
  : boleto *m* de ida
ongoing *adj* : en curso, corriente
onion *n* : cebolla *f*
only *adj* : único — ～ *adv* **1** : sólo, solamente **2 if** ～ : ojalá, por lo menos — ～
  conj BUT : pero
onset *n* : comienzo *m*, llegada *f*
onslaught *n* : ataque *m*, arremetida *f*
onto *prep* : sobre
onus *n* : responsabilidad *f*
onward *adv* & *adj* : hacia adelante
onyx *n* : ónix *m*
ooze *v* **oozed; oozing** : rezumar
opal *n* : ópalo *m*
opaque *adj* : opaco
open *adj* **1** : abierto **2** AVAILABLE : vacante,
  libre **3 an** ～ **question** : una cuestión pendiente — ～ *vt* : abrir — *vi* **1** : abrirse **2**
  BEGIN : comenzar — ～ *n* **in the** ～ **1**
  OUTDOORS : al aire libre **2** KNOWN : sacado
  a la luz — **open-air** *adj* : al aire libre —
  opener *n* **1** : abridor *m* **2** *or* **bottle** ～
  : abrebotellas *m* **3** *or* **can** ～ : abrelatas *m*
  — **opening** *n* **1** : abertura *f* **2** BEGINNING
  : comienzo *m*, apertura *f* **3** OPPORTUNITY
  : oportunidad *f* — **openly** *adv* : abiertamente
opera *n* : ópera *f*
operate *v* **-ated; -ating** *vi* **1** FUNCTION : funcionar **2** ～ **on s.o.** : operar a algn — *vt* **1**
  : hacer funcionar (una máquina) **2** MANAGE
  : dirigir, manejar — **operation** *n* **1** : op-
  eración *f* **2** FUNCTIONING : funcionamiento
  m — **operational** *adj* : operacional — **op-
  erative** *adj* : en vigor — **operator** *n* **1** : operador *m*, -dora *f* **2** *or* **machine** ～ : oper-
  ario *m*, -ria *f*
opinion *n* : opinión *f* — **opinionated** *adj*
  : dogmático
opium *n* : opio *m*
opossum *n* : zarigüeya *f*, oposum *m*
opponent *n* : adversario *m*, -ria *f*; contrincante *mf* (en deportes)
opportunity *n, pl* **-ties** : oportunidad *f* —
  opportune *adj* : oportuno — **opportunist**
  n : oportunista *mf*
oppose *vt* **-posed; -posing** : oponerse a —
  opposed *adj* **to** : en contra de
opposite *adj* **1** FACING : de enfrente **2** CON-
  TRARY : opuesto — ～ *n* **the** ～ : lo contrario, lo opuesto — ～ *adv* : enfrente — ～
  prep : enfrente de, frente a — **opposition** *n*
  1 : oposición *f* **2 in** ～ **to** : en contra de
oppress *vt* : oprimir — **oppression** *n*
  : opresión *f* — **oppressive** *adj* **1** : opresivo

2 STIFLING : agobiante — **oppressor** *n* : opresor *m*, -sora *f*
opt *vi* ~ **for** : optar por
optic *or* **optical** *adj* : óptico — **optician** *n* : óptico *m*, -ca *f*
optimism *n* : optimismo *m* — **optimist** *n* : optimista *mf* — **optimistic** *adj* : optimista
optimum *n, pl* -**ma** : lo óptimo, lo ideal
option *n* **1** : opción *f* **2 have no** ~ : no tener más remedio — **optional** *adj* : facultativo, opcional
opulence *n* : opulencia *f* — **opulent** *adj* : opulento
or *conj* **1** (*indicating an alternative*) : o (u *before* o- *or* ho-) **2** (*following a negative*) : ni **3** ~ **else** : si no
oracle *n* : oráculo *m*
oral *adj* : oral
orange *n* **1** : naranja *f* (fruta) **2** : naranja *m* (color)
orator *n* : orador *m*, -dora *f*
orbit *n* : órbita *f* — ~ *vt* : girar alrededor de — *vi* : orbitar
orchard *n* : huerto *m*
orchestra *n* : orquesta *f*
orchid *n* : orquídea *f*
ordain *vt* **1** : ordenar (un sacerdote, etc.) **2** DECREE : decretar
ordeal *n* : prueba *f* dura
order *vt* **1** : ordenar **2** : pedir (mercancías, etc.) — *vi* : hacer un pedido — ~ *n* **1** ARRANGEMENT : orden *m* **2** COMMAND : orden *f* **3** REQUEST : pedido *m* **4** : orden *f* (religiosa) **5 in** ~ **that** : para que **6 in** ~ **to** : para **7 out of** ~ : averiado, descompuesto *Lat* — **orderly** *adj* : ordenado — ~ *n, pl* -**lies** **1** : ordenanza *m* (en el ejército) **2** : camillero *m* (en un hospital)
ordinary *adj* **1** : normal, corriente **2** MEDIOCRE : ordinario — **ordinarily** *adv* : generalmente
ore *n* : mena *f*
oregano *n* : orégano *m*
organ *n* : órgano *m* — **organic** *adj* : orgánico — **organism** *n* : organismo *m* — **organist** *n* : organista *mf* — **organize** *vt* -**nized; -nizing** : organizar — **organization** *n* : organización *f* — **organizer** *n* : organizador *m*, -dora *f*
orgasm *n* : orgasmo *m*
orgy *n, pl* -**gies** : orgía *f*
Orient *n* **the** ~ : el Oriente — **orient** *vt* : orientar — **oriental** *adj* : del Oriente, oriental — **orientation** *n* : orientación *f*
orifice *n* : orificio *m*
origin *n* : origen *m* — **original** *n* : original *m* — ~ *adj* : original — **originality** *n* : originalidad *f* — **originally** *adv* : originariamente — **originate** *v* -**nated; -nating** *vt*

: originar — *vi* **1** : originarse **2** ~ **from** : provenir de — **originator** *n* : creador *m*, -dora *f*
ornament *n* : adorno *m* — ~ *vt* : adornar — **ornamental** *adj* : ornamental, de adorno — **ornate** *adj* : elaborado, adornado
ornithology *n, pl* -**gies** : ornitología *f*
orphan *n* : huérfano *m*, -na *f* — ~ *vt* : dejar huérfano — **orphanage** *n* : orfelinato *m*, orfanato *m*
orthodox *adj* : ortodoxo — **orthodoxy** *n, pl* -**doxies** : ortodoxia *f*
orthopedic *adj* : ortopédico
oscillation *n* : oscilación *f* — **oscillate** *vi* -**lated; -lating** : oscilar
ostensible *adj* : aparente, ostensible
ostentation *n* : ostentación *f* — **ostentatious** *adj* : ostentoso
osteopath *n* : osteópata *f*
ostracism *n* : ostracismo *m* — **ostracize** *vt* -**cized; -cizing** : aislar
ostrich *n* : avestruz *m*
other *adj* **1** : otro **2 every** ~ **day** : cada dos días **3 on the** ~ **hand** : por otra parte, por otro lado — ~ *pron* **1** : otro, otra **2 the** ~**s** : los otros, las otras, los demás, las demás — **other than** *prep* : aparte de, fuera de — **otherwise** *adv* **1** : eso aparte, por lo demás **2** DIFFERENTLY : de otro modo **3** OR ELSE : si no
otter *n* : nutria *f*
ought *v aux* **1** : deber **2 you** ~ **to have done it** : deberías haberlo hecho
ounce *n* : onza *f*
our *adj* : nuestro — **ours** *pron* **1** : (el) nuestro, (la) nuestra, (los) nuestros, (las) nuestras **2 a friend of** ~ : un amigo nuestro — **ourselves** *pron* **1** (*used reflexively*) : nos **2** (*used after prepositions*) : nosotros, nosotras **3** (*used for emphasis*) : nosotros mismos, nosotras mismas
oust *vt* : desbancar
out *adv* **1** OUTSIDE : fuera, afuera **2 cry** ~ : gritar **3 eat** ~ : comer afuera **4 go** ~ : salir **5 look** ~ : mirar para afuera **6 run** ~ **of** : agotar **7 turn** ~ : apagar (una luz) **8 take** ~ REMOVE : sacar — ~ *prep* → **out of** — ~ *adj* **1** ABSENT : ausente **2** UNFASHIONABLE : fuera de moda **3** EXTINGUISHED : apagado **4 the sun is** ~ : hace sol
outboard motor *n* : motor *m* fuera de borde
outbreak *n* : brote *m* (de una enfermedad), comienzo *m* (de guerra)
outburst *n* : arranque *m*, arrebato *m*
outcast *n* : paria *mf*
outcome *n* : resultado *m*
outcry *n, pl* -**cries** : protesta *f*
outdated *adj* : anticuado

outdo *vt* **-did; -done; -doing; -does** : superar

outdoor *adj* : al aire libre — **outdoors** *adv* : al aire libre

outer *adj* : exterior — **outer space** *n* : espacio *m* exterior

outfit *n* **1** EQUIPMENT : equipo *m* **2** CLOTHES : conjunto *m* — ~ *vt* **-fitted; -fitting** EQUIP : equipar

outgoing *adj* **1** SOCIABLE : extrovertido **2** ~ **mail** : correo *m* (para enviar) **3** ~ **president** : presidente *m*, -ta *f* saliente

outgrow *vt* **-grew; -grown; -growing** : crecer más que

outing *n* : excursión *f*

outlandish *adj* : estrafalario

outlast *vt* : durar más que

outlaw *n* : forajido *m*, -da *f* — ~ *vt* : declarar ilegal

outlay *n* : desembolso *m*

outlet *n* **1** EXIT : salida *f* **2** RELEASE : desahogo *m* **3** *or* **electrical** ~ : toma *f* de corriente **4** *or* **retail** ~ : tienda *f* al por menor

outline *n* **1** CONTOUR : contorno *m* **2** SKETCH : bosquejo *m*, boceto *m* **3** SUMMARY : esquema *m* — ~ *vt* **-lined; -lining 1** SKETCH : bosquejar **2** EXPLAIN : delinear, esbozar

outlive *vt* **-lived; -living** : sobrevivir a

outlook *n* **1** PROSPECTS : perspectivas *fpl* **2** VIEWPOINT : punto *m* de vista

outlying *adj* : alejado, distante

outmoded *adj* : pasado de moda, anticuado

outnumber *vt* : superar en número a

out of *prep* **1** FROM : de **2** THROUGH : por **3** WITHOUT : sin **4** ~ **curiosity** : por curiosidad **5** ~ **control** : fuera de control **6** **one** ~ **four** : uno de cada cuatro — **out–of–date** *adj* : anticuado — **out–of–door** *or* **out–of–doors** *adj* → **outdoor**

outpatient *n* : paciente *m* externo

outpost *n* : puesto *m* avanzado

output *n* **1** : producción *f*, rendimiento *m* **2** : salida *f* (informática) — ~ *vt* **-putted** *or* **-put; -putting** : producir

outrage *n* **1** : atrocidad *f*, escándalo *m* **2** ANGER : ira *f*, indignación *f* — ~ *vt* **-raged; -raging** : ultrajar — **outrageous** *adj* : escandaloso

outright *adv* **1** COMPLETELY : por completo **2** INSTANTLY : en el acto — ~ *adj* : completo, absoluto

outset *n* : comienzo *m*, principio *m*

outside *n* **1** : exterior *m* **2 from the** ~ : desde fuera, desde afuera — ~ *adj* **1** : exterior, externo **2 an** ~ **chance** : una posibilidad remota — ~ *adv* : fuera, afuera — ~ *prep or* ~ **of** : fuera de — **outsider** *n* : forastero *m*, -ra *f*

outskirts *npl* : afueras *fpl*, alrededores *mpl*

outspoken *adj* : franco, directo

outstanding *adj* **1** UNPAID : pendiente **2** EXCELLENT : excepcional

outstretched *adj* : extendido

outstrip *vt* **-stripped** *or* **-stript; -stripping** : aventajar

outward *adj* **1** : hacia afuera **2** EXTERNAL : externo, external — ~ *or* **outwards** *adv* : hacia afuera — **outwardly** *adv* APPARENTLY : aparentemente

outweigh *vt* : pesar más que

outwit *vt* **-witted; -witting** : ser más listo que

oval *n* : óvalo *m* — ~ *adj* : ovalado

ovary *n, pl* **-ries** : ovario *m*

ovation *n* : ovación *f*

oven *n* : horno *m*

over *adv* **1** ABOVE : por encima **2** AGAIN : otra vez, de nuevo **3** MORE : más **4 all** ~ : por todas partes **5 ask** ~ : invitar **6** ~ **cross** ~ : cruzar **7 fall** ~ : caerse **8** ~ **and** ~ : una y otra vez **9** ~ **here** : aquí **10** ~ **there** : allí — ~ *prep* **1** ABOVE, UPON : encima de, sobre **2** ACROSS : por encima de, sobre **3** DURING : en, durante **4 fight** ~ : pelearse por **5** ~ **$5** : más de $5 **6** ~ **the phone** : por teléfono — ~ *adj* : terminado, acabado

overall *adv* GENERALLY : en general — *adj* : total, en conjunto — **overalls** *npl* : overol *m Lat*

overbearing *adj* : dominante, imperioso

overboard *adv* **fall** ~ : caer al agua

overburden *vt* : sobrecargar

overcast *adj* : nublado

overcharge *vt* **-charged; -charging** : cobrar demasiado

overcoat *n* : abrigo *m*

overcome *v* **-came; -come; -coming** *vt* **1** CONQUER : vencer **2** OVERWHELM : agobiar — *vi* : vencer

overcook *vt* : cocer demasiado

overcrowded *adj* : abarrotado de gente

overdo *vt* **-did; -done; -doing; -does 1** : hacer demasiado **2** EXAGGERATE : exagerar **3** → **overcook**

overdose *n* : sobredosis *f*

overdraw *vt* **-drew; -drawn; -drawing** : girar en descubierto — **overdraft** *n* : sobregiro *m*, descubierto *m*

overdue *adj* : fuera de plazo (dícese de pagos, libros, etc.)

overeat *vi* **-ate; -eaten; -eating** : comer demasiado

overestimate *vt* **-mated; -mating** : sobreestimar

overflow *vt* : desbordar — *vi* : desbordarse — ~ *n* : desbordamiento *m* (de un río)

overgrown *adj* : cubierto (de malas hierbas, etc.)
overhand *adv* : por encima de la cabeza
overhang *v* **-hung; -hanging** : sobresalir
overhaul *vt* : revisar (un motor, etc.)
overhead *adv* : por encima — ~ *adj* : de arriba — ~ *n* : gastos *mpl* generales
overhear *vt* **-heard; -hearing** : oír por casualidad
overheat *vt* : calentar demasiado — *vi* : recalentarse
overjoyed *adj* : encantado
overland *adv* & *adj* : por tierra
overlap *v* **-lapped; -lapping** *vt* : traslapar — *vi* : traslaparse
overload *vt* : sobrecargar
overlook *vt* **1** : dar a (un jardín, el mar, etc.) **2** MISS : pasar por alto
overly *adv* : demasiado
overnight *adv* **1** : por la noche **2** SUDDENLY : de la noche a la mañana — ~ *adj* **1** : de noche **2** SUDDEN : repentino
overpass *n* : paso *m* elevado
overpopulated *adj* : superpoblado
overpower *vt* **1** SUBDUE : dominar **2** OVERWHELM : agobiar, abrumar
overrated *adj* : sobreestimado
override *vt* **-rode; -ridden; -riding 1** : predominar sobre **2** : anular (una decisión, etc.)
overrule *vt* **-ruled; -ruling** : anular (una decisión), rechazar (una protesta)
overrun *vt* **-ran; -running 1** INVADE : invadir **2** EXCEED : exceder
overseas *adv* : en el extranjero — ~ *adj* : extranjero, exterior
oversee *vt* **-saw; -seen; -seeing** : supervisar
overshadow *vt* : eclipsar
oversight *n* : descuido *m*

oversleep *vi* **-slept; -sleeping** : quedarse dormido
overstep *vt* **-stepped; -stepping** : sobrepasar
overt *adj* : manifiesto
overtake *vt* **-took; -taken; -taking 1** PASS : adelantar **2** SURPASS : superar
overthrow *vt* **-threw; -thrown; -throwing** : derrocar
overtime *n* **1** : horas *fpl* extras (de trabajo) **2** : prórroga *f* (en deportes)
overtone *n* SUGGESTION : tinte *m*, insinuación *f*
overture *n* : obertura *f* (en música)
overturn *vt* **1** : dar la vuelta a **2** NULLIFY : anular — *vi* : volcar
overweight *adj* : demasiado gordo
overwhelm *vt* **1** : abrumar, agobiar **2** : aplastar (a un enemigo) — **overwhelming** *adj* : abrumador, apabullante
overwork *vt* : hacer trabajar demasiado — *vi* : trabajar demasiado
overwrought *adj* : alterado, sobreexitado
owe *vt* **owed; owing** : deber — **owing to** *prep* : debido a
owl *n* : búho *m*
own *adj* : propio — ~ *vt* : poseer, tener — *vi* ~ **up** : confesar — ~ *pron* **1** my (your, his/her/their, our) ~ : el mío, la mía; el tuyo, la tuya; el suyo, la suya; el nuestro, la nuestra **2 be on one's** ~ : estar solo **3 to each his** ~ : cada uno a lo suyo — **owner** *n* : propietario *m*, -ria *f* — **ownership** *n* : propiedad *f*
ox *n, pl* **oxen** : buey *m*
oxygen *n* : oxígeno *m*
oyster *n* : ostra *f*
ozone *n* : ozono *m*

P

p *n, pl* **p's** *or* **ps** : p *f*, decimosexta letra del alfabeto inglés
pace *n* **1** STEP : paso *m* **2** RATE : ritmo *m* **3 keep** ~ **with** : andar al mismo paso que — ~ *vi* **paced; pacing** *or* ~ **up and down** : caminar de arriba para abajo
pacify *vt* **-fied; -fying** : apaciguar — **pacifier** *n* : chupete *m* — **pacifist** *n* : pacifista *mf*
pack *n* **1** BUNDLE : fardo *m* **2** BACKPACK : mochila *f* **3** PACKAGE : paquete *m* **4** : baraja *f* (de naipes) **5** : manada *f* (de lobos, etc.), jauría *f* (de perros) — ~ *vt* **1**

PACKAGE : empaquetar **2** FILL : llenar **3** : hacer (una maleta) — *vi* : hacer las maletas — **package** *vt* **-aged; -aging** : empaquetar — ~ *n* : paquete *m* — **packet** *n* : paquete *m*
pact *n* : pacto *m*, acuerdo *m*
pad *n* **1** CUSHION : almohadilla *f* **2** TABLET : bloc *m* (de papel) **3** *or* **ink** ~ : tampón *m* **4 launching** ~ : plataforma *f* (de lanzamiento) — ~ *vt* **padded; padding** : rellenar — **padding** *n* **1** : relleno *m* **2** : paja *f* (en un discurso, etc.)

                                                  parasite

paddle *n* **1** : canalete *m* (de una canoa) **2** : pala *f*, paleta *f* (en deportes) — ~ *vt* **-dled; -dling** : hacer avanzar (una canoa) con canalete

padlock *n* : candado *m* — ~ *vt* : cerrar con candado

pagan *n* : pagano *m*, -na *f* — ~ *adj* : pagano

page[1] *vt* **paged; paging** : llamar por altavoz

page[2] *n* : página *f* (de un libro, etc.)

pageant *n* : espectáculo *m* — **pageantry** *n* : pompa *f*, boato *m*

paid → **pay**

pail *n* : cubo *m Spain*, cubeta *f Lat*

pain *n* **1** : dolor *m* **2** : pena *f* (mental) **3** ~**s** *npl* EFFORT : esfuerzos *mpl* — ~ *vt* : doler — **painful** *adj* : doloroso — **painkiller** *n* : analgésico *m* — **painless** *adj* : indoloro, sin dolor — **painstaking** *adj* : meticuloso, esmerado

paint *v* : pintar — ~ *n* : pintura *f* — **paintbrush** *n* : pincel *m* (de un artista), brocha *f* (para pintar casas, etc.) — **painter** *n* : pintor *m*, -tora *f* — **painting** *n* : pintura *f*

pair *n* **1** : par *m* **2** COUPLE : pareja *f* — ~ *vt* : emparejar

pajamas *npl* : pijama *m*, piyama *mf Lat*

Pakistani *adj* : paquistaní

pal *n* : amigo *m*, -ga *f*

palace *n* : palacio *m*

palate *n* : paladar *m* — **palatable** *adj* : sabroso

pale *adj* **paler; palest** **1** PALLID : pálido **2** : claro (dícese de los colores, etc.) — ~ *vi* — **paled; paling** : palidecer — **paleness** *n* : palidez *f*

Palestinian *adj* : palestino

palette *n* : paleta *f*

pallbearer *n* : portador *m*, -dora *f* del féretro

pallid *adj* : pálido — **pallor** *n* : palidez *f*

palm[1] *n* : palma *f* (de la mano)

palm[2] *or* ~ **tree** : palmera *f* — **Palm Sunday** *n* : Domingo *m* de Ramos

palpitate *vi* **-tated; -tating** : palpitar — **palpitation** *n* : palpitación *f*

paltry *adj* **-trier; -est** : mísero, mezquino

pamper *vt* : mimar

pamphlet *n* : panfleto *m*, folleto *m*

pan *n* **1** SAUCEPAN : cacerola *f* **2** FRYING PAN : sartén *mf* — ~ *vt* **panned; panning** CRITICIZE : poner por los suelos

pancake *n* : crepe *mf*, panqueque *m Lat*

panda *n* : panda *mf*

pandemonium *n* : pandemonio *m*

pander *vi* ~ **to** : complacer a

pane *n* : cristal *m*, vidrio *m*

panel *n* **1** : panel *m* **2** GROUP : jurado *m* **3** *or* **instrument** ~ : tablero *m* (de instrumentos) — ~ *vt* **-eled** *or* **-elled; -eling** *or*

-elling : adornar con paneles — **paneling** *n* : paneles *mpl*

pang *n* : punzada *f*

panic *n* : pánico *m* — ~ *v* **-icked; -icking** *vt* : llenar del pánico — *vi* : ser presa del pánico — **panicky** *adj* : presa de pánico

panorama *n* : panorama *m* — **panoramic** *adj* : panorámico

pansy *n*, *pl* **-sies** : pensamiento *m*

pant *vi* : jadear, resoplar

panther *n* : pantera *f*

panties *npl* : bragas *fpl Spain*, calzones *mpl Lat*

pantomime *n* : pantomima *f*

pantry *n*, *pl* **-tries** : despensa *f*

pants *npl* TROUSERS : pantalón *m*, pantalones *mpl*

papa *n* : papá *m fam*

papal *adj* : papal

papaya *n* : papaya *f*

paper *n* **1** : papel *m* **2** DOCUMENT : documento *m* **3** NEWSPAPER : periódico *m* — ~ *vt* WALLPAPER : empapelar — ~ *adj* : de papel — **paperback** *n* : libro *m* en rústica — **paper clip** *n* : clip *m*, sujetapapeles *m* — **paperweight** *n* : pisapapeles *m* — **paperwork** *n* : papeleo *m*

paprika *n* : pimentón *m*

par *n* **1** : par *m* (en golf) **2 below** ~ : debajo de la par **3 on a** ~ **with** : al nivel de

parable *n* : parábola *f*

parachute *n* : paracaídas *m* — ~ *vi* **-chuted; -chuting** : lanzarse en paracaídas

parade *n* **1** : desfile *m* **2** DISPLAY : alarde *m* — ~ *v* **-raded; -rading** *vi* MARCH : desfilar — *vt* DISPLAY : hacer alarde de

paradise *n* : paraíso *m*

paradox *n* : paradoja *f* — **paradoxical** *adj* : paradójico

paraffin *n* : parafina *f*

paragraph *n* : párrafo *m*

Paraguayan *adj* : paraguayo

parakeet *n* : periquito *m*

parallel *adj* : paralelo — ~ *n* **1** : paralelo *m* (en geografía) **2** SIMILARITY : paralelismo *m*, semejanza *f* — ~ *vt* : ser paralelo a

paralysis *n*, *pl* **-yses** : parálisis *f* — **paralyze** *or Brit* **paralise** *vt* **-lyzed** *or Brit* **-lised; -lyzing** *or Brit* **-lising** : paralizar

parameter *n* : parámetro *m*

paramount *adj* **of** ~ **importance** : de suma importancia

paranoia *n* : paranoia *f* — **paranoid** *adj* : paranoico

paraphernalia *ns & pl* : parafernalia *f*

paraphrase *n* : paráfrasis *f* — ~ *vt* **-phrased; -phrasing** : parafrasear

paraplegic *n* : parapléjico *m*, -ca *f*

parasite *n* : parásito *m*

paratrooper *n* : paracaidista *mf* (militar)
parcel *n* : paquete *m*
parch *vt* : resecar
parchment *n* : pergamino *m*
pardon *n* **1** : perdón *m* **2** REPRIEVE : indulto *m* **3 I beg your ~** : perdone Ud., disculpe Ud. *Lat* — **~** *vt* **1** : perdonar **2** REPRIEVE : indultar (a un delincuente)
parent *n* **1** : madre *f,* padre *m* **2 ~s** *npl* : padres *mpl* — **parental** *adj* : de los padres
parenthesis *n, pl* **-theses** : paréntesis *m*
parish *n* : parroquia *f* — **parishioner** *n* : feligrés *m,* -gresa *f*
parity *n, pl* **-ties** : igualdad *f*
park *n* : parque *m* — **~** *v* : estacionar, parquear *Lat*
parka *n* : parka *f*
parking *n* : estacionamiento *m*
parliament *n* : parlamento *m* — **parliamentary** *adj* : parlamentario
parlor *or Brit* **parlour** *n* : salón *m*
parochial *adj* **1** : parroquial **2** PROVINCIAL : de miras estrechas
parody *n, pl* **-dies** : parodia *f* — **~** *vt* **-died; -dying** : parodiar
parole *n* : libertad *f* condicional
parrot *n* : loro *m,* papagayo *m*
parry *vt* **-ried; -rying 1** : parar (un golpe) **2** EVADE : eludir (una pregunta, etc.)
parsley *n* : perejil *m*
parsnip *n* : chirivía *f*
parson *n* : clérigo *m*
part *n* **1** : parte *f* **2** PIECE : pieza *f* **3** ROLE : papel *m* **4** : raya *f* (del pelo) — **~** *vi* **1** *or* **~ company** : separarse **2 ~ with** : deshacerse de — *vt* SEPARATE : separar
partake *vi* **-took; -taken; -taking ~ in** : participar en
partial *adj* **1** : parcial **2 be ~ to** : ser aficionado a
participate *vi* **-pated; -pating** : participar — **participant** *n* : participante *mf*
participle *n* : participio *m*
particle *n* : partícula *f*
particular *adj* **1** : particular **2** FUSSY : exigente — **~** *n* **1 in ~** : en particular, en especial **2 ~s** *npl* DETAILS : detalles *mpl* — **particularly** *adv* : especialmente
partisan *n* : partidario *m,* -ria *f*
partition *n* **1** DISTRIBUTION : partición *f* **2** DIVIDER : tabique *m* — **~** *vt* : dividir
partly *adv* : en parte
partner *n* **1** : pareja *f* (en un juego, etc.) **2** *or* **business ~** : socio *m,* -cia *f* — **partnership** *n* : asociación *f*
party *n, pl* **-ties 1** : partido *m* (político) **2** GATHERING : fiesta *f* **3** GROUP : grupo *m*
pass *vi* **1** : pasar **2** CEASE : pasarse **3** : aprobar (en un examen) **4** *or* **~ away** DIE

: morir **5 ~ for** : pasar por **6 ~ out** FAINT : desmayarse — *vt* **1** : pasar **2** *or* **~ in front of** : pasar por **3** OVERTAKE : adelantar **4** : aprobar (un examen, una ley, etc.) **5 ~ down** : transmitir — **~** *n* **1** PERMIT : pase *m,* permiso *m* **2** : pase *m* (en deportes) **3** *or* **mountain ~** : paso *m* de montaña —
passable *adj* **1** ADEQUATE : adecuado **2** : transitable (dícese de un camino, etc.) —
passage *n* **1** : paso *m* **2** CORRIDOR : pasillo *m* (dentro de un edificio), pasaje *m* (entre edificios) **3** VOYAGE : travesía *f* (por el mar) — **passageway** *n* : pasillo *m,* corredor *m*
passenger *n* : pasajero *m,* -ra *f*
passerby *n, pl* **passersby** : transeúnte *mf*
passion *n* : pasión *f* — **passionate** *adj* : apasionado
passive *adj* : pasivo
Passover *n* : Pascua *f* (en el judaísmo)
passport *n* : pasaporte *m*
password *n* : contraseña *f*
past *adj* **1** : pasado **2** FORMER : anterior **3 the ~ few months** : los últimos meses — **~** *prep* **1** IN FRONT OF : por delante de **2** BEYOND : más allá de **3 half ~ two** : las dos y media — **~** *n* : pasado *m* — **~** *adv* : por delante
pasta *n* : pasta *f*
paste *n* **1** : pasta *f* **2** GLUE : engrudo *m* — **~** *vt* **pasted; pasting** : pegar
pastel *n* : pastel *m* — **~** *adj* : pastel
pasteurize *vt* **-ized; -izing** : pasteurizar
pastime *n* : pasatiempo *m*
pastor *n* : pastor *m,* -tora *f*
pastry *n, pl* **-ries** : pasteles *mpl*
pasture *n* : pasto *m*
pasty *adj* **pastier; -est 1** DOUGHY : pastoso **2** PALLID : pálido
pat *n* **1** : palmadita *f* **2 a ~ of butter** : una porción de mantequilla — **~** *vt* **patted; patting** : dar palmaditas a — **~** *adv* **have down ~** : saberse de memoria — **~** *adj* GLIB : fácil
patch *n* **1** : parche *m,* remiendo *m* (para la ropa) **2** SPOT : mancha *f,* trozo *m* **3** PLOT : parcela *f* (de tierra) — **~** *vt* **1** MEND : remendar **2 ~ up** : arreglar — **patchy** *adj* **patchier; -est 1** : desigual **2** INCOMPLETE : parcial, incompleto
patent *adj* **1** *or* **patented** : patentado **2** OBVIOUS : patente, evidente — **~** *n* : patente *f* — **~** *vt* : patentar
paternal *adj* **1** FATHERLY : paternal **2 ~ grandmother** : abuela *f* paterna — **paternity** *n* : paternidad *f*
path *n* **1** TRACK, TRAIL : camino *m,* sendero *m* **2** COURSE : trayectoria *f*
pathetic *adj* : patético

pathology *n, pl* **-gies** : patología *f*
pathway *n* : camino *m*, sendero *m*
patience *n* : paciencia *f* — **patient** *adj* : paciente — ~ *n* : paciente *mf* — **patiently** *adv* : con paciencia
patio *n, pl* **-tios** : patio *m*
patriot *n* : patriota *mf* — **patriotic** *adj* : patriótico
patrol *n* : patrulla *f* — ~ *v* **-trolled; -trolling** : patrullar
patron *n* **1** SPONSOR : patrocinador *m*, -dora *f* **2** CUSTOMER : cliente *m*, -ta *f* — **patronage** *n* **1** SPONSORSHIP : patrocinio *m* **2** CLIENTELE : clientela *f* — **patronize** *vt* **-ized; -izing 1** : ser cliente de (una tienda, etc.) **2** : tratar (a algn) con condescencia
patter *n* : tamborileo *m* (de la lluvia), correteo *m* (de los pies)
pattern *n* **1** MODEL : modelo *m* **2** DESIGN : diseño *m* **3** STANDARD : pauta *f*, modo *m* **4** : patrón *m* (en costura) — ~ *vt* : basar (en un modelo)
paunch *n* : panza *f*
pause *n* : pausa *f* — ~ *vi* **paused; pausing** : hacer una pausa
pave *vt* **paved; paving** : pavimentar — **pavement** *n* : pavimento *m*
pavilion *n* : pabellón *m*
paw *n* **1** : pata *f* **2** : garra *f* (de un gato) — ~ *vt* : tocar con la pata
pawn[1] *n* : peón *m* (en ajedrez)
pawn[2] *vt* : empeñar — **pawnbroker** *n* : prestamista *mf* — **pawnshop** *n* : casa *f* de empeños
pay *v* **paid; paying** *vt* **1** : pagar **2** ~ **attention** : prestar atención **3** ~ **back** : devolver **4** ~ **one's respects** : presentar uno sus respetos **5** ~ **a visit** : hacer una visita — *vi* **1** : pagar **2 crime doesn't** ~ : no hay crimen sin castigo — ~ *n* : paga *f* — **payable** *adj* : pagadero — **paycheck** *n* : cheque *m* del sueldo — **payment** *n* **1** : pago *m* **2** INSTALLMENT : plazo *m*, cuota *f* *Lat* — **payroll** *n* : nómina *f*
PC *n, pl* **PCs** *or* **PC's** : PC *mf*, computadora *f* personal
pea *n* : guisante *m*, arveja *f Lat*
peace *n* : paz *f* — **peaceful** *adj* **1** : pacífico **2** CALM : tranquilo
peach *n* : melocotón *m*, durazno *m Lat*
peacock *n* : pavo *m* real
peak *n* **1** SUMMIT : cumbre *f*, cima *f*, pico *m* (de una montaña) **2** APEX : nivel *m* máximo — ~ *adj* : máximo — ~ *vi* : alcanzar su nivel máximo
peal *n* **1** : repique *m* **2** ~**s of laughter** : carcajadas *fpl*
peanut *n* : cacajuete *m*, maní *m Lat*
pear *n* : pera *f*

pearl *n* : perla *f*
peasant *n* : campesino *m*, -na *f*
peat *n* : turba *f*
pebble *n* : guijarro *m*
pecan *n* : pacana *f*, nuez *f Lat*
peck *vt* : picar, picotear — ~ *n* **1** : picotazo *m* (de un pájaro) **2** KISS : besito
peculiar *adj* **1** DISTINCTIVE : peculiar, característico **2** STRANGE : extraño, raro — **peculiarity** *n, pl* **-ties 1** : peculiaridad *f* **2** ODDITY : rareza *f*
pedal *n* : pedal *m* — ~ *vi* **-aled** *or* **-alled; -aling** *or* **-alling** : pedalear
pedantic *adj* : pedante
peddle *vt* **-dled; -dling** : vender en las calles — **peddler** *n* : vendedor *m*, -dora *f* ambulante
pedestal *n* : pedestal *m*
pedestrian *n* : peatón *m*, -tona *f* — ~ *adj* **~ crossing** : paso *m* de peatones
pediatrics *ns & pl* : pediatría *f* — **pediatrician** *n* : pediatra *mf*
pedigree *n* : pedigrí *m* (de un animal), linaje *m* (de una persona)
peek *vi* : mirar a hurtadillas — ~ *n* : miradita *f* (furtiva)
peel *vt* : pelar (fruta, etc.) — *vi* : pelarse (dícese de la piel), desconcharse (dícese de la pintura) — ~ *n* : piel *f*, cáscara *f*
peep[1] *vi* CHEEP : piar — ~ *n* : pío *m* (de un pajarito)
peep[2] *vi* **1** PEEK : mirar a hurtadillas **2** *or* ~ **out** : asomar — ~ *n* GLANCE : mirada *f* (furtiva)
peer[1] *n* : par *mf*
peer[2] *vi* : mirar (con atención)
peeve *vt* : irritar — **peevish** *adj* : malhumorado
peg *n* **1** : clavija *f* **2** HOOK : gancho *m*
pelican *n* : pelícano *m*
pellet *n* **1** : bolita *f* **2** SHOT : perdigón *m*
pelt[1] *n* : piel *f* (de un animal)
pelt[2] *vt* : lanzar (algo a algn)
pelvis *n, pl* **-vises** *or* **-ves** : pelvis *f* — **pelvic** *adj* : pélvico
pen[1] *vt* **penned; penning** ENCLOSE : encerrar — ~ *n* : corral *m*, redil *m*
pen[2] *n* **1** *or* **ballpoint** ~ : bolígrafo *m* **2** *or* **fountain** ~ : pluma *f*
penal *adj* : penal — **penalize** *vt* **-ized; -izing** : penalizar — **penalty** *n, pl* **-ties 1** : pena *f*, castigo *m* **2** : penalty *m* (en deportes)
penance *n* : penitencia *f*
pencil *n* : lápiz *m* — **pencil sharpener** *n* : sacapuntas *m*
pendant *n* : colgante *m*
pending *adj* : pendiente — ~ *prep* : en espera de
penetrate *v* **-trated; -trating** : penetrar —

penguin

penetrating *adj* : penetrante — **penetration** *n* : penetración *f*
penguin *n* : pingüino *m*
penicillin *n* : penicilina *f*
peninsula *n* : península *f*
penis *n*, *pl* **-nes** *or* **-nises** : pene *m*
penitentiary *n*, *pl* **-ries** : penitenciaría *f*
pen name *n* : seudónimo *m*
pennant *n* : banderín *m*
penny *n*, *pl* **-nies** *or* **pence** : centavo *m* (de los Estados Unidos), penique *m* (del Reino Unido) — **penniless** *adj* : sin un centavo
pension *n* : pensión *m*, jubilación *f*
pensive *adj* : pensativo
pentagon *n* : pentágono *m*
penthouse *n* : ático *m*
pent–up *adj* : reprimado
people *ns* & *pl* **1 people** *npl* : gente *f*, personas *fpl* **2** *pl* **~s** : pueblo *m*
pep *n* : energía *f*, vigor *m* — **~** *vt or* **~ up** : animar
pepper *n* **1** : pimienta *f* (condimento) **2** : pimiento *m* (fruta) — **peppermint** *n* : menta *f*
per *prep* **1** : por **2** ACCORDING TO : según **3** **~ day** : al día **4 miles ~ hour** : millas *fpl* por hora
perceive *vt* **-ceived; -ceiving** : percibir
percent *adv* : por ciento — **percentage** *n* : porcentaje *m*
perception *n* : percepción *f* — **perceptive** *adj* : perspicaz
perch[1] *n* : percha *f* (para los pájaros) — **~** *vi* : posarse
perch[2] *n* : perca *f* (pez)
percolate *vi* **-lated; -lating** : filtrarse — **percolator** *n* : cafetera *f* de filtro
percussion *n* : percusión *f*
perennial *adj* : perenne — **~** *n* : planta *f* perenne
perfect *adj* : perfecto — **~** *vt* : perfeccionar — **perfection** *n* : perfección *f* — **perfectionist** *n* : perfeccionista *mf*
perforate *vt* **-rated; -rating** : perforar
perform *vt* **1** CARRY OUT : realizar, hacer **2** : representar (una obra teatral), interpretar (una obra musical) — *vi* **1** FUNCTION : funcionar **2** ACT : actuar — **performance** *n* **1** : realización *f* **2** INTERPRETATION : interpretación *f* **3** PRESENTATION : representación *f* — **performer** *n* : actor *m*, -triz *f*; intérprete *mf* (de música)
perfume *n* : perfume *m*
perhaps *adv* : tal vez, quizá, quizás
peril *n* : peligro *m* — **perilous** *adj* : peligroso
perimeter *n* : perímetro *m*
period *n* **1** : período *m* (de tiempo) **2** : punto *m* (en puntuación) **3** ERA : época *f*

290

periodic *adj* : periódico — **periodical** *n* : revista *f*
peripheral *adj* : periférico
perish *vi* : perecer — **perishable** *adj* : perecedero — **perishables** *npl* : productos *mpl* perecederos
perjury *n* : perjurio *m*
perk *vi* **~ up** : animarse, reanimarse — **~** *n* : extra *m* — **perky** *adj* perkier; -est : alegre
permanence *n* : permanencia *f* — **permanent** *adj* : permanente — **~** *n* : permanente *f*
permeate *v* **-ated; -ating** : penetrar
permission *n* : permiso *m* — **permissible** *adj* : permisible — **permissive** *adj* : permisivo — **permit** *vt* **-mitted; -mitting** : permitir — **~** *n* : permiso *m*
peroxide *n* : peróxido *m*
perpendicular *adj* : perpendicular
perpetrate *vt* **-trated; -trating** : cometer — **perpetrator** *n* : autor *m*, -tora *f* (de un delito)
perpetual *adj* : perpetuo
perplex *vt* : dejar perplejo — **perplexing** *adj* : desconcertante — **perplexity** *n*, *pl* **-ties** : perplejidad *f*
persecute *vt* **-cuted; -cuting** : perseguir — **persecution** *n* : persecución *f*
persevere *vi* **-vered; -vering** : perseverar — **perseverance** *n* : perseverancia *f*
persist *vi* : persistir — **persistence** *n* : persistencia *f* — **persistent** *adj* : persistente
person *n* : persona *f* — **personal** *adj* : personal — **personality** *n*, *pl* **-ties** : personalidad *f* — **personally** *adv* : personalmente, en persona — **personnel** *n* : personal *m*
perspective *n* : perspectiva *f*
perspiration *n* : transpiración *f* — **perspire** *vi* **-spired; -spiring** : transpirar
persuade *vt* **-suaded; -suading** : persuadir — **persuasion** *n* : persuasión *f*
pertain *vi* **~ to** : estar relacionado con —
pertinent *adj* : pertinente
perturb *vt* : perturbar
Peruvian *adj* : peruano
pervade *vt* **-vaded; -vading** : penetrar — **pervasive** *adj* : penetrante
perverse *adj* **1** CORRUPT : perverso **2** STUBBORN : obstinado — **pervert** *n* : pervertido *m*, -da *f*
peso *n*, *pl* **-sos** : peso *m*
pessimism *n* : pesimismo *m* — **pessimist** *n* : pesimista *mf* — **pessimistic** *adj* : pesimista
pest *n* **1** : insecto *m* nocivo, animal *m* nocivo **2** : peste *f* fam (persona)
pester *vt* **-tered; -tering** : molestar
pesticide *n* : pesticida *m*

pet *n* **1** : animal *m* doméstico **2** FAVORITE : favorito *m*, -ta *f* — ~ *vt* **petted; petting** : acariciar
petal *n* : pétalo *m*
petite *adj* : chiquita
petition *n* : petición *f* — ~ *vt* : dirigir una petición a
petrify *vt* **-fied; -fying** : petrificar
petroleum *n* : petróleo *m*
petticoat *n* : enagua *f*, fondo *m Lat*
petty *adj* **-tier; -est 1** UNIMPORTANT : insignificante, nimio **2** MEAN : mezquino — **pettiness** *n* : mezquindad *f*
petulant *adj* : irritable, de mal genio
pew *n* : banco *m* (de iglesia)
pewter *n* : peltre *m*
phallic *adj* : fálico
phantom *n* : fantasma *m*
pharmacy *n, pl* **-cies** : farmacia *f* — **pharmacist** *n* : farmacéutico *m*, -ca *f*
phase *n* : fase *f* — ~ *vt* **phased; phasing 1** ~ **in** : introducir progresivamente **2** ~ **out** : retirar progresivamente
phenomenon *n, pl* **-na** *or* **-nons** : fenómeno *m* — **phenomenal** *adj* : fenomenal
philanthropy *n, pl* **-pies** : filantropía *f* — **philanthropist** *n* : filántropo *m*, -pa *f*
philosophy *n, pl* **-phies** : filosofía *f* — **philosopher** *n* : filósofo *m*, -fa *f*
phlegm *n* : flema *f*
phobia *n* : fobia *f*
phone → **telephone**
phonetic *adj* : fonético
phony *or* **phoney** *adj* **-nier; -est** : falso — ~ *n, pl* **-nies** : farsante *mf*
phosphorus *n* : fósforo *m*
photo *n, pl* **-tos** : foto *f* — **photocopier** *n* : fotocopiadora *f* — **photocopy** *n, pl* **-copies** : fotocopia *f* — ~ *vt* **-copied; -copying** : fotocopiar — **photograph** *n* : fotografía *f*, foto *f* — ~ *vt* : fotografiar — **photographer** *n* : fotógrafo *m*, -fa *f* — **photographic** *adj* : fotográfico — **photography** *n* : fotografía *f*
phrase *n* : frase *f* — ~ *vt* **phrased; phrasing** : expresar
physical *adj* : físico — ~ *n* : reconocimiento *m* médico
physician *n* : médico *m*, -ca *f*
physics *ns & pl* : física *f* — **physicist** *n* : físico *m*, -ca *f*
physiology *n* : fisiología *f*
physique *n* : físico *m*
piano *n, pl* **-anos** : piano *m* — **pianist** *n* : pianista *mf*
pick *vt* **1** CHOOSE : escoger **2** GATHER : recoger **3** REMOVE : quitar (poco a poco) **4** ~ **a fight** : buscar camorra — *vi* **1** ~ **and choose** : ser exigente **2** ~ **on** : me-

terse con — ~ *n* **1** CHOICE : selección *f* **2** *or* **pickax** : pico *m* **3 the** ~ **of** : lo mejor de
picket *n* **1** STAKE : estaca *f* **2** *or* ~ **line** : piquete *m* — ~ *v* : piquetear
pickle *n* **1** : pepinillo *m* (encurtido) **2** JAM : lío *m fam*, apuro *m* — ~ *vt* **-led; -ling** : encurtir
pickpocket *n* : carterista *mf*
pickup *n* **1** IMPROVEMENT : mejora *f* **2** *or* ~ **truck** : camioneta *f* — **pick up** *vt* **1** LIFT : levantar **2** TIDY : arreglar, ordenar — *vi* IMPROVE : mejorar
picnic *n* : picnic *m* — ~ *vi* **-nicked; -nicking** : ir de picnic
picture *n* **1** PAINTING : cuadro *m* **2** DRAWING : dibujo *m* **3** PHOTO : fotografía *f* **4** IMAGE : imagen *f* **5** MOVIE : película *f* — ~ *vt* **-tured; -turing 1** DEPICT : representar **2** IMAGINE : imaginarse — **picturesque** *adj* : pintoresco
pie *n* : pastel *m* (con fruta o carne), empanada *f* (con carne)
piece *n* **1** : pieza *f* **2** FRAGMENT : trozo *m*, pedazo *m* **3 a** ~ **of advice** : un consejo — ~ *vt* **pieced; piecing** *or* ~ **together** : juntar, componer — **piecemeal** *adv* : poco a poco — ~ *adj* : poco sistemático
pier *n* : muelle *m*
pierce *vt* **pierced; piercing** : perforar — **piercing** *adj* : penetrante
piety *n, pl* **-eties** : piedad *f*
pig *n* : cerdo *m*, -da *f*; puerco *m*, -ca *f*
pigeon *n* : paloma *f* — **pigeonhole** *n* : casilla *f*
piggyback *adv & adj* : a cuestas
pigment *n* : pigmento *m*
pigpen *n* : pocilga *f*
pigtail *n* : coleta *f*, trenza *f*
pile¹ *n* HEAP : montón *m*, pila *f* — ~ *v* **piled; piling** *vt* : amontonar, apilar — *vi* ~ **up** : amontonarse, acumularse
pile² *n* NAP : pelo *m* (de telas)
pilfer *vt* : robar, hurtar
pilgrim *n* : peregrino *m*, -na *f* — **pilgrimage** *n* : peregrinación *f*
pill *n* : pastilla *f*, píldora *f*
pillage *n* : saqueo *m* — ~ *vt* **-laged; -laging** : saquear
pillar *n* : pilar *m*, columna *f*
pillow *n* : almohada *f* — **pillowcase** *n* : funda *f* (de almohada)
pilot *n* : piloto *mf* — ~ *vt* : pilotar, pilotear — **pilot light** *n* : piloto *m*
pimp *n* : proxeneta *m*
pimple *n* : grano *m*
pin *n* **1** : alfiler *m* **2** BROOCH : broche *m* **3** *or* **bowling** ~ : bolo *m* — ~ *vt* **pinned; pinning 1** FASTEN : prender, sujetar (con alfileres) **2** *or* ~ **down** : inmovilizar

pincers *npl* : tenazas *fpl*
pinch *vt* **1** : pellizcar **2** STEAL : robar — *vi* : apretar — **~** *n* **1** : pellizco *m* **2** BIT : pizca *f* **3 in a ~** : en caso necesario
pine[1] *n* : pino *m* (árbol)
pine[2] *vi* **pined; pining 1** LANGUISH : languidecer **2 ~ for** : suspirar por
pineapple *n* : piña *f*, ananás *m*
pink *n* : rosa *m*, rosado *m* — **~** *adj* : rosa, rosado
pinnacle *n* : pináculo *m*
pinpoint *vt* : localizar, precisar
pint *n* : pinta *f*
pioneer *n* : pionero *m*, -ra *f*
pious *adj* : piadoso
pipe *n* **1** : tubo *m*, caño *m* **2** : pipa *f* (para fumar) — **pipeline** *n* **1** : conducto *m*, oleoducto *m* (para petróleo)
piquant *adj* : picante
pique *n* : resentimiento *m*
pirate *n* : pirata *mf*
pistachio *n*, *pl* **-chios** : pistacho *m*
pistol *n* : pistola *f*
piston *n* : pistón *m*
pit *n* **1** HOLE : hoyo *m*, fosa *f* **2** MINE : mina *f* **3** : hueso *m* (de una fruta) **4 ~ of the stomach** : boca *f* del estómago — **~** *vt* **pitted; pitting 1** : marcar de hoyos **2** : deshuesar (una fruta) **3 ~ against** : enfrentar a
pitch *vt* **1** : armar (una tienda) **2** THROW : lanzar — *vi* **1** *or* **~ forward** : caerse **2** LURCH : cabecear (dícese de un barco o un avión) — **~** *n* **1** DEGREE, LEVEL : grado *m*, punto *m* **2** TONE : tono *m* **3** THROW : lanzamiento *m* **4** *or* **sales ~** : presentación *f* (de un vendedor)
pitcher *n* **1** JUG : jarro *m* **2** : lanzador *m*, -dora *f* (en béisbol, etc.)
pitchfork *n* : horquilla *f*, horca *f*
pitfall *n* : riesgo *m*, dificultad *f*
pith *n* **1** : médula *f* (de un hueso, etc.) **2** CORE : meollo *m* — **pithy** *adj* **pithier; -est** : conciso y sustancioso
pity *n*, *pl* **pities 1** COMPASSION : compasión *f* **2 what a ~!** : ¡qué lástima! — **~** *vt* **pitied; pitying** : compadecerse de — **pitiful** *adj* : lastimoso — **pitiless** *adj* : despiadado
pivot *n* : pivote *m* — **~** *vi* **1** : girar sobre un eje **2 ~ on** : depender de
pizza *n* : pizza *f*
placard *n* POSTER : cartel *m*, póster *m*
placate *vt* **-cated; -cating** : apaciguar
place *n* **1** : sitio *m*, lugar *m* **2** SEAT : asiento *m* **3** POSITION : puesto *m* **4** ROLE : papel *m* **5 take ~** : tener lugar **6 take the ~ of** : sustituir a — **~** *vt* **placed; placing 1** PUT, SET : poner, colocar **2** IDENTIFY : iden-

tificar, recordar **3 ~ an order** : hacer un pedido — **placement** *n* : colocación *f*
placid *adj* : plácido, tranquilo
plagiarism *n* : plagio *m* — **plagiarize** *vt* **-rized; -rizing** : plagiar
plague *n* **1** : plaga *f* (de insectos, etc.) **2** : peste *f* (en medicina)
plaid *n* : tela *f* escocesa — **~** *adj* : escocés
plain *adj* **1** SIMPLE : sencillo **2** CLEAR : claro, evidente **3** CANDID : franco **4** HOMELY : poco atractivo **5 in ~ sight** : a la vista (de todos) — **~** *n* : llanura *f*, planicie *f* — **plainly** *adv* **1** CLEARLY : claramente **2** FRANKLY : francamente **3** SIMPLY : sencillamente
plaintiff *n* : demandante *mf*
plan *n* **1** : plan *m*, proyecto *m* **2** DIAGRAM : plano *m* — **~** *v* **planned; planning** *vt* **1** : planear, proyectar **2** INTEND : tener planeado — *vi* : hacer planes
plane[1] *n* **1** LEVEL : plano *m*, nivel *m* **2** AIRPLANE : avión *m*
plane[2] *n* *or* **carpenter's ~** : cepillo *m*
planet *n* : planeta *f*
plank *n* : tabla *f*
planning *n* : planificación *f*
plant *vt* : plantar (flores, árboles), sembrar (semillas) — **~** *n* **1** : planta *f* **2** FACTORY : fábrica *f*
plantain *n* : plátano *m* (grande)
plantation *n* : plantación *f*
plaque *n* : placa *f*
plaster *n* : yeso *m* — **~** *vt* **1** : enyesar **2** COVER : cubrir — **plaster cast** *n* : escayola *f*
plastic *adj* **1** : de plástico **2** FLEXIBLE : plástico, flexible **3 ~ surgery** : cirugía *f* plástica — **~** *n* : plástico *m*
plate *n* **1** SHEET : placa *f* **2** DISH : plato *m* **3** ILLUSTRATION : lámina *f* — **~** *vt* **plated; plating** : chapar (en metal)
plateau *n*, *pl* **-teaus** *or* **-teaux** : meseta *f*
platform *n* **1** : plataforma *f* **2** : andén *m* (de una estación de ferrocarril) **3** *or* **political ~** : programa *m* electoral
platinum *n* : platino *m*
platitude *n* : lugar *m* común
platoon *n* : sección *f* (en el ejército)
platter *n* : fuente *f*
plausible *adj* : creíble, verosímil
play *n* **1** : juego *m* **2** DRAMA : obra *f* de teatro — **~** *vi* **1** : jugar **2 ~ in a band** : tocar en un grupo — *vt* **1** : jugar (deportes, etc.), jugar a (juegos) **2** : tocar (música o un instrumento) **3 ~ the role of** : representar el papel de — **player** *n* **1** : jugador *m*, -dora *f* **2** ACTOR : actor *m*, actriz *f* **3** MUSICIAN : músico *m*, -ca *f* — **playful** *adj* : juguetón — **playground** *n* : patio *m* de recreo — **playing card** *n* : naipe *m*, carta *f* — **play-**

mate *n* : compañero *m*, -ra *f* de juego — **play–off** *n* : desempate *m* — **playpen** *n* : corral *m* (para niños) — **plaything** *n* : juguete *m* — **playwright** *n* : dramaturgo *m*, -ga *f*

plea *n* **1** : acto *m* de declararse (en derecho) **2** APPEAL : ruego *m*, súplica *f* — **plead** *v* **pleaded** *or* **pled; pleading** *vi* **1** ~ **for** : suplicar **2** ~ **guilty** : declararse culpable **3** ~ **not guilty** : negar la acusación — *vt* **1** : alegar, pretextar **2** ~ **a case** : defender un caso

pleasant *adj* : agradable, grato — **please** *v* **pleased; pleasing** *vt* **1** GRATIFY : complacer **2** SATISFY : satisfacer — *vi* **1** : agradar **2 do as you** ~ : haz lo que quieras — ~ *adv* : por favor — **pleased** *adj* : contento — **pleasing** *adj* : agradable — **pleasure** *n* : placer *m*, gusto *m*

pleat *vt* : plisar — ~ *n* : pliegue *m*

pledge *n* **1** SECURITY : prenda *f* **2** PROMISE : promesa *f* — ~ *vt* **pledged; pledging 1** PAWN : empeñar **2** PROMISE : prometer

plenty *n* **1** : abundancia *f* **2** ~ **of time** : tiempo *m* de sobra — **plentiful** *adj* : abundante

pliable *adj* : flexible

pliers *npl* : alicates *mpl*

plight *n* : situación *f* difícil

plod *vi* **plodded; plodding 1** : caminar con paso pesado **2** DRUDGE : trabajar laboriosamente

plot *n* **1** LOT : parcela *f* **2** : argumento *m* (de una novela, etc.) **3** CONSPIRACY : complot *m*, intriga *f* — ~ *v* **plotted; plotting** *vt* : tramar (un plan), trazar (una gráfica, etc.) — *vi* CONSPIRE : conspirar

plow *or* **plough** *n* **1** : arado *m* **2** → **snowplow** — ~ *v* : arar

ploy *n* : estratagema *f*

pluck *vt* **1** : arrancar **2** : desplumar (un pollo, etc.) **3** : recoger (flores) **4** ~ **one's eyebrows** : depilarse las cejas

plug *n* **1** STOPPER : tapón *m* **2** : enchufe *m* (eléctrico) — ~ *vt* **plugged; plugging 1** BLOCK : tapar **2** ADVERTISE : dar publicidad a **3** ~ **in** : enchufar

plum *n* : ciruela *f*

plumb *adj* : a plomo, vertical — **plumber** *n* : fontanero *m*, -ra *f*; plomero *m*, -ra *f* *Lat* — **plumbing** *n* **1** : fontanería *f*, plomería *f* *Lat* **2** PIPES : cañerías *fpl*

plume *n* : pluma *f*

plummet *vi* : caer en picado

plump *adj* : rechoncho *fam*

plunder *vi* : saquear, robar — ~ *n* : botín *m*

plunge *v* **plunged; plunging** *vt* **1** IMMERSE : sumergir **2** THRUST : hundir — *vi* **1** : zambullirse (en el agua) **2** DESCEND : descender

en picada — ~ *n* **1** DIVE : zambullida *f* **2** DROP : descenso *m* abrupto

plural *adj* : plural — ~ *n* : plural *m*

plus *adj* : positivo — ~ *n* **1** *or* ~ **sign** : signo *m* (de) **2** ADVANTAGE : ventaja *f* — ~ *prep* : más — ~ *conj* : y, además

plush *n* : felpa *f* — ~ *adj* **1** : de felpa **2** LUXURIOUS : lujoso

plutonium *n* : plutonio *m*

ply *vt* **plied; plying 1** : ejercer (un oficio) **2** ~ **with questions** : acosar con preguntas

plywood *n* : contrachapado *m*

pneumatic *adj* : neumático

pneumonia *n* : pulmonía *f*

poach[1] *vt* : cocer a fuego lento

poach[2] *vt or* ~ **game** : cazar ilegalmente — **poacher** *n* : cazador *m* furtivo, cazadora *f* furtiva

pocket *n* : bolsillo *m* — ~ *vt* : meterse en el bolsillo — **pocketbook** *n* : cartera *f*, bolsa *f* *Lat* — **pocketknife** *n*, *pl* -**knives** : navaja *f*

pod *n* : vaina *f*

poem *n* : poema *m* — **poet** *n* : poeta *mf* — **poetic** *or* **poetical** *adj* : poético — **poetry** *n* : poesía *f*

poignant *adj* : conmovedor

point *n* **1** : punto *m* **2** PURPOSE : sentido *m* **3** TIP : punta *f* **4** FEATURE : cualidad *f* **5 be beside the** ~ : no venir al caso **6 there's no** ~ ... : no sirve de nada... — ~ *vt* **1** AIM : apuntar **2** *or* ~ **out** : señalar, indicar — *vi* ~ **at** : señalar (con el dedo) — **point–blank** *adv* : a quemarropa — **pointer** *n* **1** NEEDLE : aguja *f* **2** : perro *m* de muestra **3** TIP : consejo *m* — **pointless** *adj* : inútil — **point of view** *n* : perspectiva *f*, punto *m* de vista

poise *n* **1** : elegancia *f* **2** COMPOSURE : aplomo *m*

poison *n* : veneno *m* — ~ *vt* : envenenar — **poisonous** *adj* : venenoso (dícese de una culebra, etc.), tóxico (dícese de una sustancia)

poke *vt* **poked; poking 1** JAB : golpear (con la punta de algo), dar **2** THRUST : introducir, asomar — ~ *n* : golpe *m* abrupto (con la punta de algo)

poker[1] *n* : atizador *m* (para el fuego)

poker[2] *n* : póquer *m* (juego de naipes)

polar *adj* : polar — **polar bear** *n* : oso *m* blanco — **polarize** *vt* -**ized; -izing** : polarizar

pole[1] *n* : palo *m*, poste *m*

pole[2] *n* : polo *m* (en geografía)

police *vt* -**liced; -licing** : mantener el orden en — ~ *ns & pl* **the** ~ : la policía — **policeman** *n*, *pl* -**men** : policía *m* — **police officer** *n* : policía *mf*, agente *mf* de policía — **policewoman** *n*, *pl* -**women** : (mujer *f*) policía *f*

policy *n, pl* **-cies** **1** : política *f* **2** *or* **insurance** ~ : póliza *f* de seguros
polio *or* **poliomyelitis** *n* : polio *f*, poliomielitis *f*
polish *vt* **1** : pulir **2** : limpiar (zapatos), encerar (un suelo) — ~ *n* **1** LUSTER : brillo *m*, lustre *m* **2** : betún *m* (para zapatos), cera *f* (para suelos y muebles), esmalte *m* (para las uñas)
Polish *adj* : polaco — ~ *n* : polaco *m* (idioma)
polite *adj* **-liter; -est** : cortés — **politeness** *n* : cortesía *f*
political *adj* : político — **politician** *n* : político *m*, -ca *f* — **politics** *ns & pl* : política *f*
polka *n* : polka *f* — **polka dot** *n* : lunar *m*
poll *n* **1** : encuesta *f*, sondeo *m* **2 the** ~**s** : las urnas — ~ *vt* **1** : obtener (votos) **2** CANVASS : encuestar, sondear
pollen *n* : polen *m*
pollute *vt* **-luted; -luting** : contaminar — **pollution** *n* : contaminación *f*
polyester *n* : poliéster *m*
polygon *n* : polígono *m*
pomegranate *n* : granada *f*
pomp *n* : pompa *f* — **pompous** *adj* : pomposo
pond *n* : charca *f* (natural), estanque *m* (artificial)
ponder *vt* : considerar — *vi* ~ **over** : reflexionar sobre
pony *n, pl* **-nies** : poni *m* — **ponytail** *n* : cola *f* de caballo
poodle *n* : caniche *m*
pool *n* **1** PUDDLE : charco *m* **2** : fondo *m* común (de recursos) **3** BILLIARDS : billar *m* **4** *or* **swimming** ~ : piscina *f* — ~ *vt* : hacer un fondo común de
poor *adj* **1** : pobre **2** INFERIOR : malo **3 the** ~ : los pobres — **poorly** *adv* : mal
pop[1] *v* **popped; popping** *vt* **1** : hacer reventar **2** ~ **sth into** : meter algo en — *vi* **1** BURST : reventarse, estallar **2** ~ **in** : entrar (un momento) **3** ~ **out** : saltar (dícese de los ojos) **4** ~ **up** APPEAR : aparecer — ~ *n* **1** : ruido *m* seco **2** → **soda pop**
pop[2] *n or* ~ **music** : música *f* popular
popcorn *n* : palomitas *fpl*
pope *n* : papa *m*
poplar *n* : álamo *m*
poppy *n, pl* **-pies** : amapola *f*
popular *adj* : popular — **popularity** *n* : popularidad *f* — **popularize** *vt* **-ized; -izing** : popularizar
populate *vt* **-lated; -lating** : poblar — **population** *n* : población *f*
porcelain *n* : porcelana *f*
porch *n* : porche *m*

porcupine *n* : puerco *m* espín
pore[1] *vi* **pored; poring** ~ **over** : estudiar esmeradamente
pore[2] *n* : poro *m*
pork *n* : carne *f* de cerdo
pornography *n* : pornografía *f* — **pornographic** *adj* : pornográfico
porous *adj* : poroso
porpoise *n* : marsopa *f*
porridge *n* : avena *f* (cocida), gachas *fpl* (de avena)
port[1] *n* HARBOR : puerto *m*
port[2] *n or* ~ **side** : babor *m*
port[3] *n* : oporto *m* (vino)
portable *adj* : portátil
portent *n* : presagio *m*
porter *n* : maletero *m*, mozo *m* (de estación)
portfolio *n, pl* **-lios** : cartera *f*
porthole *n* : portilla *f*
portion *n* : porción *f*
portrait *n* : retrato *m*
portray *vt* **1** : representar, retratar **2** : interpretar (un personaje)
Portuguese *adj* : portugués — ~ *n* : portugués *m* (idioma)
pose *v* **posed; posing** *vt* : plantear (una pregunta, etc.), representar (una amenaza) — *vi* **1** : posar **2** ~ **as** : hacerse pasar por — ~ *n* : pose *f*
posh *adj* : elegante, de lujo
position *n* **1** : posición *f* **2** JOB : puesto *m* — ~ *vt* : colocar, situar
positive *adj* **1** : positivo **2** CERTAIN : seguro
possess *vt* : poseer — **possession** *n* **1** : posesión *f* **2** ~**s** *npl* BELONGINGS : bienes *mpl* — **possessive** *adj* : posesivo
possible *adj* : posible — **possibility** *n, pl* **-ties** : posibilidad *f* — **possibly** *adv* : posiblemente
post[1] *n* POLE : poste *m*, palo *m*
post[2] *n* POSITION : puesto *m*
post[3] *n* MAIL : cartas *fpl* — ~ *vt* **1** : echar al correo **2 keep** ~**ed** : tener al corriente — **postage** *n* : franqueo *m* — **postal** *adj* : postal — **postcard** *n* : tarjeta *f* postal
poster *n* : cartel *m*
posterity *n* : posteridad *f*
posthumous *adj* : póstumo
postman → **mailman** — **post office** *n* : oficina *f* de correos
postpone *vt* **-poned; -poning** : aplazar — **postponement** *n* : aplazamiento *m*
postscript *n* : posdata *f*
posture *n* : postura *f*
postwar *adj* : de (la) posguerra
pot *n* **1** : olla *f* (de cocina) **2** FLOWERPOT : maceta *f* **3** ~**s and pans** : cacharros *mpl*
potassium *n* : potasio *m*
potato *n, pl* **-toes** : patata *f*, papa *f* *Lat*

potent *adj* **1** POWERFUL : poderoso **2** EFFECTIVE : eficaz

potential *adj* : potencial — ~ *n* : potencial *m*

pothole *n* : bache *m*

potion *n* : poción *f*

pottery *n, pl* **-teries** : cerámica *f*

pouch *n* **1** BAG : bolsa *f* pequeña **2** : bolsa *f* (de un animal)

poultry *n* : aves *fpl* de corral

pounce *vi* **pounced; pouncing** : abalanzarse

pound¹ *n* : libra *f* (unidad de dinero o de peso)

pound² *n or* **dog** ~ : perrera *f*

pound³ *vt* **1** CRUSH : machacar **2** HIT : golpear — *vi* : palpitar (dícese del corazón)

pour *vt* : verter — *vi* **1** FLOW : fluir, salir **2** **it's** ~**ing** : está lloviendo a cántaros

pout *vi* : hacer pucheros — ~ *n* : puchero *m*

poverty *n* : pobreza *f*

powder *vt* **1** : empolvar **2** CRUSH : pulverizar — ~ *n* **1** : polvo *m* **2** *or* **face** ~ : polvos *mpl* — **powdery** *adj* : polvoriento

power *n* **1** CONTROL : poder *m* **2** ABILITY : capacidad *f* **3** STRENGTH : fuerza *f* **4** : potencia *f* (política) **5** ENERGY : energía *f* **6** ELECTRICITY : electricidad *f* — ~ *vt* : impulsar — **powerful** *adj* : poderoso — **powerless** *adj* : impotente

practical *adj* : práctico — **practically** *adv* : casi, prácticamente

practice *or* **practise** *v* **-ticed** *or* **-tised; -ticing** *or* **-tising** *vt* **1** : practicar **2** : ejercer (una profesión) — *vi* : practicar — **practice** *n* **1** : práctica *f* **2** CUSTOM : costumbre *f* **3** : ejercicio *m* (de una profesión) **4** **be out of** ~ : no estar en forma — **practitioner** *n* **1** : profesional *mf* **2** **general** ~ : médico *m*, -ca *f* de medicina general

pragmatic *adj* : pragmático

prairie *n* : pradera *f*

praise *vt* **praised; praising** : elogiar, alabar — ~ *n* : elogio *m*, alabanza *f* — **praiseworthy** *adj* : loable

prance *vi* **pranced; prancing** : hacer cabriolas

prank *n* : travesura *f*

prawn *n* : gamba *f*

pray *vi* **1** : rezar **2** ~ **for** : rogar — **prayer** *n* : oración *f*

preach *v* : predicar — **preacher** *n* MINISTER : pastor *m*, -tora *f*

precarious *adj* : precario

precaution *n* : precaución *f*

precede *vt* **-ceded; -ceding** : preceder a — **precedence** *n* : precedencia *f* — **precedent** *n* : precedente *m*

precinct *n* **1** DISTRICT : distrito *m* **2** ~**s** *npl* : recinto *m*

precious *adj* : precioso

precipice *n* : precipicio *m*

precipitate *vt* **-tated; -tating** : precipitar — **precipitation** *n* **1** HASTE : precipitación *f* **2** : precipitaciones *fpl* (en meteorología)

precise *adj* : preciso — **precisely** *adv* : precisamente — **precision** *n* : precisión *f*

preclude *vt* **-cluded; -cluding** **1** PREVENT : impedir **2** EXCLUDE : excluir

precocious *adj* : precoz

preconceived *adj* : preconcebido

predator *n* : depredador *m*

predecessor *n* : antecesor *m*, -sora *f*; predecesor *m*, -sora *f*

predicament *n* : apuro *m*

predict *vt* : pronosticar, predecir — **predictable** *adj* : previsible — **prediction** *n* : pronóstico *m*, predicción *f*

predispose *vt* **-posed; -posing** : predisponer

predominant *adj* : predominante

preeminent *adj* : preeminente

preempt *vt* : adelantarse a (un ataque, etc.)

preen *vt* **1** : arreglarse (las plumas) **2** ~ **oneself** : acicalarse

prefabricated *adj* : prefabricado

preface *n* : prefacio *m*, prólogo *m*

prefer *vt* **-ferred; -ferring** : preferir — **preferable** *adj* : preferible — **preference** *n* : preferencia *f* — **preferential** *adj* : preferente

prefix *n* : prefijo *m*

pregnancy *n, pl* **-cies** : embarazo *m* — **pregnant** *adj* : embarazada

prehistoric *or* **prehistorical** *adj* : prehistórico

prejudice *n* **1** BIAS : prejuicio *m* **2** HARM : perjuicio *m* — ~ *vt* **-diced; -dicing** **1** BIAS : predisponer **2** HARM : perjudicar — **prejudiced** *adj* : parcial

preliminary *adj* : preliminar

prelude *n* : preludio *m*

premarital *adj* : prematrimonial

premature *adj* : prematuro

premeditated *adj* : premeditado

premier *adj* : principal — ~ *n* PRIME MINISTER : primer ministro *m*, primera ministra *f*

premiere *n* : estreno *m*

premise *n* **1** : premisa *f* (de un argumento) **2** ~**s** *npl* : recinto *m*, local *m*

premium *n* **1** : premio *m* **2** *or* **insurance** ~ : prima *f* (de seguro)

preoccupied *adj* : preocupado

prepare *v* **-pared; -paring** *vt* : preparar — *vi* : prepararse — **preparation** *n* **1** : preparación *f* **2** ~**s** *npl* ARRANGEMENTS : preparativos *mpl* — **preparatory** *adj* : preparatorio

prepay *vt* **-paid; -paying** : pagar por adelantado

preposition *n* : preposición *f*
preposterous *adj* : absurdo, ridículo
prerequisite *n* : requisito *m* previo
prerogative *n* : prerrogativa *f*
prescribe *vt* **-scribed; -scribing 1** : prescribir **2** : recetar (en medicina) — **prescription** *n* : receta *f*
presence *n* : presencia *f*
present[1] *adj* **1** CURRENT : actual **2 be ~ at** : estar presente en — **~** *n* **1** : presente *m* **2 at ~** : actualmente
present[2] *n* GIFT : regalo *m* — **~** *vt* **1** INTRODUCE : presentar **2** GIVE : entregar — **presentation** *n* **1** : presentación *f* **2** *or* **~ ceremony** : ceremonia *f* de entrega
presently *adv* **1** SOON : dentro de poco **2** NOW : actualmente
preserve *vt* **-served; -serving 1** : conservar **2** MAINTAIN : mantener — **~** *n* **1** JAM : confitura *f* **2** *or* **game ~** : coto *m* de caza — **preservation** *n* : preservación *f*, conservación *f* — **preservative** *n* : conservante *m*
president *n* : presidente *m*, -ta *f* — **presidency** *n*, *pl* **-cies** : presidencia *f* — **presidential** *adj* : presidencial
press *n* : prensa *f* — **~** *vt* **1** : apretar **2** IRON : planchar — *vi* **1** : apretar **2** URGE : presionar — **pressing** *adj* : urgente — **pressure** *n* : presión *f* — **~** *vt* **-sured; -suring** : presionar, apremiar
prestige *n* : prestigio *m* — **prestigious** *adj* : prestigioso
presume *vt* **-sumed; -suming** : presumir — **presumably** *adv* : es de suponer, supuestamente — **presumption** *n* : presunción *f* — **presumptuous** *adj* : presuntuoso
pretend *vt* CLAIM : pretender **2** FEIGN : fingir — *vi* : fingir — **pretense** *or* **pretence** *n* **1** CLAIM : pretensión *f* **2 under false ~s** : con pretextos falsos — **pretentious** *adj* : pretencioso
pretext *n* : pretexto *m*
pretty *adj* **-tier; -est** : lindo, bonito — **~** *adv* FAIRLY : bastante
pretzel *n* : galleta *f* salada
prevail *vi* **1** TRIUMPH : prevalecer **2** PREDOMINATE : predominar **3 ~ upon** : persuadir — **prevalent** *adj* : extendido
prevent *vt* : impedir — **prevention** *n* : prevención *f* — **preventive** *adj* : preventivo
preview *n* : preestreno *m*
previous *adj* : previo, anterior — **previously** *adv* : anteriormente
prey *n*, *pl* **preys** : presa *f* — **prey on** *vt* **1** : alimentarse de **2 ~ on one's mind** : atormentar a algn
price *n* : precio *m* — **~** *vt* **priced; pricing** : poner un precio a — **priceless** *adj* : inestimable

prick *n* : pinchazo *m* — **~** *vt* **1** : pinchar **2 ~ up one's ears** : levantar las orejas —
prickly *adj* : espinoso
pride *n* : orgullo *m* — **~** *vt* **prided; priding ~ oneself on** : enorgullecerse de
priest *n* : sacerdote *m* — **priesthood** *n* : sacerdocio *m*
prim *adj* **primmer; primmest** : remilgado
primary *adj* **1** FIRST : primario **2** PRINCIPAL : principal — **primarily** *adv* : principalmente
prime[1] *vt* **primed; priming 1** : cebar (un arma de fuego, etc.) **2** PREPARE : preparar
prime[2] *n* **the ~ of one's life** : la flor de la vida — **~** *adj* **1** MAIN : principal, primero **2** EXCELLENT : excelente — **prime minister** *n* : primero ministro *m*, primera ministra *f*
primer[1] *n* : base *f* (de pintura)
primer[2] *n* READER : cartilla *f*
primitive *adj* : primitivo
primrose *n* : primavera *f*
prince *n* : príncipe *m* — **princess** *n* : princesa *f*
principal *adj* : principal — **~** *n* : director *m*, -tora *f* (de un colegio)
principle *n* : principio *m*
print *n* **1** MARK : huella *f* **2** LETTERING : letra *f* **3** ENGRAVING : grabado *m* **4** : estampado *m* (de tela) **5** : copia *f* (en fotografía) **6 out of ~** : agotado — **~** *vt* : imprimir (libros, etc.) — *vi* : escribir con letra de molde — **printer** *n* **1** : impresor *m*, -sora *f* (persona) **2** : impresora *f* (máquina) — **printing** *n* **1** : impresión *f* **2** : imprenta *f* (profesión) **3** LETTERING : letras *fpl* de molde
prior *adj* **1** : previo **2 ~ to** : antes de — **priority** *n*, *pl* **-ties** : prioridad *f*
prison *n* : prisión *f*, cárcel *f* — **prisoner** *n* **1** : preso *m*, -sa *f* **2 ~ of war** : prisionero *m*, -ra *f* de guerra
privacy *n*, *pl* **-cies** : intimidad *f* — **private** *adj* **1** : privado **2** SECRET : secreto — **~** *n* : soldado *m* raso — **privately** *adv* : en privado
privilege *n* : privilegio *m* — **privileged** *adj* : privilegiado
prize *n* : premio *m* — **~** *adj* : premiado — **~** *vt* **prized; prizing** : valorar, apreciar — **prizefighter** *n* : boxeador *m*, -dora *f* profesional — **prizewinning** *adj* : premiado
pro *n* **1** → **professional 2 the ~s and cons** : los pros y los contras
probability *n*, *pl* **-ties** : probabilidad *f* — **probable** *adj* : probable — **probably** *adv* : probablemente
probation *n* **1** : período *m* de prueba (de un empleado, etc.) **2** : libertad *f* condicional (de un preso)

probe n 1 : sonda f (en medicina, etc.) 2 IN-VESTIGATION : investigación f — ~ vt
probed; probing 1 : sondar 2 INVESTI-GATE : investigar
problem n : problema m
procedure n : procedimiento m
proceed vi 1 ACT : proceder 2 CONTINUE : continuar 3 ADVANCE : avanzar — **proceedings** npl 1 EVENTS : actos mpl 2 : proceso m (en derecho) — **proceeds** npl : ganancias fpl
process n, pl -cesses 1 : proceso m 2 in the ~ of : en vías de — ~ vt : procesar — **procession** n : desfile m
proclaim vt : proclamar — **proclamation** n : proclamación f
procrastinate vi -nated; -nating : demorar, aplazar
procure vt -cured; -curing : obtener
prod vt **prodded; prodding** : pinchar, aguijonear
prodigal adj : pródigo
prodigy n, pl -gies : prodigio m
produce vt -duced; -ducing 1 : producir 2 CAUSE : causar 3 SHOW : presentar, mostrar 4 : poner en escena (una obra de teatro) — ~ n : productos mpl agrícolas — **producer** n : productor m, -tora f — **product** n : producto m — **productive** adj : productivo
profane adj 1 : profano 2 IRREVERENT : blasfemo — **profanity** n, pl -ties : blasfemia f
profess vt : profesar — **profession** n : profesión f — **professional** adj : profesional — ~ n : profesional mf — **professor** n : profesor m, -sora f
proficiency n : competencia f — **proficient** adj : competente
profile n 1 : perfil m 2 keep a low ~ : no llamar la atención
profit n : beneficio m, ganancia f — ~ vi : sacar provecho (de), beneficiarse (de) — **profitable** adj : provechoso
profound adj : profundo
profuse adj : profuso — **profusion** n : profusión f
prognosis n, pl -noses : pronóstico m
program n : programa m — ~ vt -grammed or -gramed; -gramming or -graming : programar
progress n 1 : progreso m 2 ADVANCE : avance m — ~ vi : progresar, avanzar — **progressive** adj 1 : progresista (dícese de la política, etc.) 2 INCREASING : progresiva
prohibit vt : prohibir — **prohibition** n : prohibición f
project n : proyecto m — ~ vt : proyectar — vi PROTRUDE : sobresalir — **projectile** n : proyectil m — **projection** n 1 : proyec-

ción f 2 PROTRUSION : saliente m — **projector** n : proyector m
proliferate vi -ated; -ating : proliferar — **proliferation** n : proliferación f — **prolific** adj : prolífico
prologue n : prólogo m
prolong vt : prolongar
prom n : baile m formal (en un colegio)
prominent adj : prominente — **prominence** n 1 : prominencia f 2 IMPORTANCE : eminencia f
promiscuous adj : promiscuo
promise n : promesa f — ~ v -ised; -ising : prometer — **promising** adj : prometedor
promote vt -moted; -moting 1 : ascender (a un alumno o un empleado) 2 FURTHER : promover, fomentar 3 ADVERTISE : promocionar — **promoter** n : promotor m, -tora f; empresario m, -ria f (en deportes) — **promotion** n 1 : ascenso m (de un alumno o un empleado) 2 ADVERTISING : publicidad f, propaganda f
prompt vt 1 INCITE : provocar (una cosa), inducir (a una persona) 2 : apuntar (a un actor, etc.) — ~ adj 1 : rápido 2 PUNCTUAL : puntual
prone adj 1 : boca abajo, decúbito prono 2 be ~ to : ser propenso a
prong n : punta f, diente m
pronoun n : pronombre m
pronounce vt -nounced; -nouncing : pronunciar — **pronouncement** n : declaración f — **pronunciation** n : pronunciación f
proof n : prueba f — ~ adj ~ against : a prueba de — **proofread** vt -read; -reading : corregir
prop n 1 SUPPORT : puntal m, apoyo m 2 : accesorio m (en teatro) — ~ vt **propped; propping** 1 ~ against : apoyar contra 2 ~ up SUPPORT : apoyar
propaganda n : propaganda f
propagate v -gated; -gating vt : propagar — vi : propagarse
propel vt -pelled; -pelling : propulsar — **propeller** n : hélice f
propensity n, pl -ties : propensión f
proper adj 1 SUITABLE : apropiado 2 REAL : verdadero 3 CORRECT : correcto 4 GENTEEL : cortés 5 ~ name : nombre m propio — **properly** adv : correctamente
property n, pl -ties 1 : propiedad f 2 BUILDING : inmueble m 3 LAND, LOT : parcela f
prophet n : profeta m, profetisa f — **prophecy** n, pl -cies : profecía f — **prophesy** v -sied; -sying vt : profetizar — vi : hacer profecías — **prophetic** adj : profético
proportion n 1 : proporción f 2 SHARE : parte f — **proportional** adj : proporcional — **proportionate** adj : proporcional

proposal *n* : propuesta *f*

propose *v* **-posed; -posing** *vt* **1** SUGGEST : proponer **2** ~ **to do sth** : pensar hacer algo — *vi* : proponer matrimonio — **proposition** *n* : proposición *f*

proprietor *n* : propietario *m*, -ria *f*

propriety *n*, *pl* **-eties** : decencia *f*, decoro *m*

propulsion *n* : propulsión *f*

prose *n* : prosa *f*

prosecute *vt* **-cuted; -cuting** : procesar — **prosecution** *n* **1** : procesamiento *m* **2 the** ~ : la acusación — **prosecutor** *n* : acusador *m*, -dora *f*

prospect *n* **1** : perspectiva *f* **2** POSSIBILITY : posibilidad *f* — **prospective** *adj* : futuro, posible

prosper *vi* : prosperar — **prosperity** *n* : prosperidad *f* — **prosperous** *adj* : próspero

prostitute *n* : prostituta *f* — **prostitution** *n* : prostitución *f*

prostrate *adj* : postrado

protagonist *n* : protagonista *mf*

protect *vt* : proteger — **protection** *n* : protección *f* — **protective** *adj* : protector — **protector** *n* : protector *m*, -tora *f*

protégé *n* : protegido *m*, -da *f*

protein *n* : proteína *f*

protest *n* : protesta *f* — ~ *vt* : protestar — *vi* ~ **against** : protestar contra — **Protestant** *n* : protestante *mf* — **protester** *or* **protestor** *n* : manifestante *mf*

protocol *n* : protocolo *m*

prototype *n* : prototipo *m*

protract *vt* : prolongar

protrude *vi* **-truded; -truding** : sobresalir

proud *adj* : orgulloso

prove *v* **proved; proved** *or* **proven; proving** *vt* : probar — *vi* : resultar

proverb *n* : proverbio *m*, refrán *m* — **proverbial** *adj* : proverbial

provide *v* **-vided; -viding** *vt* : proveer — *vi* ~ **for** SUPPORT : mantener — **provided** *or* ~ **that** *conj* : con tal (de) que, siempre que — **providence** *n* : providencia *f*

province *n* **1** : provincia *f* **2** SPHERE : campo *m*, competencia *f* — **provincial** *adj* : provinciano

provision *n* **1** : provisión *f*, suministro *m* **2** STIPULATION : condición *f* **3** ~**s** *npl* : víveres *mpl* — **provisional** *adj* : provisional — **proviso** *n*, *pl* **-sos** *or* **-soes** : condición *f*

provoke *vt* **-voked; -voking** : provocar — **provocation** *n* : provocación *f* — **provocative** *adj* : provocador, provocativo

prow *n* : proa *f*

prowess *n* **1** BRAVERY : valor *m* **2** SKILL : habilidad *f*

prowl *vi* : merodear, rondar — *vt* : merodear por — **prowler** *n* : merodeador *m*, -dora *f*

proximity *n* : proximidad *f* — **proxy** *n*, *pl* **proxies by** ~ : por poder

prude *n* : mojigato *m*, -ta *f*

prudence *n* : prudencia *f* — **prudent** *adj* : prudente

prune[1] *n* : ciruela *f* pasa

prune[2] *vt* **pruned; pruning** : podar (arbustos, etc.)

pry *v* **pried; prying** *vi* ~ **into** : entrometerse en — *vt or* ~ **open** : abrir (a la fuerza)

psalm *n* : salmo *m*

pseudonym *n* : seudónimo *m*

psychiatry *n* : psiquiatría *f* — **psychiatric** *adj* : psiquiátrico — **psychiatrist** *n* : psiquiatra *mf*

psychic *adj* : psíquico

psychoanalysis *n*, *pl* **-yses** : psicoanálisis *m* — **psychoanalyst** *n* : psicoanalista *mf* — **psychoanalyze** *vt* **-lyzed; -lyzing** : psicoanalizar

psychology *n*, *pl* **-gies** : psicología *f* — **psychological** *adj* : psicológico — **psychologist** *n* : psicólogo *m*, -ga *f*

psychopath *n* : psicópata *mf*

psychotherapy *n*, *pl* **-pies** : psicoterapia *f*

psychotic *adj* : psicótico

puberty *n* : pubertad *f*

pubic *adj* : púbico

public *adj* : público — ~ *n* : público *m* — **publication** *n* : publicación *f* — **publicity** *n* : publicidad *f* — **publicize** *vt* **-cized; -cizing** : publicitar, divulgar

publish *vt* : publicar — **publisher** *n* **1** : editor *m*, -tora *f* (persona) **2** : casa *f* editorial (negocio)

pucker *vt* : fruncir, arrugar — *vi* : arrugarse

pudding *n* : budín *m*, pudín *m*

puddle *n* : charco *m*

pudgy *adj* **pudgier; -est** : rechoncho *fam*

Puerto Rican *adj* : puertorriqueño

puff *vi* **1** BLOW : soplar **2** PANT : resoplar **3** ~ **up** SWELL : hincharse — *vt* ~ **out** : hinchar — ~ *n* **1** : bocanada *f* (de humo) **2** : chupada *f* (a un cigarrillo) **3** *or* **cream** ~ : pastelito *m* de crema **4** *or* **powder** ~ : borla *f* — **puffy** *adj* **puffier; -est** : hinchado

pull *vt* **1** : tirar de **2** EXTRACT : sacar **3** TEAR : desgarrarse (un músculo, etc.) **4** ~ **off** REMOVE : quitar **5** ~ **oneself together** : calmarse **6** ~ **up** : levantar, subir — *vi* **1** : tirar **2** ~ **through** RECOVER : reponerse **3** ~ **together** COOPERATE : reunir **4** ~ **up** STOP : parar — ~ *n* **1** : tirón *m* **2** INFLUENCE : influencia *f* — **pulley** *n*, *pl* **-leys** : polea *f* — **pullover** *n* : suéter *m*

pulp *n* **1** : pulpa *f* (de frutas, etc.) **2** *or* **wood** ~ : pasta *f* de papel
pulpit *n* : púlpito *m*
pulsate *vi* -**sated**; -**sating** : palpitar —
pulse *n* : pulso *m*
pulverize *vt* -**ized**; -**izing** : pulverizar
pummel *vt* -**meled**; -**meling** : aporrear
pump[1] *n* : bomba *f* — ~ *vt* **1** : bombear **2** ~ **up** : inflar
pump[2] *n* SHOE : zapato *m* de tacón
pumpernickel *n* : pan *m* negro de centeno
pumpkin *n* : calabaza *f*, zapallo *m* *Lat*
pun *n* : juego *m* de palabras — ~ *vi* **punned**; **punning** : hacer juegos de palabras
punch[1] *vt* **1** : dar un puñetazo a **2** PERFORATE : perforar (papeles, etc.), picar (un boleto) — ~ *n* **1** : golpe *m*, puñetazo *m* **2** *or* **paper** ~ : perforadora *f*
punch[2] *n* : ponche *m* (bebida)
punctual *adj* : puntual — **punctuality** *n* : puntualidad *f*
punctuate *vt* -**ated**; -**ating** : puntuar —
punctuation *n* : puntuación *f*
puncture *n* : pinchazo *m*, ponchadura *f* *Lat* — ~ *vt* -**tured**; -**turing** : pinchar, ponchar *Lat*
pungent *adj* : acre
punish *vt* : castigar — **punishment** *n* : castigo *m* — **punitive** *adj* : punitivo
puny *adj* -**nier**; -**est** : enclenque
pup *n* : cachorro *m*, -rra *f* (de un perro); cría *f* (de otros animales)
pupil[1] *n* : alumno *m*, -na *f* (de colegio)
pupil[2] *n* : pupila *f* (del ojo)
puppet *n* : títere *m*
puppy *n*, *pl* -**pies** : cachorro *m*, -rra *f*
purchase *vt* -**chased**; -**chasing** : comprar — ~ *n* : compra *f*
pure *adj* **purer**; **purest** : puro
puree *n* : puré *m*
purely *adv* : puramente
purgatory *n*, *pl* -**ries** : purgatorio *m* —
purge *vt* **purged**; **purging** : purgar — ~ *n* : purga *f*
purify *vt* -**fied**; -**fying** : purificar — **purification** *n* : purificación *f*
puritanical *adj* : puritano

purity *n* : pureza *f*
purple *n* : morado *m*
purport *vt* ~ **to be** : pretender ser
purpose *n* **1** : propósito *m* **2** RESOLUTION : determinación *f* **3** **on** ~ : a propósito — **purposeful** *adj* : resuelto — **purposely** *adv* : a propósito
purr *n* : ronroneo *m* — ~ *vi* : ronronear
purse *n* **1** *or* **change** ~ : monedero *m* **2** HANDBAG : cartera *f*, bolso *m* *Spain*, bolsa *f* *Lat* — ~ *vt* **pursed**; **pursing** : fruncir
pursue *vt* -**sued**; -**suing** **1** CHASE : perseguir **2** SEEK : buscar — **pursuer** *n* : perseguidor *m*, -dora *f* — **pursuit** *n* **1** CHASE : persecución *f* **2** SEARCH : búsqueda *f* **3** OCCUPATION : actividad *f*
pus *n* : pus *m*
push *vt* **1** SHOVE : empujar **2** PRESS : apretar **3** URGE : presionar **4** ~ **around** BULLY : mangonear — *vi* **1** : empujar **2** ~ **for** : presionar para — ~ *n* **1** SHOVE : empujón *m* **2** DRIVE : dinamismo *m* **3** EFFORT : esfuerzo *m* — **pushy** *adj* **pushier**; -**est** : mandón, prepotente
pussy *n*, *pl* **pussies** : gatito *m*, -ta *f*; minino *m*, -na *f*
put *v* **put**; **putting** *vt* **1** : poner **2** INSERT : meter **3** EXPRESS : decir **4** ~ **one's mind to sth** : proponerse hacer algo — *vi* ~ **up with** : aguantar — **put away** *vt* **1** STORE : guardar **2** *or* ~ **aside** : dejar a un lado — **put down** *vt* **1** SUPPRESS : aplastar, sofocar **2** ATTRIBUTE : atribuir — **put off** *vt* DEFER : aplazar, posponer — **put on** *vt* **1** ASSUME : adoptar **2** PRESENT : presentar (una obra de teatro, etc.) **3** WEAR : ponerse — **put out** *vt* INCONVENIENCE : incomodar — **put up** *vt* **1** BUILD : construir **2** LODGE : alojar **3** PROVIDE : poner (dinero)
putrefy *vi* -**fied**; -**fying** : pudrirse
putty *n*, *pl* -**ties** : masilla *f*
puzzle *v* -**zled**; -**zling** *vt* : confundir, dejar perplejo — *vi* ~ **over** : tratar de descifrar — ~ *n* **1** : rompecabezas *m* **2** MYSTERY : enigma *m*
pylon *n* : pilón *m*
pyramid *n* : pirámide *f*
python *n* : pitón *f*

Q

q *n, pl* **q's** *or* **qs** : q *f*, decimoséptima letra del alfabeto inglés

quack[1] *vi* : graznar (dícese del pato) — ~ *n* : graznido *m*

quack[2] *n* CHARLATAN : charlatán *m*, -tana *f*

quadruple *v* **-pled; -pling** *vt* : cuadruplicar — *vi* : cuadruplicarse

quagmire *n* : atolladero *m*

quail *n, pl* **quail** *or* **quails** : codorniz *f*

quaint *adj* **1** ODD : curioso **2** PICTURESQUE : pintoresco

quake *vi* **quaked; quaking** : temblar — ~ *n* → **earthquake**

qualify *v* **-fied; -fying** *vt* **1** LIMIT : matizar **2** : calificar (en gramática) **3** EQUIP : habilitar — *vi* **1** : titularse (de abogado, etc.) **2** : clasificarse (en deportes) — **qualification** *n* **1** REQUIREMENT : requisito *m* **2** ~s *npl* ABILITY : capacidad *f* **3** **without** ~ : sin reservas — **qualified** *adj* : capacitado

quality *n, pl* **-ties** **1** : calidad *f* **2** PROPERTY : ~ualidad *f*

qualm *n* **1** DOUBT : duda *f* **2** **have no** ~s **about** : no tener ningún escrúpulo en

quandary *n, pl* **-ries** : dilema *m*

quantity *n, pl* **-ties** : cantidad *f*

quarantine *n* : cuarentena *f* — ~ *vt* **-tined; -tining** : poner en cuarentena

quarrel *n* : pelea *f*, riña *f* — ~ *vi* **-reled** *or* **-relled; -reling** *or* **-relling** : pelearse, reñir — **quarrelsome** *adj* : pendenciero

quarry[1] *n, pl* **quarries** PREY : presa *f*

quarry[2] *n, pl* **quarries** EXCAVATION : cantera *f*

quart *n* : cuarto *m* de galón

quarter *n* **1** : cuarto *m* (en matemáticas) **2** : moneda *f* de 25 centavos **3** DISTRICT : barrio *m* **4** ~ **after three** : las tres y cuarto **5** ~s *npl* LODGING : alojamiento *m* — ~ *vt* **1** : dividir en cuatro partes **2** : acuartelar (tropas) — **quarterly** *adv* : cada tres meses — ~ *adj* : trimestral — ~ *n, pl* **-lies** : publicación *f* trimestral

quartet *n* : cuarteto *m*

quartz *n* : cuarzo *m*

quash *vt* **1** ANNUL : anular **2** SUPPRESS : aplastar, sofocar

quaver *vi* : temblar

quay *n* : muelle *m*

queasy *adj* **-sier; -est** : mareado

queen *n* : reina *f*

queer *adj* ODD : extraño

quell *vt* SUPPRESS : sofocar, aplastar

quench *vt* **1** EXTINGUISH : apagar **2** ~ **one's thirst** : quitar la sed

query *n, pl* **-ries** : pregunta *f* — ~ *vt* **-ried; -rying** **1** ASK : preguntar **2** QUESTION : cuestionar

quest *n* : búsqueda *f*

question *n* **1** QUERY : pregunta *f* **2** ISSUE : cuestión *f* **3** **be out of the** ~ : ser indiscutible **4** **call into** ~ : poner en duda **5** **without** ~ : sin duda — ~ *vt* **1** ASK : preguntar **2** DOUBT : cuestionar **3** INTERROGATE : interrogar — *vi* : preguntar — **questionable** *adj* : discutible — **question mark** *n* : signo *m* de interrogación — **questionnaire** *n* : cuestionario *m*

queue *n* : cola *f* — ~ *vi* **queued; queuing** *or* **queueing** : hacer cola

quibble *vi* **-bled; -bling** : discutir, quejarse por nimiedades

quick *adj* **1** : rápido **2** CLEVER : agudo — ~ *n* **to the** ~ : en lo vivo — ~ *adv* : rápidamente — **quicken** *vt* : acelerar — **quickly** *adv* : rápidamente — **quicksand** *n* : arena *f* movediza — **quick-tempered** *adj* : irascible — **quick-witted** *adj* : agudo

quiet *n* **1** : silencio *m* **2** CALM : tranquilidad *f* — ~ *adj* **1** : silencioso **2** CALM : tranquilo **3** RESERVED : callado **4** : discreto (dícese de colores, etc.) — ~ *vt* **1** SILENCE : hacer callar **2** CALM : calmar — *vi or* ~ **down** : calmarse — **quietly** *adv* **1** : silenciosamente **2** CALMLY : tranquilamente

quilt *n* : edredón *m*

quintet *n* : quinteto *m*

quip *n* : ocurrencia *f*, salida *f* — ~ *vt* **quipped; quipping** : decir bromeando

quirk *n* : peculiaridad *f*

quit *v* **quit; quitting** *vt* **1** LEAVE : dejar, abandonar **2** ~ **doing** : dejar de hacer — *vi* **1** STOP : parar **2** RESIGN : dimitir, renunciar

quite *adv* **1** COMPLETELY : completamente **2** RATHER : bastante

quits *adj* **call it** ~ : quedar en paz

quiver *vi* : temblar

quiz *n, pl* **quizzes** TEST : prueba *f* — ~ *vt* **quizzed; quizzing** : interrogar

quota *n* : cuota *f*, cupo *m*

quotation *n* **1** : cita *f* **2** ESTIMATE : presupuesto *m* — **quotation marks** *npl* : comillas *fpl* — **quote** *vt* **quoted; quoting** **1** CITE : citar **2** : cotizar (en finanzas) — ~ *n* **1** → **quotation** **2** ~s *npl* → **quotation marks**

quotient *n* : cociente *m*

R

r *n, pl* **r's** *or* **rs** : r *f*, decimoctava letra del alfabeto inglés
rabbi *n* : rabino *m*, -na *f*
rabbit *n, pl* **-bit** *or* **-bits** : conejo *m*, -ja *f*
rabble *n* : chusma *f*, populacho *m*
rabies *ns & pl* : rabia *f* — **rabid** *adj* 1 : rabioso 2 FANATIC : fanático
raccoon *n, pl* **-coon** *or* **-coons** : mapache *m*
race¹ *n* 1 : raza *f* 2 **human** ~ : género *m* humano
race² *n* : carrera *f* (competitiva) — ~ *vi* **raced; racing** 1 : correr (en una carrera) 2 RUSH : ir corriendo — **racehorse** *n* : caballo *m* de carreras — **racetrack** *n* : pista *f* (de carreras)
racial *adj* : racial — **racism** *n* : racismo *m* — **racist** *n* : racista *mf*
rack *n* 1 SHELF : estante *m* 2 **luggage** ~ : portaequipajes *m* — ~ *vt* 1 ~**ed with** : atormentado por 2 ~ **one's brains** : devanarse los sesos
racket¹ *n* : raqueta *f* (en deportes)
racket² *n* 1 DIN : alboroto *m*, bulla *f* 2 SWINDLE : estafa *f*
racy *adj* **racier; -est** : subido de tono, picante
radar *n* : radar *m*
radiant *adj* : radiante — **radiance** *n* : resplandor *m* — **radiate** *v* **-ated; -ating** *vt* : irradiar — *vi* 1 : irradiar 2 *or* ~ **out** : extenderse (desde un centro) — **radiation** *n* : radiación *f* — **radiator** *n* : radiador *m*
radical *adj* : radical — ~ *n* : radical *mf*
radii → **radius**
radio *n, pl* **-dios** : radio *mf* (aparato), radio *f* (medio) — ~ *vt* : transmitir por radio — **radioactive** *adj* : radioactivo, radiactivo
radish *n* : rábano *m*
radius *n, pl* **radii** : radio *m*
raffle *vt* **-fled; -fling** : rifar — ~ *n* : rifa *f*
raft *n* : balsa *f*
rafter *n* : cabrio *m*
rag *n* 1 : trapo *m* 2 ~**s** *npl* TATTERS : harapos *mpl*, andrajos *mpl*
rage *n* 1 : cólera *f*, rabia *f* 2 **be all the** ~ : hacer furor — ~ *vi* **raged; raging** 1 : estar furioso 2 : bramar (dícese del viento, etc.)
ragged *adj* 1 UNEVEN : irregular 2 TATTERED : andrajoso, harapiento
raid *n* 1 : invasión *f* (militar) 2 : asalto *m* (por delincuentes), redada *f* (por la policía) — ~ *vt* 1 INVADE : invadir 2 ROB : asaltar 3 : hacer una redada en (dícese de la policía) — **raider** *n* ATTACKER : asaltante *mf*

rail¹ *vi* ~ **at s.o.** : recriminar a algn
rail² *n* 1 BAR : barra *f* 2 HANDRAIL : pasamanos *m* 3 TRACK : riel *m* 4 **by** ~ : por ferrocarril — **railing** *n* 1 : baranda *f* (de un balcón), pasamanos *m* (de una escalera) 2 RAILS : reja *f* — **railroad** *n* : ferrocarril *m* — **railway** → **railroad**
rain *n* : lluvia *f* — ~ *vi* : llover — **rainbow** *n* : arco *m* iris — **raincoat** *n* : impermeable *m* — **rainfall** *n* : precipitación *f* — **rainy** *adj* **rainier; -est** : lluvioso
raise *vt* **raised; raising** 1 : levantar 2 COLLECT : recaudar 3 REAR : criar 4 GROW : cultivar 5 INCREASE : aumentar 6 : sacar (objeciones, etc.) — ~ *n* : aumento *m*
raisin *n* : pasa *f*
rake *n* : rastrillo *m* — ~ *vt* **raked; raking** : rastrillar
rally *v* **-lied; -lying** *vi* 1 : unirse, reunirse 2 RECOVER : recuperarse — *vt* : conseguir (apoyo), unir a (la gente) — ~ *n, pl* **-lies** : reunión *f*, mitin *m*
ram *n* : carnero *m* (animal) — ~ *vt* **rammed; ramming** 1 CRAM : meter con fuerza 2 *or* ~ **into** : chocar contra
RAM *n* : RAM *f*
ramble *vi* **-bled; -bling** 1 WANDER : pasear 2 *or* ~ **on** : divagar — ~ *n* : paseo *m*, excursión *f*
ramp *n* : rampa *f*
rampage *vi* **-paged; -paging** : andar arrasando todo — ~ *n* : frenesí *m* (de violencia)
rampant *adj* : desenfrenado
rampart *n* : muralla *f*
ramshackle *adj* : destartalado
ran → **run**
ranch *n* : hacienda *f* — **rancher** *n* : hacendado *m*, -da *f*
rancid *adj* : rancio
rancor *n* : rencor *m*
random *adj* 1 : aleatorio 2 **at** ~ : al azar
rang → **ring**
range *n* 1 GRASSLAND : pradera *f* 2 STOVE : cocina *f* 3 VARIETY : gama *f* 4 SCOPE : amplitud *f* 5 *or* **mountain** ~ : cordillera *f* — ~ *vi* **ranged; ranging** 1 EXTEND : extenderse 2 ~ **from...to...** : variar entre...y... — **ranger** *n or* **forest** ~ : guardabosque *mf*
rank¹ *adj* 1 SMELLY : fétido 2 OUTRIGHT : completo
rank² *n* 1 ROW : fila *f* 2 : rango *m* (militar) 3 ~**s** *npl* : soldados *mpl* rasos 4 **the** ~

and file : las bases — ~ *vt* RATE : clasificar — *vi* : clasificarse

rankle *vi* **-kled; -kling** : causar rencor, doler

ransack *vt* **1** SEARCH : registrar **2** LOOT : saquear

ransom *n* : rescate *m* — ~ *vt* : rescatar

rant *vi or* ~ **and rave** : despotricar

rap¹ *n* KNOCK : golpecito *m* — ~ *v* **rapped; rapping** : golpear

rap² *n or* ~ **music** : rap *m*

rapacious *adj* : rapaz

rape *vt* **raped; raping** : violar — ~ *n* : violación *f*

rapid *adj* : rápido — **rapids** *npl* : rápidos *mpl*

rapist *n* : violador *m*, -dora *f*

rapport *n* **have a good** ~ : entenderse bien

rapt *adj* : absorto, embelesado

rapture *n* : éxtasis *m*

rare *adj* **rarer; rarest 1** FINE : excepcional **2** UNCOMMON : raro **3** : poco cocido (dícese de la carne) — **rarely** *adv* : raramente — **rarity** *n, pl* **-ties** : rareza *f*

rascal *n* : pillo *m*, -lla *f*; pícaro *m*, -ra *f*

rash¹ *adj* : imprudente, precipitado

rash² *n* : sarpullido *m*, erupción *f*

rasp *vt* SCRAPE : raspar — ~ *n* : escofina *f*

raspberry *n, pl* **-ries** : frambuesa *f*

rat *n* : rata *f*

rate *n* **1** PACE : velocidad *f*, ritmo *m* **2** : tipo *m*, tasa *m* (de interés, etc.) **3** PRICE : tarifa *f* **4 at any** ~ : de todos modos **5 birth** ~ : índice *m* de natalidad — ~ *vt* **rated; rating 1** REGARD : considerar **2** DESERVE : merecer

rather *adv* **1** FAIRLY : bastante **2 I'd** ~… : prefiero… **3 or** ~ : o mejor dicho

ratify *vt* **-fied; -fying** : ratificar — **ratification** *n* : ratificación *f*

rating *n* **1** : clasificación *f* **2** ~**s** *npl* : índice *m* de audiencia

ratio *n, pl* **-tios** : proporción *f*

ration *n* **1** : ración *f* **2** ~**s** *npl* PROVISIONS : víveres *mpl* — ~ *vt* **rationed; rationing** : racionar

rational *adj* : racional — **rationale** *n* : lógica *f*, razones *fpl* — **rationalize** *vt* **-ized; -izing** : racionalizar

rattle *v* **-tled; -tling** *vi* : traquetear — *vt* **1** SHAKE : agitar **2** UPSET : desconcertar **3** ~ **off** : decir de corrido — ~ *n* **1** : traqueteo *m* **2 or baby's** ~ : sonajero *m* — **rattlesnake** *n* : serpiente *f* de cascabel

raucous *adj* **1** HOARSE : ronco **2** BOISTEROUS : bullicioso

ravage *vt* **-aged; -aging** : estragar, asolar — **ravages** *npl* : estragos *mpl*

rave *vi* **raved; raving 1** : delirar **2** ~ **about** : hablar con entusiasmo sobre

raven *n* : cuervo *m*

ravenous *adj* **1** HUNGRY : hambriento **2** VORACIOUS : voraz

ravine *n* : barranco *m*

ravishing *adj* : encantador

raw *adj* **rawer; rawest 1** UNCOOKED : crudo **2** INEXPERIENCED : inexperto **3** CHAFED : en carne viva **4** : frío y húmedo (dícese del tiempo) **5** ~ **deal** : trato *m* injusto **6** ~ **materials** : materias *fpl* primas

ray *n* : rayo *m*

rayon *n* : rayón *m*

raze *vt* **razed; razing** : arrasar

razor *n* : maquinilla *f* de afeitar — **razor blade** *n* : hoja *f* de afeitar

reach *vt* **1** : alcanzar **2** *or* ~ **out** : extender **3** : llegar a (un acuerdo, un límite, etc.) **4** CONTACT : contactar — *vi* **1** : extenderse **2** ~ **for** : tratar de agarrar — ~ *n* **1** : alcance *m* **2 within** ~ : al alcance

react *vi* : reaccionar — **reaction** *n* : reacción *f* — **reactionary** *adj* : reaccionario — ~ *n, pl* **-ries** : reaccionario *m*, -ria *f* — **reactor** *n* : reactor *m*

read *v* **read; reading** *vt* **1** : leer **2** INTERPRET : interpretar **3** SAY : decir **4** INDICATE : marcar — *vi* **1** : leer **2 it** ~**s as follows** : dice lo siguiente — **readable** *adj* : legible — **reader** *n* : lector *m*, -tora *f*

readily *adv* **1** WILLINGLY : de buena gana **2** EASILY : fácilmente

reading *n* : lectura *f*

readjust *vt* : reajustar — *vi* : volverse a adaptar

ready *adj* **readier; -est 1** : listo, preparado **2** WILLING : dispuesto **3** AVAILABLE : disponible **4 get** ~ : prepararse — ~ *vt* **readied; readying** : preparar

real *adj* **1** : verdadero, real **2** GENUINE : auténtico — ~ *adv* VERY : muy — **real estate** *n* : propiedad *f* inmobiliaria, bienes *mpl* raices — **realism** *n* : realismo *m* — **realist** *n* : realista *mf* — **realistic** *adj* : realista — **reality** *n, pl* **-ties** : realidad *f*

realize *vt* **-ized; -izing 1** : darse cuenta de **2** ACHIEVE : realizar — **realization** *n* **1** : comprensión *f* **2** FULFILLMENT : realización *f*

really *adv* : verdaderamente

realm *n* **1** KINGDOM : reino *m* **2** SPHERE : esfera *f*

ream *n* : resma *f* (de papel)

reap *v* : cosechar

reappear *vi* : reaparecer

rear¹ *vt* **1** RAISE : levantar **2** : criar (niños, etc.) — *vi or* ~ **up** : encabritarse

rear² *n* **1** BACK : parte *f* de atrás **2** BUTTOCKS : trasero *m fam* — ~ *adj* : trasero, posterior

rearrange *vt* **-ranged; -ranging** : reorganizar, cambiar
reason *n* : razón *f* — ~ *vt* THINK : pensar — *vi* : razonar — **reasonable** *adj* : razonable — **reasoning** *n* : razonamiento *m*
reassure *vt* **-sured; -suring** : tranquilizar — **reassurance** *n* : (palabras *fpl* de) consuelo *m*
rebate *n* : reembolso *m*
rebel *n* : rebelde *mf* — ~ *vi* **-belled; -belling** : rebelarse — **rebellion** *n* : rebelión *f* — **rebellious** *adj* : rebelde
rebirth *n* : renacimiento *m*
rebound *vi* : rebotar — ~ *n* : rebote *m*
rebuff *vt* : rechazar — ~ *n* : desaire *m*
rebuild *vt* **-built; -building** : reconstruir
rebuke *vt* **-buked; -buking** : reprender — ~ *n* : reprimenda *f*
rebut *vt* **-butted; -butting** : rebatir — **rebuttal** *n* : refutación *f*
recall *vt* **1** : llamar (al servicio, etc.) **2** REMEMBER : recordar **3** REVOKE : revocar — ~ *n* **1** : retirada *f* **2** MEMORY : memoria *f*
recant *vi* : retractarse
recapitulate *v* **-lated; -lating** : recapitular
recapture *vt* **-tured; -turing 1** : recobrar **2** RELIVE : revivir
recede *vi* **-ceded; -ceding** : retirarse
receipt *n* **1** : recibo *m* **2** ~s *npl* : ingresos *mpl*
receive *vt* **-ceived; -ceiving** : recibir — **receiver** *n* **1** : receptor *m* (de radio, etc.) **2** *or* **telephone** ~ : auricular *m*
recent *adj* : reciente — **recently** *adv* : recientemente
receptacle *n* : receptáculo *m*, recipiente *m*
reception *n* : recepción *f* — **receptionist** *n* : recepcionista *mf* — **receptive** *adj* : receptivo
recess *n* **1** ALCOVE : hueco *m* **2** : recreo *m* (escolar) **3** ADJOURNMENT : suspensión *f* de actividades *Spain*, receso *m* *Lat* — **recession** *n* : recesión *f*
recharge *vt* **-charged; -charging** : recargar — **rechargeable** *adj* : recargable
recipe *n* : receta *f*
recipient *n* : recipiente *mf*
reciprocal *adj* : recíproco
recite *vt* **-cited; -citing 1** : recitar (un poema, etc.) **2** LIST : enumerar — **recital** *n* : recital *n*
reckless *adj* : imprudente — **recklessness** *n* : imprudencia *f*
reckon *vt* **1** COMPUTE : calcular **2** CONSIDER : considerar — **reckoning** *n* : cálculos *mpl*
reclaim *vt* **1** : reclamar **2** RECOVER : recuperar
recline *vi* **-clined; -clining** : reclinarse — **re-**
clining *adj* : reclinable (dícese de un asiento, etc.)
recluse *n* : solitario *m*, -ria *f*
recognition *n* : reconocimiento *m* — **recognizable** *adj* : reconocible — **recognize** *vt* **-nized; -nizing** : reconocer
recoil *vi* : retroceder — ~ *n* : culatazo *m* (de un arma de fuego)
recollect *v* : recordar — **recollection** *n* : recuerdo *m*
recommend *vt* : recomendar — **recommendation** *n* : recomendación *f*
reconcile *v* **-ciled; -ciling** *vt* **1** : reconciliar (personas), conciliar (datos, etc.) **2** ~ **oneself to** : resignarse a — *vi* MAKE UP : reconciliarse — **reconciliation** *n* : reconciliación *f*
reconnaissance *n* : reconocimiento *m* (militar)
reconsider *vt* : reconsiderar
reconstruct *vt* : reconstruir
record *vt* **1** WRITE DOWN : anotar, apuntar **2** REGISTER : registrar **3** : grabar (música, etc.) — ~ *n* **1** DOCUMENT : documento *m* **2** REGISTER : registro *m* **3** HISTORY : historial *m* **4** : disco *m* (de música, etc.) **5** **criminal** ~ : antecedentes *mpl* penales **6** **world** ~ : récord *m* mundial — **recorder** *n* **1** : flauta *f* dulce **2** *or* **tape** ~ : grabadora *f* — **recording** *n* : disco *m* — **record player** *n* : tocadiscos *m*
recount¹ *vt* NARRATE : narrar, relatar
recount² *vt* : volver a contar (votos, etc.) — ~ *n* : recuento *m*
recourse *n* **1** : recurso *m* **2** **have** ~ **to** : recurrir a
recover *vt* : recobrar — *vi* RECUPERATE : recuperarse — **recovery** *n, pl* **-eries** : recuperación *f*
recreation *n* : recreo *m* — **recreational** *adj* : de recreo
recruit *vt* : reclutar — ~ *n* : recluta *mf* — **recruitment** *n* : reclutamiento *m*
rectangle *n* : rectángulo *m* — **rectangular** *adj* : rectangular
rectify *vt* **-fied; -fying** : rectificar
rector *n* **1** : parroco *m* (clérigo) **2** : rector *m*, -tora *f* (de una universidad) — **rectory** *n, pl* **-ries** : rectoría *f*
rectum *n, pl* **-tums** *or* **-ta** : recto *m*
recuperate *v* **-ated; -ating** *vt* : recuperar — *vi* : recuperarse — **recuperation** *n* : recuperación *f*
recur *vi* **-curred; -curring** : repetirse — **recurrence** *n* : repetición *f* — **recurrent** *adj* : que se repite
recycle *vt* **-cled; -cling** : reciclar
red *adj* : rojo — ~ *n* : rojo *m* — **redden** *vt*

redecorate

: enrojecer — *vi* : enrojecerse — **reddish** *adj* : rojizo
redecorate *vt* **-rated; -rating** : pintar de nuevo
redeem *vt* **1** SAVE : salvar, rescatar **2** : desempeñar (de un monte de piedad) **3** : canjear (cupones, etc.) — **redemption** *n* : redención *f*
red–handed *adv or adj* : con las manos en la masa
redhead *n* : pelirrojo *m*, -ja *f*
red–hot *adj* : al rojo vivo
redness *n* : rojez *f*
redo *vt* **-did; -done; -doing** : hacer de nuevo
redouble *vt* **-bled; -bling** : redoblar
red tape *n* : papeleo *m*
reduce *v* **-duced; -ducing** *vt* : reducir — *vi* SLIM : adelgazar — **reduction** *n* : reducción *f*
redundant *adj* : redundante
reed *n* **1** : caña *f* **2** : lengüeta *f* (de un instrumento)
reef *n* : arrecife *m*
reek *vi* : apestar
reel *n* : carrete *m* (de hilo, etc.) — ~ *vt* **1** ~ **in** : enrollar (un sedal), sacar (un pez) del agua **2** ~ **off** : enumerar — *vi* **1** SPIN : dar vueltas **2** STAGGER : tambalearse
reestablish *vt* : restablecer
refer *v* **-ferred; -ferring** *vt* **1** DIRECT : enviar, mandar **2** SUBMIT : remitir — *vi* **1** MENTION : referirse a **2** CONSULT : consultar
referee *n* : árbitro *m*, -tra *f* — ~ *v* **-eed; -eeing** : arbitrar
reference *n* **1** : referencia *f* **2** CONSULTATION : consulta *f* **3** *or* ~ **book** : libro *m* de consulta **4** **in** ~ **to** : con referencia a
refill *vt* : rellenar — ~ *n* : recambio *m*
refine *vt* **-fined; -fining** : refinar — **refined** *adj* : refinado — **refinement** *n* : refinamiento *m* — **refinery** *n*, *pl* **-eries** : refinería *f*
reflect *vt* : reflejar — *vi* **1** : reflejarse **2** ~ **badly on** : desacreditar **3** ~ **upon** : reflexionar sobre — **reflection** *n* **1** : reflexión *f* **2** IMAGE : reflejo *m* — **reflector** *n* : reflector *m*
reflex *n* : reflejo *m*
reflexive *adj* : reflexivo
reform *vt* : reformar — *vi* : reformarse — ~ *n* : reforma *f* — **reformer** *n* : reformador *m*, -dora *f*
refrain[1] *vi* ~ **from** : abstenerse de
refrain[2] *n* : estribillo *m* (en música)
refresh *vt* : refrescar — **refreshments** *npl* : refrigerio *m*
refrigerate *vt* **-ated; -ating** : refrigerar — **refrigeration** *n* : refrigeración *f* — **refrigera-**

tor *n* : nevera *f*, refrigerador *m* *Lat*, frigorífico *m* *Spain*
refuel *v* **-eled** *or* **-elled; -eling** *or* **-elling** *vt* : llenar de carburante — *vi* : repostar
refuge *n* : refugio *m* — **refugee** *n* : refugiado *m*, -da *f*
refund *vt* : reembolsar — ~ *n* : reembolso *m*
refurbish *vt* : renovar, restaurar
refuse[1] *v* **-fused; -fusing** *vt* **1** : rehusar, rechazar **2** ~ **to do sth** : negarse a hacer algo — *vi* : negarse — **refusal** *n* : negativa *f*
refuse[2] *n* : residuos *mpl*, desperdicios *mpl*
refute *vt* **-futed; -futing** : refutar
regain *vt* : recuperar, recobrar
regal *adj* : regio, majestuoso — **regalia** *n* : ropaje *m*, insignias *fpl*
regard *n* **1** : consideración *f* **2** ESTEEM : estima *f* **3** **in this** ~ : en este sentido **4** ~**s** *npl* : saludos *mpl* **5** **with** ~ **to** : respecto a — ~ *vt* **1** : mirar (con recelo, etc.) **2** HEED : tener en cuenta **3** ESTEEM : estimar **4** **as** ~**s** : en lo que se refiere a **5** ~ **as** : considerar — **regarding** *prep* : respecto a — **regardless** *adv* : a pesar de todo — **regardless of** *prep* **1** : sin tener en cuenta **2** IN SPITE OF : a pesar de
regent *n* : regente *mf*
regime *n* : régimen *m* — **regimen** *n* : régimen *m*
regiment *n* : regimiento *m*
region *n* : región *f* — **regional** *adj* : regional
register *n* : registro *m* — ~ *vt* **1** : registrar (a personas), matricular (vehículos) **2** SHOW : marcar, manifestar **3** : certificar (correo) — *vi* ENROLL : inscribirse, matricularse — **registrar** *n* : registrador *m*, -dora *f* oficial — **registration** *n* **1** : inscripción *f*, matriculación *f* **2** *or* ~ **number** : número *m* de matrícula — **registry** *n*, *pl* **-tries** : registro *m*
regret *vt* **-gretted; -gretting** : lamentar — ~ *n* **1** REMORSE : arrepentimiento *m* **2** SORROW : pesar *m* — **regrettable** *adj* : lamentable
regular *adj* **1** : regular **2** CUSTOMARY : habitual — ~ *n* : cliente *mf* habitual — **regularity** *n*, *pl* **-ties** : regularidad *f* — **regularly** *adv* : regularmente — **regulate** *vt* **-lated; -lating** : regular — **regulation** *n* **1** CONTROL : regulación *f* **2** RULE : regla *f*
rehabilitate *vt* **-tated; -tating** : rehabilitar — **rehabilitation** *n* : rehabilitación *f*
rehearse *v* **-hearsed; -hearsing** : ensayar — **rehearsal** *n* : ensayo *m*
reign *n* : reinado *m* — ~ *vi* : reinar
reimburse *vt* **-bursed; -bursing** : reembolsar — **reimbursement** *n* : reembolso *m*
rein *n* : rienda *f*

reincarnation n : reencarnación f
reindeer n : reno m
reinforce vt -forced; -forcing : reforzar —
  reinforcement n : refuerzo m
reinstate vt -stated; -stating 1 : restablecer
  2 : restituir (a algn en su cargo)
reiterate vt -ated; -ating : reiterar
reject vt : rechazar — **rejection** n : rechazo m
rejoice vi -joiced; -joicing : regocijarse
rejuvenate vt -nated; -nating : rejuvenecer
rekindle vt -dled; -dling : reavivar
relapse n : recaída f — ~ vi -lapsed; -laps-
  ing : recaer
relate v -lated; -lating vt 1 TELL : relatar 2
  ASSOCIATE : relacionar — vi ~ to 1 CON-
  CERN : estar relacionado con 2 UNDER-
  STAND : identificarse con 3 : relacionarse
  con (socialmente) — **related** adj ~ to
  : emparentado con — **relation** n 1 CONNEC-
  TION : relación f 2 RELATIVE : pariente mf 3
  in ~ to : en relación con 4 ~s npl : relaciones fpl — **relationship** n 1 : relación f 2
  KINSHIP : parentesco m — **relative** n : pariente mf — ~ adj : relativo — **relatively**
  adv : relativamente
relax vt : relajar — vi : relajarse — **relaxation** n 1 : relajación f 2 RECREATION : es-
  parcimiento m
relay n 1 : relevo m 2 or ~ race : carrera f
  de relevos — ~ vt -layed; -laying : transmitir
release vt -leased; -leasing 1 FREE : liberar,
  poner en libertad 2 : soltar (un freno, etc.) 3
  EMIT : despedir 4 : sacar (un libro, etc.), estrenar (una película) — ~ n 1 : liberación f
  2 : estreno m (de una película), publicación f
  (de un libro) 3 : fuga f (de gases)
relegate vt -gated; -gating : relegar
relent vi : ceder — **relentless** adj : implacable
relevant adj : pertinente — **relevance** n
  : pertinencia f
reliable adj : fiable (dícese de personas),
  fidedigno (dícese de información, etc.) —
  reliability n, pl -ties : fiabilidad f (de una
  cosa), responsabilidad f (de una persona) —
  reliance n 1 : dependencia f 2 TRUST
  : confianza f — **reliant** adj : dependiente
relic n : reliquia f
relief n 1 : alivio m 2 AID : ayuda f 3 : relieve m (en la escultura) 4 REPLACEMENT
  : relevo m — **relieve** vt -lieved; -lieving 1
  : aliviar 2 REPLACE : relevar (a algn) 3 ~
  s.o. of : liberar a algn de
religion n : religión f — **religious** adj : religioso
relinquish vt : renunciar a, abandonar
relish n 1 : salsa f (condimento) 2 with ~
  : con gusto — ~ vt : saborear

relocate vt -cated; -cating : trasladar — vi
  : trasladarse — **relocation** n : traslado m
reluctance n : reticencia f, desgana f — re-
  luctant adj : reacio, reticente — **reluctantly**
  adv : a regañadientes
rely vi -lied; -lying ~ on 1 DEPEND ON
  : depender de 2 TRUST : confiar (en)
remain vi 1 : quedar 2 STAY : quedarse 3
  CONTINUE : seguir, continuar — **remainder**
  n : resto m — **remains** npl : restos mpl
remark n : comentario m, observación f —
  ~ vt : observar — vi ~ on : observar —
  remarkable adj : extraordinario, notable
remedy n, pl -dies : remedio m — ~ vt
  -died; -dying : remediar — **remedial** adj
  : correctivo
remember vt 1 : acordarse de, recordar 2
  ~ to : acordarse de — vi : acordarse, recordar — **remembrance** n : recuerdo m
remind vt : recordar — **reminder** n : recordatorio m
reminiscence n : recuerdo m, reminiscencia
  f — **reminisce** vi -nisced; -niscing : rememorar los viejos tiempos — **reminiscent**
  adj be ~ of : recordar
remiss adj : negligente, remiso
remit vt -mitted; -mitting 1 PARDON : perdonar 2 : enviar (dinero) — **remission** n
  : remisión f
remnant n 1 : resto m 2 TRACE : vestigio m
remorse n : remordimiento m — **remorse-
  ful** adj : arrepentido
remote adj -moter; -est 1 : remoto 2
  ALOOF : distante 3 ~ from : apartado de,
  alejado de — **remote control** n : control m
  remoto — **remotely** adv SLIGHTLY : remotamente
remove vt -moved; -moving 1 : quitar (una
  tapa, etc.), quitarse (ropa) 2 EXTRACT
  : sacar 3 DISMISS : destituir 4 ELIMINATE
  : eliminar — **removable** adj : separable, de
  quita y pon — **removal** n 1 : eliminación f
  2 EXTRACTION : extracción f
remunerate vt -ated; -ating : remunerar
render vt 1 : rendir (homenaje), prestar
  (ayuda) 2 MAKE : hacer 3 TRANSLATE : traducir
rendezvous ns & pl : cita f
rendition n : interpretación f
renegade n : renegado m, -da f
renew vt 1 : renovar 2 RESUME : reanudar
  — **renewal** n : renovación f
renounce vt -nounced; -nouncing : renunciar a
renovate vt -vated; -vating : renovar — **renovation** n : renovación f
renown n : renombre m — **renowned** adj
  : célebre, renombrado
rent n 1 : alquiler m, arrendamiento m, renta

f **2 for** ~ : se alquila — ~ *vt* : alquilar —
rental *n* : alquiler *m* — ~ *adj* : de alquiler
— **renter** *n* : arrendatario *m*, -ria *f*
renunciation *n* : renuncia *f*
reopen *vt* : volver a abrir
reorganize *vt* **-nized; -nizing** : reorganizar
— **reorganization** *n* : reorganización *f*
repair *vt* : reparar, arreglar — ~ *n* **1**
: reparación *f*, arreglo *m* **2 in bad** ~ : en
mal estado
repay *vt* **-paid; -paying 1** : devolver
(dinero), pagar (una deuda) **2** : corresponder a (un favor, etc.)
repeal *vt* : abrogar, revocar — ~ *n* : abro-
gación *f*, revocación *f*
repeat *vt* : repetir — ~ *n* : repetición *f* — **repeatedly** *adv* : repetidas veces
repel *vt* **-pelled; -pelling** : repeler — **repellent** *n* : repelente *m*
repent *vi* : arrepentirse — **repentance** *n* : arrepentimiento *m*
repercussion *n* : repercusión *f*
repertoire *n* : repertorio *m*
repetition *n* : repetición *f* — **repetitious** *adj*
: repetitivo — **repetitive** *adj* : repetitivo
replace *vt* **-placed; -placing 1** : reponer **2**
SUBSTITUTE : reemplazar, sustituir **3** EX-
CHANGE : cambiar — **replacement** *n* **1**
: sustitución *f* **2** : sustituto *m*, -ta *f* (persona)
3 *or* ~ **part** : repuesto *m*
replenish *vt* **1** : reponer **2** REFILL : rellenar
replete *adj* ~ **with** : repleto de
replica *n* : réplica *f*
reply *vi* **-plied; -plying** : contestar, responder — ~ *n, pl* **-plies** : respuesta *f*
report *n* **1** : informe *m* **2** RUMOR : rumor *m*
3 *or* **news** ~ : reportaje *m* **4 weather** ~
: boletín *m* meteorológico — ~ *vt* **1** RE-
LATE : anunciar **2** ~ **a crime** : denunciar
un delito **3** *or* ~ **on** : informar sobre — *vi*
1 : informar **2** ~ **for duty** : presentarse —
report card *n* : boletín *m* de calificaciones
— **reportedly** *adv* : según se dice — **reporter** *n* : periodista *mf*; reportero *m*, -ra *f*
repose *vi* **-posed; -posing** : reposar — ~ *n*
: reposo *m*
reprehensible *adj* : reprensible
represent *vt* **1** : representar **2** PORTRAY
: presentar — **representation** *n* : representación *f* — **representative** *adj* : representativo — ~ *n* : representante *mf*
repress *vt* : reprimir — **repression** *n*
: represión *f*
reprieve *n* : indulto *m*
reprimand *n* : reprimenda *f* — ~ *vt*
: reprender
reprint *vt* : reimprimir — ~ *n* : reedición *f*
reprisal *n* : represalia *f*
reproach *n* **1** : reproche *m* **2 beyond** ~

: irreprochable — ~ *vt* : reprochar — **re-
proachful** *adj* : de reproche
reproduce *v* **-duced; -ducing** *vt* : reproducir — *vi* : reproducirse — **reproduction** *n*
: reproducción *f* — **reproductive** *adj* : reproductor
reproof *n* : reprobación *f*
reptile *n* : reptil *m*
republic *n* : república *f* — **republican** *n* : republicano *m*, -na *f* — ~ *adj* : republicano
repudiate *vt* **-ated; -ating** : repudiar
repugnant *adj* : repugnante, asqueroso —
repugnance *n* : repugnancia *f*
repulse *vt* **-pulsed; -pulsing** : repeler, rechazar — **repulsive** *adj* : repulsivo
reputation *n* : reputación *f* — **reputable** *adj*
: de confianza, acreditado — **reputed** *adj*
: supuesto
request *n* : petición *f* — ~ *vt* : pedir
requiem *n* : réquiem *m*
require *vt* **-quired; -quiring 1** CALL FOR
: requerir **2** NEED : necesitar — **requirement** *n* **1** NEED : necesidad *f* **2** DEMAND
: requisito *m* — **requisite** *adj* : necesario
resale *n* : reventa *f*
rescind *vt* : rescindir (un contrato), revocar
(una ley, etc.)
rescue *vt* **-cued; -cuing** : rescatar, salvar —
~ *n* : rescate *m* — **rescuer** *n* : salvador *m*,
-dora *f*
research *n* : investigación *f* — ~ *vt* : investigar — **researcher** *n* : investigador *m*,
-dora *f*
resemble *vt* **-sembled; -sembling** : parecerse a — **resemblance** *n* : parecido *m*
resent *vt* : resentirse de, ofenderse por — **resentful** *adj* : resentido — **resentment** *n*
: resentimiento *m*
reserve *vt* **-served; -serving** : reservar —
~ *n* **1** : reserva *f* **2** ~ **s** *npl* : reservas *fpl*
(militares) — **reservation** *n* : reserva *f* —
reserved *adj* : reservado — **reservoir** *n*
: embalse *m*
reset *vt* **-set; -setting** : volver a poner (un
reloj, etc.)
residence *n* : residencia *f* — **reside** *vi*
-sided; -siding : residir — **resident** *adj*
: residente — ~ *n* : residente *mf* — **residential** *adj* : residencial
residue *n* : residuo *m*
resign *vt* **1** QUIT : dimitir **2** ~ **oneself to**
: resignarse a — **resignation** *n* **1** : dimisión
f **2** ACCEPTANCE : resignación *f*
resilient *adj* **1** : resistente (dícese de personas) **2** ELASTIC : elástico — **resilience** *n*
1 : resistencia *f* **2** ELASTICITY : elasticidad *f*
resin *n* : resina *f*
resist *vt* : resistir — *vi* : resistirse — **resist-**

ance *n* : resistencia *f* — **resistant** *adj* : resistente
resolve *vt* **-solved; -solving** : resolver — ∼ *n* : resolución *f* — **resolution** *n* 1 : resolución *f* 2 DECISION, INTENTION : propósito *m* — **resolute** *adj* : resuelto
resonance *n* : resonancia *f* — **resonant** *adj* : resonante
resort *n* 1 RECOURSE : recurso *m* 2 *or* **tourist** ∼ : centro *m* turístico — ∼ *vi* ∼ **to** : recurrir a
resounding *adj* 1 RESONANT : resonante 2 ABSOLUTE : rotundo
resource *n* : recurso *m* — **resourceful** *adj* : ingenioso
respect *n* 1 ESTEEM : respeto *m* 2 **in some** ∼**s** : en algún sentido 3 **pay one's** ∼**s** : presentar uno sus respetos 4 **with** ∼ **to** : (con) respecto a — *vt* : respetar — **respectable** *adj* : respetable — **respectful** *adj* : respetuoso — **respective** *adj* : respectivo — **respectively** *adv* : respectivamente
respiration *n* : respiración *f* — **respiratory** *adj* : respiratorio
respite *n* : respiro *m*
response *n* : respuesta *f* — **respond** *vi* : responder — **responsibility** *n, pl* **-ties** : responsabilidad *f* — **responsible** *adj* : responsable — **responsive** *adj* : sensible, receptivo
rest[1] *n* 1 : descanso *m* 2 SUPPORT : apoyo *m* 3 : silencio *m* (en música) — ∼ *vi* 1 : descansar 2 LEAN : apoyarse 3 ∼ **on** DEPEND ON : depender de — *vt* 1 RELAX : descansar 2 LEAN : apoyar
rest[2] *n* REMAINDER : resto *m*
restaurant *n* : restaurante *m*
restful *adj* : tranquilo, apacible
restitution *n* : restitución *f*
restless *adj* : inquieto, agitado
restore *vt* **-stored; -storing** 1 RETURN : devolver 2 REESTABLISH : restablecer 3 REPAIR : restaurar — **restoration** *n* 1 : restablecimiento *m* 2 REPAIR : restauración *f*
restrain *vt* 1 : contener 2 ∼ **oneself** : contenerse — **restrained** *adj* : comedido, moderado — **restraint** *n* 1 : restricción *f* 2 SELF-CONTROL : moderación *f*, control *m* de sí mismo
restriction *n* : restricción *f* — **restrict** *vt* : restringir — **restricted** *adj* : restringido — **restrictive** *adj* : restrictivo
result *vi* : resultar — ∼ *n* 1 : resultado *m* 2 **as a** ∼ **of** : como consecuencia de
resume *v* **-sumed; -suming** *vt* : reanudar — *vi* : reanudarse
résumé *or* **resume** *or* **resumé** *n* : currículum *m* (vitae)
resumption *n* : reanudación *f*

resurgence *n* : resurgimiento *m*
resurrection *n* : resurrección *f* — **resurrect** *vt* : resucitar
resuscitate *vt* **-tated; -tating** : resucitar
retail *vt* : vender al por menor — ∼ *n* : venta *f* al por menor — ∼ *adj* : detallista, minorista — ∼ *adv* : al detalle, al por menor — **retailer** *n* : detallista *mf*, minorista *mf*
retain *vt* : retener
retaliate *vi* **-ated; -ating** : tomar represalias — **retaliation** *n* : represalias *fpl*
retard *vt* : retardar, retrasar — **retarded** *adj* : retrasado
retention *n* : retención *f*
reticence *n* : reticencia *f* — **reticent** *adj* : reticente
retina *n, pl* **-nas** *or* **-nae** : retina *f*
retinue *n* : séquito *m*
retire *vi* **-tired; -tiring** 1 WITHDRAW : retirarse 2 : jubilarse, retirarse (de un trabajo) 3 : acostarse (en la cama) — **retirement** *n* : jubilación *f* — **retiring** *adj* SHY : retraído
retort *vt* : replicar — ∼ *n* : réplica *f*
retrace *vt* **-traced; -tracing** ∼ **one's steps** : volver sobre sus pasos
retract *vt* 1 WITHDRAW : retirar 2 : retraer (garras, etc.) — *vi* : retractarse
retrain *vt* : reciclar
retreat *n* 1 : retirada *f* 2 REFUGE : refugio *m* — ∼ *vi* : retirarse
retribution *n* : castigo *m*
retrieve *vt* **-trieved; -trieving** 1 : cobrar, recuperar 2 RESCUE : salvar — **retrieval** *n* : recuperación *f* — **retriever** *n* : perro *m* cobrador
retroactive *adj* : retroactivo
retrospect *n* **in** ∼ : mirando hacia atrás — **retrospective** *adj* : retrospectivo
return *vi* 1 : volver, regresar 2 REAPPEAR : reaparecer — *vt* 1 : devolver 2 YIELD : producir — ∼ *n* 1 : regreso *m*, vuelta *f* 2 : devolución *f* (de algo prestado) 3 YIELD : rendimiento *m* 4 **in** ∼ **for** : a cambio de 5 *or* **tax** ∼ : declaración *f* de impuestos — ∼ *adj* : de vuelta
reunite *vt* **-nited; -niting** : reunir — **reunion** *n* : reunión *f*
revamp *vt* : renovar
reveal *vt* 1 : revelar 2 SHOW : dejar ver
revel *vi* **-eled** *or* **-elled; -eling** *or* **-elling** ∼ **in** : deleitarse en
revelation *n* : revelación *f*
revelry *n, pl* **-ries** : jolgorio *m*, regocijos *mpl*
revenge *vt* **-venged; -venging** : vengar — ∼ *n* 1 : venganza *f* 2 **take** ∼ **on** : vengarse de
revenue *n* : ingresos *mpl*
reverberate *vi* **-ated; -ating** : retumbar, resonar

reverence *n* : reverencia *f*, veneración *f* —
revere *vt* **-vered; -vering** : venerar — **reverend** *adj* : reverendo — **reverent** *adj* : reverente
reverie *n, pl* **-eries** : ensueño *m*
reverse *adj* : inverso, contrario — ~ *v*
-versed; -versing *vt* **1** : invertir **2** : cambiar (una política), revocar (una decisión) **3**
: dar marcha atrás a (un automóvil) — *vi*
: invertirse — ~ *n* **1** BACK : dorso *m*, revés
m **2** *or* ~ **gear** : marcha *f* atrás **3 the** ~
: lo contrario — **reversible** *adj* : reversible
— **reversal** *n* **1** : inversión *f* **2** CHANGE
: cambio *m* total **3** SETBACK : revés *m* — **revert** *vi* : revertir
review *n* **1** : revisión *f* **2** OVERVIEW : resumen *m* **3** CRITIQUE : reseña *f*, crítica *f* **4**
: repaso *m* (para un examen) — ~ *vt* **1** EXAMINE : examinar **2** : repasar (una lección)
3 CRITIQUE : reseñar — **reviewer** *n* : crítico
m, -ca *f*
revile *vt* **-viled; -viling** : injuriar
revise *vt* **-vised; -vising 1** : modificar (una política, etc.) **2** : revisar, corregir (una publicación) — **revision** *n* : corrección *f*, modificación *f*
revive *v* **-vived; -viving** *vt* **1** : reanimar, reactivar **2** : resucitar (a una persona) **3** RESTORE : restablecer — *vi* **1** : reanimarse, reactivarse **2** COME TO : volver en sí —
revival *n* : reanimación *f*, reactivación *f*
revoke *vt* **-voked; -voking** : revocar
revolt *vi* : rebelarse, sublevarse — *vt* : dar
asco a — ~ *n* : revuelta *f*, sublevación *f* —
revolting *adj* : asqueroso
revolution *n* : revolución *f* — **revolutionary**
adj : revolucionario — ~ *n, pl* **-aries** : revolucionario *m*, -ria *f* — **revolutionize** *vt*
-ized; -izing : revolucionar
revolve *v* **-volved; -volving** *vt* : hacer girar
— *vi* : girar
revolver *n* : revólver *m*
revue *n* : revista *f* (teatral)
revulsion *n* : repugnancia *f*
reward *vt* : recompensar — ~ *n* : recompensa *f*
rewrite *vt* **-wrote; -written; -writing** : volver
a escribir
rhetoric *n* : retórica *f* — **rhetorical** *adj*
: retórico
rheumatism *n* : reumatismo *m* — **rheumatic** *adj* : reumático
rhino *n, pl* **-no** *or* **-nos** → **rhinoceros** — **rhinoceros** *n, pl* **-noceroses** *or* **-noceros** *or*
-noceri : rinoceronte *m*
rhubarb *n* : ruibarbo *m*
rhyme *n* **1** : rima *f* **2** VERSE : verso *m* (en
rima) — ~ *vi* **rhymed; rhyming** : rimar

rhythm *n* : ritmo *m* — **rhythmic** *or* **rhythmical** *adj* : rítmico
rib *n* : costilla *f* — ~ *vt* TEASE : tomar el
pelo a
ribbon *n* : cinta *f*
rice *n* : arroz *m*
rich *adj* **1** : rico **2** ~ **foods** : comidas *fpl*
pesadas — **riches** *npl* : riquezas *fpl* — **richness** *n* : riqueza *f*
rickety *adj* : desvencijado, destartalado
ricochet *n* : rebote *m* — ~ *vi* **-cheted** *or*
-chetted; -cheting *or* **-chetting** : rebotar
rid *vt* **rid; ridding 1** : librar **2 get** ~ **of** : deshacerse de — **riddance** *n* **good** ~!
: ¡adiós y buen viaje!
riddle[1] *n* : acertijo *m*, adivinanza *f*
riddle[2] *vt* **-dled; -dling 1** : acribillar **2 riddled with** : lleno de
ride *v* **rode; ridden; riding** *vt* **1** : montar (a
caballo, en bicicleta), ir (en autobús, etc.) **2**
TRAVERSE : recorrer — *vi* **1** *or* ~ **horseback** : montar a caballo **2** : ir (en auto, etc.)
— ~ *n* **1** : paseo *m*, vuelta *f* **2** : aparato *m*
(en un parque de diversiones) — **rider** *n* **1**
: jinete *mf* (a caballo) **2** CYCLIST : ciclista
mf, motociclista *mf*
ridge *n* : cadena *f* (de montañas)
ridiculous *adj* : ridículo — **ridicule** *n* : burlas *fpl* — ~ *vt* **-culed; -culing** : ridiculizar
rife *adj* **1** : extendido **2 be** ~ **with** : estar
plagado de
rifle[1] *vi* **-fled; -fling** ~ **through** : revolver
rifle[2] *n* : rifle *m*, fusil *m*
rift *n* **1** : grieta *f* **2** : ruptura *f* (entre personas)
rig[1] *vt* : amañar (una elección)
rig[2] *vt* **rigged; rigging 1** : aparejar (un
barco) **2** EQUIP : equipar **3** *or* ~ **out**
DRESS : vestir **4** *or* ~ **up** CONSTRUCT
: construir — ~ *n* **1** : aparejo *m* (de un
barco) **2** *or* **oil** ~ : plataforma *f* petrolífera
— **rigging** *n* : aparejo *m*
right *adj* **1** JUST : bueno, justo **2** CORRECT
: correcto **3** APPROPRIATE : apropiado, adecuado **4** STRAIGHT : recto **5 be** ~ : tener
razón **6** → **right–hand** — ~ *n* **1** GOOD
: bien *m* **2** ENTITLEMENT : derecho *m* **3 on
the** ~ : a la derecha **4** *or* ~ **side** : derecha
f — ~ *adv* **1** WELL : bien **2** PRECISELY
: justo **3** DIRECTLY : derecho **4** IMMEDIATELY : inmediatamente **5** COMPLETELY
: completamente **6** *or* **to the** ~ : a la
derecha — ~ *vt* **1** STRAIGHTEN : enderezar
2 ~ **a wrong** : reparar un daño — **right
angle** *n* : ángulo *m* recto — **righteous** *adj*
: recto, honrado — **rightful** *adj* : legítimo —
right–hand *adj* : derecho — **right–handed**
adj : diestro — **rightly** *adv* **1** : justamente **2**
CORRECTLY : correctamente — **right–wing**
adj : derechista

rigid *adj* : rígido
rigor *or Brit* **rigour** *n* : rigor *m* — **rigorous** *adj* : riguroso
rim *n* **1** EDGE : borde *m* **2** : llanta *f* (de una rueda) **3** : montura *f* (de anteojos)
rind *n* : corteza *f*
ring[1] *v* **rang; rung; ringing** *vi* **1** : sonar (dícese de un timbre, etc.) **2** RESOUND : resonar — *vt* : tocar (un timbre, etc.) — ~ *n* **1** : toque *m* (de un timbre, etc.) **2** CALL : llamada *f* (por teléfono)
ring[2] *n* **1** : anillo *m*, sortija *f* **2** BAND, HOOP : aro *m* **3** CIRCLE : círculo *m* **4** *or* **boxing** ~ : cuadrilátero *m* **5** NETWORK : red *f* — ~ *vt* : cercar, rodear — **ringleader** *n* : cabecilla *mf*
ringlet *n* : rizo *m*, bucle *m*
rink *n* : pista *f* (de patinaje)
rinse *vt* **rinsed; rinsing** : enjuagar — ~ *n* : enjuague *m*
riot *n* : disturbio *m* — ~ *vi* : causar disturbios — **rioter** *n* : alborotador *m*, -dora *f*
rip *v* **ripped; ripping** *vt* **1** : rasgar, desgarrar **2** ~ **off** : arrancar — *vi* : rasgarse — ~ *n* : rasgón *m*, desgarrón *m*
ripe *adj* **riper; ripest** **1** : maduro **2** ~ **for** : listo por — **ripen** *v* : madurar — **ripeness** *n* : madurez *f*
rip-off *n* : timo *m fam*
ripple *v* **-pled; -pling** *vi* : rizarse (dícese de agua) — *vt* : rizar — ~ *n* : onda *f*, rizo *m*
rise *vi* **rose; risen; rising** **1** GET UP : levantarse **2** : salir (dícese del sol, etc.) **3** ASCEND : subir **4** INCREASE : aumentar **5** ~ **up** REBEL : sublevarse — ~ *n* **1** ASCENT : subida *f* **2** INCREASE : aumento *m* **3** SLOPE : cuesta *f* — **riser** *n* **1** **early** ~ : madrugador *m*, -dora *f* **2** **late** ~ : dormilón *m*, -lona *f*
risk *n* : riesgo *m* — ~ *vt* : arriesgar — **risky** *adj* **riskier; -est** : arriesgado, riesgoso *Lat*
rite *n* : rito *m* — **ritual** *adj* : ritual — ~ *n* : ritual *m*
rival *n* : rival *mf* — ~ *adj* : rival — ~ *vt* **-valed** *or* **-valled; -valing** *or* **-valling** : rivalizar con — **rivalry** *n*, *pl* **-ries** : rivalidad *f*
river *n* : río *m*
rivet *n* : remache *m* — ~ *vt* **1** : remachar **2** FIX : fijar (los ojos, etc.) **3** **be** ~**ed by** : estar fascinado con
roach → **cockroach**
road *n* **1** : carretera *f* **2** STREET : calle *f* **3** PATH : camino *m* — **roadblock** *n* : control *m* — **roadside** *n* : borde *m* de la carretera — **roadway** *n* : carretera *f*
roam *vi* : vagar — *vt* : vagar por
roar *vi* **1** : rugir **2** ~ **with laughter** : reírse a carcajadas — *vt* : decir a gritos — ~ *n* : rugido *m* (de un animal), estruendo *m* (de un avión, etc.)

roast *vt* : asar (carne, etc.), tostar (café, etc.) — *vi* : asarse — ~ *n* : asado *m* — ~ *adj* : asado — **roast beef** *n* : rosbif *m*
rob *v* **robbed; robbing** *vt* **1** : robar **2** ~ **of** : privar de — *vi* : robar — **robber** *n* : ladrón *m*, -drona *f* — **robbery** *n*, *pl* **-beries** : robo *m*
robe *n* **1** : toga *f* (de un magistrado, etc.) **2** → **bathrobe**
robin *n* : petirrojo *m*
robot *n* : robot *m*
robust *adj* : robusto
rock[1] *vt* **1** : acunar (a un niño), mecer (una cuna) **2** SHAKE : sacudir — *vi* : mecerse — ~ *n or* **music** : música *f* rock
rock[2] *n* **1** : roca *f* (sustancia) **2** BOULDER : peña *f*, peñasco *m* **3** STONE : piedra *f*
rocket *n* : cohete *m*
rocking chair *n* : mecedora *f*
rocky *adj* **rockier; -est** **1** : rocoso **2** SHAKY : tambaleante
rod *n* **1** : varilla *f* **2** *or* **fishing** ~ : caña *f* de pescar
rode → **ride**
rodent *n* : roedor *m*
rodeo *n*, *pl* **-deos** : rodeo *m*
roe *n* : hueva *f*
rogue *n* : pícaro *m*, -ra *f*
role *n* : papel *m*
roll *n* **1** : rollo *m* (de película, etc.) **2** LIST : lista *f* **3** : redoble *m* (de un tambor) **4** SWAYING : balanceo *m* **5** BUN : pancito *m Lat*, panecillo *m Spain* — ~ *vt* **1** : hacer rodar **2** *or* ~ **out** : estirar (masa) **3** ~ **up** : enrollar (papel, etc.), arremangar (una manga) — *vi* **1** : rodar **2** SWAY : balancearse **3** ~ **around** : revolcarse **4** ~ **over** : darse la vuelta — **roller** *n* **1** : rodillo *m* **2** CURLER : rulo *m* — **roller coaster** *n* : montaña *f* rusa — **roller-skate** *vi* **-skated; -skating** : patinar (sobre ruedas) — **roller skate** *n* : patín *m* (de ruedas)
Roman *adj* : romano — **Roman Catholic** *adj* : católico
romance *n* **1** : novela *f* romántica **2** AFFAIR : romance *m*
Romanian *adj* : rumano — ~ *n* : rumano *m* (idioma)
romantic *adj* : romántico
romp *n* : retozo *m* — ~ *vi* : retozar
roof *n*, *pl* **roofs** **1** : tejado *m*, techo *m* **2** ~ **of the mouth** : paladar *m* — **roofing** *n* : techumbre *f* — **rooftop** *n* : tejado *m*, techo *m*
rook[1] *n* : grajo *m* (ave)
rook[2] *n* : torre *f* (en ajedrez)
rookie *n* : novato *m*, -ta *f*
room *n* **1** : cuarto *m*, habitación *f* **2** BEDROOM : dormitorio *m* **3** SPACE : espacio *m* **4**

OPPORTUNITY : posibilidad *f* — **roommate** *n* : compañero *m*, -ra *f* de cuarto — **roomy** *adj* **roomier; -est** : espacioso

roost *n* : percha *f* — ~ *vi* : posarse — **rooster** *n* : gallo *m*

root¹ *n* : raíz *f* — ~ *vt* ~ **out** : extirpar

root² *vi* ~ **around in** : hurgar en

root³ *vi* ~ **for** SUPPORT : alentar

rope *n* : cuerda *f* — ~ *vt* **roped; roping 1** : atar (con cuerda) **2** ~ **off** : acordonar

rosary *n*, *pl* **-ries** : rosario *m*

rose¹ → **rise**

rose² *n* : rosa *f* (flor), rosa *m* (color) — ~ *adj* : rosa — **rosebush** *n* : rosal *m*

rosemary *n*, *pl* **-maries** : romero *m*

Rosh Hashanah *n* : el Año Nuevo judío

roster *n* : lista *f*

rostrum *n*, *pl* **-tra** *or* **-trums** : tribuna *f*

rosy *adj* **rosier; -est 1** : sonrosado **2** PROMISING : halagüeno

rot *v* **rotted; rotting** *vi* : pudrirse — *vt* : pudrir — ~ *n* : putrefacción *f*

rotary *adj* : rotativo — ~ *n* : rotonda *f*, glorieta *f Spain*

rotate *v* **-tated; -tating** *vi* : girar — *vt* **1** : girar **2** ALTERNATE : alternar — **rotation** *n* : rotación *f*

rote *n* **by** ~ : de memoria

rotor *n* : rotor *m*

rotten *adj* **1** : podrido **2** BAD : malo

rouge *n* : colorete *m*

rough *adj* **1** COARSE : áspero **2** RUGGED : accidentado **3** CHOPPY : agitado **4** DIFFICULT : duro **5** FORCEFUL : brusco **6** APPROXIMATE : aproximado **7** UNREFINED : tosco **8** ~ **draft** : borrador *m* — ~ *vt* **1** → **roughen 2** ~ **up** BEAT : dar una paliza a — **roughage** *n* : fibra *f* — **roughen** *vt* : poner áspero — *vi* : ponerse áspero — **roughly** *adv* **1** : bruscamente **2** ABOUT : aproximadamente — **roughness** *n* COARSENESS : aspereza *f*

roulette *n* : ruleta *f*

round *adj* : redondo — ~ *adv* → **around** — ~ *n* **1** : círculo *m* **2** : ronda *f* (de bebidas, negociaciones, etc.) **3** : asalto *m* (en boxeo), vuelta *f* (en juegos) **4** ~ **of applause** : aplauso *m* **5** ~**s** *npl* : visitas *fpl* (de un médico), rondas *fpl* (de un policía, etc.) — ~ *vt* **1** TURN : doblar **2** ~ **off** : redondear **3** ~ **off** *or* ~ **out** COMPLETE : rematar **4** ~ **up** GATHER : reunir (personas), rodear (ganado) — ~ *prep* → **around** — **roundabout** *adj* : indirecto — **round–trip** *n* : viaje *m* de ida y vuelta — **roundup** *n* : rodeo *m* (de animales), redada *f* (de delincuentes, etc.)

rouse *vt* **roused; rousing 1** AWAKEN : despertar **2** EXCITE : excitar

rout *n* : derrota *f* aplastante — ~ *vt* : derrotar

route *n* **1** : ruta *f* **2** *or* **delivery** ~ : recorrido *m*

routine *n* : rutina *f* — ~ *adj* : rutinario

rove *v* **roved; roving** *vi* : errar, vagar — *vt* : errar por

row¹ *vt* **1** : llevar a remo **2** ~ **a boat** : remar — *vi* : remar

row² *n* **1** : fila *f* (de gente o asientos), hilera *f* (de casas, etc.) **2 in a** ~ SUCCESSIVELY : seguido

row³ *n* **1** RACKET : bulla *f* **2** QUARREL : pelea *f*

rowboat *n* : bote *m* de remos

rowdy *adj* **-dier; -est** : escandaloso, alborotador — ~ *n*, *pl* **-dies** : alborotador *m*, -dora *f*

royal *adj* : real — **royalty** *n*, *pl* **-ties 1** : realeza *f* **2 royalties** *npl* : derechos *mpl* de autor

rub *v* **rubbed; rubbing** *vt* **1** : frotar **2** CHAFE : rozar **3** ~ **in** : aplicar frotando — *vi* **1** ~ **against** : rozar **2** ~ **off** : salir (al frotar) — ~ *n* : frotamiento *m*

rubber *n* **1** : goma *f*, caucho *m* **2** ~**s** *npl* : chanclos *mpl* — **rubber band** *n* : goma *f* (elástica) — **rubber stamp** *n* : sello *m* (de goma) — **rubbery** *adj* : gomoso

rubbish *n* **1** : basura *f* **2** NONSENSE : tonterías *fpl*

rubble *n* : escombros *mpl*

ruby *n*, *pl* **-bies** : rubí *m*

rudder *n* : timón *m*

ruddy *adj* **-dier; -est** : rubicundo

rude *adj* **ruder; rudest 1** IMPOLITE : grosero, mal educado **2** ABRUPT : brusco — **rudely** *adv* : groseramente — **rudeness** *n* : mala educación *f*

rudiment *n* : rudimento *m* — **rudimentary** *adj* : rudimentario

rue *vt* **rued; ruing** : lamentar — **rueful** *adj* : triste, arrepentido

ruffle *vt* **-fled; -fling 1** : despeinar (pelo), erizar (plumas) **2** VEX : alterar, contrariar — ~ *n* : volante *m* (de un vestido, etc.)

rug *n* : alfombra *f*, tapete *m*

rugged *adj* **1** : escabroso (dícese del terreno), escarpado (dícese de montañas) **2** HARSH : duro **3** STURDY : fuerte

ruin *n* : ruina *f* — ~ *vt* : arruinar

rule *n* **1** : regla *f* **2** CONTROL : dominio *m* **3 as a** ~ : por lo general — ~ *v* **ruled; ruling** *vt* **1** GOVERN : gobernar **2** : fallar (dícese de un juez) **3** ~ **out** : descartar — *vi* : gobernar, reinar — **ruler** *n* **1** : gobernante *mf*; soberano *m*, -na *f* **2** : regla *f* (para medir) — **ruling** *n* VERDICT : fallo *m*

rum *n* : ron *m*

Rumanian → **Romanian**

rumble *vi* **-bled; -bling 1** : retumbar **2** : hacer ruidos (dícese del estómago) — ∼ *n* : retumbo *m*, estruendo *m*

rummage *vi* **-maged; -maging** : hurgar

rumor *n* : rumor *m* — ∼ *vt* **be** ∼**ed** : rumorearse

rump *n* **1** : grupa *f* (de un animal) **2** ∼ **steak** : filete *m* de cadera

rumpus *n* : lío *m*, jaleo *m fam*

run *v* **ran; run; running** *vi* **1** : correr **2** FUNCTION : funcionar **3** LAST : durar **4** : desteñir (dícese de colores) **5** EXTEND : correr, extenderse **6** : presentarse (como candidato) **7** ∼ **away** : huir **8** ∼ **into** ENCOUNTER : tropezar con **9** ∼ **into** HIT : chocar contra **10** ∼ **late** : ir retrasado **11** ∼ **out of** : quedarse sin **12** ∼ **over** : atropellar — *vt* **1** : correr **2** OPERATE : hacer funcionar **3** : hacer correr (agua) **4** MANAGE : dirigir **5** ∼ **a fever** : tener fiebre — ∼ *n* **1** : carrera *f* **2** TRIP : viaje *m*, paseo *m* (en coche) **3** SERIES : serie *f* **4 in the long** ∼ : a la larga **5 in the short** ∼ : a corto plazo — **runaway** *n* : fugitivo *m*, -va *f* — ∼ *adj* : fugitivo — **rundown** *n* : resumen *m* — **run–down** *adj* **1** : destartalado **2** EXHAUSTED : agotado

rung[1] → **ring**[1]

rung[2] *n* : peldaño *m* (de una escalera, etc.)

runner *n* **1** : corredor *m*, -dora *f* **2** : patín *m* (de un trineo), riel *m* (de un cajón, etc.) —

runner–up *n, pl* **runners–up** : subcampeón *m*, -peona *f* — **running** *adj* **1** FLOWING : corriente **2** CONTINUOUS : continuo **3** CONSECUTIVE : seguido

runt *n* : animal *m* más pequeño (de una camada)

runway *n* : pista *f* de aterrizaje

rupture *n* : ruptura *f* — ∼ *v* **-tured; -turing** *vt* : romper — *vi* : reventar

rural *adj* : rural

ruse *n* : ardid *m*

rush[1] *n* : junco *m* (planta)

rush[2] *vi* : ir de prisa — *vt* **1** : apresurar, apurar **2** ATTACK : asaltar **3** : llevar rápidamente (al hospital, etc.) — ∼ *n* **1** : prisa *f*, apuro *m* **2** : ráfaga *f* (de aire), torrente *m* (de agua) — ∼ *adj* : urgente — **rush hour** *n* : hora *f* punta

russet *n* : color *m* rojizo

Russian *adj* : ruso — ∼ *n* : ruso *m* (idioma)

rust *n* : herrumbre *f*, óxido *m* — ∼ *vi* : oxidarse — *vt* : oxidar

rustic *adj* : rústico

rustle *v* **-tled; -tling** *vt* **1** : hacer susurrar **2** : robar (ganado) — *vi* : susurrar — ∼ *n* : susurro *m*

rusty *adj* **rustier; -est** : oxidado

rut *n* **1** : surco *m* **2 be in a** ∼ : ser esclavo de la rutina

ruthless *adj* : despiadado, cruel

rye *n* : centeno *m*

S

s *n, pl* **s's** *or* **ss** : s *f*, decimonovena letra del alfabeto inglés

Sabbath *n* **1** : sábado *m* (día santo judío) **2** : domingo *m* (día santo cristiano)

sabotage *n* : sabotaje *m* — ∼ *vt* **-taged; -taging** : sabotear

saccharin *n* : sacarina *f*

sack *n* : saco *m* — ∼ *vt* **1** FIRE : despedir **2** PLUNDER : saquear

sacrament *n* : sacramento *m*

sacred *adj* : sagrado

sacrifice *n* : sacrificio *m* — ∼ *vt* **-ficed; -ficing** : sacrificar

sacrilege *n* : sacrilegio *m* — **sacrilegious** *adj* : sacrílego

sad *adj* **sadder; saddest** : triste — **sadden** *vt* : entristecer

saddle *n* : silla *f* (de montar) — ∼ *vt* **-dled;**

-dling 1 : ensillar (un caballo, etc.) **2** ∼ **s.o. with sth** : cargar a algn con algo

sadistic *adj* : sádico

sadness *n* : tristeza *f*

safari *n* : safari *m*

safe *adj* **safer; safest 1** : seguro **2** UNHARMED : ileso **3** CAREFUL : prudente **4** ∼ **and sound** : sano y salvo — ∼ *n* : caja *f* fuerte — **safeguard** *n* : salvaguarda *f* — ∼ *vt* : salvaguardar — **safely** *adv* **1** : sin peligro **2 arrive** ∼ : llegar sin novedad — **safety** *n, pl* **-ties** : seguridad *f* — **safety belt** *n* : cinturón *m* de seguridad — **safety pin** *n* : imperdible *m*

saffron *n* : azafrán *m*

sag *vi* **sagged; sagging 1** : combarse **2** GIVE : aflojarse **3** FLAG : flaquear

saga *n* : saga *f*

sage[1] *n* : salvia *f* (planta)
sage[2] *adj* **sager; -est** : sabio — ∼ *n* : sabio *m*, -bia *f*
said → **say**
sail *n* **1** : vela *f* (de un barco) **2 go for a** ∼ : salir a navegar **3 set** ∼ : zarpar — ∼ *vi* : navegar — *vt* : gobernar (un barco), navegar (el mar) — **sailboat** *n* : velero *m* — **sailor** *n* : marinero *m*
saint *n* : santo *m*, -ta *f* — **saintly** *adj* **saintlier; -est** : santo
sake *n* **1 for goodness'** ∼**!** : ¡por Dios! **2 for the** ∼ **of** : por (el bien de)
salad *n* : ensalada *f*
salamander *n* : salamandra *f*
salami *n* : salami *m*
salary *n*, *pl* **-ries** : sueldo *m*
sale *n* **1** : venta *f* **2 for** ∼ : se vende **3 on** ∼ : de rebaja — **salesman** *n*, *pl* **-men** : vendedor *m*, dependiente *m* — **saleswoman** *n*, *pl* **-women** : vendedora *f*, dependienta *f*
salient *adj* : saliente
saliva *n* : saliva *f*
sallow *adj* : amarillento, cetrino
salmon *ns & pl* : salmón *m*
salon *n* → **beauty salon**
saloon *n* : bar *m*
salsa *n* : salsa *f* mexicana, salsa *f* picante
salt *n* : sal *f* — ∼ *vt* : salar — **saltwater** *adj* : de agua salada — **salty** *adj* **saltier; -est** : salado
salute *v* **-luted; -luting** *vt* : saludar — *vi* : hacer un saludo — ∼ *n* : saludo *m*
salvage *n* : salvamento *m* — ∼ *vt* **-vaged; -vaging** : salvar
salvation *n* : salvación *f*
salve *n* : ungüento *m*
same *adj* **1** : mismo **2 be the** ∼ **(as)** : ser igual (que) **3 the** ∼ **thing (as)** : la misma cosa (que) — ∼ *pron* **1 all the** ∼ : igual **2 the** ∼ : lo mismo — ∼ *adv* **the** ∼ : igual
sample *n* : muestra *f* — ∼ *vt* **-pled; -pling** : probar
sanatorium *n*, *pl* **-riums** *or* **-ria** : sanatorio *m*
sanctify *vt* **-fied; -fying** : santificar
sanction *n* : sanción *f* — ∼ *vt* : sancionar
sanctity *n*, *pl* **-ties** : santidad *f*
sanctuary *n*, *pl* **-aries** : santuario *m*
sand *n* : arena *f* — ∼ *vt* : lijar (madera)
sandal *n* : sandalia *f*
sandpaper *n* : papel *m* de lija — ∼ *vt* : lijar
sandwich *n* : sandwich *m*, bocadillo *m* Spain — ∼ *vt* ∼ **between** : meter entre
sandy *adj* **sandier; -est** : arenoso
sane *adj* **saner; sanest 1** : cuerdo **2** SENSIBLE : sensato
sang → **sing**

sanitarium *n*, *pl* **-iums** *or* **-ia** → **sanatorium**
sanitary *adj* **1** : sanitario **2** HYGIENIC : higiénico — **sanitary napkin** *n* : compresa *f* (higiénica) — **sanitation** *n* : sanidad *f*
sanity *n* : cordura *f*
sank → **sink**
Santa Claus *n* : Papá *m* Noel
sap[1] *n* **1** : savia *f* (de una planta) **2** SUCKER : inocentón *m*, -tona *f*
sap[2] *vt* **sapped; sapping** : minar (la fuerza, etc.)
sapphire *n* : zafiro *m*
sarcasm *n* : sarcasmo *m* — **sarcastic** *adj* : sarcástico
sardine *n* : sardina *f*
sash *n* : faja *f* (de un vestido), fajín *m* (de un uniforme)
sat → **sit**
satanic *adj* : satánico
satchel *n* : cartera *f*
satellite *n* : satélite *m*
satin *n* : raso *m*
satire *n* : sátira *f* — **satiric** *or* **satirical** *adj* : satírico
satisfaction *n* : satisfacción *f* — **satisfactory** *adj* : satisfactorio — **satisfy** *v* **-fied; -fying** *vt* **1** : satisfacer **2** CONVINCE : convencer — **satisfying** *adj* : satisfactorio
saturate *vt* **-rated; -rating 1** : saturar **2** DRENCH : empapar — **saturation** *n* : saturación *f*
Saturday *n* : sábado *m*
Saturn *n* : Saturno *m*
sauce *n* : salsa *f* — **saucepan** *n* : cacerola *f* — **saucer** *n* : platillo *m* — **saucy** *adj* **saucier; -est** IMPUDENT : descarado
sauna *n* : sauna *mf*
saunter *vi* : pasear
sausage *n* : salchicha *f*
sauté *vt* **-téed** *or* **-téd; -téing** : saltear, sofreír
savage *adj* : salvaje, feroz — ∼ *n* : salvaje *mf* — **savagery** *n*, *pl* **-ries** : ferocidad *f*
save *v* **saved; saving 1** RESCUE : salvar **2** RESERVE : guardar **3** : ahorrar (dinero, tiempo, etc.) — ∼ *prep* EXCEPT : salvo
savior *n* : salvador *m*, -dora *f*
savor *vt* : saborear — **savory** *adj* : sabroso
saw[1] → **see**
saw[2] *n* : sierra *f* — ∼ *vt* **sawed; sawed** *or* **sawn; sawing** : serrar — **sawdust** *n* : serrín *m*, aserrín *m*
saxophone *n* : saxofón *m*
say *v* **said; saying; says** *vt* **1** : decir **2** INDICATE : marcar (dícese de relojes, etc.) — *vi* **1** : decir **2 that is to** ∼ : es decir — ∼ *n*, *pl* **says 1 have no** ∼ : no tener ni voz ni voto **2 have one's** ∼ : dar su opinión — **saying** *n* : refrán *m*

scab *n* 1 : costra *f* (en una herida) 2 STRIKE-
BREAKER : esquirol *mf*
scaffold *n* : andamio *m* (en construcción)
scald *vt* : escaldar
scale¹ *n* : balanza *f* (para pesar)
scale² *n* : escama *f* (de un pez, etc.) — ~ *vt*
scaled; scaling : escamar
scale³ *vt* scaled; scaling 1 CLIMB : escalar
2 ~ down : reducir — ~ *n* : escala *f* (musical, salarial, etc.)
scallion *n* : cebolleta *f*
scallop *n* : vieira *f*
scalp *n* : cuero *m* cabelludo
scam *n* : estafa *f*, timo *m fam*
scamper *vi* ~ away : irse corriendo
scan *vt* scanned; scanning 1 : escandir
(versos) 2 EXAMINE : escudriñar 3 SKIM
: echar un vistazo a 4 : escanear (en informática)
scandal *n* 1 : escándalo *m* 2 GOSSIP : habla-
durías *fpl* — scandalous *adj* : escandaloso
Scandinavian *adj* : escandinavo
scant *adj* : escaso
scapegoat *n* : chivo *m* expiatorio
scar *n* : cicatriz *f* — ~ *v* scarred; scarring
vt : dejar una cicatriz en — *vi* : cicatrizar
scarce *adj* scarcer; -est : escaso —
scarcely *adv* : apenas — scarcity *n, pl*
-ties : escasez *f*
scare *vt* scared; scaring 1 : asustar 2 be
~d of : tener miedo a — ~ *n* 1 FRIGHT
: susto *m* 2 ALARM : pánico *m* — scarecrow *n* : espantapájaros *m*, espantajo *m*
scarf *n, pl* scarves *or* scarfs 1 : bufanda *f*
2 KERCHIEF : pañuelo *m*
scarlet *adj* : escarlata — scarlet fever *n* : escarlatina *f*
scary *adj* scarier; -est : que da miedo
scathing *adj* : mordaz
scatter *vt* 1 STREW : esparcir 2 DISPERSE
: dispersar — *vi* : dispersarse
scavenger *n* : carroñero *m*, -ra *f* (animal)
scenario *n, pl* -ios 1 : guión *m* (cinemático)
2 the worst-case ~ : el peor de los casos
scene *n* 1 : escena *f* 2 behind the ~s
: entre bastidores 3 make a ~ : armar un
escándalo — scenery *n, pl* -eries 1 : decorado *m* 2 LANDSCAPE : paisaje *m* — scenic
adj : pintoresco
scent *n* 1 : aroma *m* 2 PERFUME : perfume
m 3 TRAIL : rastro *m* — scented *adj* : per-
fumado
sceptic → skeptic
schedule *n* 1 : programa *m* 2 TIMETABLE
: horario *m* 3 behind ~ : atrasado, con retraso 4 on ~ : según lo previsto — ~ *vt*
-uled; -uling : planear, programar
scheme *n* 1 PLAN : plan *m* 2 PLOT : intriga

f 3 DESIGN : esquema *f* — ~ *vi* schemed;
scheming : intrigar
schism *n* : cisma *m*
schizophrenia *n* : esquizofrenia *f* — schizophrenic *adj* : esquizofrénico
scholar *n* : erudito *m*, -ta *f* — scholarly *adj*
: erudito — scholarship *n* 1 : erudición *f* 2
GRANT : beca *f*
school¹ *n* : banco *m* (de peces)
school² *n* 1 : escuela *f* 2 COLLEGE : universidad *f* 3 DEPARTMENT : facultad *f* — ~ *vt*
: instruir — schoolboy *n* : colegial *m* —
schoolgirl *n* : colegiala *f* — schoolteacher
n → teacher
science *n* : ciencia *f* — scientific *adj* : científico — scientist *n* : científico *m*, -ca *f*
scissors *npl* : tijeras *fpl*
scoff *vi* ~ at : burlarse de, mofarse de
scold *vt* : regañar
scoop *n* 1 : pala *f* 2 : noticia *f* exclusiva (en
periodismo) — ~ *vt* 1 : sacar (con pala) 2
~ out : ahuecar 3 ~ up : recoger
scoot *vi* : ir rápidamente — scooter *n* 1
: patinete *m* 2 *or* motor ~ : escúter *m*
scope *n* 1 RANGE : alcance *m* 2 OPPORTU-
NITY : posibilidades *fpl*
scorch *vt* : chamuscar
score *n, pl* scores 1 : tanteo *m* (en deportes)
2 RATING : puntuación *f* 3 : partitura *f* (musical) 4 *or pl* score TWENTY : veintena *f* 5
keep ~ : llevar la cuenta 6 on that ~ : en
ese sentido — ~ *v* scored; scoring *vt* 1
: marcar, anotarse *Lat* (un tanto) 2 : sacar
(una nota) — *vi* : marcar (en deportes)
scorn *n* : desdén *m* — ~ *vt* : desdeñar —
scornful *adj* : desdeñoso
scorpion *n* : alacrán *m*, escorpión *m*
Scot *n* : escocés *m*, -cesa *f* — Scotch *adj* →
Scottish — ~ *n or* whiskey : whisky
m escocés — Scottish *adj* : escocés
scoundrel *n* : sinvergüenza *mf*
scour *vt* 1 SCRUB : fregar 2 SEARCH : registrar
scourge *n* : azote *m*
scout *n* : explorador *m*, -dora *f*
scowl *vi* : fruncir el ceño — ~ *n* : ceño *m*
fruncido
scram *vi* scrammed; scramming : largarse
scramble *v* -bled; -bling *vi* 1 CLAMBER
: trepar 2 ~ for : pelearse por — *vt*
: mezclar — ~ *n* : rebatiña *f*, pelea *f* —
scrambled eggs *npl* : huevos *mpl* revueltos
scrap¹ *n* 1 PIECE : pedazo *m* 2 *or* ~ metal
: chatarra *f* 3 ~s *npl* : sobras — ~ *vt*
scrapped; scrapping : desechar
scrap² *n* FIGHT : pelea *f*
scrapbook *n* : álbum *m* de recortes
scrape *v* scraped; scraping *vt* 1 : rascar 2
: rasparse (la rodilla, etc.) 3 *or* ~ off : ras-

par **4** ～ **together** : reunir — *vi* **1** RUB : rozar **2** ～ **by** : arreglárselas — ～ *n* **1** : rasguño *m* **2** PREDICAMENT : apuro *m*
scratch *vt* **1** CLAW : arañar **2** MARK : rayar **3** : rascarse (la cabeza, etc.) **4** ～ **out** : tachar — ～ *n* **1** : arañazo *m* **2** MARK : rayón *m* **3 start from** ～ : empezar desde cero
scrawl *v* : garabatear — ～ *n* : garabato *m*
scrawny *adj* **scrawnier; -est** : escuálido
scream *vi* : gritar, chillar — ～ *n* : grito *m*, chillido *m*
screech *n* **1** : chillido *m* (de personas) **2** : chirrido *m* (de frenos, etc.) — ～ *vi* **1** : chillar **2** : chirriar (dícese de los frenos, etc.)
screen *n* **1** : pantalla *f* **2** PARTITION : mampara *f* **3** *or* **window** ～ : mosquitero *m* — ～ *vt* **1** SHIELD : proteger **2** HIDE : ocultar **3** : seleccionar (candidatos, etc.)
screw *n* : tornillo *m* — ～ *vt* **1** : atornillar **2** ～ **up** RUIN : fastidiar — **screwdriver** *n* : destornillador *m*
scribble *v* **-bled; -bling** : garabatear — ～ *n* : garabato *m*
script *n* **1** HANDWRITING : escritura *f* **2** : guión *m* (de cine, etc.) — **scripture** *n* **1** : escritos *mpl* sagrados **2 the Scriptures** *npl* : las Escrituras *fpl*
scroll *n* : rollo *m* (de pergamino, etc.)
scrounge *v* **scrounged; scrounging** *vt* : gorrear *fam* — *vi* ～ **around for sth** : andar buscando algo
scrub[1] *n* UNDERBRUSH : maleza *f*
scrub[2] *vt* **scrubbed; scrubbing** SCOUR : fregar — ～ *n* : fregado *m*
scruff *n* **by the** ～ **of the neck** : por el pescuezo
scruple *n* : escrúpulo *m* — **scrupulous** *adj* : escrupuloso
scrutiny *n*, *pl* **-nies** : análisis *m* cuidadoso — **scrutinize** *vt* **-nized; -nizing** : escudriñar
scuff *vt* : raspar, rayar
scuffle *n* : refriega *f*
sculpture *n* : escultura *f* — **sculpt** *v* : esculpir — **sculptor** *n* : escultor *m*, -tora *f*
scum *n* **1** FROTH : espuma *f* **2** : escoria *f* (dícese de personas)
scurry *vi* **-ried; -rying** : corretear
scuttle[1] *n* : cubo *m* (para carbón)
scuttle[2] *vt* **-tled; -tling** : hundir (un barco)
scuttle[3] *vi* SCAMPER : corretear
sea *n* **1** : mar *mf* **2 at** ～ : en el mar — ～ *adj* : del mar — **seafarer** *n* : marinero *m* — **seafood** *n* : mariscos *mpl* — **seagull** *n* : gaviota *f*
seal[1] *n* : foca *f* (animal)
seal[2] *n* **1** STAMP : sello *m* **2** CLOSURE : cierre *m* (hermético) — ～ *vt* : sellar

seam *n* **1** : costura *f* **2** VEIN : veta *f*
seaman *n*, *pl* **-men** : marinero *m*
seamy *adj* **seamier; -est** : sórdido
seaplane *n* : hidroavión *m*
seaport *n* : puerto *m* marítimo
search *vt* : registrar — *vi* ～ **for** : buscar — ～ *n* **1** : registro *m* **2** HUNT : búsqueda *f* — **searchlight** *n* : reflector *m*
seashell *n* : concha *f* (marina) — **seashore** *n* : orilla *f* del mar — **seasick** *adj* **1** : mareado **2 be** ～ : marearse — **seasickness** *n* : mareo *m*
season *n* **1** : estación *f* (del año) **2** : temporada *f* (en deportes, etc.) — ～ *vt* **1** FLAVOR : sazonar **2** : secar (madera) — **seasonal** *adj* : estacional — **seasoned** *adj* EXPERIENCED : veterano — **seasoning** *n* : condimento *m*
seat *n* **1** : asiento *m* **2** : fondillos *mpl* (de un pantalón) **3** BUTTOCKS : trasero *m* **4** CENTER : sede *f* — ～ *vt* **1 be** ～**ed** : sentarse **2 the bus** ～**s 30** : el autobús tiene cabida para 30 — **seat belt** *n* : cinturón *m* de seguridad
seaweed *n* : alga *f* marina
secede *vi* **-ceded; -ceding** : separarse (de una nación, etc.)
secluded *adj* : aislado — **seclusion** *n* : aislamiento *m*
second *adj* : segundo — ～ *or* **secondly** *adv* : en segundo lugar — ～ *n* **1** : segundo *m*, -da *f* **2** MOMENT : segundo *m* **3 have** ～**s** : repetir (en una comida) — ～ *vt* : secundar — **secondary** *adj* : secundario — **secondhand** *adj* : de segunda mano — **second–rate** *adj* : mediocre
secret *adj* : secreto — ～ *n* : secreto *m* — **secrecy** *n*, *pl* **-cies** : secreto *m*
secretary *n*, *pl* **-taries 1** : secretario *m*, -ria *f* **2** : ministro *m*, -tra *f* (del gobierno)
secretion *n* : secreción *f* — **secrete** *vt* **-creted; -creting** : secretar
secretive *adj* : reservado — **secretly** *adv* : en secreto
sect *n* : secta *f*
section *n* : sección *f*, parte *f*
sector *n* : sector *m*
secular *adj* : secular
security *n*, *pl* **-ties 1** : seguridad *f* **2** GUARANTEE : garantía *f* **3 securities** *npl* : valores *mpl* — **secure** *adj* **-curer; -est** : seguro — ～ *vt* **-cured; -curing 1** FASTEN : asegurar **2** GET : conseguir
sedan *n* : sedán *m*
sedate *adj* : sosegado
sedative *adj* : sedante — ～ *n* : sedante *m*
sedentary *adj* : sedentario
sediment *n* : sedimento *m*
seduce *vt* **-duced; -ducing** : seducir — **se-**

duction *n* : seducción *f* — **seductive** *adj* : seductor

see *v* **saw; seen; seeing** *vt* **1** : ver **2** UNDERSTAND : entender **3** ESCORT : acompañar **4** ~ **s.o. off** : despedirse de algn **5** ~ **sth through** : llevar algo a cabo **6** ~ **you later!** : ¡hasta luego! — *vi* **1** : ver **2** UNDERSTAND : entender **3 let's** ~ : vamos a ver **4** ~ **to** : ocuparse de

seed *n, pl* **seed** *or* **seeds 1** : semilla *f* **2** SOURCE : germen *m* — **seedy** *adj* **seedier; -est** SQUALID : sórdido

seek *v* **sought; seeking** *vt* **1** *or* ~ **out** : buscar **2** REQUEST : pedir **3** ~ **to** : tratar de — *vi* SEARCH : buscar

seem *vi* : parecer

seep *vi* : filtrarse

seesaw *n* : balancín *m*

seethe *vi* **seethed; seething** : rabiar, estar furioso

segment *n* : segmento *m*

segregate *vt* **-gated; -gating** : segregar — **segregation** *n* : segregación *f*

seize *v* **seized; seizing** *vt* **1** GRASP : agarrar **2** CAPTURE : tomar **3** : aprovechar (una oportunidad) — *vi or* ~ **up** : agarrotarse — **seizure** *n* **1** CAPTURE : toma *f* **2** : ataque *m* (en medicina)

seldom *adv* : pocas veces, raramente

select *adj* : selecto — ~ *vt* : seleccionar — **selection** *n* : selección *f* — **selective** *adj* : selectivo

self *n, pl* **selves 1** : ser *m* **2 her better** ~ : su lado bueno — **self–addressed** *adj* : con la dirección del remitente — **self–assured** *adj* : seguro de sí mismo — **self–centered** *adj* : egocéntrico — **self–confidence** *n* : confianza *f* en sí mismo — **self–confident** *adj* : seguro de sí mismo — **self–conscious** *adj* : cohibido — **self–control** *n* : dominio *m* de sí mismo — **self–defense** *n* : defensa *f* propia — **self–employed** *adj* : que trabaja por cuenta propia — **self–esteem** *n* : amor *m* propio — **self–evident** *adj* : evidente — **self–help** *n* : autoayuda *f* — **self– important** *adj* : presumido — **self–interest** *n* : interés *m* personal — **selfish** *adj* : egoísta — **selfishness** *n* : egoísmo *m* — **selfless** *adj* : desinteresado — **self–pity** *n, pl* **-ties** : autocompasión *f* — **self–portrait** *n* : autorretrato *m* — **self– respect** *n* : amor *m* propio — **self–righteous** *adj* : santurrón — **self–service** *adj* : de autoservicio — **self–sufficient** *adj* : autosuficiente — **self– taught** *adj* : autodidacta

sell *v* **sold; selling** *vt* : vender — *vi* : venderse — **seller** *n* : vendedor *m*, **-dora** *f*

selves → **self**

semantics *ns & pl* : semántica *f*

semblance *n* : apariencia *f*

semester *n* : semestre *m*

semicolon *n* : punto y coma *m*

semifinal *n* : semifinal *f*

seminary *n, pl* **-naries** : seminario *m* — **seminar** *n* : seminario *m*

senate *n* : senado *m* — **senator** *n* : senador *m*, **-dora** *f*

send *vt* **sent; sending 1** : mandar, enviar **2** ~ **away for** : pedir **3** ~ **back** : devolver (mercancías, etc.) **4** ~ **for** : mandar a buscar — **sender** *n* : remitente *mf*

senile *adj* : senil — **senility** *n* : senilidad *f*

senior *n* **1** SUPERIOR : superior *m* **2** : estudiante *mf* de último año (en educación) **3** *or* ~ **citizen** : persona *f* mayor **4 be s.o.'s** ~ : ser mayor que algn — ~ *adj* **1** : superior (en rango) **2** ELDER : mayor — **seniority** *n* : antigüedad *f*

sensation *n* : sensación *f* — **sensational** *adj* : sensacional

sense *n* **1** : sentido *m* **2** FEELING : sensación *f* **3** COMMON SENSE : sentido *m* común **4 make** ~ : tener sentido — ~ *vt* **sensed; sensing** : sentir — **senseless** *adj* **1** : sin sentido **2** UNCONSCIOUS : inconsciente — **sensible** *adj* : sensato, práctico — **sensibility** *n, pl* **-ties** : sensibilidad *f* — **sensitive** *adj* **1** : sensible **2** TOUCHY : susceptible — **sensitivity** *n, pl* **-ties** : sensibilidad *f* — **sensual** *adj* : sensual — **sensuous** *adj* : sensual

sent → **send**

sentence *n* **1** : frase *f* **2** JUDGMENT : sentencia *f* — ~ *vt* **-tenced; -tencing** : sentenciar

sentiment *n* **1** : sentimiento *m* **2** BELIEF : opinión *f* — **sentimental** *adj* : sentimental — **sentimentality** *n, pl* **-ties** : sentimentalismo *m*

sentry *n, pl* **-tries** : centinela *m*

separation *n* : separación *f* — **separate** *v* **-rated; -rating** *vt* **1** : separar **2** DISTINGUISH : distinguir — *vi* : separarse — ~ *adj* **1** : separado **2** DETACHED : aparte **3** DISTINCT : distinto — **separately** *adv* : por separado

September *n* : septiembre *m*, setiembre *m*

sequel *n* **1** : continuación *f* **2** CONSEQUENCE : secuela *f*

sequence *n* **1** ORDER : orden *m* **2** : secuencia *f* (de números o escenas)

Serb *or* **Serbian** *adj* : serbio

serene *adj* : sereno — **serenity** *n* : serenidad *f*

sergeant *n* : sargento *mf*

serial *adj* : seriado — ~ *n* : serial *m* — **series** *n, pl* **series** : serie *f*

serious *adj* : serio — **seriously** *adv* **1** : seriamente **2** GRAVELY : gravemente **3 take** ~ : tomar en serio

sermon *n* : sermón *m*

serpent *n* : serpiente *f*

servant *n* : criado *m*, -da *f*

serve *v* **served; serving** *vi* **1** : servir **2** : sacar (en deportes) **3** ~ **as** : servir de — *vt* **1** : servir **2** ~ **time** : cumplir una condena — **server** *n* **1** WAITER : camarero *m*, -ra *f* **2** : servidor *m* (en informática)

service *n* **1** : servicio *m* **2** CEREMONY : oficio *m* **3** MAINTENANCE : revisión *f* **4** **armed** ~**s** : fuerzas *fpl* armadas — ~ *vt* **-viced; -vicing** : revisar (un vehículo, etc.) — **serviceman** *n*, *pl* **-men** : militar *m* — **service station** *n* : estación *f* de servicio — **serving** *n* : porción *f*, ración *f*

session *n* : sesión *f*

set *n* **1** : juego *m* (de platos, etc.) **2** : set *m* (en tenis, etc.) **3** *or* **stage** ~ : decorado *m* **4 television** ~ : aparato *m* de televisión — ~ *v* **set; setting** *vt* **1** *or* ~ **down** : poner **2** : poner en hora (un reloj) **3** FIX : fijar (una fecha, etc.) **4** ~ **fire to** : prender fuego a **5** ~ **free** : poner en libertad **6** ~ **off** : hacer sonar (una alarma), hacer estallar (una bomba) **7** ~ **out to (do sth)** : proponerse (hacer algo) **8** ~ **up** ASSEMBLE : montar, armar **9** ~ **up** ESTABLISH : establecer — *vi* **1** : cuajarse (dícese de la gelatina, etc.), fraguar (dícese del cemento) **2** : ponerse (dícese del sol, etc.) **3** ~ **in** BEGIN : empezar **4** ~ **off** *or* ~ **out** : salir (de viaje) — ~ *adj* **1** FIXED : fijo **2** READY : listo, preparado — **setback** *n* : revés *m* — **setting** *n* **1** : posición *f* (de un control) **2** MOUNTING : engaste *m* (de joyas) **3** SCENE : escenario *m*

settle *v* **settled; settling** *vi* **1** : asentarse (dícese de polvo, colonos, etc.) **2** ~ **down** RELAX : calmarse **3** ~ **for** : conformarse con **4** ~ **in** : instalarse — *vt* **1** DECIDE : fijar, decidir **2** RESOLVE : resolver **3** PAY : pagar **4** CALM : calmar **5** COLONIZE : colonizar — **settlement** *n* **1** PAYMENT : pago *m* **2** COLONY : colonia *f*, poblado *m* **3** AGREEMENT : acuerdo *m* — **settler** *n* : colono *m*, -na *f*

seven *adj* : siete — ~ *n* : siete *m* — **seven hundred** *adj* : setecientos — ~ *n* : setecientos *m* — **seventeen** *adj* : diecisiete — ~ *n* : diecisiete *m* — **seventeenth** *adj* : decimoséptimo — ~ *n* **1** : decimoséptimo *m*, -ma *f* (en una serie) **2** : diecisieteavo *m* (en matemáticas) — **seventh** *adj* : séptimo — ~ *n* **1** : séptimo *m*, -ma *f* (en una serie) **2** : séptimo *m* (en matemáticas) — **seventieth** *adj* : septuagésimo — ~ *n* **1** : septuagésimo *m*, -ma *f* (en una serie) **2** : setentavo *m* (en matemáticas) — **seventy** *adj* : setenta — ~ *n*, *pl* **-ties** : setenta *m*

sever *vt* **-ered; -ering** : cortar, romper

several *adj* : varios — ~ *pron* : varios, varias

severance *n* : ruptura *f*

severe *adj* **severer; -est 1** : severo **2** SERIOUS : grave — **severely** *adv* **1** : severamente **2** SERIOUSLY : gravemente — **severity** *n* **1** : severidad *f* **2** SERIOUSNESS : gravedad *f*

sew *v* **sewed; sewn** *or* **sewed; sewing** : coser

sewer *n* : cloaca *f* — **sewage** *n* : aguas *fpl* negras

sewing *n* : costura *f*

sex *n* **1** : sexo *m* **2** INTERCOURSE : relaciones *fpl* sexuales — **sexism** *n* : sexismo *m* — **sexist** *adj* : sexista — **sexual** *adj* : sexual — **sexuality** *n* : sexualidad *f* — **sexy** *adj* **sexier; -est** : sexy

shabby *adj* **shabbier; -est 1** WORN : gastado **2** UNFAIR : malo, injusto

shack *n* : choza *f*

shackle *n* : grillete *m*

shade *n* **1** : sombra *f* **2** : tono *m* (de un color) **3** NUANCE : matiz *m* **4** *or* **lampshade** : pantalla *f* **5** *or* **window** ~ : persiana *f* — ~ *vt* **shaded; shading** : proteger de la luz — **shadow** *n* : sombra *f* — **shadowy** *adj* INDISTINCT : vago — **shady** *adj* **shadier; -est 1** : sombreado **2** DISREPUTABLE : sospechoso

shaft *n* **1** : asta *f* (de una flecha, etc.) **2** HANDLE : mango *m* **3** AXLE : eje *m* **4** : rayo *m* (de luz) **5** *or* **mine** ~ : pozo *m*

shaggy *adj* **shaggier; -est** : peludo

shake *v* **shook; shaken; shaking** *vt* **1** : sacudir **2** MIX : agitar **3** ~ **hands with s.o.** : dar la mano a algn **4** ~ **one's head** : negar con la cabeza **5** ~ **up** UPSET : afectar — *vi* : temblar — ~ *n* **1** : sacudida *f* **2** → **handshake** — **shaker** *n* **1 salt** ~ : salero *m* **2 pepper** ~ : pimentero *m* — **shaky** *adj* **shakier; -est 1** : tembloroso **2** UNSTABLE : poco firme

shall *v aux*, *past* **should**; *pres sing & pl* **shall 1** (*expressing volition or futurity*) → **will 2** (*expressing possibility or obligation*) → **should 3** ~ **we go?** : ¿nos vamos?

shallow *adj* **1** : poco profundo **2** SUPERFICIAL : superficial

sham *n* : farsa *f* — ~ *v* **shammed; shamming** : fingir

shambles *ns & pl* : caos *m*, desorden *m*

shame *n* **1** : vergüenza *f* **2 what a** ~**!** : ¡qué lástima! — ~ *vt* **shamed; shaming** : avergonzar — **shameful** *adj* : vergonzoso — **shameless** *adj* : desvergonzado

shampoo *vt* : lavar (el pelo) — ~ *n*, *pl* **-poos** : champú *m*

shamrock n : trébol m
shan't (contraction of **shall not**) → **shall**
shape v **shaped; shaping** vt 1 : formar 2 DETERMINE : determinar 3 be ~d like : tener forma de — vi or ~ **up** : tomar forma — ~ n 1 : forma f 2 **get in** ~ : ponerse en forma — **shapeless** adj : informe
share n 1 : porción f 2 : acción f (en una compañía) — ~ v **shared; sharing** vt 1 : compartir 2 DIVIDE : dividir — vi : compartir — **shareholder** n : accionista mf
shark n : tiburón m
sharp adj 1 : afilado 2 POINTY : puntiagudo 3 ACUTE : agudo 4 HARSH : duro, severo 5 CLEAR : nítido 6 : sostenido (en música) 7 a ~ **curve** : una curva cerrada — ~ adv at **two o'clock** ~ : a las dos en punto — ~ n : sostenido (en música) — **sharpen** vt : afilar (un cuchillo, etc.), sacar punta a (un lápiz) — **sharpener** n 1 or **knife** ~ : afilador m 2 or **pencil** ~ : sacapuntas m — **sharply** adv : bruscamente
shatter vt 1 : hacer añicos 2 DEVASTATE : destrozar — vi : hacerse añicos
shave v **shaved; shaved** or **shaven; shaving** vt 1 : afeitar 2 SLICE : cortar — vi : afeitarse — ~ n : afeitada f — **shaver** n : máquina f de afeitar
shawl n : chal m
she pron : ella
sheaf n, pl **sheaves** 1 : gavilla f 2 : fajo m (de papeles)
shear vt **sheared; sheared** or **shorn; shearing** : esquilar — **shears** npl : tijeras fpl (grandes)
sheath n, pl **sheaths** : funda f, vaina f
shed¹ v **shed; shedding** vt 1 : derramar (lágrimas, etc.) 2 : mudar (de piel, etc.), quitarse (ropa) 3 ~ **light on** : aclarar
shed² n : cobertizo m
she'd (contraction of **she had** or **she would**) → **have, would**
sheen n : brillo m, lustre m
sheep n, pl **sheep** : oveja f — **sheepish** adj : avergonzado
sheer adj 1 THIN : transparente 2 PURE : puro 3 STEEP : escarpado
sheet n 1 : sábana f (de la cama) 2 : hoja f (de papel) 3 : capa f (de hielo, etc.) 4 PLATE : placa f, lámina f
shelf n, pl **shelves** : estante m
shell n 1 : concha f 2 : caparazón m (de un crustáceo, etc.) 3 : cáscara f (de un huevo, etc.) 4 : armazón mf (de un edificio, etc.) 5 POD : vaina f 6 MISSILE : proyectil m — ~ vt 1 : pelar (nueces, etc.) 2 BOMBARD : bombardear
she'll (contraction of **she shall** or **she will**) → **shall, will**

shellfish n : marisco m
shelter n 1 : refugio m 2 **take** ~ : refugiarse — ~ vt 1 PROTECT : proteger 2 HARBOR : albergar
shelve vt **shelved; shelving** DEFER : dar carpetazo a
shepherd n : pastor m — ~ vt GUIDE : conducir, guiar
sherbet n : sorbete m
sheriff n : sheriff mf
sherry n, pl **-ries** : jerez m
she's (contraction of **she is** or **she has**) → **be, have**
shield n : escudo m — ~ vt : proteger
shier, shiest → **shy**
shift vt 1 MOVE : mover 2 SWITCH : transferir — vi 1 CHANGE : cambiar 2 MOVE : moverse 3 or ~ **gears** : cambiar de velocidad — ~ n 1 CHANGE : cambio m 2 : turno m (de trabajo) — **shiftless** adj : holgazán — **shifty** adj **shiftier; -est** : sospechoso
shimmer vi : brillar, relucir
shin n : espinilla f
shine v **shone** or **shined; shining** vi : brillar — vt 1 : alumbrar (una luz) 2 POLISH : sacar brillo a — ~ n : brillo m
shingle n : teja f plana y delgada (en construcción) — ~ vt **-gled; -gling** : techar
shingles npl : herpes m
shiny adj **shinier, -est** : brillante
ship n 1 : barco m, buque m 2 → **spaceship** — ~ vt **shipped; shipping** : transportar, enviar (por barco) — **shipbuilding** n : construcción f naval — **shipment** n : envío m — **shipping** n 1 : transporte m 2 SHIPS : barcos mpl — **shipshape** adj : ordenado — **shipwreck** n : naufragio m — ~ vt **be ~ed** : naufragar — **shipyard** n : astillero m
shirk vt : esquivar
shirt n : camisa f
shiver vi : temblar (del frío, etc.) — ~ n : escalofrío m
shoal n : banco m
shock n 1 IMPACT : choque m 2 SURPRISE, UPSET : golpe m emocional 3 : shock m (en medicina) 4 or **electric** ~ : descarga f (eléctrica) — ~ vt : escandalizar — **shock absorber** n : amortiguador m — **shocking** adj : escandaloso
shoddy adj **shoddier; -est** : de mala calidad
shoe n : zapato m — ~ vt **shod; shoeing** : herrar (un caballo) — **shoelace** n : cordón m (de zapato) — **shoemaker** n : zapatero m, -ra f
shone → **shine**
shook → **shake**
shoot v **shot; shooting** vt 1 : disparar 2 : echar (una mirada) 3 PHOTOGRAPH : foto-

grafiar **4** FILM : rodar — *vi* **1** : disparar **2**
~ by : pasar como una bala — **~** *n* : brote
m, retoño *m* (de una planta) — **shooting
star** *n* : estrella *f* fugaz
shop *n* **1** : tienda *f* **2** WORKSHOP : taller *m*
— **~** *vi* **shopped; shopping 1** : hacer
compras **2 go shopping** : ir de compras —
shopkeeper *n* : tendero *m*, -ra *f* — **shoplift**
vi : hurtar mercancía (en tiendas) — **shop-
lifter** *n* : ladrón *m*, -drona *f* (que roba en
tiendas) — **shopper** *n* : comprador *m*, -dora
f
shore *n* : orilla *f*
shorn → **shear**
short *adj* **1** : corto **2** : bajo (de estatura) **3**
CURT : brusco **4 a ~ time ago** : hace poco
5 be ~ of : estar corto de — **~** *adv* **1 stop
~** : parar en seco **2 fall ~** : quedarse corto
— **shortage** *n* : escasez *f*, carencia *f* —
shortcake *n* : tarta *f* de fruta — **shortcom-
ing** *n* : defecto *m* — **shortcut** *n* : atajo *m* —
shorten *vt* : acortar — **shorthand** *n*
: taquigrafía *f* — **short–lived** *adj* : efímero
— **shortly** *adv* : dentro de poco — **shortness** *n* **1** : lo corto (de una cosa), baja estatura *f* (de una persona) **2 ~ of breath**
: falta *f* de aliento — **shorts** *npl* : shorts
mpl, pantalones *mpl* cortos — **short-
sighted** → **nearsighted**
shot *n* **1** : disparo *m*, tiro *m* **2** : tiro *m* (en
deportes) **3** ATTEMPT : intento *m* **4** PHOTO-
GRAPH : foto *f* **5** INJECTION : inyección *f* **6**
: trago *m* (de licor) — **shotgun** *n* : escopeta
f
should *past of* **shall 1 if she ~ call** : si
llama **2 I ~ have gone** : debería haber ido
3 they ~ arrive soon : deben llegar pronto
4 what ~ we do? : ¿qué hacemos?
shoulder *n* **1** : hombro *m* **2** : arcén *m* (de
una carretera) — **~** *vt* : cargar con (la responsabilidad, etc.) — **shoulder blade** *n*
: omóplato *m*
shouldn't (*contraction of* **should not**) →
should
shout *v* : gritar — **~** *n* : grito *m*
shove *v* **shoved; shoving** : empujar — **~** *n*
: empujón *m*
shovel *n* : pala *f* — **~** *vt* **-veled** *or* **-velled;
-veling** *or* **-velling 1** : mover (tierra, etc.)
con una pala **2** DIG : cavar (con una pala)
show *v* **showed; shown** *or* **showed; showing** *vt* **1** : mostrar **2** TEACH : enseñar **3**
PROVE : demostrar **4** ESCORT : acompañar
5 : proyectar (una película), dar (un programa de televisión) **6 ~ off** : hacer alarde
de — *vi* **1** : notarse, verse **2 ~ off** : lucirse
3 ~ up ARRIVE : aparecer — **~** *n* **1**
: demostración *f* **2** EXHIBITION : exposición
f **3** : espectáculo *m* (teatral), programa *m*

(de televisión, etc.) — **showdown** *n* : confrontación *f*
shower *n* **1** : ducha *f* **2** : chaparrón *m* (en
meteorología) **3** PARTY : fiesta *f* — **~** *vt* **1**
SPRAY : regar **2 ~ s.o. with** : colmar a algn
de — *vi* **1** : ducharse **2** RAIN : llover
showy *adj* **showier; -est** : llamativo, ostentoso
shrank → **shrink**
shrapnel *ns & pl* : metralla *f*
shred *n* **1** : tira *f* (de tela, etc.) **2** IOTA : pizca
f — **~** *vt* **shredded; shredding 1** : hacer
tiras **2** GRATE : rallar
shrewd *adj* : astuto
shriek *vi* : chillar — **~** *n* : chillido *m*, alarido *m*
shrill *adj* : agudo, estridente
shrimp *n* : camarón *m*
shrine *n* **1** TOMB : sepulcro *m* **2** SANCTU-
ARY : santuario *m*
shrink *v* **shrank; shrunk** *or* **shrunken;
shrinking** *vt* : encoger — *vi* **1** : encogerse
(dícese de ropa), reducirse (dícese de
números, etc.) **2 ~ back** : retroceder
shrivel *vi* **-veled** *or* **-velled; -veling** *or* **-vel-
ling** *or* **~ up** : arrugarse, marchitarse
shroud *n* **1** : sudario *m*, mortaja *f* **2** VEIL
: velo *m* — **~** *vt* : envolver
shrub *n* : arbusto *m*, mata *f*
shrug *vi* **shrugged; shrugging** : encogerse
de hombros
shrunk → **shrink**
shudder *vi* : estremecerse — **~** *n* : estremecimiento *m*
shuffle *v* **-fled; -fling** *vt* : barajar (naipes),
revolver (papeles, etc.) — *vi* : caminar ar-
rastrando los pies
shun *vi* **shunned; shunning** : evitar, esquivar
shut *v* **shut; shutting** *vt* **1** CLOSE : cerrar **2**
~ off *or* **turn off 3 ~ up** CONFINE : encerrar — *vi* **1** *or* **~ down** : cerrarse **2 ~ up!**
: ¡cállate! — **shutter** *n* **1** *or* **window ~**
: contraventana *f* **2** : obturador *m* (de una
cámara)
shuttle *n* **1** : lanzadera *f* (para tejer) **2** *or* **~
bus** : autobús *m* (de corto recorrido) **3** →
space shuttle — **~** *v* **-tled; -tling** *vt*
: transportar — *vi* : ir y venir
shy *adj* **shier** *or* **shyer; shiest** *or* **shyest**
: tímido — **~** *vi* **shied; shying** *or* **~ away**
: retroceder — **shyness** *n* : timidez *f*
sibling *n* : hermano *m*, hermana *f*
sick *adj* **1** : enfermo **2 be ~** VOMIT : vomitar **3 be ~ of** : estar harto de **4 feel ~**
: tener náuseas — **sicken** *vt* DISGUST : dar
asco a — **sickening** *adj* : nauseabundo
sickle *n* : hoz *f*
sickly *adj* **sicklier; -est 1** UNHEALTHY : en-

fermizo 2 → **sickening — sickness** *n* : enfermedad *f*

side *n* 1 : lado *m* 2 : costado *m* (de una persona), ijada *f* (de un animal) 3 : parte *f* (en una disputa, etc.) 4 ~ **by** ~ : uno al lado de otro 5 **take** ~s : tomar partido — ~ *vi* ~ **with** : ponerse de parte de — **sideboard** *n* : aparador *m* — **sideburns** *npl* : patillas *fpl* — **side effect** *n* : efecto *m* secundario — **sideline** *n* : línea *f* de banda (en deportes) — **sidestep** *vt* -**stepped**; -**stepping** : eludir, esquivar — **sidetrack** *vt* **get** ~ed : distraerse — **sidewalk** *n* : acera *f* — **sideways** *adj & adv* : de lado — **siding** *n* : revestimiento *m* exterior

siege *n* : sitio *m*

sieve *n* : tamiz *m*, cedazo *m*

sift *vt* 1 : cerner, tamizar 2 *or* ~ **through** : pasar por el tamiz

sigh *vi* : suspirar — ~ *n* : suspiro *m*

sight *n* 1 : vista *f* 2 SPECTACLE : espectáculo *m* 3 : lugar *m* de interés (turístico) 4 **catch** ~ **of** : avistar — ~ *vt* : avistar — **sightseer** *n* : turista *mf*

sign *n* 1 : signo *m* 2 NOTICE : letrero *m* 3 GESTURE : seña *f*, señal *f* — ~ *vt* : firmar (un cheque, etc.) — *vi* 1 : firmar 2 ~ **up** ENROLL : inscribirse

signal *n* : señal *f* — ~ *v* -**naled** *or* -**nalled**; -**naling** *or* -**nalling** *vt* 1 : hacer señas a 2 INDICATE : señalar — *vi* 1 : hacer señas 2 : señalizar (en un vehículo)

signature *n* : firma *f*

significance *n* 1 : significado *m* 2 IMPORTANCE : importancia *f* — **significant** *adj* : importante — **signify** *vt* -**fied**; -**fying** : significar

sign language *n* : lenguaje *m* gestual — **signpost** *n* : poste *m* indicador

silence *n* : silencio *m* — ~ *vt* -**lenced**; -**lencing** : silenciar — **silent** *adj* 1 : silencioso 2 MUM : callado 3 : mudo (dícese de películas y letras)

silhouette *n* : silueta *f* — ~ *vt* -**etted**; -**etting be** ~**d against** : perfilarse contra

silicon *n* : silicio *m*

silk *n* : seda *f* — **silky** *adj* **silkier**; -**est** : sedoso

sill *n* : alféizar *m* (de una ventana), umbral *m* (de una puerta)

silly *adj* **sillier**; -**est** : tonto, estúpido

silt *n* : cieno *m*

silver *n* 1 : plata *f* 2 → **silverware** — ~ *adj* : de plata — **silverware** *n* : plata *f* — **silvery** *adj* : plateado

similar *adj* : similar, parecido — **similarity** *n*, *pl* -**ties** : semejanza *f*, parecido *m*

simmer *v* : hervir a fuego lento

simple *adj* **simpler**; -**plest** 1 : simple 2 EASY : sencillo — **simplicity** *n* : simplicidad *f*, sencillez *f* — **simplify** *vt* -**fied**; -**fying** : simplificar — **simply** *adv* 1 : sencillamente 2 ABSOLUTELY : realmente

simulate *vt* -**lated**; -**lating** : simular

simultaneous *adj* : simultáneo

sin *n* : pecado *m* — ~ *vi* **sinned**; **sinning** : pecar

since *adv* 1 *or* ~ **then** : desde entonces 2 **long** ~ : hace mucho — ~ *conj* 1 : desde que 2 BECAUSE : ya que, como 3 **it's been years** ~... : hace años que... — ~ *prep* : desde

sincere *adj* -**cerer**; -**est** : sincero — **sincerely** *adv* : sinceramente — **sincerity** *n* : sinceridad *f*

sinful *adj* : pecador (dícese de las personas), pecaminoso (dícese de las acciones)

sing *v* **sang** *or* **sung**; **sung**; **singing** : cantar

singe *vt* **singed**; **singeing** : chamuscar

singer *n* : cantante *mf*

single *adj* 1 : solo, único 2 UNMARRIED : soltero 3 **every** ~ **day** : cada día, todos los días — ~ *n* 1 : soltero *m*, -ra *f* 2 *or* ~ **room** : habitación *f* individual — ~ *vt* -**gled**; -**gling** ~ **out** SELECT : escoger 2 DISTINGUISH : señalar — **single-handed** *adj* : sin ayuda, solo

singular *adj* : singular — ~ *n* : singular *m*

sinister *adj* : siniestro

sink *v* **sank** *or* **sunk**; **sunk**; **sinking** *vi* 1 : hundirse (en un líquido) 2 DROP : bajar, caer — *vt* 1 : hundir 2 ~ **sth into** : clavar algo en — ~ *n* 1 *or* **kitchen** ~ : fregadero *m* 2 *or* **bathroom** ~ : lavabo *m*, lavamanos *m*

sinner *n* : pecador *m*, -dora *f*

sip *v* **sipped**; **sipping** *vt* : sorber — *vi* : beber a sorbos — ~ *n* : sorbo *m*

siphon *n* : sifón *m* — ~ *vt* : sacar con sifón

sir *n* 1 (*in titles*) : sir *m* 2 (*as a form of address*) : señor *m* 3 **Dear Sir** : Estimado señor

siren *n* : sirena *f*

sirloin *n* : solomillo *m*

sissy *n*, *pl* -**sies** : mariquita *mf fam*

sister *n* : hermana *f* — **sister-in-law** *n*, *pl* **sisters-in-law** : cuñada *f*

sit *v* **sat**; **sitting** *vi* 1 *or* ~ **down** : sentarse 2 LIE : estar (ubicado) 3 MEET : estar en sesión 4 *or* ~ **up** : incorporarse — *vt* : sentar

site *n* 1 : sitio *m*, lugar *m* 2 LOT : solar *m*

sitting room → **living room**

sitter → **baby-sitter**

situated *adj* : ubicado, situado — **situation** *n* : situación *f*

six *adj* : seis — ~ *n* : seis *m* — **six hundred**
adj : seiscientos — ~ *n* : seiscientos *m* —
sixteen *adj* : dieciséis — ~ *n* : dieciséis *m*
— **sixteenth** *adj* : decimosexto — ~ *n* 1
: decimosexto *m*, -ta *f* (en una serie) 2
: dieciseisavo *m*, dieciseisava parte *f* —
sixth *adj* : sexto — ~ *n* 1 : sexto *m*, -ta *f*
(en una serie) 2 : sexto *m* (en matemáticas)
— **sixtieth** *adj* : sexagésimo — ~ *n* 1
: sexagésimo *m*, -ma *f* (en una serie) 2
: sesentavo *m* (en matemáticas) — **sixty** *adj*
: sesenta — ~ *n, pl* **-ties** : sesenta *m*
size *n* 1 : tamaño *m*, talla *f* (de ropa),
número *m* (de zapatos) 2 EXTENT : magnitud *f* — ~ *vt* **sized; sizing** — **up** : evaluar
— **sizable** *or* **sizeable** *adj* : considerable
sizzle *vi* **-zled; -zling** : chisporrotear
skate[1] *n* : raya *f* (pez)
skate[2] *n* : patín *m* — ~ *vi* **skated; skating**
: patinar — **skateboard** *n* : monopatín *m* —
skater *n* : patinador *m*, -dora *f*
skeleton *n* : esqueleto *m*
skeptic *n* : escéptico *m*, -ca *f* — **skeptical**
adj : escéptico — **skepticism** *n* : escepticismo *m*
sketch *n* 1 : esbozo *m*, bosquejo *m* 2 SKIT
: sketch *m* — ~ *vt* : bosquejar — *vi* : hacer
bosquejos — **sketchy** *adj* **sketchier; -est**
: incompleto
skewer *n* : brocheta *f*, broqueta *f*
ski *n, pl* **skis** : esquí *m* — ~ *vi* **skied; skiing** : esquiar
skid *n* : derrape *m*, patinazo *m* — ~ *vi* **skid-
ded; skidding** : derrapar, patinar
skier *n* : esquiador *m*, -dora *f*
skill *n* 1 : habilidad *f*, destreza *f* 2 TECH-
NIQUE : técnica *f* — **skilled** *adj* : hábil
skillet *n* : sartén *mf*
skillful *adj* : hábil, diestro
skim *vt* **skimmed; skimming** 1 : espumar
(sopa, etc.), descremar (leche) 2 : pasar
rozando (una superficie) 3 *or* ~ **through**
: echar un vistazo a — ~ *adj* : descremado
skimp *vi* ~ **on** : escatimar — **skimpy** *adj*
skimpier; -est 1 : exiguo, escaso 2
: brevísimo (dícese de ropa)
skin *n* : piel *f* — ~ *vt* **skinned; skinning**
: despellejar — **skin diving** *n* : buceo *m*,
submarinismo *m* — **skinny** *adj* **skinnier;
-est** : flaco
skip *v* **skipped; skipping** *vi* : ir brincando
— *vt* OMIT : saltarse — ~ *n* : brinco *m*,
salto *m*
skipper *n* : capitán *m*, -tana *f*
skirmish *n* : escaramuza *f*
skirt *n* : falda *f* — ~ *vt* 1 BORDER : bordear
2 EVADE : eludir
skull *n* : cráneo *m* (de una persona viva),
calavera *f* (de un esqueleto)

skunk *n* : mofeta *f*, zorrillo *m Lat*
sky *n, pl* **skies** : cielo *m* — **skylight** *n*
: claraboya *f*, tragaluz *m* — **skyline** *n* : horizonte *m* — **skyscraper** *n* : rascacielos *m*
slab *n* : bloque *m* (de piedra, etc.)
slack *adj* 1 LOOSE : flojo 2 CARELESS : descuidado — ~ *n* 1 **take up the** ~ : tensar
(una cuerda, etc.) 2 ~**s** *npl* : pantalones
mpl — **slacken** *vt* : aflojar — *vi* : aflojarse
slain → **slay**
slam *n* : golpe *m*, portazo *m* (de una puerta)
— ~ *v* **slammed; slamming** *vt* 1 *or* ~
down : tirar, plantar 2 *or* ~ **shut** : cerrar
de golpe 3 ~ **the door** : dar un portazo —
vi 1 : cerrarse de golpe 2 ~ **into** : chocar
contra
slander *vt* : calumniar, difamar — ~ *n* : calumnia *f*, difamación *f*
slang *n* : argot *m*
slant *n* : inclinación *f* — ~ *vi* : inclinarse
slap *vt* **slapped; slapping** 1 : dar una bofetada a 2 ~ **s.o. on the back** : dar una palmada en la espalda a algn — ~ *n* : bofetada
f, cachetada *f Lat*
slash *vt* 1 : hacer un tajo en 2 : rebajar (precios) drásticamente — ~ *n* : tajo *m*
slat *n* : tablilla *f*
slate *n* : pizarra *f*
slaughter *n* : matanza *f* — ~ *vt* 1 : matar
(animales) 2 MASSACRE : masacrar —
slaughterhouse *n* : matadero *m*
slave *n* : esclavo *m*, -va *f* — ~ *vi* **slaved;
slaving** : trabajar como un burro — **slavery**
n : esclavitud *f*
Slavic *adj* : eslavo
slay *vt* **slew; slain; slaying** : asesinar
sleazy *adj* **sleazier; -est** : sórdido
sled *n* : trineo *m*
sledgehammer *n* : almádena *f*
sleek *adj* : liso y brillante
sleep *n* 1 : sueño *m* 2 **go to** ~ : dormirse
— ~ *vi* **slept; sleeping** : dormir —
sleeper *n* **be a light** ~ : tener el sueño
ligero — **sleepless** *adj* **have a** ~ **night**
: pasar la noche en blanco — **sleepwalker** *n*
: sonámbulo *m*, -la *f* — **sleepy** *adj* **sleepier;
-est** 1 : somnoliento, soñoliento 2 **be** ~
: tener sueño
sleet *n* : aguanieve *f* — ~ *vi* : caer aguanieve
sleeve *n* : manga *f* — **sleeveless** *adj* : sin
mangas
sleigh *n* : trineo *m*
slender *adj* : delgado
slew → **slay**
slice *vt* **sliced; slicing** : cortar — ~ *n*
: trozo *m*, rebanada *f* (de pan, etc.), tajada *f*
(de carne)
slick *adj* SLIPPERY : resbaladizo, resbaloso
Lat

                         smooth

slide v **slid; sliding** vi : deslizarse — vt : deslizar — ~ n 1 : deslizamiento m 2 : tobogán m (para niños) 3 : diapositiva f (fotográfica) 4 DECLINE : descenso m

slier, sliest → **sly**

slight adj 1 : ligero, leve 2 SLENDER : delgado — ~ vt : desairar — **slightly** adv : ligeramente, un poco

slim adj **slimmer; slimmest** 1 : delgado 2 a ~ **chance** : escasas posibilidades fpl — ~ v **slimmed; slimming** : adelgazar

slime n 1 : baba f (de un caracol, etc.) 2 MUD : limo m — **slimy** adj **slimier; -est** : viscoso

sling vt **slung; slinging** 1 THROW : lanzar 2 HANG : colgar — ~ n 1 : honda f 2 : cabestrillo m (en medicina) — **slingshot** n : tirachinas m

slink vi **slunk; slinking** : andar furtivamente

slip¹ v **slipped; slipping** vi 1 SLIDE : resbalarse 2 **let sth** ~ : dejar escapar algo 3 ~ **away** : escabullirse 4 ~ **up** : equivocarse — vt 1 : deslizar 2 ~ **into** : ponerse (una prenda) 3 **it slipped my mind** : se me olvidó — ~ n 1 MISTAKE : error m, desliz m 2 ~ **of the tongue** : lapsus m 3 PETTICOAT : enagua f

slip² n ~ **of paper** : papelito m

slipper n : zapatilla f, pantufla f

slippery adj **slipperier; -est** : resbaladizo, resbaloso Lat

slit n 1 OPENING : rendija f 2 CUT : corte m, raja f — ~ vt **slit; slitting** : cortar

slither vi : deslizarse

sliver n : astilla f

slogan n : eslogan m

slop v **slopped; slopping** vt : derramar — vi : derramarse

slope vi **sloped; sloping** : inclinarse — ~ n : pendiente f, declive m

sloppy adj **sloppier; -est** 1 CARELESS : descuidado 2 UNKEMPT : desaliñado

slot n : ranura f

sloth n : pereza f

slouch vi : andar con los hombros caídos (en una silla)

slovenly adj : desaliñado

slow adj 1 : lento 2 **be** ~ : estar atrasado (dícese de un reloj) — ~ adv → **slowly** — ~ vt : retrasar, retardar — vi or ~ **down** : ir más despacio — **slowly** adv : lentamente, despacio — **slowness** n : lentitud f

sludge n SEWAGE : aguas fpl negras

slug¹ n 1 : babosa f (molusco) 2 BULLET : bala f 3 TOKEN : ficha f

slug² vt **slugged; slugging** : pegar un porrazo a

sluggish adj : lento

slum n : barrio m bajo

slumber vi : dormir — ~ n : sueño m

slump vi 1 DROP : bajar 2 COLLAPSE : dejarse caer 3 → **slouch** — ~ n : bajón m

slung → **sling**

slunk → **slink**

slur¹ n ASPERSION : calumnia f, difamación f

slur² vt **slurred; slurring** : arrastrar (las palabras)

slurp v : beber haciendo ruido — ~ n : sorbo m (ruidoso)

slush n : nieve f medio derretida

sly adj **slier; sliest** 1 : astuto, taimado 2 **on the** ~ : a escondidas

smack¹ vi ~ **of** : oler a

smack² vt 1 : pegar una bofetada a 2 KISS : besar 3 ~ **one's lips** : relamerse — ~ n 1 SLAP : bofetada f 2 KISS : beso m — ~ adv : justo, exactamente

small adj : pequeño, chico — **smallpox** n : viruela f

smart adj 1 : listo, inteligente 2 STYLISH : elegante — ~ vi STING : escocer — **smartly** adv : elegantemente

smash n 1 BLOW : golpe m 2 COLLISION : choque m 3 BANG, CRASH : estrépito m — ~ vt 1 BREAK : romper 2 DESTROY : aplastar — vi 1 SHATTER : hacerse pedazos 2 ~ **into** : estrellarse contra

smattering n : nociones fpl

smear n 1 : mancha f — ~ vt 1 : embadurnar (de pinta, etc.), untar (de aceite, etc.) 2 SMUDGE : manchar

smell v **smelled** or **smelt; smelling** : oler — ~ n 1 : (sentido m del) olfato m 2 ODOR : olor m — **smelly** adj **smellier; -est** : maloliente

smelt vt : fundir

smile vi **smiled; smiling** : sonreír — ~ n : sonrisa f

smirk vi : sonreír con suficiencia — ~ n : sonrisa f satisfecha

smitten adj **be** ~ **with** : estar enamorado de

smith n : blacksmith

smock n : blusón m, bata f

smog n : smog m

smoke n : humo m — ~ v **smoked; smoking** vi 1 : humear (dícese de fuegos, etc.) 2 : fumar (dícese de personas) — vt 1 : ahumar (carne, etc.) 2 : fumar (cigarrillos) — **smoker** n : fumador m, -dora f — **smokestack** n : chimenea f — **smoky** adj **smokier; -est** 1 : lleno de humo 2 : a humo (dícese de sabores, etc.)

smolder vi : arder (sin llama)

smooth adj 1 : liso (dícese de superficies), suave (dícese de movimientos), tranquilo (dícese del mar) 2 : sin grumos (dícese de salsas, etc.) — ~ vt : alisar — **smoothly** adv : suavemente — **smoothness** n : suavidad f

smother

smother *vt* : asfixiar (a algn), sofocar (llamas, etc.)

smudge *v* smudged; smudging *vt* : emborronar — *vi* : correrse — ~ *n* : mancha *f*, borrón *m*

smug *adj* smugger; smuggest : suficiente

smuggle *vt* -gled; -gling : pasar de contrabando — **smuggler** *n* : contrabandista *mf*

snack *n* : refrigerio *m*, tentempié *m fam*

snag *n* : problema *m* — ~ *v* snagged; snagging *vt* : enganchar — *vi* : engancharse

snail *n* : caracol *m*

snake *n* : culebra *f*, serpiente *f*

snap *v* snapped; snapping *vi* 1 BREAK : romperse 2 : intentar morder (dícese de un perro, etc.) 3 ~ at : contestar bruscamente a — *vt* 1 BREAK : romper 2 ~ one's fingers : chasquear los dedos 3 ~ open/shut : abrir/cerrar de golpe — ~ *n* 1 : chasquido *m* 2 FASTENER : broche *m* (de presión) 3 be a ~ : ser facilísimo — **snappy** *adj* snappier; -est 1 FAST : rápido 2 STYLISH : elegante — **snapshot** *n* : instantánea *f*

snare *n* : trampa *f* — ~ *vt* snared; snaring : atrapar

snarl[1] *vi* TANGLE : enmarañar, enredar — ~ *n* : enredo *m*, maraña *f*

snarl[2] *vi* GROWL : gruñir — *n* : gruñido *m*

snatch *vt* : arrebatar

sneak *vi* : ir a hurtadillas — *vt* : hacer furtivamente — ~ *n* : soplón *m*, -plona *f fam* — **sneakers** *npl* : tenis *mpl*, zapatillas *fpl* — **sneaky** *adj* sneakier; -est : solapado

sneer *vi* : sonreír con desprecio — ~ *n* : sonrisa *f* de desprecio

sneeze *vi* sneezed; sneezing : estornudar — ~ *n* : estornudo *m*

snide *adj* : sarcástico

sniff *vi* : oler — *vt* 1 : oler 2 → sniffle — ~ *n* : aspiración *f* por la nariz — **sniffle** *vi* -fled; -fling : sorberse la nariz — **sniffles** *npl* have the ~ : estar resfriado

snip *n* : tijeretada *f* — ~ *vt* snipped; snipping : cortar (con tijeras)

snivel *vi* -veled *or* -velled; -veling *or* -velling : lloriquear

snob *n* : esnob *mf* — **snobbish** *adj* : esnob

snoop *vi* : husmear — ~ *n* : fisgón *m*, -gona *f*

snooze *vi* snoozed; snoozing : dormitar — ~ *n* : siestecita *f*, siestita *f*

snore *vi* snored; snoring : roncar — ~ *n* : ronquido *m*

snort *vi* : bufar — ~ *n* : bufido *m*

snout *n* : hocico *m*, morro *m*

snow *n* : nieve *f* — ~ *vi* : nevar — **snowfall** *n* : nevada *f* — **snowflake** *n* : copo *m* de nieve — **snowman** *n* : muñeco *m* de nieve — **snowplow** *n* : quitanieves *m* — **snow-**

shoe *n* : raqueta *f* (para nieve) — **snowstorm** *n* : tormenta *f* de nieve — **snowy** *adj* snowier; -est 1 a ~ day : un día nevoso 2 ~ mountains : montañas *fpl* nevadas

snub *vt* snubbed; snubbing : desairar — ~ *n* : desaire *m*

snuff *vt or* ~ out : apagar

snug *adj* snugger; snuggest 1 : cómodo 2 TIGHT : ajustado — **snuggle** *vi* -gled; -gling : acurrucarse

so *adv* 1 LIKEWISE : también 2 THUS : así 3 THEREFORE : por lo tanto 4 *or* ~ much : tanto 5 *or* ~ very : tan 6 and ~ on : etcétera 7 I think ~ : creo que sí 8 I told you ~ : te lo dije — ~ *conj* 1 THEREFORE : así que 2 *or* ~ that : para que 3 ~ what? : ¿y qué? — ~ *adj* TRUE : cierto — ~ *pron or* ~ : más o menos

soak *vi* : estar en remojo — *vt* 1 : poner en remojo 2 ~ up : absorber — ~ *n* : remojo *m*

soap *n* : jabón *m* — ~ *vt or* ~ up : enjabonar — **soapy soapier; -est** *adj* : jabonoso

soar *vi* 1 : planear 2 SKYROCKET : dispararse

sob *vi* sobbed; sobbing : sollozar — ~ *n* : sollozo *m*

sober *adj* 1 : sobrio 2 SERIOUS : serio — **sobriety** *n* 1 : sobriedad *f* 2 SERIOUSNESS : seriedad *f*

so-called *adj* : supuesto, presunto

soccer *n* : futbol *m*, fútbol *m*

social *adj* : social — ~ *n* : reunión *f* social — **sociable** *adj* : sociable — **socialism** *n* : socialismo *m* — **socialist** *n* : socialista *mf* — ~ *adj* : socialista — **socialize** *v* -ized; -izing *vt* : socializar — *vi* ~ with : alternar con — **society** *n*, *pl* -eties : sociedad *f* — **sociology** *n* : sociología *f*

sock[1] *n*, *pl* socks *or* sox : calcetín *m*

sock[2] *vt* : pegar, golpear — ~ *n* PUNCH : puñetazo *m*

socket *n* 1 *or* electric ~ : enchufe *m*, toma *f* de corriente 2 *or* eye ~ : órbita *f*, cuenca *f* 3 : glena *f* (de una articulación)

soda *n* 1 *or* ~ pop : refresco *m*, gaseosa *f* 2 *or* ~ water : soda *f*

sodium *n* : sodio *m*

sofa *n* : sofá *m*

soft *adj* 1 : blando 2 SMOOTH : suave — **softball** *n* : softbol *m* — **soft drink** *n* : refresco *m* — **soften** *vt* 1 : ablandar 2 EASE, SMOOTH : suavizar — *vi* 1 : ablandarse 2 EASE : suavizarse — **softly** *adv* : suavemente — **software** *n* : software *m*

soggy *adj* soggier; -est : empapado

soil *vt* : ensuciar — ~ *n* DIRT : tierra *f*

solace *n* : consuelo *m*

solar *adj* : solar

sold → **sell**

solder *n* : soldadura *f* — ~ *vt* : soldar

soldier *n* : soldado *mf*

sole[1] *n* : lenguado *m* (pez)

sole[2] *n* : planta *f* (del pie), suela *f* (de un zapato)

sole[3] *adj* : único — **solely** *adv* : únicamente, sólo

solemn *adj* : solemne — **solemnity** *n, pl* -ties : solemnidad *f*

solicit *vt* : solicitar

solid *adj* 1 : sólido 2 UNBROKEN : continuo 3 ~ **gold** : oro *m* macizo 4 **two** ~ **hours** : dos horas seguidas — ~ *n* : sólido *m* — **solidarity** *n* : solidaridad *f* — **solidify** *v* -**fied**; -**fying** *vt* : solidificar — *vi* : solidificarse — **solidity** *n, pl* -**ties** : solidez *f*

solitary *adj* : solitario — **solitude** *n* : soledad *f*

solo *n, pl* **solos** : solo *m* — **soloist** *n* : solista *mf*

solution *n* : solución *f* — **soluble** *adj* : soluble — **solve** *vt* **solved**; **solving** : resolver — **solvent** *n* : solvente *m*

somber *adj* : sombrío

some *adj* 1 (*of unspecified identity*) : un 2 (*of an unspecified amount*) : algo de, un poco de 3 (*of an unspecified number*) : unos 4 CERTAIN : algunos 5 **that was** ~ **game!** : ¡fue un partidazo! — ~ *pron* 1 SEVERAL : algunos, unos 2 PART : un poco, algo — ~ *adv* ~ **twenty people** : unas veinte personas — **somebody** *pron* : alguien — **someday** *adv* : algún día — **somehow** *adv* 1 : de algún modo 2 ~ **or other** : de alguna manera u otra — **someone** *pron* : alguien — **somersault** *n* : voltereta *f*, salto *m* mortal — **something** *pron* 1 : algo 2 ~ **else** : otra cosa — **sometime** *adv* 1 : algún día, en algún momento 2 ~ **next month** : (durante) el mes que viene — **sometimes** *adv* : a veces — **somewhat** *adv* : algo — **somewhere** *adv* 1 : en alguna parte, en algún lado 2 ~ **around** : alrededor de 3 ~ **else** → **elsewhere**

son *n* : hijo *m*

song *n* : canción *f*

son-in-law *n, pl* **sons-in- law** : yerno *m*

sonnet *n* : soneto *m*

soon *adv* 1 : pronto 2 SHORTLY : dentro de poco 3 **as** ~ **as** : en cuanto 4 **as** ~ **as possible** : lo más pronto posible 5 ~ **after** : poco después 6 ~**er or later** : tarde o temprano 7 **the** ~**er the better** : cuanto antes mejor

soot *n* : hollín *m*

soothe *vt* **soothed**; **soothing** 1 CALM : calmar 2 RELIEVE : aliviar

sop *vt* **sopped**; **sopping** ~ **up** : absorber

sophistication *n* : sofisticación *f* — **sophisticated** *adj* : sofisticado

sophomore *n* : estudiante *mf* de segundo año

soprano *n, pl* -**nos** : soprano *mf*

sorcerer *n* : hechicero *m*, brujo *m* — **sorcery** *n* : hechicería *f*, brujería *f*

sordid *adj* : sórdido

sore *adj* **sorer**; **sorest** 1 : dolorido 2 ANGRY : enfadado 3 ~ **throat** : dolor *m* de garganta 4 **I have a** ~ **throat** : me duele la garganta — ~ *n* : llaga *f* — **sorely** *adv* : muchísimo — **soreness** *n* : dolor *m*

sorrow *n* : pesar *m*, pena *f* — **sorry** *adj* **sorrier**; -**est** 1 PITIFUL : lamentable 2 **feel** ~ **for** : compadecer 3 **I'm** ~ : lo siento

sort *n* 1 : tipo *m*, clase *f* 2 **a** ~ **of** : una especie de — ~ *vt* : clasificar — **sort of** *adv* 1 SOMEWHAT : algo 2 MORE OR LESS : más o menos

SOS *n* : SOS *m*

so-so *adj & adv* : así así *fam*

soufflé *n* : suflé *m*

sought → **seek**

soul *n* : alma *f*

sound[1] *adj* 1 HEALTHY : sano 2 FIRM : sólido 3 SENSIBLE : lógico 4 **a** ~ **sleep** : un sueño profundo 5 **safe and** ~ : sano y salvo

sound[2] *n* : sonido *m* — *vt* : hacer sonar, tocar (una trompeta, etc.) — *vi* 1 : sonar 2 SEEM : parecer

sound[3] *n* CHANNEL : brazo *m* de mar — ~ *vt* 1 : sondar (en navegación) 2 *or* ~ **out** : sondear

soundly *adv* 1 SOLIDLY : sólidamente 2 DEEPLY : profundamente

soundproof *adj* : insonorizado

soup *n* : sopa *f*

sour *adj* 1 : agrio 2 ~ **milk** : leche *f* cortada — ~ *vt* : agriar

source *n* : fuente *f*, origen *m*

south *adv* 1 : al sur — ~ *adj* : (del) sur — ~ *n* : sur *m* — **South African** *adj* : sudafricano — **South American** *adj* : sudamericano — **southeast** *adv* : hacia el sureste — ~ *adj* : (del) sureste — ~ *n* : sureste *m*, sudeste *m* — **southeastern** *adj* → **southeast** — **southerly** *adv & adj* : del sur — **southern** *adj* : del sur, meridional — **southwest** *adv* : hacia el suroeste — ~ *adj* : (del) suroeste — ~ *n* : suroeste *m*, sudoeste *m* — **southwestern** *adj* → **southwest**

souvenir *n* : recuerdo *m*

sovereign *n* : soberano *m*, -na *f* — ~ *adj* : soberano — **sovereignty** *n, pl* -**ties** : soberanía *f*

Soviet *adj* : soviético
sow[1] *n* : cerda *f*
sow[2] *vt* **sowed; sown** *or* **sowed; sowing**
  : sembrar
sox → **sock**
soybean *n* : soya *f*, soja *f*
spa *n* : balneario *m*
space *n* **1** : espacio *m* **2** ROOM, SPOT : sitio
  m, lugar *m* — ⁓ *vt* **spaced; spacing** : espaciar — **spaceship** *n* : nave *f* espacial —
  space shuttle *n* : transbordador *m* espacial
  — **spacious** *adj* : espacioso, amplio
spade[1] *n* SHOVEL : pala *f*
spade[2] *n* : pica *f* (naipe)
spaghetti *n* : espaguetis *mpl*
span *n* **1** PERIOD : espacio *m* **2** : luz *f* (entre
  dos soportes) — ⁓ *vt* **spanned; spanning**
  1 : abarcar (un período) **2** CROSS : extenderse sobre
Spaniard *n* : español *m*, -ñola *f*
spaniel *n* : spaniel *m*
Spanish *adj* : español — ⁓ *n* : español *m*
  (idioma)
spank *vt* : dar palmadas a (en las nalgas)
spar *vi* **sparred; sparring** : entrenarse (en
  boxeo)
spare *vt* **spared; sparing 1** PARDON : perdonar **2** SAVE : ahorrar **3 can you** ⁓ **a**
  dollar? : ¿me das un dólar? **4 I can't** ⁓
  the time : no tengo tiempo **5** ⁓ **no ex-**
  pense : no reparar en gastos **6 to** ⁓ : de
  sobra — ⁓ *adj* **1** : de repuesto **2** EXCESS
  : de más **3** LEAN : delgado — ⁓ *n or* ⁓
  part : repuesto *m* — **spare time** *n* : tiempo
  m libre — **sparing** *adj* : parco, económico
spark *n* : chispa *f* — ⁓ *vi* : chispear, echar
  chispas — *vt* : despertar (interés), provocar
  (crítica) — **sparkle** *vi* **-kled; -kling** : destellar, centellear — ⁓ *n* : destello *m*, centelleo
  m — **spark plug** *n* : bujía *f*
sparrow *n* : gorrión *m*
sparse *adj* **sparser; -est** : escaso
spasm *n* : espasmo *m*
spat[1] → **spit**
spat[2] *n* QUARREL : disputa *f*, pelea *f*
spatter *vt* : salpicar
spawn *vi* : desovar — *vt* : engendrar, producir — ⁓ *n* : hueva *f*
speak *v* **spoke; spoken; speaking** *vi* **1**
  : hablar **2** ⁓ **out against** : denunciar **3** ⁓
  up : hablar más alto **4** ⁓ **up for** : defender
  — *vt* **1** : decir **2** : hablar (un idioma) —
  speaker *n* **1** ORATOR : orador *m*, -dora *f* **2**
  : hablante *mf* (de un idioma) **3** LOUD-
  SPEAKER : altavoz *m*
spear *n* : lanza *f* — **spearhead** *n* : punta *f* de
  lanza — ⁓ *vt* : encabezar — **spearmint** *n*
  : menta *f* verde
special *adj* : especial — **specialist** *n* : espe-

cialista *mf* — **specialization** *n* : especial-
  ización *f* — **specialize** *vi* **-ized; -izing** : especializarse — **specially** *adv* : especialmente — **specialty** *n*, *pl* **-ties** : especialidad
  f
species *ns* & *pl* : especie *f*
specify *vt* **-fied; -fying** : especificar — **spe-**
  cific *adj* : específico — **specifically** *adv* **1**
  : específicamente **2** EXPLICITLY : expresamente — **specification** *n* : especificación *f*
specimen *n* : espécimen *m*
speck *n* **1** SPOT : mancha *f* **2** BIT : mota *f* —
  speckled *adj* : moteado
spectacle *n* **1** : espectáculo *m* **2** ⁓**s** *npl*
  GLASSES : gafas *fpl*, lentes *fpl*, anteojos *mpl*
  — **spectacular** *adj* : espectacular — **spec-**
  tator *n* : espectador *m*, -dora *f*
specter *or* **spectre** *n* : espectro *m*
spectrum *n*, *pl* **-tra** *or* **-trums 1** : espectro *m*
  2 RANGE : gama *f*
speculation *n* : especulación *f*
speech *n* **1** : habla *f* **2** ADDRESS : discurso
  m — **speechless** *adj* : mudo
speed *n* **1** : rapidez *f* **2** VELOCITY : velocidad *f* — ⁓ *v* **sped** *or* **speeded; speeding**
  vi **1** : conducir a exceso de velocidad **2** ⁓
  off : irse a toda velocidad **3** ⁓ **up** : acelerarse — *vt or* ⁓ **up** : acelerar — **speed limit**
  n : velocidad *f* máxima — **speedometer** *n*
  : velocímetro *m* — **speedy** *adj* **speedier,**
  -est : rápido
spell[1] *vt* **1** : escribir (las letras de) **2** *or* ⁓
  out : deletrear **3** MEAN : significar
spell[2] *n* ENCHANTMENT : hechizo *m*
spell[3] *n* : período *m* (de tiempo)
spellbound *adj* : embelesado
spelling *n* : ortografía *f*
spend *vt* **spent; spending 1** : gastar
  (dinero) **2** : pasar (las vacaciones, etc.) **3**
  ⁓ **time on** : dedicar tiempo a
sperm *n*, *pl* **sperm** *or* **sperms** : esperma *mf*
spew *vt* : vomitar, arrojar (lava, etc.)
sphere *n* : esfera *f* — **spherical** *adj* : esférico
spice *n* : especia *f* — ⁓ *vt* **spiced; spicing**
  : condimentar, sazonar — **spicy** *adj* **spicier;**
  -est : picante
spider *n* : araña *f*
spigot *n* : grifo *m* *Spain*, llave *f* *Lat*
spike *n* **1** : clavo *m* (grande) **2** POINT : punta
  f — **spiky** *adj* : puntiagudo
spill *vt* : derramar — *vi* : derramarse
spin *v* **spun; spinning** *vi* : girar — *vt* **1**
  : hilar (lana, etc.) **2** TWIRL : hacer girar —
  ⁓ *n* **1** : vuelta *f*, giro *m* **2 go for a** ⁓ : dar
  una vuelta (en auto)
spinach *n* : espinacas *fpl*
spinal cord *n* : médula *f* espinal

spindle *n* : huso *m* (para hilar) — **spindly** *adj* : larguirucho *fam*
spine *n* **1** : columna *f* vertebral **2** QUILL : púa *f* **3** THORN : espina *f* **4** : lomo *m* (de un libro)
spinster *n* : soltera *f*
spiral *adj* : de espiral, en espiral — ~ *n* : espiral *f* — ~ *vi* -**raled** *or* -**ralled**; -**raling** *or* -**ralling** : ir en espiral
spire *n* : aguja *f*
spirit *n* **1** : espíritu *m* **2 in good** ~**s** : animado **3** ~**s** *npl* : licores *mpl* — **spirited** *adj* : animado — **spiritual** *adj* : espiritual — **spirituality** *n, pl* -**ties** : espiritualidad *f*
spit[1] *n* ROTISSERIE : asador *m*
spit[2] *v* **spit** *or* **spat**; **spitting** : escupir — *n* SALIVA : saliva *f*
spite *n* **1** : rencor *m* **2 in** ~ **of** : a pesar de — ~ *vt* **spited**; **spiting** : fastidiar — **spiteful** *adj* : rencoroso
spittle *n* : saliva *f*
splash *vt* : salpicar — *vi* **1** : salpicar **2** *or* ~ **about** : chapotear — ~ *n* **1** : salpicadura *f* **2** : mancha *f* (de color, etc.)
splatter → **spatter**
spleen *n* : bazo *m* (órgano)
splendor *n* : esplendor *m* — **splendid** *adj* : espléndido
splint *n* : tablilla *f*
splinter *n* : astilla *f* — *vi* : astillarse
split *v* **split**; **splitting** *vt* **1** : partir **2** BURST : reventar **3** *or* ~ **up** : dividir — *vi* **1** : partirse, rajarse **2** *or* ~ **up** : dividirse — ~ *n* **1** CRACK : rajadura *f* **2** *or* ~ **seam** : descosido *m* **3** DIVISION : división *f*
splurge *vi* **splurged**; **splurging** : derrochar dinero
spoil *vt* **spoiled** *or* **spoilt**; **spoiling 1** RUIN : estropear **2** PAMPER : consentir, mimar — **spoils** *npl* : botín *m*
spoke[1] → **speak**
spoke[2] *n* : rayo *m* (de una rueda)
spoken → **speak**
spokesman *n, pl* -**men** : portavoz *mf* — **spokeswoman** *n, pl* -**women** : portavoz *f*
sponge *n* : esponja *f* — ~ *vt* **sponged**; **sponging** : limpiar con una esponja — **spongy** *adj* **spongier**; -**est** : esponjoso
sponsor *n* : patrocinador *m*, -dora *f* — ~ *vt* : patrocinar — **sponsorship** *n* : patrocinio *m*
spontaneity *n* : espontaneidad *f* — **spontaneous** *adj* : espontáneo
spooky *adj* **spookier**; -**est** : espeluznante
spool *n* : carrete *m*
spoon *n* : cuchara *f* — **spoonful** *n* : cucharada *f*
sporadic *adj* : esporádico
spore *n* : espora *f*

sport *n* **1** : deporte *m* **2 be a good** ~ : tener espíritu deportivo — **sportsman** *n, pl* -**men** : deportista *m* — **sportswoman** *n, pl* -**women** : deportista *f* — **sporty** *adj* **sportier**; -**est** : deportivo
spot *n* **1** : mancha *f* **2** DOT : punto *m* **3** PLACE : lugar *m*, sitio *m* **4 in a tight** ~ : en apuros **5 on the** ~ INSTANTLY : en ese mismo momento — ~ *vt* **spotted**; **spotting 1** STAIN : manchar **2** DETECT, NOTICE : ver, descubrir — **spotless** *adj* : impecable — **spotlight** *n* **1** : foco *m*, reflector *m* **2 be in the** ~ : ser el centro de atención — **spotty** *adj* **spottier**; -**est** : irregular
spouse *n* : cónyuge *mf*
spout *vi* : salir a chorros — ~ *n* **1** : pico *m* (de una jarra, etc.) **2** STREAM : chorro *m*
sprain *n* : esguince *m* — ~ *vt* : sufrir un esguince en
sprawl *vi* **1** : repantigarse (en un sillón, etc.) **2** EXTEND : extenderse — ~ *n* : extensión *f*
spray[1] *n* BOUQUET : ramillete *m*
spray[2] *n* **1** MIST : rocío *m* **2** *or* **aerosol** ~ : spray *m* **3** *or* ~ **bottle** : atomizador *m* — ~ *vt* : rociar (una superficie), pulverizar (un líquido)
spread *v* **spread**; **spreading** *vt* **1** : propagar (enfermedades), difundir (noticias, etc.) **2** *or* ~ **out** : extender **3** : untar (con mantequilla, etc.) — *vi* **1** : propagarse, difundirse **2** *or* ~ **out** : extenderse — ~ *n* **1** : propagación *f*, difusión *f* **2** PASTE : pasta *f* (para untar) — **spreadsheet** *n* : hoja *f* de cálculo
spree *n* **go on a** ~ : ir de juerga *fam*
sprig *n* : ramito *m*
sprightly *adj* **sprightlier**; -**est** : vivo
spring *v* **sprang** *or* **sprung**; **sprung**; **springing** *vi* **1** : saltar **2** ~ **from** : surgir de **3** ~ **up** : surgir — *vt* **1** ACTIVATE : accionar **2** ~ **a leak** : hacer agua **3** ~ **sth on s.o.** : sorprender a algn con algo — ~ *n* **1** : manantial *m* (de aguas) **2** : primavera *f* (estación) **3** LEAP : salto *m* **4** RESILIENCE : elasticidad *f* **5** : resorte *m* (mecanismo) **6** *or* **bedspring** : muelle *m* — **springboard** *n* : trampolín *m* — **springtime** *n* : primavera *f* — **springy** *adj* **springier**; -**est** : mullido
sprinkle *vt* -**kled**; -**kling 1** : salpicar, rociar **2** DUST : espolvorear — ~ *n* : llovizna *f* — **sprinkler** *n* : aspersor *m*
sprint *vi* **1** : correr **2** : esprintar (en deportes) — ~ *n* : esprint *m* (en deportes)
sprout *vi* : brotar — ~ *n* : brote *m*
spruce[1] *vt* **spruced**; **sprucing** ~ **up** : arreglar
spruce[2] *n* : picea *f* (árbol)
spry *adj* **sprier** *or* **spryer**; **spriest** *or* **spryest** : ágil, activo
spun → **spin**

spur *n* **1** : espuela *f* **2** STIMULUS : acicate *m* **3 on the ~ of the moment** : sin pensarlo — **~** *vi* **spurred; spurring** *or* **~ on 1** : espolear (un caballo) **2** MOTIVATE : motivar

spurn *vt* : desdeñar, rechazar

spurt¹ *vi* : salir a chorros — **~** *n* : chorro *m*

spurt² *n* **1** : arranque *m* (de energía, etc.) **2 work in ~s** : trabajar por rachas

spy *v* **spied; spying** *vt* : ver, divisar — *vi* **~ on s.o.** : espiar a algn — **~** *n* : espía *mf*

squabble *n* : riña *f*, pelea *f* — **~** *vi* **-bled; -bling** : reñir, pelearse

squad *n* : pelotón *m* (militar), brigada *f* (de policías)

squadron *n* : escuadrón *m* (de soldados), escuadra *f* (de aviones o naves)

squalid *adj* : miserable

squall *n* : turbión *m*

squalor *n* : miseria *f*

squander *vt* : derrochar (dinero, etc.), desperdiciar (oportunidades, etc.)

square *n* **1** : cuadrado *m* **2** : plaza *f* (de una ciudad) — **~** *adj* **squarer; -est 1** : cuadrado **2** HONEST : justo **3** EVEN : en paz **4 a ~ meal** : una comida decente — **~** *vt* **squared; squaring 1** : elevar al cuadrado (un número) **2** : saldar (una cuenta) — **square root** *n* : raíz *f* cuadrada

squash¹ *vt* **1** : aplastar **2** : acallar (protestas, etc.) — **~** *n* : squash *m* (deporte)

squash² *n*, *pl* **squashes** *or* **squash** : calabaza *f* (vegetal)

squat *vi* **squatted; squatting 1** *or* **~ down** : ponerse en cuclillas **2** : ocupar un lugar sin derecho — **~** *adj* **squatter; squattest** : achaparrado

squawk *n* : graznido *m* — **~** *vi* : graznar

squeak *vi* **1** : chillar **2** CREAK : chirriar — **~** *n* **1** : chillido *m* **2** CREAK : chirrido *m* — **squeaky** *adj* **squeakier; -est** : chirriante

squeal *vi* **1** : chillar (dícese de personas, etc.), chirriar (dícese de frenos, etc.) **2** PROTEST : quejarse — **~** *n* : chillido *m* (de una persona), chirrido *m* (de frenos, etc.)

squeamish *adj* : impresionable, delicado

squeeze *vt* **squeezed; squeezing 1** : apretar **2** : exprimir (frutas, etc.) **3** : extraer (jugo, etc.) — **~** *n* : apretón *m*

squid *n*, *pl* **squid** *or* **squids** : calamar *m*

squint *vi* : entrecerrar los ojos — **~** *n* : estrabismo *m*

squirm *vi* : retorcerse

squirrel *n* : ardilla *f*

squirt *vt* : lanzar un chorro de — *vi* : salir a chorros — **~** *n* : chorrito *m*

stab *n* **1** : puñalada *f* **2 ~ of pain** : pinchazo *m* **3 take a ~ at** : intentar — **~** *vt* **stabbed; stabbing 1** KNIFE : apuñalar **2** STICK : clavar

stable *n* **1** : establo *m* (para ganado) **2** *or* **horse ~** : caballeriza *f* — **~** *adj* **-bler; -blest** : estable — **stability** *n*, *pl* **-ties** : estabilidad *f* — **stabilize** *vt* **-lized; -lizing** : estabilizar

stack *n* : montón *m*, pila *f* — **~** *vt* : amontonar, apilar

stadium *n*, *pl* **-dia** *or* **-diums** : estadio *m*

staff *n*, *pl* **staffs** *or* **staves 1** : bastón *m* **2** *pl* **staffs** PERSONNEL : personal *m* **3** *pl* **staffs** : pentagrama *m* (en música) — **~** *vt* : proveer de personal

stag *n*, *pl* **stags** *or* **stag** : ciervo *m*, venado *m* — **~** *adj* : sólo para hombres — **~** *adv* **go ~** : ir solo

stage *n* **1** : escenario *m* (de un teatro) **2** PHASE : etapa *f* **3 the ~** : el teatro — **~** *vt* **staged; staging 1** : poner en escena **2** ARRANGE : montar — **stagecoach** *n* : diligencia *f*

stagger *vi* : tambalearse — *vt* **1** : escalonar (turnos, etc.) **2 be ~ed by** : quedarse estupefacto por — **~** *n* : tambaleo *m* — **staggering** *adj* : asombroso

stagnant *adj* : estancado — **stagnate** *vi* **-nated; -nating** : estancarse

stain *vt* **1** : manchar **2** : teñir (madera) — **~** *n* **1** : mancha *f* **2** DYE : tinte *m*, tintura *f* — **stainless steel** *n* : acero *m* inoxidable

stair *n* STEP : escalón *m*, peldaño *m* **2 ~s** *npl* : escalera(s) *f(pl)* — **staircase** *n* : escalera(s) *f(pl)* — **stairway** *n* : escalera(s) *f(pl)*

stake *n* **1** POST : estaca *f* **2** BET : apuesta *f* **3** INTEREST : intereses *mpl* **4 be at ~** : estar en juego — **~** *vt* **staked; staking 1** : estacar **2** BET : jugarse **3 ~ a claim to** : reclamar

stale *adj* **staler; stalest 1** : duro (dícese del pan) **2** OLD : viejo **3** STUFFY : viciado

stalk¹ *n* : tallo *m* (de una planta)

stalk² *vt* : acechar — *vi* *or* **~ off** : irse con altivez

stall¹ *n* **1** : compartimiento *m* (de un establo) **2** STAND : puesto *m* — **~** *vt* : parar (un motor) — *vi* : pararse

stall² *vt* DELAY : entretener — *vi* : andar con rodeos

stallion *n* : caballo *m* semental

stalwart *adj* **1** STRONG : fornido **2 ~ supporter** : partidario *m* leal

stamina *n* : resistencia *f*

stammer *vi* : tartamudear — **~** *n* : tartamudeo *m*

stamp *n* **1** SEAL : sello *m* **2** DIE : cuño *m* **3** *or* **postage ~** : sello *m*, estampilla *f* Lat, timbre *m* Lat — **~** *vt* **1** : franquear (una carta) **2** IMPRINT : sellar **3** MINT : acuñar **4 ~ one's foot** : dar una patada (en el suelo)

stampede n : estampida f — ~ vi **-peded; -peding** : salir en estampida

stance n : postura f

stand v **stood; standing** vi **1** : estar de pie, estar parado Lat **2** BE : estar **3** CONTINUE : seguir vigente **4** LIE, REST : reposar **5** ~ **aside** or ~ **back** : apartarse **6** ~ **out** : sobresalir **7** or ~ **up** : ponerse de pie, pararse Lat — vt **1** PLACE : poner, colocar **2** ENDURE : soportar **3** ~ **a chance** : tener una posibilidad — **stand by** vt **1** : mantener (una promesa, etc.) **2** SUPPORT : apoyar — **stand for** vt **1** MEAN : significar **2** PERMIT : permitir — **stand up** vi **1** ~ **for** : defender **2** ~ **up to** : resistir a — ~ n **1** RESISTANCE : resistencia f **2** STALL : puesto m **3** BASE : base f **4** POSITION : posición f **5** ~**s** npl : tribuna f

standard n **1** : norma f **2** BANNER : estandarte m **3** CRITERION : criterio m **4** ~ **of living** : nivel m de vida — ~ adj : estándar — **standardize** vt **-ized; -izing** : estandarizar

standing n **1** RANK : posición f **2** DURATION : duración f

standpoint n : punto m de vista

standstill n **1 be at a** ~ : estar paralizado **2 come to a** ~ : pararse

stank → **stink**

stanza n : estrofa f

staple[1] n : producto m principal — ~ adj : principal, básico

staple[2] n : grapa f (para papeles) — ~ vt **-pled; -pling** : grapar, engrapar Lat — **stapler** n : grapadora f, engrapadora f Lat

star n : estrella f — ~ v **starred; starring** vt FEATURE : estar protagonizado por — vi ~ **in** : protagonizar

starboard n : estribor m

starch vt : almidonar — ~ n **1** : almidón m **2** : fécula f (comida)

stardom n : estrellato m

stare vi **stared; staring** : mirar fijamente — ~ n : mirada f fija

starfish n : estrella f de mar

stark adj **1** PLAIN : austero **2** HARSH : severo, duro **3** SHARP : marcado — ~ adv **1** : completamente **2** ~ **naked** : en cueros (vivos)

starlight n : luz f de las estrellas

starling n : estornino m

starry adj **starrier; -est** : estrellado

start vi **1** : empezar, comenzar **2** SET OUT : salir **3** JUMP : sobresaltarse **4** or ~ **up** : arrancar — vt **1** : empezar, comenzar **2** CAUSE : provocar **3** or ~ **up** ESTABLISH : montar **4** or ~ **up** : arrancar (un motor, etc.) — ~ n **1** : principio m **2 get an early** ~ : salir temprano **3 give s.o. a** ~ : asus-

tar a algn — **starter** n : motor m de arranque (de un vehículo)

startle vt **-tled; -tling** : asustar

starve v **starved; starving** vi : morirse de hambre — vt : privar de comida — **starvation** n : inanición f, hambre f

stash vt : esconder

state n **1** : estado m **2 the States** : los Estados Unidos — ~ vt **stated; stating 1** SAY : decir **2** REPORT : exponer — **stately** adj : decir **2** REPORT : exponer — **stately** adj : majestuoso — **statement** n **1** : declaración f **2** or **bank** ~ : estado m de cuenta — **statesman** n, pl **-men** : estadista mf

static adj : estático — ~ n : estática f

station n **1** : estación f (de trenes, etc.) **2** RANK : condición f (social) **3** : canal m (de televisión), emisora f (de radio) **4** → **fire station, police station** — vt : apostar, estacionar — **stationary** adj : estacionario

stationery n : papel m y sobres mpl (para cartas)

station wagon n : camioneta f (familiar)

statistic n : estadística f — **statistical** adj : estadístico

statue n : estatua f

stature n : estatura f, talla f

status n **1** : situación f **2** or **social** ~ : estatus m **3 marital** ~ : estado m civil

statute n : estatuto m

staunch adj : leal

stave vt **staved** or **stove; staving 1** ~ **in** : romper **2** ~ **off** : evitar

staves → **staff**

stay[1] vi **1** REMAIN : quedarse, permanecer **2** LODGE : alojarse **3** ~ **awake** : mantenerse despierto **4** ~ **in** : quedarse en casa — vt : suspender (una ejecución, etc.) — ~ n **1** : estancia f, estadía f Lat **2** SUSPENSION : suspensión f

stay[2] n SUPPORT : soporte m

stead n **1 in s.o.'s** ~ : en lugar de algn **2 stand s.o. in good** ~ : ser muy útil a algn — **steadfast** adj **1** FIRM : firme **2** LOYAL : leal, fiel — **steadily** adv **1** : progresivamente **2** INCESSANTLY : sin parar **3** FIXEDLY : fijamente — **steady** adj **steadier; -est 1** FIRM, SURE : firme, seguro **2** FIXED : fijo **3** DEPENDABLE : responsable **4** CONSTANT : constante — ~ vt **steadied; steadying 1** : mantener firme **2** : calmar (los nervios)

steak n : bistec m, filete m

steal v **stole; stolen; stealing** vt : robar — vi **1** : robar **2** ~ **away** : escabullirse

stealth n : sigilo m — **stealthy** adj **stealthier; -est** : furtivo, sigiloso

steam n **1** : vapor m **2 let off** ~ : desahogarse — ~ vi : echar vapor — vt **1** : cocer al vapor **2 ~ up** : empañar — **steam engine** *n* : motor *m* de vapor — **steamship** *n* : (barco *m* de) vapor *m* — **steamy** *adj* **steamier; -est 1** : lleno de vapor **2** PASSIONATE : tórrido

steel *n* : acero — **~** *vt* **~ oneself** : armarse de valor — **~** *adj* : de acero

steep¹ *adj* **1** : empinado **2** CONSIDERABLE : considerable **3** : muy alto (dícese de precios)

steep² *vt* : dejar (té, etc.) en infusión

steeple *n* : aguja *f*, campanario *m*

steer¹ *n* : buey *m*

steer² *vt* : dirigir (un auto, etc.), pilotear (un barco) — **steering wheel** *n* : volante

stem¹ *n* : tallo *m* (de una planta), pie *m* (de una copa) — **~** *vi* **~ from** : provenir de

stem² *vt* **stemmed; stemming** : contener, detener

stench *n* : hedor *m*, mal olor *m*

stencil *n* : plantilla *f* (para marcar)

step *n* **1** : paso *m* **2** RUNG, STAIR : escalón *m* **3 ~ by ~** : paso por paso **4 take ~s** : tomar medidas **5 watch your ~** : mira por dónde caminas — **~** *vi* **stepped; stepping 1** : dar un paso **2 ~ back** : retoceder **3 ~ down** RESIGN : retirarse **4 ~ in** : intervenir **5 ~ out** : salir (por un momento) **6 ~ this way** : pase por aquí — **step up** *vt* INCREASE : aumentar

stepbrother *n* : hermanastro *m* — **stepdaughter** *n* : hijastra *f* — **stepfather** *n* : padrastro *m*

stepladder *n* : escalera *f* de tijera

stepmother *n* : madrastra *f* — **stepsister** *n* : hermanastra *f* — **stepson** *n* : hijastro *m*

stereo *n*, *pl* **stereos** : estéreo *m* — **~** *adj* : estéreo

stereotype *vt* **-typed; -typing** : estereotipar — **~** *n* : estereotipo *m*

sterile *adj* : estéril — **sterility** *n* : esterilidad *f* — **sterilization** *n* : esterilización *f* — **sterilize** *vt* **-ized; -izing** : esterilizar

sterling *adj* : excelente — **sterling silver** *n* : plata *f* de ley

stern¹ *adj* : severo, adusto

stern² *n* : popa *f*

stethoscope *n* : estetoscopio *m*

stew *n* : estofado *m*, guiso *m* — **~** *vt* : estofar, guisar — **~** *vi* **1** : cocer **2** FRET : preocuparse

steward *n* **1** : administrador *m*, -dora *f* **2** : auxiliar *m* de vuelo (en un avión) **3** : camarero *m* (en un barco) — **stewardess** *n* **1** : auxiliar *f* de vuelo, azafata *f* (en un avión) **2** : camarera *f* (en un barco)

stick¹ *n* **1** : palo *m* **2** TWIG : ramita *f* (suelta) **3** WALKING STICK : bastón *m*

stick² *v* **stuck; sticking** *vt* **1** : pegar **2** STAB : clavar **3** PUT : poner **4 ~ out** : sacar (la lengua, etc.) — **~** *vi* **1** : pegarse **2** JAM : atascarse **3 ~ around** : quedarse **4 ~ out** PROTRUDE : sobresalir **5 ~ out** SHOW : asomar **6 ~ up** : sobresalir **7 ~ up for** : defender — **sticker** *n* **1** : etiqueta *f* adhesiva — **stickler** *n* **be a ~ for** : insistir mucho en — **sticky** *adj* **stickier; -est** : pegajoso

stiff *adj* **1** RIGID : rígido, tieso **2** STILTED : forzado **3** STRONG : fuerte **4** DIFFICULT : difícil **5** : entumecido (dícese de músculos) — **stiffen** *vt* : fortalecer, hacer más duro — **~** *vi* **1** HARDEN : endurecerse **2** : entumecerse (dícese de músculos) — **stiffness** *n* : rigidez *f*

stifle *vt* **-fled; -fling** : sofocar

stigmatize *vt* **-tized; -tizing** : estigmatizar

still *adj* **1** : inmóvil **2** SILENT : callado — **~** *adv* **1** : todavía, aún **2** NEVERTHELESS : de todos modos, aún así **3 sit ~!** : ¡quédate quieto! — **~** *n* : quietud *f*, calma *f* — **stillborn** *adj* : nacido muerto — **stillness** *n* : calma *f*, silencio *m*

stilt *n* : zanco *m* — **stilted** *adj* : forzado

stimulate *vt* **-lated; -lating** : estimular — **stimulant** *n* : estimulante *m* — **stimulation** *n* : estimulación *f* — **stimulus** *n*, *pl* **-li** : estímulo *m*

sting *v* **stung; stinging** : picar — **~** *n* : picadura *f* — **stinger** *n* : aguijón *m*

stingy *adj* **stingier; -est** : tacaño — **stinginess** *n* : tacañería *f*

stink *vi* **stank** *or* **stunk; stunk; stinking** : apestar, oler mal — **~** *n* : hedor *m*, peste *f* fam

stint *vi* **~ on** : escatimar — **~** *n* : período *m*

stipulate *vt* **-lated; -lating** : estipular

stir *v* **stirred; stirring** *vt* **1** : remover, revolver **2** MOVE : mover **3** INCITE : incitar **4** *or* **~ up** : despertar (memorias, etc.), provocar (ira, etc.) — **~** *vi* : moverse, agitarse — **~** *n* COMMOTION : revuelo *m*

stirrup *n* : estribo *m*

stitch *n* **1** : puntada *f* **2** PAIN : punzada *f* (en el costado) — **~** *v* : coser

stock *n* **1** INVENTORY : existencias *fpl* **2** SECURITIES : acciones *fpl* **3** ANCESTRY : linaje *m*, estirpe *f* **4** BROTH : caldo *m* **5 out of ~** : agotado **6 take ~ of** : evaluar — **~** *vt* : surtir, abastecer — **~** *vi* **~ up on** : abastecerse — **stockbroker** *n* : corredor *m*, -dora *f* de bolsa

stocking *n* : media *f*

stock market *n* : bolsa *f* — **stockpile** *n* : reservas *fpl* — **~** *vt* **-piled; -piling** : almacenar — **stocky** *adj* **stockier; -est** : robusto, fornido

stodgy *adj* **stodgier; -est 1** DULL : pesado **2** OLD-FASHIONED : anticuado

stoic n : estoico m, -ca f — ~ or **stoical** adj : estoico — **stoicism** n : estoicismo m

stoke vt **stoked; stoking** : echar carbón o leña a

stole[1] → **steal**

stole[2] n : estola f

stolen → **steal**

stomach n : estómago m — ~ vt : aguantar, soportar — **stomachache** n : dolor m de estómago

stone n 1 : piedra f 2 : hueso m (de una fruta) — ~ vt **stoned; stoning** : apedrear — **stony** adj **stonier; -est** 1 : pedregoso 2 a ~ **silence** : un silencio sepulcral

stood → **stand**

stool n : taburete m

stoop vi 1 : agacharse 2 ~ **to** : rebajarse a — ~ n **have a** ~ : ser encorvado

stop v **stopped; stopping** vt 1 PLUG : tapar 2 PREVENT : impedir 3 HALT : parar, detener 4 CEASE : dejar de — vi 1 : detenerse, parar 2 CEASE : cesar, dejar 3 ~ **by** : visitar — ~ n 1 : parada f, alto m 2 **come to a** ~ : pararse, detenerse 3 **put a** ~ **to** : poner fin a — **stopgap** n : arreglo m provisorio — **stoplight** n : semáforo m — **stoppage** n or **work** ~ : paro m — **stopper** n : tapón m

store vt **stored; storing** : guardar (comida, etc.), almacenar (datos, mercancías, etc.) — ~ n 1 SUPPLY : reserva f 2 SHOP : tienda f — **storage** n : almacenamiento m — **storehouse** n : almacén m — **storekeeper** n : tendero m, -ra f — **storeroom** n : almacén m

stork n : cigüeña f

storm n : tormenta f, tempestad f — ~ vi 1 RAGE : ponerse furioso 2 ~ **in/out** : entrar/salir furioso — vt ATTACK : asaltar — **stormy** adj **stormier; -est** : tormentoso

story[1] n, pl **stories** 1 TALE : cuento m 2 ACCOUNT : historia f 3 RUMOR : rumor m

story[2] n FLOOR : piso m, planta f

stout adj 1 BRAVE : valiente 2 RESOLUTE : tenaz 3 STURDY : fuerte 4 FAT : corpulento

stove[1] n 1 : estufa f (para calentar) 2 RANGE : cocina f

stove[2] → **stave**

stow vt 1 : guardar 2 LOAD : cargar — vi ~ **away** : viajar de polizón — **stowaway** n : polizón m

straddle vt **-dled; -dling** : sentarse a horcajadas sobre

straggle vi **-gled; -gling** : rezagarse, quedarse atrás — **straggler** n : rezagado m, -da f

straight adj 1 : recto, derecho 2 : lacio (dícese del pelo) 3 HONEST : franco 4 TIDY : arreglado — ~ adv 1 DIRECTLY : derecho 2 EXACTLY : justo 3 CLEARLY : con claridad 4 FRANKLY : con franqueza — **straightaway** adv : inmediatamente — **straighten** vt 1 : enderezar 2 ~ **up** : arreglar — **straightforward** adj 1 FRANK : franco 2 CLEAR : claro, sencillo

strain[1] n 1 LINEAGE : linaje m 2 STREAK : veta f 3 VARIETY : variedad f 4 ~**s** npl : acordes mpl (de música)

strain[2] vt 1 : forzar (la vista o la voz) 2 FILTER : colar 3 : tensar (relaciones, etc.) 4 ~ **a muscle** : sufrir un esguince 5 ~ **oneself** : hacerse daño — vi : esforzarse (por) — ~ n 1 STRESS : tensión f 2 SPRAIN : esguince m — **strainer** n : colador m

strait n 1 : estrecho m 2 **in dire** ~**s** : en grandes apuros

strand[1] vt **be** ~**ed** : quedar(se) varado

strand[2] n 1 : hebra f 2 **a** ~ **of hair** : un pelo

strange adj **stranger; -est** 1 : extraño, raro 2 UNFAMILIAR : desconocido — **strangely** adv : de manera extraña — **strangeness** n 1 : rareza f 2 UNFAMILIARITY : lo desconocido — **stranger** n : desconocido m, -da f

strangle vt **-gled; -gling** : estrangular

strap n 1 : correa f 2 or **shoulder** ~ : tirante m — ~ vt **strapped; strapping** : sujetar con una correa — **strapless** n : sin tirantes — **strapping** adj : robusto, fornido

strategy n, pl **-gies** : estrategia f — **strategic** adj : estratégico

straw n 1 : paja f 2 or **drinking** ~ : pajita f 3 **the last** ~ : el colmo

strawberry n, pl **-ries** : fresa f

stray n : animal m perdido — ~ vi 1 : perderse, extraviarse 2 : apartarse (de un grupo, etc.) 3 DEVIATE : desviarse — ~ adj : perdido

streak n 1 : raya f 2 VEIN : veta f 3 ~ **of luck** : racha f de suerte — vi ~ **by** : pasar como una flecha

stream n 1 : arroyo m, riachuelo m 2 FLOW : chorro m, corriente f — ~ vi : correr — **streamer** n 1 PENNANT : banderín m 2 : serpentina f (de papel) — **streamlined** adj 1 : aerodinámico 2 EFFICIENT : eficiente

street n : calle f — **streetcar** n : tranvía m — **streetlight** n : farol m

strength n 1 : fuerza f 2 FORTITUDE : fortaleza f 3 TOUGHNESS : resistencia f, solidez f 4 INTENSITY : intensidad f 5 ~**s and weaknesses** : virtudes y defectos — **strengthen** vt 1 : fortalecer 2 REINFORCE : reforzar 3 INTENSIFY : intensificar

strenuous adj 1 : enérgico 2 ARDUOUS : duro, riguroso

stress n 1 : tensión f 2 EMPHASIS : énfasis m 3 : acento m (en lingüística) — ~ vt 1

stretch

EMPHASIZE : enfatizar **2** *or* ~ **out** : estresar — **stressful** *adj* : estresante
stretch *vt* **1** : estirar (músculos, elástico, etc.) **2** EXTEND : extender **3** ~ **the truth** : forzar la verdad — *vi* **1** : estirarse **2** EXTEND : extenderse — ~ *n* **1** : extensión *f* **2** ELASTICITY : elasticidad *f* **3** EXPANSE : tramo *m* **4** : período *m* (de tiempo) — **stretcher** *n* : camilla *f*
strew *vt* **strewed; strewed** *or* **strewn; strewing** : esparcir (semillas, etc.), desparramar (papeles, etc.)
stricken *adj* ~ **with** : aquejado de (una enfermedad), afligido por (tristeza, etc.)
strict *adj* : estricto — **strictly** *adv* ~ **speaking** : en rigor
stride *vi* **strode; stridden; striding** : ir dando zancadas — ~ *n* **1** : zancada *f* **2 make great** ~**s** : hacer grandes progresos
strident *adj* : estridente
strife *n* : conflictos *mpl*
strike *v* **struck; struck; striking** *vt* **1** HIT : golpear **2** *or* ~ **against** : chocar contra **3** *or* ~ **out** DELETE : tachar **4** : dar (la hora) **5** IMPRESS : impresionar **6** : descubrir (oro o petróleo) **7 it** ~**s me as...** : me parece... **8** ~ **up** START : entablar — *vi* **1** : golpear **2** ATTACK : atacar **3** : declararse en huelga **4** : sobrevenir (dícese de una enfermedad, etc.) — ~ *n* **1** BLOW : golpe *m* **2** : huelga *f*, paro *m* *Lat* (de trabajadores) **3** ATTACK : ataque *m* — **strikebreaker** *n* : esquirol *mf* — **striker** *n* : huelgista *mf* — **striking** *adj* : notable, llamativo
string *n* **1** : cordel *m* **2** : sarta *f* (de perlas, insultos, etc.), serie *f* (de eventos, etc.) **3** ~**s** *npl* : cuerdas *fpl* (en música) — ~ *vt* **strung; stringing 1** : ensartar **2** *or* ~ **up** : colgar — **string bean** *n* : habichuela *f* verde
stringent *adj* : estricto, severo
strip[1] *v* **stripped; stripping** *vt* **1** REMOVE : quitar **2** UNDRESS : desnudar **3** ~ **s.o. of sth** : despojar a algn de algo — *vi* UNDRESS : desnudarse
strip[2] *n* : tira *f*
stripe *n* : raya *f*, lista *f* — **striped** *adj* : a rayas, rayado
strive *vi* **strove; striven** *or* **strived; striving 1** ~ **for** : luchar por **2** ~ **to** : esforzarse por
strode → **stride**
stroke *vt* **stroked; stroking** : acariciar — ~ *n* **1** : golpe *m* **2** : derrame *m* cerebral (en medicina)
stroll *vi* : pasearse — ~ *n* : paseo *m* — **stroller** *n* : cochecito *m* (para niños)
strong *adj* : fuerte — **stronghold** *n* : bastión *m* — **strongly** *adv* **1** DEEPLY : profunda-

mente **2** WHOLEHEARTEDLY : totalmente **3** VIGOROUSLY : enérgicamente
strove → **strive**
struck → **strike**
structure *n* : estructura *f* — **structural** *adj* : estructural
struggle *vi* **-gled; -gling 1** : forcejear **2** STRIVE : luchar — ~ *n* : lucha *f*
strum *vt* **strummed; strumming** : rasguear
strung → **string**
strut *vi* **strutted; strutting** : pavonearse — ~ *n* : puntal *m* (en construcción)
stub *n* : colilla *f* (de un cigarillo), cabo *m* (de un lápiz, etc.), talón *m* (de un cheque) — ~ *vt* **stubbed; stubbing** ~ **one's toe** : darse en el dedo
stubble *n* : barba *f* de varios días
stubborn *adj* **1** : terco, obstinado **2** PERSISTENT : tenaz
stucco *n, pl* **stuccos** *or* **stuccoes** : estuco
stuck → **stick** — **stuck–up** *adj* : engreído, creído *fam*
stud[1] *n* : semental *m* (animal)
stud[2] *n* **1** NAIL, TACK : tachuela *f*, tachón *m* **2** *or* ~ **earring** : arete *m* *Lat*, pendiente *m* *Spain* **3** : montante *m* (en construcción)
student *n* : estudiante *mf; alumno *m*, -na *f* (de un colegio) — **studio** *n, pl* **studios** : estudio *m* — **study** *n, pl* **studies** : estudio *m* — ~ *v* **studied; studying** : estudiar — **studious** *adj* : estudioso
stuff *n* **1** : cosas *fpl* **2** MATTER, SUBSTANCE : cosa *f* **3 know one's** ~ : ser experto — ~ *vt* **1** FILL : rellenar **2** CRAM : meter — **stuffing** *n* : relleno *m* — **stuffy** *adj* **stuffier; -est 1** STODGY : pesado, aburrido **2** : tapado (dícese de la nariz) **3** ~ **rooms** : salas *fpl* mal ventiladas
stumble *vi* **-bled; -bling 1** : tropezar **2** ~ **across** *or* **upon** : tropezar con
stump *n* **1** : muñón *m* (de una pierna, etc.) **2** *or* ~ **tree** : tocón *m* — ~ *vt* : dejar perplejo
stun *vt* **stunned; stunning 1** : aturdir (con un golpe) **2** ASTONISH : dejar atónito
stung → **sting**
stunk → **stink**
stunning *adj* **1** : increíble, sensacional **2** STRIKING : imponente
stunt[1] *vt* : atrofiar
stunt[2] *n* : proeza *f* (acrobática)
stupendous *adj* : estupendo
stupid *adj* **1** : estúpido **2** SILLY : tonto, bobo — **stupidity** *n* : tontería *f*, estupidez *f*
sturdy *adj* **sturdier; -est 1** : fuerte, resistente **2** ROBUST : robusto
stutter *vi* : tartamudear — ~ *n* : tartamudeo *m*

sty *n* **1** *pl* **sties** PIGPEN : pocilga *f* **2** *pl* **sties** *or* **styes** : orzuelo *m* (en el ojo)
style *n* **1** : estilo *m* **2** FASHION : moda *f* **3 be in** ~ : estar de moda — ~ *vt* **styled; styling** : peinar (pelo), diseñar (vestidos, etc.) — **stylish** *adj* : elegante, chic — **stylist** *n* : estilista *mf*
suave *adj* : refinado y afable
sub¹ *vi* **subbed; subbing** → **substitute** — ~ *n* → **substitute**
sub² *n* → **submarine**
subconscious *adj* : subconsciente — ~ *n* : subconsciente *m*
subdivide *vt* **-vided; -viding** : subdividir — **subdivision** *n* : subdivisión *f*
subdue *vt* **-dued; -duing** **1** CONQUER : sojuzgar **2** CONTROL : dominar **3** SOFTEN : atenuar — **subdued** *adj* : apagado
subject *n* **1** : sujeto *m* **2** : súbdito *m*, -ta *f* (de un gobierno) **3** TOPIC : tema *m* — ~ *adj* **1** : sometido **2** ~ **to** : sujeto a — ~ *vt* ~ **to** : someter a — **subjective** *adj* : subjetivo
subjunctive *n* : subjuntivo *m* — **subjunctive** *adj* : subjuntivo
sublime *adj* : sublime
submarine *adj* : submarino — ~ *n* : submarino *m*
submerge *v* **-merged; -merging** *vt* : sumergir — *vi* : sumergirse
submit *v* **-mitted; -mitting** *vi* **1** YIELD : rendirse **2** ~ **to** : someterse a — *vt* : presentar — **submission** *n* **1** : sumisión *f* **2** PRESENTATION : presentación *f* — **submissive** *adj* : sumiso
subordinate *adj* : subordinado — ~ *n* : subordinado *m*, -da *f* — ~ *vt* **-nated; -nating** : subordinar
subpoena *n* : citación *f*
subscribe *vi* **-scribed; -scribing** ~ **to** : suscribirse a (una revista, etc.), suscribir (una opinión, etc.) — **subscriber** *n* : suscriptor *m*, -tora *f* (de una revista, etc.); abonado *m*, -da *f* (de un servicio) — **subscription** *n* : suscripción *f*
subsequent *adj* **1** : subsiguiente **2** ~ **to** : posterior a — **subsequently** *adv* : posteriormente
subservient *adj* : servil
subside *vi* **-sided; -siding** **1** SINK : hundirse **2** : amainar (dícese de tormentas, pasiones, etc.), remitir (dícese de fiebres, etc.)
subsidiary *adj* : secundario — ~ *n*, *pl* **-ries** : filial *f*
subsidy *n*, *pl* **-dies** : subvención *f* — **subsidize** *vt* **-dized; -dizing** : subvencionar
subsistence *n* : subsistencia *f* — **subsist** *vi* : subsistir
substance *n* : sustancia *f*
substandard *adj* : inferior

substantial *adj* **1** CONSIDERABLE : considerable **2** STURDY : sólido **3** : sustancioso (dícese de una comida, etc.) — **substantially** *adv* : considerablemente
substitute *n* : sustituto *m*, -ta *f* (de una persona); sucedáneo *m* (de una cosa) — ~ *vt* **-tuted; -tuting** : sustituir — **substitution** *n* : sustitución *f*
subterranean *adj* : subterráneo
subtitle *n* : subtítulo *m*
subtle *adj* **-tler; -tlest** : sutil — **subtlety** *n*, *pl* **-ties** : sutileza *f*
subtraction *n* : resta *f* — **subtract** *vt* : restar
suburb *n* **1** : barrio *m* residencial, suburbio *m* **2 the** ~**s** : las afueras — **suburban** *adj* : de las afueras (de una ciudad)
subversion *n* : subversión *f* — **subversive** *adj* : subversivo
subway *n* : metro *m*
succeed *vt* : suceder a — *vi* : tener éxito (dícese de personas), dar resultado (dícese de planes, etc.) — **success** *n* : éxito *m* — **successful** *adj* : de éxito, exitoso *Lat* — **successfully** *adv* : con éxito
succession *n* **1** : sucesión *f* **2 in** ~ : sucesivamente, seguidos — **successive** *adj* : sucesivo — **successor** *n* : sucesor *m*, -sora *f*
succinct *adj* : sucinto
succulent *adj* : suculento
succumb *vi* : sucumbir
such *adj* **1** : tal **2** ~ **as** : como **3** ~ **a pity!** : ¡qué lástima! — ~ *pron* **1** : tal **2 and** ~ : y cosas por el estilo **3 as** ~ : como tal — ~ *adv* **1** VERY : muy **2** ~ **a nice man!** : ¡qué hombre tan simpático! **3** ~ **that** : de tal manera que
suck *vt* **1** *or* ~ **on** : chupar **2** *or* ~ **up** : sorber (bebidas), aspirar (con una máquina) — **sucker** *n* **1** SHOOT : chupón *m* **2** FOOL : imbécil *mf* — **suckle** *vt* **-led; -ling** : amamantar — **suction** *n* : succión *f*
sudden *adj* **1** : repentino **2 all of a** ~ : de repente — **suddenly** *adv* : de repente
suds *npl* : espuma *f* (de jabón)
sue *vt* **sued; suing** : demandar (por)
suede *n* : ante *m*, gamuza *f*
suet *n* : sebo *m*
suffer *vi* : sufrir — *vt* **1** : sufrir **2** BEAR : tolerar — **suffering** *n* : sufrimiento *m*
suffice *vi* **-ficed; -ficing** : bastar — **sufficient** *adj* : suficiente — **sufficiently** *adv* : (lo) suficientemente
suffix *n* : sufijo *m*
suffocate *v* **-cated; -cating** *vt* : asfixiar — *vi* : asfixiarse — **suffocation** *n* : asfixia *f*
suffrage *n* : sufragio *m*
sugar *n* : azúcar *mf* — **sugarcane** *n* : caña *f* de azúcar — **sugary** *adj* : azucarado

suggestion *n* **1** : sugerencia *f* **2** TRACE : indicio *m* — **suggest** *vt* **1** : sugerir **2** INDICATE : indicar

suicide *n* **1** : suicidio *m* (acto) **2** : suicida *mf* (persona) — **suicidal** *adj* : suicida

suit *n* **1** LAWSUIT : pleito *m* **2** : traje *m* (ropa) **3** : palo *m* (de naipes) — ~ *vt* **1** ADAPT : adaptar **2** BEFIT : ser apropiado para **3** ~ s.o. : convenir a algn (dícese de fechas, etc.), quedar bien a algn (dícese de ropa) — **suitable** *adj* : apropiado — **suitcase** *n* : maleta *f*, valija *f Lat*

suite *n* **1** : suite *f* (de habitaciones) **2** : juego *m* (de muebles)

suitor *n* : pretendiente *m*

sulfur *n* : azufre *m*

sulk *vi* : enfurruñarse *fam* — **sulky** *adj* **sulkier; -est** : malhumorado

sullen *adj* : hosco

sultry *adj* **sultrier; -est** **1** : bochornoso **2** SENSUAL : sensual

sum *n* : suma *f* — ~ *vt* **summed; summing** ~ **up** : resumir — **summarize** *v* **-rized; -rizing** : resumir — **summary** *n, pl* **-ries** : resumen *m*

summer *n* : verano *m*

summit *n* : cumbre *f*

summon *vt* **1** : llamar (a algn), convocar (una reunión) **2** : citar (en derecho) — **summons** *n, pl* **summonses** SUBPOENA : citación *f*

sumptuous *adj* : suntuoso

sun *n* : sol *m* — **sunbathe** *vi* **-bathed; -bathing** : tomar el sol — **sunbeam** *n* : rayo *m* de sol — **sunburn** *n* : quemadura *f* de sol

Sunday *n* : domingo *m*

sundry *adj* : varios, diversos

sunflower *n* : girasol *m*

sung → **sing**

sunglasses *npl* : gafas *fpl* de sol, lentes *mpl* de sol

sunk → **sink** — **sunken** *adj* : hundido

sunlight *n* : (luz *f* del) sol *m* — **sunny** *adj* **-nier; -est** : soleado — **sunrise** *n* : salida *f* del sol — **sunset** *n* : puesta *f* del sol — **sunshine** *n* : sol *m*, luz *f* del sol — **suntan** *n* : bronceado *m*

super *adj* : súper *fam*

superb *adj* : magnífico, espléndido

superficial *adj* : superficial

superfluous *adj* : superfluo

superimpose *vt* **-posed; -posing** : sobreponer

superintendent *n* **1** : superintendente *mf* (de policía) **2** *or* **building** ~ : portero *m*, -ra *f* **3** *or* **school** ~ : director *m*, -tora *f* (de un colegio)

superior *adj* : superior — ~ *n* : superior *m* — **superiority** *n, pl* **-ties** : superioridad *f*

superlative *adj* **1** : superlativo (en gramática) **2** EXCELLENT : excepcional — ~ *n* : superlativo *m*

supermarket *n* : supermercado *m*

supernatural *adj* : sobrenatural

superpower *n* : superpotencia *f*

supersede *vt* **-seded; -seding** : reemplazar, suplantar

supersonic *adj* : supersónico

superstition *n* : superstición *f* — **superstitious** *adj* : supersticioso

supervisor *n* : supervisor *m*, -sora *f* — **supervise** *vt* **-vised; -vising** : supervisar — **supervision** *n* : supervisión *f* — **supervisory** *adj* : de supervisor

supper *n* : cena *f*, comida *f*

supplant *vt* : suplantar

supple *adj* **-pler; -plest** : flexible

supplement *n* : suplemento *m* — ~ *vt* : complementar — **supplementary** *adj* : suplementario

supply *vt* **-plied; -plying** **1** : suministrar **2** ~ **with** : proveer de — ~ *n, pl* **-plies** **1** : suministro *m*, provisión *f* **2** ~ **and demand** : oferta y demanda **3 supplies** *npl* PROVISIONS : provisiones *fpl*, víveres *mpl* — **supplier** *n* : proveedor *m*, -dora *f*

support *vt* **1** BACK : apoyar **2** : mantener (una familia, etc.) **3** PROP UP : sostener — ~ *n* **1** : apoyo *m* (moral), ayuda *f* (económica) **2** PROP : soporte *m* — **supporter** *n* : partidario *m*, -ria *f*

suppose *vt* **-posed; -posing** **1** : suponer **2 be ~d to (do sth)** : tener que (hacer algo) — **supposedly** *adv* : supuestamente

suppress *vt* **1** : reprimir **2** : suprimir (noticias, etc.) — **suppression** *n* **1** : represión *f* **2** : supresión *f* (de información)

supreme *adj* : supremo — **supremacy** *n, pl* **-cies** : supremacía *f*

sure *adj* **surer; -est** **1** : seguro **2 make ~ that** : asegurarse de que — ~ *adv* **1** OF COURSE : por supuesto, claro **2 it ~ is hot!** : ¡qué calor! — **surely** *adv* : seguramente

surfing *n* : surf *m*, surfing *m*

surface *n* : superficie *f* — ~ *v* **-faced; -facing** *vi* : salir a la superficie — *vt* : revestir

surfeit *n* : exceso *m*

surfing *n* : surf *m*, surfing *m*

surge *vi* **surged; surging** **1** SWELL : hincharse (dícese del mar) **2** SWARM : moverse en tropel — ~ *n* **1** : oleaje *m* (del mar), oleada *f* (de gente) **2** INCREASE : aumento *m* (súbito)

surgeon *n* : cirujano *m*, -na *f* — **surgery** *n, pl* **-geries** : cirugía *f* — **surgical** *adj* : quirúrgico

surly *adj* **surlier; -est** : hosco, arisco
surmount *vt* : superar
surname *n* : apellido *m*
surpass *vt* : superar
surplus *n* : excedente *m*
surprise *n* **1** : sorpresa *f* **2 take by** ~ : sorprender — ~ *vt* **-prised; -prising** : sorprender — **surprising** *adj* : sorprendente
surrender *vt* : entregar, rendir — *vi* : rendirse — ~ *n* : rendición *m* (de una ciudad, etc.), entrega *f* (de posesiones)
surrogate *n* : sustituto *m*
surround *vt* : rodear — **surroundings** *npl* : ambiente *m*
surveillance *n* : vigilancia *f*
survey *vt* **-veyed; -veying 1** : medir (un solar) **2** INSPECT : inspeccionar **3** POLL : sondear — ~ *n*, *pl* **-veys 1** INSPECTION : inspección *f* **2** : medición *f* (de un solar) **3** POLL : encuesta *f*, sondeo *m* — **surveyor** *n* : agrimensor *m*, -sora *f*
survive *v* **-vived; -viving** *vi* : sobrevivir — *vt* : sobrevivir a — **survival** *n* : supervivencia *f* — **survivor** *n* : superviviente *mf*
susceptible *adj* ~ **to** : propenso a — **susceptibility** *n*, *pl* **-ties** : propensión *f* (a enfermedades, etc.)
suspect *adj* : sospechoso — ~ *n* : sospechoso *m*, -sa *f* — ~ *vt* : sospechar (algo), sospechar de (algn)
suspend *vt* : suspender — **suspense** *n* **1** : incertidumbre *m* **2** : suspenso *m* Lat, suspense *m* Spain (en el cine, etc.) — **suspension** *n* : suspensión *f*
suspicion *n* : sospecha *f* — **suspicious** *adj* **1** QUESTIONABLE : sospechoso **2** DISTRUSTFUL : suspicaz
sustain *vt* **1** : sostener **2** SUFFER : sufrir
swagger *vi* : pavonearse
swallow¹ *v* : tragar — ~ *n* : trago *m*
swallow² *n* : golondrina *f* (pájaro)
swam → **swim**
swamp *n* : pantano *m*, ciénaga *f* — ~ *vt* : inundar — **swampy** *adj* **swampier; -est** : pantanoso, cenagoso
swan *n* : cisne *f*
swap *vt* **swapped; swapping 1** : intercambiar **2** ~ **sth for sth** : cambiar algo por algo **3** ~ **sth with s.o.** : cambiar algo a algn — ~ *n* : cambio *m*
swarm *n* : enjambre *m* — ~ *vi* : enjambrar
swat *vt* **swatted; swatting** : aplastar (un insecto)
sway *n* **1** : balanceo *m* **2** INFLUENCE : influjo *m* — ~ *vi* : balancearse — *vt* : influir en
swear *v* **swore; sworn; swearing** *vi* **1** : jurar **2** CURSE : decir palabrotas — *vt* : jurar — **swearword** *n* : palabrota *f*

sweat *vi* **sweat** *or* **sweated; sweating** : sudar — ~ *n* : sudor *m* — **sweater** *n* : suéter *m* — **sweatshirt** *n* : sudadera *f* — **sweaty** *adj* **sweatier; -est** : sudado
Swedish *adj* : sueco — ~ *n* : sueco *m* (idioma)
sweep *v* **swept; sweeping** *vt* **1** : barrer **2** ~ **aside** : apartar **3** ~ **through** : extenderse por — *vi* : barrer — ~ *n* **1** : barrido *m* **2** : movimiento *m* circular (de la mano, etc.) **3** SCOPE : alcance *m* — **sweeping** *adj* **1** WIDE : amplio **2** EXTENSIVE : extenso — **sweepstakes** *ns* & *pl* : lotería *f*
sweet *adj* **1** : dulce **2** PLEASANT : agradable — ~ *n* : dulce *m* — **sweeten** *vt* : endulzar — **sweetener** *n* : endulzante *m* — **sweetheart** *n* **1** : novio *m*, -via *f* **2** (*used as a form of address*) : cariño *m* — **sweetness** *n* : dulzura *f* — **sweet potato** *n* : batata *f*, boniato *m*
swell *vi* **swelled; swelled** *or* **swollen; swelling 1** *or* ~ **up** : hincharse **2** INCREASE : aumentar, crecer — ~ *n* : oleaje *m* (del mar) — **swelling** *n* : hinchazón *f*
sweltering *adj* : sofocante
swept → **sweep**
swerve *vi* **swerved; swerving** : virar bruscamente
swift *adj* : rápido — **swiftly** *adv* : rápidamente
swig *n* : trago *m* — ~ *vi* **swigged; swigging** : beber a tragos
swim *vi* **swam; swum; swimming 1** : nadar **2** REEL : dar vueltas — ~ *n* **1** : baño *m* **2 go for a** ~ : ir a nadar — **swimmer** *n* : nadador *m*, -dora *f*
swindle *vt* **-dled; -dling** : estafar, timar — ~ *n* : estafa *f*, timo *m fam*
swine *ns* & *pl* : cerdo *m*, -da *f*
swing *v* **swung; swinging** *vt* **1** : balancear, hacer oscilar **2** MANAGE : arreglar — *vi* **1** : balancearse, oscilar **2** SWIVEL : girar — ~ *n* **1** : vaivén *m*, balanceo *m* **2** SHIFT : cambio *m* **3** : columpio *m* (para niños) **4 in full** ~ : en pleno proceso
swipe *v* **swiped; swiping** *vt* STEAL : birlar *fam*, robar — ~ *vt* ~ **at** : intentar pegar
swirl *vi* : arremolinarse — ~ *n* **1** EDDY : remolino *m* **2** SPIRAL : espiral *f*
swish *vt* : agitar (haciendo un sonido) — *vi* **1** RUSTLE : hacer frufrú **2** ~ **by** : pasar silbando
Swiss *adj* : suizo
switch *n* **1** WHIP : vara *f* **2** CHANGE : cambio *m* **3** : interruptor *m*, llave *f* (de la luz, etc.) — ~ *vt* **1** CHANGE : cambiar de **2** EXCHANGE : intercambiar **3** ~ **on** : encender, prender *Lat* **4** ~ **off** : apagar — *vi* **1** : sacudir (la cola, etc.) **2** CHANGE : cambiar

3 SWAP : intercambiarse — **switchboard** *n* : centralita *f*, conmutador *m* *Lat*
swivel *vi* **-veled** *or* **-velled; -veling** *or* **-velling** : girar (sobre un pivote)
swollen → **swell**
swoon *vi* : desvanecerse
swoop *vi* ~ **down on** : abatirse sobre — ~ *n* : descenso *m* en picada
sword *n* : espada *f*
swordfish *n* : pez *m* espada
swore, sworn → **swear**
swum → **swim**
swung → **swing**
syllable *n* : sílaba *f*
syllabus *n*, *pl* **-bi** *or* **-buses** : programa *m* (de estudios)
symbol *n* : símbolo *m* — **symbolic** *adj* : simbólico — **symbolism** *n* : simbolismo *m* — **symbolize** *vt* **-ized; -izing** : simbolizar
symmetry *n*, *pl* **-tries** : simetría *f* — **symmetrical** *adj* : simétrico
sympathy *n*, *pl* **-thies** **1** COMPASSION : compasión *f* **2** UNDERSTANDING : comprensión *f* **3** CONDOLENCES : pésame *m* **4 sympathies** *npl* LOYALTY : simpatías *fpl* — **sympathize** *vi* **-thized; -thizing** **1** ~ **with** PITY : com-

padecerse de **2** ~ **with** UNDERSTAND : comprender — **sympathetic** *adj* **1** COMPASSIONATE : compasivo **2** UNDERSTANDING : comprensivo
symphony *n*, *pl* **-nies** : sinfonía *f*
symposium *n*, *pl* **-sia** *or* **-siums** : simposio *m*
symptom *n* : síntoma *m* — **symptomatic** *adj* : sintomático
synagogue *n* : sinagoga *f*
synchronize *vt* **-nized; -nizing** : sincronizar
syndrome *n* : síndrome *m*
synonym *n* : sinónimo *m* — **synonymous** *adj* : sinónimo
synopsis *n*, *pl* **-opses** : sinopsis *f*
syntax *n* : sintaxis *f*
synthesis *n*, *pl* **-theses** : síntesis *f* — **synthesize** *vt* **-sized; -sizing** : sintetizar — **synthetic** *adj* : sintético
syphilis *n* : sífilis *f*
Syrian *adj* : sirio
syringe *n* : jeringa *f*, jeringuilla *f*
syrup *n* : jarabe *m*
system *n* **1** : sistema *m* **2** BODY : organismo *m* **3 digestive** ~ : aparato *m* digestivo — **systematic** *adj* : sistemático

T

t *n*, *pl* **t's** *or* **ts** : t *f*, vigésima letra del alfabeto inglés
tab *n* **1** TAG : etiqueta *f* **2** FLAP : lengüeta *f* **3** ACCOUNT : cuenta *f* **4 keep** ~**s on** : vigilar
table *n* **1** : mesa *f* **2** LIST : tabla *f* **3** ~ **of contents** : índice *m* de materias — **tablecloth** *n* : mantel *m* — **tablespoon** *n* **1** : cuchara *f* grande **2** : cucharada *f* (cantidad)
tablet *n* **1** PAD : bloc *m* **2** PILL : pastilla *f* **3** *or* **stone** ~ : lápida *f*
tabloid *n* : tabloide *m*
taboo *adj* : tabú — ~ *n* : tabú *m*
tacit *adj* : tácito
taciturn *adj* : taciturno
tack *vt* **1** : fijar con tachuelas **2** ~ **on** ADD : añadir — ~ *n* **1** : tachuela *f* **2 change** ~ : cambiar de rumbo
tackle *n* **1** GEAR : aparejo *m* **2** : placaje *m*, tacle *m* *Lat* (acción) — ~ *vt* **-led; -ling** **1** : placar, taclear *Lat* **2** CONFRONT : abordar
tacky *adj* **tackier; -est** **1** : pegajoso **2** GAUDY : de mal gusto

tact *n* : tacto *m* — **tactful** *adj* : diplomático, discreto
tactical *adj* : táctico — **tactic** *n* : táctica *f* — **tactics** *ns* & *pl* : táctica *f*
tactless *adj* : indiscreto
tadpole *n* : renacuajo *m*
tag¹ *n* LABEL : etiqueta *f* — ~ *v* **tagged; tagging** *vt* : etiquetar — *vi* ~ **along with** s.o. : acompañar a algn
tag² *vt* : tocar (en varios juegos)
tail *n* **1** : cola *f* **2** ~**s** *npl* : cruz *f* (de una moneda) — ~ *vt* FOLLOW : seguir
tailor *n* : sastre *m*, -tra *f* — ~ *vt* **1** : confeccionar (ropa) **2** ADAPT : adaptar
taint *vt* : contaminar
take *v* **took; taken; taking** *vt* **1** : tomar **2** BRING : llevar **3** REMOVE : sacar **4** BEAR : soportar, aguantar **5** ACCEPT : aceptar **6 I** ~ **it that...** : supongo que... **7** ~ **a bath** : bañarse **8** ~ **a walk** : dar un paseo **9** ~ **back** : retirar (palabras, etc.) **10** ~ **in** ALTER : achicar **11** ~ **in** GRASP : entender **12** ~ **in** TRICK : engañar **13** ~ **off** REMOVE : quitar, quitarse (ropa) **14** ~ **on**

: asumir (una responsabilidad, etc.) **15** ~ **out** : sacar **16** ~ **over** : tomar el poder de **17** ~ **place** : tener lugar **18** ~ **up** SHORTEN : acortar **19** ~ **up** OCCUPY : ocupar — *vi* **1** : prender (dícese de una vacuna, etc.) **2** ~ **off** : despegar (dícese de aviones, etc.) **3** ~ **over** : asumir el mando — ~ *n* **1** PROCEEDS : ingresos *mpl* **2** : toma *f* (en el cine) — **takeoff** *n* : despegue *m* (de un avión, etc.) — **takeover** *n* : toma *f* (de poder, etc.), adquisición *f* (de una empresa)

talcum powder *n* : polvos *mpl* de talco

tale *n* : cuento *m*

talent *n* : talento *m* — **talented** *adj* : talentoso

talk *vi* **1** : hablar **2** ~ **about** : hablar de **3** ~ **to/with** : hablar con — *vt* **1** SPEAK : hablar **2** ~ **over** : hablar de, discutir — ~ *n* **1** CHAT : conversación *f* **2** SPEECH : charla *f* — **talkative** *adj* : hablador

tall *adj* **1** : alto **2 how** ~ **are you?** : ¿cuánto mides?

tally *n, pl* **-lies** : cuenta *f* — ~ *v* **-lied; -lying** *vt* RECKON : calcular — *vi* MATCH : concordar, cuadrar

talon *n* : garra *f*

tambourine *n* : pandereta *f*

tame *adj* **tamer; -est 1** : domesticado **2** DOCILE : manso **3** DULL : insípido, soso — ~ *vt* **tamed; taming** : domar

tamper *vi* ~ **with** : forzar (una cerradura), amañar (documentos, etc.)

tampon *n* : tampón *m*

tan *v* **tanned; tanning** *vt* : curtir (cuero) — *vi* : broncearse — ~ *n* **1** SUNTAN : bronceado *m* **2** : (color *m*) café *m* con leche

tang *n* : sabor *m* fuerte

tangent *n* : tangente *f*

tangerine *n* : mandarina *f*

tangible *adj* : tangible

tangle *v* **-gled; -gling** *vt* : enredar — *vi* : enredarse — ~ *n* : enredo *m*

tango *n, pl* **-gos** : tango *m*

tank *n* **1** : tanque *m*, depósito *m* **2** : tanque *m* (militar) — **tanker** *n* **1** : buque *m* tanque **2** *or* ~ **truck** : camión *m* cisterna

tantalizing *adj* : tentador

tantrum *n* **throw a** ~ : hacer un berrinche

tap[1] *n* FAUCET : llave *f*, grifo *m* *Spain* — ~ *vt* **tapped; tapping 1** : sacar (un líquido, etc.), sangrar (un árbol) **2** : intervenir (un teléfono)

tap[2] *vt* **tapped; tapping** STRIKE : tocar, dar un golpecito en — ~ *n* : golpecito *m*, toque *m*

tape *n* : cinta *f* — ~ *vt* **taped; taping 1** : pegar con cinta **2** RECORD : grabar — **tape measure** *n* : cinta *f* métrica

taper *n* : vela *f* (larga) — ~ *vi* **1** NARROW : estrecharse **2** *or* ~ **off** : disminuir

tapestry *n, pl* **-tries** : tapiz *m*

tar *n* : alquitrán *m* — ~ *vt* **tarred; tarring** : alquitranar

tarantula *n* : tarántula *f*

target *n* **1** : blanco *m* **2** GOAL : objetivo *m*

tariff *n* : tarifa *f*, arancel *m*

tarnish *vt* **1** : deslustrar **2** : empañar (una reputación, etc.) — *vi* : deslustrarse

tart[1] *adj* SOUR : ácido, agrio

tart[2] *n* : pastel *m*

tartan *n* : tartán *m*

task *n* : tarea *f*

tassel *n* : borla *f*

taste *v* **tasted; tasting** *vt* TRY : probar — *vi* **1** : saber **2** ~ **like** : saber a — ~ *n* **1** FLAVOR : gusto *m*, sabor *m* **2 have a** ~ **of** : probar **3 in good/bad** ~ : de buen/mal gusto — **tasteful** *adj* : de buen gusto — **tasteless** *adj* **1** : sin sabor **2** COARSE : de mal gusto — **tasty** *adj* **tastier; -est** : sabroso

tatters *npl* : harapos *mpl* — **tattered** *adj* : harapiento

tattle *vi* **-tled; -tling** ~ **on s.o.** : acusar a algn

tattoo *vt* : tatuar — ~ *n* : tatuaje *m*

taught → **teach**

taunt *n* : pulla *f*, burla *f* — ~ *vt* : mofarse de, burlarse de

taut *adj* : tirante, tenso

tavern *n* : taberna *f*

tax *vt* **1** : gravar **2** STRAIN : poner a prueba — ~ *n* **1** : impuesto *m* **2** BURDEN : carga *f* — **taxable** *adj* : imponible — **taxation** *n* : impuestos *mpl* — **tax– exempt** *adj* : libre de impuestos

taxi *n, pl* **taxis** : taxi *m* — ~ *vi* **taxied; taxiing** *or* **taxying; taxis** *or* **taxies** : rodar por la pista (dícese de un avión)

taxpayer *n* : contribuyente *mf*

tea *n* : té *m*

teach *v* **taught; teaching** *vt* : enseñar, dar clases de (una asignatura) — *vi* : dar clases — **teacher** *n* : profesor *m*, -sora *f;* maestro *m*, -tra *f* (de niños pequeños) — **teaching** *n* : enseñanza *f*

teacup *n* : taza *f* de té

team *n* : equipo *m* — ~ *vi* *or* ~ **up** : asociarse — **teammate** *n* : compañero *m*, -ra *f* de equipo — **teamwork** *n* : trabajo *m* de equipo

teapot *n* : tetera *f*

tear[1] *v* **tore; torn; tearing** *vt* **1** : romper, rasgar **2** ~ **apart** : destrozar **3** ~ **down** : derribar **4** ~ **off** *or* ~ **out** : arrancar **5** ~ **up** : romper (papel, etc.) — *vi* **1** : romperse, rasgarse **2** RUSH : ir a toda velocidad — ~ *n* : desgarro *m*, rasgón *m*

tear² *n* : lágrima *f* — **tearful** *adj* : lloroso

tease *vt* **teased; teasing 1** : tomar el pelo a, burlarse de **2** ANNOY : fastidiar

teaspoon *n* **1** : cucharita *f* **2** : cucharadita *f* (cantidad)

technical *adj* : técnico — **technicality** *n, pl* **-ties** : detalle *m* técnico — **technically** *adv* : técnicamente — **technician** *n* : técnico *m*, -ca *f*

technique *n* : técnica *f*

technological *adj* : tecnológico — **technology** *n, pl* **-gies** : tecnología *f*

teddy bear *n* : oso *m* de peluche

tedious *adj* : tedioso, aburrido — **tedium** *n* : tedio *m*

tee *n* : tee *m* (en deportes)

teem *vi* **1** POUR : llover a cántaros **2** be ~**ing with** : estar repleto de

teenage *or* **teenaged** *adj* : adolescente — **teenager** *n* : adolescente *mf* — **teens** *npl* : adolescencia *f*

teepee → **tepee**

teeter *vi* : tambalearse

teeth → **tooth** — **teethe** *vi* **teethed; teething** : echar los dientes

telecommunication *n* : telecomunicación *f*

telegram *n* : telegrama *m*

telegraph *n* : telégrafo *m* — ~ *v* : telegrafiar

telephone *n* : teléfono *m* — ~ *v* **-phoned; -phoning** : llamar por teléfono

telescope *n* : telescopio *m*

televise *vt* **-vised; -vising** : televisar — **television** *n* : televisión *f*

tell *v* **told; telling** *vt* **1** : decir **2** RELATE : contar **3** DISTINGUISH : distinguir **4** ~ **s.o. off** : regañar a algn — *vi* **1** : decir **2** KNOW : saber **3** SHOW : tener efecto **4** ~ **on s.o.** : acusar a algn — **teller** *n or* **bank** ~ : cajero *m*, -ra *f*

temp *n* : empleado *m*, -da *f* temporal

temper *vt* MODERATE : temperar — ~ *n* **1** MOOD : humor *m* **2** have a bad ~ : tener mal genio **3** lose one's ~ : perder los estribos — **temperament** *n* : temperamento *m* — **temperamental** *adj* : temperamental — **temperate** *adj* **1** : moderado **2** ~ **zone** : zona *f* templada

temperature *n* **1** : temperatura *f* **2** have a ~ : tener fiebre

tempest *n* : tempestad *f*

temple *n* **1** : templo *m* **2** : sien *f* (en anatomía)

tempo *n, pl* **-pi** *or* **-pos 1** : tempo *m* **2** PACE : ritmo *m*

temporarily *adv* : temporalmente — **temporary** *adj* : temporal

tempt *vt* : tentar — **temptation** *n* : tentación *f*

ten *adj* : diez — ~ *n* : diez *m*

tenacity *n* : tenacidad *f* — **tenacious** *adj* : tenaz

tenant *n* : inquilino *m*, -na *f;* arrendatario *m*, -ria *f*

tend¹ *vt* MIND : cuidar

tend² *vi* ~ **to** : tender a — **tendency** *n, pl* **-cies** : tendencia *f*

tender¹ *adj* **1** : tierno **2** PAINFUL : dolorido

tender² *vt* : presentar — ~ *n* **1** : oferta *f* **2** legal ~ : moneda *f* de curso legal

tenderloin *n* : lomo *f* (de cerdo o vaca)

tenderness *n* : ternura *f*

tendon *n* : tendón *m*

tenet *n* : principio *m*

tennis *n* : tenis *m*

tenor *n* : tenor *m*

tense¹ *n* : tiempo *m* (de un verbo)

tense² *v* **tensed; tensing** *vt* : tensar — *vi* : tensarse — ~ *adj* **tenser; tensest** : tenso — **tension** *n* : tensión *f*

tent *n* : tienda *f* de campaña

tentacle *n* : tentáculo *m*

tentative *adj* **1** HESITANT : vacilante **2** PROVISIONAL : provisional

tenth *adj* : décimo — ~ *n* **1** : décimo *m*, -ma *f* (en una serie) **2** : décimo *m* (en matemáticas)

tenuous *adj* : tenue, endeble

tepid *adj* : tibio

term *n* **1** WORD : término *m* **2** PERIOD : período *m* **3** be on good ~s : tener buenas relaciones **4** in ~s of : con respecto a — ~ *vt* : calificar de

terminal *adj* : terminal — ~ *n* **1** : terminal *m* **2** *or* **bus** ~ : terminal *f*

terminate *v* **-nated; -nating** *vi* : terminar(se) — *vt* : poner fin a — **termination** *n* : terminación *f*

termite *n* : termita *f*

terrace *n* : terraza *f*

terrain *n* : terreno *m*

terrestrial *adj* : terrestre

terrible *adj* : espantoso, terrible — **terribly** *adv* : terriblemente

terrier *n* : terrier *mf*

terrific *adj* **1** HUGE : tremendo **2** EXCELLENT : estupendo

terrify *vt* **-fied; -fying** : aterrar, aterrorizar — **terrifying** *adj* : aterrador

territory *n, pl* **-ries** : territorio *m* — **territorial** *adj* : territorial

terror *n* : terror *m* — **terrorism** *n* : terrorismo *m* — **terrorist** *n* : terrorista *mf* — **terrorize** *vt* **-ized; -izing** : aterrorizar

terse *adj* **terser; tersest** : seco, lacónico

test *n* **1** TRIAL : prueba *f* **2** EXAM : examen *m*, prueba *f* **3** : análisis *m* (en medicina) — ~ *vt* **1** TRY : probar **2** QUIZ : examinar **3**

: analizar (la sangre, etc.), examinar (los ojos, etc.)

testament *n* **1** WILL : testamento *m* **2 the Old/New Testament** : el Antiguo/Nuevo Testamento

testicle *n* : testículo *m*

testify *v* **-fied; -fying** : testificar

testimony *n, pl* **-nies** : testimonio *m*

test tube *n* : probeta *f*, tubo *m* de ensayo

tetanus *n* : tétano *m*

tether *vt* : atar

text *n* : texto *m* — **textbook** *n* : libro *m* de texto

textile *n* : textil *m*

texture *n* : textura *f*

than *conj & prep* : que, de (con cantidades)

thank *vt* **1** : agradecer, dar (las) gracias a **2** ～ **you!** : ¡gracias! — **thankful** *adj* : agradecido — **thankfully** *adv* **1** : con agradecimiento **2** FORTUNATELY : gracias a Dios — **thanks** *npl* **1** : agradecimiento *m* **2** ～**!** : ¡gracias!

Thanksgiving *n* : día *m* de Acción de Gracias

that *pron, pl* **those 1** : ése, ésa, eso **2** (*more distant*) : aquél, aquélla, aquello **3 is** ～ **you?** : ¿eres tú? **4 like** ～ : así **5** ～ **is...** : es decir... **6 those who...** : los que... — ～ *conj* : que — ～ *adj, pl* **those 1** : ese, esa **2** (*more distant*) : aquel, aquella **3** ～ **one** : ése, ésa — ～ *adv* : tan

thatched *adj* : con techo de paja

thaw *vt* : descongelar (alimentos), derretir (hielo) — *vi* **1** : descongelarse **2** MELT : derretirse — ～ *n* : deshielo *m*

the *art* **1** : el, la, los, las **2** PER : por — ～ *adv* **1** ～ **sooner** ～ **better** : cuanto más pronto, mejor **2 I like this one** ～ **best** : éste es el que más me gusta

theater *or* **theatre** *n* : teatro *m* — **theatrical** *adj* : teatral

theft *n* : robo *m*, hurto *m*

their *adj* : su, sus, de ellos, de ellas — **theirs** *pron* **1** : (el) suyo, (la) suya, (los) suyos, (las) suyas **2 some friends of** ～ : unos amigos suyos, unos amigos de ellos

them *pron* **1** (*used as direct object*) : los, las **2** (*used as indirect object*) : les, se **3** (*used as object of a preposition*) : ellos, ellas

theme *n* **1** : tema *m* **2** ESSAY : trabajo *m* (escrito)

themselves *pron* **1** (*used reflexively*) : se **2** (*used emphatically*) : ellos mismos, ellas mismas **3** (*used after a preposition*) : sí (mismos), sí (mismas)

then *adv* **1** : entonces **2** NEXT : luego, después **3** BESIDES : además — ～ *adj* : entonces

thence *adv* : de ahí (en adelante)

theology *n, pl* **-gies** : teología *f* — **theological** *adj* : teológico

theorem *n* : teorema *m* — **theoretical** *adj* : teórico — **theory** *n, pl* **-ries** : teoría *f*

therapeutic *adj* : terapéutico — **therapist** *n* : terapeuta *mf* — **therapy** *n, pl* **-pies** : terapia *f*

there *adv* **1** *or* **over** ～ : allí, allá **2** *or* **right** ～ : ahí **3 in** ～ : ahí (dentro) **4** ～, **it's done!** : ¡listo! **5 up/down** ～ : ahí arriba/abajo **6 who's** ～**?** : ¿quién es? — ～ *pron* **1** ～ **is/are** : hay **2** ～ **are three of us** : somos tres — **thereabouts** *or* **thereabout** *adv or* ～ : por ahí — **thereafter** *adv* : después — **thereby** *adv* : así — **therefore** *adv* : por lo tanto

thermal *adj* : térmico

thermometer *n* : termómetro *m*

thermos *n* : termo *m*

thermostat *n* : termostato *m*

thesaurus *n, pl* **-sauri** *or* **-sauruses** : diccionario *m* de sinónimos

these → **this**

thesis *n, pl* **theses** : tesis *f*

they *pron* **1** : ellos, ellas **2 where are** ～**?** : ¿dónde están? **3 as** ～ **say** : como dicen — **they'd** (*contraction of* **they had** *or* **they would**) → **have, would** — **they'll** (*contraction of* **they shall** *or* **they will**) → **shall, will** — **they're** (*contraction of* **they are**) → **be** — **they've** (*contraction of* **they have**) → **have**

thick *adj* **1** : grueso **2** DENSE : espeso **3 a** ～ **accent** : un acento marcado **4 it's two inches** ～ : tiene dos pulgadas de grosor — ～ *n* **in the** ～ **of** : en medio de — **thicken** *vt* : espesar — *vi* : espesarse — **thicket** *n* : matorral *m* — **thickness** *n* : grosor *m*, espesor *m*

thief *n, pl* **thieves** : ladrón *m*, -drona *f*

thigh *n* : muslo *m*

thimble *n* : dedal *m*

thin *adj* **thinner; -est 1** : delgado **2** : ralo (dícese del pelo) **3** WATERY : claro, aguado **4** FINE : fino — ～ *v* **thinned; thinning** *vt* DILUTE : diluir — *vi* : ralear (dícese del pelo)

thing *n* **1** : cosa *f* **2 for one** ～ : en primer lugar **3 how are** ～**s?** : ¿qué tal? **4 it's a good** ～ **that...** : menos mal que... **5 the important** ～ **is...** : lo importante es...

think *v* **thought; thinking** *vt* **1** : pensar **2** BELIEVE : creer **3** ～ **up** : idear — *vi* **1** : pensar **2** ～ **about** *or* ～ **of** CONSIDER : pensar en **3** ～ **of** REMEMBER : acordarse de **4 what do you** ～ **of it?** : ¿qué te parece? — **thinker** *n* : pensador *m*, -dora *f*

third *adj* : tercero — ～ *or* **thirdly** *adv* : en tercer lugar — ～ *n* **1** : tercero *m*, -ra *f* (en

thirst *n* : sed *f* — **thirsty** *adj* **thirstier; -est 1** : sediento **2 be ~** : tener sed

thirteen *adj* : trece — ~ *n* : trece *m* — **thirteenth** *adj* : décimo tercero — ~ *n* **1** : decimotercero *m*, -ra *f* (en una serie) **2** : treceavo *m* (en matemáticas)

thirty *adj* : treinta — ~ *n*, *pl* **thirties** : treinta *m* — **thirtieth** *adj* : trigésimo — ~ *n* **1** : trigésimo *m*, -ma *f* (en una serie) **2** : treintavo *m* (en matemáticas)

this *pron*, *pl* **these 1** : éste, ésta, esto **2** like ~ : así — ~ *adj*, *pl* **these 1** : este, esta **2** ~ **one** : éste, ésta **3** ~ **way** : por aquí — ~ *adv* ~ **big** : así de grande

thistle *n* : cardo *m*

thong *n* **1** : correa *f* **2** SANDAL : chancla *f*

thorn *n* : espina *f* — **thorny** *adj* : espinoso

thorough *adj* **1** : meticuloso **2** COMPLETE : completo — **thoroughly** *adv* **1** : a fondo **2** COMPLETELY : completamente — **thoroughbred** *adj* : de pura sangre — **thoroughfare** *n* : vía *f* pública

those → **that**

though *conj* : aunque — ~ *adv* **1** : sin embargo **2 as** ~ : como si

thought → **think** — ~ *n* **1** : pensamiento *m* **2** IDEA : idea *f* — **thoughtful** *adj* **1** : pensativo **2** KIND : amable — **thoughtless** *adj* **1** CARELESS : descuidado **2** RUDE : desconsiderado

thousand *adj* : mil — ~ *n*, *pl* **-sands** *or* **-sand** : mil *m* — **thousandth** *adj* : milésimo — ~ *n* **1** : milésimo *m*, -ma *f* (en una serie) **2** : milésimo *m* (en matemáticas)

thrash *vt* : dar una paliza a — *vi* *or* ~ **around** : agitarse, revolcarse

thread *n* **1** : hilo *m* **2** : rosca *f* (de un tornillo) — ~ *vt* : enhilar (una aguja), ensartar (cuentas) — **threadbare** *adj* : raído

threat *n* : amenaza *f* — **threaten** *v* : amenazar — **threatening** *adj* : amenazador

three *adj* : tres — ~ *n* : tres *m* — **three hundred** *adj* : trescientos — ~ *n* : trescientos *m*

threshold *n* : umbral *m*

threw → **throw**

thrift *n* : frugalidad *f* — **thrifty** *adj* **thriftier; -est** : económico, frugal

thrill *vt* : emocionar — ~ *n* : emoción *f* — **thriller** *n* : película *f* de suspense *Spain*, película *f* de suspenso *Lat* — **thrilling** *adj* : emocionante

thrive *vi* **throve** *or* **thrived; thriven 1** FLOURISH : florecer **2** PROSPER : prosperar

throat *n* : garganta *f*

throb *vi* **throbbed; throbbing 1** PULSATE : palpitar **2** VIBRATE : vibrar **3** ~ **with** **pain** : tener un dolor punzante

throes *npl* **1** PANGS : agonía *f* **2 in the** ~ **of** : en medio de

throne *n* : trono *m*

throng *n* : muchedumbre *f*, multitud *f*

throttle *vt* **-tled; -tling** : estrangular — ~ *n* : válvula *f* reguladora

through *prep* **1** : por, a través de **2** BETWEEN : entre **3** BECAUSE OF : a causa de **4** DURING : durante **5** → **throughout 6 Monday** ~ **Friday** : de lunes a viernes — ~ *adv* **1** : de un lado a otro (en el espacio), de principio a fin (en el tiempo) **2** COMPLETELY : completamente — ~ *adj* **1 be** ~ : haber terminado **2** ~ **traffic** : tráfico *m* de paso —

throughout *prep* : por todo (un lugar), a lo largo de (un período de tiempo)

throw *v* **threw; thrown; throwing** *vt* **1** : tirar, lanzar **2** : proyectar (una sombra) **3** CONFUSE : desconcertar **4** ~ **a party** : dar una fiesta **5** ~ **away** *or* ~ **out** : tirar, botar *Lat* — *vi* ~ **up** VOMIT : vomitar — ~ *n* : tiro *m*, lanzamiento *m*

thrush *n* : tordo *m*, zorzal *m*

thrust *vt* **thrust; thrusting 1** : empujar (bruscamente) **2** PLUNGE : clavar **3** ~ **upon** : imponer a — ~ *n* **1** : empujón *m* **2** : estocada *f* (en esgrima)

thud *n* : ruido *m* sordo

thug *n* : matón *m*

thumb *n* : (dedo *m*) pulgar *m* — ~ *vt* *or* ~ **through** : hojear — **thumbnail** *n* : uña *f* del pulgar — **thumbtack** *n* : tachuela *f*, chinche *f* *Lat*

thump *vt* : golpear — *vi* : latir con fuerza (dícese del corazón) — ~ *n* : ruido *m* sordo

thunder *n* : truenos *mpl* — ~ *vi* : tronar — *vt* SHOUT : bramar — **thunderbolt** *n* : rayo *m* — **thunderous** *adj* : atronador — **thunderstorm** *n* : tormenta *f* eléctrica

Thursday *n* : jueves *m*

thus *adv* **1** : así **2** THEREFORE : por lo tanto

thwart *vt* : frustrar

thyme *n* : tomillo *m*

thyroid *n* : tiroides *mf*

tiara *n* : diadema *f*

tic *n* : tic *m* (nervioso)

tick[1] *n* : garrapata *f* (insecto)

tick[2] *n* **1** : tictac *m* (sonido) **2** CHECK : marca *f* — ~ *vi* : hacer tictac — *vt* **1** *or* ~ **off** CHECK : marcar **2** ~ **off** ANNOY : fastidiar

ticket *n* **1** : pasaje *m* (de avión), billete *m* *Spain* (de tren, avión, etc.), boleto *m* *Lat* (de tren o autobús) **2** : entrada *f* (al teatro, etc.) **3** FINE : multa *f*

tickle *v* **-led; -ling** *vt* **1** : hacer cosquillas a **2** AMUSE : divertir — *vi* : picar — ~ *n* : cosquilleo *m* — **ticklish** *adj* **1** : cosquilloso **2** TRICKY : delicado

tidal wave *n* : maremoto *m*
tidbit *n* MORSEL : golosina *f*
tide *n* : marea *f* — ~ *vt* **tided; tiding** ~ **over** : ayudar a superar un apuro
tidy *adj* **-dier; -est** : ordenado, arreglado — ~ *vt* **-died; -dying** *or* ~ **up** : ordenar, arreglar
tie *n* **1** : atadura *f*, cordón *m* **2** BOND : lazo *m* **3** : empate *m* (en deportes) **4** NECKTIE : corbata *f* — ~ *v* **tied; tying** *or* **tieing** *vt* **1** : atar, amarrar *Lat* **2** ~ **a knot** : hacer un nudo — *vi* : empatar (en deportes)
tier *n* : nivel *m*, piso (de un pastel), grada *f* (de un estadio)
tiger *n* : tigre *m*
tight *adj* **1** : apretado **2** SNUG : ajustado, ceñido **3** TAUT : tirante **4** STINGY : agarrado **5** SCARCE : escaso **6 a** ~ **seal** : un cierre hermético **7 a** ~ **spot** : un aprieto — ~ *adv* **closed** ~ : bien cerrado — **tighten** *vt* **1** : apretar **2** TENSE : tensar **3** : hacer más estricto (reglas, etc.) — **tightly** *adv* : bien, fuerte — **tightrope** *n* : cuerda *f* floja — **tights** *npl* : leotardo *m*, mallas *fpl*
tile *n* **1** : azulejo *m*, baldosa *f* (de piso) **2** *or* **roofing** ~ : teja *f* — ~ *vt* **tiled; tiling 1** : revestir de azulejos, embaldosar (un piso) **2** : tejar (un techo)
till¹ *prep & conj* → **until**
till² *vt* : cultivar
till³ *n* : caja *f* (registradora)
tilt *n* **1** : inclinación *f* **2 at full** ~ : a toda velocidad — ~ *vt* : inclinar — *vi* : inclinarse
timber *n* **1** : madera *f* (para construcción) **2** BEAM : viga *f*
timbre *n* : timbre *m*
time *n* **1** : tiempo *m* **2** AGE : época *f* **3** : compás *m* (en música) **4 at** ~**s** : a veces **5 at this** ~ : en este momento **6 for the** ~ **being** : por el momento **7 from** ~ **to** ~ : de vez en cuando **8 have a good** ~ : pasarlo bien **9 many** ~**s** : muchas veces **10 on** ~ : a tiempo **11** ~ **after** ~ : una y otra vez **12 what** ~ **is it?** : ¿qué hora es? — ~ *vt* **timed; timing** : tomar el tiempo a (algn), cronometrar (una carrera, etc.) — **timeless** *adj* : eterno — **timely** *adj* **-lier; -est** : oportuno — **timer** *n* : temporizador *m*, avisador *m* (de cocina) — **times** *prep* **3** ~ **4 is 12** : 3 por 4 son 12 — **timetable** *n* : horario *m*
timid *adj* : tímido
tin *n* **1** : estaño *m* **2** CAN : lata *f*, bote *m* *Spain* — **tinfoil** *n* : papel *m* (de) aluminio
tinge *vt* **tinged; tingeing** *or* **tinging** : matizar — ~ *n* **1** TINT : matiz *m* **2** TOUCH : dejo *m*

tingle *vi* **-gled; -gling** : sentir (un) hormigueo — ~ *n* : hormigueo *m*
tinker *vi* ~ **with** : intentar arreglar (con pequeños ajustes)
tinkle *vi* **-kled; -kling** : tintinear — ~ *n* : tintineo *m*
tint *n* : tinte *m* — ~ *vt* : teñir
tiny *adj* **-nier; -est** : diminuto, minúsculo
tip¹ *v* **tipped; tipping** *vt* **1** TILT : inclinar **2** *or* ~ **over** : volcar — *vi* : inclinarse
tip² *n* END : punta *f*
tip³ *n* ADVICE : consejo *m* — ~ *vt* ~ **off** : avisar
tip⁴ *vt* : dar una propina a — ~ *n* GRATUITY : propina *f*
tipsy *adj* **-sier; -est** : achispado
tiptoe *n* **on** ~ : de puntillas — ~ *vi* **-toed; -toeing** : caminar de puntillas
tip–top *adj* : excelente
tire¹ *n* : neumático *m*, llanta *f* *Lat*
tire² *v* **tired; tiring** *vt* : cansar — *vi* : cansarse — **tired** *adj* **1** ~ **of** : cansado de, harto de **2** ~ **out** : agotado — **tireless** *adj* : incansable — **tiresome** *adj* : pesado
tissue *n* **1** : pañuelo *m* de papel **2** : tejido *m* (en biología)
title *n* : título *m* — ~ *vt* **-tled; -tling** : titular
to *prep* **1** : a **2** TOWARD : hacia **3** IN ORDER TO : para **4** UP TO : hasta **5 a quarter** ~ **seven** : las siete menos cuarto **6 be nice** ~ **them** : trátalos bien **7 ten** ~ **the box** : diez por caja **8 the mate** ~ **this shoe** : el compañero de este zapato **9 two** ~ **four years old** : entre dos y cuatro años de edad **10 want** ~ **do** : querer hacer — ~ *adv* **1 come** ~ : volver en sí **2** ~ **and fro** : de un lado a otro
toad *n* : sapo *m*
toast *vt* **1** : tostar (pan, etc.) **2** : brindar por (una persona) — ~ *n* **1** : pan *m* tostado, tostadas *fpl* **2** DRINK : brindis *m* — **toaster** *n* : tostador *m*
tobacco *n, pl* **-cos** : tabaco *m*
toboggan *n* : tobogán *m*
today *adv* : hoy — ~ *n* : hoy *m*
toddler *n* : niño *m* pequeño, niña *f* pequeña (que comienza a caminar)
toe *n* : dedo *m* (del pie) — **toenail** *n* : uña *f* (del pie)
together *adv* **1** : juntos **2** ~ **with** : junto con
toil *n* : trabajo *m* duro — ~ *vi* : trabajar duro
toilet *n* **1** BATHROOM : baño *m*, servicio *m* **2** : inodoro *m* (instalación) — **toilet paper** *n* : papel *m* higiénico — **toiletries** *npl* : artículos *mpl* de tocador
token *n* **1** SIGN : muestra *f* **2** MEMENTO : recuerdo *m* **3** : ficha *f* (para un tren, etc.)
told → **tell**

tolerable *adj* : tolerable — **tolerance** *n* : tolerancia *f* — **tolerant** *adj* : tolerante — **tolerate** *vt* -ated; -ating : tolerar

toll[1] *n* **1** : peaje *m* **2** **death** ~ : número *m* de muertos **3 take a** ~ **on** : afectar

toll[2] *vi* RING : tocar, doblar — ~ *n* : tañido *m*

tomato *n, pl* **-toes** : tomate *m*

tomb *n* : tumba *f*, sepulcro *m* — **tombstone** *n* : lápida *f*

tome *n* : tomo *m*

tomorrow *adv* : mañana — ~ *n* : mañana *m*

ton *n* : tonelada *f*

tone *n* : tono *m* — ~ *vt* **toned; toning** or ~ **down** : atenuar

tongs *npl* : tenazas *fpl*

tongue *n* : lengua *f*

tonic *n* **1** : tónico *m* **2** or ~ **water** : tónica *f*

tonight *adv* : esta noche — ~ *n* : esta noche *f*

tonsil *n* : amígdala *f*

too *adv* **1** ALSO : también **2** EXCESSIVELY : demasiado

took → **take**

tool *n* : herramienta *f* — **toolbox** *n* : caja *f* de herramientas

toot *vt* : sonar (un claxon, etc.) — ~ *n* **1** WHISTLE : pitido *m* **2** HONK : bocinazo *m*

tooth *n, pl* **teeth** : diente *m* — **toothache** *n* : dolor *m* de muelas — **toothbrush** *n* : cepillo *m* de dientes — **toothpaste** *n* : pasta *f* de dientes, pasta *f* dentífrica

top[1] *n* **1** : parte *f* superior **2** SUMMIT : cima *f*, cumbre *f* **3** COVER : tapa *f*, cubierta *f* **4 on** ~ **of** : encima de — ~ *vt* **topped; topping 1** COVER : rematar (un edificio, etc.), bañar (un pastel, etc.) **2** SURPASS : superar **3** ~ **off** : llenar — ~ *adj* **1** : de arriba, superior **2** BEST : mejor **3 a** ~ **executive** : un alto ejecutivo

top[2] *n* : trompo *m* (juguete)

topic *n* : tema *m* — **topical** *adj* : de interés actual

topmost *adj* : más alto

topple *v* **-pled; -pling** *vi* : caerse — *vt* **1** OVERTURN : volcar **2** OVERTHROW : derrocar

torch *n* : antorcha *f*

tore → **tear**[1]

torment *n* : tormento *m* — ~ *vt* : atormentar

torn → **tear**[1]

tornado *n, pl* **-does** or **-dos** : tornado *m*

torpedo *n, pl* **-does** : torpedo *m* — ~ *vt* : torpedear

torrent *n* : torrente *m*

torrid *adj* : tórrido

torso *n, pl* **-sos** or **-si** : torso *m*

tortilla *n* : tortilla *f*

tortoise *n* : tortuga *f* (terrestre) — **tortoiseshell** *n* : carey *m*, concha *f*

tortuous *adj* : tortuoso

torture *n* : tortura *f* — ~ *vt* **-tured; -turing** : torturar

toss *vt* **1** : tirar, lanzar **2** : mezclar (una ensalada) — *vi* ~ **and turn** : dar vueltas — ~ *n* : lanzamiento *m*

tot *n* : pequeño *m*, -ña *f*

total *adj* : total — ~ *n* : total *m* — ~ *vt* **-taled** or **-talled; -taling** or **-talling 1** : ascender a **2** or ~ **up** : totalizar, sumar

totalitarian *adj* : totalitario

tote *vt* **toted; toting** : llevar

totter *vi* : tambalearse

touch *vt* **1** : tocar **2** MOVE : conmover **3** AFFECT : afectar **4** ~ **up** : retocar — *vi* : tocarse — ~ *n* **1** : tacto *m* (sentido) **2** HINT : toque *m* **3** BIT : pizca *f* **4 keep in** ~ : mantenerse en contacto **5 lose one's** ~ : perder la habilidad — **touchdown** *n* : touchdown *m* — **touchy** *adj* **touchier; -est 1** : delicado **2 be** ~ **about** : picarse a la mención de

tough *adj* **1** : duro **2** STRONG : fuerte **3** STRICT : severo **4** DIFFICULT : difícil — **toughen** *vt* or ~ **up** : endurecer — *vi* : endurecerse — **toughness** *n* : dureza *f*

tour *n* **1** : viaje *m* (por un país, etc.), visita *f* (a un museo, etc.) **2** : gira *f* (de un equipo, etc.) — ~ *vi* **1** TRAVEL : viajar **2** : hacer una gira (dícese de equipos, etc.) — *vt* : viajar por, recorrer — **tourist** *n* : turista *mf*

tournament *n* : torneo *m*

tousle *vt* **-sled; -sling** : despeinar

tout *vt* : promocionar

tow *vt* : remolcar — ~ *n* : remolque *m*

toward or **towards** *prep* : hacia

towel *n* : toalla *f*

tower *n* : torre *f* — ~ *vi* ~ **over** : descollar sobre — **towering** *adj* : altísimo

town *n* **1** VILLAGE : pueblo *m* **2** CITY : ciudad *f* — **township** *n* : municipio *m*

tow truck *n* : grúa *f*

toxic *adj* : tóxico

toy *n* : juguete *m* — ~ *vi* ~ **with** : juguetear con

trace *n* **1** SIGN : rastro *m*, señal *f* **2** HINT : dejo *m* — ~ *vt* **traced; tracing 1** : calcar (un dibujo, etc.) **2** DRAW : trazar **3** FIND : localizar

track *n* **1** : pista *f* **2** PATH : sendero *m* **3** or **railroad** ~ : vía *f* (férrea) **4 keep** ~ **of** : llevar la cuenta de — ~ *vt* TRAIL : seguir la pista de

tract[1] *n* **1** EXPANSE : extensión *f* **2** : tracto *m* (en anatomía)

tract[2] *n* PAMPHLET : folleto *m*

traction *n* : tracción *f*

tractor *n* **1** : tractor *m* **2** *or* ~ **-trailer** : camión *m* (con remolque)
trade *n* **1** PROFESSION : oficio *m* **2** COMMERCE : comercio *m* **3** INDUSTRY : industria *f* **4** EXCHANGE : cambio *m* — ~ *v* **traded; trading** *vi* : comerciar — *vt* ~ **sth with s.o.** : cambiar algo a algn — **trademark** *n* : marca *f* registrada
tradition *n* : tradición *f* — **traditional** *adj* : tradicional
traffic *n* : tráfico *m* — ~ *vi* **trafficked; trafficking** ~ **in** : traficar con — **traffic light** *n* : semáforo *m*
tragedy *n*, *pl* **-dies** : tragedia *f* — **tragic** *adj* : trágico
trail *vi* **1** DRAG : arrastrar **2** LAG : rezagarse **3** ~ **off** : apagarse — *vt* **1** DRAG : arrastrar **2** PURSUE : seguir la pista de — ~ *n* **1** : rastro *m*, huellas *fpl* **2** PATH : sendero *m* — **trailer** *n* **1** : remolque *m* **2** : caravana *f* (vivienda)
train *n* **1** : tren *m* **2** : cola *f* (de un vestido) **3** SERIES : serie *f* **4** ~ **of thought** : hilo *m* (de las ideas) — ~ *vt* **1** : adiestrar, entrenar (atletas, etc.) **2** AIM : apuntar — *vi* : prepararse, entrenarse (en deportes, etc.) — **trainer** *n* : entrenador *m*, -dora *f*
trait *n* : rasgo *m*
traitor *n* : traidor *m*, -dora *f*
tramp *vi* : caminar (pesadamente) — ~ *n* VAGRANT : vagabundo *m*, -da *f*
trample *vt* **-pled; -pling** : pisotear
trampoline *n* : trampolín *m*
trance *n* : trance *m*
tranquillity *or* **tranquility** *n* : tranquilidad *f* — **tranquil** *adj* : tranquilo — **tranquilize** *vt* **-ized; -izing** : tranquilizar — **tranquilizer** *n* : tranquilizante *m*
transaction *n* : transacción *f*
transatlantic *adj* : transatlántico
transcend *vt* **1** : ir más allá de **2** OVERCOME : superar
transcribe *vt* **-scribed; -scribing** : transcribir — **transcript** *n* : transcripción *f*
transfer *v* **-ferred; -ferring** *vt* **1** : transferir (fondos, etc.) **2** : trasladar (a un empleado, etc.) — *vi* **1** : cambiarse (de escuelas, etc.) **2** : hacer transbordo (entre trenes, etc.) — ~ *n* **1** : transferencia *f* (de fondos, etc.), traslado *m* (de una persona) **2** : boleto *m* (para hacer transbordo) **3** DECAL : calcomanía *f*
transform *vt* : transformar — **transformation** *n* : transformación *f*
transfusion *n* : transfusión *f*
transgression *n* : transgresión *f* — **transgress** *vt* : transgredir
transient *adj* : pasajero
transit *n* **1** : tránsito *m* **2** TRANSPORTATION

: transporte *m* — **transition** *n* : transición *f* — **transitive** *adj* : transitivo — **transitory** *adj* : transitorio
translate *vt* **-lated; -lating** : traducir — **translation** *n* : traducción *f* — **translator** *n* : traductor *m*, -tora *f*
translucent *adj* : translúcido
transmit *vt* **-mitted; -mitting** : transmitir — **transmission** *n* : transmisión *f* — **transmitter** *n* : transmisor *m*
transparent *adj* : transparente — **transparency** *n*, *pl* **-cies** : transparencia *f*
transpire *vi* **-spired; -spiring** **1** TURN OUT : resultar **2** HAPPEN : suceder
transplant *vt* : trasplantar — ~ *n* : trasplante *m*
transport *vt* : transportar — ~ *n* : transporte *m* — **transportation** *n* : transporte *m*
transpose *vt* **-posed; -posing** **1** : trasponer **2** : transportar (en música)
trap *n* : trampa *f* — ~ *vt* **trapped; trapping** : atrapar — **trapdoor** *n* : trampilla *f*
trapeze *n* : trapecio *m*
trappings *npl* : adornos *mpl*, atavíos *mpl*
trash *n* : basura *f*
trauma *n* : trauma *m* — **traumatic** *adj* : traumático
travel *vi* **-eled** *or* **-elled; -eling** *or* **-elling** **1** : viajar **2** MOVE : desplazarse — ~ *n* : viajes *mpl* — **traveler** *or* **traveller** *n* : viajero *m*, -ra *f*
traverse *vt* **-versed; -versing** : atravesar
travesty *n*, *pl* **-ties** : parodia *f*
trawl *vi* : pescar (con red de arrastre) — **trawler** *n* : barco *m* de pesca
tray *n* : bandeja *f*
treachery *n*, *pl* **-eries** : traición *f* — **treacherous** *adj* **1** : traidor **2** DANGEROUS : peligroso
tread *v* **trod; trodden** *or* **trod; treading** *vt* **1** *or* ~ **on** : pisar **2** ~ **water** : flotar — *vi* **1** STEP : pisar **2** WALK : caminar — ~ *n* **1** STEP : paso *m* **2** : banda *f* de rodadura (de un neumático) — **treadmill** *n* : rueda *f* de andar
treason *n* : traición *f* (a la patria)
treasure *n* : tesoro *m* — ~ *vt* **-sured; -suring** : apreciar — **treasurer** *n* : tesorero *m*, -ra *f* — **treasury** *n*, *pl* **-suries** : erario *m*, tesoro *m*
treat *vt* **1** : tratar **2** CONSIDER : considerar **3** ~ **s.o. to (dinner, etc.)** : invitar a algn (a cenar, etc.) — ~ *n* **1** : gusto *m*, placer *m* **2** **it's my** ~ : invito yo
treatise *n* : tratado *m*
treatment *n* : tratamiento *m*
treaty *n*, *pl* **-ties** : tratado *m*
treble *adj* **1** TRIPLE : triple **2** : de tiple (en música) — ~ *vt* **-bled; -bling** : triplicar — **treble clef** : clave *f* de sol

tree 342

tree *n* : árbol *m*
trek *vi* **trekked; trekking** : viajar (con dificultad) — ∼ *n* : viaje *m* difícil
trellis *n* : enrejado *m*
tremble *vi* **-bled; -bling** : temblar
tremendous *adj* : tremendo
tremor *n* : temblor *m*
trench *n* **1** : zanja *f* **2** : trinchera *f* (militar)
trend *n* **1** : tendencia *f* **2** FASHION : moda *f* — **trendy** *adj* **trendier; -est** : de moda
trepidation *n* : inquietud *f*
trespass *vi* : entrar ilegalmente (en propiedad ajena)
trial *n* **1** : juicio *m*, proceso *m* **2** TEST : prueba *f* **3** ORDEAL : dura prueba *f* — ∼ *adj* : de prueba
triangle *n* : triángulo *m* — **triangular** *adj* : triangular
tribe *n* : tribu *f* — **tribal** *adj* : tribal
tribulation *n* : tribulación *f*
tribunal *n* : tribunal *m*
tribute *n* : tributo *m* — **tributary** *n, pl* **-taries** : afluente *m*
trick *n* **1** : trampa *f* **2** PRANK : broma *f* **3** KNACK, FEAT : truco *m* **4** : baza *f* (en naipes) — ∼ *vt* : engañar — **trickery** *n* : engaño *m*
trickle *vi* **-led; -ling** : gotear — ∼ *n* : goteo *m*
tricky *adj* **trickier; -est 1** SLY : astuto, taimado **2** DIFFICULT : difícil
tricycle *n* : triciclo *m*
trifle *n* **1** TRIVIALITY : nimiedad *f* **2 a** ∼ : un poco — ∼ *vi* **-fled; -fling** ∼ **with** : jugar con — **trifling** *adj* : insignificante
trigger *n* : gatillo *m* — ∼ *vt* : causar, provocar
trill *n* : trino *m* — ∼ *vi* : trinar
trillion *n* : billón *m*
trilogy *n, pl* **-gies** : trilogía *f*
trim *vt* **trimmed; trimming 1** : recortar **2** ADORN : adornar — ∼ *adj* **trimmer; trimmest 2** SLIM : esbelto **2** NEAT : arreglado — ∼ *n* **1** : recorte *m* **2** DECORATION : adornos *mpl* **3 in** ∼ : en buena forma — **trimming** *npl* **1** : adornos *mpl* **2** GARNISH : guarnición *f*
Trinity *n* : Trinidad *f*
trinket *n* : chuchería *f*
trio *n, pl* **trios** : trío *m*
trip *v* **tripped; tripping** *vi* **1** : caminar (a paso ligero) **2** STUMBLE : tropezar **3** ∼ **up** : equivocarse — *vt* **1** ACTIVATE : activar **2** ∼ **s.o.** : hacer una zancadilla a algn **3** ∼ **s.o. up** : hacer equivocar a algn — ∼ *n* **1** : viaje *m* **2** STUMBLE : traspié *m*
tripe *n* **1** : mondongo *m*, callos *mpl* **2** NONSENSE : tonterías *fpl*
triple *vt* **-pled; -pling** : triplicar — ∼ *n*

: triple *m* — ∼ *adj* : triple — **triplet** *n* : trillizo *m*, -za *f* — **triplicate** *n* : triplicado *m*
tripod *n* : trípode *m*
trite *adj* **triter; tritest** : trillado
triumph *n* : triunfo *m* — ∼ *vi* : triunfar — **triumphal** *adj* : triunfal — **triumphant** *adj* : triunfante
trivial *adj* : trivial — **trivia** *ns & pl* : trivialidades *fpl* — **triviality** *n, pl* **-ties** : trivialidad *f*
trod, trodden → **tread**
trolley *n, pl* **-leys** : tranvía *m*
trombone *n* : trombón *m*
troop *n* **1** : escuadrón *m* (de caballería), compañía *f* (de soldados) **2** ∼**s** *npl* : tropas *fpl* — ∼ *vi* ∼ **in/out** : entrar/salir en tropel — **trooper** *n* **1** : soldado *m* **2** *or* **state** ∼ : policía *mf* estatal
trophy *n, pl* **-phies** : trofeo *m*
tropic *n* **1** : trópico *m* **2 the** ∼**s** : el trópico — ∼ *or* **tropical** *adj* : tropical
trot *n* : trote *m* — ∼ *vi* **trotted; trotting** : trotar
trouble *v* **-bled; -bling** *vt* **1** WORRY : preocupar **2** BOTHER : molestar — *vi* : molestarse — ∼ *n* **1** PROBLEMS : problemas *mpl* **2** EFFORT : molestia *f* **3 be in** ∼ : estar en apuros **4 get in** ∼ : meterse en problemas **5 I had** ∼ **doing it** : me costó hacerlo — **troublemaker** *n* : alborotador *m*, -dora *f* — **troublesome** *adj* : problemático
trough *n, pl* **troughs 1** : depresión *f* **2** *or* **feeding** ∼ : comedero *m* **3** *or* **drinking** ∼ : bebedero *m*
troupe *n* : compañía *f* (de teatro)
trousers *npl* : pantalón *m*, pantalones *mpl*
trout *n, pl* **trout** : trucha *f*
trowel *n* : paleta *f* (de albañil), desplantador *m* (de jardinero)
truant *n* : alumno *m*, -na *f* que falta a clase
truce *n* : tregua *f*
truck *vt* : transportar en camión — ∼ *n* **1** : camión *m* **2** CART : carro *m* — **trucker** *n* : camionero *m*, -ra *f*
trudge *vi* **trudged; trudging** : caminar a paso pesado
true *adj* **truer; truest 1** : verdadero **2** LOYAL : fiel **3** GENUINE : auténtico **4 be** ∼ : ser cierto, ser verdad
truffle *n* : trufa *f*
truly *adv* : verdaderamente
trump *n* : triunfo *m* (en naipes)
trumpet *n* : trompeta *f*
trunk *n* **1** STEM, TORSO : tronco *m* **2** : trompa *f* (de un elefante) **3** : baúl *m* (equipaje) **4** : maletero *m* (de un auto) **5** ∼**s** *npl* : traje *m* de baño (de hombre)
truss *n* **1** FRAMEWORK : armazón *m* **2** : braguero *m* (en medicina)

trust n **1** CONFIDENCE : confianza f **2** HOPE : esperanza f **3** CREDIT : crédito m **4** : trust m (en finanzas) **5 in** ~ : en fideicomiso — ~ vi **1** : confiar **2** HOPE : esperar — vt **1** : confiar en, fiarse de (en frases negativas) **2** ~ **s.o. with sth** : confiar algo a algn — **trustee** n : fideicomisario m, -ria f — **trustworthy** adj : digno de confianza

truth n, pl **truths** : verdad f — **truthful** adj : sincero, veraz

try v **tried; trying** vt **1** ATTEMPT : tratar (de), intentar **2** : juzgar (un caso, etc.) **3** TEST : poner a prueba **4** or ~ **out** : probar **5** ~ **on** : probarse (ropa) — vi **1** : hacer un esfuerzo — ~ n, pl **tries** : intento m — **trying** adj **1** ANNOYING : irritante, pesado **2** DIFFICULT : duro — **tryout** n : prueba f

tsar → **czar**

T–shirt n : camiseta f

tub n **1** : cuba f, tina f **2** CONTAINER : envase m **3** BATHTUB : bañera f

tuba n : tuba f

tube n **1** : tubo m **2** or **inner** ~ : cámara f **3 the** ~ : la tele

tuberculosis n, pl **-loses** : tuberculosis f

tubing n : tubería f — **tubular** adj : tubular

tuck vt **1** : meter **2** ~ **away** : guardar **3** ~ **in** : meter por dentro (una blusa, etc.) **4** ~ **s.o. in** : arropar a algn — ~ n : jareta f

Tuesday n : martes m

tuft n : mechón m (de pelo), penacho m (de plumas)

tug vt **tugged; tugging** or ~ **at** : tirar de, jalar de — ~ n : tirón m, jalón m — **tugboat** n : remolcador m — **tug–of–war** n, pl **tugs–of–war** : tira y afloja m

tuition n **1** : enseñanza f **2** or ~ **fees** : matrícula f

tulip n : tulipán m

tumble vi **-bled; -bling** : caerse — ~ n : caída f — **tumbler** : vaso m (sin pie)

tummy n, pl **-mies** : barriga f, panza f

tumor n : tumor m

tumult n : tumulto m — **tumultuous** adj : tumultuoso

tuna n, pl **-na** or **-nas** : atún m

tune n **1** MELODY : melodía f **2** SONG : tonada f **3 in** ~ : afinado **4 out of** ~ : desafinado — ~ v **tuned; tuning** vt : afinar — vi ~ **in** : sintonizar — **tuner** n **1** : afinador m, -dora f (de pianos, etc.) **2** : sintonizador m (de un receptor)

tunic n : túnica f

tunnel n : túnel m — ~ vi **-neled** or **-nelled; -neling** or **-nelling** : hacer un túnel

turban n : turbante m

turbine n : turbina f

turbulent adj : turbulento — **turbulence** n : turbulencia f

turf n **1** GRASS : césped m **2** SOD : tepe m

turgid adj : ampuloso (dícese de prosa, etc.)

turkey n, pl **-keys** : pavo m

turmoil n : confusión f

turn vt **1** : hacer girar (una rueda, etc.), volver (la cabeza, una página, etc.) **2** : dar la vuelta a (una esquina) **3** SPRAIN : torcer **4** ~ **down** REFUSE : rechazar **5** ~ **down** LOWER : bajar **6** ~ **in** : entregar **7** ~ **off** : cerrar (una llave), apagar (la luz, etc.) **8** ~ **on** : abrir (una llave), encender, prender Lat (la luz, etc.) **9** ~ **out** EXPEL : echar **10** ~ **out** PRODUCE : producir **11** ~ **out** → **turn off 12** or ~ **over** FLIP : dar la vuelta a, voltear Lat **13** ~ **over** TRANSFER : entregar **14** ~ **s.o.'s stomach** : revolver el estómago a algn **15** ~ **sth into sth** : convertir algo en algo **16** ~ **up** RAISE : subir — vi **1** ROTATE : girar, dar vueltas **2** BECOME : ponerse **3** SOUR : agriarse **4** RESORT : recurrir **5** or ~ **around** : darse la vuelta, volverse **6** ~ **into** : convertirse en **7** ~ **left** : doblar a la izquierda **8** ~ **out** COME : acudir **9** ~ **out** RESULT : resultar **10** ~ **up** APPEAR : aparecer — ~ n **1** : vuelta f **2** CHANGE : cambio m **3** CURVE : curva f **4 do a good** ~ : hacer un favor **5 whose** ~ **is it?** : ¿a quién le toca?

turnip n : nabo m

turnout n : concurrencia f — **turnover** n **1** : tartaleta f (postre) **2** : volumen m (de ventas) **3** : movimiento f (de personal) — **turnpike** n : carretera f de peaje — **turntable** n : plato m giratorio

turpentine n : trementina f

turquoise n : turquesa f

turret n **1** : torrecilla f **2** : torreta f (de un tanque, etc.)

turtle n : tortuga f (marina) — **turtleneck** n : cuello m de tortuga

tusk n : colmillo m

tussle n : pelea f — ~ vi **-sled; -sling** : pelearse

tutor n : profesor m, -sora f particular — vt : dar clases particulares a

tuxedo n, pl **-dos** or **-does** : esmoquin m, smoking m

TV → **television**

twang n **1** : tañido m **2** : acento m nasal (de la voz)

tweak vt : pellizcar — ~ n : pellizco m

tweed n : tweed m

tweet n : gorjeo m, pío m — ~ vi : piar

tweezers npl : pinzas fpl

twelve adj : doce — ~ n : doce m — **twelfth** adj : duodécimo — ~ n **1** : duodécimo m, -ma f (en una serie) **2** : doceavo m (en matemáticas)

twenty adj : veinte — ~ n, pl **-ties** : veinte

m — **twentieth** *adj* : vigésimo — ~ *n* **1** : vigésimo *m*, -ma *f* (en una serie) **2** : veinteavo *m* (en matemáticas)
twice *adv* **1** : dos veces **2** ~ **as much/ many as** : el doble de (algo), el doble que (algn)
twig *n* : ramita *f*
twilight *n* : crepúsculo *m*
twin *n* : gemelo *m*, -la *f;* mellizo *m*, -za *f* — ~ *adj* : gemelo, mellizo
twine *n* : cordel *m*, bramante *m Spain*
twinge *n* : punzada *f*
twinkle *vi* **-kled; -kling 1** : centellear **2** : brillar (dícese de los ojos) — ~ *n* : centelleo *m*, brillo *m* (de los ojos)
twirl *vt* : girar, dar vueltas a — *vi* : girar, dar vueltas — ~ *n* : giro *m*, vuelta *f*
twist *vt* **1** : retorcer **2** TURN : girar **3** SPRAIN : torcerse **4** : tergiversar (palabras) — *vi* **1** : retorcerse **2** COIL : enrollarse **3** : serpentear (entre montañas, etc.) — ~ *n* **1** BEND : vuelta *f* **2** TURN : giro *m* **3** ~ **of**

lemon : rodajita *f* de limón — **twister** →
tornado
twitch *vi* : moverse (espasmódicamente) — ~ *n* **nervous** ~ : tic *m* nervioso
two *adj* : dos — ~ *n, pl* **twos** : dos *m* —
twofold *adj* : doble — ~ *adv* : al doble —
two hundred *adj* : doscientos — ~ *n* : doscientos *m*
tycoon *n* : magnate *mf*
tying → **tie**
type *n* : tipo *m* — ~ *v* **typed; typing** : escribir a máquina — **typewritten** *adj* : escrito a máquina — **typewriter** *n* : máquina *f* de escribir
typhoon *n* : tifón *m*
typical *adj* : típico, característico — **typify** *vt* **-fied; -fying** : tipificar
typist *n* : mecanógrafo *m*, -fa *f*
typography *n* : tipografía *f*
tyranny *n, pl* **-nies** : tiranía *f* — **tyrant** *n* : tirano *m*, -na *f*
tzar → **czar**

U

u *n, pl* **u's** *or* **us** : u *f,* vigésima primera letra del alfabeto inglés
udder *n* : ubre *f*
UFO (*unidentified flying object*) *n, pl* **UFO's** *or* **UFOs** : ovni *m*, OVNI *m*
ugly *adj* **uglier; -est** : feo — **ugliness** *n* : fealdad *f*
ulcer *n* : úlcera *f*
ulterior *adj* ~ **motive** : segunda intención *f*
ultimate *adj* **1** FINAL : final, último **2** UTMOST : máximo **3** FUNDAMENTAL : fundamental — **ultimately** *adv* **1** FINALLY : por último, finalmente **2** EVENTUALLY : a la larga
ultimatum *n, pl* **-tums** *or* **-ta** : ultimátum *m*
ultraviolet *adj* : ultravioleta
umbilical cord *n* : cordón *m* umbilical
umbrella *n* : paraguas *m*
umpire *n* : árbitro *m*, -tra *f* — ~ *vt* **-pired; -piring** : arbitrar
umpteenth *adj* : enésimo
unable *adj* **1** : incapaz **2 be** ~ **to** : no poder
unabridged *adj* : íntegro
unacceptable *adj* : inaceptable
unaccountable *adj* : inexplicable
unaccustomed *adj* **be** ~ **to** : no estar acostumbrado a

unadulterated *adj* : puro
unaffected *adj* **1** : no afectado **2** NATURAL : sin afectación, natural
unafraid *adj* : sin miedo
unaided *adj* : sin ayuda
unanimous *adj* : unánime
unannounced *adj* : sin dar aviso
unarmed *adj* : desarmado
unassuming *adj* : modesto, sin pretensiones
unattached *adj* **1** : suelto **2** UNMARRIED : soltero
unattractive *adj* : poco atractivo
unauthorized *adj* : no autorizado
unavailable *adj* : no disponible
unavoidable *adj* : inevitable
unaware *adj* **1** : inconsciente **2 be** ~ **of** : ignorar — **unawares** *adv* **catch s.o.** ~ : agarrar a algn desprevenido
unbalanced *adj* : desequilibrado
unbearable *adj* : inaguantable, insoportable
unbelievable *adj* : increíble
unbending *adj* : inflexible
unbiased *adj* : imparcial
unborn *adj* : aún no nacido
unbreakable *adj* : irrompible
unbridled *adj* : desenfrenado
unbroken *adj* **1** INTACT : intacto **2** CONTINUOUS : continuo

unbutton vt : desabrochar, desabotonar
uncalled–for adj : inapropiado, innecesario
uncanny adj -nier; -est : extraño, misterioso
unceasing adj : incesante
unceremonious adj 1 INFORMAL : poco ceremonioso 2 ABRUPT : brusco
uncertain adj 1 : incierto 2 in no ~ terms : de forma vehemente — **uncertainty** n, pl -ties : incertidumbre f
unchanged adj : igual, sin alterar — **unchanging** adj : inmutable
uncivilized adj : incivilizado
uncle n : tío m
unclear adj : poco claro
uncomfortable adj 1 : incómodo 2 DISCONCERTING : inquietante, desagradable
uncommon adj : raro
uncompromising adj : intransigente
unconcerned adj : indiferente
unconditional adj : incondicional
unconscious adj : inconsciente
unconstitutional adj : inconstitucional
uncontrollable adj : incontrolable
unconventional adj : poco convencional
uncouth adj : grosero
uncover vt 1 : destapar 2 REVEAL : descubrir
undecided adj : indeciso
undeniable adj : innegable
under adv 1 : debajo 2 LESS : menos 3 or ~ anesthetic : bajo los efectos de la anestesia — ~ prep 1 BELOW, BENEATH : debajo de, abajo de 2 ~ 20 minutes : menos de 20 minutos 3 ~ the circumstances : dadas las circunstancias
underage adj : menor de edad
underclothes → underwear
undercover adj : secreto
undercurrent n : tendencia f oculta
underdeveloped adj : subdesarrollado
underestimate vt -mated; -mating : subestimar
underfoot adv : bajo los pies
undergo vt -went; -gone; -going : sufrir, experimentar
undergraduate n : estudiante m universitario, estudiante f universitaria
underground adv 1 : bajo tierra 2 go ~ : pasar a la clandestinidad — ~ adj 1 : subterráneo 2 SECRET : secreto, clandestino — ~ n : movimiento m clandestino
undergrowth n : maleza f
underhanded adj SLY : solapado
underline vt -lined; -lining : subrayar
underlying adj : subyacente
undermine vt -mined; -mining : socavar, minar
underneath adv : debajo, abajo — ~ prep : debajo de, abajo de Lat

underpants npl : calzoncillos mpl, calzones mpl Lat
underpass n : paso m inferior
underprivileged adj : desfavorecido
underrate vt -rated; -rating : subestimar
undershirt n : camiseta f
understand v -stood ; -standing : comprender, entender — **understandable** adj : comprensible — **understanding** adj : comprensivo, compasivo — ~ n 1 : comprensión f 2 AGREEMENT : acuerdo m
understatement n that's an ~ : decir sólo eso es quedarse corto
understudy n, pl -dies : sobresaliente mf (en el teatro)
undertake vt -took; -taken; -taking : emprender (una tarea), encargarse de (una responsabilidad) — **undertaker** n : director m, -tora f de una funeraria — **undertaking** n : empresa f, tarea f
undertone n 1 : voz f baja 2 SUGGESTION : matiz m
undertow n : resaca f
underwater adj : submarino — ~ adv : debajo (del agua)
under way adv get ~ : ponerse en marcha
underwear n : ropa f interior
underwent → undergo
underworld n the ~ CRIMINALS : la hampa, los bajos fondos
underwriter n : asegurador m, -dora f
undesirable adj : indeseable
undeveloped adj : sin desarrollar
undignified adj : indecoroso
undisputed adj : indiscutible
undo vt -did; -done; -doing 1 UNFASTEN : deshacer, desatar 2 : reparar (daños, etc.)
undoubtedly adv : indudablemente
undress vt : desnudar — vi : desnudarse
undue adj : indebido, excesivo
undulate vi -lated; -lating : ondular
unduly adv : excesivamente
undying adj : eterno
unearth vt : desenterrar
unearthly adj -lier; -est : sobrenatural, de otro mundo
uneasy adj -easier; -est 1 AWKWARD : incómodo 2 WORRIED : inquieto 3 RESTLESS : agitado — **uneasily** adv : inquietamente — **uneasiness** n : inquietud f
uneducated adj : inculto
unemployed adj : desempleado — **unemployment** n : desempleo m
unerring adj : infalible
unethical adj : poco ético
uneven adj 1 : desigual 2 : impar (dícese de un número)
unexpected adj : inesperado

unfailing *adj* **1** CONSTANT : constante **2** IN-EXHAUSTIBLE : inagotable

unfair *adj* : injusto — **unfairly** *adv* : injustamente — **unfairness** *n* : injusticia *f*

unfaithful *adj* : infiel — **unfaithfulness** *n* : infidelidad *f*

unfamiliar *adj* **1** : desconocido **2 be ~ with** : desconocer

unfasten *vt* **1** : desabrochar (ropa, etc.) **2** UNDO : desatar (una cuerda, etc.)

unfavorable *adj* : desfavorable

unfeeling *adj* : insensible

unfinished *adj* : sin terminar

unfit *adj* **1** UNSUITABLE : impropio **2** UN-SUITED : no apto, incapaz

unfold *vt* **1** : desplegar, desdoblar **2** REVEAL : revelar (un plan, etc.) — *vi* **1** : extenderse, desplegarse **2** DEVELOP : desarrollarse

unforeseen *adj* : imprevisto

unforgettable *adj* : inolvidable

unforgivable *adj* : imperdonable

unfortunate *adj* **1** UNLUCKY : desgraciado, desafortunado **2** INAPPROPRIATE : inoportuno — **unfortunately** *adv* : desgraciadamente

unfounded *adj* : infundado

unfriendly *adj* **-lier; -est** : poco amistoso

unfurl *vt* : desplegar

unfurnished *adj* : desamueblado

ungainly *adj* : desgarbado

ungodly *adj* **1** : impío **2 an ~ hour** : una hora intempestiva

ungrateful *adj* : desagradecido

unhappy *adj* **-pier; -est 1** SAD : infeliz, triste **2** UNFORTUNATE : desafortunado — **unhappily** *adv* **1** SADLY : tristemente **2** UNFORTUNATELY : desgraciadamente — **unhappiness** *n* : tristeza *f*

unharmed *adj* : salvo, ileso

unhealthy *adj* **-thier; -est 1** : malsano **2** SICKLY : enfermizo

unheard–of *adj* : sin precedente, insólito

unhook *vt* : desenganchar

unhurt *adj* : ileso

unicorn *n* : unicornio *m*

unification *n* : unificación *f*

uniform *adj* : uniforme — **~** *n* : uniforme *m* — **uniformity** *n, pl* **-ties** : uniformidad *f*

unify *vt* **-fied; -fying** : unificar

unilateral *adj* : unilateral

unimaginable *adj* : inconcebible

unimportant *adj* : insignificante

uninhabited *adj* : deshabitado, despoblado

uninjured *adj* : ileso

unintentional *adj* : involuntario

union *n* **1** : unión *f* **2** *or* **labor ~** : sindicato *m*, gremio *m Lat*

unique *adj* : único — **uniquely** *adv* EXCEPTIONALLY : excepcionalmente

unison *n* **in ~** : al unísono

unit *n* **1** : unidad *f* **2** : módulo *m* (de un mobiliario)

unite *v* **united; uniting** *vt* : unir — *vi* : unirse — **unity** *n, pl* **-ties 1** : unidad *f* **2** HARMONY : acuerdo *m*

universe *n* : universo *m* — **universal** *adj* : universal

university *n, pl* **-ties** : universidad *f*

unjust *adj* : injusto — **unjustified** *adj* : injustificado

unkempt *adj* **1** : descuidado, desaseado **2** : despeinado (dícese del pelo)

unkind *adj* : poco amable, cruel — **unkindness** *n* : falta *f* de amabilidad, crueldad *f*

unknown *adj* : desconocido

unlawful *adj* : ilegal

unless *conj* : a menos que, a no ser que

unlike *adj* : diferente — **~** *prep* : a diferencia de — **unlikelihood** *n* : improbabilidad *f* — **unlikely** *adj* **-lier; -est** : improbable

unlimited *adj* : ilimitado

unload *v* : descargar

unlock *vt* : abrir (con llave)

unlucky *adj* **-luckier; -est 1** UNFORTUNATE : desgraciado **2** : de mala suerte (dícese de un número, etc.)

unmarried *adj* : soltero

unmask *vt* : desenmascarar

unmistakable *adj* : inconfundible

unnatural *adj* **1** : anormal **2** AFFECTED : afectado, forzado

unnecessary *adj* : innecesario — **unnecessarily** *adv* : innecesariamente

unnerving *adj* : desconcertante

unnoticed *adj* : inadvertido

unobtainable *adj* : inasequible

unobtrusive *adj* : discreto

unofficial *adj* : no oficial

unorthodox *adj* : poco ortodoxo

unpack *vt* **1** : desempaquetar, desempacar *Lat* (un paquete, etc.) **2** : deshacer (una maleta) — *vi* : deshacer las maletas

unparalleled *adj* : sin igual

unpleasant *adj* : desagradable

unplug *vt* **-plugged; -plugging** : desconectar, desenchufar

unpopular *adj* : poco popular

unprecedented *adj* : sin precedente

unpredictable *adj* : imprevisible

unprepared *adj* **1** : no preparado **2** UNREADY : desprevenido

unqualified *adj* **1** : no calificado, sin título **2** COMPLETE : absoluto

unquestionable *adj* : indiscutible — **unquestioning** *adj* : incondicional

unravel *v* **-eled** *or* **-elled; -eling** *or* **-elling** *vt* : desenmarañar — *vi* : deshacerse

unreal *adj* : irreal — **unrealistic** *adj* : poco realista
unreasonable *adj* **1** : irrazonable **2** EXCESSIVE : excesivo
unrecognizable *adj* : irreconocible
unrelated *adj* : no relacionado
unrelenting *adj* : implacable
unreliable *adj* : que no es de fiar
unrepentant *adj* : impenitente
unrest *n* **1** : inquietud *f*, malestar *m* **2** *or* **political** ~ : disturbios *mpl*
unripe *adj* : verde, no maduro
unrivaled *or* **unrivalled** *adj* : incomparable, sin par
unroll *vt* : desenrollar — *vi* : desenrollarse
unruly *adj* : indisciplinado
unsafe *adj* : inseguro
unsaid *adj* : sin decir
unsanitary *adj* : antihigiénico
unsatisfactory *adj* : insatisfactorio
unscathed *adj* : ileso
unscrew *vt* : destornillar
unscrupulous *adj* : sin escrúpulos
unseemly *adj* **-lier; -est** : indecoroso
unseen *adj* **1** : no visto **2** UNNOTICED : inadvertido
unselfish *adj* : desinteresado
unsettle *vt* **-tled; -tling** DISTURB : perturbar — **unsettled** *adj* **1** CHANGEABLE : inestable **2** DISTURBED : agitado, inquieto **3** : variable (dícese del tiempo)
unsightly *adj* : feo
unskilled *adj* : no calificado — **unskillful** *adj* : torpe, poco hábil
unsociable *adj* : poco sociable
unsound *adj* **1** : defectuoso, erróneo **2** of ~ **mind** : demente
unspeakable *adj* **1** : indecible **2** TERRIBLE : atroz
unstable *adj* : inestable
unsteady *adj* **1** : inestable **2** SHAKY : tembloroso
unsuccessful *adj* **1** : fracasado **2 be** ~ : no tener éxito
unsuitable *adj* **1** : inadecuado **2** INCONVENIENT : inconveniente
unsure *adj* : inseguro
unsuspecting *adj* : confiado
unsympathetic *adj* : indiferente
unthinkable *adj* : inconcebible
untidy *adj* : desordenado (dícese de una sala, etc.), desaliñado (dícese de una persona)
untie *vt* **-tied; -tying** *or* **-tieing** : desatar
until *prep* : hasta — ~ *conj* : hasta que
untimely *adj* **1** PREMATURE : prematuro **2** INOPPORTUNE : inoportuno
untold *adj* : incalculable
untoward *adj* **1** ADVERSE : adverso **2** IMPROPER : indecoroso

untroubled *adj* **1** : tranquilo **2 be** ~ **by** : no estar afectado por
untrue *adj* : falso
unused *adj* **1** NEW : nuevo **2 be** ~ **to** : no estar acustumbrado a
unusual *adj* : poco común, insólito — **unusually** *adv* : excepcionalmente
unveil *vt* : descubrir, revelar
unwanted *adj* : superfluo (dícese de un objeto), no deseado (dícese de un niño, etc.)
unwarranted *adj* : injustificado
unwelcome *adj* : inoportuno, molesto
unwell *adj* **be** ~ : sentirse mal
unwieldy *adj* : difícil de manejar
unwilling *adj* : poco dispuesto — **unwillingly** *adv* : de mala gana
unwind *v* **-wound; -winding** *vt* : desenrollar — *vi* **1** : desenrollarse **2** RELAX : relajarse
unwise *adj* : imprudente
unworthy *adj* **be** ~ **of** : no ser digno de
unwrap *vt* **-wrapped; -wrapping** : desenvolver
up *adv* **1** ABOVE : arriba **2** UPWARDS : hacia arriba **3 ten miles farther** ~ : diez millas más adelante **4** ~ **here/there** : aquí/allí arriba **5** ~ **north** : en el norte **6** ~ **until** : hasta — ~ *adj* **1** AWAKE : levantado **2** FINISHED : terminado **3 be** ~ **against** : enfrentarse con **4 be** ~ **on** : estar al corriente de **5 it's** ~ **to you** : depende de tí **6 prices are** ~ : los precios han aumentado **7 the sun is** ~ : ha salido el sol **8 what's** ~? : ¿qué pasa? — ~ *prep* **1 go** ~ **the river** : ir río arriba **2 go** ~ **the stairs** : subir la escalera **3** ~ **the coast** : a lo largo de la costa — ~ *v* **upped; upping; ups** *vt* : aumentar — *vi* **she** ~ **and left** : agarró y se fue
upbringing *n* : educación *f*
upcoming *adj* : próximo
update *vt* **-dated; -dating** : poner al día, actualizar — ~ *n* : puesta *f* al día
upgrade *vt* **-graded; -grading** : elevar la categoría de (un puesto, etc.), mejorar (una facilidad, etc.)
upheaval *n* : trastorno *m*
uphill *adv* : cuesta arriba — ~ *adj* **1** : en subida **2 be an** ~ **battle** : ser muy difícil
uphold *vt* **-held; -holding** : sostener, apoyar
upholstery *n, pl* **-steries** : tapicería *f*
upkeep *n* : mantenimiento *m*
upon *prep* **1** : en, sobre **2** ~ **leaving** : al salir
upper *adj* : superior — ~ *n* : parte *f* superior (del calzado, etc.)
uppercase *adj* : mayúsculo
upper class *n* : clase *f* alta
upper hand *n* : ventaja *f*, dominio *m*
uppermost *adj* : más alto

upright *adj* **1** VERTICAL : vertical **2** ERECT : derecho **3** JUST : recto, honesto — ~ *n* : montante *m*, poste *m*
uprising *n* : insurrección *f*, revuelta *f*
uproar *n* COMMOTION : alboroto *m*
uproot *vt* : desarraigar
upset *vt* **-set; -setting** **1** OVERTURN : volcar **2** DISTRESS : alterar, inquietar **3** DISRUPT : trastornar — ~ *adj* **1** DISTRESSED : alterado **2 have an ~ stomach** : estar mal del estómago — ~ *n* : trastorno *m*
upshot *n* : resultado *m* final
upside down *adv* **1** : al revés **2 turn ~** : volver — **upside-down** *adj* : al revés
upstairs *adv* : arriba — ~ *adj* : de arriba — ~ *ns & pl* : piso *m* de arriba
upstart *n* : advenedizo *m*, -za *f*
upstream *adv* : río arriba
upswing *n* **be on the ~** : estar mejorándose
up-to-date *adj* **1** : corriente, al día **2** MODERN : moderno
uptown *adv* : hacia la parte alta de la ciudad, hacia el distrito residencial
upturn *n* : mejora *f*, auge *m* (económico)
upward *or* **upwards** *adv* : hacia arriba — **upward** *adj* : ascendente, hacia arriba
uranium *n* : uranio *m*
urban *adj* : urbano
urbane *adj* : urbano, cortés
urge *vt* **urged; urging** **1** PRESS : instar, exhortar **2 ~ on** : animar — ~ *n* : impulso *m*, ganas *fpl* — **urgency** *n*, *pl* **-cies** : urgencia *f* — **urgent** *adj* **1** : urgente **2 be ~** : urgir
urine *n* : orina *f* — **urinate** *vi* **-nated; -nating** : orinar
urn *n* : urna *f*
Uruguayan *adj* : uruguayo

us *pron* **1** (*as direct or indirect object*) : nos **2** (*as object of a preposition*) : nosotros, nosotras **3 both of ~** : nosotros dos **4 it's ~!** : ¡somos nosotros!
usage *n* : uso *m*
use *v* **used; using** *vt* **1** : usar **2** CONSUME : consumir, tomar (drogas, etc.) **3 ~ up** : agotar, consumir — *vi* **1 she ~d to dance** : acostumbraba bailar **2 winters ~d to be colder** : los inviernos solían ser más fríos — ~ *n* **1** : uso *m* **2 have no ~ for** : no necesitar **3 have the ~ of** : poder usar, tener acceso a **4 it's no ~!** : ¡es inútil! — **used** *adj* **1** SECONDHAND : usado **2 be ~ to** : estar acostumbrado a — **useful** *adj* : útil, práctico — **usefulness** *n* : utilidad *f* — **useless** *adj* : inútil — **user** *n* : usuario *m*, -ria *f*
usher *vt* **1** : acompañar, conducir **2 ~ in** : hacer entrar — ~ *n* : acomodador *m*, -dora *f*
usual *adj* **1** : habitual, usual **2 as ~** : como de costumbre — **usually** *adv* : usualmente
usurp *vt* : usurpar
utensil *n* : utensilio *m*
uterus *n*, *pl* **uteri** : útero *m*, matriz *f*
utility *n*, *pl* **-ties** **1** : utilidad *f* **2** *or* **public ~** : empresa *f* de servicio público
utilize *vt* **-lized; -lizing** : utilizar
utmost *adj* **1** FARTHEST : extremo **2 of the ~ importance** : de suma importancia — ~ *n* **do one's ~** : hacer todo lo posible
utopia *n* : utopía *f* — **utopian** *adj* : utópico
utter[1] *adj* : absoluto, completo
utter[2] *vt* : decir, pronunciar (palabras) — **utterance** *n* : declaración *f*, expresión *f*
utterly *adv* : completamente, totalmente

V

v *n*, *pl* **v's** *or* **vs** : v *f*, vigésima segunda letra del alfabeto inglés
vacant *adj* **1** AVAILABLE : libre **2** UNOCCUPIED : desocupado **3** : vacante (dícese de un puesto) **4** : ausente (dícese de una mirada) — **vacancy** *n*, *pl* **-cies** **1** : (puesto *m*) vacante *f* **2** : habitación *f* libre (en un hotel, etc.)
vacate *vt* **-cated; -cating** : desalojar, desocupar
vacation *n* : vacaciones *fpl*
vaccination *n* : vacunación *f* — **vaccinate** *vt*

-nated; -nating : vacunar — **vaccine** *n* : vacuna *f*
vacuum *n*, *pl* **vacuums** *or* **vacua** : vacío *m* — ~ *vt* : pasar la aspiradora por — **vacuum cleaner** *n* : aspiradora *f*
vagina *n*, *pl* **-nae** *or* **-nas** : vagina *f*
vagrant *n* : vagabundo *m*, -da *f*
vague *adj* **vaguer; -est** : vago, indistinto
vain *adj* **1** CONCEITED : vanidoso **2 in ~** : en vano
valentine *n* : tarjeta *f* del día de San Valentín
valiant *adj* : valiente, valeroso

valid adj : válido — **validate** vt -dated; -dating : validar — **validity** n : validez f
valley n, pl -leys : valle m
valor n : valor m, valentía f
value n : valor m — ~ vt -ued; -uing : valorar — **valuable** adj : valioso — **valuables** npl : objetos mpl de valor
valve n : válvula f
vampire n : vampiro m
van n : furgoneta f, camioneta f
vandal n : vándalo m — **vandalism** n : vandalismo m — **vandalize** vt : destrozar, destruir
vane n or **weather** ~ : veleta f
vanguard n : vanguardia f
vanilla n : vainilla f
vanish vi : desaparecer
vanity n, pl -ties **1** : vanidad f **2** or ~ **table** : tocador m
vantage point n : posición f ventajosa
vapor n : vapor m
variable adj : variable — ~ n : variable f — **variance** n **at** ~ **with** : en desacuerdo con — **variant** n : variante f — **variation** n : variación f — **varied** adj : variado — **variegated** adj : abigarrado, multicolor — **variety** n, pl -ties **1** : variedad f **2** ASSORTMENT : surtido m **3** SORT : clase f — **various** adj : varios, diversos
varnish n : barniz f — ~ vt : barnizar
vary v **varied; varying** : variar
vase n **1** : jarrón m **2** or **flower** ~ : florero m
vast adj : vasto, enorme — **vastness** n : inmensidad f
vat n : cuba f
vault[1] vi LEAP : saltar — ~ n : salto m
vault[2] n **1** DOME : bóveda f **2** or **bank** ~ : cámara f acorazada, bóveda f de seguridad Lat **3** CRYPT : cripta f
VCR (videocassette recorder) n : video m
veal n : (carne f de) ternera f
veer vi : virar
vegetable adj : vegetal — ~ n **1** : vegetal m (planta) **2** ~**s** npl : verduras fpl — **vegetarian** n : vegetariano mf — **vegetation** n : vegetación f
vehemence n : vehemencia f — **vehement** adj : vehemente
vehicle n : vehículo m
veil n : velo m — ~ vt **1** : cubrir con un velo **2** CONCEAL : velar
vein n **1** : vena f **2** : veta f (de un mineral, etc.)
velocity n, pl -ties : velocidad f
velvet n : terciopelo m — **velvety** adj : aterciopelado
vending machine vt : máquina f expendedora

vendor n : vendedor m, -dora f
veneer n **1** : chapa f **2** FACADE : apariencia f
venerable adj : venerable — **venerate** vt -ated; -ating : venerar — **veneration** n : veneración f
venereal adj : venéreo
venetian blind n : persiana f veneciana
Venezuelan adj : venezolano
vengeance n **1** : venganza f **2 take** ~ **on** : vengarse de — **vengeful** adj : vengativo
venison n : (carne f de) venado m
venom n : veneno m — **venomous** adj : venenoso
vent vt : desahogar — ~ n **1** or **air** ~ : rejilla f de ventilación **2** OUTLET : desahogo m — **ventilate** vt -lated; -lating : ventilar — **ventilation** n : ventilación f — **ventilator** n : ventilador m
ventriloquist n : ventrílocuo m, -cua f
venture v -tured; -turing vt **1** RISK : arriesgar **2** : aventurar (una opinión, etc.) — vi : atreverse — ~ n or **business** ~ : empresa f
venue n : lugar m
Venus n : Venus m
veranda or **verandah** n : veranda f
verb n : verbo m — **verbal** adj : verbal — **verbatim** adv : palabra por palabra — ~ adj : literal — **verbose** adj : verboso
verdict n **1** : veredicto m **2** OPINION : opinión f
verge n **1** : borde m **2 on the** ~ **of** : a punto de (hacer algo), al borde de (algo) — ~ vi **verged; verging** ~ **on** : rayar en
verify vt -fied; -fying : verificar — **verification** n : verificación f
vermin ns & pl : alimañas fpl
vermouth n : vermut m
versatile adj : versátil — **versatility** n : versatilidad f
verse n **1** LINE : verso m **2** POETRY : poesía f **3** : versículo m (en la Biblia) — **versed** adj **be well** ~ **in** : ser muy versado en
version n : versión f
versus prep : versus
vertebra n, pl -**brae** or -bras : vértebra f
vertical adj : vertical — ~ n : vertical f
vertigo n, pl -goes or -gos : vértigo m
verve n : brío m
very adv **1** : muy **2 at the** ~ **least** : por lo menos **3 the** ~ **same thing** : la misma cosa **4** ~ **much** : mucho **5** ~ **well** : muy bien — ~ adj **verier; -est 1** PRECISE, SAME : mismo **2** MERE : solo, mero **3 the** ~ **thing** : justo lo que hacía falta
vessel n **1** CONTAINER : recipiente m **2** SHIP : nave f, buque m **3** or **blood** ~ : vaso m sanguíneo

vest *n* **1** : chaleco *m* **2** *Brit* UNDERSHIRT : camiseta *f*
vestibule *n* : vestíbulo *m*
vestige *n* : vestigio *m*
vet *n* **1** → **veterinarian 2** → **veteran**
veteran *n* : veterano *m*, -na *f*
veterinarian *n* : veterinario *m*, -ria *f* — **veterinary** *adj* : veterinario
veto *n*, *pl* -**toes** : veto *m* — ~ *vt* : vetar
vex *vt* ANNOY : irritar
via *prep* : por, vía
viable *adj* : viable
viaduct *n* : viaducto *m*
vial *n* : frasco *m*
vibrant *adj* : vibrante — **vibrate** *vi* -**brated; -brating** : vibrar — **vibration** *n* : vibración *f*
vicar *n* : vicario *m*, -ria *f*
vicarious *adj* : indirecto
vice *n* : vicio *m*
vice president *n* : vicepresidente *m*, -ta *f*
vice versa *adv* : viceversa
vicinity *n*, *pl* -**ties 1** : inmediaciones *fpl* **2 in the** ~ **of** ABOUT : alrededor de
vicious *adj* **1** SAVAGE : feroz **2** MALICIOUS : malicioso
victim *n* : víctima *f*
victor *n* : vencedor *m*, -dora *f*
victory *n*, *pl* -**ries** : victoria *f* — **victorious** *adj* : victorioso
video *n* : video *m*, vídeo *m* *Spain* — ~ *adj* : de video — **videocassette** *n* : videocasete *m* — **videotape** *n* : videocinta *f* — ~ *vt* -**taped; -taping** : videograbar
vie *vi* **vied; vying** : competir
Vietnamese *adj* : vietnamita
view *n* **1** : vista *f* **2** OPINION : opinión *f* **3 come into** ~ : aparecer **4 in** ~ **of** : en vista de (que) — ~ *vt* **1** : ver **2** CONSIDER : considerar — **viewer** *n* *or* **television** ~ : televidente *mf* — **viewpoint** *n* : punto *m* de vista
vigil *n* : vela *f* — **vigilance** *n* : vigilancia *f* — **vigilant** *adj* : vigilante
vigor *or Brit* **vigour** *n* : vigor *m* — **vigorous** *adj* **1** : enérgico **2** ROBUST : vigoroso
Viking *n* : vikingo *m*, -ga *f*
vile *adj* **viler; vilest 1** : vil **2** REVOLTING : asqueroso **3** TERRIBLE : horrible
villa *n* : casa *f* de campo
village *n* : pueblo *m* (grande), aldea *f* (pequeña) — **villager** *n* : vecino *m*, -na *f* (de un pueblo), aldeano *m*, -na *f* (de una aldea)
villain *n* : villano *m*, -na *f*
vindicate *vt* -**cated; -cating 1** : vindicar **2** JUSTIFY : justificar
vindictive *adj* : vengativo
vine *n* **1** : enredadera *f* **2** GRAPEVINE : vid *f*
vinegar *n* : vinagre *m*
vineyard *n* : viña *f*, viñedo *m*

vintage *n* **1** : cosecha *f* (de vino) **2** ERA : época *f* — ~ *adj* **1** : añejo (dícese de un vino) **2** CLASSIC : de época
vinyl *n* : vinilo
viola *n* : viola *f*
violate *vt* -**lated; -lating** : violar — **violation** *n* : violación *f*
violence *n* : violencia *f* — **violent** *adj* : violento
violet *n* : violeta *f* (flor), violeta *m* (color)
violin *n* : violín *m* — **violinist** *n* : violinista *mf* — **violoncello** → **cello**
VIP *n*, *pl* **VIPs** : VIP *mf*
viper *n* : víbora *f*
virgin *n* : virgen *mf* — ~ *adj* **1** : virgen (dícese de la lana, etc.) **2** CHASTE : virginal — **virginity** *n* : virginidad *f*
virile *adj* : viril — **virility** *n* : virilidad *f*
virtual *adj* : virtual — **virtually** *adv* : prácticamente
virtue *n* **1** : virtud *f* **2 by** ~ **of** : en virtud de
virtuoso *n*, *pl* -**sos** *or* -**si** : virtuoso *m*, -sa *f*
virtuous *adj* : virtuoso
virulent *adj* : virulento
virus *n* : virus *m*
visa *n* : visado *m*, visa *f Lat*
vis-à-vis *prep* : con respecto a
viscous *adj* : viscoso
vise *n* : torno *m* de banco
visible *adj* **1** : visible **2** NOTICEABLE : evidente — **visibility** *n*, *pl* -**ties** : visibilidad *f*
vision *n* **1** : visión *f* **2 have** ~**s of** : imaginarse — **visionary** *adj* : visionario — ~ *n*, *pl* -**ries** : visionario *m*, -ria *f*
visit *vt* : visitar — *vi* **1** : hacer una visita **2 be** ~**ing** : estar de visita — ~ *n* : visita *f* — **visitor** *n* **1** : visitante *mf* **2** GUEST : visita *f*
visor *n* : visera *f*
vista *n* : vista *f*
visual *adj* : visual — **visualize** *vt* -**ized; -izing** : visualizar
vital *adj* **1** : vital **2** CRUCIAL : esencial — **vitality** *n*, *pl* -**ties** : vitalidad *f*, energía *f*
vitamin *n* : vitamina *f*
vivacious *adj* : vivaz, animado
vivid *adj* : vivo (dícese de colores), vívido (dícese de sueños, etc.)
vocabulary *n*, *pl* -**laries** : vocabulario *m*
vocal *adj* **1** : vocal **2** OUTSPOKEN : vociferante — **vocal cords** *npl* : cuerdas *fpl* vocales — **vocalist** *n* : cantante *mf*, vocalista *mf*
vocation *n* : vocación *f* — **vocational** *adj* : profesional
vociferous *adj* : vociferante, ruidoso
vodka *n* : vodka *m*
vogue *n* **1** : moda *f*, boga *f* **2 be in** ~ : estar de moda, estar en boga

voice *n* : voz *f* — ~ *vt* **voiced; voicing** : expresar
void *adj* **1** INVALID : nulo **2** ~ **of** : falto de — ~ *n* : vacío *m* — ~ *vt* : anular
volatile *adj* : volátil — **volatility** *n* : volatilidad *f*
volcano *n, pl* **-noes** *or* **-nos** : volcán *m* — **volcanic** *adj* : volcánico
volition *n* **of one's own** ~ : por voluntad propia
volley *n, pl* **-leys 1** : descarga *f* (de tiros) **2** : torrente *m* (de insultos, etc.) **3** : volea *f* (en deportes) — **volleyball** *n* : voleibol *m*
volt *n* : voltio *m* — **voltage** *n* : voltaje *m*
voluble *adj* : locuaz
volume *n* : volumen *m* — **voluminous** *adj* : voluminoso
voluntary *adj* : voluntario — **volunteer** *n* : voluntario *m*, -ria *f* — ~ *vt* : ofrecer — *vi* ~ **to** : ofrecerse a

voluptuous *adj* : voluptuoso
vomit *n* : vómito *m* — ~ *v* : vomitar
voracious *adj* : voraz
vote *n* **1** : voto *m* **2** SUFFRAGE : derecho *m* al voto — ~ *vi* **voted; voting** : votar — **voter** *n* : votante *mf* — **voting** *n* : votación *f*
vouch *vi* ~ **for** : responder de (algo), responder por (algn) — **voucher** *n* : vale *m*
vow *n* : voto *m* — ~ *vt* : jurar
vowel *n* : vocal *m*
voyage *n* : viaje *m*
vulgar *adj* **1** COMMON : ordinario **2** CRUDE : grosero, vulgar — **vulgarity** *n, pl* **-ties** : vulgaridad *f*
vulnerable *adj* : vulnerable — **vulnerability** *n, pl* **-ties** : vulnerabilidad *f*
vulture *n* : buitre *m*
vying → **vie**

W

w *n, pl* **w's** *or* **ws** : w *f*, vigésima tercera letra del alfabeto inglés
wad *n* : taco *m* (de papel, etc.), fajo *m* (de billetes)
waddle *vi* **-dled; -dling** : andar como un pato
wade *v* **waded; wading** *vi* : caminar por el agua — *vt or* ~ **across** : vadear
wafer *n* : barquillo *m*
waffle *n* : gofre *m* Spain, wafle *m* Lat
waft *vt* : llevar por el aire — *vi* : flotar
wag *v* **wagged; wagging** *vt* : menear — *vi* : menearse
wage *n or* **wages** *npl* : salario *m* — ~ *vt* **waged; waging** ~ **war** : hacer la guerra
wager *n* : apuesta *f* — ~ *v* : apostar
wagon *n* **1** CART : carrito *m* **2** → **station wagon**
waif *n* : niño *m* abandonado
wail *vi* : lamentarse — ~ *n* : lamento *m*
waist *n* : cintura *f* — **waistline** *n* : cintura *f*
wait *vi* : esperar — *vt* **1** AWAIT : esperar **2** ~ **tables** : servir a la mesa — ~ *n* **1** : espera *f* **2 lie in** ~ : estar al acecho — **waiter** *n* : camarero *m*, mozo *m* Lat — **waiting room** *n* : sala *f* de espera — **waitress** *n* : camarera *f*, moza *f* Lat
waive *vt* **waived; waiving** : renunciar a — **waiver** *n* : renuncia *f*
wake[1] *v* **woke; woken** *or* **waked; waking**
vi or ~ **up** : despertarse — *vt* : despertar — ~ *n* : velatorio *m* (de un difunto)
wake[2] *n* **1** : estela *f* (de un barco) **2 in the** ~ **of** : tras, como consecuencia de
waken *vt* : despertar — *vi* : despertarse
walk *vi* **1** : caminar, andar **2** STROLL : pasear **3 too far to** ~ : demasiado lejos para ir a pie — *vt* **1** : caminar por **2** : sacar a pasear (a un perro) — ~ *n* **1** : paseo *m* **2** PATH : camino *m* **3** GAIT : andar *m* — **walker** *n* **1** : paseante *mf* **2** HIKER : excursionista *mf* — **walking stick** *n* : bastón *m* — **walkout** *n* STRIKE : huelga *f* — **walk out** *vi* **1** STRIKE : declararse en huelga **2** LEAVE : salir, irse **3** ~ **on** : abandonar
wall *n* : muro *m* (exterior), pared *f* (interior), muralla *f* (de una ciudad)
wallet *n* : billetera *f*, cartera *f*
wallflower *n* **be a** ~ : comer pavo
wallop *vt* : pegar fuerte — ~ *n* : golpe *m* fuerte
wallow *vi* : revolcarse
wallpaper *n* : papel *m* pintado — ~ *vt* : empapelar
walnut *n* : nuez *f*
walrus *n, pl* **-rus** *or* **-ruses** : morsa *f*
waltz *n* : vals *m* — ~ *vi* : valsar
wan *adj* **wanner; -est** : pálido
wand *n* : varita *f* (mágica)
wander *vi* **1** : vagar, pasear **2** STRAY : diva-

gar — vt : pasear por — **wanderer** n : vagabundo m, -da f — **wanderlust** n : pasión f por viajar
wane vi **waned; waning** : menguar — ~ n **be on the** ~ : estar disminuyendo
want vt **1** DESIRE : querer **2** NEED : necesitar **3** LACK : carecer de — ~ n **1** NEED : necesidad f **2** LACK : falta f **3** DESIRE : deseo m — **wanting** adj **be** ~ : carecer
wanton adj **1** LEWD : lascivo **2** ~ **cruelty** : crueldad f despiadada
war n : guerra f
ward n **1** : sala f (de un hospital, etc.) **2** : distrito m electoral **3** : pupilo m, -la f (de un tutor, etc.) — ~ vt ~ **off** : protegerse contra — **warden** n **1** : guardián m, -diana f **2** or **game** ~ : guardabosque mf **3** or **prison** ~ : alcaide m
wardrobe n **1** CLOSET : armario m **2** CLOTHES : vestuario m
warehouse n : almacén m, bodega f Lat —
wares npl : mercancías fpl
warfare n : guerra f
warily adv : cautelosamente
warlike adj : belicoso
warm adj **1** : caliente **2** LUKEWARM : tibio **3** CARING : cariñoso **4** I feel ~ : tengo calor **5** ~ **clothes** : ropa f de abrigo — ~ vt or ~ **up** : calentar — vi **1** or ~ **up** : calentarse **2** ~ **to** : tomar simpatía a (algn), entusiasmarse con (algo) — **warmblooded** adj : de sangre caliente — **warmhearted** adj : cariñoso — **warmly** adv **1** : calurosamente **2 dress** ~ : abrigarse —
warmth n **1** : calor m **2** AFFECTION : cariño m, afecto m
warn vt : advertir, avisar— **warning** n : advertencia f, aviso m
warp vt **1** : alabear (madera, etc.) **2** DISTORT : deformar — vi : alabearse
warrant n **1** : autorización f **2 arrest** ~ : orden f judicial — ~ vt : justificar — **warranty** n, pl **-ties** : garantía f
warrior n : guerrero m, -ra f
warship n : buque m de guerra
wart n : verruga f
wartime n : tiempo m de guerra
wary adj **warier; -est** : cauteloso
was → **be**
wash vt **1** : lavar(se) **2** CARRY : arrastrar **3** ~ **away** : llevarse **4** ~ **over** : bañar — vi : lavarse — ~ n **1** : lavado m **2** LAUNDRY : ropa f sucia — **washable** adj : lavable — **washcloth** n : toallita f (para lavarse) — **washed—out** adj **1** : desvaído (dícese de colores) **2** EXHAUSTED : agotado — **washer** n **1** → **washing machine 2** : arandela f (de una llave, etc.) — **washing machine** n : máquina f de lavar, lavadora f —

washroom n : servicios mpl (públicos), baño m
wasn't (contraction of **was not**) → **be**
wasp n : avispa f
waste v **wasted; wasting** vt **1** : desperdiciar, derrochar, malgastar **2** ~ **time** : perder tiempo — vi or ~ **away** : consumirse — ~ adj : de desecho — ~ n **1** : derroche m, desperdicio m **2** RUBBISH : desechos mpl **3** a ~ **of time** : una pérdida de tiempo — **wastebasket** n : papelera f — **wasteful** adj : derrochador — **wasteland** n : yermo m
watch vi **1** : mirar **2** or **keep** ~ : velar **3** ~ **out!** : ¡ten cuidado!, ¡ojo! — vt **1**: mirar **2** or ~ **over** : vigilar, cuidar **3** ~ **what you do** : ten cuidado con lo que haces — ~ n **1** reloj m **2** SURVEILLANCE : vigilancia f **3** LOOKOUT : guardia mf — **watchdog** n : perro m guardián — **watchful** adj : vigilante — **watchman** n, pl **-men** : vigilante m, guarda m — **watchword** n : santo m y seña
water n : agua f — ~ vt **1** : regar (el jardín, etc.) **2** ~ **down** DILUTE : diluir, aguar — vi **1** : lagrimar (dícese de los ojos) **2 my mouth is** ~**ing** : se me hace agua la boca — **watercolor** n : acuarela f — **watercress** n : berro m — **waterfall** n : cascada f, salto m de agua — **water lily** n : nenúfar m — **waterlogged** adj : lleno de agua, empapado — **watermelon** n : sandía f — **waterpower** n : energía f hidráulica — **waterproof** adj : impermeable — **watershed** n **1** : cuenca f (de un río) **2** : momento m crítico — **waterskiing** n : esquí m acuático — **watertight** adj : hermético — **waterway** n : vía f navegable — **waterworks** npl : central f de abastecimiento de agua — **watery** adj **1** : acuoso **2** DILUTED : aguado, diluido **3** WASHED-OUT : desvaído (dícese de colores)
watt n : vatio m — **wattage** n : vataje m
wave v **waved; waving** vi **1** : saludar con la mano **2** : flotar (dícese de una bandera) — vt **1** SHAKE : agitar **2** CURL : ondular **3** SIGNAL : hacer señas (con la mano) — ~ n **1** : ola f (de agua) **2** CURL : onda f **3** : onda f (en física) **4** : señal f (con la mano) **5** SURGE : oleada f — **wavelength** n : longitud f de onda
waver vi : vacilar
wax[1] vi : crecer (dícese de la luna)
wax[2] n : cera f (para pisos, etc.) — ~ vt : encerar — **waxy** adj **waxier; -est** : ceroso
way n **1** : camino m **2** MEANS : manera f, modo m **3 by the** ~ : a propósito, por cierto **4 by** ~ **of** : vía, pasando por **5 come a long** ~ : hacer grandes progresos **6 get in the** ~ : meterse en el camino **7 get one's own** ~ : salirse uno con la suya **8**

whale

mend one's ∼s : dejar las malas costumbres 9 out of the ∼ REMOTE : remoto, recóndito 10 which ∼ did he go? : ¿por dónde fue?
we *pron* : nosotros, nosotras
weak *adj* 1 : débil 2 DILUTED : aguado 3 a ∼ excuse : una excusa poco convincente — weaken *vt* : debilitar — *vi* : debilitarse — weakling *n* : debilucho *m*, -cha *f* — weakly *adv* : débilmente — ∼ *adj* weaklier; -est : enfermizo — weakness *n* 1 : debilidad *f* 2 FLAW : flaqueza *f*, punto *m* débil
wealth *n* : riqueza *f* — wealthy *adj* wealthier; -est : rico
wean *vt* : destetar
weapon *n* : arma *f*
wear *v* wore; worn; wearing *vt* 1 : llevar (ropa, etc.), calzar (zapatos) 2 *or* ∼ away : desgastar 3 ∼ oneself out : agotarse 4 ∼ out : gastar — *vi* 1 LAST : durar 2 ∼ off : desaparecer 3 ∼ out : gastarse — *n* 1 USE : uso *m* 2 CLOTHING : ropa *f* 3 be the worse for ∼ : estar deteriorado — wear and tear *n* : desgaste *m*
weary *adj* -rier; -est : cansado — ∼ *v* -ried; -rying *vt* : cansar — *vi* : cansarse — weariness *n* : cansancio *m* — wearisome *adj* : cansado
weasel *n* : comadreja *f*
weather *n* : tiempo *m* — ∼ *vt* 1 WEAR : erosionar, desgastar 2 ENDURE, OVERCOME : superar — weather-beaten *adj* : curtido — weatherman *n*, *pl* -men : meteorólogo *m*, -ga *f* — weather vane *n* : valeta *f*
weave *v* wove *or* weaved; woven *or* weaved; weaving *vt* 1 : tejer (tela) 2 INTERLACE : entretejer 3 ∼ one's way : abrirse camino — *vi* : tejer — ∼ *n* : tejido *m* — weaver *n* : tejedor *m*, -dora *f*
web *n* 1 : telaraña *f* (de araña) 2 : membrana *f* interdigital (de aves) 3 NETWORK : red *f*
wed *v* wedded; wedding *vt* : casarse con — *vi* : casarse
we'd (*contraction of* we had, we should, *or* we would) → have, should, would
wedding *n* : boda *f*, casamiento *m*
wedge *n* 1 : cuña *f* 2 PIECE : porción *f*, trozo *m* — ∼ *vt* wedged; wedging 1 : apretar (con una cuña) 2 CRAM : meter
Wednesday *n* : miércoles *m*
wee *adj* 1 : pequeñito 2 in the ∼ hours : a las altas horas
weed *n* : mala hierba *f* — ∼ *vt* 1 : desherbar 2 ∼ out : eliminar
week *n* : semana *f* — weekday *n* : día *m* laborable — weekend *n* : fin *m* de semana — weekly *adv* : semanalmente — ∼ *adj* : semanal — ∼ *n*, *pl* -lies : semanario *m*

weep *v* wept; weeping : llorar — weeping willow *n* : sauce *m* llorón — weepy *adj* weepier; -est : lloroso
weigh *vt* 1 : pesar 2 CONSIDER : sopesar 3 ∼ down : sobrecargar (con una carga), abrumar (con preocupaciones, etc.) — *vi* : pesar
weight *n* 1 : peso *m* 2 gain ∼ : engordar 3 lose ∼ : adelgazar — weighty *adj* weightier; -est 1 HEAVY : pesado 2 IMPORTANT : importante, de peso
weird *adj* 1 : misterioso 2 STRANGE : extraño
welcome *vt* -comed; -coming : dar la bienvenida a, recibir — ∼ *adj* 1 : bienvenido 2 you're ∼ : de nada — ∼ *n* : bienvenida *f*, acojida *f*
weld *v* : soldar
welfare *n* 1 WELL-BEING : bienestar *m* 2 AID : asistencia *f* social
well[1] *adv* better; best 1 : bien 2 CONSIDERABLY : bastante 3 as ∼ : también 4 as ∼ as : además de — ∼ *adj* : bien — ∼ *interj* 1 (*used to introduce a remark*) : bueno 2 (*used to express surprise*) : ¡vaya!
well[2] *n* : pozo *m* — ∼ *vi or* ∼ up : brotar, manar
we'll (*contraction of* we shall *or* we will) → shall, will
well-being *n* : bienestar *m* — well-bred *adj* : fino, bien educado — well-done *adj* 1 : bien hecho 2 : bien cocido (dícese de la carne, etc.) — well-known *adj* : famoso, bien conocido — well-meaning *adj* : bienintencionado — well-off *adj* : acomodado — well-rounded *adj* : completo — well-to-do *adj* : próspero, adinerado
Welsh *adj* : galés — ∼ *n* 1 : galés *m* (idioma) 2 the ∼ : los galeses
went → go
wept → weep
were → be
we're (*contraction of* we are) → be
weren't (*contraction of* were not) → be
west *adv* : al oeste — ∼ *adj* : oeste, del oeste — ∼ *n* 1 : oeste *m* 2 the West : el Oeste, el Occidente — westerly *adv* & *adj* : del oeste — western *adj* 1 : del oeste 2 Western : occidental — Westerner *n* : habitante *mf* del oeste — westward *adv* & *adj* : hacia el oeste
wet *adj* wetter; wettest 1 : mojado 2 RAINY : lluvioso 3 ∼ paint : pintura *f* fresca — ∼ *vt* wet *or* wetted; wetting : mojar, humedecer
we've (*contraction of* we have) → have
whack *vt* : golpear fuertemente — ∼ *n* : golpe *m* fuerte
whale *n*, *pl* whales *or* whale : ballena *f*

wharf *n, pl* **wharves** : muelle *m*, embarcadero *m*
what *adj* **1** (*used in questions and exclamations*) : qué **2** WHATEVER : cualquier — ~
pron **1** (*used in questions*) : qué **2** (*used in indirect statements*) : lo que, que **3** ~
does it cost? : ¿cuánto cuesta? **4** ~ **for?**
: ¿por qué? **5** ~ **if** : y si — **whatever** *adj* **1**
: cualquier **2 there's no chance** ~ : no hay ninguna posibilidad **3 nothing** ~
: nada en absoluto — ~ *pron* **1** ANYTHING
: lo que **2** (*used in questions*) : qué **3** ~ **it may be** : sea lo que sea — **whatsoever** *adj*
& pron → **whatever**
wheat *n* : trigo *m*
wheedle *vt* **-dled; -dling** : engatusar
wheel *n* **1** : rueda *f* **2** *or* **steering** ~
: volante *m* (de automóviles, etc.), timón *m*
(de barcos) — ~ *vt* : empujar (algo sobre ruedas) — *vi or* ~ **around** : darse la vuelta
— **wheelbarrow** *n* : carretilla *f* — **wheelchair** *n* : silla *f* de ruedas
wheeze *vi* **wheezed; wheezing** : resollar —
~ *n* : resuello *m*
when *adv* : cuándo — ~ *conj* **1** : cuando **2**
the days ~ **I clean the house** : los días
(en) que limpio la casa — ~ *pron* : cuándo
— **whenever** *adv* : cuando sea — ~ *conj* **1**
: cada vez que **2** ~ **you like** : cuando quieras
where *adv* **1** : dónde **2** ~ **are you going?**
: ¿adónde vas? — ~ *conj & pron* : donde
— **whereabouts** *adv* : (por) dónde — ~ *ns*
& pl : paradero *m* — **wherever** *adv* **1** : en
cualquier parte **2** WHERE : dónde, adónde
— ~ *conj* : dondequiera que
whet *vt* **whetted; whetting** **1** : afilar **2** ~
the appetite : estimular el apetito
whether *conj* **1** : si **2 we doubt** ~ **he'll show up** : dudamos que aparezca **3** ~ **you like it or not** : tanto si quieras como si no
which *adj* **1** : qué, cuál **2 in** ~ **case** : en cuyo caso — ~ *pron* **1** (*used in questions*)
: cuál **2** (*used in relative clauses*) : que, el (la) cual — **whichever** *adj* : cualquier — ~
pron : el (la) que, cualquiera que
whiff *n* **1** PUFF : soplo *m* **2** SMELL : olorcillo *m*
while *n* **1** : rato *m* **2 be worth one's** ~
: valer la pena **3 in a** ~ : dentro de poco —
~ *conj* **1** : mientras **2** WHEREAS : mientras que **3** ALTHOUGH : aunque — ~ *vt* **whiled; whiling** ~ **away the time** : matar el tiempo
whim *n* : capricho *m*, antojo *m*
whimper *vi* : lloriquear — ~ *n* : quejido *m*
whimsical *adj* : caprichoso, fantasioso
whine *vi* **whined; whining** **1** : gimotear **2**
COMPLAIN : quejarse — ~ *n* : quejido *m*, gemido *m*

whip *v* **whipped; whipping** *vt* **1** : azotar **2**
BEAT : batir (huevos, crema, etc.) **3** ~ **up**
AROUSE : avivar, despertar — *vi* FLAP : agitarse — ~ *n* : látigo *m*
whir *vi* **whirred; whirring** : zumbar — ~ *n*
: zumbido *m*
whirl *vi* **1** : dar vueltas, girar **2** *or* ~ **about**
: arremolinarse — ~ *n* **1** : giro *m* **2** SWIRL
: torbellino *m* — **whirlpool** *n* : remolino *m*
— **whirlwind** *n* : torbellino *m*
whisk *vt* **1** : batir **2** ~ **away** : llevarse —
~ *n or* **egg** ~ : batidor *m* — **whisk broom** *n* : escobilla *f*
whisker *n* **1** : pelo *m* (de la barba) **2** ~**s**
npl : bigotes *mpl* (de animales)
whiskey *or* **whisky** *n, pl* **-keys** *or* **-kies**
: whisky *m*
whisper *vi* : cuchichear, susurrar — *vt*
: susurrar — ~ *n* : susurro *m*
whistle *v* **-tled; -tling** *vi* **1** : silbar, chiflar
Lat **2** : pitar (dícese de un tren, etc.) — *vt*
: silbar — ~ *n* **1** : silbido *m*, chiflido *m*
(sonido) **2** : silbato *m*, pito *m* (instrumento)
white *adj* **whiter; -est** : blanco — ~ *n* **1**
: blanco *m* (color) **2** : clara *f* (de huevos) **3**
or ~ **person** : blanco *m*, -ca *f* — **white-collar** *adj* **1** : de oficina **2** ~ **worker**
: oficinista *mf* — **whiten** *vt* : blanquear —
whiteness *n* : blancura *f* — **whitewash** *vt*
1 : enjalbegar **2** CONCEAL : encubrir (un escándalo, etc.) — ~ *n* **1** : jalbegue *m*,
lechada *f* **2** COVER-UP : encubrimiento *m*
whittle *vt* **-tled; -tling** **1** : tallar (madera) **2**
or ~ **down** : reducir
whiz *or* **whizz** *vi* **whizzed; whizzing** **1**
BUZZ : zumbar **2** ~ **by** : pasar muy rápido
— ~ *or* **whizz** *n, pl* **whizzes** : zumbido *m*
— **whiz kid** *n* : joven *m* prometedor
who *pron* **1** (*used in direct and indirect questions*) : quién **2** (*used in relative clauses*)
: que, quien — **whodunit** *n* : novela *f*
policíaca — **whoever** *pron* **1** : quienquiera
que, quien **2** (*used in questions*) : quién
whole *adj* **1** : entero **2** INTACT : intacto **3 a**
~ **lot** : muchísimo — ~ *n* **1** : todo *m* **2 as**
a ~ : en conjunto **3 on the** ~ : en general
— **wholehearted** *adj* : sincero — **wholesale** *n* : venta *f* al por mayor — ~ *adj* **1** : al
por mayor **2** ~ **slaughter** : matanza *f*
sistemática — ~ *adv* : al por mayor —
wholesaler *n* : mayorista *mf* — **wholesome** *adj* : sano — **whole wheat** *adj* : de
trigo integral — **wholly** *adv* : completamente
whom *pron* **1** (*used in direct questions*) : a
quién **2** (*used in indirect questions*) : de
quién, con quién, en quién **3** (*used in relative clauses*) : que, a quien
whooping cough *n* : tos *f* ferina

whore *n* : puta *f*
whose *adj* **1** (*used in questions*) : de quién **2** (*used in relative clauses*) : cuyo — ~ *pron* : de quién
why *adv* : por qué — ~ *n, pl* **whys** : porqué *m* — ~ *conj* : por qué — ~ *interj* (*used to express surprise*) : ¡vaya!, ¡mira!
wick *n* : mecha *f*
wicked *adj* **1** : malo, malvado **2** MISCHIEVOUS : travieso **3** TERRIBLE : terrible, horrible — **wickedness** *n* : maldad *f*
wicker *n* : mimbre *m* — ~ *adj* : de mimbre
wide *adj* **wider; widest** **1** : ancho **2** VAST : amplio, extenso **3** *or* ~ **of the mark** : desviado — ~ *adv* **1** ~ **apart** : muy separados **2 far and** ~ : por todas partes **3** ~ **open** : abierto de par en par — **wide-awake** *adj* : (completamente) despierto — **widely** *adv* : extensivamente — **widespread** *adj* : extendido
widow *n* : viuda *f* — ~ *vt* : dejar viuda — **widower** *n* : viudo *m*
width *n* : ancho *m*, anchura *f*
wield *vt* **1** : usar, manejar **2** EXERT : ejercer
wiener → **frankfurter**
wife *n, pl* **wives** : esposa *f*, mujer *f*
wig *n* : peluca *f*
wiggle *v* **-gled; -gling** *vt* : menear, contonear — *vi* : menearse — ~ *n* : meneo *m*
wigwam *n* : wigwam *m*
wild *adj* **1** : salvaje **2** DESOLATE : agreste **3** UNRULY : desenfrenado **4** RANDOM : al azar **5** FRANTIC : frenético **6** OUTRAGEOUS : extravagante — ~ *adv* **1** → **wildly 2 run** ~ : volver al estado silvestre (dícese de las plantas), desmandarse (dícese de los niños) — **wildcat** *n* : gato *m* montés — **wilderness** *n* : yermo *m*, desierto *m* — **wildfire** *n* **1** : fuego *m* descontrolado **2 spread like** ~ : propagarse como un reguero de pólvora — **wildflower** *n* : flor *f* silvestre — **wildlife** *n* : fauna *f* — **wildly** *adv* **1** FRANTICALLY : frenéticamente **2** EXTREMELY : locamente
will[1] *v past* **would**; *pres sing & pl* **will** *vi* WISH : querer — *v aux* **1 tomorrow we** ~ **go shopping** : mañana iremos de compras **2 he** ~ **get angry over nothing** : se pone furioso por cualquier cosa **3 I** ~ **go despite them** : iré a pesar de ellos **4 I won't do it** : no lo haré **5 that** ~ **be the mailman** : eso ha de ser el cartero **6 the couch** ~ **hold three people** : en el sofá cabrán tres personas **7 accidents** ~ **happen** : los accidentes ocurrirán **8 you** ~ **do as I say** : harás lo que digo
will[2] *n* **1** : voluntad *f* **2** TESTAMENT : testamento *m* **3 free** ~ : libre albedrío *m* —
willful *or* **wilful** *adj* **1** OBSTINATE : terco **2** INTENTIONAL : intencional — **willing** *adj*

1 : complaciente **2 be** ~ **to** : estar dispuesto a — **willingly** *adv* : con gusto — **willingness** *n* : buena voluntad *f*
willow *n* : sauce *m*
willpower *n* : fuerza *f* de voluntad
wilt *vi* : marchitarse
wily *adj* **wilier; -est** : artero, astuto
win *v* **won; winning** *vi* : ganar — *vt* **1** : ganar, conseguir **2** ~ **over** : ganarse a — ~ *n* : triunfo *m*, victoria *f*
wince *vi* **winced; wincing** : hacer una mueca de dolor — ~ *n* : mueca *f* de dolor
winch *n* : torno *m*
wind[1] *n* **1** : viento *m* **2** BREATH : aliento *m* **3** FLATULENCE : flatulencia *f* **4 get** ~ **of** : enterarse de
wind[2] *v* **wound; winding** *vi* : serpentear — *vt* **1** COIL : enrollar **2** ~ **a clock** : dar cuerda a un reloj
windfall *n* : beneficio *m* imprevisto
winding *adj* : tortuoso
wind instrument *n* : instrumento *m* de viento
windmill *n* : molino *m* de viento
window *n* : ventana *f* (de un edificio o una computadora), ventanilla *f* (de un vehículo), vitrina *f* (de una tienda) — **windowpane** *n* : vidrio *m* — **windowsill** *n* : repisa *f* de la ventana
windpipe *n* : tráquea *f*
windshield *n* **1** : parabrisas *m* **2** ~ **wiper** : limpiaparabrisas *m*
window-shop *vi* **-shopped; -shopping** : mirar las vitrinas
wind up *vt* : terminar, concluir — *vi* : terminar, acabar — **windup** *n* : conclusión *f*
windy *adj* **windier; -est 1** : ventoso **2 it's** ~ : hace viento
wine *n* : vino *m* — **wine cellar** *n* : bodega *f*
wing *n* **1** : ala *f* **2 under s.o.'s** ~ : bajo el cargo de algn — **winged** *adj* : alado
wink *vi* : guiñar — ~ *n* **1** : guiño *m* **2 not sleep a** ~ : no pegar el ojo
winner *n* : ganador *m*, -dora *f* — **winning** *adj* **1** : ganador **2** CHARMING : encantador — **winnings** *npl* : ganancias *fpl*
winter *n* : invierno *m* — ~ *adj* : invernal, de invierno — **wintergreen** *n* : gaulteria *f* — **wintertime** *n* : invierno *m* — **wintry** *adj* **wintrier; -est** : invernal, de invierno
wipe *vt* **wiped; wiping 1** : limpiar **2** ~ **away** : enjugar (lágrimas), borrar (una memoria) **3** ~ **out** : aniquilar, destruir — ~ *n* : pasada *f* (con un trapo, etc.)
wire *n* **1** : alambre *m* **2** CABLE *m* (eléctrico o telefónico) **3** TELEGRAM : telegrama *m* — ~ *vt* **-wired; wiring 1** : instalar el cableado en (una casa, etc.) **2** BIND : atar con alambre **3** TELEGRAPH : enviar un telegrama a — **wireless** *adj* : inalámbrico

— **wiring** *n* : cableado *m* — **wiry** *adj* **wirier;** **-est** **1** : hirsuto, tieso (dícese del pelo) **2** : esbelto y musculoso (dícese del cuerpo)

wisdom *n* : sabiduría *f* — **wisdom tooth** *n* : muela *f* de juicio

wise *adj* **wiser; wisest** **1** : sabio **2** SENSI-BLE : prudente — **wisecrack** *n* : broma *f,* chiste *m* — **wisely** *adv* : sabiamente

wish *vt* **1** : desear **2** ~ **s.o. well** : desear lo mejor a algn — *vi* **1** : pedir (como deseo) **2** **as you** ~ : como quieras — ~ *n* **1** : deseo *m* **2** **best** ~**es** : muchos recuerdos — **wishbone** *n* : espoleta *f* — **wishful** *adj* **1** : deseoso **2** ~ **thinking** : ilusiones *fpl*

wishy-washy *adj* : insípido, soso

wisp *n* **1** : mechón *m* (de pelo) **2** : voluta *f* (de humo)

wistful *adj* : melancólico

wit *n* **1** CLEVERNESS : ingenio *m* **2** HUMOR : agudeza *f* **3** **at one's** ~**'s end** : desesperado **4** **scared out of one's** ~**s** : muerto de miedo

witch *n* : bruja *f* — **witchcraft** *n* : brujería *f,* hechicería *f*

with *prep* **1** : con **2** **I'm going** ~ **you** : voy contigo **3** **it varies** ~ **the season** : varía según la estación **4** **the girl** ~ **red hair** : la muchacha de pelo rojo **5** ~ **all his work, the business failed** : a pesar de su trabajo, el negocio fracasó

withdraw *v* **-drew; -drawn; -drawing** *vt* : retirar — *vi* : apartarse — **withdrawal** *n* **1** : retirada *f* **2** : abandono (de drogas, etc.) — **withdrawn** *adj* : introvertido

wither *vi* : marchitarse

withhold *vt* **-held; -holding** : retener (fondos), negar (permiso, etc.)

within *adv* : dentro — ~ *prep* **1** : dentro de **2** (*in expressions of distance*) : a menos de **3** (*in expressions of time*) : dentro de, en menos de **4** ~ **reach** : al alcance de la mano

without *adv* **do** ~ : pasar sin algo — ~ *prep* : sin

withstand *vt* **-stood; -standing** **1** BEAR : aguantar **2** RESIST : resistir

witness *n* **1** : testigo *mf* **2** EVIDENCE : testimonio *m* **3** **bear** ~ : atestiguar — ~ *vt* **1** SEE : ser testigo de **2** : atestiguar (una firma, etc.)

witticism *n* : agudeza *f,* ocurrencia *f*

witty *adj* **-tier; -est** : ingenioso, ocurrente

wives → **wife**

wizard *n* **1** : mago *m,* brujo *m* **2** **a math** ~ : un genio de matemáticas

wizened *adj* : arrugado

wobble *vi* **-bled; -bling** **1** : tambalearse **2** : temblar (dícese de la voz, etc.) — **wobbly** *adj* : cojo

woe *n* **1** : aflicción *f* **2** ~**s** *npl* TROUBLES : penas *fpl* — **woeful** *adj* : triste

woke, woken → **wake**

wolf *n, pl* **wolves** : lobo *m,* -ba *f* — ~ *vt or* ~ **down** : engullir

woman *n, pl* **women** : mujer *f* — **womanly** *adj* : femenino

womb *n* : útero *m,* matriz *f*

won → **win**

wonder *n* **1** MARVEL : maravilla *f* **2** AMAZE-MENT : asombro *m* — ~ *v* : preguntarse — **wonderful** *adj* : maravilloso, estupendo

won't (*contraction of* will not) → **will**

woo *vt* **1** COURT : cortejar **2** : buscar el apoyo de (clientes, votantes, etc.)

wood *n* **1** : madera *f* (materia) **2** FIREWOOD : leña *f* **3** *or* ~**s** *npl* FOREST : bosque *m* — ~ *adj* : de madera — **woodchuck** *n* : marmota *f* de América — **wooded** *adj* : arbolado, boscoso — **wooden** *adj* : de madera — **woodpecker** *n* : pájaro *m* carpintero — **woodshed** *n* : leñera *f* — **woodwind** *n* : instrumento *m* de viento de madera — **woodwork** *n* : carpintería *f*

wool *n* : lana *f* — **woolen** *or* **woollen** *adj* : de lana — ~ *n* : lana *f* (tela) **2** ~**s** *npl* : prendas *fpl* de lana — **woolly** *adj* **-lier; -est** : lanudo

word *n* **1** : palabra *f* **2** NEWS : noticias *fpl* **3** ~**s** *npl* : letra *f* (de una canción, etc.) **4** **have** ~**s with** : reñir con **5** **just say the** ~ : no tienes que decirlo **6** **keep one's** ~ : cumplir su palabra — ~ *vt* : expresar — **word processing** *n* : procesamiento *m* de textos — **word processor** *n* : procesador *m* de textos — **wordy** *adj* **wordier; -est** : prolijo

wore → **wear**

work *n* **1** LABOR : trabajo *m* **2** EMPLOYMENT : trabajo *m,* empleo *m* **3** : obra *f* (de arte, etc.) **4** ~**s** *npl* FACTORY : fábrica *f* **5** ~**s** *npl* MECHANISM : mecanismo *m* — ~ *v* **worked** *or* **wrought; working** *vt* **1** : hacer trabajar (a una persona) **2** : manejar, operar (una máquina, etc.) — *vi* **1** : trabajar **2** FUNCTION : funcionar **3** : surtir efecto (dícese de una droga), resultar (dícese de una idea, etc.) — **worked up** *adj* : nervioso — **worker** *n* : trabajador *m,* -dora *f;* obrero *m,* -ra *f* — **working** *adj* **1** : que trabaja (dícese de personas), de trabajo (dícese de la ropa, etc.) **2** **be in** ~ **order** : funcionar bien — **working class** *n* : clase *f* obrera — **workingman** *n, pl* **-men** : obrero *m* — **workman** *n, pl* **-men** **1** : obrero *m* **2** ARTISAN : artesano *m* — **workmanship** *n* : artesanía *f,* destreza *f* — **workout** *n* : ejercicios *mpl* (físicos) — **work out** *vt* **1** DEVELOP : elaborar **2** SOLVE : resolver — *vi* **1** TURN

OUT : resultar **2** SUCCEED : lograr, salir bien **3** EXERCISE : hacer ejercicio — **workshop** *n* : taller *m* — **work up** *vt* **1** EXCITE : ponerse como loco **2** GENERATE : desarrollar

world *n* : mundo *m* **2 think the** ~ **of s.o.** : tener a algn en alta estima — ~ *adj* : mundial, del mundo — **worldly** *adj* : mundano — **worldwide** *adv* : en todo el mundo — ~ *adj* : global, mundial

worm *n* **1** : gusano *m*, lombriz *f* **2** ~**s** *npl* : lombrices *fpl* (parásitos)

worn → **wear** — **worn–out** *adj* **1** USED : gastado **2** TIRED : agotado

worry *v* -**ried; -rying** *vt* : preocupar, inquietar — *vi* : preocuparse, inquietarse — ~ *n, pl* -**ries** : preocupación *f* — **worried** *adj* : preocupado — **worrisome** *adj* : inquietante

worse *adv* (*comparative of* **bad** *or of* **ill**) : peor — ~ *adj* (*comparative of* **bad** *or of* **ill**) **1** : peor **2 from bad to** ~ : de mal en peor **3 get** ~ : empeorar — ~ *n* **1 the** ~ : el (la) peor, lo peor **2 take a turn for the** ~ : ponerse peor — **worsen** *v* : empeorar

worship *v* -**shiped** *or* -**shipped; -shiping** *or* -**shipping** *vt* : adorar — *vi* : practicar una religión — ~ *n* : adoración *f*, culto *m* — **worshiper** *or* **worshipper** *n* : adorador *m*, -dora *f*

worst *adv* (*superlative of* **ill** *or of* **bad** *or* **badly**) : peor — ~ *adj* (*superlative of* **bad** *or of* **ill**) : peor — ~ *n* **the** ~ : lo peor, el (la) peor

worth *n* **1** : valor *m* (monetario) **2** MERIT : mérito *m*, valía *f* **3 ten dollars'** ~ **of gas** : diez dólares de gasolina — ~ *prep* **1 it's** ~ **$ 10** : vale $ 10 **2 it's** ~ **doing** : vale la pena hacerlo — **worthless** *adj* **1** : sin valor **2** USELESS : inútil — **worthwhile** *adj* : que vale la pena — **worthy** *adj* -**thier; -est** : digno

would *past of* **will 1 he** ~ **often take his children to the park** : solía llevar a sus hijos al parque **2 I** ~ **go if I had the money** : iría yo si tuviera el dinero **3 I** ~ **rather go alone** : preferiría ir sola **4 she** ~ **have won if she hadn't tripped** : habría ganado si no hubiera tropezado **5** ~ **you kindly help me with this?** : ¿tendría la bondad de ayudarme con esto? — **would–be** *adj* **a** ~ **poet** : un aspirante a poeta — **wouldn't** (*contraction of* **would not**) → **would**

wound[1] *n* : herida *f* — ~ *vt* : herir
wound[2] → **wind**
wove, woven → **weave**
wrangle *vi* -**gled; -gling** : reñir — ~ *n* : riña *f*, disputa *f*
wrap *vt* **wrapped; wrapping 1** : envolver **2**

~ **up** FINISH : dar fin a — ~ *n* **1** : prenda *f* que envuelve (como un chal) **2** WRAPPER : envoltura *f* — **wrapper** *n* : envoltura *f*, envoltorio *m* — **wrapping** *n* : envoltura *f*, envoltorio *m*

wrath *n* : ira *f*, cólera *f* — **wrathful** *adj* : iracundo

wreath *n, pl* **wreaths** : corona *f* (de flores, etc.)

wreck *n* **1** WRECKAGE : restos *mpl* **2** RUIN : ruina *f*, desastre *m* **3 be a nervous** ~ : tener los nervios destrozados — ~ *vt* : destrozar (un automóvil), naufragar (un barco) — **wreckage** *n* : restos *mpl* (de un buque naufragado, etc.), ruinas *fpl* (de un edificio)

wren *n* : chochín *m*

wrench *vt* **1** PULL : arrancar (de un tirón) **2** SPRAIN, TWIST : torcerse — ~ *n* **1** TUG : tirón *m*, jalón *m* **2** SPRAIN : torcedura *f* **3** *or* **monkey** ~ : llave *f* inglesa

wrestle *vi* -**tled; -tling** : luchar — **wrestler** *n* : luchador *m*, -dora *f* — **wrestling** *n* : lucha *f*

wretch *n* : desgraciado *m*, -da *f* — **wretched** *adj* **1** : miserable **2** ~ **weather** : tiempo *m* espantoso

wriggle *vi* -**gled; -gling** : retorcerse, menearse

wring *vt* **wrung; wringing 1** *or* ~ **out** : escurrir (el lavado, etc.) **2** TWIST : retorcer **3** EXTRACT : arrancar (información, etc.)

wrinkle *n* : arruga *f* — ~ *v* -**kled; -kling** *vt* : arrugar — *vi* : arrugarse

wrist *n* : muñeca *f* — **wristwatch** *n* : reloj *m* de pulsera

writ *n* : orden *f* (judicial)

write *v* **wrote; written; writing** : escribir — **write down** *vt* : apuntar, anotar — **write off** *vt* CANCEL : cancelar — **writer** *n* : escritor *m*, -tora *f*

writhe *vi* **writhed; writhing** : retorcerse

writing *n* : escritura *f*

wrong *n* **1** INJUSTICE : injusticia *f*, mal *m* **2** : agravio *m* (en derecho) **3 be in the** ~ : haber hecho mal — ~ *adj* **wronger; wrongest 1** : malo **2** UNSUITABLE : inadecuado, inapropiado **3** INCORRECT : incorrecto, equivocado **4 be** ~ : no tener razón — ~ *adv* : mal, incorrectamente — ~ *vt* **wronged; wronging** : ofender, ser injusto con — **wrongful** *adj* **1** UNJUST : injusto **2** UNLAWFUL : ilegal — **wrongly** *adv* **1** UNJUSTLY : injustamente **2** INCORRECTLY : mal

wrote → **write**

wrought iron *n* : hierro *m* forjado

wrung → **wring**

wry *adj* **wrier; wriest** : irónico, sardónico (dícese del humor)

XYZ

x *n, pl* **x's** *or* **xs** : x *f,* vigésima cuarta letra del alfabeto inglés
xenophobia *n* : xenofobia *f*
Xmas *n* : Navidad *f*
X ray *n* **1** : rayo *m* X **2** *or* ~ **photograph** : radiografía *f* — **x-ray** *vt* : radiografiar
xylophone *n* : xilófono *m*
y *n, pl* **y's** *or* **ys** : y *f,* vigésima quinta letra del alfabeto inglés
yacht *n* : yate *m*
yam *n* **1** : ñame *m* **2** SWEET POTATO : batata *f,* boniato *m*
yank *vt* : tirar de, jalar *Lat* — ~ *n* : tirón *m,* jalón *m Lat*
Yankee *n* : yanqui *mf*
yap *vi* **yapped; yapping** : ladrar — ~ *n* : ladrido *m*
yard *n* **1** : yarda *f* (medida) **2** COURTYARD : patio *m* **3** : jardín *m* (de una casa) — **yardstick** *n* **1** : vara *f* (de medir) **2** CRITERION : criterio *m*
yarn *n* **1** : hilado *m* **2** TALE : historia *f,* cuento *m*
yawn *vi* : bostezar — ~ *n* : bostezo *m*
year *n* **1** : año *m* **2 she's ten ~s old** : tiene diez años **3 I haven't seen them in ~s** : hace siglos que no los veo — **yearbook** *n* : anuario *m* — **yearling** *n* : animal *m* menor de dos años — **yearly** *adv* **1** : anualmente **2 three times ~** : tres veces al año — ~ *adj* : anual
yearn *vi* : anhelar — **yearning** *n* : anhelo *m,* ansia *f*
yeast *n* : levadura *f*
yell *vi* : gritar, chillar — *vt* : gritar — ~ *n* : grito *m,* chillido *m*
yellow *adj* : amarillo — ~ *n* : amarillo *m* — **yellowish** *adj* : amarillento
yelp *n* : gañido *m* — ~ *vi* : dar un gañido
yes *adv* **1** : sí **2 say ~** : decir que sí — ~ *n* : sí *m*
yesterday *adv* : ayer — ~ *n* **1** : ayer *m* **2 the day before ~** : anteayer
yet *adv* **1** : aún, todavía **2 has he come ~?** : ¿ya ha venido? **3 not ~** : todavía no **4 ~ more problems** : más problemas aún **5** NEVERTHELESS : sin embargo — ~ *conj* : pero
yield *vt* **1** PRODUCE : producir **2 ~ the right of way** : ceder el paso — *vi* : ceder — ~ *n* : rendimiento *m,* rédito *m* (en finanzas)
yoga *n* : yoga *m*
yogurt *n* : yogur *m,* yogurt *m*
yoke *n* : yugo *m*

yolk *n* : yema *f* (de un huevo)
you *pron* **1** (*used as subject—familiar*) : tú; vos (*in some Latin American countries*); ustedes *pl;* vosotros, vosotras *pl Spain* **2** (*used as subject—formal*) : usted, ustedes *pl* **3** (*used as indirect object—familiar*) : te, les *pl* (se *before lo, la, los, las*), os *pl Spain* **4** (*used as indirect object—formal*) : lo (*Spain sometimes* le), la; los (*Spain sometimes* les), las *pl* **5** (*used after a preposition—familiar*) : ti; vos (*in some Latin American countries*); ustedes *pl;* vosotros, vosotras *pl Spain* **6** (*used after a preposition—formal*) : usted, ustedes *pl* **7 with ~** (*familiar*) : contigo; con ustedes *pl;* con vosotros, con vosotras *pl Spain* **8 with ~** (*formal*) : con usted, con ustedes *pl* **9 ~ never know** : nunca se sabe — **you'd** (*contraction of* **you had** *or* **you would**) → **have, would** — **you'll** (*contraction of* **you shall** *or* **you will**) → **shall, will**
young *adj* **younger; youngest** **1** : joven **2 my ~er brother** : mi hermano menor **3 she is the ~est** : es la más pequeña **4 the ~** : los jóvenes — *npl* : jóvenes *mfpl* (de los humanos), crías *fpl* (de los animales) — **youngster** *n* : chico *m,* -ca *f;* joven *mf*
your *adj* **1** (*familiar singular*) : tu **2** (*familiar plural*) su, vuestro *Spain* **3** (*formal*) : su **4 on ~ left** : a la izquierda
you're (*contraction of* **you are**) → **be**
yours *pron* **1** (*belonging to one person—familiar*) : (el) tuyo, (la) tuya, (los) tuyos, (las) tuyas **2** (*belonging to more than one person—familiar*) : (el) suyo, (la) suya, (los) suyos, (las) suyas; (el) vuestro, (la) vuestra, (los) vuestros, (las) vuestras *Spain* **3** (*formal*) : (el) suyo, (la) suya, (los) suyos, (las) suyas
yourself *pron, pl* **yourselves** **1** (*used reflexively—familiar*) : te, se *pl,* os *pl Spain* **2** (*used reflexively—formal*) : se **3** (*used for emphasis*) : tú mismo, tú misma; usted mismo, usted misma; ustedes mismos, ustedes mismas *pl;* vosotros mismos, vosotras mismas *pl Spain*
youth *n, pl* **youths** **1** : juventud *f* **2** BOY : joven *m* **3 today's ~** : los jóvenes de hoy — **youthful** *adj* **1** : juvenil, de juventud **2** YOUNG : joven
you've (*contraction of* **you have**) → **have**
yowl *vi* : aullar — ~ *n* : aullido *m*
yucca *n* : yuca *f*
Yugoslavian *adj* : yugoslavo

yule *n* CHRISTMAS : Navidad *f* — **yuletide** *n* : Navidades *fpl*

z *n, pl* **z's** *or* **zs** : z *f*, vigésima sexta letra del alfabeto inglés

zany *adj* **-nier; -est** : alocado, disparatado

zeal *n* : fervor *m*, celo *m* — **zealous** *adj* : entusiasta

zebra *n* : cebra *f*

zenith *n* **1** : cenit *m* (en astronomía) **2** PEAK : apogeo *m*

zero *n, pl* **-ros** : cero *m*

zest *n* **1** : gusto *m* **2** FLAVOR : sazón *f*

zigzag *n* : zigzag *m* — ~ *vi* **-zagged; -zagging** : zigzaguear

zinc *n* : cinc *m*, zinc *m*

zip *v* **zipped; zipping** *vt or* ~ **up** : cerrar la cremallera de, cerrar el cierre de *Lat* — *vi* SPEED : pasarse volando — **zip code** *n* : código *m* postal — **zipper** *n* : cremallera *f*, cierre *m Lat*

zodiac *n* : zodíaco *m*

zone *n* : zona *f*

zoo *n, pl* **zoos** : zoológico *m*, zoo *m* — **zoology** *n* : zoología *f*

zoom *vi* : zumbar, ir volando — ~ *n* **1** : zumbido *m* **2** *or* ~ **lens** : zoom *m*

zucchini *n, pl* **-ni** *or* **-nis** : calabacín *m*, calabacita *f Lat*

Common Spanish Abbreviations

SPANISH ABBREVIATION AND EXPANSION		ENGLISH EQUIVALENT	
abr.	abril	Apr.	April
A.C., a.C.	antes de Cristo	BC	before Christ
a. de J.C.	antes de Jesucristo	BC	before Christ
admon., admón.	administración	—	administration
a/f	a favor	—	in favor
ago.	agosto	Aug.	August
Apdo.	apartado (de correos)	—	P.O. box
aprox.	aproximadamente	approx.	approximately
Aptdo.	apartado (de correos)	—	P.O. box
Arq.	arquitecto	arch.	architect
A.T.	Antiguo Testamento	O.T.	Old Testament
atte.	atentamente	—	sincerely
atto., atta.	atento, atenta	—	kind, courteous
av., avda.	avenida	ave.	avenue
a/v.	a vista	—	on receipt
BID	Banco Interamericano de Desarrollo	IDB	Interamerican Development Bank
Bo	banco	—	bank
BM	Banco Mundial	—	World Bank
c/, C/	calle	st.	street
C	centígrado, Celsius	C	centigrade, Celsius
C.	compañía	Co.	company
CA	corriente alterna	AC	alternating current
cap.	capítulo	ch., chap.	chapter
c/c	cuenta corriente	—	current account, checking account
c.c.	centímetros cúbicos	cu. cm	cubic centimeters
CC	corriente continua	DC	direct current
c/d	con descuento	—	with discount
Cd.	ciudad	—	city
CE	Comunidad Europea	EC	European Community
CEE	Comunidad Económica Europea	EEC	European Economic Community
cf.	confróntese	cf.	compare
cg.	centígramo	cg	centigram
CGT	Confederación General de Trabajadores o del Trabajo	—	confederation of workers, workers' union
CI	coeficiente intelectual o de inteligencia	IQ	intelligence quotient
Cía.	compañía	Co.	company
cm.	centímetro	cm	centimeter
Cnel.	coronel	Col.	colonel
col.	columna	col.	column
Col. Mex	colonia	—	residential area
Com.	comandante	Cmdr.	commander
comp.	compárese	comp.	compare
Cor.	coronel	Col.	colonel
C.P.	código postal	—	zip code
CSF, c.s.f.	coste, seguro y flete	c.i.f.	cost, insurance, and freight
cta.	cuenta	ac., acct.	account
cte.	corriente	cur.	current

SPANISH ABBREVIATION AND EXPANSION		ENGLISH EQUIVALENT	
c/u	cada uno, cada una	ea.	each
CV	caballo de vapor	hp	horsepower
D.	Don	—	—
Da., D.ª	Doña	—	—
d.C.	después de Cristo	AD	anno Domini (in the year of our Lord)
dcha.	derecha	—	right
d. de J.C.	después de Jesucristo	AD	anno Domini (in the year of our lord)
dep.	departamento	dept.	department
DF, D.F.	Distrito Federal	—	Federal District
dic.	diciembre	Dec.	December
dir.	director, directora	dir.	director
dir.	dirección	—	address
Dña.	Doña	—	—
do.	domingo	Sun.	Sunday
dpto.	departamento	dept.	department
Dr.	doctor	Dr.	doctor
Dra.	doctora	Dr.	doctor
dto.	descuento	—	discount
E, E.	Este, este	E	East, east
Ed.	editorial	—	publishing house
Ed., ed.	edición	ed.	edition
edif.	edificio	bldg.	building
edo.	estado	st.	state
EEUU, EE.UU.	Estados Unidos	US, U.S.	United States
ej.	por ejemplo	e.g.	for example
E.M.	esclerosis multiple	MS	multiple sclerosis
ene.	enero	Jan.	January
etc.	etcétera	etc.	et cetera
ext.	extensión	ext.	extension
F	Fahrenheit	F	Fahrenheit
f.a.b.	franco a bordo	f.o.b.	free on board
FC	ferrocarril	RR	railroad
feb.	febrero	Feb.	February
FF AA, FF.AA.	Fuerzas Armadas	—	armed forces
FMI	Fondo Monetario Internacional	IMF	International Monetary Fund
g.	gramo	g., gm, gr.	gram
G.P.	giro postal	M.O.	money order
gr.	gramo	g., gm, gr.	gram
Gral.	general	Gen.	general
h.	hora	hr.	hour
Hnos.	hermanos	Bros.	brothers
I + D, I & D, I y D	investigación y desarrollo	R & D	research and development
i.e.	esto es, es decir	i.e.	that is
incl.	inclusive	incl.	inclusive, inclusively
Ing.	ingeniero, ingeniera	eng.	engineer
IPC	índice de precios al consumo	CPI	consumer price index
IVA	impuesto al valor agregado	VAT	value-added tax
izq.	izquierda	l.	left
juev.	jueves	Thurs.	Thursday
jul.	julio	Jul.	July

SPANISH ABBREVIATION AND EXPANSION		ENGLISH EQUIVALENT	
jun.	junio	**Jun.**	June
kg.	kilogramo	**kg**	kilogram
km.	kilómetro	**km**	kilometer
km/h	kilómetros por hora	**kph**	kilometers per hour
kv, kV	kilovatio	**kw, kW**	kilowatt
l.	litro	**l, lit.**	liter
Lic.	licenciado, licenciada	—	—
Ltda.	limitada	**Ltd.**	limited
lun.	lunes	**Mon.**	Monday
m	masculino	**m**	masculine
m	metro	**m**	meter
m	minuto	**m**	minute
mar.	marzo	**Mar.**	March
mart.	martes	**Tues.**	Tuesday
mg.	miligramo	**mg**	milligram
miérc.	miércoles	**Wed.**	Wednesday
min	minuto	**min.**	minute
mm.	milímetro	**mm**	millimeter
M-N, m/n	moneda nacional	—	national currency
Mons.	monseñor	**Msgr.**	monsignor
Mtra.	maestra	—	teacher
Mtro.	maestro	—	teacher
N, N.	Norte, norte	**N, no.**	North, north
n/o	nuestro	—	our
n.º	número	**no.**	number
N. de (la) R.	nota de (la) redacción	—	editor's note
NE	nordeste	**NE**	northeast
NN.UU.	Naciones Unidas	**UN**	United Nations
NO	noroeste	**NW**	northwest
nov.	noviembre	**Nov.**	November
N.T.	Nuevo Testamento	**N.T.**	New Testament
ntra., ntro.	nuestra, nuestro	—	our
NU	Naciones Unidas	**UN**	United Nations
núm.	número	**num.**	number
O, O.	Oeste, oeste	**W**	West, west
oct.	octubre	**Oct.**	October
OEA, O.E.A.	Organización de Estados Americanos	**OAS**	Organization of American States
OMS	Organización Mundial de la Salud	**WHO**	World Health Organization
ONG	organización no gubernamental	**NGO**	non-governmental organization
ONU	Organización de las Naciones Unidas	**UN**	United Nations
OTAN	Organización del Tratado del Atlántico Norte	**NATO**	North Atlantic Treaty Organization
p.	página	**p.**	page
P, P.	padre	**Fr.**	father
pág.	página	**pg.**	page
pat.	patente	**pat.**	patent
PCL	pantalla de cristal líquido	**LCD**	liquid crystal display
P.D.	post data	**P.S.**	postscript
p. ej.	por ejemplo	**e.g.**	for example
PNB	Producto Nacional Bruto	**GNP**	gross national product
pº	paseo	**Ave.**	avenue
p.p.	porte pagado	**ppd.**	postpaid

Common Spanish Abbreviations

SPANISH ABBREVIATION AND EXPANSION		ENGLISH EQUIVALENT	
PP, p.p.	por poder, por poderes	p.p.	by proxy
prom.	promedio	av., avg.	average
ptas., pts.	pesetas	—	—
q.e.p.d.	que en paz descanse	R.I.P.	may he/she rest in peace
R, R/	remite	—	sender
RAE	Real Academia Española	—	—
ref., ref.ᵃ	referencia	ref.	reference
rep.	república	rep.	republic
r.p.m.	revoluciones por minuto	rpm.	revolutions per minute
rte.	remite, remitente	—	sender
s.	siglo	c., cent.	century
s/	su, sus	—	his, her, your, their
S, S.	Sur, sur	S, so.	South, south
S.	san, santo	St.	saint
S.A.	sociedad anónima	Inc.	incorporated (company)
sáb.	sábado	Sat.	Saturday
s/c	su cuenta	—	your account
SE	sudeste, sureste	SE	southeast
seg.	segundo, segundos	sec.	second, seconds
sep., sept.	septiembre	Sept.	September
s.e.u.o.	salvo error u omisión	—	errors and omissions excepted
Sgto.	sargento	Sgt.	sergeant
S.L.	sociedad limitada	Ltd.	limited (corporation)
S.M.	Su Majestad	HM	His Majesty, Her Majesty
s/n	sin número	—	no (street) number
s.n.m.	sobre el nivel de mar	a.s.l.	above sea level
SO	sudoeste/suroeste	SW	southwest
S.R.C.	se ruega contestación	R.S.V.P.	please reply
ss.	siguientes	—	the following ones
SS, S.S.	Su Santidad	H.H.	His Holiness
Sta.	santa	St.	Saint
Sto.	santo	St.	saint
t, t.	tonelada	t., tn	ton
TAE	tasa anual efectiva	APR	annual percentage rate
tb.	también	—	also
tel., Tel.	teléfono	tel.	telephone
Tm.	tonelada métrica	MT	metric ton
Tn.	tonelada	t., tn	ton
trad.	traducido	tr., trans., transl.	translated
UE	Unión Europea	EU	European Union
Univ.	universidad	Univ., U.	university
UPC	unidad procesadora central	CPU	central processing unit
Urb.	urbanización	—	residential area
v	versus	v., vs.	versus
v	verso	v., ver., vs.	verse
v.	véase	vid.	see
Vda.	viuda	—	widow
v.g., v.gr.	verbigracia	e.g.	for example
vier., viern.	viernes	Fri.	Friday
V.M.	Vuestra Majestad	—	Your Majesty
VᵒBᵒ, V.ᵒB.ᵒ	visto bueno	—	OK, approved
vol, vol.	volumen	vol.	volume
vra., vro.	vuestra, vuestro	—	your

Spanish Numbers

Cardinal Numbers

1	uno	28	veintiocho
2	dos	29	veintinueve
3	tres	30	treinta
4	cuatro	31	treinta y uno
5	cinco	40	cuarenta
6	seis	50	cincuenta
7	siete	60	sesenta
8	ocho	70	setenta
9	nueve	80	ochenta
10	diez	90	noventa
11	once	100	cien
12	doce	101	ciento uno
13	trece	200	doscientos
14	catorce	300	trescientos
15	quince	400	cuatrocientos
16	dieciséis	500	quinientos
17	diecisiete	600	seiscientos
18	dieciocho	700	setecientos
19	diecinueve	800	ochocientos
20	veinte	900	novecientos
21	veintiuno	1,000	mil
22	veintidós	1,001	mil uno
23	veintitrés	2,000	dos mil
24	veinticuatro	100,000	cien mil
25	veinticinco	1,000,000	un millón
26	veintiséis	1,000,000,000	mil millones
27	veintisiete	1,000,000,000,000	un billón

Ordinal Numbers

1st	primero, -ra	17th	decimoséptimo, -ma
2nd	segundo, -da	18th	decimoctavo, -va
3rd	tercero, -ra	19th	decimonoveno, -na; or
4th	cuarto, -ta		decimonono, -na
5th	quinto, -ta	20th	vigésimo, -ma
6th	sexto, -ta	21st	vigésimoprimero,
7th	séptimo, -ta		vigésimaprimera
8th	octavo, -ta	30th	trigésimo, -ma
9th	noveno, -na	40th	cuadragésimo, -ma
10th	décimo, -ma	50th	quincuagésimo, -ma
11th	undécimo, -ca	60th	sexagésimo, -ma
12th	duodécimo, -ma	70th	septuagésimo, -ma
13th	decimotercero, -ra	80th	octogésimo, -ma
14th	decimocuarto, -ta	90th	nonagésimo, -ma
15th	decimoquinto, -ta	100th	centésimo, -ma
16th	decimosexto, -ta	1,000th	milésimo, -ma

English Numbers

Cardinal Numbers

1	one	20	twenty
2	two	21	twenty-one
3	three	30	thirty
4	four	40	forty
5	five	50	fifty
6	six	60	sixty
7	seven	70	seventy
8	eight	80	eighty
9	nine	90	ninety
10	ten	100	one hundred
11	eleven	101	one hundred and one
12	twelve	200	two hundred
13	thirteen	1,000	one thousand
14	fourteen	1,001	one thousand and one
15	fifteen	2,000	two thousand
16	sixteen	100,000	one hundred thousand
17	seventeen	1,000,000	one million
18	eighteen	1,000,000,000	one billion
19	nineteen	1,000,000,000,000	one trillion

Ordinal Numbers

1st	first	16th	sixteenth
2nd	second	17th	seventeenth
3rd	third	18th	eighteenth
4th	fourth	19th	nineteenth
5th	fifth	20th	twentieth
6th	sixth	21st	twenty-first
7th	seventh	30th	thirtieth
8th	eighth	40th	fortieth
9th	ninth	50th	fiftieth
10th	tenth	60th	sixtieth
11th	eleventh	70th	seventieth
12th	twelfth	80th	eightieth
13th	thirteenth	90th	ninetieth
14th	fourteenth	100th	hundredth
15th	fifteenth	1,000th	thousandth